<table>
<tr><td>

1850–1890

Childhood Seen as an Adventure, Not a Training Ground for Adulthood

Fantasy and Nonsense

Edward Lear's *A Book of Nonsense* (1846)

Lewis Carroll's *Alice's Adventures in Wonderland* (1865)

Adventure

Jules Verne's *Twenty-Thousand Leagues Under the Sea* (1869)

Robert Louis Stevenson's *Treasure Island* (1883)

Howard Pyle's *The Merry Adventures of Robin Hood* (1883)

Real People

Margaret Sidney's *The Five Little Peppers and How They Grew* (1880)

Louisa May Alcott's *Little Women* (1868)

Johanna Spyri's *Heidi* (1884)

Mark Twain's *The Adventures of Huckleberry Finn* (1884)

</td></tr>
</table>

1850–
1890

Childhood Seen as an Adventure, Not a Training Ground for Adulthood

Fantasy and Nonsense

  Edward Lear's *A Book of Nonsense* (1846)

  Lewis Carroll's *Alice's Adventures in Wonderland* (1865)

Adventure

  Jules Verne's *Twenty-Thousand Leagues Under the Sea* (1869)

  Robert Louis Stevenson's *Treasure Island* (1883)

  Howard Pyle's *The Merry Adventures of Robin Hood* (1883)

Real People

  Margaret Sidney's *The Five Little Peppers and How They Grew* (1880)

  Louisa May Alcott's *Little Women* (1868)

  Johanna Spyri's *Heidi* (1884)

  Mark Twain's *The Adventures of Huckleberry Finn* (1884)

1900

Great Animal Fantasy

  Beatrix Potter's *The Tale of Peter Rabbit* (1901)

  Rudyard Kipling's *The Just So Stories* (1902)

  Kenneth Grahame's *The Wind in the Willows* (1908)

1922

The Newbery Medal First Awarded to an Outstanding Author of Children's Literature

  Willem Van Loon's *The Story of Mankind*

  Honor Books:

    Charles Hawes's *The Great Quest*

    Bernard Marshall's *Cedric the Forester*

    William Bowen's *The Old Tobacco Shop*

    Padraic Colum's *The Golden Fleece and the Heroes Who Lived Before Achilles*

    Cornelia Meigs's *Windy Hill*

1924

The Horn Book Magazine **First Published**

1938

The first Caldecott Medal was presented to the illustrator of the most distinguished picture book published in the United States

  Animals of the Bible by Helen Dean Fish, ill. by Dorothy P. Lathrop

  Honor Books:

    Seven Simeon: A Russian Tale by Boris Artzybasheff

    Four and Twenty Blackbirds: Nursery Rhymes of Yesterday Recalled for Children of To-Day by Helen Dean Fish, ill. by Robert Lawson

1940s

A Time of Happy Family Stories

  Elizabeth Enright's *Thimble Summer* (1938)

  Eleanor Estes's *The Moffats* (1941)

  Sydney Taylor's *All-of-a-Kind Family* (1951)

1957

Soviet Union Launches Sputnik—An Abundance of Nonfictional Books Considered Necessary for a Better Education

  Irving Adler's *Tools in Your Life* (1956)

  Isaac Asimov's *Building Blocks of the Universe* (1957) and *Words of Science: and the History Behind Them* (1959)

  Franklyn M. Branley's *Mickey's Magnet* (1956)

  Katherine Shippen's *Men, Microscopes, and Living Things* (1955)

1960s

A Time of Popular High Fantasy

  C. S. Lewis's *The Lion, the Witch, and the Wardrobe* (1961) First of the "Chronicles of Narnia"

  Lloyd Alexander's *The Book of Three* (1964) First of the "Prydain Books"

  Susan Cooper's *Over Sea, Under Stone* (1965)

Lavish Full-Color Books Emphasize Excellence in Design. Many Gifted Illustrators Enter Field of Children's Books

  Leo Lionni's *Inch by Inch* (1960)

  Maurice Sendak's *Where the Wild Things Are* (1963)

  Ezra Jack Keats's *The Snowy Day* (1963)

  Blair Lent's *The Wave* (1964)

  Evaline Ness's *Sam, Bangs & Moonshine* (1967)

  Ed Emberley's *Drummer Hoff* (1967)

1965

Beginning of an Increased Sensitivity to Racial Perspectives in Children's Books

  Nancy Larrick's *Saturday Review* article "The All-White World of Children's Books"

1970s

Authors and Illustrators Representing Ethnic Minorities Make Major Contributions to Children's Literature

  Virginia Hamilton's *The Planet of Junior Brown* (1972) and *M. C. Higgins, the Great* (1974)

  Lawrence Yep's *Dragonwings*

  Jamake Highwater's *Anpao: An American Indian Odyssey* (1977)

  Illustrators—Leo and Diane Dillon's *Why Mosquitoes Buzz in People's Ears* (1975)

1982

First Newbery Medal Awarded to a Book of Poetry

  Nancy Willard's *A Visit to William Blake's Inn*

THROUGH THE EYES OF A CHILD

An Introduction to Children's Literature

Children are always drawn to the statue of Hans Christian Andersen in Central Park.

THROUGH THE EYES OF A CHILD

An Introduction to Children's Literature

DONNA E. NORTON
Texas A&M University

CHARLES E. MERRILL PUBLISHING COMPANY
A Bell & Howell Company
Columbus ■ Toronto ■ London ■ Sydney

Published by Charles E. Merrill Publishing Co.
A Bell & Howell Company
Columbus, Ohio 43216

This book was set in Korinna
Cover illustration and design by Tony Faiola
Text Design: Ann Mirels
Chapter Opening Art: Chapters 1, 2, 3, 4, 5, 6, 7, 8, 11 by Tony
                       Faiola
                       Chapters 9, 10, 12 by Steve Botts and
                       Tony Faiola
Production Coordination: Linda Hillis Bayma

Library of Congress Catalog Card Number: 82-062479
International Standard Book Number: 0-675-09832-7
1 2 3 4 5 6 7 8 9—88 87 86 85 84 83

Printed in the United States of America

FOLLOWING THE COMPLE-
tion of her doctorate at the
University of Wisconsin, Madison, Donna E. Norton joined the
College of Education faculty at Texas
A&M University where she teaches
courses in children's literature, language arts, and reading. Dr. Norton
is the 1981–1982 recipient of the
Texas A&M Faculty Distinguished
Achievement Award in Teaching.
This award is given "in recognition
and appreciation of ability, personality, and methods which have resulted
in distinguished achievements in the
teaching and in the inspiration of students." She is listed in *Who's Who of
American Women.*

Dr. Norton is the author of two
books: *The Effective Teaching of
Language Arts* and *Language Arts Activities for Children.* She is a frequent contributor to journals and presenter at professional conferences. The focus of her
current research is multiethnic literature and comparative education. In conjunction with this research, she has developed a graduate course that enables
students to study children's literature and reading instruction in England and
Scotland.

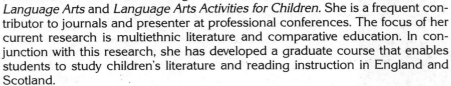

Prior to her college teaching experience, Dr. Norton was an elementary
teacher in River Falls, Wisconsin and in Madison, Wisconsin. She was a Language Arts/Reading Consultant for federally funded kindergarten through adult
basic education programs. In this capacity she developed, provided inservice instruction, and evaluated kindergarten programs, summer reading and library
programs, remedial reading programs, learning disability programs for middle
school children, elementary and secondary literature programs for the gifted,
and diagnostic and intervention programs for reading disabled adults. Dr. Norton's continuing concern for literature programs results in frequent consultations with educators from various disciplines, librarians, and school administrators and teachers.

CREDITS

Photos

Flashback Illustrations

Other Illustrations
The chapter opening illustration on pages 104–5 adapted from "The Frog Prince" in Walter Crane's *Goody Two Shoes' Picture Books*. London, New York, Boston: George Routledge & Sons, 1875
Page 590, Figure 12–2, courtesy OCLC, Inc., Dublin, Ohio
Page 57, lower right, from the collection of Julia Estadt

Development of Textbook Concept and Organization
Martha Barclay, Northern Iowa Area Community College; Delorys Blume, University of Central Florida; Robert O. Boord, University of Nevada, Las Vegas; N. Boraks, Virginia Commonwealth University; Maxine Burress, University of Wisconsin; Gertrude B. Camper, Roanoke College; Delila Caselli, Sioux Falls College; Virginia Chirbart, College of St. Benedict; Eileen Cunningham, St. Thomas Aquinas College; Douglas L. Decker, Virginia State University; Lois Elendine, Oklahoma Christian College; Marjorie L. Farmer, Pembroke State University; Kay E. Fisher, Simpson College; E.W. Freeman, LeMoyne-Owen College; Margaret Gunn, Delta State University; C. Hooker-Schrader, Longwood College; Louise M. Hulst, Dordt College; Betty Kingery, Westmar College; Eleanor W. Lofquist, Western Carolina Univesity; Mary Maness, Bartlesville Wesleyan College; Charles Matthews, College of Charleston; Rita E. Meadows, Lakeland, Florida; D.D. Miller, Univesity of Missouri - St. Louis; Dorothy Z. Mills, East Carolina University; Martha L. Morris, Indiana Central University; Joan S. Nist, Auburn University; Olga M. Santora, State University of New York; Ronnie Sheppard, Georgia College; Richard J. Sherry, Asbury College; Sidney W. Shnayer, California State University at Chico; Dorothy Spethmann, Dakota State College; John Stinson, Jr., Miami, Florida; Emilie P. Sullivan, University of Arkansas; Lola Jiles Sullivan, Florida International University; Marilyn C. Teele, Loma Linda University; Barbara Townsend, Salisbury State College; Marion Turkish, William Paterson College; Linda Western, University of Wisconsin — Milwaukee; Marilyn Yoder, Grace College; Collette Zerba, Cardinal Stritch College.

PREFACE

THIS TEXT IS INTENDED FOR any adult who is interested in evaluating, selecting, and sharing children's literature. Its focus and organization are designed for children's literature classes taught in the departments of English, Education, and Library Science. *Through the Eyes of a Child* is written in the hope that adults who work with children and literature will discover and share with children the enchantment in books and help children develop a lifetime appreciation for literature and a respect for our literary heritage. It is my hope that my own love for literature and enthusiasm for books will be transmitted to the reader of this text.

HIGHLIGHTS

Extensive and Current Selection of Children's Books

The selection of books from the thousands of books available is a major concern for writers of children's literature textbooks. To determine the most suitable selections, I personally read over five thousand books. The ones discussed in *Through the Eyes of a Child* were chosen for their quality of literature, balance of content, variety of authors, and balance between new books and those which have passed the test of time or are considered classics in the field. *Approximately twenty-five percent of the books included in each chapter were published within the two years prior to the publication of Through the Eyes of a Child.* Thus, most of the books discussed in the text are in print. A few out-of-print books are included when they are the best examples for a specific discussion or when the books are just too good to be ignored. Most of these are still available in libraries.

Two-Part Chapter Organization

This unique feature of the text, beginning in chapter five and extending through chapter twelve, places the characteristics, history, and titles of each genre right next to the appropriate strategies for involving children in that genre. Thus, genre and involvement can be taught together, sequentially, or independently. The involvement strategies have been field tested at the university, elementary, and secondary school levels, and during inservice training for teachers and librarians.

Emphasis on Criteria for Book Evaluation and Selection

Each chapter builds a model for evaluating and selecting books based upon literary and artistic characteristics which readers can then use themselves. The importance of child development in this process is also stressed.

Issues

Each chapter identifies important issues that are related to the genre or content of the chapter and which are designed to introduce teachers, librarians, and parents to current concerns. Most of these issue highlights are referenced to current periodicals and professional journals and are written to encourage readers' contemplation and further investigation. For this reason, they are presented as open-ended discussions.

Flashbacks

Also included in each chapter, these illustrated features highlight important people, works, and events in the history of children's literature. They are designed to provide a more complete understanding of the genre.

Through the Eyes of . . .

Beginning with chapter three, each chapter includes a personal statement by a well-known author or illustrator which provides a special glimpse into their "view" of the creation of children's books.

Annotated Bibliographies of Children's Literature
These extensive bibliographies include readability by grade level and interest by age range.

Text Teaching Aids
Each chapter concludes with two groups of suggested activities designed to foster adult understanding of and children's appreciation for the genre. Special web diagrams are used throughout the text to highlight the interrelationships in literature, the many values of literature, and the multiple learning possibilities available. Webs are also used to illustrate the development of instructional activities and oral discussions about literature. The webbing process, according to my students, helps them clarify concepts, visualize relationships, and identify numerous values for sharing literature with children.

Chapter on Multiethnic Literature
This material was organized as a separate chapter to make it more accessible to librarians, teachers, and students of children's literature.

Annual Update
Due to the many additions and changes in this field, I will prepare for adopters of *Through the Eyes of a Child* a list of the new children's books and award winners, the new professional publications, and discuss current issues or new developments in the field. This free update will be distributed by the publisher when requested by instructors who have adopted the text for their class.

Donna E. Norton

ACKNOWLEDGMENTS

A massive project such as writing and publishing a children's literature text would not be possible without the enthusiasm, critical evaluation, suggestions, and hard work of many people. My appreciation is extended to my children's literature students, teachers, and librarians who discussed books with me, created enthusiasm for books, and shared books with children. The multiethnic literature chapter was enhanced by research conducted by Sue Mohrmann and Blanche Lawson; field testing in the Bryan, Texas schools; teachers and librarians across Texas who took part in the research; and support by curriculum coordinator Barbara Erwin and principal Marge Hazlet. The children's librarians at the Houston Public Library and the Houston Library archives deserve a special thank-you. They discussed reactions to books, searched for hard-to-locate literature, and allowed me to check out hundreds of books at one time. The writing of a text also requires typing expertise; the long hours of work performed by Loretta Johnson made a finished manuscript possible.

The children's librarians at the Public Library of Columbus and Franklin County; Grandview, Ohio Public Library; Bexley, Ohio Public Library; and Westerville, Ohio Public Library provided much assistance in locating numerous children's books.

I would like to thank the people at Merrill—Linda Bayma, who, as production editor, spent an enormous amount of time polishing and tying together the countless loose ends of such a project; free-lancers Linda Krieg, Barbara Longstreth, and Marikay Schwartz; Cynthia Donaldson for her help with photo acquisition; Marcia Earnest for tracking down numerous library books; Julie Estadt, developmental editor, for her work with the initial draft; Tony Faiola and Steve Botts for the spectacular cover and chapter opening artwork; Ann Mirels for the wonderful text design; George McCann for the effective promotion coordination; Ken Montavon for the excellent advertising support; Shirley Rudolph for her untiring secretarial effort; Roger Williams, Executive Editor; Alan Borne, Editor-in-Chief; and, finally, Gil Imholz, former Administrative Editor, for the inception of this project, and Rich Wohl, his successor—for carefully guiding *Through the Eyes of a Child* to its completion, which is now in your hands.

My sincere appreciation is also extended to Patricia Clapp, Beverly Cleary, Sandra B. Cohen, Tomie de Paola, Jean Fritz, Virginia Hamilton, Jamake Highwater, Madeleine L'Engle, Jack Prelutsky, Martin and Alice Provensen, and Jack Denton Scott for the time and creativity they were able to share with us during their very busy schedules. The insights, personal statements, and viewpoints of these authors, illustrators, and educators are especially rewarding in a textbook about children's literature.

I wish to deeply thank Patricia Cianciolo at Michigan State, Donald J. Bissett at Wayne State, Shirley Lukenbill at the University of Texas, and Linda Western for their extensive and insightful reviews of the various manuscript drafts of *Through the Eyes of a Child*. Their efforts have been invaluable in my goal of creating an accurate, timely, and lively text. And, finally, special gratitude goes to Patricia Cianciolo and Wendy K. Sutton for their co-authoring the excellent Instructor's Resource Manual which accompanies the text.

**CONTENTS
IN
BRIEF**

SPECIAL FEATURES

CONTENTS

CHAPTER SEVEN

Modern Fantasy 256

CHAPTER ELEVEN

Multiethnic Literature   486

CHAPTER TWELVE

Nonfiction: Informational Books and Biographies   546

THROUGH THE EYES
OF A CHILD

An Introduction to Children's Literature

ONE
The Child and Children's Literature

VALUES OF LITERATURE FOR
CHILDREN

PROMOTING DEVELOPMENT
THROUGH LITERATURE

LITERATURE entices, motivates, and develops. It opens doors of discovery and provides endless hours of adventure and enjoyment. How else can children follow a rabbit down a hole, find an enchanted kingdom inside a wardrobe, save a wild herd of mustangs from slaughter, masquerade as men and fight in the Revolutionary War, grow up on a homestead in frontier America, learn about a new hobby that will provide many enjoyable hours, or model themselves after a real-life hero? Children need not be tied to the whims of television programming or wait in line at the neighborhood theater—these adventures are as close as the nearest bookshelf or library.

Not only should children become aware of the enchantment in books, but the adults in their lives also have a responsibility. As Bernice Cullinan (7) has suggested, "Books can play a significant role in the life of the young child, but the extent to which they do depends entirely upon adults. Adults are responsible for providing books and transmitting the literary heritage contained in nursery rhymes, traditional tales, and great novels" (p. 1).

As you read this book you will gain knowledge about literature so that you can share stimulating books and book-related experiences with children.

This chapter discusses the various values of sharing literature with children in order to help you search for books that can play a significant role in children's lives. It also focuses on the importance of considering the child when selecting children's literature. Developmental characteristics are described

ISSUE

The Publisher's Responsibility in a Pluralistic Society

ROBERT F. BAKER, WRITing from a publisher's viewpoint, presents literature students with a thoughtful overview of the multiple issues facing publishers of children's literature and other reading materials for children.[1] He states that most Americans believe that reading materials selected to be used with children should provide a balance reflecting the pluralistic, multicultural, multivalued mosaic of American life. While many people agree that a literature program should be nonracist and nonsexist, offer children insights into varied patterns of family life, allow children to experience literature of many kinds, and introduce them to a rich and diverse heritage, there are issues related to the execution of these guidelines. A few of the representative issues and concerns mentioned by Baker include the following: (1) What is the range of skin colors that must appear in illustrations to avoid giving children the impression that all blacks look alike? (2) How does one convey the range of occupational choices open to women? (3) How does one cope with mothers who are unhappy with the current portrait of the American family? (4) How should one determine what is excessive violence? (5) Should the Polynesian boy in *Call It Courage* be seen in his loincloth or should he be fully clothed? (6) How should one handle the demands for greater reliance on standard English? Additional sensitive issues identified by Baker for today's publishers include attitudes toward American values and ideals, theories of evolution and creation, viewpoints on business and labor, relationships between parents and children, treatments of religion, and political attitudes. Baker concludes that "in the final analysis, the publisher must make the final decision, weighing conflicting recommendations from a variety of well-meaning and well-informed sources."

1 Baker Robert F. "A Publisher Views the Development and Selection of Reading Programs" in *Indoctrinate or Educate?* edited by Thomas C. Hatcher and Lawrence G. Erickson, pp. 25-30. Newark, Del.: International Reading Association, 1979.

along with the importance of literature in promoting language, cognitive, personality, and social development. Finally, a few books that exemplify children's needs during different stages of development are suggested.

VALUES OF LITERATURE FOR CHILDREN

Following a rabbit down a rabbit hole or walking through a wardrobe into a mythical kingdom sounds like a lot of fun. There is nothing wrong with admitting that one of the primary values of literature is pure pleasure, and there is nothing wrong with turning to a book to escape or to enjoy an adventure with new or old book friends. Time is enriched, not wasted, when children look at beautiful pictures and imagine themselves in new places. When children discover enjoyment in books, they develop favorable attitudes toward them that usually extend into a lifetime of appreciation. Doris Roettger (14) offers a strong rationale for allowing children many opportunities to read for enjoyment. In interviewing a large number of children, she asked them how school and reading could be made more enjoyable. The students recommended that (1) children should be given a chance to read books each day; (2) teachers should ask them about their interests and help them find books on those subjects, and (3) teachers should tell children about books and should give them time to talk about books with each other and with the teacher. This is good advice—librarians, teachers, parents, or anyone who works with children should heed it.

While the primary value of literature may be pleasure, there are other benefits to be gained from books. They are the major resource transmitting our literary heritage from one generation to the next. Each new generation can enjoy the words of Lewis Carroll, Edward Lear, Robert Louis Stevenson, Mark Twain, and Louisa May Alcott and, through the work of such storytellers as the Brothers Grimm, can also experience the folktales originally told through the oral tradition.

Literature plays a strong role in understanding and valuing our cultural heritage in addition to understanding and enjoying our literary heritage. Developing positive attitudes toward our own culture and those of others is necessary for both social and personal development. Carefully selected literature can illustrate the contributions and values of the many cultures found in the child's world. This is especially critical in fostering an appreciation of the heritage of the ethnic minorities. A positive self-concept is not possible unless we have respect for others as well as ourselves; literature can contribute considerably toward this understanding.

The vicarious experiences of literature result in personal development as well as pleasure. Without literature, children could not relive the colonists' experiences as they cross the ocean and shape a new land; they could not experience solitude and fear as they fight for survival on an isolated island; and most of them could not travel to distant places in the galaxy. Historical fiction provides children with an opportunity to live in the past. Science fiction allows them to speculate about the "what ifs" of science, and contemporary realistic fiction encourages them to experience relationships with people and the environment. Because children can learn from literature how other people handle their problems, vicarious experiences with the characters in books can help them deal with similar problems; these experiences can also help children understand other people's feelings.

Another value of literature is illustrated by a television interview with a high school sophomore who was considered a promising young scientist. When asked how he had become so knowledgeable, the boy replied, "I read a lot." Books had opened doors to knowledge and expanded his interests. Don't educators and parents want this respect for knowledge to be transmitted to all children? The many books available can do this. Information books relay new knowledge; biographies and autobiographies tell about the people who gained this knowledge or made discoveries. Information books are written about all content areas and at all levels of difficulty. Photographs and illustrations show the wonders of nature or depict the step-by-step process required to master a new hobby. Realistic stories from a specific time bring history to life. Even for very young children, cognitive development may be stimulated through the use of concept books that illustrate colors, numbers, shapes, and sizes.

No discussion about the values of literature can be concluded without stressing the role literature plays in nurturing and expanding the imagination. Books take children into imaginative worlds that stimulate additional creative experiences as they tell or write their own stories and interact with each other during creative drama. Both well-written literature and the illustrations found in picture storybooks can stimulate children's aesthetic development. Children enjoy and evaluate these illustrations as well as explore the media used as they create their own illustrations.

Finally, literature and literature-related activities nurture child development. The rest of this chapter discusses how appropriate children's literature can promote language development, cognitive development, personality development, and social development.

PROMOTING DEVELOPMENT THROUGH LITERATURE

Research in child development has shown that there are recognizable stages in language and social development. Children do not progress through these stages at the same rate, but there is an order through which they mature. The characteristics of children demonstrated during each stage provide clues that can be used in selecting appropriate literature; this literature can benefit them during that stage of development, helping them progress to the next stage. Understanding these stages will be useful to anyone who works with children. Each of the four child development topics concludes with a chart listing the stages, the characteristics of average children during that stage, the implications of those characteristics, and suggested literature selections that can be used with children who demonstrate those characteristics.

Language Development

Preschool Children. Children during their first few years show dramatic changes in language ability, and most learn language very rapidly. They usually speak their first words at about one year of age; at about eighteen months, they begin to put two words together. (These two-word combinations are called *telegraphic speech.*) Speech during this stage of language development is made up mostly of nouns, verbs, and adjectives; usually there are no prepositions, articles, auxiliary verbs, or pronouns. When children say "pretty flower" or "all gone milk," they are using telegraphic speech. The number of different two-word combinations increases slowly, then shows a sudden upsurge around the age of two.

Martin Braine (5) recorded the speech of three children from the ages of eighteen months and reported that the cumulative number of different two-word combinations for one child in successive months was 14, 24, 54, 89, 350, 1,400, 2,500 + . This is a rapid expansion of speech in a very short time.

All children seem to go through the same stages of language development, although the rate of development varies from child to child. A longitudinal study conducted by Roger Brown (6) showed great variance among children. For example, one child successfully used six grammatical morphemes by the age of two years, three months; a second child did not master them until the age of three years, six months; and a third was four years old before reaching an equivalent stage in language development. The average language developmental stage, then, refers to characteristics demonstrated by a large number, but not all, children in this age group.

Speech becomes more complex by the age of three years, and most children have added adverbs, pronouns, prepositions, and additional adjectives. They also enjoy playing with the sounds of language in this stage of development. By the age of four, they produce grammatically correct sentences; this stage is a questioning one during which language is used to ask "why" and "how."

Literature and literature-related experiences can encourage language development in these preschool children. Book experiences in the home, library, and/or nursery school can help them use language to discover their world, to identify and name actions and objects, to gain more complex speech, and to enjoy the wonder of language. Children's first book experiences are frequently with large picture books and Mother Goose rhymes, and as these books are read to children or the pictures are discussed, they add new words to their vocabularies. The picture books help them give meaning to their expanding vocabularies. For example, children who are just learning to identify their hands and other parts of their bodies may find these parts in large drawings of children such as those found in Satomi Ichikawa's *Let's Play.* Parents of very young children may share Helen Oxenbury's excellent "Baby Board Books." *Dressing,* for example, includes a picture of baby's clothing followed by a picture of the child dressed in that item. The illustrations are sequentially developed; they can encourage talking about the steps in dressing. Other books in this series include *Friends, Playing, Working,* and *Family.*

About this time, young children also learn to identify actions in pictures, and they enjoy recognizing and naming familiar actions such as those in Eve Rice's *Oh, Lewis!* In this picture book, Lewis is going shopping with his mother, but first he must find his mittens, have his jacket zipped, his boots buckled, and his hood tied. *Richard Scarry's The Best Word Book Ever* appeals to young children and provides practice in naming common objects.

There are many excellent books that allow children to listen to the sounds of language and experiment with these sounds. For example, *Over in the Meadow,* by Ezra Jack Keats, is a popular picture book illustrating the old nursery song. Children may respond in both Spanish and English when they interact with the rhymes in *Tortillitas Para Mama* by Margot C. Griego et al. Rhyming books are especially appealing to young children. Both the colorful pictures and rhyming words in Barbara Emberley's *Drummer Hoff* fascinate them—they love to join in with the rhyming elements, "parriage"—"carriage," "farrell"—"barrel," and "bammer"—"rammer."

The loving environment captured by the illustrations and the accompanying nursery rhymes encourage language development. From *Tortillitas Para Mama* selected and translated by Margot C. Griego, Betsy L. Bucks, Sharon S. Gilbert, and Laurel H. Kimball. Illustrated by Barbara Cooney. Copyright © 1981 by Margot Griego, Betsy Bucks, Sharon Gilbert, Laurel Kimball. Copyright © 1981 by Barbara Cooney. Reproduced by permission of Holt, Rinehart and Winston, Publishers.

Elementary-Age Children. Language development continues as children progress through the grades. Walter Loban conducted the most extensive, longitudinal study of language development in school-age children, examining the language development of the same group of over two hundred children from the age of five to eighteen (11). He found that children's power over language increases through successive control over forms of language, including the ability to handle pronouns, verb tenses, and connectors.

Like younger children, school-age children apparently go through similar stages in language development, although their rate of development varies widely. Loban identified several major differences between children ranking high in language proficiency and those ranking low. Those who demon-

strated high proficiency excelled in the control of expressed ideas, and both speech and writing showed unity and planning. Students spoke freely, fluently, and easily, using a rich variety of vocabulary and adjusting the pace of their words to their listeners. The difference was dramatic: the higher group reached a level of oral proficiency in first grade that the lower group did not attain until sixth grade. The lower group's oral communication was characterized by rambling and unpurposeful dialogue showing a meager vocabulary.

In the area of written language, the high group was more fluent, used more words per sentence, showed a richer vocabulary, and was superior in using connectors such as *meanwhile* and *unless* in their writing. They also used more subordination in combining thoughts into complex forms. The high group again showed greater proficiency at a much younger age, fourth-grade level, than the low one; the proficiency shown by the high group was not shown by the low group until the tenth grade. Students superior in oral language also ranked highest on listening and were both attentive and creative listeners. Children who were superior in oral language in kindergarten and first grade also excelled in reading and writing in the sixth grade. Loban concluded that greater attention should be given to the development and instruction of oral language. Discussion should be a vital part of elementary and library programs because children need that kind of instruction to help them organize ideas and illustrate complex generalizations.

Due to the fact that literature provides both a model for language and stimulation for oral and written activities, it excels in developing language. Throughout this text, we will present literature suggestions to be read aloud to children; literature to provide a model for expanding language proficiency; and literature to stimulate oral discussion, creative dramatics, creative writing, and listening enjoyment.

Literature provides stimulation for the dramatic play and creative dramatics that children in the primary grades so enjoy. For example, Maurice Sendak's *Where the Wild Things Are* tells the story of Max who gets into so much mischief when he is wearing his wolf suit that his mother sends him to his room without any supper; his vivid imagination turns the room into a forest inhabited by wild things. Max stays in the kingdom and becomes king but finally gets lonely and wants to return to the land where someone loves him. Children can relate to Max's experience and use it to stimulate their own wild experiences through creative drama. Marco, in Dr. Seuss's *And to Think That I Saw It on Mulberry Street,* is another boy who uses his imagination when he is in a normal environment. The setting is the street on which Marco walks home from school. The only thing Marco sees is a horse drawing a wagon, but this does not stifle his storytelling ability as he envisions what he would like to see on plain old Mulberry Street. Children enjoy using their imagination and turning the common occurrences of their streets into creative experiences. Chapters five, six, and seven present books that involve children in enchantment.

Wordless picture books are excellent stimulators for oral and written language. Tomie de Paola's *Pancakes for Breakfast* presents a series of humorous incidents related to preparing pancakes. *The Ballooning Adventures of Paddy Pork,* by John Goodall, illustrates the adventures of a pig when he leaves home to join the circus. Mitsumasa Anno's *Anno's Britain* may stimulate language as children discover literary characters and present-day personalities among the British landmarks. Some wordless books are more complex and show sequences or changes brought on because of time. John Goodall's *The Story of an English Village* shows what happens in a village beginning in the fourteenth century and continuing into the twentieth century. Wordless books such as the latter may stimulate the oral language of older children. Chapter five presents wordless picture books and stimulating activities that are useful with them.

Stages in Language Development. Chart 1–1 lists the characteristics in language development that are associated with these stages, the educational implications of these characteristics, and several literature selections that may be used to stimulate children's development in those language skills. Approximate ages are shown in the chart, but they should not be considered absolute. The reader should look instead at the stages in development, because research has shown that recognizable stages exist, and there is an order through which children mature, although they do not progress at the same rate or at the same age. The characteristics and implications presented were compiled from studies by Brown (6) and Loban (11), a report by Bartel (2), and texts by Braga and Braga (4) and Gage and Berliner (9).

Cognitive Development

The factors related to developing the strategies that will aid children to remember, anticipate, integrate perceptions, and develop concepts fill numerous textbooks and have been the subject of both research and conjecture. Jean Piaget stated that the order in which children's thinking matures is the same for all, although the pace varies from child to child. Early stimulation is also necessary if cognitive development is to occur; it appears to be so important that children who grow up in isola-

ted areas without a variety of experiences may be three to five years behind other children in developing the mental strategies that aid recall.

Books and related literature experiences are frequently mentioned as a means of stimulating cognitive development. It is necessary to know the exact meaning of cognition before stages in cognitive development can be presented and literature selections provided. According to the child development authorities Mussen, Conger, and Kagan (12), cognition refers to the processes involved in "(1) perception—the detection, organization, and interpretation of information from both the outside world and the internal environment, (2) memory—the storage and retrieval of the perceived information, (3) reasoning—the use of knowledge to make inferences and draw conclusions, (4) reflection—the evaluation of the quality of ideas and solutions, and (5) insight—the recognition of new relationships between two or more segments of knowledge" (pp. 234–35). All of these processes are extremely important and are essential for success during both school and adult life. Each is also closely related to understanding and enjoying literature: without visual and auditory perception, literature could not be read or heard; without memory, there would be no way to see the relationships among literary works and to recognize new relationships as experiences are extended. The cognitive processes can be stimulated by carefully selecting literature and literature experiences that can encourage the oral exchange of ideas and the development of thought processes.

In order to use literature to provide stimulation for developing thought processes, Dorothy Strickland (18) recommends that you should "capitalize on every opportunity to develop the child's ability to handle basic operations associated with thinking" (p. 55). She identifies these operations that can be developed through the use of literature: observing, comparing, classifying, hypothesizing, organizing, summarizing, applying, and criticizing. Each operation will be examined and some suggestions made so that literature and literature-related activities may be used to stimulate thinking processes.

Observing. Picture books containing large, colorful pictures are excellent for developing observational skills. For example, children can describe the actions of the family and the contents of the rooms in Tomie de Paola's illustrations for *The Night Before Christmas.* They can describe the family bringing in the tree, decorating the tree with popcorn and paper chains, and then nestling into their beds. The objects in the 1840s New England house, St. Nicholas and the sleigh filled with

CHART 1–1
Language Development

Characteristics	Implications	Literature Suggestions
Preschool: Ages two–three		
1 Very rapid language growth occurs. By the end of this period, children have vocabularies of about nine hundred words.	1 Provide many activities to stimulate language growth including picture books and Mother Goose rhymes.	Chorao, Kay. *The Baby's Lap Book.* Wezel, Peter. *The Good Bird.*
2 They learn to identify and name actions in pictures.	2 Read books that contain clear, familiar action pictures; encourage children to identify actions.	Oxenbury, Helen. *Playing.* Polushkin, Maria. *Who Said Meow?* Rice, Eve. *Oh, Lewis!*
3 They learn to identify large and small body parts.	3 Allow children to identify familiar body parts in picture books.	Berger, Terry, and Kandell, Alice. *Ben's ABC Day.* Ichikawa, Satomi. *Let's Play.*
Preschool: Ages three–tour		
1 Vocabularies have increased to about fifteen hundred words. Children enjoy playing with sound and rhythm in language.	1 Include opportunities to listen to and say rhymes, poetry, and riddles.	Chute, Marchette. *Rhymes About Us.* Emberley, Barbara. *Drummer Hoff.* Griego, Margot, et al. *Tortillitas Para Mama.* Martin, Sarah Catherine. *The Comic Adventures of Mother Hubbard and Her Dog.*
2 They develop the ability to use past tense but may overgeneralize the *ed* and *s* markers.	2 Allow children to talk about what they did yesterday, discuss actions in books.	Hill, Eric. *Spot's First Walk.* Kraus, Robert. *Milton the Early Riser.*
3 Language is used as a tool to help children find out about their world.	3 Read picture storybooks to allow children to find out about and discuss pets, families, people, the environment.	Ahlberg, Janet, and Ahlberg, Allen. *Peek-a-boo!* Barton, Byron. *Where's Al.* Nakatani, Chiyoko. *The Zoo in My Garden.* Spier, Peter. *Bill's Service Station.* Spier, Peter. *Food Market.*
4 Speech becomes more complex, with more adjectives, adverbs, pronouns, and prepositions.	4 Expand the use of descriptive words through detailed picture books and picture storybooks. Allow children to tell stories and describe characters and their actions.	Crews, Donald. *Harbor.* Crews, Donald. *Freight Train.* Garelick, May. *Down to the Beach.*
Preschool: Ages four–five		
1 Language is more abstract; children produce gramatically correct sentences. Their vocabularies include approximately twenty-five hundred words.	1 Children enjoy books with slightly more complex plots. They can tell longer and more detailed stories, enjoy retelling folktales, and can tell stories using wordless books.	Aruego, Jose. *Look What I Can Do.* Brown, Marcia. *The Bun: A Tale from Russia.* Cauley, Lorinda Bryan. *Goldilocks and the Three Bears.* Duff, Maggie. *Rum Pum Pum.* Hutchinson, Veronica. *Henny Penny.*
2 They understand the prepositions *over, under, in, out, in front of,* and *behind.*	2 Use concept books or other picture books in which these terms can be reinforced.	Bancheck, Linda. *Snake In, Snake Out.* Hutchins, Pat. *Rosie's Walk.*
3 They enjoy asking many questions, especially those related to *why* and *how.*	3 Take advantage of this natural curiosity and find books to help answer their questions. Allow them to answer each others' questions.	Barton, Byron. *Airport.* Showers, Paul. *Look at Your Eyes.*

CHART 1–1 *(cont.)*
Language Development

Characteristics	Implications	Literature Suggestions
Preschool—Kindergarten: Ages five–six 1 Most children use complex sentences frequently and begin to use correct pronouns and verbs in present and past tense. They understand approximately six thousand words.	1 Give them many opportunities for oral language activities connected with literature.	Aardema, Verna. *Bringing the Rain to Kapiti Plain.* Aardema, Verna. *Why Mosquitoes Buzz in People's Ears: A West African Tale.* Bennett, Jill. *Tiny Tim: Verses For Children.* Langstaff, John. *Oh, A-Hunting We Will Go.*
2 Children enjoy taking part in dramatic play and producing dialogue about everyday functions such as home situations, and grocery store experiences.	2 Read stories about the home and community. Allow children to act out their own stories.	Hurd, Edith Thacher. *I Dance in My Red Pajamas.* Kroll, Steven. *If I Could Be My Grandmother.* Mayer, Mercer. *The Great Cat Chase.* Seuss, Dr. *And to Think That I Saw It on Mulberry Street.* Spier, Peter. *Fire House: Hook and Ladder Company Number Twenty-Four.*
3 They are curious about the written appearance of their own language.	3 Write chart stories using the children's own words; have them dictate descriptions of pictures.	Briggs, Raymond. *The Snowman.* Krahn, Fernando. *Who's Seen the Scissors.* Spier, Peter. *Rain.*
Early Elementary: Ages six–eight 1 Language development continues; many new words are added to their vocabularies.	1 Provide daily time for reading to children and allow for oral interaction.	de Paola, Tomie. *Fin M'Coul: The Giant of Knockmany Hill.* Galbraith, Kathryn. *Spots Are Special!* Galdone, Paul. *Puss in Boots.* Kellogg, Steven. *A Rose for Pinkerton.* Silverstein, Shel. *A Light in the Attic.*
2 Most children use complex sentences with adjectival clauses and conditional clauses beginning with *if*. The average oral sentence length is seven and one-half words.	2 Read stories that provide models for children's expanding language structure.	Rose, Anne. *As Right as Right Can Be.* Severo, Emöke de Papp. *The Good-Hearted Youngest Brother.* Skorpen, Liesel M. *His Mother's Dog.* Asian Cultural Centre for UNESCO. *Folktales from Asia for Children Everywhere.*
Middle Elementary: Ages eight–ten 1 Children begin to relate concepts to general ideas. They use connectors such as *meanwhile* and *unless*.	1 Supply books as models. Let children use these terms during oral language activities.	Belpre, Pura. *The Rainbow-Colored Horse.* Hill, Donna. *Ms. Glee Was Waiting.*
2 The subordinating connector *although* is used correctly by 50 percent of children. Present participle active and perfect participle appear. The average number of words in sentence is nine.	2 Use written models and oral models to help children master these language skills. Literature discussions allow many opportunities for oral sentence expansion.	de Paola, Tomie. *The Quicksand Book.* Gilchrist, Theo. *Halfway up the Mountain.*
Upper Elementary: Ages ten–twelve 1 Children use complex sentences with subordinate clauses of concession introduced by *nevertheless* and *in spite of.* Auxiliary verbs *might, could,* and *should* appear frequently.	1 Encourage oral language and written activities so children can use more complex sentence structures.	Anderson, Margaret. *In the Keep of Time.* Ellis, Mel. *The Wild Horse Killers.* Konigsburg, E. L. *Journey to an 800 Number.* L'Engle, Madeleine. *A Swiftly Tilting Planet.*

toys, and pictures of the living room after Santa leaves the toys encourage observation.

Both younger and older children may observe details in picture books. In *Lentil*, by Robert McCloskey, there are excellent drawings of a midwestern town in the early 1900s. The pictures include details associated with the town square, houses on the streets, the interior of the schoolhouse, the train depot, and a parade. This book contains single lines under each picture, but the details of the pictures illustrate the life-style and the emotions of the characters in the story.

The humorous illustrations for *Hilary Knight's The Twelve Days of Christmas* contain pages crowded with animals as a generous bear presents his true love with fiddling foxes, milking kittens, drumming rabbits, and dancing pigs. The final illustration showing the Christmas Fair stimulates considerable discussion. Older children enjoy searching for the art objects and literature characters in Mitsumasa Anno's *Anno's Italy*. Anno's detailed wordless books are excellent sources for developing observational skills.

Comparing. Picture books and other literature selections provide many opportunities for comparing. Young children,

for example, can compare the various attributes of the hats illustrated in Stan and Janice Berenstain's *Old Hat, New Hat*. The hats include ones that are heavy, light, loose, tight, flat, tall, big, small, shiny, frilly, fancy, silly, and lumpy. These new hats could also be compared with the old hat, still considered the best one of all. Wordless books are also excellent for comparisons. *Changes, Changes*, by Pat Hutchins, opens with a picture of two doll figures who have built a house from blocks. The book continues to illustrate their adventures: when the house catches on fire, they change the structure of the blocks to form a fire truck; the fire truck puts out the fire but causes an abundance of water; the dolls then change the blocks into a boat and sail safely to shore; on shore they build a truck and then a train; finally, they reach their preferred location and rebuild their house of blocks. Children could be asked to make comparisons and notice the changes in this book by first examining the pictures, deciding on what is being built and why, and then describing the changes that occur between pictures. Because there is one difference between the second house and the original, they can make a final comparison. Additional comparisons could be made as children build their own structures out of blocks and try to change the purpose of the structure by using only the original blocks.

Knight's active animals and considerable detail provide a rich source for observation and discussion.
Reprinted with permission of Macmillan Publishing Co., Inc. from *The Twelve Days of Christmas* illustrated by Hilary Knight. Copyright © 1981 by Hilary Knight.

Older children can also use pictures to compare. Peter Spier, in *Tin Lizzie*, using both words and illustrations, tells of a 1909 Model T touring car better known as a Tin Lizzie. The car is purchased new from a factory in Detroit and sent by rail to a small midwestern town. The Tin Lizzie progresses through several owners until it is finally found rusting in a modern-day farmyard. A businessman buys and restores the car to its original glory and then takes his family for rides through the city and countryside. This book shows the many changes that have taken place in the last seventy years, and children could make comparisons between the clothing, transportation, homes, towns, and streets shown in the different periods represented. The illustrations include advertisements such as a sandwich board showing a haircut for 10 cents, a sign on a building asking $400 for a High Wheel motor vehicle produced by W. H. McIntyre, and a sign in front of the Model T touring car stating a price of $850. Comparisons could be made between those prices and the current cost of similar goods and services.

Books written around the same setting, subject, or theme can also be compared. For example, Robert McCloskey's *Time of Wonder* and Golden MacDonald's *The Little Island* take place on islands. The islands could be compared and special attention given to the differences in the storm sequences illustrated and described in both books: a family experiences a hurricane in *Time of Wonder* and then explores the island to discover changes that have occurred following the storm; in *The Little Island*, the storm occurs on an isolated island. Another beach-related book, *Down to the Beach*, by May Garelick, illustrates only happy times. The experiences of characters in the other two island books can be compared with those developed in this nonthreatening environment.

Another excellent comparison activity may be encouraged as children read different editions of the same folktale. For example, they may compare the soft, glowing illustrations in Ilse Plume's version of *The Bremen Town Musicians* with Donna Diamond's black and white scenes in her book, *The Bremen Town Musicians: A Grimm's Fairy Tale*. They may consider their responses toward both the illustrations and the written text.

Upper elementary children can make comparisons between the main characters, their struggles for survival, and their growing up in such books as Scott O'Dell's *Island of the Blue Dolphins* and Armstrong Sperry's *Call It Courage*. They are especially good for comparisons; the main character is a girl in the first book and a boy in the other. Additional books describing special kinds of courage include Maia Wojciechowska's *Shadow of a Bull*, Jean George's *My Side of the Mountain*, and Elizabeth George Speare's *The Bronze Bow*.

Classifying. Children must be able to classify objects or ideas before they can see or understand the relationships between them. Concept books are useful because they introduce children to such things as color, shape, use, or size. Color concept books, for example, include those that develop color concepts at differing levels of abstractness. *My Very First Book of Colors*, by Eric Carle, allows children to match blocks of color with the color shown in the illustration. In Carle's *The Mixed-up Chameleon*, the chameleon wants to change his appearance so he can look like the other animals in the zoo. The eight basic colors, as well as simple addition and subtraction, are developed in Carle's *Let's Paint a Rainbow*. Roger Duvoisin's *See What I Am* is a more difficult color concept book that introduces the primary colors and then mixes them to produce the secondary colors. The artist also shows how colors are used to make color illustrations in picture books.

Size concepts are also found in books that range in difficulty level for the concept introduced. In Carle's *My Very First Book of Shapes*, children match black shapes with similar shapes in color; John Reiss's *Shapes* presents both the shapes and their names as well as their three-dimensional forms; and Tana Hoban's *Circles, Triangles, and Squares* illustrates shapes found in the children's environment. These include such objects as cookies, eyeglasses, and bubbles.

Many other books develop classification skills. For example, after listening to the folktale "The Three Bears," children classify the bears according to their size, then classify the porridge bowls, chairs, and beds, and finally, they can identify the character in the story who would use these items. (Flannelgraph characters and objects will make classification more concrete for young children.) Stories can be classified using categories such as animals, wild animals, pets; boy or girl as the main character; country or city setting. Characteristics of the story or characters can also be used for classification: realistic, unrealistic; likable, unlikable; happy, sad; funny, serious.

Hypothesizing. Helping children to hypothesize about the subject, plot, or characters in a story assists them in developing cognitive skills and also develops their interests, motivating them to read or listen to a selection. For example, children could look at the cover illustration of Russell Hoban's *Best Friends for Frances* and guess what they believe the book will be about. They could answer questions such as Who will be in the story? What do you think they will do? The sad faces on the cover of Hoban's *Nothing to Do* could also be used for considerable speculation about what is in the book. In this story, Father gives Walter a "something-to-do stone." Children can guess what he will do with the stone and can decide what they would do if they had a similar stone.

Older children also benefit from hypothesizing. Descriptive chapter titles are excellent sources for verbal or written speculations. For example, before reading or listening to Ann McGovern's *Runaway Slave: The Story of Harriet Tubman*, children can discuss the title and then guess what they think will appear in each of the following chapters: "Who Was Harriet Tubman?"; "At Miss Susan's"; "Follow the North Star"; "Trouble"; "I'm Going to Leave You"; "Harriet Tubman, Conductor"; "Nightime, Daytime"; "Go On—Or Die"; "A Sad Christmas"; and "The War Years." After each chapter is read, they can review the accuracy of their predictions to see if new information changes some of their ideas about what has not yet happened.

Organizing. Young children experience difficulty understanding time concepts, sequence of time, and when things happen. Illustrated books about the seasons or different times of the day allow children to consider what happens in their own environment. Robert Welber's *Song of the Seasons* could encourage discussion about the changes in a year.

Plot development in literature requires some form of logical organization. After children have listened to or read a literature selection, they interpret this organization and improve their ability to put ideas into sequential order when they retell a story or develop a creative drama. With their strong sequential plots, folktales are especially appropriate for developing organizational skills. "The Three Little Pigs," for example, develops a plot by progressing from the flimsiest building materials to the strongest. "The Little Red Hen" uses chronological order as the story progresses from the seed, to the planting, to the tilling, to the harvesting, to the baking, and finally to the eating. Several folktales organize plot according to size. In "The Three Billy Goats Gruff," the goats cross the bridge and confront the troll in a size ordering that goes from small, to medium, to large. The Yiddish folktale, "It Could Always Be Worse," is about the discontented owner of a small, crowded hut who takes his rabbi's advice and brings a series of larger and larger animals into his hut. When he finally clears out the animals, he appreciates his house.

Cumulative folktales are also excellent for reinforcing the organization of the plot, because they repeat the sequence each time a new experience is added to the story. In the Russian version of the "Gingerbread Man," a bun comes to life and successively outwits a series of animals until he is outwitted by the fox. "Henny Penny" has a series of animals who join Penny to inform the King that the sky is falling. The King in Maggie Duff's *Rum Pum Pum* steals Blackbird's wife and thus causes a series of animals to try to get even with him.

"Why" tales also frequently depict a series of events to explain something. For example, Verna Aardema's *Why Mosquitoes Buzz in People's Ears: A West African Tale* describes the sequence of events that prevented the owl from waking the sun and bringing in a new day.

These kinds of folktales make excellent selections for flannelboard stories. When children retell the stories using the flannelgraphs, they develop and reinforce organizational skills. These stories are excellent, too, for creative drama or for storytelling because both strengthen children's organizational abilities.

Summarizing. Summarizing skills can be developed with any genre of literature or literature from any level of difficulty. Summaries may follow after listening to or reading literature, and an oral or a written format may be used. Oral summaries may also motivate other children to read a selection. After a recreational reading period in the classroom, library, or home, members of the group can retell the story, the part of the story they liked best, the most important information learned, the funniest part of the story, the most exciting part, and the actions of the most or least admired character. Frequently, other children become interested in reading the same book.

Applying. Young children need many opportunities to apply the skills, concepts, information, or ideas they learn about in books. When they read concept books, for example, they should see and manipulate concrete examples, not merely look at pictures. Children who read Carle's *1, 2, 3 to the Zoo* or *My Very First Book of Numbers* can count and group objects. Manipulative experiences can also be used beyond the concept of one-to-one correspondence when children read books such as Giulio Maestro's *One More and One Less* or John Reiss's *Numbers*. The first book develops addition and subtraction concepts, while the second introduces the concept of grouping objects in sets of five or ten.

Pat Hutchins's wordless book *Changes, Changes*, previously discussed as a means to develop comparisons, also provides opportunities for application. Children can look at the colorful pictures and try to duplicate the structures of the house, fire truck, boat, truck, and train using their own blocks.

Information books also offer application opportunities. For example, middle and upper elementary students can apply the information found in Eve and Glenn Bunting's *Skateboards: How to Make Them, How to Ride Them* when they ride and repair their own skateboards; *Cactus in the Desert*, by Phyllis Busch, can be used by children as they try to grow their own cactus gardens; *Freshwater Fish and Fishing* by Jim Arnosky provides information on fishing as a sport; and Sam Savitt's

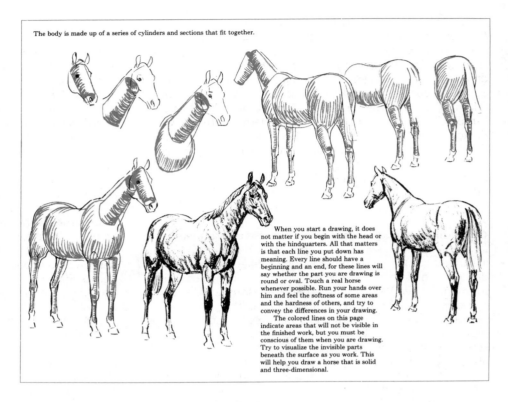

The body is made up of a series of cylinders and sections that fit together.

When you start a drawing, it does not matter if you begin with the head or with the hindquarters. All that matters is that each line you put down has meaning. Every line should have a beginning and an end, for these lines will say whether the part you are drawing is round or oval. Touch a real horse whenever possible. Run your hands over him and feel the softness of some areas and the hardness of others, and try to convey the differences in your drawing.

The colored lines on this page indicate areas that will not be visible in the finished work, but you must be conscious of them when you are drawing. Try to visualize the invisible parts beneath the surface as you work. This will help you draw a horse that is solid and three-dimensional.

The sequentially detailed illustrations encourage children to apply the artist's suggestions to their own drawings. From *Draw Horses with Sam Savitt* by Sam Savitt. Copyright © 1981 by Sam Savitt. Reprinted by permission of the author and Viking Penguin Inc.

Draw Horses with Sam Savitt provides detailed directions and drawings that help children draw horses standing or in motion. Numerous "how-to" books stimulate children's interests in hobbies, crafts, and sports.

Criticizing. Neither adults nor children should be required or encouraged to accept everything they hear or read without criticism. Children should be given many opportunities to evaluate critically what they read or listen to. Critical evaluation skills are developed when children sense the appropriateness, reliability, value, and authenticity of what they read. Historical fiction selections are excellent for investigating and discussing the authenticity of the characters, settings, and plots.

Research indicates that the level and type of questioning strategies used with children affect their levels of thinking and development of critical evaluative skills. Consequently, oral discussion skills and possible questioning strategies that will stimulate critical evaluation are discussed. Ways of developing these skills by using specific books are developed throughout this text.

Stages in Cognitive Development. Chart 1–2 suggests the characteristics in cognitive development associated with developmental stages, the educational implications of these characteristics, and several literature selections that may be used to stimulate children's development in those cognitive skills. The characteristics and implications in this chart were compiled from studies by Piaget (13) and from texts by Mussen, Conger, and Kagan (12) and Braga (4). (Ages are approximate and not absolute.)

Personality Development

Children go through many stages of personality development as they try to achieve the ability to express emotions acceptably, express empathy toward others, and develop feelings of self-worth and self-esteem. Young children experience difficulty understanding and expressing their emotions. Infants cry whenever they are unhappy, angry, or uncomfortable. Slowly, with guidance, children learn to handle their emotions productively rather than disruptively. Expanded experiences, adult and sibling models, and personal success show them other ways of dealing with emotions. Overcoming fears, developing trust, overcoming the desire to have only their own way, and developing acceptable interaction with both peers and adults inevitably involve traumatic experiences. Progressing through the stages of personality development is part of the maturing process; books can play a very important role in this development.

Bibliotherapy, an interaction between reader and literature in which the ideas inherent in the reading materials can have a therapeutic effect upon the reader, is frequently suggested as a means of helping children through various times of stress. Joanne Bernstein's *Books to Help Children Cope with Separation and Loss* (3), provides an introduction to bibliotherapy and annotated bibliographies of books in various areas of childhood adjustment such as hospitalization, loss of a friend, and parents' divorce. Rhea Joyce Rubin's *Using Bibliotherapy* (16) and the *Bibliotherapy Source Book* (15) discuss the theoretical and practical aspects of designing a program for using books in therapy. Although most of the emotional problems young children experience will not be as severe as coping with

CHART 1–2
Cognitive Development

Characteristics	Implications	Literature Suggestions
Preschool: Ages two–three		
1 Children learn new ways to organize and classify their worlds by putting together things that they perceive to be alike.	1 Provide opportunities for them to discuss and group things that are alike: color, shape, size, use. Use picture concept books with large, colorful pictures.	Ichikawa, Satomi. *Let's Play.*
2 They begin to remember two or three items.	2 Exercise children's short-term memories by providing opportunities to recall information.	Alexander, Martha. *Out! Out! Out!* Carroll, Ruth. *What Whiskers Did.*
Preschool: Ages three–four		
1 Children develop an understanding of how things relate to each other: how parts go together to make a whole, and how they are arranged in space in relation to each other.	1 Give children opportunities to find the correct part of a picture to match another picture. Simple picture puzzles may be used.	Hoban, Tana. *Look Again!* Hoban, Tana. *Take Another Look.* Hutchins, Pat. *Changes, Changes.*
2 They begin to understand relationships and classify things according to certain attributes that they share, such as color, size, shape, and what they are used for. These classifications are perceptual.	2 Share concept books on color, size, shape, and use. Provide opportunities for children to group and classify objects and pictures.	Carle, Eric. *My Very First Book of Colors.*
3 They begin to understand how objects relate to each other in terms of number and amount.	3 Give picture counting books to children. Allow them to count.	Carle, Eric. *My Very First Book of Numbers.* Hutchins, Pat. *I Hunter.*
4 Children begin to compare two things and tell which is bigger and which is smaller.	4 Share and discuss books that allow comparisons in size, such as a giant and a boy, a big item and a small item, or a series of animals.	Asbjornsen, P. C., and Moe, J. E. *The Three Billy Goats Gruff.*
Preschool: Ages four–five		
1 Children remember to do three things told to them or retell a short story if the material is presented in a meaningful sequence.	1 Tell short, meaningful stories and allow children to retell them; flannelboard and picture stories help them organize the story. Give them practice in following three-step directions.	Galdone, Paul. *The Gingerbread Boy.* Galdone, Paul. *What's in Fox's Sack? An Old English Tale.* Ginsburg, Mirra. *How the Sun Was Brought Back to the Sky.*

CHART 1–2 *(cont.)*
Cognitive Development

Characteristics	Implications	Literature Suggestions
2 They increase their ability to group objects according to important characteristics but still base their rules on how things look to them.	2 Provide many opportunities to share concept books and activities designed to develop ideas of shape, color, size, feel, and use.	Carle, Eric. *My Very First Book of Shapes.* Hoban, Tana. *Circles, Triangles, and Squares.* Hoban, Tana. *Is It Red? Is It Yellow? Is It Blue?* Welber, Robert. *Song of the Seasons.*
3 They pretend to tell time but do not understand the concept. Things happen "now" or "before now."	3 Share books to help them understand sequence of time and when things happen, such as the seasons of the year, and what happens during different times of the day or different days of the week.	

Preschool—Kindergarten: Ages five–six

Characteristics	Implications	Literature Suggestions
1 Children learn to follow one type of classification (e.g., color, shape) through to completion without changing the main characteristic partway through the task.	1 Continue to share concept books and encourage activities that allow children to group and classify.	Emberley, Ed. *Ed Emberley's ABC.* Lobel, Arnold. *On Market Street.*
2 They count to ten and discriminate ten objects.	2 Reinforce developing counting skills with counting books and other counting activities.	Carle, Eric. *My Very First Book of Numbers.* Carle, Eric. *1, 2, 3 to the Zoo.* Carle, Eric. *The Very Fussy Monkey.* Knight, Hilary. *Hilary Knight's The Twelve Days of Christmas.*
3 They identify primary colors.	3 Reinforce color identification through the use of color concept books and by discussing colors found in other picture books.	Carle, Eric. *Let's Paint a Rainbow.* Hutchins, Pat. *Changes, Changes.*
4 They learn to distinguish between "a lot of" something or "a little of" something.	4 Provide opportunities for children to identify and discuss the differences between these concepts.	Gág, Wanda. *Millions of Cats.* Zemach, Margot. *It Could Always Be Worse.*
5 Children require trial and error before they can arrange things in order from smallest to biggest.	5 Share books that progress from smallest to largest. Have children retell stories using flannelboard characters drawn in appropriate sizes.	Galdone, Paul. *The Three Billy Goats Gruff.* Zemach, Margot. *It Could Always Be Worse.*
6 They still have vague concepts of time.	6 Share books to help them understand time sequence.	Clifton, Lucille. *Everett Anderson's Year.*

Early Elementary: Ages six–eight

Characteristics	Implications	Literature Suggestions
1 Children are learning to read; they enjoy reading easy books and demonstrating their new abilities.	1 Provide easy-to-read books geared to children's developing reading skills.	Griffith, Helen. *Alex and the Cat.* Kraus, Robert. *Leo the Late Bloomer.* Lobel, Arnold. *Frog and Toad All Year.* Lobel, Arnold. *Uncle Elephant.* Seuss, Dr. *The Cat in the Hat.*
2 They are learning to write and enjoy creating their own stories.	2 Allow children to write, illustrate, and share their own picture books. Wordless books can be used to suggest plot.	de Paola, Tomie. *The Hunter and the Animals: A Wordless Picture Book.* Goodall, John. *The Ballooning Adventures of Paddy Pork.* Waber, Bernard. *The Snake: A Very Long Story.*
3 The attention span is increasing and children enjoy longer stories than they did when they were five.	3 They enjoy listening to longer story books. They are starting to enjoy longer stories if the chapters can be completed each story time.	Grahame, Kenneth. *Wayfarers All: From the Wind in the Willows.* Hague, Kathleen. *The Man Who Kept House.* Oakley, Graham. *The Church Mouse.* Oakley, Graham. *Hetty and Harriet.*

CHART 1–2 *(cont.)*
Cognitive Development

Characteristics	Implications	Literature Suggestions
4 Children under seven still base their rules on immediate perception and learn through real situations.	4 Provide experiences which allow them to see, discuss, and verify information and relationships.	Duvoisin, Roger. *See What I Am.* Maestro, Giulio. *One More and One Less.* Reiss, John J. *Shapes.* Simon, Seymour. *Animal Fact/Animal Fable.*
5 Sometime during this age they pass into the stage Piaget refers to as concrete operational.	5 Children have developed a new set of rules called groupings. They don't have to see all objects to group; they can understand relationships among categories.	Anno, Mitsumasa. *Anno's Counting Book.* Feelings, Muriel. *Moja Means One: Swahili Counting Book.*
Middle Elementary: Ages eight–ten 1 Reading skills improve rapidly, although there are wide variations in reading ability among children within the same age group.	1 Children enjoy independent reading. Provide books for appropriate reading levels. Allow them opportunities to share experiences with books with peers, parents, teachers, and other adults.	Blume, Judy. *Tales of a Fourth Grade Nothing.* Cleary, Beverly. *Ramona and Her Father.* Cleary, Beverly. *Ramona Quimby, Age 8.* Wilder, Laura Ingalls. *Little House in the Big Woods.*
2 The interest level of literature may still be above the reading level for many children.	2 Children need a daily time during which they can listen to a variety of books being read aloud.	Arkhurst, Joyce Cooper. *The Adventures of Spider.* King-Smith, Dick. *Pigs Might Fly.* Lewis, C. S. *The Lion, the Witch and the Wardrobe.* White, E. B. *Charlotte's Web.* White, E. B. *Stuart Little.*
3 Memory improves as they learn to attend to certain stimuli and to ignore others.	3 Help children set purposes for listening or reading before the actual literature experience.	Dallinger, Jane. *Grasshoppers.* Nance, John. *Lobo of the Tasaday.* Scott, Jack Denton. *The Book of the Pig.* Selsam, Millicent. *Tyrannosaurus Rex.*
Upper Elementary: Ages ten–twelve 1 Children develop an understanding of the chronological ordering of past events.	1 Historic fiction and books showing historic changes helps them understand differing viewpoints and historical perspective.	Bess, Clayton. *Story for a Black Night.* British Museum of Natural History. *Man's Place in Evolution.* Forbes, Esther. *Johnny Tremain.* Hickman, Janet. *The Valley of the Shadow.* Sutcliff, Rosemary. *Sun Horse, Moon Horse.*
2 They apply logical rules, reasoning, and formal operations to abstract problems and propositions.	2 Use questioning and discussion strategies designed to develop higher level thought processes. Children enjoy more complex books.	Alexander, Lloyd. *Westmark.* Hall, Lynn. *Danza!* Raskin, Ellen. *The Westing Game.* Schlee, Ann. *Ask Me No Questions.*

loss and separation, there are numerous adjustments they must face.

According to Rosalind Engle (8), "Image readiness begins at birth and involves all the actions and interactions between children and the members of their environment. Literature becomes an influence in the child's life as soon as others are willing to share it and the child responds" (p. 892). It can be used to help children understand their feelings, identify with characters who experience similar feelings, and gain new insights into how others have coped with those same problems. Joan Glazer (10) identifies four ways in which literature contributes to emotional growth. First, it shows children that many of their feelings are also common to other children and that they are both normal and natural. Second, literature explores the feeling from several viewpoints, giving a fuller picture and providing the basis for naming that emotion. Third, actions of various characters show options for ways to deal with particular emotions. Fourth, it makes clear that one person experiences many emotions, and that these sometimes conflict.

Characters in literature experience emotions similar to those felt by most children. For example, jealousy is a common occurrence when a new baby comes into the home. Books about new babies can help children express their fears and realize their parents still love them—that it is not unusual to feel fearful about a new relationship. Ezra Jack Keats's *Peter's Chair* shows how one child handles these feelings when he not only gets an unwanted baby sister but also sees his own furniture painted pink for the new arrival. Overcoming feelings of jealousy can also be a theme in stories about animals. In Jenny Wagner's *John Brown, Rose and the Midnight Cat,* the dog fears that a cat coming into his home will disturb his very comfortable life with a nice widow.

Fear is another emotion found both in real life and in books, and overcoming it is a common theme in children's books. Many children fear going to school for the first time or moving

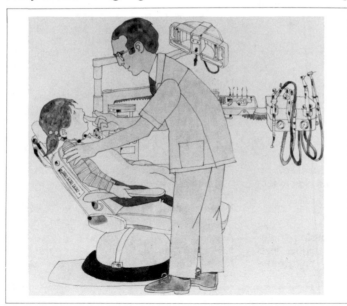

Illustrations of realistic situations provide a preview of a visit to a dentist; children's fears might be reduced through discussion. Illustration (my dentist wiggles my loose tooth) in *My Dentist* by Harlow Rockwell. Copyright © 1975 by Harlow Rockwell. By permission of Greenwillow Books (A Division of William Morrow & Company.)

into a new school or neighborhood. Eric Carle's *Do You Want to Be My Friend?,* Miriam Cohen's *Will I Have a Friend?,* and Rosemary Wells's *Timothy Goes to School* have heroes who successfully cope with this problem. Other fears can occur when children must experience unknown situations; books may help them anticipate what it will be like to go to the doctor or dentist or to take a trip. Harlow Rockwell has written and illustrated two books to help answer young children's questions about physical checkups. *My Doctor* describes a visit to a pediatrician and includes a description of the equipment that will be used. In a similar way, *My Dentist* shows through pictures and text what happens when children get their teeth cleaned. Older children have many of their questions answered in James Howe's *The Hospital Book.* Barbara Greenberg's *The Bravest Babysitter* illustrates the common childhood fears of thunder and storms and turns the normal situation around when the babysitter becomes frightened during a thunderstorm; it is the younger child who tries to distract the fearful older one. In Robert McCloskey's *Time of Wonder,* a family copes with a hurricane while living in a summer cottage on the coast.

Even a short separation from a parent may be the most feared experience of all. Patricia MacLachlan's *Mama One, Mama Two* suggests the warm, loving relationship that can develop between a foster mother and a child. The author uses a shared story to allow readers to understand the love for both parents.

Children must learn to deal with emotions such as anger and must understand and use other ways to handle such feelings. Literature again provides many examples of how to handle problems. Books can act as a stimulus for discussing how children handled or could have handled similar situations. Young children, for example, can certainly identify with Judith Viorst's Alexander in *Alexander and the Terrible, Horrible, No Good, Very Bad Day* or with Patricia Giff's Ronald in *Today was a Terrible Day.* Many children have days when absolutely nothing goes right. *The Quarreling Book* by Charlotte Zolotow develops a similar theme: the day starts out all wrong because Father forgets to kiss Mother. The consequences of this act are a series of quarrels that continue until a dog finally breaks the cycle. Edna Mitchell Preston and Rainey Bennett's *The Temper Tantrum Book* shows that even animals can have tantrums when they have experiences similar to those of young children. The animals explain what makes them angry. The book can prompt children to share what makes them angry and how they deal with this problem. Teasing may cause crying or other emotions. Several books develop this theme and describe how children react to, and overcome, this situation. Jim is *The*

Smallest Boy in the Class in Jerrold Beim's book. He misbehaves when he is teased and called "Tiny." An understanding teacher helps him overcome the problem, develop his own feelings of self-worth, and improve his behavior. Animals in children's books have similar problems when it comes to size. In Robert Kraus's *The Littlest Rabbit,* bullies tease the rabbit.

In addition to the ability to handle their emotions, children must have positive and realistic self-concepts and feelings of self-esteem; their self-concepts are what they believe they are. Infants do not think of themselves as individuals. Slowly, children realize that they have an identity separate from other members of the family, and between the ages of two and three, they develop this concept. By the age of three, with the assistance of a warm, loving environment, most have developed a set of feelings about themselves; they consider themselves "I." Egocentric feelings continue for several years, and children consider that they are the center of their universe. If the development of self-esteem is to progress positively, they need to know that their families, friends, and the larger society value them. All children must feel pride in their accomplishments and cultural heritage and must develop positive sex-role identifications. Those who have developed positive feelings of self-worth will be able to assume personal responsibility for their own successes and failures. Aliki Brandenberg's *The Two of Them,* for example, develops a strong relationship between a girl and her grandfather; this relationship helps her accept his eventual death and be responsible for an orchard they both loved.

Literature can play a dramatic role in developing self-concept and feelings of self-worth. Young children can discover the capabilities that they have; they also realize that acquiring some skills takes considerable time. For example, Peter, in Ezra Jack Keats's *Whistle for Willie,* tries and tries to whistle. After considerable practice, he finally learns this skill. Books such as Jean Holzenthaler's *My Hands Can* and Ann and Paul Rand's *I Know a Lot of Things* help young children develop the realization that they can do many things. Positive attitudes toward one's heritage can be reinforced through reading and doing things that their cultural group favors and that show the many positive contributions of the people who belong to it. (This is especially important for ethnic minority groups, and chapter eleven discusses these implications.) If selected carefully, books provide excellent self-role models and illustrate that both males and females can function successfully in many different roles. (This is a topic that chapter nine covers in detail.)

Several excellent books for older children are based on the themes of overcoming problems and developing full maturity.

Text and illustrations convey the love expressed between a child and a foster parent.
Specified illustration from *Mama One, Mama Two* by Patricia MacLachlan. Pictures by Ruth Lercher Bornstein. Illustrations copyright © 1982 by Ruth Lercher Bornstein.

Scott O'Dell's *Island of the Blue Dolphins* is about a girl who survives alone on an island off the coast of California. She is not rescued for eighteen years and must overcome loneliness, develop weapons that violate a taboo of her society, and create a life for herself. Another survival book is *Call It Courage,* by Armstrong Sperry. In this story, Mafatu must overcome his fear of the sea before he can return home.

Feelings of self-worth may also be influenced by levels of reading achievement. Alexander and Filler (1) reviewed the research in the area of reading achievement and self-concept development and they concluded that "(1) A low self-concept may be caused by the child's poor evaluation of his reading performance or by evaluations of those individuals whom he likes, such as parents, peers, and/or teachers. (2) A learner who feels that he may not be successful in the eyes of individuals important to him may attempt to avoid the reading act. He may use such avoidance behaviors as disinterest in or hatred of reading, apparent lack of effort, or refusal to read. (3) The learner may reinforce his own self-concept. If he believes he

Text and illustrations develop a close relationship between a child and her grandfather.
From *The Two of Them* by Aliki Brandenberg. Copyright © 1979 by Aliki Brandenberg. By permission of Greenwillow Books (A Division of William Morrow & Co.).

will not succeed in reading because of some previous experience, he actually may not succeed. (4) Because of his self-concept, the reader may become progressively better or poorer with reading. Success generally leads to greater effort; failure tends to cause less effort, which results in progressively poorer performance as the learner advances in school" (pp. 6–7).

Children's personality development is extremely important. If they do not understand themselves and believe that they are important, how can they value anyone else? Many literary selections and literature-related experiences developed throughout this text will reinforce positive personality development through such experiences as reading orally in a warm and secure environment, discussing and acting out various roles from literature, enhancing self-worth by learning new skills

through literature, increasing knowledge of cultural contributions, and enjoying a wide variety of reading.

Chart 1–3 lists the characteristics of personality development associated with developmental stages, the educational implications of these characteristics, and literature selections that may be used to stimulate children's personality development. The characteristics and implications in this chart were compiled from texts by Mussen, Conger, and Kagan (12) and Sarafino and Armstrong (17).

Social Development

According to child development authorities, the term *socialization* refers to the process by which children acquire behavior, beliefs, standards, and motives valued by their families and their cultural groups. Socialization is said to occur when children learn the ways of their groups so that they can function acceptably within them. They must learn to exert control over aggressive and hostile behavior if they are to have acceptable relationships with family members, friends, and the larger world community. These acceptable relationships require that children develop an understanding of the feelings and viewpoints of others.

Quite obviously, socialization is a very important part of child development. Understanding the processes that influence social development is essential for anyone who works with children. Three processes have been identified as being the most influential for socialization. First, there is the process of reward and punishment. Parents or other adults reward behavior they wish to strengthen and punish responses they wish to eliminate or reduce. For example, refusing to share a toy with another child may lead to punishment; the offender is not allowed to play with a favorite toy. In contrast, appropriate sharing behavior may be rewarded with a hug and a favorable comment. Second, children acquire many of their responses, behaviors, and beliefs by observing others. They imitate the behavior or other responses of adults or peers. During this observation, children also learn about other appropriate behavior within the culture. For example, a girl may observe that her mother has a certain role in the family and try to copy her. She is learning about sex-role behavior within her culture. Children also observe what other members of the family fear and how members of their group react to people who belong to different racial or cultural groups. The third process, identification, may be the most important for socialization. Identification requires emotional ties with the model; children believe they are like these models and their thoughts, feelings, and characteristics become similar to them.

Preschool children start to develop concepts of right or wrong when they identify with their parents and with parental values, attitudes, and standards of conduct. The two-year-old

CHART 1–3
Personality Development

Characteristics	Implications	Literature Suggestions
Preschool: Ages two–three		
1 Children begin to think that they have their own identity separate from other members of the family.	1 Help children understand that they are people who have their own identity and their own worth.	Holzenthaler, Jean. *My Hands Can.* Wolde, Gunilla. *This is Betsy.*
2 They feel the need for security.	2 Holding a child during lap reading can add to a sense of security and enjoyment of books.	Burningham, John. *The Snow.* Lindgren, Barbro. *The Wild Baby.* Zemach, Margot. *Hush Little Baby.*
Preschool: Ages three–four		
1 Children have developed a fairly steady self-concept; they identify themselves as "I" and have a set of feelings about themselves.	1 Children's self-concepts are affected by attitudes and behavior of those around them; they must feel that others care about them, accept them, and think they are worthy.	Iwasaki, Chihiro. *What's Fun Without a Friend?* Jonas, Ann. *When You Were A Baby.* Krauss, Ruth. *The Carrot Seed.* Rand, Ann, and Rand, Paul. *I Know A Lot of Things.* Williams, Barbara. *Someday, Said Mitchell.*
2 Children require warm and secure environments.	2 Share books with children in a warm atmosphere in classrooms, libraries, or at home.	Adoff, Arnold. *Black Is Warm Is Tan.* Dabcovich, Lydia. *Sleepy Bear.* Hill, Eric. *Spot's Birthday Party.* Rice, Eve. *Benny Bakes a Cake.* Sharmat, Marjorie. *A Big Fat Enormous Lie.*
3 Children hide from unhappy situations by withdrawing, suggesting that problems don't exist, or by blaming someone else.	3 Special guidance should help children accept mistakes without decreasing their feelings of self-worth.	
4 They begin to become aware of their cultural heritage.	4 They need to be proud of who they are. Provide literature to stress cultural contributions and the contributions of the home and neighborhood.	Adoff, Arnold. *Black Is Warm Is Tan.* Clark, Ann Nolan. *Along Sandy Trails.*
Preschool: Ages four–five		
1 They continue to be egocentric; they talk in first person and consider themselves the center of the world.	1 Present literature in which they can identify with the character and the story.	Pearson, Susan. *Izzie.* Sonneborn, Ruth. *I Love Gram.*
2 They improve in their ability to handle their own emotions in productive ways.	2 Help children identify other ways to handle problems. Use literature to help them see how others handle their emotions.	Keats, Ezra Jack. *Peter's Chair.* Keats, Ezra Jack. *Regards to the Man in the Moon.* Viorst, Judith. *Alexander and the Terrible, Horrible, No Good, Very Bad Day.* Wagner, Jenny. *John Brown, Rose and the Midnight Cat.*
3 Fears of unknown situations may cause children to lose confidence and to lose control of their emotions.	3 Help children understand what is new to them and help them feel comfortable with their ability to handle unknown situations. Read about and discuss new situations.	Carle, Eric. *Do You Want to Be My Friend?* Rockwell, Harlow. *My Dentist.* Rockwell, Harlow. *My Doctor.*
4 They begin to respond to intrinsic motivation.	4 Children require good models for intrinsic motivation. Books are sources of models.	Wahl, Jan. *Jamie's Tiger.* Williams, Barbara. *Chester Chipmunk's Thanksgiving.*
5 Children require warm and secure environments.	5 Continue reading to children in a loving atmosphere.	Buckley, Helen. *Grandfather and I.* Buckley, Helen. *Grandmother and I.* Gammell, Stephen. *Wake Up, Bear ... It's Christmas!*

CHART 1–3 *(cont.)*
Personality Development

Characteristics	Implications	Literature Suggestions
Preschool—Kindergarten: Ages five–six		
1 Five-year-olds are usually outgoing, sociable, and friendly.	1 They enjoy stories showing similar characteristics in the main characters.	Hoffman, Phyllis. *Steffie and Me.* Marshall, James. *George and Martha One Fine Day.* Small, David. *Eulalie and the Hopping Head.*
2 Children are quite stable and adjusted in their emotional life; they are developing self-assurance and confidence in others.	2 These characteristics should be encouraged. Opportunities should allow children to expand self-assurance—it is closely related to self-worth.	Brandenberg, Aliki. *The Two of Them.* Lexau, Joan. *Benjie on His Own.* Ormerod, Jan. *Sunshine.*
3 They require warmth and security in adult relationships even though self-assurance increases.	3 Continue to provide warm relationships through a close association during story time.	Brown, Margaret Wise. *The Runaway Bunny.* Murphy, Jill. *Peace at Last.* Zolotow, Charlotte. *My Grandson Lew.*
Early Elementary: Ages six–eight		
1 Six-year-olds are not as emotionally stable as five-year-olds; they show more tension, may strike out against a teacher or parent.	1 Help children discover acceptable ways to handle their tensions. Read stories to illustrate how other children handle their tensions.	Ehrlich, Amy. *Leo, Zack, and Emmie.* Preston, Edna Mitchell. *The Temper Tantrum Book.* Sharmat, Marjorie. *Gladys Told Me to Meet Her Here.*
2 Children seek independence from adults but continue to require warmth and security from the adults in their lives.	2 Provide opportunities for them to demonstrate independence; allow them to choose books and activities for sharing. Supply books in which characters develop independence.	Cleary, Beverly. *Ramona Quimby, Age 8.* Greene, Carol. *Hinny Winny Bunco.* Jewell, Nancy. *Bus Ride.* Schulman, Janet. *Jenny and the Tennis Nut.*
Middle Elementary: Ages eight–ten		
1 The personality characteristic of cooperation is highly valued by fourth graders but declines in later grades.	1 Encourage literature activities that allow for cooperation; provide books stressing cooperation as the theme.	Goffstein, M. B. *Family Scrapbook.*
2 Children have fewer fears about immediate and possible dangers but may have strong fears about remote or impossible situations, such as ghosts, lions, and witches.	2 Literature selections describing children's fears may be used for discussion and developing understanding of unrealistic fears.	Johnston, Tony. *Four Scary Stories.* Terris, Susan. *No Boys Allowed.*
Upper Elementary: Ages ten–twelve		
1 Many children have internalized their control; they believe that they are in control of what happens and assume more personal responsibility for successes and failures.	1 Reinforce responsibility, organizing, and making decisions. Provide books that illustrate the development of internalized control.	Blume, Judy. *It's Not the End of the World.* Lowry, Lois. *Anastasia Again!* Salassi, Otto R. *On the Ropes.*
2 Independence is a valued personality trait.	2 Supply literature to illustrate developing independence for both male and female characters.	Corcoran, Barbara. *The Trick of Light.* O'Dell, Scott. *Island of the Blue Dolphins.* Park, Ruth. *Playing Beatie Bow.* Sperry, Armstrong. *Call It Courage.*
3 Rapid changes in physical growth may cause some children to become self-conscious and self-critical; others may be preoccupied with their appearance.	3 Stories of other children who experience problems growing up may be especially appealing during this time.	Blume, Judy. *Are You There God? It's Me, Margaret.* Cleaver, Vera, and Cleaver, Bill. *Me Too.*

knows certain acts are wrong. According to Piaget (13), children younger than seven or eight have rigid and inflexible ideas of right and wrong that they learn from their parents. Piaget suggests that between the ages of eight and eleven considerable changes occur in children's moral development. They start to develop a sense of equality and to take into account the situation in which the wrong action occurs. Children become more flexible and realize that there are exceptions to their original strict rules of behavior; at this time, the peer group begins to influence their conduct.

Children's first relationships are usually within the immediate family; next they extend to a few friends, then to school, and finally to the broader world of the adult. Literature and literature-related activities can aid in the development of these relationships by encouraging children to become sensitive to the feelings of others. For example, Ann Herbert Scott's *Sam* is very unhappy when the members of his family are too busy to play with him. When they realize what is wrong, members of Sam's family remember to include him in their activities. The four-year-old in Eve Rice's *Benny Bakes a Cake* helps his mother in the kitchen but faces disappointment when his dog eats the cake. Overcoming problems related to sibling rivalry is a frequent theme in children's books and is one that children can understand. In Charlotte Zolotow's *Big Brother,* a little sister is constantly teased by her older brother. *Stevie,* by John Steptoe, tells of Robert's reactions when his mother takes care of a young child; Robert is upset when Stevie plays with his things but discovers that he actually misses Stevie when he leaves. The frustration and satisfaction experienced by the smallest child in the family is described in Clyde Bulla's *Keep Running, Allen!* When Allen has difficulty keeping up with his older brothers and sisters, he discovers the pleasure of observing nature. He feels even greater enjoyment when older siblings join in his nature explorations.

Children may empathize with Benny when he experiences a series of emotions, including elation, disappointment, and renewed happiness.
From *Benny Bakes a Cake* by Eve Rice. Copyright © 1981 by Eve Rice. By permission of Greenwillow Books (A Division of William Morrow & Co.).

Many books for preschool and early primary children deal with various emotions related to friendship. Satomi Ichikawa's *Let's Play* illustrates children playing together in a variety of settings. Best friends may have strong attachments for each other as shown in Miriam Cohen's *Best Friends* and Russell Hoban's *Best Friends for Frances*. In contrast, they may also experience problems as Crosby Bonsall demonstrates in *It's Mine!—A Greedy Book*. In this book, best friends quarrel when one of them wants to play with the other's toys. Many emotions related to friendship are developed in Marjorie Sharmat's *Gladys Told Me to Meet Her Here*. When Irving's friend is late for a day at the zoo, he feels disappointment, worry, and finally anger.

Social development includes becoming aware of and understanding the different roles played by people. One of the greatest contributions made by literature and literature-related discussions is the realization that both boys and girls can achieve in a wide range of roles. Books that emphasize nonstereotyped sex roles and achievement are excellent models and stimuli for discussion. For example, Margery Facklam's *Wild Animals, Gentle Women* includes information on the lives and contributions of eleven women who have studied animal behavior. The author also shows how a student can prepare for this profession. The autobiography by Phyllis Reynolds Naylor, *How I Came to Be a Writer*, describes how the author became a professional writer. An unusual book that tells the story of a role uncommon to women is Patricia Clapp's *I'm Deborah Sampson: A Soldier in the War of the Revolution:* Deborah disguises herself as a man in order to fight. Books are also being written that stress the nonstereotyping of emotions. Charlotte Zolotow's *William's Doll,* a book for young children,

Learning to play with other children is important for social development. Illustration from *Let's Play* by Satomi Ichikawa reprinted by permission of Philomel Books, a division of The Putnam Publishing Group. *Let's Play,* copyright © 1981 by Satomi Ichikawa.

Are Children's Picture Books Transmitting Images That Will Foster Children's Social Development?

THIS TEXTBOOK AND texts by Huck and Cullinan suggest that young children's literature appreciation and social development can be fostered through a careful selection of picture storybooks that encourage children to become sensitive to the feelings of others, to be aware and understand the various roles played by people, and to be aware and understand differing viewpoints and attitudes. Social science educator Joe Hurst, however, is very critical of the social images portrayed in many children's picture books.[1]

Hurst analyzed the participatory images found in Caldecott Medal winners published between 1958 and 1978 and in an equal number of non-award winning picture books published during the same time period. In the area of participatory behavior Hurst concluded: "The picture books sampled provide a bland, passive view of life. Their illustrations, quoted dialogue, and author narratives present no role models of democratic participation or participatory

behaviors. All the characters are portrayed in situations where few important decisions are made and where active participation is unnecessary" (p. 139).

Hurst's conclusions and recommendations are critical. His main concern deals with decision making, active participation in the plots, and social issues. He recommends that children, teachers, and parents apply criteria relative to active, participatory role models and unprejudicial treatment of groups; librarians order, display, and encourage children to read books related to active participation; and publishers make an effort toward producing books that present a more realistic, active, unbiased view of America and the world. Hurst does not consider literary quality, integration of illustration and text, or enhancement of children's enjoyment in the literature analyzed. When educators and parents are choosing picture books to share with young children, these issues related to social development will need to be considered.

1 Hurst, Joe B. "Images in Children's Picture Books." *Social Education* (February 1981): 138-43.

relates a young boy's experiences when he wants a doll. His brother and neighbor consider him a sissy; his father buys him masculine toys. It is his grandmother, however, who explains that it is perfectly all right for boys to have dolls.

An important part of socialization is to become aware of different views, and literature is an excellent way of accomplishing this. They may sympathize with the native American girl who loves her family but longs for a free life among the wild horses in *The Girl Who Loved Wild Horses* by Paul Goble. Children may also understand the slave's viewpoint and the consequences of prejudice when they read F. N. Monjo's *The Drinking Gourd.* Likewise, older children discover the consequences of prejudice when they read Mildred Taylor's *Let the*

Circle Be Unbroken. Contemporary realistic fiction shows many differing viewpoints developed in books such as Judy Blume's *It's Not the End of the World* in which Karen faces the problem of divorcing parents. At first she is very upset and tries to get them back together but finally realizes that, while it is actually happening, her world will not end because her parents still love her. *The Saving of P.S.,* by Robbie Branscum, a very popular book with older elementary students, tells the story of a girl who doesn't seem to fit in with her family. She is a "sinner" in the family of a preacher. Ecological viewpoints are developed in several books. Mel Ellis's *The Wild Horse Killers* describes the hazards faced by a teenager when she leads a herd of wild horses across mountains and deserts in order to

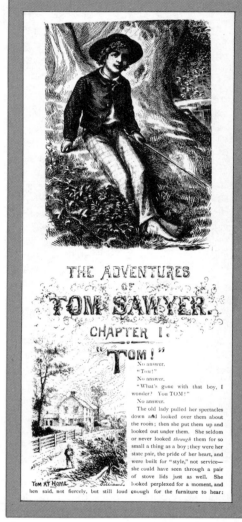

THE *ADVENTURES OF TOM SAWYER* BY MARK TWAIN (Samuel Clemens) is considered one of the first adventure stories that is American in tone. In *The Adventures of Tom Sawyer* and the *Adventures of Huckleberry Finn*, Mark Twain captured the human, cultural, and geographical influences that affect a boy's life. The author wrote from his own experiences living in the river town of Hannibal, Missouri in the 1800s. Here is an environment in which boys can explore the countryside, swim in the river, fish in a leisurely flowing stream, and plan all types of mischief. In Twain's books, there is not only the leisurely, adventurous life of childhood, there is also Tom's discoveries about himself and those around him. There is the horror of a churchyard murder that is accidentally witnessed by Tom Sawyer and Huckleberry Finn. There is racial bias expressed by some characters toward minorities. The characters express both the best and worst of human qualities.

Twain's books became popular reading with children who wanted to read adventures about real people in real locations. The popularity of the American adventure story set in a definite region may be seen by listing a few of the books written by Twain's contemporaries. Thomas Aldrich, in *The Story of a Bad Boy*, places his characters in a New England town. Noah Brooks's *The Boy Emigrants* is set in the Great Plains. Kate Douglas Wiggin's *Rebecca of Sunnybrook Farm* has a Maine setting.

save them from slaughter. Conflicts over pollution are the central theme of Jean Craighead George's *Who Really Killed Cock Robin?* in which a scientific investigation results when a robin, a symbol for a pollution-free city, dies. Chapter nine, "Contemporary Realistic Fiction" and chapter eleven, "Multiethnic Literature" present these and other selections; they also develop suggestions for children's interaction with this literature.

Chart 1– 4 lists social development characteristics associated with developmental stages, the educational implications of these characteristics, and literature possibilities that may be used to foster children's social development. The characteristics and implications in this chart were compiled from studies by Piaget (13) and texts by Mussen, Conger, and Kagan (12) and Braga (4).

CHART 1—4
Social Development

Characteristics	Implications	Literature Suggestions
Preschool: Ages two–three		
1 Children learn to organize and represent their world; they imitate actions and behaviors they have observed.	1 Encourage children to role play so they can begin to take others' points of view and learn about behavior.	Carle, Eric. *The Mixed-up Chameleon.* Kraus, Robert. *The Littlest Rabbit.* Oxenbury, Helen. *Family.*
2 They transform things into make-believe: a yard-long ruler may be a horse.	2 Provide objects and books that suggest creative interpretations.	Ayal, Ora. *Ugbu.* Hutchins, Pat. *Changes, Changes.* Lionni, Leo. *Let's Make Rabbits.*
Preschool: Ages three–four		
1 They begin to realize that other people have feelings just as they do.	1 Encourage children to talk about how they felt when something similar happened to them; provide books that show feelings.	Alexander, Martha. *Nobody Asked Me If I Wanted a Baby Sister.* Keats, Ezra Jack. *Peter's Chair.*
2 Children enjoy playing together and develop strong attachments to other children.	2 Encourage growing social skills of sharing, taking turns, and playing cooperatively.	Cohen, Miriam. *Best Friends.* Hoban, Russell. *Best Friends for Frances.* Ichikawa, Satomi. *Let's Play.*
3 They begin to enjoy participating in group activities and group games.	3 Let children be both leaders and followers during group activities after reading a book.	Bulla, Clyde. *Keep Running, Allen!* Scott, Ann Herbert. *Sam.*
4 They begin to identify others' feelings by observing facial expressions.	4 Encourage them to become sensitive to their own and others' feelings by talking about feelings that accompany different facial expressions in books.	Berger, Terry. *I Have Feelings.* Bonsall, Crosby. *It's Mine!—A Greedy Book.* Hoban, Russell. *The Little Brute Family.*
Preschool: Ages four–five		
1 Children start to avoid aggression when angry and to look for a compromise. They are, however, frequently bossy, assertive, and prone to using alibis.	1 Praise children for talking out anger, help them to calm down and talk about the situation, direct them toward finding solutions. Choose books in which aggression is avoided.	Viorst, Judith. *I'll Fix Anthony.* Zolotow, Charlotte. *The Quarreling Book.*
2 They begin to understand consequences of good and bad and may engage in unacceptable behavior to elicit reactions.	2 Explain actions in their terms. Let children discuss alternative actions.	Beim, Jerrold. *The Smallest Boy in the Class.* Galdone, Paul. *The Little Red Hen.*
3 Children seldom play alone but begin to work by themselves.	3 Encourage persistence; let them work at something until it is completed to their satisfaction. This is crucial for problem solving and self-directed learning.	Burton, Virginia Lee. *Mike Mulligan and His Steam Shovel.*
4 They increase their awareness of the different roles people play—nurse, police officer, grocery clerk, man, woman, etc.	4 Provide opportunities to meet different kinds of people through real life and books; encourage dramatic play around different roles.	Klein, Norma. *Girls Can Be Anything.* Rockwell, Harlow. *My Doctor.* Zolotow, Charlotte. *William's Doll.*
5 They may exhibit unreasonable fears such as fear of the dark, thunder, animals, etc.	5 Help children overcome fears by sharing experiences of others who had fears but overcame them.	Greenberg, Barbara. *The Bravest Babysitter.*
Preschool—Kindergarten: Ages five–six		
1 Children like to help parents around the house; they are developing dependable behavior.	1 Allow children to be responsible for jobs that they can realistically complete. Read stories about children helping.	Rice, Eve. *Benny Bakes a Cake.* Rylant, Cynthia. *When I Was Young in the Mountains.*

CHART 1—4 *(cont.)*
Social Development

Characteristics	Implications	Literature Suggestions
2 They protect younger brothers and sisters and other children.	2 Let them help and read to younger children, encourage them to become aware that they are growing into independent people. Share reasons why all people need security.	Kepes, Juliet. *Cock-a-Doodle-Doo.* Lisker, Sonia O. *Lost.*
3 They are proud of their accomplishments; they take pride in going to school and in their possessions.	3 Encourage a feeling of self-worth: praise accomplishments, encourage children to share school and home experiences, and allow them to talk about their possessions.	Fassler, Joan. *Howie Helps Himself.* Felt, Sue. *Rosa-Too-Little.* Udry, Janice. *What Mary Jo Shared.*
4 They continue to show anxiety and unreasonable fear.	4 Help children overcome their fears and anxieties; stress that these are normal.	Buckley, Helen. *Michael Is Brave.* Waber, Bernard. *Ira Sleeps Over.* Wells, Rosemary. *Timothy Goes to School.*
5 Children enjoy playing outside on their favorite toys: tricycles and sleds.	5 Provide opportunities for play, discussions about play, reading and drawing about outside play, and dictating stories about outside play.	Keats, Ezra Jack. *The Snowy Day.* McLeod, Emilie Warren. *The Bear's Bicycle.*
6 Children enjoy excursions to new and familiar places.	6 Plan trips to zoos, fire stations, etc. Read about these places, encourage children to tell about family trips.	Felt, Sue. *Rosa-Too-Little.* Gretz, Susanna. *The Bears Who Went to the Seaside.*
7 They enjoy dressing up, role playing, and creative play.	7 Provide opportunities for them to dress up and play different roles. Read stories that can be used for creative play.	Cauley, Lorinda Bryan. *Goldilocks and the Three Bears.* Galdone, Paul. *The Amazing Pig: An Old Hungarian Tale.*
Early Elementary: Ages six–eight		
1 Children may defy parents when they are under pressure; they have difficulty getting along with younger siblings.	1 Encourage them to become more sensitive to family needs, to talk and read stories about situations, and direct them toward finding solutions.	Blume, Judy. *The One in the Middle is the Green Kangaroo.* Ness, Evaline. *Sam, Bangs, and Moonshine.* Sendak, Maurice. *Where the Wild Things Are.* Zolotow, Charlotte. *Big Brother.*
2 They want to play with other children but frequently insist on being first.	2 Encourage children both to lead and follow, read books in which children overcome similar problems.	Udry, Janice May. *Let's Be Enemies.*
3 Children respond to teachers' help or praise. They try to conform and please teachers.	3 Allow them to share work and receive praise. "Show and tell" is especially enjoyable for six- and seven-year-olds. Praise their reading and sharing of books.	Lobel, Arnold. *Frog and Toad All Year.* Schwartz, Alvin. *There is a Carrot in My Ear and Other Noodle Tales.* Van Leeuwen, Jean. *More Tales of Oliver Pig.*
4 They enjoy sitting still and listening to stories read at school, at home, or in the library.	4 Provide frequent storytelling and story-reading times.	de Paola, Tomie. *The Clown of God.* Galdone, Paul. *Cinderella.* Rabe, Berniece. *The Balancing Girl.* Turkle, Brinton. *Do Not Open.*
5 Children have definite inflexible ideas of right and wrong.	5 They identify with the values, attitudes, and standards of conduct their parents accept.	Lobel, Arnold. *Grasshopper on the Road.* Ness, Evaline. *Sam, Bangs, & Moonshine.* Williams, Jay. *The Reward Worth Having.*

CHART 1–4 *(cont.)*
Social Development

Characteristics	Implications	Literature Suggestions
6 They are curious about differences between boys and girls.	6 They ask questions about differences between boys and girls and where babies come from. Books help answer such questions.	Andry, Andrew, and Schepp, Steven. *How Babies Are Made* (plants and animals). Isenbart, Hans-Heinrich. *A Duckling Is Born.* Sheffield, Margaret, and Bewley, Sheila. *Where Do Babies Come From?* (human).

Middle Elementary: Ages eight–ten

Characteristics	Implications	Literature Suggestions
1 Concepts of right and wrong become more flexible; the situation in which the wrong action occurred is taken into consideration.	1 Experiences and books help them relate to different points of view; they begin to realize there are different attitudes, values, and standards from those their parents stress.	Branscum, Robbie. *The Saving of P.S.* Goble, Paul. *The Girl Who Loved Wild Horses.*
2 Children begin to be influenced by their peer groups.	2 Acceptance of the peer group becomes more important; this group can influence attitudes, values, and interests.	Allard, Harry. *Miss Nelson Is Missing.* Delton, Judy. *Kitty in the Middle.*
3 Thinking is becoming socialized; they can understand other people's points of view. They feel that their reasoning and solutions to problems should agree with others.	3 Provide many opportunities for them to investigate differing points of view. Literature is an excellent source.	Byars, Betsy. *The Animal, the Vegetable, and John D. Jones.* Monjo, F. N. *The Drinking Gourd.* Sandin, Joan. *The Long Way to a New Land.*

Upper Elementary: Ages ten–twelve

Characteristics	Implications	Literature Suggestions
1 Children have developed racial attitudes; low-prejudiced children increase in perception of nonracial characteristics; high-prejudiced children increase in perception of racial characteristics.	1 Literature and instructional activities must develop multiethnic values and stress contributions of ethnic minorities.	Adoff, Arnold. *All the Colors of the Race.* Adoff, Arnold. *Malcolm X.* Glubok, Shirley. *The Art of Africa.* Highwater, Jamake. *Anpao—An American Indian Odyssey.* White, Florence. *Cesar Chavez: Man of Courage.*
2 They want to do jobs well instead of starting and exploring them; feelings of inferiority and inadequacy may result if they feel they cannot measure up to their own personal standards.	2 Encourage expansion of knowledge in high-interest areas; provide books in these areas; provide assistance and encouragement to allow them to finish jobs that meet expectations.	Bunting, Glenn, and Bunting, Eve. *Skateboards: How to Make Them, How to Ride Them.* Cobb, Vicki, and Darling, Kathy. *Bet You Can't! Science Impossibilities to Fool You.* Cresswell, Helen. *Absolute Zero: Being the Second Part of the Bagthorpe Saga.*
3 They have a sense of justice and resist imperfections in the world.	3 Idealistic concerns increase interest in stories where people overcome injustice, improve some aspect of life, or raise questions about life.	Barry, Scott. *The Kingdom of Wolves.* George, Jean Craighead. *Who Really Killed Cock Robin?* Lasky, Kathryn. *The Night Journey.* Riskind, Mary. *Apple Is My Sign.* Yates, Elizabeth. *Amos Fortune, Free Man.*
4 Peer groups exert strong influences on children; conformity to parents decreases and conformity to peers increases in social situations. May challenge parent.	4 If differences between peer and family values are too great, children may experience conflicts. Literature selections and discussions can help.	Byars, Betsy. *The Cybil War.* Greenberg, Jan. *The Iceberg and Its Shadow.*

CHART 1—4 *(cont.)*
Social Development

Characteristics	Implications	Literature Suggestions
5 Boys and girls accept the identity of the opposite sex.	5 Girls more than boys begin to feel that marriage would be desirable; books that develop relationships with the opposite sex interest girls especially.	Benjamin, Carol Lea. *The Wicked Stepdog.* L'Engle, Madeleine. *A Ring of Endless Light.* Wilder, Laura Ingalls. *The First Four Years.* Wilder, Laura Ingalls. *These Happy Golden Years.*
6 Children have developed strong associations with gender-typed expectations: girls may fail in "masculine" tasks; boys in "feminine" tasks.	6 Provide books and discussions that avoid sex-stereotyped roles; emphasize that both sexes can succeed in many roles.	Clapp, Patricia. *I'm Deborah Sampson: A Soldier in the War of the Revolution.* Facklam, Margery. *Wild Animals, Gentle Women.* Paige, David. *A Day in the Life of a Marine Biologist.* Tobias, Tobi. *Arthur Mitchell.* Yates, Elizabeth. *My Diary — My World.*

SUMMARY

Literature opens doors of discovery and adventure for children. Its values provide enjoyment, transmit our literary heritage, allow understanding and valuing of our cultural heritage, provide vicarious experiences, transmit knowledge, nurture and expand imagination, foster language development, stimulate cognitive development, foster personality development, and encourage social development.

There are recognizable stages in child development: children do not progress through these stages at the same rate, but there is an order in which their development matures. Knowing the characteristics of children during these different stages can benefit parents, teachers, librarians, or other adults who are concerned with selecting appropriate literature and literature-related activities. This chapter described four aspects of child development: language development, cognitive development, personality development, and social development. Cognitive development included observing, comparing, classifying, hypothesizing, organizing, summarizing, applying, and criticizing. Stages, characteristics, educational and developmental implications, and literature suggestions were developed for each aspect.

Throughout this text, the reader will discover numerous books that are beneficial to children during their different developmental stages. Many child development implications will be suggested as these books are discussed in the following chapters.

Selected Activities for Understanding the Child and Children's Literature

■ Ask several children how school and reading literature could be made more enjoyable. Compare the responses you receive with those obtained by Doris Roettger (p. 5).
■ Select several books such as Eve Rice's *Oh Lewis* that could encourage young children to identify familiar actions in books. Share these with a few preschool children and let them interact orally with the text.
■ Listen to the language of several children who are the same age. Do you notice any differences in their language development? Are these differences similar to those identified by Walter Loban (p. 7)?
■ Select several books that you believe would stimulate children's language development. Present the books and your rationale for choosing them to your literature class.
■ With a group of your peers, compile an additional list of picture books that would be useful when developing one of the following cognitive skills: observing, comparing, hypothesizing, organizing, summarizing, applying, and criticizing. Share your findings with your class.
■ Read several books in which young children must overcome problems such as jealousy, fear, or anger. Compare the ways the authors have allowed children to handle their problems. Do the feelings seem normal and natural? Is more than one aspect of a feeling developed? Are options shown for handling the emotion?

References

1 Alexander, J. Estill, and Filler, Ronald Claude. *Attitudes and Reading*. Newark, Del.: International Reading Association, 1976.
2 Bartel, Nettie. "Assessing and Remediating Problems in Language Development." In *Teaching Children with Learning and Behavior Problems*, edited by Donald Hammill and Nettie Bartel. Boston: Allyn & Bacon, 1975.
3 Bernstein, Joanne. *Books to Help Children Cope with Separation and Loss*. New York: Bowker, 1977.
4 Braga, Laurie, and Braga, Joseph. *Learning and Growing: A Guide to Child Development*. Englewood Cliffs, N.J.: Prentice-Hall, 1975.
5 Braine, Martin. "The Ontogeny of English Phrase Structure: The First Phase." In *Readings in Language Development*, edited by Lois Bloom. New York: John Wiley, 1978.
6 Brown, Roger. *A First Language/The Early Stages*. Cambridge, Mass.: Harvard University, 1973.
7 Cullinan, Bernice E. "Books in the Life of the Young Child." In *Literature and Young Children*, edited by Bernice Cullinan and Carolyn Carmichael. Urbana, Ill.: National Council of Teachers of English, 1977.
8 Engel, Rosalind. "Literature Develops Children's I's for Reading." *Language Arts* 53 (November/December, 1976): 892–98.
9 Gage, N. L., and Berliner, David C. *Educational Psychology*. Chicago: Rand McNally, 1979.
10 Glazer, Joan. *Children's Literature for Early Childhood*. Columbus, Ohio: Merrill, 1981.
11 Loban, Walter. *Language Development: Kindergarten through Grade Twelve*. Urbana, Ill.: National Council of Teachers of English, 1976.
12 Mussen, Paul Henry; Conger, John Janeway; and Kagan, Jerome. *Child Development and Personality*. New York: Harper & Row, 1979.
13 Piaget, Jean, and Inhelder, B. *The Psychology of the Child*. New York: Basic Books, 1969.
14 Roettger, Doris. "Reading Attitudes and the Estes Scale." Paper presented at the Twenty-third Annual Convention of the International Reading Association, Houston, Texas, 1978.
15 Rubin, Rhea Joyce. *Bibliotherapy Source Book*. Phoenix, Arizona: Oryx Press, 1978.
16 Rubin, Rhea Joyce. *Using Bibliotherapy: A Guide to Theory and Practice*. Phoenix, Arizona: Oryx Press, 1978.
17 Sarafino, Edward P., and Armstrong, James W. *Child and Adolescent Development*. Glenview, Ill.: Scott, Foresman, 1980.
18 Strickland, Dorothy S. "Promoting Language and Concept Development." In *Literature and Young Children*, edited by Bernice Cullinan and Carolyn Carmichael. Urbana, Ill.: National Council of Teachers of English, 1977.

Additional References

de Villiers, Peter, and de Villiers, Jill G. *Language Acquisition*. Boston: Harvard University Press, 1980.
Ginsburg, Herbert, and Opper, Sylvia. *Piaget's Theory of Intellectual Development: An Introduction*. Englewood Cliffs, N.J.: Prentice-Hall, 1969.
Kagan, Jerome, and Brim, Orville G. *Constancy and Change in Human Development*. Boston: Harvard University Press, 1980.
Keil, Francis. *Semantic and Conceptual Development*. Boston: Harvard University Press, 1980.

CHILDREN'S LITERATURE

Aardema, Verna. *Bringing the Rain to Kapiti Plain*. Illustrated by Beatriz Vidal. Dial, 1981.

———, *Why Mosquitoes Buzz in People's Ears: A West African Tale*. Illustrated by Leo and Diane Dillon. Dial, 1975.

Adoff, Arnold. *All of the Colors of the Race*. Illustrated by John Steptoe. Lothrop, Lee & Shepard, 1982.

———. *Black Is Warm Is Tan*. Harper & Row, 1973.

———. *Malcolm X*. Crowell, 1970.

———, ed. *My Black Me: A Beginning Book of Black Poetry*. Dutton, 1974.

Ahlberg, Janet, and Ahlberg, Allen. *Peek-a-boo!* Viking, 1981.

Alexander, Lloyd. *Westmark*. Dutton, 1981.

Alexander, Martha. *Nobody Asked Me If I Wanted a Baby Sister*. Dial, 1971.

———. *Out! Out! Out!* Dial, 1968.

Allard, Harry. *Miss Nelson Is Missing*. Illustrated by James Marshall. Houghton Mifflin, 1977.

Anderson, Margaret. *In the Keep of Time*. Knopf, 1977.

Andry, Andrew, and Schepp, Steven. *How Babies Are Made*. Time-Life, 1968.

Anno, Mitsumasa. *Anno's Britain*. Philomel, 1982.

———. *Anno's Counting Book*. Crowell, 1977.

———. *Anno's Italy*. Collins, 1980.

Ardizzone, Edward. *The Wrong Side of the Bed*. Doubleday, 1970.

Arkhurst, Joyce Cooper. *The Adventures of Spider*. Illustrated by Jerry Pinkney. Little, Brown, 1964.

Arnosky, Jim. *Freshwater Fish and Fishing*. Four Winds, 1982.

Aruego, Jose. *Look What I Can Do*. Scribner's, 1971.

Asbjornsen, P. C., and Moe, J. E. *The Three Billy Goats Gruff*. Illustrated by Marcia Brown. Harcourt Brace Jovanovich, 1957.

Asian Cultural Centre for UNESCO. *Folktales from Asia for Children Everywhere*. 1977, 1978, 1979.

Ayal, Ora. *Ugbu*. Harper & Row, 1979.

Banchek, Linda. *Snake In, Snake Out*. Crowell, 1978.

Barry, Scott. *The Kingdom of Wolves*. Putnam, 1979.

Barton, Byron. *Airport*. Crowell, 1982.

———. *Where's Al*. Houghton Mifflin, 1972.

Beim, Jerrold. *The Smallest Boy in the Class*. Morrow, 1949.

Belpre, Pura. *The Rainbow-Colored Horse*. Warne, 1978.

Benjamin, Carol Lea. *The Wicked Stepdog*. Crowell, 1982.

Bennett, Jill. *Tiny Tim: Verses For Children*. Illustrated by Helen Oxenbury. Delacorte, 1982.

Berenstain, Stan, and Berenstain, Janice. *Old Hat, New Hat*. Random House, 1970.

Berger, Terry. *I Have Feelings*. Human Science, 1971.

Berger, Terry, and Kandell, Alice. *Ben's ABC Day*. Lothrop, Lee & Shepard, 1982.

Bess, Clayton. *Story for a Black Night*. Houghton Mifflin, 1982.

Blume, Judy. *Are You There God? It's Me, Margaret*. Bradbury, 1970.

———. *It's Not the End of the World*. Bradbury, 1972.

———. *The One in the Middle is the Green Kangaroo*. Bradbury, 1981.

———. *Tales of a Fourth Grade Nothing*. Dutton, 1972.

Bonsall, Crosby. *It's Mine—A Greedy Book*. Harper & Row, 1964.

Brandenberg, Aliki. *The Two of Them*. Morrow, 1979.

Branscum, Robbie. *The Saving of P.S.* Doubleday, 1977.

Briggs. Raymond. *The Snowman*. Random House, 1978.

British Museum of Natural History. *Man's Place in Evolution*. Cambridge, 1981.

Brown, Marcia. *The Bun: A Tale from Russia*. Harcourt Brace Jovanovich, 1972.

Brown, Margaret Wise. *The Runaway Bunny*. Harper & Row, 1972.

Buckley, Helen E. *Grandfather and I*. Lothrop, Lee & Shepard, 1959.

———. *Grandmother and I*. Lothrop, Lee & Shepard, 1961.

———. *Michael Is Brave*. Lothrop, Lee & Shepard, 1971.

Bulla, Clyde. *Keep Running, Allen!* Crowell, 1978.

Bunting, Eve, and Bunting, Glenn. *Skateboards: How to Make Them, How to Ride Them*. Harvey, 1977.

Burningham, John. *The Rabbit*. Crowell, 1975.

———. *The Snow*. Crowell, 1975.

Burton, Virginia Lee. *Mike Mulligan and His Steam Shovel*. Houghton Mifflin, 1939.

Busch, Phyllis. *Cactus in the Desert*. Crowell, 1979.

Byars, Betsy. *The Animal, the Vegetable, and John D. Jones*. Illustrated by Ruth Sanderson. Delacorte, 1982.

———. *The Cybil War*. Viking, 1981.

Carle, Eric. *Do You Want to Be My Friend?* Crowell, 1971.

———. *Let's Paint a Rainbow*. Philomel, 1982.

———. *The Mixed-up Chameleon*. Crowell, 1975.

———. *My Very First Book of Colors*. Crowell, 1974.

———. *My Very First Book of Numbers*. Crowell, 1974.

———. *My Very First Book of Shapes*. Crowell, 1974.

Most of these titles are annotated in the chapters in which they are discussed in depth.

————. *1, 2, 3 to the Zoo.* Philomel, 1968.

————. *The Very Fussy Monkey.* Philomel, 1982.

Carroll, Ruth. *What Whiskers Did.* Walck, 1965.

Cauley, Lorinda Bryan. *Goldilocks and the Three Bears.* Putnam, 1981.

Chorao, Kay. *The Baby's Lap Book.* Dutton, 1977.

Chute, Marchette. *Rhymes About Us.* Dutton, 1974.

Clapp, Patricia. *I'm Deborah Sampson: A Soldier in the War of the Revolution.* Lothrop, Lee & Shepard, 1977.

Clark, Ann Nolan. *Along Sandy Trails.* Photographs by Alfred A Cohn. Viking, 1969.

Cleary, Beverly. *Ramona and Her Father.* Illustrated by Alan Tiegreen. Morrow, 1977.

————. *Ramona Quimby, Age 8.* Morrow, 1981.

Cleaver, Vera, and Cleaver, Bill. *Me Too.* Lippincott, 1973.

Clifton, Lucille. *Everett Anderson's Year.* Holt, Rinehart & Winston, 1974.

Cobb, Vicki, and Darling, Kathy. *Bet You Can't! Science Impossibilities to Fool You.* Illustrated by Martha Weston. Lothrop, Lee & Shepard, 1980.

Cohen, Miriam. *Best Friends.* Macmillan, 1971.

————. *Will I Have a Friend?* Macmillan, 1971.

Corcoran, Barbara. *The Trick of Light.* Atheneum, 1972.

Cresswell, Helen. *Absolute Zero: Being the Second Part of the Bagthorpe Saga.* Macmillan, 1978.

Crews, Donald. *Freight Train.* Greenwillow, 1978.

————. *Harbor.* Greenwillow, 1982.

Dabcovich, Lydia. *Sleepy Bear.* Dutton, 1982.

Dallinger, Jane. *Grasshoppers.* Photographed by Uko Sato. Lerner, 1981.

Delton, Judy. *Kitty in the Middle.* Dell, 1980.

de Paola, Tomie. *The Clown of God.* Harcourt Brace Jovanovich, 1978.

————. *Fin M'Coul: The Giant of Knockmany Hill.* Holiday, 1981.

————. *The Hunter and the Animals: A Wordless Picture Book.* Holiday, 1981.

————. *Pancakes for Breakfast.* Harcourt Brace Jovanovich, 1978.

————. *The Quicksand Book.* Holiday, 1977.

Duff, Maggie. *Rum Pum Pum.* Macmillan, 1978.

Duvoisin, Roger. *See What I Am.* Lothrop, Lee & Shepard, 1974.

Ehrlich, Amy. *Leo, Zack and Emmie.* Dial, 1981.

Ellis, Mel. *The Wild Horse Killers.* Holt, Rinehart & Winston, 1976.

Emberley, Barbara. *Drummer Hoff.* Illustrated by Ed Emberley. Prentice-Hall, 1967.

Emberley, Ed. *Ed Emberley's ABC.* Little, Brown, 1978.

Facklam, Margery. *Wild Animals, Gentle Women.* Harcourt Brace Jovanovich, 1978.

Fassler, Joan. *Howie Helps Himself.* Illustrated by Joe Lasker. Whitman, 1975.

Feelings, Muriel. *Moja Means One: Swahili Counting Book.* Illustrated by Tom Feelings. Dial, 1971.

Felt, Sue. *Rosa-Too-Little.* Doubleday, 1950.

Forbes, Esther. *Johnny Tremain.* Illustrated by Lynd Ward. Houghton Mifflin, 1943.

Gág, Wanda. *Millions of Cats.* Coward-McCann, 1928.

Galbraith, Kathryn. *Spots Are Special!* Atheneum, 1976.

Galdone, Paul. *The Amazing Pig: An Old Hungarian Tale.* Houghton Mifflin, 1981.

————. *Cinderella.* McGraw-Hill, 1978.

————. *The Gingerbread Boy.* Seabury, 1975.

————. *The Little Red Hen.* Houghton Mifflin, 1973.

————. *Puss in Boots.* Houghton Mifflin, 1976.

————. *The Three Billy Goats Gruff.* Houghton Mifflin, 1973.

————. *What's in Fox's Sack? An Old English Tale.* Clarion, 1982.

Gammell, Stephen. *Wake Up, Bear . . . It's Christmas!* Lothrop, Lee & Shepard, 1981.

Garelick, May. *Down to the Beach.* Scholastic, 1976.

George, Jean Craighead. *My Side of the Mountain.* Dutton, 1975.

————. *Who Really Killed Cock Robin?* Dutton, 1971.

Giff, Patricia. *Today was a Terrible Day.* Viking, 1980.

Gilchrist, Theo. *Halfway up the Mountain.* Lippincott, 1978.

Ginsburg, Mirra. *How the Sun Was Brought Back to the Sky.* Macmillan, 1975.

Glubok, Shirley. *The Art of Africa.* Harper & Row, 1965.

Goble, Paul. *The Girl Who Loved Wild Horses.* Bradbury, 1978.

Goffstein, M.B. *Family Scrapbook.* Farrar, Straus & Giroux, 1978.

Goodall, John. *The Ballooning Adventures of Paddy Pork.* Harcourt Brace Jovanovich, 1969.

————. *The Story of an English Village.* Atheneum, 1979.

Grahame, Kenneth. *Wayfarers All: From the Wind in the Willows.* Illustrated by Beverly Gooding. Scribner's, 1981.

Greenberg, Barbara. *The Bravest Babysitter.* Dial, 1977.

Greenberg, Jan. *The Iceberg and Its Shadow.* Farrar, Straus & Giroux, 1980.

Greene, Carol. *Hinny Winny Bunco.* Illustrated by Jeanette Winter. Harper & Row, 1982.

Gretz, Susanna. *The Bears Who Went to the Seaside.* Follett, 1973.

Griego, Margot C.; Bucks, Betsy L.; Gilbert, Sharon S.; and Kimball, Laurel H. *Tortillitas Para Mama.* Illustrated by Barbara Cooney. Holt, Rinehart & Winston, 1981.

Griffith, Helen. *Alex and the Cat.* Illustrated by Joseph Low. Greenwillow, 1982.

Grimm, Brothers. *The Bremen Town Musicians.* Retold and Illustrated by Ilse Plume. Doubleday, 1980.

————. *The Bremen Town Musicians: A Grimm's Fairy Tale.* Retold and illustrated by Donna Diamond. Delacorte, 1981.

Hague, Kathleen, and Hague, Michael. *The Man Who Kept House.* Harcourt Brace Jovanovich, 1981.

Hall, Lynn. *Danza!* Scribner's, 1981.

Hickman, Janet. *The Valley of the Shadow.* Macmillan, 1974.

Highwater, Jamake. *Anpao—An American Indian Odyssey.* Harper & Row, 1980.

Hill, Donna. *Ms. Glee Was Waiting.* Atheneum, 1978.

Hill, Eric. *Spot's Birthday Party.* Putnam, 1981.

————. *Spot's First Walk.* Putnam, 1981.

Hoban, Russell. *Best Friends for Frances.* Harper & Row, 1976.

————. *The Little Brute Family.* Macmillan, 1966.

————. *Nothing to Do.* Harper & Row, 1964.

Hoban, Tana. *Circles, Triangles, and Squares.* Macmillan, 1974.

————. *Is It Red? Is It Yellow? Is It Blue?* Greenwillow, 1978.

————. *Look Again!* Macmillan, 1971.

————. *Take Another Look.* Greenwillow, 1981.

Hoffman, Phyllis. *Steffie and Me.* Harper & Row, 1970.

Holzenthaler, Jean. *My Hands Can.* Dutton, 1978.

Howe, James. *The Hospital Book.* Photographs by Mal Warshaw. Crown, 1981.

Hurd, Edith Thacher. *I Dance in My Red Pajamas.* Illustrated by Emily Arnold McCully. Harper & Row, 1982.

Hutchins, Pat. *Changes, Changes.* Macmillan, 1971.

————. *I Hunter.* Greenwillow, 1982.

————. *Rosie's Walk.* Macmillan, 1968.

Hutchinson, Veronica. *Henny Penny.* Little, Brown, 1976.

Ichikawa, Satomi. *Let's Play.* Putnam, 1981.

Isenbart, Hans-Heinrich. *A Duckling is Born.* Photographed by Othmar Baumli. Putnam, 1981.

Iwasaki, Chihiro. *What's Fun Without a Friend?* McGraw-Hill, 1975.

Jewell, Nancy. *Bus Ride.* Harper & Row, 1978.

Johnston, Tony. *Four Scary Stories.* Putnam, 1978.

Jonas, Ann. *When You Were A Baby.* Greenwillow, 1982.

Keats, Ezra Jack. *Over in the Meadow.* Four Winds, 1972.

————. *Peter's Chair.* Harper & Row, 1967.

————. *Regards to the Man in the Moon.* Four Winds, 1982.

_____. *The Snowy Day*. Viking, 1962.

_____. *Whistle for Willie*. Viking, 1964.

Kellogg, Steven. *A Rose for Pinkerton*. Dial, 1981.

Kepes, Juliet. *Cock-a-Doodle-Doo*. Pantheon, 1978.

King-Smith, Dick. *Pigs Might Fly*. Illustrated by Mary Rayner. Viking, 1982.

Klein, Norma. *Girls Can Be Anything*. Dutton, 1975.

Knight, Hilary. *Hilary Knight's The Twelve Days of Christmas*. Macmillan, 1981.

Konigsburg, E. L. *Journey to an 800 Number*. Atheneum, 1982.

Krahn, Fernando. *Who's Seen the Scissors?* Dutton, 1975.

Kraus, Robert. *Leo the Late Bloomer*. Illustrated by Jose Aruego. Windmill, 1971.

_____. *The Littlest Rabbit*. Scholastic, 1975.

_____. *Milton the Early Riser*. Illustrated by Jose and Ariane Aruego. Windmill, 1972.

Krauss, Ruth. *The Carrot Seed*. Harper & Row, 1945.

Kroll, Steven. *If I Could Be My Grandmother*. Pantheon, 1977.

Langstaff, John. *Oh, A-Hunting We Will Go*. Atheneum, 1974.

Lasky, Kathryn. *The Night Journey*. Warne, 1981.

L'Engle, Madeleine. *A Ring of Endless Light*. Farrar, Straus & Giroux, 1980.

_____. *A Swiftly Tilting Planet*. Farrar, Straus & Giroux, 1978.

Lewis, C.S. *The Lion, the Witch, and the Wardrobe*. Macmillan, 1951.

Lexau, Joan. *Benjie on His Own*. Dial, 1970.

Lindgren, Barbro. *The Wild Baby*. Illustrated by Eva Eriksson. Greenwillow, 1981.

Lionni, Leo. *Let's Make Rabbits*. Pantheon, 1982.

Lisker, Sonia O. *Lost*. Harcourt Brace Jovanovich, 1975.

Lobel, Arnold. *Frog and Toad All Year*. Harper & Row, 1976.

_____. *Grasshopper on the Road*. Harper & Row, 1978.

_____. *On Market Street*. Illustrated by Anita Lobel. Greenwillow, 1981.

_____. *Uncle Elephant*. Harper & Row, 1981.

Lowry, Lois. *Anastasia Again!* Houghton Mifflin, 1981.

McCloskey, Robert. *Lentil*. Viking, 1940.

_____. *Time of Wonder*. Viking, 1957.

MacDonald, Golden. *The Little Island*. Illustrated by Leonard Weisgard. Doubleday, 1946.

McGovern, Ann. *Runaway Slave: The Story of Harriet Tubman*. Illustrated by R.M. Powers. Four Winds, 1965.

MacLachlan, Patricia. *Mama One, Mama Two*. Illustrated by Ruth Lercher Bornstein. Harper & Row, 1982.

McLeod, Emilie Warren. *The Bear's Bicycle*. Little, Brown, 1975.

Maestro, Giulio. *One More and One Less*. Crown, 1974.

Marshall, James. *George and Martha One Fine Day*. Houghton Mifflin, 1978.

Martin, Sarah Catherine. *The Comic Adventures of Old Mother Hubbard and Her Dog*. Illustrated by Tomie de Paola. Harcourt Brace Jovanovich, 1981.

Mayer, Mercer. *The Great Cat Chase*. Four Winds, 1975.

Miles, Miska. *Noisy Gander*. Dutton, 1978.

Monjo, F.N. *The Drinking Gourd*. Harper & Row, 1969.

Moore, Clement Clarke. *The Night Before Christmas*. Illustrated by Tomie de Paola. Holiday, 1980.

Murphy, Jill. *Peace at Last*. Dial, 1980.

Nakatani, Chiyoko. *The Zoo in My Garden*. Crowell, 1973.

Nance, John. *Lobo of the Tasaday*. Pantheon, 1982.

Naylor, Phyllis Reynolds. *How I Came to Be a Writer*. Atheneum, 1978.

Ness, Evaline. *Sam, Bangs, & Moonshine*. Holt, Rinehart & Winston, 1966.

Oakley, Graham. *The Church Mouse*. Atheneum, 1972.

_____. *Hetty and Harriet*. Atheneum, 1982.

O'Dell, Scott. *Island of the Blue Dolphins*. Houghton Mifflin, 1960.

Ormerod, Jan. *Sunshine*. Lothrop, Lee & Shepard, 1981.

Oxenbury, Helen. *Dressing*. Simon & Schuster, 1981.

_____. *Family*. Simon & Schuster, 1981.

_____. *Friends*. Simon & Schuster, 1981.

_____. *Playing*. Simon & Schuster, 1981.

_____. *Working*. Simon & Schuster, 1981.

Paige, David. *A Day in the Life of a Marine Biologist*. Photographed by Roger Ruhlin. Troll Associates, 1981.

Park, Ruth. *Playing Beatie Bow*. Atheneum, 1982.

Pearson, Susan. *Izzie*. Dial, 1975.

Polushkin, Maria. *Who Said Meow?* Crown, 1975.

Preston, Edna Mitchell, and Bennett, Rainey. *The Temper Tantrum Book*. Penguin, 1976.

Rabe, Berniece. *The Balancing Girl*. Illustrated by Lillian Hoban. Dutton, 1981.

Rand, Ann, and Rand, Paul. *I Know a Lot of Things*. Harcourt Brace Jovanovich, 1956.

Raskin, Ellen. *The Westing Game*. Dutton, 1978.

Reiss, John J. *Numbers*. Bradbury, 1971.

_____. *Shapes*. Bradbury, 1974.

Rice, Eve. *Benny Bakes a Cake*. Greenwillow, 1981.

_____. *Oh, Lewis!* Macmillan, 1974.

Riskind, Mary. *Apple Is My Sign*. Houghton Mifflin, 1981.

Rockwell, Harlow. *My Dentist*. Greenwillow, 1975.

_____. *My Doctor*. Macmillan, 1973.

Rose, Anne. *As Right As Right Can Be*. Dial, 1976.

Rylant, Cynthia. *When I Was Young in the Mountains*. Illustrated by Diane Goode. Dutton, 1982.

Salassi, Otto R. *On the Ropes*. Greenwillow, 1981.

Sandin, Joan. *The Long Way to a New Land*. Harper & Row, 1981.

Savitt, Sam. *Draw Horses with Sam Savitt*. Viking, 1981.

Scarry, Richard. *Richard Scarry's The Best Word Book Ever*. Western, 1963.

Schlee, Ann. *Ask Me No Questions*. Holt, Rinehart & Winston, 1982.

Schulman, Janet. *Jenny and the Tennis Nut*. Greenwillow, 1978.

Schwartz, Alvin. *There is a Carrot in My Ear and Other Noodle Tales*. Illustrated by Karen Ann Weinhaus. Harper & Row, 1982.

Scott, Ann Herbert. *Sam*. Illustrated by Symeon Shimin. McGraw-Hill, 1967.

Scott, Jack Denton. *The Book of the Pig*. Putnam, 1981.

Selsam, Millicent. *Tyrannosaurus Rex*. Harper & Row, 1978.

Sendak, Maurice. *Where the Wild Things Are*. Harper & Row, 1963.

Seuss, Dr. *And to Think That I Saw It on Mulberry Street*. Vanguard, 1937.

_____. *The Cat in the Hat*. Beginner, 1957.

Severo, Emöke de Papp. *The Good-Hearted Youngest Brother*. Illustrated by Diane Goode. Bradbury, 1981.

Sharmat, Marjorie. *A Big Fat Enormous Lie*. Dutton, 1978.

_____. *Gladys Told Me to Meet Her Here*. Harper & Row, 1970.

Sheffield, Margaret, and Bewley, Sheila. *Where Do Babies Come From?* Knopf, 1973.

Showers, Paul. *Look at Your Eyes*. Crowell, 1962.

Silverstein, Shel. *A Light in the Attic*. Harper & Row, 1981.

Simon, Seymour. *Animal Fact/Animal Fable*. Crown, 1979.

Skorpen, Liesel M. *His Mother's Dog*. Harper & Row, 1978.

Small, David. *Eulalie and the Hopping Head*. Macmillan, 1982.

Sonneborn, Ruth. *I Love Gram*. Viking, 1971.

Speare, Elizabeth George. *The Bronze Bow*. Houghton Mifflin, 1961.

Sperry, Armstrong. *Call It Courage*. Macmillan, 1940.

Spier, Peter. *Bill's Service Station*. Doubleday, 1981.

_____. *Food Market*. Doubleday, 1981.

_____. *Fire House: Hook and Ladder Company Number Twenty-Four*. Doubleday, 1981.

———. *Rain*. Doubleday, 1982.

———. *The Star-Spangled Banner*. Doubleday, 1973.

———. *Tin Lizzie*. Doubleday, 1975.

Steptoe, John. *Stevie*. Harper & Row, 1969.

Sutcliff, Rosemary. *Sun Horse, Moon Horse*. Illustrated by Shirley Felts. Dutton, 1978.

Taylor, Mildred. *Let the Circle Be Unbroken*. Dial, 1981.

Terris, Susan. *No Boys Allowed*. Doubleday, 1976.

Tobias, Tobi. *Arthur Mitchell*. Illustrated by Carol Byard. Crowell, 1975.

Turkle, Brinton. *Do Not Open*. Dutton, 1981.

Udry, Janice May. *Let's Be Enemies*. Harper & Row, 1961.

———. *What Mary Jo Shared*. Whitman, 1966.

Van Leeuwen, Jean. *More Tales of Oliver Pig*. Dial, 1981.

Viorst, Judith. *Alexander and the Terrible, Horrible, No Good, Very Bad Day*. Illustrated by Ray Cruz. Atheneum, 1972.

———. *I'll Fix Anthony*. Harper & Row, 1969.

Waber, Bernard. *Ira Sleeps Over*. Houghton Mifflin, 1972.

———. *The Snake: A Very Long Story*. Houghton Mifflin, 1978.

Wagner, Jenny. *John Brown, Rose and the Midnight Cat*. Bradbury, 1978.

Wahl, Jan. *Jamie's Tiger*. Harcourt Brace Jovanovich, 1977.

Welber, Robert. *Song of the Seasons*. Pantheon, 1973.

Wells, Rosemary. *Timothy Goes to School*. Dial, 1981.

Wezel, Peter. *The Good Bird*. Harper & Row, 1966.

White, E.B. *Charlotte's Web*. Harper & Row, 1952.

———. *Stuart Little*. Harper & Row, 1945.

White, Florence M. *Cesar Chavez: Man of Courage*. Garrard, 1973.

Wilder, Laura Ingalls, *The First Four Years*. Illustrated by Garth Williams. Harper & Row, 1971.

———. *Little House in the Big Woods*. Harper & Row, 1932.

———. *These Happy Golden Years*. Harper & Row, 1943.

Williams, Barbara. *Chester Chipmunk's Thanksgiving*. Dutton, 1978.

———. *Someday, Said Mitchell*. Dutton, 1976.

Williams, Jay. *The Reward Worth Having*. Illustrated by Mercer Mayer. Four Winds, 1977.

Wojciechowska, Maia. *Shadow of a Bull*. Illustrated by Alvin Smith. Atheneum, 1964.

Wolde, Gunilla. *This is Betsy*. Random House, 1975.

Yates, Elizabeth. *Amos Fortune, Free Man*. Aladdin, 1950.

———. *My Diary—My World*. Westminister, 1981.

Zemach, Margot. *Hush Little Baby*. Dutton, 1976.

———. *It Could Always Be Worse*. Farrar, Straus & Giroux, 1977.

Zolotow, Charlotte. *Big Brother*. Illustrated by Mary Chalmers. Harper & Row, 1966.

———. *My Grandson Lew*. Illustrated by William Pène du Bois. Harper & Row, 1974.

———. *The Quarreling Book*. Illustrated by Arnold Lobel. Harper & Row, 1963.

———. *William's Doll*. Illustrated by William Pène du Bois. Harper & Row, 1972.

TWO
History of Children's Literature

MILESTONES IN THE HISTORY OF
CHILDREN'S LITERATURE
CHANGING VIEWS OF CHILDREN AND
FAMILY IN LITERATURE

IT MAY BE surprising to many readers to discover that childhood has not always been considered an important time of life. When students of children's literature look at the beautiful books published to meet children's needs, interests, and reading levels, many are amazed to learn that not too long ago books written specifically for children were not available.

Tracing the history of children's literature uncovers some fascinating milestones that created changes in attitudes toward children and their books. Changes in printing technology provided affordable books; more importantly, there were changes in the attitudes of society toward children. When society looked upon children as little adults who must rapidly step into the roles of their parents, there was little time or need to read books about a nonexistent childhood. In contrast, when childhood is viewed as a special part of life, and children are encouraged to develop as well as have free time for themselves, then literature written specifically for children becomes very important.

When viewed across the history of the human race, the history of children's literature is very short. Neither earlier tales told through the oral tradition nor early books were created specifically for children. When such books were eventually written, they often mirrored a societal or religious concern. Consequently, a study of children's literature from the early books of the fifteenth century through contemporary times reflects concerns and values of the society and the changing roles that have been placed upon both children and the family.

Literature researchers are beginning to view children's literature as a viable vehicle for studying social values and changing attitudes. Winkler, in the *Chronicle of Higher Education* (35) says that the 1970s and 1980s are characterized by an ever-increasing interest in the scholarly study of children's literature. She identifies 1978 as a turning point in the publication of research that is concerned with viewing children's literature as an index to the social attitudes of the time. This is suggested in Robert Kelly's publication, "Mother Was a Lady: Self and Society in Selected American Children's Periodicals, 1865-1890" (16), and in the sociology of children's books as found in Mary Lystad's *From Dr. Mather to Dr. Seuss: Two Hundred Years of American Books for Children* (24).

The increasing number of doctoral dissertations that critically evaluate certain aspects of children's literature also suggests the current importance of children's literature as a research subject. For example, from the 1930s until 1970, there were approximately two hundred theses written. In contrast, the 1970s produced nearly eight hundred dissertations. Sev-

eral of these studies suggest the relationship that exists between social, cultural, and economic influences and various story themes or values expressed by characters in children's literature of the time period.

This chapter views the history of children's literature in two ways. First, it considers some milestones in the development of literature as they relate to books for children. Second, it focuses on the changing view of children and the family as reflected in the literature from early books for children through contemporary stories.

Chart 2–1 provides a brief overview of those early milestones. Chart 2–2 lists important events in the history of children's book illustration and Chart 2–3 provides additional notable authors of children's literature. Charts 2–4, 2–5, and 2–6 provide an overview of literature as a reflector of the culture.

MILESTONES IN THE HISTORY OF CHILDREN'S LITERATURE

The Oral Tradition

Long before the recorded history of mankind, family units and tribes conveyed the traditions and values of the group through stories told around the campfire. These stories accounted for many of the tribes' unanswerable questions, allowed ancient people to speculate about their beginnings, and emphasized ethical truths of the group. When hunters returned from their adventures, they probably told of the perils of the hunt and of hostile encounters with other tribes. Heroic deeds were certainly told and retold until they became a part of the groups' heritage. The oral tradition has existed from the beginning of oral communication among human beings; it goes back to the very roots of every civilization throughout the world. These tales were not told specifically for children; they were surely there, however, listening, watching, and learning.

In the Middle Ages the heroic tales of "Beowulf" were told in the great halls of Europe, while simpler tales such as "Jack the Giant Killer" were repeated around cottage hearths or campfires. Often called *castle* and *cottage* tales because of their locations, these stories provided our ancestors with literature long before they were written down or printed by the first printing press. In the castle halls, wandering minstrels or bards told their tales to the lords of the land. Many heroic stories were accompanied by the lyre or harp and varied little in form. They were memorized and handed down from generation to generation. The ruling classes favored poetic epics about the reputed deeds of the lord of the manor or his ancestors. Conse-

CHART 2–1
Historic Milestones in Children's Literature

	Oral Tradition
	"Beowulf"
	"Jack the Giant Killer"
1400s	Early Books
	Hornbooks
	Caxton's Printing Press - 1476
1500s	Chapbooks Introduced
	"Jack the Giant Killer"
1600s	The Puritan Influence
	Spiritual Milk for Boston Babes in either England, drawn from the Breasts of both Testaments for their Souls' Nourishment
	Pilgrim's Progress
1693	View of Childhood Changes
	John Locke's *Some Thoughts Concerning Education*
1698	First Fairy Tales Written for Children
	Charles Perrault's *Tales of Mother Goose*
1719	Great Adventure Stories
	Daniel Defoe's *Robinson Crusoe*
	Jonathan Swift's *Gulliver's Travels*
1744	Children's Literature: A True Beginning
	John Newbery's *A Little Pretty Pocket Book* and *History of Little Goody Two Shoes*
1762	Children Should Be Guided in Their Search for Knowledge
	Jean Jacques Rousseau's *Emile*

1789	Poetry about Children
	William Blake's *Songs of Innocence*
1800s	The Romantic Movement in Europe
	The Brothers Grimm
	Hans Christian Andersen
1800s	Illustrators Make Their Impact on Children's Books
	Walter Crane
	Randolph Caldecott
	Kate Greenaway
1860	The Victorian Influence
	Charlotte Yonge's *The Daisy Chain* and *The Clever Woman of the Family*
1850-1900	Childhood Seen as an Adventure, Not a Training Ground for Adulthood
	Fantasy
	Lewis Carroll's *Alice's Adventures in Wonderland*
	Edward Lear's *A Book of Nonsense*
	Adventure
	Robert Louis Stevenson's *Treasure Island*
	Howard Pyle's *The Merry Adventures of Robin Hood*
	Jules Verne's *Twenty-Thousand Leagues under the Sea*
	Real People
	Margaret Sidney's *The Five Little Peppers and How They Grew*
	Louisa May Alcott's *Little Women*
	Johanna Spyri's *Heidi*

quently, many heroes were regal as Beowulf or King Arthur, or they lived in princely or queenly surroundings as those in the French version of Cinderella.

In contrast, the oral tales told around cottage fires or at country fairs had quite different heroes and plots. These stories were often about simple people such as the peasants themselves who had to try to overcome daily problems and the unknown forces of nature or the spiritual world. The storyteller often told stories about the peasant outwitting the great lord. It was possible for the youngest, poorest, and simplest lad to use resourcefulness or kindness to win the hand of the princess and go from rags to riches; his reward was his ability to live happily ever after in great splendor. Because peasants also had to live with daily threats from nature and the animal kingdom, many tales dealt with man's overcoming the evils of the predator world. Wolves, foxes, and even dragons had to be slain or outwitted.

The invaders of England and western Europe also brought their legacy to this oral tradition. Roman conquerors brought the legends and myths of the Roman and Greek gods. People heard stories that tried to explain the spiritual world in which gods controlled the fate of man; Atlas supported the heavens on his shoulders, Zeus ruled the heavens and earth, and Pluto ruled Hades. The Danes and invaders from northern Europe also brought their own legends about heroes and gods.

By whatever name they were known—bards, minstrels, or devisers of tales—these early storytellers were entertainers: if they did not entertain, they lost their audiences or even their meals and lodging. Consequently, they learned to tell stories that had rapid plot development and easily identifiable characters. These storytellers also possessed considerable power. Their tales, whether woven from their imaginations or retold from legends and stories of old, could influence people who heard them. Because of this, if a minstrel's story offended or discredited the lord, the minstrel could be punished or imprisoned. By the end of the fourteenth century, feudal authority sought to control the tale and often jailed a storyteller who angered either a ruler or the church.

The oral tradition, according to Leeson (19), reached its climax in the feudal age. At this time, stories were told either by older members of the community or by traveling minstrels. The same stories were told to audiences of all ages. Sidney (30) described the storyteller as able to hold children from their play and old men from the chimney corner. Many of these early folktales, myths, and legends are today considered ideal for sharing with children, but this was not the attitude of feudal Europe. A child was considered a small adult who should enter into adult life as quickly as possible. It was not considered necessary to make up stories primarily for a younger population. Consequently, the stories about giants, heroes, and simpletons that relieved the strain of adult life also entertained the children.

These favorite tales that may have been told and retold for a thousand years were logical choices for early manuscripts. The heroic tales such as the epics and legends that perpetuated the reputations of a great lord or his ancestors were handwritten into medieval manuscripts. When printing finally became possible, the popular tales and fables from this oral tradition were among the first books printed.

Early Books—1400s

In the 1400s, hornbooks, printed sheets of text mounted on wood and covered with translucent animal horn, were introduced to teach reading and numbers. The books, which were in the shape of a paddle, usually included the alphabet, a syllabary, numerals, and the Lord's Prayer. These texts remained popular into the 1700s when a variant of the hornbook, the battledore, became popular. These later lesson books consisted of folded paper or cardboard. Like the hornbooks, battledores usually contained an alphabet, numerals, and proverbs or prayers.

Prior to 1476, the literary heritage consisted either of the oral tradition or handwritten manuscripts. Each manuscript was usually handlettered by a monk or scribe and required hundreds of hours of laborious work to complete. If these rare, early books were meant for children, they were usually designed to provide instruction in rhetoric, grammar, and music for privileged children who attended monastery schools. Because manuscripts were both rare and valuable, children usually wrote on slates as the monks dictated the lessons.

A significant event took place in the 1450s when Johann Gutenberg discovered a practical method for using movable metal type, making it possible to mass-produce books. William Caxton went to Germany to learn the printing trade and established England's first printing press in 1476.

The hornbook, which was used for instruction, usually contained the alphabet, numerals, and the Lord's Prayer.
Photo courtesy of The Horn Book, Inc.

Caxton, in addition to being a printer and seller of books, was considered a reputable translator of literature. These translations, "along with his concern for 'hardening' [standardizing] the form of the English language, his writing of prologues and epilogues, his skill in selecting titles, and his literary style, secure him a lasting place in English literature" (3, p. 25).

When Caxton opened his printing business in 1476, most of the books used with children were not written for their interest but adhered to the sentiment that young readers should read only what would improve their manners or instruct their minds. *Caxton's Book of Curtesye* printed in 1477 (11), for example, contained directions for drawing readers away from vice and turning them toward a life of virtue. In order to do this, verses guided readers toward personal cleanliness: comb your hair, clean your ears, clean your nose but don't pick it; taught them how to behave: look pleasantly at folk, don't quarrel with dogs, and look people straight in the face when speaking; informed them how to act in church: kneel before the cross, don't chatter but be silent; and instructed them in table manners: don't be ravenous, don't blow on your food or put your knife to your face, and don't undo your girdle at the table. A similar book printed by Caxton, *The Babees Book,* subtitled *A Little Report of How Young People Should Behave,* was translated from Latin and described how pages should act in a lord's household.

The majority of books published by Caxton were not meant to be read by children, but three of his publications are now considered classics in children's literature. In 1481, he published the beast fable *Reynart the Foxe* (The History of Reynard the Fox), a satire of oppression and tyranny. This tale of a clever fox who could outwit all his adversaries became popular with both adults and children. Caxton's most important publication may be *The Book of the subtyl historyes and fables of Esope* (The Fables of Aesop), published in 1484. He translated this text from a manuscript by Machault, a French monk.

Caxton's edition of cautionary animal tales was divided into seven parts: information about Aesop's life; the Romulus collection of Aesop's fables; seventeen fables that had not been included in the Romulus collection; seventeen newly translated fables; twenty-seven fables of Avianus, a Roman fabulist; thirteen tales from a Spanish fabulist; and thirteen tales written by an Italian humorist (20). These fables about the weakness of men and animals were popular with readers of various ages and are still enjoyed by children today. Darton (7) says that *"Caxton's Aesop,* with infinitely little modernization, is the best text for children today" (p. 10).

Caxton's publication in 1485 of Sir Thomas Malory's *Le Morte d'Arthur* (The Death of Arthur) preserved the legendary story of King Arthur and his knights. This story has been published in many versions suitable for young readers.

There is no doubt that Caxton's publications had a major impact upon the world of literature. Lenaghan (20) says that there are at least eight of Caxton's books in the Famous Prefaces volume of *The Harvard Classics.* Meigs et al. (27) also stress Caxton's importance and evaluate his contributions to literature in this way: "His volumes, the first printed books which Englishmen and English children were to have offered to them in their own language, were in outward form of a standard not easily equalled. The ample pages, the broad margins, the black-letter type which suggested manuscript, all contributed to their beauty and dignity, to their worthiness to be England's first widespread realization of her own literature" (p. 31).

Caxton's books are described as beautiful, but they were still too expensive for the common people. The problem of providing inexpensive reading material was overcome, however, with the development of chapbooks, which sold for pennies. (Chapbooks did not compare with the higher literary quality of

Caxton's books.) They were first printed in England in the 1500s and even earlier in France. Some of the first chapbooks were based on ballads such as "The Two Children in the Wood," and traditional tales such as "Jack the Giant Killer" were also found in early versions and became very popular.

Chapbooks were available from two sources. Customers could go directly to the printer and select their choice from displays of large uncut sheets of as many as sixteen pages of text; the text would then be bound into a hard-cover book. Chapbooks were also available from peddlers (or "chapmen") who sold the books along with ribbons, patent medicines, and other wares at markets and fairs.

These inexpensive chapbooks with their crude woodcuts were very popular and included stories on many subjects. According to McCulloch (25), they could be classified into the following categories: religious instruction, supernatural interpretation, romantic legends, ballad tales, and historic narratives. The titles found in John Ashton's *Chap-Books of the Eighteenth Century* (2) include such religious titles as "The History of Joseph and his Brethren," "The Unhappy Birth, Wicked Life, and Miserable Death of the Vile Traytor and Apostle Judas Iscariot," and "The Holy Disciple." There were also traditional tales, including "Reynard the Fox," "Tom Thumb," and "A True

This lesson book, or battledore, was made from folded paper or cardboard.
Courtesy of The Horn Book, Inc.

Tale of Robin Hood." Supernatural tales such as "The Portsmouth Ghost" and "The Guilford Ghost" were also found.

Chapbooks were widely enjoyed in both England and the United States during the 1700s, but their popularity rapidly declined during the early 1800s. They were especially important, according to McCulloch (25), because they were a forerunner to many modern literary forms: children's books, western tales, and even comic books.

The Puritan Influence

Both censorship and the growing Puritan influence affected the literature of the 1600s. According to Bingham and Scholt (3), "The political-religious upheavals of seventeenth-century England brought many restrictions; one of the most affecting was censorship of the press" (p. 49). As both printing and literacy spread, the Crown realized the power of the press and in 1637 decreed that only London, Oxford, Cambridge, and York could have printing establishments.

The beliefs of the Puritans, who were growing in strength and numbers in England and America, also influenced literature of the period. Puritans considered traditional tales about giants, fairies, and witches found in chapbooks to be impious and corrupting. Consequently, they urged that children should not be allowed to read these materials and should be provided with literature that would instruct and reinforce their moral development. Lonsdale and Macintosh (23) describe the Puritan philosophy toward children and literature: "They wanted their descendants to be staunch Puritans to perpetuate the Puritan beliefs. The elders demanded that the children live according to Puritan rules as children of God. Family worship, admonitions from elders, home instruction, strict attendance at school, and close attention to lessons all were aimed at perpetuating those ideals and values for which the parents themselves had sacrificed so much. To the elders, the important part of education was learning to read, write, and figure. Only literature that would instruct and warn was tolerated" (p. 161).

Awesome titles for books that stressed the importance of instructing children in moral concerns were common in Puritan times. In 1649, the grandfather of Cotton Mather (The Puritan who was so influential during the New England witch-hunts) wrote a book called *Spiritual Milk for Boston Babes in either England, Drawn from the Breasts of Both Testaments for Their Souls' Nourishment.* In 1671, the leading Puritan writer James Janeway published a series of stories about children who died at an early age but led saintly lives. His *A Token for Children, Being an Exact Account of the Conversion, Holy and Exemplary Lives, and Joyful Deaths of Several Young Children* was

Peddlers sold inexpensive chapbooks between the sixteenth and nineteenth centuries.
From *Chapbooks of the Eighteenth Century* by John Ashton. Published by Chatti and Windus, 1882. From the John G. White Collection, Cleveland Public Library.

not meant for enjoyment but to instruct Puritan children in moral development.

The most influential piece of literature written during this period was John Bunyan's *Pilgrim's Progress,* published in 1678. This book was written to teach moral development, but it also contained bold action that appealed both to children and to older readers. Bunyan's hero, Christian, experiences many perilous adventures as he searches for salvation. Christian begins his journey alone and progresses through the Slough of Despond and into the Valley of Humiliation. His journey is not without danger. He must battle and overcome the monster who blocks the road. He overcomes this obstacle, and a companion, Faithful, joins him. When Faithful is executed in the town of Vanity Fair, another companion, Hopeful, joins Christian on his journey and helps him fight the giant Despair and finally reach salvation. The characters have such names as Mr.

Greatheart, Mr. Valiant-for-Truth, Ignorance, and Mrs. Timorous. The settings are equally well named — the Valley of the Shadow of Death, the Delectable Mountains, and the Eternal City. This story was not originally written for children, but it had such vivid actions and descriptions that children adopted it for its entertainment value.

Pilgrim's Progress and the *Spiritual Milk for Boston Babes in either England* were required reading for colonial children in America. In addition, the dominant book in colonial homes was *The New England Primer,* a combination ABC and catechism designed to teach Puritan ideals. The ABCs were written in such a way that spiritual instruction was the main theme. For example, the 1727 edition of the primer contained ABCs that followed this format:

The New England primer taught both Puritan ideals and the alphabet.
From *The New England Primer, Enlarged,* Boston, 1727 edition. From the Rare Books and Manuscript Division, The New York Public Library, Astor, Lenox, and Tilden Foundations.

The *New England Primer* appeared around 1690 and continued in various editions until 1830. According to Meigs et al. (27), the power and the influence of the primer lasted through at least a hundred editions. "The idea of early death and the necessity of preparing for it was a theme that was never laid to rest. . . . It was not the idea that the good die young, which they wished to keep always in mind, but the tragic fact that in that age the chance of life for young children was cruelly small and that parents must teach their children to be ready for death among the first things that they must know" (p. 114). The Puritan beliefs and the literature of this period were a major influence in England and America for a considerable length of time.

John Locke Influences the View of Childhood

Because children living in sixteenth- and seventeenth-century England were expected to assume adult roles early in life, teaching and books were designed accordingly. Even in behavior, a child was expected to act like an adult. In this strict climate, there was little consideration for child development, special educational needs, or literature written especially for children's interests.

Much of the enlightenment that considered the child as a person has been credited to the philosophy and writings of John Locke. Locke envisioned the child's mind at birth as a *tabula rasa,* a blank page on which ideas were to be imprinted. Consequently, he advocated milder ways of teaching and bringing up children than had been previously recommended. His philosophy, described in *Some Thoughts Concerning Education* (22), published in 1693, stressed the relationship between a healthy physical and mental development.

The experiences suggested by Locke were quite different from those recommended by the Puritans. According to Townsend (33), Locke believed that children who could read should be provided with easy, pleasant books suited to their capacities. These books should encourage them to read, reward them for their experiences, but not fill their heads with useless "trumpery" or encourage the principles of vice. Locke found a grave shortage of books that could provide pleasure or reward, but he could recommend *Aesop's Fables* and *Reynard the Fox.* He believed that *Aesop's Fables,* in addition to delighting and entertaining children, could provide useful reflections for adults. If the fables also had pictures, Locke felt that they could further entertain and provide encouragement for reading. Locke stated his concern for the materials available to children when he wrote in *Some Thoughts Concerning Education:* "Some easy pleasant book suited to his capacity, should be put into his hands, wherein the entertainment that he finds might draw him on, and reward his pains in reading. . . . To this purpose I think Aesop's Fables the best, which being stories apt to delight and entertain a child. . . . If Aesop has pictures in it, it will entertain him much the better, and encourage him to read . . . *Reynard the Fox* is another book I think may be made use of to the same purpose . . . . What other books there are in English of the kind of those above-mentioned, fit to engage the liking of children, and tempt him to read? I do not know" (pp. 140–41).

Locke's philosophy did provide the first glimmer of hope that children should go through a period of childhood rather than immediately assume the same roles as their parents. While there were few appropriate books for children, this was a beginning of the realization that they might benefit from books written to encourage their reading.

Charles Perrault's Tales of Mother Goose—1698

An exciting step in children's literature took place in seventeenth-century France. This literature was quite different from that written and recommended by the Puritans. Charles Perrault, a gifted member of the Académie Française, published a book called *Contes de ma Mère l'Oye* (Tales of Mother Goose). The stories in this collection were not those which are normally referred to as Mother Goose rhymes but were well-known fairy tales such as "Cinderella," "Sleeping Beauty," "Puss in Boots," "Little Red Riding Hood," "Blue Beard," "Little Thumb," "Requet with the Tuft," and "Diamond and the Toads." These tales were not his original writings but were the same stories that had been told to French children and had provided entertainment in the elegant salons of the Parisian aristocracy. Heroines such as Cinderella and Sleeping Beauty befitted the castle influence on the oral tradition. Perrault retold rather than wrote original tales, but he is considered one of the first writers to recognize that fairy tales belong to the world of children. Readers can thank Perrault or, as many scholars now believe, his son Pierre Perrault d'Armancour (28), for collecting these tales that have been translated and retold by many different contemporary writers and illustrators of children's books. Here, at last, was the beginning of entertainment written for children rather than adopted by them because nothing else was available.

Defoe and Swift—Great Adventure Writers

Children love adventure stories, but thus far the investigation of the history of children's literature has not revealed any adventure stories written for them. Two adventure books that appeared in the early eighteenth century were written for adults but were quickly embraced by children.

A political climate that rewarded dissenters by placing them into prison molded the author of the first great adventure story, *Robinson Crusoe,* in 1719. Defoe was condemned to Newgate Prison after he wrote a fiery pamphlet responding to the political and religious controversies of his time. His prison experiences, however, did not deter his writing; he wrote constantly even while in jail.

Defoe was motivated to write *Robinson Crusoe* when he read the personal accounts of a Scottish sailor, Alexander Selkirk, who had been marooned on one of the Juan Fernandez islands, located off the coast of Chile. This Scottish sailor disagreed with the captain of his ship, deserted, and lived alone on the island for four years. He was discovered by an English sea captain and brought back to England. Defoe was so captivated by the man's problems and those connected with long-term survival on an island that he began an adventure story that answered his questions about how a man might provide himself with food, clothing, and shelter if he were shipwrecked on an island.

The resulting tale first appeared in serial publication and then in a book. Children and adults enjoyed the exciting and suspenseful story about Robinson Crusoe and how he coped with his problems. The book was so influential that thirty-one years after Defoe's death Jean Jacques Rousseau, the founder of modern education, said that *Robinson Crusoe* would be the first book read by his son, Emile. Alderson (1) describes the influence of Defoe upon Rousseau: "Such is the beginning of a long discussion by Rousseau in the second part of *Emile,* in which he portrays the exemplary behavior and development of Robinson Crusoe, the man uninfluenced by corrupt civilization, the man who, thrown back entirely upon himself, experiences once again evolution in the highest sense. He receives as his companion the still unspoiled savage, who is a symbolic figure for his age which has started to believe in the natural goodness of mankind and which thinks to see corruption only in the influence of the surrounding world" (pp. 102–3).

Robinson Crusoe became so popular in the eighteenth century that it stimulated a whole group of books written about the same subject, which came to be known as *Robinsonades.* The most popular Robinsonade was Johann Wyss's *The Swiss Family Robinson.*

The second major adventure story written during the early eighteenth century also dealt with the subject of shipwreck. Jonathan Swift's *Gulliver's Travels,* published in 1726, included realistic adventures with strange beings encountered in mysterious lands. Like Defoe, Swift did not write for children.

In fact, Swift wrote *Gulliver's Travels* as a satire about the human race. Children, however, thought of the story as an enjoyable adventure. Gulliver was considered a hero when he was captured by the Lilliputians, the tiny people who lived in the land of Lilliput, whom he rescued from a series of mishaps. Seventeenth-century children enjoyed Gulliver's other adventures: he went into the land of the Brobdingnag, the realm of giants; onto the flying island of Laputa; and finally, into the land of the Houyhnhnms, the talking horses.

These adventure stories must have seemed truly remarkable to children surrounded otherwise by literature written only to instruct or to moralize. The impact of these eighteenth-century writers is still seen today, as twentieth-century children enjoy versions of these first adventure stories.

Newbery Publishes the First Books for Children

Townsend (33) describes the 1740s as the decade commonly regarded as the time when the idea of children's books began. New ways of thought emerged as the middle classes began to strengthen. Because a larger number of people had the time, the money, and the education to read, books became more important. Middle-class life also began to center around the home and family rather than around the street or great house. With this growing emphasis on family life, a realization that children should be children rather than small adults began.

Into this climate came John Newbery, an admirer of Locke. This advocate of a milder way of educating children was also a writer and publisher, so it was not surprising that he published books designed for children. Bingham and Scholt (3) suggest the importance of Newbery's publications: "It was his 1744 publication of *A Little Pretty Pocket Book* that ostensibly began a new line of books for children. Although his work reflected the didactic tone of the time, his books were not intended to be textbooks. Their gilt-paper covers, attractive pages, engaging stories and verses—and sometimes toys which were offered with the books—provided 'diversion' for children of the English-speaking world" (p. 86). *A Little Pretty Pocket Book* included a letter from Jack the Giant Killer written both to instruct and entertain children. Readers would not consider this early book for children to be very entertaining when compared with books written to amuse today's children, but it must have been revolutionary for its time. Newbery published a more famous book in 1765, *History of Little Goody Two Shoes,* a fictitious story written by Oliver Goldsmith.

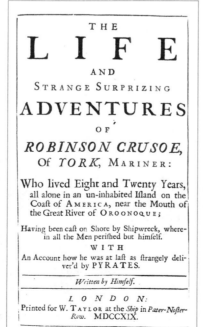

Although not written for children, Defoe's adventure became popular with eighteenth century children.
Courtesy of Lilly Library, Indiana University, Bloomington. Indiana.

Newbery's company, set up in London, became a success. His accomplishments are often attributed to his bustling energy, his interest in literature and writers, his love for children, and his taking note of the chapbooks and children's tastes as measured by the popularity of their favorite stories. He did not publish the drab chapbooks, however; his books had "gilt and embossed paper covers which were to be the mark of Newbery's taste, his understanding, and his astute business sense" (27, p. 59). In addition to *A Little Pretty Pocket Book* and *History of Little Goody Two Shoes,* Newbery's publications included *Nurse Truelove's New Year's Gift, Mother Goose, Tom Thumb's Folio,* and the old favorites such as *Aesop's Fables, Robinson Crusoe,* and *Gulliver's Travels.* Because of Newbery's success, publishers realized that there *was* a market for books written specifically for children. It is fitting that the coveted Newbery Award given annually to the outstanding author of a children's literature selection should bear his name.

Rousseau Advocates Natural Development

While Locke had advocated a milder and more rational approach for educating children, Rousseau recommended a totally new approach. Locke believed that children should be led in their search for knowledge, but Rousseau said that they should be accompanied in this search. According to his philosophy, children needed a wise adult who could supply necessary information and gently guide their education. Gillespie (12) maintains, "At a time when the major emphasis was on sharpening the muscles of the mind and filling it to the brim with all the knowledge in the world it could absorb, Jean Jacques Rousseau's exhortations to 'retournez à la nature' had a strong impact on the complacency of educators of this period" (p. 21).

Rousseau felt that children should grow naturally. In his *Emile,* in 1762, he described the growth and developmental stages of children and stressed the importance of experiences that would be in harmony with physical and mental development. Rousseau's stages progressed from early sensory motor development, through a concrete learning period, and into a period where intellectual conceptualization was possible. The major piece of literature that Rousseau felt both emphasized the roles of humans who must use their own ideas to cope with their environment and provided worthwhile reading for children was *Robinson Crusoe.*

Gillespie (12) summarizes Rousseau's importance to children and their literature by saying, "His impact on the attitude of parents toward children was forceful and unmistakable. Now children were looked upon as 'little angels' who could do

no wrong. They were permitted to be children rather than 'little adults'. They became the center of the educational scene rather than satellites around the curriculum" (p. 23).

William Blake's Poetry About Children

William Blake, who is credited with writing verses as if a child had written them, published his *Songs of Innocence* in 1789. Darton (7) characterizes Blake in the spiritual sense as "a child happy on a cloud, singing and desiring such songs as few but he could write" (p. 185). Blake's introductory poem to *Songs of Innocence* is often quoted and provides the reader an opportunity to visualize this happy child. (The punctuation and spelling are from the engraved first edition cited in Darton, 1932.)

Introduction

Piping down the valleys wild
Piping songs of pleasant glee
On a cloud I saw a child.
And he laughing said to me.

Pipe a song about a Lamb:
So I piped with merry chear,
Piper pipe that song again—
So I piped, he wept to hear.

Drop thy pipe thy happy pipe
Sing thy songs of happy chear.
So I sung the same again
While he wept with joy to hear

Piper sit thee down and write
In a book that all may read—
So he vanish'd from my sight.
And I pluck'd a hollow reed

And I made a rural pen,
And I stain'd the water clear,
And I wrote my happy songs,
Every child may joy to hear

Blake's second book of poetry, which has been used with children, was *Songs of Experience* published in 1794.

The Tales of the Brothers Grimm and Andersen

Sir Walter Scott novels, enthusiasm for Gothic architecture, respect for the Middle Ages, lyrical ballads, and Rousseau's philosophy of a return to nature were all characteristic of the Romantic Movement. In this atmosphere grew a desire to explore folk literature.

In the early 1800s, two German scholars, Jakob and Wilhelm Grimm, became interested in collecting German folktales that reflected the ancient German language and tradition. In researching their subject, the brothers listened to the tales told by Dortchen and Gretchen Wild, the Wilds' maid Marie, a farmer's wife called Frau Viehmännin, and other storytellers from throughout Germany. Although scholars disagree about the exact replication of the language in these tales, Hürlimann (15) describes the transcribing of tales in this way: "Naturally (and now comes the most important part of it all) the brothers, delighted as they may have been about the story-telling of these lovely young girls and others, did not just write down what they heard. Even for the first edition they did a lot of revising, comparing with other sources, and trying to find a simple language which was at the same time full of character. With time and with later editions it became clear that Jakob, the more scholarly, tried to keep the tales in the most simple, original form, more or less as they had heard them, and that Wilhelm, more of a poet, was for retelling them in a new form with regard to the children" (p. 71).

The first volume, published in 1812, contained eighty-five tales, including "Cinderella," "Hansel and Gretel," "Little Red Riding Hood," and "The Frog Prince." The second edition, published in 1815, was the book that was to become popular throughout the world of children. Hürlimann says that "Second edition changes were chiefly concessions to the children: some pictures by Ludwig Grimm were added, and the learned commentary was removed or banished to the third volume of the second edition which was a scholarly affair" (p. 72).

In 1823, the tales collected by the Brothers Grimm were translated into English and were published under the title *German Popular Stories*. Since that time, tales such as "Snow White and the Seven Dwarfs," "Rumpelstiltskin," and "The Elves and the Shoemaker" have been illustrated by hundreds of artists in many countries and have become part of our literary heritage. (Chapter six discusses some of the editions of these tales that have been either translated or rewritten for children.)

Most of the published folktales and fairy tales that have been discussed thus far were either written down by Perrault or the Brothers Grimm. The stories had been told in castles and cottages for many generations. Hans Christian Andersen is generally credited as being the first to create an original fairy tale, using his own experiences to stimulate his writing. Andersen

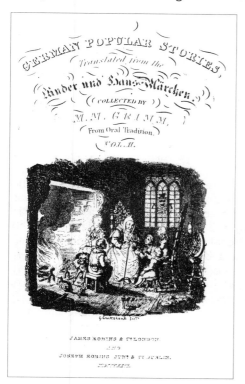

German Popular Stories, such as this 1826 edition, introduced the Grimms' folktales to English-speaking children. Courtesy of Lilly Library, Indiana University, Bloomington, Indiana.

was born to a poor but happy family in Odense, Denmark. His cobbler father shared stories with him and even built a puppet theater for his son's enjoyment. This theater gave Hans many hours of pleasure as he made up plays and put on puppet shows. Even when his father died and it seemed that he would have to learn a trade, he retained his dream of becoming an actor. During these poverty-stricken years, he often tried to forget his troubles by putting on shows and telling stories to children. Because Andersen wanted to write stories and plays, he returned to school to improve his writing skills. While there, he suffered from cruel jokes about his looks; he was thin and had large feet and a large nose. (Doesn't this sound like a theme for one of his fairy tales?) In 1828, when Andersen was twenty-three, he began to write stories and poems. Five years later, he was recognized by the Danish government as a promising writer; its financial support allowed him to travel and write about his experiences. When his *Life in Italy* was published, Andersen at last started to make money. His next book was far different from this more scholarly work: it was written in the same language used to tell stories and was the first of his famous fairy tale books. When his *Fairy Tales Told for Children* was published, a friend told him that his *Life in Italy* would make him famous but the fairy tales would make people remember him forever. Although Andersen did not believe his fairy tales were as good as his other books, he enjoyed writing them. Andersen wrote a new fairy tale book each Christmas as a gift to children of all ages.

When Andersen was sixty-two, he was invited back to Odense, the town in which he had known happiness, poverty, and then sadness. This time he was the honored guest at a celebration that lasted for an entire week. Andersen's fairy stories are still popular; newly illustrated versions are published every year. These colorful picture book versions, as well as tales in anthologies, are still enjoyed by children of many ages. (See chapter seven for a discussion of these modern fantasy books.)

Early Illustrators of Children's Books

Johann Amos Comenius, a Moravian teacher and former bishop of the Bohemian Brethren, is credited with writing the first picture book for children. Hürlimann (15) describes Comenius as a great humanist who wanted children to observe God's creations—plants, stars, clouds, rain, sun, and geography—rather than memorize abstracted knowledge. In order to achieve this goal, he took children out of the classroom and then wrote their experiences in simple sentences using both Latin and the children's own language. These simple sentences and accompanying woodcuts were published in 1658

Illustrated is a typical woodcut from *Orbis Pictus,* the first picture book for children.
A reprint of the *Orbis Pictus* has been published by Singing Tree Press, Gale Research Company, Detroit, Michigan.

as *Orbis Pictus* (Painted World). There is disagreement about whether Comenius drew these illustrations himself or whether he instructed artists in their execution. Bingham and Scholt (3) credit the woodcuts in the 1658 edition to Paul Kreutzberger and the wood engravings in the 1810 American edition to Alexander Anderson. Hürlimann, however, emphasizes the significance of this book by saying, "The pictures are in wonderful harmony with the text, and the book was to become for more than a century the most popular book with children of all classes" (p. 67).

Most illustrations before the 1800s, especially those in the inexpensive chapbooks, were crude woodcuts. If color was used, it was usually applied by hand by amateurs who filled in the colors according to a guide. Thomas Bewick is credited with being one of the earliest artists to illustrate books for children. His skillfully executed woodcuts graced *The New Lottery Book of Birds and Beasts,* published in 1771, and *A Pretty Book of Pictures for Little Masters and Misses; or Tommy Trip's History of Beasts and Birds,* published in 1779.

Three nineteenth-century English artists made an enormous impact on illustrations for children's books. Ruth Hill Viguers (9), in the introduction to *The Kate Greenaway Treasury,* says that the work of these artists "represents the best to be found in picture books for children in any era: the strength of design and richness of color and detail of Walter Crane's pictures; the eloquence, humor, vitality, and movement of Randolph Caldecott's art; and the tenderness, dignity, and grace of the very personal intepretation of Kate Greenaway's enchanted land of childhood" (p. 13).

Crane's *The House That Jack Built,* published in 1865, was the first of his series of *toy books,* the name used for picture books published for young children. These books, engraved by Edmund Evans, are credited with marking the beginning of the modern era in color illustrations. From 1865 through 1898, Crane illustrated over forty books, including folktales such as *The Three Bears, Cinderella,* and *Jack and the Bean-stalk* and alphabet books such as *The Railroad Alphabet, The Farmyard Alphabet,* and *The Absurd ABC.* Many of Crane's illustrations reflect his appreciation of Japanese color prints.

Caldecott's talent was discovered by the printer Evans when he saw Caldecott's illustrations for Washington Irving's *Old Christmas.* His first endeavor in 1878, *The History of John Gilpin,* demonstrated his ability to depict robust characters, action, and humor. (The Caldecott Medal, named for the artist, is embossed with the picture of Gilpin galloping through an English village.) Caldecott's lively and humorous figures jump fences, dance to the fiddler, and flirt with milkmaids in such picture books as *The Fox Jumps over the Parson's Gate, Come Lasses and Lads,* and *The Milkmaid.* Caldecott's picture books have been reissued by Frederick Warne.

Kate Greenaway, the third prominent illustrator of this period, was also encouraged and supported in her work by Evans. Delighted by Greenaway's drawings and verses, Evans printed her first book, *Under the Window,* in 1878. It was so successful that 70,000 English editions and over 30,000 French and German editions were sold. Greenaway continued illustrating books reflecting happy days of childhood and the blossoming apple trees and primroses that dotted the English countryside of her youth. In letters to her friend John Ruskin, she described her view of the world: "I go on liking things more and more, seeing them more and more beautiful. Don't you think it is a great possession to be able to get so much joy out of things that are always there to give it, and do not change? What a great pity my hands are not clever enough to do what my mind and eyes see, but there it is!" (9, p. 19).

Some other picture books illustrated by Greenaway are *Kate Greenaway's Birthday Book* (1880), *Mother Goose* (1881), *The Language of Flowers* (1884), *Marigold Garden* (1885), and *Kate Greenaway's Book of Games* (1889). One of Greenaway's best-known illustrated texts is Robert Browning's *Pied Piper of Hamelin* (1880).

Greenaway's name, like Caldecott's, has been given to an award honoring distinguished artistic accomplishment in the field of children's books. The Kate Greenaway Medal is given annually to the most distinguished British illustrator of children's books.

By the late 1800s when Crane, Caldecott, and Greenaway began drawing for children, the attitude toward children was also changing. According to Laws (18), these three artists "were under no public compulsion to be morally edifying or factually informative. Children were no longer supposed to

Caldecott's figures suggest action, movement, and vitality.
From *The Hey Diddle Diddle Picture Book* by Randolph Caldecott. Reproduced by permission of Frederick Warne & Co., Inc., Publishers.

CHART 2–2
Milestones in the History of Children's Illustration

1484	William Caxton, *Aesop's Fables*, contained over one hundred woodcuts.
1658	Johann Amos Comenius, *Orbis Pictus* (Painted World), considered by many to be the first picture book for children.
1771	Thomas Bewick, *The New Lottery Book of Birds and Beasts*.
1784	Thomas and John Bewick, *The Select Fables of Aesop and Others*.
1789	William Blake, *Songs of Innocence*.
1823	George Cruikshank, translation of Grimms' *Fairy Tales*.
1853	George Cruikshank, *Fairy Library*.
1865	John Tenniel, illustrations for Lewis Carroll's *Alice's Adventures in Wonderland*.
1865	Walter Crane, *The House That Jack Built*, the first of the toy books engraved by Evans.
1878	Randolph Caldecott, *The Diverting History of John Gilpin*, the first of sixteen picture books.
1878	Kate Greenaway, *Under the Window*.
1883	Howard Pyle, *Robin Hood*.
1900	Arthur Rackham, illustrations for Grimms' *Fairy Tales*.
1901	Beatrix Potter, *The Tale of Peter Rabbit*.
1924	E. H. Shepard, illustrations for A. A. Milne's *When We Were Very Young*.
1933	Kurt Wiese, illustrations for Marjorie Flack's *The Story of Ping*.
1933	E. H. Shepard, illustrations for Kenneth Grahame's *The Wind in the Willows*.
1937	Dr. Seuss, *And to Think That I Saw It on Mulberry Street*.

be 'young persons' whose taste would be much the same whether they were five or fifteen. So long as they pleased children artists were free; indeed Crane wrote that 'in a sober and matter-of-fact age Toybooks afford perhaps the only outlet for unrestricted flights of fancy open to the modern illustrator who likes to revolt against the depotism of facts'" (p. 318).

This brief discussion of illustrators does not mention all the artists who made contributions in the nineteenth century, but it does outline the relatively short history of children's book illustration. (Chapter four discusses many twentieth-century artists.) Chart 2–2 summarizes some milestones in illustration from the fifteenth century into the early twentieth century.

Victorian Influences on Literature

If literature is a product of its time, readers would expect the Victorian period to influence literature just as the Puritans influenced the literature of the 1600s and the Romantic Movement influenced the literature in the early 1800s. Kelly (17) describes the social factors that influenced children's literature of the Victorian period. He analyzed children's literature that appeared in children's periodicals of the time and concluded that "The ideal defined a social identity, a concept of selfhood that was peculiarly adapted to the realities of American life and its promise. The gentleman and lady offered models for negotiating the difficult and precarious passage from childhood to adulthood as well as for moderating the economic competition between free men that was the most important social fact of American life in the nineteenth century" (p. 42). This ideal represented a defensive stance appropriate in a precarious

world, and it offered children a definition of experience in which they could interpret events and find meaning in pain and suffering.

Kelly identified two types or patterns of stories in which children experienced this precarious world. In the first type, identified as *ordeal*, the child becomes isolated for a short time from the protection and influence of parents or other adults. Circumstances force the child to act decisively; the situations often seem contrived to emphasize that sound character rather than sound reasoning is involved. The child demonstrates the expected behaviors, then returns to the safety of the family and is justly rewarded. Courage, self-reliance, and presence of mind are the characteristics most often emphasized in this type of literature. For example, the heroine in "Nellie in the Light House," published in an 1877 edition of *St. Nicholas* magazine, exemplifies these qualities. She is a seven-year-old daughter of a lighthouse keeper. When her father goes to the mainland for supplies, the housekeeper is called away to nurse a neighbor, the housekeeper's husband collapses from a stroke, a storm causes high winds, and the beacon light is extinguished. Now alone, Nellie must overcome her fear and find a way to rekindle the beacon. She remembers a hymn her mother sang to her and rekindles the light; this light then saves her father who was caught in the storm.

The second type of story is *change of heart*. This type of story involves a child who has not as yet reached the ideal of self-discipline and sound moral character. At some point, the main character exhibits behavior that is not only unacceptable but often harmful; the child realizes this and resolves to change. An example of a change of heart story is "Charlie

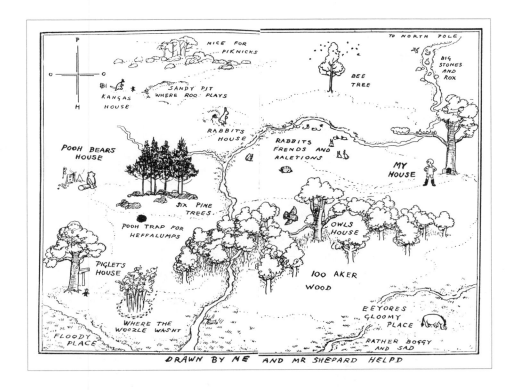

E. H. Shepard's illustrations provided a believable setting for Winnie-the-Pooh. Illustration by E. H. Shepard. From *Winnie-the-Pooh* by A. A. Milne. Published by Methuen & Co., 1926.

Balch's Metamorphosis," which appeared in an 1867 edition of the *Riverside Magazine for Young People.* Charlie is a sullen and lazy boy who has withdrawn after his mother's death. His father sends him to a boarding school where he joins a rough crowd of boys. Charlie realizes the errors of his ways during a sermon; the rest of the story places him in situations that test his resolution for change of heart. By the end of the story, Charlie has a cheerful disposition and better manners.

Kelly summarizes this Victorian literature by saying that fortitude, temperance, prudence, justice, liberality, courtesy, courage, self-reliance, and presence of mind are all social realities depicted in these stories. In fact, "So great was the emphasis on a self-control that one author warned that 'carelessness is worse than stealing'; and Louisa May Alcott assured the youthful readers of *Jack and Jill:* 'Our actions are in our own hands, but the consequences of them are not. Remember that . . . and think twice before you do anything'" (p. 41).

Victorian literature also reflected the intense interest in family and childhood that was a growing concern of the time. Many stories described life in the large families that were common in Victorian times. These families were more self-contained than families of today; the stories reflected their interests and aspirations. Religion was also a major part of family life, and consequently, was an important factor in Victorian literature.

Charlotte Yonge was one of the most prolific authors of the Victorian period who wrote about family life. Her childhood involved close family ties with her brother and many cousins. She often wrote down conversations among the people in her extended family that later provided her with realistic settings and dialogue. In addition to close family settings, her stories also reflected the Christian ethic of the Victorian period. *The Daisy Chain,* for example, told about a husband and wife who became missionaries and traveled to the Loyalty Islands.

Women are usually portrayed in Victorian novels as inferior to men. In *The Daisy Chain,* the hero's sister is advised not to compete with her brother at the university because a woman cannot equal a man scholastically. In Yonge's *The Clever Woman of the Family,* published in 1865, the heroine thinks for herself, but whenever there is a disagreement between her ideas and a man's ideas, she must adhere to the superior wisdom of a brother, father, or husband. Stark, in her introduction to *Florence Nightingale* (32), says that Victorian England was

MRS. EWING'S STORIES.

"What's your name, boy?" — PAGE 247.

JAN OF THE WINDMILL.
A STORY OF THE PLAINS.
By Mrs. EWING.   Price, $1.00.

ROBERTS BROTHERS, Publishers,
BOSTON

JULIANA HORATIA EWING WAS ONE OF THE MOST PROLIFIC authors of the Victorian period. Many of her popular tales first appeared in English periodicals such as *The Monthly Packet* and *Aunt Judy's Magazine for Young People*. Her first three stories appeared in *The Monthly Packet* in 1861. The following year these stories titled *Melchior's Dream and Other Stories* were published in book form by the Society for the Promotion of Christian Knowledge. Among her other books were *Mrs. Overtheway's Remembrances* (1869), *Jan of the Windmill* (1876), *Brothers of Pity, and Other Tales* (1882), *Jackanapes* (1884), and *Daddy Darwin's Dovecot* (1884). The last two books in this list were illustrated by Randolph Caldecott.

Literary critics of the time considered Mrs. Ewing's writing to be among the best of the Victorian period. Their comments also reflected the concerns and values of the times. For example, a critic for the Worcester Spy described Mrs. Ewing as a genius whose writing touched the heart, excited tender and noble emotion, encouraged religious feeling, and deepened the scorn for the mean and the cowardly. This same critic recommended that children read Mrs. Ewing's stories because they nourished everything that was lovely in children's characters. Consequently, their influence was considered "refining" and "ennobling." Mrs. Ewing's stories were popular for many years, remaining in print until the 1930s.

in the grip of an ideology that worshiped women in the home. They were viewed as wives and mothers or as failed wives or mothers. She declares, "Woman was the center of the age's cult of the family, 'The angel in the house,' tending to domestic altar. She was viewed as man's inferior—less rational, weaker, needing his protection; but at the same time, she was exalted for her spirituality, her moral influence. Man was the active one, the doer; woman was the inspirer and the nurturer. The spheres of work in the world and in the home were rigidly divided between the sexes" (p. 4). Consequently, middle- and upper-class women were encouraged to devote themselves to getting married and being a credit to their husbands; their education prepared them to oversee the education and moral

training of their children, command their servants, grace their husbands' tables, dress to please their husbands, do needlework, write letters, and dabble in drawing and music. They were also expected to visit the sick and do other charitable work that extended their nurturing female qualities. The majority of the books of the time stressed this same Victorian ideology.

The Victorian period provided a genteel life for children in the middle and upper classes, but there were still large groups of children who worked in coal mines and factories for long hours every day. In 1862, the poet Elizabeth Barrett Browning wrote of these children's woes in her poem, "The Cry of the Children." She described the children as weeping while other children played. Another well-known author of the period, Charles Dickens, also stirred the Victorian conscience and illustrated the plight of the less fortunate children of the time.

The values presented in most of the literature, however, were those of the upper middle classes. Erisman (8) investigated the values presented in American children's literature in the late nineteenth and early twentieth centuries and concluded that a dual world existed. The first world was nonfiction; it was realistic and dealt with the social, technological, and biographical topics of an urban society. The second world was fiction; it presented ideal middle-class values, implying that they were the typical American values. Likewise, Kelly's (16) research into the values found in children's literature for the last half of the nineteenth century concluded that fiction tended to provide models of the social types considered appropriate for emulation. Kelly also found evidence of unresolved tensions about America's growing cities, a beginning emphasis on the responsibilities of a cultural elite, and changing ideas about childhood.

Fantasy, Adventure, and Real People

As previously noted, changes were taking place that affected society's and the family's view of childhood. Childhood was considered a desirable time, at least for children in the middle and upper classes. There were also growing conflicts between upper- and middle-class values and the realities of a working-class society. Still more conflicts resulted between science and religion as people tried to cope with Darwin's theory of evolution. Women such as Florence Nightingale were trying to fight social attitudes and find a place for themselves in a world that considered them inferior. This world also provided a desire for glorious adventure as explorers brought the polar regions into world view, a railroad was built across the United States, and steamships were closing the distance gap between the United States and the continents of the world. All these changes influenced the world of children's literature.

Fantasy. By the mid-1800s, the resistance to fantasy in children's literature was finally removed. Children had been reading and enjoying the Grimms' and Perrault's folktales, and Andersen's stories had been translated into English. In addition, there was the growing belief that literature should entertain children during their extended period of childhood rather than merely instruct them. Fantasy in the Victorian period created a world, according to Chapman (6), where fears could be projected into impossible creatures, but there was safety because the fears were formed from imagination. Although

growing to maturity seemed dangerous, the happiest people acquired new knowledge while retaining childlike qualities. This description of fantasy leads readers directly into the works of the two most imaginative writers of this time.

Lewis Carroll and Edward Lear created landmarks in fantasy and nonsense. The details about the creation of Carroll's (pseudonym for Charles Dodgson) *Alice's Adventures in Won-*

The illustrations and text for *Alice's Adventures in Wonderland* were designed to give pleasure, not to teach a lesson. Illustration by John Tenniel. From *Alice's Adventures in Wonderland* by Lewis Carroll. Published by Macmillan and Co., 1865. Courtesy of Lilly Library, Indiana University, Bloomington, Indiana.

derland help readers understand why this book has become a classic in children's literature. Alderson (1) describes the scene in 1862: "One summer's day on the river at Oxford a thirty-year-old lecturer in mathematics at Christ Church was taking the three daughters of his Dean, Edith, Lorina, and Alice, out for a row. His name was Charles Lutwidge Dodgson. The day was hot and the children wanted to have a story told them, a thing they had come to expect from Mr. Dodgson. So the young lecturer complied, his mind relaxing in the drowsy heat and his thoughts, which did not tire so easily, following paths of their own making" (p. 64). The paths led directly down the rabbit hole and into adventures with fantasy creatures such as the white rabbit and the Cheshire cat. The story told that afternoon made such an impression on the real Alice that she pestered Dodgson to write it down. He wrote it for her, gave it to her as a gift, and after it was thoroughly enjoyed by many people, had it published for others.

The revolutionary quality of *Alice's Adventures in Wonderland* and the later *Through the Looking Glass* is, according to Meigs et al. (27), to be found "in the fact that they were written purely to give pleasure to children; moreover they were written purely for pleasure on the part of the author, too, for thus is a masterpiece made. Here, then, for the first time we find a story designed for children without a trace of a lesson or moral" (p. 194). When compared with earlier books written for children, this was truly a milestone in children's literature. (Chapter seven discusses the stories themselves.)

The second great fantasy writer, Edward Lear, wrote his fantasy in the form of nonsense verses. His absurd and delightful characters appeared for the first time in 1846 in *A Book of Nonsense; More Nonsense* was published in 1872. Lear's *Nonsense Songs, Botany and Alphabets,* published in 1871, contained his "Nonsense Stories," his "Nonsense Geography," "Natural History," and his "Nonsense Alphabets." Lear's *Laughable Lyrics,* published in 1877, contained such nonsense verses as "The Quangle-Wangle's Hat," "The Dong with the Luminous Nose," and "The Youghy-Bonghy-Bo."

Like Carroll's fantasy, Lear's verses were enjoyed both by younger and older readers. In addition, both writers are often quoted and enjoyed today as much as they were when their works were created. (Chapter eight discusses Lear's nonsense verses.)

Adventure. Real-life adventures were taking place: the North Pole was being discovered, Stanley and Livingston were exploring Africa, and a railroad was being constructed across the United States. If a person could not go to a remote region and

THERE WAS AN OLD MAN OF KILDARE,
WHO CLIMBED INTO A VERY HIGH CHAIR;
WHEN HE SAID, — "HERE I STAYS, —
TILL THE END OF MY DAYS,
THAT IMMOVABLE MAN OF KILDARE.

Lear's illustrations heightened the humor of his limericks. From *A Book of Nonsense* by Edward Lear. Published by Heinrich Hoffman, 1846. Courtesy of Lilly Library, Indiana University, Bloomington, Indiana.

overcome the perils lurking there, the next best adventure was the vicarious one offered through books.

Robert Louis Stevenson was the master of adventure stories written during this time. When *Treasure Island* was published, it was considered the greatest adventure story for children since *Robinson Crusoe*. Alderson (1) says that Robert Louis Stevenson "is the man whose influence on subsequent children's literature has been greatest" (p. 256).

Stevenson was born in Edinburgh, Scotland, the son of a lighthouse engineer. When he was a young boy, his father told him bedtime tales filled with "blood and thunder" and his nurse told him stories of body snatchers, ghosts, and martyrs. As an adult, he traveled extensively and sailed to many lands, but he still loved the lochs, islands, and misty forests of his home. All these early experiences are evident in Stevenson's two most famous adventure stories, *Treasure Island* and *Kidnapped*.

Treasure Island had an interesting beginning. While trying to entertain his stepson, Stevenson drew a water-color map of an island; he followed his drawing with the now famous story of pirates, buried treasure, and a young boy's adventures. Stevenson believed that an adventure story should have a specific effect on the reader. He felt that the readers should be absorbed in and delighted by a book; their minds should be filled with a kaleidoscope of images. In addition, stories should satisfy the readers' nameless longings. Stevenson believed that Crusoe's recoiling from the footprint on the beach, Achilles shouting against the Trojans, and Ulysses bending over the great bow were culminating moments that have been printed on the mind's eye forever (23). This was also the quality that children and adults should demand in their literature. Stevenson expertly created this quality in literature for children.

Alderson (1) describes *Treasure Island* as a boy's adventure par excellence. In his rationale for his belief, he says: "Call to mind for a moment the opening of this marvelous tale of treasure and treachery: the inn in the lonely cover, the comings and goings of the old pirates, the ominous hints of the fearful events which are to come. It is a superb overture, reaching its climax with the appearance of John Silver, stumping in on his wooden leg, as sympathetic a ship's cook as you ever wish to meet" (p. 257).

Treasure Island and *Kidnapped* have the ingredients of outstanding adventure: action, mystery, and pursuit and evasion. In addition to realistic action, they contain authentic historic settings. With such attributes, readers can easily see why Stevenson was described as the man who had great influence on subsequent children's literature.

While Stevenson wrote of pirates, buried treasure, and adventures on mysterious islands, Howard Pyle's books took readers back to an earlier time when it was possible to fight evil, overcome the king's injustice, and have a rollicking good time in the green depths of Sherwood Forest. Pyle's *The Merry Adventures of Robin Hood,* published in 1883, retold the old English ballad about Robin Hood, Little John, Friar Tuck, and the merry men who robbed the rich to give to the poor and constantly thwarted the evil plans of the Sheriff of Nottingham. Here was swashbuckling entertainment that also provided children with a glimpse of an earlier period in history. (See *The Merry Adventures of Robin Hood,* p. 233 in chapter six.)

The Industrial Revolution, the invention of the steam engine, and new, undreamed-of possibilities that must be just around the corner laid the groundwork for a new kind of adventure story in the last half of the nineteenth century. Jules Verne's science fiction adventure stories can certainly be classified as another bench mark in children's literature. Here was a writer who could envision a submarine, guided missiles, and dirigibles long before such things were possible. His first science fiction book, *Five Weeks in a Balloon,* was published in France in 1863. His two most famous books, *Twenty-Thousand Leagues under the Sea,* published in 1869, and *Around the World in Eighty Days,* published in 1872, have been immortalized in film. Consequently, the heroes of these books, Captain Nemo and Phileas Fogg, are well known both to readers and movie fans. It is interesting that Verne was stimulated to write because he admired the writing of an earlier author, Daniel Defoe. *The Mysterious Island,* published in 1875, was written because of Verne's interest in *Robinson Crusoe.*

The tribute to Verne's genius can be seen in the popularity of his works even today after his glorious inventions have become reality. The details and descriptions are so believable that they seem as modern now as they did when they were published in the 1800s. The popularity of Verne's literature also caused other authors to write science fiction and expand this new genre.

Real People. While some books written during this period dealt with fantasy and fantastic adventures, many others were written around realistic situations and real people. During the latter nineteenth and early twentieth centuries, a type of book that Fraser (10) calls a *local-color story* came into its own. This type of story, in which place, story, and characters are tightly integrated, is of major interest because, according to Fraser, "This integration which reveals the complex involvement of human, cultural, and geographical influences, produces a rich literature—peculiarly rich for the student of American culture, and extraordinarily rich for the young persons fortunate enough to read it" (p. 55). During this time, authors wrote about such diverse areas as Edward Eggleston's *The Hoosier School Boy* (boyhood days in rural Indiana), Thomas Bailey Aldrich's *The Story of a Bad Boy* (New England seafaring town), Kate Douglas Wiggin's *Rebecca of Sunnybrook Farm* (rural Maine), Mark Twain's *Huckleberry Finn* (Mississippi River town), and Frances Courtenay Baylor's *Juan and Juanita* (Southwest). The diverse qualities of American geography and people are found in these books. Fraser maintains that these local-color stories also transmit a conservative, traditional view of American life to the next generation. He says, "The stories convey a sentimental view of human life. Despite the stories' surface reality in language and setting, their young readers encounter in them citizens of a country notably different from that in which the tales are being told. Far from being representative of modern types, these characters are often carry-overs

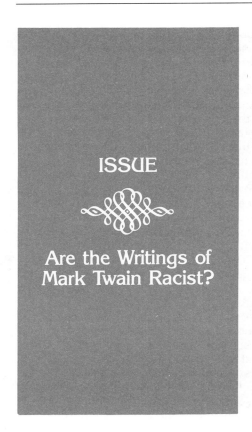

ISSUE

Are the Writings of Mark Twain Racist?

WRITINGS OF MARK Twain (Samuel Clemens), especially the *Adventures of Huckleberry Finn,* are under protest in the 1980s because of Twain's use of language and imagery to depict black people. Those who suggest that the *Adventures of Huckleberry Finn* should be banned or rewritten point to the numerous use of "nigger" and instances in which black Americans are stereotyped rather than presented as individual, well-rounded characters.

Twain might find this 1980s protest ironic; in the 1880s he was accused of going too far in his cause for human equality and justice. Robert Scott Kellner,[1] a recognized Twain scholar, believes, however, that "a close examination of Twain's writing reveals an element of satire in his seemingly racist language, a satire directed at the reader who would choose to agree with the stereotyped image. Twain's language and imagery about the blacks in his stories work together as a mirror in which bigoted readers ultimately see themselves." Kellner stresses that in the relationships between Huckleberry Finn and Jim, Twain makes it clear that a black man is capable of earning a trust that withstands the pressures of an anti-black heritage. In addition, he can give love and loyalty, strive for physical emancipation, and be a wise father figure for a misinformed boy.

As students of children's literature read the writings of Mark Twain, they should consider if the writings reflect a belief in the inequality of man or if they suggest that people of all races share a common humanity.

1 Kellner, Robert Scott. "Defending Mark Twain." *The Eagle,* Bryan-College Station, Texas, 11 April 1982, p. 1D.

from an earlier age, persons whose thoughts reflect the ideals of a preindustrial, apolitical, largely rural America. So even as the stories acquaint their readers with new locales, they transmit the attitudes of an earlier time" (p. 59).

The greatest American realistic adventure writer of this period was Mark Twain (Samuel Clemens). While Stevenson was writing about adventures on far-off islands, Twain was immortalizing life on the Mississippi River. Twain grew up in the river town of Hannibal, Missouri, where he lived many of the adventures about which he later wrote. He explored the river and its islands, raided melon patches, and used a cave as a rendezvous to plan further adventures and mischief with his friends. These adventures made Tom Sawyer and Huckleberry Finn live for many adventure-loving children. Twain's heroes did not leave the continent, but they did run away from home, have exciting adventures on a nearby island, return in time to hear plans for their own funeral, and then attend this momentous occasion. Characters such as Injun Joe, Aunt Polly, Tom Sawyer, Becky Thatcher, and Huckleberry Finn still provide hours of reading pleasure for children and adults today.

Many books reflected the American family of the Victorian period, and series stories dealing with the everyday lives of large families became popular. Margaret Sidney, for example, wrote a series of books about the five little Peppers. The first book, *The Five Little Peppers and How They Grew,* published in 1881, was followed by *The Five Little Peppers Midway* and *The Five Little Peppers Grown Up.*

The most famous author of family stories was certainly ahead of her time. Louisa May Alcott's account of family life in *Little Women,* published in 1868, is so real that readers feel that they know each member of the March family intimately; this relationship is especially strong with Jo, the main character. This book that shows the warm family ties and everyday struggles of a family of meager means is actually about Alcott's own family. In many ways, her life was quite different from the usual Victorian model. Her father, Bronson Alcott, be-

Mark Twain wrote adventures about life in an environment in which he lived.
From *Adventures of Huckleberry Finn* by Mark Twain. Published by Charles L. Webster and Co., 1885. Courtesy of Lilly Library, Indiana University, Bloomington, Indiana.

that made Alcott herself such an unusual woman. She was courageous, warm, and honest, but she had a quick temper that often got her into difficulty. Alcott did not believe in the inferiority of women. *Little Women* was so popular that she wrote a sequel in 1869, *Little Women, Part II.* She also wrote such favorites as *An Old-Fashioned Girl, Little Men,* and *Eight Cousins.*

One very popular realistic story published during this period had a foreign background. When foreign travel was just becoming possible, the lure of foreign lands was strong in books. Mountains that climb into the sky, sheepherders, tinkling bells, rushing streams, flower-strewn meadows, a hut with a bed of fresh hay, and the freedom to wander in these delightful Swiss surroundings were found in Johanna Spyri's *Heidi,* published in 1880 and translated into English in 1884. Spyri was born in a Swiss village where her father was the doctor. While she was growing up, she and her family made many trips to the moun-

lieved in educating his daughters; consequently, she was first educated at home by her father and then went to the district school. Alcott's life was very similar to Jo's in *Little Women.* She went to Boston where she tried to earn a living so that her family would not have to support her. While there, she wrote constantly. Her early melodramatic stories were published in magazines, and she began to earn her living as a writer. Alcott left Boston to nurse her sister during a terminal illness. (This incident became Beth's illness and subsequent death in *Little Women.*) When the Civil War came, Alcott left home to nurse soldiers until poor health forced her to return to her family.

In 1867, a publisher asked her to write a book for girls, and she decided to write about her own family. The resulting *Little Women* was an overwhelming success. Readers enjoyed the intimate details of a warm, loving, and very human family. The most popular character, Jo, showed all of the characteristics

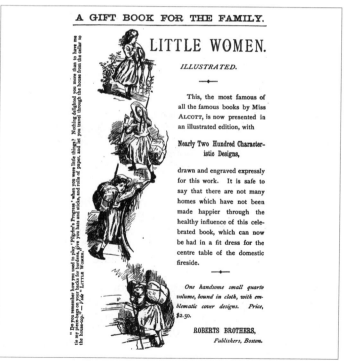

An advertisement for *Little Women* suggests the happy family influence of the book.
From *Jo's Boys and How They Turned Out* by Louisa M. Alcott. Published by Roberts Brothers, 1886.

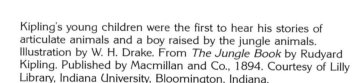

Kipling's young children were the first to hear his stories of articulate animals and a boy raised by the jungle animals. Illustration by W. H. Drake. From *The Jungle Book* by Rudyard Kipling. Published by Macmillan and Co., 1894. Courtesy of Lilly Library, Indiana University, Bloomington, Indiana.

tain village of Maienfeld where they played in the meadows and brooks and had picnic lunches at the herdsman's hut. Later, when she wrote *Heidi,* these earlier experiences created a setting and a heroine that were real to her readers. Haviland (13) says that "In an era when so much children's literature was burdened with dead dialogue and moral content, the freshness of this story must have come as a breath of mountain air; today, Heidi holds her own with carefree heroines of any of the best modern children's books because she is real" (p. 79).

Space does not allow a complete discussion of all the books that were written for children or were written for adults and read by children. Chart 2–3 lists some previously discussed books and some additional milestones in literature that bring the world of children's books into the twentieth century.

CHANGING VIEWS OF CHILDREN AND FAMILY IN LITERATURE

Attitudes toward children have changed considerably since the early centuries when many children were not greatly valued, infanticide was practiced, and children were believed to be undeveloped adults who must be brought quickly into the adult world. Likewise, the family has changed from the Middle Ages, when poor children shared the poverty and hard work of their parents and children from upper classes and nobility were separated from their families for long periods. During this time, upper-class children were often cared for by a nurse until the age of six or seven and then sent to a monastery school or exchanged with children from other households where a boy

CHART 2–3
Notable Authors of Children's Literature

Year	Author, Title	Year	Author, Title
1477	William Caxton, *Caxton's Book of Curtesye*	1908	Kenneth Grahame, *The Wind in the Willows*
1484	William Caxton, *The Fables of Aesop*	1911	Frances Hodgson Burnett, *The Secret Garden*
1485	William Caxton, *Le Morte d'Arthur*	1913	Eleanor H. Porter, *Pollyanna*
1678	John Bunyan, *Pilgrim's Progress*	1918	O. Henry, *The Ransome of Red Chief*
1698	Charles Perrault or Pierre Perrault d'Armancour, *Tales of Mother Goose*	1921	Hendrik Willem Van Loon, *The Story of Mankind* (One of the first informational books attempting to make learning exciting; first Newbery Medal, 1922)
1719	Daniel Defoe, *Robinson Crusoe*	1922	Margery Williams Bianco, *The Velveteen Rabbit*
1726	Jonathan Swift, *Gulliver's Travels*	1924	A. A. Milne, *When We Were Very Young*
1744	John Newbery, *A Little Pretty Pocket Book*	1926	A. A. Milne, *Winnie-the-Pooh*
1789	William Blake, *Songs of Innocence*	1928	Wanda Gág, *Millions of Cats*
1812	First volume of Grimm Brothers' fairy tales, *Kinder-und Hausmärchen*		Carl Sandburg, *Abe Lincoln Grows Up*
	Johann Wyss, *Swiss Family Robinson*	1929	Rachel Field, *Hitty, Her First Hundred Years*
1820	Sir Walter Scott, *Ivanhoe: A Romance*	1932	Laura Ingalls Wilder, *Little House in the Big Woods*
1823	Clement G. Moore, *A Visit from St. Nicholas*		Laura E. Richards, *Tirra Lirra: Rhymes Old and New*
1826	James Fenimore Cooper, *The Last of the Mohicans*	1933	Jean de Brunhoff, *The Story of Babar*
1843	Charles Dickens, *A Christmas Carol*	1937	Dr. Seuss, *And to Think That I Saw It on Mulberry Street*
1846	Edward Lear, *A Book of Nonsense*		John Ronald Reuel Tolkien, *The Hobbit*
	Hans Christian Andersen's fairy tales in English translations	1939	James Daugherty, *Daniel Boone*
1851	John Ruskin, *King of the Golden River*	1940	Armstrong Sperry, *Call It Courage*
1856	Charlotte Yonge, *The Daisy Chain*		Doris Gates, *Blue Willow*
1862	Christina Georgina Rossetti, *Goblin Market*	1941	Lois Lenski, *Indian Captive, The Story of Mary Jemison*
1863	Charles Kingsley, *The Water Babies*		Robert McCloskey, *Make Way for Ducklings*
1865	Lewis Carroll, *Alice's Adventures in Wonderland*	1942	Virginia Lee Burton, *The Little House*
	Mary Elizabeth Mapes Dodge, *Hans Brinker, or the Silver Skates, a Story of Life in Holland*	1944	Robert Lawson, *Rabbit Hill*
1868	Louisa May Alcott, *Little Women*	1946	Esther Forbes, *Johnny Tremain*
1870	Thomas Bailey Aldrich, *The Story of a Bad Boy*	1947	Marcia Brown, *Stone Soup*
1871	George MacDonald, *At the Back of the North Wind*	1950	Beverly Cleary, *Henry Huggins*
1872	Jules Verne, *Around the World in Eighty Days*	1951	Olivia Coolidge, *Legends of the North*
1873	*St. Nicholas: Scribner's Illustrated Magazine for Girls and Boys*, edited by Mary Mapes Dodge	1952	Lynd Ward, *The Biggest Bear*
1876	Mark Twain, *The Adventures of Tom Sawyer*		E. B. White, *Charlotte's Web*
1877	Anna Sewell, *Black Beauty*		David McCord, *Far and Few*
1880	Margaret Sidney, *The Five Little Peppers and How They Grew*	1953	Mary Norton, *The Borrowers*
1881	Joel Chandler Harris, *Uncle Remus; His Songs and Sayings: The Folklore of the Old Plantation*	1954	Rosemary Sutcliff, *The Eagle of the Ninth*
1883	Howard Pyle, *Merry Adventures of Robin Hood of Great Renown, in Nottinghamshire*	1955	L. M. Boston, *The Children of Green Knowe*
	Robert Louis Stevenson, *Treasure Island*	1957	Else Holmelund Minarik, *Little Bear*
1884	Johanna Spyri, *Heidi; Her Years of Wandering and Learning*	1958	Jean Fritz, *The Cabin Faced West*
1885	Robert Louis Stevenson, *A Child's Garden of Verses*		Elizabeth George Speare, *The Witch of Blackbird Pond*
1886	Frances Hodgson Burnett, *Little Lord Fauntleroy*	1959	Leo Lionni, *Little Blue and Little Yellow*
1889	Andrew Lang, *The Blue Fairy Book*		Jean George, *My Side of the Mountain*
1892	Carlo Collodi, *The Adventures of Pinocchio*	1960	Michael Bond, *A Bear Called Paddington*
	Arthur Conan Doyle, *The Adventures of Sherlock Holmes*		Scott O'Dell, *Island of the Blue Dolphins*
1894	Rudyard Kipling, *The Jungle Books*	1961	C. S. Lewis, *The Lion, the Witch, and the Wardrobe*
1901	Beatrix Potter, *The Tale of Peter Rabbit*	1962	Ronald Syme, *African Traveler, The Story of Mary Kingsley*
1903	L. Leslie Brooke, *Johnny Crow's Garden*		Madeleine L'Engle, *A Wrinkle in Time*
	Kate Douglas Wiggin, *Rebecca of Sunnybrook Farm*		Ezra Jack Keats, *The Snowy Day*
	J. M. Barrie, *Peter Pan; or The Boy Who Would Not Grow Up*	1964	Louise Fitzhugh, *Harriet the Spy*
1904	Howard Garis, *The Bobbsey Twins; or Merry Days Indoors and Out* (There are over seventy books in the series.)		Irene Hunt, *Across Five Aprils*
			Lloyd Alexander, *The Book of Three*
		1967	John Christopher, *The White Mountains*
			E. L. Konigsburg, *Jennifer, Hecate, MacBeth, William McKinley and Me, Elizabeth*
			Virginia Hamilton, *Zeely*

CHART 2–3 *(cont.)*
Notable Authors of Children's Literature

1969	John Steptoe, *Stevie*	1976	Mildred Taylor, *Roll of Thunder Hear My Cry*
	William H. Armstrong, *Sounder*	1977	Jamake Highwater, *Anpao: An Indian Odyssey*
	Theodore Taylor, *The Cay*		Patricia Clapp, *I'm Deborah Sampson: A Soldier in the War of the Revolution*
	Vera and Bill Cleaver, *Where the Lilies Bloom*		Katherine Paterson, *Bridge to Terabithia*
	William Steig, *Sylvester and the Magic Pebble*		Jane Yolen, *The Seeing Stick*
1970	Betsy Byars, *Summer of the Swans*		Margaret Musgrove, *Ashanti to Zulu: African Traditions*
	Judy Blume, *Are You There God? It's Me, Margaret*	1978	Tomie de Paola, *The Clown of God*
1971	Arnold Lobel, *Frog and Toad Are Friends*	1979	José Aruego and Ariane Dewey, *We Hide, You Seek*
	Muriel Feelings, *Moja Means One: Swahili Counting Book*	1981	Nancy Willard, *A Visit to William Blake's Inn*
	Robert Kraus, *Leo, the Late Bloomer*	1982	Graham Oakley, *Hetty and Harriet*
1972	Judith Viorst, *Alexander and the Terrible, Horrible, No Good, Very Bad Day*		Clayton Bess, *Story for a Black Night*
			Nina Bawden, *Kept in the Dark*
1973	Doris Smith, *A Taste of Blackberries*		Laurence Pringle, *Water: The Next Great Resource Battle*
1974	Janet Hickman, *The Valley of the Shadow*		Cynthia Rylant, *When I Was Young in the Mountains*
1975	Lawrence Yep, *Dragonwings*		

might train for knighthood or a girl could learn etiquette, music, and household management.

Authors of literature written for children or adopted by children often write books that reflect the views of childhood and the family that are common for the time. Researchers are increasingly viewing children's literature as a vehicle for looking at these changing attitudes. Bingham and Scholt (3), in *Fifteen Centuries of Children's Literature: An Annotated Chronology of British and American Works in Historical Context,* present the history of children's literature according to the historical background, the development of books, the attitudes toward and treatment of children, and an annotated chronology of books. Kelly (16), in *Mother Was a Lady: Self and Society in Selected American Children's Periodicals, 1865–1890,* considers the social values reflected in children's stories of that time period. Lystad (24) considers the sociology of children's books over two centuries in *From Dr. Mather to Dr. Seuss: Two Hundred Years of American Books for Children.*

Other researchers have analyzed children's literature over time: Shaw (29) studied themes in books published between 1850 and 1964, Carmichael (5) analyzed social values reflected in contemporary realistic fiction, Townsend (33) contrasted the relationships between generations depicted in the literature of the 1950s and the 1960s, Homze (14) analyzed the changing interpersonal relationships depicted in realistic fiction published between 1920 and 1960, and Cadogan and Craig (4) looked at the changing role of females in *You're a Brick, Angela! A New Look at Girls' Fiction from 1839 to 1975.*

There is a considerable body of children's literature written around children and their relationships within the family. This section of the chapter considers the changing view of children and the family by comparing examples of literature published from 1865 to 1903, 1938 to 1960, and 1969 to 1980. Charts show examples of social values, family life, and personal relationships and feelings expressed by the child characters or family members. Space does not permit an extensive search of many volumes, but five or six examples have been chosen for discussion from each time period. These books illustrate many of the changing viewpoints toward children and the family. The books can be located easily by children's literature students who would like to read them. The older books are available in reproductions published by Garland Publishing of New York and London.

The Child and the Family, 1865–1903

The Victorian period with its stress on developing duty to God and parents, the rise of the public school and Sunday School movements, and the beginning of a belief that children are individuals in their own right are all viewpoints that are identifiable in the literature of the time. Much literature suggests the development of conscience, the merit of striving for perfection, and the male and female roles exemplified by the family members. *The Daisy Chain* (Charlotte Yonge), *Little Women* (Louisa M. Alcott), *The Story of a Bad Boy* (Thomas Bailey Aldrich), *Five Little Peppers and How They Grew* (Margaret Sidney), and *Rebecca of Sunnybrook Farm* (Kate Douglas Wiggin) provide examples of the literature during this period.

Similarities and differences in social values are expressed by the authors. All indicate the acceptance of responsibility,

Changing Issues Affect Book Publishing in the Twentieth Century

THE TWENTIETH CENTURY, like other historic periods, produced issues that affected books published for children. A brief look at major issues in the 1950s, 1960s, and 1970s indicates that children's book publishers must respond to the issues of the times. Ann Durell identifies some of these changing issues in two articles published in *The Horn Book*.[1,2]

Durell identifies the 1950s as a time when publishing was fun. The taboos of the 1900s were still in place: no lying or stealing unless suitably punished, no drinking, no bad language. In the late 1950s, the library market took on new significance as Russia launched Sputnik. Although attacks were made against our educational system, books were considered a means for improving education. A major controversy over one book may suggest the feelings of the times. Racial prejudice was exemplified by the protests and even book burnings that followed the publication of Garth Williams's *The Rabbits' Wedding* (One rabbit was black and the other was white).

Durell categorizes the 1960s as a time of rapidly expanding school libraries. Title II of the Elementary and Secondary School Act mandated funds for the purchase of nontextbooks for schools. Both the sale of nonfiction and easy-to-read book titles and school libraries expanded rapidly. New issues were, however, entering the publishing trade as the country was polarized by the Vietnam War and the new demands of the Great Society. The all-white world of children's books was challenged; editors started searching for black authors. For the most part, however, children's books did not reflect the social upheavals of the time.

The 1970s brought additional issues and literature that reflected the social upheavals. Reactions to two books in the early 1970s exemplify these changing issues. When a white author won the Newbery Medal for writing about a black family (*Sounder*), protests and demands were made which intensified editors' search for authors and illustrators who represented ethnic minorities. In another book, Mickey's nudity in Maurice Sendak's *In the Night Kitchen* resulted in actions ranging from covering the nudity before the book was placed on the shelf to actual banning of the book. As the 1970s continued, concern was raised about the sex roles portrayed in children's books; lists of taboos in children's books were reduced; and books reflected a positive image of ethnic minorities. Durell emphasizes the paradox created by these changes and the new pressures exerted on publishers. On the one hand, the only criterion for allowing books to be published was the portrayal of a positive picture of females, minority groups, senior citizens, and handicapped. On the other hand, groups demanding conservative standards insisted on returning to the 1950s taboos. Consequently, censorship, but for different reasons, became an issue on both sides.

Many of these issues have not been resolved. The various sides of the issues will be discussed in appropriate chapters throughout this book.

1 Durell, Ann. "There Is No Happy Ending: Children's Book Publishing — Past, Present, and Future." *The Horn Book* 58 (Feb. 1982): 23-30.

2 Durell, Ann. "There Is No Happy Ending: Children's Book Publishing — Past, Present, and Future." *The Horn Book* 58 (April 1982): 145-50.

whether to the family, or to the improvement of life for the poor, or for one's own improvement. For example, the older family members in *The Daisy Chain* take over raising the younger children when their mother dies; their greatest concerns are instilling Christian goodness and the ability to live up to their father's wishes. Likewise, the children in *Little Women* and *Five Little Peppers and How They Grew* feel responsible for their siblings and their mothers. Rebecca, in *Rebecca of Sunnybrook Farm,* feels this responsibility to such an extent that she completes four years of work at the academy in three years. She wants to earn a living so that she can help educate her siblings.

There are definite ideas about sex roles connected with equality of opportunity, ambition, and the importance of education and knowledge. Male characters in *The Daisy Chain* and *Little Women* attend the university; males and females attend separate schools in *The Story of a Bad Boy.* Education may also stress different objectives for males and females. Yonge's heroine secretly completes assignments related to her brother's classical education and is not expected to understand mathematical concepts. Drawing, writing, and music are desired accomplishments for females in *Little Women;* piano lessons are sought by the oldest female Pepper, and writing is Rebecca's desire. In contrast, the males in *The Daisy Chain* receive a classical education, while Aldrich's hero wants training in such "manly arts" as boxing, riding, and rowing.

All the characters respect adult authority. Children strive to live up to their parents' ideals or want the acceptance and respect of their parents. The hero in *The Story of a Bad Boy* may not always ask for or follow his grandfather's advice, but he admits that he deserves the terrible things that usually happen to him when he disobeys.

A religious emphasis is a consistent characteristic of family life in these books. *The Daisy Chain* family reads the Bible together, discusses the meaning of the minister's sermons, debates the relative importance of the temptations in their lives, and organizes a church and school for the poor. The *Little Women* receive strength from prayer and Bible reading. Sundays, in *The Story of a Bad Boy,* are described as solemn days in which the family attends church, reads the Scriptures, and eats food prepared the day before. *The Five Little Peppers* voice considerable admiration for the clergy and want to become "good." Rebecca's aunt and her father before her are influential church members.

Alcott's illustration reinforces the vision of a warm, loving Victorian family.
Illustration by May Alcott. From *Little Women or, Meg, Jo, Beth and Amy* by Louisa M. Alcott. Published by Roberts Brothers, 1868. Courtesy of Lilly Library, Indiana University, Bloomington, Indiana.

The relationships within the family show many similarities. There are definite male and female roles: the females usually run the household and make decisions dealing with everyday life. The father is usually the undisputed head of the family. The author may state this viewpoint so there is no misunderstanding on the part of the reader. Alcott expresses this view as she describes the March family after Mr. March returns from the war:

To outsiders, the five energetic women seemed to rule the house, and so they did in many things; but the quiet scholar, sitting among his books, was still the head of the family, the household conscience, anchor, and comforter: to him the busy, anxious women always turned in troublous times, finding him, in the truest sense of those sacred words, husband and father. (p. 294)

Children in several of these stories have enjoyable play experiences. The *Little Women* act out plays, sing, go on excursions, and play their own version of *Pilgrim's Progress*. In addition to plays, the boys in *The Story of a Bad Boy* form a boys' club that provides an organizational focus for their outings and pranks. The Pepper children entertain each other by telling stories.

Considerable insights about these children and their families are gained by viewing the types of problems experienced by the heroes and heroines. Yonge's heroine strives to raise the family and help the poor. She works to keep the youngest baby an "unstained jewel" until the baby will return to her mother. In addition, she and her brother face the problems concerned with providing spiritual guidance to the poor. Many of Jo's problems in *Little Women* are related to strengthening her self-control. Alcott describes Jo's remorse and personal development as she turns to her mother:

Jo's only answer was to hold her mother close, and, in the silence which followed, the sincerest prayer she had ever prayed left her heart without words; for in that sad, yet happy hour, she had learned not only the bitterness of remorse and despair, but the sweetness of self-denial and self-control; and, led by her mother's hand, she had drawn nearer to the Friend who welcomes every child with a love stronger than that of any father, tenderer than that of any mother. (p. 103)

The problems created by Aldrich for his hero allow the boy to consider and strengthen his own moral code. Although there are several unhappy and even disastrous experiences, the hero does not dwell upon them but suggests that they have caused him to become more manly and self-reliant.

Overcoming problems related to poverty and growing up without a father are major concerns of the Pepper children. Their mother often answers them in this way: "You keep on a-tryin', and the Lord'll send some way; don't you go to botherin' your head about it now, Polly—it'll come when it's time" (p. 256). The family's financial problems are finally solved when a wealthy old gentleman invites them to share his home. The man's daughter reveals their faith in the Pepper family when she says: "I do believe they'll repay you; for I do think there's good blood there; these children have a look about them that shows them worthy of trust" (p. 292).

Many of Rebecca's problems are caused by the conflicts between her aunt's strict views on children's behavior and her own high-spirited actions. Rebecca also experiences personal misgivings when her actions do not live up to her desire to be good. The advantages of these conflicts are stated by her English teacher at the academy: "Luckily she attends to her own development. . . . In a sense she is independent of everything and everybody; she follows her saint without being conscious of it" (p. 255). Her teacher continues to admire her aunt's uncompromising New England grit and what it has done for Rebecca: "I don't regret one burden that Rebecca has borne or one sorrow that she has shared. Necessity has only made her brave; poverty has only made her daring and self-reliant" (p. 255).

Chart 2–4 illustrates the similarities and differences found in the literature of this time period.

The Child and the Family, 1938–1960

The 1900s brought considerable change to children's lives: many states passed child labor laws; John Dewey's theories stressed socialization of children (the Progressive Education Association was formed in 1918); the educational system expanded rapidly (aims for secondary education were enacted by the National Education Association in 1918); and religious training put less emphasis on sinfulness and began to stress the importance of moral development and responsibility toward others.

McElderry (26) says, "With the end of World War II in 1948, another period of expansion began and children's book departments achieved major status in trade publishing. Prior to this time they had been pleasant and respected adjuncts, but

CHART 2—4

Social Values, Family Life, and Personal Relationships, 1865-1903

	SOCIAL VALUES						
Book, Author, Date, Setting	Dignity of Human Beings	Acceptance of Responsibility	Belief in Equality of Opportunity	Ambition	Obedience to Law, Patriotism	Importance of Education and Knowledge	Respect for Adult Authority
Yonge, *The Daisy Chain*, 1856, 1868. Rural England. Middle class.	Concern for family members. Some poor described as uncivilized. Wanted to improve role of poor by building church.	Duty to tend to poor. Founded and taught in school for poor. Each member accepted responsibility to younger siblings after mother's death.	Boys had advanced education. Girls not expected to understand mathematical concepts. Girls trained to guide family. Poor children worked at early ages.	Charity, humility, devotion to good works. Development of Christian goodness.	Respect stated for military profession.	Both sexes read many books. Read Bible in Greek and English. Males attended university. Asked not to use slang.	Children wanted to live up to their father's wishes and ideals. Asked mother's permission at home.
Alcott, *Little Women*, 1868. New England city suburb; Large gardens, quiet streets.	More important to have personal dignity, self-respect, and peace than wealth. Concern for ill and poor.	Duty to poor; gave their Christmas breakfast to a poor family. Strong duty to family.	Girls were educated but not at the university. Males attended university.	Heroine, Jo, wanted to write. Other sisters: drawing, music. Work ethic stressed by son-in-law.	Mother encouraged her husband to serve in the Union army. Mother devoted time to Soldiers Aid Society.	Jo loved Aunt March's large library. They all read. Felt humiliated when punished at school. Father described as scholar. Jo asked not to use slang.	Children wanted their parents' acceptance. Looked up to a "noble" mother and turned to the "quiet scholar" who helped them during "troublesome times."
Aldrich, *The Story of a Bad Boy*, 1870. New Orleans then to small New Hampshire town.	In New Orleans Tom kicked a "negro boy" who was in his way. Tom believed Indians scalp children. In New Hampshire household, aunt and servant were friends. No social criticism mentioned.	Main character did not dwell on unhappy events in story but believed in accepting reality.	Stressed Puritan ethic of diligence and common sense. Veneer of well being. Main character thought all adults had money when they wanted it.	Males should learn "manly arts" and become self-reliant. Tom did not want to be lowest in his class. No single drive expressed by the main character.	Generally, yes. Boys escaped from jail so father would not learn about their prank. Military experience held in high esteem.	Gained enjoyment and escaped by reading. Attended boys' academy. Wanted to be promoted to higher position in class.	Respected adults but did not always ask permission. Tom did not mention something when he knew grandfather would disapprove.
Sidney, *Five Little Peppers and How They Grew*, 1880. Poverty level. United States.	Peppers were proud and believed they had a good life, although they were poor.	Each member expressed responsibility for siblings and mother. Polly almost ruined her eyes sewing for mother when Polly had measles.	Family said their ship would come in and hard times would be over.	Members wanted to help mother. Polly wanted to play the piano. Ann wanted their ship to come in. To be "good."	No disrespect stated.	Polly wanted to learn. Wealthy cousins had tutor. Wealthy old gentleman promised to educate Polly.	Children always respected their widowed mother. Jasper wanted his father's respect.
Wiggin, *Rebecca of Sunnybrook Farm*, 1903. Small New England town.	Prejudice stated by neighbor against being "dark complected." Aunt Miranda disowned her sister when she married against her wishes. Rebecca respected many people.	Rebecca worked hard to complete the academy in three years instead of four.	Rebecca thought boys could do more exciting things than girls. Teacher stressed that girls could have a profession. Brother hoped to become a doctor.	Rebecca wanted an education to help her family. To become a writer.	No disrespect stated.	Reading gave pleasure. Education could make it possible to improve position in life. Rebecca respected intelligence.	Rebecca respected knowledge of English teacher and sought her advice.

FAMILY LIFE				PERSONAL RELATIONSHIPS AND FEELINGS				
Description	Religion Stability	Numbers in Family	Extended Family	Relationships Within Family	Independent Male or Female	Dependent Male or Female	Types of Problems	Friendships
Warm, close, and self-sufficient. Family center of heroine's existence. Cleanliness of home considered a virtue.	Stressed responsibility for raising good and holy children. Family read Bible and discussed meaning of Sunday services.	Eleven children. Father. Mother (died early in story).	Prim, middle-aged governess. Nurse. Servants.	Definite male and female roles. Children relied upon mother in the home. Father, head of household. Children respected each other.	Mother: at home, gentle power, strong authority. Father: skillful, clever, sensitive but showed vexation and sarcasm. Ethel: secretly kept up with brother's classical studies.	Mother: reserved and shrinking from society. Males made major decisions. Girls clung to males.	Concerned with not living up to parents' expectations and God's desire. Love of glory considered a temptation.	Mainly with family members or people in own class.
Warm, filled with laughter and singing. Children made their own fun; played "Pilgrim's Progress" and acted out plays. At 9:00, stopped work and sang before going to bed.	Father asked his wife to pray for the girls each evening. They turned to God to help them overcome troubles and temptations.	Four girls. Mother. Father (away in Army in Part I).	Housekeeper.	Mother guided the heart. Father guided the soul. Father, head of family. Strong ties among sisters. Oldest sister's gentle advice influenced her sisters.	Jo: didn't want to grow up to be a lady. Jo: wanted to do something extraordinary. Jo: said her quick temper and restless spirit got her in trouble. Mother: managed household while husband was away.	Mother: worried about guiding children to meet husband's ideals. Children turned to parents for guidance. Beth: too bashful to attend school.	Overcoming problems that led to "sweetness of self-denial and self-control."	Greatest among sisters. Neighbor boy.
Family and main character generally cheerful and affectionate. "Old Puritan austerity cropped but once a week." Main character interacted more with friends as they put on plays, formed a club, attended school, and played pranks.	Nutter house had been in the family nearly one hundred years. Attic with its treasures was symbolic of the long residence of one family. Sundays were solemn. Attended church, read Bible, and ate cold meals.	One child living with grandfather in the north. Parents living in New Orleans.	Grandfather. Maiden aunt. Servant.	Grandfather understood boy; he had once run away to sea. Grandfather showed pride when Tom won fight with a bully who harassed smaller boys.	Grandfather lived at ease on money invested in shipping. A maiden sister managed the household with her brother and servant. Tom had freedom to explore the countryside. Tom stressed male need to "learn to box, to ride, to pull an oar, and to swim."	Girls attended separate school and were graduated by "a dragon of watchfulness." Pony's vanities compared to female "weaknesses."	Problems allowed main character to consider his moral code. When he disobeyed something usually went wrong.	A group of boys at the academy. The Centipede Club—all boys. Tom and older seaman. Aunt and female servant were friends.
Close, happy family who told stories and expressed love and concern for each other. Boys argued with new cousins.	Stable because of closeness but grew up under considerable pressure. Expressed great respect for minister.	Five children, widowed mother.	Wealthy old gentleman, his son, his daughter, and her children.	Everyone pampered Phronsie, the pretty baby in the family. Phronsie and Polly brought changes in others' lives because of the influence of their personalities.	Mother made family decisions but often had no idea about how they would manage. Boys got into more trouble than girls.	Mother eventually accepted help from a wealthy gentleman who brought the family out of poverty. Polly, although plucky, often fainted.	Concerned with being good. Problems connected with survival in poverty.	Mainly each other in the family. A wealthy boy who rescued Phronsie and was impressed with the warm family. Phronsie and the wealthy gentleman whom she changed.
Rebecca had a happy-go-lucky family led by father who had difficulty making money. Two aunts led a very conservative life.	Contrasts drawn between the two families. Rebecca's parents moved often. Aunts lived in the same home as their father.	One of seven children. Father died, mother had difficulties.	Two spinster sisters. Rebecca lived with them.	Aunt Jane was warmer and more understanding. Aunt Miranda was strict, head of household and respected traditional values.	Rebecca was "plucky," "dauntless," and "intelligent." Aunt Miranda was strong-willed, managed their lives. Rebecca usually self-reliant.	Aunt Jane infrequently spoke out against Miranda. Aunts wanted dependent, obedient child.	Tried to live up to the traditional behavioral ideals of a strict aunt and Rebecca's desire to be "respectably, decently good."	Rebecca was friendly. Liked many adults and children. They also liked her.

adult departments were considered more prestigious. . . . Family stories like those of Eleanor Estes and Elizabeth Enright, biographies like Genevieve Foster's, natural science books like Herbert Zim's all flourished. The world had once again been saved, and ever optimistic, children's book editors saw a bright future ahead for the children of this country and the world" (p. 89).

This optimistic future is reflected in the views of children and the family depicted in literature of the late 1930s through the beginning of the 1960s. Townsend's (33) analysis of the generations depicted in the literature of the 1950s concluded that this decade exemplified traditional values: children lived in a stable community in which there was an orderly succession between generations, the older generations were wise and respected, and childhood was meant to be happy and secure.

The following books, written by award-winning authors, characterize the social values, the stability of family life, and the types of personal relationships depicted during this time period: *Thimble Summer* (Elizabeth Enright); *The Moffats* (Eleanor Estes); *All-of-a-Kind Family* (Sydney Taylor); and *Meet the Austins* (Madeleine L'Engle).

The locations of these families range from a rural Wisconsin farm to a New York City neighborhood and their economic levels range from lower to upper middle class, but the values depicted in the stories are similar. Accepting responsibility for one's own actions and for those of other family members are important in all of the stories. The children in *Thimble Summer* finish farm chores without complaining, while the older Moffats care for younger brothers and sisters. This responsibility extends to actions beyond the family. When a library book is lost in *All-of-a-Kind Family,* the child who loses it offers to pay for the book although it will take weeks to accumulate the pennies; her sisters sympathize and offer some of their own meager allowances. The responsibility of every member of the family is especially important to the Austins; one child is not allowed to disrupt the family.

Dignity of human beings is stressed in all these stories. The family in *Thimble Summer* brings an orphan boy into their home without checking his identification; they accept him on trust. The children in *All-of-a-Kind Family* are told to accept people and not to ask them about their personal lives. The Austin family feels empathy toward others' problems, and the parents include their children in serious discussions.

Other traditional social values are also respected. All the families show respect for the law or patriotism through their actions. Education is considered important; children enjoy reading, go to school with the anticipation that it will increase

their understanding, or finish their homework before playing. Families may prize collections of books or consider their few books among their most honored possessions. The work ethic is a powerful force in all the stories. Children may talk about saving their money to buy a farm, mother may take in sewing to keep the family together, or father may work long hours, saving for the day when he can make life better for his family. Children respect adult wisdom or authority; they enjoy listening to older neighbors tell about their experiences, they are told to listen to their teachers, and to comply with parental desires.

Family life is characterized by happy, secure relationships complemented by mutual respect, warmth, and humor. Religious values are suggested by Sunday School attendance, preparing for the Sabbath, or saying prayers before meals. Stability may also be suggested by the number of years spent in an area.

Children living in families in the literature of this time have few emotional problems. They usually feel good about themselves and their families. Their actions suggest dependence upon the family but independence in their daily actions. The independence of movement without fear around a neighborhood, city, or countryside is especially striking. For example, when Garnet in *Thimble Summer* hitchhikes into town, her only fear is that someone she knows will pick her up and return her to the farm before she can carry out her reasons for going to town. Likewise, the Moffats explore their city with the understanding that they can always find their way home. When the children do go beyond the city, they expect a stranger to help them find their way home.

The family is very important to each member's stability. The authors, through their characters, suggest children's reliance upon the family. Garnet thinks about her family and concludes that she has a nice mother and family. She feels safe and warm to know that she belongs to them and they to her. The actions of the Moffats express confidence in, and trust for, the family unit. The children in *All-of-a-Kind Family* cannot imagine what it would be like not to have a family. Likewise, Vicky, in *Meet the Austins,* is pleased because her mother looks just the way a mother should look. This total family stability is often instrumental in changing the lives of those who come into contact with the family. Chart 2–5 illustrates the similarities and differences found in the literature of this time period.

The Child and the Family, 1969–1980

Researchers who have analyzed children's literature over time have identified the 1960s and 1970s as a period in which traditional social, family, and personal values may be changing. Townsend (33) concluded that the literature of the 1960s began to suggest an erosion of adult authority and a widening of the generation gap. Homze's (14) study substantiated these findings: she found that adults were shown as less authoritarian and critical in their relationships with children. Children in turn were more outspoken and critical of the adult characters in the stories. They also asserted their independence while portraying less affectionate and more competitive natures.

Binnie Tate Wilkin (34) says that trends in the 1960s and 1970s "can almost too easily be linked to educational, social and political and economic concerns" (p. 21). She continues, "Social and political unrest in America and the world during the sixties and seventies exposed and actively involved many young people in violence in the streets, protest movements, and political advocacy. They witnessed the quest by minorities for respect and equality. They saw the assassination of a president and other political leaders. Many revolted against American involvement in the Vietnam War. . . . Almost all levels of society were challenged to respond to the activism. Book publishers responded with new materials reflecting dominant concerns. Distress about children's reading problems, federal responses to urban unrest, the youth movements, new openness about sexuality, religious protest, etc. were reflected in children's books" (p. 21).

Sociological researchers have also been interested in the changing values expressed by the American people. Stacks (31) reports that "in the late 1960s, and through most of the 1970s, some fundamental and widely shared cultural views changed in the U.S. With the economy booming, many Americans were liberated from the old anxieties about material success. The belief that hard work, self-denial and moral rectitude were their own rewards gave way to a notion . . . that the 'self' and the realization of its full 'potential' were all-important pursuits" (p. 18). Polls quoted by Stacks stated that about 20 percent of Americans express belief in traditional values of hard work, family loyalty, and sacrifice, while 63 percent embrace some traditional values but are tolerant about abortion, premarital sex, remaining single, and not having children. Stacks concludes that the people who believe in the traditional values are an increasingly vocal group who "could set to a significant degree the moral tone for the 1980s" (p. 18).

Some researchers indicate, however, that the American family has experienced far more continuity than change over the last fifty years. Lobsenz (21) reports these findings from *Middletown Families: 50 Years of Change and Continuity* that reflect retention of some traditional values and changes in certain others:

1 Families feel optimistic about their personal future although they express pessimism about the prospects of pollution, inflation, and war.
2 Marriage is seen as important and rewarding although divorce is accepted without criticism.
3 While half of Middletown's wives work, they continue to be responsible for most of the housework and child care.
4 There seems to be no breakdown of family ties because couples spend more time with relatives than with friends.

When literature written between the 1930s and early 1960s is compared with that written in the 1970s and early 1980s, readers can identify the similarities and changes that have taken place in the characterization of the American family. A happy, stable unit is often depicted in the earlier literature. but the later literature frequently reflects a family in turmoil as it adjusts to a new culture, faces the prospects of surviving without one or both parents, handles the disruption resulting from divorce, or deals with the extended family exemplified by grandparents or a foster home. This later literature suggests that there are many acceptable family units other than the traditional family.

While many books could be selected for this discussion, the following books exemplify some of these diverse attitudes toward family and children: *Where the Lilies Bloom* (Vera and Bill Cleaver); *The Changeling* (Zilpha Snyder); *The Bears' House* (Marilyn Sachs); *Mom, the Wolf Man, and Me* (Norma Klein); *Call Me Danica* (Winifred Madison); and *The Night Swimmers* (Betsy Byars).

The two strongest stories related to the dignity of human beings and acceptance of responsibility are found in the Cleaver and Madison books. *Where the Lilies Bloom* is about the proud, independent mountain people who earn their living through wildcrafting. The father, before he dies, asks his daughter to keep the family together without accepting charity and to instill in the children pride in having the name of Luther. In *Call Me Danica*, Danica's father tells the other members of the family to have pride in themselves and not be ashamed even if they are poor. Both these fathers die, but they leave their families a heritage of pride and dignity; the families work together and eventually build new lives.

An opposite condition is found in *The Bears' House*; here, the father deserts his children and sick wife. The children want to stay together so much that they apply for welfare and lie to the authorities about their parents. The father in *The Night Swimmers* works evenings, and his daughter is responsible for her younger brothers. He says that fatherhood is a burden; he wants to write country music lyrics.

CHART 2–5

Social Values, Family Life, and Personal Relationships, 1938-1960

Book, Author, Date, Setting	SOCIAL VALUES						
	Dignity of Human Beings	Acceptance of Responsibility	Belief in Equality of Opportunity	Ambition	Obedience to Law, Patriotism	Importance of Education and Knowledge	Respect for Adult Authority
Enright, *Thimble Summer*, 1938. Rural Wisconsin farm.	An orphan boy was given love and respect of the family.	Children accepted farm chores without complaining.	Father believed his daughter could be the farmer in the family.	Strong work ethic: Children talk about saving money to buy a farm.	Yes. No. Conflicts mentioned.	Reading important to the girls as a means of escape.	Children respected parents. Enjoyed listening to friends, great-grandmother tell stories about her life.
Estes, *The Moffats*, 1941. Middle-sized New England city. Poor family.	They trusted each other and strangers. They expected strangers to give them help when they were lost.	Older members responsible for younger brothers and sisters. Joe felt terrible when he lost coal money, and his mother would need to work late. He searched until he found it.	Family worked together. Males and females did many things together. Positive mood.	Mother worked hard to keep family. Took in sewing. Traded sewing for free dancing lessons.	Nine-year-old always walked cautiously by police chief's house; never stood on his lawn.	Five-year-old Rufus looked forward to school. "Go to school or be a dunce." All children had dancing lessons.	Girl worried about mimicking new superintendent of schools. Mother: "Do as the teacher says." Mother was voice of authority; they went to her to ask questions.
Taylor, *All-Of-A-Kind Family*, 1951. New York, East Side (1912). Jewish family.	You accept people. "You don't ask them about their personal lives."	Child felt responsible for lost library book; her sisters offered their few pennies. They tried to avoid household chores. A promise was considered important.	Father believed his work and savings would make it possible to have a better life.	Father wanted more for his family than he could give them. Worked and saved for the day he could make their lives better.	Father did not want the U.S. flag placed on the floor.	Great excitement because Friday was library day. Books were treasured.	Children obediently followed parents. Called themselves "Mama's children."
L'Engle, *Meet the Austins*, 1960. Country home. Father M.D.	Family felt empathy toward others' problems. Children included in serious discussions.	Consideration for others was essential. One child could not disrupt the family.	Yes. Aunt Elena was a well-known concert pianist.	Scientific experiments were considered important. Education was important.	Family rules were stressed.	Homework was to be finished before playing. Grandfather collected books.	"When daddy speaks that way we hop." Children did not want their parents to come home and find work not finished.

Families in literature of this period may express concern for equal opportunities and express different feelings about their respect for law, the importance of education, and respect for adult authority. The mountaineer father in *Where the Lilies Bloom,* for example, has a strong distrust for anyone who offers assistance, since they could be placed in bondage if they accept help. His daughter, although she respects her father's wishes, realizes that she must overcome her ignorance and even accept help if the family is to stay together. Sachs's heroine expresses a negative feeling toward equal opportunity. The children are afraid to ask for assistance because they fear authorities would separate the family and place them in foster homes. This book illustrates a stereotypic attitude toward education: the father, before he leaves, calls the oldest boy a sissy because he likes to read books rather than take part in sports. The mother and daughter in *Call Me Danica* have difficulties because their ambitions are not seen as appropriate for women. In contrast, the mother in *Mom, the Wolf Man, and Me* is a successful photographer and allows her daughter to accompany her on women's rights and peace marches.

Family life varies considerably in these stories. The most traditional family values are expressed by the characters and actions in *Call Me Danica.* Love is considered the most valuable family characteristic; the family demonstrates respect for religious and moral values by attending church, saying prayers, and stating that marriage is the only appropriate life-style for

FAMILY LIFE					PERSONAL RELATIONSHIPS AND FEELINGS			
Description	Religion Stability	Numbers in Family	Extended Family	Relationships Within Family	Independent Male or Female	Dependent Male or Female	Types of Problems	Friendships
Very happy and secure family. Garnet had a nice mother and a nice family. Considerable trust of others.	Families had lived in the valley for generations. No strong religious emphasis.	Three children. Mother. Father.	Brought an orphan boy to work on farm without checking I.D.	Strong, trusting. Slight brother and sister friction.	Independent female who loved her family. Hitchhiked to town without fear. Angry when brother suggested she do women's work.		No real problems.	Next-door girl whose family had lived there for generations.
Family was happy and secure in their relationships, although their rented house had a "for sale" sign on it. Mother didn't really share children's experiences but listened to them.	Worked together for good of the family, even when Rufus had scarlet fever and they were quarantined. Went to Sunday school.	Four children. Widowed mother.		Had fun together. Humorous experiences. Mother was supportive and loving. Not critical except about getting clothes dirty.	Children could travel around town. Always found their way back.	They relied upon each other and upon their mother to answer questions.	Their house was for sale, and they accepted the possibility of moving. Some problems because of family illness or need for money. Problems overcome in humorous ways.	Family members. Neighbors. They made friends with strangers around town.
Happy secure family: a "gentle, soft" father; a loving, but strong mother. After five girls, father cried with happiness when boy was born.	Very stable; could not imagine what it would be like not to have a family. Law of the Sabbath carefully observed.	Six children. Father. Mother.	Mother's brother was a frequent visitor.	Mother planned games for children to make them enjoy dusting. Children were proud of their mother; wanted to introduce her to new librarian.	Strong mother who took care of the family. Father owned his own business: a "junk shop." Children hid their candy from their mother.	Children gave in to firm mother.	No major problems. Saved for lost library book, hid candy.	Very close to each other: no other children mentioned. Neighborhood peddlers and librarian were friends.
Spontaneous family love. Mutual respect and understanding. Warmth and humor. Strong father who made them accept the consequences when they didn't do their homework.	Strong family ties. Sunday school and church important. Family prayed before meals and at other times in their day.	Four children. Father. Mother.	Orphaned ten-year-old daughter of a friend.	Children disagreed with each other but always made up. Father and mother talked over family problems with children.	Children were individual thinkers.	Vicky believed her older brother always knew what to say and could get her out of difficulties. Family depended on each other.	Maggy, an orphaned girl, was disturbed because she had never known love. Problems centered around helping her make adjustments.	Children close friends. Uncle Douglas always understood them and knew how to make them feel good about themselves.

men and women. The greatest family instability is expressed in *The Bears' House:* the mother is emotionally and physically ill, the father has left, and the children fearfully argue about their actions. Religious values are not discussed in the book.

While children in the literature of the 1940s and 1950s had few personal and emotional problems, children in this time period may have considerable responsibility and may experience emotional problems as they try to survive. The strongest character in *Where the Lilies Bloom* attempts to hold the family together but discovers that she needs people outside her immediate family. Snyder's heroine experiences conflicts between her individual needs and unique abilities and those of her capable family. The oldest boy in *The Bears' House* tries to organize his family, while his nine-year-old sister escapes into the imaginative world of a dollhouse family. Klein's heroine fears her life will change if her mother marries. The characters in *Call Me Danica* must overcome problems related to the death of a strong father, adjust to a new culture, and gain self-confidence. Byars's characters must look after themselves while their father works. In addition, the daughter experiences conflicting emotions: she feels unappreciated, is jealous about a brother's attachment to a new friend, and realizes that the family needs help. Her personal problems increase because she is unsure of her place in the family.

Chart 2–6 presents the various social, family, and personal values expressed by the characters in these books.

CHART 2–6
Social Values, Family Life, and Personal Relationships, 1969-1980

	SOCIAL VALUES						
Book, Author, Date, Setting	Dignity of Human Beings	Acceptance of Responsibility	Belief in Equality of Opportunity	Ambition	Obedience to Law, Patriotism	Importance of Education and Knowledge	Respect for Adult Authority
Cleaver, *Where the Lilies Bloom*, 1969. Smoky Mountains. Poor wildcrafters.	Father took pride in family name of Luther; wanted to instill pride in family. Wanted to keep family together and not accept charity.	Fourteen-year-old promised her father she would keep family together. Kept her older sister from marrying their neighbor.	Father stressed that you don't thank people who put you in bondage. You hate them or get out.	Daughter wanted to overcome her ignorance and keep the family together.	Father disliked people in authority who might place him in bondage.	Daughter knew books would give her answers that she wanted.	Children respected their father. Tried to do his wishes.
Snyder, *The Changeling*, 1970. Upper-class white and lower-class white families.	Conflicts between individual rights and family values. Daughter's friend's family described as drifters.	Martha's brother told the truth and saved her from trouble, although he got into trouble with the law.	Heroine discovered appreciation for her own individuality and her special talents.	Parents excelled in everything they did. Father: lawyer. Mother: charity worker. Expected daughter to share their traditional values and goals.	One family respected law. The other often ran from the law.	Very important in Martha's family. Martha's brother and sister attended college.	The girls from the two families were different. One respected authority more than the other.
Sachs, *The Bears House*, 1971. Poor city neighborhood.	Father deserted the family. Children felt a strong longing to stay together. Applied for welfare.	Strong responsibility for each other. Oldest boy schemed to keep them together. Nine-year-old Fran Ellen had strong attachment for the baby.	No. Fran Ellen was positive that she didn't have a chance of winning.	To survive together as a family.	They were afraid of the law; it would separate their family and place them in a foster home.	Father considered Fletcher a sissy because he read books all the time. Mother defended Fletcher; he was something special.	Children expressed fear of adults in power.
Klein. *Mom, The Wolf Man, and Me*.1972. Middle class.	Daughter sometimes bragged about her illegitimacy to see people's reactions. A best friend did not ask about her father.	Mother had a nontraditional schedule. They were not constrained by time and other more conventional family living styles. Mother responsible for care of daughter.	Mother was a professional photographer. Took her daughter on marches for women's rights and peace.	Profession important to mother.	Strong feelings against war.	Not stressed.	Eleven-year-old had frank discussions with her mother. Some disagreement.
Madison, *Call Me Danica*, 1977. Moved from Yugoslavia to Vancouver.	Father proud of his heritage: "Have pride in yourself. . . . Even if you are poor, don't get ashamed."	Daughter tried to help mother adjust to a new culture and develop confidence. Children tried to earn money for clothes.	Mother: "Women get the worst of it." She believed in women's role. Mother: "Men don't like to see a woman chef—they think I should be washing dishes."	Danica studied hard. She wanted to become a doctor. Mother wanted her own restaurant.	Father expressed strong feelings about need to fight against an enemy who would take over his country.	Studying came before work. Twelve-year-old Danica knew she would need to study very hard to reach her goal.	Children showed surprise when friends disobeyed parents or did things they knew their parents would not allow. Danica had strong guilt when "Never before had I lied to Mama or deceived her."
Byars, *The Night Swimmers*, 1980. Suburbs.	Children believed people "run you off" their property to make you feel so bad that you won't come back.	Father let his daughter take over responsibility for the family. Father expressed feelings about burdens related to fatherhood: he would rather write lyrics.	The children felt they could grow up and have their dreams. Didn't say how they would do it.	Children wanted to do things that rich people did. Father wanted a hit recording. Retta wanted to grow up and be important.	Children waited until wealthier family had gone to bed and then swam in their pool. They knew they were trespassing.	Not stressed.	Children's father paid little attention to his children. The older sister tried to manage her brothers, not always successfully.

FAMILY LIFE				PERSONAL RELATIONSHIPS AND FEELINGS				
Description	Religion Stability	Numbers in Family	Extended Family	Relationships Within Family	Independent Male or Female	Dependent Male or Female	Types of Problems	Friendships
proud independent mily who learned to ather medicinal ants on slopes of moky Mountains.	Long-time mountain resident.	Four children. Father died early in the story.		Strong family ties.	Mary Call was very resourceful. Found a way to earn money wildcrafting.	The children were dependent upon fourteen-year-old Mary who tried to hold family together.	After father died, they tried to survive as a family. Mary discovered that she needed other people.	People could not trust friends when they had secrets.
ne family with rong conventional lues whose mem- rs, except for Mar- a, always suc- eded. Martha felt t of place and con- rned because she as different.	Martha's family was stable. Her friend's family moved often because of problems.	Three children. Two parents. Friend's family: Eight children, two parents.	Grandmother sometimes lived with family.	Martha went outside of her family and created a world of imagination and friendship. Her own family didn't understand her.	Ivy Carson, Martha's friend, was creative and imaginative.	Shy Martha was dependent upon her friend for enjoyable experiences. Martha cried easily.	Overcoming problems that allowed shy girl to appreciate her own individuality and special talents.	Upper-middle-class girl and an unusual daughter of a drifter.
ather deserted them; other was sick. The ildren argued and pressed fear of sep- ation.	Unstable. Religion not mentioned.	Five children. Sick mother. Father deserted.		Love between Fran Ellen and baby. Argued but tried to stay together. Mother ineffectual.	Children decided to look after themselves.	Fran Ellen sucked her thumb. Worried about the baby. Escaped in her imagination to a doll- house. Mother dependent.	Tried to overcome problems related to parents' desertion and illness. Emotional problems: nine-year-old tried to solve her own problems.	No friends at school; they teased Fran Ellen.
other and daughter d enjoyable rela- onship; they had fun gether.	Mother did not set household sched- ule. They enjoyed this freedom. They were Jewish but never talked about it.	One child. Mother.	Mother's boyfriend lived with them on weekends.	Daughter loved her unconventional life with her unmarried mother. Mother, daughter had frank discussions.	Mother had strong character. Daughter self-assured but worried about possible changes in their lives.		Daughter feared how her life might change if her mother married.	Daughter's best friend was a boy whose father was a rabbi. He never asked her questions about her father.
proud loving family o stressed that real ve is priceless and it important to believe oneself. They devel- ed difficulty com- unicating when they ced new culture.	They had lived in a small village for many years. Father's death changed sta- bility. Church impor- tant in their lives. Mother: Marriage was the only way for two people to live to- gether.	Three children. Mother. Father died before they moved to Canada.		Strong love but at times difficulty con- fiding worries.	Father: Strong, inde- pendent. Danica had spirit, helped mother gain hope.	Mother: Worried and dependent upon her husband. It was terri- ble for the children to see mother lose confidence.	Overcoming family problems after death of strong father. Overcoming prob- lems adjusting to a new culture and gaining belief in one- self.	Danica made friends with the doc- tor; she walked his dogs. He encour- aged her to strive for her dream.
ather was a country nger who worked at ght. Daughter was sponsible for two ys. She considered erself a social di- ctor. She tried to anage their lives and ys rebelled. She as hurt because she t unappreciated.	They had moved from old neighbor- hood and friends. Neighbors disap- proved of a father who wore rhine- stones and high- gloss boots and let his children "run loose at night like dogs." Religion not mentioned.	Three children. Fa- ther. Mother had died.		Father rarely inter- fered with or helped children. Retta learned her role model as a mother from T.V. Boys ex- pected her to act like T.V. and grocery- store mothers.	Retta planned exciting experiences like swimming at night in a private pool five blocks from house. She learned to cook from school cafeteria and watching T.V. commercials.	Retta knew she had problems with the house and the boys. Didn't know what to do about them.	Tried to raise a motherless family when father worked at night and slept in daytime. Conflicts showed difficulty for a young girl trying to find her own place in the family.	One boy took pride in a male friend; he tried not to share friend with family.

The charts showing the social values, family life, and personal relationships and feelings depicted by characters in the books over the three time periods illustrate the changing views toward children and the family that have occurred during the last one hundred twenty years. Students of children's literature will be interested in extending these viewpoints as future authors write about children and the family.

SUMMARY

Literature that is enjoyed by children and adults has its roots in the distant past when stories were told around cottage hearths, campfires, or in great castle halls. With the establishment of the printing press in 1476, it was possible to mass-produce books. Many folktales became popular books. The Puritans in the 1600s criticized the traditional stories about giants and fairies and stressed the publication of books that would instruct children in moral concerns. These attitudes changed with John Locke's writings; Locke believed that children should not be treated as young adults but should have a period of childhood. In 1698, a great milestone for children's literature occurred: Charles Perrault's *Tales of Mother Goose* was published. John Newbery, in 1744, is credited as being the writer whose books were a true beginning for children's literature. The research of the Brothers Grimm provided a collection of folktales that are still children's favorites. The Victorian period produced literature in which the gentleman and lady characters offered models for negotiating the precarious passage from childhood to adulthood. The chapter concluded with an analysis of the changing view of children and the family as found in the literature published from 1865 to 1903, 1938 to 1960, and 1969 to 1980.

Suggested Activities for Understanding the History of Children's Literature

■ Investigate the life and contributions of William Caxton. What circumstances led to his opening a printing business in 1476? Why were *Reynart the Fox, The Book of the Subtyle Historyes and Fables of Esope,* and *Le Morte d'Arthur* considered such important contributions to children's literature?

■ Compare the literary quality of William Caxton's books with the literary quality of a reproduction of a chapbook.

Why do you believe the chapbooks have been identified as forerunners of children's books, western tales, and comic books?

■ Trace the development of the hornbook from its introduction in the 1400s until it was superseded by the battledores in the 1700s. Consider any changes in the lesson books and how they might have influenced the development of children's literature.

■ Read John Bunyan's *Pilgrim's Progress*. Identify the characteristics that would make it acceptable Puritan reading. Compare these characteristics with the characteristics of the book that would appeal to children.

■ Choose a tale published by Charles Perrault in his *Tales of Mother Goose*: "Cinderella," "Sleeping Beauty," "Puss in Boots," "Little Red Riding Hood," "Blue Beard," or "Little Thumb." Compare the language and style of this early edition with the language and style in a twentieth century version of the same tale. What differences did you find? Why do you believe any changes were made?

■ Select one of the "Robinsonades" published after the successful publication of Defoe's *Robinson Crusoe*. Compare the plot development, characterization, and setting with Defoe's text.

■ Investigate the impact of John Newbery's publications on the history of children's literature. State why you do or do not believe that the Newbery Award should bear his name.

■ Compare the backgrounds, possible motivations, and probable recording techniques of Jakob and Wilhelm Grimm with those of Charles Perrault. Can you identify any reasons for possible differences or similarities in their tales?

■ Choose one of the following great nineteenth-century English artists who made an impact on children's illustrations: Kate Greenaway, Walter Crane, or Randolph Caldecott. Read biographical information and look at examples of their illustrations. Share your information and reactions with your literature class.

■ Victorian literature is frequently characterized as depicting fortitude, temperance, prudence, justice, and self-reliance. In addition, there is a strong emphasis on the interests and aspirations of the large Victorian family. Read a Victorian novel such as Charlotte Yonge's *The Daisy Chain*; identify the Victorian standards reflected in the literature.

■ Read Mark Twain's *Adventures of Tom Sawyer* or *Huckleberry Finn*. Consider the issue discussed on page 56. How would you evaluate Mark Twain's writing for the nineteenth century and for the twentieth century?

References

1 Alderson, Brian W., ed. and trans. *Three Centuries of Children's Books in Europe.* Cleveland: World, 1959.

2 Ashton, John. *Chap-Books of the Eighteenth Century.* London: Chatto and Windus, 1882.

3 Bingham, Jane, and Scholt, Grayce. *Fifteen Centuries of Children's Literature: An Annotated Chronology of British and American Works in Historical Context.* Westport, Conn.; Greenwood, 1980.

4 Cadogan, Mary, and Craig, Patricia. *You're a Brick, Angela! A New Look at Girls' Fiction from 1839 to 1975.* London: Gollancz, 1976.

5 Carmichael, Carolyn Wilson. "A Study of Selected Social Values as Reflected in Contemporary Realistic Fiction for Children." East Lansing, Mich.: Michigan State University, 1971, University Microfilm No. 71–31, 172.

6 Chapman, Raymond. *The Victorian Debate, English Literature and Society 1832–1901.* New York: Basic Books, 1968.

7 Darton, F. J. Harvey. *Children's Books in England, Five Centuries of Social Life.* Cambridge: At the University Press, 1932, 1966.

8 Erisman, Fred Raymond. "There Was a Child Went Forth: A Study of St. Nicholas Magazine and Selected Children's Authors, 1890–1915." Minneapolis: University of Minnesota, 1966, University Microfilm No. 66-12, 197.

9 Ernest, Edward. *The Kate Greenaway Treasury.* Cleveland: World, 1967.

10 Fraser, James H., ed. *Society and Children's Literature.* Boston: Godine, 1978.

11 Furnivall, Frederick J., ed. *Caxton's Book of Curtesye.* London: Oxford University Press, 1868. Reprinted from Caxton's 1477 text.

12 Gillespie, Margaret C. *Literature for Children: History and Trends.* Dubuque, Iowa: Brown, 1970.

13 Haviland, Virginia. *Children and Literature, View and Reviews.* Glenview, Ill.: Scott, Foresman, 1973.

14 Homze, Alma Cross. "Interpersonal Relationships in Children's Literature, 1920 to 1960." University Park, Pa.: Pennsylvania State University, 1963, University Microfilm No. 64-5366.

15 Hürlimann, Bettina. "Fortunate Moments in Children's Books." In *The Arbuthnot Lectures, 1970–1979,* compiled by Zena Sutherland, pp. 61–80. Chicago: American Library Association, 1980.

16 Kelly, Robert Gordon. "Mother Was a Lady: Self and Society in Selected American Children's Periodicals, 1865–1890." Iowa City, Iowa: University of Iowa, 1970, University Microfilm No. 71-5770.

17 Kelly, Robert Gordon. "Social Factors Shaping Some Nineteenth-Century Children's Periodical Fiction." In *Society and Children's Literature,* edited by James H. Fraser. Boston: Godine, 1978.

18 Laws, Frederick. "Randolph Caldecott." In *Only Connect: Readings on Children's Literature,* edited by Sheila Egoff, G. T. Stubbs, and L. F. Ashley. 2d ed. Toronto: Oxford University, 1980.

19 Leeson, Robert. *Children's Books and Class Society.* London: Writers and Readers, 1977.

20 Lenaghan, R. T., ed. *Caxton's Aesop.* Cambridge, Mass.: Harvard University, 1967.

21 Lobsenz, Norman. "News from the Home Front." *Family Weekly,* August 2, 1981, p. 9.

22 Locke, John. "Some Thoughts Concerning Education." In *English Philosophers,* edited by Charles W. Eliot. Harvard Classics, vol. 37. New York: Villier, 1910.

23 Lonsdale, Bernard J., and Macintosh, Helen K. *Children Experience Literature.* New York: Random House, 1973.

24 Lystad, Mary. *From Dr. Mather to Dr. Seuss: Two Hundred Years of American Books for Children.* Boston: G. K. Hall, 1980.

25 McCulloch, Lou J. *An Introduction to Children's Literature, Children's Books of the 19th Century.* Des Moines, Iowa: Wallace-Honestead, 1979.

26 McElderry, Margaret. "The Best Times, The Worst Times, Children's Book Publishing 1917–1974." *The Horn Book Magazine,* October 1974, pp. 85–94.

27 Meigs, Cornelia; Nesbitt, Elizabeth; Eaton, Anne Thaxter; and Hill, Ruth. *A Critical History of Children's Literature: A Survey of Children's Books in English.* New York: Macmillan, 1969.

28 Muir, Percy. *English Children's Books, 1600 to 1900.* New York: Praeger, 1954.

29 Shaw, Jean Duncan. "An Historical Survey of Themes Recurrent in Selected Children's Books Published in America Since 1850." Philadelphia: Temple University, 1966, University Microfilm No. 67-11, 437.

30 Sidney, Sir Philip. *An Apologie for Poetrie.* London: 1595.

31 Stacks, John F. "Aftershocks of the 'Me' Decade." *Time,* August 3, 1981, p. 18.

32 Stark, Myra. *Florence Nightingale.* New York: Feminist, 1979.

33 Townsend, John Rowe. *Written for Children: An Outline of English-Language Children's Literature.* New York: Lippincott, 1975.

34 Wilkin, Binnie Tate. *Survival Themes in Fiction for Children and Young People.* Metuchen, N.J.: Scarecrow, 1978.

35 Winkler, Karen J. "Academe and Children's Literature: Will They Live Happily Ever After?" *Chronicle of Higher Education,* June 15, 1981.

Additional References

Andrews, Siri, ed. *The Hewins Lectures 1947-1962.* Boston: Horn Book, 1963.

Aries, Philippe. *Centuries of Childhood: A Social History of Family Life.* New York: Knopf, 1962.

Avery, Gillian. *Nineteenth Century Children, Heroes and Heroines in English Children's Stories, 1780-1900.* Ontario, Canada: Hodder, 1965.

Cable, Mary. *The Little Darlings: A History of Child Rearing in America.* New York: Scribner's, 1975.

Eames, Wilberforce. *Early New England Catechisms: A Bibliographical Account of Some Catechisms Published before the Year 1800, for Use in New England.* New York: Watts, 1964.

Egoff, Sheila; Stubbs, G. T.; and Ashley, L. F., eds. *Only Connect, Readings on Children's Literature.* 2d ed. Toronto: Oxford University, 1980.

Feaver, William. *When We Were Young: Two Centuries of Children's Book Illustration.* New York: Holt, Rinehart & Winston, 1977.

Gottlieb, Gerald, ed. *Early Children's Books and Their Illustrations.* Boston: Godine, 1975.

Haviland, Virginia. *The Travelogue Storybook of the Nineteenth Century.* Boston: Horn Book, 1950.

Hürlimann, Bettina. *Three Centuries of Children's Books in Europe.* Cleveland: World, 1968.

LaBeau, Dennis, ed. *Children's Authors and Illustrators: An Index to Biographical Dictionaries.* Detroit: Gale, 1976.

MacLeod, Ann Scott. *A Moral Tale: Children's Fiction and American Culture, 1820-1860.* London: Archon, 1975.

Mahoney, Bertha E.; Latimer. Louise Payson; and Folmsbee, Beulah. *Illustrators of Children's Books 1744-1945.* Boston: Horn Book, 1947.

Neuburg, Victor E., ed. *The Penny Histories: A Study of Chapbooks for Young Readers over Two Centuries.* New York: Harcourt Brace Jovanovich, 1969.

Sutherland, Zena, comp. *The Arbuthnot Lectures, 1970-1979.* Chicago: American Library Association, 1980.

Temple, Nigel, ed. *Seen and Not Heard: A Garland of Fancies for Victorian Children.* New York: Dial, 1970.

Thomas, Alan G. *Great Books and Book Collectors.* New York: Putnam, 1975.

Thwaite, Mary F. *From Primer to Pleasure in Reading: An Introduction to the History Children's Books in England from the Invention of Printing to 1914 with an Outline of Some Developments in Other Countries.* Boston: Horn Book, 1972.

Whalley, Joyce Irene. *Cobwebs to Catch Flies: Illustrated Books for the Nursery and Schoolroom, 1700-1900.* Berkeley: University of California, 1975.

THREE
Selecting Literature for Children

WHEN the thousands of books that have been published for children are considered, it seems an awesome task to select appropriate ones to meet the needs of children. These selections must be shared with groups of children as well as with the individual child. Books need to be chosen to provide balance in the school or public library. The objectives of the literature program have to be considered in order to evaluate literature and then select appropriate books.

The literature program, according to Helen Huus (10), should have five objectives. First, it should help students realize that literature is for entertainment and can be enjoyed throughout their lives. This literature should cater to children's interests as well as create new interests in topics they did not know about. Consequently, adults must know these interests and understand ways to stimulate new ones. Second, the literature program should acquaint children with their literary heritage. To accomplish this, literature that fosters the preservation of knowledge and allows its transmission to future generations must be provided. Adults have to know fine literature from the past and share it with children. Third, the literature program should help students understand the nature of literature and lead them to prefer the best it has to offer. Children need to listen to and read fine literature and appreciate that authors not only have something to say but also that they say it extremely well. Adults must be able to identify the best in literature and share these books with children. Fourth, the literature program should help children to grow up and understand humanity. They see book characters who overcome the same problems they have and learn other ways to cope with these problems. Literature introduces children to people from other times and nations, and through literature they can see both themselves and their world in a new perspective. Fifth, the literature program should help children evaluate their own reading and extend their appreciation and imagination. To do this, students need to learn to compare, relate, question, and evaluate.

If children are to gain enjoyment, knowledge of their heritage, a recognition of what constitutes good literature, an understanding of self and others, and appreciation, they should be provided with a balanced literature selection. It should include classics and contemporary stories, stories that are fanciful or realistic, prose as well as poetry, biographies, and books containing information. In order to provide this balance, adults need to know about many kinds of literature; this text will provide them with a wide knowledge of numerous types of books written for children.

This chapter focuses on evaluating books written for children by presenting and discussing the literary elements associated with plot development, characterization, setting, theme, style, and point of view. It also discusses children's literature interests, procedures for their evaluation, and characteristics of literature found in books chosen by children.

EVALUATING BOOKS WRITTEN FOR CHILDREN

One of the issues in children's book selection according to Sheila Egoff (4) is the mediocrity found in many of them. She concluded that about 2.5 percent of these books are excellent, about 35 percent are extremely poor, and the rest are mediocre. Egoff maintains that if the role of literature is to help develop the individual, then a good book will promote an awareness of life. Ruth Kearney Carlson (1) feels strongly about the issue of mediocrity: "Mediocrity in books provides certain outlooks which are commonplace. We underestimate children. Slow learners and poor readers are just as interested in ideas as are quick readers. Mediocre books are rarely challenged by adults. They have commonplace, dully written pages and seldom take strong stands for certain causes. Mediocre books build laziness in young readers" (p. 18).

If merit rather than mediocrity is to be part of the literature experience, both children and adults need opportunities to read, discuss, discover, and evaluate literature. The criteria usually used to evaluate children's fiction include elements of plot, characterization, setting, theme, style, and point of view. Also, it is necessary to be concerned with other characteristics: relevance, suitability, potential popularity, and the development of nonstereotypes in the literature.

Plot Development

When a child is asked to tell about a favorite story, usually the story's plot or plan of action is retold. Children want a book to have a good plot: a good story means action, excitement, some suspense, and enough conflict to develop interest. It also allows them to become involved with the action, to feel the conflict developing, to recognize the climax when it occurs, and to respond to a satisfactory ending. Children's expectations for, and enjoyment of, conflict vary according to their ages and the types of books they read. Young children are satisfied with simple plots dealing with everyday happenings, but as children mature, they expect and enjoy more complex plots. Following the plot of a story is like following a path or a thread winding through it, allowing the action to develop naturally. If the plot is well developed, the book should be difficult to put down unfinished; if the plot is not well developed, it will not sustain interest, or it will be so prematurely predictable that the story will end long before it should. The way the author develops this action assists children in their enjoyment of the story.

Developing Order of Events. A story is expected to have a good beginning; the beginning introduces the action, the characters, and entices the reader. A story should have a good middle section that develops the conflict. Finally, the reader wants the story to have a recognizable climax and an appropriate ending. If any element is missing, the book is unsatisfactory and a waste of time. Authors have several approaches for presenting the events in a credible plot. In children's literature, chronological order is the most common way to develop events. The author reveals the plot by presenting the first happening, followed by the second happening, and so forth, until the story is completed. Illustrations frequently reinforce the chronological order in picture storybooks for younger children. In *Sleepy Bear*, for example, Lydia Dabcovich follows a bear as he watches the birds fly away in the fall, finds a cave and sleeps through the snow, and finally rouses in the spring as the bees return.

One very strong and visible example of chronological order is found in cumulative folktales. The happenings are related to each other in sequential order and are repeated each time a new experience, action, or character is introduced. Children who enjoy the cumulative style of the nursery rhyme "The House That Jack Built" will also enjoy a similar cumulative rhythm in Verna Aardema's *Bringing the Rain to Kapiti Plain: A Nandi Tale.* The Danish folktale *The Fat Cat,* translated and illustrated by Jack Kent, is an example of a text developed totally on the cumulative approach. As the hungry cat encounters each prospective victim, he repeats his previous actions until finally the cat restates all of his previous nine encounters. This repetition is very effective with young children, as it encourages them to join in during the storytelling and allows them to anticipate the style of the folktale.

In contrast to *The Fat Cat,* which uses the cumulative approach for the total story, *Why Mosquitoes Buzz in People's Ears,* by Verna Aardema, first develops the story through sequential order and then reviews the actions by going back over the details; this time the actions proceed from last to first and are presented in a cumulative format.

In addition to proceeding from the first to last happening, the order of events may follow the maturing process of the main character. In *The Clown of God,* the author, Tomie de Paola, introduces a small beggar boy who is happy because he has a wonderful gift: he can juggle. His fortune changes as time passes, and he even juggles before royalty. Years go by and the juggler becomes old and unable to perform; he is re-

The plot development follows the main character as he progresses from a talented young juggler to an old man. From *The Clown of God,* copyright © 1978 by Tomie de Paola. Reproduced by permission of Harcourt Brace Jovanovich, Inc.

jected by the crowd and wearily heads home. His journey ends in the sanctuary of the church of the Little Brothers where he performs his final juggling act. This magnificent performance results in his death but also causes a miracle.

Authors of biographies frequently use this method of plot development. Jean Fritz, for example, traces the life of a Revolutionary War personage in *Traitor: The Case of Benedict Arnold.* The plot follows Arnold from about his fourteenth birthday, through his ascent as a hero, and concludes with his conspiracy against the Americans. Dates in the text help the reader follow the chronological order.

Books written for older readers sometimes use flashbacks in addition to chronological order. At the point when the reader has many questions about a character's background, or wonders why a character is acting in a certain way, the author may interrupt the order of the story and reveal information about a previous time or experience. Flashbacks are effectively used in *Mrs. Frisby and the Rats of NIMH* by Robert C. O'Brien. Without flashbacks, the reader would not know why the rats feel indebted to the mouse, Mrs. Frisby. The plot progresses to the point where both the reader and Mrs. Frisby have many unanswered questions, and the wise rat Nicodemus responds, "To answer that I would have to tell you quite a long story about us, and Nimh, and Jonathan, and how we came here" (p. 97). The chronology of the story is now interrupted and the reader discovers why the rats were taken to the laboratory, how their intelligence was drastically increased, how they learned to read, what method they used to escape from the laboratory, what techniques increased their knowledge, and the circumstances under which rat society was developed. After the reader and Mrs. Frisby understand the circumstances behind the development of this superior rat society, the chronological order continues. Without these flashbacks, the reader would have so many unanswered questions that a logical plot development would not be possible. This technique is more complex than simple chronological order and is not usually used in the shorter plots written for younger children.

Patricia MacLachlan, however, uses flashbacks to provide background information in a picture storybook for younger children, *Mama One, Mama Two.* The plot begins as a young foster child has difficulty sleeping. The reasons for her separation from her mother, her love for her mother, and her hopes for the future are developed as she and her foster mother share a warm bedtime story. In this case, the flashback is one that could be understood by younger readers. In addition, young children enjoy hearing about other young children during storytelling.

Developing Conflict. Excitement in a story occurs when the main characters experience a struggle or overcome conflict. When conflict is added to the sequence of events, the result is called *plot.* According to Rebecca Lukens (12), four kinds of conflict are found in children's literature: person-against-person, person-against-society, person-against-nature, and person-against-self. Plots written for younger children usually develop only one kind of conflict, but many of the more complex plots written for older children may use several conflicting situations.

Person Against Person. One very early conflict of person against person enjoyed by young children is the tale of the world's most famous bunny, *Peter Rabbit,* by Beatrix Potter. In this story, Peter's disobedience and greed quickly bring him into conflict with the owner of the garden, Mr. McGregor. Excitement and suspense develop as Peter and Mr. McGregor proceed through a series of encounters. This is a life-and-death matter because the reader has been previously warned about Peter's fate: Mrs. McGregor will put him into a pie. This knowledge increases the suspense when Mr. McGregor discovers Peter and chases him with a rake; Peter unfortunately becomes tangled in a gooseberry net, and Mr. McGregor tries to trap him inside a sieve. Thankfully, Peter escapes each time; the excitement is intensified, however, as he narrowly misses being caught. Readers appreciate Peter's fear when he leaves a piece of clothing behind after each escape attempt. There is also great relief as Peter finally escapes, leaving both Mr. McGregor and a large white cat behind the garden gate. Children usually sympathize with Peter when his disobedience results in a stomachache and a dose of camomile tea.

Several antagonists provide the conflict in *Mrs. Frisby and the Rats of NIMH.* First, Mrs. Frisby and her family are in danger from Farmer Fitzgibbon and his house-destroying tractor. Contact with a human would not result in a tense situation but Mrs. Frisby's young son had been ill with pneumonia, and the family could not move from its winter home in the garden to a summer home in the woods. The need to overcome this problem forces Mrs. Frisby to seek the aid of a group of extraordinary rats. These rats also have antagonists. Both the conflict and identity of the antagonists now become more complex. First, there is the conflict between the rats and their possible discovery by the farmer. Another conflict develops between the rats and scientists of NIMH: the scientists want to recapture or kill the rats. In addition to these person-against-person conflicts, a more subtle conflict is suggested when the rats speculate about human society's probable refusal to accept a self-supporting rat society. Both person-against-society and person-against-self conflicts are suggested when one group of rats worries about what could happen to the rat society if it does not work hard to develop its own civilization but merely lives on the edge of human civilization. Mrs. Frisby's conflict is easily resolved; the rats' is not.

In these two examples, conflicts developed between animals and humans. While this type of conflict frequently occurs in children's literature, there are many examples of conflicts resulting between two human or two animal antagonists. In folktales, it is common for plots to be developed around conflicts between a beautiful young girl and her wicked stepmother ("Cinderella," "Sleeping Beauty") or between good humans and the wicked witch ("Rapunzel," "Hansel and Gretel"). An Italian version of the Rapunzel tale, Giambattista Basile's *Petrosinella: A Neapolitan Rapunzel,* develops the conflict between an ogress and a heroine who is imprisoned because the girl's mother craves parsley from the garden of the ogress. The heroine in this tale does not wait for the prince to rescue her; instead she discovers the reason for her enchantment and makes it possible for the prince and herself to escape the ogress's power. A series of fierce animals who help the heroine and the prince escape add to the conflict as they battle the ogress.

A humorous person-against-person conflict provides the story line in Beverly Cleary's *Ramona and Her Father.* Seven-year-old Ramona's life changes drastically when her father loses his job; her mother must work full-time while her father spends more time with Ramona. Their time together, however, is not as enjoyable as Ramona envisions. Her father becomes tense and irritable as his period of unemployment lengthens. When his smoking increases, Ramona decides that his life is in danger and devises a plan to save him. Her campaign includes putting signs around the house, notes in her father's clothing, and even fake cigarettes that turn out to be "no smoking" messages. Ramona and her father survive their experience and by the end of the story have returned to their normal warm, personal relationship.

Illustrations and plot relate a humorous conflict between a seven-year-old and her father.
Illustration by Allan Tiegreen on page 99 in *Ramona and Her Father* by Beverly Cleary. Copyright © 1975, 1977 by Beverly Cleary. By permission of William Morrow and Company.

Ellen Raskin develops a more complex person-against-person plot in *The Westing Game.* This mystery for older children places eight couples in a complex game, with each team trying to solve the mystery of Samuel Westing's will; the reward for the winning team is Mr. Westing's millions. The teams play the game even when a blizzard, a bomber, and the suspicion that one of them may be a killer threatens their existence. In a surprising, involved plot, the reader learns that the teams are playing the game not with the pre-arranged clues written by a dead millionaire but with clues written by a brilliant master of disguise. The ending is satisfactory; the youngest team member is the only one to unravel the clues and discover the secret.

Another complex person-against-person conflict develops in Katherine Paterson's *Jacob Have I Loved.* The conflict develops as one twin believes she is the despised biblical Esau while her sister is the adored favorite of the family. The unhappy heroine's descriptions of her early experiences with her sister, her growing independence as she works with her father, and her final discovery that she, not her sister, is the strong twin create a strong plot and memorable characters.

Animal-against-animal plots are also common in children's stories. Three Little Pigs are in conflict with a wicked wolf, Three Billy Goats Gruff must overcome the long-nosed troll who lives under the bridge, and proud, beautiful Chanticleer, the rooster, must outwit the clever fox. In Barbara Cooney's adaptation of Chaucer's *Chanticleer and the Fox,* Chanticleer, the rooster with a superior crowing voice, and the sly wicked fox are in conflict. Chanticleer is doomed when the fox flatters him and convinces him to try to sing as well as his father. Unfortunately, when Chanticleer sings, he stretches his neck and closes his eyes, exactly what the fox has waited for. With one jump, the rooster is captured and taken to the woods; all is not lost, however, for Chanticleer tricks the fox into opening his mouth. As the conflict ends, Chanticleer learns a lesson: "Never again shall you with your flattery get me to sing with my eyes closed. For he who closes his eyes when he watch, God let him never prosper" (p. 30 unnumbered). Trickery is also involved in the animal-against-animal conflicts found in Priscilla Jaquith's *Bo Rabbit Smart For True: Folktales from the Gullah.* In a humorous conflict, Bo Rabbit tricks a whale and an elephant into a pulling contest; both animals believe Bo Rabbit is at the end of the rope. Beast tales from many lands develop plots in which animals are rewarded for courage, loyalty, or intelligence or are punished for foolishness, wickedness, or ignorance.

Person Against Society. Part of the struggle in *Mrs. Frisby and the Rats of NIMH* results because society is not ready for a superior, self-supporting rat civilization. Conflicts may also develop when the main character's actions or desires differ from the values held by the society of a historical period. The *Witch*

Complex person-against-person conflict develops between twin sisters.
Jacket by Kinoko Craft from *Jacob Have I Loved* by Katherine Paterson (Thomas Y. Crowell Co.) Copyright © 1980 by Katherine Paterson.

of Blackbird Pond, by Elizabeth George Speare, shows an example of this. The heroine, Kit Taylor, leaves a colorful and carefree island home to live in Puritan Connecticut. Her former way of life immediately conflicts with this austere society when she jumps into the water to rescue a child's doll (only witches can float) and continues to wear the colorful dresses of her homeland. Kit befriends an old woman suspected of being a witch and is arrested and tried for witchcraft.

Patricia Clapp develops a similar person-against-society conflict in *Witches' Children: A Story of Salem.* Told from the perspective of a bound girl, the plot develops rapidly as village girls are overcome by mysterious "seizures" and the villagers search for the person or persons responsible. Again, the conflict results because of the beliefs of the people during a specific time period.

Deborah, the heroine in Patricia Clapp's *I'm Deborah Sampson,* is also out of step with her time. She heads out to work for a farm family when her poverty-stricken mother can't take care of her. This experience causes Deborah to grow strong and determined. The American Revolution begins, and she sees the boys she has come to love leave home to fight for their country. When her friend Robbie is killed, she wants only to commemorate the lost life. Women are not allowed to join the army, so Deborah disguises herself as a boy and volunteers for service. The next three years find her hiding her identity and surviving in a masculine society. The pace of the story increases when Deborah is caught trying to join the Continental army; this does not deter her, for she goes to a recruiting office farther from home. She changes her name to Robert Shurtlieff and lives in the barracks, marches as a foot soldier, and even encounters the enemy. For three years, she successfully fools a society that would be shocked at such unladylike behavior. Throughout her experience, Deborah fears not death but discovery: "It was not until then that I realized I had caught a British ball in my right shoulder. I was terrified! Not by the wound itself, nor by the pain, but at the thought of a doctor's examination" (p. 115).

Person Against Nature. Instead of focusing on another person or a whole society as an antagonist, the plots of many memorable books for older children develop around conflicts occurring between humans and nature. When the author thoroughly describes the environment, the reader vicariously travels into a world ruled by nature's harsh law of survival. This is the case in Jean Craighead George's *Julie of the Wolves.* Miyax (Julie is her English name), a thirteen-year-old Eskimo girl, is lost and without food on the North Slope of Alaska. She is introduced lying on her stomach and peering at a pack of wolves. It is not the wolves, however, who are her enemy. It is the desperate predicament of being lost in a land that stretches for hundreds of miles without human presence. Consider the impact of this antagonist as described by the author: "No roads cross it; ponds and lakes freckle its immensity. Winds scream across it, and the view in every direction is exactly the same. Somewhere in this cosmos was Miyax; and the very life in her body, its spark and warmth, depended upon these wolves for survival. And she was not so sure they would help" (p. 6). She is not only lost, she is lost during the continual daylight when there is no North Star to guide her. The author describes Miyax's plight as she is lost in a land so harsh that no berry bushes point to the south, and no birds fly overhead so that she can follow. Nature must be considered even when taking care of clothing; if she doesn't use the traditional Eskimo ways to protect her clothes from moisture, the dampness could bring death. The constant wind, empty sky, cold and deserted earth are ever present as she searches for food, protects herself from the elements, and makes friends with the wolves. These animals must bring her food if she is to survive. Miyax crosses the Arctic and makes friends with the wolves. The author encourages readers to visualize the power and beauty of this harsh land as well as the girl's sorrow as human destruction makes its impress upon the land, the animals, and the Eskimo way of life.

Another book that places a young person against the elements of nature is Armstrong Sperry's *Call It Courage*. Here, the enemy is the crashing, stormy sea. The hero's conflict with his adversary begins when the canoe young Mafatu and his mother are in capsizes during a hurricane; his mother drowns. As a consequence of this earlier experience, Mafatu is in great fear of the sea. The author describes the antagonist as "a monster livid and hungry. Higher and higher it rose, until it seemed that it must scrape at the low-hanging clouds. Its crest heaved over with a vast sigh. The boy saw it coming. He tried to cry out. No sound issued from his throat. Suddenly the wave was upon him. Down it crashed. Chaos! Mafatu felt the paddle torn from his hands. Thunder in his ears. Water strangled him. Terror in his soul" (p. 24). From this quote, it is clear that there are two adversaries in the story: the hero is in conflict with nature and also in conflict with self, for Mafatu battles to overcome his own terror and develop courage. The two adversaries are interwoven in the plot as Mafatu leaves his island in order to prove that he is not a coward. Quite rapidly the reader learns that the sea is not his only enemy; he is swept ashore on an alien, forbidden island used by eaters-of-men to perform their terrible sacrifices. He must overcome his fear of the "spirit" and wild boars that inhabit the island. Each time that Mafatu wins against nature he also comes closer to his goal—victory over himself.

Person Against Self. Mafatu's greatest victory is his ability to overcome the fear within himself. Without this victory, he cannot be called by his rightful name Mafatu, Stout Heart, nor can he have the respect of his father, his Polynesian people, or him-self. His need for courage is interwoven with the values of these early Polynesians who worship courage. This need for courage is made believable by an author who carefully describes the attitudes of the Polynesian people as well as the circumstances that cause Mafatu's fear.

Children must overcome many natural fears and problems while growing up; consequently, this person-against-self conflict is a popular plot device used by children's authors. Lying is a problem that often gets children into difficulty. Sam, in *Sam, Bangs & Moonshine,* by Evaline Ness, does not mean to do any harm with her fibs, but they do cause her problems and almost cost her friend's life. Sam convinces her friend Thomas that she has a mermaid mother and a baby kangaroo. Thomas believes the story and goes out to Blue Rock to search for Sam's mother and the kangaroo. Unfortunately, the tide almost covers the rock before Thomas is rescued. When Sam realizes what she has done, her father asks her to tell herself the difference between real and "moonshine." She discovers that a mermaid mother, her baby kangaroo, and a dragon-drawn chariot are all "flummadiddle." Her father, her cat Bangs, and her friend Thomas are the real things. Sam overcomes her person-against-self conflict as she learns that there is good as well as bad moonshine.

Jean Fritz's *The Cabin Faced West* shows how a girl's love for her former home and way of life can cause her to be discontented with her new surroundings. Ten-year-old Ann does not understand why anyone would give up neighbors, school, and a church for a lot of uncleared land. Throughout the story, she looks longingly down the road toward her old home in Gettysburg, dreams about the excitement of her life there, and hopes that she will be able to return. The road becomes a symbol of her dreams and the author describes her thoughts about the road: "Nothing ever happened at this end of the road; everything exciting was at the other end—the Gettysburg end. Certainly there was nothing exciting about the road itself. Ann shuddered when she remembered the long, weary miles the road took up each of those dreadful mountains and the slipping, sliding miles down the other sides. Yet when Ann was alone, she usually came right here. It was almost as if the road held some kind of special promise for her" (p. 19). Ann starts to see Hamilton Hill and the frontier in a new way when the family is visited by General George Washington who tells Ann that the future is traveling west with people like herself and that the best opportunities are on the frontier. The author encourages readers to understand Ann's changing feelings by having her remember the glorious times her family has had and decide that nothing is as beautiful as their new home and the rolling farmland cleared from the forest. At this point, she has an

The illustrations suggest Sam's imaginary world of "moonshine."
From *Sam, Bangs & Moonshine* written and illustrated by Evaline Ness. Copyright © 1966 by Evaline Ness. Reproduced by permission of Holt, Rinehart and Winston, Publishers.

opportunity to travel east but decides she would rather stay with her family and plan for tomorrow.

Authors of contemporary realistic fiction frequently develop plots around children facing and overcoming problems related to family disturbances. For example, the cause of the person-against-self conflict in Carol Lea Benjamin's *The Wicked Stepdog* is the fear of a girl who believes she is losing her father's love. By describing the heroine's initial reactions to her new stepmother and her feelings about the actions of her father, the author develops Louise's personal conflicts. The first person narrative provides insights into Louise's changing attitudes and her feelings about herself and her family.

These plots tell credible stories without relying on contrivance or coincidence. Many of the same conflicts may occur in children's lives; consequently, the plots seem real to them. Credibility is an important consideration in evaluating plot in children's books. Although authors of adult books often rely on considerable tension or sensational conflict to create interest, writers of children's books like to focus more on the characters and how they overcome problems. The next section shows how plot and characters are related in a memorable book.

Characterization

A believable, enjoyable story needs a strong plot and main characters who seem lifelike and develop throughout the story. The characters remembered fondly from childhood usually have several sides to their characters; like real people they are not all good or all bad. Laura, from the various Little House books, demonstrates a wide range of human characteristics as she grows up. She is honest, trustworthy, and courageous but can also be jealous, frightened, or angry. One child described Laura this way: "I would like Laura for my best friend. She would be fun to play with but she would also understand when I was hurt or angry. I could tell Laura my secrets without being afraid she would laugh at me or tell them to someone else." Any writer who can develop such a friend for children is a master at developing characterization.

Laura is an example of what is referred to as a "round character" in literature. Her character is not only fully developed throughout the story but also changes during its course. Characters should have more than one side just as real people do, and they should be expected to change as they overcome their problems. How does an author develop such a memorable character? How can this author show the many sides of the character as well as demonstrate believable change as this character matures?

Revealing Character. According to Charlotte Huck (9), the credibility of characters depends upon the writer's ability to reveal their natures, strengths, and weaknesses. She states that this may be done by (1) telling about characters through narration, (2) recording their conversations with others, (3) describing their thoughts, (4) showing the thoughts of others about them, or (5) showing them in action (p. 9).

Armstrong Sperry, in *Call It Courage*, uses all these methods to reveal Mafatu's character and the changes that take place as he overcomes his fears. The author first tells the reader that Mafatu fears the sea. Narration reveals how the young child clung to his mother's back as a stormy sea and sharks tried to end both their lives. His memories of this experience make him "useless" in his Polynesian tribe, and through narration, the writer also shows that Mafatu's fear is so terrible that he wants to escape to a world far away. Next, the author reveals through dialogue others' thoughts about him. Mafatu's former friend gives the verdict of the tribe when he states the following: "That is woman's work. Mafatu is afraid of the sea. He will never be a warrior" (p. 12). The laughter of the tribe follows, and the author then indicates how Mafatu feels when he describes his thoughts: "Suddenly a fierce resentment stormed through him. He knew in that instant what he must do: he must prove his courage to himself, and to the others, or he could no longer live in their midst. He must face Moana, the Sea God—face him and conquer him" (p. 13). Mafatu's battle for courage is now shown through a combination of actions and thoughts. When terror raises its cruel head and Mafatu is sure he will die at sea, his loyal dog gives him assurance. When he realizes he is on a forbidden island used for human sacrifice, at first he cannot move, but later he dares to take a ceremonial spear even though it may mean death. Then he is elated because he has won a victory over himself. He becomes terror stricken again as a hammerhead shark encircles his raft; he overcomes his fear and attacks the shark to save his dog. He realizes, however, that he could not have killed the shark just to save himself. Mafatu celebrates a final victory when he kills the wild boar whose teeth symbolize courage. Mafatu's tremendous victory over fear is shown as the author describes the feelings of Mafatu's father who can now hold his head high with pride: "Here is my son come home from the sea. Mafatu, Stout Heart. A brave name for a brave boy" (p. 115).

The previous discussion of Patricia Clapp's *I'm Deborah Sampson* mentioned that Deborah's conflict causes her to grow both in strength and determination. Clapp's development of Deborah's consistency and continual ability to grow stronger each time she overcomes a problem is one reason why she is such a memorable character. The author suggests the heroine's search for her own identity and her determination by allowing her to say a rhyme when she needs help in believing in herself:

I'm Deborah Sampson, I'm strong and I'm free.
My forefathers handed their strength down to me.
John Alden, Miles Standish, helped settle this land,
And Governor Bradford ruled well that small band.
Abraham Sampson, he followed ere long,
And all of these names make me loyal and strong. (p. 14)

Deborah's strength and determination are tested when her father dies and she must be bound to a family for eight years. She responds characteristically in shock and then with tears because she cannot believe that anyone could treat her this way: "The tears had run dry, but never had I felt such a weight of abject woe. I was nothing and no one—simply a creature to be bandied round by grown-ups, to be housed wherever someone could be found to take me in" (p. 34). Deborah's dejection does not last for long, however, as she discovers that the family with whom she must live and work is actually warm and loving. The author suggests the respect and love demonstrated by the family toward Deborah. The boys are impressed because she doesn't act like a girl; she learns to shoot a rifle, races against and beats the boys, and plants and cultivates her own garden. As Deborah lives her three extraordinary years in the Continental army, she remains true to herself and calls upon the strength built up through her many experiences; whenever she is terrified or unsure, she reminds herself that she is strong, free, and has a purpose.

As the reader progresses through this text, many memorable characters will be discovered. Through picture storybooks, old favorites will be found, such as Frances the badger (*Best Friends for Frances*), who has very human needs that are easily identified and understood by young children. Modern fantasy introduces that wonderful, faithful spider Charlotte (*Charlotte's Web*) and a terrific pig named Wilbur. Stuart Little, Peter Rabbit, and Winnie the Pooh are additional examples of articulate animal characters who live in the pages of modern fantasy. Some beloved fantasy characters are remembered because of their eccentric behavior or the strange worlds in which they

And a River went out of Eden.

THIS FRONTISPIECE BY GRAHAM ROBERTSON IN Kenneth Grahame's 1908 *The Wind in the Willows* suggests an idyllic woodland setting for an animal fantasy. It may also hint that all may not go well if the inhabitants leave this Eden.

The author's description of the river, the river bank, the changing seasons, and the wild wood and the wide world creates a visual feeling for the location. The descriptions of wandering streams, whispering reeds and willows, and smells of marshlands also create a mood in which animal characters have the freedom to explore an enticing environment. In the opening chapter, for example, the author describes an early spring setting; a time when animals such as Rat and Mole are called by the simple pleasures of springtime.

There are other settings, however, that may be less desirable, settings that go beyond the river bank. In the wild wood are weasels, sloats, and foxes who attack the peaceful inhabitants of the river bank. Beyond the wild wood is the wide world that may also entice some inhabitants and may even create danger. There is a feeling, however, that this more alien world does not really matter to the characters who enjoy living on the isolated river bank.

live. Mary Poppins and Alice in Wonderland are just two. In realistic fiction, there are interesting people: Jess Aarons in *Bridge to Terabithia,* Karana as she overcomes tremendous problems to survive her experiences on *The Island of the Blue Dolphins,* and Cassie as she grows in strength and character in *Roll of Thunder, Hear My Cry.* Old favorites emerge in historical fiction; for example, Laura Ingalls and Caddie Woodlawn as they grow up on the frontier. A new heroine, Catherine Hall from *A Gathering of Days,* will no doubt take her place alongside the other heroes and heroines of frontier America. These characters are all believable and have the capacity to be remembered long after other details of their stories are forgotten.

Setting

Thus far, these stories have developed a story line by integrating plot and characterization. But how does the reader become aware of the way characters see, smell, hear, or touch? Is it possible to know how they might talk and act, or understand the values that they might hold? These questions cannot be answered unless the geographic location of the story and the time when the story took place are recognized. In literature, this time and place is called the *setting.* As in adult

stories, children's stories may take place in the past, present, or future; both plot and characterization should be consistent with what actually occurred or could have occurred during that period. In addition, if the geographic location is identifiable, it should be presented accurately. The combination of plot, characterization, and setting make a story credible.

Purpose of Setting. In some books, setting is such an important part of the story that the plot and characters' actions cannot be developed without understanding time and place. In other stories, however, the setting provides only a background. In fact, some settings are so well known that just a few words place the reader immediately into the expected location. Consider, for example, the introduction, "Once upon a time." Of course, the story takes place in times of yore or a very long time ago when it was possible for magical spells to transform princes into beasts or to change pumpkins into glittering carriages. This is such a common setting for traditional folklore that thirty of the thirty-seven fairy tales in *The Red Fairy Book* begin with the phrase, "Once upon a time." In *Chanticleer and the Fox,* the author says that the story takes place "Once upon a time" and also happens during the days when birds and beasts could sing and talk. Magical spells cannot happen everywhere; they usually occur in "a certain kingdom," "deep in the forest," in "the humble hut of a wise and good peasant," or "far, far away, in a warm and pleasant land." Children are so familiar with these settings that additional details and descriptions are not necessary.

The setting has a more important purpose than providing an instant background in most stories, however. Stories that use setting to create a mood, develop the setting as an antagonist, provide a historical background, or are symbolic are considered next.

Mood. The epic story of Attila the Hun, *The White Stag,* takes place a long time ago when pagan voices were in the wind and fairies danced in the moonlight. The author, Kate Seredy, depicts a setting to create a mood in which a white stag could miraculously appear or moonmaidens seem natural. The first time the stag appears, the leader of the tribe stands before a sacrificial altar in a cold, rocky, and barren land. He waits to hear the voice of Hadur, who will lead his starving people to the promised land. At this time, the white stag appears and leads the Huns on the first stage of their travels to a land rich in game, sheltered from the cold, and filled with green pastures.

Two Huns, Hunor and Magyar, see the white stag again, and he leads them through the "ghost hour" onto a grassy hill cov-

ered with white birch; they hear a brook tinkling like silver bells and a breeze sounding like minstrels' flutes. The reader would expect magic in this place, and is not disappointed as the author describes the vision: "Moonmaidens, those strange changeling fairies who lived in white birch trees and were never seen in the daylight; Moonmaidens who, if caught by the gray-hour of dawn, could never go back to fairyland again; Moonmaidens, who brought good luck to men" (p. 34). The stag appears each time the people need guidance or delivery, and a setting is described in which the stag's appearance is believable.

When the future, formidable leader Attila is born, the setting is not one of gentle magic. Attila's father has just challenged his god, and the result is terrifying: "Suddenly, without warning it [the storm] was upon them with lightning and thunder that roared and howled like an army of furious demons. Trees groaned and crashed to the ground to be picked up again and sucked into the spinning dark funnel of the whirlwind" (p. 64). The author uses this setting to introduce Red Eagle, Attila, the scourge of god, who leads his people onward. The author finally describes a setting in which Attila and his Huns have an impenetrable mountain in front of them and enemies behind them. The stag appears, leads the group through a pass, and into the promised land.

The appearance of a mythical white stag seems believable in this setting. From *The White Stag,* written and illustrated by Kate Seredy. Copyright © 1937 by Kate Seredy. Copyright renewed 1965 by Kate Seredy. Reprinted by permission of Viking Penguin, Inc.

Setting as Antagonist. Two books have been discussed that develop conflict through a person-against-nature antagonist. The descriptions of the Arctic setting in *Julie of the Wolves* are essential; without them, it would be difficult to understand the life-and-death peril facing Miyax. These descriptions make it possible to comprehend Miyax's love for the Arctic, her admiration of and dependence on the wolves, and her preference for the old Eskimo ways.

In *Call It Courage,* the sea as antagonist must be thoroughly described in order to understand the traumatic and disabling nature of Mafatu's fear. Without understanding the setting, the magnitude of Mafatu's victory over his own fear could not be understood.

Historical Background. Accuracy in setting is extremely important in historical fiction. Unless the author describes the location and the time period carefully, children cannot comprehend unfamiliar historical periods. Both the characters' actions and the conflict in the story may be influenced by the time period. It is, therefore, essential to understand the setting.

A Gathering of Days, by Joan Blos, is an example of historical fiction that develops the setting—a small New Hampshire farm in the 1830s. Life in rural America is brought alive by descriptions of little things such as home remedies, country pleasures, and country hardships. The author describes in detail the preparation of a cold remedy as the character goes to pump for water, blows up the fire, heats a kettle of water over the flames, wrings out a flannel in hot water, sprinkles the flannel with turpentine, and places it on the patient's chest. The joys and difficulties of winter are developed by contrasting Father's and the children's reactions during the breaking out from the snow. It is so cold that Father places himself between the team of oxen in order to benefit from the warmth of their bodies; the children, however, compare the same experience to the Fourth of July. The author also describes discipline and school life in the 1830s: disobedience might result in a thrashing; girls, because of their sex, are excused from all but the simplest arithmetic. The joys of farm life are described, and the reader vicariously shares in the excitement and taste during tapping the maple sugar trees and collecting nuts. This last experience is described by the author: "O, I do think, as has been said, that if getting in the corn and potatoes are the prose of a farm child's life, then nutting's the poetry" (p. 131).

Ann Schlee, in *Ask Me No Questions,* develops a historical setting in which her characters must consider if feeding hungry children justifies stealing food. In order to develop a credible setting for this moral issue, Schlee places her characters in nineteenth century England as they are forced to move from their London home to avoid a cholera epidemic. The author describes Victorian attitudes toward children and the children's discovery of an asylum where children are forced to eat pig slop in their efforts to avoid starvation. The plot develops as two children leave their home, move in with their aunt who expresses very Victorian attitudes, and discover the horrible conditions in the asylum near their aunt's home. The author's detailed descriptions of settings and characterizations encourage readers to understand the issues and conflicts experienced by the characters.

The author of historical fiction must not only depict the time and the location but must also be aware of speech patterns, vocabulary usage, and values consistent with the time and location. To do this, the author must be immersed in the past and do considerable research. Joan Blos, author of *A Gathering of Days,* said that she researched her subject at the New York Public Library, the Graduate and William C. Clements libraries on the University of Michigan campus, and the town library of Holderness, New Hampshire. She also consulted town and county records in New Hampshire and discussed the story with faculty in the Department of History.

Symbolic Settings. The settings that have already been discussed in traditional literature are symbolic. The deep dark woods and the magical kingdom from once upon a time are places where anything can happen. Writers of contemporary, realistic literature may also use symbolic settings to allow their characters to live their secret wishes and become stronger.

A secret kingdom in the woods is the setting for part of Katherine Paterson's *Bridge to Terabithia.* The author develops a need for a secret kingdom as she describes the two main characters: a boy, Jess, who would rather be an artist than follow the more masculine aspirations of his father; and a girl, Leslie, who doesn't fit in with the rural Virginia values of her peers. This need is increased as specific actions lead to their friendship: Jess's father accuses the school of turning his son into a sissy; the boys refuse to let Leslie race with them until Jess intervenes; Jess writes about football, which he hates, because he knows that everyone will laugh at him if he writes about drawing; the class hisses at Leslie because she doesn't have a television set (her home is filled with books). Jess and Leslie find that they have much in common, including a love for books and art. They believe they need a secret place where they could be joint rulers, and even the entrance to their secret country is symbolic: "I know—she was getting excited—it could be a magic country like Narnia, and the only way you can get in is by swinging across on this enchanted rope" (p. 39).

A boy and girl create a secret kingdom in which they can escape the problems of the real world.
Drawing by Donna Diamond from *Bridge to Terabithia* by Katherine Paterson. Copyright © 1977 by Katherine Paterson. A Newbery Medal winner. By permission of Thomas Y. Crowell, Publishers.

They grab the old rope, swing across the creek, and search the woods for a place to build their stronghold. The author describes the setting covered with dogwood, red bud, oaks, and evergreens as a nonfrightening place filled with streams of light dancing through the leaves. Within the kingdom, anything is possible: "Between the two of them they owned the world and no enemy, Gary Fulcher, Wanda Kay Moore, Janice Avery, Jess's own fears and insufficiencies, nor any of the foes whom Leslie imagined attacking Terabithia could ever really defeat them" (p. 40). The author develops two credible worlds as Jess and Leslie go from the world of school and home to the one that they make for themselves in Terabithia.

Real magic can also happen in an English garden surrounded by a high wall. The setting of the children's classic, *The Secret Garden,* by Frances Hodgson Burnett, is a garden that has been locked for ten years—the key is even buried and the gate hidden behind vines. The first change in the life of a lonely, unhappy girl occurs when she discovers the garden: "It was the sweetest, most mysterious-looking place anyone could imagine. The high walls which shut it in were covered with the leafless stems of climbing roses which were so thick that they were matted together" (p. 76). Finding the garden, working in it, and watching it grow brings happiness to the girl and restores health to a sick boy. Good magic is portrayed in the tiny growing things, the description of a secret kingdom, and the mystic circle found under the plum tree. The greatest magic of all, however, occurs as working in the garden results in a reunion between a previously unhappy father and his ten-year-old son.

A setting can supply only background for the story, or it can be so significant that both plot and characterization could not be developed without a thorough description and understanding of the setting. This text will provide a clearer understanding of specific requirements of setting as it is developed in literature types such as picture storybooks, fantasy, historical fiction, and biography.

Theme

The theme of a story is the underlying idea that ties the plot, characterization, and setting together into a meaningful whole. When themes are evaluated in children's books, several questions should be asked: What did the author want to convey about life or society? Is this theme worthwhile for children? Themes in children's books are frequently stated rather than implied, as they may be in adult books. Some themes are influenced by historical periods while others are universal.

Themes Recurrent in History. Researchers have found the study of relationships between social, cultural, and economic influences and various story themes a fascinating subject. Jean Shaw (17) investigated themes found in children's books published in the United States between 1850 and the 1960s and concluded that literature themes were related to the social, cultural, and economic influences of these times. She identified the following themes and their most influential time periods: (1) search for values was common from 1850–65, 1914–19, and from 1936 through the 1960s; (2) problems concerned with growing up were popular from 1865–1905, during the early 1930s, and after World War II; (3) books about travel and understanding people in other lands were most popular from 1918 until the depression; (4) lives of heroes dominated pre-World War I years and remained strong through the late 1950s; (5) fantasy themes found in fairy tales reflected periods of prosperity, reaching peaks around 1910, from 1917–29, and from the 1950s into the 1960s; (6) the urge to acquire more knowledge on subjects was common around the early 1900s and during World War II. (See chapter nine for a dicussion of contemporary themes and chapter ten for time line of historical fiction themes.)

Adults and older children can have a better understanding of historical values as well as social, cultural, and economic influences of the times by identifying popular themes written by authors of children's books and investigating the history of the time period. Chapter two investigated this relationship between theme and historical period and discussed examples.

Developing Understanding. Literature offers children an opportunity to live vicariously and to understand the struggles of growing up; consequently, the themes of many children's books deal with developing self-understanding. Gretchen Hayden (8) investigated personal development themes found in children's books that had been awarded the Newbery medal and concluded that the following were most popular: (1) difficulties in establishing good relationships between adults and children; (2) need for morality to guide one's actions; (3) importance of support from other people; (4) acceptance of self and others; (5) respect for authority; (6) ability to handle problems; and (7) necessity for cooperation.

Many of these themes are found in the books previously discussed. The difficulty of establishing a good relationship between adults and a child, for example, is developed in a humorous way in Beverly Cleary's *Ramona and Her Father*. The author indicates that Ramona usually has a good relationship with her family, but it rapidly deteriorates when her father loses his job. The feelings of frustration are enhanced as Ramona ponders the new difficulties of getting along with adults when she "never wanted to annoy her father or her mother either, just Beezus, although sometimes without even trying she succeeded in annoying her whole family" (p. 29). Cleary describes her efforts to help her family and her frustration when her actions do not work out as she hopes. For example, after the cat destroys the jack-o-lantern the family has made together, her father mistakenly thinks Ramona's sadness is due to the loss of the pumpkin: "Didn't grown-ups think children worried about anything but jack-o-lanterns? Didn't they know children worried about grown-ups?" (p. 85).

In Robert O'Brien's *Mrs. Frisby and the Rats of NIMH*, a group of superior rats search for a morality to guide their actions. They have studied the human race and do not wish to make the same mistakes; they also worry about their easy life. After evaluating their life, they decide that using the equipment found in the Toy Tinker's truck was their first error. This discovery made it possible for them to steal electricity as well as food and water from the human society. The author reveals their new understanding as the rats conclude: "It was this, of course, that made life so easy that it seemed pointless. We did not have enough work to do because a thief's life is always based on somebody else's work" (p. 171). They search for an answer to their moral dilemma and conclude, "We could not find any easy answer—because there was none. There was, however, a hard answer" (p. 171). At this point, they decide that they must choose the hard answer, move into an isolated valley, and work to develop their own civilization.

One book that develops the importance of support from another human being is Theodore Taylor's *The Cay*. When Phillip and his mother leave Curaçao in order to find safety in the United States, they do not expect to have their boat torpedoed by a German submarine. This causes Phillip and a West Indian named Timothy to be isolated first on a life raft and then on a tiny Caribbean island. Their isolation, as well as their need for each other, is increased when a blow to Phillip's head causes blindness. Although Phillip looks down on Timothy because he has black skin, he must rely on him to make their hut, provide their food, and prepare a means for rescuers to find them. Timothy shows that he understands both Phillip's feelings and the importance of human support when he says, "Young bahss, be an outrageous mahn if you like, but 'ere I'm all you got" (p. 70). As Phillip learns to rely more and more on Timothy, his attitude changes. First, he asks Timothy to call him Phillip and not young boss; next, he moves closer to him and discovers that Timothy's skin feels neither black nor white; he then helps Timothy through malaria; later, when he tries to remember Timothy's face, he asks him if he is still black; and, finally, Phillip realizes that Timothy has given his life to protect him during a hurricane. At this point, Phillip admits his total need for another person, he worries about what would happen if another storm comes or if he should become ill, and he finally concludes, "I could never survive alone" (p. 133). After Phillip is rescued, he realizes that both his life and attitudes have changed; he thinks fondly of the legacy left to him by his wonderful black friend.

The Cay contains a theme that stresses acceptance of self and others. Through their need for each other, the white boy and the black West Indian develop total acceptance. The hero-

Superior rats consider the morality of their actions in a complex plot.
From Robert C. O'Brien, *Mrs. Frisby and the Rats of NIMH,* illustrated by Zena Bernstein. Copyright © 1971 by Robert C. O'Brien. (New York: Charles Scribner's Sons, 1971). Reprinted with the permission of Atheneum Publishers.

ine in *A Gathering of Days,* Catherine Hall, also learns to accept herself and others. She experiences injustice for the first time when she and her friends secretly help a runaway slave. Two traumatic experiences increase her acceptance of others as well as influence her own maturity. Catherine has been responsible for the well-being of her little sister and widowed father for many years. When her father remarries and a stepmother (and step-brother) enter their home, the women must learn to respect each other. The other experience is one of grief when Catherine's best friend dies. She tries to understand her father's explanation that country life is hard and country folk need to learn to accept this or they will be broken.

Catherine learns not only the meaning of authority but also to respect it. Throughout her journal, she frequently says that she experiences difficulty when asked to do something against her will. After she learns to respect her new mother, however, she concludes, "I know I shall find good consequence in whatever is decided by Father and Mammann. Thus it now appears

to me that trust, and not submission, defines obedience" (p. 139).

The conflicts in the majority of books already discussed deal in some way with overcoming problems. The characters may overcome problems within themselves or in their relationships with others or problems caused by society or nature. Characters have faced their adversaries, and through a maturing process, have learned to handle their own difficulties. Handling problems may be as dramatic and preplanned as Mafatu's search for courage in *Call It Courage* or may result from an accidental experience as that found in *The Cay.* Few characters have to handle more problems than Deborah in *I'm Deborah Sampson.* She grows in strength even when she must leave her mother and work for a cousin at the age of five and later when she is bound to a family for eight years. She keeps her identity secret during three years in the Continental army, and finally, after her marriage, she solves financial problems by touring the country and talking about her military experiences.

Many minor difficulties are also used to develop themes in children's books. Sam in *Sam, Bangs & Moonshine* must overcome her tendency to lie; Ann in *The Cabin Faced West* learns to love her new home on the frontier.

The Cay develops a theme stressing the need for cooperation in order to overcome problems of survival. While Phillip must use Timothy's eyes to see, Timothy needs Phillip's ability to write in order to form the rocks into the word "HELP." They also need each other for companionship. Most of the stories with settings in isolated areas, such as the frontier, stress cooperation. All of the families cooperate to open the snow-clogged roads in *A Gathering of Days.* They also work together to tap the maple sugar trees. The family and the larger community cooperate throughout the Laura Ingalls Wilder books. Without this, families living on the frontier could not survive; the pioneer spirit is one of adventure in the unknown and requires cooperation.

The themes in memorable books are usually ones that children, because of their own needs, can understand. This text has also shown that authors frequently express more than one theme in a story.

Style

Authors have a wide choice of words to select from and numerous ways to arrange words in order to create plots, settings, and characterizations; the way they use words and sentences to develop a story is referred to as *style.* One effective way to evaluate style is to read a selection aloud. The style should sound both pleasing and appropriate for the story. The language should bring characters to life, enhance plot development, and create the mood. This section considers some of the devices of style used by award-winning authors.

Appeal to the Senses. *The Girl Who Loved Wild Horses,* by Paul Goble, was picked as a Children's Choice selection (see page 96); children's reasons for choosing this book most often referred to the author's use of language. Goble uses words to create the image of the wild horses racing through the canyons and the spirit of the Indian girl who loves them. For example, during a storm, this scene is described: "The horses galloped faster and faster, pursued by thunder and lightning. They swept like a brown flood across hills and through valleys. Fear drove them on and on, leaving their familiar grazing grounds far behind" (p. 12 unnumbered). The author uses descriptive verbs to create an image and similes to develop the image of horses moving like a brown flood. Other similes in

the book compare one stallion's eyes to "cold stars" and the floating of his mane and tail to "wispy clouds." The author's style complements the illustrations, and together they form a story recreating a world of moonlit cliffs, beautiful wild horses, and an Indian girl who must share their freedom.

Another author who paints a setting with words is Kate Seredy. The text has already described the setting of *The White Stag* where moonmaidens appear and another where the wrath of the pagan god descends upon the challenging Hun (p. 87). Like Goble, Seredy uses similes to enhance her descriptions. For example, the white stag leaps away "as lightly as sunlight leaps over running water" (p. 20) and his slender legs are compared to the branches of white birch. The softness of the moonmaiden's voice is compared to the downy wing of a bird. The Huns are both closely related to, and dependent upon, the whims of nature. It is therefore realistic to have the comparisons taken from the environment of animals, plants, and weather.

Authors may also depict a leisurely, unhurried setting or one filled with tension and excitement. Through specific selection of words and sentence patterns, Armstrong Sperry creates two quite different moods for Mafatu in *Call It Courage.* As Mafatu goes through the jungle, he is preoccupied and moves at a leisurely pace. Sperry also uses a long sentence pattern to develop this mood: "His mind was not in this business at all: he was thinking about the rigging of his canoe, planning how he could strengthen it here, tighten it there" (p. 77). This dreamy preoccupation changes rapidly as Mafatu senses danger. Likewise, Sperry's sentence structure changes and tension builds through short choppy sentences and harsh verbs: "The boar charged. Over the ground it tore. Foam flew back from its tusks. The boy braced himself" (p. 78).

Many of the stories enjoyed by young children contain repetition of words, phrases, or sentences. Repetition is especially appealing because it encourages children to join in during the reading. Kent's cumulative tale *The Fat Cat,* for example, repeats phrases such as "I ate the gruel/and the pot" each time the cat encounters a new victim. Repetition provides a pleasing rhythm in *When I Was Young in the Mountains* by Cynthia Rylant. The author introduces memories such as Grandfather's kisses, Grandmother's cooking, and listening to frogs singing at dusk with the phrase "When I was young in the mountains." Rylant's style seems especially appropriate for a story that suggests love for a way of life.

Other literary devices such as alliteration and rhyming are also used. Chapter five discusses these style choices and examples from the literature.

Point of View

An incident may be described in different terms by several people who have the same experience. The details they choose to describe, the feelings they experience, and their beliefs in the right or wrong of an incident may vary because of their backgrounds, values, and other perspectives. Consequently, the same story may change drastically depending on the point of view of the storyteller. Consider, for example, how *Mrs. Frisby and the Rats of NIMH*, by Robert O'Brien, would change if told from the viewpoint of a laboratory technician rather than that of articulate rodents. How would Peter Rabbit's story change if Beatrix Potter had told it from the viewpoint of mother rabbit? How would Armstrong Sperry's *Call It Courage* differ if told from the viewpoint of a Polynesian tribesman who loves the sea rather than from the viewpoint of a boy who fears it?

An author has several options when selecting point of view. First, should the story be told from the first person point of view (I) of one of the characters? If the author chooses a first person point of view, whose actions and feelings should influence the plot development, characterization, and theme? Second, should the story be told from an objective point of view in which the actions speak for themselves? In this case the author describes the actions and the reader infers the meaning or thoughts of the characters. Third, should the story be told from an omniscient point of view in which the author tells the story in third person (they, he, she)? The author in this case is not restricted to knowledge, experience, and feelings of one person. Every detail, feeling, and thought of all characters can be revealed. Finally, should the story be told from a limited omniscient point of view? In this case, the author can concentrate on the experience of one character, but has the option to be all-knowing about other characters. (A limited omniscient point of view may help the author clarify the subject for the reader.)

Although there is no preferred point of view for children's literature, the credibility and enjoyment of a story for a specific age group may be affected by the author's choice. Contemporary realistic fiction for eight- to ten-year-olds and for older children is frequently told from a first person point of view, or at least from the viewpoint of a child. This may be successful because children of this age often empathize with the character if they have had similar experiences. Carol Lea Benjamin introduces her twelve-year-old character in *The Wicked Stepdog* with these thoughts: "I think most parents are pretty phony. Take my dad for example" (p. 1). The actions in the story are then interpreted through the viewpoint of the twelve-year-old. Likewise, Beverly Cleary's popular Ramona stories are told from the viewpoint of a seven- or eight-year-old precocious child. In *Ramona Quimby, Age 8* the author describes Ramona's third grade experiences and her efforts to help at home through Ramona's frequently humorous viewpoint.

The consistency of point of view encourages readers to believe in the characters and the plot development. This is especially crucial in modern fantasy; authors must encourage readers to suspend disbelief if another world, unusual characters, or magical incidents are to be believed. A writer, for example, may describe a setting as if it is being viewed by a character only a few inches tall. To be believable, however, the story cannot stray from the viewpoint of the tiny character. The character's actions, the responses of others toward the character, and the setting must be consistent. Chapter seven discusses the importance of point of view in modern fantasy.

The literary elements are all important when evaluating and selecting literature. Plot development, characterization, setting, theme, style, and point of view all interact in outstanding children's literature.

Nonstereotypes

Stereotypes must be considered when evaluating literature for young children; stereotypic views of both race and sex have been highly criticized by educators. Of particular concern in the areas of racism and bias are literary selections that represent minority groups in a way that is insensitive or demeaning. In addition, the literature collection may inadequately represent minorities. Under these circumstances, there may be a shortage of quality stories with minority characters; a limited number of works by authors who write from a minority perspective; and a shortage of materials that depict the literary, cultural, and historical influence of minorities.

To remedy these deficiencies, literature must be offered that lacks negative stereotypes and presents an honest, authentic picture of the people and their cultural and historical contributions. Because ethnic culture is so important, chapter eleven is devoted to multiethnic literature. There are discussions about multiethnic literature values, the images of ethnic groups found in literature of the past, criteria for evaluating multiethnic literature, and the authors and their works. In addition to evaluating literature, chapter eleven also investigates approaches that adults can use to evaluate children's attitudes toward ethnic literature, develop a multiethnic literature program, improve self-concepts, and develop an appreciation for this literature. Understanding these approaches is essential because research indicates that, if attitudes and self-concepts are to change, reading positive multiethnic literature must be

ISSUE

❧❧❧

Evaluation of Children's Literature: Literary Merit Versus Popularity Versus Social Significance

CHILDREN'S LITERATURE is evaluated not only by children who are potential readers of each selection but also by literary critics, teachers, librarians, parents, and publishers. Questions related to literary quality, social philosophy, and suitability of content are debated along with the potential or proven popularity of a book to attract children's interests. The evaluation criteria used for book awards, criticism, and recommendations for book purchases frequently reflect the standards of diverse groups. The adult-selected award winners, exemplified by the Newbery Medal, Caldecott Medal, Notable Children's Books, and Boston Globe-Horn Book Award, suggest that the highest literary value should be a primary consideration when choosing books for children. In contrast, the various readers' choice awards, which are compiled from young readers' preferences, imply that children's interests and the popularity of books among children themselves should be an essential consideration. A third position represented by groups such as the Council on Interracial Books for Children suggests that books should be evaluated according to human values with a book selection policy that stems from child development and psychology, cultural pluralism, and aesthetic standards.

The selection standards reflected by these three positions may or may not identify the same books as literature worthy of sharing with children. The merits of each type of evaluation are debated in professional literature, in college classrooms, and during professional conferences. Reviewers of children's books may emphasize one or more of these positions when they evaluate new books or compile lists of recommended books. It is helpful if readers can identify any particular bias of a reviewer so that they can interpret and use recommendations to meet their own individual needs.

Carolyn Bauer and LaVonne Sanborn[1] maintain that both literary quality and popularity are important. They suggest that books which have won both types of awards deserve considerable emphasis because this indicates that children do enjoy some books with literary value. From a list of 193 books that have won readers' choice awards, Bauer and Sanborn have identified 39 that were also literary merit award winners. Of these, *Mrs. Frisby and the Rats of NIMH, The Mouse and the Motorcycle, Old Yeller, Rascal,* and *The Trumpet of the Swan* have each won four readers' choice awards. Authors Beverly Cleary, George Selden, and E. B. White each have two titles that have won awards for literary value and popularity.

Increased sensitivity to the human values expressed in books may result in debates about the merit of previously acclaimed literature. For example, Walter Edmonds's *The Matchlock Gun* won the Newbery Medal in 1942. The same book, however, was criticized in the 1970s because of insensitive descriptions of Native Americans.

When evaluating literature and reading literature critiques, students of children's literature may consider each selection standard. How would the book be evaluated according to literary merit, popularity, and social significance?

1 Bauer, Carolyn J., and Sanborn, LaVonne H. "The Best of Both Worlds: Children's Books Acclaimed by Adults and Young Readers." *Top of the News* 38 (Fall 1981): 53-56.

followed by discussions or other activities that allow interaction between children and adults.

Another consideration when evaluating children's literature is the role portrayed by females. Sadker and Sadker (15) maintain that "blatant quotes denigrating one sex, usually women, are relatively common in children's books, and it is not at all difficult to find statements that girls are dumb, silly, unable to keep secrets, and generally incompetent" (p. 232). These authors claim that if the material contains quotes that group all males or all females together and make insulting remarks about either sex as a whole, the book may be sexist. The total book, however, must be read before this decision can be reached, because isolated quotes should not be judged out of context.

Of equal concern to both educators and parents are books that stereotype males and suggest that they do not have a wide range of options. Chapter nine evaluates sexism in books and considers other controversial issues in literature. That chapter also discusses controversial issues related to contemporary realistic fiction, suggests guidelines for choosing it, presents authors and their books, and suggests ways to expand children's reactions to realistic fiction.

THE RIGHT BOOK FOR THE INDIVIDUAL CHILD

Chapter one considered the different stages of children's development as well as the role that literature can play in encouraging language growth, intellectual development, personality development, social development, and creative development. Because of these developmental stages, children may have different personal and literary needs at various times. In addition to different needs, they also have diverse interests and reading abilities that must be considered when selecting the right book for the individual.

It is necessary to understand why and what children read in order to help them select materials that stimulate their interests and enjoyment. John Guthrie (7) investigated studies that researched why people read. He concluded that the two most important reasons given were to obtain general knowledge and to provide relaxation and enjoyment. Additional answers to questions of what adults read are provided by Jeanne Chall and Emily Marston (2); they found that the most powerful determinants of adult reading are accessibility, readability, and interest. These factors influence children's reading as well. If developing enjoyment through literature is a major objective of the program, it is essential that many excellent books be available to children, that their readability level be considered, and

that adults know how to gain and use information about children's interests.

Accessibility

A very important determinant for leisure reading is accessibility of materials. In order to know what books interest them, to gain knowledge of their heritage, to recognize good literature, to understand themselves and others, and to develop an appreciation for what they read, children must have opportunities to read and listen to many books. As suggested previously, the literature program should include a wide variety of high quality literature, both old and new.

The Child's Ability

Readability was the second consideration for determining selections identified by Chall and Marston (2). Readability level is a concern when selecting literature for children to read independently; they enjoy reading books that do not have so many unknown words that they become frustrated. This independent level of reading is the level at which a child is able to pronounce about 98–100 percent of the words in a selection and can answer 90–100 percent of comprehension questions asked about it. There are wide ranges in reading abilities in any one age group or grade level, and an adult working with children must provide, and be familiar with, an equally wide range of literature. For this reason, readability grade levels are presented for the books listed in the annotated bibliographies at the end of each chapter. (See appendix E, page 000, for a readability graph and directions for computing readability.)

Many children have reading levels lower than their interest levels; it is important to provide many opportunities for them to listen to, and interact with, fine literature. Chapter five presents comparisons between books designed to be read *by* young children and those designed to be read *to* young children.

The Child's Interests

Adults can learn more about children's interests in several ways. First, studies of interests can be reviewed, and second, interests can be evaluated through interest inventories. Attention should be given to information gained from each source.

For many years, researchers have investigated factors related to leisure time reading and reading interests of children at different age levels. A recent study by Vincent Greaney (6) identified some of these factors: (1) American and British studies have indicated that the time and amount of leisure reading varies with age; children at the end of primary school read the most, and a decrease in leisure reading follows this period (this decrease does not occur, however, with high-ability readers); (2) girls read more books than boys, although boys read more nonfiction than girls; (3) children from working-class homes do not read as much as those from higher socioeconomic backgrounds or educational levels; and (4) there is a relationship between the amount of leisure reading and the level of student achievement; good readers read more and also read higher quality materials.

Several studies have investigated specific literature interests of children at different ages. For example, Gordon Peterson (14) studied library books selected by second graders in a midwestern city and found that both boys and girls were more interested in fanciful stories than in realistic ones; these included modern fantasy stories about animals, fanciful humorous stories, and fantasy stories about people. Both sexes reported that their main reasons for selecting and liking a book had to do with its subject and illustrations. This portion of the study indicated similarities between boys and girls, but there were also some differences. Boys read more informational books, while girls read larger portions of the books; both completed more than half of the books they checked out.

Other researchers have studied reading interests of children in grades three through five. Thomas Dowan (3) researched children in Florida schools and concluded that boys in grades three through five are more interested in adventure, tall tales, historical nonfiction, how-to-do-it, sports, and science. Girls are more interested in animals, fairy tales, modern fantasy, children of the United States, and children from other lands. Similar results were found by Joan Feeley (5), who concluded that fourth- and fifth-grade boys like sports, excitement, and informational content; girls prefer social empathy, fantasy, and content dealing with their recreational interests.

While this information can provide some general ideas about what subjects children of a particular age prefer, stereotypes of children's preferences must not be developed. Without asking questions about interests, for example, there was no way to learn that a fourth grader was a Shakespeare buff, as the interest research does not indicate that he should like Shakespeare's plays. A first-grade girl's favorite subject was dinosaurs and she could identify them by name; it was impossible to discover this without an interview. Research does not indicate that first-grade girls should be interested in factual, scientific subjects. These two cases point to the need to discover children's interests before helping them select books that will entice and stimulate.

There are several ways to uncover children's interests. One of the simplest is informal conversation: ask the child to describe what he likes to do and read about. When working with a number of children, however, some way of recording the information is usually needed. An interest inventory can be developed in which students answer questions about their favorite hobbies, books, sports, television shows, and other interests. After the questions, an adult can either read them and write in answers for children too young to read and write or give the inventory to a group of older children who can write their own responses. Such an inventory might include some of the questions asked in Chart 3–1. (Changes would need to be made according to children's age levels, and additional information can be discovered if they tell why they like certain books.) After the interest inventory is given, pertinent information should be used to help children select books and extend their enjoyment of literature.

CHILDREN'S PREFERENCES IN BOOKS—THE CHILD AS CRITIC

This text has discussed children's interests, abilities, and needs as they relate to selecting books for children. It has also considered evaluating books according to plot, characterization, setting, theme, and style. Children are the ultimate critics of what they read, and their preferences should be considered when evaluating and selecting books to share with them.

For the last few years, the International Reading Association and the Children's Book Council have had a joint project that allow approximately 10,000 children from throughout the United States to evaluate children's books published during a given year. Each year their reactions are recorded; a research team uses this information to determine the "Children's Choices" for that year. A list of books is then compiled for the following levels: beginning independent reading, younger children, middle grades, older readers, informational books, and poetry. This very useful annotated bibliography is published each year in the October issue of *The Reading Teacher,* or it may be obtained from the Children's Book Council, 67 Irving Place, New York, N.Y. 10003.

A look at these lists of children's favorites also gives a better understanding of the elements in books that appeal to children. In order to identify characteristic elements found in the Children's Choices, Sam Sebesta (16) evaluated the books listed and tried to discover if these characteristics were different from those found in books not chosen by children. His evaluation produced the following:

1 Plots of the Children's Choices are faster paced than those found in books not chosen as favorites.
2 Young children enjoy reading about nearly any topic if the information is presented in a specific way. The topic may

CHART 3–1
An Informal Interest Inventory

1 Do you have a hobby? _____
   If you do, what is your hobby? _____
2 Do you have a pet? _____
   What kind of a pet do you have? _____
3 What is your favorite book that someone has read to you? _____
4 What kinds of books do you like to have read to you?

real animals _____	fantasy animals _____	fairy tales _____
real children _____	family stories _____	poetry _____
science fiction _____	picture books _____	historical fiction _____
funny stories _____	information books _____	science books _____
sports stories _____	mysteries _____	adventures _____
true stories _____		

5 What is your favorite book that you have read by yourself? _____
6 What kinds of books do you like to read by yourself? (Similar to 4) _____
7 What sports do you like? _____
8 Who are your favorite sports stars? _____
9 What do you do when you get home from school? _____
10 What do you like to do on Saturday? _____
11 Do you like to collect things? _____
   What do you like to collect? _____
12 What are your favorite subjects in school? _____
13 Would you rather read a book by yourself or have someone read it to you? _____
14 Name a book you read this week. _____
15 Where would you like to go on vacation? _____
16 Do you go to the library? _____
   If you do, how often do you go? _____
   Do you have a library card? _____
17 Do you watch television? _____
18 If you do, what kinds of programs do you like?

comedies _____	specials _____	mysteries _____
sports _____	news _____	detective shows _____
animal programs _____	cartoons _____	science fiction _____
family stories _____	westerns _____	other _____
educational TV _____	music _____	
true stories _____	game shows _____	

19 Name your favorite television programs. _____
20 Who are your favorite characters on TV? _____
21 Name several subjects you would like to know more about. _____

be less important than interest studies have indicated; specifics rather than topics seem to underlie preferences.

3 Children like detailed descriptions of settings. They want to know exactly how the place looks and feels before the main action occurs.

4 One type of plot structure does not dominate Children's Choices. Some stories have a central focus with a carefully arranged cause-and-effect plot; others have plots that meander with episodes showing no connection.

5 Children do not like sad books.

6 Many books explicitly teach a lesson. Critics usually frown on didactic literature, but children seem to like some of it.

7 Warmth was the most outstanding quality found in the books. Children enjoy books where the characters like each other, express their feelings in things they say and do, and sometimes act selflessly.

Sebesta believes this information should be used to help children select books and to stimulate reading and discussions. For example, attention can be called to the warmth,

THROUGH THE EYES OF AN EDUCATOR

The Role of Literature in the Mainstreamed Classroom

Sandra B. Cohen

Associate professor of education in the Department of Special Education, University of Virginia, and co-author of *Language Arts for the Mildly Handicapped*, SANDRA B. COHEN discusses values, selection, and use of children's literature in mainstreamed classrooms.

ALTHOUGH MAINSTREAMing, the integration of handicapped and nonhandicapped children, has been federally mandated in P.L. 94-142 (Education for All Handicapped Children Act), it is disconcerting that it is not, in many cases, successfully accomplished in educational practice. Handicapped children who are placed in regular education classrooms are often separated socially and instructionally from their normal peers. The barriers that hinder successful mainstreaming are lack of understanding of handicapping conditions, feelings of isolation and differences, and an unwillingness by some teachers to try new instructional approaches.

Social and instructional integration of handicapped and nonhandicapped children is at the core of the mainstreaming concept and is very difficult to achieve. Teachers must incorporate strategies into their lessons that will allow them to appropriately manage the heterogeneous groups of children found in mainstreamed classrooms.

One subject that is very adaptable for use with mainstreamed children is literature. Experiences with literature allow children of different abilities, both cognitively and emotionally, to mutually enjoy stories, discuss viewpoints, and understand how people who are different from them can also be so much like they are. For the nonhandicapped, literature can be used as an introduction to the needs, feelings, and lives of disabled persons. In addition to the obvious concern for readability, teachers should select stories about disabled persons that accurately portray the handicapping condition.

Exceptional children, who are much like their normal peers in many ways, do have some specific needs and feelings which differentiate them. In some cases, handicapped children may feel alone and may be unable to express themselves in a manner which will allow others to appreciate what they are going through. Literature can fill a void by reflecting the handicapped child's feelings in stories about real or literary disabled characters. The handicapped can differ as much from one another as they do from nonhandicapped youngsters. The type of instructional program will vary according to the disability and the child's past experiences. Teachers should recognize individual differences and select appropriate literature. By understanding themselves and others, all handicapped children can become more socially accepting of and acceptable to others.

Some mainstreaming programs separate children with different ability levels. Handicapped children need not be isolated during instructional periods; rather, teachers should develop learning experiences which integrate a variety of ability levels. For instance, when listening to a story a heterogeneous group of children can apply interpretations according to their own cognitive levels, and all can participate in a class discussion. One way of integrating children instructionally is to present stories adjusted according to readability but which express the same content. The illustrations and comprehension questions can remain the same and act as motivators and learning checkpoints for all children. In other situations literature may be used as a tool for children to work cooperatively. Literature may also form the basis of concept teaching in many content areas such as math, history, and science.

Used in a variety of ways, literature can break down barriers and allow all children to better understand each other and learn together. Handicapped mainstreamed children need not be treated separately from their nonhandicapped peers. The use of literature to successfully achieve mainstreaming's goal of social and instructional integration is limited only by the skills and creativity of the teacher.

pace, or descriptions in a story to heighten the interaction between the book and the reader.

The 1982 Children's Choices list (11) suggests types of stories that appeal to readers. At the beginning independent level are comical stories about more or less realistic family situations, humorous animal stories, stories that develop emotional experiences, action-filled fantasies, traditional stories, counting books, rhymes, and riddles. Stories chosen by younger readers include realistic stories about families, friends, school, and personal problems; animal stories; fantasies; fast-paced adventures; folktales; and humorous stories. Stories chosen by children in the middle grades include realistic stories about sibling rivalry, peer acceptance, fears, and not conforming to stereotypes; fantasies; suspense; and humorous stories. Popular informational books include factual and nonsensical advice about human health, factual information about animals, and biographical information about sports stars. Popular poetry includes collections by Judith Viorst, Shel Silverstein, and William Cole.

The books that children choose are from a wide variety of genres. Some are on highly recommended lists of children's books; others are not. Many educators and children's literature authorities are concerned with the quality of books children read. Children can, according to Glenna Sloan (18), make valid judgments about good books if they are taught to do so. She believes that they can be trained to consider these questions: Did the story end the way you expected? Did the author prepare you for the ending? How? If you could make up a different ending, how would you change the rest of the story?

If children are to improve in their ability to make valid judgments, they must experience good books and investigate and discuss what it is about a book that makes it memorable. Young children usually just enjoy and talk about books, but older ones can start to evaluate what they do and do not like about literature.

A sixth-grade teacher encouraged her students to make judgments and to develop a list of selection criteria by developing a literature study with the class (13). The motivation for the study began when the students wondered about what favorite books their parents might have read when they were in the same grade. To answer this question, the children interviewed their parents and other adults and asked them which books and characters were their favorites. The books, characters, and number of people who recommended them were listed on a large chart. Each student then read a book that a parent or another respected adult had enjoyed. (Many adults also reread these books.) Following their reading, the children discussed the book with the adult and discussed what made or did not make the book memorable for them. At this time, the teacher introduced the concepts of plot, characterization, setting, theme, style, and format; the children searched the books they had read for examples of each element. Finally, they listed questions that they should ask themselves when evaluating a book:

Questions to Ask Myself When I Judge a Book

1 Is this a good story?
2 Is the story about something I think could really happen?
3 Did the main character overcome the problem, but not too easily?
4 Did the climax seem natural?
5 Did the characters seem real?
6 Did the characters in the story grow?
7 Did I find out about more than one side of the characters?
8 Did the setting present what is actually known about that time or place?
9 Did the characters fit into the setting?
10 Did I feel that I was really in that time or place?
11 What did the author want to tell me in the story?
12 Was the theme worthwhile?
13 When I read the book aloud, did the characters sound like real people actually talking?
14 Did the rest of the language sound natural?

A review of these fourteen evaluative questions shows how closely they correspond with the criteria that should be used in evaluating the plot, characterization, setting, theme, and style found in literature. When children are given the opportunity and are encouraged to share, discuss, and evaluate books, they are able to expand their enjoyment and select worthwhile stories and characters. Sharing and discussion can take place in the library, in a classroom, or in the home.

SUMMARY

The literature program should help students to enjoy books, understand their heritage, recognize good literature, understand themselves and others, and develop appreciation. To develop these objectives, a balanced literature selection is required that contains classic and contemporary stories, fanciful and realistic stories, prose and poetry, biographies, and informational books. Therefore, adults working with children must acquire knowledge of many types of literature.

When selecting literature for children, the first consideration should be given to the child who will be reading the book. Children have different personal and literary needs at various times. In addition to these needs, they also have diverse interests and reading abilities that must be considered when selecting the right book for each individual.

If literary merit and not mediocrity is to be a part of the literary experience, both children and adults need opportunities to read, discuss, and evaluate literature. The criteria usually used to evaluate children's literature include such elements as plot, characterization, setting, theme, style, and point of view.

Plot is the story's plan of action; a good plot lets children share the action, feel the conflict, recognize the climax, and respond to a satisfactory ending. Children's expectations for, and enjoyment of, conflict vary with their ages and what kinds of books they read. A good story has a beginning, a middle, and an end. Chronological order is the most common way to present events in children's literature. Plot develops when the main character overcomes conflict. There are four kinds of conflict in children's literature: person against person, person against society, person against nature, and person against self.

Characters should seem believable and should develop throughout the course of a story. Characterization is developed when the author tells about the characters, records their conversations, describes their thoughts, shows others their thoughts, or shows the characters in action.

Setting is the geographic location and the time—either past, present, or future—during which the story takes place. Both plot and characterization should be consistent with what actually occurred during that period of history. Setting may be used to provide an instant background, create a mood, develop a conflict, suggest symbolism, or depict a complete historical background.

The theme is the underlying idea of the story that ties plot, characterization, and setting together in a meaningful whole. It should be worthwhile for children. Many themes found in children's books deal with developing self-understanding, including problems in establishing good relationships between adult and child; need for morality to guide actions; importance of support from other people; acceptance of self and others; respect for authority; ability to handle problems; and necessity for cooperation.

Style is the way an author arranges words to create plots, settings, and characterizations. This language should bring the characters to life, enhance plot development, and create the mood of the setting.

Point of view in literature is the viewpoint through which the author chooses to tell the story. The author may select a first person point of view, an objective point of view, an omniscient point of view, or a limited omniscient point of view.

Suggested Activities for Understanding the Selection and Evaluation of Children's Literature

- Administer an interest inventory to children, tabulate the results, select several books that would appeal to their interests, and share the books with the children. What were their responses to the books?
- Compare the plots of several books written for younger children with plots in books written for older children. Compare the way events are ordered, the conflict that is developed, the amount of suspense or tension, and the climax of the stories.
- Find examples of person-against-person, person-against-self, person-against-society, and person-against-nature conflicts found in literature. Do some books develop more than one type of conflict? What makes it believable? Share these examples with your class.
- Read a Little House book. Do you agree with the child who said she would like Laura for her best friend? How has the author developed Laura into a believable character? Give examples of techniques the author used to reveal her character.
- Compare the main character in a fairy tale such as Cinderella or Snow White with one in a book such as I'm Deborah Sampson, Island of the Blue Dolphins, or Call It Courage. Describe each character. Do they change in the course of the story? How does the author show that change?
- Find descriptions of settings that (1) are used to create a mood, (2) develop conflict, (3) are symbolic, and (4) describe a historic period. What is the importance of each setting? Close your eyes and try to picture the setting. If it is realistic, what did the author do to make it real? If it does not seem real, what is wrong? How would you improve it?
- Investigate themes found in children's literature published during the 1960s, 1970s, and 1980s. Which ones are common? Can you draw any conclusions about the social, cultural, and economic influences of the times? Make a time line to summarize the results.
- Find several examples of writing in which the author's style has created a specific image. Read each selection to an audience. How does it respond to the author's use of style?
- Review the books in the most recent list of Children's Choices. What are some characteristics of books chosen by younger, middle elementary, and older readers?

References

1 Carlson, Ruth Kearney. "Book Selection for Children of a Modern World." In *Developing Active Readers: Ideas for Parents, Teachers, and Librarians,* edited by Dianne L. Monson and Day Ann K. McClenathan, pp. 16–29. Newark Del.: International Reading Association, 1979.

2 Chall, Jeanne S., and Marston, Emily W. "The Reluctant Reader: Suggestions from Research and Practice." *Catholic Library World* 47 (February 1976): 274–75.

3 Dowan, Thomas William. "Personal Reading Interests as Expressed by Children in Grades Three, Four, and Five in Selected Florida Public Schools." Tallahassee, Fla.: Florida State University, 1971. University Microfilm no. 72–13,502. 140 pp.

4 Egoff, Sheila. "If That Don't Do No Good, That Won't Do No Harm: The Uses and Dangers of Mediocrity in Children's Reading." *Issues in Children's Book Selection: A School Library Journal/Library Journal Anthology,* pp. 4–5, 7. New York: Bowker, 1973.

5 Feeley, Joan T. "Interest Patterns and Media Preferences of Boys and Girls in Grades 4 and 5." New York: New York University, 1972. University Milcrofilm no. 72–20,628. 180 pp.

6 Greaney, Vincent. "Factors Related to Amount and Type of Leisure Time Reading." *Reading Research Quarterly* 15 (1980): 337–57.

7 Guthrie, John T. "Why People (Say They) Read." *The Reading Teacher* 32 (March 1979): 752–55.

8 Hayden, Gretchen Purtell. "A Descriptive Study of the Treatment of Personal Development in Selected Children's Fiction Books Awarded the Newbery Medal." Detroit: Wayne State University, 1969. University Microfilm no. 70–19, 060. 303 pp.

9 Huck, Charlotte S. *Children's Literature in the Elementary School.* New York: Holt, Rinehart & Winston, 1979.

10 Huus, Helen. "Teaching Literature at the Elementary School Level." *The Reading Teacher* 26 (May 1973): 795–801.

11 International Reading Association. "Children's Choices for 1982." *The Reading Teacher* 35 (October 1982): 53–72.

12 Lukens, Rebecca J. *A Critical Handbook of Children's Literature.* Glenview, Ill.: Scott, Foresman, 1981.

13 Norton, Donna E. *The Effective Teaching of Language Arts.* Columbus, Oh.: Merrill, 1980.

14 Peterson, Gordon Charles. "A Study of Library Books Selected by Second Grade Boys and Girls in the Iowa City, Iowa Schools." Iowa City, Iowa: University of Iowa, 1971. University Microfilm no. 72–8307. 200 pp.

15 Sadker, Myra Pollack, and Sadker, David Miller. *Now upon a Time, A Contemporary View of Children's Literature.* New York: Harper & Row, 1977.

16 Sebesta, Sam Leaton. "What Do Young People Think about the Literature They Read?" *Reading Newsletter,* no. 8. Rockleigh, N.J.: Allyn & Bacon, 1979.

17 Shaw, Jean Duncan. "An Historical Survey of Themes Recurrent in Selected Children's Books Published in America since 1850." Philadelphia, Pa.: Temple University, 1966, University Microfilm no. 67–11. 437 pp.

18 Sloan, Glenna Davis. *The Child as Critic: Teaching Literature in the Elementary School.* New York: Teachers College Press, 1975, p. 78.

CHILDREN'S
LITERATURE

Aardema, Verna. *Bringing the Rain to Kapiti Plain: A Nandi Tale*. Illustrated by Beatriz Vidal. Dial, 1981 (I:5–8). A cumulative tale from Kenya.

_____. *Why Mosquitoes Buzz in People's Ears*. Illustrated by Leo and Diane Dillon. Dial, 1975 (I:5–9 R:6). An African folktale that tells in a cumulative tale the humorous reason for mosquitoes' buzzing.

Andersen, Hans Christian. *The Wild Swans*. Retold by Amy Ehrlich. Illustrated by Susan Jeffers. Dial, 1981 (ch. 7).

Basile, Giambattista. *Petrosinella: A Neapolitan Rapunzel*. Illustrated by Diane Stanley. Warne, 1981 (ch. 6).

Benjamin, Carol Lea. *The Wicked Stepdog*. Crowell, 1982 (I:9–12 R:4). A 12-year-old girl believes she has lost her father when he remarries. She changes her mind about life when she meets a boy.

Blos, Joan W. *A Gathering of Days*. Scribner's, 1979 (I:8–14 R:6). Thirteen-year-old Catherine Hall lives on a farm in New Hampshire; the year is 1830. This journal tells her experiences as she cares for the family, goes to school, goes through the turmoil of her father's remarriage, and is saddened by the death of her best friend.

Burnett, Frances Hodgson. *The Secret Garden*. Illustrated by Tasha Tudor. Lippincott, 1911, 1938, 1962 (I:8–12 R:7). A garden that hasn't been seen by anybody for ten years works its magic spell on a lonely girl, a sick boy, and an unhappy father.

Clapp, Patricia. *I'm Deborah Sampson: A Soldier in the War of the Revolution*. Lothrop, Lee & Shepard, 1977 (I:9+ R:6). Deborah is shifted from home to home until she is bound to a farm family. At eighteen, she disguises herself as a man and fights in the Revolutionary War.

_____. *Witches' Children: A Story of Salem*. Lothrop, Lee & Shepard, 1982 (I:9+ R:6). Witchcraft is feared in 1692. The story tells how a small group of girls creates hysteria.

Cleary, Beverly. *Ramona and Her Father*. Illustrated by Alan Tiegreen. Morrow, 1977 (I:7–12 R:6). Ramona, a second grader, tries to help her father through a trying period after he loses his job. A warm, humorous story.

_____. *Ramona Quimby, Age 8*. Illustrated by Alan Tiegreen. Morrow, 1981 (I:7–12 R:6). A third grader helps her family when her father returns to college. The humor appeals to children.

Cooney, Barbara. *Chanticleer and the Fox* (original by Geoffrey Chaucer). Crowell, 1958 (I:5–10 R:4). Chanticleer, the rooster with the most superior crow, is tricked by the fox. He, in turn, tricks the fox.

Dabcovich, Lydia. *Sleepy Bear*. Dutton, 1982 (I:3–6 R:1). Illustrations and text follow a bear as he hibernates and wakes up in the spring.

de Paola, Tomie. *The Clown of God*. Harcourt Brace Jovanovich, 1978 (I:all R:4). A legend about a juggler who offers the gift of his talent, and a miracle results.

Fritz, Jean. *The Cabin Faced West*. Illustrated by Feodor Rojankousky. Coward-McCann, 1958 (I:7–10 R:5). Ann and her family move from Gettysburg to a cabin on the other side of the mountains. Ann dreams of leaving the frontier and going back home until she begins to see the frontier with new eyes.

_____. *Traitor: The Case of Benedict Arnold*. Putnam, 1981 (ch. 12).

George, Jean Craighead. *Julie of the Wolves*. Illustrated by John Schoenherr. Harper & Row, 1972 (I:10–13 R:7). An Eskimo girl is lost on the North Slope of Alaska; she cannot survive unless she is accepted and helped by wolves.

Goble, Paul. *The Girl Who Loved Wild Horses*. Bradbury, 1978 (I:6–10 R:5). An American Indian girl loves wild horses, joins them in a flight during a storm, and finally goes to live with them.

Jaquith, Priscilla. *Bo Rabbit Smart For True: Folktales From the Gullah*. Illustrated by Ed Young. Philomel, 1981 (ch. 11).

Kent, Jack. *The Fat Cat: a Danish Folktale*. Scholastic, 1971 (I:5–8). A Danish cumulative folktale.

Konigsburg, E. L. *Journey to an 800 Number*. Atheneum, 1982 (I:10+ R:6). A boy's life-style and ideas change drastically when he accompanies his father and a camel act.

Lang, Andrew. *The Red Fairy Book*. Illustrated by H. J. Ford and Lancelot Speed. McGraw-Hill, 1967 (1890).

MacLachlan, Patricia. *Mama One, Mama Two*. Illustrated by Ruth Lercher Bornstein. Harper & Row, 1982 (I:5–7 R:2). A foster mother shares a story about a girl's real mother.

Ness, Evaline. *Sam, Bangs & Moonshine*. Holt, Rinehart & Winston, 1966 (I:5–9 R:3). Sam leads a double life. She almost costs a friend his life.

O'Brien, Robert C. *Mrs. Frisby and the Rats of NIMH*. Illustrated by Zena Bernstein. Atheneum, 1971 (I:8–12 R:4). Mrs. Frisby, a mouse, asks for help from a superior group of rats who are able to read. The rats, however, have a far more difficult problem of their own.

I = Interest by age range;
R = Readability by grade level.

O'Dell, Scott. *Island of the Blue Dolphins*. Houghton Mifflin, 1960 (ch. 9).

Paterson, Katherine. *Bridge to Terabithia*. Illustrated by Donna Diamond. Crowell, 1977 (I:10–14 R:6). Terabithia is the special kingdom of a boy who wishes to be an artist and a girl different from the rest of her classmates.

————. *Jacob Have I Loved*. Crowell, 1980. (I:10 R:6). A girl overcomes the belief that her younger twin sister has stolen her birthright.

Potter, Beatrix. *A Treasury of Peter Rabbit and Other Stories*. Avenel, 1979 (I:2–7). Peter has an unhappy experience in Mr. McGregor's garden.

Raskin, Ellen. *The Westing Game*. Dutton, 1978 (I:10–14 R:5). Sixteen heirs are invited to solve the riddle surrounding the death of an eccentric millionaire. The person who solves the mystery will claim the inheritance.

Rylant, Cynthia. *When I Was Young in the Mountains*. Illustrated by Diane Goode. Dutton, 1982 (I:4–7 R:3). A young girl remembers some special experiences such as Grandmother's corn bread and going to the swimming hole.

Schlee, Ann. *Ask Me No Questions*. Holt, 1982 (I:10+ R:6). Two children discover the harsh reality of nineteenth century England when they learn about hundreds of children who live in an asylum.

Seredy, Kate. *The White Stag*. Viking, 1937; Puffin, 1979 (I:10–14 R:7). Epic story of the Huns and Magyars as they migrate from Asia to Europe. Concludes with Attila and the Hun and their entrance into the promised land.

Speare, Elizabeth George. *The Witch of Blackbird Pond*. Houghton Mifflin, 1958 (I:9–14 R:4). Kit Tyler leaves her island home and lives with relatives in Puritan New England. She rapidly comes in conflict with the Puritan way of life and is suspected of being a witch.

Sperry, Armstrong. *Call It Courage*. Macmillan, 1940 (I:9–13 R:6). A Polynesian boy travels alone in an outrigger canoe to overcome his fear of the sea.

Taylor, Mildred. *Roll of Thunder, Hear My Cry*. Dial, 1976 (ch. 11).

Taylor, Theodore. *The Cay*. Doubleday, 1969 (I:8–12 R:6). A young boy and a West Indian are shipwrecked on a barren Caribbean island. The boy, who dislikes blacks, becomes blind and is dependent upon the West Indian.

Wilder, Laura Ingalls. *Little House in the Big Woods*. Harper, 1932 (ch. 10).

FOUR
Artists and Their Illustrations

WHEN young children are asked what attracts them to a book, they frequently mention the illustrations. The bright colors of an East African setting may entice them into an explorer's role as they search for camouflaged animals. Jagged lines and dark colors may depict the terror associated with a storm; delicate lines and pastel colors may suggest a mythical fairyland setting. The textures in the illustrations may invite children to visualize the fur of a wild bear or the feathers of an eagle ready for flight. The lines and colors may focus children's attention on the main character and encourage them to follow the plot with more enjoyment, excitement, and understanding. Detailed drawings may allow children to visualize a setting, understand the time period, and visualize the characters.

This chapter considers these visual elements of a picture, the artist's choice of media, the artist's style, and criteria to consider when evaluating illustrations. The chapter concludes with a discussion of some of the outstanding illustrators and considers how they use the elements and media to create memorable picture books.

THE VISUAL ELEMENTS—THE GRAMMAR OF THE ARTIST

When literary elements and literature evaluations were discussed in chapter three, the narrative portions of literature were considered as well as how an author creates plot, characterization, setting, themes, and style using words. This chapter considers the visual elements of a picture book. How does an artist create an appropriate visualization of the techniques used by the author? Chapter three showed that there are various devices available that let an author develop a credible story; an artist also uses specific techniques to create a picture that will totally complement the story. The writer develops style by arranging words, but the artist relies on a different form of grammar to create a picture. While this grammar is not a strict set of rules, there is, according to Edmund Feldman (4), "a visual grammar based on artistic usage" (p. 218) that consists of the elements of line, color, shape, and texture. When they are organized into a whole, the artist has created a picture composition designed to be seen and to convey a feeling; each element is considered in discovering how outstanding artists have used them to convey meaning in picture books.

Line

Artists use line to suggest direction, motion, and energy. Lines can be thin, wide, light, heavy, feathery, jagged, straight, or curved and can suggest mood as well as movement. According to Feldman (4), line is the most crucial visual element. He gives the following reasons:

1 Line is familiar to everyone because of our almost universal experience with writing and drawing.
2 Line is definite, assertive, intelligible (although its windings and patterning may be infinitely complex); it is precise and unambiguous; it commits the artist to a specific statement.
3 Line conveys meaning through its identification with natural phenomena.
4 Line leads the viewer's eye and involves him in its "destiny."
5 Line permits us to do with our eyes what we did as children in getting to know the world: we handled objects and felt their contours. By handling an object we trace its outlines, with our fingers. In our growth toward maturity, the outlines of things eventually become more important for identification than color, size, or texture. (p. 293)

Feldman's discussion of the relationship between line and natural phenomena is especially interesting to people involved with children and with illustrations found in their literature. Because children experience these basic natural phenomena, they may relate more meaningfully to drawings because of their experiences. Vertical lines, for example, look like trees in a windless landscape or like people who stand rather than move. Consequently, they suggest lack of movement. Horizontal lines such as those found on a placid lake surface or a flat horizon imply calm, sleep, and an absence of strife. Children also use a baseline in drawings to convey the idea of the ground upon which they walk. When vertical and horizontal lines join at a right angle, artificial elements are introduced that differ considerably from the natural world of irregular and approximate shapes. If two vertical lines are connected by a horizontal line at the top, they give the feeling of a solid, safe place: a doorway, house, or building. In contrast, diagonal lines suggest loss of balance and uncontrolled motion, but they can suggest safety if they form a triangle that rests on a horizontal base. In both man-made design and nature, jagged lines symbolize breakdown and destruction. Consequently, catastrophic danger is suggested by jagged diagonal lines. Curved lines are considered fluid because of their resemblance to the eddies, whirlpools, and concentric circles found in flowing water. Because of this, circular and curved lines are considered less definite and predictable than straight lines.

Paul Goble, who illustrated *The Girl Who Loved Wild Horses*, used line effectively to depict the mood and setting of the story and to enhance plot development (see p. 4 of color insert). Since this story is a Native American folktale, the relationships between lines and natural phenomena are striking. The reader is introduced to the Indian girl as she goes down to the river at sunrise to watch the wild horses. It is a calm, nonthreatening scene. The lines of the horses' legs are all vertical as the horses are quietly drinking from the river. The calm is enhanced by their reflections in the water; not even a ripple breaks the tranquility. On the next page, the girl rests in a meadow close to home. The homes are tepees and their triangular shapes and flat bases sit securely on the ground. The text relates, however, that a rumble of thunder can be heard while she sleeps. The cloud lines suggest this break in a peaceful afternoon; they are heavy, circular, with softly jagged lines jutting into the sky. The pace of the story increases rapidly—lightning flashes and the horses rear and snort in terror. The illustrations also show this change: sharp lines of lightning are drawn from the black rolling clouds down to the ground. The pace and fear increase; the lines of the horses show running movement as they gallop in front of the storm. Even the lines of the plants are diagonal, suggesting the power of the dangerous wind. As the storm disappears and stars come out, the narration tells that the tired horses and the girl stop to rest. The illustration shows the hills drawn in vertical lines with horizontal lines connecting them. The horses and girl quietly watch the moon shining over the hills, and their lines show lack of motion. This book is an excellent example of how an artist uses lines to depict the setting and plot development of a story.

In contrast, the soft, delicate curving lines found in Marcia Brown's illustrations in Perrault's *Cinderella* create a mood suggestive of a mythical kingdom that could only exist "once upon a time." These lines are not bold and dark, but only suggest form. The delicate drawings of Cinderella transformed into a beautiful princess by her fairy godmother contain a magical quality. Because they do not show a definite path or form, anything can happen, and no one is disappointed when the pumpkin turns into a coach and the rat into a coachman. Even the architecture has this magical quality. Delicately curved windows, softly flowing draperies, and lightly traced pillars provide the background for a favorite fairy tale. These artists have demonstrated how lines can be used to suggest motions, moods, and settings.

Color

A combination of line and color may be the visual element artists use most frequently to convey mood and emotion in a picture book. Modernistic artists feel so strongly about the communicative ability of color that they often rely only on color to provide meaning and emotion through nonobjective art. Many feelings about color and line may be associated with natural phenomena. The warm colors—reds, yellows, oranges—are most associated with fire, sun, and blood. In contrast, the cool colors—blues, greens, and some violets—suggest ice.

The artist's use of delicate lines and colors suggests a magical setting.
From Marcia Brown, *Cinderella.* Copyright 1954 by Marcia Brown (New York: Charles Scribner's Sons, 1954). Reprinted with the permission of Charles Scribner's Sons.

Looking at the colors used in picture book illustrations one can determine whether the color language of the artist complements the written language of the author. When evaluating color in illustrations, the reader should ask if the color is appropriate for the mood, setting, characterization, and theme of the story. The following examples show how artists have used the visual language of color in picture books. The fine lines used by Marcia Brown in *Cinderella* are complemented by her choice of colors. Soft pastels—pinks, yellows, blues, and greens—bring a light, shimmering radiance to the fairy tale quality of the pictures. If she had chosen bright, harsh colors, the mood could have been destroyed. In contrast, Paul Goble relied upon heavier lines and deep black to convey the idea of threatening storm clouds in *The Girl Who Loved Wild Horses.*

Color selection can depict the total mood of a story. Barbara Cooney is an artist who used color to translate a gentle story about a quieter time in American life, and her illustrations for Donald Hall's *Ox-Cart Man* complement the mood, setting, and characterization of the narrative. These illustrations reflect the mood of a quiet New England in the early 1800s. The hills are gentle curves painted in soft greens, grays, and blues. The deep rusts, blues, and greens of the clothing look authentic for the time period. Cooney's color choices also show the passing of time. When the farmer is first introduced, the trees are covered with the orange, yellow, and brown leaves of autumn; as he travels over the hills and past villages, the whole hillside is aflame with rusts and oranges; by the time he reaches Portsmouth, the trees have only a few brown leaves. As he returns home, a soft, brown land is seen, creating the feeling of waiting for snow. White now becomes a dominant color—the hills are covered with snow. The season changes, and soft greens next cover the hills; the trees explode with white and pink apple blossoms. The brown used for the garden almost gives a promise of the new life cycle that is beginning. The colors all suggest the peaceful life possible in the early nineteenth century, and many viewers of this book express this feeling of tranquillity. One child said the pictures made her feel homesick; she had lived in an area that had hills, valleys, quiet farms, and changing seasons (see p. 6 of color insert).

The bright colors of East Africa are used by Jose Aruego and Ariane Dewey in their *We Hide, You Seek* (see p. 9 of color insert). Colors are shown in these illustrations in the same way they are used in Africa, to camouflage the animals when they need to hide. The artists first researched animals living in Africa, then drew pictures that used the animal's spots, stripes, patterns, and colors in its natural environment. To show bush animals hiding, for example, the artists used the reddish browns of the giraffe's markings to hide him among reddish brown vines. Likewise, the tigers' spots make them hard to see against tree limbs, and yellow and green birds look just like leaves covered with sunlight. On the following page, the artists reveal the animals; now color is employed to expose differences between the animals and their environment. Camouflaged pictures encourage children to search for the hidden animals before they turn the page to discover their locations. The mother of a two-year-old said that her son was so excited by this book that he woke her up at midnight to read it again. This child appreciated color used as a puzzle for him to solve. These illustrators also used a combination of line and color to create prancing rabbits and a hungry fox that appeal to preschool children in George Shannon's *Dance Away.*

Aruego and Dewey researched African animals before they drew their illustrations; artists Leo and Diane Dillon and author Margaret Musgrove researched African people before working on *Ashanti to Zulu: African Traditions.* This book presents in beautiful color the traditions of twenty-six different African peoples. The artists used line effectively to combine the illustrations into a central theme of searching; each illustration is surrounded by a frame of gold and black, and each corner has an interwoven design based on the Kano knot that symbolizes endless searching. (This design originated in Nigeria during the sixteenth and seventeenth centuries.) The artists have used color to depict the life-styles, artifacts, ceremonial traditions, climates, and animals found in the different sections of Africa. The colors used in the clothing, artifacts, and traditional dance costumes are so complete that they present a vision of people who are proud of their heritage (see p. 9 of color insert).

Vivid watercolors and colorful borders reflecting patterns from antique quilts depict an early American Christmas in Tomie de Paola's illustrations for Clement Moore's *The Night Before Christmas* (see p. 16 of color insert). The geometric borders in blues, greens, reds, and yellows enhance the setting and form a visual continuity.

Maurice Sendak used alternating pages of color and black and white drawings in his illustrations for Janice Udry's *The Moon Jumpers.* The author relates that the sun has set, and cool night shadows surround the house. The sun is not important in this story, and is shown in black and white. The next page, however, reveals a colorful world of cool shadows as the reader experiences deep green grass, a forest with feathery leaves, and a violet house bathed in the first glow from the pale yellow moon. When the lights go on in the house, the children come out with their arms raised toward the rising moon. The text relates that they dance barefooted in the grass, and the wind gently stirs their hair. The illustrations show children frolicking across the shadowy green grass and jumping toward the large, pale yellow moon. A slight tension enters when they see a giant coming toward them, but it is only Father's shadow as he walks across the grass. Here there are light and dark tones that seem slightly menacing. The mood does not persist, however, as the children discover the giant's identity and see Mother outlined within the safety of the doorway. Aside from print, color effectively suggests mood, emotion, and sensation.

Shape

Lines join and intersect to form outlines of shapes and blocks, and areas of color meet to produce shapes. Shapes have been influential in art, as they provide the foundation for work by artists such as Cezanne, Seurat, and Mondrian. The use of shapes by these artists has influenced many other artists and book illustrators, and may be used to create different moods. MacCann and Richard (10) state that shapes ranging from free form and imaginative to rigidly geometric and precise can suggest awkwardness, delicacy and grace, or complexity. Perfect geometric shapes have a tendency to imply mechanical origin; irregularity and variation characterize handmade forms. For example, the blurred, irregular, and indefinite shapes found in Stephen Gammell's illustrations for Olaf Baker's *Where the Buffaloes Begin* suggest a mystical mood where it would be possible for shaggy buffaloes to rise out of the mists of a legendary lake and save a tribe of Plains Indians from an attack by their enemies. The soft shapes and wispy lines seem to reinforce the close relationship between the buffaloes and the lake shrouded in mist. The pictures also demonstrate that black and white illustrations can be just as powerful as color.

Gerald McDermott, illustrator and author of *Arrow to the Sun,* combines shapes and color so that the reader can enter the world of the pueblo, the kiva, and the sun god. Rich yellow, orange, and brown rectangles depict the pueblo which is separated by a black void from the orange and yellow circular sun. The spark of life traveling from the sun to the pueblo moves across this void upon a rectangular ray from the sun. This spark of life becomes the sun god's earthly son. He is illustrated as a black and yellow rectangle, while his mother's form has a more circular appearance. These colors remain dominant in the geometric shapes until the sun god's son decides to search for his father, is transformed into an arrow, and returns. He takes on the sun's power as well as the colors availa-

Soft, indefinite shapes capture the folktale quality of this Native American tale.
From *Where the Buffaloes Begin* by Olaf Baker, illustrated by Stephen Gammell. Copyright © 1981 by Frederick Warne & Co., Inc. Reprinted with permission of the publisher.

ble to the sun after he enters the kivas of lions, serpents, bees, and lightning and endures these trials. The colors of the rainbow are added to his geometric design, he returns to earth as an arrow, and his people celebrate with the dance of life. The artist now illustrates the forms of the earth people with the colors brought to earth. Shapes and colors are used to create not only the setting, but also the plot of the story. The artist's choice of color helps readers feel the Indian reverence for the solar fire—the source of all life. Similar uses of color and shape are seen in McDermott's *Sun Flight*. The colors change from blues and greens to oranges and reds as Icarus flies closer and closer to the sun. Finally, his wings and body become aflame with deep reds, oranges, and browns. These colors dominate until Icarus plunges into the sea; at this point, cool greens and blues dominate.

Geometric shapes and sun colors give a powerful feeling to a tale from the southwestern United States.
From *Arrow to the Sun* by Gerald McDermott Copyright © 1974 by Gerald McDermott. Reprinted by permission of Viking Penguin, Inc.

Ben Shahn's *The Shape of Content* (17) provides additional information on shape as an element in graphic arts.

Texture

A child looks at an object for the first time and usually wants to touch it to know exactly how it feels. It is smooth, rough, sharp, soft. People experience the texture of such items as tree bark, leaves, brick, stones, skin, hair, and fur and learn how something feels without actually touching it. Sculptors can create works of art with texture, but book illustrators must manipulate other visual elements such as line, color, shape, and light and dark patterning to create a textural sensation. Some illustrators have effectively used their art to satisfy our curiosity about how something feels. By looking at these pictures, one can imagine how the objects would feel if they could be touched.

Brian Wildsmith, in his *ABC*, manipulates line, color, and light and dark to create objects and animals with a visual texture. His drawing of a nest has short dark lines projecting from the outside; they look and visually feel like the twigs and grasses surrounding a nest. The inside of the nest, however, is painted in solid deep purple and resembles the soft lining that birds might place there. In another picture, short curling lines, drawn in white and shades of green and black, create fur for the illustration of a yak. Children frequently touch this picture to see if it is real.

Owls with soft-textured feathers and big round eyes, peacocks ablaze with color, and roosters ready to fight are all found in Celestino Piatti's *The Happy Owls*. Piatti's forms are simple, but the colors and lines used within the forms create a feeling of layered feathers. Contrasts within the forms create a highly satisfactory visual design. The owls, for example, have fronts consisting of white feathers on a brown background, and wings and backs of brown, blue, and green feathers. In contrast, their eyes are large circular white orbs with red centers that stare directly at the viewer. Two thicknesses of black line assist in developing texture, form, and contrast. The owls' bodies and dominant eyes are outlined with wide black lines, while the lines in the feathers become finer and more delicate. Color, form, and line also create a peacock that spreads a fan-shaped plumage with preening pride. Leonard Baskin's illustrations for Ted Hughes's *Under the North Star* suggest the fur, feathers, and dispositions of northern animals. The snowy owl blends in magnificently with an icy background, the overlapping lines of a grizzly bear suggest a realistic encounter with this king of the wilderness, and the broad strokes on the eagle's feathers produce a fierce hunter ready for flight.

The artist's strong use of line and color creates a feeling of texture.
From Celestino Piatti, *The Happy Owls.* Copyright © 1964 by Celestino Piatti (New York: Atheneum, 1964). Reprinted with the permission of Atheneum Publishers.

Organizing the Visual Elements—Design

When writing is organized into a narrative form, it is called *style;* when visual elements of line, color, shape, and texture are organized into a unified picture, it is known as *design* or *composition.* Design is the way the artist brings unity, balance, and a sense of rhythm into the illustration. When an artist combines the visual elements into a unified whole, viewers experience aesthetic appreciation; in contrast, when the development of unity is ignored, viewers often feel that they are looking at an incomplete or inferior picture.

Authors of picture books emphasize certain characters, develop main ideas, and also provide background information. Artists also organize their illustrations so that the viewer can identify the most important element in a picture and follow a visual sequence within the picture. Artists, according to Feldman (4), show dominance in their work by emphasizing size (the largest form is seen first); using color intensity (an intense area of warm color dominates an intense area of cool color of the same size); placing the most important item in the center; using strong lines to suggest a visual path; and achieving dominance through nonconformity (the viewer's eye travels to the exception or the item that is different). When evaluating picture storybooks, viewers are also concerned whether this dominance complements the emphasis of the story.

Both lines and warm colors focus attention and lead to a visual path in Uri Shulevitz's illustrations for *The Fool of the World and the Flying Ship,* by Arthur Ransome. The Fool is first introduced walking along a winding path. The viewer follows this path up a hill until the Fool's father and the family cottage is seen. In several other illustrations, the line of a pointing arm and hand lead to the main emphasis. The Fool's mother is pointing at something; when this direction is followed, the Fool is seen on top of the fireplace. Another illustration shows a ship pointed toward a man on the ground, with the man's arm extended toward the ship. The man is a prominent figure because he is dressed in warm pink against a light brown background. The text tells that the Fool falls asleep, wakes up, and

Lines and color create a realistic texture for the snowy owl of the far north.
From *Under the North Star* by Ted Hughes. Drawings by Leonard Baskin. Illustrations Copyright © 1981 by Leonard Baskin. Reprinted with permission of Viking Penguin Inc.

Lines and color attract the viewer's attention to the ship.
Illustration from *The Fool of the World and the Flying Ship*, retold by Arthur Ransome, Pictures by Uri Shulevitz. Pictures copyright © 1968 by Uri Shulevitz. Reprinted by permission of Farrar, Straus and Giroux, Inc.

sees a ship where a tree once stood. An area of warm yellow surrounded by cool green attracts attention. The yellow forms a slight hill that focuses attention upon the major emphasis in the picture and the text page: the marvelous flying ship.

Lines forming a pathway also play an important role in Barbara Cooney's illustrations for Donald Hall's *Ox-Cart Man*. The first illustration shows the man and the ox cart standing in the center of a lightly colored, curved roadway. One end of the roadway goes back to the barn; the other end becomes a country lane that meanders across the hills. The lane is very important to the farmer, because it is his means of reaching the market town. This path continues through a majority of the pictures as the farmer travels over the hills, through the valleys, into Portsmouth, back over the hills, and past the farms until he finally returns to his own home.

Artists also must provide balance in their illustrations. Several drawings in Tomie de Paola's *Helga's Dowry: A Troll Love Story,* for example, achieve balance through symmetry: two trees on either side of one illustration frame the central characters of Helga and Lars; in another drawing, a double-page spread shows the house in the center with Helga and the King on one side and another view of Helga and the King on the other side. In this drawing, even the house is symmetrical, with seven curved windows on each side. The symmetry in this book gives a primitive feeling to the illustrations which complement the mood of this story. Symmetry also suggests a primitive feeling in de Paola's *The Friendly Beasts: An Old English Christmas Carol.*

Sendak's drawings for *The Moon Jumpers* show several examples of balance in the contrast of light versus darker shadows. The light also focuses attention on the children who are having a joyous experience in the moonlight. In one picture, attention is drawn to a boy standing in a doorway; there is yellow light in the background, but the rest of the house is shrouded in shadow. In another drawing, the light from the moon is balanced with the dark shadows covering the forest.

Viewers first center on the children who are surrounded by moonlight; their eyes then travel outward to the shadowy unknown. Light versus dark also provides balance seen in the giant shadow crossing the lawn. Lighter tones in a later picture provide a stage for the mother as she comes out of the house. In this picture, the brighter yellow created by the electric light forms a background for the doorway and also provides a center of light for a picture otherwise surrounded by shadow. The vertical lines, with a horizontal line over the top, suggest a sense of security when the viewer looks at the mother outlined in the doorway.

Repetition is a favorite stylistic element used by authors of children's books; it is also a favorite visual element used by artists. When repetition is used, it can create a sense of rhythm and provide a visual direction. Virginia Lee Burton's illustrations are excellent examples of this technique. In *The Little House* for example, the little house sits on a hill surrounded by rows of trees. The trees recede into the background and become smaller and smaller but produce a rhythmical pattern that proceeds from the house back into the distant space. Wanda Gág is another illustrator who uses repetition effectively. Her cats, in *Millions of Cats,* cover hills and fill roadways until the world is literally filled with millions and billions and trillions of cats!

These illustrations exemplify the elements of line, color, shape, and texture; elements have been combined to create a visual composition that also complements the mood, plot, and characterization. An artist has other choices to make in creating a picture book that integrates story and pictures; these are discussed next.

MEDIA—THE ARTIST'S CHOICE

The elements of line, color, shape, and texture will all be influenced by the materials that the artist uses in illustrating. Quite different moods and effects are created when watercolors, collages, or woodcuts are used. Artists may also mix media to create a desired composition. There are two concerns when evaluating picture books: Is the medium used appropriate for the story? Has it been used effectively? When selecting media, according to Harry Borgman (2), the artist should try to use each medium to its best advantage. Borgman states his own preferences: "If I want a bright, translucent wash tone, I would either use watercolor or dyes. For an opaque paint that is water resistant, I would use acrylics. If I want to draw a line that will dissolve a bit when water is washed over it, I would use a Pentel Sign pen" (p. 113). The following discussion of various media

The artist's effective use of repetition complements the story line.
Reprinted by permission of Coward, McCann & Geoghegan, Inc. from *Millions of Cats* by Wanda Gág. Copyright 1928; renewed © 1956 by Wanda Gág.

will indicate how each specific form chosen helps to convey the artist's intentions.

Woodcuts

Woodcuts are among the oldest illustration media. Paul Gauguin was the first major artist to work in woodcuts; his work encouraged others to experiment with the full potential of this medium. In a woodcut, the image is first drawn on a woodblock and the areas around the design cut away. Inks are then rolled onto this raised surface; the woodblock is pressed onto paper, transferring the image from the block to the paper. A different woodblock is cut for each color in a figure. Woodcuts can be printed in many colors or tones with varying degrees of transparency, and the wood grains and textures can add to the effect of the composition. Consequently, the nature of the wood itself can be used to create a forceful and haunting style.

The bold colors and lines produced by woodcuts create a simplicity frequently desired by illustrators of folktales. Gail Haley, for example, used woodcuts to illustrate her African folktale *A Story, a Story*. Strong lines are seen in the drawings of native huts, foliage, and Ananse, the spider man. The texture of the woodblocks adds to the primitive mood. Lines of the wood grains show on a woven background and even on Ananse's body when he captures the hornets and reaches boldly for the fairy-whom-no-man-sees.

Wood texture is very apparent in Marcia Brown's illustrations for *Once a Mouse,* a fable from India. Wood grains appear in the background and in drawings of the old hermit, the animals, and the trees. These lines are especially powerful in an illustration where the hermit reprimands the proud, ungrateful tiger. The woodcut's potential for developing a haunting style is depicted in an illustration of the tiger being changed into a mouse. The wood grains add to the fable quality of the story.

Both the strong lines and bright colors that can be created from woodcuts are appropriate for Ed Emberley's illustrations in *Drummer Hoff,* by Barbara Emberley. Black lines outline the strong greens, blues, purples, reds, and yellows in the soldiers' uniforms. This cumulative rhyme ends with a big "kahbah-bloom"; therefore the bold brightness seems very suitable for the comical characters in the story (see p. 12 of color insert).

Collage

Collage, derived from the French word *coller,* which means "to paste" or "stick," is a recent addition to the world of illustration. Pasting and sticking are exactly what artists do when using this technique. Literally any substance that can be attached to a surface is used to develop the design. Artists can use many artificial and natural substances in a collage composition: cardboard, paper, cloth, glass, leather, and metal; and wood, leaves, bark, or even butterflies. In addition, they may cut up and rearrange their own paintings or use oils or other media to add background. A collage can be soft and subtle or can give a definite feeling of texture to an illustration.

Eric Carle, a popular artist of young children's picture books, develops his collages through a three-step process (7). He begins with tissue paper that he paints over with acrylic paints. Next, he uses rubber cement to paste down the paper into the desired designs. Finally, he applies colored crayon to provide any needed accents. Carle is known for his striking, colorful storybooks—*The Very Hungry Caterpillar* won the American Institute of Graphic Art's award for 1970. His painted collages add vibrant colors to *Twelve Tales From Aesop.* His most recent books, in addition to brightly colored collage illustrations, include pop-up or other features that encourage children to interact with the book. Readers work tabs that move a honeybee's wings, stinger, and tongue in *The Honeybee and the Robber.* His board books for young children, *Catch the Ball, Let's Paint a Rainbow,* and *The Very Fussy Monkey,* invite interaction and attract children's attention through color.

Another artist who illustrates primarily with collage is Ezra Jack Keats. In *Peter's Chair,* lace looks very realistic as it cascades from the inside of a cloth-covered bassinet. On the same page, pink wallpaper with large flowers provides the background for baby sister's room. Keats also combines paints and collage in his illustrations, a combination effectively used in *The Trip.* These illustrations have a three-dimensional quality appropriate for a story about a boy who builds his old neighborhood within a box and then visits it in his imagination. Photographs are used in the collage illustrations in Keats's *Regards to the Man in the Moon.* These illustrations suggest the diversity that can be found in one medium.

A heavily textured look results when leaves, wood, grasses, shells, and fur are used in collage illustrations. Jeannie Baker's illustrations for *Grandmother* use these items, plus many other natural and artificial substances, to create a story about a garden that is almost a jungle, a house full of treasures, and a grandmother and child who share many experiences.

Collage is discussed again on pages 181–82 to show how the collage medium and collage-illustrated books can be used to stimulate children's interest in literature and art experiences.

Line and Wash

Many illustrations that have been discussed rely on lines drawn in ink to convey meaning and develop the mood of the story.

Ink is a versatile medium that may be applied with a brush, pen, sponge, cloth, or even with the artist's fingers. What emerges, according to Laliberté and Mogelon (8) is "a terribly direct, strong, and uncompromising statement of the nature of our time and the talent of the artist. The very character of ink is challenging, demanding and a spur to experimentation and creativity. It is a bold form of expression, sparkling clean because it is so definite and positive" (p. 43).

The creation of the author usually inspires the creation of the artist and encourages this expression in ink; these roles, however, have been reversed in *Something on My Mind*. Tom Feelings's sensitive drawings of children inspired the accompanying poetry written by Nikki Grimes. The drawings, printed in black, portray the loneliness, fear, sorrow, and hope that children experience while they are growing up. The backgrounds are also superb: heavy black wrought-iron gates, lighter picket fences, an old Victorian house, and apartment house steps provide a believable atmosphere for wishful thinking.

Varying line qualities can also be used to convey human emotions corresponding to characterizations in books. Ray Cruz's drawings for Judith Viorst's *Alexander and the Terrible, Horrible, No Good, Very Bad Day* exemplify the very essence of a boy who experiences unhappy and frustrating emotions. The scowling expressions and the hair standing up convey the spirit of a boy who has gum in his hair, has lost his best friend, and doesn't have any dessert in his lunch box. Maurice Sendak's children, in Ruth Krauss's *A Hole Is to Dig,* also depict a variety of emotions as the children joyfully have a party, dreamily look at the moon, or mischievously startle other children. The ink lines in these small drawings seem just right for the mood of the book.

Varying lines can create detailed backgrounds for storybooks. A whole forest of pen-and-ink drawings is the background for Susan Jeffers's *Three Jovial Huntsmen.* Heavier lines create the texture of tree trunks; lighter lines hide animals camouflaged from the shortsighted hunters. Lines on the dog give the impression of hair.

Detailed lines provide a valuable background in many books written and illustrated by Mitsumasa Anno. In *Anno's Italy,* for example, lines create the bricks, stones, wood, and artwork seen by the artist during a journey through Italy. Likewise, lines depict distinctive British landmarks such as Big Ben and the Tower of London in *Anno's Britain.* A huge castle, oversized toothbrushes, common household tools, and small people are outlined in black in Anno's *The King's Flower.* The drawings of the King's out-of-scale possessions add humor to a tale that also teaches a valuable lesson.

Varying shades of water-thinned ink, sparely drawn figures, and textured paper suggest a traditional Japanese setting ap-

Varying line qualities create a woodland background and hide the animals.
Copyright © 1973 from the book *Three Jovial Huntsmen* by Susan Jeffers. Reprinted with permission of Bradbury Press, Inc. Scarsdale, NY 10583.

propriate for Sumiko Yagawa's *The Crane Wife.* Illustrator Suekichi Akaba's traditional Japanese painting techniques complement the story of a transformed crane who rewards a poor farmer for his care, but returns to animal form when the young man becomes greedy and breaks his promise.

Earlier it was indicated that line is the most crucial visual element used by the artist. When line is combined with the artist's skills, a memorable picture that complements the mood of the story or the characters can result.

Color—Watercolors, Acrylics, Pastels

Ink and various paint media are usually found in children's book illustrations. Watercolor can be applied in various ways

Textured paper and traditional Japanese painting techniques enhance this Japanese folktale.
Illustration p. 23 (unnumbered) by Suekichi Akaba. Copyright © 1979 by Suekichi Akaba from *The Crane Wife* by Sumiko Yagawa. By permission of William Morrow & Company.

—from thin, transparent washes to thick applications of pure pigment. The choice depends upon the effect the artist desires. For example, watercolors and pen and ink create vivid illustrations in Goble's *The Girl Who Loved Wild Horses.* Pure colors of red, deep black, bright yellow, and warm brown depict the energy of stampeding horses, the terror of the oncoming storm, and the beauty of an Indian girl whose wish comes true when she joins the wild horses. Pure pigment complemented the action of this story far more than pale colors could have.

Tomie de Paola's illustrations for *The Clown of God* demonstrate additional qualities that can be achieved with watercolors. In some of the pictures, the texture of heavy watercolor paper shows through the paint and creates the feeling of cloudy skies, rough landscapes, and plastered church interiors. In another illustration, a pale blue stream has such a transparent appearance that stones in the streambed can be seen.

The effects of three color media—watercolors, pastels, and acrylics—are seen in Leo and Diane Dillon's illustrations for *Ashanti to Zulu.* Vibrant jewelry and designs on artifacts contrast with the soft shades of the flowing garments. The river in the illustration that depicts the Lozi people is so transparent that the bottom of the boat shimmers through the water. In other pictures, the sky vibrates with heat from the sun, or jewel-like tones express the breathtaking beauty of exotic birds and plants. The choice of media in these illustrations suggests the differing moods and effects that can be developed using woodcuts, collage, line, and wash, or various paint media. Artists, as will be discussed later, frequently select media to correspond with the story line of the book.

THE ARTIST'S STYLE

Some picture books present the world in realistic terms; others show subjects in such a way that imagination must be used to envision the world from the artist's view. The style of the picture, whether realistic or abstract, is another choice the artist makes.

Realistic Art

Illustrations that depict subjects as they are commonly seen in nature and ordinary life are referred to as *realistic* art (14). Realistic artists do not try to develop an exact image of their subject; instead, through use of texture, line, shape, and color, they create a composition that is possible and not highly unrealistic. Lynd Ward's illustrations for *The Biggest Bear* are excellent examples of realistic art creating the details of a realistic story. Lines are very important in these drawings: the texture of shingles on the roof and rough, unpainted siding on the buildings make the farm seem real; lines create wheat that looks ripe enough to harvest, and bear fur that looks thick and heavy. These drawings also show motion. When the bear cub runs in to claim the mash prepared for the chickens, several frightened chickens look as if they will fly off the page. In a later drawing, one almost feels the pull on Johnny as the grown bear drags him rapidly through the woods.

Realistic animals are Clare Newberry's trademark. Her cat drawings not only suggest a cat's appearance but its temperament as well. In *Marshmallow,* the drawings create a cat who is master of the house, contented, suspicious, excited, curious, and warmly affectionate.

The panorama of the northern wilderness and the Great Lakes region is presented through Holling Clancy Holling's illustrations for *Paddle-to-the-Sea.* When an Indian boy carves a canoe complete with a wooden Indian occupant and places the canoe on a snowbank overlooking Lake Superior, both a narrative and visual adventure begin. When spring arrives, the

The artist uses realistic art to develop the North Woods setting. From *Paddle-to-the-Sea,* by Holling C. Holling. Copyright 1941 and 1969 by Holling Clancy Holling. Reprinted by permission of the publisher, Houghton Mifflin Company.

viewer sees water rushing past a beaver dam, the drawing is so realistic that teeth marks can be seen on the birch stumps. Danger is sensed as Paddle is caught between two large logs on a white-water river; the rough texture of the logs and foaming quality of the water creates realistic peril. As Paddle reaches Lake Superior and starts his journey to the sea, the illustrations show sawmills, white-capped waves, a northern marsh, and a forest fire. In several pictures, there is almost a feeling of cool spray as waves crash over jagged rocks. The illustrations complement a story that also provides factual information about the Great Lakes and the lumber and shipping industries.

Impressionism

Artists have been fascinated by the scintillating effect of light on landscapes. Monet was one of the most influential painters who, working from outdoor subjects, experimented with breaking up colors and shapes to create an impression of light. To "capture the momentary visual experience of a particular time of day Monet returned again and again to the same subject with different canvases in order to record the qualities of light and mood of each changing hour" (16).

The term *impressionist* was used by a critic who objected to the sketchy quality of some landscapes. Consequently, this light and airy style of art was called *impressionism.*

Illustrators of children's stories have been influenced by impressionism. The magical mood of certain stories lends itself extremely well to its shimmering quality. An airy atmosphere and impression of light are expressed in Maurice Sendak's illustrations for Charlotte Zolotow's *Mr. Rabbit and the Lovely Present.* A rabbit and a little girl experience nature as they search the outdoors to find objects that are red, yellow, green, and blue. Their search takes them across a shimmering yellow

The shimmering quality of impressionism is seen in Sendak's outdoor setting.
Specified illustration from *Mr. Rabbit and the Lovely Present* by Charlotte Zolotow, Pictures by Maurice Sendak. Pictures copyright © 1962 by Maurice Sendak.

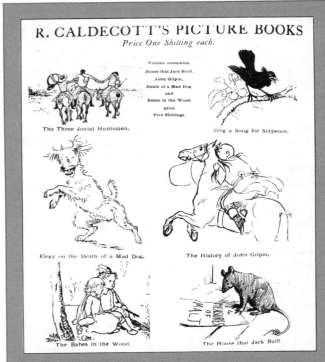

ILLUSTRATOR RANDOLPH CALDECOTT IS CREDITED with being the forefather of the modern picture book. Caldecott's illustrations made an enormous impact in nineteenth century England. His expert use of line created robust characters who depicted humor, vitality, and action.

The books pictured in this flashback are from a series of sixteen picture books, or toy books, illustrated by Caldecott. The first, William Cowper's *The History of John Gilpin*, was published in 1878. The Caldecott Medal is embossed with a picture from this book. The remaining five books shown were published between 1879 and 1900. Caldecott also illustrated books by the top writers of the period including Juliana Horatia Ewing (*Jackanapes*) and Washington Irving (*Old Christmas, Washington Irving's Sketch Book*). Caldecott's toy books, however, signaled the beginning of the high-quality picture books that would eventually be available for children.

meadow, through an emerald green world of dappled light, by a glowing apple tree, and through the light-speckled woods. Effects of light on the landscapes also progress from bright afternoon into the early evening glow. The mood is one of relaxation and quiet happiness that may best be expressed through the impressionist style.

Expressionistic Art

Abstract art began, according to Thomas Munro (14), with "some representational image and eliminated more and more of its details until nothing recognizable as such remained" (p. 208). This description resembles artist Beverly Brodsky McDermott's approach in illustrating the Jewish legend *The Golem*. She says, "As I explored the mysteries of the Golem an evolution took place. At first, he resembled something human. Then he was transformed. His textured body became a powerful presence lurking in dark corners, spilling out of my paintings. In the end he shatters into pieces of clay-color and returns to the earth. All that remains is the symbol of silence" (Foreword). Her illustrations, instead of recreating a natural-istic setting, use strong shapes and colors to symbolize the powerful legend of a rabbi who uses a magic spell to create a man out of clay. Since the setting is Prague's ghetto, the time is one when Jewish people lived in fear. The choice of somber colors and dark lines helps create this mood.

Cubism

In contrast to *The Golem,* McDermott's illustrations for *The Crystal Apple* use bright colors and shapes to create a story about a girl who sees the world through her imagination. Her world is not one of somber moods, but one of rainbows, cathedral spires, and visions of forests. Since these are only visions through "a crystal apple," the abstraction of art creates this mood (see p. 12 of color insert).

The content of a picture storybook is enhanced through the artist's style. A realistic style can capture a mood suggesting even the smallest probable detail of a setting, a magical mood may be created through the shimmering quality of the impressionists, or strong symbolism through the use of expressionistic art.

EVALUATING THE ILLUSTRATIONS IN CHILDREN'S BOOKS

Artists who illustrate books have unique demands placed upon them; they must consider plot, characterization, setting, and theme as well as the demands of their chosen media. When a picture book is evaluated, both the narrative portion and the illustrations are viewed. The following criteria summarize the main points in the preceding material:

1 The artist's use of line should depict the setting, create a mood, suggest appropriate motion, and reinforce the plot development of the story.
2 The color language of the artist should reinforce the written language of the author; the color should be appropriate for the mood, setting, characterization, and theme of the story.
3 The artist's use of shape should enhance the mood of the text and may create desired expressions of awkwardness, delicacy, or complexity.
4 The artist's use of texture should assist the viewer in visualizing how an object would feel if touched.
5 The design should bring unity, balance, and a sense of rhythm to the illustration. It should reinforce the story and provide aesthetic appreciation.
6 The media selected should reinforce the mood, setting, theme, characterization, and plot of the story.
7 The artist's style should enhance the author's style.
8 The illustrations should help the reader anticipate both the action of the story and the climax.
9 The illustrations should portray convincing character delineation and development.
10 The illustrations should be accurate and consistent with the text.

OUTSTANDING ILLUSTRATORS OF CHILDREN'S PICTURE BOOKS: A FEW EXAMPLES

Many outstanding illustrators of children's books have been mentioned during the discussion of the visual elements, choice of media, and the artist's style. This section discusses specific artists in more detail so that the scope of their work

ISSUE

Are Children's Book Illustrators Creating Books for Adults, Rather Than for Children?

IN A RECENT ISSUE OF *Children's Literature in Education*, Eric A. Kimmel[1] contends that a noticeable trend in children's literature is "the appearance of a growing number of exotically illustrated, high-priced picture books that appear to be far too unusual or sophisticated to attract many children" (p. 41). In this category of picture books he identifies Wayne Anderson's *Ratsmagic;* Chris Van Allsburg's *The Garden of Abdul Gasazi* and *Jumanji;* Molly Bang's *The Grey Lady and the Strawberry Snatcher;* Graham Oakley's *Magical Changes;* David Macauley's *Unbuilding;* most of Harlin Guin's books; and Maurice Sendak's *Outside Over There.* Kimmel argues that books such as these are being written and illustrated to appeal to adult critics rather than to children. He speculates that children will ignore these books in favor of books by Ezra Jack Keats, Leo Lionni, and Tomie de Paola and books such as Virginia Lee Burton's *Mike Mulligan and His Steam Shovel,* Robert McCloskey's *Blueberries for Sal,* and Maurice Sendak's *Where the Wild Things Are.*

Students of children's literature may look at these books, talk to librarians about children's preferences, and share the books with children. How do children of different ages respond to pictures and text? Does it make a difference how illustrated books are shared with children? What do children like about the pictures and text? What do you like about the pictures and text?

1 Kimmel, Eric A. "Children's Literature Without Children." *Children's Literature in Education* 13 (Spring 1982): 38-43.

may be better understood. They will be discussed according to their major emphasis upon line, color, or a major medium such as woodcut or collage. (This is not meant to suggest that an artist does not use various techniques; it is only a means to expand and reinforce the previous discussion of the grammar of the artist.)

Line—A Crucial Visual Element

This section discusses artists who use line to create strong designs, create character (both animal and human), develop detail, and suggest setting and mood. While the artists may use all of the visual elements well, their use of line is especially effective.

Virginia Lee Burton.   Movement, rhythm, line, repetition, and contrast are all elements of design found in Virginia Lee Burton's illustrations. Lee Kingman (6) says "this sense of movement, whether derived from the action inherent in an illustration, or from the changes and contrasts in a design, is an essential quality in all Virginia Lee Burton's work" (p. 449). It is interesting to note that she studied ballet and was fascinated with the spatial concepts of dance; this interest may suggest why she has been so successful in capturing motion on paper. Kingman also credits her ability to see movement, as well as draw it, to her art study with husband George Demetrios: "As he urges his students to draw, 'Faster, faster, faster!—sometimes making the model change poses every minute—they must learn to see the figure in its entirety and put it on the paper rapidly" (p. 450).

Both text and illustrations become part of Burton's design, and the page conveys a feeling of total unity between the visual and written elements. This design technique was used very effectively in *The Little House.* As an introduction to the little house on top of a green hill, the written text forms a pathway up the hill toward the house. Later, a repetition of trees is seen that causes the viewer's eyes to travel back toward the horizon. This movement is strengthened with brown dirt roads circling the hill and fields plowed on the hillsides; each field has a progressively smaller figure of a farmer plowing. This spring scene is followed by three illustrations depicting the changing seasons; rows of field crops add to the repetition in the summer picture; shocks of corn cover the fields in autumn; snow and children playing are seen in winter. This idealistic scene is jarringly shattered as a dirty line of highway equipment brings civilization, a blacktopped road, to the country. Now, rows of brown houses cover the hills with repetitive rhythm; the clouds are even black.

Repetition and line provide visual paths and suggest movement. Illustration from *The Little House* by Virginia Lee Burton. Copyright 1942 by Virginia Lee Demetrios. Copyright © renewed 1969 by George Demetrios. Reprinted by permission of the publisher, Houghton Mifflin Company.

Repetition in larger and larger buildings progresses until the little house is finally rescued and moved to a new hill in the country.

Robert Lawson.   It is highly unusual for an artist or author to win the Caldecott *and* the Newbery awards. The first artist-author to win this distinction was Robert Lawson. (This text will discuss his writing when it looks at the world of fantasy and considers such books as *Rabbit Hill* and *Ben and Me.*) Lawson's philosophy about children's illustrations may suggest the reasons for his success. According to Annette Weston (19): "He had never seen in the work of any illustrator whom children have loved for generations the slightest indication that they were catering to limited tastes or limited understanding" (p. 256). In contrast, he believed that children were less limited than adults, and consequently, "They are, for a pitifully few short years, honest and sincere, clear-eyed and open minded.

To give them anything less than the utmost that we possess of frankness, honesty and sincerity is, to my mind, the lowest possible crime" (p. 257).

His illustrations are both witty and honest. He researched Spanish landscapes, architecture, bullfighting, and costumes before illustrating Munro Leaf's *The Story of Ferdinand*. This amusing story which parallels human problems connected with being different is complemented by the illustrations. Strong dark lines show the Spanish landscape and a young bull who would rather smell flowers then prepare to fight in the bullring. Powerful lines show a bull who is fierce and full of movement; this occurs only because Ferdinand sits on a bee. The matador is shown in strutting pride, while the picadores are cringing in terror. The drawings depict human emotions as Ferdinand sits, refusing to fight, and the angry picadores and matador are losing face with the crowd. A totally tranquil ending leaves Ferdinand sitting under his favorite tree and smelling the flowers.

Ludwig Bemelmans. Strong design and patterns and lines suggesting movement are found in Ludwig Bemelmans's illustrations. In *Madeline,* twelve little girls dressed in similar coats, hats, or dresses provide continuity throughout and permit balanced illustrations; six little girls are on each side of the table, six are on each side of a row of sinks, six little girls in six little beds and so on. Even the expressions on their faces are similar.

The majority of Bemelmans's illustrations are filled with details of people, plants, and architectural interest. In *Madeline,* lines create intricate architectural detail for backgrounds that include the Eiffel Tower, the Opera, the Place Vendome, Notre Dame, and the Tuileries Gardens. Diagonal lines produce a feeling of movement in several illustrations. The reader can feel the force of the rain as the transparent diagonal lines strike the ground and the slanted bodies of the pedestrians try to protect themselves. In another drawing, the girls glide across the ice; later, Dr. Cohn's form is drawn in a diagonal position when he rushes toward the phone; and finally, Miss Clavel is drawn at an angle to make her appear as though she is running rapidly toward the girls' bedroom.

Illustrations in other Bemelmans books show similar techniques, but the detailed backgrounds present different locations. In *Madeline in London,* for example, the girls are drawn in locations such as the Houses of Parliament, Trafalgar Square, the Tower Bridge, and Buckingham Palace.

Roger Duvoisin. Drawings with strong black lines interspersed with pages highlighted in warm colors have proven successful for Roger Duvoisin. This flair for staging and design results from his varied art background. First, he specialized in mural painting and stage scenery, then began designing posters and illustrations. Next, he became involved in textile design and finally entered the world of children's illustrations.

Duvoisin uses wide sweeping lines to draw a happy lion with a long mane and switching tail, who has become a favorite with children. Several pages in Louise Fatio's *The Happy Lion* resemble staging for a play. A slightly opened door reveals the face of a curious, surprised lion. He peeks out and walks down a pathway perfectly balanced with trees and scalloped wire hedging on either side; as the path widens, the lion seems to be walking directly toward the reader. When he enters the town, the detail increases, adding streets, stories, and people. The drawings show motion as ladies run with purses in the air, groceries are flung around, and frightened pedestrians run in diagonal lines away from the lion.

The artist creates balance with trees and path hedging; the lion seems to have center stage.
From *The Happy Lion* by Louise Fatio, illustrated by Roger Duvoisin, copyright © 1954 by McGraw-Hill Book Company. Reprinted with permission of the publisher.

Duvoisin's illustrations for Alvin Tresselt's *White Snow Bright Snow* use strong lines, colors, and shapes to depict a world waiting for the season's first snowfall. Black trees wait to be covered; yellow, red, and green rectangular houses sit on a gray background; and large, irregular white shapes fill the night sky with flakes of snow. Children enjoy Duvoisin's illustrations of animals and nature.

Nicolas Mordvinoff. The power of line to express characterization, suggest objects, develop detail, build texture, and provide balance and a sense of design in a composition is seen in Nicolas Mordvinoff's illustrations. Line used with minimal color develops the characters and setting in his illustrations for William Lipkind's *Two Reds.* The boy, who is one of the reds, is drawn as a simple black outline. His most distinguishing feature, however, is in the bright red lines, sometimes outlined in black, that create an impression of tousled hair. The other red, a rather devious cat with the name of Furpatto Purrcatto, is outlined in black but colored in red. Lines create the texture of fur. A complete wash of pale red covers several of the drawings. One detailed drawing of a city street depicts a scene that rattles and rumbles and sounds like the roar of a waterfall. The warm red helps to develop this mood. In another drawing, the Signal Senders have seen Red spying on them. Now they race and try to capture him. The red wash again heightens the plot development and ties the illustrations into the narrative action.

In Lipkind's *Finders Keepers,* lines create animal characterization. There is a marvelous goat complete with curly hair on his head, massive curved horns, and fresh, succulent hay hanging out of his mouth. A horse appears to have a mane, and a farmer's cart is filled with a stack of stiff, prickly hay. In several of the drawings, line is used to create a pathway for visual attention. For example, a trail meanders from the farmer off into the distance; the next character to be introduced, the goat, is walking down the lane. In another illustration, a wide red road begins at the bottom left of the drawing and becomes narrower as it disappears over the hill. Here, the reader's eye travels from the dogs who are trotting along on the wider section of the road up to the barber who is walking toward them. In *The Little Tiny Rooster,* also by Lipkind, a divided roadway extending in two directions is a symbol of the indecision felt by the tiny rooster. Mordvinoff again uses lines to suggest animal characterization. The tiny rooster may be small, but he is powerful. In one drawing, lines and the white outline of the rooster create the feeling of movement as the rooster moves into a swallow's nest in the barn. Pride can be felt in the stretch of his neck and the radiance of his tail feathers.

Susan Jeffers. Texture, motion, mood, and differences between reality and fantasy are all suggested by Susan Jeffers's detailed illustrations. Her various uses of line are especially apparent in Hans Christian Andersen's *The Wild Swans.* Numerous fine lines suggest the layered texture of eleven enchanted swans, owls hidden in a forest, and tree trunks dappled with light and moss (see p. 7 of color insert). In one illustration, short black curved lines interspersed with jagged white lines depict a stormy sea. Circular white shapes create the feeling of spray covering the huddled brothers as they protect their sister. The setting of the text changes from one in which the heavens blaze with lightning and angry waves reach out, to one filled with the fragrance of cedar woods, sunshine, and delicate green plants. It is in this setting that a beautiful fairy enters the girl's dreams, and she learns how to free her brothers. Jeffers's accompanying illustration implies the division between the reality of the characters sleeping on the ground and the fantasy of the palace in the clouds. Heavier, dark lines create the forest, the hillside, and the sleeping characters. Light, fluffy clouds divide the page and suggest a separation from this reality to the realm of a fairy and castle drawn in light, almost transparent lines in the top portion of the picture.

Other books in which Jeffers develops mood, setting, and texture through her detailed line drawings include *Three Jovial Huntsmen,* Robert Frost's *Stopping By Woods on a Snowy Evening,* the Grimms' *Hansel and Gretel,* Hans Christian Andersen's *The Snow Queen,* and Eugene Field's *Wynken, Blynken and Nod.*

Robert McCloskey. Robert McCloskey's illustrations present the real world of boys, girls, families, animals, and islands. Strong lines and detailed drawings depict the settings in most of his books; colors, however, are used for the many moods in *Time of Wonder.*

The illustrations for *Time of Wonder* seem to depict the very essence of an island that is susceptible to the whims of nature. Watercolors present a serene world and even show the shadow of a white cloud as it covers the land. When gentle rain approaches, McCloskey's watercolors are so transparent that the first thing seen is a thin mist descending; later, diagonal lines of drops break the peaceful water. The light fog surrounds two children as they experience the whispering sound of growing ferns. The island is not always serene, however. As the storm and excitement increase, the lines of the trees bend and the illustrations become alive with movement. These illustrations correspond to the changing narrative style of the author.

Lines, contrasts, and shapes develop a setting and story about a child who looks as if she could walk off the page in *Blueberries for Sal.* The child, whether walking with her mother, stealing berries from a pail, wandering off in search of more berries, or following the wrong mother, is totally believa-

THE·PEACOCK'S·COMPLAINT

THE Peacock con-
-sidered it wrong
That he had not the nightingale's
song;
So to Juno he went,
She replied "Be content
With thy having, & hold thy
fool's tongue!"

·DO·NOT·QUARREL·WITH·NATURE·

1.

2.

J JUMPED FOR IT

KC

3.

1. Walter Crane's illustrated texts, characterized by subdued colors, strong design, and rich detail, are credited with marking the beginning of the modern era in color illustrations. From *The Baby's Own Aesop*.

2. Caldecott's illustrations are noted for robust characters, humor, and movement. From Randolph Caldecott's *The Farmer's Boy*.

3. Kate Greenaway's drawings portray tenderness, beauty, and grace. From *Apple Pie*.

4. This engraving of *A Continuation of the Comic Adventures of Old Mother Hubbard and Her Dog* is an example of the illustrations found in early books for children.

4.

In an instant the herd was galloping away like the wind. She called to the horses to stop, but her voice was lost in the thunder. Nothing could stop them. She hugged her horse's neck with her fingers twisted into his mane. She clung on, afraid of falling under the drumming hooves.

6.

5. Line and color combine to create a feeling of impending danger and terror. Notice the heavy black clouds with circular lines and jagged lightning. The diagonal lines of the horses' legs and manes complement the mood. Copyright © 1978 from the book *The Girl Who Loved Wild Horses* by Paul Goble. Reprinted with permission of Bradbury Press, Inc., Scarsdale, N.Y. 10583.

6. Use of color and line draws the reader's attention to the farmer and the ox. From *The Ox-Cart Man* by Donald Hall, illustrated by Barbara Cooney. Illustrations copyright © 1979 by Barbara Cooney Porter. Reprinted by permission of Viking Penguin, Inc.

7. Finely detailed lines enhance the dreamlike quality of this fairy tale setting. Excerpted from *The Wild Swans*, retold by Amy Ehrlich, illustrated by Susan Jeffers. Illustrations copyright © 1981 by Susan Jeffers. Used by permission of The Dial Press.

7.

9.

10.

11.

8. Maurice Sendak was inspired by the watercolors in William Blake's paintings in creating his illustrations for this book. Illustration from *Outside Over There* by Maurice Sendak. Copyright © 1981 by Maurice Sendak. By permission of Harper & Row, Publishers, Inc.

9. Three color media—pastels, watercolors, and acrylics—create vibrant designs and artifacts. Excerpted from *Ashanti to Zulu: African Traditions* by Margaret Musgrove, illustrated by Leo and Diane Dillon. Illustrations copyright © 1976 by Leo and Diane Dillon. Used by permission of The Dial Press.

10. Warm, vivid colors of red, yellow, orange are appropriate for an African setting. The color contrasts help readers locate the hidden animals. Illustration "Ready or not, here I come!" from *We Hide, You Seek* by Jose Aruego and Ariane Dewey. Copyright © 1979 by Jose Aruego and Ariane Dewey. Reprinted by permission of Greenwillow Books (A Division of William Morrow & Company).

11. Vivid colors and simple shapes attract the reader's attention in this wordless picture book. Reprinted with permission of Macmillian Publishing Co., Inc. from *Changes, Changes* by Pat Hutchins. Copyright © 1971, Pat Hutchins.

13.

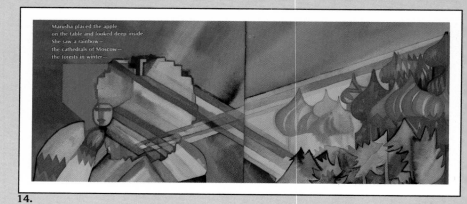

Marusha placed the apple
on the table and looked deep inside.
She saw a rainbow —
the cathedrals of Moscow —
the forests in winter —

14.

15.

16.

12. The fragile beauty of a forest scene is shown in the artist's delicate use of line. Illustration from *The Nightingale* by Hans Christian Andersen, translated by Eva Le Gallienne, illustrated by Nancy Ekholm Burkert. Pictures copyright © 1965 by Nancy Ekholm Burkert. By permission of Harper & Row, Publishers, Inc.

13. Strong lines of the woodcuts and bold colors enhance the folklore quality of this cumulative tale. From the book *Drummer Hoff* by Barbara and Ed Emberley. Copyright © 1967 by Edward R. Emberley and Barbara Emberley. Published by Prentice-Hall, Inc., Englewood Cliffs, N.J. 07632.

14. Cubism is an appropriate style for illustrations portraying a girl's imaginative vision. From *The Crystal Apple* by Beverly Brodsky McDermott. Copyright © 1974 by Beverly Brodsky McDermott. Reprinted by permission of Viking Penguin, Inc.

15. The artist's style recaptures the muted colors and rich textures of old tapestry in this folktale by the Brothers Grimm. Copyright © 1977 from the book *Thorn Rose, or the Sleeping Beauty* by the Brothers Grimm, illustrated by Errol LeCain. Reprinted with permission of Bradbury Press, Inc., Scarsdale, N.Y. 10583.

16. Tony Chen uses watercolors and pen and ink to illustrate this Vietnamese variation of "Cinderella." From *In the Land of Small Dragon* by Ann Nolan Clark, illustrated by Tony Chen. Illustrations copyright © 1979 by Tony Chen. Reprinted by permission of Viking Penguin, Inc.

17.

18.

17. Reproductions of Boris Zvorykin's original gouache paintings (a method of painting with opaque watercolors) enrich this Russian folktale. An illustration from *The Firebird and Other Russian Fairy Tales.* Copyright © 1978 by Viking Penguin Inc. Reproduced by permission of Viking Penguin Inc.

18. Bright, jeweled tones suggest the magical abilities of an unusual fish in this German folktale. Illustration from *The Fisherman and His Wife* by the Brothers Grimm, translated by Elizabeth Shub, illustrated by Monika Laimgruber. Copyright © 1978 by Artemis Verlag. Reprinted by permission of Greenwillow Books (A Division of William Morrow & Company).

19. de Paola achieves balance through symmetry. Notice the lines of the trees in the painting, the pictures on either side of the fireplace, and the fireplace decorations. Copyright © 1980 by Tomie de Paola. Reprinted from *The Night Before Christmas* by permission of Holiday House, Inc.

20. Use of color photography and magnification help clarify the content of this informational book. Reprinted by permission of G. P. Putnam's Sons from *Nature's Way: The Butterfly Cycle* by Oxford Scientific Films. Copyright © 1976 by Oxford Scientific Films.

21. Some informational books present concepts through cartoonlike illustrations. Taken from *Animal Fact/Animal Fable* by Seymour Simon. Illustrations by Diane de Groat. Copyright © 1979 text by Seymour Simon; illustrations by Diane de Groat. Used by permission of Crown Publishers, Inc.

19.

20.

21.

ble. McCloskey has created an inquisitive child who shows her berries to a surprised mother bear.

Chris Van Allsburg. Chris Van Allsburg's *The Garden of Abdul Gasazi* and *Jumanji* demonstrate the effectiveness of black and white illustrations. Line, shading, and symmetry of design suggest a formal garden setting and create a visual path in several illustrations for *The Garden of Abdul Gasazi.* For example, the viewer is led into the garden through a rectangular doorway surrounded by a vine-covered wall. Two statues pointing toward the door provide symmetry and emphasize the visual path. Inside the doorway, the path is balanced with an arbor of trees. Shading enhances the picture and encourages the viewer to focus upon the distant garden: the tunnel of dark trees leads to a small circle of white. This circle represents the garden where the story line develops.

Tomie de Paola. Tomie de Paola has illustrated, or written and illustrated, over seventy books, including traditional folktales, informational books, and realistic fiction. His folktales use stories from Italian, Scandinavian, and Mexican folklore. In *The Clown of God,* the influence of two pre-Renaissance artists, Giotto and Fra Angelico, is seen. According to de Paola (5), he uses this influence in its absolute simplicity: "I almost reduce features to a symbol. And yet I think of my faces as good and

Symmetry of design directs the viewer's eye toward the distant garden.
From *The Garden of Abdul Gasazi* by Chris Van Allsburg. Copyright © 1979 by Chris Van Allsburg. Reprinted by permission of Houghton Mifflin Company.

The artist's black and white illustrations create a moment of surprise for human and animal characters.
From *Blueberries for Sal* by Robert McCloskey. Copyright 1948, © renewed 1976 by Robert McCloskey. Reprinted by permission of Viking Penguin Inc.

warm. I try to show expression in very few lines" (p. 299). These lines, however, are one of de Paola's most important elements. In the illustrations for *The Clown of God,* he first penciled in the lines, then went over these sketches with raw sienna waterproof ink, followed by a second brown pencil line. Finally, he went over the drawings with brown ink. Watercolors and inks were then used to complete the artwork. Simple lines in features are also very important in *Songs of the Fog Maiden* and *When Everyone Was Fast Asleep.* When cool shades of blue and green are added to the illustrations, a magic mood is created in which a fog maiden could easily move from her day garden to her night one and accomplish magic along the way.

de Paola's theater experience is also evident in his illustrations. He states, "I think theater training is very good for an illustrator. There are so many ways picture books are like theater-scenes, settings, characterization. A double page spread can be like a stage" (p. 300). Consequently, many of the actions in his illustrations appear to take place in front of a setting or a backdrop. *Giorgio's Village,* for example, is itself a stage-like setting in which windows open and tabs allow movement. This pop-up recreates an Italian Renaissance Village. Staging is also important in de Paola's illustrations for Sarah Martin's *The Comic Adventures of Old Mother Hubbard and Her Dog.* On center stage are the various scenes with Old

THROUGH THE EYES OF AN ILLUSTRATOR

Dan O'Connor

Illustrating and Books

Tomie dePaola

TOMIE DE PAOLA, illustrator of over seventy books and winner of the Caldecott honor award, discusses early art experiences and the importance of doodling.

I AM A DOODLER. IN FACT, I *love* to doodle. I always have. I keep pads of scratch paper and black and red fine-line markers by the telephones, at my drawing table, on my desk, in my carry-on bag when I fly, and when I was teaching, I never went to a meeting (faculty, committee, etc.) without my handy pad and markers.

Growing up, coloring books were absent from our house . . . at least, in my room. My tools were plain paper, pencils and my trusty crayolas. After all, I was going to be an artist when I grew up. And besides, my own drawings and doodles seemed to be far more interesting to me, and those around me, than the simple coloring book images. (My mother also admitted recently that plain paper was lots cheaper.)

I learned at an early age that there was a definite difference between out-in-out drawing and serious doodling. A drawing had more structure, more direction. A definite idea was usually the beginning of a drawing. For example, I might say, "I think I will do a drawing of a girl ice skating, wearing a fancy Ice Follies-type costume." (Yes, the Ice Follies were around way back then.) Then, the problem would be to try to do a drawing that coincided with my original idea or vision.

Doodles were (and are) totally different. I would just put pencil to paper and see what happened. All sorts of interesting images would result. I might start out not really concentrating on my doodle but on what else I was doing at the time. Talking on the phone was a very good activity for doodling. Late at night under the covers with a flashlight and listening to the radio was another activity that produced more terrific doodles — some actually on sheets rather than on paper. The "state of the art" doodles of this early period though appeared as if by magic on my arithmetic papers. There would be columns of figures copied from the blackboard and before I knew it, the paper would be covered with pictures with no room for the answers. My teachers — well, at least, a few of them — were *not* amused. They warned me. I'd never learn to add, subtract, multiply, etc. They were right, but for me as an artist, the doodling proved to be a far more important activity. I was able to buy a calculator with a royalty check, and now, I have an accountant.

"Meeting doodles," especially faculty meeting doodles, proved to be among the most valuable for me. It was during a college faculty meeting that was about the same issues the previous dozen meetings had been about, that "Strega Nona" appeared on my pad. I didn't know who she was at that moment, but a few months on my studio wall, and she soon let me know all about herself.

I've just opened a drawer and found some doodles that were done several years ago. (I stash doodles in different drawers so they can show up later and surprise me. My assistant saves all the phone-call doodles for me. My mother and an old friend both have doodles of mine in special drawers, waiting for the day they can cash in on them.)

The new found doodles are on the wall of my studio. There is a rather fetching sheep and two classy cats, dressed to kill. Who knows . . . someday . . . But remember! You read about them here first!

Mother Hubbard and her prancing poodle. Each illustration is surrounded by an arch resembling side panels of a stage; drawings on the panels show other Mother Goose characters.

Two books also show the influence of films. In *Watch Out for the Chicken Feet in Your Soup* and *Charlie Needs a Cloak,* the action of the story and in the illustrations starts before the title page. The title page then becomes both a part of the narrative and part of the illustrated action. de Paola believes that children should be given many options in visual imagery. This belief is expressed in his various books and the way he has incorporated the elements of art, theater, and film into his illustrations.

Peter Spier. Carefully drawn lines can recreate each stone in London Bridge, express the excitement symbolized by the United States flag after a battle, depict an ark filled with animals, or present the changing American scene. Peter Spier creates detailed, authentic drawings that depict historic settings. In *Noah's Ark,* every illustration is filled with details concerned with building, loading, and living on the ark. Children can find new details each time they look. Comparing an early drawing with a later illustration, for example, shows that two snails are the last animals to board the ark; later, these same snails are the last animals to leave. Spier's *The Fox Went Out on a Chilly Night* recreates a country setting filled with farms, covered bridges, cemeteries, town squares, and colonial buildings. The heritage of *The Star-Spangled Banner* is recreated on a ship deck, through rockets glaring in the sky, developed in all the color and movement of the battlefield, and shown in scenes from the American past as well as contemporary America. Another bit of American history is presented in his *Tin Lizzie;* this time the illustrations begin in 1909 and continue through modern times. Spier's illustrations involve considerable research and touring of historic sites before the books are completed.

Spier uses lines drawn in pen and ink and full-color wash illustrations to create a series of village books, each designed in the shape of a building, including: *Bill's Service Station, Fire House: Hook and Ladder Company Number Twenty-Four, Food Market, My School, The Pet Store,* and *The Toy Shop.* The detailed drawings provide excellent sources for stimulating discussions as young children explore their own community and identify familiar objects.

Maurice Sendak. Maurice Sendak has been labeled "The Picasso of children's books" by *Time* magazine. This chapter has already noted his artistic versatility. It discussed his use of color, line, and balance in *The Moon Jumpers;* an ink medium in *A Hole Is to Dig;* and impressionism in *Mr. Rabbit and the Lovely Present.* Sendak's philosophy of illustration is probably the most important clue as to why his work has been so successful in creating the mood of the story. One of his primary aims in illustrating a text is to make "the pictures so organically akin to the text, so reflective of its atmosphere, that they look as if they could have been done in no other way. They should help create the special world of the story . . . creating the air for a writer" (13, p. 352).

This special relationship between text and illustration may be most apparent in *Outside Over There* and *Where the Wild Things Are.* The steps in creating the illustrations for *Outside Over There,* which Sendak considers his best and most significant children's book, are described by the artist (3). One of his first concerns was drawing ten-year-old Ida holding a baby. In order to produce realistic positions, he took pictures of a child holding a baby. The real baby kept slipping out of the child's arms; consequently, the clothes on both children became disheveled and drooped with the body movements. This flow of movement is found in the illustrations of Ida holding both the real and ice babies. In order to create the desired colors for the mood and setting of the story, Sendak referred to watercolors by William Blake. Sendak describes his choice of colors: "The colors belong to Ida. She is rural, of the time in the country when winter sunsets have that certain yellow you never see in other seasons. There's a description of women's clothing, watered silk, and that's what those skies are like—moist, sensuous, silken, almost transparent—the color I copied in the cape Ida wears and in other things showing up against soft mauve, blue, green, tan—all part of the story's feeling" (3, p. 46). Line and color suggest the mood, setting, and characterization in the book (see p. 8 of color insert).

The illustrations for *Where the Wild Things Are* are totally integrated with the text, plot development, characterization, and setting. When Max enters his room, the room gradually becomes the wild kingdom, trees seem to grow naturally out of the bedposts, and the door is balanced with a tree on either side. The shag of the rug is even incorporated into the fantasy as it grows longer and longer until it becomes grass. Contrasting light forms a stage for Max as he dances in the moonlight. The illustrations, as the plot progresses, also cover more and more of the page; by the time Max reaches the island and becomes king of the wild things, they cover six pages without being interrupted by text. The characterization depicted in the text is also shown in the illustrations. Max looks like a boy who would be sent to his room because he is mischievous. The wild things have terrible eyes, claws, and teeth. They look as if they could roar grisly roars and gnash horrible teeth. Sendak uses line, color, and an interest in European folklore to create memorable books integrating author's style and artist's techniques.

Color—Creating Mood, Setting, and Characterization

A combination of color and line creates the mood, setting, and characterization in a majority of picture book illustrations. Many of the illustrators discussed under the topic of line also use color in their illustrations. This section discusses several artists who use color to create effects such as the feeling of fur on animals or a shimmering effect of sunlight, to create balance within an illustration, and to develop the story's mood.

Clare Turlay Newberry. Creating the many moods and temperaments of cats requires both a remarkable understanding of their spirit and long, careful hours of observation. Children frequently say that Clare Newberry must have watched cats for a long time in order to draw them so lovingly. These children are correct. Newberry spent many hours observing and doing quick sketches before she could capture the moods illustrated in her humorous books about cats. In *Drawing a Cat* (15), she relates that cats do not stay in the same position for long; consequently, the artist must make hundreds of sketches before the desired effect is achieved. She states that concentrated observation must accompany the act of drawing; this observation is the only way to gain knowledge of the cat.

Newberry's cat illustrations suggest the feeling of fur. This effect is created by painting with charcoal gray watercolor on wet paper, then adding details with crayons after the paper was dry. This technique and Newberry's ability to depict the essence of a cat or another animal create the totally believable *Widget;* her hair can be as fluffy as the hair on a contented kitten or it can stand on end when danger in the form of a teddy bear or a dog named Pudge threatens her well-being. While Newberry's illustrations are in grays, blacks, and browns, they explode with the characterization of the animals in the narrative portion of the text.

Taro Yashima. An illuminating use of color, a balance of colored shapes and white spaces, and shimmering lines are all used by Taro Yashima to create pictures that exemplify the mood, setting, and characterizations for his stories. For example, *Crow Boy* is a small Japanese boy who feels frightened by and alienated from his schoolmates. Yashima draws Crow Boy as a small child isolated by white space from his class and his teacher. Even the position of his arms suggest his fear; he covers his head to protect himself from the stares of the teacher and his classmates. When Crow Boy has an understanding teacher, he is no longer shown in isolation; as his confidence increases, so does his size and stature. As he starts to gain confidence, Yashima has illuminated him with a feeling of shimmering light; his form is outlined with shades of white. This same illumination is seen in Yashima's landscapes, where trees are drawn as if sunlight is outlining the forms in warmth and shadow.

Contrasting dark and light colors also create a mood for *Umbrella.* The viewer can almost feel the raindrops making wonderful music when they strike a little girl's prized umbrella. The inside of the umbrella is a dark, solid color; the outside has thick horizontal lines painted in deep blue; and rain falls in transparent blue vertical lines. A delightful sense of balance results as the happy child is outlined with shimmering lines of rain.

Nancy Ekholm Burkert. According to Michael Danoff (9), Nancy Burkert "is an artist whose work is rooted in the particulars of nature. Her drawings capture the specifics of the natural world with awe-inspiring precision and clarity. For her, the natural world is as miraculous as any realm of fantasy. . . . In her eyes, currents of the metaphysical flow through the particulars of the physical world; the natural is one with the super-natural" (p. 1). Flow, vitality, and rhythm produced by brush and colored inks are terms that can be used to describe the visual elements of Burkert's illustrations.

Before she illustrated Grimms' *Snow White and the Seven Dwarfs,* Burkert visited Germany's Black Forest and researched books about the Middle Ages. Consequently, her illustrations for the book reflect this research and create the mood of the Black Forest. In one picture, a once-upon-a-time mood is recreated by drawing the mysterious forest; the light sifts through the trees on Snow White as she carefully walks through the wood and is observed by the creatures in the shadows. Intricate details recapture the mood of the dwarf's home (research for this room was completed at the Unterlinden Museum in Colmar). Here are carved wood, pewter utensils, woven rugs, and a warm fireplace. This homely scene can be contrasted with another that takes place in the dark castle when the wicked stepmother concocts a poisoned apple. Now, the details include herbs, spider's webs, and partial skeletons.

A softer and gentler world is created in her illustrations for Lear's *The Scroobious Pip.* When the beasts of the world appear to try to discover the nature of the scroobious pip, soft brush lines and colored inks create a horse with a flowing mane, fragile transparent butterflies, a mountain goat with curly hair, and the mythical scroobious pip with translucent wings, shimmering scaly tail, and softly feathered head.

Burkert's love for line creates an oriental mood in her illustrations for Eva LeGalliene's translation of Hans Christian Andersen's *The Nightingale.* The text tells that the emperor lives in a beautiful palace, built of finest porcelain, but so delicate that one must move carefully so as not to disturb its fragility. Burkert's illustrations help to create this environment. Soft pink and white blossoms cover the trees, and mist rises gently from the sea to create the background for the detailed drawings of the palace. She developed a unity for the whole book by illustrating pages of text with blossoms, branches, and plants that gently curve on the page margins (see p. 10 of color insert).

Leo and Diane Dillon. The oral tradition of the folktale is complemented by the illustrations drawn by Leo and Diane Dillon. An interest in African and North American folktales and people is evident in their beautifully illustrated, award-winning books. Their work reflects careful research into the decorative motif of various cultures and helps to recreate the heritage of a culture.

Both Indian and African illustrations set the mood for the narrative portion of the text. For example, the text for the North American Indian tale by Natalia Belting, *Whirlwind Is a Ghost Dancing,* is rich in imagery. The wind is a ghost, the moon smokes a pipe and creates the clouds with his smoke, the sun's rays are earthmaker's eyelashes, and the stars are bright-breasted birds. The Dillons' illustrations, drawn in a combination of pastels and bright acrylics, create a world where such images are possible. Cool greens and blues entwine in a design depicting the ghost wind, an Indian sits on the surface of the moon smoking a pipe, the daughters of the wind wear icicle pendants and frost-feather head-dresses drawn in cool hues, and the sun is a warm red and orange porcupine shape floating through the sky. Their illustrations for Verna Aardema's African folktale, *Why Mosquitoes Buzz in People's Ears,* create the feeling of a traditional cumulative tale. The cutout effect outlining the animals and the sun seems appropriate for a story that would usually be told rather than read. (This text has already discussed the Dillons' use of watercolors, pastels, and acrylics to create the vibrant illustrations for Musgrove's *Ashanti to Zulu.*) Whether these artists are illustrating Indian or African folktales, considerable research has preceded their drawings.

Barbara Cooney. Barbara Cooney's illustrations for Donald Hall's *Ox-Cart Man* differ considerably from the earlier *Chanticleer and the Fox.* In illustrations for Chanticleer, her use of line creates a strutting, vain rooster in the earlier portion of the book and a frightened, humble one as the story reaches its climax. The use of line also suggests the life and death struggle between Chanticleer and his enemy, the fox. In *Ox-Cart Man,* the harsher, bolder black lines have disappeared; colors and gentler shapes create the setting for a New England farmer

and his family who live in the peaceful countryside of the early nineteenth century. Colors also suggest seasonal changes and the passage of time; the blaze of a New England autumn, the bleakness before the first snowfall, the cheery warmth of the hearthside, the snow-covered stillness of the sugar tree, and the renewal of a springtime promise.

Cooney's illustrations for Margot Griego's *Tortillitas Para Mama* recreate the varied settings associated with Spanish nursery rhymes. Warm browns depict the interior of a Mexican home and the family making tortillas, cool blues warmed by the shining moon suggest a village by the water, and warm fuchsias reflect the warmth of a mother and father sharing a quiet time with their baby.

Color also creates the mood in her illustrations for Delmore Schwartz's *"I Am Cherry Alive," The Little Girl Sang.* Shades of one color depict a golden mood as the little girl observes a tree covered with autumn leaves; a green moon is created as she looks at her reflection in a green pond surrounded by gentle green trees; there is a blue mood as she looks over a blue mist-covered valley seen by the light of a pale moon; and finally a new mood is set as crocuses explode against a white snowy backdrop. Cooney uses all art elements in her illustrations.

Specialized Media

The majority of the artists discussed use inks, paints, watercolors, or pastels to create their colorful illustrations or depict movement in their drawings. Others work primarily in one medium such as woodcuts, cardboard cuts, or collage. This final section discusses several artists whose major contributions have been in these media.

Antonio Frasconi. Strong designs created by woodcuts and vivid colors are found in Antonio Frasconi's illustrations. Frasconi is a well-known woodcut artist who uses this medium effectively when illustrating children's books. The textures possible with woodcuts create several dramatic pictures in Doris Dana's *The Elephant and His Secret.* One page is dramatically divided with vivid purple as background for the top half of the page and bright red as the background for the lower half. A woodcut of a mountain is on the top, while a woodcut depicting the mountain's shadow in the form of an elephant is on the red background. The texture of the wood shows horizontal and vertical lines and folds creating the feeling of a heavy mass of stone mountain. In contrast, solid black with lightly grained red lines creates the elephant shadow. In the South American folk rhyme, *The Snow and the Sun,* Frasconi's woodcuts produce a feeling of conflict between the natural elements of sun and snow. The strong lines create the image of cold wind blowing across the land. This feeling is heightened by the choice of colors; the power of the sun is shown in red; the snow and wind are black and white. Woodcuts also bring a simple power to the Mother Goose characters found in Frasconi's *The House That Jack Built.* (Several artists have chosen to illustrate this nursery rhyme; interesting comparisons can be made between media used and mood created.) Frasconi combines woodcuts, watercolor, and collage in Jan Wahi's *The Little Blind Goat* to capture a story told in the style of a folktale.

Blair Lent. A total unity of illustration with story, delicate lines, cardboard cuts, Japanese art, and folktales are all associated with Blair Lent's illustrations. This combination is clearly seen in his beautiful cardboard cuts for *The Wave* by Margaret Hodges. He has captured the once-upon-a-time quality of a fragile Japanese village on the seashore. Even the title page introduces the significance of the sea; curving waves in delicate gold, gray, and brown lines roll gently across the page. On the next page, the same waves roll on, but three fishing boats now glide upon them. In this way, viewers are introduced to a village dependent upon the whims of a calm or angry sea. The delicate lines produced by the cardboard cuts emphasize the fragility of the homes that will soon feel the ravage of the tidal wave. The mounting tension is also accompanied by changes in the illustrations. Instead of delicate shades of gold and gray, a sky filled with rich brown from the blazing rice field is seen, and the sea has changed from a gentle curve to an angry black swirl of line that becomes almost black as the wave meets the land. As the climax is reached, double pages are filled with circular waves and water-tossed buildings. The colors revert to gentler golds and grays as the wave recedes, and the people are shown safe on the hill. The final picture shows the rebuilt village with a new temple built in honor of the wise farmer who burned his crops in order to warn the people of danger. There is an almost cloudlike quality to the final illustration in which the island is shown on top of a gently rolling sea.

Leo Lionni. Stylized shapes, color, and texture are all part of the animal fable world of Leo Lionni's stories and illustrations. Soft muted watercolors, textured collage, and thickly painted surfaces are also apparent in his work. Lionni's main involvement with illustration, according to MacCann and Richard, is "with the surface appearance of forms and with the arrangement of these textured forms on the picture page" (10, p. 58).

Lionni's experiences as architect, painter, mosaic artist, and graphics artist and art director for *Fortune* have all involved shape, color, and texture. His use of these elements to recreate the feeling of a watery world is apparent in *Swimmy.* This is not a realistic world of discernible water plants and fish;

Cardboard cuts create curving waves and fragile homes that will experience a tidal wave.
Illustration from *The Wave* by Margaret Hodges, illustrated by Blair Lent. Copyright © 1964 by Margaret Hodges. Copyright © 1964 by Blair Lent. Reprinted by permission of the publisher, Houghton Mifflin Company.

it is a world of seaweed that has the texture of painted doilies against a pale blue, watercolor background, fish that are only suggestive outlines, and transparent pink jellyfish.

In contrast to the muted watercolors in *Swimmy,* vivid colors and strong shapes are predominant in *Pezettino,* the story of a small orange shape who is convinced that he is a piece of someone else. His search takes him to larger shapes who are composed of many smaller squares of bold color. The visual and textural interest that is possible from collage is shown in Lionni's illustrations for *Alexander and the Wind-up Mouse.* The real mouse, for example, has a furry texture created by tearing paper; the wind-up mouse has a smooth surface that could only be achieved by a cutting instrument. Texture is also given to a teddy bear when paper is torn rather than cut. The illustrations demonstrate the variety of materials and designs that can be used in collage. There are paisley and flowered prints, furry substances, scraps of newspaper, and tissue paper.

Ezra Jack Keats. Color, texture, and an understanding of children's needs and emotions are all evident in the illustrations of Ezra Jack Keats. Keats combines collage and paints in compositions that portray the inner-city of the small child. Sometimes this environment is peaceful, as in *The Snowy Day;* at other times, it can be frightening, as in *Goggles!* Sometimes a child is lonely, as in *Louie* or *The Trip;* a child may dream, as in *Dreams;* or a child may be jealous, as in *Peter's Chair.*

The majority of books illustrated by Keats use both collage and paints to develop design and create mood. In *The Snowy Day,* brilliantly white torn paper provides the snow covering for chimneys and rooftops as Peter looks out on a fresh white world. As he goes out into this world, however, the huge snowbanks have been shaded with pastel colors; the pristine whiteness has been disturbed by man and machine. Blue shadowy footprints combine the text and illustrations as the reader is asked to look at Peter's footprints in the snow. Simple, rounded shapes depict snowbanks, and buildings are rectangles of color in the background. The simple red-clad figure of Peter stands out against the snowy background.

Quite a different mood is created with collage and paints in *Goggles!* The scene is not a peaceful city after a snowfall; instead, it is the harsher reality of two children who must escape from bigger boys who want their possessions. The colors are dark and the collages include thrown-away items that might be in back alleys. The big boys are to be feared and Keats has shown them in almost featureless, black silhouettes. In one picture, a hole in a piece of wood is used to frame the scene as the two small boys look through it and try to plan how to get home.

Shadows and vivid swirls of colors provide contrasts in *Dreams.* The hot evening sky is painted in warm reds, oranges, and yellows; as it grows darker and cooler, deep blues and blacks cover the sky until finally it is black. When the paper mouse figure falls, its shadow becomes bigger and bigger until it is so big that it frightens the dog away. Keats illustrates a dark shadow that almost covers a two-page spread. Now, the danger to the cat has passed and Roberto can fall asleep; his room is filled with comforting shades of pinks and grays.

Looking through illustrations by Keats indicates the many different moods and designs that can be created when an artist uses collage and paint.

SUMMARY

A quality picture book must be concerned with both art and writing. Consequently, both media must bear the burden of narration. The illustrations should help the reader anticipate action, the pictures should help create the basic mood of the story, there should be convincing character delineation, and pictures should be accurate and consistent with the text.

While the writer develops style by arranging words, the artist uses visual elements to create composition designed to be seen and convey meaning. Lines, since they are used to suggest direction, motion, and energy, are considered the most crucial visual element used by artists. In addition, they have a very close relationship with various natural phenomena; lines can suggest lack of movement, calmness or an absence of strife, a safe place, motion, or danger. Lines can also create the mood of a story. While strong lines can suggest natural phenomena, soft delicate lines create a mythical kingdom of magical once upon a time.

A combination of line and color may be the visual element that artists use most frequently to convey mood and emotion in picture books. Color is also related to natural phenomena; warm reds, yellows, and oranges are associated with fire and sun, while cool blues and greens suggest ice. When evaluating color in illustrations, the viewer should ask if the color is appropriate for the mood, setting, characterization, and theme of the story.

Shapes can also be used to create many different moods. Ranging from free form and imaginative to rigidly geometric and precise, shapes can imply delicacy and grace, awkwardness, or complexity. When an illustrator manipulates shape, line, color, and light and dark patterning, a feeling of texture may also be created.

When authors organize their writing into a narrative form, it is called style; when artists organize visual elements into a unified picture, this is referred to as design or composition. Artists can organize their illustrations to identify the most important element in a picture and follow the visual sequence within it. Size, color intensity, central location, strong lines, and nonconformity can all be used to emphasize desired dominance.

The elements of line, color, shape, and texture are influenced by the materials that artist chooses to create the illustrations. Different moods are created by woodcuts, collage, inks, watercolors, or other paints. In addition to media, the artist may also choose to represent the story in realistic terms, or the style may be very imaginative. Realistic artists depict a setting that is highly possible; impressionists experiment with breaking colors and shapes to give an impression of light; abstract artists represent a mood or image with few details of the original object. All styles can be found in children's book illustrations.

The chapter concluded with a discussion of some of the outstanding picture book artists and considered how they have used these elements and media to create memorable illustrations that integrate story and pictures.

Selected Activities for Understanding Artists and Their Illustrations

■ With some of your peers, select one of the following criteria for evaluating the illustrations and narrative portions of a picture book: *(a)* The illustrations should help the reader anticipate both the action of the story and the climax (for example, Blair Lent's illustrations for Hodges's *The Wave* or Maurice Sendak's illustrations for *Where the Wild Things Are). (b)* The pictures should help create the basic mood of the story (Paul Goble's *The Girl Who Loved Wild Horses* or Marcia Brown's illustrations for Perrault's *Cinderella). (c)* The illustrations should portray convincing character delineation and development (Taro Yashima's *Crow Boy). (d)* All pictures should be accurate and consistent with text (Barbara Cooney's illustrations for Donald Hall's *Ox-Cart Man).* Find examples of books that clearly exemplify the criteria and share them with the class.

■ Feldman has suggested that lines are related to natural phenomena (p. 106). Look carefully at the illustrations in several books. Are there examples in which vertical lines suggest lack of movement, horizontal lines suggest calmness or an absence of strife, vertical and horizontal lines connected at the top suggest a solid, safe place, diagonal lines suggest motion, and jagged lines symbolize danger? Compare the moods and settings suggested by the use of color in American Indian folktales (for example, McDermott's *Arrow to the Sun,* Goble's *The Girl Who Loved Wild Horses,* or Belting's *Whirlwind Is a Ghost Dancing)* with the moods and settings suggested in fairy tales (Brown's *Puss in Boots* and LeGalliene's translation of Andersen's *The Nightingale).*

■ Select a fairy tale such as *Cinderella* or *Snow-White* that has been illustrated by several artists. Compare the artists' use of line, color, and shape to create the mood and setting of the story.

■ Read the narrative portion of several picture storybooks. Evaluate whether or not the dominance of the illustrations complements the emphasis of the narrative portion of the text. Choose an example that complements the text and one that does not; share the examples and rationale with the class.

■ With a group of your peers, select one media choice available to artists—woodcuts, collage, inks, watercolors, acrylics, pastels, and so forth. Investigate how the medium is used in illustrations and select several picture books in which the artist uses this medium. Share your findings with the class.

■ With some of your peers, select a style choice available to artists—realistic, impressionistic, abstract, and so forth. Investigate how this style is used by artists and select several picture books in which the artist uses that style. Does the style complement the intended mood of the text? Share your findings with the class.

■ Choose an outstanding illustrator of children's books. Find as many of the illustrator's works as you can. Search for the artists' use of the elements of art—line, color, shape, and texture—and the various media and styles used by the artist. Compare the books. Does the artist use a similar style in all works, or does this style change with the subject matter of the text? Compare earlier works with later ones. Are there any changes in the use of elements, style, or media?

References

1 Bader, Barbara. *American Picture Books from Noah's Art to the Beast Within.* New York: Macmillan, 1976.

2 Borgman, Harry. *Art and Illustration Techniques.* New York: Watson-Guptill, 1979.

3 Davis, Joann. "Trade News: Sendak on Sendak." As told to Jean F. Mercier. *Publishers Weekly.* April 10, 1981, pp. 45–6.

4 Feldman, Edmund Burke. *Varieties of Visual Experience.* New York: Abrams, 1972.

5 Hepler, Susan Ingrid. "Profile, Tomie de Paola: A Gift to Children." *Language Arts* 56 (March 1979): 269–301.

6 Kingman, Lee. "Virginia Lee Burton's Dynamic Sense of Design." *Horn Book* 46 (October 1970): 449–60.

7 Klingberg, Delores. "Profile—Eric Carle." *Language Arts* 54 (April 1977): 445–52.

8 Laliberté, Norman, and Mogelon, Alex. *The Reinhold Book of Art Ideas.* New York: Van Nostrand Reinhold, 1976.

9 Larkin, David, ed. *The Art of Nancy Ekholm Burkert.* New York: Harper & Row, 1977.

10 MacCann, Donnarae, and Richard, Olga. *The Child's First Books: A Critical Study of Pictures and Texts.* New York: Wilson, 1973.

11 McDermott, Beverly Brodsky. *The Golem.* Philadelphia: Lippincott, 1976.

12 Mahony, Bertha E; Latimer, Louise Payson; and Folmsbee, Beulah. *Illustrations of Children's Books, 1744–1945.* Boston: Horn Book, 1947.

13 Moritz, Charles. *Current Biography Yearbook.* New York: Wilson, 1968.

14 Munro, Thomas. *Form and Style in the Arts, an Introduction to Aesthetic Morphology.* Cleveland: Case Western Reserve, 1970.

15 Newberry, Clare Turlay. *Drawing a Cat.* London: The Studio Limited, 1940.

16 Preble, Duane. *Art Forms.* New York: Harper & Row, 1978.

17 Shahn, Ben. *The Shape of Content.* Boston: Harvard University Press, 1957.

18 Townsend, John Rowe. *Written for Children.* New York: Lippincott, 1975.

19 Weston, Annette H. "Robert Lawson: Author and Illustrator." *Elementary English* 47 (January 1970): 74–84.

CHILDREN'S LITERATURE

Aardema, Verna. *Why Mosquitoes Buzz in People's Ears.* Illustrated by Leo and Diane Dillon. Dial, 1975 (I:5–9   R:6) An African cumulative tale.

Andersen, Hans Christian. *The Snow Queen.* Retold by Amy Ehrlich. Illustrated by Susan Jeffers. Dial, 1982 (ch. 7).

———. *The Wild Swans.* Retold by Amy Ehrlich. Illustrated by Susan Jeffers. Dial, 1981 (ch. 7).

Anno, Mitsumasa. *Anno's Britain.* Philomel, 1982 (ch. 5).

———. *Anno's Italy.* Collins, 1980 (ch. 5).

———. *The King's Flower.* Collins, 1979 (I:5–8   R:6). A king has the biggest castle, knife, fork, etc., but cannot command a flower to grow bigger than nature intended.

Aruego, Jose, and Dewey, Ariane. *We Hide, You Seek.* Greenwillow, 1979 (I:2–6). The rhino plays hide and seek with many African animals. Colors and lines create a camouflage book that allows children to look for hidden animals.

Baker, Jeannie. *Grandmother.* Deutsch, 1978 (ch. 5).

Baker, Olaf. *Where the Buffaloes Begin.* Illustrated by Stephen Gammell. Warne, 1981 (I:8 +   R:7). Soft, irregular shapes add power to a Prairie Indian legend.

Belting, Natalia. *Whirlwind Is a Ghost Dancing.* Illustrated by Leo and Diane Dillon. Dutton, 1974 (I:6–12   R:3). North American Indian lore is recreated in verse format.

Bemelmans, Ludwig. *Madeline.* Viking, 1939, 1977 (I:4–9   R:5). Madeline and eleven other little girls live in Paris. She visits the sights but also has an appendectomy.

———. *Madeline in London.* Viking, 1961, 1977 (I:4–9   R:3). Madeline and eleven little girls visit London.

Brown, Marcia. *Once a Mouse.* Scribner's, 1961. (I:3–7   R:6). Woodcuts provide powerful illustrations for a fable from India that retells what happens when a hermit turns a frightened mouse first into a cat, then a dog, and finally a tiger.

———. *Puss in Boots.* Scribner's, 1952 (ch. 5).

Burton, Virginia Lee. *The Little House.* Houghton Mifflin, 1942 (I:3–7 and R:3). Repetition creates a sense of rhythm in illustrations. A little house watches progress in the form of the city come closer and closer until she is finally surrounded by tall buildings. She is happy again when she is moved to the country.

Carle, Eric. *Catch the Ball.* Philomel, 1982 (I:3–6). A string attached to a ball encourages children's vocabulary development.

———. *The Honeybee and the Robber: A Moving/ Picture Book.* Philomel, 1981 (I:3–6). A brightly colored pop-up allows children to move the wings of a bee and a butterfly.

———. *Let's Paint a Rainbow.* Philomel, 1982 (I:3–6). Rainbow colors help children learn eight basic colors

———. *Twelve Tales From Aesop.* Philomel, 1980 (I:4–8). Painted collage illustrations enhance tales for young listeners.

———. *The Very Fussy Monkey.* Philomel, 1982 (I:3–6). Brightly colored illustrations encourage counting from one through ten.

———. *The Very Hungry Caterpillar.* Crowell, 1971 (I:2–7). A colorful collage picture book that presents the life cycle of the caterpillar who eats his way through the pages.

Cooney, Barbara. *Chanticleer and the Fox.* Adapted from Geoffrey Chaucer. Crowell, 1958 (ch. 3).

———. *The Little Juggler.* Adapted and illustrated by Cooney. Hastings, 1982 (I:all). An orphan offers his juggling talent as a Christmas gift to the Virgin Mary.

Dana, Doris. *The Elephant and His Secret.* Illustrated by Antonio Frasconi. Atheneum, 1974 (I:3–7   R:4). The elephant takes the shadow of a mountain for his body. The animals are at first afraid, but he finally saves their lives. This is written in both Spanish and English.

de Paola, Tomie. *Big Anthony and the Magic Ring.* Harcourt Brace Jovanovich, 1979 (I:5–9   R:3). Big Anthony uses Strega Nona's magic ring to turn himself into a handsome young man. The results, however, are different from those he imagined.

———. *Charlie Needs a Cloak.* Prentice-Hall, 1973 (I:3–6   R:4). A simple information book tells in a humorous way how a shepherd shears sheep, cards and spins wool, weaves and dyes the cloth, and then sews a cloak.

———. *The Clown of God.* Harcourt Brace Jovanovich, 1978 (ch. 3).

———. *The Friendly Beasts: An Old English Christmas Carol.* Putnam, 1981 (I:3–8   R:2). The Christmas carol is illustrated in large colorful drawings.

———. *Giorgio's Village.* Putnam, 1982 (ch. 5).

———. *Helga's Dowry: A Troll Love Story.* Harcourt Brace Jovanovich, 1977 (I:5–9   R:4). Helga leaves the world of trolls to earn a dowry. She discovers, however that her original heart's desire is not worthy of her efforts.

———. *Songs of the Fog Maiden.* Holiday, 1979 (I:3–8   R:5). The fog maiden lives in a castle between the sun and the cold. She sings to both her day garden and her night garden.

———. *Watch Out for the Chicken Feet in Your Soup.* Prentice-Hall, 1974 (I:3–7   R:2). Joey and his friend visit Joey's Italian grandmother. Joey is embarrassed by her old-fashioned ways until his friend shows great admiration for her.

I = Interest by age range;
R = Readability by grade level.

_____. *When Everyone Was Fast Asleep.* Holiday, 1976 (I:3–8 R:6). The fog maiden's cat brings two children out into an enchanted night. They are returned safely to their homes by the fog maiden.

Emberley, Barbara. *Drummer Hoff.* Illustrated by Ed Emberley. Prentice-Hall, 1967 (I:3–7 R:6). A cumulative rhyme depicting all the people associated with firing a cannon. Woodcuts and bright colors add impact.

Fatio, Louise. *The Happy Lion.* Illustrated by Roger Duvoisin. McGraw-Hill, 1954 (ch. 5).

Field, Eugene. *Wynken, Blynken and Nod.* Illustrated by Susan Jeffers. Dutton, 1982 (ch. 8).

Frasconi, Antonio. *The House That Jack Built.* Crowell, 1958 (I:3–6). A cumulative folktale.

_____. *The Snow and the Sun.* Harcourt Brace Jovanovich, 1961 (I:5–10 R:3). A South American folk rhyme written in Spanish and English.

Gág, Wanda. *Millions of Cats.* Coward-McCann, 1928 (ch. 5).

_____. *Snow White and the Seven Dwarfs.* Coward-McCann, 1938 (I:5–9 R:6). The popular fairy tale.

_____. *Tales from Grimm.* Coward-McCann, 1936 (I:6–9 R:4). Sixteen tales from Grimm including "Hansel and Gretel," "Rapunzel," and "The Frog Prince."

Goble, Paul. *The Girl Who Loved Wild Horses.* Bradbury, 1978 (ch. 3).

Griego, Margot C.; Bucks, Betsy L.; Gilbert, Sharon S.; and Kimball, Laurel H. *Tortillitas Para Mama.* Illustrated by Barbara Cooney. Holt, Rinehart and Winston, 1981 (I:3–7). Nursery rhymes in Spanish and English.

Grimes, Nikki. *Something on My Mind.* Illustrated by Tom Feelings. Dial, 1978 (I:all). Poems about the joys, fears, hopes, and sorrows of growing up.

Grimm, Brothers. *Hansel and Gretel.* Illustrated by Susan Jeffers. Dial, 1980 (ch. 6).

_____. *Snow-White and the Seven Dwarfs.* Illustrated by Nancy Ekholm Burkert. Farrar, Straus & Giroux, 1972 (ch. 6).

Haley, Gail E. *A Story, a Story.* Atheneum, 1970 (ch. 5).

Hall, Donald. *Ox-Cart Man.* Illustrations by Barbara Cooney. Viking, 1979 (I:3–8 R:5). Colors, lines, and design are dominant elements in a tale about a New Englander who travels by ox cart, sells his products, and returns home to make more goods.

Hodges, Margaret. *The Wave.* Illustrated by Blair Lent. Houghton Mifflin, 1964 (I:5–9 R:5). Woodcuts illustrate a Japanese folktale about a wise old man who saves his people from a tidal wave.

Holling, Holling Clancy. *Paddle-to-the-Sea.* Houghton Mifflin, 1941 (I:7–12 R:4). An Indian boy carves a canoe and places it where it will flow into Lake Superior. The book tells of the boat's adventures as it goes through the Great Lakes into the Atlantic Ocean.

Hughes, Ted. *Under the North Star.* Illustrated by Leonard Baskin. Viking, 1981 (ch. 8).

Jeffers, Susan. *Three Jovial Huntsmen.* Bradbury, 1973 (ch. 5).

Keats, Ezra Jack. *Dreams.* Macmillan, 1974 (ch. 5).

_____. *Goggles!* Macmillan, 1969 (ch. 5).

_____. *Louie.* Greenwillow, 1975 (ch. 5).

_____. *Peter's Chair.* Harper & Row, 1967 (ch. 5).

_____. *Regards to the Man in the Moon.* Scholastic Four Winds, 1981 (ch. 5).

_____. *The Snowy Day.* Viking, 1962 (I:2–6 R:2). Peter experiences a great snowfall; he makes footprints, angels, and a snowman.

_____. *The Trip.* Greenwillow, 1978 (ch. 5).

Krauss, Ruth. *A Hole Is to Dig.* Illustrated by Maurice Sendak. Harper & Row, 1952 (I:2–6 R:2). Illustrations of children depict children's definitions for such things as brothers, holes, mud, principals, and mountains.

Lawson, Robert. *Ben and Me.* Little, Brown, 1939 (ch. 7).

_____. *Rabbit Hill.* Viking, 1944 (ch. 7).

Leaf, Munro. *The Story of Ferdinand.* Illustrated by Robert Lawson. Viking, 1936 (I:4–10 R:6). Is there anything wrong with being different? Ferdinand proves that he'd rather smell the flowers than fight the matador.

Lear, Edward, and Nash, Ogden. *The Scroobious Pip.* Illustrated by Nancy Ekholm Burkert. Harper & Row, 1968 (ch. 8).

LeGalliene, Eva (Hans Christian Andersen). *The Nightingale.* Illustrated by Nancy Ekholm Burkert. Harper & Row, 1965 (I:6–12 R:8). The Hans Christian Andersen tale about an Emperor who learns that a beautiful live nightingale is preferable to a jeweled mechanical bird.

Lionni, Leo. *Alexander and the Wind-up Mouse.* Pantheon, 1969 (ch. 5).

_____. *A Color of His Own.* Random House, 1975 (I:2–7 R:5). An animal fable in which the chameleon looks for his own color.

_____. *The Greentail Mouse.* Random House, 1973 (I:3–7 R:4). When field mice plan a Mardi Gras they forget that life is not filled with frightening masks. Seeing a mouse without a mask changes them back to their good natured selves.

_____. *Pezzettino.* Pantheon, 1975 (I:2–6 R:3). Pezzettino, or Little Piece, is so small that he believes he must be a piece of someone else. The wise one helps him learn that he is himself.

_____. *Swimmy.* Pantheon, 1963 (I:2–6 R:3). A little fish learns about the marvels of the sea and teaches other little fish to swim in the shape of a big fish so they can frighten their predators.

Lipkind, William. *Finders Keepers.* Illustrated by Nicolas Mordvinoff. Harcourt Brace Jovanovich, 1951 (I:2–7 R:1). Two dogs find a bone and try to decide the bone's ownership. They ask passersby but do not receive any useful suggestions.

_____. *The Little Tiny Rooster.* Illustrated by Nicolas Mordvinoff. Harcourt Brace Jovanovich, 1960 (I:3–7 R:3). The chickens and roosters believe the tiniest rooster is too small to be useful until he saves the eggs from a prowling fox.

_____. *Two Reds.* Illustrated by Nicolas Mordvinoff. Harcourt Brace Jovanovich, 1950 (I:2–7 R:3). A boy and a cat are enemies until they save each other from capture.

MacLachlan, Patricia. *The Sick Day.* Illustrations by William Pène Du Bois. Pantheon, 1979 (I:2–7 R:2). Father entertains Emily when she gets sick; then he gets sick and she entertains him.

Martin, Sarah Catherine. *The Comic Adventures of Old Mother Hubbard and Her Dog.* Illustrated by Tomie de Paola. Harcourt Brace Jovanovich, 1981 (ch. 5).

McCloskey, Robert. *Blueberries for Sal.* Viking, 1948 (ch. 5).

_____. *Lentil.* Viking, 1940 (ch. 5).

_____. *Make Way for Ducklings.* Viking, 1941 (ch. 5).

_____. *One Morning in Maine.* Viking, 1952 (ch. 5).

_____. *Time of Wonder.* Viking, 1957 (ch. 5).

McDermott, Beverly Brodsky. *The Crystal Apple.* Viking, 1974 (I:4–9 R:4). A Russian tale about three sisters who ask their father for special gifts, including a crystal apple. Cubism and bright colors dominate.

_____. *The Golem.* Lippincott, 1976 (I:9–14 R:5). Expressionistic art captures the magic spell that creates the Golem from a lump of clay. The Golem is destroyed when he becomes too powerful.

McDermott, Gerald. *Arrow to the Sun.* Viking, 1974 (I:3–9 R:2). Strong shape and color add to a Pueblo Indian tale about the time when an Indian boy searches for his father who is lord of the sun.

_____. *Sun Flight.* Four Winds, 1980 (ch. 6).

Moore, Clement. *The Night Before Christmas.* Illustrated by Tomie de Paola. Holiday, 1980 (ch. 8).

Mosel, Arlene. *Tikki Tikki Tembo.* Illustrated by Blair Lent. Holt, Rinehart & Winston, 1968 (I:5–9 R:7). A Chinese folktale explaining why Chinese children now have shorter names.

Musgrove, Margaret. *Ashanti to Zulu: African Traditions* Illustrated by Leo and Diane Dillon. Dial, 1976 (ch. 5).

Newberry, Clare Turlay. *Marshmallow.* Harper & Row, 1942 (ch. 5).

_____. *Widget.* Harper & Row, 1958. (ch. 5).

Perrault, Charles. *Cinderella.* Illustrated by Marcia Brown. Harper & Row, 1954 (I:5–8 R:5). Fine lines suggest the mood of the fairy tale.

Piatti, Celestino. *The Happy Owls.* Atheneum, 1964 (I:3–7 R:4). The owls try to explain why they are happy; a group of fowls does not understand.

Ransome, Arthur. *The Fool of the World and the Flying Ship.* Illustrated by Uri Shulevitz. Farrar, Straus & Giroux, 1968 (I:6–10 R:6). Lines and warm colors focus attention in a Russian tale about a simple lad who overcomes enormous obstacles in order to marry the Czar's daughter.

Schwartz, Delmore. *"I Am Cherry Alive," The Little Girl Sang.* Illustrated by Barbara Cooney. Harper & Row, 1979. An illustrated poem about a little girl who is celebrating being alive.

Sendak, Maurice. *In the Night Kitchen.* Harper & Row, 1970 (ch. 5).

_____. *Outside Over There.* Harper & Row, 1981 (I:5–8 R:5). Goblins steal a baby sister.

_____. *Where the Wild Things Are.* Harper & Row, 1963 (ch. 5).

Shannon, George. *Dance Away.* Illustrated by Jose Aruego and Ariane Dewey. Greenwillow, 1982 (I:2–6). Line and color complement the repetitive language as a rabbit outwits a hungry fox.

Singer, Isaac B. *Zlateh the Goat.* Illustrated by Maurice Sendak. Harper & Row, 1966 (I:6–10 R:6). A collection of Jewish folktales.

Spier, Peter. *Bill's Service Station.* Doubleday, 1981 (I:3–7). One of the "Village Book" series, cut in the shape of a building.

_____. *The Erie Canal.* Doubleday, 1970 (ch. 5).

_____. *Fire House: Hook and Ladder Company Number Twenty-Four.* Doubleday, 1981 (I:3–7). Detailed drawings of a fire house.

_____. *Food Market.* Doubleday, 1981 (I:3–7). Detailed drawings depict a food market.

_____. *The Fox Went Out on a Chilly Night.* Doubleday, 1961. (ch. 5).

_____. *London Bridge Is Falling Down!* Doubleday, 1967 (ch. 5).

_____. *My School.* Doubleday, 1981 (I:3–7). Activities associated with a school.

_____. *Noah's Ark.* Doubleday, 1977 (ch. 5).

_____. *The Pet Store.* Doubleday, 1981 (I:3–7). Detailed drawings of a pet store.

_____. *The Star-Spangled Banner.* Doubleday, 1973. (ch. 5).

_____. *Tin Lizzie.* Doubleday, 1975 (ch. 5).

_____. *The Toy Shop.* Doubleday, 1981 (I:3–7). Detailed drawings of a toy store.

Tresselt, Alvin. *White Snow Bright Snow.* Illustrated by Roger Duvoisin. Lothrop, Lee & Shepard, 1947 (I:2–7 R:4). The snow falls, the people prepare for it, and the children enjoy it.

Udry, Janice May. *The Moon Jumpers.* Illustrated by Maurice Sendak. Harper & Row, 1959 (I:3–9 R:2). Colors create a mood as children go out in the evening to play in the moonlight.

Van Allsburg, Chris. *The Garden of Abdul Gasazi.* Houghton Mifflin, 1979 (I:5–8 R:5). A boy has a magical experience in a magician's garden.

_____. *Jumanji.* Houghton Mifflin, 1981 (I:5–8 R:6). An unusual game creates a jungle environment.

Viorst, Judith. *Alexander and the Terrible, Horrible, No Good, Very Bad Day.* Illustrated by Ray Cruz. Atheneum, 1972 (ch. 5).

Wahl, Jan. *The Little Blind Goat.* Illustrated by Antonio Frasconi. Stemmer, 1981 (I:5–9 R:3). A blind goat is taught to overcome his handicap.

Ward, Lynd. *The Biggest Bear.* Houghton Mifflin, 1952 (ch. 5).

Wildsmith, Brian. *Brian Wildsmith's ABC.* Watts, 1963 (ch. 5).

_____. *Hunter and His Dog.* Oxford, 1979 (I:3–7 R:3). A hunting dog cares for wounded ducks.

Yagawa, Sumiko. *The Crane Wife.* Translated by Katherine Paterson. Illustrated by Suekichi Akaba. Morrow, 1981 (I:all R:6). A traditional Japanese tale expressing the dangers of greed.

Yashima, Taro. *Crow Boy.* Viking, 1955 (I:4–8 R:4). Chibi, the tiny boy, is a lonely outcast at school. An understanding teacher finally recognizes his potential and helps Chibi gain respect.

_____. *Umbrella.* Viking, 1958 (I:3–7 R:7). Momo receives an umbrella for her third birthday and then waits impatiently for the rain to come.

Zolotow, Charlotte. *Mr. Rabbit and the Lovely Present.* Illustrated by Maurice Sendak. Harper & Row, 1962 (I:3–8 R:2). A little girl, with the help of a rabbit, searches for a gift for her mother's birthday.

FIVE
Picture Books

A Book Is More Than Words
Involving Children in Picture Books

A Book Is More Than Words

MANY adults thinking of a child, a lap, and a picture book experience warm feelings, either from remembering their own early experiences with books or remembering a time when they shared books with a child. These early experiences allow children to value books and appreciate the enchantment found in them. When this is shared with a loving adult, both the child and the adult benefit.

The books included under the genre of picture books provide many values in addition to pleasure. When children are encouraged to interact with picture books, the values are numerous and varied. The rhythm and repetition found in nursery rhymes stimulate language development in young children. Rhymes also develop auditory discrimination and attentive listening skills. Alphabet books reinforce children's ability to identify letter/sound relationships and help expand their vocabularies. Concept books enhance intellectual development by fostering understanding associated with abstract ideas. Wordless books develop observational skills and descriptive vocabularies and increase children's ability to create a story characterized by a logical sequence. Illustrations found in picture books develop sensitivity to art and beauty, and the well-written text of a storybook develops appreciation for language style. All of these values make picture books a very important contribution to the development of the young child.

This chapter suggests criteria that should be considered when evaluating picture books. The literary elements in Mother Goose rhymes are discussed and appropriate Mother Goose books identified. Additional picture books, including toy books, alphabet books, counting books, wordless books, concept books, and easy-to-read books, are suggested. The chapter concludes with a discussion of specific storybooks and the elements that make them memorable.

EVALUATING PICTURE BOOKS

The term *picture books* covers a wide variety of selections ranging from Mother Goose books and toy books for young children to picture storybooks that contain sufficient plot development to satisfy much older children. Younger children respond to stories presented visually as well as verbally. Many of the picture books discussed rely heavily upon the illustrations to present content. Some have each scene or rhyme illustrated; others contain a more highly developed story line and do not rely as heavily upon pictures to develop the plot.

Because of this reliance upon both text and illustrations, picture books have a unique requirement: the illustrations and narrative portions must complement each other. Consequently, the illustrations, the text, and the relationship between the two must be considered in any evaluation. The following questions can help in selecting picture books for children.

1 Are the illustrations accurate, and do they correspond to the content of the story?
2 Do the illustrations complement the setting, plot, and mood of the story?
3 Is characterization enhanced through the illustrations?
4 Do both text and illustrations avoid stereotypes of race and sex?
5 Is the plot one that will appeal to children?
6 Is the theme worthwhile?
7 What is the purpose for sharing this book with children or recommending that they read it?
8 Is the author's style and language appropriate for children's interests and age levels?

Many picture books have another unique characteristic not shared by many other books. The writer and the illustrator may or may not be the same person. Picture books are frequently illustrated by well-known artists. Chapter four concentrated upon artists and their media. This chapter places heavier emphasis upon authors and their literature.

MOTHER GOOSE BOOKS

Mother Goose rhymes have been frequently identified as the earliest literature enjoyed by young children; the rhymes, rhythms, and pleasing sound effects of the jingles appeal to young children who are experimenting with their own language patterns. As discussed in chapter one, experimentation with sounds and interacting with nursery rhymes is recommended for language development. A brief review of the literary elements in nursery rhymes suggests why children enjoy them and indicates why the jingles add to children's language development.

Literary Elements in Mother Goose

The rhythm in many nursery rhymes almost forces children to react to the verse. For example, they may clap their hands or jump up and down to the rhythm of this jingle:

> Handy dandy, Jack-a-Dandy
> Loves plum cake and sugar candy;
> He bought some at a grocer's shop
> And out he came, hop, hop, hop.

In addition to the appeal of the rhythm in this verse, children also enjoy listening and responding to the rhyming elements. Words such as *dandy-candy, shop-hop* invite them to join in and add the rhyming word or make up their own rhymes. Rhyming is a common literary element found in Mother Goose verses. The adventures of many favorite characters are enhanced by rhymes such as those found in "Little Miss Muffet sat on a tuffet"; "Jack and Jill went up the hill"; "Hickory, dickory, dock, the mouse ran up the clock"; "Bobby Shafto's gone to sea, Silver buckles on his knee"; or "Rub a dub, dub, three men in a tub". Many of these verses rhyme at the end of each line; they also use internal rhyming elements such as those found in "hickory, dickory, dock" or in "rub, a dub, dub." An easy way to test the long-lasting influence of many of these rhyming verses is to ask older children to share one of their favorite Mother Goose rhymes. They can probably say several though they may not have heard or recited them for years.

Children also respond to the repetition of sounds in a phrase or line of poetry. Alliteration, defined as a common consonant used in consecutive words, provides phrases that children enjoy repeating. "A misty, moisty, morning," for example, may become a favorite phrase, or children may sing "Sing a song of sixpence" or "Diddle, diddle dumpling" just to experience the marvelous feeling that results from the repetition of beginning sounds. If the alliteration in one sentence is excessive, tongue twisters are the result. Children love the challenge of this jingle:

> Peter Piper picked a peck of pickled peppers.
> A peck of pickled peppers Peter Piper picked.
> If Peter Piper picked a peck of pickled peppers,
> Where's the peck of pickled peppers Peter Piper picked?

One great appeal of Mother Goose verses for children is the humorous circumstances illustrated in many rhymes. There is great humor in

> Hey, diddle, diddle!
> The cat and the fiddle,
> The cow jumped over the moon;
> The little dog laughed
> To see such sport,
> And the dish ran away with the spoon.

This verse is an example of hyperbole. Hyperbole is defined as the use of exaggeration for effect and is frequently found in Mother Goose rhymes.

Additional Appeals of Mother Goose

The rhyme, rhythm, and exaggerated comparisons of Mother Goose verses foster language development and enjoyment of literature. The humor and comical situations in the verses apparently have great appeal for young children. They appreciate the ridiculous situations found when an old woman lives in a shoe and has so many children she doesn't know what to do, when a barber tries to shave a pig, or when Simple Simon goes fishing in his mother's pail. Simple Simon's foolishness continues to amuse children when he tries unsuccessfully to catch a bird by placing salt on its tail, or with this final indignity:

> He went for water with a sieve,
> But soon it ran all through:
> And now poor Simple Simon
> Bids you all adieu.

A search through Mother Goose verses reveals that there are both good and bad little girls and boys in nursery rhyme land; in fact, the same children may be both good and bad. These characteristics have a strong appeal for young children, who are also good and bad at different times. Good children in nursery rhymes are depicted frequently as sleeping when they are supposed to sleep. Little Fred is this ideal child:

> When little Fred went to bed,
> He always said his prayers,
> He kissed mamma and then pappa,
> And straightway went upstairs.

Good children are also kind to animals; this child even describes how not to treat them:

> I like Little Pussy,
> Her coat is so warm,
> And if I don't hurt her
> She'll do me no harm;
> So I'll not pull her tail,
> Nor drive her away,
> But Pussy and I
> Very gently will play.

All children, however, are not so nice to animals:

> Ding, dong, bell,
> Pussy's in the well!
> Who put her in?
> Little Tommy Green.
> Who pulled her out?
> Little Johnny Stout.
> What a naughty boy was that,
> To try to drown poor pussy cat,
> Who never did him any harm,
> But killed the mice in his father's barn!

Nineteenth-century children and the English countryside highlight Greenaway's illustrations for this early Mother Goose edition. From *Mother Goose: Or, the Old Nursery Rhymes* by Kate Greenaway. Reproduced by permission of Frederick Warne & Co., Inc., Publishers.

Animals may also portray naughty behavior in nursery rhymes. The raven is certainly bad when he attacks a farmer and his daughter who are riding a mare:

A raven cried croak! and they all tumbled down,
    Bumpety, bumpety, bump!
The mare broke her knees, and the farmer his crown,
    Lumpety, lumpety, lump!
The mischievous raven flew laughing away,
    Bumpety, bumpety, bump!
And vowed he would serve them the same the next day,
    Lumpety, lumpety, lump!

While nursery rhymes may not explicitly state what behavior is either good or bad, children have no difficulty relating to many Mother Goose characters.

There are many different editions of Mother Goose that appeal to children. Some contain many rhymes in one text, some develop a longer version of one Mother Goose rhyme in a picture storybook format, and others present insights into the universality of children by presenting verses enjoyed by children in foreign lands. The next section looks at a few examples of each type of Mother Goose edition and discusses some characteristics that make them appropriate for sharing with one child; others are suitable for sharing with a group.

Mother Goose Collections

While the verses in the various collections may be practically the same, the formats, sizes of the books, and illustrations are quite different. Some editions contain several hundred verses in large-book format; others have fewer verses and are just large enough to hold; some have illustrations reminiscent of eighteenth-century England; and others have very modern illustrations.

Many adult students in university classes prefer the Mother Goose editions with settings in the England of the 1600s and 1700s. These editions may be reissues of the original publications or may be published in the twentieth century. Two popular early editions, John Newbery's *The Original Mother Goose's Melody* (6) and Kate Greenaway's *Mother Goose: Or, the Old Nursery Rhymes* have been reissued. Newbery's edition may be of greater interest to adults (the text contains a history of Mother Goose), although many older children enjoy looking at the earlier orthography and comparing the verses and illustrations with twentieth-century editions. Another interesting comparison for both older children and adults to view and discuss is Newbery's tendency to add a moral to the close of each verse, while the twentieth-century editions ignore the moral. For example, in Newbery's edition, the Mother Goose rhyme "Ding dong Bell, The Cat is in the Well," is followed by this maxim: "He that injures one threatens a Hundred" (p. 25).

The second popular early Mother Goose edition, *Mother Goose: Or, the Old Nursery Rhymes,* was first published in 1881. The illustrator, Kate Greenaway, was a well-known author/illustrator of children's books during the 1800s. Her book, published by Frederick Warne, is a small text suitable for sharing with one child. Greenaway's nursery rhymes are illustrated with pictures of delicate children. (See page 49 for a discussion of Kate Greenaway's illustrations.) These children would certainly appeal to the sentiment of any reader.

A modern twentieth-century Mother Goose edition, also with illustrations of appealing children and an earlier English setting, is *Marguerite De Angeli's Book of Nursery and Mother Goose Rhymes.* In the foreword to her book, De Angeli states that her writing and illustrations are influenced by her first memories of nursery rhymes and how her English grandfather read them aloud. She also says that when she visited England the earlier memories came alive, and she sought appropriate models for her nursery rhymes; consequently, flowering fields, blossoming hedgerows, stone walls, castles, cobblestone streets, and the chalky cliffs of Dover are all found in the illustrations. The children in her illustrations are reminiscent of Greenaway's models; smiling, frolicking, and wondering children are shown playing in muted backgrounds of soft greens, browns, and golds. De Angeli also admits in the foreword to her book that although the setting is an earlier England, the models for the children are her own children and grandchildren. This is a large book and contains 376 rhymes with several verses printed on each page.

Arnold Lobel's *Gregory Griggs and Other Nursery Rhyme People* tells the tales of such lesser-known characters as Theophilus Thistle, the successful thistle sifter; Gregory Griggs who had twenty-seven different wigs; Charley, Charley who stole the barley; Michael Finnegan who grew a long beard right on his chinnigan; and Terence McDiddler, the three-stringed fiddler. The language and strong rhyming patterns found in the verses make the book appropriate for reading aloud. The humorous, nonsensical verses are enriched by Lobel's soft pastel illustrations; each rhyme is illustrated with a large picture, making it especially good for sharing with a group of children.

Human characters are not always the models for nursery rhymes. A large, colorful edition by Wallace Tripp, *Granfa' Grig Had a Pig and Other Rhymes Without Reason from Mother Goose,* depicts many of the characters as animals. In his series of illustrations for the rhyme "Old King Cole," the king is a jolly lion; the fiddlers are a cat, a bear, and a heavyset man; the fifers are a rabbit and a hippopotamus; and the trumpeters are elephants. The drawings are humorous and the added dialogue in a cartoon-bubble format provides interest and amusement for older readers. The series of pictures that illustrate some longer rhymes may also be used to stimulate oral language activities, especially those developing sequential order.

Picture Books That Illustrate One Mother Goose Rhyme or Tale

The humor, simple plots, characters, and jingles found in nursery rhymes lend themselves to expansion into picture storybook format. Children frequently want to know more about their favorite nursery rhyme characters; books illustrated by several artists allow children to share longer versions of nursery rhymes. These versions may also stimulate creative interpretations as children think about what might happen if they expanded and illustrated the plots in other nursery rhymes.

Three well-known authors and illustrators have used picture book format to extend nursery rhymes into humorous stories. Several books by Paul Galdone especially appeal to young children. There is something compelling about rhymes such as "This is the cat, That killed the rat, That ate the malt, That lay in the house that Jack built." As the cumulative tale progresses and each new character is added, children also enter into the fun by repeating the lines. Paul Galdone's *The House That Jack Built* illustrates the characters as they become a part of the story. These humorous illustrations are large enough to be shared with a group of children who will enjoy joining in and "reading" the story. *Old Mother Hubbard and Her Dog* is another story Galdone based on nursery rhymes.

Sarah Martin's *The Comic Adventures of Old Mother Hubbard* is another humorous edition that appeals to children. Tomie de Paola's illustrations add a hilarious touch. Old Mother Hubbard is dressed in a full skirt, bustle, high collar, and ribboned hat. Her dog is an orange, smartly trimmed poodle. The illustrations encourage additional interaction with the text as children identify other nursery rhyme characters drawn as a border on each page.

In Maurice Sendak's *Hector Protector and as I Went over the Water,* children are introduced to the familiar Hector from the nursery rhyme:

> Hector Protector was dressed all in green;
> Hector Protector was sent to the Queen.
> The Queen did not like him,
> No more did the King;
> So Hector Protector was sent back again.

This rhyme, however, does not say why the Queen doesn't like Hector Protector. Sendak's version shows exactly why Hector returns so rapidly to his home as the Queen is not pleased when Hector thrusts his snake-wrapped sword at her. The few words and large, humorous pictures appeal to the imaginations of young children.

Two expanded nursery rhyme stories have enough detail and accurate information to interest older readers as well as younger children. Peter Spier's *London Bridge Is Falling Down* tells in pictures the story that accompanies the favorite nursery game song. Each line of the song is illustrated in pictures that show the London of an earlier era. These pictures are so detailed that architecture, transportation, and dress are all illustrated. Of interest to the older reader is an account of the history of London Bridge, beginning with the Romans building the first bridge in 43 B.C., and extending through the completion of the newest bridge in the 1970s. Spier's second book, *To Market! to Market,* contains rhymes and pictures that depict farm and market life such as that found in the rhyme "To market, to market, to buy a fat pig, Home again, home again, jiggety-jig." The final two pages give a description and history of the historic town of New Castle, Delaware; they also describe the numerous trips that Spier took through Delaware, Maryland, and Pennsylvania when sketching and collecting the details for the book. These concerns for accuracy and detail provide a book that may be used to foster oral language discussion skills with older children and to develop a historical perspective as well.

Mother Goose and Other Rhymes in Foreign Lands

Traditional nursery rhymes and children's jingles are found in many different lands. The language and style may differ, but there are similarities in content. According to Robert Wyndham in *Chinese Mother Goose Rhymes,* nursery rhymes are amazingly alike and it is correct to refer to them as universal. There are rhymes about good and bad children, tall and short people, animals, and nature. There are, however, unique characteristics in these rhymes that allow children to develop appreciation for the values and contributions of other cultures.

The Prancing Pony: Nursery Rhymes from Japan, translated by Charlotte B. De Forest, is an example of a children's book that combines the traditional nursery rhymes of Japan with the Japanese art of *kusa-e* (collage). The nursery rhymes were collected in the early 1900s by the Japanese educator Tasuku Harada and later translated by De Forest. Because rhyme and meter are not devices found in Japanese verse, adults, rather than children, appreciated the original English translations; the rhymes were "transmuted" by adding both rhyme and meter to the originals in order to appeal more to English-speaking children. The resulting rhymes illustrate the Japanese love for nature, as the verses are frequently about flowers, cherry trees,

師傅騎馬沿街走我騎蛟龍水上游

太陽出來一點紅師傅騎馬我騎龍

As the sun came up, a ball of red,
I followed my friend wherever he led.
He thought his fast horse would leave me
*   behind,*
But I rode a dragon as swift as the wind!

The Chinese orthography and illustrations suggest the oriental settings for these nursery rhymes.
From *Chinese Mother Goose Rhymes* by Robert Wyndham, with the permission of Philomel Books, a division of the Putnam Publishing Group. Copyright © 1968 by Robert Wyndham.

nightingales, and other birds. The love for cherry blossoms is felt in this verse:

The Prancing Pony

Your prancing, dancing pony—
    Oh, please don't tie him here.
This cherry tree's in blossom—
    Oh, dear, dear, dear!
He'll prance and dance and whinny,
    He'll neigh and stamp and call,
And down the soft, pink blossoms
    Will fall, fall, fall! (p. 31)

Snowmen apparently appeal to both Japanese and American children. This poem shows how much fun making a snowman can be:

Snowman

Quilly-quo,
A quart of snow.
Pilly-pail,
A pint of hail.
Oh, see the snowflakes fall!

Telly-toll,
The snowballs roll
To make a snowman tall!

With charcoal eyes,
He looks so wise—
And thinks he knows it all! (p. 32)

The illustrations in *The Prancing Pony* also depict a Japanese setting. The illustrator, Keiko Hida, has used natural plant dyes to color the handmade textured rice paper used in the collages: browns are from cedar bark, red from madder roots, black from persimmon juice, yellow from the fruit of the cape jasmine, purple from the wood of the Judas tree, and indigo from the indigo plant. The resulting illustrations are simple geometric shapes, but they provide the feeling of running, flying, and prancing.

Chinese nursery rhymes have also been translated into an English version designed to appeal to, and entertain, English-speaking readers and listeners. Robert Wyndham's *Chinese Mother Goose Rhymes* are about dragons, Buddhas, carriage chairs, and the Milky Way and have counting, rocking, and twirling rhymes as well. Each page shows a rhyme in English and the same rhyme written in Chinese orthography. Simple, colorful drawings illustrate each rhyme. A child is fascinated with a lady bug in this verse:

Lady bug, lady bug,
Fly away, do!
Fly to the mountain
To feed upon dew.

Feed upon dew
And when you are through,
Lady bug, lady bug,
Fly home again, do! (p. 3 unnumbered)

Turning games and nonsense words apparently have universal appeal for young children. The following is a Chinese version of a turning jingle:

Gee lee, gu lu, turn the cake,
Add some oil, the better to bake.
Gee lee, gu lu, now it's done;
Give a piece to everyone. (p. 40 unnumbered)

Danish nursery rhymes have been translated and illustrated in N. M. Bodecker's *It's Raining, Said John Twaining*. Some subjects in these rhymes are quite different from those found in the oriental rhymes. Wooden shoes, kings, queens, princes, and princesses are common characters in the Danish verses, and there are fewer references to nature. Like the familiar English Mother Goose verses, the Danish nursery rhymes use rhyming elements, tongue-twisting nonsense words, and riddles. Young children enjoy repeating nonsense words, and the names of some characters in the rhymes such as Skat Skratterat Skrat Skrirumskrat, should appeal to them. This Danish nursery rhyme book is appropriate for reading to young children or sharing with a larger group because each rhyme is illustrated with a colorful, full-page picture.

Margot C. Griego has collected nursery rhymes and lullabies from the Spanish-speaking communities in Mexico and the United States. *Tortillitas Para Mama* contains finger plays, counting rhymes, and clapping rhymes written in both Spanish and English.

The traditional nursery rhymes from many nations are an important contribution to our cultural heritage. Sharing them with children fosters the self-esteem of children who are part of that ethnic heritage and develops understanding of values and contributions of other cultures for children who are not a part of that heritage.

TOY BOOKS

Within the category of picture books are a growing number of board, pop-up, flap, cloth, and plastic books that entice young children to interact with the text, develop vocabularies, count, identify colors, and discuss content with an adult. These books are valuable additions to children's literature because they stimulate language, cognitive, personal, and social development of preschool-age children. They also provide a happy experience with books that it is hoped will extend into later childhood and adulthood.

Board books range in content from identifying baby's clothing to exploring the neighborhood and alphabet and counting books. Helen Oxenbury's board books are especially appropriate for the younger child. Each page contains an easily identifiable picture of a baby's actions as he or she gets dressed, interacts with family members, or accomplishes a new skill. There are five appealing books in this set including *Dressing, Family, Friends, Playing* and *Working*. Another series of board books that uses familiar items and one simple object per page is illustrated by Zokeisha. *Things I Like to Eat; Things I Like to Look At; Things I Like to Play With;* and *Things I Like to Wear* should enhance vocabulary development and identification of familiar objects. Likewise Richard Scarry's *Richard Scarry's Lowly Worm Word Book* identifies familiar objects such as food, bath, and parts of the body.

Several board books develop concepts related to counting, the alphabet, and seasonal changes. For example, Helen Craig's *The Mouse House 1, 2, 3* is a miniature foldout board book that relies on humorous illustrations of mice forming the numbers. Rosemary Wells's *Max's Toys: A Counting Book* also develops simple concepts related to numbers. Eric Carle's *The Very Fussy Monkey* develops counting ability and vocabulary as a monkey turns down one coconut, two apples, and three pears, etc., until he reaches ten bananas. The alphabet is introduced in Helen Craig's *The Mouse House ABC.* This time the mice are busy forming the letters from a variety of objects including wood, paint, and rope. Monika Beisner's *A Folding Alphabet Book* develops the alphabet as animals or other objects form the letter they represent. Helen Craig's *Mouse House Months* shows a tree as it goes through its seasonal changes; there is an illustration appropriate for each month.

Board books also develop understandings about children's expanding environment. Common animals in the environment are illustrated and discussed in one or two simple sentences in the following books: Lisa Bonforte's *Farm Animals;* Tony Chen's *Wild Animals;* and Michele Roosevelt's *Animals in the Woods.*

Children's curiosity about their neighborhood and various buildings in their town can motivate exciting discussions and discovery using Peter Spier's various board books shaped like the buildings they represent. There is enough detail in each illustration that children can name objects, equipment, or other items that are found in each of these books: *Bill's Service Station; Fire House: Hook and Ladder Company Number Twenty-Four; Food Market; My School; The Pet Store;* and *The Toy Shop.* Parents, librarians, and nursery school or kindergarten teachers may use the books to stimulate discussions and motivate interest in the environment. A librarian, for example, asked a small group of young children to describe the details in the *Food Market* and then tell how their own food market was the same or different.

Pop-ups may introduce children to beloved story-book characters, tell simple stories, or create fascinating three-dimensional settings. For example, Michael Bond's *Paddington's Pop-Up Book* introduces children to a popular modern fantasy character. Likewise, Nicola Bayley's *Puss in Boots* tells a pop-up version of the folktale. John Goodall's Paddy Pig is also introduced through a pop-up. *Paddy Finds A Job* and *Shrewbettina Goes to Work* tell humorous wordless stories that stimulate language development and may encourage children to seek other books about the characters.

THROUGH THE EYES OF AN ILLUSTRATOR TEAM

© Hilary Masters 1981

Creating Picture Books

Alice and Martin Provensen

ALICE and MARTIN PROVENSEN, whose work has won the New York Times Best Illustrative Children's Book award, the Brooklyn Museum's Art Books for Children Citation, and the Caldecott honor award, discuss the challenges of illustrating a new manuscript.

OUR WORK IS CONCENtrated on book illustration and starting each new book is still, after having worked together for thirty-seven years, an exhilarating experience. It is not surprising that there are so many husband and wife teams in the children's book field. Our marriages must surely have been enhanced by the enchantment of this shared experience. In addition to the actual illustration of a book, there is much craft, much measuring, calculation and minutae and many decisions in its making. It is a welcome thing to have a reliable, able, sympathetic (if sometimes critical), person working alongside.

Publishing a book is in many ways similar to producing a movie or a play. It is not done by one person. The illustrator's part in its production has most in common with the actor's performance. We approach each new book as a new role and have never developed a style or mannerisms that would suit every text.

A brilliant player, such as Alec Guiness, creates a new persona for each new part he plays, trying to find the inner and outer guise which will best express the texture of the character and the meaning of the play. Each new role presents him with a new challenge. For us, each new manuscript does the same.

The illustrator's task if one really is an *illustrator* (that is to say "illuminator") is to do the text full justice, trying as the actor does, to find the right line, the right tone and rhythm and the right spirit with which to bring a manuscript written or edited for children to the fulfillment of its intended purpose — a children's book.

Before we begin our search for what we hope will be this inevitable "rightness" in the finished illustrations, we try to choose a format (shape) for the book which will be suitable for the subject matter and the age group of its readers. Then, too, there is the length of the book (the number of pages), based not only on the length of the manuscript but also on the size of the type used, the number of lines on each page, the size and number of illustrations, all again relating to the age level of its audience and increasingly the cost of its production, to be considered.

At this stage we often have several and separate opinions about what the appearance of the finished book should be. We work toward the solution by making rough layouts and actually constructing crude dummies. It is now that the first rough sketches, by either of us, are drawn. We decide which scenes or characters are the most important, which will make the most vital pictures, which, in the case of a narrative manuscript, will forward the story line and in the case of diverse subject matter, as in a Mother Goose book, how the pages can be designed to unify the text visually.

It is always easy to find the wrong solutions. The right ones emerge through a process of experimentation, but once we have decided on a format, ordered the type set, agreed on what the spirit and appearance of the book should be, we try to set aside our individual egos and place our individual drawing styles and painting skills to the service of that image.

We have been given the opportunity to draw Bibles and books of nonsense, warriors and lions, mythological landscapes and modern city streets. We have illustrated alphabet books and music books, cookbooks and books of poetry and yet are always astonished and pleased to discover how much there is still to be done.

Eric Carle's bright, colorful illustrations and pop-up techniques enhance a simple story line in *The Honeybee and the Robber: A Moving/Picture Book.* The plot follows a honeybee as she tries to gather nectar but encounters a bird, a fish, and a frog who all wish to eat her for breakfast. Children enjoy the action when they can make the bee move her wings, a bear cross his eyes, a flower open its petals, and a butterfly spread his wings. Tomie de Paola's *Giorgio's Village* is a fascinating book consisting of six three-dimensional fold-down spreads that resemble a stage setting of an Italian Renaissance village. Children of all ages are intrigued as they follow the action in the village from early morning until evening.

Flap books and other mechanical books encourage children's interaction with the text as they speculate about what is under a flap and then open it to discover if they were correct. Eric Hill has written and illustrated an excellent series of books for preschool children. In *Where's Spot?* the plot revolves around Spot's full dinner bowl and discovering where the dog could be. Children join Spot's mother as they open a door or lift a covering in search of Spot. Each opening reveals a different animal. A similar approach is used in *Spot's First Walk* as children lift flaps to discover what Spot finds behind each door. For example, behind the door in the coop Spot discovers a hen who says "Have a nice day!" Likewise, children lift the flaps in *Spot's Birthday Party* to discover the location of the animals who play hide and seek at his party. The lettering is large and clear against a white background and the illustrations are both colorful and humorous. Young children return many times to rediscover what is behind each flap.

Another book that provides a unique guessing game for children is Bruno Munari's *Who's There? Open the Door.* The author/illustrator uses pages of varying size beginning with a giraffe who brought a crate with a zebra inside. Each panel decreases in size until the last little door opens.

Robert Crowther has designed two mechanical books that stimulate interaction with the text as well as develop concepts related to the alphabet and counting. *The Most Amazing Hide-And-Seek Alphabet Book* has clear capital and lower case letters that conceal an object beginning with the letter. *The Most Amazing Hide-And-Seek Counting Book* uses pictures that rotate or lift to uncover objects for counting.

Cloth and plastic books may develop concepts and stimulate language development of very young children. John E. Johnson's *The Sky Is Blue, the Grass Is Green* develops color identification through familiar objects such as a red fire engine and white milk. J. P. Miller's *The Cow Says Moo* identifies sounds made by farm animals. Peggy Parish identifies a series of activities in four books that progress in difficulty. Her *I Can - Can You?* asks such questions as "Can you catch your toes?" to the more difficult "Can you put your toys away?"

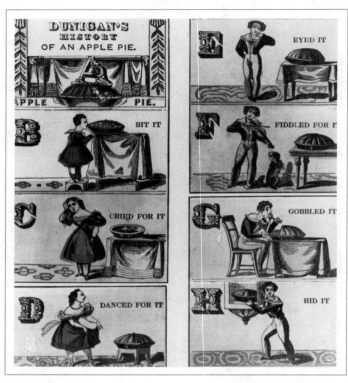

An early nursery rhyme traces the "History of an Apple Pie" using alphabetical order.

From *One Hundred Nineteenth-Century Rhyming Alphabets in English* by Ruth Baldwin. Carbondale, Ill: Southern Illinois University Press, 1972. From the John G. White Collection, Cleveland Public Library.

The books discussed in this section provide "reading" and sharing materials for very young children. There is apparently a trend toward publishing more material for very young children; a visit to a book store or a search through publishers' catalogues will show students of children's literature the increasing numbers of available texts. In addition, *Booklist*, the journal for the American Library Association is reviewing toy books as part of its coverage of children's books.

ALPHABET BOOKS

Like Mother Goose rhymes, alphabet books are frequently shared with young children. Alphabet books can stimulate vocabulary development, and item identification. They may be shared with children in the expectation that children will learn

Costumes and occupations in the illustrations show the Shaker influence on American children's literature.
From *A Peaceable Kingdom,* illustrated by Alice and Martin Provensen. Copyright © 1978 by Alice and Martin Provensen. Reprinted by permission of Viking Penguin Inc.

to identify the letters and their sounds. If letter/sound identification is a major concern, then the letters and corresponding illustrations should be easily identifiable. In addition, the pictured objects should not have more than one commonly used name or include pictures that are difficult for children to identify. For example, young children often call a rabbit a bunny. Consequently, rabbit might not be the best choice for illustrating the letter *r* in an alphabet book for very young children. If young children use the book independently, the pages should not be cluttered with numerous objects that could confuse letter/sound identification.

Alphabet books may, however, be used with adult guidance or with older children to develop observational and discussion skills. In this case, a page rich with detail and numerous objects may be preferred to the simple presentation of one letter and one object found in the books designed for younger children. Evaluating any alphabet book depends on the age of the children and the desired objective. Some alphabet books provide historical insights, some are appropriate for young children, and some contain enough rich detail to interest even the older child.

Early Editions of Alphabet Books

Like Mother Goose rhymes, alphabet books were among the early books published for children. Some of them have been reissued or new books reminiscent of earlier texts have been published. One very early rhyme using an ABC format was *A–Apple Pie* which tells the tale of an apple pie as "B bit it" and "C cut it" until the end of the alphabet and pie are finally

reached. Greenaway illustrated the rhyme in 1886, and her original woodblock designs have been used in a reissue of this charming text.

Ruth Baldwin's *One Hundred Nineteenth-Century Rhyming Alphabets in English* contains a version of "History of an Apple Pie" as well as other early alphabets (1). The 296 pages of the large text are filled with colorful reproductions depicting the original pictures and verses. Each rhyme is identified according to title, illustrator, publisher, and date of publication.

A recent publication of another early ABC is Alice and Martin Provensen's *A Peaceable Kingdom: The Shaker Abecedarius.* It was first published in the Shaker Manifesto of July 1882 under the title, "Animal Rhymes." According to Richard Barsam (2), it was written for the purpose of teaching reading. While teachers were strict disciplinarians, singing and dancing were part of children's school life. The rhyme and meter of these verses must have appealed to them and helped them learn not only their ABCs but also animal identification. The charming illustrations in the twentieth-century version are reminiscent of an earlier time in American history. Each animal in the verse is illustrated above its name and people are shown in typical Shaker occupations, wearing the dress of these earlier times. These alphabet books suggest a link with the past; today's children discover settings from the past and share an experience that children living in an earlier time also enjoyed.

Animal Themes in ABCs

The animal themes popular in the Shaker ABC are still very popular in current ABCs. These animal alphabet books range

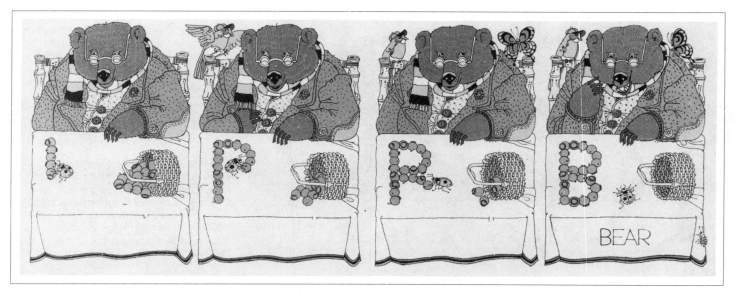

More detailed illustrations show several animals and objects beginnning with each letter.
From *Ed Emberley's ABC* by Ed Emberley. Copyright © 1978 By Edward R. Emberley. By
permission of Little, Brown, and Company.

in complexity: some show one letter and a single animal for each entry; some have a single letter, a single animal, and a rhyming phrase; some have very descriptive phrases with each letter; and some develop an integrated story in alphabetical order.

Ed Emberley's ABC is a more complex book that would be appropriate for a slightly older child. This publication not only shows the letter, but also demonstrates, in a series of four pictures, how each letter is formed. The illustration from the *B* page of the text shows why these humorous drawings appeal to children. It is also clear that the double page contains considerable information. Bear, bird, butterfly, basket, and blueberries all begin with the letter *B*. This book is worthwhile to share with children as they learn to print letters and can motivate them to develop their own alphabet books.

Two very colorful, large-format alphabet books use a series of descriptive words or verses to accompany the letters and illustrations. Each illustration of two animals in Leonard Baskin's *Hosie's Alphabet* covers a full page with lovely watercolors. The accompanying words are to be listened to, rather than read by, the younger child. For example, an iguana that illustrates the letter *I* is "an incredible scaly iguana," while a spider on the *S* page is "a gangling entangling spider." The bold, bright illustrations in *Celestino Piatti's Animal ABC* almost jump off the page! Bears, elephants, giraffes, lions, and tigers

are all outlined in vivid black, and appropriate bright oranges, browns, and greens add to the illustrations. Each letter and illustration is accompanied by a verse.

Alphabetical order is used in several books in order to develop a story line. An older alphabet book that is still popular with young children tells the adventures of a bunny in alphabetical sequence. In Wanda Gág's *The ABC Bunny* children can follow the adventures of the bunny as an apple falling wakes him up from his snug bed. On his journey he meets the appropriate animals such as a frog, a jay, and a lizard. He also experiences a gale and is hit by hail before he finally reaches the safety of his hole again. Large black and white illustrations appeal to children. The only color on the page is the letter drawn in red. A more complex story is developed in Roger Duvoisin's alphabet tale, *A for the Ark*.

Other ABC Books

Anno's Alphabet: An Adventure in Imagination is a beautifully illustrated book by Mitsumasa Anno. The title is an excellent introduction to what is in store for observant readers. A first glance indicates a simple, attractively illustrated ABC Book using large wood cutouts for each letter and large simple objects that show the beginning sound of each letter. While the book can be used at this level, a large part of the fun and imaginative experience will be lost if readers are not observant. Anno has cleverly entangled numerous objects that begin with each sound into the black and white border circling each page. For example, the *B* pages are entwined with bean stalks and include buttons, bees, bells, birds, and beans hidden behind the leaves. A similar search through the *P* pages reveals poppies, peas, pumpkins, and parrots. Children enjoy discovering these picture puzzles and searching for the hidden objects. Another alphabet book by Anno that captures children's imaginations is *Anno's Magical ABC: An Anamorphic Alphabet.* The book contains distorted pictures which viewers must see reflected in a shiny cylindrical object if they are to focus and identify the picture. Animals and other objects accompany upper- and lowercase letters.

A buying excursion down a market street of an earlier time provides an enjoyable trip through the alphabet in Arnold and Anita Lobel's *On Market Street.* The child buys gifts from the shopkeepers who are covered with objects from their respective wares: apples, books, clocks, doughnuts . . . through zippers. The colorful illustrations are also good for concept development as children see and discuss the various objects categorized in each group.

Terry Berger and Alice Kandell use familiar activities to develop the alphabet in *Ben's ABC Day.* Children can identify the actions in color photographs as Ben awakens, brushes his teeth, combs his hair, dresses and performs additional activities that complete the alphabet. Each letter is displayed in large uppercase print; the activity words are printed in lowercase. This book stimulates discussion as children identify activities that they also perform.

Several alphabet books are designed to provide information to older students rather than teach letter/sound relationships to younger ones. Two award-winning books present information about African life. *Ashanti to Zulu: African Traditions,* by Margaret Musgrove, depicts important customs from each of the twenty-six African peoples. A map of Africa at the end of the book shows each tribe's location. The illustrations by Leo and Diane Dillon are vividly portrayed in pastels, watercolors, and acrylics. Each page is surrounded by a gold and black frame; the interwoven corners of the framework symbolize endless searching. *Jambo Means Hello: Swahili Alphabet Book* introduces Swahili words and customs. The author, Muriel Feelings, expresses the hope that the book will stimulate children of African ancestry to learn more about their heritage. These beautiful books could encourage children of all cultural backgrounds to learn more about African people. Rural American activities are depicted in Mary Azarian's *A Farmer's Alphabet.* The text, originally designed as a set of posters, uses black and white woodcuts.

These examples of alphabet books show that one can be found for almost every purpose and age, but each needs to be selected and evaluated carefully.

COUNTING BOOKS

Counting books, like alphabet books, are frequently shared with children for specific learning experiences. If their purpose is to develop young children's concepts of one-to-one correspondence and to develop the ability to count sequentially from one through ten, then counting books must have several characteristics. First, the numbers and corresponding objects must be easily identifiable. Effective number books for

toys,

Detailed illustrations may enhance discussion and concept development.
From *On Market Street* by Arnold Lobel. Copyright © 1981 by Anita Lobel. By permission of Greenwillow Books (A Division of William Morrow & Co.).

younger children frequently show one large number, the corresponding number word, and one large object or the appropriate number of the same object. Books that stimulate manipulation of concrete objects are especially good. For example, a counting book showing the number two and two blocks might encourage a child to count two real blocks. Likewise, one that shows a photograph of ten clearly identifiable buttons might stimulate the child to count out ten real buttons. Second, the numbers and corresponding objects should be clearly separated so that children are not confused and distracted by an abundance of detail. For young children, it is preferable that a page contain one number and the corresponding number of objects. If, for example, a child looks at the number one and then sees five different objects, his concept of one may be quite confused. In addition, the actual number represented by an object should be easily identifiable.

One star showing five points may be a poor choice for depicting the number five as the child may not understand that five, not one, is being depicted. If counting and developing number concepts are the primary reasons for choosing the book, the pictures must clearly illustrate this information.

There are also counting books for older children. They may develop the concept of sets of numbers or of addition or subtraction, or may encourage children to search for many groups of the same number on a single page. The range of difficulty is quite wide; therefore, children's abilities must be considered when selecting a counting or number concept book.

One very simple counting book for younger children, Eric Carle's *My Very First Book of Numbers,* is a small manipulative book that uses a divided page format. Children are to match the squares on the top portion of the book with the corre-

A counting book for older children develops groupings and a number mystery.
From Russell Hoban, *Ten What? A Mystery Counting Book.* Text copyright © 1974 by Russell Hoban; illustrations copyright © 1974 by Sylvie Selig (New York: Charles Scribner's Sons, 1974). Reprinted with permission of Charles Scribner's Sons.

6 **sita**
(see·tah)

The clothing East Africans wear includes the kanga, busuti, lapa, kanzu, and dashiki.

East African culture is depicted in this unusual counting book.
Excerpted from the book *Moja Means One* by Muriel Feelings, Illustrated by Tom Feelings.
Illustrations Copyright © 1971 by Tom Feelings. Used by permission of The Dial Press.

sponding pictures on the bottom portion. There are no words in this text; even a young child could match pictures that show equal amounts.

Several counting books for young children use photographs to develop number concepts. Dick Rowan's *Everybody In! A Counting Book* shows ten black and white photographs of children playing in a swimming pool. The concepts of numbers from one through ten are easily seen even by young children, because the number and word are printed on one side, and a full-page photograph of the appropriate number of children is pictured on the other side of the double-page spread.

Numbers from one through ten as well as concepts of addition and subtraction are developed in Mitsumasa Anno's *Anno's Counting House.* On alternating double pages the illustrator shows the interiors and exteriors of two houses. In the old house ten people are preparing to move. Then there are only nine people in the old house and one in the new house. The process continues until the new house is furnished. Then children may go backwards in the text and discover what happens to the people.

Count and See, by Tana Hoban, is a simple counting book with easy-to-identify number concepts that also extend to sets and higher numbers. The numbers, their corresponding written words, and a circle or circles illustrating the number are presented in white on a black background. On the opposite page, a photograph illustrates the number. The photographs include familiar items found in many children's environments: one fire hydrant, two children, . . . twenty watermelon seeds, . . . forty peanuts shown in groups of ten, . . . and one hundred peas shown in pods of ten each. The book could also be used for counting and grouping concrete items or making counting books that use the items shown in the pictures. (Counting and grouping objects help cognitive development.)

A more complex counting book designed for older children is Russell Hoban's *Ten What? A Mystery Counting Book.* A mystery is added to the number concepts as two bird secret agents receive an urgent message to get ten of something. Their search takes them through a landscape with just the right numbers of animals, objects, and people to illustrate each successive number from one through ten. There are several groupings of each number on a single page. For example, the ten page shows ten oriental acrobats, ten pastry cooks, ten beehives, and so on. While this book depicts numbers up through ten, it is considerably more difficult to identify and differentiate the objects than in Carle's, Rowan's, or Tana Hoban's counting books.

Hilary Knight's *The Twelve Days of Christmas* may also be used as a counting book. The humorous illustrations show the gifts given on each of the twelve days. Older children can count the accumulated objects on the final two-page spread. Are there twelve lords a-leaping, twenty two ladies dancing, thirty fiddlers fiddling . . . and twelve partridges in pear trees?

The African landscape is used to camouflage animals in Pat Hutchins's *I Hunter*. This book for younger children encourages interaction with the text as children follow the progress of a safari hunter; the animals remain camouflaged until the hunter leaves. Then children can discover and count the easily seen animals. Lines and colors develop illustrations that encourage children to search for the hidden animals, then discover if they were correct.

One of the most unusual counting books is designed not only to teach the number concepts from one through ten but also to inform American children about some basic aspects of East African life. Muriel Feelings's text, accompanied by Tom

Feelings's illustrations, presents the Swahili numbers in *Moja Means One, Swahili Counting Book*. The introduction presents a map of Africa showing where Swahili is spoken; it also provides additional information about the African people and the author. Each double-page spread shows the numeral, the Swahili word for the number, a sentence providing information about the illustration, and soft brown and white paintings depicting animal or village life. This book may be more appropriate for stimulating interest in an African culture or providing information for older children than it is for presenting number concepts to younger children.

The counting books discussed here range from simple one-to-one correspondence for younger children to more complex books that stress the concept of sets. Manipulative experiences, encouraged by counting books, can stimulate children's cognitive development.

CONCEPT BOOKS

Many of the books suggested in chapter one for stimulating young children's cognitive development are also concept

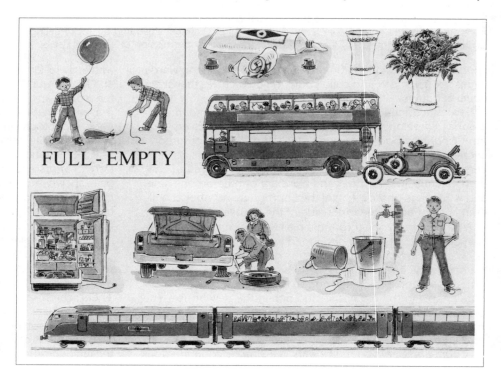

Several detailed illustrations show what is meant by full and empty.
Illustrations from *Fast-Slow, High-Low* by Peter Spier. Copyright © 1972 by Peter Spier. Reprinted by permission of Doubleday & Company, Inc.

books. Some concepts such as red, yellow, and green or triangle, square, circle, and rectangle are easily shown in concrete form or in picture book format. Other concepts, however, are much more difficult for children to understand. How can terms such as *over-under, in-out, on-off, big-biggest,* and *ten o'clock* be pictured or described. All these terms are used with young children who may not understand what they mean. Concept books ask children to put a mark under the picture, to select a red color crayon, to find the triangle in a picture, to identify the biggest tree, or to find the smallest bear. They are designed to help children understand the meaning of these difficult words. Like number books, concept books can be found at various levels of difficulty: both children's understanding and the book's level of abstraction should be considered in selecting appropriate books.

Large, clearly identifiable, black and white photographs illustrate the concept of *opposite* in Tana Hoban's *Push-Pull, Empty-Full: A Book of Opposites.* Even young children can see the meaning in a group of antonyms pictured in this text. Large photographs and their related words are shown in nearly full-page size. *Empty* is illustrated by showing a photograph of an empty produce basket; the basket is filled with mushrooms to depict *full.* Other examples of photographs and their corresponding concepts include a boy *pushing* and a girl *pulling* a wagon, a puddle for *wet* and leaves on the street for *dry,* a turtle *in* and *out* of his shell.

Unlike Hoban's book, Spier's *Fast-Slow, High-Low: A Book of Opposites* shows numerous colorful drawings depicting *opposite* and is more detailed and complex. Hoban depicts *full* and *empty* in one large photograph showing the object first full, then empty; Spier's two full-empty pages show drawings such as *full* and *empty* balloons, toothpaste tubes, flower vases, busses, refrigerators, tires, and pails. There is considerably more to observe and discuss in Spier's book, and the illustrations of the concepts are better for older children.

Tana Hoban's *Circles, Triangles and Squares* can stimulate oral discussion and observation. Common shapes are presented in black and white photographs. Circles are illustrated by a girl blowing various sized bubbles; a boy wearing glasses, holding a lollipop, and wearing beads and round buttons; a pile of round pipes; a girl rolling a hoop; bicycle and automobile tires; roller skates; and cookies. Triangles and squares are illustrated in a similar way. Each picture provides many opportunities for shape identification and discussion that can allow children to observe and identify shapes in their own environments.

Several concepts are developed in Donald Crews's *Freight Train.* Large, colorful illustrations take children into the world of trains and color. The names of eight colors and the identification of the various freight cars are seen as drawings show a yellow hopper car, a red caboose, and a blue gondola car. The train starts, and the blurred illustration gives the reader a feeling of motion as it proceeds through tunnels, by cities, and across trestles. The concepts of *darkness* and *daylight* are shown when the train goes from a dark page into the light. Young children are naturally fascinated by trains and enjoy the feeling of strength, movement, and sound developed in this book. Another concept book illustrated by Crews is Robert Kalan's *Blue Sea.* This simply illustrated book pictures various-sized fish to show the concepts of *little, big, bigger,* and *biggest.* The blue background on each page resembles the ocean. In *Harbor,* Crews takes children on an exploratory visit to a harbor where they can discover tugboats, freighters, and barges going in and out. Concepts and vocabulary that may be developed on a carousel ride are illustrated in *Carousel.*

Concepts related to shape are developed through real-life photographs.
Reprinted with permission of Macmillan Publishing Co., Inc. from *Circles, Triangles, and Squares* by Tana Hoban. Copyright © 1974 by Tana Hoban.

Photographs illustrate spatial concepts in Tana Hoban's *Over, Under, and Through.* The large black and white photographs show children stepping *over* puddles, crawling *through* large pipes, jumping *over* fire hydrants, and walking *under* outstretched arms. A humorously illustrated small book that develops spatial concepts is Linda Banchek's *Snake In, Snake Out.* Is there a more enticing way to teach the concepts of *on, in, out, up, over, off, down,* and *under,* than to have a friendly snake crawl out of a box and proceed to be chased *over, in, out,* and so forth, as an old lady tries to remove him from the house? The book also has a happy ending when the two become friends, and he curls up near the lady who happily rocks in her chair.

The size concepts of *big* and *little* are presented in delightful photographs of zoo animals in Tana Hoban's *Big Ones, Little Ones.* Each photograph illustrates differences in size by picturing a mother animal and her baby. This book is also excellent for identifying animals and stimulating discussion about zoo animals or going to a zoo. The photographs include a bear, hippo, sheep, baboon, zebra, elephant, and other animals.

Several concept books can help develop color concepts. A simple book for the young child is Eric Carle's *My Very First Book of Colors.* This is a manipulation book that allows a child to match a block of color with a picture of an object illustrated in that color. There are no words; the child can either match the colors or identify or describe the objects if the book is shared with an adult. A larger storybook that may also be used for color identification is Carle's *The Mixed-up Chameleon.* The chameleon in the story is confused when he sees so many beautifully colored animals. Consequently, each time he sees one, a part of him turns the color of the other animal. This book has a happy ending when the chameleon discovers that his own color and shape are the best.

Tana Hoban's *Take Another Look* encourages interaction with the text and careful observation. A circular cutout over each photograph requires children to look carefully, guess

ISSUE

Are Picture Books Controversial?

SEVERAL OF THE BOOKS discussed in this chapter have stirred controversy and were subsequently removed from library shelves. Other books have had illustrations altered to meet specific standards. When Maurice Sendak's *In the Night Kitchen* was published in 1970, the nudity of the child was criticized. Several incidents occurred in which the nudity was covered with a drawn-on wash-cloth or the book was removed from the shelf. Garth Williams's *The Rabbit's Wedding* was criticized in the 1960s because the illustrations showed the marriage of a black and a white rabbit. In 1969 *Sylvester and the Magic Pebble* was criticized for two reasons: some parents objected to police officers being portrayed as pigs; others objected to the portrayal of the mother doing housework while Sylvester and his father relaxed. *Changes, Changes,* by Pat Hutchins, was criticized in the 1970s because the man has a more active role; he drives and decides what to make from the blocks, while the woman pulls the train whistle and hands him the blocks. An earlier book not discussed in this chapter illustrates changing sensitivity. Helen Bannerman's *Little Black Sambo* (1899) was popular for many years until the crudely drawn features of the characters and the story line were considered offensive and resulted in the book being taken off many library shelves.

As you evaluate picture books consider which books might be controversial and the reasons for the controversy. Do controversial picture books change with the times? What subjects might have caused controversy in picture books published in the 1950s, 1960s, or 1970s? Are those subjects still controversial in the 1980s? Are there any new areas of controversy developing today?

what they are viewing, and then turn the page to see if their observations were right. A daisy center provides the first question. Oral language development may be stimulated as children tell why they think the circle is a certain object. They also discover that their eyes may fool them.

WORDLESS PICTURE BOOKS

A new type of picture book uses a different format in which the illustrations tell the whole story without the addition of words. Because these books have no words, they are excellent for promoting both oral and written language development; children enjoy the opportunity to become authors and provide the missing text. These experiences are valuable for stimulating creative thinking, language development, and cognitive development. Dorothy Strickland (7) says "experiences with books that are thoughtfully planned to promote active verbal exchanges of ideas will have lasting positive effects upon both the communicative mode and the cognitive structure of the child" (p. 53). Wordless books that invite individual interpretations are especially good for stimulating cognitive and language development. In addition, visual literacy abilities are enhanced as children watch the pages for clues to the action. Wordless books are especially valuable because they allow children of different backgrounds to enjoy the same book. The second part of this chapter suggests several ways of using wordless books to develop discussion skills, oral interpretation, and creative writing.

Although they have no text, various levels of detail and plot complexity are found in wordless books. Some develop easily identifiable plots, some have considerable details, and others can have many interpretations. Consequently, wordless books are suitable for a wide range of age and interest levels. In addition, some of them are large, making them appropriate for sharing with a group, while others are small and lend themselves to individual interpretation, or lap "reading." All of these characteristics should be considered when choosing wordless books for children. Pat Hutchins's *Changes, Changes* is a simple wordless book that appeals to children in preschool and kindergarten who enjoy building with blocks. Helen Sewell's illustrations show two wooden dolls as they choose blocks, build a house, cope with a fire by turning the house into a fire truck, solve the problem of too much water by building a boat, reach land by constructing a truck, change the truck into a train, and eventually rebuild their home. The pictures are large and colorful and the actions easily identifiable; the book is therefore appropriate for stimulating oral language. It is also excellent for stimulating manipulation and problem solving (see p. 9 of color insert).

Martha Alexander's small wordless book *Out! Out! Out!* appeals to preschool children. The plot of the story is easily followed, the home setting is familiar, the episodes are humorous, there is enough detail for discussion, and best of all a small child solves a problem that has eluded several adults. Another familiar setting is found in Jan Ormerod's *Sunshine*. The child in the wordless book not only wakes up her parents but she also helps them prepare for their day. The action-filled, color illustrations can stimulate oral discussions, creative dramatics, and writing.

Realistic humor is a popular theme of wordless books for young children. A series of wordless books by Mercer Mayer tell the humorous adventures of a boy, a dog, and a frog. In the first book, *A Boy, a Dog, and a Frog,* the boy tries to catch the frog with a fishnet, trips, and lands in the water with the pail on his head. Both the boy and the dog try to catch the frog, but only the dog is caught. As they head home dejectedly, the frog decides to follow and joins them for a rollicking good time in the bathtub. Additional adventures occur in *Frog, Where Are You?* and *A Boy, a Dog, a Frog, and a Friend.* The next book, *Frog Goes to Dinner,* illustrates the humorous disruptions that can occur if a frog hides in a boy's pocket and accompanies the family to a very fancy restaurant. The pictures show the frog jumping into a saxophone, diving into a lettuce salad, swimming in champagne, and finally causing the family to be asked to leave. (This is the most detailed of the series, and children frequently think it is the funniest.) Each book is small, just the right size for individual enjoyment or for sharing with an adult. The illustrations are expressive and contain sufficient detail to stimulate language development and enjoyment.

Several wordless books develop plots describing the antics of animals from the world of fantasy. Paula Winter's *Sir Andrew* revolves around a donkey who is so busy admiring himself that he has an accident and causes accidents to others. Children enjoy the final consequence as he approaches an unseen banana peel. Tomie de Paola's *The Hunter and the Animals: A Wordless Picture Book* follows a hunter as he enters the forest and frightens the animals into hiding. (Children can look for the hidden animals in the illustrations.) When he falls asleep the animals emerge, take his belongings, and change the environment. There is an anti-hunting message in this book as the animals help the confused hunter after he awakes; as a gesture of understanding, he breaks his gun. John S. Goodall's *Paddy Goes Traveling* follows the humorous antics of Paddy Pork as he goes to the beach. There is enough plot development in

A wordless book for older children provides sufficient details for numerous viewings.
From *Anno's Italy* by Mitsumasa Anno. Copyright © 1980 by Philomel Books, a division of the Putnam Publishing Group. Reprinted by permission of the publisher.

these illustrations to stimulate the creation of narrative even by older children.

Some wordless books are exceptional because of their detail. John S. Goodall's *The Story of an English Village* illustrates the changes that occur in a village over several centuries. It is detailed enough to appeal to older children who can make comparisons between the time periods shown in the illustrations. Spier's *Noah's Ark* is another excellent example of a detailed wordless picture book. (Jacob Revius's poem, "The Flood," was translated from the Dutch by Spier.) The only words occur at the beginning of the book. The pictures tell the story of the building of the ark, the boarding of all of the animals, the long wait, and the starting of life again as the land is plowed and cultivated. These pictures contain so much detail

that something new may be discovered each time a child reads the book.

Anno's Journey, by Mitsumasa Anno, is also appropriate for oral discussion and storytelling by older children. The drawings are the result of the artist's travels through Europe. The journey begins when a figure alights from a rowboat and starts to follow a path. This path continues through each illustration, tracing the journey through the countryside, past busy farms and churches, and through villages and larger towns. Anno adds to the enjoyment by suggesting that the reader look for certain details in the pictures such as details in paintings and characters from children's literature. The pictures are detailed enough to keep even older children or adults occupied. Another wordless book by Anno takes the viewer on a journey through Italy. In *Anno's Italy*, a path again wanders through the countryside, past farms, and through villages. This time the illustrator shows figures from well-known stories, paintings, sculptures, and landmarks. *Anno's Britain* follows the same format. Detailed drawings allow children to identify St. Paul's Cathedral, Big Ben, The Tower of London, and Stonehenge. Historical and literary characters such as Shakespeare, Isaac Newton, Winnie-the-Pooh and Alice in Wonderland are found in the illustrations.

Many wordless books are ideal for promoting oral language development. Others, however, are so obscure in story line that children may be frustrated when asked to tell the story. When choosing wordless books, the adult should consider the following questions:

1 Is there a sequentially organized plot that provides a framework for children who are just developing their own organizational skills?
2 Is the depth of detail appropriate for the children's age level? (Too much detail will overwhelm younger children, while not enough detail may bore older ones.)
3 Do the children have enough experiential background to understand and interpret the illustrations? Can they interpret the book during individual reading or would adult interaction be necessary?
4 Is the size of the book appropriate for the purpose? (Larger books are necessary for group sharing.)
5 Is the subject one that will appeal to the children?

The varied levels of complexity found in wordless books indicate that appropriate selections can be found for young children and more advanced students. This same complexity, however, means that selection of materials will need careful consideration.

EASY-TO-READ BOOKS

Another specialized picture book is the easy-to-read book, designed to be read by children with beginning reading skills. Like picture storybooks, these books contain many pictures designed to suggest the story line; unlike picture storybooks, however, the authors must use a controlled vocabulary that the young reader can manage independently. The process of controlling the vocabulary to fit the needs of beginning readers may result in contrived language; it is quite difficult to write stories that sound natural if all of the words must be selected from the easiest level of readability.

The difference between easy-to-read books and other picture storybooks may be more readily illustrated by comparing the readability levels of two books designed for first-grade children; one is an easy-to-read book, while the other is a picture

Humorous illustrations enhance an unexpected experience in a favorite easy-to-read book.
From *The Cat in The Hat,* by Dr. Seuss. Copyright © 1957 by Dr. Seuss. Reprinted by permission of Random House, Inc.

storybook. There are several readability formulas that may be used by authors, teachers, and librarians in determining the approximate level of reading skill required to read a selection. The Fry Readability Formula (3), for example, measures the level by averaging the number of sentences and the number of syllables per 100 words. These averages are plotted on a graph that identifies the corresponding grade level for the book. (This technique is explained in Appendix E.) It is assumed that easier books have short sentences and more monosyllabic words. As the readability level increases, the sentences become longer and more multisyllable words are used.

If we compare the readability levels of an easy-to-read book and a picture storybook designed to meet the interest levels of first graders, we can understand the uniqueness of these books. A 100-word selection analyzed from a popular easy-to-read book, Dr. Seuss's (Theodor Geisel) *The Cat in the Hat,* showed sixteen sentences and 100 syllables for those 100 words. The sentences were very short and all words were one syllable. Plotting these two findings on Fry's graph indicates a first-grade readability level. In contrast, another book also written for first-grade interests by Dr. Seuss, *And to Think That I Saw It on Mulberry Street,* has seven and one-half sentences and 126 syllables in a 100-word selection. The resulting readability level of this book is fifth grade. While both appeal to children of about the same age, there is considerable difference between the ability needed to read them. Consequently, the first book is usually read by children; the second is usually selected to be read aloud by an adult.

Even though easy-to-read books may not meet all standards for literary quality, they do meet the needs of beginning readers. Because children need independent experiences with books that allow them to reinforce their reading skills and to develop pride in their accomplishments, easy-to-read books should be included in every book collection for primary-age children. In addition, easy-to-read books provide materials for students who need successful experiences in remedial reading classes. Because of their controlled use of language and sentence structure, they should seldom be used for read-aloud literary experiences.

Animal antics appeal to young elementary children, and many favorite easy-to-read books have animals as the main characters. One of the most whimsical and beloved animals is the cat in Dr. Seuss's *The Cat in the Hat.* This cat amazes and entertains two children when he balances a fish bowl, milk, and a cake simultaneously. Thing One and Thing Two add to the destruction when they fly kites in the house. The cat, however, saves the situation when he brings in a multiarmed machine that picks up the mess before Mother returns. Seuss's humor-

Soft woodland colors and animals with human characteristics combine in a memorable easy-to-read book.
Illustration from *Grasshopper on the Road,* written and illustrated by Arnold Lobel. Copyright © 1978 by Arnold Lobel. By permission of Harper & Row, Publishers, Inc.

ous illustrations and rhyming dialogue appeal to children. The cat emphasizes this enjoyment as he encourages the children:

> Look at me!
> Look at me!
> Look at me Now!
> It is fun to have fun
> But you have to know how. (p. 8)

Several enchanting easy-to-read books have been written and illustrated by Arnold Lobel. The soft brown and green illustrations in the various Frog and Toad stories create a feeling of a woodland setting and show the friendship felt by these two characters. In the first book, *Frog and Toad Are Friends,* read-

ers are introduced to the two friends as Frog tries to entice Toad out of his home in order to enjoy the new spring season. Children enjoy Toad's reactions when Frog knocks on the door:

> "Toad, Toad," shouted Frog,
> "wake up. It is spring!"
> "Blah," said a voice
> from inside the house.

Frog, however, convinces Toad that it really is spring and he should get up. The book contains five adventure stories as these two friends explore spring, try to cheer each other up, search for a lost button, go swimming, and wait for the mail. Their adventures continue in *Frog and Toad Together* and *Frog and Toad All Year.*

Illustrations in soft woodland colors and a grasshopper who decides to follow a winding country lane just to discover where it leads provide an appealing combination in Lobel's *Grasshopper on the Road.* Lobel develops more characterization than is found in many easy-to-read books by having the grasshopper encounter other rural inhabitants and then try to change each behavior pattern. Lobel offers a satisfying conclusion when Grasshopper decides that he is the one who has a very interesting life.

Helen V. Griffith develops a memorable animal character who may be experiencing feelings similar to those of her youthful readers. When the dog in *Alex and the Cat* is dissatisfied with himself he attempts to be a cat, a wolf, and a rescuer of baby birds. After his adventures he concludes that he is better off being himself, a house pet.

Other animals in easy-to-read books that appeal to children include Syd Hoff's *Chester* and *Sammy the Seal,* Bernard Wiseman's *Morris Goes to School* and *Morris Has a Cold,* and Arnold Lobel's *Uncle Elephant.*

Easy-to-read books are also designed to appeal to children's special interests—in mysteries, sports, science, history, or magic, for example. For children who enjoy simple mysteries, Crosby Bonsall's gang of boy private eyes solves several mysteries. In *The Case of the Cat's Meow,* they solve the case of the missing cat. A sequel to the book, *The Case of the Scaredy Cats,* tells what happens when girls invade the boys' private-eye clubhouse. The boys' plans to scare them away do not materialize, and the girls prove that they are just as good as boys. Easy-to-read books meet the needs of children who are excited by the opportunity to read a book independently. Many of them also enjoy reading these books aloud to an appreciative parent.

PICTURE STORYBOOKS—A SHARED EXPERIENCE

A common characteristic of many picture books discussed thus far is considerable reliance on illustrations with only a brief narrative. All or most of the contents are presented through illustrations. This reliance on pictures is especially crucial in concept books, counting books, a majority of the alphabet books, and all of the wordless picture books. Many of these books do not have a continuous story line; instead, the illustrations are grouped according to a common theme or are in a specific order because of numerical or alphabetical sequence.

All picture books, however, do not have the above characteristics. Picture storybooks contain many illustrations, but they also develop a definite story line. In a well-written picture storybook, the illustrations and narrative complement each other; children cannot deduce the whole story line merely by viewing the pictures.

When adults think about the enjoyable book experiences shared between adults and children during story hour or at bedtime, it is usually the picture storybook that is remembered. Childhood would not be as exciting without such friends as Mike Mulligan, Ferdinand, or Babar. What is it that makes these books memorable and creates an enjoyable experience for both children and adults? The answer to this question will be approached by discussing the elements of imagination, plot, characterization, humor, and style that contribute to outstanding picture storybooks and then by sharing some books that illustrate this unique combination between writer and artist.

Elements in Picture Storybooks

Originality and Imagination. The clever cat actually saves his friends the church mice from an invasion of rats, a boy gets his wishes from a charge card company whose machine goes mad, and a boy's bedroom becomes the kingdom for all the wild things. Where else but in the world of picture books can children find such original ideas and imagination?

As an example of originality, Sampson, the church cat in Graham Oakley's *The Church Mice Adrift,* does not behave in the usual manner. When rats invade the church, Sampson actually develops a plan to outwit them and save the mice from their enemies. In another original tale, *The Wish Card Ran Out,* James Stevenson gives his hero wishes by creating a spoof on credit cards. When Charlie does not get a baseball glove for his birthday, he is unhappy until he finds a lost International Wish card issued by a big corporation that took over from wishing wells and fairy godmothers. Charlie, however, discovers that the wish card does not give him the results he wants. Consequently, he travels to Wish Center where the cleaning woman, a former fairy godmother, helps him out of his dilemma. The cartoon illustrations, witty lines, and turnabout on credit cards create a humorous, imaginative tale.

A child's imagination structures the delightful story in Maurice Sendak's *Where the Wild Things Are.* Only in picture book fantasy can a young child who is being disciplined turn his room into a forest, then extend it into the whole world, and finally sail away for weeks until he reaches the kingdom where all the wild things live. Only in picture book fantasy can that same boy rule over all of the wild things and still return to his own room before his supper gets cold. Picture storybooks and their accompanying illustrations are filled with imaginative episodes such as the ones described. They provide many hours of enjoyment during story hours and are excellent for stimulating children's imagination during creative play, storytelling, and creative writing.

Plot. The characteristics of both the shorter picture storybooks and the children who read or hear the stories place special demands on plot development. Because many of these books are designed to be shared with, or read by, young children who have short attention spans, the plots are usually simple, clearly developed, and quite brief. The shorter story formats lack the space either to develop subplots or to describe several characters. Consequently, they usually allow children to become involved with the action, identify the problem, and solve it rapidly. For example, in the first three pages of *Where the Wild Things Are,* children know that Max has got into so much trouble that he has been sent to bed without supper. Even though the thirty-seven words used thus far do not reveal what Max has done, the pictures explain his problems. Children can see him standing on books, using a large nail to attach a homemade clothesline to the wall, and chasing the dog with a fork. The plot is swiftly paced, and children rapidly join Max in his imaginary world as the room becomes wilder and wilder. Additional conflict is introduced when Max encounters the wild things, and children feel the excitement as he confronts these monsters and overcomes them with a magic trick. There is sympathy for Max after he has played long enough and sends his new subjects off to bed without their suppers; at this point, he wants someone to love him. This problem of unrequited love is resolved rapidly, and Max returns to his own room and his own supper. The author uses only thirty-eight words to tell what happens between the time he leaves the wild things and returns home. This book is an excellent example of the important relationship between illustrations and plot development; the illustrations become larger and larger as the drama increases and then become smaller again as Max returns to his world.

In addition to overcoming imaginary conflicts in fantasies, plots in picture storybooks frequently deal with children who overcome realistic family or personal problems. Lucille Clifton's *Amifika* lives in a small apartment with his mother. Amifika's conflict begins when he hears his mother tell cousin Katy that his father is coming home from the army. Instead of being happy, Amifika is frightened; his mother confides that because of the tiny apartment she will have to get rid of something his father does not remember. Because Amifika cannot remember his father, he is convinced that he will be eliminated. The plot and tension develop as the reader follows and sympathizes with Amifika's attempts to hide from his mother and recall his father. The conflict is quickly and pleasantly resolved

when Amifika feels warm arms around him. Not only is he found by his father but he also remembers him:

And all of a sudden the dark warm plce came together in Amifika's mind and he jumped in the man's arms and squeezed his arms around the man's neck just like his arms remembered something. "You my own Daddy! My Daddy!" he hollered at the top of his voice and kept hollering as his Daddy held him and danced and danced all around the room. (pp. 24–25)

Another characteristic of plots in storybooks for young children is this happy and emotionally satisfying ending. Whether they are fantasy or realistic fiction, the stories have a rapid introduction to the action, a fast pace, and a strong, satisfying climax.

Characterization. The characters found in picture storybooks must also have specific traits that make them appeal to younger children and meet the demands of the shorter picture story format. These characters must be presented so that they

The need for love between adult and child characters is suggested in the illustrations. Illustrations by Clement Hurd from *The Runaway Bunny* by Margaret Wise Brown. Copyright 1942 by Harper & Row, Publishers, Inc. Illustrations renewed © 1970 by Clement C. Hurd. By permission of Harper & Row, Publishers, Inc.

are credible, even though the shorter story does not allow for the fully developed characters preferred in literature for older children and adults. One way that picture books develop characterization is through illustrations. Maurice Sendak, for example, did not need to describe Max, the wild things, or the rumpus that takes place between them. His illustrations show these effectively. The expressions and actions show how Max reacts to his mother's punishment, how he reacts during his first encounter with the wild things, how they react to him, how he subdues them, how he feels when he is lonely, and how he must return to receive his mother's love. Through these illustrations, the reader has an excellent understanding of the main character; without them, this book would require many more words to develop the characters of Max and his wild things.

Like Max, many main characters in picture storybooks are human; unlike Max, many develop credibility through realistic experiences rather than fantasy. Any child can sympathize with, and understand the reactions of, Judith Viorst's hero in *Alexander and the Terrible, Horrible, No Good, Very Bad Day.*

Wouldn't anyone have a horrible day if, like Alexander, he awoke with gum in his hair, if he didn't get a prize in his cereal when everyone else did, if he received reprimands from the teacher, if his best friend said he wasn't his best friend, if his mother didn't give him dessert, if the dentist found a cavity in his tooth, if the only sneakers available were white, if he was responsible for the mess in his dad's office, if he had to eat lima beans for dinner, and if even the cat ignored him and went to sleep with his brother? If all of these things happened in one day, anyone might decide, like Alexander, to move to Australia. The illustrations in this book complement the text and show Alexander's reactions as well as the reactions of others toward him.

In addition to human characters, storybooks for children also contain many animal main characters who may either act and speak like humans or retain their animal natures. Margaret Brown's *The Runaway Bunny* is a book that reflects the animal's and the child's need for independence and love. A credible little bunny demonstrates characteristics that relate closely to young children's needs. The dialogue between mother rabbit and the baby bunny (they talk like humans) stresses the bunny's desire to experience some freedom by running away. Each time that he suggests ways that he could run away, however, mother rabbit counters with actions she would take to get him back. The love between the two animals is visible in both dialogue and pictures; the bunny decides it would be better to stay with the mother who loves him.

An animal that acts more like an animal is Clare Newberry's delightful kitten *Widget.* The actions and illustrations depict recognizable kitten actions as Widget insists on climbing out of her box, pounces at a slipper, curls up in the slipper, inquisitively approaches a teddy bear, and sneaks out of an open door for the first time. She explores the outside world, sniffs flowers, plays with a bug, tries to catch butterflies, and encounters a puppy. When mother cat hears her spit at the puppy, she comes to the rescue and returns Widget to her box. The illustrations are so reminiscent of a real kitten's actions that children touch the pictures and describe times when their own kittens performed the same way.

Humor. Selecting and sharing books that contribute to children's merriment is a major goal of any literature program. There are elements in many picture storybooks that can cause children to laugh aloud. In order to investigate the sources of humor found in some storybooks, Sue Anne Martin (5) analyzed the sources of humor found in Caldecott Medal books. She concluded that their humor had the following five general sources: (1) word play and nonsense, (2) surprise and the unexpected, (3) exaggeration, (4) the ridiculous and caricature, and (5) superiority. Some examples of humor found in picture storybooks are considered next.

Word Play and Nonsense. Theodor Geisel, better known as Dr. Seuss, is an undisputed authority in the area of word play and nonsense. Seuss's heroes frequently make up totally new words and names to describe and identify the animals found in their imagination. While a zoo normally contains lions and tigers, these animals would not be found in the zoo if Gerald McGrew were the zookeeper. In *If I Ran the Zoo,* there are such nonsensical animals as an elephant-cat, a bird known as a Bustard, a beast called Flustard, and bugs identified as thwerlls and chugs. Of course, no one could find such animals in the usual jungles, so Gerald must search in Motta-fa-Potta-fa-Pell, in the wilds of Nantasket, and on the Desert of Zind. Children not only enjoy the nonsense found in the rhyming text but also respond to the totally imaginative illustrations of these strange animals.

Surprise and the Unexpected. Margot Zemach's *It Could Always Be Worse* is an excellent example of the unexpected found in many picture storybooks. If a man lived in a small one-room hut with his wife and six children, and living conditions became so miserable that he went to the Rabbi for advice, how might the Rabbi respond to the problem? Children are certainly surprised when the Rabbi suggests that the man bring his chickens, a rooster, and a goose into the hut. When conditions do not improve, the Rabbi suggests adding the

ONE OF THE EARLIER Mother Goose rhymes, *The Original Mother Goose's Melody*, was first printed in London by John Newbery in 1760. (The first known English nursery rhyme book for children, *Tommy Thumb's Song Book for all little Masters and Misses*, was published in London in 1744.) It is believed by many that Goldsmith was the collector of the rhymes and prepared them for the press. The copyright for the Mother Goose edition was secured in 1780 by Thomas Carnan, John Newbery's stepson. The rhymes, which contained maxims or morals, were popular in both London and America. Soon after the American Revolution Isaiah Thomas of Worcester, Massachusetts copied many of Newbery's books, including *The Original Mother Goose's Melody*. In the early 1800s the printers Munroe and Francis of Boston published a Mother Goose edition that closely resembled John Newbery's version.

Mother GOOSE's Melody. 37

JACK and *Gill*
　Went up the Hill,
　To fetch a Pail of Water;
Jack fell down
And broke his Crown,
　And *Gill* came tumbling after.

Maxim.

The more you think of dying, the better you will live.

ARISTOTLE's

38 Mother GOOSE's Melody.

ARISTOTLE's STORY.

THERE were two Birds sat on
　a Stone,
　Fa, la, la, la, lal, de;　[one,
One flew away, and then there was
　Fa, la, la, la, lal, de;
The other flew after,
And then there was none,
　Fa, la, la, la, lal, de;
And so the poor Stone
　Was left all alone,
　Fa, la, la, la, lal, de.

This may serve as a Chapter of Consequence in the next new Book of Logick.

goat and the cow to the group. By now, conditions are so difficult that the Rabbi suggests that the animals leave the hut immediately. The poor man now discovers he has plenty of room in the hut—it is even quite peaceful.

Exaggeration. Children's imaginations are often filled with exaggerated tales about what they can or would like to do. In James Stevenson's *Could Be Worse!* it is not the children, but Grandpa, who exaggerates. He always does the same thing and always says the same thing day after day. Whenever any one complains, Grandpa responds with "could be worse." When he overhears his grandchildren commenting on his dull existence, he tells them what happened the previous evening. In one night, he is captured by a large bird and dropped in the snowy mountains. In rapid succession, he encounters the Abominable Snowman, crosses the burning desert, escapes from a giant animal, lands in the ocean, and returns home on a paper airplane. After the grandchildren hear his story, they respond with his favorite expression, "could be worse."

The Ridiculous and Caricature. Is there anything more ridiculous than pondering about what could be worse than sitting on a prickly cactus? A great deal, according to Dr. Seuss's *Did I Ever Tell You How Lucky You Are?* The imaginative, humorous pictures and text let readers know that it would actually be much worse if they worked on the Bunglebung Bridge that crosses Boober Bay, if they had to sit on a wamel when they were riding a camel, or if they were Poogle Horn Players who must go down Poogle Horn Stairs to wake up the Prince of Poo-Boken.

The ridiculous situation in Steven Kellogg's *A Rose For Pinkerton* results when a girl thinks her Great Dane needs a friend and she chooses a kitten. The kitten, however, jumps at the dog and eats his dinner. In contrast, Pinkerton takes on the characteristics of the cat as he tries to sit on his owner's lap. The illustrations complement the absurd situation. While Pinkerton sits on his owner's lap, he is thinking he is small. On the same page the cat thinks of herself as a dog and holds the leash begging for a walk.

Human foolishness provides a ridiculous situation in *The Three Wishes*, a folktale picture book by Paul Galdone. A woodcutter's problems begin when he is offered three wishes by a fairy. An accidental wish for a sausage causes such an argument with his wife that he wishes it were attached to her nose. He ponders the advisability of wishing for a barrel of gold, but finally relents and wishes for the sausage to be removed. Consequently, the only wealth received by the foolish woodcutter and his wife is the long sausage that they share for supper.

Superiority. When the town simpleton beats not only his clever brothers but also the Czar of the land, the result is an unusual tale of humorous superiority. Arthur Ransome's *The Fool of the World and the Flying Ship* is a Russian tale in which the good deeds performed by a simple lad allow him to obtain a flying ship, discover companions who have marvelous powers, overcome obstacles placed in his path by the Czar, win the hand of the Czar's daughter, and live happily ever after. This type of story appeals to young children who frequently feel the need to overcome many problems. The fact that the humble lad is a hero must be very reassuring.

Style. Because there are fewer words in a picture storybook than in a novel, the writer must select those words very carefully. In addition, the picture storybook is more frequently read aloud to children rather than read silently by them. Consequently, its style must add to the oral rendition of the story. A way to evaluate the effectiveness of style is to read the book orally.

One reason that folktales are so popular with children is their tendency to use repetition. Prior to printing, this repetition made the story easier to remember when it was retold. Young children also enjoy repetition because it provides them with an opportunity to join in with the dialogue. Today's writers and illustrators of folktales in picture book format also use repetition. For example, in Verna Aardema's *Why Mosquitoes Buzz in People's Ears*, the author uses the repetition of a cumulative tale. Through repetition, the tale adds a new incident with each telling until the story is complete.

Repetition of the same series of words is also used by authors of modern fiction. In *Alexander and the Terrible, Horrible, No Good, Very Bad Day*, the author repeats the phrase "terrible, horrible, no good, very bad day" seven times. Each description of an unhappy experience concludes with a sentence incorporating those words. This book is excellent for sharing aloud because children quickly understand the story structure and join in with the repeated phrase. (Chapter one recommends books that stimulate oral language development.)

Repeating single words in a sentence is also used to develop stronger oral interpretations. This writing style is found often in African folktales; words are repeated several times to give them stronger meaning. In Gail Haley's *A Story, A Story*, for example, the Sky God describes Ananse, the spider man, as "so small, so small, so small" to convey the idea that he is very, very small. Similar use of repetition conveys the impression of a dancing fairy, rain on a hornet's nest, and securing a man-eating leopard firmly by the feet. This form of repetition is also used to denote a stronger statement in *Why Mosquitoes Buzz in People's Ears*. When a mother owl finds her dead baby, she is "so sad, so sad, so sad." The night that doesn't end is described as "long, long, long."

Younger children enjoy listening to words that create vivid images. In *Where the Wild Things Are*, Sendak vividly creates an image of the wild things who roar terrible roars, gnash terrible teeth, and roll terrible eyes. Children can visualize and recreate the actions during activities designed to encourage their own creative interpretations of the wild things. In addition, sounds of unknown words may be used to suggest meaning and visualize a setting. In the preface to *A Story, A Story*, Haley says that many African words will be found in the book; the listeners are then instructed to listen carefully so they can tell what the sounds of the words mean. Many unknown words are used to describe the animals' movements. A python slithers "wasawusu, wasawusu, wasawusu" down a rabbit hole; a rabbit bounds "krik, krik, krik" across an open space; and sticks go "purup, purup" as they are pulled out of the iguana's ears.

Words are selected to suggest moods in well-written picture storybooks. Jane Yolen, in *The Seeing Stick*, creates a mood of wonder as Hwei Ming, the unhappy, blind daughter of a Chinese emperor, is guided to "see" by touching an old man's carvings on a walking stick. The text and illustrations are closely coordinated: when Yolen describes the sad girl and introduces the old man who will eventually help her, Remy Charlip's and Demetra Maraslis's illustrations are in soft black and white. When the young girl touches the marvelous carvings and is guided in exploring them by the old man, the illustrations become soft pastels. Yolen creates a tender mood as Hwei Ming turns to her father and "sees" him for the first time:

The longing for a life-style different from his parents' brings a young animal to this setting.
From *Charlie the Tramp* by Russell Hoban. Text copyright © 1966 by Russell Hoban. Illustrations copyright © 1966 by Lillian Hoban. Reprinted by permission of Four Winds Press, a division of Scholastic Inc.

"She reached out and her fingers ran eagerly through his hair and down his nose and cheek and rested curiously on a tear they found there. And that was strange, indeed, for had not the emperor given up crying over such things when he ascended the throne?" (p. 19 unnumbered). Yolen saves the greatest miracle until last; it is on the final page that she reveals that the old man is also blind.

Creators of outstanding picture storybooks use imagination, plot, characterization, humor, and style to write stories that appeal to the imagination and sensitivity of young children.

Outstanding Picture Storybooks—A Unique Coexistence Between Writer and Artist

Children's picture storybooks include stories about people in disguise as animals, talking animals with human emotions,

personification, family life and real situations, and humorous and inventive fantasies. This section discusses stories by some outstanding authors who have written books on these subjects.

People in Disguise as Animals. Many of the stories with animal characters are so closely associated with human life-styles, behavior patterns, and emotions that it is difficult to separate them from other family stories. If these stories are read without reference to the illustrations or a specific animal name, children might assume the stories are about a human family. These stories may be so popular with children because they can easily identify with the character, the resulting emotions, and the overcoming of the problem.

Consider, for example, the plots in Russell Hoban's *Bread and Jam for Frances* and *A Baby Sister for Frances*. In the first book, Frances, a badger, has an understanding audience when she refuses to eat anything but bread and jam. Hoban allows her parents, like good human parents, to carefully guide Frances into her decision that bread and jam are boring; in fact, it is pleasant to try different foods. In the second book, Hoban encourages Frances to cope with jealousy as she faces the arrival of a baby and a mother who is too busy. Increasing unhappiness is projected as Frances decides to run away and packs a lunch. Her real need for her family is suggested when she runs away to the next room and looks longingly at her family. Hoban creates a warm ending and solves Frances's problems when she decides to return to her family and accept her sister. This warmth is expressed in Hoban's language:

Big sisters really have to stay
At home, not travel far away,
Because everybody misses them
And wants to hug-and-kisses them. (p. 26 unnumbered)

In *Charlie the Tramp,* Hoban develops a plot around a desire to rebel against parental authority. After Charlie is allowed to experience his desired life-style, he happily reverts to the behavior of his parents.

Robert Kraus in *Leo the Late Bloomer* develops a credible character through realistic experiences shared by many children: Leo, a young tiger, cannot read, write, draw, talk, or even eat neatly. The author develops another credible situation as one parent worries while the other suggests that Leo is merely a late bloomer. Kraus uses repetition in dialogue as the seasons go by, "But Leo still wasn't blooming" (p. 16). A satisfactory ending results in both text and illustrations as Leo discovers he can read, write, draw, eat neatly, and even speak in whole sentences. The text concludes with the illustration of a happy father, mother, and child, as Leo declares, "I made it!" (p. 28 unnumbered).

Another animal who experiences very human problems is Rosemary Wells's Timothy in *Timothy Goes to School*. A credible character emerges as Timothy Raccoon makes many mistakes during his first week in school: he wears the wrong clothes, a classmate does everything right while Timothy does everything wrong. The author develops a warm, satisfying ending as Timothy discovers a friend and both "animals" are now happy. These stories are examples of selections that are really about people in the guise of animals.

Talking Animals with Human Emotions. While the previous "animals" lived in very human settings, there are also animal stories in which animals talk like humans but live in traditional animal settings such as meadows, barnyards, jungles, and zoos. The animals in these stories may display a mixture of animal and human traits.

The main character in Munro Leaf's *The Story of Ferdinand*, for example, dwells in a meadow where he lives with his mother and the other bulls. Contrasts are developed between the bulls who run, jump, and butt their heads together and Ferdinand who sits under his favorite cork tree, smelling the flowers. The author develops a strong theme, suggesting that everyone should be his own person—it is not wrong to be different. This theme is enhanced as Ferdinand tells his worried mother that he would rather sit quietly under the tree than romp with other bulls. Leaf allows Ferdinand to remain true to his individual nature: when he is taken to the bullring, he merely sits and smells the flowers.

Jean de Brunhoff uses both a variety of emotional experiences and ridiculous situations to develop characters and plots in the various Babar books. Emotionally, Babar grows up, grieves when his mother dies, runs away to the city, returns to the jungle where he is crowned King, and raises a family. There is also the incongruity of an elephant wearing shoes with spats, doing sit-up exercises with a little old lady, taking a bath in a people-sized tub, and driving a small car.

Possible ridiculous situations that could result when animals either misunderstand objects valued by humans or leave the security of their environments are developed by Roger Duvoisin and Louise Fatio. Duvoisin's *Petunia* becomes conceited and believes she is wise when she finds a book. Her advice creates an uproar in the barnyard when she states that the firecrackers discovered in the meadow are candy and are consequently good to eat. Her true wisdom occurs when she discovers that books have words; she will need to learn to read if she really wants to be wise. Fatio also takes her main character beyond the world he knows. *The Happy Lion* develops problems when he leaves his zoo cage to visit his good friends in town. To his wonderment, they respond with fright, screams, and running rather than with the "bonjour" he had expected. It is François, the keeper's son, who welcomes him as a friend and the two walk happily back to the zoo.

Many young children like a combination of fast, slapstick adventures and an animal with easily identifiable human characteristics, such as Hans Rey's *Curious George*. The reader is introduced to this comedic monkey as he observes a large yellow hat lying on the jungle floor. His curiosity gets the better of him, he is captured by the man with the yellow hat, and his adventures begin. The text and illustrations develop one mishap after another, as George tries to fly but falls in the ocean, grabs a bunch of balloons and is whisked away by the wind, and is finally rescued again by the man with the yellow hat. These rapid verbal and visual adventures appeal to young children who may be curious about their own worlds and would like to try some of these same activities. The Curious George books all bring delight to children.

In addition to acting like humans, animals in picture storybooks may be humorous, fanciful, and become involved with magic. William Steig creates stories about talking bones, magical pebbles, and men transformed into dogs. In *Farmer Palmer's Wagon Ride,* Steig relies on the absurdity of the situation and descriptive words to provide amusement. The ridiculous plot begins as Farmer Palmer the pig loads his wagon, hitches it to Ebenezer the donkey, and heads for home. The author's skillful use of words that visualize the setting is shown as a tree falls across their trail and Farmer Palmer must saw it with a "thuck-thwuck and a whoosh-sheesh, whoosh-sheesh" (p. 12 unnumbered). Next the wheel falls off, and it "quivered, ribbled and dibbled around" (p. 12 unnumbered). When Ebenezer sprains his hock, Farmer Palmer puts him into the wagon and proceeds to pull the wagon himself until "there was a bib-biblidy-rib-ribbidy-rip as the wheels ricketed over rocks and ruts and tore loose from the wagon" (p. 21 unnumbered). The illustrations show the final absurdity as Farmer Palmer arrives home peddling a bicycle with Ebenezer strapped to his back. This exaggeration and absurdity have a slapstick humor that appeals to children.

Magic enters into the plots of two Steig picture storybooks. In *Sylvester and the Magic Pebble* the plot is introduced as Sylvester discovers a flaming red pebble that contains extraordinary powers. The author develops the ordeal for Sylvester and his parents as the donkey accidentally changes himself into a rock and is then unable to reach the pebble. The ordeal continues as the grieving parents search for Sylvester who is experiencing the changing seasons as a rock. Steig creates a suspenseful conclusion as Sylvester's parents spread a picnic lunch on top of the large rock and the donkey tries to communicate with them. The story concludes satisfactorily as the parents place the pebble on the rock and Sylvester wishes to become himself. The magical transformation in *Caleb & Kate* proceeds as a mischievous witch transforms a sleeping carpenter into a dog. The spell is broken when the dog rescues his wife from robbers.

Personification. The technique of giving human characteristics to inanimate objects is called *personification.* Children usually see nothing wrong with a house that thinks, a doll that feels, or a steam shovel that responds to emotions. Virginia Lee Burton, a favorite writer for small children, is a master of personification. In *Mike Mulligan and His Steam Shovel,* Burton creates a credible personality for a steam shovel because Mike names her and believes in her. The author creates drama as the two friends try to dig the basement of Popperville's town hall in only one day. The author provides suspense as mean old Henry B. Swap hopes that Mary Anne, the steam shovel, will fail; if she does, Mike will not be paid. The suspense builds as more and more people come to watch: "Now the girl who answers the telephone called up the towns of Bangerville and Bopperville and Kipperville and Kopperville and told them what was happening in Popperville" (p. 28 unnumbered). The illustrations show more and more people coming to watch Mary Anne dig. Sympathy for the steam shovel is enhanced as she works faster and faster when people cheer for her. The sun is setting; will she succeed? As the dirt flies, a little boy finally thinks of a way to rescue her from the finished cellar and outwit the plans of Henry B. Swap.

Two other books by Burton have personified objects as main characters. Katy, an extraordinary red crawler tractor, is the heroine in *Katy and the Big Snow.* Credibility for the tractor is created as snow reaches the second floor windows in Geopolis and the chief of police calls for help. Katy says, "Sure," and then, "Follow me." She responds the same way to the postmaster, the telephone company, the water department, the hospital, the fire chief, and the airport. When such real city departments believe in her, it is easy for the reader to believe also. In *The Little House* Burton creates a heroine who is both strong and needs love. Burton's descriptions and illustrations of the changes around the house as she watches the city lights come closer and closer seem real. When the house feels sad and lonely, Burton shows her with cracked paint and broken windows. The house proceeds, like a real person, through a series of emotions until she is moved away from the city and happily settles down on her new foundation where she can watch the sun, moon, and stars and the seasons come and go. "Once again she was lived in and taken care of" (p. 39).

Credibility is developed in Leo Lionni's *Alexander and the Windup Mouse,* when a windup mouse and a real mouse become friends. Like many children who want to be something else, the real mouse is envious of the windup mouse, who is certain that everyone loves him. The real mouse is so envious that he wishes to be transformed into a play mouse until he learns that the windup mouse is to be discarded. Then the real mouse uses his wish to transform his friend into a real mouse. Like many children, the real mouse learns that he would rather be himself. This is a theme found in many picture storybooks; it corresponds with young children's self-discovery.

Family Life and Real Situations. Young children enjoy sharing stories about other children who may have the same concerns, problems, experiences, or pleasures as they have. The numerous books by Ezra Jack Keats, for example, have plots and characters that are easily identifiable. When the stories are read and the pictures are viewed, readers relate to the young child's private world. In *Peter's Chair,* Peter experiences the normal jealousy that may accompany the arrival of a baby. When he see his old furniture being painted pink, he even considers running away. When he discovers that his favorite chair is really too small for him and realizes that his family still loves him, he offers to paint the chair pink. In *A Letter to Amy,* Peter writes a birthday party invitation to a girl and then wonders what the boys will say when they see her at his party. Another of Keats's very realistic heroes is *Louie,* a shy boy who usually does not talk to anyone. He responds, however, to a puppet when the neighborhood children present a show, and a warm feeling results when they secretly give the puppet to him. In another book, Louie is very lonely when his family moves to a new neighborhood. He solves his problems in *The Trip* by building a shoe box model of his old neighborhood, and goes on a soaring trip of imagination and adventure as he revisits old friends. In *Regards to the Man in the Moon,* Louie is teased because his father is a junkman. His father's advice, a spacecraft built from junk, and his imagination allow Louie and a friend to experience space flight. When the other children hear of these adventures, they want to take part in them also.

While books by Keats usually have an inner-city setting, the settings of another well-known children's author are frequently in the country or on the Maine coast. Warm family relationships and a love of the seashore are experienced in Robert McCloskey's books. *Blueberries for Sal* introduces a charming little girl and her mother. This delightful story allows readers to share a berry-picking expedition between two sets of parents: mother and daughter, and bear and cub. McCloskey develops drama when the youngsters get mixed up and start following the wrong parent. The story has a warm satisfying ending as both children are reunited with their respective parents. *One Morning in Maine* reintroduces an older Sal and the rest of her

A realistic story shows that it is normal for a boy to want a doll. Illustration by William Pène du Bois from *William's Doll* by Charlotte Zolotow. Pictures copyright © 1972 by William Pène du Bois. By permission of Harper & Row, Publishers Inc.

family. This time the major part of Sal's day is spent with her father as they dig for clams, discuss the implications of her first loose tooth, and row across the bay to the little town of Buck's Harbor. McCloskey's detailed drawings add to the reality of the settings.

Loving relationships are popular themes in books for young children. Edith Hurd contrasts parents' views of what grandparents want on their visit with the granddaughter's opinion in *I Dance in My Red Pajamas*. What the grandparents really want develops as they play, bake, and dance together, Grandfather finally concludes that it was a lovely, beautiful, noisy day. The illustrations enhance the feeling of a lovely holiday shared by the family.

Warm emotional experiences between children and adults are frequently the subject of Charlotte Zolotow's small books. Feelings about a dead grandfather are shared between mother and son in *My Grandson Lew*. Zolotow creates a warm relationship between mother and son when six-year-old Lewis wakes up and informs his mother that he misses his grandfather. They share loving memories of such experiences as "eye hugs," a scratching beard, a tune that rumbles in the chest, strong arms, and a tobacco smell.

Small boys often wish for dolls; this wish may cause friction between them and their fathers or brothers. Zolotow's *William's Doll* tells about a young boy who wants a doll to hug, cradle, and play with. Because of these feelings, his brother calls him a creep and his neighbor calls him a sissy. His father tries to interest him in "masculine" toys and brings him a basketball and an electric train. William enjoys both toys but still wants a doll. When his grandmother visits, he explains his wish to her, shows her he can shoot baskets, and tells her that his father does not want him to play with a doll. Grandmother understands William's need, buys him a baby doll, and then explains beautifully and with understanding to his upset father that William wants and needs a doll so that he can practice being a father just like his own father. This book can suggest to children that there is nothing wrong with nonstereotypic behavior.

Two picture storybooks by Tomie de Paola also deal with the subjects of the death of a beloved grandparent and a boy who must overcome sex-role bias. In *Nana Upstairs & Nana Downstairs*, readers experience Tommy's warm relationship with a grandmother and a great-grandmother. When his great-grandmother dies, he feels a great loss until he sees a falling star and his mother suggests, "perhaps that was a kiss from Nana Upstairs" (p. 23 unnumbered). This idea is very reassuring to him; years later, when his grandmother dies, he sees another falling star and decides that both grandmothers are now "Nana Upstairs." In *Oliver Button Is a Sissy,* readers discover a boy who would rather walk in the woods, read books, dress in costumes, and dance than be active in sports. When Oliver takes dancing lessons, the boys in the school write "Oliver Button is a sissy" on the wall; however, after he performs in a talent show, the message changes to "Oliver Button is a star." Again, children can discover that nonstereotypic behavior is all right.

Aliki Brandenberg's *The Two of Them* describes the warm relationships developed between a girl and her grandfather. An understanding of the strength of their love is developed as the author shares their experiences: he made her a ring, he made her a bed and sang her lullabies, he took her to the beach, he told her stories, she helped him in his store, she wheeled him in a wheelchair when he became old, and then she told him stories. After he dies, caring for the apple tree they both loved helps her overcome her sorrow.

Arnold Adoff's *Black Is Brown Is Tan* tells in poetic form about relationships in a family with a black mother and a white father. The world of their two children is filled with hugs, a "chocolate mama," cooking out, singing, and sitting on laps. On special occasions when both grandmothers come to visit the family shares stories about long ago and gathers together to sing. Books such as this can relay important messages to children as they discover warm, loving relationships between black and white adults and children.

Real experiences with special children are found increasingly in picture storybooks. These books tend to show that children with special educational needs or handicaps are similar to other children. One very appealing book is Jeanne Peterson's *I Have a Sister, My Sister Is Deaf.* The author tells in poetic form what it was like to grow up with her own sister. The author describes how her sister plays the piano by feeling the rumbling cords, climbs monkey bars, stalks deer by watching movements in the grass, lip-reads, and enjoys life. Bernard Wolf's *Anna's Silent World* takes the reader into the educational world of the deaf. In this book, children receive a special glimpse of a happy child as she learns to talk, read, join her classmates for stories and playground fun, and enjoy Saturday with her family and friends. Teachers report that this book helps sensitize children to the needs of the handicapped.

Humorous and Inventive Fantasies. Dr. Seuss is one of the most popular authors of children's books; he develops characters who are original, humorous, and talk with a style that children enjoy. Seuss credits his advertising experience with helping him write concisely and draw illustrations that "marry pictures with books." In addition, he states: "My fantastic creatures probably come into existence because I actually do not draw very well and have trouble putting together conventional animals" (9, p. 118).

One of Seuss's most popular books, *The 500 Hats of Bartholomew Cubbins,* develops as a peasant discovers he is wearing a magical hat; humor and conflict result when the King orders him to remove it. But alas, every time Bartholomew tries, another hat appears. Seuss increases suspense and humor as the King calls in Sir Snipps, the maker of fine hats; Nad, the wise man; the Father of Nad; Grand Duke Wilfred; the Yoman of the Bowmen; the magicians; and the executioner—all try unsuccessfully to remove the hat. When the number reaches 157 hats, the magicians cast a spell:

Dig a hole five furlongs deep,
Down to where the night snakes creep,
Mix and mold the mystic mud,
Malber, Balber, Tidder, Tudd. (p. 31 unnumbered)

When the number of hats reaches 233, Bartholomew is marched down to the dungeon to meet the executioner. When the number reaches 346, he is taken to the highest turret to be pushed off. Happily, with number 451, the hats begin to change and become increasingly fancy; number 500 is so beautiful that the King offers to buy it for 500 gold pieces. With that offer, the spell is broken and a rich Bartholomew returns home.

In addition to being humorous and original, several of Seuss's characters must face moral issues. Horton the elephant is one. In *Horton Hatches the Egg,* readers learn what it means to be faithful—one hundred percent. Horton is laughed at and jeered when he takes seriously his promise to sit on the egg of a lazy bird named Mayzie. Horton faithfully sits on the nest in a tree through the winter, while being transported across the ocean, and when being gawked at in a circus. He gains his reward, however, when the egg hatches and it is an

A home becomes the site of an unexpected situation in this inventive fantasy.
From *Jumanji* by Chris Van Allsburg. Copyright © 1981 by Chris Van Allsburg. Reprinted by permission of Houghton Mifflin Company.

elephant-bird. The people all respond to his loyalty; "And it should be, it should be, it should be like that! Because Horton was faithful! He sat and he sat! He meant what he said and he said what he meant . . . And they sent him home Happy. One hundred percent!" (p. 51 unnumbered). Again, in *Horton Hears a Who,* there is a moral tale presented in a humorous way. This time readers learn that no one is unimportant as Horton tries to save the Whos, a group that lives on a dust particle in the village of Whoville.

Authors of humorous and inventive fantasies frequently rely on unexpected situations to introduce and to develop the plot. Chris Van Allsburg's *Jumanji* begins with the reality of two bored children who are asked to keep the house neat until their parents return with guests. Their boredom entices them to make a mess with their toys and then to go to the park. It is in the park that Van Allsburg introduces the unexpected: a jungle adventure game with the warning that once the game is started it cannot be ended until one player reaches the golden city. When the children take the game to their home, they realize the consequences of the rules: a lion appears on the piano and chases Peter through the house. Additional jungle animals or jungle-related action appears with each frantic throw of the dice. Van Allsburg ends the story on a note of suspense and speculation. The children return the game, but two other children, who are notorious for never reading directions, pick up the game and run through the park.

John Burningham develops a humorous and unexpected situation in *Avocado Baby* when the weakling baby of weakling parents refuses to eat. The situation reverses when he eats an avocado. Now the parents put "Beware of the Baby" on the gate as he demonstrates his strength by carrying a piano upstairs, breaking his cot, and outmatching bullies. Another unexpected situation results in Trinka Noble's *The Day Jimmy's Boa Ate the Wash.* A series of catastrophes occur on a class trip to a farm. The climax results when Jimmy drops his pet boa in the hen house. The plot twists, however, as Jimmy goes home with a pig under his arm and the farmer's wife is shown happily knitting a sweater for the boa. There is exaggerated humor in both text and illustrations.

These picture storybooks can provide adults and children with many sharing experiences. The elements in outstanding picture books enhance children's enjoyment through their originality, imaginative plots, characterization, humor, and style.

SUMMARY

Picture books, in addition to providing pleasure for children, stimulate language development, expand intellectual development, develop observational skills and descriptive vocabularies, increase sensitivity to art and beauty, and develop appreciation for language style.

When evaluating picture books, readers must consider if the text and illustrations complement each other. The pictures should be an integral part of the text, and the action reflected in the illustrations; the pictures should show the mood of the story and should be accurate and authentic.

Literary elements found in Mother Goose books include rhyming, repetition, metaphors, and similes. In addition to rhymes and sounds, the humor in the verses appeals to young children. There are many different Mother Goose collections that may be shared with children. The appropriateness of a book depends upon the age of the children and whether it is to be shared with one child or with a group.

Toy books include board, pop-up, flap, cloth, and plastic books. They are designed to be shared with very young children and may encourage children to interact with the text, develop vocabularies, count, identify colors, and discuss content with an adult.

Alphabet books are frequently shared with children in the expectation that the children will learn to identify the letters and corresponding alphabet sounds. They may, in addition, be used to develop observational and discussion skills.

Counting books also range in complexity from those that show one large number and a drawing of the corresponding object to those that show numerous objects on one page or extend to number concepts through 100. Counting and grouping objects are beneficial for children's cognitive development.

Concept books are written to stimulate children's cognitive development and to promote understanding of difficult ideas as well as colors, shapes, opposites, spatial concepts, and size.

In wordless books, illustrations tell the whole story without adding words. These books are especially good for stimulating ideas and language, since they invite individual interpretations. Some wordless books develop easily identifiable plots, some have considerable detail, and others could have numerous interpretations.

Easy-to-read books are designed to be read by children with beginning reading skills; therefore, authors use a controlled vocabulary. Children may increase their feelings of self-esteem and accomplishment as they complete successful reading experiences.

Picture storybooks, unlike picture books such as Mother Goose rhymes, develop a definite story line. In a well-written picture storybook, the illustrations and narrative complement each other. Memorable storybooks contain elements of originality and imagination, plot, characterization, humor, and style.

Many attractively illustrated books with appealing story lines are found in traditional literature, discussed in chapter six.

Suggested Activities for Adult Understanding of Picture Books

- Choose several different Mother Goose editions that contain the same nursery rhymes. Compare the artists' interpretations of these characters. For example, comparisons could be made between Jack Sprat illustrations found in *Marguerite De Angeli's Book of Nursery and Mother Goose Rhymes,* Paul Galdone's *Jack Sprat His Wife & His Cat,* Kate Greenaway's *Mother Goose,* and Wallace Tripp's *Granfa' Grig Had a Pig.*
- Select a common animal or object frequently written about in children's books. Find several picture books that develop a story about that animal or object. Compare the ways the different artists depict the animals through the illustrations, and the ways the writers describe the animals and develop plots about them.
- Select several alphabet books that might be appropriate for young children and choose several that might be more beneficial for older children, Evaluate each group of books, share the books, the rationale, and the evaluation with the class.
- Find examples of rhythm, rhyme, repetition of sounds, hyperbole, metaphor, and simile found in Mother Goose.
- Select several wordless books that might be appropriate for stimulating oral language development with young children and several that are more appropriate for use with older children. Compare the details and plot development found in each book.
- Begin a collection of nursery rhymes from other lands that illustrate the universal nature of children and rhymes that illustrate the unique characteristics of people living in these countries.
- Find examples of humor in picture storybooks. Look for wordplay and nonsense, the unexpected, exaggeration, the ridiculous, and superiority.
- Choose a picture storybook that develops characterization through the illustrations. Try to depict this same characterization through narration. Compare the length of the two stories.

References

1 Baldwin, Ruth M. *100 Nineteenth-Century Rhyming Alphabets in English.* Carbondale, Ill.: Southern Illinois University, 1972.
2 Barsam, Richard. Foreword to *A Peaceable Kingdom.* New York: Viking, 1978.
3 Fry, Edward. "Fry's Readability Graph: Clarifications, Validity, and Extension." *Journal of Reading* 21 (December 1977): 249.
4 MacCann, Donnarae, and Richard, Olga. *The Child's First Books: A Critical Study of Pictures and Texts.* New York: Wilson, 1973.
5 Martin, Sue Anne Gillespi. "The Caldecott Medal Award Books, 1938–1968: Their Literary and Oral Characteristics as They Relate to Storytelling." Wayne State University, 1969. University Microfilm No. 72–16, 219.
6 Newbery, John, et al., eds. *The Original Mother Goose's Melody.* Circa 1760. Reissue. Detroit: Gale, 1969.
7 Strickland, Dorothy S. "Prompting Language and Concept Development." In *Literature and Young Children,* edited by Bernice Cullinan. Urbana, Ill.: The National Conference of Teachers of English, 1977.
8 Townsend, John Rowe. *Written for Children.* New York: Lippincott, 1975.
9 Wintle, Justin, and Fisher, Emma. *The Pied Pipers, Interviews With the Influential Creators of Children's Literature.* New York: Paddington, 1974.

Additional References

Cianciolo, Patricia, ed. *Picture Books for Children.* Chicago: American Library Association, 1973.
Coody, Betty. *Using Literature With Young Children.* Dubuque, Ia.: Brown, 1979.
Hoffman, Miriam, and Samuels, Eva, eds. *Authors and Illustrators of Children's Books: Writings on Their Lives and Works.* New York: Bowker, 1972.
Hopkins, Lee Bennett. *The Best of Book Bonanza.* New York: Holt, Rinehart & Winston, 1980.
Jacobs, Leland B., ed. *Using Literature With Young Children.* New York: Columbia University, Teachers College, 1965.
Kingman, Lee, ed. *Newbery and Caldecott Medal Books, 1966–1975.* Boston: Horn Book, 1975.
Moore, Vardine. *Preschool Story Hour.* Metuchen, N.J.: Scarecrow. 1972.
Peterson, Linda Kauffman, and Solt, Marilyn Leathers. *Newbery and Caldecott Medal and Honor Books: An Annotated Bibliography.* Boston, Mass.: G.K. Hall, 1982.
Sartain, Harry W., ed. *Mobilizing Family Forces for Worldwide Reading Success.* Newark, Del.: International Reading Association, 1981.

Involving Children in Picture Books

I F PICTURE BOOKS are to be truly a shared experience, there must be an adult who cares enough to make it stimulating and enjoyable. Providing these experiences, however, requires careful selection and preparation. These picture books may be nursery rhymes shared with young children to stimulate oral language and dramatization; alphabet books selected for developing knowledge of the alphabet or discussion skills; lap books that encourage children to find objects in pictures or make predictions; wordless books selected to stimulate storytelling and creative writing; picture storybooks ideal for reading aloud; books containing illustrations that encourage aesthetic development; or picture books that encourage children to join in with songs and movement. Whatever the book, if it is worth sharing, the sharing experience is worth thoughtful preparation. This section discusses some effective ways to increase children's enjoyment and learning during these experiences.

Picture books may be used in a variety of ways with children, and the examples in this chapter suggest only a few ways in which they can stimulate creativity and aesthetic interpretations. Mother Goose may be used with young children to promote language development, dramatization, and art interpretation. With older students, the rhymes may stimulate research; interest in history, old customs, manners, and beliefs; and creative interpretations. Alphabet books, wordless books, and concept books may be used to develop intellectual growth, language growth, and creative writing. Reading orally to children is also a valuable experience, and oral reading is enhanced by carefully selecting books, preparing for reading, and considering the audience. This chapter also suggests techniques that encourage aesthetic experiences in visual art and ways to stimulate aesthetic development.

SHARING MOTHER GOOSE WITH YOUNGER CHILDREN

Mother Goose rhymes are a natural source for stimulating language development and listening appreciation in very young children. They can also be used with five- through eight-year-olds for stimulating creative drama skills through pantomime and role playing, introducing children to the concept of plot development, expanding language and literature interpretive skills through choral speaking, and encouraging story telling.

The web shown in Figure 5–1 lists some potentially important child development benefits related to sharing Mother Goose rhymes with children.

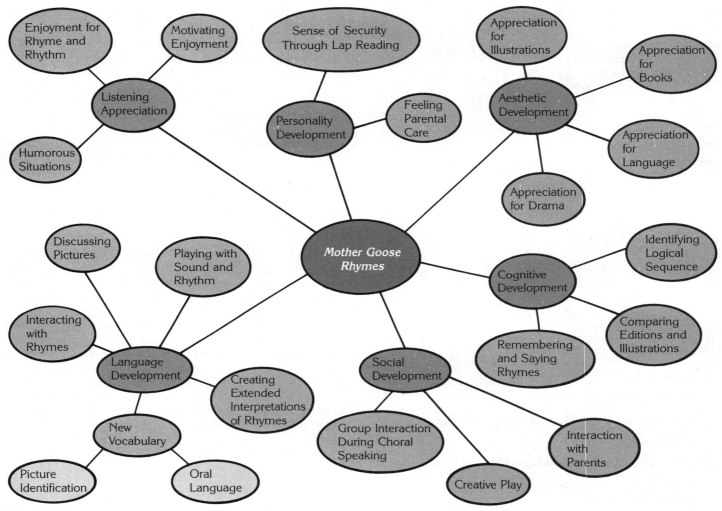

FIGURE 5–1

There are some approaches that can be used to stimulate language development and appreciative listening in preschool children. Even two- and three-year-olds thoroughly enjoy and respond to the rhyme, rhythm, and nonsense found in nursery rhymes. Because passive listening may not encourage language development, it is necessary for adults to add experiences that motivate children to interact with the verses in enjoyable ways. Once the simpler Mother Goose books have been read repeatedly, children usually know the rhymes from memory. At this time, they can help the adult finish the verses by filling in the missing word or rhyming elements as in "Jack and Jill, went up the _____, to fetch a pail of water, Jack fell down, and broke his _____, and Jill came tumbling after." In addition to providing enjoyment during a shared experience, this activity encourages auditory discrimination and attentive listening; these skills are necessary for later successes in reading and language arts.

Another approach that encourages interaction with nursery rhymes and picture interpretations is to substitute an incorrect word within a known rhyme and have children correct the error. This is especially enjoyable if the nursery rhyme book has large, colorful illustrations that allow children to point out what is wrong with the adult version. The adult could say, "Jack be nimble, Jack be quick, Jack jump over a pumpkin." or "Little Boy Blue come blow your horn. The pig's in the meadow, the chick's in the corn." Many children enjoy trying to trick the adult by making up their own incorrect versions.

Young children enjoy creative play and will spontaneously dramatize many of their favorite rhymes. Dramatization allows children to explore body movements, develop an awareness of their senses, expand their imaginations and language development, and experiment with characterization (13). One of the first adult-led creative drama activities recommended for beginning school-age children encourages development of a sense of movement and interpretation of a situation without the use of words. The adult can read or tell various nursery rhymes while children pretend to be each character in the rhyme and perform the action expressed in the verse. Enough time should be allowed following each line so that they can act out the part. Nursery rhymes are ideal for developing these pantomime skills. Children especially enjoy acting out action rhymes such as "Little Miss Muffet," "Jack Be Nimble," and "The Cat and the Fiddle." After children have experiences with a number of multiple roles in the nursery rhymes, they can be led in the development of cooperative pantomimes. For example, "Little Miss Muffet" has two characters, a girl and a spider; "The Cat and the Fiddle" has four. Children can form small groups and informally interact with others as they pantomime the action. Games can also be played during which a child or a group of children pantomimes the action of a nursery rhyme character while another group guesses the identity of the character.

Geraldine Siks (13) believes that nursery rhymes are excellent to introduce children to the concept that a drama has several parts—a beginning, a middle, and an end. (She recommends this as an introductory activity for both older and younger children.) The simple plots in many nursery rhymes make them ideal for this purpose. In the rhyme "Humpty Dumpty," there are three definite actions that cannot be interchanged and still retain a logical sequence: (1) beginning—"Humpty Dumpty sat on a wall"; (2) middle—"Humpty Dumpty had a great fall"; and (3) end—"All the King's horses and all the King's men couldn't put Humpty Dumpty together again." Children can listen to the rhyme, identify the actions, discuss the reasons for the order, and finally act out each part. They can be encouraged to extend their parts by adding dialogue or characters that might be active in their creative extensions of beginning, middle, or ending incidents. Other nursery rhymes illustrating sequential plot development include "Jack and Jill," "Pat-a Cake, Pat-a Cake, Baker's Man," and "Rock-a-Bye Baby."

Children frequently memorize their favorite nursery rhymes, and they can be used for choral-speaking arrangements, even though the children may not have developed reading skills. Chapter eight suggests ways to stimulate oral language and appreciation through choral speaking.

Finally, there are several delightful picture books that illustrate one Mother Goose rhyme or tale. (Several were discussed earlier in this chapter.) Books such as Paul Galdone's *The House that Jack Built* or Sarah Martin's *The Comic Adventures of Old Mother Hubbard and Her Dog* can be used to encourage children's interpretations of their own extended Mother Goose tales. After sharing these books with children, the adult could ask them if there are any Mother Goose characters they would like to know more about. A discussion with first graders, for example, revealed that several children wanted to know what it would be like to live in a pumpkin. They talked about how they might decorate its interior, what they could do inside a pumpkin, what they would do in order to keep a "wife very

well," and how neighbors might react to a pumpkin in the neighborhood. They dictated their story to the teacher and then divided it into separate sentences, each illustrated by one child. The illustrations and corresponding sentences were drawn and written on tagboard, then placed in the classroom library. This book was one of the most popular picture storybooks in the classroom. When more children created their own books, the children's librarian developed a library display of both commercially published Mother Goose books and books printed and illustrated by the children. Other Mother Goose rhymes that lend themselves to extended oral, written, or artistic versions include "Old Mother Hubbard," "Old King Cole," and "Simple Simon."

Older Children and Mother Goose

One stimulating and exciting experience using Mother Goose rhymes occurred not with young children but with sixth graders. These students were discussing their favorite early childhood stories, and one child asked if there was a real Mother Goose. This question led to library research, debate, and the creative writing of nursery rhymes about incidents and people in history and current events.

First, the children researched the question: Who was the real Mother Goose? They discovered that there were conflicting answers. For example, some sources indicated that the original Mother Goose was Dame Goose of Boston; another resource said that she was goose-footed Bertha, wife of Robert II of France; still others referred to Charles Perrault's *Tales of Mother Goose,* published in 1697. And many others stated that there never was a Mother Goose. Following this research, the individuals chose the version they favored and debated the issue.

Next, their research revealed that some verses were believed to have been written for adults rather than for children. They discovered that while there was not agreement about this, several sources indicated that some Mother Goose rhymes were supposedly based upon the lives of real people. This idea was fascinating, and they wondered who or what incident might have caused "Little Miss Muffet," "Little Jack Horner" or "Humpty Dumpty." A search for possible personages and situations resulted in the information shown in Chart 5–1.

Finally, the children wrote their own Mother Goose rhymes about people and situations in the news or in history. In addition to oral language, research, and writing, they learned about old customs, manners, and beliefs.

Other stimulating ways of using Mother Goose with older children have been used by university students in children's literature classes. The illustrations in the nursery rhyme books have been used to increase aesthetic appreciation and knowl-

Mother Goose rhymes stimulate language development and enjoyment when shared with an appeciative child.

edge about art media. Children compared the illustrations in different Mother Goose editions, discussed art media used by the illustrator, discussed their personal responses to the art, discovered more information about art media, demonstrated the techniques to the group, and then illustrated their picture books to be shared with younger children.

SHARING ALPHABET BOOKS WITH CHILDREN

The most common way to share an alphabet book with children is to read it to them or have them identify objects shown in the pictures to reinforce their ability to identify letter/sound relationships. According to John Stewig (16), however, the alphabet book should be used for additional learning; he thinks the ABC books are neglected. He suggests that the book should be used as a source of materials for developing visual literacy (the ability to look analytically at a picture and interpret it) and verbal literacy (the ability to talk clearly about one's observations, comparisons, and reactions). To develop both visual and verbal literacy, Stewig recommends a three-step sequence of activities that begins with children describing the object in the picture, then comparing two different objects using common descriptions, and finally saying which picture

CHART 5—1
Mother Goose Personages

Mother Goose Rhyme	Personages	Situations
There was an old woman who lived in a shoe.	Parliament James VI of Scotland and I of England	Geographic location of parliament. England had many people. This disliked monarch was not English, but Parliament told the people to get along as well as they could.
Old King Cole was a merry old soul.	Third century—King Cole	He was a brave and popular monarch.
Humpty Dumpty sat on a wall.	Richard III—1483	The "usurper" when he lay slain upon Bosworth Field.
I love sixpence, pretty little sixpence.	Henry VII—1493 Charles of France	Miserliness of Henry resulted in public jest. French ruler pacified Henry with £149,000 when Henry signed the treaty of Etaples.
Little Jack Horner sat in a corner eating his Christmas pie.	Jack Horner, an emissary of the Bishop of Glastonbury	Jack lived at Horner Hall and was taking twelve deeds to church-owned estates to Henry VIII. The deeds were hidden in a pie. On his way, he pulled out the deed to Mells Park estate and kept it.
Sing a song of sixpence, a pocket full of rye,	Henry VIII	Henry's humming over the confiscated revenues from the friars' rich grainfields.
Four and twenty blackbirds baked in a pie	The friars and monks	The title deeds to twenty-four estates owned by the church were put into a pie and delivered to Henry VIII.
When the pie was opened, The birds began to sing;	The friars and monks	The monks put their choicest treasures in chests and hid them in a lake.
Wasn't that a dainty dish To set before a king?	Henry VIII	Henry picked the deeds he wanted and bestowed others as payment.
The King was in the counting house Counting out his money	Henry VIII	Henry was counting his revenues.
The Queen was in the pantry Eating bread and honey;	Katherine of Aragon	She was eating the bread of England, spread with Spain's assurances that the King could not divorce her.
The maid was in the garden, Hanging out the clothes,	Anne Boleyn	Anne had dainty frocks from France and was smiling at the King in the garden of Whitehall Palace.
When down flew a blackbird, And snipped off her nose.	Anne Boleyn, Cardinal Wolsey, and the royal headsman.	Cardinal Wolsey broke Anne's engagement to Lord Percy. After marrying Henry VIII, the royal headsman executed Anne—1563.
To market, to market to buy a fat pig.	Henry VIII	Henry VIII declared himself head of the Church of England to obtain a divorce from Katherine of Aragon.
Needles and pins, needles and pins, When a man marries his trouble begins.	Katherine Howard and Henry VIII	After her marriage to Henry, she introduced pins from France to the English court. Ladies had to begin a separate allowance for this luxury.
Punch and Judy fought for a pie; Punch gave Judy a sad blow in the eye.	Punch—England Judy—France	England and France fought over Italy.
Little Boy Blue	Cardinal Wolsey	The cardinal was too busy with pleasant dreams about his fame to be aware of danger.
Hey diddle, diddle, The cat and the fiddle.	The cat—Queen Elizabeth I—1561	Queen Elizabeth played with her ministers as if they were mice. She liked to dance.
A frog he would a-wooing go,	Duke of Anjou and Queen Elizabeth I—1577	A satire about the wooing of forty-nine-year-old Elizabeth by the twenty-three-year-old French prince.
I saw a ship a sailing, A sailing on the sea,	Sir Francis Drake	Drake brought back potatoes and other foods that were introduced to England.
Mistress Mary, quite contrary. How does your garden grow?	Mary Queen of Scots and her royal maids	She wore flashing jewels and gowns from Paris.

CHART 5—1 (cont.)

Mother Goose Rhyme	Personages	Situations
Little Miss Muffet sat on a tuffet Eating her curds and whey; When along came a spider, and sat down beside her,	Mary Queen of Scots John Knox	At eighteen (1560), she was made monarch of Scotland. She laughed with her maids. John Knox denounced the frivolous Mary from the pulpit of St. Giles.
Little Bo-Peep has lost her sheep.	Mary Queen of Scots	Tells about Mary's problems as the clans rose and prepared for battle.
Jack Spratt could eat no fat, His wife could eat no lean.	Charles I Henrietta Maria of France	After their marriage, they each went their heedless ways and plundered England.
Yankee Doodle came to town, Riding on a pony; He stuck a feather in his hat, and called it macaroni.	Prince Rupert of the Palatinate, Royalist General of the Civil Wars—1653	Prince Rupert had a large following; he could lead men and showed great endurance. The feather signified that the wearer was one of his soldiers. Rupert could steal into an enemy's camp and take the horses.

they prefer and why. Since there are alphabet books illustrated and written at several levels of complexity, this activity could be used with children of all ages.

Butterflies are illustrated in different settings in three ABC books appropriate for younger children. The butterfly in *Brian Wildsmith's ABC* is a colorful full-page painting that shows a single butterfly in vivid pinks, purples, whites, greens, and yellows drawn against a deep purple background. The butterfly in *Ed Emberley's ABC* is part of a larger picture and is interacting with a bear and a bird, both dressed as people. Marcia Brown's butterflies, in *All Butterflies: An ABC,* are shown ascending into an outdoor setting of blues, blacks, and whites.

During a discussion of these three books, the adult could use the following sequence in order to increase visual and verbal literacy. First, children could be asked to look at each picture and answer questions such as the following: What has the artist drawn in this picture? What colors are used in this picture of the butterfly? How large is the butterfly? What is the butterfly doing in this picture? Where is the butterfly in this picture? Is it in a field? After the children have described each picture by using as much detail as they can, they should compare the butterfly illustrations in the three ABC books. The discussion should focus on both similarities and differences. Discussion could include some of the following questions: Are the butterflies all the same size? What words could be used to tell someone the size of each butterfly? Look at the three butterflies. What colors are the same? What colors are different? In order to find these butterflies, would one look for them in the same kind of place? How is the place that these butterflies live (country scene) different from the place this butterfly lives (indoor scene with table and chair)? Which butterfly acts more like a real butterfly? Why? Finally, children can relate which picture they prefer and why they prefer it.

It is very important to allow children to think about and articulate their reasons for choosing a picture. This requires careful leadership by an adult, because the adult's opinion should not be used to sway children into forming one opinion. When children were asked to talk about their preferences and reasons for choosing these pictures, they answered in many different ways. One child preferred the Wildsmith butterfly because it had beautiful purple and pink colors and resembled one he had painted. His mother had framed the painting for his room, and it had brought him considerable pleasure. Another child preferred Marcia Brown's butterflies: when she looked at them, she felt as if she were walking in a beautiful meadow through wild flowers and watching the butterflies flying up ahead of her. A third child liked Emberley's butterfly because it was part of a humorous picture, and she liked the idea of a butterfly sharing an experience with a bear and a bird. All the children gave divergent answers, but they had valid reasons for their preferences. To increase language skills further, children might pretend they were one of the butterflies and tell a story about what they would do if they were that butterfly. They could paint and describe butterfly pictures of their own to increase aesthetic and visual skills.

USING PICTURE BOOKS THAT ENCOURAGE CHILD AND TEXT INTERACTION

Several books for young children encourage them to find hidden objects or to predict what is going to happen next. Language development, cognitive development, and enjoyment are stimulated by actively involving children during a story experience. Young children love to play "I spy" and look for hidden objects in pictures. Familiar folktale and nursery rhyme characters are illustrated and hidden in Janet and Allen Ahlberg's *Each Peach Pear Plum.* The two lines that precede each picture tell who is in the picture; the text also suggests a hidden figure. Children enjoy searching the pastel watercolor drawings for such story favorites as Tom Thumb, Mother Hubbard, Cinderella, The Three Bears, Baby Bunting, Bo-Peep, Jack and Jill, a wicked witch, and Robin Hood. When this book is used, time should be provided for children, not an adult, to locate the hidden characters. *Peek-a-boo!* by the same authors also encourages interaction.

Another excellent book for interaction and discovery is *We Hide, You Seek* by Jose Aruego and Ariane Dewey. A great deal of potential enjoyment would be missed if the twenty-six words of the text were read without trying to find and identify the animals in the pictures. The colorful illustrations tell the story of what happens when a group of African animals challenges a rhino to a game of hide and seek. The artists have camouflaged the animals so well that children need to search for spotted leopards and giraffes hidden in the bush, reptiles and birds hidden in the desert, alligators and birds hidden in the swamp, zebras and lions camouflaged on the plains, and hip-

pos and crocodiles hidden in the river. Humor is added when rhino searches unsuccessfully for the animals; by turning the page, the viewer sees that rhino finds the animals because he is clumsy, not clever. His clumsy moves startle the animals and reveal their hiding places. The rhino gets even, however, when it's his turn and he hides in a herd of his own kind. Children should be encouraged to identify the hiding places and identify and describe the animals.

Eric Carle's *Watch Out! A Giant!* is a book that can be used to encourage predictions. Large, colorful illustrations show two children trying to escape from a giant. On each page, they find an object such as a box or a gate that they can go through; these objects open to allow children to peek into the next page. Readers then decide what they think will happen before they turn the page and discover if they were right. Another book that encourages children to make predictions is Tana Hoban's *Take Another Look.* This fascinating text allows the reader to peek through a hole and see a portion of the photograph found on the following page. Children should be encouraged to tell what they think the picture is, and why, before they turn the page to see if their predictions were correct. The strength of each book lies partly in the adult's ability to stimulate active participation and oral interaction from the readers or listeners. This kind of book is especially good for lap reading or for sharing with a small group.

SHARING WORDLESS PICTURE BOOKS

Wordless books are ideal for encouraging language growth, stimulating intellectual development, motivating creative writing, and evaluating language. The children's ages and the complexity of the plot or details should be considered when choosing appropriate books. Some have considerable detail and are excellent for developing observational skills and descriptive vocabularies; others are more appropriate for encouraging understanding and interpretation of sequential plot development.

Stimulating Cognitive and Language Development

Chapter one discussed the advisability of promoting cognitive development through literature. Several skills associated with the thinking process—observing, comparing, and organizing—can be developed through the use of wordless books. Children can describe what is happening in each picture and what details they observe, compare pictures or changes that occur as the result of the wordless plot, and organize their thoughts

Sharing stories in the classroom or library allows children to discover the pleasure in books.

into a sequentially well-organized story. In addition, the describing, oral comparing, and storytelling encourage language expansion.

Wordless books, such as Peter Spier's *Noah's Ark,* are good for developing observational skills and descriptive language. Children can describe the action in each picture as they follow the building of the ark, the loading of food, utensils, and the animals, the problems that develop inside the ark, and the final landing and starting life anew. Each picture has enough detail to encourage considerable discussion. The following list includes examples of the observational and descriptive discussion developed with a group of seven-year-olds:

1 After looking at a double-page spread showing animals boarding the ark, children identified animals they recognized.
2 Children described the color, size, mode of traveling, and natural habitat of the animals.
3 Humorous details in the illustrations were identified.
4 Noah's problems were identified and their possible causes and/or solutions were suggested.
5 Children speculated about Noah's feelings as he tried to rid the roof of too many birds, dealt with a reluctant donkey, and finally closed the doors.
6 Children thought of descriptive words for the animals. Examples included: slithering snakes, leaping frogs, a stubborn donkey, swiftly hopping rabbits, lazy brown monkeys, and tiny creeping snails.
7 Children compared the position of the snails in the illustrations at the beginning of the book with the illustrations at the end.
8 Each child chose one picture and told or wrote a detailed description of the picture.

The wordless books illustrated by Mitsumasa Anno are excellent to develop observational skills in older children. *Anno's Journey, Anno's Italy,* and *Anno's Britain* contain fascinating details that could be discovered during a visual trip through Europe. At the end of the books, there are lists of details that a reader should look for, such as characters from folktales or well-known paintings or people. There are, however, many other details that the illustrator does not mention. These details are intriguing enough to keep an adult interested; a librarian who looked at *Anno's Italy* indicated that she enjoyed searching the pictures for identifiable objects and found Mary, Joseph, and the donkey strolling along a country lane. These three books could also be used to make oral comparisons. A path is used to guide the visitor on the journey: *Anno's Journey* begins with a boatman landing his boat and starting his journey; in contrast, *Anno's Italy* ends with the boatman boarding his boat and rowing away from the shore.

The humorous wordless book by Mercer Mayer, *Frog Goes to Dinner,* is excellent for encouraging before and after comparisons: people are enjoying a leisurely meal in one picture; the next one shows what happens when Frog interrupts their dining. Each picture can be described and then comparisons made between the two. A first grader gave the following oral comparison when he discussed the two pictures of the band: "The band was playing beautifully. They had their eyes closed and were enjoying the music. All of a sudden the frog jumped in the saxophone. Now the saxophone player tried to play but couldn't. His face puffed out and he looked funny. The other players jumped. The frog made the drum player fall into his drum. The horn player thought it was funny."

Motivating Writing

With their colorful illustrations wordless books are ideal for motivating writing or dictating picture captions, composing group stories, and writing individual stories.

Dictation of Picture Captions. One very early writing or dictating activity is to have children write captions to accompany pictures. Younger children frequently enjoy having their parents or a teacher write down their brief descriptions or captions for the pictures in wordless books. The children first look at the books and any accompanying story or details are discussed. Next, the adult writes down exactly what the child dictates about the picture. If reading readiness is also a goal, the adult should repeat each word as it is being written. When the captions are finished, the children and adult can read them in sequence while the children follow the illustrations and the printing. Such sentences can also be used to reinforce sequential development as the captions can be mixed and then placed into sequential order.

Wordless books that are simple enough for younger children and also have a plot development that encourages children to dictate sequentially ordered sentences or picture captions include Fernando Krahn's *Who's Seen The Scissors?;* Martha Alexander's *Out! Out! Out!;* Pat Hutchins's *Changes, Changes;* and Mercer Mayer's various book adventures with Boy, Dog, and Frog.

Dictation of Group or Individual Stories. Educators in reading and language arts such as Roach Van Allen (1) and Russell Stauffer (15) recommend the use of language experiences that stimulate children's oral language and writing through discussing, exploring ideas, and expressing feelings. These experiences in turn provide the content for group and individual stories composed by children and recorded by an adult. Many teachers introduce students to the language experience approach through a group chart story. This can be done with any age group, although it is a frequent readiness or early-reading activity in kindergarten or first grade.

The chart story is usually written by an entire group (guided by the teacher) following a shared motivational experience such as a field trip, an art project, observing an animal, a film, or pictures, or listening to music or a story. Many of the wordless books discussed in this text provide excellent sources for the motivational activity.

If a wordless book is to motivate the writing of a chart story, an adult first shares the book with the group. Following oral discussion, the adult records the child-dictated story on poster board, chalkboard, or large sheet of newsprint. It is essential that children can see each word as it is written. As the chart story is written, children will see that sentences flow from top to bottom on the page, follow a left-to-right sequence, and begin with capital letters and end with periods.

As the children dictate the story, an adult writes each word, repeating the word aloud as it is being written. (Some adults identify each child's contribution on the chart story by placing his or her name after the contribution.) Following the completion of the chart story, the adult reads the whole story. Next, the children reread the story with the adult. Following this experience, some children may choose to read the story individually while others read their own contributions.

Wordless books and their accompanying chart stories should be placed in an area easily accessible to children, so that they can enjoy reading the stories by themselves. Some teachers tape record the children's reading of the chart stories and then place the recording, the chart story, and the wordless book in a listening center. (Additional information on using the language experience method is found in the Stauffer or Allen texts.)

The sequentially developed wordless books may also be used to stimulate children to tell or write stories with improved plot and sequence. John Goodall's *The Adventures of Paddy Pork* contains greater plot development than many wordless books. When the book was used with a group of fourth graders, the primary purpose was to encourage them to write a sequentially developed story. The teacher first shared the book orally with the children. They discussed the setting, characters in the story, and the probable events that occurred. Children were encouraged to give their own interpretations for the pictures and then share their reasons for those interpretations.

Finally, they wrote their own stories to accompany the pictures in the book. The stories may also be placed on tapes in a listening center, read to children in other classes, or added to the library.

READING TO CHILDREN

The adult who reads to children accepts an opportunity and a responsibility for sharing a marvelous experience. Kay Vandergrift (17) states this dual role very well: "Through reading aloud, the reader re-creates for children not only their own world seen through other eyes but leads them also to worlds beyond the eye. Reading aloud is a way to let children enter, vicariously, into a larger world—both real and fanciful—in company with an adult who cares enough to take them on the literary journey" (p. 11). This section expands upon the value of reading to children, and explores characteristics of appropriate books and the important preparation for reading orally.

The Values of Reading Orally

There is probably no better way to interest children in the world of books than to read to them. It is a way for them to learn that literature is a form of pleasure. Without parents, librarians, or other adults, a very young child would not experience nursery rhymes or stories such as *Peter Rabbit* or *The Runaway Bunny*. For children just struggling to learn to read, a book may not be a source of happiness. In fact, books may actually arouse negative feelings in many children. Being read to helps them develop an appreciation for literature that they could not manage with their own reading ability. Without the adult, younger elementary children would not be able to experience the marvelous verses and stories of A. A. Milne or share in the joyous world of Dr. Seuss.

A second value of oral reading is found in the motivational activity of the listening experience. If children enjoy listening to the book, they usually want to read it themselves. Very young children frequently ask for a book to be reread so many times that they memorize the content. At this point, they feel proud of being able to "read" their own book. Older children also enjoy rereading a selection. Whenever a particularly enjoyable selection was read to children in one classroom, all copies would be checked out of the class or school library. Reading aloud also motivates older elementary children. A study with fifth graders showed that reading aloud to them for twenty to thirty minutes a day affected both the quantity and quality of their voluntary reading (14). Unfortunately, research also indicates that the amount of time a teacher spends reading stories usually decreases in the upper elementary grades, and is almost nonexistent in middle schools and high schools.

A third value of reading aloud is the improvement it often brings to related areas such as reading achievement and language and vocabulary development. A study by Cohen (4) demonstrated that seven-year-olds who were read aloud to for twenty minutes each day gained significantly in vocabulary and reading scores. Cohen's results are not surprising; listening to and discussing stories afford opportunities to learn new meanings of familiar words, new synonyms for known words, and new words and concepts.

A fourth value of reading aloud is to develop readiness for formal reading instruction. According to Mary Jett-Simpson (7), "Parents are the most important resource for developing readiness for formal reading instruction. Parents can establish an attitude toward reading by giving books an important place in their own daily lives as well as in the lives of their children" (p. 73). She maintains that for a parent to set aside twenty to thirty minutes each evening for holding a child and reading is the most powerful sharing technique available.

In order to gain all of these benefits from reading, the adult must select appropriate literature, prepare the selection carefully, and read with enthusiasm and enjoyment.

Choosing the Books

Choosing the appropriate book depends, of course, upon the ages of the children, their interests, the desire to balance the types of literature presented, their experience, the number of children who will share the experience, and the quality of the literature.

Style and illustrations are both considerations when choosing books to read aloud. The language in A.A. Milne's *Winnie the Pooh* and Dr. Seuss's *The 500 Hats of Bartholomew Cubbins* appeals to young listeners. Likewise, young children enjoy illustrations that are an integral part of the story. For example, illustrations in Robert McCloskey's *Lentil* help children visualize the midwestern town of the early 1900s, and Maurice Sendak's *Where the Wild Things Are* show Max's exceptional adventure.

Other books, such as Tomie de Paola's *The Clown of God,* have such beautiful illustrations that they should be shared for aesthetic appreciation. Many books discussed in chapter four and in this chapter require that the illustrations be shared with children.

In addition to the style and illustrations, a book selected for reading aloud should be worthy of the time spent by both reader and listeners. It should not be something picked up hurriedly to fill in time. Children's reading ability should also be considered when selecting these stories. The books chosen should challenge children to grow in appreciation and interest. The numerous easy-to-read books should usually be left for children to read independently.

Children's ages and attention spans must also be considered. Young children respond to short stories; in fact, the four- or five-year-old may benefit from several short story times a day rather than a twenty- or thirty-minute period. Books such as *Happy Birthday, Sam* or *The Wind Blew* by Pat Hutchins, and *Leo the Late Bloomer* by Robert Kraus, are brief and have large, colorful pictures. These books also have other elements that appeal to young children: *The Wind Blew,* for example, uses rhyming words to tell the story; *Happy Birthday, Sam* tells the story of a young child who cannot reach the switch in his room, his clothes in his closet, or the water faucet until a birthday present makes it possible for him to do so; *Leo the Late Bloomer* relates the problems of a young tiger who cannot do anything right until, all at once, he finally blooms. As children enter kindergarten and advance into first grade, they begin to enjoy longer picture storybooks. Robert McCloskey's *Make Way for Ducklings* and the various Dr. Seuss books are favorites with beginning elementary school children. The longer picture storybooks, with more elaborate plots, are enjoyed by children in first and second grades. Books such as William Steig's *Sylvester and the Magic Pebble* or *Caleb & Kate,* and Graham Oakley's *The Church Mice Adrift* have enough plot development to appeal to second-grade children. By the time children reach third grade, they are ready for continued stories, although an entire chapter should be completed during each story time. Third graders usually enjoy E. B. White's *The Trumpet of the Swan, Charlotte's Web,* and *Stuart Little.* Fourth and fifth graders often respond to books like Madeleine L'Engle's *A Wrinkle in Time* and C. S. Lewis's *The Lion, the Witch and the Wardrobe.* Armstrong Sperry's *Call It Courage* and Esther Forbes's *Johnny Tremain* often appeal to sixth- and seventh-grade students. (These books will be discussed in later chapters.)

Preparing for Reading Aloud

Many adults mistakenly believe that children's stories are so simple that it is unnecessary to preread a selection before reading it to children. Ramon Ross (12) states his view with considerable force: "If I were to lay down for you one single cardinal rule that must never be broken, it would be that you never, never read a story aloud to an audience unless you have first read it aloud to yourself." Many embarrassing situations, such as being unable to pronounce a word or selecting an inappropriate book, can be avoided if the adult reads the story silently in order to understand it, identify the sequence of events, recognize the mood, and identify any problems with vocabulary or concepts.

After the silent reading, the adult should read the story aloud in order to practice pronunciation, pacing, and voice characterization. It is helpful if beginning readers listen to themselves on a tape recorder before reading to children.

Finally, the adult should consider how to introduce the story and decide what type of discussion or other activity, if any, might follow the reading. (Ideas for both discussions and other activities are included throughout this text.)

Sharing the Oral Reading with an Audience

What makes the story hour a time of magic or an insignificant part of the day? In addition to an enthusiastic reader and a carefully selected story, research conducted by Linda Lamme (8) concludes that the following factors contribute to the quality of the reading performance:

1 Child involvement, including reading parts of a selection with an adult, predicting what will happen next, or filling in missing words, is the most influential factor during oral reading.
2 Eye contact between the reader and the audience is essential.
3 Adults who read with expression are more effective than those who use a monotonous tone.
4 Good oral readers try to put variety into their voices, using neither too high nor too low a pitch or too loud nor too soft a volume.
5 Readers who point to meaningful words or pictures in the book as they read are better oral readers than those who just read the story and show the pictures.
6 Adults who know the story and do not need to read the text verbatim are more effective during the presentation.
7 Readers who select picture books large enough for children to see and appealing enough to hold their interest or elicit comments are effective.
8 Grouping is important so that all the children can see the pictures and hear the story.
9 Adults who highlight the words and language of the story by making the rhymes apparent, discussing unusual vocabulary words, and highlighting any repetition found in the text are better readers.

All of these factors should be considered and practiced when an adult prepares for the oral presentation or reads a story to an appreciative audience. Properly prepared, the adult is ready to take children on a literary journey.

CHILDREN'S DEVELOPMENT RELATED TO A PICTURE STORYBOOK

Picture storybooks and Mother Goose rhymes have considerable potential for stimulating many aspects of children's development. By reading to children, interacting with them, and encouraging them to read independently, the adult increases this potential. Child development authority Barbara Borusch (2) suggests that books such as Robert McCloskey's *Time of Wonder* be used to stimulate language, cognitive, moral, and social development as well as motivate interest in additional books. The *Time of Wonder* web (see Figure 5-2) is designed around Borusch's recommendations.

Time of Wonder is especially appropriate for stimulating language appreciation and development. There are wildlife-related words such as porpoises, lobsters, gulls, cormorants, loons, and barnacles; area-related words such as bay, island, cove, schooner, and driftwood; sound descriptions such as a silently gliding ripple, buzzing outboards, rustling birch leaves, heavy stillness, slamming rain, and screaming wind.

McCloskey's language style may encourage children to observe nature and make their own comparisons as he compares the sound of growing ferns pushing through dead leaves to half a whisper or the sound of a gentle wind to a lullaby. Sharp contrasts are also made between a gentle first rain and wind and the sharp, choppy waves that accompany the approaching storm. The author's verbs are descriptive and can encourage children to make similar observations as they listen to mice nibble, spiders scurry, and the tide ripple.

Cognitive development can be enhanced by encouraging children to make comparisons between similarities and differences in the island before and after the hurricane, islands in different parts of the world, and the island in the book and the children's own environment. Children can be encouraged to observe storms in their own environment and changes that result because of the storms. They can consider the vocabulary as it relates to such concepts as color, size, and time.

The family in *Time of Wonder* prepares for the storm and gives each other comfort as they endure the hurricane. McCloskey's children play together in the water, on the beach, and in their search for treasures after the storm. Children can consider what they or their families might do under similar circumstances. They can evaluate the responsibilities and the possible feelings of each family member. They can also consider how they would feel if they were experiencing the events in the story.

One of the most important values can be found in the book's potential to motivate, as children may be stimulated to

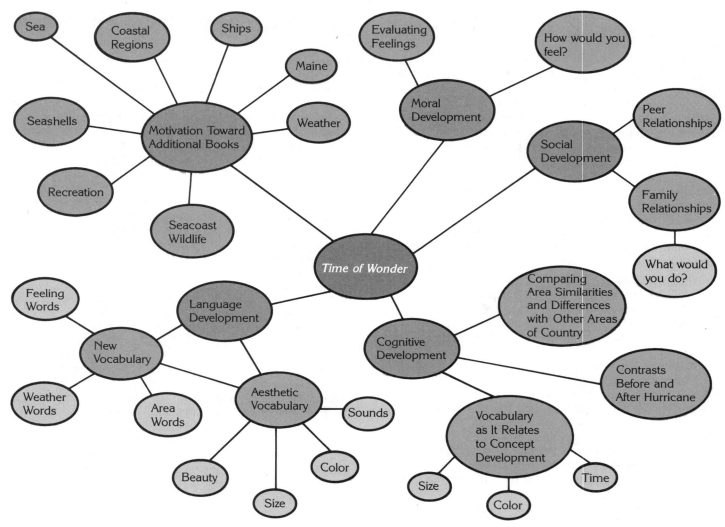

FIGURE 5–2

read or listen to other fictional or informational books about the Maine coast, storms, weather, coastal regions, water recreation, treasures from the sea, and water birds and other wildlife.

STIMULATING AESTHETIC DEVELOPMENT

If "aesthetic" means being sensitive to art and beauty, then looking at many of the beautiful illustrations in children's books must provide an aesthetic experience. This experience is important, according to H. S. Broudy (3), because "it is a primary source of experience on which all cognition, judgment, and action depend. It furnishes the raw material for concepts and ideals, for creating a world of possibility" (p. 636). Broudy believes that aesthetic experience is so vital that it should be considered a basic in children's education. Consequently, if adults concentrate on the skills of aesthetic expression and impression, they can improve the sensitivity of the learner, just as when they concentrate on reading skills they improve the reading ability of the learner. He believes that the best method to improve the aesthetic sensitivity of children is through the manipulation of materials in the various media.

Children as Artists

Aesthetic development requires both stimulation and a time to create personal interpretations. The varied illustrations found in children's literature provide many ideas and stimulation for both art development and appreciation. Linda Lamme and Frances Kane (9), like Broudy, suggest that children can learn to appreciate the art media in literature by becoming actively involved in making their own illustrations. Even though some art media are too complex for younger children, Lamme and Kane state that collage is an ideal media for creative interpretations, stimulating language through oral discussion, developing fine motor skills, and developing an appreciation for the collage illustrations used in children's literature. Their work with young children has identified the following procedures that should be used when working with collage: (1) introduce the idea of collage by having children tear designs from paper and then paste them onto a larger sheet of paper, (2) allow children to experience and experiment with textural differences,

(3) encourage them to create collage illustrations and share their accompanying stories orally, and (4) introduce and discuss literature illustrations that use collage.

Several well-known illustrators of children's books use this technique. The illustrations of artists such as Ezra Jack Keats, Jeannie Baker, and Leo Lionni can be used first to provide an adult reference and later as a source of material for children to discuss and compare. The following paragraphs show how this four-step process might be followed using either Jeannie Baker's *Grandmother* or *Grandfather*.

First, encourage children to experiment with the collage technique by having them tear and cut shapes and pictures from plain paper or magazines; then have them paste the shapes onto another piece of paper.

Following this experience, provide opportunities for children to experience and experiment with texture. (Baker's illustrations are a fine source of inspiration for the adult, because she uses many different textures to create large, colorful pictures.) Baker's illustrations show both garden and inside scenes, so one could take children on a texture exploration walk. During this walk, they should feel and describe the characteristics of, and differences in, the textures found in such items as tree bark, leaves, sidewalks, flowers, brick walls, grass, all types of fabrics, all types of paper, buttons, dried foods, and so forth. After they have discussed and experienced textures, have them collect items with different textural qualities. These items could be developed into charts and texture collages as children experiment with the differences produced by using different kinds of paper, materials, and objects. Oral language should be encouraged as they feel and look at the different textural characteristics and resulting charts.

Following their experimentation with the collage media and textures, encourage children to create their own pictures or series of pictures using the collage technique and as many different textures as they wish. After they have created their own illustrations, have them share the illustrations and their accompanying stories or descriptions.

Finally, share the books *Grandmother* and *Grandfather* with the children. As the stories are read, have the children tell what kinds of art media the illustrator used, discuss the feelings produced by each collage object and why they think the illustrator chose the material to represent the subject, discuss the texture they would feel if they could touch the original collage, and let them decide if the illustrations make the story better.

Artists may combine other art media with collage when they illustrate books. The work of Ezra Jack Keats is an excellent example of combining collage with painting. His illustrations in *The Trip, Maggie and the Pirate,* and *Pet Show!* are brightly colored combinations of collage and painting. His *Regards to the*

ISSUE

How Much "Pizzazz" Is Necessary to Entice Children Into a Library Reading Program?

ARE SUMMER READING programs more successful if they develop programs that motivate reading by utilizing the techniques of the mass media and Madison Avenue or are they more successful if they use knowledge of child development to facilitate an interplay between children's inquiries, the librarian, and the library materials? The content of library reading programs is debated by two librarians in *Top of the News*. Mary Somerville builds a case for programs that begin "with a bang, not lag in the middle, and end with skyrockets" (p. 271).[1] She believes that programming must appeal to "media babies" who will not respond to a more traditional program. In her article she identifies the following principles that make an effective summer reading program: pick a theme with dramatic possibilities, reinforce the theme in every aspect of the program, dramatize the theme with costumed actors, embody the theme in graphic figures, coordinate library materials with the theme, create a folder with pizzazz, offer prizes for program completion, include "razzle-dazzle" games, reduce clerical work, be a creative catalyst, and publicize the program.

Pete Giacoma is critical of the above programming: he believes that educators and researchers in the field of children's librarianship should consider children's psychology and cognitive development rather than think of children as consumers whose attention is vied for according to rules established by advertisers.[2] Giacoma asks that developers of library programs consider the following questions: Will students who take part in the program remain enthusiastic readers? Will the students be library patrons when they reach adolescence and young adulthood? What is the quality of the relationship between the librarian as a professional librarian and the child? Giacoma concludes that the best library program correlates "thoughtfully designed professional quality offerings, freshened with creativity, and the personalities of commited librarians with the best innate desires of children to learn more details about this place — the world of ideas, facts, imaginings, words, visuals, and sounds to which they are still awakening" (p. 66).

1 Somerville, Mary. "How to Knock the Stuffings Out of Your Summer Reading Program." *Top of the News* 37 (Spring 1981): 265-274.

2 Giacoma, Pete. "The Stuffings and Nonsense of Summer Reading Programs: A Response." *Top of the News* 38 (Spring 1981): 64-67.

Man in the Moon uses bits of photography. *The Trip* even illustrates a young boy working with various colors and shapes of paper as he creates his own neighborhood within a box. This work could be used to stimulate children's experimentation with both collage and painting.

Other art forms and illustrations may also be used to stimulate aesthetic development. Children greatly enjoy watching Peanuts and Charlie Brown cartoons, and when the cartoons are in book format they are usually in constant library circulation. Well-known cartoonists have written books describing how they draw cartoons and illustrate picture storybooks for children. Syd Hoff, for example, has written two books that provide some simple directions for young cartoonists. Both his *Jokes to Enjoy, Draw, and Tell* (6) and *How to Draw Cartoons* (5) illustrate such skills as drawing men's and ladies' faces, and how to depict the desired expressions on those faces; drawing figures that show movement and different physical characteristics; and drawing animals. Children can experiment with these simple cartoon techniques and try to depict various emotions and actions in their own characters.

After experimenting with people, animals, and other objects, children can look with new understanding and appreciation at some picture storybooks illustrated by well-known cartoonists. Children may compare Syd Hoff's cartoon illustrations in *Chester* and *Sammy the Seal* with his directions for drawing cartoons. Illustrations by James Stevenson could be viewed and discussed. His book, *Could Be Worse!* shows Grandpa experiencing numerous actions and predicaments. In two other books, Stevenson draws cartoon characters and also writes much of the text in cartoon bubble format. Children can look at the animals in *Monty* and decide whether the cartoon characters demonstrate the emotions and humor of the text. The more detailed drawings in *The Sea View Hotel* allow children to observe and discuss the settings as well as the animal characters. The humorous illustrations for *The Wish Card Ran Out!* are also excellent for appreciation.

Other books by cartoonists that can be shared and discussed with children include William Steig's *Caleb & Kate* and *Sylvester and the Magic Pebble*. These cartoons can also be compared with illustrations of people and animals in books that do not use cartoonlike illustrations. Children can discuss their reactions to each form of illustration and decide whether one type might be more appropriate or effective than another.

After children have drawn cartoons and viewed cartoonists' illustrations, they can draw not only their own cartoons but also write stories. Children enjoy putting their short cartoons together in newspaper format or writing and illustrating their own books.

There are many other art forms and works of illustrators that may be used to stimulate aesthetic development. Chapter four discussed many artists and their works; there are examples of such media as watercolors, oil paintings, and pencil sketches as well as examples of representational, impressionistic, and expressionistic art that can be used to stimulate children.

ACTIVITIES POSSIBLE WITH A PICTURE STORYBOOK

The numerous ways of sharing picture books with children recommended in this chapter suggest only a few of the possibilities for providing stimulating and enjoyable experiences with books. This chapter will conclude with some of the varied experiences that teachers, librarians, and other adults have developed around Maurice Sendak's *Where the Wild Things Are.* The following list (11) suggests a few of the stimulating activities that increase children's interaction with the book:

1 Appreciative Listening—Read the story orally to children; share the pictures and your enthusiasm.
2 Oral Language—After reading the book discuss with children how they might also daydream and make themselves heroes or heroines in a story. What kinds of activities would they dream about? Where would they go? What would they do? Ask children to pantomime their dreams.
3 Oral Language–Art Interpretation—Have children create masks depicting the Wild Things. Perform a creative drama of the story and other adventures that Max might have during another visit to the fantasy land.
4 Oral Language–Art Interpretation—Have children create puppets of the Wild Things and depict their adventures through a puppet production.
5 Art Interpretation—At one time in his career Maurice Sendak constructed papier-mâché models of storybook characters. Have children select a favorite Sendak character and make a papier-mâché model.
6 Art Interpretation—At one time, Maurice Sendak designed window displays for new books. Have a group of children design a bulletin board as if it were a window display advertising *Where the Wild Things Are.*
7 Art Interpretation–Oral Language—Ask children to design a colorful poster that could be used to promote the sale of Sendak's book. Use the poster to convince someone else that he or she should read it.
8 Art Interpretation–Oral Language—Have children create a travel poster or travel brochure that advertises Max's fantasy land or that illustrates a new fantasy land of their own. Use the poster to convince someone that he or she would enjoy visiting the fantasy land.
9 Creative Writing–Appreciative Listening—Maurice Sendak states that he enjoys listening to Mozart, Beethoven, and Wagner while he works. Have children listen to a recording of one of these composers, describe what they visualize as they listen, and draw a series of pictures stimulated by the listening experience. Have them write a story that accompanies the pictures.
10 Picture–Mood Interpretation—Older children may also discover the relationship between illustration and text achieved by Sendak's book. Encourage them to look carefully at the illustrations while reading or listening to the text. Discuss the enlargement of illustrations as the plot advances. Use the following quote from an interview with Sendak (18) to stimulate the discussion: "One of the reasons why the picture book is so fascinating is that there are devices to make the form itself more interesting. In *Where the Wild Things Are* the device is really a matching of shapes. I used it to describe Max's moods pictorially: his

anger, which is more or less normal in the beginning; its expansion into rage; then the explosion of fantasy as a release from that particular anger; and finally the collapse of that, when the fantasy goes and it's all over. The smell of food brings Max back to reality and he's a little boy again. A book is inert. What I try to do is animate it, and make it move emotionally" (p. 23). After children have discussed Sendak's devices that animate the text, encourage them to try animating their own writing.

11 Motivation—Enjoyment—Create a Maurice Sendak reading center in the classroom or school library. Place in the center books written and illustrated by Sendak as well as books written by other authors and illustrated by Sendak. Decorate the center with posters, papier-mâché characters, puppets, and other art work created by children. Include in the center any Sendak-motivated stories written and illustrated by children. Encourage children to use the center.

While these activities are written for one book, they suggest the multiple experiences that could accompany many picture storybooks. It should always be remembered, however, that enjoyment of books and reading is the major goal. Books can be shared and savored without planning any accompanying activities.

SUMMARY

Sharing picture books with children provides adults and children with opportunities for enjoyable and rewarding experiences. If these experiences are worth sharing, they are also worthy of careful preparation. When selecting materials for the shared experiences, adults need to consider the nature of the picture book and the purpose for sharing the book with children.

Mother Goose books can be used for language enrichment, dramatization, role playing, choral speaking, artistic interpretations, research projects, and creative writing. Researching the origins of Mother Goose rhymes can inspire library research, oral language, and creative writing when the verses are used with older children.

Alphabet books that reinforce letter/sound relationships can be used as source material for developing visual and verbal literacy. Wordless books are ideal for encouraging language growth, stimulating intellectual development, and motivating creative writing.

One very enjoyable way of sharing picture books with children is by oral reading. Through shared experiences, children learn that literature is a pleasurable experience and are motivated to read books independently, expand language competencies, and develop readiness skills. Age, attention span, and interest should all be considered when selecting books for oral reading.

Interaction activities with picture books can be designed to stimulate aesthetic development. Appreciation for the art media in literature will be enhanced by having children become actively involved in making their own illustrations and encouraging them to experience and value the diverse art styles available in picture books.

Suggested Activities for Children's Appreciation of Picture Books

■ Choose a nursery rhyme book appropriate for sharing with young children. Share the book with a child and encourage the child to interact with the rhymes by supplying missing words, making up rhyming games, or role playing the characters found in the nursery rhymes.

■ Choose several nursery rhymes that have a definite beginning, middle, and end. Use them with children to help them develop an understanding of plot development.

■ Select several alphabet books that would be appropriate for encouraging visual and verbal literacy. Develop a series of questions that would encourage children to describe the pictures, compare the pictures, and evaluate their personal preferences for the pictures. Share the alphabet books and questions with a group of children.

■ Select a wordless book appropriate for use with younger children, and one with enough detail to appeal to older children. Carefully plan the interaction to be used with each book. Share the books with the two different age groups. Compare the responses received from each group.

■ Select a picture storybook appropriate for sharing orally with children. Prepare the story for reading, and share the book with a group of children or a peer group.

■ Compile a list of picture storybooks appropriate for sharing with five-, six-, seven-, and eight-year-old children.

■ Choose an art medium used to illustrate children's books. Research the methods used by illustrators who use that medium. Develop a series of activities that allow children to experience and experiment with the medium, create their own illustrations, and discuss literature illustrations that use that medium.

■ Compile a list of picture book illustrators and their illustrations that could be used to stimulate an understanding of watercolors, collage, pencil drawings, and so forth.

- Choose a picture book that illustrates a nursery song, animal song or holiday song. Plan an interaction activity that encourages children to sing, accompany the song with rhythm instruments, play a singing game, or do a counting activity. Share the activity with a group of children or a peer group.
- Develop a web illustrating the child development potential related to an ABC, concept book, or wordless picture book.
- Choose a children's picture storybook other than the one developed in the chapter; list the multiple uses of the book.

References

1 Allen, Roach Van. *Language Experiences in Communication.* Boston: Houghton Mifflin, 1976.

2 Borusch, Barbara. Personal Correspondence. Eastern Michigan University, Dec. 1, 1980.

3 Broudy, H. S. "How Basic Is Aesthetic Education? or Is It the Fourth R?" *Language Arts* V. 54 (September 1977): 631–37.

4 Cohen, Dorothy. "The Effect of Literature on Vocabulary and Reading Achievement." *Elementary English* 45 (February 1968): 209–13, 217.

5 Hoff, Syd. *How to Draw Cartoons.* New York: Scholastic, 1975.

6 Hoff, Syd. *Jokes to Enjoy, Draw, and Tell.* New York: Putnam, 1974.

7 Jett-Simpson, Mary. "Parents and Teachers Share Books with Young Children." In *Developing Active Readers: Ideas for Parents, Teachers and Librarians,* edited by Dianne L. Monson and Day Ann K. McClenathan. Newark, Del.: International Reading Association, 1979.

8 Lamme, Linda Leonard. "Reading Aloud to Young Children." *Language Arts* 53 (November–December, 1976):886–88.

9 Lamme, Linda Leonard, and Kane, Frances. "Children, Books, and Collage." *Language Arts* 53 (November–December, 1976): 902–5.

10 Loban, Walter. *Language Development: Kindergarten through Grade Twelve.* Urbana, Ill.: National Council of Teachers of English, 1976.

11 Norton, Donna. *Language Arts Activities for Children.* Columbus, Ohio: Merrill, 1980.

12 Ross, Ramon R. *Storyteller.* 2d ed. Columbus, Ohio: Merrill, 1980.

13 Siks, Geraldine Brain. *Drama with Children.* New York: Harper & Row, 1977.

14 Sirota, Beverly S. "The Effect of a Planned Literature Program of Daily Oral Reading by the Teacher on the Voluntary Reading of Fifth Grade Children." New York University, 1971. University Microfilm No. 71–28, 560.

15 Stauffer, Russell. *The Language-Experience Approach to the Teaching of Reading.* New York: Harper & Row, 1980.

16 Stewig, John Warren. "Alphabet Books: A Neglected Genre." *Language Arts* 55 (January 1978): 6–11.

17 Vandergrift, Kay. "Reading Aloud to Young Children." In *Using Literature with Young Children,* edited by Leland B. Jacobs, pp. 11–14. Columbia University, Teachers College, 1974.

18 Wintle, Justin and Fisher, Emma. *The Pied Pipers, Interviews with the Influential Creators of Children's Literature.* New York: Paddington, 1974.

CHILDREN'S LITERATURE

Mother Goose

Blegvad, Lenore. *This Little Pig-a-Wig and Other Rhymes about Pigs.* Atheneum, 1978 (I:3–6). Twenty-two nursery rhymes about pigs are presented in a small book. One verse and corresponding illustration are on each page.

Bodecker, N. M. *It's Raining, Said John Twaining.* Atheneum, 1973 (I:4–7). Fourteen Danish nursery rhymes are translated and illustrated.

De Angeli, Marguerite. *Marguerite De Angeli's Book of Nursery and Mother Goose Rhymes.* Doubleday, 1954 (I:4–7). A large 192-page book that has 376 illustrated nursery rhymes. The pictures have an early English setting.

De Forest, Charlotte B. *The Prancing Pony: Nursery Rhymes from Japan.* Illustrations by Keiko Hida. Walker/Weatherhill, 1968 (I:5–10). Traditional Japanese nursery rhymes were collected by Tasuku Harada and translated by the author. Illustrated with a form of collage called *kusa-e.*

Frasconi, Antonio. *The House That Jack Built.* Harcourt Brace Jovanovich, 1958 (I:3–7). The popular nursery rhyme written in both English and French.

Galdone, Paul. *The House That Jack Built.* McGraw-Hill, 1961 (I:3–7). The cumulative nursery rhyme is retold in large, humorous illustrations.

————. *Old Mother Hubbard and Her Dog.* McGraw-Hill, 1961 (I:3–7). Humorous illustrations tell the complete story of Old Mother Hubbard.

Greenaway, Kate. *Mother Goose: Or, the Old Nursery Rhymes.* Warne, 1881 (I:3–7). A small Mother Goose illustrated with charming Greenaway children.

Griego, Margot C.; Bucks, Betsy L.; Gilbert, Sharon S.; and Kimball, Laurel H. *Tortillitas Para Mama.* Illustrated by Barbara Cooney. Holt, Rinehart & Winston, 1981 (ch. 4).

Jeffers, Susan. *Three Jovial Huntsmen.* Bradbury, 1973 (I:4–7). Muted colors show hundreds of animals peeking out at three hunters who are unable to find any animals when they go on a hunting trip.

Lobel, Arnold. *Gregory Griggs and Other Nursery Rhyme People.* Greenwillow, 1978 (I:4–7). Thirty-four lesser known nursery rhymes about the humorous predicaments of ladies and gentlemen are presented.

Marshall, James. *James Marshall's Mother Goose.* Farrar, Straus & Giroux, 1979 (I:3–7). Large humorous illustrations accompany each of the 33 nursery rhymes in this collection.

Martin, Sarah Catherine. *The Comic Adventures of Old Mother Hubbard and Her Dog.* Harcourt

I = Interest by age range;
R = Readability by grade level.

Brace Jovanovich, 1981 (I:3–7). A humorously illustrated edition of one nursery rhyme.

Miller, Mitchell. *One Misty Moisty Morning.* Farrar, Straus & Giroux, 1971 (I:3–7). A small collection of the more unusual nursery rhymes. Soft pencil drawings illustrate each rhyme.

Provensen, Alice, and Provensen, Martin. *The Mother Goose Book.* Random House, 1976 (I:all). Traditional illustrations are used in a large collection of Mother Goose rhymes. The rhymes are grouped according to topics.

Sendak, Maurice. *Hector Protector and as I Went over the Water.* Harper & Row, 1965 (I:3–7). Two nursery rhymes are told predominately through the use of illustrations.

Spier, Peter. *London Bridge Is Falling Down.* Doubleday, 1967 (I:all). Each line of the nursery rhyme and song is illustrated in detailed drawings. A history of the bridge dating from 1209 is presented on the last two pages.

————. *To Market, to Market.* Doubleday, 1967 (I:5–12). Drawings depicting New Castle, Delaware, as it might have appeared in 1826 are used to illustrate a nursery tale of pigs, animals, farms, and markets. The last two pages tell the history of the town from 1638 through modern times.

Tarrant, Margaret. *Nursery Rhymes.* Crowell, 1978 (I:3–7). Forty-eight popular nursery rhymes are illustrated with traditional drawings.

Tripp, Wallace. *Granfa' Grig Had a Pig and Other Rhymes Without Reason from Mother Goose.* Little, Brown, 1976 (I:4–8). Humorous animal drawings are used to illustrate 121 nursery rhymes in a large book format.

Tudor, Tasha. *Mother Goose.* Walck, 1972 (I:3–7). Seventy-seven popular Mother Goose rhymes are illustrated in a smaller book format. One rhyme and one illustration are on each page.

Wyndham, Robert. *Chinese Mother Goose Rhymes.* Illustrated by Ed Young. World, 1968; Philomel, 1982 (paperback) (I:4–7). Traditional Chinese rhymes are translated into English. The illustrations and Chinese orthography provide the setting for oriental rhymes.

Zuromskis, Diane. *The Farmer in the Dell.* Little, Brown, 1978 (I:3–6). Colorful eighteenth-century pictures illustrate the song.

Toy Books

Bayley, Nicola. *Puss in Boots.* Greenwillow, 1977 (I:4–8). Pop-up version of the folktale.

Beisner, Monika. *A Folding Alphabet Book.* Farrar, Straus & Giroux, 1981 (I:4–6). A long folded book in which animals and other objects form the letters.

Bond, Michael. *Paddington's Pop-Up Book*. Illustrated by Igor Wood. Price, Stern, Sloan, 1977 (I:3–8). A humorous pop-up that introduces children to Paddington Bear.

Bonforte, Lisa. *Farm Animals*. Random House, 1981 (I:2–4). A board book illustrating and describing common farm animals.

Bruna, Dick. *My Toys*. Methuen, 1980 (I:1–3). A foldout board book illustrates familiar toys.

_____. *Out and About*. Methuen, 1980 (I:1–3). A foldout board book.

Carle, Eric. *Catch the Ball*. Philomel, 1982 (ch. 4).

_____. *The Honeybee and the Robber: A Moving Picture Book*. Philomel, 1981 (ch. 4).

_____. *Let's Paint a Rainbow*. Philomel, 1982 (ch. 4).

_____. *The Very Fussy Monkey*. Philomel, 1982 (ch. 4).

Chen, Tony. *Wild Animals*. Random House, 1981 (I:2–4). One or two sentences describe each illustration of a wild animal.

Craig, Helen. *The Mouse House ABC*. Random House, 1979 (I:3–6). A miniature foldout board book in which mice form the letters.

_____. *Mouse House Months*. Random House, 1981 (I:3–6). A miniature foldout board book follows a tree through the seasons and shows a scene for each month.

_____. *The Mouse House 1, 2, 3*. Random House, 1980 (I:3–6). A miniature foldout board book in which mice form the numbers.

Crowther, Robert. *The Most Amazing Hide-and-Seek Alphabet Book*. Viking, 1978 (I:3–6). A mechanical book with each letter concealing an object that begins with that letter.

_____. *The Most Amazing Hide-and-Seek Counting Book*. Viking, 1981 (I:3–6). Colorful pages have pictures that pull, lift, or rotate to introduce counting.

de Paola, Tomie. *Giorgio's Village*. Putnam, 1982 (I:all). A pop-up of an Italian Renaissance village.

Goodall, John S. *Paddy Finds a Job*. Atheneum, 1981 (I:4–6). A wordless pop-up about Goodall's familiar character.

_____. *Shrewbettina Goes to Work*. Atheneum, 1981 (I:4–6). Amusing plot in wordless pop-up.

Hill, Eric. *Spot's Birthday Party*. Putnam, 1982 (I:2–4). In a "lift the flap" book Spot, the dog, plays hide and seek with the guests at his party.

_____. *Spot's First Walk*. Putnam, 1981 (I:2–4). Readers discover what Spot sees on his walk when they lift each flap.

_____. *Where's Spot?* Putnam, 1980 (I:2–4). Spot is missing and children may search for him under the flaps.

Johnson, John E. *The Sky is Blue, the Grass is Green*. Random House, 1980 (I:2–4). A cloth color concept book.

Keussen, Gudren. *This Is How We Live in the Country*. Ars Edition, 1981 (I:3–5). This board book illustrates a European country setting.

_____. *This Is How We Live in Town*. Ars Edition, 1981 (I:3–5). This board book illustrates a European urban setting.

Miller, J. P. *The Cow Says Moo*. Random House, 1979 (I:2–4). A cloth book identifies sounds made by farm animals.

Munari, Bruno. *Who's There? Open the Door*. Philomel, 1980 (I:3–6). A guessing game as readers try to identify what is in decreasingly smaller parcels.

Oxenbury, Helen. *Dressing*. Wanderer Books, 1981 (I:1–3). A board book follows step-by-step dressing.

_____. *Family*. Wanderer Books, 1981 (I:1–3). A board book shows baby with family.

_____. *Friends*. Wanderer Books, 1981 (I:1–3). A board book illustrates baby and friends.

_____. *Playing*. Wanderer Books, 1981 (I:1–3). A board book shows baby playing.

_____. *Working*. Wanderer Books, 1981 (I:1–3). A board book showing familiar work.

Parish, Peggy. *I Can-Can You?* Illustrated by Marylin Hafner. Greenwillow, 1980 (I:1–3). A plastic book demonstrating accomplishments.

Roosevelt, Michele Chopin. *Animals in the Woods*. Random House, 1981 (I:2–4). One or two sentences describe pictures of woodland animals.

Scarry, Richard. *Richard Scarry's Lowly Worm Word Book*. Random House, 1981 (I:1–3). Lowly demonstrates familiar objects such as bath, body parts, and food.

Spier, Peter. *Bill's Service Station*. Doubleday, 1981 (ch. 4).

_____. *Fire House: Hook and Ladder Company Number Twenty-Four*. Doubleday, 1981 (ch. 4).

_____. *Food Market*. Doubleday, 1981 (ch. 4).

_____. *My School*. Doubleday, 1981 (ch. 4).

_____. *The Pet Store*. Doubleday, 1981 (ch. 4).

_____. *The Toy Shop*. Doubleday, 1981 (ch. 4).

Wells, Rosemary. *Max's First Word*. Dial, 1979 (I:2–4). A board book for young children.

_____. *Max's New Suit*. Dial, 1979 (I:2–4). A short board book story.

_____. *Max's Ride*. Dial, 1979 (I:2–4). Humorous board book.

_____. *Max's Toys: A Counting Book*. Dial, 1979 (I:2–4). A simple counting board book.

Zokeisha. *Things I Like to Eat*. Simon & Schuster, 1981 (I:1–3). One object per page of familiar foods.

_____. *Things I Like to Look At*. Simon & Schuster, 1981 (I:1–3). Pictures of familiar objects.

_____. *Things I Like To Play With*. Simon & Schuster, 1981 (I:1–3). Colorful pictures of familiar toys.

_____. *Things I Like To Wear*. Simon & Schuster, 1981 (I:1–3). Illustrations that help young children identify names of clothing.

Alphabet Books

Anno, Mitsumasa. *Anno's Alphabet: An Adventure in Imagination*. Crowell, 1975 (I:5–7). A wordless alphabet book that shows a single letter on one page and a single object beginning with that letter on the opposite page.

_____. *Anno's Magical ABC: An Anamorphic Alphabet*. Lettering by Masaichiro Anno. Philomel, 1981 (I:4–7). A distorted picture is viewed by looking into a shiny object.

Azarian, Mary. *A Farmer's Alphabet*. Godine, 1981 (I:5–8). Wood cuts present images of rural Vermont.

Baldwin, Ruth M. *One Hundred Nineteenth-Century Rhyming Alphabets in English*. Southern Ill. University, 1972 (I:all). A collection of older alphabets.

Baskin, Leonard. *Hosie's Alphabet*. Words by Hosea Tobias and Lisa Baskin. Viking, 1972 (I:6–8). Each double page has one letter of the alphabet, a short descriptive phrase (i.e., an incredibly scaly iguana), and a full-page picture of the object.

Berger, Terry, and Kandell, Alice S. *Ben's ABC Day*. Lothrop, Lee & Shepard, 1982 (I:3–6). A child's familiar activities illustrate each letter.

Brown, Marcia. *All Butterflies: An ABC*. Scribner's, 1974 (I:3–7). Two-word phrases that also correspond with two letters of the alphabet are illustrated on each double page. They progress from "All Butterflies" through "Your Zoo."

Craft, Kinuko. *Mother Goose ABC*. Platt & Munk, 1977 (I:4–8). Mother Goose rhymes are presented in alphabetical order from "a diller, a dollar," through "X, Y, and tumble down Z." Large full-page illustrations are included for each rhyme.

Duvoisin, Roger. *A for the Ark*. Lothrop, Lee & Shepard, 1952 (I:6–8). A theme ABC illustrating the animals entering the ark. There is considerable writing in this text.

Eichenberg, Fritz. *Ape in a Cape: An Alphabet of Odd Animals*. Harcourt Brace Jovanovich, 1952 (I:3–8). Each page presents one letter, a rhyming phrase about the illustration (kitten with a mitten), and one large picture.

Emberley, Ed. *Ed Emberley's ABC*. Little, Brown, 1978 (I:5–8). An amusing alphabet that shows the formation of the letters and an animal representation for each letter.

Feelings, Muriel. *Jambo Means Hello: Swahili Alphabet Book.* Dial, 1974 (I:all). A beautiful book using the Swahili alphabet and drawings depicting the Swahili culture.

Gág, Wanda. *The ABC Bunny.* Coward-McCann, 1933 (I:3–6). A bunny is shown in numerous adventures related to letters of the alphabet. Two colors are used: the black and white illustrations are lithographs; the letters are shown in red.

Greenaway, Kate. *A–Apple Pie.* Warne, 1886 (I:3–8). The old rhyme that was first referenced in 1671. The letters of the alphabet are used to develop a tale describing what happened following the baking of an apple pie.

Hoban, Tana. *A, B, See!* Greenwillow, 1982 (I:4–6). Photographs illustrate objects that begin with the uppercase letters.

Lobel, Arnold. *On Market Street.* Illustrated by Anita Lobel. Greenwillow, 1981 (I:4–7). Tradespeople show their wares from A to Z.

Mendoza, George. *Norman Rockwell's Americana ABC.* Dell, 1975 (I:all). Norman Rockwell paintings are used to illustrate each letter of the alphabet. Pictures are excellent for oral discussion.

Milne, A. A. *Pooh's Alphabet Book.* Illustrations by E. H. Shepard. Dutton, 1975 (I:6–10). A small alphabet book using quotations and illustrations from the Pooh books to introduce each letter of the alphabet.

Munari, Bruno. *Bruno Munari's ABC.* World, 1960 (I:3–6). Large letters and pictures are appropriate for sharing and discussing with younger children.

Musgrove, Margaret. *Ashanti to Zulu: African Traditions.* Illustrated by Leo and Diane Dillon. Dial, 1976 (I:7–12). Traditions and customs from twenty-six African tribes are presented in alphabetical order.

Nedobeck, Don. *Nedobeck's Alphabet Book.* Childrens Press, 1981 (I:3–6). Illustrations and words depict the letters.

Newberry, Clare Turlay. *The Kitten's ABC.* Harper & Row, 1965 (I:3–6). Newberry's delightful kittens experience each letter of the alphabet.

Nicholson, William. *An Alphabet.* Wofsy, 1975 (I:all). A copy of an alphabet first published in 1897. Different professions illustrate each letter.

Niland, Deborah. *ABC of Monsters.* McGraw-Hill, 1978 (I:3–6). A small humorous alphabet that shows monsters doing funny things at a monster party: annoying apes, bothering bees, and cuddling cats.

Piatti, Celestino. *Celestino Piatti's Animal ABC.* Atheneum, 1966 (I:4–7). Brightly illustrated animals and short verses accompany letters.

Provensen, Alice, and Provensen, Martin. *A Peaceable Kingdom: The Shaker Abecedarius.* Viking, 1978 (I:all). This collection of illustrated alphabet animal rhymes was first published in the Shaker Manifesto of July 1882.

Ruben, Patricia. *Apples to Zippers: An Alphabet Book.* Doubleday, 1976 (I:4–8). Photographs are used to illustrate objects that begin with the various letters of the alphabet.

Tudor, Tasha. *A Is for Annabelle.* Walck, 1954 (I:3–7). Annabelle is Grandmother's doll. All of the letters and corresponding verses tell about, and illustrate playing with or dressing, Annabelle.

Wildsmith, Brian. *Brian Wildsmith's ABC.* Watts, 1962 (I:3–6). A beautifully illustrated ABC. The text contains the letter in small and capital letters, a word that represents the letter, and one picture illustrating the word.

Counting Books

Anno, Mitsumasa. *Anno's Counting Book.* Crowell, 1977 (I:3–7). Large detailed drawings of landscapes illustrate each number. Number 6: six blocks, six buildings, six ducks, six children, six adults, six pine trees, six railroad cars, etc.

———. *Anno's Counting House.* Philomel, 1982 (I:3–7). Cut out windows show ten little people who demonstrate counting, adding, and subtracting.

Carle, Eric. *My Very First Book of Numbers.* Crowell, 1974 (I:3–6). A simple matching book in which the child matches black squares with an illustration of fruits showing the appropriate numbers.

———. *1, 2, 3, to the Zoo.* World, 1968 (I:3–7). Zoo animals are presented, along with corresponding numbers. The book progresses from one elephant to ten birds.

———. *The Very Hungry Caterpillar.* Crowell, 1971 (ch. 4).

Feelings, Muriel. *Moja Means One, Swahili Counting Book.* Illustrations by Tom Feelings. Dial, 1971 (I:all). The numbers from one through ten are shown in numbers and written in Swahili. The illustrations show Swahili scenes.

Hoban, Russell. *Ten What? A Mystery Counting Book.* Illustrated by Sylvie Selig. Scribner's, 1974 (I:6–9). Two bird detectives set out with the urgent message to "get ten." They progress through pages of numerous pictures of two, three, etc., until they solve the riddle.

Hoban, Tana. *Count and See.* Macmillan, 1972 (I:4–7). Photographs depict the numbers from 1 through 15, and numbers 20, 30, 40, 50, and 100.

Hutchins, Pat. *1 Hunter.* Greenwillow, 1982 (I:3–5). Camouflaged animals encourage children to find and count the African animals.

Keats, Ezra Jack. *Over in the Meadow.* Scholastic, 1972 (I:5–8). The poem by Wadsworth is illustrated with animals that can be counted.

Knight, Hilary. *Hilary Knight's The Twelve Days of Christmas.* Macmillan, 1981 (I:all). A bear gives his friend the gifts listed in the English folksong.

Maestro, Giulio. *One More and One Less: A Number Concept Book.* Crown, 1974 (I:4–8). The first part of the book develops the concept of *one more* by adding one animal per page up to the number ten; words and numerals are also shown. The last part shows the subtraction process as one animal is subtracted on each page.

Milne, A. A. *Pooh's Counting Book.* Illustrated by E. H. Shepard. Dutton, 1982 (I:6–10). Numbers from 1 through 10 are developed through quotes from various Pooh stories.

Nedobeck, Don. *Nedobeck's Numbers Books.* Childrens Press, 1981 (I:3–6). Clearly illustrated objects show number concepts.

Reiss, John J. *Numbers.* Bradbury, 1971 (I:4–7). Objects are shown that illustrate the number concepts from 1–20. The concept of 20–100 are shown by grouping objects in sets of 5 or 10.

Rowan, Dick. *Everybody In! A Counting Book.* Bradbury, 1968 (I:3–6). Photographs of children swimming in a pool are used to illustrate the numbers and words from one through ten.

Concept Books

Banchek, Linda. *Snake In, Snake Out.* Illustrated by Elaine Arnold. Crowell, 1978 (I:3–7). Eight words—(up, down, in, out, over, under, on, off) —are presented through a picture book that describes a grandmother who finds herself the owner of a snake.

Carle, Eric. *The Grouchy Ladybug.* Crowell, 1971 (I:4–7). A ladybug progresses through the day from six in the morning to six at night. Along the way, she encounters colorful insects and animals.

———. *The Mixed-up Chameleon.* Crowell, 1975 (I:2–6). A chameleon wishes to be a bear, fox, flamingo, fish, deer, elephant, turtle, giraffe, and seal. He finally wants to be himself again. The book may be used for color identification.

———. *My Very First Book of Colors.* Crowell, 1974 (I:3–6). Nine colors are shown in half-page blocks. Colors are to be matched with illustrations.

———. *My Very First Book of Shapes.* Crowell, 1974 (I:4–7). Children match black shapes with a similar shape represented in a colored illustration.

Crews, Donald. *Carousel.* Greenwillow, 1982 (I:4–8). Illustrations take reader on a carousel ride.

_____. *Freight Train*. Greenwillow, 1978 (I:3–7). Colors, the names of the various cars on a freight train, and concepts such as *through, daylight,* and *darkness* are developed.

_____. *Harbor*. Greenwillow, 1982 (I:3–7). Children discover names of harbor ships—tugboats, freighters, liners, tankers, and barges—as they go in and out of the harbor.

Duvoisin, Roger. *See What I Am*. Lothrop, Lee & Shepard, 1974 (I:5–9 and older children interested in art). The primary colors are introduced and then mixed to produce the secondary colors—purple, green, brown, and orange. The artist shows how colors are used to make color illustrations in picture books.

Hoban, Tana. *Big Ones, Little Ones*. Greenwillow, 1976 (I:2–7). Photographs of zoo animals compare the adult and the baby to develop the concept of *big* and *little*.

_____. *Circles, Triangles, and Squares*. Macmillan, 1974 (I:4–8). This wordless book presents the shapes found around us. Photographs include bubbles, squares, triangular signs, circular pipes, circular glasses, hoops, and tires.

_____. *Dig, Drill, Dump, Fill*. Greenwillow, 1975 (I:5–10). Photographs presenting the world of heavy machinery include scoop shovels, drills, dump trucks and cement mixers.

_____. *Over, Under & Through and Other Spatial Concepts*. Macmillan, 1973 (I:3–7). Photographs illustrate the spatial concepts related to *over, under, through, on, in, around, across, between, beside, below, against,* and *behind.*

_____. *Push–Pull, Empty–Full: A Book of Opposites*. Macmillan, 1972 (I:3–7). Photographs and the descriptive words illustrate the opposite meanings of terms such as *push-pull, empty-full, wet-dry, in-out, up-down,* and *thick-thin.*

_____. *Take Another Look*. Greenwillow, 1981 (I:4–8). Viewers look at an object through a circular cutout, guess what it is, and turn the page to see if they were correct.

Kalan, Robert. *Blue Sea*. Illustrated by Donald Crews. Greenwillow, 1979 (I:3–7). Large illustrations of fish show size concepts.

Spier, Peter. *Crash! Bang! Boom!* Doubleday, 1972 (I:4–9). Detailed pictures show items that make various noises. The word depicting the sound is printed next to each picture.

_____. *Fast-Slow, High-Low: A Book of Opposites*. Doubleday, 1972 (I:5–10). Numerous detailed pictures illustrate the concept of *opposites.*

Wordless Books

Alexander, Martha. *Bobo's Dream*. Dial, 1970 (I:3–7). Bobo dreams that he becomes large and rescues his master's football from a group of bigger boys.

_____. *Out! Out! Out!* Dial, 1968 (I:3–7). A little boy coaxes a bird out of a house by creating a trail of cereal.

Anno, Mitsumasa. *Anno's Britain*. Philomel, 1982 (I:all). The illustrations follow a traveler through Great Britain as he visits landmarks.

_____. *Anno's Italy*. Collins, 1980 (I:all). Illustrations take the viewer on a trip through Italy.

_____. *Anno's Journey*. Philomel, 1978 (I:6–12). Illustrations record the journey of the artist as he journeys through the countryside, the small towns, and cities of Europe.

_____. *Topsy-Turvies—Pictures to Stretch the Imagination*. Walker/Weatherhill, 1970 (I:all). Children are instructed to use their imaginations, think for themselves, and decide what the little men are doing in the pictures.

Aruego, Jose. *Look What I Can Do*. Scribner's, 1971 (I:3–7). Two carabaos try to outdo each other and get into funny situations.

Briggs, Raymond. *The Snowman*. Random House, 1978 (I:3–7). A snowman comes to life and takes his young creator on a tour of strange lands. He also explores the house.

Carle, Eric. *Do You Want to Be My Friend?* Crowell, 1971 (I:3–7). (Received first prize for picture books at the International Children's Book Fair, Bologna, Italy.) A mouse searches for a friend throughout the illustrations.

Carroll, Ruth. *What Whiskers Did*. Walck, 1965 (I:3–7). A puppy first breaks his leash, then chases a rabbit, and finally makes friends with the rabbits in their hole.

de Paola, Tomie. *The Hunter and the Animals: A Wordless Picture Book*. Holiday, 1981 (I:5–9). The forest animals convince the hunter to break his gun.

_____. *Pancakes for Breakfast*. Harcourt Brace Jovanovich, 1978 (I:3–7). The procedures for making pancakes are shown in a humorous wordless book.

Goodall, John. *The Adventures of Paddy Pork*. Harcourt Brace Jovanovich, 1968 (I:5–9). A pig named Paddy leaves home and joins the circus. After a series of experiences, he decides to return home.

_____. *The Story of an English Village*. Atheneum, 1979 (I:all). This wordless book illustrates the changes in an English village that occur beginning in the fourteenth century and continuing into the twentieth.

_____. *Paddy Goes Traveling*. Atheneum, 1982 (I:5–9). Paddy Pork has an adventure on the beach.

Hutchins, Pat. *Changes, Changes*. Macmillan, 1971 (I:2–6). Two doll figures are shown in a house made of blocks. They rearrange the blocks when the house catches on fire in order to build a fire truck, a boat, and other structures.

Keats, Ezra Jack. *Clementina's Cactus*. Viking, 1982 (I:all). The wordless book explores the world of the desert.

Krahn, Fernando. *Who's Seen the Scissors?* Dutton, 1975 (I:4–8). A pair of scissors leaves a tailor shop and flies around the town cutting various items.

Mayer, Mercer. *A Boy, a Dog and a Frog*. Dial, 1967 (I:5–9). A boy and a dog try unsuccessfully to catch a frog. He finally follows them home and happily gets into the bathtub.

_____. *Frog Goes to Dinner*. Dial, 1974 (I:6–9). Boy secretly puts Frog into his pocket and takes him along when the family goes to a fancy restaurant. Frog jumps out, and causes all kinds of disruptions until the family is asked to leave.

_____. *Frog, Where Are You?* Dial, 1969 (I:5–9). The boy and dog search for the missing frog. They run into bees, an owl, and a deer.

_____. *The Great Cat Chase*. Four Winds, 1974 (I:5–7). A cat dressed up as a baby runs away and children try to catch him.

_____. *A Boy, a Dog, a Frog, and a Friend*. Dial, 1971 (I:5–9). The frog's son accompanies the boy and the dog when they find a turtle. The turtle tricks them but then becomes a friend.

Mayer, Mercer, and Mayer, Marianna. *One Frog Too Many*. Dial, 1975 (I:5–9). Frog becomes jealous when Boy receives a new frog for his birthday.

Ormerod, Jan. *Sunshine*. Lothrop, Lee & Shepard, 1981 (I:4–8). A child wakes up and helps her parents leave the house on time.

Spier, Peter. *Noah's Ark*. Doubleday, 1977 (I:3–9). Illustrates Jacobris Revius's poem *The Flood*. The illustrations of animals and ark are filled with considerable detail.

_____. *Rain*. Doubleday, 1982 (I:4–9). Two children walk in the rain, splash in puddles, and watch ducks enjoy the rain.

Winter, Paula. *Sir Andrew*. Crown, 1980 (I:5–9). A conceited donkey goes for a walk and breaks a leg; his conceit continues as he views himself hobbling in his cast.

Easy-to-Read Books

Benchley, Nathaniel. *Oscar Otter*. Illustrations by Arnold Lobel. Harper & Row, 1966 (I:5–9 R:2). Oscar is building a slide in the woods. He gets lost and is chased by a fox, a wolf, and a moose.

_____. *Small Wolf*. Illustrations by Joan Sandin. Harper & Row, 1972 (I:6–10 R:3). This "I can read" history book tells the story of how an Indian family had to move west from Manhattan Island in order to avoid conflict with the white man.

Bonsall, Crosby. *The Case of the Cat's Meow*. Harper & Row, 1965 (I:5–9 R:2). The Wizard

Private Eyes try to solve the mystery of Mildred the missing cat.

———. *The Case of the Scaredy Cats.* Harper & Row, 1971 (I:5–9 R:1). Girls invade the club-house of the boy private eyes. The girls prove that girls are as good as boys.

Brenner, Barbara. *Wagon Wheels.* Illustrated by Don Bolognese. Harper & Row, 1978 (I:6–9 R:1). An easy-to-read history book based on the true story of Ed Muldie and his family as they move from Kentucky to Kansas in 1878.

Bulla, Clyde Robert. *Daniel's Duck.* Illustrations by Joan Sandin. Harper & Row, 1979 (I:6–9 R:2). Daniel lives in the mountains of Tennessee and admires the carving of a famous neighbor.

Bunting, Eve. *The Big Red Barn.* Illustrated by Howard Knotts. Harcourt Brace Jovanovich, 1979 (I:6–9 R:2). Craig's grandpa teaches him to accept changes in his life; he has both a new stepmother, and the old red barn on the farm is destroyed.

Chenery, Janet. *The Toad Hunt.* Illustrations by Ben Shecter. Harper & Row, 1967 (I:5–9 R:2). An entertaining information book about toads and frogs.

Ehrlich, Amy. *Leo, Zack and Emmie.* Dial, 1981 (I:5–8 R:2). A new girl affects the friendship of two boys.

Flower, Phyllis. *Barn Owl.* Illustrations by Cherryl Pape. Harper & Row, 1978 (I:5–8 R:1). An "I can read" science book describes the barn owls' hunting methods.

Gage, Wilson. *Squash Pie.* Illustrated by Glen Rounds. Greenwillow, 1976 (I:5–8 R:3). A humorous story about a farmer who plants squash because he wants squash pie; unfortunately, something keeps stealing his squash.

Gray, Genevieve. *How Far, Felipe?* Illustrated by Ann Grifalconi. Harper & Row, 1978 (I:6–9 R:2). An "I can read" history book tells the story of Felipe and his donkey when they join Colonel Anzos's caravan in 1775 and travel to California.

Griffith, Helen V. *Alex and the Cat.* Illustrations by Joseph Low. Greenwillow, 1982 (I:5–8 R:1). A dog tries to realize his great dreams but discovers that he is better off as a house pet.

Hoff, Syd. *Chester.* Harper & Row, 1961 (I:5–8 R:1). Chester is a wild horse who wants to belong to someone.

———. *Sammy the Seal.* Harper & Row, 1959 (I:5–8 R:1). Sammy lives in a zoo but wants to see what it would be like on the outside. He has his chance and even attends school.

Kessler, Leonard. *Kick, Pass, and Run.* Harper & Row, 1966 (I:5–8 R:1). Football is explained in simple terms when Rabbit, Duck, Cat, Owl, and Frog find a football and try to discover what it is.

Leeuwen, Jean Van. *Tales of Oliver Pig.* Illustrated by Arnold Lobel. Dial, 1979 (I:5–7 R:2). Oliver pig has five short adventures.

———. *More Tales of Oliver Pig.* Dial, 1981 (I:5–7 R:2). Further adventures of Oliver.

Lobel, Anita. *The Pancake.* Greenwillow, 1978 (I:5–8 R:3). The folktale of the pancake is told in an easier to read version.

Lobel, Arnold. *Frog and Toad All Year.* Harper & Row, 1976 (I:5–8 R:1). Frog and Toad have some funny adventures throughout the various seasons of the year.

———. *Frog and Toad Are Friends.* Harper & Row, 1970 (I:5–8 R:1). Frog and Toad share five short stories about spring, a story, a lost button, a swim, and a letter.

———. *Frog and Toad Together.* Harper & Row, 1972 (I:5–8 R:1). Five short stories about the adventures of Frog and Toad as they make a list of activities, plant a garden, eat cookies, experience an adventure with a snake and a hawk, and dream.

———. *Grasshopper on the Road.* Harper & Row, 1978 (I:5–8 R:2). Grasshopper sets out on a trip and meets some insects who don't like to do something different every day.

———. *Owl at Home.* Harper & Row, 1975 (I:5–8 R:2). Five easy-to-read stories explore Owl's adventures when he invites winter into his house, sees strange lumps, makes tear-water tea, tries to be both upstairs and downstairs, and makes friends with the moon.

———. *Uncle Elephant.* Harper & Row, 1981 (I:5–8 R:2). Uncle Elephant takes care of his nephew when the parents are lost at sea.

Miles, Miska. *Noisy Gander.* Illustrated by Leslie Merrill. Unicorn/Dutton, 1978 (I:5–8 R:2). A small gosling makes the discovery that loud honking can be very useful.

Rice, Eve. *Once in a Wood. Ten Tales from Aesop.* Greenwillow, 1979 (I:6–9 R:2). Ten Aesop fables are retold in an easier-to-read version.

Ryder, Joanne. *Fireflies.* Illustrations by Don Bolognese. Harper & Row, 1977 (I:6–9 R:1). The life cycle of a firefly is developed in words and pictures.

Seuss, Dr. *The Cat in the Hat.* Random House, 1957 (I:4–7 R:1). A very unusual cat causes both amusement and mischief when he entertains two bored children on a rainy day.

———. *The Cat in the Hat Comes Back.* Random House, 1958 (I:4–7 R:1). The cat returns and brings with him little cats A through Z.

Wiseman, Bernard. *Morris Goes to School.* Harper & Row, 1970 (I:5–8 R:1). Morris cannot count so he decides to go to school.

———. *Morris Has a Cold.* Dodd, Mead, 1978 (I:5–8 R:1). Boris Bear tries to help Morris Moose get rid of a cold. They try both old and new remedies in a comical story.

Yolen, Jane. *The Giants Go Camping.* Illustrated by Tomie de Paola. Seabury, 1979 (I:6–8 R:2). Five giants go camping; each has an adventure in one of the book's five chapters.

Picture Storybooks

Aardema, Verna. *Why Mosquitoes Buzz in People's Ears.* Illustrated by Leo and Diane Dillon. Dial, 1975 (ch. 4).

Adoff, Arnold. *Black Is Brown Is Tan.* Illustrated by Emily Arnold McCully. Harper & Row, 1973 (I:3–7). A happy family with a black mother and a white father share their experiences.

Ahlberg, Janet, and Ahlberg, Allen. *Each Peach Pear Plum: An I-Spy Story.* Viking, 1978 (I:3–7). Two short lines introduce each page and suggest what the reader should find in a picture "I Spy" story.

———. *Peek-a-boo!* Viking, 1981 (I:2–6). A baby peeks through an opening on a page to discover the family's activities.

Anderson, Lonzo. *Izzard.* Illustrated by Adrienne Adams. Scribner's, 1973 (I:6–10 R:4). Jamie, a boy who lives in the Virgin Islands, adopts a lizard for a pet. He takes responsibility for his pet until Izzard grows up and returns to his natural surroundings.

Aruego, Jose, and Dewey, Ariane. *We Hide, You Seek.* Greenwillow, 1979 (ch 4).

Asch, Frank. *Moon Bear.* Scribner's, 1978 (I:2–7 R:5). Little bear is afraid that the moon will disappear and never come back. He discovers new friends when he tries to help the moon.

Baker, Jeannie. *Grandfather.* Deutsch, 1980 (I:5–8). Collage illustrations depict a visit with Grandfather.

———. *Grandmother.* Deutsch, 1979 (I:5–8). Collage illustrations show a visit with Grandmother.

Brandenberg, Aliki. *The Two of Them.* Greenwillow, 1979 (I:3–8 R:7). A girl and her grandfather develop a close relationship before he dies.

Brown, Margaret Wise. *Fox Eyes.* Illustrated by Garth Williams. Pantheon, 1977 (I:2–7 R:5). The red fox is observing an opossum family and other animals; his "whiskerchew!" cough warns the animals of his presence.

———. *The Runaway Bunny.* Illustrated by Clement Hurd. Rev. ed. Harper & Row, 1972 (I:2–7 R:6). A beautiful children's story that emphasizes the need for both independence and love.

Burningham, John. *Avocado Baby.* Crowell, 1982 (I:3–6 R:4). A weakling baby becomes strong after eating an avocado.

———. *The Rabbit.* Crowell, 1975 (I:2–5). In this colorful small book, a young boy describes the behavior of his pet rabbit.

———. *The Snow.* Crowell, 1975 (I:2–5). A small boy plays outside with his mother.

Burton, Virginia Lee. *Katy and the Big Snow.* Houghton Mifflin, 1943, 1971 (I:2–6 R:4). Katy is the strongest crawler tractor in Geoppolis; she saves the town after a heavy snow fall.

———. *The Little House.* Houghton Mifflin, 1942 (ch. 4).

———. *Mike Mulligan and His Steam Shovel.* Houghton Mifflin, 1939 (I:2–6 R:4). Mary Anne, the steam shovel, proves that she can dig in one day more than 100 men can dig in a week.

Carle, Eric. *The Secret Birthday Message.* Crowell, 1972 (I:3–7). Basic shapes are shown in a birthday message. The child follows these shapes in the message and discovers his birthday present.

———. *Watch Out! A Giant!* Collins, 1978 (I:3–7). Two children go through a series of openings in the book pages as they try to escape from a giant. A large, brightly illustrated book.

Clifton, Lucille. *Amifika.* Illustrated by Thomas Di Grazia. Dutton, 1977 (I:3–7 R:3). A small black boy fears his father's return because he can't remember him.

de Brunhoff, Jean. *The Story of Babar.* Random House, 1933, 1961 (I:3–9 R:4). The original Babar story in which Babar loses his mother, is befriended by a little old lady, learns the ways of humans, and is crowned King of the elephants.

———, and de Brunhoff, Laurent. *Babar's Anniversary Album: 6 Favorite Stories.* Random House, 1981 (I:3–9 R:4). Contains *The Story of Babar, The Travels of Babar, Babar the King, Babar's Birthday Surprise, Babar's Mystery,* and *Babar and the Wully-Wully.*

de Paola, Tomie. *The Clown of God.* Harcourt Brace Jovanovich, 1978 (ch. 3).

———. *Nana Upstairs & Nana Downstairs.* Putnam, 1973 (I:3–7 R:6). Tommy has two beloved grandmothers; a great-grandmother upstairs and a grandmother downstairs.

———. *Oliver Button Is a Sissy.* Harcourt Brace Jovanovich, 1979 (I:5–8 R:2). Oliver likes to dance, read books, and dress in costumes. The boys consider him a sissy until he performs in a talent show.

———. *The Quicksand Book.* Holiday, 1977 (I:5–9 R:4). A humorous story; it also discusses the composition of quicksand and how to rescue someone who falls into quicksand.

———. *Strega Nona's Magic Lessons.* Harcourt Brace Jovanovich, 1982 (I:5–9 R:6). Disaster results when Big Anthony tries to use Strega Nona's magic.

Duvoisin, Roger. *Petunia.* Knopf, 1950 (I:3–6 R:6). Petunia, the silly goose, learns that she has to do more than carry a book to gain wisdom.

Emberley, Barbara. *Drummer Hoff.* Illustrated by Ed Emberley. Prentice-Hall, 1967 (ch. 4).

Fatio, Louise. *The Happy Lion.* Illustrated by Roger Duvoisin. McGraw-Hill, 1954 (I:3–7 R:7). A lion who lives in a zoo discovers people are not so friendly when he goes to town to visit them.

Flora, James. *Sherwood Walks Home.* Harcourt Brace Jovanovich, 1966 (I:3–8 R:2). Robert, the windup bear, is left in the park. A humorous cumulative tale tells what happens as he tries to get home before his motor runs down.

Gág, Wanda. *Millions of Cats.* Coward-McCann, 1929 (I:3–7 R:3). The little old woman's desire for a pretty cat results in a fight between trillions of cats. She gets one scraggly kitten who turns out to be the best one of all.

Galdone, Paul. *The Three Wishes.* McGraw-Hill, 1967. (I:3–7 R:2). A humorous illustrated folktale about foolish actions.

Gammell, Stephen. *Wake Up Bear . . . It's Christmas!* Lothrop, Lee & Shepard 1981 (I:5–8 R:4). A Christmas story accompanied by humorous illustrations.

Garelick, May. *Down to the Beach.* Illustrated by Barbara Cooney. Four Winds, 1973 (I:3–7). A thoroughly enjoyable time is had at the beach where there are boats, birds, fishermen, waves, shells, and fog horns.

Hader, Berta and Hader, Elmer. *The Big Snow.* Macmillan, 1948 (I:3–7 R:4). The wild animals prepare for winter and experience the big snow.

Haley, Gail E. *A Story, A Story.* Atheneum, 1970 (I:6–10 R:6). An African tale that tells how Ananse, the spider man, bargained with the Sky God.

Hoban, Russell. *A Baby Sister for Frances.* Illustrated by Lillian Hoban. Harper & Row, 1964 (I:5–8 R:4). Frances the badger has a new baby sister, and things just aren't the same.

———. *A Bargain for Frances.* Illustrated by Lillian Hoban. Harper & Row, 1970 (I:4–8 R:2). This easy-to-read book tells the story of Frances and her friend Thelma.

———. *Best Friends for Frances.* Illustrated by Lillian Hoban. Harper & Row, 1969 (I:4–8 R:4). When Frances discovers that her friend Albert would rather go wandering by himself and play ball with the boys, she learns that her little sister is a lot of fun and can also be a best friend.

———. *Bread and Jam for Frances.* Illustrated by Lillian Hoban. Harper & Row, 1964 (I:4–8 R:4). Frances wants bread and jam, not eggs or anything else that is new.

———. *Charlie the Tramp.* Illustrated by Lillian Hoban. Four Winds, 1966 (I:4–8 R:4). A young animal, with human characteristics, tries to rebel against his parents.

———. *Nothing to Do.* Illustrations by Lillian Hoban. Harper & Row, 1964 (I:4–8 R:4). Walter Possum complains that he has nothing to do. Father solves his problem.

Hurd, Edith Thacher. *I Dance In My Red Pajamas.* Illustrated by Emily Arnold. McCully Harper, 1982 (I:3–7 R:3). Text develops the warm relationship between a girl and her visiting grandparents.

Hutchins, Pat. *Happy Birthday, Sam.* Greenwillow, 1978 (I:3–6 R:4). Sam cannot reach the switch, his clothes in the closet, the water faucet, or the knob of the front door. Grandpa's birthday present solves his problem.

———. *The Wind Blew.* Macmillan, 1974 (I:3–6 R:4). A short, rhyming story that tells with colorful pictures what happened when the wind blew objects away from people.

Jonas, Ann. *When You Were A Baby.* Greenwillow, 1982 (I:2–5 R:2). The author reminds children about things they could not do as babies but can do as growing children.

Keats, Ezra Jack. *Dreams.* Macmillan, 1974 (I:3–8 R:3). Robert makes a mouse at school; everyone else dreams his mouse saves Archie's cat from a dog.

———. *Goggles!* Macmillan, 1969 (I:5–9 R:3). When Archie and Willie find a pair of motorcycle goggles, some bigger boys try to take the goggles away from them. By crawling through a pipe, they outwit the bullies and reach home safely.

———. *A Letter to Amy.* Harper & Row, 1968 (I:3–8 R:3). Peter writes a birthday party invitation to his friend Amy.

———. *Louie.* Greenwillow, 1975. (I:3–8 R:2). Louie responds to a puppet in a play and later is given the puppet by the children who put on the show.

———. *Maggie and the Pirate.* Four Winds, 1979 (I:4–8 R:3). Maggie's pet cricket is stolen by a "pirate." When she tries to retrieve the cricket, he is accidentally drowned. The pirate feels very bad about her loss and gives her a new cricket.

———. *Peter's Chair.* Harper & Row, 1967 (I:3–8 R:2). Peter overcomes jealousy when his furniture is painted for his sister.

———. *Pet Show!* Macmillan, 1972 (I:4–8 R:2). (Beautiful bright colors and collage form pictures.) All the children bring pets to the local pet show. When Archie can't find his cat, he brings a germ in a jar and is awarded a prize for the quietest pet.

———. *Regards to the Man in the Moon.* Four Winds, 1981 (I:4–8 R:3). Two children build a spaceship from junk and fuel it with their imaginations.

_____. *The Trip*. Greenwillow, 1978 (I:3–8 R:2). Louie has moved into a new neighborhood and is lonesome for his old friends. He constructs a shoe box scene and can visit his friends again.

Kepes, Juliet. *Cock-a-Doodle-Doo*. Pantheon, 1978 (I:3–7). A tiger takes care of a baby chick and hopes it will make a good dinner. The tiger, of course, does not eat the chick.

Kellogg, Steven. *A Rose for Pinkerton*. Dial, 1981 (I:4–8 R:3). A girl chooses a kitten as a friend for her great dane. Humor develops as the two try to act like each other.

_____. *Tallyho, Pinkerton!* Dial, 1982 (I:4–8 R:3). The great dane, Rose, and her owner go on a hilarious trip to the woods.

Kraus, Robert. *The King's Trousers*. Illustrated by Fred Gwynne. Simon & Schuster, 1981 (I:4–8 R:4). Cartoonlike illustrations and ridiculous situations create a humorous book.

_____. *Leo the Late Bloomer*. Illustrated by Jose and Ariane Aruego. Windmill, 1971 (I:2–6 R:4). A large, colorful picture book tells the story of a tiger who can't do anything right. Suddenly, he blooms.

_____. *Milton the Early Riser*. Illustrated by Jose and Ariane Aruego. Windmill/Dutton, 1972 (I:3–8). Milton, a Panda bear, wakes up early, and there is no one to play with because everyone is asleep. He plays by himself until he falls asleep; at that time everyone else gets up.

Leaf, Munro. *The Story of Ferdinand*. Illustrated by Robert Lawson. Viking, 1936 (ch. 4).

Lexau, Joan M. *Benjie on His Own*. Dial, 1970 (I:4–8). Benjie's grandmother is ill and needs to go to the hospital. Benjie gets help for her and stays with neighbors while she is in the hospital.

Lionni, Leo. *Alexander and the Wind-up Mouse*. Pantheon, 1969 (I:3–6 R:3). A real mouse thinks it would be better to be like Willy the windup mouse because everyone loves the toy. He learns it's better to be real.

_____. *The Biggest House in the World*. Pantheon, 1968 (I:3–6 R:7). A small snail's father tells him a story about a snail who wanted and got the biggest snail shell in the world. The small snail decides it's better to be himself.

Marshall, James. *George and Martha One Fine Day*. Houghton Mifflin, 1978 (I:3–8). Two hippos have a thoroughly delightful day as they walk on a tightrope and visit an amusement park.

Mayer, Mercer. *There's A Nightmare in My Closet*. Dial, 1969 (I:3–7 R:3). A young boy decides to get rid of his nightmare by confronting the monster.

McCloskey, Robert. *Blueberries for Sal*. Viking, 1948 (I:4–8 R:6). Two families go picking berries on blueberry hill: one is Sal and her mother, the other is a bear and her cub. The

two youngsters get mixed up and start following the wrong mother.

_____. *Lentil*. Viking, 1940 (I:4–9 R:7). The town of Alto, Ohio, prepares for the return of their town hero. Lentil saves the homecoming when Old Sneep tries to wreck the welcome.

_____. *One Morning in Maine*. Viking, 1952 (I:4–8 R:3). Sal and her family experience the joys of living on an island as they search for clams and boat across to the village.

_____. *Time of Wonder*. Viking, 1957 (I:5–8 R:4). We see an island as a family explores it in the spring, during a hurricane, and after the storm has passed.

Nakatani, Chiyoko. *The Zoo in My Garden*. Crowell, 1973 (I:3–7 R:2). A young boy describes the zoo in his own garden. It includes dogs, pigeons, butterflies, snails, and insects.

Ness, Evaline. *Sam, Bangs & Moonshine*. Holt, Rinehart & Winston, 1966 (ch. 3).

Newberry, Clare. *Barkis*. Harper & Row, 1938 (I:3–8 R:6). A new birthday puppy at first causes problems because two children do not want to share him.

_____. *Marshmallow*. Harper & Row, 1942 (I:2–7 R:7). Oliver the cat is introduced to a new apartment mate, Marshmallow, a rabbit.

_____. *Widget*. Harper & Row, 1958 (I:2–7 R:2). A kitten explores the outside world, and mother comes to the rescue.

Noble, Trinka Hakes. *The Day Jimmy's Boa Ate the Wash*. Illustrated by Steven Kellogg. Dial, 1980 (I:5–8 R:4). Havoc results when a boy drops his pet boa in the hen house.

Oakley, Graham. *The Church Mice Adrift*. Atheneum, 1977 (I:5–10 R:6). The church cat saves the church mice from an invasion of rats. A more detailed plot will interest older primary children.

_____. *The Church Mice Spread Their Wings*. Atheneum, 1975 (I:5–10 R:6). Sampson and the mice of Wortlehorpe Church try to resist the pressures of the rat race by exploring nature; they discover that nature is not so placid.

_____. *The Church Mouse*. Atheneum, 1972 (I:5–10 R:6). Arthur lives peacefully and enjoyably in a church. The church cat has listened to so many sermons about brotherhood that he treats Arthur accordingly.

_____. *Hetty and Harriet*. Atheneum, 1982 (I:5–10 R:6). A discontented hen and her meek friend leave the security of their barnyard for a series of adventures.

Pearson, Susan. *Izzie*. Illustrations by Robert Andrew Parker. Dial, 1975 (I:4–9). Izzie, a favorite toy, starts to show the effects of all the loving activities.

Peet, Bill. *Cyrus the Unsinkable Sea Serpent*. Houghton Mifflin, 1975. (I:5–9 R:7). A sailing

ship is rescued from squalls and pirates by a not so fierce sea serpent.

_____. *The Gnats of Knotty Pine*. Houghton Mifflin, 1975 (I:5–9 R:6). Hunting season brings problems to the animals of the forest; when they try to form a plan, none can agree. Only the gnats are able to save the doubting animals.

_____. *How Droofus the Dragon Lost His Head*. Houghton Mifflin, 1971 (1:5–9 R:5). The tale of a good kind dragon who cannot eat animals, who befriends a poor family, and allows his head to be used on the castle wall during special occasions.

Peterson, Jeanne Whitehouse. *I Have a Sister, My Sister Is Deaf*. Illustrations by Deborah Ray. Harper & Row, 1977 (I:3–8 R:1). The author shares her enjoyable experiences with her deaf sister.

Provensen, Alice, and Provensen, Martin. *The Year at Maple Hill Farm*. Atheneum, 1978 (I:4–9 R:3). Large illustrations and text trace the seasons of the year and how the animals change with the seasons.

Ransome, Arthur. *The Fool of The World and the Flying Ship*. Illustrated by Uri Shulevitz. Farrar Straus & Giroux, 1968 (ch. 4)

Rayner, Mary. *Garth Pig and the Ice Cream Lady*. Atheneum, 1977 (I:5–9 R:4). The wolf uses an ice cream truck in order to capture a pig.

Rey, Hans. *Curious George*. Houghton Mifflin, 1941. 1969 (I:2–7 R:2). George begins his slapstick adventures when he leaves the jungle with the man who has a yellow hat.

Schatell, Brian. *Farmer Goff and His Turkey Sam*. Lippincott, 1982 (I:4–7 R:5). A prize-winning turkey who performs tricks is not allowed to eat pie. He runs away and wins a pie-eating contest.

Sendak, Maurice. *In the Night Kitchen*, Harper & Row, 1970 (I:5–7). A young child dreams that he is in the world of the night kitchen.

_____. *Seven Little Monsters*. Harper & Row, 1977 (I:5–8). An illustrated account of the actions of Sendak's monsters.

_____. *The Sign on Rosie's Door*. Harper & Row, 1960 (I:5–9 R:2). Rosie pretends she is Alinda, the lady singer, and tries to stage a show.

_____. *Where the Wild Things Are*. Harper & Row, 1963 (I:4–8 R:6). Max's vivid imagination turns his room into a forest inhabited by wild things.

Seuss, Dr. *And To Think That I Saw It on Mulberry Street*. Vanguard, 1937 (I:3–9 R:5). A young boy imagines all the fantastic things that could be on his street.

_____. *Did I Ever Tell You How Lucky You Are?* Random House, 1973 (I:4–10 R:3). Is there anything worse than sitting on a prickly cactus? According to this book, a whole series of things are worse.

_____. *Dr. Seuss's Sleep Book*. Random House, 1962 (I:4–10   R:5). What would it be like if ninety-nine zillion creatures were sleeping? Dr. Seuss gives the reader a humorous, "Who's-Asleep-Score."

_____. *The 500 Hats of Bartholomew Cubbins*. Vanguard, 1938 (I:4–9   R:4). Bartholomew has a bewitched hat that keeps reappearing as he tries to take off his hat before the King.

_____. *Horton Hatches the Egg*. Random House, 1940, 1968 (I:3–9   R:4). Horton replaces lazy Mayzie on her nest and finally hatches an elephant bird.

_____. *Hunches in Bunches*. Random House, 1982 (I:6-10   R:4). A young boy has problems deciding on his hunches.

_____. *I Can Lick 30 Tigers Today!* Random House, 1969 (I:4–10   R:4). Three short stories in addition to the title: "King Looie Katy," and the "Glunk That Got Thunk."

_____. *If I Ran the Zoo*. Random House, 1950 (I:4–10   R:3). A boy is not satisfied with the plain old animals in the zoo and searches in odd places for some unusual animals.

Skorpen, Liesel Moak. *His Mother's Dog*. Illustrated by M. E. Mullin. Harper & Row, 1978 (I:4–9   R:5). Jealousy results when both his dogs prefer his mother and a new baby arrives.

Small, David. *Eulalie and the Hopping Head*. Macmillan, 1982 (I:4–7   R:5). A toad and her daughter find an abandoned doll in the woods. The doll gives them the opportunity to make the fox change her opinion.

Spier, Peter. *Bored—Nothing To Do!* Doubleday, 1978 (I:3–9). When two boys become bored, they build and fly their own airplane.

_____. *The Legend of New Amsterdam*. Doubleday, 1979 (I:all). The illustrations and text show the city of New Amsterdam (New York) in the 1660s.

_____. *Oh, Were They Ever Happy!* Doubleday, 1978 (I:4–9). Children surprise their parents when they paint the house; they use all the various leftover paint they can find.

_____. *The Star-Spangled Banner*. Doubleday, 1973 (I:8 +). The words of the national anthem are illustrated in accurate details from history.

Steig, William. *The Amazing Bone*. Farrar, Straus & Giroux, 1976 (I:6–9   R:3). A pig and a talking bone escape from robbers and from a hungry fox.

_____. *Caleb & Kate*. Farrar, Straus & Giroux, 1977 (I:6–9   R:3). Caleb the carpenter goes to sleep in the woods and is changed into a dog by Yedida the witch. He returns to his wife; she

likes the dog but continues to search for her husband.

_____. *Farmer Palmer's Wagon Ride*. Farrar, Straus & Giroux, 1974 (I:6–9 and   R:5). A humorous story in which the pig and his donkey have one misfortune after another.

_____. *Sylvester and the Magic Pebble*. Simon & Schuster, 1969 (I:6–9   R:5). A magical pebble causes a donkey to turn into a rock.

Stevenson, James. *Could Be Worse!* Greenwillow, 1977 (I:5–9   R:3). Grandpa always responds with "Could be worse" until his grandchildren decide nothing interesting ever happens to him. He responds with a whopper.

_____. *Monty*. Greenwillow, 1979 (I:5–9). Three animals boss an alligator as he takes them across the river, but one day he isn't there. Cartoon format is used.

_____. *The Sea View Hotel*. Greenwillow, 1978 (I:5–10   R:3). A mouse can't find anything to do in an adult resort until he meets the caretaker. Illustrations resemble cartoons.

_____. *The Wish Card Ran Out!* Greenwillow, 1981 (I:6–10   R:4). Cartoon illustrations enhance a humorous spoof on credit cards.

_____. *We Can't Sleep*. Greenwillow, 1982 (I:4–8   R:4). Grandpa tells a story when Louie and Mary Anne cannot sleep.

Turkle, Brinton. *Do Not Open*. Elsevier-Dutton, 1981 (I:4–7   R:4). A monster pops out of a bottle marked "Do not open." The lady tricks the monster into changing its shape and is saved by her cat.

Ungerer, Tomi. *The Beast of Monsieur Racine*. Farrar, Straus & Giroux, 1971 (I:5–9   R:5). A strange beast steals prized pears and becomes a friend of Monsieur Racine. The beast's identity causes a riot at the Academy of Sciences.

Van Allsburg, Chris. *Jumanji*. Houghton Mifflin, 1981 (ch. 4)

Viorst, Judith. *Alexander and the Terrible, Horrible, No Good, Very Bad Day*. Illustrated by Ray Cruz. Atheneum, 1972 (I:3–8   R:6). A boy decides he's going to move to Australia when a series of bad incidents happen to him. Very good for reading aloud.

Waber, Bernand. *The Snake: A Very Long Story*. Houghton Mifflin, 1978 (I:3–8). Collages of scenery and a traveling snake provide an around-the-world adventure. (Creative writing and dramatization.)

Wagner, Jenny. *John Brown, Rose and the Midnight Cat*. Illustrated by Ron Brooks. Bradbury, 1978 (I:4–8). A dog fears that a cat will disturb his life in the home of a nice widow lady.

Ward, Lynd. *The Biggest Bear*. Houghton Mifflin, 1952 (I:5–8   R:4). A boy searches for a bear because he wants a bearskin for the outside of his barn.

Wells, Rosemary. *A Lion for Lewis*. Dial, 1982 (I:3–7   R:4). Lewis, the youngest brother, discovers a way to gain his brother's and sister's attention.

_____. *Timothy Goes to School*. Dial, 1981 (I:4–7   R:4). Timothy Raccoon goes through many trials during his first week in school.

Willard, Nancy. *Simple Pictures Are Best*. Illustrated by Tomie de Paola. Harcourt Brace Jovanovich, 1977 (I:5–9). A shoemaker and his wife frustrate a photographer when they keep adding items that they want included in a photograph for their wedding anniversary. The photographer argues that simple pictures are best.

Williams, Barbara. *Chester Chipmunk's Thanksgiving*. Illustrated by Kay Charao. Dutton, 1978 (I:3–7). Chester wants to share Thanksgiving with his friends who are all busy.

_____. *Someday, Said Mitchell*. Illustrated by Kay Charao. Dutton, 1976 (I:2–7). Mitchell is a small boy who wants to provide his mother with various labor-saving devices.

Williams, Jay. *Everyone Knows What a Dragon Looks Like*. Illustrated by Mercer Mayer. Four Winds, 1976 (I:5–10). The town of Wie is threatened by the Wild Horseman of the North. The town leaders pray for help from the Great Cloud Dragon who saves the town.

_____. *The Reward Worth Having*. Illustrated by Mercer Mayer. Four Winds, 1977 (I:5–10). Three soldiers of the king help an old man; each gets to choose his own reward.

Wolf, Bernard. *Anna's Silent World*. Lippincott, 1977 (I:5–10   R:6). The reader follows Anna's day in school, at recess, and with friends; Anna is deaf.

Yolen, Jane. *The Seeing Stick*. Illustrated by Remy Charlip and Demetra Maraslis. Crowell, 1977 (I:5–8   R:6). An old man carves pictures on a stick; the carvings help a blind girl see in this story set in ancient Peking.

Zemach, Margot. *It Could Always Be Worse: A Yiddish Folk Tale*. Farrar, Straus & Giroux, 1976 (I:5–9   R:2). The Rabbi, in this Yiddish folk tale, gives advice to a man who lives in a crowded hut.

Zolotow, Charlotte. *My Grandson Lew*. Illustrated by William Péne du Bois. Harper & Row, 1974 (I:5–8   R:2). Lewis and his mother share some beautiful memories about Lewis's grandfather who had died four years before.

_____. *The Quarreling Book*. Illustrated by Arnold Lobel. Harper & Row, 1963 (I:4–8). The day starts out all wrong when father forgets to kiss his wife good-bye.

_____. *William's Doll*. Illustrations by William Péne du Bois. Harper & Row, 1972 (I:4–8   R:4). William's desire for a doll results in various responses from his family.

SIX
Traditional Literature

Of Castle and Cottage

Involving Children in Traditional Literature

Of Castle and Cottage

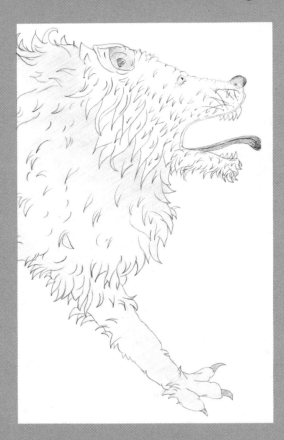

ENCHANTED swans who are returned to human form because of a sister's devotion, a brave boy who climbs into the unknown world at the top of a beanstalk, and a girl who finds refuge in the forest home of seven little men are all brought to life in traditional literature. This literature contains something that appeals to all interests. There are humorous stories, magical stories, and stories about great heroes and their wondrous deeds. The stories have settings from throughout the world. Some take place on the warm, lofty heights of Mount Olympus; others happen on the cold, icy summit of Asgard; still others occur in mythical forests or in magical castles. Regardless of location or subject, these tales include some of the most beloved and remembered stories from childhood.

This chapter discusses the traditional literature heritage, the values of sharing folktales with children, the types of traditional literature, the characteristics of folktales found in various cultures, and the reasons for presenting folktales. Characteristics and examples of fables, myths, and legends are also presented.

THE TRADITIONAL LITERATURE HERITAGE

The quest for our traditional literary heritage takes students of children's literature to a time before the beginning of recorded history and to all parts of the world. They find tales of religious significance that allowed ancient people to speculate about their beginnings; they find heroes from all cultures who overcame supernatural adversaries to gain their rewards; and they find tales of heroic deeds that probably gratified the rulers of ancient tribes. Similarities in tale types, narrative motifs, and content found in stories from varied peoples throughout the world constitute tangible evidence, according to folklorist Stith Thompson (19), that traditional tales are both universal and ancient.

The art of the traditional storyteller has been cultivated in every rank of society and reflects the culture, the nature of the land, and the social contacts of the people. For example, when stories were told in ancient European castles, storytellers related great deeds of noblemen. The English court heard about King Arthur and his Knights of the Round Table, and the French court heard princely stories such as "The Song of Roland." Likewise in China, stories for the ruling classes often portrayed a benevolent dragon, the symbol of Han imperial authority.

Stories told to and by the peasants were in contrast to those told to the nobility. Their life was quite different from that of the noblemen. It was often cruel, harsh, and unjust, and the peasants' stories reflected a need to overcome inequality and dream of a better life. The poorest lad might outwit the noble-man, win his daughter in marriage, and gain lifelong wealth. This theme is found in "The Flying Ship," a Russian tale; in "The Golden Goose," a German tale; and in "The Princess and the Glass Hill," a Norwegian tale. Other stories, such as the English tale, "Jack the Giant Killer" told of overcoming horrible adversaries with cunning and bravery. The peasants in these stories are not always clever. Consequences of stupidity are told in the Norwegian tale, "The Husband Who Has to Mind the House"; in the Russian tale, "The Falcon under the Hat"; and in the fable, "The Miller, the Boy, and the Donkey." In place of the benevolent imperial dragon, stories for the common people in China often developed a cruel and evil dragon and reflected the hero's overcoming this power.

In earlier times, traditional tales were told to all listeners, old and young. With the coming of a strong Puritan influence in England and the colonies, folktales were considered immoral; stories were considered appropriate only if they instructed children and reinforced their moral development. Tales of giants, witches, and enchantment were not regarded highly; in fact, these tales were often condemned. Two occurrences helped advance folktales and guarantee their availability for all time. In France, Charles Perrault published a group of folktales called *Tales of Mother Goose*. This 1698 publication included "Cinderella" and "Sleeping Beauty." Over one hundred years later, the Romantic Movement in Europe generated enthusiasm for exploring folklore to discover more about the roots of the language. In Germany, the Brothers Grimm carefully collected the oral tales from the storytellers themselves. These tales have been retold or adapted by many contemporary writers. This work also influenced collectors in other countries as well as writers of literature.

By the end of the ninteenth century, as discussed in chapter two, childhood was considered a necessary and valuable experience for children. More leisure hours created a need for literature to entertain children, and folktales became a valuable part of this childhood experience. Today, folk literature is considered a part of every child's heritage. It would be difficult to imagine early childhood without "The Little Red Hen," and "The Three Bears." Likewise, it would be hard to think of literature for the nine- or ten-year-old without "Snow White and the Seven Dwarfs." Older children's literary experiences would not be complete without tales of Greek or Norse mythology.

TYPES OF TRADITIONAL LITERATURE

Traditional tales have been handed down from generation to generation by word of mouth. In contrast to a modern story, there is no identified original author. Instead, the storyteller tells what he has received from previous tellers of tales. Folklorists and others interested in collecting and analyzing traditional literature do not always agree on definitions and subtypes for tales. For purposes of definition, this text will use the definitions of folktales, myths, and legends identified and recommended by William Bascom (4).

Folktales

Folktales, according to Bascom, are "prose narratives which are regarded as fiction. They are not considered as dogma or history, they may or may not have happened, and they are not taken seriously" (4, p. 4). Because the tales are set in any time or any place, they are considered almost timeless and placeless. Folktales usually tell the adventures of animal or human characters. Within these tales are certain motifs or patterns such as supernatural adversaries (ogres, witches, and giants), supernatural helpers, magic and marvels, tasks and quests, faithfulness or unfaithfulness, and justice. (Not all motifs are found within one tale.)

Even within folktales there are subcategories or subtypes such as cumulative tales, humorous tales, beast tales, magic and wonder tales, pourquoi tales, and realistic tales.

Cumulative Tales. Tales that build upon the action, characters, or speeches within the story until a climax is reached are found among all cultures. Most of the tales give their main characters, whether animal, vegetable, human, or inanimate object, intelligence and reasoning ability. These stories are frequently shared with younger children because the structure of the tale allows them to join in with the story as each new happening occurs. A runaway baked food is a popular, culturally diverse subject for cumulative tales; it is found not only in the "Gingerbread Boy" but also in the Norwegian version, "The Pancake," the English version, "Johnny Cake," and the Russian version, "The Bun." In all of these tales, the repetition builds until a climax is reached. Other familiar cumulative tales include "Henny Penny" and "The Fat Cat," a Danish tale and "Why Mosquitoes Buzz in People's Ears," an African tale.

Humorous Tales. Folktales allow people to laugh at themselves as well as at others. In Russian tales such as "The Peasant's Pea Patch" and "The Falcon under the Hat," the humor results from absurd situations or the stupidity of the character. Human foolishness resulting from unwise decisions provides the humor and a moral in the English folktale, "Mr. and Mrs. Vinegar," and in the Norwegian tale, "The Husband Who Has to Mind the House." Humor and the need to laugh at oneself as well as at others appear to be universal.

Beast Tales. Beast tales are among the most universal folktales, being found in all cultures. For example, the coyote is a popular animal in Native American tales, while the fox and wolf are found in many European tales. The rabbit and the bear are main characters in the American Black Uncle Remus stories. Beasts in folktales frequently talk and act quite like people. In some stories, such as "The Bremen Town Musicians," the animal main characters use their wits to frighten away the robbers and claim the wealth. In other tales, such as "The Three Billy Goats Gruff," the animals may first use their wits and finally their strength to overcome the enemy. Still other animals win through industrious actions such as those found in "The Little Red Hen." Finally, tales about talking animals may show the cleverness of one animal and the stupidity of another character. The animal character in "Puss in Boots" helps his master by outwitting the ogre and placing his master into the ogre's realm.

Magic and Wonder Tales. The majority of these tales contain some element of magic. The fairy godmother transforms the kind, lovely, mistreated girl into a beautiful princess ("Cinderella"); the peasant boy is rewarded with a cloth that provides food ("The Lad Who Went to the Northwind"); a kindhearted simpleton is rewarded with a magical ship ("The Fool of the World and the Flying Ship"); or the evil witch transforms the handsome prince into a beast ("Beauty and the Beast"). Good or bad magic can be performed; when it is good, the person who benefits has usually had misfortune or is considered inferior by a parent or society. When it is bad, love and diligence usually overcome the magic. This type of magic is found in the German tale "The Six Swans" and in the Norwegian tale "East of the Sun and West of the Moon."

Pourquoi Tales. These tales are told to answer a question, explain the existence of something; or explain the characteristics of animals, plants, or humans. For example, why does an animal or a human act in a certain way? Kathleen Arnott's (1) collection, *Animal Folk Tales around the World* contains several stories that are characteristic of this type of tale. "Why Siberian Birds Migrate in Winter" tells why some birds migrate and also why "the brown owl and his relatives stay behind, spending the winter months in Siberia and struggling to keep alive until the spring comes round again" (p. 96). A West Indies folktale tells "Why You Find Spiders in Banana Bunches"; an American tale suggests "Why Rabbits Have Short Tails." Children enjoy these tales and like to make up their own *pourquoi* stories about animal or human characteristics.

Realistic Tales. The majority of folktales include supernatural characters, magic, or other exaggerated incidents. A few tales, however, are about plots that could have happened and people who could have existed. One such tale is "Dick Whittington," who comes to London looking for streets paved with gold. He doesn't find gold, but he does find work with an honest merchant. When the merchant sends a ship abroad, he asks each employee to place an item on the ship. Dick's only possession is his cat, whose ability brings Dick a fortune. Some versions of this story suggest that at least parts of it are true; there was a Dick Whittington who was lord mayor of London.

Many folktales that are included in these categories will be discussed later. The folktales are presented according to country of origin to enhance understanding of the types of folktales characteristic of a certain culture.

Fables

A second type of traditional literature is a fable. Fables are brief moral tales in which animals usually appear as characters who talk and act like humans. The fable uses the animal tale to indicate a moral lesson or to satirize human conduct. For example, in the familiar "The Hare and the Tortoise," the hare taunts the tortoise about her slow movements and boasts about his own speed. The tortoise then challenges the hare to a race. The hare starts rapidly and is soon far ahead; but, he becomes tired, and in his confidence, he decides to nap. Meanwhile, the tortoise, keeping at her slow and steady pace, plods across the finish line. When the hare awakens he discovers that the tortoise has reached the goal. The moral of this fable indicates that perseverance and determination may compensate for the lack of other attributes. (Both the early fables of Aesop and the modern picture storybook versions of fables are discussed in a later section.)

Myths

"Myths are prose narratives which, in the society in which they are told, are considered to be truthful accounts of what happened in the remote past. They are accepted on faith; they are taught to be believed; and they can be cited as authority in answer to ignorance, doubt, or disbelief. Myths are the embodiment of dogma; they are usually sacred; and they are often associated with theology and ritual" (4, p. 4). Myths account for such things as natural phenomena and the origin of the world, mankind, and death. The main characters in myths may be animals, deities, or cultural heroes, whose actions take place in an earlier world or in another world such as the underworld or the sky. Greek myths, for example, frequently explain the creation of the world, the creation of the gods and goddesses who ruled from Mount Olympus, and the reasons for natural phenomena. A myth about the warrior goddess Athena describes how she sprang, fully grown, from the head of Zeus, father of gods. The myth "Demeter and Persephone" explains why there are seasonal changes.

Legends

"Legends are prose narratives which, like myths, are regarded as true by the narrator and his audience, but they are set in a period considered less remote, when the world was much as it is today. Legends are more often secular than sacred, and their principal characters are human. They tell of migrations, wars and victories, deeds of past heroes, chiefs, and Kings, and succession in ruling dynasties" (4, p. 4). Legends from the British Isles tell about King Arthur and his Knights of the Round Table and Robin Hood. Legends from the Ukraine tell how Prince Vladimir of Kiev established the Knights of the Golden Table. Hungarian legends report the westward migration of tribes as they left Asia and established a new nation in the promised land of Hungary.

Distinctions Between Folktale, Myth, and Legend

To summarize and clarify the differences between folktale, myth, and legend, consider Chart 6–1 which includes Bascom's terminology along with several examples from each type of traditional literature:

CHART 6–1
Characteristics of Folktale, Myth, and Legend

Form and Examples	Belief	Time	Place	Attitude	Principal Characters
Folktale 1. "Snow White and Seven Dwarfs" (European)	**Fiction** fiction	**Anytime** "once upon a time"	**Anyplace** "in the great forest"	**Secular** secular	**Human or Nonhuman** human girl and dwarfs
2. "The Crane Wife" (Asian)	fiction	long ago	"in a faraway mountain village"	secular	human man, supernatural wife
3. "Why Mosquitoes Buzz in People's Ears" (African)	fiction	"one morning"	in a forest	secular	animals
Myth 1. "The Warrior Goddess: Athena" (European)	**Considered Fact** considered fact	**Remote Past** remote past	**Other World or Earlier World** Olympus	**Sacred** deities	**Nonhuman** Greek goddess
2. "Zuñi Creation Myth" (Native American)	considered fact	before and during creation	sky, earth and lower world	deities	Creator Awonawilona, Sun Father, Earth Mother
Legend 1. "King Arthur Tales" (European)	**Considered Fact** considered fact	**Recent Past** recent past	**World of Today** Britain	**Secular or Sacred** secular	**Human** king
2. "The White Archer" (Native American)	considered fact	recent past	Land of Eskimos	secular	Indian who wanted to avenge parents' death

VALUES OF TRADITIONAL LITERATURE FOR CHILDREN

One strong rationale for using traditional tales with children is provided by Bruno Bettelheim in *The Uses of Enchantment: The Meaning and Importance of Fairy Tales* (5). Bettelheim claims, in his psychoanalytic approach to traditional tales, that nothing is as enriching to both children and adults as the traditional tale. To reinforce this claim, he argues that these tales allow children to learn about human progress and about possible solutions to human problems. Children can understand the problem in a tale because it is stated briefly and pointedly. In addition, tales provide situations that subtly convey the advantages of moral behavior. Children learn that struggling against difficulties is unavoidable; however, if they meet the unexpected and unjust hardships, they can emerge victorious. Traditional tales present characters who are both good and bad. Children gain the conviction, according to Bettelheim, that crime does not pay. The simple and straightforward characters in traditional tales allow children to identify with the good characters and reject the bad. Consequently, they identify with the hero and all of his struggles, thus learning that while they too may experience rejection, like the hero, they will be given help and guidance when needed.

In addition to enriching children's lives by allowing them to learn about human problems, traditional tales also provide a means for advancing world understanding. Ruth Kearney Carlson (6) lists eight ways that traditional tales can develop world understanding.

First, through the use of traditional tales, children can better understand the cultural traditions of the nonscientific view of early humanity. The way these people approached the mysteries of their creation and that of the universe and then tried to provide rational answers to their questions provides insight into understanding them. The Greek, Roman, and Norse myths tell how early people tried to explain creation and nature through the powers of gods, giants, and demons. These myths were taken so seriously that religions grew up around them; gods were worshiped and sacrifices were made to them. Children can learn the Greek beliefs about the beginning of the universe in *A Book of Myths;* Thomas Bulfinch's insights into Norse beliefs on creation are found in Olivia Coolidge's *Legends of the North.* Children can learn how Greeks answered the mysteries of drought, crop failure, and starvation by reading Penelope Proddow's *Demeter and Persephone.* These tales, in addition to providing lively entertainment, fill readers with admiration for the people who developed such answers for unanswerable questions.

Second, a study of traditional tales can show children the relatedness of various story types and motifs among the people of the world. For example, the tale of a girl who loses her mother, acquires a jealous or evil stepmother, is mistreated (but remains gentle and kind), and finally is rewarded for her goodness is found in folk literature throughout the world. This text discusses four versions of the Cinderella tale. The French version collected by Perrault develops a Cinderella who has a fairy godmother to help her. The German version, collected by the Brothers Grimm, presents a Cinderella who plants a tree on her mother's grave and is granted wishes by a bird who dwells in the branches. In the English version, Tattercoats, a gooseherd eventually creates a beautiful gown for her when he blows on his pipe. In the Vietnamese tale, Tam is rewarded when the cherished bones of her beloved fish are replaced by a beautiful gown. While these stories have different characters, types of enchantment, and backgrounds, the underlying themes are the same. (Scholars have identified more than 500 versions of the Cinderella tale found in cultures throughout the world.)

Third, children learn about diffusion as they observe how different versions of the same tale or trickster hero are dispersed throughout different parts of the world. Anyone who has ever tried to categorize traditional literature according to country of origin is amazed at the similarity found among tales. It is sometimes difficult to classify the location of the tale if the author who is retelling it does not specify the translation's source. The similarities among these tales indicate the movement of people and conquests that have occurred throughout history; they also emphasize that humans throughout the world have had similar needs and problems. Some folktales from different countries are almost identical. For example, the German tale, "The Table, the Donkey and the Stick," is very similar to the Norwegian tale, "The Lad Who Went to the North Wind." Kathleen Arnott (1), in *Animal Folk Tales around the World,* states that while researching animal tales she discovered that "almost every country has its traditional trickster, such as the fox in Palestine and the mouse-deer in Malaysia; its stupid, easily fooled creature, such as the bear in Lapland or the giraffe in West Africa; and its benevolent, goodnatured animal, such as the kangaroo in Australia" (introduction). The tales are very similar, although the animals and the settings are characteristic of the countries in which they are told.

Fourth, traditional tales can develop an appreciation for the music, art, literature, and dance of different countries. If the artist has carefully researched the culture, using authentic backgrounds, clothing, and art objects to illustrate the tales, children gain appreciation for the cultural contributions of a country. For the picture storybooks recreating the Greek myths *Demeter and Persephone* and *Dionysos and the Pirates* by Proddow, illustrator Barbara Cooney went to Greece to do research. The illustrations of the cliffs, temples, sailing vessels, and gods and goddesses help develop an appreciation for this ancient culture. Likewise, Nancy Ekholm Burkert visited museums and the Black Forest in Germany to research the medieval period before illustrating the Grimms' *Snow White and the Seven Dwarfs.* Boris Zvorykin's illustrations in *The Firebird and Other Russian Fairy Tales,* beautifully recreate the spiraling, onion-shaped architecture of Czarist Russia as well as the clothing and art work characteristic of the time. Likewise, Leo and Diane Dillon researched African cultures before illustrating *Why Mosquitoes Buzz in People's Ears: A West African Tale.*

Fifth, traditional tales provide information about different countries, such as which animals are revered or disliked in a country, its geography, and the ancient holidays celebrated by its people. The wolf, for example, feared in the woodlands and mountains of Europe, became the villain in the German tale, "Little Red Riding Hood," and the Hungarian tale, "One Little Pig and Ten Wolves." In contrast, the hen is considered industrious in the English tale, "The Little Red Hen;" the fish is a symbol of good luck, wealth, and happiness in Chinese folktales; and the buffalo herd helps a Native American tribe in Olaf Baker's *Where the Buffaloes Begin.* Contrasts in weather and geography are evident in the Greek and Norse myths; illustrations and stories about them suggest the extremes between the warm lands of Mount Olympus and the colder regions of Asgard. Descriptions of holidays and other celebrations are also found in traditional literature. Ruth Robins's *Taliesin and King Arthur* describes and illustrates the festival of the Yule; Howard Pyle's *The Story of King Arthur and His Knights* describes great tournaments that included prancing horses, lovely ladies, and gallant knights; wedding celebrations are presented in such tales as Perrault's *Cinderella.*

Sixth, traditional tales contribute to a better understanding of the languages and dialects found in various countries. Children find the names in folktales from different countries fascinating. For example, they enjoy hearing stories about Russian Maria Morevna, the beautiful Tsarevna; Vietnamese Tam, the girl who lived in the Land of Small Dragon; and Mazel and Shlimazel, who have a wager in the Yiddish folktale. Many tales include language or dialects characteristic of a country or time period. Howard Pyle's *The Story of King Arthur and His Knights* contains dialogue written in an earlier English: "Sir Knight, I demand of thee why thou didst smite that shield. Now let me tell thee, because of thy boldness, I shall take away from thee thine own shield, and shall hang it upon yonder appletree,

where thou beholdest all those other shields to be hanging" (p. 44). Reading this prose may be difficult even for older elementary children, but they do enjoy hearing it. Irish dialect is included in Joseph Jacob's *Guleesh;* phrases such as "there was neither cark nor care" add to the realism of the story.

Seventh, traditional tales encourage children to identify with the imagination of people from a different time and place, and provide marvelous stimulation for creative drama, writing or other artistic expression. When they listen to traditional tales and then interact with their own imagination, they gain respect for the people who themselves created such wondrous tales.

Finally, traditional tales encourage children to realize that heroes from all over the world have inherent qualities of goodness, mercy, courage, and industry. For example, heroic King Arthur is described as the most honorable, gentlest knight who ever lived; Robin Hood is the hero of the commoners because he helped the poor; Beowulf had such a shining light of goodness that even the evil Grendel was overcome by his presence.

FOLKTALES

Characteristics of Folktales

Because folktales differ from other types of literature, they have characteristics related to setting, plot development, characterization, style, and theme that may differ from other types of children's stories.

Setting. Setting in literature includes both time and place. The time in folktales is always the far-distant past, usually introduced by some version of "once upon a time." The first line of a folktale usually places the listener immediately into a time when anything might happen to peasant or nobleman. "Gazelle Horn," a tale from Tibet, places the setting in very remote times, in a forest free from villages. A Russian tale, Zvorykin's *The Firebird,* begins "Long ago, in a distant kingdom, in a distant land, lived Tsar Vyslar Andronovich" (p. 112). Native American folktales may begin with some version of "when all was new, and the gods dwelt in the ancient places, long, long before the time of our ancients." A French tale is placed "on a day of days in the time of our fathers," while a German tale begins "in the olden days when wishing still helped one." With these introductions, the listener knows that enchantment and overcoming obstacles are both possible.

Setting also includes place. Chapter three discussed the symbolic settings found in many folktales. These settings are not carefully described because there is no need for description. One knows immediately that magic can happen in the forest or in the mystical castle. The action in the Grimms' "Snow White and the Seven Dwarfs" takes place "in the great forest," while the setting for de Beaumont's *Beauty and the Beast* is "a great castle." The title itself, for a Romanian tale, "The Land Where Time Stood Still," suggests the symbolic setting. Forests and castles are in the realm of the unknown; imaginations allow readers to accept and expect unusual occurrences.

The introduction that places the folktale in the far-distant past may also briefly sketch the location. A setting that puts children immediately into the time and mood for a wondrous experience appears in Isaac Bashevis Singer's introduction to *Mazel and Shlimazel*. It takes place "In a faraway land, on a sunny day, [when] the sky was as blue as the sea, and the sea was as blue as the sky, and the earth was green and in love with them both" (p. 1). A Chinese tale, "The Cinnamon Tree in the Moon," also suggests a nature setting "where not even a soft breeze stirs the heavens and one can see the shadows in the moon." After introducing these briefly described settings, the tales proceed immediately into identifying the characters and developing the conflict.

Characterization. Folktale characters are less completely developed than those in other types of stories. Just as the oral storyteller did not have time to describe the setting fully, he also lacked the time to develop his characters fully. Thus, folktale characters are essentially symbolic and are usually referred to as *flat*—that is, they do not change in the course of the story. A witch is always wicked, whether she is in the German tale "Hansel and Gretel" or whether she is Baba Yaga in the Russian "Maria Morevna." Other evil characters include giants, ogres, trolls, or stepmothers. Just as there are characters who are easily typed as bad, there are those who are always good. The young heroine is fair, kind, and loving. The youngest son is honorable, kind, and unselfish, even if he is considered foolish. Characteristic differences are shown, for example, between the good and bad characters in Singer's *Mazel and Shlimazel*. Mazel, the spirit of good luck, is young, tall, and slim, with pink cheeks and a jaunty stride. In contrast, Shlimazel, the spirit of bad luck, is an old man with a wan face, angry eyes, and a nose that is crooked and red from drinking. His beard is as gray as a spider's web, he wears a long black coat, and walks with a slumping stride.

The characters' natures are frequently introduced early in the tale. The first paragraph in Perrault's "Cinderella: or The Little Glass Slipper" from his *Histories or Tales of Past Times* (15) is an example:

There was once upon a time, a gentleman who married for his second wife the proudest and most haughty woman that ever was known. She had been a widow, and had by her former husband two daughters of her own humor, who were exactly like her in all things. He had also by a former wife a young daughter, but of an unparalleled goodness and sweetness of temper, which she took from her mother, who was the best creature in the world. (p. 73)

Children have no trouble identifying the good or the bad characters in folktales. This easy identification as well as the development of action allows them to identify with their heroes or heroines and may account for their popularity with young children.

Plot Development. Conflict and action abound in folktales. The nature of the oral tradition made it imperative that listeners be brought quickly into the action and identify with the characters. Consequently, even in written versions readers are immersed into the major conflict within the first few opening sentences. For example, the conflict in Paul Galdone's *The Little Red Hen* is between laziness and industriousness. The first sentence introduces the animals who live together in a little house. The second sentence introduces the conflict, that is, that the cat, dog, and mouse are lazy. Then the industrious hen is introduced. The remainder of the story develops the conflict between the lazy and industrious animals. It is quickly resolved, when the hen eats her own baking. Similarly, in "The Three Billy Goats Gruff," the goats want to get to the other side of the bridge. The conflict comes rapidly when they discover a troll living under the bridge. The action increases as each goat approaches the bridge, confronts the troll, and convinces the troll to allow him to cross. This cannot go on indefinitely; with each crossing, the tension increases until the largest billy goat and the troll must settle their differences. The conflict quickly reaches a climax when the largest goat knocks the troll off the bridge and crosses to the other side. The goats eat happily forever after.

This character-to-character conflict between good and evil is a characteristic of the majority of folktales. Even though the odds are often uneven, the hero overcomes the giant in "Jack the Giant Killer," the children outsmart the witch in "Hansel and Gretel," the intelligent animal outwits the ogre in "Puss in Boots," and a brother saves his sister from a dragon in "The Golden Sheng."

The recurring actions found in folktales have been the focus of several researchers. Vladimir Propp (17) analyzed one hundred Russian folktales and identified thirty-one actions accounting for uniformity and repetitiveness. While all tales did not possess all actions, he noted that the actions that did exist were in the same sequence. More importantly, he discovered that similar patterns were apparent in non-Russian tales. He concluded that it was not the country of origin that made the tales consistent, but the degree to which the tales remained true to the folk tradition.

F. André Favat (10) summarized Propp's findings and analyzed French and German tales according to their actions. The following list of recurring actions that may be found in various combinations is adapted from Favat:

1. One family member absents himself from home.
2. The hero is forbidden to do some action.
3. The hero violates a forbidden order.
4. The villain attempts to survey the situation.
5. The villain receives information about the victim.
6. The villain attempts to trick or deceive his victim in order to possess him or his belongings.
7. The victim submits to deception and unwittingly helps his enemy.
8. The villain causes harm or injury to a member of a family.
9. One family member either lacks or desires to have something.
10. A misfortune or lack is made known; the hero is approached with a request or command; he is allowed to go or is sent on a mission.
11. The seeker agrees to or decides upon a counteraction.
12. The hero leaves home.
13. The hero is tested, interrogated, or attacked, which prepares the way for him to receive a magical agent or a helper.
14. The hero reacts to the actions of the future donor.
15. The hero acquires a magical agent.
16. The hero is transferred, delivered, or led to the whereabouts of an object.
17. The hero and the villain join in direct combat.
18. The hero is marked.
19. The villain is defeated.
20. The initial misfortune or lack is eliminated.
21. The hero returns.
22. The hero is pursued.
23. The hero is rescued from pursuit.
24. The hero, unrecognized, arrives home or in another country.
25. A false hero presents unfounded claims.
26. A difficult task is proposed to the hero.
27. The task is resolved.
28. The hero is recognized.
29. The false hero or villain is exposed.
30. The hero is given a new appearance.
31. The villain is punished.
32. The hero is married and ascends the throne.

These patterns or various combinations of these patterns can be found in many of the folktales discussed in this chapter. Just as there are similarities in the beginnings of tales and in plot development, there are also similar endings, usually some version of "and they lived happily ever after."

Style. Perrault believed "that the best stories are those that imitate best the style and the simplicity of children's verses" (15, p. viii). This style has few distracting details or unnecessary descriptions. This simplicity is especially apparent in the thoughts and dialogues carried on by the characters: they think and talk like people. The dialogue, for example, in the Grimms' "The Golden Goose" sounds as if the listener were overhearing a conversation. The little old gray man welcomes the first son with: "Good morning. Do give me a piece of that cake you have got in your pocket, and let me have a draught of your wine—I am so hungry and thirsty." The clever, selfish son immediately answers: "If I give you my cake and wine I shall have none left for myself: you just go your own way." (Disaster rapidly follows this interchange.) When Dullhead, the youngest, simplest son, begs to go into the woods, his father's response reflects his opinion of his son's ability: "Both your brothers have injured themselves. You had better leave it alone; you know nothing about it." Dullhead begs very hard, and father replies: "Very well, then—go. Perhaps when you have hurt yourself, you may learn to know better." This German folktale is filled with rapid interchanges as Dullhead is rewarded with the golden goose and moves humorously on toward his destiny with the king and the beautiful princess.

The language of folktales is frequently enriched through rhymes and verses. In "Jack and the Beanstalk," the giant chants:

> Fee, fi-fo-fum,
> I smell the blood of an Englishman,
> Be he alive, or be he dead
> I'll have his bones to grind my bread.

The enchanted frog from the Grimms' "The Frog King" approaches the princess's door with these words:

> Princess! Youngest princess!
> Open the door for me!
> Dost thou not know what thou saidst to me
> Yesterday by the cool waters of the fountain?
> Princess, youngest princess!
> Open the door for me!

Likewise, "Hansel and Grethel" are asked by the witch:

> Nibble, nibble, gnaw,
> Who is nibbling at my little house?

As the story nears its end, another rhyme asks the duck for help:

> Little duck, little duck, dost thou see
> Hansel and Grethel are waiting for thee?
> There's never a plank or bridge in sight,
> Take us across on thy back so white.

The language style of the folktale, the easily identifiable characters, and rapid plot development make the stories very appropriate for sharing orally with children. Storytelling techniques are suggested on pages 236–39.

Themes in Folktales

Folktales contain universal truths and reflect the traditional values of the people. The characters and their actions and the rewards and punishments in folktales provide for considerable reflection about human nature and society. Within folktales are themes that reflect the highest human hopes as well as moral and material attainment: good will overcome evil, justice will triumph, unselfish love will conquer, kindness will result in rewards, intelligence will win over physical strength, diligence and hard work will result in rewards. In contrast to moral and material attainment, the tales also reflect what will happen and why it will happen to those who do not meet the traditional standards: the jealous queen is punished, the wicked stepsisters are blinded by birds, the foolish king loses part of his fortune or his daughter, the greedy man loses the source of his success or his well being.

The universality of these themes suggests that people throughout the world have responded to similar ideals and beliefs. For example, consider the universality of two of these themes, the superiority of intelligence and the loss of rewards because of foolishness. The hero in the English "Jack and the Giant Killer" outwits the much larger and less intelligent giant. Spider, in the African tale "A Story, A Story" outwits a series of animals and wins his wager with the being who controls stories. The hero in the Jewish "The Fable of the Fig Tree" is rewarded because he considers long-range consequences of his actions. The heroine in the Chinese "The Clever Wife" uses her wits to bring the family power. In contrast to rewarded behavior, "Mr. and Mrs. Vinegar" in the English tale lose their possessions because of foolish actions. "The Fisherman and His Wife" in the German tale return to their humble position because of foolish choices and greed. The Russian characters in "The Falcon Under the Hat" lose their possessions because of foolish actions. The husband in the Japanese "The Crane Wife" loses his wife and his means of support when he listens to foolish advice and allows his greed to outweigh his wife's ad-

vice. These themes may be found in traditional literature collected throughout the world.

Motifs in Folktales

Cruel stepmothers, cloaks of invisibility and enchanted youths who must wait for the love of a maiden to break the spell are all elements in folktales that take them out of the ordinary and encourage folk to remember and repeat the tales. Folklorists have identified hundreds of such elements, or motifs, found in folktales. These motifs are used to analyze folktales and identify similar elements in other tales. This analysis is especially rewarding when investigating folktales from various cultures. Some motifs are practically universal, suggesting similar thought processes in people living in different parts of the world. Others help folklorists trace a tale as it proceeded from one culture to another or to identify tales that may be traced to a common source.

Some of the most common motifs concern supernatural beings such as ogres, witches, giants, dwarfs, fairies, and extraordinary animals; supernatural helpers and remarkable beasts; magical objects and powers; and magical transformations.

Supernatural Adversaries and Deceitful Beasts. Supernatural beings in folktales may be adversaries or helpers. The wicked beings such as the ogres and witches may find children, entice them into their cottages or castles, and make preparations to feast upon them. Luckily, they are outwitted and the children are saved. Such wicked adversaries are found in the German "Hansel and Gretel" and the English "Jack and the Beanstalk." The encounter with the evil being may be the result of an unlucky chance meeting as in "Hansel and Gretel" or it may be deliberately sought as in "Jack the Giant Killer" and in the Chinese tale "Li Chi Slays the Serpent." In addition to being evil, these adversaries are usually rather stupid; consequently, they are overcome by characters who use wit and trickery.

Deceitful animals are motifs in tales from many countries. In the English and French versions of "Little Red Riding Hood" the wolf plays the role of the ogre, deceives a child, and is eliminated. The wolf is also a deceitful creature in "The Three Little Pigs." In Japanese folklore, the fox has a malicious nature, can assume human shape, and has the power to bewitch humans.

Supernatural Helpers and Remarkable Beasts. Folklore heroes and heroines are frequently helped in their quests by dwarfs, fairy godmothers, and extraordinary beasts. Seven dwarfs help Snow White in her battle against her evil stepmother. A little old man causes hardships to the selfish older brothers and rewards the generous younger brother in the Russian "The Fool of the World and the Flying Ship." This same motif is found in tales from western Asia, eastern Europe, and India. A fairy godmother makes it possible for the French "Cinderella" to appear at the ball. Supernatural beings assist various maidens in more than 500 versions of this story found in cultures throughout the world.

Just as there are deceitful animals in most cultures, there are also animals who are extraordinary companions and help the deserving human characters. The cat in the French "Puss in Boots" outwits an ogre and provides riches for his human master. Horses climb the glass mountain and help the deserving lad win the princess in the Norwegian "Princess on the Glass Hill." A horse grants three favors in the Puerto Rican "The Rainbow-Colored Horse" and allows the hero to win the nobleman's daughter. Animals, like other supernatural creatures in folktales, usually help the deserving characters who are, and remain, noble of heart.

Magical Objects and Powers. The possession of a magical object or power is a crucial factor in many folktales. When all seems lost, the hero may don the cloak of invisibility and follow "The Twelve Dancing Princesses" down a winding stair or command his companions to produce an army from twigs or change the seasons as in "The Fool of the World and the Flying Ship." Magical objects are frequently obtained in an extraordinary manner, may be lost or stolen, and must be recovered. This sequence occurs in the Norwegian "The Lad Who Went to the North Wind" and the German "The Donkey, the Table, and the Stick." A lad goes to the North Wind demanding the return of his meal; he is given a magical object; a dishonest innkeeper steals the object; after the action is repeated three times, the dishonest innkeeper is punished. Stealing a magical object may result in considerable problems for the thief. In the Norwegian tale, "The Magic Mill," the mill grinds salt on command, but only the rightful owner can command it to stop.

Magical Transformations. Beasts who are enchanted humans, cranes who become supernatural wives, and frogs who are enchanted royalty illustrate the popular motif of magical transformation. The cycle found in beast marriage stories usually follows a pattern in which a prince is magically transformed into a beast or monster and a gentle, unselfish youngest daughter breaks the enchantment when she falls in love with the beast. "Beauty and the Beast" (French) is the best known of these tales. Other versions include a Basque tale in which the beast is a huge serpent, a Magyar tale with a pig, and a Lithuanian tale with a white wolf.

"The Crane Wife," a Japanese folktale, exemplifies the transformation from animal to human. In this tale, a poor farmer is rewarded for his care of a wounded crane. The crane transforms herself into a lovely woman, marries the farmer, and provides for his needs by mysteriously weaving beautiful fabrics. This tale, however, does not suggest a "happily ever after" conclusion. Instead, the farmer becomes greedy, listens to bad advice, disobeys his wife, and causes the transformed crane to return to her previous form.

Native American tales frequently include humans transformed into animals. "The Ring in the Prairie," a Shawnee Indian tale, includes transformations of humans and sky dwellers: a human hunter transforms himself into a mouse to capture a girl who descends from the sky; the sky dwellers secure part of an animal and are transformed into that specific animal. Many of the native American transformation stories suggest a close relationship between humans and animals.

Multiple Motifs. The preceding motifs suggest only a few of the motifs found in folktales. Although a folktale may be remembered for one extraordinary motif, there are usually multiple motifs within the tale. As an example of this characteristic, consider the following motifs found in "Jack and the Beanstalk": (1) a foolish bargain, (2) the hero acquires a magical object, (3) a plant with extraordinary powers grows to the sky, (4) the ogre or giant repeats "fee-fi-fo-fum," (5) the hero is hidden by the ogre's wife, (6) the hero steals a magical object from the ogre, (7) the magical object possesses the power of speech, (8) the hero summons the ogre. Listing such common elements provides folklorists with a means of analyzing folktales across cultures.

Universality of Motifs. Chart 6–2 summarizes the discussion of motifs and suggests that folktale motifs are found in folktales collected from many parts of the world. The search for common motifs is an enlightening and rewarding activity for children as well as adults. Many of the values of sharing folktales with children are gained through comparative and cross-cultural study of traditional literature.

Folktales from the British Isles

English folktales about ogres, giants, and clever heroes were among the first stories published as inexpensive chapbooks in the 1500s. Even though not written especially for children, tales of folk heroes rapidly became popular with younger readers. These fast plots and rather unpromising heroes are still popular with the children. The various "Jack tales," for example, develop plots around villainous ogres or giants who terror-

CHART 6–2
Common Motifs in Folktales from Different Cultures

Common Motif	Culture	Folktale
Supernatural Adversaries		
Ogre	England	"Jack the Giant Killer"
Ogress	Italy	"Petrosinella"
Troll	Norway	"Three Billy Goats Gruff"
Giant	Germany	"The Valiant Little Tailor"
Dragon	China	"The Golden Sheng"
Witch	Africa	"Marandenboni"
Deceitful or Ferocious Beasts		
Wolf	Germany	"The Wolf and the Seven Little Kids"
Wolf	France	"Little Red Riding Hood"
Wolf	England	"The Three Little Pigs"
Wild hog, unicorn, and lion	United States	"Jack and the Varmints"
Supernatural Helpers		
Fairies	France and Germany	"The Sleeping Beauty"
Fairy Godmother	Vietnam	"The Land of Small Dragon"
Jinni	Arabia	"The Woman of the Well"
Cat (fairy in disguise)	Italy	"The Cunning Cat"
Magical Objects		
Cloak of invisibility	Germany	"The Twelve Dancing Princesses"
Magical cloth	Norway	"The Lad Who Went to the North Wind"
Magical lamp	Arabia	"Aladdin and the Magic Lamp"
Magical mill	Norway	"Why the Sea is Salt"
Magical Powers		
Granted wishes	Germany	"The Fisherman and His Wife"
Wish for a child	Russia	"The Snow Maiden"
Humans with extraordinary powers	Mexico	"The Riddle of the Drum"
Humans with extraordinary powers	Russia	"The Fool of the World and the Flying Ship"

Common Motif	Culture	Folktale
Magical Transformations		
Prince to bear	Norway	"East of the Sun and West of the Moon"
Prince to beast	France	"Beauty and the Beast"
Bird to human	Japan	"The Crane Wife"
Human to animal	Native American	"The Ring in the Prairie"

ize the kingdom and heroes who overcome their adversaries with trickery and cleverness rather than magical powers. This cycle, found in "Jack the Giant Killer" begins when even the king cannot subdue the giant. Characteristically, the hero, accompanied by a pickax, a shovel, a horn, and his wit, proceeds to the giant's cave. There, he digs a pit, covers it with sticks and straw, blows loudly on the horn, and traps the enraged giant when he charges out of the cave. A similar hero and villain are found in another Jack tale, "Jack and the Beanstalk."

The villains in English folktales may not always be ogres or giants, but they may play a similar role. For example, "Three Little Pigs" must outwit a wolf, and a young girl is frightened by "The Three Bears."

In addition to clearly defined good and bad characters, the repetitive language in "The Three Little Pigs" and "The Three Bears" appeals to storytellers and listeners. In The "Three Little Pigs" there is the wolf's threat, "I'll huff and I'll puff and I'll blow your house in," as well as the pig's reply "Not by the hair on my chinny chin chin." In "The Three Bears" there is first the repetition of three chairs, three bowls of porridge, and three beds. Later there is language repetition as each of the bears say: "Who has been sitting in my chair? Who has been eating my porridge? Who has been sleeping in my bed?" There are several versions of this folktale that appeal to young children. Paul Galdone's *The Three Bears* has large pictures that differentiate sizes of bears, bowls, beds, and chairs. Consequently, the book may be used to develop size concepts. Lorinda Bryan Cauley's *Goldilocks and the Three Bears,* with its compelling illustrations, is also an excellent version to share with children.

Repetitive language in "The Little Red Hen" also appeals to young children. They often join in as the little red hen asks each question and is given an answer: " 'Not I,' said the cat," " 'Not I,' said the dog," " 'Not I,' said the mouse." Galdone's

The Little Red Hen is a good choice for younger children. The contrasts between the lazy cat, dog, and mouse and the busy hen are developed through the illustrations.

Two other tales illustrated by Galdone depict characteristic British folklore themes. For example, clever heroes frequently win over villainous foes. In *What's in Fox's Sack? An Old English Tale,* the villain is a sly fox who manages to get a boy into his sack. A clever woman outsmarts the fox by placing a large bulldog inside the sack. The humor resulting from ridiculous human actions is emphasized in *The Three Sillies.* In this tale, a man searches for three people who are sillier than his future wife and her parents. (Compare this English tale with the Russian "The Falcon Under the Hat.")

Impossible tasks created by foolish boasting, a bargain with a supernatural helper, magical spinning, the importance of a secret name, and revealing a name in a riddle are all motifs found in Harve Zemach's *Duffy and the Devil.* In this Cornish tale resembling "Rumpelstiltskin," an inefficient maid misleads her employer about her spinning ability, and makes an agreement with the devil who promises to do the knitting for three years. At the end of this time she must produce his name or go with him. When the time arrives, the squire goes hunting and overhears the festivities of the witches and the devil. The folktale style includes a verse sung by the little man with the long tail:

Tomorrow! Tomorrow! Tomorrow's the day!
I'll take her! I'll take her! I'll take her away!

Let her weep, let her cry, let her beg, let her pray-
She'll never guess my name is . . . Tarraway! (p. 30 unnumbered)

Thus, Duffy learns the magic name and cheats the devil from claiming her soul. (The importance of a secret name is reflected in folktales from many cultures. In the English tale the name is Tim Tit Tot; a Scottish secret name is Whuppity Stoories; a tale from Nigeria is "The Hippopotamus called Isantim.")

In Flora Annie Steel's English version of the Cinderella tale, *Tattercoats,* the heroine is ignored and despised not by a stepmother, but by her grandfather, who mourns his daughter's death in childbirth and rejects the child who survived. In this version, there are no cruel stepsisters, but the servants mock and mistreat her.

Her only friends are an old nurse and the crippled gooseherd. In this version, Tattercoats does not become beautifully dressed before she meets the prince. Instead, she meets him in the forest, and he accompanies her and the gooseherd to the town. Along the way, the prince realizes what a fine and beautiful person Tattercoats is, and he invites her to attend the ball dressed just as she is. At the stroke of midnight, Tattercoats, the gooseherd, and the flock of noisy geese walk into the ballroom and approach the startled king. Taking her hand, the prince introduces her as his bride. As the gooseherd plays a special tune on his pipe, Tattercoats is transformed into a beautifully dressed girl, and the geese become pages who bear her long train.

And so she did,
to the very last crumb.

After that,

The industrious hen is contrasted with the lazy animals in Galdone's English folktale. From the book *The Little Red Hen* by Paul Galdone, published by Clarion Books, Ticknor & Fields: A Houghton Mifflin Company, New York. Copyright © 1973 by the author/illustrator.

English folk literature is filled with humorous tales that stress human foolishness, frequently making a point about human foibles. "Mr. and Mrs. Vinegar" exemplify comical characters who are foolish because they are discontent (9). Even when the Vinegars gain wealth, they cannot keep it. After a series of absurd trades in which Mr. Vinegar succeeds in losing everything, he realizes the error of his ways: "I was not content with what I had in the first place. And because of it I ended up with nothing" (p. 27). His wife tells him, however, that he really does not have nothing because "You have just spoken with new-found wisdom. And is wisdom not better than all the gold pieces in the world?" (p. 27).

Folktales from Ireland are filled with fairies and other little people; one example is William Stobb's rendition of Joseph Jacob's *Guleesh*. Guleesh is a boy who enjoys sitting outside on moon-lit nights. On one such night, he discovers and follows the little sheehogues, the fairy hosts of Ireland. He imitates their words and suddenly finds himself riding a horse as fast as the wind. He accompanies the sheehogues as they cross the sea and kidnap the daughter of the king of France, but tricks the fairies into releasing her. The fairies cannot take the princess away from Guleesh, but they cast a spell making her mute. Guleesh discovers an herb that ends the spell, the princess can speak, and they are married. This tale ends not with "and they lived happily ever after" but with one more characteristic of Irish folk literature:

there was neither cark nor care, sickness nor sorrow, mishap nor misfortune on them till the hour of their death, and may the same be with me, and with us all! (p. 32)

There are fewer grand stories of mystical enchantment in British folktales than in French or German stories. Peasants rather than royalty are usually the heroes. Consequently, one can learn about the problems, beliefs, values, and humor of common people. Themes in British folktales suggest that intelligence will win over physical strength, hard work and diligence will be rewarded, and love and loyalty are important. Adversaries include ogres, giants, wolves, and the devil.

French Folktales

The majority of French folktales portray the splendor of the French court rather than the more humble peasant cottage. The original tales were collected and written down by Charles Perrault, a member of the Académie Française. In 1698, he published a collection of folktales called *Tales of Mother Goose,* that included "Cinderilla" (original spelling), "Sleeping Beauty," "Puss in Boots," "Little Red Riding Hood," "Blue Beard," "Little Thumb," "Requet with the Tuft," and "Diamond

and the Toads." These stories had entertained children and adults of the Parisian aristocracy and, consequently, are quite different from tales that stress wicked, dishonest kings being outwitted by simple peasants. A new edition of Perrault's tales, *The Glass Slipper: Charles Perrault's Tales of Time Past* includes eight tales highlighted by elegant illustrations that capture the formality of the early French court.

Many illustrators and translators of French fairy tales depict royal French settings. For example, Marcia Brown's interpretation of Perrault's *Cinderella* is quite different from the German version. In this French tale, Cinderella has a fairy godmother who grants her wishes. A pumpkin is transformed into a gilded carriage, six mice become beautiful horses, a rat becomes a coachman with an elegant mustache, and lizards turn into footmen complete with fancy livery and lace. Cinderella is dressed in a beautiful gown embroidered with rubies, pearls, and diamonds. This version also has the magical hour of midnight when everything returns to normal. Perrault's *Cinderella* contains stepsisters who are rude and haughty, but they are not as cruel as in the German version. Cinderella even finds it possible to forgive them:

Now her stepsisters recognized her. Cinderella was the beautiful personage they had seen at the ball! They threw themselves at her feet and begged forgiveness for all their bad treatment of her. Cinderella asked them to rise, embraced them and told them she forgave them with all her heart. She begged them to love her always. (p. 27)

Cinderella not only forgives them but also provides them with a home at the palace and marries them to the lords of the court. Brown's illustrations, drawn with fine lines and colored with pastels, depict a magical kingdom where life in the court is a marvelous existence.

Another book beautifully illustrated by Marcia Brown is Perrault's *Puss in Boots.* Its drawings reflect the mythical world that would be appropriate for oral tales in the French court. The hero creates a royal environment for his poor young master by tricking an ogre out of his fields and castle. With Puss's help, the new Marquis of Carabas impresses the King, marries the princess, and lives with Puss who becomes an honored lord.

The Sleeping Beauty appears in both French and German versions. The virtues bestowed upon the baby suggest German and French values. In the German version, eleven good fairies present baby Beauty with virtue, beauty, wealth, and everything one could wish for. In the French version, seven fairies bestow intelligence, beauty, kindness, generosity, gaiety, and grace. Each version has a wicked fairy who gives Beauty the gift of death on her sixteenth birthday, and each has the fairy reduce the wicked gift to a hundred-year sleep. David

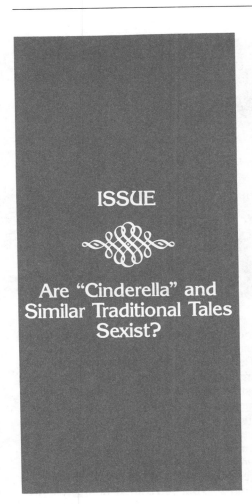

ISSUE

Are "Cinderella" and Similar Traditional Tales Sexist?

PURITANS IN ENGLAND and the United States considered many of the traditional tales too violent to be shared with children. Today the tales are being attacked by groups who consider the actions of the beautiful, often helpless females, and the clever, handsome princes who rescue them to be sexist. Ethel Johnston Phelps is an author who believes the image of the good, obedient, meek, and submissive heroine is harmful and should be altered. She has published two books that depict brave and clever heroines: *Tatterhood and Other Tales*[1] and *The Maid of the North*.[2] *Time* magazine's review of these books concludes: "Though Phelps celebrates females who have brains and energy, her feminist lens at times distorts the drama beneath the surface of the folk tales" (3, p. 60). In defense of this criticism the *Time* writer provides two examples. In "The Twelve Huntsmen" Phelps has the prince collapse at the appropriate moment; in the original story the girl demonstrates this behavior. In "The Maid of the North" Phelps changes the dialogue from the original in which the maid fends off a suitor by describing the disadvantages of leaving home to join a stranger's household. In Phelps's version the maid expresses this viewpoint against marriage: "A wife is like a house dog tied with a rope. Why should I be a servant and wait upon a husband?"

Should these stories be rewritten to reflect changing attitudes of the times or will rewriting distort the value of the traditional tale? Are children harmed by the male and female stereotypes developed in traditional literature? If stories are tampered with, will children lose their identification with characters like themselves, who are often bewildered and feel like underdogs in traditional tales?

1 Phelps, Ethel Johnston. *Tatterhood and Other Tales*. Feminist Press, 1978.

2 Phelps, Ethel Johnston. *The Maid of the North*. Holt, Rinehart & Winston, 1981.

3 "Sexes: Feminist Folk and Fairy Tales." *Time,* 20 July 1981, p. 60.

Walker's illustrations for the French *Sleeping Beauty* show his background in theatrical set and costume design. They create the feeling of a stage setting with fairies dancing lightly across the stage. The lighting enhances the view of the great hall and emphasizes the beautiful princess. (It is interesting to compare this version of *The Sleeping Beauty* with Beni Montresor's *Cinderella,* a picture storybook that depicts the Italian opera by Gioacchino Rossini.)

A newer version of Madame de Beaumont's *Beauty and the Beast* has been translated and illustrated by Diane Goode. Meant originally for the wealthier classes, it is introduced in this way:

Once upon a time there lived a merchant who was extremely rich. He had six children, three sons and three daughters. And since he was a sensible man, he spared no expense upon their education, but gave them all kinds of tutors. (p. 1)

This longer tale provides more information about Beauty: not only is she prettier than her two older sisters, but she is also nicer. She loves her father and gladly accompanies him when, due to changing fortunes, he must move to the country. In her free time, Beauty enjoys reading, playing the harpsichord, and singing while she spins. These things are important to her; even when she enters the Beast's castle, she is provided with a library, a harpsichord, and music books. Goode's illustrations create a magical setting in which the Beast, lacking beauty and wit, is eventually loved for his virtue and can be transformed back into a handsome prince.

The regal surroundings of a castle are emphasized in a tale of an enchanted beast.
© 1978 from *Beauty and the Beast* by Madame de Beaumont, trans. and illustrated by Diane Goode. Reprinted with permission of Bradbury Press, Inc.

These tales contain more enchantment than do tales from other countries. The motifs in French tales include fairy godmothers, fairies, remarkable beasts who help their young masters, unselfish girls who break enchantments, and deceitful beasts.

German Folktales

> Mirror, mirror on the wall.
> Who is the fairest of them all?

These words bring to mind one of the most popular childhood tales. German traditional tales, whether they are about enchanted princesses, clever animals, or poor but honest peasants, are among the most enjoyed folktales in the world. Their modern accessibility is owed to Wilhelm and Jacob Grimm, German professors who researched the roots of the German language through the traditional tales that had been told orally for generations. After listening to the tales being told by the village storyteller, they wrote them down and initially published them as *Kinder-und Hausmärchen*. The stories ultimately were translated into many languages and became popular throughout Europe and the United States.

In German folklore, the wolf is the cunning and treacherous villain in several translations written for younger children. Paul Galdone's *Little Red Riding Hood*, for example, shows the little maiden putting on her red velvet cloak, taking a basket of food, and traveling through the woods to visit her grandmother. On the way, she meets the sly wolf who stops her for a chat; he then hurries ahead of her, gobbles up grandmother, and does the same thing to Little Red Riding Hood. In this version, the huntsman rescues grandmother and Red Riding Hood from inside the wolf and places stones in the wolf's stomach. Galdone's illustrations are not frightening, and they present a story that is appropriate for younger children.

The wolf in German folk tales is cunning, dangerous, and receives just punishment. In Anne Rogers's version of the Grimms' *The Wolf and the Seven Little Kids,* the mother goat specifically warns her children about the deceitful wolf: "He may try to disguise himself, but you'll know him by his gruff voice and his black feet" (p. 1). The wolf, however, comes to an end similar to the wolf in Little Red Riding Hood. After he has tricked and eaten the kids, the mother goat cuts him open, saves her children, and places rocks inside the wolf. When awakened, the wolf feels terrible, loses his balance, and falls into the well.

Not all animals in German folklore are as fearsome as the wolf. The Bremen Town Musicians, for example, even though old and ready to be destroyed by their owners, are still clever. In Hans Fischer's version of the Grimms' *The Traveling Musicians,* the donkey, hound, cat, and rooster set out to seek their fortunes as musicians. They give only one concert, but this is sufficient to frighten away a band of robbers whose house and treasures they can claim for themselves. Fischer's illustrations add to the humorous quality of the text. Ilse Plume's softly colored illustrations for the Grimms' *The Bremen Town Musi-*

cians suggest the gentle nature of the animals and the setting in a sunlit forest.

The poor peasant or soldier is a frequent hero in German folklore. The peasant may not be cunning, but he is usually good. In the *Grimms' Golden Goose,* for example, the youngest son is even called Simpleton. When his brothers leave home, they are given a fine rich cake and a bottle of wine. In contrast, Simpleton is despised by his parents and is given a cinder cake and sour beer. His kind heart is rewarded, however, and he overcomes these injustices: when his brothers refuse to share their food with an old man, they cut themselves with an ax; Simpleton shares his food and it becomes cake and wine. He is further rewarded with a golden goose who has magical powers that allow the lad to marry the princess. This tale tells exactly why Simpleton is rewarded. The old man tells him, "I have done all this for you because you were kind and merciful to me" (p. 23). Many of the actions identified by Propp are found in this tale.

Penniless soldiers are frequent heroes in the Grimms' tales. The soldier in *The Bearskinner,* illustrated by Felix Hoffman, outwits the devil. The soldier accepts a challenge to wear a bearskin, neither wash nor shave, and not pray for seven years. If he dies during this time, he would belong forever to the devil; if he lives, he would be free—and rich—for the rest of his life. He roams the world doing good deeds and asking people to pray for him. At the end of the seven years, he has successfully outwitted the devil and claims his reward. Three soldiers receive rewards of magical gifts when they share their campfire with a stranger in Warwick Hutton's *The Nose Tree.* The soldiers, however, are tricked out of their possessions by a princess. This action does not go unpunished. In a humorous ending, she tricks the soldiers out of an additional object: an apple that causes her nose to grow. Her growing nose suggests an important theme in German folktales—human greed is punishable.

Peasants in German folktales are not always generous; they may be greedy and discontented. When this happens, however, they are punished. One such character is the unhappy wife in the Grimms' *The Fisherman and His Wife,* illustrated by Monika Laimgruber (see p. 15 of color insert). In this humorous tale, a fisherman catches an enchanted flounder, releases it back to the sea, and returns home to tell his wife. She is furious because he did not ask for a reward and sends him back to ask the flounder for a nice cottage. Rhyme enhances the folktale style as the fisherman calls to the flounder:

> Flounder, flounder, in the sea,
> Hear my words and come to me.
> Grant the wish of Ilsebill,
> Though her wish is not my will. (p. 5 unnumbered)

The flounder grants the wife's wish, but she is not happy for long. Next, she asks for a large stone palace, then to be made king of the land, then emperor, then pope, and finally God. This final request causes the flounder to send the discontented wife back to her humble pot on the edge of the sea.

Many of the best-loved German folktales are stories of princesses who sleep for a hundred years, have wicked stepmothers, or are enchanted by witches. One very lovely version of the Grimms' "Snow White" is translated by Randall Jarrell and illustrated by Nancy Ekholm Burkert. Considerable research on medieval times went into her drawings for *Snow White and the Seven Dwarfs.* Burkert visited museums in Europe and journeyed through the Black Forest in search for authenticity. The book is one that thoroughly portrays every aspect of the mystical forest, the dwarfs' cottage, and the wicked stepmother's secret tower room.

Two other Brothers Grimm books depicting the medieval beauty of the original fairy tales are illustrated by Errol Le Cain. *The Twelve Dancing Princesses* is the tale of twelve girls who wear out their slippers every night. This tale is told from the viewpoint of a poor soldier who is given a cloak of invisibility after he helps an old woman. With her gift and warning he proceeds to the palace, follows the princesses down a winding stair, and watches them dance the night away with twelve princes. After the soldier proves where they have been, the king rewards him with a bride of his choice. Errol Le Cain has also illustrated *Thorn Rose, or the Sleeping Beauty.* The opulence of the magical kingdom is recreated in drawings of rich ladies, good fairies who fly on beautifully plumed birds, an evil fairy who flies on an orange dragon, and resplendent castle scenes. Each page is surrounded by a rich border resembling a design from a medieval tapestry (see p. 12 of color insert).

A German version of the Grimms' *Cinderella,* illustrated by Otto S. Svend, is different from the French one. There is no fairy godmother; instead, white doves and other birds help Cinderella complete her stepmother's impossible tasks. When the stepmother and the stepsisters leave for the ball, Cinderella goes to the hazel tree growing by her mother's grave and says:

> Shake and shiver, hazel tree,
> Throw gold and silver down to me. (p. 11 unnumbered)

The bird in the tree gives her a dress made of gold and silver and a pair of satin slippers. She goes to the ball, dances with the prince, and returns home. The same thing happens three evenings in a row; on the last evening, the bird gives her slippers made from pure gold. On the way home from the palace, Cinderella loses her left slipper on the stair, sending the prince on a search of the kingdom for the girl who can wear the slipper. When he arrives at Cinderella's home, one stepsister chops off her toe to squeeze into the shoe. This deceit does not work, however; as the prince and stepsister ride by the grave, two doves tell the prince that there is blood in the shoe. Cinderella is finally called in from the cinders, her foot fits into the shoe, and she rides away with the prince. The stepsisters are not forgiven as they were in the French version. On Cinderella's wedding day, the sisters join the bridal procession; the doves, who are perched peacefully on Cinderella's shoulders, peck out the sisters' eyes.

Breaking enchantments through unselfish love is a popular theme in German folklore. This theme is found in the Grimms' *The Six Swans*. The sister is the heroine of the story as only she can restore their human form by sewing six shirts out of starwort. However, she cannot speak for the six years required for her task. The girl goes through many ordeals before she is successful. This same theme is found in Elizabeth Crawford's translation of the Grimms' *The Seven Ravens*. In this version the young girl seeks to free her seven brothers from a raven enchantment.

Another lovely maiden who must go through considerable unhappiness before she is rescued by her prince is the Grimms' *Rapunzel*. Bernadette Watts creates a version of the beautiful girl who is shut into the high tower by the wicked witch and remains there until she and the prince are discovered. When the prince is blinded by his jump from the tower, Rapunzel's tears drop into his eyes, and he is no longer blind. Again, love has overcome wickedness. A newer version of this story, *Rapunzel: From the Brothers Grimm,* is enhanced by Trina Hyman's settings illustrating rustic interiors and lush woodlands. An interesting comparison may be made between these versions of the German "Rapunzel" and Giambattista Basile's Neapolitan version, *Petrosinella,* illustrated by Diane Stanley. The witch in this version is an ogress. The couple is saved when Petrosinella (parsley) discovers three acorns that are the cause of her enchantment and uses her knowledge to free herself and the prince.

German folktales are popular for storytelling. They contain quick openings, fast plots, and enough excitement to keep listeners entertained story after story. Many of the folktale motifs discussed earlier are found in these tales. Supernatural adversaries include devils and witches. Wolves are often beast adversaries. The good-hearted youngest child is often rewarded, while selfishness, greed, and discontent are punished. The noble character frequently wins as a result of intervention by supernatural helpers; this character may, however, be required to pass a test before winning the reward. Magical objects such as wands and cloaks of invisibility and magical spells such as the long sleep are recurring motifs.

The heroine plays a more active role in this Italian version of "Rapunzel."
From *Petrosinella* by Giambattista Basile. Illustrated by Diane Stanley. Copyright © 1981 by Frederick Warne & Co., Inc. Reprinted with permission of the publisher.

Norwegian Folktales

Pat Shaw Iverson (12) states that "If Norway were to show the world a single work of art which would most truly express the Norwegian character, perhaps the best choice would be the folktales, published for the first time more than a hundred years ago and later illustrated by Erik Werenskiold and Theodor Kittelsen" (p. 5). These folktales, collected by Norwegian scholars Peter Christian Asbjörnsen and Jörgen E. Moe, were published under the title *Norwegian Folk Tales* in 1845. Their interest in collecting the original traditional tales of the Norwegian people was stimulated by reading the Grimms' *Kinder- und Hausmärchen*. They were also interested in the "National Renaissance" then sweeping Europe, and folklore and folk music were considered excellent sources for studying early traditions and the history of the people.

It is interesting to compare supernatural adversaries, remarkable helpers, magical objects, and similar plots found in folktales from other European cultures with the motifs in Norwegian tales. Consider, for example, Mercer Mayer's version of *East of The Sun and West of the Moon*. First, this tale has motifs that are similar to the French "Beauty and the Beast" and other tales of human enchantment and lost loves: an enchanted human demands a promise in return for a favor, the promise is at first honored, the maiden disenchants the human, he must leave because she does not honor her promise, she searches for him, and finally saves him. The adversaries and helpers in this tale reflect a northern climate and culture. The human is enchanted by a troll princess who lives in a distant kingdom inhabited by trolls. The maiden is helped in her journey by Salamander, who knows the fiery heart of the world;

Father Forest, who understands the body of earth and stone; Great Fish, who knows the blood of salt and water; and North Wind, who understands the mind of the earth, the moon, and the sun. The gifts given to her by each helper allow her to overcome the trolls and free the prince: a tinder box makes it possible to melt the ice encasing the youth, a shot from the bow and arrow causes the troll princess to turn to wood, and reflections in the fish scale cause the remaining trolls to turn to stone. Mayer's illustrations of snowy winters, creatures frozen in ice, icy mountains, and tree-covered landscapes also help to set the scene.

It is interesting to contrast Mayer's version with Asbjörnsen and Moe's *East of the Sun and West of the Moon*. In this tale, a white bear offers the family riches if the youngest daughter is allowed to live in his castle.

Norwegian folktale collections provide many excellent stories for retelling. Several favorites are found in Virginia Haviland's *Favorite Fairy Tales Told in Norway*. Young children love to listen to, and dramatize, "Three Billy Goats Gruff." The plot is a classic Norwegian folktale filled with action and appealing language. Another favorite for storytelling and creative drama is "Taper Tom," whose hero is the characteristic youngest son

The North Wind is important in this tale from Norwegian folklore.
Reprinted by permission of Four Winds Press, a division of Scholastic Inc. from *East of the Sun and West of the Moon* by Mercer Mayer. Copyright © 1980 by Mercer Mayer.

who sits in a chimney corner amusing himself by grubbing in the ashes and splitting tapers for lights. His family laugh at his belief that he can win the princess's hand in marriage and half the kingdom by making her laugh. With the assistance of the magical golden goose who does not relinquish anyone who touches her, Tom forms a parade of unwilling followers: an old woman, an angry man who kicks at the woman, a smithy who waves a pair of tongs, and a cook who runs after them waving a ladle of porridge. At this ridiculous scene, the sad princess bursts into laughter. Tom wins the princess and half the kingdom. (Compare this tale with the *Grimms' Golden Goose*.)

This last tale suggests the humorous incidents found in some Norwegian tales. Absurd situations provide the humor in Kathleen and Michael Hague's retelling of Asbjörnsen and Moe's *The Man Who Kept House*. One comical experience after another occurs when a husband tries to prove that his wife's housework is easier than his farm work. After they ex-

Many Norwegian tales are about humorous incidents. From *Favorite Fairy Tales Told in Norway*, retold by Virginia Haviland. Illustrations Copyright © 1961 by Leonard Weisgard. By permission of Little, Brown and Company.

change jobs, the baby tosses oatmeal onto the ceiling, the clean laundry is soiled, the goat gets into the house and creates chaos, and the husband almost hangs himself and the cow. Fast paced action and large, humorous illustrations are appreciated by younger children.

Motifs in Norwegian folktales include magical objects, supernatural adversaries, and human enchantment. The consequences of broken promises are suggested when a girl loses her loved one because of her actions; unselfish love, however, can intervene. Themes suggest the rewarding of unselfish love and the punishment of greed. These tales help children appreciate the Norwegian heritage. The sharp humor, the trolls, and the poor boys who overcome adversity are all excellent subjects for storytelling.

Russian Folktales

Heroes who may be czars (tsars) or peasants; settings that reflect the snow in winter, the dense, dark forest, the wooden huts of the peasants, or the gilded towers of the noblemen's palaces; and villains who may be the long-nosed witch Baba Yaga or a dishonest nobleman or peasant are all found in Russian folktales. Two types of folktales are considered common in Russian traditional literature. First, there are merry tales characterized by rapid, humorous dialogue. These tales are short, and the plot frequently becomes more absurd for the poor hero before things improve. Second, there are folktales that include serious stories of enchantment and magic.

An example of a merry tale written in picture storybook format for younger children is Guy Daniels's *The Peasant's Pea Patch*. The tale builds upon the absurd acts of a foolish person and suggests that the remedy for a problem may be worse than the problem. This peasant feeds honey and vodka to the cranes eating his peas, waits until they are asleep, ties them to his cart, and tries to drag them home. When they awake they take the peasant on a wild ride through the sky. Again, the peasant solves his problem with another foolish act. He cuts the rope from the cranes and plunges into a treacherous quagmire where he is stuck; when a strong duck lands on his head, he grabs the duck and is finally freed. His problems continue, however, as he has additional adventures with a bear and beehives before he limps home. Many other merry tales are found in Guy Daniels's *The Falcon under the Hat, Russian Merry Tales and Fairy Tales*.

Humans in Russian folktales may be judged fools by their actions or by their speech. Saying the wrong thing at the wrong time to the wrong person constitutes foolish actions in Leo Tolstoy's *The Fool*.

A gigantic rooster, or troll bird, is a ferocious adversary in this Norwegian folktale about trolls.
Illustration from *The Terrible-Troll Bird* by Ingri and Edgar Parin D'Aulaire. Copyright © 1933, 1976 by Ingri and Edgar Parin D'Aulaire. Reprinted by permission of Doubleday & Company, Inc.

Many Russian folktales are complex stories of quests, human longing, and human greed. *The Firebird and other Russian Fairy Tales,* beautifully illustrated by Boris Zvorykin, contains four such folktales. The title story introduces the firebird who has golden wings and eyes like oriental crystals. She plucks the golden apples from Tsar Vyslav's garden, beginning the quest by the Tsar's three sons to capture her. The youngest son meets a wolf who accompanies him on his search and offers advice, which the young Tsarevich does not take. He must capture a horse with the golden mane from the realm of Tsar Afron and capture the royal Tsarevna, Elena the Fair, before he can return to his father with the beautiful firebird (see p. 14 of color insert).

A desire for children is a universal theme found in "The Snow Maiden." In the Russian version, a woodcutter and his wife are unhappy because they do not have a child, so they create a *snegurochka* (a snow child). They wish so strongly that a miracle happens: "They looked at their snow maiden, and were amazed at what they saw. The eyes of the snow maiden twinkled; a diadem studded with precious stones sparkled like fire on her head; a cape of brocade covered her shoulders; embroidered boots appeared on her feet" (p. 53).

"Vassilissa The Fair" tells about the universal problem of the most beautiful child whose stepmother and stepsisters hate her. This girl has an enchanted doll, given her by her mother, who helps her do impossible chores, retrieve fire from the terrible witch Baba Yaga, and weave cloth so fine it must be made into shirts for the Tsar. Vassilissa's talents and her beauty greatly impress the Tsar, and they are married. This story, along with six traditional tales, is found in Aleksandr Nikolaevich Afanasér's *Russian Folk Tales.* The illustrations drawn by Ivan Bilibin, the late nineteenth century Russian illustrator, depict traditional costumes and earlier Russian settings.

Alexander Pushkin was one of the first Russian writers to capture the national folktales in written form. Patricia Tracy Lowe has translated and retold his stories in picture storybook formats. *The Tale of Czar Saltan or the Prince and the Swan Princess* is the story of a czar who marries the youngest, loveliest daughter of peasants. Problems arise when the czar leaves for war, and the girl's jealous sisters plot against her. A message from the czar is changed, and the lovely czarina and her baby are cast into a barrel which is thrown into the ocean. Instead of drowning, the baby rapidly matures, lands on a barren island with his mother, and saves a lovely swan. The island mysteriously turns into a wonderland, the boy saves his mother from her enemies, and they are reunited with his father, the czar. In *The Tale of The Golden Cockerel,* a fable is retold in which the czar is not honorable. He makes a promise he is unwilling to keep and must pay a heavy penalty. These tales reflect the importance of keeping promises and the consequences of jealousy and greed. Another tale of good versus evil and the consequences of jealousy and greed is found in Yūzō Otsuka's *Suho and the White Horse: A Legend of Mongolia.*

Themes of rewarding kindness and motifs of magical powers and rather foolish, kindhearted peasants are found in Arthur Ransome's *The Fool of the World and the Flying Ship* and Rosemary Harris's *The Flying Ship.* The peasant sets out to win the hand of the czar's daughter; he has offered her hand in marriage to anyone who can build a flying ship. Kindness to an old man provides the magical ship. Companions with extraordinary powers are required before the peasant wins his reward. This tale infers that the czar does not want the peasant to marry his daughter.

Russian tales reflect a vast country with numerous cultures. The themes imply that humans desire their own children; that talent, beauty, and kindness are appreciated and rewarded; and that people must pay the consequences for foolish actions, greed, broken promises, and jealousy. The humor suggests the universal need to laugh at oneself and others.

Jewish Folktales

Jewish folktales, according to Charlotte Huck (11), "have a poignancy, wit, and ironic humor that is not matched by any other folklore" (p. 194). An excellent example of this wit and humor is found in Margot Zemach's *It Could Always Be Worse.* This Yiddish folktale tells of nine unhappy people who share a small one-room hut. The father desperately seeks the advice of the Rabbi, who suggests that he bring a barnyard animal inside. A pattern of complaint and advice continues until most of the livestock is in the house. When the Rabbi tells the farmer to clear the animals out of the hut, the whole family appreciates its large, peaceful home.

Isaac Bashevis Singer's *Mazel and Shlimazel or the Milk of a Lioness* is longer and more complex. It pits Mazel, the spirit of good luck, against Shlimazel, the spirit of bad luck. To test the strength of good luck versus bad, they choose to manipulate the life of Tam, a bungler who lives in the poorest hut in the village. As soon as Mazel stands behind Tam, he succeeds at everything he tries. He fixes the king's carriage wheel and is invited to court where he accomplishes impossible tasks; even Princess Nesika is in love with him. Just as Tam is about to successfully complete his greatest challenge, the year is over and an old, bent man with spiders in his beard stands beside Tam. With one horrible slip of the tongue, Tam is in disfavor and condemned to death. Shlimazel has won! But wait! Mazel pre-

sents Shlimazel with the wine of forgetfulness, which causes Shlimazel to forget poor Tam. Mazel rescues Tam from hanging, Tam redeems himself with the king, marries the Princess and becomes the wisest of prince consorts. Tam's success is more than good luck, however: "Tam had learned that good luck follows those who are diligent, honest, sincere and helpful to others. The man who has these qualities is indeed lucky forever" (p. 42).

Folktales suggest the human qualities valued by the people; sincerity, unselfishness, and wisdom, for example, are handsomely rewarded in Michael Gross's *The Fable of the Fig Tree.* In this warm Hebrew folktale, the king asks Elisha how he knows that he will live long enough to eat the figs of the tree he is planting. Elisha's answer pleases the king: "If the Lord desires it, I hope to do so. If not, my children will gather the fruit. My parents, and their parents before them, and all the generations of parents before them, planted trees for their children. Thus it is my duty to plant trees for my children" (p. 3 unnumbered). Elisha lives to reap a harvest, takes a basket of figs to the king, and is handsomely rewarded with a basket of gold pieces. An envious villager decides to claim an equal reward by taking both good and bad figs to the king; the king commands that the soldiers tie him to a post and allow passersby to throw the figs at him. The man's unsympathetic wife tells her husband that he should be thankful—that it would have been worse if he had given the king hazelnuts.

The Golem is a deeply perceptive story that, according to the author Beverly Brodsky McDermott, "evokes centuries of hope for a better world—hope that must in the end be tempered with the reality of man's limitations" (introduction to text). This tale reveals the ancient belief of the sacred clay. The setting is the ghetto of Prague where the gates are fastened tightly, locking the Jews inside. Rabbi Lev has a dream that convinces him to mold a clay man to protect his people. Rabbi Lev and two men go to the attic where the clay is hidden under ancient prayer books. They circle the clay and chant secret names. As the flames glow and water flows, a man is made. Their man, the Golem, does not always act appropriately. When the ghetto is attacked, he grows into a giant, crushes the mob, and scorches the earth. Lamenting over his imperfect creation, Rabbi Lev turns him back into clay. McDermott's two years of research in developing this book included the study of Hebrew symbols and their corresponding magical qualities according to Cabalists (Jewish mystics). The book is also appreciated by older students; one fifteen-year-old boy, after reading it said he enjoyed it because "*The Golem* shows that man cannot be like God. When he tries to make God his peer his efforts will fail. What man creates will never be completely flawless, because man is not flawless." Compare this version with Isaac Bashevis Singer's text and Uri Shulevitz's illustrations for *The Golem.*

Themes in Jewish folktales suggest that sincerity, unselfishness, and true wisdom are rewarded; these attributes, however, may be difficult to find. The tales reflect human foibles as people face and overcome dissatisfaction and realize the dangers of excessive power.

Folktales from Asia and the East

Magical dragons, jackals, and cranes; legends describing the discovery of salt, the birth of Confucius, and two lovers turned

Daylight flooded the attic and four men descended the narrow stairway.

The dangers of excessive power are emphasized in this Jewish tale.
An illustration from *The Golem: A Jewish Legend,* written and illustrated by Beverly Brodsky McDermott. Copyright © 1976 by Beverly Brodsky McDermott. By permission of J. B. Lippincott, Publishers.

into doves to escape the wrath of the mandarin; tales of clever people, wise ancestors, and people who wish for good fortune; and exotic tales from Baghdad are all found in the folklore of the East. Collections and individual folktales from China, Japan, and other Eastern countries will be discussed here.

China. "A teacher can open the door, but the pupil must go through by himself" or "The home which has an old grandparent in it contains a precious jewel" (20) are all sayings handed down through Chinese tradition that suggest traditional Chinese philosophy and values. Chinese folktales tell of the ruling classes, the common people, and various Chinese tribes who lived on the perimeter of China. According to Louise and Yuanhsi Kuo (13), "The true feelings of the common man, his inner thoughts and aspirations were conveyed by such tales. Joy, sorrow, hardship, greed, fear, and varied emotions were portrayed simply yet skillfully; often with roguish humor. Religious beliefs, superstitions, morals, ethics, and philosophy were popular topics that showed the social conditions, manners, customs, and thoughts of people during a particular era" (p. 9).

A dislike for Han imperial authority is reflected in several tales told by the peasants. In these tales the dragon, the symbol of authority, is usually evil and is overcome by a peasant's wit. Such a tale is retold by Louise and Yuan-hsi Kuo in their collection of *Chinese Folk Tales.* "The Golden Sheng" is about a little girl who is captured by a flying dragon and taken to his cave. This is not a benevolent dragon:

Your sister is suffering; your sister is suffering,
In the evil dragon's cave.
Tears cover her face;
Blood stains her back;
Her hand drills the rock.
Your sister is suffering; your sister is suffering. (p. 18)

Two common motifs, reward for unselfish action and a magical object, allow her brother to rescue her and dispose of the beast. Enroute, he moves a dangerous boulder out of the path and is rewarded with a dazzling golden *sheng* that creates a melodious sound when blown into; the sound is so hypnotic that even earthworms and lizards are forced to dance. The boy rescues his sister by forcing the dragon to dance; the dancing continues until the dragon collapses into a pond and whirls with increasing speed for seven days and seven nights.

Other tales in the Kuos' collection reveal the ancestor worship, the supernatural quality of certain animals, early beliefs about the creation of the world, and the importance of knowledge and cleverness. One story, for example, tells about "The Clever Wife" who uses her wits to bring her family power in a

China predominantly controlled by men. A man is terrified when a magistrate demands that he must weave a cloth as long as the road, brew enough wine to match the quantity of water in the ocean, and raise a pig as heavy as the mountain. His wife tells him to return to the magistrate with a ruler, a measuring bowl, and a kitchen scale; inform the magistrate that he will finish the tasks as soon as the magistrate uses the ruler to measure the road so that he will know how long to weave the cloth; he will brew the wine after the magistrate measures the ocean with a measuring bowl; and he will raise the pig after the magistrate weighs the mountain with the scale. The magistrate wonders how such a foolish-looking fellow could respond so cleverly. When the man admits it was his wife's idea, the magistrate says that he had good counsel and that he will not bother the family again.

Robert Wyndham's *Tales the People Tell in China* includes myths, legends, folktales, and anecdotes that help people understand Chinese traditions. One humorous story for storytelling, "The Marvelous Pear Seed," tells how a thief is placed in a dank prison cell after he steals and eats a pear. He eats all the evidence except one seed. After days and days of imprisonment, the thief tells the jailor that he has a rare gift for the emperor. He has an audience with the emperor and tells him that he has a magical seed that will produce a tree bearing pears of pure gold. However, the tree will not bear golden fruit unless the seed is planted by a person who has neither stolen or cheated. No one will accept the seed, and the thief is pardoned by the emperor.

Cleverness also rewards a courageous general in "The Borrowing of 100,000 Arrows." This general must produce an impossible number of arrows in three days. Instead of trying to manufacture them, he stacks bundles of straw on the decks of twenty fast ships and lashes additional bundles of straw to their sides. He heads the ships through dense fog toward the enemy's camp with his crew pounding drums and yelling as they approach. The enemy general, thinking he is under attack by hundreds of sailors, orders his archers to attack. Too late, he realizes that he has been tricked; at least 100,000 arrows are stuck into the bundles of straw.

Japan. Many Japanese tales are similar to the Chinese stories. Stories of the dragon are found in tales from both countries. The tiger also came to Japan as a legendary creature. Frequently found in Japanese tales, this animal usually is considered a symbol of power. These and other animal tales are found in Pratt and Kula's *Magic Animals of Japan*. This book contains short stories about the mysterious and beautiful mermaid who inhabits the sea and animals such as the fox who

Wisdom is an important traditional value as shown in the theme for "The Borrowing of 100,000 Arrows."
From *Tales People Tell in China* by Robert Wyndham. Copyright © 1971 by Robert Wyndham. Reprinted by permission of Julian Messner, a Simon & Schuster division of Gulf & Western Corporation.

may be either a symbol of abundance or a mischief maker able to transform himself and the cat, a symbol of friendliness and prosperity.

Several Japanese folktales have been chosen for retelling in picture storybook format. Margaret Hodges's *The Wave* tells in words and beautiful cardboard cuts by Blair Lent what happens when a tidal wave sweeps over a small Japanese village; the village is saved because the man living on the mountain intentionally burns his crops to attract the people. His unselfish deed saves their lives. Another Japanese tale illustrated by Blair Lent is Arlene Mosel's *The Funny Little Woman*.

Allen Say's *Once Under the Cherry Blossom Tree* is an ancient traditional tale that was used by storytellers to set the mood for the longer stories that would follow. It is the tale of a miserly landlord who hates spring and loves to overcharge his tenants. One day, he accidentally swallows a cherry pit, causing a cherry tree to grow from the top of his head. When the villagers laugh at him, he furiously uproots the tree. This does not end his problems, however; a hole remains on his head. The rains of summer fill the hole, and magnificent fish swim in the water. The miser becomes so angry when children steal his fish that he jumps into the air, his feet sink into the hole on his head, his body disappears into the hole, and a lovely pond is the only thing that remains. This pond becomes the happiest place in the valley.

The unhappy consequences of greed and unwise counsel are common themes in Japanese folktales. Consider, for example, the motifs in a tale of a supernatural wife, Sumiko Yagawa's *The Crane Wife*. There are motifs common to tales of transformed wives or husbands in other cultures: there is a reward for kindness when a poor farmer rescues a wounded crane (the crane is tranformed into a lovely wife), a prohibition is set by the enchanted wife (she asks her husband not to look upon her when she weaves cloth); the husband breaks his promise and the prohibition; this act forces the enchanted one to leave. Unlike many of the transformation tales discussed earlier, the loved one does not search for the disenchanted being. Instead, after the poor farmer accepts unwise advice, becomes greedy, and looks at his wife, he loses her and her helpful ability forever. Illustrator Suekichi Akaba's sparsely drawn figures and line and wash drawings on textured papers complement this traditional tale.

Another Japanese tale about a crane suggests the desirability of friendship between humans and the crane of enchantment. Anne Laurin's *The Perfect Crane* tells about a lonely magician who creates a crane from rice paper. A strong friendship then develops between the two characters.

Other Asian and Eastern Folktales.   The Asian Cultural Centre for UNESCO has published a series of five books called *Folk Tales from Asia for Children Everywhere* that contain stories from many countries. Many of these stories are appreciated by storytellers. A tale from Afghanistan, for example, is similar to the story of Aladdin. In "The Carpenter's Son," the magic item is not a lamp but a ruby. A story from Burma, "The Four Puppets," stresses the harm that wealth and power can bring if they are not tempered with wisdom and love. There are also stories of wicked genies, tricky and clever animals, and wise and evil men.

A Vietnamese variation of the Cinderella tale develops both motifs that are common in other versions and culturally related adaptations. Similar motifs in Ann Nolan Clark's *In the Land of Small Dragon* include the death of the mother, a cruel stepmother and stepsister, a persecuted heroine, magical assistance, a difficult task, meeting the prince, and proof of identity. The illustrations (see p. 13 of color insert) and the text develop a strong cultural identity, however. For example, the father's second wife is the wicked adversary; the girl's tasks (catching fish, working in the rice paddies, separating rice from husks) are culturally related; her fairy godmother gives her jeweled slippers (hai); and the prince is an Emperor's son. The language, as shown by the following description of the maiden, makes it a good choice for sharing orally:

> Tam's face was a golden moon,
> Her eyes dark as a storm cloud,
> Her feet delicate flowers
> Stepping lightly on the wind.
> No envy lived in her heart,
> Nor bitterness in her tears. (p. 2)

The tales supposedly told by Shahrazad to King Shahryar to keep him from marrying a maiden each evening and beheading her in the morning are among the best known Arabian tales. An anthology of romances, fables, and jests told throughout the Near East made up the original *The Thousand Nights and a Night.* One of the best known of these tales, *Aladdin and the Wonderful Lamp,* has been illustrated by Errol LeCain. The illustrations for Andrew Lang's retelling depict the richness of a Persian setting.

The consequences of miserliness and the intervention of fate are suggested in Pamela Travers's *Two Pairs of Shoes.* In these two Persian tales worn slippers reflect the characters of the men who own them. In one tale tattered slippers are the outward symbol of a merchant's miserliness. In the other, worn slippers are the symbol of the humble roots of the king's chief adviser. The lesson learned by the merchant reflects traditional wisdom: nothing lasts forever; when an object is no longer useful it should be relinquished.

Many folktales from India were included in a series of animal stories known as the *Panchatantra.* The original tales were moralistic and included tales about the reincarnations of the Buddha. English translations, however, usually deleted the morals and references to the Buddha. Consequently, the stories have characteristics of folktales. Characteristic animal folktales are included in Nancy De Roin's *Jataka Tales.* Virginia Haviland's *Favorite Fairy Tales Told in India* is a fine source for additional Indian folktales.

THROUGH THE EYES OF AN AUTHOR

Traditional Native American Tales

Expert in traditional Native American literature and culture and collector of traditional tales, JAMAKE HIGHWATER, author of *Anpao: An American Indian Odyssey*, discusses his own feelings and beliefs.

I N A VERY REAL SENSE, I AM the brother of the fox. My whole life revolves around my kinship with four-legged things. I am rooted in the natural world. I'm two people joined into one body. The contradiction doesn't bother me. But people always assume the one they're talking to is the only one there is. That bothers me. There is a little of the legendary Anpao in me, but also a little of John Gardner. I stand in both those worlds, not between them. I'm very much a twentieth century person, and yet I'm traditional Northern Plains Indian.

I've always had an enormous regard for the intellect. Still, I like to go home to my people, who are in touch with the beginning of things. At home, people are carpenters; some are poets, painters, and teachers; some work on construction jobs. They are people who perceive the importance of small things that are easily missed by those of us who move much too quickly.

I came to terms with the solemn aspects of life very early. I was always among Indians, for we traveled the powwow circuit. I was always listening to some older person telling stories. They are nameless to me now, and countless, because there were so many. I was introduced to the Indian world as children in my tribe were in the 1870s when we were a nomadic people. I was rootless, yet connected to a vital tradition. The elders talked to me and gave me a sense of the meaning of my existence.

I talk and think as a poet, but I don't want to perpetuate the romantic notion of the Indian as watching chipmunks his entire life, waiting to see which side of the tree the moss grows on. For the Indian, art is not reserved for a leisure class, as it is in Anglo society. It is part of our fundamental way of thinking. We are an aesthetic people. Most primal people are. We represent a constant chord that's been resounding ever since man began. While those Cro-Magnon people in the caves of southern France (at least according to Western mentality) should have been out worrying about the great likelihood that they wouldn't survive, they were building scaffolds fifty or sixty feet high and with tiny oil lamps were painting the ceilings of their caves with marvelous magical images. These images were an implicit and important part of their lives. For us, this aesthetic reality is a continuous process. The kiva murals of the Hopi and the Mimbres pottery rival the finest accomplishments of Western art. This idea of life as art is part of being Indian. It's not quaint or curious or charming. It's fundamental, like plowing a field. There's great beauty in plowing a field.

I think Indians have become a metaphor for a larger idea. We are building bridges toward cultures. Some people in white society are also building bridges toward us, and they sometimes join together. That means that it's possible for everyone to find the Indian in himself. It's a kind of sensibility that I'm talking about.

Drawn from an interview with Jane B. Katz, 1980.

Eastern folktales contain such universal motifs as reward for unselfishness, assistance from magical objects, cruel adversaries, and punishment for dishonesty. The tales also emphasize the traditional values of the people: homage is paid to ancestors, knowledge and cleverness are rewarded, and greed and miserly behavior are punished.

African Folktales

African folktales are characterized by a highly developed oral tradition. Repetitive language and styles that encourage interaction with the storyteller make them excellent choices for sharing with children. Many of the stories are "why" tales that explain animal and human characteristics. Verna Aardema's *Why Mosquitoes Buzz in People's Ears* uses cumulative language to explain the buzz. *The Third Gift* by Jan Carews explains how the Jubas acquired work, beauty and imagination. Personified animals, who are frequently tricksters, are popular subjects. The hare, the tortoise, and Ananse the spider use wit and trickery to gain their objectives. These tales and others that reflect traditional values of the African people are discussed on pages 493–95 in chapter eleven, "Multiethnic Literature."

American Folktales

American folktales are discussed last because a large body of the literature has roots in the heritage of the old world. In addition, many of the tales were influenced by written literature and story heroes were fostered by professional writers. Consequently, it is more difficult, if not in some cases impossible, to identify tales that began in the oral tradition.

Folklorists identify four types of folktales found in the United States. First, there are the Native American tales that were handed down through centuries of tribal storytelling. Second, there are black folktales that reflect African and European themes but were changed as slaves faced difficulties in a new land. Third, there are variants of earlier folktales. These tales have traditional themes, motifs, and characters, but were changed to meet the needs of a robust, rural America. Finally, there are the boisterous and boastful tall tales.

Native American Folktales. These tales are usually considered the only traditional tales that are truly indigenous to the United States. Any study of Native American tales reveals that there is not one group of folktales; instead, the tales differ from region to region and tribe to tribe. There are, however, a few commonalities. Many of the tales are nature tales that reveal why or how animals obtain specific characteristics. For example, Margaret Hodges's *The Fire Bringer* tells how the coyote received his markings and how an Indian tribe obtained fire. Likewise, William Toye's *The Loon's Necklace* explains how the loon received the characteristic markings. As in other cultures, animal trickster tales are popular. The tricksters are often ravens, rabbits, or coyotes, and they often have powers of transformation. Transformation may also be used by a hero as he begins his quest. Gerald McDermott's hero is transformed into an arrow as he searches for his father and the creator in *Arrow to the Sun: A Pueblo Indian Tale.*

The importance of the folktale as a means of passing on tribal beliefs is revealed in Olaf Baker's *Where the Buffaloes Begin.* It is from Nawa, the tribal storyteller, that a young Prairie Indian learns about a sacred spot where the buffaloes rise out of a lake. After he finds the lake and waits quietly in the night, he hears the words of the storyteller singing in his mind:

Do you hear the noise that never ceases?
It is the Buffaloes fighting far below.
They are fighting to get out upon the prairie.
They are born below the Water but are fighting for the Air.
In the great lake in the Southland where the Buffaloes begin!
  (p. 20 unnumbered)

The diversity of Native American folktales, cultures, and customs are illustrated in Jamake Highwater's *Anpao: An Indian Odyssey.* Highwater's book emphasizes the importance of traditional tales in transmitting the culture. These tales and others are discussed on pages 503–5 in chapter eleven.

Black Folktales. Many black American folktales reflect both an African origin and an adaptation to a new environment and harsh reality. A rabbit trickster, for example, who triumphs over more powerful animals, is popular in African folklore. (The tortoise and Anansi, the spider, play similar trickster roles.) He is also one of the most popular characters in tales collected from blacks on southern plantations. This popularity is believed to be associated with the role of slavery in which cunning, wit, and deception were often the only weapons available against oppression.

Rabbit trickster tales are included in the various Brer Rabbit Stories collected by Joel Chandler Harris (*Uncle Remus and His Friends,* 1892; *Told By Uncle Remus,* 1905). While Harris collected his tales in Georgia, a similar trickster rabbit is found in West Virginia folklore and tales from coastal South Carolina. Consider, for example, the motifs and characteristics of the hero found in a West Virginian "Tar Baby" tale: (1) The large animals need a well; (2) Little Mr. Rabbit refuses to help dig the well and brags that he will drink without working; (3) The more powerful animals become angry and guard the well; (4) Mr.

Rabbit outsmarts Mr. Bear by singing and causing him to dance away from the well; (5) The animals ridicule Mr. Bear for being tricked; (6) Mr. Monkey guards the well and is tricked in the same way; (7) The animals make a tar man to guard the well; (8) Mr. Rabbit strikes and kicks the tar man and is captured; and (9) Mr. Rabbit outwits the less intelligent powerful animals by convincing them that he wants to have his head cut off or be shot, but he does not want to be fed large amounts of food and thrown into the thicket.

An excellent example of the infusion of a culture, language, and environment into tales from an earlier time is found in Priscilla Jaquith's *Bo Rabbit Smart For True: Folktales From the Gullah.* These tales collected from the Sea Islands off the coast of Georgia and South Carolina combine African words (*cooter* for *tortoise*), Elizabethan English, and dialect from the British provinces (*bittles* for *victuals*). In the African tradition, the stories repeat key words to increase their significance: "Alligator, Miz Alligator and all the little alligators slither into the field, KAPUK, kapuk, kapuk, kapuk, kapuk, kapuk, kapuk" (p. 27).

Jaquith's stories about a small, witty rabbit who outsmarts such powerful animals as a whale and an elephant are excellent to share with children. They also exemplify the changes in the oral tradition as storytellers modify the setting and the language. The moral of one of the stories, "Alligator's Sunday Suit" also suggests a serious theme found in some of the Black American folklore: "Don't go looking for trouble, else you might find it" (p. 30).

Variants of European Tales. The best-known variants of European tales belong to the Jack tale cycle in which a seemingly nonheroic person overcomes severe obstacles and outwits adversaries. "Jack and the Varmits," for example, is similar to "The Brave Little Tailor." In the European tradition, Jack is rewarded by a king. Instead of a giant, Jack must overcome a wild hog, a unicorn, and a lion. The influences of rural America are found in both the setting and language. The lion, who was killing cattle, horses, and humans, came over the mountains from Tennessee. Both the king and Jack speak in frontier dialect.

Boastful frontier humor is also found in tall tales that reflect settlers' hardships as they face severe climatic changes, unknown lands, and people whose lives reflect an unknown and frequently unappreciated culture.

Tall Tales. Exaggerated claims in tall tales may declare that the American soil is so rich that fast-growing vines damage the pumpkins by dragging them on the ground; frontiersmen are so powerful that they can lasso and subdue a cyclone; and a king of the rivermen can outshoot, outfight, outrun, and outbrag everyone in the world. The heroes who faced extremes in weather, conquered humans and beasts, and subdued the wilderness are not the godlike heroes of European mythology. Instead, their lives reflect more primitive virtues of brute force, animal cunning, and courage. The characters and situations also infer frontier idealism: the heroes are free to travel, live self-sufficient lives, and are extremely resourceful. There are several types of heroes in American tall tales. There are the hard-working, persevering characters of endurance and duty such as Johnny Appleseed. This hero considered it his mission to plant apple trees across the country. There are the boisterous, bragging, roughnecks such as Davy Crockett, Mike Fink, Paul Bunyan, and Pecos Bill, who, according to their exploits, conquered mountains, rivers, forests, and deserts. Finally, there are the characters who reflect a country changing from a rural to an urban orientation and mechanization. Such a hero is John Henry.

Comparisons of Folktales

The folktales discussed in this section have many similarities in plot, characterization, and style. They also reflect cultural differences. Chart 6–3 summarizes some of these similarities and differences by comparing one tale from each of the cultures. Students of children's literature may analyze other tales from each culture to identify common characteristics.

The Appeal of Folktales for Children

It is difficult to suggest any literature more appealing to children than folktales. F. Andre Favat (10) reviewed the relevant research and reached some interesting conclusions about children's ages and their interest in folktales:

1 Children between the ages of five and ten, or from kindergarten through the fifth grade, are interested in folktales, whether they select books voluntarily or are presented with books and asked for their opinion.
2 This interest follows what might be called a *curve of reading preference;* that is, children's interest in folktales emerges at a prereading age and gradually rises to a peak between the approximate ages of six and eight. It then gradually declines.
3 Concurrent with this decline in interest in folktales, there is an emergence of interest in stories of reality.

Folktales appeal to a wide range of interest and age levels. Animal tales such as "The Three Little Pigs," "The Little Red

CHART 6–3

Comparisons of Folktales from Different Cultures

Culture and Examples	Protagonist— Main Character	Portrayal of Hero	Characteristics of Other Characters	Setting	Intended Audience	Dominant Plot Situation	Qualities Admired	Conclusion Indication of Characters' Fate
British "Jack the Giant Killer"	Simple peasant lad.	Simple peasant lad who is brave and outwits villains.	Evil giants. Weak king who cannot solve problem.	Rural mountain cave.	Common people.	Hero sets out to rid kingdom of giants.	Intelligence, bravery.	Happy ending. Villains slain. Hero rewarded with knighthood.
French "Sleeping Beauty"	Adolescent girl who is also a princess (about fifteen).	Prince "pursued on by love and honor"; "valiant."	Wicked fairy who gives gift of death. Father who cannot protect his daughter. (He was away when the girl fell asleep.)	Castle. Prince goes through series of rooms similar to Versailles.	Nobility.	Threatened girl is rescued by a prince.	Values admired at court: beauty, wit of an angel, grace, dancing, and singing.	Happy ending. Prince and Princess are married.
German "Hansel and Gretel"	Boy and girl, woodcutter's children.	Hansel cares for his sister, but Gretel outwits witch.	Stepmother who wants to leave the children in the woods. Weak father who cannot care for his children. Wicked witch.	The forest.	Common people.	Abandoned children outwit a wicked witch.	Outwitted witch.	Wicked witch punished by burning to death. Stepmother dead. Children rewarded with jewels. Happy ending.
Norwegian "The Lad Who Went to the Northwind"	Simple peasant lad.	Simple, but honest, peasant lad who finally realizes he has been tricked.	Powerful northwind. Scolding mother. Dishonest, greedy innkeeper.	Rural, far north.	Common people.	Hero sets out to retrieve lost object.	Honesty, kindness.	Dishonest innkeeper beaten. Boy rewarded with magical objects. Happy ending.
Russian "The Fool of the World and the Flying Ship"	Simple young peasant.	Foolish, kindhearted young peasant.	Dishonorable Czar who tries to trick hero. Four companions with great powers.	Rural countryside. Czar's palace.	Common people.	Simple boy sets out on a quest; he is aided by acquiring magical ship and companions.	Kindness, honesty.	Unhappy Czar gains an unwanted son-in-law. Peasant marries royalty. Happy ending.
Jewish "Mazel and Shlimazel"	Poor peasant.	Ne'er-do-well bungler before good luck intercedes.	Spirit of good luck is happy and attractive. Spirit of bad luck is slumped and angry.	King's court and countryside.	Common people.	Simple boy, accompanied by good luck then bad luck, sets out on a series of quests.	Diligence, honesty, sincerity, helpfulness.	Bad luck forgets about his victim. Good luck stays with him. Hero marries the princess, and eventually becomes wisest of prince consorts. Happy ending.
Chinese "The Golden Sheng"	Poor adolescent girl stolen by dragon.	Boy who grew up very rapidly.	Evil, cruel dragon.	Rural.	Common people.	A young boy goes on a quest to save his sister from a dragon.	Helpfulness, diligence, loyalty.	Dragon whirls himself to death. Brother and sister return to mother where they use remains of the dragon to help their work. Happy ending.
African "How Spider Got a Thin Waist"	Tricky and greedy spider.	Greedy spider who does not work but plays in the sun.	Hard-working villagers.	Forest and village.	Common people.	Hero tries to get food without working.	Greed is punished.	Greedy spider gains a thin waist.
Native American "The Fire Bringer"	Young Paiute Indian boy.	Boy who is concerned about his people.	Intelligent coyote, swift runners	Mesa and mountain.	Common people	Boy and coyote set out to get fire for the Paiutes.	Intelligence, swiftness, bravery.	Boy and coyote honored.

Hen," and "The Three Bears" have been illustrated in picture book format for young children while some versions of fairy tales such as "Beauty and the Beast" are of interest to upper elementary school children.

Favat's research also showed some possible reasons for children's interest in folktales. He states that the characteristics of folktales correspond with the characteristics Piaget ascribed to children. First, children believe that objects, actions, thoughts, and words can exercise magical influence over events in their own lives. Folktales are filled with such actions; the prince kisses the sleeping princess to awaken her, or a devoted sister throws shirts over her enchanted brothers to change them from swans back into humans. Second, children believe that many inanimate objects are living or have a consciousness. In folktales, sticks or mills can appear to have life. Children also award human consciousness to animals; consequently, the animals in folktales and fables who act like people are consistent with the children's belief. Third, young children believe in justice and punishment for wrongdoing and rewards for good behavior. Folktales contain retribution and justice; the good Goose Girl is rewarded by marrying the prince and her deceitful maid is punished harshly. Fourth, the relationship between the hero and his world is much the same as the relationship between children and their own world: children are at the center of their universe; the heroes or heroines are the centers of their folktale world. The world, for example, centers around Sleeping Beauty. She sleeps for a hundred years and so does the whole castle.

In addition to the relationships between children and folktales, children enjoy the fast-paced plots, the easily identifiable good or bad characters, and a plot development that allows them to identify with their heroes.

FABLES

The origin of the fable is credited by legend to a Greek slave named Aesop who lived in the sixth century B.C., whose nimble wit supposedly got his master out of numerous difficulties. It is not certain, however, that Aesop was one man, and several critics attribute these early fables to various sources. Fables are found worldwide; fables similar to Aesop's have come from China and India. Whatever their origin, fables are excellent examples of stories handed down through centuries of oral and written tradition.

Characteristics of Fables

The fable, according to R. T. Lenaghan (14) in his introduction to *Caxton's Aesop,* has the following characteristics: "(1) it is fiction in the sense that it did not really happen; (2) it is literary entertainment; (3) it is poetic fiction with double or allegorical significance; and (4) it is a moral tale, usually with animal characters" (p. 12). In addition, although the main characters are usually animals, they frequently talk, behave like humans, and possess human traits. Fables are short, usually having no more than two or three characters who perform simple, straightforward actions that result in a single climax. There is also a human lesson to be learned by reading about the foibles of the animals.

These characteristics apparently appealed to storytellers in the early centuries and to publishers and readers in the fifteenth century. Fables were among the earliest materials printed by William Caxton on his printing press. Lenaghan credits the fable's popularity at that time to its generic ambiguity; it could be a tale, a pedagogical device, a sermon, and a literary genre. Also, it could reach a wide range of intelligence; it could be bluntly assertive or cleverly ironic; or it could be didactic or skeptical. Readers could, consequently, emphasize whatever function of the fable they chose.

The popularity of the fable continued, and it was a subject chosen for writing and illustrating by Randolph Caldecott. Caldecott's 1883 edition of *The Caldecott Aesop,* reissued in 1978, provides modern readers with an opportunity to enjoy a reproduction of his original fables and hand-colored illustrations. It is interesting to note how Caldecott illustrated the fables, with the first illustration corresponding to the animal in the fable followed by a version in which people replace the animals.

Collections of Fables

Fables are popular subjects for modern storytellers and illustrators. Young children like the animals who talk and the often humorous climaxes. Brian Wildsmith has chosen several fables originally translated by Jean de La Fontaine to develop into picture storybook format. The fable of the rat who is captured by a lion, released, and then saves the lion from capture by persistently gnawing an entrapping net is pictured vividly in *The Lion and the Rat.* In this version for young children, each sentence is illustrated with a large, colorful two-page drawing. The characteristics of the animals are developed through the illustrations, and children can see that both patience and hard work can bring success when size, strength, and anger cannot. Wildsmith has also illustrated each line in La Fontaine's translation of *The Miller, the Boy and the Donkey,* the humorous tale of a miller who follows everyone's advice when he takes his donkey to market. The illustrations show the donkey being carried on a litter, the boy riding the donkey, and the man riding the donkey, both riding the donkey, and finally no one riding the donkey. The miller finally realizes that he should make up his own mind and then stick with it. (It is interesting to compare this version with others; the donkey does not drown in Wildsmith's picture storybook as he does in the original Aesop fable.) How success can be achieved through gentleness and warmth rather than through strength and fury is demonstrated in a third picture story fable by Wildsmith. *The North Wind and the Sun* illustrates the challenge between the North Wind and the sun as each one tries to remove the cloak from a horseman.

Numerous collections of Aesop fables have also been compiled and illustrated for slightly older children. It is interesting to compare these various editions to see how the fables have been interpreted and illustrated. Anne Terry White's version contains forty fables. She introduces them by saying that Aesop made his animals behave like humans to make a point without hurting the feelings of the great and powerful leaders who could be cruel to a slave. She also says that when he told a story about an animal, his listeners understood his meaning. White's version is written in simple narrative form with dialogue among the talking beasts. In the fable, "The Lion and the Mouse," White describes the capture of the mouse in this way:

Bang! The Lion clapped his paw to his face and felt something caught. It was furry. Lazily he opened his eyes. He lifted up one side of his huge paw just a little bit to see what was under it and was amazed to find a Mouse. (p. 5)

Each fable in this collection is followed by its moral. The moral of "The Lion and the Mouse" is simply stated:

Little friends may prove to be great friends. (p. 8)

The woodcuts by Helen Siegle complement the mood developed by White's version of Aesop's fables.

In contrast, quite a different literary style is used by Ennis Rees in *Lions and Lobsters and Foxes and Frogs*. This version retells the Aesop fables in rhyming verse. The capture of the mouse is told in this way:

He seized the mouse in his paw
And was going to eat him,
But stopped when he looked down and saw
That the mouse would entreat him.

Ruth Spriggs's large edition of *The Fables of Aesop* has 143 fables told in story format. Each fable is followed by its moral. The moral for "The Lion and the Mouse" is stated as follows:

Do not judge people's usefulness by their appearance. (p. 10)

Contemporary versions of fables differ in illustrators' style as well as literary style. Compare the illustrations in two recent editions: Heidi Holder's *Aesop's Fables* and Harold Jones's illustrations for *Tales from Aesop*. Holder's illustrations are detailed paintings surrounded by equally detailed borders. Jones's less sophisticated drawings suggest the spirited characteristics and emotions of human and animal characters.

It is interesting to compare these contemporary versions with those published in the 1400s and 1800s, noting the differences in writing style, language, spelling, and illustrations. Some fables were written for adults; others were specifically written with children in mind. Older children can learn more about their literary heritage by comparing and discussing various versions of these ancient stories.

They had not gone very far before they met a farmer.

He burst out laughing when he saw them. "How silly you are," he cried. "Fancy carrying a donkey! Why *he* should be carrying *you*, not *you* carrying *him*."

The Miller, the Boy and the Donkey is an example of a single fable that has been told in picture book format.
From *The Miller, the Boy and the Donkey* by Brian Wildsmith, published by Oxford University Press © Wildsmith 1969.

The detailed drawings, with the castle in the background, create an elegant setting for a fable.

An illustration from *Aesop's Fables* illustrated by Heidi Holder. Copyright © 1981 by Heidi Holder. Reproduced by permission of Viking Penguin Inc.

MYTHS

Each ancient culture made up stories that answered questions about the creation of the earth, the creation of people, and the reasons for natural phenomena. The Greeks called them *mythos,* which means "tales" or "stories." When the word *myth* is used today, it means, according to Isaac Asimov (2), a story containing fanciful or supernatural incidents intended to explain nature or tell about the gods and demons invented by these earlier people. Bascom's (4) definition cited earlier in this chapter defined myth as having the following characteristics: believed to be fact; had a setting reflecting a time and place—often an earlier or other world; had a setting in the remote past;

reflected a sacred attitude; and had nonhuman (divine) principal characters. The importance of these early myths is better understood when one realizes that a religion grew up about them; gods controlled natural forces so they had to be honored, and sacrifices had to be made to win their favors. Stars, planets, months, and days of the week were named after these gods and goddesses.

Myths live on in literature and provide an understanding of the rich cultural heritage that comes from the cradle of civilization. In addition, many terms used in mythology are also found in modern language. Children find these stories exciting and become interested in this rich literary heritage. Jane Yolen (21) identifies four purposes for using myths with children. First, myths provide a means for introducing allusions to children. An author describing something as being "as swift as Mercury" or "as strong as Heracles," is alluding to characteristics of the gods. Second, myths provide a knowledge of ancestral cultures, a way of looking at another culture from the inside out. Consequently, learning about Greek gods helps children understand the Greek world view; while learning about Norse gods helps them understand the Norse religious superstructure. Third, myths are tools for therapy; they offer new dimensions for imagination and suggest images that can be structured in daydreams. Fourth, myths are models for belief. They are serious statements about existence and provide a framework for understanding people and everything they did or thought.

Greek and Roman Mythology

The best-known myths are probably those originating in early Greece. When the Romans conquered Greece, they adopted many Greek gods but changed the spellings according to the Roman alphabet. In order to understand these stories, Helen Sewell (18), the author of *A Book of Myths,* says that one must be acquainted with the ideas of the structure of the universe that prevailed among these early Greeks. They believed the universe was created from unorganized matter called *chaos,* a swirling and transparent vapor. When form and shape were created, the result was *order* and *cosmos.* The Greeks believed that the first things formed out of chaos were the gods: *Gaia* (meaning "earth"; *Terra* is the Roman name) and *Ouranos* (meaning "sky"; *Uranus* is the Roman name) (2). From their offspring, the remaining Greek gods emerged. These gods lived on Mount Olympus, but they frequently came down from those lofty heights into the human world.

The Greeks believed that the earth was flat and circular, with their own country being the center. Around this flowed the

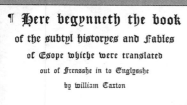

¶ Here begynneth the book of the subtyl historyes and fables of Esope whiche were translated out of Frensshe in to Englysshe by william Caxton

At Westmynstre In the yere of oure Lorde .m. cccc.lxxxiij

FLASHBACK

PUBLISHED BY CAXTON IN THE 1400s, *The book of the subtyl historyes and fables of Esope* is considered one of Caxton's most important contributions to literature. These fables, or cautionary animal tales with morals, were popular with readers in the fifteenth century. In the seventeenth century, John Locke recommended fables as ideal reading for children. Many artists since the 1400s have chosen to illustrate the fables. They are still popular today.

River Ocean. The Dawn, the Sun, and the Moon were supposed to rise out of the eastern ocean and drive through the air giving light to the gods and mortals. The majority of the stars also rose out of, and sank into, this ocean. The Greeks believed that the northern part of the earth beyond the mountains was inhabited by a race of people called *Hyperboreans.* In these mountains were the caverns from which came the piercing north winds that sometimes chilled Greece. On the south lived the Ethiopians whom the gods favored; on the west lay the Elysian Plain where mortals favored by the gods were transported to enjoy immortality.

Greek and Roman mythology includes stories about the creation of this world and its inhabitants, tales of the gods and goddesses who ruled the world, and stories about the mortal heroes and craftsmen who frequently interacted with the gods and sometimes claimed descent from the immortals.

Although there are motifs and themes in this mythology that are similar to the previously discussed folktales, the myths include Bascom's requirements for setting, time, attitude, and principal characters. Let us consider, for example, these points in two tales that have similar plots: Edna Barth's version of the myth *Cupid and Psyche* and the Norse folktale "East of the Sun and West of the Moon."

Cupid and Psyche	"East of the Sun and West of the Moon"
Setting	
Olympus, Greece	Any kingdom
An earlier world	
Time	
In a remote past when gods and goddesses dwelled on earth	Once upon a time
Attitude	
Sacred, worship of deity required or punishment resulted	Secular
Principal Characters	
Nonhuman goddess of love and her son, Cupid	Transformed human male and human girl
Mortal who becomes immortal	Troll princess
Intervention of deity important	

The plot development in the two tales is similar: a young girl breaks a promise, her loved one leaves, she searches for him, and she must overcome obstacles or perform tasks before they are reunited. The principal characters differ in important characteristics, however. Psyche, a beautiful mortal princess, is

as her wings would take her, the little bird flew up to Cupid's window. Cooing to get his attention, she urged him to go to Psyche's rescue.

Completely recovered now, Cupid was still being punished by Venus. The door of his room was still locked and his window still barred. But, such was the power of his love that he managed to bend back the bars. His wings, strong from their long rest, carried him swiftly to the spot where Psyche lay lifeless, the open box on the path beside her.

With a light touch of one of his arrows, Cupid aroused her. Then, gathering up the deadly sleep, he put it back into the box.

"Psyche, Psyche," he said. "Once again your curiosity

57

Compare the Greek setting for this tale of enchantment with the Norwegian "East of the Sun and West of the Moon."
From the book *Cupid and Psyche* by Edna Barth, published by Clarion Books, Tickner & Freeds: A Houghton Mifflin Company, New York. Copyright © 1976 by the illustrator, Ursula Arndt.

the object of a goddess's anger and jealousy. She later falls in love with a god, performs tasks stipulated by the goddess, and requires intervention from the most divine ruler, Jupiter. Edna Barth (3) believes there is a strong religious significance in *Cupid and Psyche*. She states that the myth originally represented the progress of the human soul as it travels toward perfection. Symbolized by Psyche, the soul originated in heaven where all is love, symbolized by Cupid. It is then condemned for a period of time to wander the earth and undergo hardship and misery. If the soul proves worthy, it will be returned to heaven and reunited with love.

Circumstances surrounding the creation of the gods and goddesses, their places within the Olympian family, the consequences resulting from varied personality traits, and their accomplishments create exciting tales and enjoyable reading. Chart 6–4 includes examples of Greek and Roman gods and goddesses, their area of rule, their accomplishments, and examples of texts that include myths about the deities.

There is a close interaction in mythology between gods or goddesses and heroes or craftsmen. The deities frequently help the heroes. Margaret Hodges's introduction to *The Gorgon's Head* implies the reverence felt for the heroes: "The gods

CHART 6–4
Greek and Roman Gods and Goddesses

Name	Ruler	Accomplishments	Examples of Texts
Zeus (Jupiter) (Roman names in parentheses)	Ruler of Mount Olympus King of gods and men	Used lightning to gain control of the universe	Gates's *Lord of the Sky: Zeus*
Athena (Minerva)	Goddess of wisdom and protectress in war	Established rule of law Gave olive tree to mankind	Gates's *The Warrior Goddess: Athena*
Apollo (Apollo)	God of Sun Patron of truth, music, medicine, and archery	Established the oracle (prophets who gave advice)	Gates's *The Golden God: Apollo* Bulfinch's *A Book of Myths*
Artemis (Diana)	Goddess of moon Guardian of cities, young animals, and women	Mighty huntress	Bulfinch's *A Book of Myths*
Aphrodite (Venus)	Goddess of love and beauty	Flowers sprang up where she walked Had power to beguile gods Gave birth to Fear and Terror	Gates's *Two Queens of Heaven: Aphrodite and Demeter*
Demeter (Ceres)	Goddess of crops	Giver of grain and fruit Caused famine when Hades took her daughter to the underworld	Coolidge's *Greek Myths* Gates's *Two Queens of Heaven: Aphrodite and Demeter* Proddow's *Demeter and Persephone*
Hermes (Mercury)	Messenger of the gods Protector of flocks, cattle, and mischief makers	Trickster who was named god of commerce, orators, and writers	Gates's *The Golden God: Apollo*
Poseidon (Neptune)	God of the sea and earthquakes	Gave horses to humans Answered voyager's prayers	D'Aulaires' *Book of Greek Myths*
Dionysus (Bacchus)	God of wine, fertility, the joyous life, and hospitality	Gave Greece the gift of wine	Bulfinch's *A Book of Myths* Coolidge's *Greek Myths*
Ares (Mars)	God of war	Symbol of evils and suffering caused by war	D'Aulaires' *Book of Greek Myths*
Hephaestus (Vulcan)	God of fire and artisans	From his forges came Pandora, the first mortal woman Created mechanical objects	D'Aulaires' *Book of Greek Myths*
Eros (Cupid)	God of love (son of Venus)		Barth's *Cupid and Psyche*

love a hero. As every day dawns, they show him the path that he must follow, even to the farthest ends of the earth and over the perilous sea. The gods guide him and guard him in danger, and when he dies they take him straight up into the starry heavens" (p. 7).

The deities, depending upon their moods and objectives, may punish mortals who challenge the gods. When inventors and craftsmen, for example, perform forbidden deeds or try to emulate the gods, they may be severely punished.

Chart 6–5 lists some of the heroes and craftsmen, their accomplishments, and suggested texts.

Selecting Versions of Greek and Roman Myths. The versions of myths listed in the previous charts differ in authors'

CHART 6–5
Heroes and Craftsmen

Name	Accomplishments	Examples of Texts
Heracles	Given 12 tasks in atonement — killed 9 headed hydra, captured bull of Minos, held up sky	Garfield and Blishen's *The Golden Shadow* Silverthorne's *I Heracles*
Perseus (son of Zeus)	Killed Medusa, freed princess from serpent	Hodges's *The Gorgon's Head* Kingsley's *The Heroes*
Jason	Searched for golden fleece, fought giants, fire-eating bulls	Colum's *The Golden Fleece*
Theseus	Rid the roads of giants and bandits	Kingsley's *The Heroes*
Daedalus and Icarus	Inventor, builder of labyrinth for Minotaur Icarus died when he flew too close to the sun	Farmer's *Daedalus and Icarus* McDermott's *Sun Flight* Serraillier's *A Fall From the Sky*

style, completeness of text, and inclusion of illustrations. Consequently, adults must consider these factors when choosing books for appropriate ages. Eight- or nine-year-olds, for example, may enjoy Penelope Proddow's *Demeter and Persephone*. The language, written in the form of a narrative poem, is good for sharing orally. Barbara Cooney's illustrations of Greek hillsides and temples help depict the setting for this delightful story. Edna Barth's version of *Cupid and Psyche* is also appropriate for children who enjoy such folktales as "Beauty and the Beast" and "East of the Sun and West of the Moon."

Another myth that is enjoyed by younger children is Gerald McDermott's version of the Daedalus myth, *Sun Flight*. This colorful text is based on McDermott's animated film that won the Zellerbach Award for Films as Art at the San Francisco International Film Festival. Bold colors depict the setting on Crete as the two craftsmen face the wrath of Minos and fashion their wings. The final flight sequences are told through the illustrations as McDermott changes Icarus's colors from the blues and greens of his initial flight, to orange and red as he nears the sun, to reds and browns as he falls in flames, and to greens as he is engulfed by the waves. Penelope Farmer's version, *Daedalus and Icarus,* is also appropriate for younger children.

Older children frequently enjoy the longer, more developed versions of the myths. Adults may wish to compare Ian Serraillier's version of the Daedalus myth with McDermott's and Farmer's versions. Serraillier's *A Fall From the Sky,* includes the reasons for Daedalus's jealousy, his trial, and his attempts to escape judgment. The intervention of the goddess

This highly illustrated version of a myth is appropriate for younger readers.
Reprinted by permission of Four Winds Press, a division of Scholastic Inc. from *Sun Flight* by Gerald McDermott. Copyright © 1980 by Gerald McDermott.

Athena and the symbolization of the partridge are also included in this more complex version.

Enthusiastic readers of Greek mythology enjoy comparing these three versions. A seventh grade teacher asked her students to read the three texts and discuss the strengths and the weaknesses of each version. She used the highly illustrated McDermott version to stimulate the interpretation of additional scenes from Serraillier's version into an animated film or picture book.

The remainder of the versions listed on the charts contain language and story complexity that are more appropriate for older children. Elizabeth Silverthorne's *I, Heracles* is written from the hero's viewpoint. She introduces him by having him speak to the reader and explain why he is so strong:

I hope you won't think I'm bragging when I tell you about some of the things I've done. I really do have superhuman strength, you know, but I don't take any credit for it. My mother is Alcmena—she's an earthly princess—and my father is Zeus— he is the ruler of all the other gods on Mount Olympus. Naturally that makes me half man and half god, and that accounts for my strength. (p.11)

Many children enjoy this first-person style and state that Heracles seems like a very real hero.

Doris Gates develops stories with fast-paced plots and language that suggest word pictures. Her style reads well and is an excellent choice for sharing orally. For example, her description of the goddess's creation in *The Warrior Goddess: Athena* seems appropriate for a warrior:

She sprang from the head of Zeus, father of gods. Born without a mother, she was fully grown and fully armed. Her right hand gripped a spear, while her left steadied a shield on her forearm. The awful aegis, a breast ornament bordered with serpents, hung from her neck, and from her helmeted head to her sandaled feet she was cloaked in radiance, like the flash of weaponry. So the great goddess Athena came to join the family of gods on high Olympus, and, of all Zeus's children, she was his favorite. (p. 11)

Contrast this description to Gates's description of the creation of the goddess of love and beauty in *Two Queens of Heaven: Aphrodite and Demeter:*

There appeared a gathering of foam on the water. It resembled the white spindrift that trails behind a great wave as it breaks. But this form did not trail. It formed itself into a raft rising and falling with the sea. Suddenly a woman's figure appeared atop the raft balancing on slender feet. She was young and beautiful beyond anything in human form the sun had ever shone on. (pp. 9–10)

Versions of myths told by Olivia Coolidge, Charles Kingsley, and Padraic Colum are also good choices for older children.

Norse Mythology

The warm, sunny world of Mount Olympus is far behind. A far different group of gods and heroes existed in a world of ice, glaciers, and cold mountains. The harsh conditions of the northern life helped to form their legends. Consequently, a frost giant is the first being to be created and the mythology is filled with trolls, wild beasts, and frost giants.

Just as the Greek myths influenced literature, so did those of the Norsemen. Shakespeare was influenced by an old Norse tale when he wrote Hamlet; J. R. R. Tolkien, a professor of Anglo-Saxon literature at Oxford, relied on his knowledge of the northern sagas and Beowulf when he wrote *The Hobbit* and *The Lord of the Rings.*

The tales of the northern gods were collected during the twelfth and thirteenth centuries from the earlier oral tradition. These original tales formed two volumes, the *Elder* and the *Younger Edda.* These texts are now the sources for most of our knowledge about Norse mythology. According to Olivia Coolidge (8), the earth began when a frost giant, Ymer, came out of the swirling mists. The shifting particles formed a great cow whose milk nourished Ymer. As time went by, sons and daughters were also created out of the mists. Gods were created when the cow began to lick the great ice blocks that filled the mists. As she licked, a huge god appeared. When he stood up, his descendants were formed from his warm breath. These gods knew that the frost giants were evil and vowed to destroy them. A mighty battle resulted between the gods and the frost giants, with the gods finally overpowering the giants. Ymer was destroyed, and the remaining giants fled into the outer regions and created a land of mists and mountains. The mightiest of the gods, Odin, looked at the dead frost giant, Ymer, and suggested that the gods use his body to make a land where they could live. They formed Ymer's body into the round, flat earth, and on its center they built mountains that would contain their home, Asgard. Ymer's skull was used to form the great arch of heaven; the blood was the ocean, a barrier between the earth and giantland. Sparks were stolen from the fiery regions to light the stars, and chariots were built in which the gods placed sun and moon spirits who would ride over the earth.

Olivia E. Coolidge's *Legends of the North* is an excellent source of stories about these Norse gods who lived on earth in the mighty citadel of Asgard. It includes tales of the northern gods and heroes. In "The Apples of Idun," one learns why the gods often walked on earth:

Odin smiled. "We should learn to know the earth because it is ours," he replied. "Sometimes we ride the clouds or fly on wings like the birds, but often we must travel as men do, yard by yard over stone after stone. We shall always remember these hills, their sandy soil, their sparse yellow flowers, their little dried pines, and the green valley below." (p. 20)

Thor also appears in Coolidge's text. He strides around with red hair bristling and fierce eyes ablaze; sometimes he rides in his chariot drawn by red-eyed goats, as shaggy and fierce as their master. One humorous selection that children enjoy is "The Hammer of Thor," in which he searches loudly for his missing hammer. Children probably feel close to Thor as he responds in exasperation when Freyja, the goddess of beauty, asks him where he put it. He shouts, "If I knew where I put it, I should not be looking for it now" (p. 35). Thor discovers that the giant Thyrm has stolen the hammer and wants Freyja as ransom. When the goddess vehemently refuses to become the giant's bride, the suggestion is made that Thor dress up as a bride and go to giantland to retrieve his own hammer. After considerable argument, the huge god dresses in gown and veil to cover his fierce eyes and bristling beard, and accompanied by the impish Loki, leaves for giantland. Mighty Thor remains quiet as the wedding feast progresses, and it is fast-witted Loki who answers the giant's questions and calms his suspicions. Finally, Thor is able to touch his hammer as the wedding ceremony begins. This is what he has been waiting for; he regains his hammer, overpowers the giant, removes his skirts, and leaves for home. The humor and action in this tale make it excellent for storytelling.

Other enjoyable tales for sharing include Ingri and Edgar Parin D'Aulaire's *Norse Gods and Giants* and Padraic Colum's *The Children of Odin.*

EPICS AND LEGENDS

The great epics and legends in literature are closely related to mythology. Epics are long narrative poems about the deeds of a traditional or historical hero of high station. The focus of the epic is on a human hero, not a god or goddess. Two of the better known Greek and Roman epics are the *Iliad* and the *Odyssey.* The *Iliad* tells an account of the Trojan War. The *Odyssey* reports Odysseus's (Ulysses) journey as he defeats the cyclops, overcomes the song of the sirens, and manages to survive ten long years of hazardous adventures.

"Beowulf" is usually considered the best example of Norse epic poetry. There are three main episodes in this struggle

"The Hammer of Thor" is an excellent storytelling choice from Coolidge's collection.
From *Legends of the North* by Olivia Coolidge. Copyright © 1951 and © renewed 1979 by Olivia E. Coolidge. Reprinted by permission of Houghton Mifflin Co.

against evil: (1) Beowulf fights and kills the monster Grendel. (2) Beowulf dives to the depths of the pool and attacks Grendel's mother, She. (3) Beowulf fights the dragon Firedrake, and is mortally wounded. Versions are available either in narrative or poetic form. One version, which the author Robert Nye calls a *new telling,* is written in narrative form for younger readers. Nye's *Beowulf* retells Beowulf's heroic destruction of the monsters Grendel, She, and the Firedrake long ago in the land of the Danes. Nye's description of the great hall, Heorot, seems appropriate for heroic deeds: "It stood tall and firm on the edge of the misty fen. By day, it towered above men's heads like a second sun, so bright were its walls and roofs. By night, the torchlight blazing from its high windows, it was like a huge sentinel who did not sleep" (p. 5).

While Beowulf is strong, he is also good. This characteristic is found in each retelling. Nye's version, for example, describes the hero as having real strength that "lay in the balance of his person—which is perhaps another way of saying that he was strong because he was good, and good because he had the strength to accept things in him which were bad" (p. 25). His good is so powerful that it is felt by the evil monsters and is instrumental in their defeat.

Many of the heroes in legends also reflect a strong sense of goodness as they overcome various worldly evils. The line between myth and legend, however, is often vague. The early legends usually enlarged the lives of religious figures such as martyrs and saints. In more recent times, legends developed around the lives and accomplishments of royal figures and folk heroes. The similarities and differences between myth and legend are seen when comparing them according to Bascom's (4) definition of belief, setting, time, attitude, and principal characters:

Myth: Creation of Athena	*Legend: Tales of King Arthur*
Belief	
Told as factual	Told as factual (British
Belief in gods	chieftan of 5th-6th
	century)
Setting	
Olympus, Greece	British Isles
An earlier world	
Time	
In the remote past when gods	Time of kings and knights
dwelled on earth	A recognizable world
Attitude	
Sacred, goddess sprang from	Sacred, quest for holy grail
head of Zeus, father of gods	Secular, established Round
	Table and leader of
	knights
Principal Character	
Nonhuman, assists heroes in	Human king
quests	Does not have supernatural
	powers

King Arthur, according to this definition, is a legend because there is a belief in fact, the setting has a time and place in the world as it is today, the time is in the recent past, the attitude may be sacred or secular, and the principal character is human.

Tales of this legendary British king were so popular in early England that Sir Thomas Malory's *Morte d'Arthur* was one of the first books published in England. Another early version of the tale is Howard Pyle's *The Story of King Arthur and His Knights.* The first section of Pyle's version, "The Book of King Arthur," reveals how Arthur removes the sword signifying he is rightful king of England, claims his birthright, weds Guinevere,

and establishes the Round Table. The second section, "The Book of Three Worthies," tells of Merlin the magician, Sir Pellias, and Sir Gawaine.

Rosemary Sutcliff has written several stories about King Arthur. *The Sword and The Circle: King Arthur and the Knights of the Round Table* includes thirteen tales associated with the legend.

Taliesin and King Arthur by Ruth Robbins is a charming picture book that relates the legend of a young bard who pleases King Arthur with his songs and his ability to tell of deeds to

A legendary setting is depicted in this tale about early England. *From Taliesin and King Arthur* by Ruth Robbins. Copyright © 1970 by Ruth Robbins for text and illustrations. Reprinted by permission of the publisher, Houghton Mifflin Company.

come and rites long buried. It describes the Yule festival when Druids cut the sacred mistletoe, the holiday games played in the old Roman amphitheatre, and the Grand Meeting of the Bards. During this time, poets, storytellers, minstrels, and ballad makers of the realm gather for a contest in which the greatest is honored by the king. The winner is Taliesin who accomplishes his tale with the harp. He tells a wondrous tale of magic, enchantment, and a mother who uses her powers to endow a child with wisdom and understanding.

Another legendary figure is Robin Hood, the hero of Sherwood Forest. Stories about Robin Hood were told orally for centuries and were mentioned in manuscripts as early as 1360. Legend suggests that he was born Robert Fitzooth, Earl of Huntingdon, in Nottinghamshire, in 1160. According to the tales he was a great archer. He and his band of outlaws poached the king's deer, robbed the rich, and gave money to the poor.

Stories of Robin Hood are very popular with children. Movies and television plays have been produced about his adventures. Pyle's *The Merry Adventures of Robin Hood* and the shorter version, *Some Merry Adventures of Robin Hood,* provide children with visions of what it would be like to live "in merry England in the time of old" and to interact with Little John, Will Scarlet, Friar Tuck, the Sheriff of Nottingham, and King Richard of the Lion's Heart. Children enjoy comparing the various editions and describing the strengths and weaknesses of each. For this purpose, even the Walt Disney movie that presents Robin Hood as a fox, Little John as a bear, and Prince John as a lion makes an interesting comparison and adds to a lively discussion, especially about characterization.

The setting for Nina Bawden's retelling of the *William Tell* legend is fourteenth century Europe. This famous Swiss patriot inspired his people to overthrow their oppressors and organize a new country. There is enough action in this tale, which includes the famous scene in which Tell shoots an apple off his son's head, to hold the interest of youthful readers.

Chapter three described the setting of another famous legend. Kate Seredy's *The White Stag* describes the Hun-Magyar tribes and the development of their leaders as they first see the stag and follow the animal as they leave their barren Asian land to find their longed-for home, Hungary.

These epics and legends help children understand the conditions of the times that created the need for such heroes. They are tales of adventure that stress the noblest actions of man as well as those less noble, but justice reigns over injustice. Children can feel the magnitude of the oral tradition as they listen to these tales; there is no better way to introduce them to children.

SUMMARY

Traditional literature includes stories handed down orally through centuries. Two milestones in traditional literature occurred: Charles Perrault published his French folktales, and the Brothers Grimm collected and published their traditional tales.

Four types of traditional literature are usually identified: folktales, fables, myths, and legends. Cumulative tales, humorous tales, beast tales, magic or wonder tales, pourquoi tales, and realistic tales can be categorized as types of folktales.

Traditional tales allow children to learn about problems of human beings and possible solutions. In addition, traditional tales develop world understanding by contributing to an understanding of cultural traditions and diffusion, aesthetic appreciation, informational gains, respect for other languages, and inherent qualities of goodness in heroes. Their strongest value may be the enjoyment gained by hearing and reading traditional literature.

Selected Activities for Adult Understanding of Traditional Literature

- Read the stories included in Charles Perrault's *Tales of Mother Goose* and some tales collected by the Brothers Grimm. Note the similarities and differences you discover in the characterization, setting, and action. Describe the people for whom you believe the stories were originally told.

- Choose a professional group that has been interested in researching and interpreting traditional literature (e.g., early Christian scholars, folklorists, psychologists, anthropologists). Investigate their interpretations of several folktales.

- Read an example of a cumulative tale, a humorous tale, a beast tale, a magic or wonder tale, a pourquoi tale, and a realistic tale. Compare the characterization, setting, style, and theme found in each type of folktale.

- Choose a common theme found in folktales, such as that in "Cinderella" or trickster stories. Find examples of the same story in folktales from several countries. What are the similarities and differences? How do the stories develop cultural characteristics?

- Choose an animal found frequently in traditional literature. Read stories that include that animal; choose stories from cultures throughout the world. Is the animal revered or despised? How would you account for this?

■ Select a country and several traditional tales from that country. Choose stories for which the illustrators conducted extensive research before completing the drawings. Share the discoveries about the fine arts of the country with the class.

■ Find examples of settings, plot development, or characterization found in literature from different countries. Discuss any similarities and differences with the class.

■ Choose three folktales from different countries. Compare the actions developed in the three tales using the list identified on page 203.

■ Choose several examples of folktales that are not compared in Chart 6–3. Following a similar format, analyze the tales.

■ Read a fable in *Caxton's Aesop* and *The Caldecott Aesop*. Compare it with the same fable written in a modern version. Are there any differences in writing style, language, spelling, and illustrations between the earlier and later versions? If there are, what do you believe is the reason for the differences? Share the two versions with a child. How does the child respond to each version?

■ Select numerous folktales from one country; investigate the information you can learn about the culture, people, and country with your peers. Share your findings with the class.

■ Compare the versions of creation and the characteristics of gods and goddesses in Greek and Norse mythology. Why do you believe any differences exist?

■ Choose a folktale, myth, and legend. Develop a chart using Bascom's definitions of each type of traditional literature.

References

1 Arnott, Kathleen. *Animal Folk Tales around the World.* Illustrated by Bernadette Watts. New York: Walck, 1970.

2 Asimov, Isaac. *Words from the Myths.* Boston: Houghton Mifflin, 1961.

3 Barth, Edna. *Cupid and Psyche.* Boston: Houghton Mifflin, 1976.

4 Bascom, William. "The Forms of Folklore: Prose Narratives." *Journal of American Folklore* 78 (Jan–Mar. 1965):3–20

5 Bettelheim, Bruno. *The Uses of Enchantment: The Meaning and Importance of Fairy Tales.* New York: Knopf, 1976.

6 Carlson, Ruth Kearney. "World Understanding through the Folktale." In *Folklore and Folk Tales around the World,* edited by Ruth Kearney Carlson, pp. 3–21. Newark, Del.: The International Reading Association, 1972.

7 Cook, Elizabeth. *The Ordinary and the Fabulous: An Introduction to Myths, Legends and Fairy Tales.* 2d ed. Cambridge: At the University Press, 1976.

8 Coolidge, Olivia E. *Legends of the North.* Boston: Houghton Mifflin, 1951.

9 Corcoran, Jean. *Folk Tales of England.* New York: Bobbs-Merrill, 1963.

10 Favat, F. André. *Child and Tale: The Origins of Interest.* Urbana, Ill.: The National Council of Teachers of English, 1977.

11 Huck, Charlotte S. *Children's Literature in the Elementary School.* New York: Holt, Rinehart & Winston, 1979.

12 Iverson, Pat Shaw, trans., *Norwegian Folk Tales.* New York: Viking, 1960.

13 Kuo, Louise, and Kuo, Yuan-hsi. *Chinese Folk Tales.* Millbrae, Calif.: Celestial Arts, 1976.

14 Lenaghan, R.T., ed. *Caxton's Aesop.* Cambridge: Harvard University, 1967.

15 Perrault, Charles. *Histories or Tales of Past Times.* Preface by Michael Patrick Hearn. New York: Garland, 1977. Reprint of the 1729 edition printed by J. Pote and R. Montagu, London.

16 Pratt, Davis, and Kula, Elsa. *Magic Animals of Japan.* Berkeley, Calif.: Parnassus, 1967.

17 Propp, Vladimir. *Morphology of the Folktale.* Translated by Laurence Scott. Austin, Tex.: University of Texas, 1968.

18 Sewell, Helen. *A Book of Myths, Selections from Bulfinch's Age of Fable.* New York: Macmillan, 1942.

19 Thompson, Stith. *The Folktale.* New York: The Dryden Press, 1946.

20 Wyndham, Robert. *Tales the People Tell in China.* Illustrated by Jay Yang. New York: Messner, 1971.

21 Yolen, Jane. "How Basic Is Shazam?" *Language Arts* 54 (September 1977): 645–51.

Involving Children in Traditional Literature

STORYTELLING

COMPARING FOLKTALES FROM
DIFFERENT COUNTRIES

INVESTIGATING FOLKTALES FROM A
SINGLE COUNTRY

CREATIVE DRAMATICS AND FOLKLORE

CREATIVE WRITING MOTIVATED BY
MYTHOLOGY

VISUAL IMAGES—INTERPRETED IN ART

THE STORIES and books just discussed are among children's most memorable experiences with literature. With their well-defined plots, easily identifiable characters, rapid action, and satisfactory endings, the tales lend themselves to many enjoyable experiences in the classroom, library, home, or around the campfire. This section explores ways to recapture the oral tradition through storytelling, comparing folktales from different countries, creative dramatics, creative writing, and art interpretations.

STORYTELLING

Throughout antiquity, the storyteller was a prized addition to cottage and castle alike. In Russia, storytellers applied for positions as tellers of tales in the homes. In the great halls of Europe, aristocrats listened to ballad singers and minstrels relate the deeds of Beowulf and King Arthur. In peasant cottages, the heroic conquests of "Jack the Giant Killer" entertained both young and old. Across the sea, native Americans related trickster tales around evening campfires, and in Africa, the flickering fireside was the scene for Zulu stories of magic, monsters, and animals that talked.

Because these traditional tales were handed down through the oral tradition, they are the logical sources for developing the art of storytelling. This art is well worth the effort. John Stewig (15), states that there are three important reasons to include storytelling as part of childhood experiences. First, storytelling helps children understand the oral tradition of literature. In the past, children were initiated into their literary heritage through storytelling. Unhappily, this experience does not often occur today. Second, storytelling allows the adult an opportunity to involve children in the experience. Free from dependence on the book, the storyteller can use gestures and actions to involve children in the story. Third, when an adult tells a story, children understand that it is a worthy activity and are stimulated to try telling stories themselves.

This section discusses selecting and preparing stories for telling, sharing them with an audience, and using flannelboards during the sharing.

Choosing the Story

The most important factor in choosing a story is to select one that is really enjoyable. The story should be one that the narrator would enjoy spending time on and retelling; also, it should be one that can be told with conviction and enthusiasm.

Storytelling demands an appreciative audience. Consequently, the storyteller must be aware of children's interests, ages, and experience. Young children have short attention spans so story length must be considered when selecting a tale. Children's ages will also influence the subject matter of the tale; young children like stories about familiar subjects such as animals, children, or home life. They respond to the repetitive language in cumulative tales and enjoy joining in when stories such as "Henny Penny" reach their climax. The simple folktales such as "The Three Bears," "The Three Little Pigs," and "The Three Billy Goats Gruff" are excellent stories to share with young children. Children from ages seven through ten enjoy folktales with longer plots, such as those collected by the Brothers Grimm; "Rapunzel" and "Rumpelstiltskin" are favorites. Other favorites include Jewish folktales such as "It Could Always Be Worse." Older children enjoy hero tales, myths, and legends.

Folktales contain several characteristics that make them appropriate for storytelling. They have considerable action, and strong beginnings that bring listeners rapidly into the action; they have several strong characters who are easily recognized by listeners; they contain strong climaxes that are familiar to children; and they have satisfactory endings. All these characteristics are worthwhile criteria for selecting tales.

A final consideration for story selection is the mood the adult wishes to create: a humorous, light-hearted feeling or a scary, frightening mood. If, for example, the adult wants to choose an appropriate story for Halloween, then mood is very important. Even the site for storytelling affects mood and story selection. A storyteller was asked to tell a story to a group of people who were sitting on high rocks overlooking Lake Superior. The wind was causing the waves to crash with a mighty roar onto the rocks below, and when the group looked out over the lake, there was only a wide stretch of water—there were no human beings in sight. The view to the north was one of thick forests, ferns, and distant waterfalls. Again, no human beings were visible. The Norse myth, "The Hammer of Thor," from Coolidge's *Legends of the North* seemed ideal for this setting.

After the adult has selected an enjoyable story, one that is appropriate for the audience, has appropriate characteristics, and creates the desired mood, it must be prepared for telling.

Preparing the Story for Telling

Storytelling does not require memorization, but it does require preparation. Certain steps will help the storyteller prepare for this enjoyable experience. Ramon Ross (13) recommends the following sequence of steps:

1 Read the story aloud several times. Try to get a feeling for its rhythm and style, so that when it is retold, the interpretation will be faithful to the original.
2 Think of the major actions of the story and try to find where one action or bit ends and another begins. These bits give an outline to follow in telling the story.
3 Develop a sense of the characters in the story. Envision a picture of the characters, the clothes they wear, their shapes and sizes, unusual features, personality traits, how they speak, their mannerisms, and the like.
4 Think through the setting of the story. The storyteller should be able to draw a map showing where the story took place.
5 Look for phrases to incorporate in the story when it is told. Read the story again. What phrases and language patterns should be used to tell the story?
6 Begin telling parts of the story aloud, testing different ways to say the same words. The intonation should agree with the meaning the teller hopes to convey.
7 Plan gestures that add to the story. Once gestures have been decided, they may be practiced in front of a mirror.
8 Prepare an introduction and a conclusion for the story. Give background information, share information about hearing the story for the first time, or share a related object.
9 Finally, practice the entire story. Time the telling at each practice. Record the story on audio tape. Play it back and listen for voice qualities to be cultivated and others to be discarded. Practice in front of a mirror, noting posture, gestures, and general impression.

Sharing the Story with an Audience

Considerable time has been spent in preparation, and the story should be presented effectively. This presentation is enhanced by creating an interest in the story, setting a mood, creating an environment where children can see and hear the storyteller, and presenting the story with effective eye contact and voice control.

Book jackets, giant books, miniature books, travel posters, art objects, puppets, or music may be used to stimulate children's interest in the story. The librarian or teacher who regularly tells stories to large groups of children can use any of these methods so that children will look forward to the storyhour. Colorful book jackets from folktales or myths not only entice but also help set the mood. For example, a display might be developed around the book jacket for Felix Hoffman's *The Bearskinner*, by the Brothers Grimm. In addition to the book jacket, the display could include a toy bear, a bear-skin, and a toy soldier wearing a fur cape. Accompanying questions might include the following: Would people like to wear a bearskin for seven years? What would they feel like and look like if they couldn't wash, comb their hair, or cut their nails for seven years? What could possibly be so important that they would agree to do these things?

Stories about giants lend themselves very well to displays of large books. One librarian drew huge figures of giants and beanstalks on large sheets of tagboard. The sheets were placed together to form a gigantic book, and it was used to stimulate interest in "Jack and the Beanstalk." Likewise, draw-ings of a huge hammer stimulated interest about Thor. The giant books worked very well in these cases; the children spec-ulated about the size or strength of anyone who could read such a large book.

Miniature books were used before another story hour to stimulate interest in stories about little people. When "Tom Thumb" was the story, the storyteller also included other tiny objects, many formed out of clay, that would be appropriate for a little person.

If the story has an identifiable location, travel posters can be used to stimulate interest and provide background informa-tion; they are especially appealing for folktales from other countries. Travel posters about Greece and Italy have been used with Greek and Roman mythology. Travel posters show-ing Norwegian fiords and mountains can accompany Norse myths, while posters showing pictures of the Black Forest and old European castles are appropriate for "Snow White" and "Sleeping Beauty."

Objects from the story or from the country in which the set-ting of the story is placed may also be used to increase interest. Dolls, plates, figurines, stuffed animals, or even a lariat can add to the story hour.

After interest has been generated, the storyteller can con-centrate on setting the mood for story time. Many storytellers use storyhour symbols. For example, if a small lamp is the symbol for story hour, children know that when the lamp is lit, it is time to listen. Music may also be a symbol; when a certain record, music box tune, piano introduction, or guitar selection is played, it is time for story hour to begin. These techniques are usually effective; children learn to associate them with an enjoyable listening experience.

The story has been prepared, and the storyteller has consid-ered how it will be introduced. Now it can be told to a group of children. Norton (11) has the following suggestions for telling the story:

1 Find a place in the room where all children can see and hear the presentation.

2 Either stand in front of the group or sit with them.
3 Select an appropriate introduction: use a prop, tell some-thing about the author, discuss a related event, or ask a question.
4 Maintain eye contact with the children. This engages them more fully in the story.
5 Use appropriate voice rate and volume for effect.
6 While telling the story, a short step or shift in footing will indicate a change in scene or character or heighten the suspense. A seated storyteller can lean forward or away from the children.
7 After telling the story, pause to give the audience a chance to soak in everything said. (p. 335)

Using Feltboards to Share Folktales

Storytelling does not require any props. In fact, some of the best storytellers use nothing except their voices and gestures to recapture the plots and characters found in folktales. Most storytellers, however, enjoy adding variety to their repertoire. Children also enjoy experimenting with different approaches to storytelling; the flannelboard or feltboard lends itself to storytelling by both adults and children.

A feltboard is a rectangular-shaped lightweight board cov-ered with felt, flannel cloth, or lightweight indoor-outdoor car-peting. This board acts as the backdrop for figures cut from felt, pellon, or other material backed with Velcro. Felt or pellon figures will cling directly to the feltboard, while any object, even leather, wood, or foam rubber will adhere to the felt if first

backed with a small square or strip of Velcro. Other materials such as yarn or cotton balls will also cling to the feltboard and may be used to add interest and texture to the story.

Stories that lend themselves to feltboard interpretations have only a few major characters, plots that depend upon oral telling rather than physical action, and settings that do not demand exceptional detail. All these characteristics are similar to those already stipulated for the simple folktales that are enjoyed by young children. Two very pleasing types of stories to retell on the feltboard are the folktales, "Three Billy Goats Gruff" or "The Three Bears," or the cumulative tales, "The Gingerbread Boy" or "Henny Penny." Paul Anderson (1) makes this statement in *Story Telling with the Flannel Board:*

The best stories for use on a flannel board are those that follow a repetitive refrain, those that have one major plot with no subplots, those that contain the kind of action that can be illustrated by figures on the board and can be told with a reasonable number of figures. The old stories which involve magic are especially good. The frog can change into a prince. The objects the king touches can turn to gold. The fish can swallow the tin soldier. (p. 8)

Consider the Norwegian folktale "The Three Billy Goats Gruff." First, the characters are simply portrayed. The three goats range in size from a small goat to a great big goat with curved horns. Then there is an ugly old troll with big eyes and a long, long nose. The setting is also easily shown. There must be a bridge crossing a stream; there can also be green grass on the other side of the bridge. The action can be illustrated effectively. Each goat can go "Trip, trap! Trip, trap! over the bridge." The troll can challenge each goat with, "Who's that tripping over my bridge?" The climax is also easily illustrated; the big billy goat knocks the troll off the bridge and continues to cross to the other side. The plot develops sequentially from small billy goat, to medium size billy goat, and finally to great big billy goat.

The English folktale, "The Donkey, the Table, and the Stick," is another story that makes an effective feltboard production. Children enjoy seeing the magic donkey produce gold coins when his ear is pulled; they laugh over the poor lad's exasperation as nothing happens when he pulls and pulls the common donkey's ear. They are enthusiastic over the table that can produce turkey, sausages, and other good things. They laugh when the storyteller tries to get the ordinary table to produce food. Finally, they are overjoyed when the magic stick beats the evil innkeeper. These actions can be effectively shown with feltboard characters.

Cumulative tales are excellent for feltboard presentations; as each new character in the cumulative tale is introduced, it is placed on the feltboard. Children join in the dialogue as "The Fat Cat," for example, encounters first the gruel, then the pot,

the old woman, Skahottentot, Skilinkenlot, five birds, seven dancing girls, the lady with the pink parasol, the parson, and the woodsman.

Through these presentations, children learn about sequential order and also stimulate their language development. Children's literature students who use feltboard stories with children often find that the children either ask if they can retell the stories or make up their own feltboard stories to share. If feltboards and materials are provided, children will naturally enjoy telling stories.

Whether the story is told to one child or to a group, storytelling is well worth the effort of preparation and presentation. Watching children as they respond to a magical environment and then make their own first efforts as storytellers proves that storytelling should be included in every child's experience.

COMPARING FOLKTALES FROM DIFFERENT COUNTRIES

Understanding how various story types are related, becoming aware of cultural diffusion, and learning about different countries are values gained from reading traditional literature. One way to help children gain these values is by comparing folktales from different countries. Two approaches may be used to provide valuable experiences. Several versions of the same tale may be shared and discussed, and many tales from the same country may be experienced.

Comparing Different Versions of the Same Folktale

Many older children are fascinated to discover that some tales appear in almost every culture. The names may vary, magical objects may differ, and settings may change, but the basic elements of the story remain the same. Four different versions of the Cinderella story were discussed earlier in this chapter. This number is only a beginning for an investigation. Over nine hundred versions of the Cinderella story have been found throughout the world. Mary Ann Nelson (10) claims that there are over five hundred European versions. Jane Bingham and Grayce Scholt (3) and Elinor Ross (12) suggest that older children should investigate the motifs of these tales. Questions such as the following can be compiled with the children's assistance to guide their search and discovery:

Questions to Ask about the Cinderella Tales

1 What caused Cinderella to have a lowly position in the family?
2 What shows that Cinderella has a lowly position in the household?

3 How is she related to other household members?

4 What happens to keep Cinderella away from the ball?

5 How does she receive her wishes or transformation?

6 Where does Cinderella meet the prince?

7 What is the test signifying the rightful Cinderella?

8 What happens to the stepsisters?

Sources for comparisons include the Cinderella versions listed in this book: Mary Ann Nelson's (10) anthology, Bingham and Scholt's (3) synopses of twelve variants of the Cinderella story, and folklore collections from around the world. Chart 6–6 represents some key variants found in Cinderella tales from different countries.

After children have read, listened to, and discussed many Cinderella tales, their investigations may agree with conclusions found in Bingham and Scholt's research. These investigators compared twelve Cinderella tales and concluded the following:

1 The menial position of the heroine is usually shown by describing the impossible tasks she is asked to do. These tasks reflect the culture of the story.

2 Supernatural powers aid the heroine. Many powers relate to the dead mother: she returns in the form of an animal, or a tree appears over her grave.

3 The magical clothes of the transformed heroine are usually elegant and appropriate for the culture: gold and silver, or Indian dress of leather and beads.

4 The hero and heroine usually meet in places that are important to the culture: a ball, a theater, a church, or a wigwam.

5 The male figure is in an elevated position in society. He is of noble birth in the majority of the tales, but the Chinese tale describes him as a scholar.

6 Seven of the twelve tales include cruel stepmothers. The heroine has to contend with cruel stepsisters or sisters.

7 Eight tales had some form of shoe test for identifying Cinderella. A Japanese version required the heroine to compose a song; a native American version asked the heroine to identify what the chief's sledstrings and bowstrings were made of.

8 In five of the twelve tales, the wicked stepmother or stepsisters meet violent ends.

9 All the tales reflect the societies that produced them. Native American tales refer to chiefs, wigwams, moccasins and bowstrings; Japanese stories refer to kimonos, rice, and oni.

Other tales may also be used for comparisons. P. T. Travers (16) has included five versions of the Sleeping Beauty tale and one of her own translations in *About the Sleeping Beauty*. This collection contains her own version, which is Arabian; "Dornroschen or Briar-Rose," from the Grimms' *Household Tales;* "La Belle au Bois Dormant or The Sleeping Beauty in the Wood," from Perrault; "Sole, Luna, e Talia or Sun, Moon, and

CHART 6–6

Variations Found in Cinderella Stories from Different Countries

Origin	Cause of Lowly Position	Outward Signs of Lowly Position	Cinderella's Relationship to Household	How She Receives Wishes	What Happens to Keep Her from Social Occasion	Where She Meets the Prince	What Happens to Stepsisters	Test of Rightful Cinderella
French Perrault, "Cinderilla"	Mother died. Father remarried.	Sitting in ashes. Vilest household tasks.	Stepdaughter to cruel woman. Unkind stepsisters.	Wishes to fairy godmother.	(Ball) No gown. Family won't let her go.	Castle ball. Beautifully dressed.	Forgiven. Live in palace. Marry lords.	Glass slipper.
German Grimm, "Cinderella"	Mother died. Father remarried.	Wears clogs, old dress. Sleeps in cinders. Heavy work.	Stepdaughter to cruel woman. Cruel stepsisters.	Wishes to bird on tree on mother's grave.	(Ball) Must separate lentils.	Castle ball. Beautifully dressed.	Blinded by birds.	Gold slipper.
English "Tattercoats"	Mother died at her birth. Grandfather blames her.	Ragbag clothes. Scraps for food.	Despised granddaughter. Hated by servants.	Gooseherd plays pipe.	(Ball) Grandfather refuses.	In forest. Dressed in rags.	Grandfather weeps. Hair grows into stones.	None.
Vietnamese "In the Land of Small Dragon"	Mother died. Father's number two wife hates her.	Collects wood. Cares for rice paddies.	Stepdaughter to hateful woman. Hated by halfsister.	Fairy. Bones of fish.	(Festival) Must separate rice from husks.	Festival.	Not told.	Jeweled slipper (hai).
Chinese "Beauty and Pock Face"	Mother turned into cow.	Straightens hemp. Hard work.	Stepdaughter to cruel woman. Cruel stepsister.	From bones of mother in earthenware pot.	(Theater) Straighten hemp. Separate sesame seeds.	Scholar picks up shoe from road.	Roasted in oil.	Walks on eggs. Climbs ladder of knives. Jumps into oil.

Talia," from the Italian *The Pentamerone of Giambattista Basile;* "The Queen of Tubber Tintye," from *Myths and Folklore of Ireland;* and "The Petrified Mansion," from Bengal Fairy Tales. There are also many variants of "Little Red Riding Hood" and "The Lad Who Went to the North Wind." Linda Western's "A Comparative Study of Literature through Folk Tale Variants" (17) is another source of different versions of the same tale.

A search for variant versions of the same tale is an enjoyable experience and encourages children to develop an understanding of the impact of cultural diffusion on literature. They also realize that each culture has placed the tale in a context that reflects the society of the storyteller and the audience.

INVESTIGATING FOLKTALES FROM A SINGLE COUNTRY

Children can learn a great deal about a country and its people by investigating a number of tales from that country. This investigation also increases children's understanding of the multicultural heritage of their own country and develops understanding of, and positive attitudes toward, cultures other than their own.

This fact was made clear when a group of fifth-grade children was studying folktales to learn more about the people of a country. They were reading and discussing Russian folktales at a time that relationships between Russia and the United States were strained. As they read these tales, especially the merry ones with their rapid, humorous dialogues and absurd plots, the children decided that the common people who could invent and enjoy those stories must be similar to themselves. They realized that they were laughing at the same type of story that could also bring humor to children in Russia. During this investigation and sharing of folktales, respect for many of the cultures was increased. Children commented for example, that Jewish folktales often stressed the unselfish desire for a better world or rewarded sincerity and wisdom. Also, they were impressed with the fact that the Chinese Cinderella married a scholar and not a nobleman. They learned, through the folktales, to respect the ancient values of the people who created them.

A successful folktale study of one country was conducted in a fifth-grade classroom. The web shown in Figure 6–1, "Traditional Tales from China," illustrates the related motivation, stimulating activities, and folktales that stressed personal values, disagreeable human qualities, symbols, and supernatural beings. During the first part of the unit, the children listened to, read, and discussed folktales from China. Their interest was stimulated by objects displayed throughout the room, on tables, and on bulletin boards. A large red paper dragon met the children as they entered the room. Other objects included joss sticks (incense), lanterns, Chinese flutes, a tea service, fans, statues of mythical beasts, lacquered boxes and plates, silk, samples of Chinese writing, a blue willow plate, jade, and pictures of art work, temples, pagodas, people, and animals. Many Chinese folktales were displayed on the library table. In the background, a recording of Chinese music was playing. The chalkboard contained a message, written in Chinese figures, welcoming the children to China. The students looked at the displays, listened to the music, tried to decipher the message, and discussed what they saw and heard. They located China on a map and on a globe. Next, they listed questions they had about China—questions about the people, country, values, art, music, food, houses, animals, and climate.

The teacher read aloud some of the foreword to Louise and Yuan-hsi Kuo's *Chinese Folk Tales* (6). She asked the students to close their eyes and imagine the scene, to listen carefully, and then tell when this scene took place. Did it happen in modern times or many centuries ago?

But suddenly the room echoes with an ear-splitting clash of cymbals and the sonorous boom of a drum and in the street below our window prances a splendid lion. The sound of cymbals and the beat of drums have been heard incessantly since early morning and are merely a prelude to a major part to come: a procession with gay silk banners flying, votive offerings of barbecued pigs . . . golden brown and saffron, cartloads heaped with fruit, red-colored eggs and other delicacies, giant joss sticks, candles and lanterns. A magnificent dragon, gyrating and performing with vigor and intensity to the rapid beat of a drum, will bring the procession to a climax. Throngs crowd the doorways, line the path, as excited onlookers join the ranks to mingle with those on their way to the temple . . . journey's end. This is the day of days . . . the grand finale of five days of celebration in homage to T'ien Ho, the Heavenly Goddess of the Sea . . . she who will bestow blessings on all who worship her, and protect them for the entire year. (p. 7)

After listening to the selection, the children speculated about the time period and gave their reasons for choosing either ancient or modern times. Many children were quite surprised to hear that the event was a festival held in modern Hong Kong. This discussion led into reading Chinese folktales in order to learn more about the Chinese people and a heritage that could still influence modern-day people.

Next, the teacher shared several of her favorite Chinese folktales with the children. They included the humorous "The Clever Woman" and "The Borrowing of 100,000 Arrows." She also provided brief introductions to other tales. These intro-

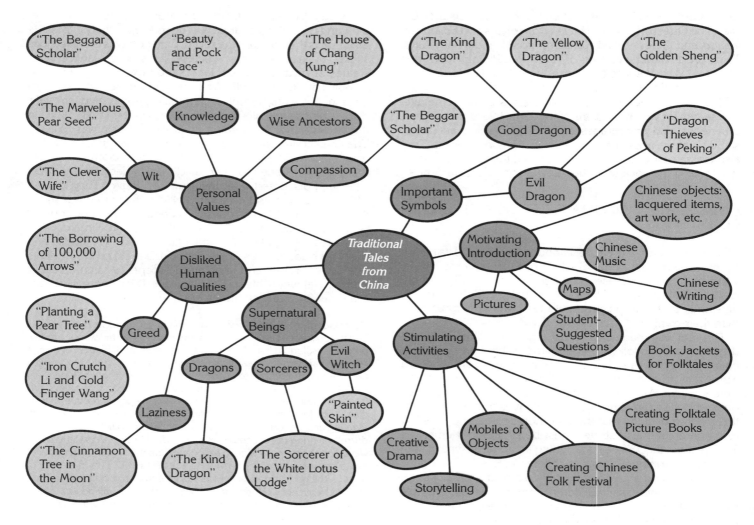

FIGURE 6–1

ductions were told to stimulate students' interest in reading the tales. Children then chose tales to read independently. As they read, they also considered their questions about China. Consequently, when they discovered information about the culture and the people, they jotted this information down so that it could be shared with the class.

After considerable information had been collected, they discussed ways of verifying whether or not the information was accurate. They compared the information with library reference materials and magazines such as *National Geographic.*

They also invited to the classroom several visitors who were either Chinese or had visited China.

The students also used their knowledge about the people, culture, and literature in art, creative drama, and writing. Travel posters, book jackets for folktales, mobiles of folk literature objects, and illustrations for folktales were drawn. One artistic activity was to create picture storybooks from single folktales. Children chose a favorite tale not already in picture book format, illustrated it with drawings, and bound the pages together. Because many of the published picture books contained information about the origin of the tale, similar information was included on the inside of the front covers. Published book jackets often tell about the illustrator and the research that was done to provide authentic pictures. The students' books also contained this information. They told about themselves and how they prepared for their drawing assignment, and described the medium they used for their illustrations. These books were shared with their own and other classes and proudly displayed in the library.

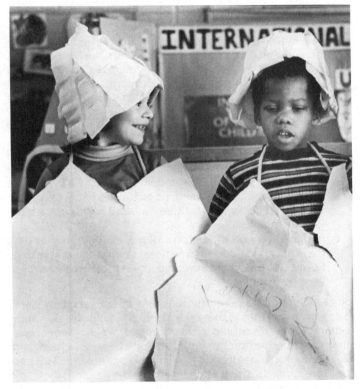

Folklore may encourage children to act out their favorite stories.

Some stories were chosen for creative drama. The class was divided into groups according to favorite folktales. Each group then chose a method for sharing the story with the rest of the class. Some groups recreated the stories as plays, others chose puppetry, and one group used pantomime with a narrator reading the lines.

Parents were invited to attend a Chinese folktale festival. Art projects, the picture storybooks, information learned, and the creative dramas were shared with an appreciative audience.

This initial unit about one country led to an interest in folktales from other countries. Folktales from Japan and other Asian countries were read next. Children discovered the similarities among many of these tales, especially in the symbolic animals found in both Chinese and Japanese folktales. They went on to detect Chinese influence on non-Asian writers when they read the beautiful version of Hans Christian Andersen's *The Nightingale,* illustrated by Nancy Ekholm Burkert.

The discovery of similar mythical animals led to another interesting search through folklore. The teacher read Winifred Miller's article "Dragons—Fact or Fantasy?" (9) and the children discovered that both Chinese and Japanese folktales had good and evil dragons; good dragons, a representation of Han nobility, were found in folktales told to ruling classes; and folktales about the common people referred to the dragon as evil. With teacher guidance, the students accomplished many of the activities suggested by Miller's article.

Folktales lend themselves well to many activities, and the teacher and librarian will find many ways to increase world understanding through literature. Chapter eleven presents a unit that includes African, Native American, Mexican American, and Asian folktales.

CREATIVE DRAMATICS AND FOLKLORE

Folklore is a natural source of materials for storytelling and also stimulates creative drama. Elizabeth Cook (4) maintains that the most exciting ways of retelling traditional tales are through drama, either in movement alone or in movement accompanied by words. Many sequences can be mimed as the adult reads them to children: children can act out individual parts or groups of children can re-create their own versions of the tales. This section considers suggestions for using folklore in pantomime and stimulating creative interpretations.

Pantomime

Pantomime is creative drama in which an actor plays a part with gestures and actions without using words. Pantomime, according to Geraldine Siks (14), should be part of a planned drama curriculum in which children learn to relax and concentrate, experiment with body movement, use their senses, stimulate their imaginations, develop language and speech, and understand and use characterization. Children's first pantomime experiences usually include activities in which they learn to relax and experiment with different ways to move their bodies. After they have an idea about what their bodies can express, pantomiming folktales can help children interpret various actions and emotions.

Familiar folktales enjoyed by young children are excellent for pantomime. For example, Paul Galdone's *The Three Bears* can be read by an adult as children pretend to be each character in the story. Children can pretend to be as small as the little wee bear, average size for the middle-sized bear, and huge for the great big bear. As bears, they can prepare their porridge, sit in their chairs, lie in their beds, and walk in the woods. Then, as Goldilocks, they can show curiosity as they peep into the window and then through the keyhole and cautiously enter the bears' home. They can react to porridge that is too hot, too cold, and just right. They can show discomfort as they try to climb into the great big chair, sink into the too soft chair, and then rock comfortably in the little chair until they surprisingly crash to the floor. They can show similar reactions to the three beds. As bears, they can return to the house, demonstrate outrage over the famous lines, "Somebody has been tasting my porridge, Somebody has been sitting in my chair," and "Somebody has been lying in my bed." Finally, they can return to the character of Goldilocks as she awakens, sees the bears, and dashes into the woods. This experience allows children to demonstrate emotions and develop believable characterization through body movement.

Other folktales that young children like to pantomime are "The Three Little Pigs," "The Three Billy Goats Gruff," and "The Little Red Hen."

When children start to enjoy longer folktales, there are many sources of materials for pantomime. They can put on their cloaks of invisibility and tiptoe behind *The Twelve Dancing Princesses* as the princesses descend the winding stairs. They can stop in fright as they accidentally step on the long dress of a princess. They can walk in wonderment through the silver forest, gold forest, and diamond forest. As prince and princess, they can dance gracefully through the night and then sleepily climb the winding stairs.

Because many magical tales show vivid contrasts between good and evil characters, children can form pairs and play opposing or complementary roles. *Cinderella* has scenes between good and evil characters: Cinderella and her stepmother, or Cinderella and her stepsisters. There are also scenes between evil characters and evil forces: the stepmother and stepsisters plot to leave Cinderella at home, force her to work, or try to fit their feet inside the slipper. In Singer's Jewish tale *Mazel and Shlimazel,* they can pantomime the opposing characters of good and bad luck.

All opposing forces are not between good and evil. Children also enjoy and learn when the opposing forces are cleverness and foolishness. In the Russian tale, "The Falcon under the Hat," they can portray these roles as the clever soldier tricks the foolish woman out of her money. There are the same opposing forces as the woman's son, Fedka, searches for a greater fool than his mother. The following scenes suggest the pantomime possibilities for this tale:

1 Fedka makes "a kow-tow—a low, humble bow—to the sow" (p. 16) in his effort to convince the baroness that the sow is to become his sister-in-law.
2 The foolish baroness responds in amusement; she orders her fur coat placed on the sow, the carriage hitched to the horses, and then watches, in laughter, as Fedka rides out of the yard with her prized belongings.
3 The baron returns home, jumps on his horse, and pursues Fedka.
4 Fedka hides the carriage and is sitting alongside the road guarding his hat when the baron approaches.
5 The baron asks Fedka about the carriage; Fedka convinces him that he could find the carriage if he could leave the valuable falcon that is under his hat. The baron offers to sit with the hat so that Fedka can find and return the carriage; he pays Fedka three hundred rubles in case the falcon escapes.
6 Fedka jumps on the baron's horse, leaves him guarding the empty hat, rides off to retrieve the carriage, and returns home. (He has found several people who are more foolish than his mother.)

After children have pantomimed these characters, they like to add words and extend this folktale into a humorous play. Many other folktales discussed in this chapter have excellent scenes that describe humorous confrontations between characters.

Scenes from Greek and Norse mythology are excellent pantomime subjects for older children. Psyche's search for Cupid and the impossible tasks of separating grain, gathering the golden fleece, and visiting the underground world of Hades may be recreated. Children can pretend to be the chariot of the sun as it trails across the sky; Perseus as he searches for the Gorgon's head; Daedalus and Icarus as they build the labyrinth, fashion wings of bird feathers held in place by hot wax, dip toward the sea, soar toward the sun, and then, as Icarus, rapidly plunge into the ocean; and Thor as he frantically searches for his missing hammer, dresses as a bride, and retrieves his hammer from the giant Thrym. Quite different movements and expressions are necessary to depict gods, goddesses, or heroes found in Greek or Norse mythology. Acting out the scenes through pantomime helps children understand the qualities of these heroes and appreciate the language found in the myths.

Creative Interpretations

As children pantomime stories such as "The Three Bears" or "The Falcon under the Hat," they usually want to add words and create their own plays. It is a natural extension of pantomime to add "Somebody has been sitting in my chair" or to create a dialogue in which the hero tries to convince the baroness that she should loan him her pig. Pantomiming provides a foundation for other creative activities; it allows children to experience the movement and emotion of the story and characters before they try to work with dialogue. Stories used to stimulate pantomime can also be used for creative interpretations requiring words. Folklore meets the criteria stated by Barbara McIntyre (8) for stories that are appropriate for dramatization. They should *(a)* have ideas worth sharing, *(b)* involve conflict, *(c)* include action in the development of the plot, *(d)* contain characters who seem real, and *(e)* have situations in which interesting dialogue can be developed. The folktales discussed in this chapter qualify in all of these areas.

Folklore can be used to stimulate creative dramatizations in two ways. The stories themselves can be recreated, and they can act as stimulators to help children create new interpretations. Usually, children first act out stories that are close to the original in plot and characterization. As they become more secure, they also enjoy making up new stories or creating additional ones about a character. Whatever the purpose for using the folktales, however, the adult needs to guide children's dramatizations. This guidance includes stimulating them into the mood for the story, presenting the story so they will have a foundation to draw from, guiding their planning, guiding their creative dramatization, and finally helping them evaluate their presentations.

Each step is considered in the following discussion of how a third-grade teacher used *Grimm's Golden Goose* to develop a creative dramatization with her students. In order to stimulate interest in the story, the teacher placed a yellow toy goose, a dry crust of bread, and a bottle of sour liquid in front of the class. She then asked the children if they thought they could acquire a fortune and a beautiful princess if they had the objects. She let them try to think of ways they might accomplish this miracle. The children decided that a little magic might help.

The teacher next told the story of "The Golden Goose," using the goose, the stale bread, and the sour liquid to assist her. This time, however, as the stale bread was transformed, she had a pastry to take its place, and as the sour liquid was changed, she had a jug of sweet grape juice to exchange.

She encouraged the class to talk about their favorite roles and favorite characters in the story. She then asked them to improvise the actions of each character, including the despised and mistreated Dummling (or Simpleton, depending upon the version used) and his parents, the arrogant older brother, the little old man who asks for food, the arrogant second brother, Dummling when he shares his food with the old man, Dummling as he cuts down the trees and discovers the golden goose, the three girls who become stuck to the goose, the parson who tries to pull the girls away from Dummling, the clerk who tries to release the parson, the laborers who try to release the parson, and the serious princess who finally laughs. The class discussed which actions they would like to include in the play and the sequence of events. They decided to use the goose, the bread, the liquid, the pastry, and the grape juice as props.

After they were satisfied with the sequence and who should play each role (at least for the first time), they acted out the story. They did not try to memorize lines but improvised the general mood. They put on their production several times so the children could play various roles and take turns being the audience.

Finally, they talked about the drama. They discussed the good things about their play: Why did they feel sorry for Dummling? How did the older brothers show that they thought they were brighter than Dummling? What did they do so that the children did not feel sorry for their bad luck? What did the old man do to let them know he was very old? Why did they laugh at Dummling? Many positive comments were made about the play, and the children then talked about how they could improve the presentation.

A Christmas Festival—Or Winter Holiday Celebration

Gallant knights show off their skills in tests of archery and outdoor games; the great hall is decorated with mistletoe; the Yule log is on the fire; plum puddings, wild boar, and roasted venison cover the banquet tables; and minstrels and storytellers prepare to enchant the holiday merrymakers. Books say this is how the Christmas season was celebrated in the days of King Arthur. Books also say that in the 1800s groups of Cornish young people traveled from house to house performing the play *Duffy and the Devil*. Children in a fifth-grade class combined these two English holiday traditions to develop their own Christmas festival. (This can be called a Winter Holiday Celebration without referring to Christmas.)

To prepare for the festival, they chose English folktales and parts of heroic tales that could be told to a gathering of people. Readings from King Arthur and Robin Hood were included along with "The Marriage of Sir Gawain," and the folktales "Jack the Giant Killer," "Mr. and Mrs. Vinegar," and "The Donkey, the Table, and the Stick."

They developed Harve Zemach's *Duffy and the Devil* into a creative dramatization to add to the traditional Christmas setting. To assist the children in developing the play, the teacher used steps similar to those described earlier for the "Golden Goose." After the story was shared with the class, they talked about their favorite parts and characters. They improvised the actions of Squire Lovel of Trovel unhappily observing his old housekeeper Jone; the old woman chasing Duffy with a broom; Duffy convincing Squire Lovel that she is a marvelous housekeeper; poor Duffy facing the impossible spinning task and meeting the devil; Squire Lovel's happiness with his new stockings; Duffy's dealing with the devil; Squire Lovel's and Duffy's wedding; the return of the devil; Squire Lovel observing the celebration of witches and the devil; Squire Lovel telling Duffy the name of the funny little man; and Duffy's outwitting of the angry devil. The class then discussed the actions and scenes they would like to include.

The group decided to retain the flavor of the language. While they did not completely memorize, they did use words such as *bufflehead, clouts, whillygogs,* and *whizamagees.* Next they chose players, practiced the sequence, and discussed what they liked about the play and how it could be improved.

On the day of the festival, the room was decorated like an Old English hall at Christmas. Every class member had some part, whether it was introducing a ballad or folktale and giving a little information about it, reading a heroic tale, telling a folktale, or being in the play *Duffy and the Devil.* Both guests and children thoroughly enjoyed their Christmas festival. All agreed that the oral tradition was alive in that fifth-grade class.

The Way of Danger—The Drama of Theseus

During a study of Greek mythology, one university student developed a creative dramatization around the adventures of the Greek hero, Theseus. With a group of fifth-grade students, she read Ian Serraillier's *The Way of Danger* and other myths about Theseus. The students located the settings for Theseus's adventures and plotted his travels on a map.

Next, with teacher guidance, the group outlined the life of Theseus into the major scenes they wished to portray, and dramatized their story. The following outline resulted from their planning:

The Life of Theseus

I. Theseus as a boy
   A. Aethra and Aegeus (his mother and father)
   B. Theseus and Aethra (his mother)
   C. Theseus and Pittheus (his grandfather)
II. Theseus journeys to Athens
   A. He meets the Club-bearer
   B. He meets the Foot-washer
   C. He meets the Stretcher
III. Theseus meets his father, the king
   A. He encounters Madea, the witch
   B. He is remembered by his father
IV. Theseus and the Minotaur
   A. He travels to Crete
   B. He encounters Minos, the wicked king
   C. Ariadne saves him from Minotaur
   D. He returns to Athens

Additional Ways to Use Traditional Literature During Creative Dramatics

Mythology and other traditional stories are filled with tales that lend themselves to creative interpretations. The following are a few ideas that have been performed successfully by children's literature students, classroom teachers, and librarians:

1 Following the reading of King Midas, the children first performed the story as *The Golden Touch*. Later, they divided into groups and chose another object as an obsession. They each performed the King Midas story as if everything the king touched turned to objects such as ice cream, chocolate, or money.

2 The story of Meleager was read to the students; the part where the queen burns the fire that kills Meleager was not read. The teacher guided the children in developing a court trial for the purpose of identifying Meleager's killer. A judge, defense lawyers, prosecution lawyers, witnesses, suspects, and jury were all identified. The class conducted a trial, and the lawyers elicited stories from each witness and suspect. These stories were developed by each person according to the facts presented in the literature. Jury members then discussed their opinions, provided rationales, and finally voted on who they believed was the guilty person. After the court trial, the adult shared the story's real ending with the group.

3 Following the reading of stories about Poseidon, god of the sea, children became interested in his challenge to Athena. In this myth, Poseidon wanted to rule Athens. The gods, however, decided that the city should be awarded to the one who could produce the gift most useful to mortals.

The gods ruled in favor of Athena who gave mortals the olive. Students accomplished several creative activities that were motivated by this myth. They debated about which gift was the most useful, Poseidon's or Athena's; they developed short plays showing the desirability of each; they created other challenges and acted out the results.

The oral tradition can be recreated and stimulated through pantomime and creative interpretations. The strong action found in the plots, the characters, the conflict, and the situations that can stimulate the development of dialogue make traditional tales especially useful for such interpretations.

CREATIVE WRITING MOTIVATED BY MYTHOLOGY

Just as the adventures of the gods, goddesses, and heroes can stimulate creative dramatics, storytelling, and artistic interpretations, they can also be used during the motivational phase of creative writing. (See pages 358–62 for a description of the steps necessary to develop creative writing with literature.) The following examples of creative writing motivated by mythology have been used effectively with children.

The heroes of Greek mythology are popular with ten-, eleven-, and twelve-year-old children. One teacher, for example, used children's enthusiasm for Elizabeth Silverthorne's *I, Heracles* to encourage them to write about similar heroes. This story is written in the first person, thus allowing Heracles to tell his own story, interpret his own feelings, and describe his own relationships with other gods. After the teacher shared the story with children (they had already read other myths), she encouraged them to pretend that they were heroes, gods, or goddesses and write a story describing themselves and their exploits. The following story was a result of this activity:

I am the lovely Psyche who is worshipped by all of the people. I have not always been this lucky, however. Let me tell you the story about how my curiosity almost made me lose my life.

Venus was very jealous of me when people started to pay more attention to me than to her. She sent her son, Cupid, to cast a spell on me. Thankfully, Cupid fell in love with me instead and he took me away to a wonderful palace. Everything went along fine until I wanted to see this man who saved me from his mother's anger. I made the mistake of lighting an oil lamp and holding it over him. I accidentally spilled a drop of oil on him. When he saw me he was angry because I had disobeyed him. He spread his wings and flew away. When he left, the beautiful palace disappeared. I was left without anything.

I decided to search for Cupid. I traveled day and night until I finally came to the temple of Venus. She was very angry with me. She made me do impossible work. I separated piles of grain, I went to terrible sheep to gather their fleece, and I even went to the underworld to bring back a box filled with beauty from Proserpine.

My curiosity almost ruined my life for me a second time. I was told not to open the box but I did it anyway. A terrible sleep started to overcome me. Thankfully, Cupid rescued me before I died. The gods forgave me and made me immortal. Cupid and I were married and we lived happily on Mount Olympus.

Other creative writing assignments motivated by mythology included asking students to pretend they were Zeus and write a story about how they would rule Mount Olympus or to pretend they had done a favor for a god and then were rewarded. In this last assignment, they were to consider what they would ask for as a reward, write a story about themselves performing the favor, and include information about the favor they asked for and the consequences, if any, of their wish.

Pourquoi Tales Motivate Writing

Many pourquoi (why) tales answer questions about why animals act or look a certain way. There are tales, for example, that tell why certain animals have short tails. Stories such as "How the Rabbit Lost His Tail," "Why the Bear Has a Little Tail," and "Why the Stork Has No Tail" may be found in traditional literature. A third-grade teacher shared Edward Dolch's *"Why" Stories from Different Countries* (5) with her children. They talked about the stories and speculated about other ways that one of these animals might have lost its tail. They wrote their own stories about why a rabbit, a bear, or a stork might have a short tail.

Other "why" stories shared included "Why the Frog Cries at Night," "Why the Woodpecker Looks for Bugs," "Why Dogs Wag Their Tails," and "Why the Squirrel Lives in Trees." Children then wrote their own versions of such problems as "Why the Chicken Cannot Fly," "Why the Horse Has a Mane," and "Why the Rabbit Hops."

VISUAL IMAGES—INTERPRETED IN ART

Traditional literature, especially versions that have not been written down into simplified language, is filled with passages that evoke visual images. Just as the tales inspire picture book illustrators to create magical settings, they can also stimulate young artists to interpret the cold, icy chasms of the Norse gods; recreate the birth of Aphrodite out of the foaming, shimmering water; or illustrate the creation of the world as the earth emerges from the swirling and transparent vapor of Greek mythology.

Children enjoy making a gingerbread house after listening to "Hansel and Gretel."

Allowing children to experience the artistic moods of traditional literature through paints, chalk, or crayons is another way to help them extend their enjoyment. For example, the following activity could be used to stimulate children to draw or paint a picture in shades of the hottest colors: What are the dancing flames that attract Sigurd to venture toward the glowing horizon? What is the circling pillar of smoke? Have robbers burned a citadel? Has a dragon breathed fire on the farmlands of a great king? These questions can introduce children to an artistic experience in which they interpret Sigurd's adventures. As "The Valkyrie" from Olivia Coolidge's *Legends of the North* is read, children can first close their eyes and try to visualize color and mood. Then they can express these images in color on paper. This passage can stimulate paintings in hot colors:

By dawn Sigurd could hear the hissing of the fire. Greyfell picked his way with care over the hot faces of the rock, which were bathed in a bright red light. The flames made a ring of flickering points, now sinking, now flaring, now parting, now shooting out over the sides of the mountain as though caught in a sudden wind. (p. 105)

In contrast to an interpretation in vivid, hot colors is the description of the creation of the world in Norse mythology. Children can recreate the world of "The First Gods and Giants" found in the D'Aulaires' *Norse Gods and Giants*. This passage can stimulate a different kind of painting or drawing.

Early in the morning of time there was no sand, no grass, no lapping wave. There was no earth, no sun, no moon, no stars. There was Niflheim, a waste of frozen fog, and Muspelheim, a place of raging flames. And in between the fog and fire there was a gaping pit— Ginungagap. For untold ages crackling embers from Niflheim whirled around in the dark and dismal pit. As they whirled together, faster and faster, fire kindled a spark of life within the ice. (p. 12)

Other myths can be used to motivate artistic interpretations. Children can illustrate Demeter's influence on the earth when she became angry because her daughter Persephone was kidnapped by Hades, and her joy when Persephone was returned.

Heroic tales contain many incidents that can be illustrated. A large mural could be drawn showing the heroic deeds of Jason as he searches for the golden fleece, Heracles as he accomplishes his twelve impossible labors, or Perseus as he ventures to retrieve Medusa's head. The Norse epic "Beowulf" contains many scenes that lend themselves to artistic activities. Children can illustrate the great hall, Heorot, which sits on the edge of the misty fen. Nye's description of the towering walls and the torchlight blazing from the windows can be used to motivate this experience. Beowulf's conquest of the monster Grendel; She, the mother of Grendel; and the firebreathing lizard, Firedrake, can all be illustrated.

Individual gods and goddesses can also be illustrated. Poseidon, god of the sea, can be pictured with his trident, the three-pronged spear, riding his golden chariot across the surface of the water or living in his golden palace at the bottom of the ocean; Zeus, the ruler of Mount Olympus, can be drawn with his powerful thunderbolt; Athena, goddess of wisdom and protectress in war, can be shown in her armor, holding her great shield; Apollo, god of truth, archery, and music, can be illustrated with a lyre and arrows; and Demeter, goddess of crops, can be depicted with grains and other growing things.

The creation and interpretation of numerous forest scenes can be stimulated by Gail E. Haley's *The Green Man.* One teacher read the legend to her third graders, encouraged them to discuss the tapestry-like illustrations, and asked them to consider possible reasons for changes in Claude's behavior. Next she quoted Haley's concluding comments about the Green Man: "Legend tells us that there will be a Lord of the Forest 'for as long as the Greenwood stands.' It is certainly easy to believe that the Green Man is there—hidden among the leaves watching to make sure that all is well" (p. 29). Finally, she asked the children to pretend to be the Green Man and illustrate the greenwood as they believe it should appear. During another art period, she asked them to illustrate two pictures; one that would make them happy if they were the Green Man, the other one that would make them sad.

Folktales and myths contain scenes, characters, and story lines that are excellent for artistic interpretations. The tales allow children's imagination to expand, and encourage them to create an imaginary world in chalk, paint, or other media.

SUMMARY

The oral tradition may be recaptured through the use of many activities in the classroom, library, or home. Storytelling is one of the most enjoyable and rewarding ways to share traditional literature. It helps children understand the oral tradition, allows the adult an opportunity to involve children in storytelling, and stimulates children to try storytelling themselves. The storyteller should enjoy the stories. The stories should meet the interests, ages, and experience of the children; have considerable action, strong beginnings, strong characters, and contain satisfactory endings. Storytelling does not require memorization, but developing an effective storytelling experience does require preparation. The storyteller must read the story aloud, think of the major actions, develop a sense of the characters, think through the setting, and look for phrases that might be incorporated into the story. A story can also be enhanced by stimulating interest in the story, setting a mood for the story, creating an appropriate environment, and presenting the story with effective eye contact and voice control.

Children learn to understand the relatedness of traditional story types, become aware of cultural diffusion, and learn about different countries when they read traditional literature. Activities that let children compare different versions of the same folktale and investigate many folktales from one country allow them to develop these values.

Drama is a most exciting way to share traditional tales. Tales may be shared through movement alone (pantomime) or in movement accompanied by words (creative dramatics). Materials for pantomime range from simple folktales to longer magical fairy tales. In addition to pantomiming whole stories, children can pantomime contrasting forces of good and evil or cleverness and foolishness. They can pantomime scenes from Greek or Norse mythology. Folklore can be used to stimulate creative dramatizations in two ways: the stories themselves can be recreated or they can act as stimulants to help children create new interpretations. Children do require guidance in their interpretations. Guidance includes stimulating their interest in the story, presenting the story, guiding their planning for the creative interpretation, directing their creative dramatization, and helping them evaluate their presentations.

Traditional literature may also be used to motivate creative writing, and several activities were suggested. The chapter concluded with suggestions for using the visual images found in traditional literature to encourage artistic interpretations.

Suggested Activities for Children's Appreciation of Traditional Literature

■ Choose a folktale of interest, prepare the story for telling, and share the story with either one child or a group of children.

■ Select a cumulative tale such as "The Gingerbread Boy" or a simple folktale such as "The Three Bears" and prepare it as a feltboard story. Share the story with either one child or a group.

■ Select a folktale that has many versions from diverse cultures. For example, "Sleeping Beauty" is found in many cultures. What questions should children ask when they investigate the tales? Develop a chart similar to the one in the text for "Cinderella." What are the key similarities and differences? How do the tales reflect the culture? Draw a list of conclusions that could be made from the folktales.

■ With a peer group, select a country to investigate. Develop a list of appropriate traditional tales and a list of related examples of art, music, and so forth, and design some activities that would help children develop an understanding of the country.

■ Choose a folktale that has rapid action appropriate for pantomiming. Lead a peer group or a group of children through the pantomime.

■ Lead a peer group or a group of children through the five steps described in this chapter for developing creative interpretations: stimulating interest, presenting the story, guiding the planning, guiding the creative dramatization, and helping the group to evaluate their presentation.

■ Compile a file of creative writing ideas that could be motivated by traditional literature.

■ Select a story from traditional literature that evokes visual images. Share the selection with a child, and allow the child to interpret the story using paints, chalk, or crayons.

■ Compile a file of folktales that contain vivid word pictures; describe how these tales could be used to help children interpret the mood of the tale through art.

References

1 Anderson, Paul S. *Story Telling with the Flannel Board.* Minneapolis: Denison, 1971.

2 Bauer, Caroline. *Handbook for Storytellers.* Chicago: American Library Association, 1977.

3 Bingham, Jane M., and Scholt, Grayce. "The Great Glass Slipper Search: Using Folk Tales with Older Children." *Elementary English* 51 (October 1974): 990–98.

4 Cook, Elizabeth. *The Ordinary and the Fabulous: An Introduction to Myths, Legends, and Fairy Tales.* 2d ed. Cambridge: At the University Press, 1976.

5 Dolch, Edward. *"Why" Stories from Different Countries.* New Canaan, Conn.: Garrard, 1958.

6 Kuo, Louise, and Kuo, Yuan-hsi. *Chinese Folk Tales.* Millbrae, Calif.: Celestial Arts, 1976.

7 Lang, Andrew. *Blue Fairy Book.* New York: David McKay, 1964.

8 McIntyre, Barbara M. *Creative Drama in the Elementary School.* Itasca, Ill.: Peacock, 1974.

9 Miller, Winifred. "Dragons—Fact or Fantasy?" *Elementary English* 52 (April 1975): 582–85.

10 Nelson, Mary Ann. *A Comparative Anthology of Children's Literature.* New York: Holt, Rinehart & Winston, 1972.

11 Norton, Donna E. *The Effective Teaching of Language Arts.* Columbus, Ohio: Merrill, 1980.

12 Ross, Elinor P. "Comparison of Folk Tale Variants." *Language Arts* 56 (April 1979): 422–26.

13 Ross, Ramon Royal. *Storyteller.* 2d ed. Columbus, Ohio: Merrill, 1980.

14 Siks, Geraldine. *Drama with Children.* New York: Harper & Row, 1977.

15 Stewig, John Warren. "Storyteller: Endangered Species?" *Language Arts* 55 (March 1978): 339–45.

16 Travers, P. T. *About the Sleeping Beauty.* Illustrated by Charles Keeping. New York: McGraw-Hill, 1975.

17 Western, Linda. "A Comparative Study of Literature through Folk Tale Variants." *Language Arts 57* (April 1980): 395–402.

18 Zinsmaster, Wanna. "Dramatizing Literature with Young Children." In *Using Literature with Young Children,* edited by Leland B. Jacobs. New York: Teachers College, 1974.

CHILDREN'S LITERATURE

FABLES

Aesop. *Aesop's Fables* Illustrated by Heidi Holder. Viking, 1981 (I:9–12 R:7). Nine fables illustrated with full-color paintings.

———. *Aesop's Fables.* Retold by Anne Terry White. Illustrated by Helen Siegle. Random House, 1964 (I:6–10 R:3). Forty of Aesop's fables told in story format.

———. *The Fables of Aesop.* Selected and edited by Ruth Spriggs. Illustrated by Frank Baber. Rand McNally, 1976 (I:6–10 R:5). A large book containing 143 fables.

———. *Lions and Lobsters and Foxes and Frogs.* Retold by Ennis Rees. Illustrated by Edward Gorey. Young Scott, 1971 (I:8–10 R:7). Seventeen Aesop fables told in verse.

———. *Tales From Aesop.* Retold and illustrated by Harold Jones. Watts/Julia MacRae, 1982 (I:all). Twenty-one fables illustrated by a leading English illustrator.

Caldecott, Randolph. *The Caldecott Aesop, A Facsimile of the 1883 Edition.* Doubleday, 1978 (I:all R:7). A reproduction of the earlier Aesop's fable written and illustrated by Caldecott.

La Fontaine, Jean de. *The Lion and the Rat.* Illustrated by Brian Wildsmith. Watts, 1963 (ch. 4).

———. *The Miller, the Boy and the Donkey.* Illustrated by Brian Wildsmith. Watts, 1969; Oxford, 1981 (ch. 4).

FOLKTALES

African—Black Literature
See pages 542–44, chapter eleven.

American—Native American
See pages 544–45, chapter eleven.

Asian and Eastern

Asian Cultural Centre for UNESCO. *Folk Tales from Asia for Children Everywhere,* Book Three. Weatherhill, 1976 (I:8–12 R:6). Stories from Afghanistan, Burma, Indonesia, Iran, Japan, Pakistan, Singapore, Sri Lanka, and Vietnam.

———. *Folk Tales from Asia for Children Everywhere,* Book Four. Weatherhill, 1976 (I:8–12 R:6). Folktales from Bangladesh, Cambodia, India, Korea, Laos, Malaysia, Nepal, Philippines and Thailand.

———. *Folk Tales from Asia for Children Everywhere,* Book Five. Weatherhill, 1977 (I:8–12 R:6). Stories from India, Philippines, Pakistan, Japan, Malaysia, Burma, and Iran.

Clark, Ann Nolan. *In the Land of Small Dragon.* Illustrated by Tony Chen. Viking, 1979 (I:7–12 R:7). A Vietnamese variation of "Cinderella."

DeRoin, Nancy (ed.) *Jataka Tales.* Illustrated by Ellen Lanyon. Houghton Mifflin, 1975 (I:7–9 R:5). Animal tales from India attributed to Buddha.

Haviland, Virginia. *Favorite Fairy Tales Told in India.* Illustrated by Blair Lent. Little, Brown, 1973 (I:8–10 R:5). A collection of characteristic tales.

———. *Favorite Fairy Tales Told in Japan.* Illustrated by George Suyeoka. Little, Brown, 1967 (I:8–10 R:5). A collection of Japanese folktales.

Hodges, Margaret. *The Wave.* Illustrated by Blair Lent (ch. 4).

Iké, Jane and Zimmerman, Baruch. *A Japanese Fairy Tale.* Warne, 1982 (I:5–8 R:5). A hunchback takes the disfiguration of his future wife, allowing her to be beautiful.

Kuo, Louise, and Kuo, Yuan-hsi. *Chinese Folk Tales.* Celestial Arts, 1976 (I:8–12 R:6). Folklore from the rulers and the minority tribes of China. Book includes an explanation about the symbolization of the tale and a history of China.

Lang, Andrew. *Aladdin and the Wonderful Lamp.* Illustrated by Errol LeCain. Viking, 1981 (I:7–9 R:6). Deep color and ornamentation appropriately illustrate a tale from *The Arabian Nights.*

Laurin, Anne. *The Perfect Crane.* Illustrated by Charles Mikolaycak. Harper & Row, 1981 (I:5–9 R:6). A Japanese tale about the friendship between a magician and the crane he creates from rice paper.

Louie, Ai-Lang. *Yeh Shen: A Cinderella Story From China.* Illustrated by Ed Young. Philomel, 1982 (I:7–9 R:6). This ancient Chinese tale has many similarities with versions from other cultures.

Mosel, Arlene. *The Funny Little Woman.* Illustrated by Blair Lent. Dutton, 1972 (I:5–8 R:5). A little woman pursues a rice dumpling and is captured by wicked people.

Pratt, Davis, and Kula, Elsa. *Magic Animals of Japan.* Parnassus, 1967 (I:8–12 R:7). Tales of the fabled creatures of Japan.

Roberts, Moss. *Chinese Fairy Tales and Fantasies.* Pantheon, 1979 (I:10 R:6). A collection of tales about enchantment, greed, animals, women, ghosts, and judges.

I = Interest by age range;
R = Readability by grade level.

Say, Allen. *Once Under the Cherry Blossom Tree.* Harper & Row, 1974 (I:6–10 R:4). A Japanese tale about the miserly landlord who swallows a cherry pit and has a cherry tree growing out of his head.

Travers, Pamela. *Two Pairs of Shoes.* Illustrated by Leo and Diane Dillon. Viking, 1980 (I:9–12 R:6). Two Persian tales reflect men's characters through their responses to their shoes.

Wyndham, Robert. *Tales the People Tell in China.* Illustrated by Jay Yang. Messner, 1971 (I:8–12 R:6). Myths, legends, and folktales from China. Includes sayings of the people and notes on each tale.

Yagawa, Sumiko. *The Crane Wife.* Illustrated by Suekichi Akaba. Morrow, 1981 (I:7–10 R:6). A wife sacrifices herself for her husband and must return to her animal form when he breaks his promise.

British

Cauley, Lorinda Bryan. *Goldilocks and the Three Bears.* Putnam, 1981 (I:3–7 R:4). Large colorful illustrations appeal to children.

Corcoran, Jean. *Folk Tales of England.* Bobbs-Merrill, 1963 (I:6–10 R:4). A collection of twenty folktales including "Mr. and Mrs. Vinegar," "Dick Whittington," "The Three Sillies," "Lazy Jack," and "Jack the Giant Killer."

de Paola, Tomie. *The Friendly Beasts: An Old English Christmas Carol.* Putnam, 1981 (I:3–9). The Bethlehem setting is depicted in this folk song.

Galdone, Paul. *The Little Red Hen.* Seabury, 1973 (I:3–7 R:3). The little red hen lives with a cat, a dog, and a mouse; only the red hen likes to work.

_____. *The Three Bears.* Seabury, 1972 (I:3–7 R:5). The traditional tale illustrated with large, humorous pictures.

_____. *The Three Sillies.* Houghton Mifflin, 1981 (I:3–7 R:2). Colorful, humorous illustrations add to tale about a man's search for three people sillier than his future in-laws.

_____. *What's in Fox's Sack? An Old English Tale.* Clarion, 1982 (I:3–7 R:2). A fox is outsmarted by a woman who puts a bulldog in his bag. Large, humorous illustrations appeal to young children.

Garner, Alan. *The Lad of the Gad.* Philomel, 1981 (I:8–10 R:6). Five Gaelic stories based on J. F. Campbell's *Popular Tales of the West Highlands* and an Irish tale.

Godden, Rumer. *The Dragon of Og.* Illustrated by Pauline Baynes. Viking, 1981 (I:9–12 R:6). Scottish tale about the new lord who refuses to give the dragon bullocks from his herd.

Jacobs, Joseph. *Guleesh.* Illustrated by William Stobbs. Follett, 1972 (I:7–12 R:5). An Irish folktale about the sheehogues, the fairy hosts of Ireland, and a boy who joins them when they capture the King's daughter.

Steel, Flora Annie. *Tattercoats.* Illustrated by Diane Goode. Bradbury, 1976 (I:7–10 R:7). The gooseherd plays the role of the fairy godmother in this English version of "Cinderella."

Zemach, Harve. *Duffy and the Devil.* Illustrated by Margot Zemach. Farrar, Straus & Giroux, 1973 (I:8–12 R:6). A Cornish tale that resembles "Rumplestiltskin," but the maid makes an agreement with the devil.

French

de Beaumont, Madame. *Beauty and the Beast.* Translated and illustrated by Diane Goode. Bradbury, 1978 (I:8–14 R:7). Lovely illustrations accompany the tale of a girl who is willing to sacrifice her own life for the love of her father.

Montresor, Beni. *Cinderella.* Knopf, 1965 (I:8–14 R:6). A version of "Cinderella" taken from the Italian opera by Gioacchino Rossini.

Perrault, Charles. *Cinderella.* Illustrated by Marcia Brown. Scribner's, 1954 (ch. 4).

_____. *The Glass Slipper: Charles Perrault's Tales of Time Past.* Translated by John Bierhorst. Illustrated by Mitchell Miller. Four Winds, 1981 (I:9–12 R:6). A new translation of *Histoires ou contes du temps passé.*

_____. *Puss in Boots.* Illustrated by Marcia Brown. Scribner's, 1952 (ch. 4).

_____. *Puss in Boots.* Illustrated by Hans Fischer, Harcourt Brace Jovanovich, 1959 (I:5–8 R:6). Line drawings of Puss make an interesting comparison to those drawn by Marcia Brown.

_____. *The Sleeping Beauty.* Translated and illustrated by David Walker. Crowell, 1976 (I:8–14 R:6). Beautifully illustrated book that resembles the stage setting for an opera or ballet.

German

deRegniers, Beatrice Schenk. *Red Riding Hood.* Illustrated by Edward Gorey. Atheneum, 1972 (I:4–8 R:2). A verse format of the story based on the Brothers Grimm version.

Galdone, Paul. *Hansel and Gretel.* McGraw-Hill, 1982 (I:5–7 R:3). A folktale appropriate for younger children.

_____. *Little Red Riding Hood.* McGraw-Hill, 1974 (I:4–8 R:4). Large, colorful pictures retell the Grimms' folktale.

_____. *The Table, the Donkey and the Stick.* McGraw-Hill, 1976 (I:3–8 R:5). A picture book version of the Grimms' folktale.

Grimm, Brothers. *The Bearskinner.* Illustrated by Felix Hoffman. Atheneum, 1978 (I:5–8 R:3). A brave soldier makes a bargain with a stranger, goes seven years without washing or shaving, and wins his freedom as well as wealth.

_____. *The Bremen Town Musicians.* Retold and illustrated by Ilse Plume. Doubleday, 1980 (I:5–8 R:5). Soft, colored illustrations show animals going through the forest.

_____. *The Bremen Town Musicians: A Grimm's Fairy Tale.* Retold and illustrated by Donna Diamond. Delacorte, 1981 (I:5–8 R:5). Black and white illustrations in a smaller sized text.

_____. *Cinderella.* Illustrated by Nonny Hogrogian. Greenwillow, 1981 (I:6–12 R:6). An attractive version of the German tale.

_____. *Cinderella.* Translated by Anne Rogers. Illustrated by Otto S. Svend. Larousse, 1978 (I:6–12 R:5). Cinderella is helped by the pigeons and turtle doves so that she can go to the ball.

_____. *Eric Carle's Storybook, Seven Tales by the Brothers Grimm.* Watts, 1976 (I:6–8 R:4). "Hans in Luck," "Three Golden Hairs," "Fisherman and His Wife," "Tom Thumb," "Seven with One Blow," "The Youth Who Wanted to Shiver," and "The Seven Swabians."

_____. *Favorite Tales From Grimm.* Retold and illustrated by Mercer Mayer. Four Winds, 1982 (I:7–10 R:6). Twenty illustrated stories.

_____. *The Fisherman and His Wife.* Translated by Elizabeth Shub. Illustrated by Monika Laimgruber. Greenwillow, 1978 (I:4–8 R:2). A discontented wife keeps asking more and more favors from an enchanted flounder until she is returned to her original humble environment.

_____. *The Goose Girl.* Illustrated by Marguerite de Angeli. Doubleday, 1964 (I:7–12 R:7). A princess is tricked by a serving maid and must become a goose girl until the King discovers her true identity.

_____. *Grimms' Golden Goose.* Illustrated by Charles Mikolaycak. Random House, 1969 (I:7–12 R:6). Simpleton, the kind younger brother, is rewarded with a golden goose. The goose provides him with a means of winning a princess.

_____. *Hansel and Gretel.* Illustrated by Anthony Browne. Watts, 1982 (I:9–12 R:5). Illustrations showing a contemporary setting should be interesting for a comparative study.

_____. *Hansel and Gretel.* Illustrated by Susan Jeffers. Dial, 1980 (I:5–9 R:6). Illustrations with strongline and a magnificent gingerbread house should appeal to readers.

_____. *The Musicians of Bremen.* Translated by Anne Rogers. Illustrated by Otto S. Svend. Larousse, 1974 (I:4–8 R:6). An old dog, donkey, cat, and rooster decide to become musicians. They use their singing voices to frighten robbers away from a cottage.

————. *The Nose Tree*. Retold and illustrated by Warwick Hutton. Atheneum, 1981 (I:5–9 R:6). Trickery and humorous illustrations are good for the story hour.

————. *Rapunzel*. Illustrated by Bernadette Watts. Crowell, 1975 (I:7–12 R:7). The lovely Rapunzel is placed in a tower where she must let down her golden hair to allow the witch and the prince to ascend.

————. *Rapunzel: From the Brothers Grimm*. Retold by Barbara Rogasky. Illustrated by Trina Hyman, Holiday, 1982 (I:6–9 R:6). The forest setting seems right for a girl imprisoned in a high tower.

————. *Rare Treasures from Grimm: Fifteen Little-Known Tales*. Translated by Ralph Manheim. Illustrated by Erik Blegvad. Doubleday, 1981 (I:9–12 R:6). Each tale is illustrated by a full-page painting.

————. *The Seven Ravens*. Translated by Elizabeth Crawford. Illustrated by Lisbeth Zwerger. Morrow, 1981 (I:6–9 R:6). A girl frees her brothers from an enchantment.

————. *The Six Swans*. Illustrated by Adrie Hospes. McGraw-Hill, 1973 (I:7–12 R:5). Six brothers are enchanted by their evil stepmother. Only their sister can save them.

————. *The Sleeping Beauty*. Illustrated by Warwick Hutton. Atheneum, 1979 (I:7–12 R:6). Watercolors illustrate the story of magic and enchantment.

————. *Snow White and the Seven Dwarfs*. Translated by Randal Jarrell. Illustrated by Nancy Ekholm Burkert. Farrar, Straus & Giroux, 1972 (I:7–12 R:6). The illustrations were carefully researched by the artist and reflect the Black Forest and German heritage.

————. *Snow White and the Seven Dwarfs*. Translated by Anne Rogers. Illustrated by Otto S. Svend. Larousse, 1975 (I:7–12 R:6). The familiar fairy tale in a picture storybook.

————. *Thorn Rose or the Sleeping Beauty*. Illustrated by Errol LeCain. Bradbury, 1977 (I:7–12 R:7). Lovely illustrations depict the opulence of a magical kingdom.

————. *Tom Thumb*. Translated by Anthea Bell. Illustrated by Otto S. Svend. Larousse, 1976 (I:5–9 R:6). The small boy who is no bigger than your thumb runs away from two strangers and two thieves.

————. *The Twelve Dancing Princesses*. Illustrated by Errol LeCain. Viking, 1978 (I:7–12 R:7). Twelve princesses dance their shoes through every night. The king offers wealth and the

hand of a princess to the man who can solve the mystery.

————. *Wanda Gág's The Six Swans*. Translated by Wanda Gág. Illustrated by Margot Tomes. Coward-McCann, 1982 (I:5–9 R:4). A newly illustrated edition of Gág's translation from *More Tales from Grimm*.

————. *The Wolf and the Seven Little Kids*. Translated by Anne Rogers. Illustrated by Otto S. Svend. Larousse, 1977 (I:4–8 R:4). Seven little goats have a conflict with the wolf when their mother leaves the house.

Jewish

Gross, Michael. *The Fable of the Fig Tree*. Illustrated by Mila Lazarevich. Walck, 1975 (I:6–10 R:7). An old man plants a tree even if he can't benefit from the fruit.

McDermott, Beverly Brodsky. *The Golem*. Lippincott, 1976 (I:8+ R:5). Rabbi Lev creates a man out of a lump of clay, but the Golem does not protect the Jewish people the way the Rabbi envisions.

Singer, Isaac Bashevis. *The Golem*. Illustrated by Uri Shulevitz. Farrar, Straus & Giroux, 1982 (I:8+ R:?). Another version of this Jewish folktale.

————. *Mazel and Shlimazel or the Milk of the Lioness*. Illustrated by Margot Zemach. Farrar, Straus & Giroux, 1967 (I:8–12 R:4). Mazel, the spirit of good luck, and Shlimazel, the spirit of bad luck, have a contest. Who will win?

Zemach, Margot. *It Could Always Be Worse*. Farrar, Straus & Giroux, 1977 (ch. 5).

Norwegian

Asbjörnsen, Peter Christian, and Moe, Jorgen E. *East of the Sun and West of the Moon and Other Tales*. Illustrated by Tom Vroman. Macmillan, 1963 (I:6–10 R:7). A collection of twelve Norwegian folk tales.

————. *The Man Who Kept House*. Retold by Kathleen and Michael Hague. Illustrated by Michael Hague. Harcourt Brace Jovanovich, 1981 (I:5–9 R:6). Humorous illustrations show the husband's problems when he takes over his wife's chores.

————. *Norwegian Folk Tales*. Illustrated by Erik Werenskiold and Theodor Kittelsen. Viking, 1960 (I:6–10 R:3). A collection of thirty-five Norwegian folktales.

————. *The Three Billy Goats Gruff*. Illustrated by Marcia Brown. Harcourt Brace Jovanovich, 1957 (I:3–7 R:5). Goats prancce across pages of this favorite tale for telling.

Galdone, Paul. *The Three Billy Goats Gruff*. Seabury, 1973 (I:5–8 R:5). A picture storybook

about the three billy goats who defeat the troll who lives under the bridge.

Hague, Kathleen, and Hague, Michael. *East of the Sun and West of the Moon*. Harcourt Brace Jovanovich, 1980. (I:7–9 R:5). A maiden lives in the castle of an enchanted white bear.

Haviland, Virginia. *Favorite Fairy Tales Told in Norway*. Illustrated by Leonard Weisgard. Little, Brown, 1961 (I:6–10 R:4). This collection includes "The Princess on the Glass Hill," "Why the Sea Is Salt," "The Three Billy Goats Gruff," "Taper Tom," "Why the Bear is Stumpy-Tailed," "The Lad and the North Wind," and "Boots and the Troll."

Mayer, Mercer. *East of the Sun and West of the Moon*. Four Winds, 1980 (I:8–10 R:4). A beautifully illustrated version of the Asbjörsen and Moe tale.

Russian

Afanasév, Aleksandr Nikolaevich. *Russian Folk Tales*. Translated by Robert Chandler. Illustrated by Ivan I. Bilibin. Random House, 1980 (I:8–12 R:7). Seven memorable tales collected by the nineteenth-century folklorist.

Bain, R. Nisbet, ed. *Cossack Fairy Tales and Folktales*. E. W. Mitchell. CORE Collection, 1976 (I:9+ R:7). Twenty-seven western Ukrainian folktales are reprinted from a 1894 edition.

Daniels, Guy. *The Falcon under the Hat, Russian Merry Tales and Fairy Tales*. Illustrated by Feodor Rojan-kovsky. Funk & Wagnalls, 1969 (I:7–12 R:4). A collection of short humorous stories and fairy tales translated from Russian folk literature.

————. *The Peasant's Pea Patch*. Illustrated by Robert Quackenbush. Delacorte, 1971 (I:5–9 R:4). A Russian merry tale about a poor peasant who tries to protect his pea patch.

Ginsburg, Mirra. *Three Rolls and One Doughnut*. Illustrated by Anita Lobel. Dial, 1970 (I:8–12 R:4). A collection of short fables and tales from Russia.

Harris, Rosemary. *The Flying Ship*. Illustrated by Errol LeCain. Faber & Faber, 1975 (I:8–12 R:5). The Czar declares that a young man, in order to marry his daughter, must produce a flying ship.

Otsuka, Yūzō. *Suho and the White Horse: A Legend of Mongolia*. Adapted from Ann Herring's translation. Illustrated by Suekichi Akaba. Viking, 1981 (I:5–8 R:6). In a tale about good versus evil, a herdsman's horse is killed because of a nobleman's greed.

Pushkin, Alexander. *The Tale of Czar Saltan or the Prince and the Swan Princess*. Translated by Patricia Tracy Lowe. Illustrated by I. Bilibin. Crowell, 1975 (I:8–12   R:6). The Czar marries the youngest daughter, but her sisters trick her into exile.

_____. *The Tale of the Golden Cockerel.* Translated by Patricia Tracy Lowe. Illustrated by I. Bilibin. Crowell, 1975 (I:8–12   R:6). A Russian Czar makes a promise to a sorcerer; misfortune results when he doesn't keep his promise.

Ransome, Arthur. *The Fool of the World and the Flying Ship.* Illustrated by Uri Shulevitz. Farrar, Straus & Giroux, 1968 (ch. 4).

Tolstoy, Leo. *The Fool.* Translated by Anthea Bell. Illustrated by Lapointe. Schocken, 1981 (I:5–8). A story in rhyme tells about a foolish man who says the wrong things to the wrong people.

Zvorykin, Boris, illustrator. *The Firebird and Other Russian Fairy Tales.* Edited by Jacqueline Onassis. Viking, 1978 (I:8–14   R:3). "The Firebird," "Maria Morevna," "The Snow Maiden," and "Vassilissa The Fair" are retold in a beautifully illustrated edition.

Other Folktales

Basile, Giambattista. *Petrosinella.* Adapted from the translation by John Edward Taylor. Illustrated by Diane Stanley. Warne, 1981 (I:7–10   R:6). An Italian version of "Rapunzel."

Blair, Walter. *Tall Tale America: A Legendary History of Our Humorous Heroes.* Illustrated by Glen Rounds. Coward-McCann, 1944 (I:8–10   R:5).

Dégh, Linda (ed). *Folktales of Hungary.* Translated by Judith Holász. University of Chicago Press. 1965 (I:10 +   R:6). A large collection of folktales; includes a foreword, introduction, glossary, and notes.

Galdone, Paul. *The Amazing Pig: An Old Hungarian Tale.* Houghton Mifflin, 1981 (I:5–8   R:3). A humorous tale about a king who promises his daughter in marriage to any man who tells him something he cannot believe.

Ginsburg, Mirra. *Two Greedy Bears.* Illustrated by Jose Aruego and Ariane Dewey. Macmillan, 1976 (I:3–6   R:4). In a Hungarian tale, two greedy bears fight over cheese; a fox solves the problem by eating the cheese.

Haviland, Virginia. *Favorite Fairy Tales Told in Czechoslovakia.* Illustrated by Trina Schart Hyman. Little, Brown, 1966 (I:6–10   R:4). A collection of folktales from Czechoslovakia.

_____. *Favorite Fairy Tales Told in Italy.* Illustrated by Evaline Ness. Little, Brown, 1967 (I:6–10   R:4). A fine source of Italian folktales.

Severo, Emoke de Papp, trans. *The Goodhearted Youngest Brother.* Illustrated by Diane Goode. Bradbury, 1981 (I:5–8   R:6). A Hungarian tale reveals how a kindhearted youngest brother releases three beautiful princesses from enchantment.

LEGENDS

Bawden, Nina. *William Tell.* Illustrated by Pascale Allamand. Lothrop, Lee & Shepard, 1981 (I:6–9   R:5). Tale of the fourteenth-century Swiss patriot who inspired his people to fight for their freedom.

Haley, Gail E. *The Green Man.* Scribner's, 1980 (I:7–10   R:6). Paintings resembling tapestries accompany the legend about a man who lived in the woods and cared for the animals.

Hastings. Selina. *Sir Gawain and the Green Knight.* Illustrated by Juan Wijngaard. Lothrop, Lee & Shepard, 1981 (I:9–12   R:4). One of King Arthur's knights is challenged by a giant adversary.

Malcolmson, Anne, ed. *The Song of Robin Hood.* Music by Grace Castagnetta. Illustrated by Virginia Lee Burton. Houghton Mifflin, 1947 (I:7–9). Lovely illustrations accompany the verses.

Pyle, Howard. *The Merry Adventures of Robin Hood.* 1883. Reprint. Scribner's, 1946 (I:10–14   R:8). The original, longer version of Robin Hood's adventures.

_____. *Some Merry Adventures of Robin Hood.* Scribner's, 1954 (I:8–12   R:7). Twelve stories selected from the original version of Robin Hood.

_____. *The Story of King Arthur and His Knights.* Scribner's, 1933 (I:12 +   R:8). The story of how Arthur becomes king of England, establishes the Round Table, and performs heroic deeds.

Riordan, James. *Tales of King Arthur.* Illustrated by Victor G. Ambrus. Rand McNally, 1982 (I:9–12   R:6). New illustrations for a classic legend about the English hero.

Robbins, Ruth. *Taliesin and King Arthur.* Parnassus, 1970 (I:8–14   R:6). A Welsh poet sings of his own past; he wins the honor of the greatest bard of all.

Seredy, Kate. *The White Stag.* Viking, 1937, 1965 (ch. 3).

Sutcliff, Rosemary. *The Road to Camlann: The Death of King Arthur.* Illustrated by Shirley Felts. Dutton, 1982 (I:10 +   R:7). Mordred attempts to destroy the kingdom by exposing Queen Guinevere and Sir Lancelot.

_____. *The Sword and the Circle: King Arthur and the Knights of the Round Table.* Dutton, 1981 (I:10 +   R:7). Includes thirteen stories associated with King Arthur.

MYTHOLOGY

Greek and Roman Myths

Barth, Edna. *Cupid and Psyche.* Illustrated by Ati Forberg. Seabury, 1976 (I:7–12   R:6). Prin-

cess Psyche is loved by Cupid but hated by Venus, the goddess of love. She must prove herself before she joins the immortals.

Bulfinch, Thomas. *A Book of Myths.* Illustrated by Helen Sewell. Macmillan, 1942, 1964 (I:10 +   R:6). A collection of Greek myths written in short story format.

_____. *Myths of Greece & Rome.* Penguin, 1981 (paperback) (I:10   R:8). A good source for the myths.

Colum, Padraic. *The Golden Fleece and the Heroes Who Lived Before Achilles.* Illustrated by Willy Pogany. Macmillan, 1921, 1949, 1962 (I:9 +   R:6). Jason and the Greek heroes search for golden fleece.

Coolidge, Olivia. *Greek Myths.* Illustrated by Edouard Sandoz. Houghton Mifflin, 1949 (I:10 +   R:7). An excellent collection of myths.

D'Aulaire, Ingri, and D'Aulaire, Edgar Parin. *D'Aulaires' Book of Greek Myths.* Doubleday, 1962 (paperback, 1980) (I:8 +   R:6). A collection of tales about gods, goddesses, and heroes.

Farmer, Penelope. *Daedalus and Icarus.* Illustrated by Chris Connor. Harcourt Brace Jovanovich, 1971 (I:8 +   R:6). Daedalus creates wings to escape from a labyrinth and is the first mortal to attempt what previously only the gods have done.

Garfield, Leon, and Blishen, Edward. *The Golden Shadow.* Illustrated by Charles Keeping. Pantheon, 1973 (I:10 +   R:7). Tells about activities of Greek gods, goddesses, and heroes.

Gates, Doris. *The Golden God: Apollo.* Illustrated by Constantinos' CoConis. Viking, 1973 (I:9 +   R:6). Story of Apollo and his associations with other gods and goddesses.

_____. *Lord of the Sky: Zeus.* Illustrated by Robert Handville. Viking, 1972 (I:10 +   R:7). The myths centering around Zeus, including Io, Daucalion's flood, Baucis and Philemon, Europa, Cadmus, Theseus, and Dionysus.

_____. *Two Queens of Heaven: Aphrodite and Demeter.* Illustrated by Trina Schart Hyman. Viking, 1974 (I:9 +   R:5). A group of myths telling the exploits of Aphrodite and Demeter.

_____. *The Warrior Goddess: Athena.* Illustrated by Don Bolognese. Viking, 1972 (I:9 +   R:6). Exploits of the goddess Athena, Zeus's daughter, as she assists the heroes in the quests.

Hodges, Margaret. *The Gorgon's Head.* Illustrated by Charles Mikolaycak. Little, Brown, 1972 (I:10 +   R:6). Perseus is sent to bring back the Medusa's head. With the help of Athena's polished shield and Mercury's winged sandals, he overcomes the Medusa.

Kingsley, Charles. *The Heroes.* Mayflower, 1980 (I:8 +   R:6). Tales of Greek heroes.

McDermott, Gerald. *Sun Flight.* Four Winds, 1980 (I:all   R:6). Daedalus the master craftsman and his son construct wings and escape from Crete.

Proddow, Penelope. *Demeter and Persephone*. Illustrated by Barbara Cooney. Doubleday, 1972 (ch. 4).

Serraillier, Ian. *A Fall From the Sky*. Illustrated by William Stobbs. Walck, 1966 (I:10+   R:6). The story of the craftsman Daedalus who rids himself of his nephew but is punished by the loss of his own son.

————. *Heracles the Strong*. Illustrated by Rocco Negri. Walck, 1970 (I:10+   R:6). The twelve labors of Heracles, plus other adventures of the Greek hero.

————. *The Way of Danger: The Story of Theseus*. Illustrated by William Stobbs. Walck, 1963 (I:10+   R:5). The son of the king of Athens kills the Minotaur and rescues Theseus from the underworld as part of his heroic deeds.

Silverthorne, Elizabeth. *I, Heracles*. Abingdon, 1978 (I:8–12   R:5). The strong half-man and half-god retells his twelve labors.

Norse Myths and Epics

Coolidge, Olivia E. *Legends of the North*. Illustrated by Edouard Sandoz. Houghton Mifflin, 1951 (I:9–14   R:6). The northern legends including the gods Thor and Baldur, the heroes Beowulf and Sigurd, and the tales from the sagas.

D'Aulaire, Ingri, and D'Aulaire, Edgar Parin. *Norse Gods and Giants*. Doubleday, 1967 (I:8–12   R:6). A collection of Norse tales, including explanations about creation, tales of Thor, Odin, and Loki.

Nye, Robert. *Beowulf*. Illustrated by Alan E. Cober. Wang, 1968 (I:9+   R:5). Beowulf overcomes the monster Grendel and other evils by using both strength and cunning.

SEVEN
Modern Fantasy

Time, Space, and Place
Involving Children in Modern Fantasy

Time, Space, and Place

**EVALUATING MODERN FANTASY
AUTHORS AND THEIR BOOKS**

I N THE TIME OF swords and periwigs and full-skirted coats with flowered lappets—when gentlemen wore ruffles, and gold-laced waistcoats of paduasoy and taffeta—there lived a tailor in Gloucester. (p. 11)

With these rhythmical words from *The Tailor of Gloucester,* one of the most popular authors of modern fantasy takes her readers into a time and a setting when the impossible becomes convincingly possible. When children escape into Beatrix Potter's world of Peter Rabbit, Squirrel Nutkin, or Benjamin Bunny, they enter the intriguing sphere of fantasy.

Authors of modern fantasy create their settings by altering one or more of the literary elements from what is expected in the real world. A new world may be created as exemplified by J. R. R. Tolkien's Middle Earth in *The Hobbit* or Ursula K. LeGuin's Earthsea in *A Wizard of Earthsea.* Other authors of fantasy may not create new worlds, but they may change their characters so they have unusual experiences in the real world. Mary Norton uses this technique in *The Borrowers* when she places her little people in the midst of adult-size humans. Authors of fantasy frequently choose to have their characters depart from what we know to be possible in our world. They may go down a rabbit hole and enter another domain as in Lewis Carroll's *Alice's Adventures in Wonderland,* take trips through time as in Margaret J. Anderson's *In the Keep of Time,* or tesseract through time and space as in Madeleine L'Engle's *A Wrinkle in Time.* The characters themselves may be contrary to reality. There are personified toys such as Margery Williams's *The Velveteen Rabbit* and A. A. Milne's *Winnie-the-Pooh.* There are articulate animals such as found in Beatrix Potter's *The Tale of Peter Rabbit,* Rudyard Kipling's *The Jungle Books,* and Michael Bond's *A Bear Called Paddington.* Authors also create eccentric characters who experience preposterous situations as found in Carl Sandburg's *Rootabaga Stories* and Astrid Lindgren's *Pippi Longstocking.*

How an author alters the literary elements, why an author alters the literary elements, and when an author should alter the literary elements are all important considerations when evaluating modern fantasy.

This chapter discusses the evaluation of modern fantasy and stresses the relationship between traditional and modern fantasy. It discusses the works of authors who bridge the world between old and new fantasy, allegory, fairy stories, good versus evil, and power and responsibility. The rest of the chapter reviews authors and their books in the following categories: articulate animals; dolls, toys, and inanimate objects; eccentric characters, preposterous situations, and exaggerations; little people; friendly presences, ghosts, and goblins; time warps; and science fiction.

EVALUATING MODERN FANTASY

Modern fantasy should be evaluated by the same criteria recommended for literature in chapter three, but the few points that follow should be emphasized: fantasy point of view, the development of a fantasy setting, fantasy character, and themes found in modern fantasy.

Point of View—Suspending Disbelief

Rebecca J. Lukens (9) says, "If fantasy is to be successful, we must willingly suspend disbelief. If the story's characters, conflict, and theme seem believable to us, we find it plausible and even natural to know the thoughts and feelings of animal characters or tiny people. In fact, the story may be so good that we wish it were true. We wish we knew Arrietty. [Arrietty is a character in *The Borrowers.*] This persuasion that the writer wishes to bring about—persuasion that 'what if' is really 'it's true'—is most successful when the writer is consistent about point of view" (p. 108).

The point of view of a story is determined by the author's choice of the person telling it. A story might be told quite differently through the view of a child, a mother, a wicked witch, a six-inch person, or an observer. While point of view is important in all literature, it is consistency of point of view and how it influences the details in the story that persuades readers to suspend disbelief in modern fantasy.

The Borrowers, by Mary Norton, seems believable because most of the story is told from the viewpoint of Arrietty who is only six inches tall. The Clock family sitting room seems authentic because the reader views it through Arrietty's eyes, envisioning the postage stamp portraits on the walls, a work of art created by a pillbox supporting a chess piece, and a padded trinket box settee. Even the reaction to a miniature book that is Arrietty's diary is dealt with through the physical capabilities of a miniature person: "Arrietty braced her muscles and heaved the book off her knees, and stood it upright on the floor" (p. 20). The reader is ready to believe the story because sights, feelings, and physical reactions are described as if a six-inch person were actually living through the experience.

Richard Shohet (14), who evaluated the functions of voice in children's literature, concluded that storytellers such as Beatrix Potter, Kenneth Grahame, and A. A. Milne tell their stories in a way that suspends disbelief. These storytellers urge the reader to consider that the events and characters might have occurred. Beatrix Potter, for example, accomplishes believable situations by telling the story from Peter Rabbit's point of view and by interjecting the storyteller's first person into the story: "I am sorry to say that Peter was not very well during the evening." Most children have eaten too much at some time and probably know that Peter would have a stomachache after overeating.

This consistency of viewpoint, whether writing about hobbits, giants, or time warps, creates a fantasy that, once accepted, encourages a vicarious experience because every point of the story is believable.

Setting—Creating a World

Settings in traditional tales are usually in magical kingdoms or deep in a mysterious woods. Children know that magic is possible—they accept an environment conducive to magic. Writers of modern fantasy often combine reality and fantasy as characters or stories go back and forth between two worlds, or they may create totally new worlds in which magic or unusual circumstances are possible. If the story is to be credible, the author must develop the setting so completely that readers can see, hear, and feel it.

The settings for the "Borrowers" books, described through the eyes of little people, are an integral part of each story. The inside of a cottage drain becomes both an escape route and an antagonist in *The Borrowers Afloat.* Readers see a new world as they visualize the drain from the inside: "There were other openings as they went along, drains that branched into darkness and ran away uphill. Where these joined the main drain a curious collection of flotsam and jetsam piled up over which they had to drag the soap lid . . . the air from that point onwards, smelled far less strongly of tea leaves" (p. 105). The setting in the drain changes from a fairly calm escape route to one filled with drumming noises and fright as a bath drain opens. Norton now describes a setting that becomes the antagonist: "A millrace of hot scented water swilled through her clothes, piling against her at one moment, falling away the next. Sometimes it bounced above her shoulders, drenching her face and hair; at others it swirled steadily about her waist and tugged at her legs and feet" (p. 110). There is so much detail that readers can see the contents of the inside of the drain as if they too were only six inches tall, they can smell the soap and tea leaves deposited in the drain, and they can hear the changing sounds as water echoes through the drain or gushes down in thundering torrents.

Other authors must create new worlds as the characters go from the world of reality to the world of fantasy. Alice, in *Alice's Adventures in Wonderland,* by Lewis Carroll, goes from a peaceful river bank, travels down a rabbit hole, and finds a unique world that is described in great detail through her viewpoint. Ten-year-old Elizabeth, in Margaret Anderson's *To Nowhere and Back,* walks down a country lane and finds a nineteenth-century world instead of the dilapidated cottage she expected. The descriptions of the same setting in two different centuries are important to the story. Authors whose characters travel in time warps must create believable, authentic settings for two time periods. These historical settings are integral parts of books such as Anderson's *In the Keep of Time* and *In the Circle of Time.*

Characterization

Characters in modern fantasy are as varied as the imaginations of creative authors. Imaginary elements enable authors to remove their heroes and heroines from the real world. They may, for example, humanize animals by granting them speech; they may reduce the size of human characters and leave them in a human world or place them in a new environment; they may give the characters magic or other unusual powers; or they may use time warps to place their characters in historical periods or into the future.

Merely giving a character unusual powers or placing the character in a fanciful world does not create a memorable character. The character must also be believable; that is, one who encourages readers to suspend disbelief. Language is one way that authors can make characters believable. Tolkien, for example, in *The Hobbit* and *The Lord of the Rings,* creates languages for many characters. Ruth Noel (11), in her evaluation of Tolkien's use of language, concludes that the musical flow of Elvish words and names implies that the Elves are noble people who love beauty and music. In contrast, the guttural, unfamiliar sounds of Dwarfish indicate that the language is isolated from that of men and Elves. Likewise, the croaked curses of the Orcs establish them as a coarse, cruel, unimaginative people, and the prolonged chants of the Ents demonstrate their peaceful life in the forest.

Characters may also seem believable because they are placed in the real world before they enter the world of fantasy. For example, C. S. Lewis in "The Chronicles of Narnia" develops normal human characters who visit a real home and enter into childhood games. When these real characters are confronted with the fantastic, they believe it is happening. If readers believe in these characters, they also suspend disbelief. Likewise, Margaret Anderson's characters in *In the Keep of Time* have a strong foundation in reality before they enter their time warp fantasies. Because normal human characters believe in what is happening to them and believe in the characters they meet, readers also believe.

The characters in Anderson's story transcend time when they encounter and believe in a tangible object. A real key allows them to walk through a door and into another time. C. S. Lewis's characters enter Narnia through a wardrobe, while Alan Garner's character in *The Weirdstone of Brisingamen* is the owner of a tear-shaped crystal. Such tangible objects often make the fantasy possible. Because the real characters believe in the power of the tangible object, the reader also believes.

When the author develops a logical framework, places characters into plausible settings, develops characters' actions that are consistent within the framework, and carefully follows the rules of his or her own creation, there is an internal consistency within the story. Magical properties seem plausible because characters follow a required order of events, behaviors seem believable because they are consistent, and plots seem credible because they are the result of logical implications. Consistency in characterization is especially important. If, for example, animals supposedly live and behave like animals, they should consistently live like animals unless the author has carefully developed why they change, when they change, and how they change. Without such internal consistency, the fantasy would not encourage the reader to suspend disbelief.

Themes

Themes found in modern fantasy include some very important human values. Ned Hedges (6) evaluated children's classics and concluded that physical traits acquired by animals tend to affirm specific human values or condemn certain human corruptions. He suggested that Kenneth Grahame, in *The Wind in the Willows,* created characters and situations that depict both personal values and corruption found in society. Writers such as George MacDonald, who wrote during the Victorian period in England, developed themes that condemned the state of civilization and stressed the need for faith.

The constant battle between good and evil and the need to be alert to the dangers of evil are popular subjects in many fantasies. The overcoming of old evil by older magic is found in works by C. S. Lewis. The importance of faith and striving for high ideals are themes developed by Lloyd Alexander, J. R. R. Tolkien, and C. S. Lewis.

The fantasies of Ursula Le Guin stress the importance of every action; one action may, in fact, influence the outcome in the battle between good and evil. Her stories suggest that power carries with it an enormous responsibility.

The power of love is important in both Margery Williams's *The Velveteen Rabbit* and Madeleine L'Engle's *A Wrinkle in Time.* The power of love and friendship are also strong themes in E. B. White's *Charlotte's Web.* Patience as a worthwhile human value is suggested by several writers of modern fairy tales.

Criteria for Selecting Modern Fantasy

When evaluating modern fantasy, the reader should consider the following questions:

1 Does the author encourage the reader to suspend disbelief by developing a point of view that is consistent in every detail, including sights, feelings, and physical reactions?
2 If several time periods are developed, are the settings authentic and an integral part of the story?
3 Is there careful attention to the details in the setting? Do these details reflect the point of view?
4 Does the author use an appropriate language or create a believable language that represents the characterization in the story?
5 How does the author's characterization allow children to suspend disbelief? Do characters begin in a real world before they travel to the world of fantasy? Does a believable character accept a fanciful world, characters, or happenings? Is every action consistent with the framework developed by the author?
6 Is the theme worthwhile for children?

These themes, imaginative characters, detailed settings, and points of view that encourage readers to suspend disbelief are found in many books that appeal to children of different ages. The rest of this chapter discusses books that are among the first stories shared with children. Many of these are also books that adults can enjoy.

AUTHORS AND THEIR BOOKS

Many authors of modern fantasy are well known for one type of fantasy or have written series or chronicles depicting one subject or a new world; consequently, this section is organized according to modern fantasy subjects and the well-known authors who write in these areas. The section begins with authors whose work contains elements of traditional literature; they bridge the world between traditional folktales and mythology and modern fantasy. It also includes authors who write about articulate animals, personified toys, eccentric characters and preposterous situations, strange and curious worlds, little people, friendly presences and ghosts, time warps, and science fiction.

Bridging the World Between Old and New Fantasy

Children and adults who enjoy traditional folktales and mythology will find authors and books to please them in the modern fantasy tales that have elements of earlier, traditional stories. The literary fairy tales of Hans Christian Andersen contain elements similar to those recorded by the Brothers Grimm. The fantasies of Lewis, Tolkien, and Alexander contain elements of mythology. The stories of Le Guin and Susan Cooper take children into the world of sorcery and wizardry.

Many authors of this type of modern fantasy develop allegorical themes, stress the consequences of the battle between good and evil, and suggest that power brings with it considerable responsibility. Other stories can be enjoyed for their elements of high adventure, memorable characters, and credible settings.

Fairy Stories. Children know that fairy tales take place "Once upon a time," the hero or heroine overcomes all obstacles and is rewarded with a happy ending, and magical powers may be used to assist prince, princess, or humble person of noble worth. In addition, fairy tales usually contain good and wicked elements that are easily identifiable; the virtuous are rewarded and the wicked punished.

Certain basic elements in traditional fairy stories may also be found in contemporary fairy tales. Dorothy De Wit (4) identifies several motifs in which magic is basic. There may be the magic of smallness as in the traditional tale "Tom Thumb" or in Andersen's *Thumbelina*. The magic of sleep is important in the folktales "Briar Rose" and "Snow White and the Seven Dwarfs"; it is also important in Washington Irving's *Rip Van Winkle*. Other motifs include a magical disguise as in the folktales "The Frog Prince," and "Beauty and the Beast," and in Andersen's "The Wild Swans," and a magical ability as in the folktale "The Fool of the World," and Jane Yolen's "The Moon Ribbon."

Beginnings: Hans Christian Andersen. Charles Perrault is usually credited with publishing the first children's book of fairy tales, but it is Andersen who, a century later, is credited with writing the first fairy tale for children. While Perrault wrote down stories from the oral tradition, Andersen created new stories for theater audiences and readers. Sutherland, Monson, and Arbuthnot (15) suggest the bridge that exists between traditional tales and Andersen's work by stating that his first stories for children were "elaborations of familiar folk and fairy tales, but he soon began to allow his imagination full rein in the invention of plot, the shaping of character, and the illumination of human condition. These later creations, solely from Andersen's fertile imagination, are called literary fairy tales, to distinguish them from the fairy tales of unknown origin, those created by common folk. Andersen's work served as inspiration for other writers" (p. 215).

Andersen's "The Wild Swans" is a fairy tale that is quite similar to the Grimms' traditional tale, "The Six Swans." There is enchantment by an evil, jealous stepmother; there is also the courage and endurance of a young girl who is willing to suffer in order to free her brothers.

Others of Andersen's literary tales have been described as being symbolic of his own life. (After learning about Andersen's background, college students enjoy theorizing about these symbolic relationships.) Andersen was born in Odense, Denmark, the son of a cobbler. His father made young Hans a puppet theater and told him many of the traditional tales that later appeared in many of his stories. These pleasant years, however, were not typical of Andersen's later youth. His early experiences at school were unpleasant, and he saw his father's frustration after a pair of silk shoes that he had worked on for long hours were angrily rejected by the lady who had ordered them. (Shoes also cause a great deal of unhappiness in Andersen's "The Red Shoes.")

Andersen was fourteen when his father died; he moved to Copenhagen where he became a pupil of the Royal Theater and later returned to school to learn the writing skills he lacked. Once again he found unhappiness at school. He was larger than the other children, and the school master poked fun at his size, his looks, and his lack of knowledge. (The Ugly Duckling is also a subject of cruel jokes as he grows into adulthood.) Andersen persevered, and at twenty-three was ready to fulfill his ambition to become a writer. He began to write stories and poems about the people he observed; after a walking trip through part of Europe, he wrote a book called *Life in Italy*. With this book, Andersen began earning a substantial living from writing and his name became well known. It was the stories he wrote for children, however, that apparently gave him the most pleasure. His first book included "The Princess and the Pea" and "The Tinder Box." After these stories were published, Andersen began writing new books of fairy tales that were published nearly every year.

Andersen's tales have been widely translated and illustrated and are available both in elaborate single editions and in collections.

The transformation of the Ugly Duckling, from being cruelly ostracized by the barnyard animals to becoming the most beautiful swan in the garden lake, has been recaptured by Lorinda Bryan Cauley. Her realistic and humorous illustrations show the lifelike agony of the barnyard; every animal seems to focus contempt upon the poor duckling. Children can follow, in pictures and text, the sorrow felt by the duckling and then his realization that he is not something to be pitied. They can observe his head emerging from under his wing, not in conceit, but in wonder, as he senses his transformation.

Cauley's humorous illustrations depict the discomfort of a swan who thinks he's an ugly duckling.
From *The Ugly Duckling: A Tale from Hans Christian Andersen,* retold and illustrated by Lorinda Bryan Cauley, copyright © 1979 by Lorinda Bryan Cauley. Reproduced by permission of Harcourt Brace Jovanovich, Inc.

Nancy Ekholm Burkert has beautifully illustrated two of Andersen's stories that reflect the beauty of natural life versus the heartbreak associated with longing for mechanical perfection or metallic glitter. *The Nightingale* tells of a Chinese emperor who turned from the voice of a faithful nightingale to a jeweled, mechanical bird. He learns, however, that only the real, unjeweled bird's song can bring comfort and truth. Burkert's other Andersen tale, *The Fir Tree,* tells of a little fir tree who learns only after he is taken from the forest the significance of what he has lost.

Illustrator Susan Jeffers and author Amy Ehrlich have combined their talents to create three beautiful versions of

Andersen's tales. Jeffers's finely detailed drawings suggest a fantasy setting in *Thumbelina* and *The Wild Swans*. Her illustrations and Amy Ehrlich's retelling of *The Snow Queen* may be contrasted with another version of the same tale retold by Naomi Lewis and illustrated by Errol LeCain.

Several collections of Andersen's tales are available for sharing with children or reading independently. Eric Carle has illustrated *Seven Stories by Hans Christian Andersen* which were chosen for their appeal to young children. *Michael*

The formal castle setting, complemented by symmetry and design, seems appropriate for a tale bridging the world between old and new fantasy.
An illustration from *Fairy Tales* by Hans Christian Andersen, illustrated by Kay Nielsen. Reproduced by permission of Viking Penguin Inc.

Hague's Favorite Hans Christian Andersen Fairy Tales includes nine stories written in larger print. More extensive collections include *Ardizzone's Hans Andersen,* illustrated by Edward Ardizzone, and *Hans Andersen: His Classic Fairy Tales,* illustrated by Michael Foreman. Kay Nielsen's illustrations from a 1924 edition of Andersen's tales found in the Metropolitan Museum of Art create an older world setting in *Fairy Tales.*

Jane Yolen. Yolen has used the format of the classical folktale to weave original stories about the power of kindness, the conquest of fear, and the madness of pride. Her settings, language, and characters are similar to those in the best traditional tales. The settings in the five tales in *The Girl Who Cried Flowers* are magical places such as "on the far side of yesterday," "far to the North, where the world is lighted only by the softly flickering snow," (p. 46) and ancient Greece. The heroines and heroes are also of fairy tale quality. The heroine of "Silent Bianca" is a strange and beautiful girl with a face as pale as snow and hair as white as a moonbeam; she is not only beautiful, she is also wise. However, she does not speak as others do; her sentences must be plucked out of the air and her fragile words warmed by the hearth fire before they can be heard. In Bianca's land, there lives a king who seeks a wife who would be both beautiful and wise. The king hears of Bianca and sends his unhappy counselors, who want a girl of noble birth, to bring her to his castle. The king creates an obstacle to measure the wisdom of both Silent Bianca and his arguing counselors. Silent Bianca proves her wisdom, tricks the king's guards, marries the king, and they live happily ever after, with the king spending many hours by the hearthstone listening to the counsel of his wise and loving queen.

Six stories of proud princesses, wicked stepmothers, fair maidens, and magical spirits are found in *The Moon Ribbon and Other Tales.* The title story has a theme of love and kindness triumphing over evil and greed. A widower with a kind-hearted daughter marries a beautiful but cruel widow with two equally cruel daughters. Life becomes very unhappy for the girl when her father dies. She is overjoyed, however, when she finds a treasure, "The Moon Ribbon of Her Mother's Hair," which has special powers. When needed, it becomes a silver river taking her to her mother, a silver highway that transports her, and finally a silver red stair that leads her evil stepmother and stepsisters into the underground from where they never return.

Two other books contain short stories written as traditional tales. *The Hundredth Dove and Other Tales* contains seven stories of ice maidens, mermen, and seal maidens. A blind gypsy storyteller spins tales in the *Dream Weaver.* These tales are fragile, gossamer dreams woven to fit a particular character. As each person approaches the Dream Weaver, she takes the thread from her basket, strings the warp, and spins her tale. As the Dream Weaver puts away her loom and threads she makes this statement:

Memory is the daughter of the ear and the eye. I know you will take the dream with you, in your memory, and it will last long past the weaving. (p. 80)

The Mermaid's Three Wisdoms is a longer story with a contemporary setting that blends fantasy with reality. The fantasy character is Melusina, a mermaid, who is expelled from her undersea home when she allows a human to see her. The "real" character is Jess, who has a hearing impairment. The author creates a believable fantasy character through the reactions of this modern girl. When old magic changes the mermaid into a girl who cannot speak, Jess learns to communicate with her and together they realize the meaning of the three wisdoms:

Have patience, like the sea. Move with the rhythm of life around you. Know that all things touch all others, as all life touches and is touched by the sea. The last, I think is the most important. (p. 87)

Yolen uses the noble quest theme and the legendary characters of traditional literature to create a humorous story in *The Acorn Quest.* This gentle spoof has animal characters who somewhat resemble their traditional human counterparts: King Earthor, Sir Runsalot, and Wizard Squirrelin. These animal characters, however, frequently quarrel and have difficulty focusing on the problem of probable famine. The plot develops around the quest for a golden acorn at the edge of the world. On the journey they confront a traditional enemy, a dragon, and the human enemy, greed.

Andersen and Yolen use the basic elements found in traditional fairy tales to create new stories that are not translations or retellings of the old stories. There are, however, many elements in common, as suggested by settings in unnamed kingdoms in the distant past, heroes and heroines who are given magical powers, noble and wicked characters, rewards for virtue and punishment for wickedness. Authors who use these elements create a strong traditional bridge between old and new fantasy.

Allegory. There is a strong religious bridge between old and new fantasy. According to Bruno Bettelheim (2), "Most fairy tales originated in periods when religion was a most important part of life; thus, they deal, directly or by inference, with religious themes. The stories of The Thousand and One Nights are full of references to Islamic religion. A great many Western fairy tales have religious content; but most of these stories are neglected today and unknown to the larger public just because, for many, these religious themes no longer arouse universally and personally meaningful associations" (p. 13).

As an illustration of a religious motif in fairy tales, Bettelheim refers to the story "Our Lady's Child," recorded by the Brothers Grimm. In this German tale, the Virgin Mary takes the three-year-old daughter of a poor woodcutter to heaven where she cares for her. At the age of fourteen, the girl is given the keys to thirteen doors, twelve of which she may open, but not the thirteenth. When she cannot resist this temptation, and then lies about her actions, she is returned to earth as a mute. On earth, she suffers severe ordeals and is finally to be burned at the stake. Because her only desire is to confess her misdeed, she regains her voice and the Virgin grants her happiness. Bettelheim states, "The lesson of the story is: a voice used to tell lies

Michael Hague's illustrations complement the traditional elements of Yolen's modern tales.
Reprinted by permission of Philomel Books from *Dream Weaver* by Jane Yolen. Illustrations copyright © 1979 by Michael Hague.

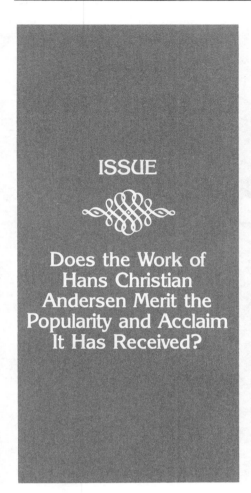

ISSUE

❧

Does the Work of Hans Christian Andersen Merit the Popularity and Acclaim It Has Received?

CRITICS DISAGREE ABOUT the literary merit of the one hundred fifty-eight fairy tales written by Hans Christian Andersen. Speaking from a favorable viewpoint, Alan Moray Williams describes the tales which have been translated into eighty-two languages: "The tales combine the freshness of vision and the innocence of childhood with the gentle irony and knowledge of human psychology that only hard experience can produce. They are racy with the homely speech of the Danish common people and warm with the beauty of the countryside" (1, p. 236). While Williams does not believe that all of the tales are equally good, he concludes "most are little masterpieces, as perfect in their way as Tanagra statuettes" (p. 237).

In contrast, Roger Sale finds little literary merit in a majority of Andersen's tales. Sale describes Andersen's work in these terms: "He aims satiric shafts, he points his morals and adorns his tales. Of all the major reputations among authors of children's literature, Andersen's is much the hardest to understand or justify . . . what is wrong with his work is, almost without exception, what is wrong with all inferior children's literature" (2, p. 64). Sale is especially critical of "The Little Mermaid" and "Thumbelina"; Sale explains that the stories are inferior because Andersen is trying to justify his own personal feelings through the actions of the characters. Sale prefers Andersen's more impersonal stories such as "The Snow Queen."

It is left to the reader and listener to decide whether Andersen's tales are magical gems which children have never quite forgotten or are inferior products of a writer's personal civil war in which the writer uses his unhappiness as an exploitable resource.

1 Williams, Alan Moray. "Hans Christian Andersen." In *Only Connect: Writings on Children's Literature,* ed. Sheila Egoff, G.T. Stubbs, and L.F. Ashley. New York: Oxford University Press, 1980.

2 Sale, Roger. *Fairy Tales and After: From Snow White to E.B. White.* Cambridge, Mass.: Harvard University Press, 1978.

leads us only to perdition; better we should be deprived of it, as is the heroine of the story. But a voice to repent, to admit our failures and state the truth, redeems us" (p. 14).

Strong religious connections may be seen in the fantasies of George MacDonald. The later works of C. S. Lewis, as well, combine mythology and theology to create a series of fantasies that may be read at several levels: there are fast-moving adventures in lands inhabited by talking animals, fauns, dwarfs, centaurs, and a wicked White Witch; there are also strong allegorical themes.

George MacDonald. The influence of the Victorian period and training as a Congregational minister combined to create a writer who used fantasy to present and condemn the state of civilization in Victorian England as well as write stories filled with religious allegory. *At the Back of the North Wind,* first published in 1871 and reissued in 1966, is about Diamond, the son of a coachman, who lives two lives. One is the harsh life of working-class London; the other is his dreamlike existence when he travels with the North Wind, a beautiful woman with long flowing hair.

MacDonald uses the North Wind to express much of his own philosophy. The North Wind tells Diamond that "Good people see good things; bad people, bad things" (p. 37). When little Diamond asks her how to reach the sweet, gentle land where it is always the month of May, the North Wind tells him that different people reach the land in different ways. Diamond clings to the back of the North Wind, with her streaming hair enfolding him, and they fly to a land filled with gentle breezes, pure water, and constant flowers. When Diamond returns, he is described as being a good boy; MacDonald tells the reader that this has occurred because Diamond has been to the back of the North Wind. MacDonald also refers to Diamond as "God's Baby." Diamond questions the reality of the North Wind, and she says, "I think . . . that if I were only a dream, you would not have been able to love me so. You love me when you are not with me, don't you?" (p. 363). The end of the story reveals Little Diamond lying quietly on the bed and suggests MacDonald's allegorical interpretation:

I walked up the winding stair, and entered his room. A lovely figure, as white and almost as clear as alabaster, was lying on the bed. I saw at once how it was. They thought he was dead. I knew that he had gone to the back of the North Wind. (p. 378)

C. S. Lewis. A professor of medieval and renaissance literature at Cambridge University, Lewis used his understanding of theology, medieval allegory, classical legend, Norse mythology, and an interest in the writings of MacDonald and E. Nesbit to create a highly acclaimed (winner of the Carnegie Medal for best children's books) and popular saga in fantasy. "The Chronicles of Narnia," beginning with *The Lion, the Witch and the Wardrobe* and ending seven books later with *The Last Battle,* tell a marvelous adventure of good versus evil. Children can enjoy the series for its high adventure, or it can be read for its allegorical significance.

While *The Lion, the Witch and the Wardrobe* is considered the first of the chronicles, it is in *The Magician's Nephew* that readers discover how the fantasy began and how the passage between the magical world of Narnia and Earth was made possible. They discover that the tree grown from the magical Narnia apple has blown over and its wood used to build a large wardrobe. This is the same wardrobe through which the daughters of Eve and the sons of Adam (*The Lion, the Witch and the Wardrobe*) enter into the kingdom, meet the wicked White Witch, and help the great lord-lion Aslan defeat the powers of evil. In *The Lion, the Witch and the Wardrobe,* readers discover the Christian allegory as Aslan gives his life to save Edmond who has betrayed them all. Aslan, however, rises from the dead and tells the startled, bereaved children that the deeper magic before the dawn of time has won. "It means that though the witch knew the Deep Magic, there is a magic deeper still which she did not know. Her knowledge goes back only to the dawn of Time. But if she could have looked a little further back, into the stillness and the darkness before Time dawned, she would have read there a different incantation. She would have known that when a willing victim who has committed no treachery was killed in a traitor's stead, the Table would

The flowing lines of the North Wind seem to enfold little Diamond.
Illustration by E. H. Shepard. *At the Back of the North Wind* by George Macdonald. Children's Illustrated Classics series. Reprinted with permission of J M Dent & Sons, Ltd.

crack and Death itself would start working backward" (pp. 132–33). From Aslan, the children learn that after they have once been crowned, they will remain kings and queens of Narnia forever.

After this initial adventure, the remaining books in the chronicle tell other fantastic tales of adventure and overcoming evil. In *The Voyage of the Dawn Treader,* three children enter the imaginary world through a picture of a ship and embark on an exciting voyage. In *The Silver Chair,* two children are called by Aslan for a special quest. They enter Narnia through a door in the wall and must overcome evil in order to free a lost prince of Narnia who is enchanted under a wicked spell.

The final Christian allegory is contained in the last book of the series, *The Last Battle*. Here the children are reunited with Aslan after their death on earth and discover "for them it was only the beginning of the real story. All their life in this world and all their adventures in Narnia had only been the cover and the title page: now at last they were beginning Chapter One of the Great Story which no one on earth has read: in which every chapter is better than the one before."

The stories in the "Chronicles of Narnia" are filled with adventures and characters that appeal to children. There are magical spells, centaurs, dwarfs, unicorns, ogres, witches, and minotaurs. Throughout the stories, there are characters who strive for high ideals and who recognize the importance of faith. People who read both mythology and the writings of Lewis will discover in his stories a strong connection with the world of traditional mythology.

Good Versus Evil. Quests for lost objects stolen by evil dragons, descents into darkness to overcome evil, and settings where lightning splinters the world and sets the stage for the battle between two opposing forces are all found in mythology and modern fantasy. Two modern authors, Tolkien and Alexander, have used their knowledge of Northern mythology to develop superb stories of good versus evil. These authors bridge the distance between the concept of the destiny of humanity as prophesied by mythical fate and the time when the old evil enchantment is finally eliminated, and humans, unaided, must guide their own destinies. With Tolkien, the reader finds himself in the Kingdom of Middle Earth where there are good and gentle hobbits who become heroes unexpectedly, cunning dwarfs, wise wizards, evil trolls, and dragons, and many other mythical creatures who have characters ranging from noble to evil. Occasionally, the hobbits show free will, but there are often feelings of fatalism as the characters dream about what is to happen or feel that a certain happening will occur. With Alexander, the reader joins humanity as the battle between the old evil and the old good enchantments is at its height. The battle revolves around the ownership of a sword that was enchanted for the good of the world. The battle between the evil Lord of Death and his forces, the Deathless Cauldron-Born, and the good Sons of Don continues until the old evil enchantment is conquered; now the enchantments can be taken away from humanity, and deeds, rather than words of prophecy, can shape its destiny.

A third author who writes about good versus evil and bridges the world between old and new mythology is Alan Garner. His writings use the magic of sun, moon, and blood from earlier, crueler times. He pits the high magic of thoughts and spells against this evil magic.

J. R. R. Tolkien. Destiny, subterranean descents out of the sunlit world, supernatural immortals, evil dragons, and rings of power are all found in Tolkien's popular stories. His writings, according to Ruth S. Noel (11), "form a continuation of the mythic tradition into modern literature . . . . In no other literary work has such careful balance of mythic tradition and individual imagination been maintained" (pp. 6–7). This balance between myth and imagination is not accidental in Tolkien's writing. Tolkien studied mythology for most of his life; he was professor of Anglo-Saxon literature at Oxford and a professor of English language and literature at Merton College. His chief interest was in the literary and linguistic tradition of the English West Midlands, especially in *Beowulf* and *Sir Gawain and the Green Knight*. Tolkien respected the quality in myths that allows evil to be unexpectedly averted and great good to succeed. This battle between good and evil is masterfully developed in the *Hobbit* and in *The Lord of the Rings,* its more complex sequel.

According to Tolkien (16), these stories were at first a philological game in which he invented languages: "The stories were made rather to provide a world for the languages than the reverse. I should have preferred to write in 'Elvish'" (p. 242). This creation of languages with their own alphabets and rules helps to make Tolkien's characters believable.

He has readers visualize, and believe in, the world of Middle Earth through careful attention to detail and vivid descriptions of setting. For example, he introduces the reluctant hobbit, Bilbo Baggins, to the challenge and promise of joining a quest to regain the dwarfs' treasures by using a dwarfs' chant:

> Far over the misty mountains cold
> To dungeons deep and caverns old
> We must away ere break of day
> To find our long-forgotten gold. (p. 37)

As the wizard Gandalf, the twelve dwarfs, and Bilbo Baggins proceed over the mountains toward the lair of the evil dragon Smaug, Tolkien describes a place where lightning splinters the peaks and rocks shiver. When Bilbo descends into the mountain dungeons to confront Smaug, Tolkien details a setting befitting the climax of a heroic quest: darkness is gradually replaced by a red light and wisps of vapor, quiet is replaced by a rumbling and gurgling noise. Ahead, in the bottommost cellar, lies a huge, red-golden dragon surrounded by precious gold and jewels.

The quest, as in traditional tales, is successful, the dragon is dead, and the goblins are overthrown. The hero retains his decency, his honor, and his pledge to help his friends.

The ring found during the hobbit's quest becomes the source for the plot in the longer, more complex *The Lord of the*

There is a strong relationship between mythology and the text and illustrations in Tolkien's books.
From *Farmer Giles of Ham* by J.R.R. Tolkien. Copyright © 1976 by George Allen & Unwin (Publishers) Ltd. Reprinted by permission of Houghton Mifflin Company.

Rings. In his foreword to *Fellowship of the Ring,* Tolkien says that he had no intention of writing a story with an inner meaning or message. The story is not meant to be allegorical. "As the story grew it put down roots (into the past) and threw out unexpected branches; but its main theme was settled from the outset by the inevitable choice of the Ring as the link between it and The Hobbit" (16, p. 6). The opposing strategies of the good wizard Gandalf versus the Dark Lord Sauron are developed in the final segment, *The Return of the King.* Many high school and college students, and other adults, have been brought back into the world of mythology through Tolkien's books.

Lloyd Alexander. The landscape and mood of Alexander's mythical land of Prydain are influenced both by vivid recollections of Wales and a knowledge of Welsh legends. Alexander's favorite boyhood stories were about King Arthur and other legends and fairy tales. When he researched the Mabinogion, a collection of traditional Welsh legends, he discovered the characters of Gwydion Son of Don, Arawn Death-Lord of Annuvin, Dallben the enchanter, and Hen Wen the oracular pig. These "Prydain Chronicles" characters present an outstanding adventure of good versus evil. Alexander tried to make the land of fantasy relevant to the world of reality. Many children may see themselves as they, like the assistant pig-keeper Taran, try to discover themselves and find their place in the world.

Alexander's books take place in a time when "Fair Folk" lived with humans, a time of enchanters and enchantments, a time before the passages were closed between the world of enchantment and the world of humans. In the first "Prydain Chronicle," *The Book of Three,* he introduces the forces of good and evil and an assistant pig-keeper, Taran, who dreams of discovering his parentage and becoming a hero. (Alexander tells the readers that people are all assistant pig-keepers at heart because their capabilities seldom match their aspirations, and they are often unprepared for what is to happen.) The forces of good include the enchanter Dallben, who reads the prophecy written in *The Book of Three,* the Sons of Don and their leader Prince Gwydion, who in ancient times voyaged from the Summer Country to stand as guardians against the evil Annuvin; and the Princess Eilonwy, descendant of enchantresses. The forces of evil are led by a warlord who "is a man of evil for whom death is a black joy. He sports with death as you might sport with a dog" (p. 22). The forces of good are aided by Hen Wen, an oracular pig who can foretell the future by pointing out ancient symbols carved on letter sticks. Alexander brings additional credibility to his characters by presenting their chronological history.

The plot of this first book is built around Hen Wen's escape and Taran and Prince Gwydion's search for her. This search is complicated by the fact that the forces of evil are also searching for Hen Wen. The war-lord wants to capture Hen Wen because she knows his secret name; this name is powerful because "Once you have the courage to look upon evil, seeing it for what it is and naming it by its true nature, it is powerless against you, and you can destroy it" (p. 209). Though evil is not destroyed, the search uncovers Dyrnwyn, the missing sword, whose power is so ancient that it was believed to be no more than a legend.

In the second book of the series, *The Black Cauldron,* Alexander reveals more about the warlord and his forces. The companions seek to find and destroy the feared cauldron in which the deathless, voiceless warriors of the evil lord are created from the bodies of warriors slain in battle. In the third book, *The Castle of Llyr,* the forces of evil try to capture Princess Eilonwy. In the fourth book, *Taran Wanderer,* Taran searches for the identity of his parents. In the final book of the chronicles, *The High King,* Alexander answers many of the reader's questions, creates the final battle between good and evil, and brings the age of enchantment to an end. Through his characters, he describes the origin of the magical harp that causes the bard Fflweddur both joy and humiliation; he develops the lineage of the enchanted sword Dyrnwyn that lies beyond the memory of living man.

Throughout his books, Alexander develops strong characters: the noble Sons of Don, the developing characters of Taran and Princess Eilonwy, and such humorous characters as the often-complaining Gurgi who brings delight with his rhymed speech—he wants no tastings of "lotions and potions" and "rumblings and crumblings." The characters gain credibility through Alexander's history of the people and of their long struggle against the forces of evil. The reader is en-

couraged to believe in the tangible objects of power because the characters place so much faith in the legend of the sword, the prophecies written in *The Book of Three,* and the fearsome black cauldron.

Interesting comparisons may be made between Alexander's Prydain Chronicles and his later adventures stressing good versus evil. The setting in *Westmark* and *The Kestrel* is later, after humanity has had an opportunity to shape its own destiny. As in the Prydain Chronicles, Alexander creates a credible world by describing the kingdom of Westmark and its rulers, drawing a detailed map of the country, and developing various characters who live in the land. The theme is also similar as the plots develop around the struggle of good versus evil and the moral dilemmas that must be faced as the characters try to find their own place in the world. The forces of good are championed by Theo, a poor printer's apprentice, who despises injustice, and Mickle, whose social conscience makes her a threat to the aristocracy. The forces of evil are represented by the king's power-hungry minister, corruption within the aristocracy, and the ultimate cruelties of war. Like the assistant pig-keeper, Taran, in the Prydain Chronicles, Theo faces both moral dilemmas and physical danger before the stories end.

Alan Garner. John Townsend (17) states that in British fantasy the most influential writer of the 1960s is Alan Garner. His stories, according to Townsend, are popular and related to traditional literature because they portray the old magic—sun,

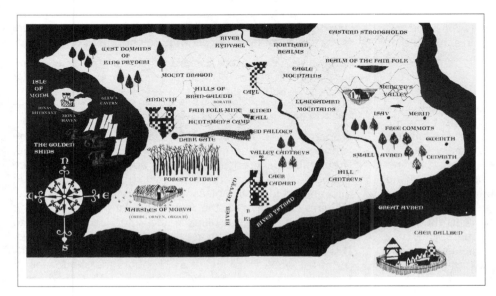

The detailed map helps develop credibility for Prydain.
From *The High King* by Lloyd Alexander. Map by Evaline Ness. Copyright © 1968 by Lloyd Alexander. Copyright © 1968 by Holt, Rinehart and Winston. Reproduced by permission of Holt, Rinehart and Winston, Publishers.

moon, and blood magic—that survives from crueler times; the high magic of thoughts and spells that checks the old magic, and the old evil against which the old magic is a potent but uncertain weapon. Garner's stories transcend time barriers by allowing present-day children to discover objects that contain ancient spells influential in old legends. The ancient masters of good and evil then emerge either to pursue or to safeguard the children.

Garner creates a believable fantasy in *The Weirdstone of Brisingamen* by placing two normal characters into the reality of an English country setting. Garner achieves credibility through the reactions of the children as they discover the powers in a tangible object, a tear-shaped piece of crystal that has been handed down through many generations. The plot then revolves around this lost weirdstone that is sought by both the forces of good and evil. The children, aided by two dwarfs, set out to return the stone to the good wizard Cadellin, its guardian. Along the way, however, they encounter the fury of the evil Grimer, the Morrigan—a shape-changing witch; giant troll women known as mara; and the wolf Managarm as they are chased through underground tunnels and across the countryside. The final confrontation reveals the power of the weirdstone.

The children meet the characters of legend and fantasy again in *The Moon of Gomrath*. Now they possess the magical "Mark of Fahla" that the evil powers of the underworld want. They are saved, however, by the intervention of the wizard Cadellin and his faithful followers.

Children who enjoy the conflicts in the traditional myths usually enjoy the continuation of the battles between good and evil and the characters who fight so diligently on either side, as represented in the modern fantasies of Tolkien, Alexander, and Garner.

Power and Responsibility. Magical words, knowing a being's or object's true name, sorcery, spells of enchantment, and the unleashing of good and evil powers are important subjects found in ancient literature as well as modern fantasy. Characters, mortal and immortal, who fight against evil must be careful not to be tempted and overcome by the powers of evil and darkness. Writers who develop stories around the theme that the greater the power, the greater the responsibility, frequently stress the importance of each action and choice as characters use magical words and cast spells of enchantment. They may develop plots suggesting that one action may influence many events either for good or for evil. These actions may be as seemingly unimportant as the choice of a correct word; but, in the world of magical powers, every word has weight and meaning.

The hero may be a fledgling wizard with the ability to speak in an ancient tongue, change his shape, or call the spirits of the dead; or he may be one born to guard the forces of good and fight against evil. Whatever their role, the characters must learn the magnitude of their own powers and realize the responsibility they have as they fight the forces of darkness. Modern fantasy stories by LeGuin and Cooper develop this theme.

Ursula K. LeGuin. Somewhere in the land of fantasy lies Earthsea, an archipelago of imaginary islands. It is a time when wizards cast their spells, and people believe in the power of enchantment. It is a time when people cannot seek the "Dragon's Run" for fear of being killed by fire-blowing winged creatures; powerful wizards, however, can speak in the dragon tongue and need not fear them. It is a precarious time when responsible wizards fear the unleashing of evil powers and try to retain a balance in the world.

LeGuin convinces the reader to suspend disbelief with her detailed descriptions of Earthsea, a world in which she places peasants, craftsmen, men who travel the sea, and a culture permeated with magic. A young boy, Sparrowhawk, who has unusual powers and great pride and jealousy lives in this world. LeGuin's series follows the life of Sparrowhawk from the time he is an apprentice until he is finally the most powerful wizard in the land.

The first book, *A Wizard of Earthsea,* tells of the young boy with powers strong enough to save his village, but with a weakness that places him in grave danger. LeGuin emphasizes the danger in pride and impatience; Gont Island's Master Wizard cautions Sparrowhawk about wanting to learn and use powers of enchantment he is not yet mature enough to understand:

Have you never thought how danger must surround power as shadow does light. This sorcery is not a game we play for pleasure or for praise. Think of this: that every act of our Art is said and is done either for good, or for evil. Before you speak or do you must know the price that is to pay! (p. 35)

Sparrowhawk, renamed Ged, does not understand the warning and goes to the School for Wizards on Roke Island. The conflict between Sparrowhawk and another apprentice leads to a duel of sorcery skills, in which Ged calls up a dead spirit and accidentally unleashes an evil being onto the world. LeGuin's description of the rent in the darkness, the blazing brightness, the hideous black shadow, and Ged's reaction to the beast help convince the reader that evil really was released. This belief in unleashed evil is important because the remainder of the book follows Ged as he hunts the shadow-beast across the islands to the farthest waters of Earthsea and develops an understanding that he is responsible for his own actions.

ISSUE

❦

Children's Reading Choices: *The Hobbit* Versus *Halloween II*

RESULTS FROM A NAtional survey of children's reading choices published in *Booklist*[1] present librarians, teachers, and parents with concerns, thought-provoking messages, some indications for satisfaction, and several reasons for dissatisfaction. Of the fifty most popular titles, eleven are modern fantasy, thirty-one are realistic fiction, two are poetry, three are picture story books, two are historical fiction, and one is traditional literature. The top ten books include two selections from modern fantasy: E. B. White's *Charlotte's Web* and Roald Dahl's *Charlie and the Chocolate Factory*. Other choices discussed in this chapter include J. R. R. Tolkien's *The Hobbit*, Madeleine L'Engle's *A Wrinkle in Time*, Beverly Cleary's *The Mouse and the Motorcycle*, C. S. Lewis's *The Lion, the Witch, and the Wardrobe*, Roald Dahl's *James and the Giant Peach*, among others.

Although these books are found on almost all recommended lists, comments made by librarians and teachers who took part in the survey should cause us to reflect upon children's choices, the quality of the library and classroom literature program, and the need to lead children into literature. The author of the article, Barbara Elleman, compares this Chosen by Children list with the 1982 juvenile best-seller list issued by Dalton Bookstores. Only three titles appeared on both lists. The Dalton list included Disney and Sesame Street spin-offs, Strawberry Shortcake, and Smurfs. Elleman concluded that the Dalton books were purchased without the guidance of teachers and librarians.

Consider the following points made in the article and conclusions reached by participants in the survey. Are these points reasons for satisfaction or dissatisfaction with the classroom and library literature program?

1. The authors on the Chosen by Children list are generally respected authors; several have won awards for literary merit.
2. In libraries where children's book interests are promoted, authors such as Aiken and L'Engle appear; it appears that children can be led to good literature.
3. Children's choices may only reflect what is being read at the time in the classroom and not actual preferences.
4. Many spin-offs from television shows and films such as *King Kong* and "Battlestar Galactica" are favorites.
5. Several librarians noted juniorhigh preference for adult horror novels such as *Halloween II*.
6. Popularity does not always mean high-quality literature.
7. Certain categories of literature are missing, including nonfiction, most classics, and fairy tales (except "Cinderella").

As you consider the implications of each of the above statements, also consider the implications of this comment by one of the adults who took part in the survey:

This survey dramatized for me the tremendous power a teacher has to raise and broaden tastes and cultural value among her students. Thirty minutes a week in the library can supplement, enrich, and stimulate a good classroom program; it cannot adequately nourish a poor one. Children who are required to read challenging books (yet encouraged to select them according to their own tastes) learn the joys of literature. Those who aren't led (or pushed) through that door may never open it on their own. (p. 508)

1 Elleman, Barbara. "Chosen By Children." *Booklist* 79 (Dec. 1, 1982): 507–9.

Older and more experienced, Ged understands the power of darkness and light in the *Tombs of Atuan*. His search for the other half of the Ring of Erreth-Akbe takes him to the labyrinth beneath the tombs of the "Nameless Ones." He meets Artha, a young priestess of these powers of evil, who keeps him captive in the tombs that can diminish his powers. The wizard changes her mind, and she and Ged discover that the only way they can leave is together. The author suggests just how much Ged has matured as he tells Artha that freedom is not easily won:

Freedom is a heavy load, a great and strange burden for the spirit to undertake. It is not easy. It is not a gift given, but a choice made, and the choice may be a hard one. The road goes upward towards the light; but the laden traveler may never reach the end of it." (p. 157)

The final adventure takes Ged to *The Farthest Shore* on a quest to discover why the springs of wizardry are running dry. He is successful, returning the vital balance of the world's equilibrium, but discovers that his power demands the ultimate responsibility if this balance is to be maintained.

LeGuin develops a character who has meaning for people living in any time or place. Ged must overcome both personal problems and outside conflicts before he reaches responsible maturity and understands the consequences of his actions.

Susan Cooper. While the great wizard of Earthsea had to learn through a nearly tragic incident that responsibility accompanies great power, Cooper's hero, Will Stanton, must learn what it means to be born with the gift of tremendous power. With Will, readers learn that the responsibility accompanying great power is a burden. Cooper, a British writer now living in the United States, weaves ancient Celtic and English traditions into her series of five books in which good must battle evil. The characters transcend time so that the battle is fought in both the present and the past. The author's technique of placing the characters on a firm foundation of contemporary reality provides a believable plot by developing characters who, when confronted with the fantastic, believe in the reality of the experience.

Quests for the objects of power (which have been made over the centuries by the craftsmen of the Light and have slept for many centuries awaiting a time when they are needed to battle against the forces of Darkness) form the thread of continuity in Cooper's stories. In her first book, *Over Sea, Under Stone,* three children visit Cornwall and find an old map disclosing a hidden treasure that could hinder the forces of Darkness. The children find the Grail but lose the manuscript that is the key to the chalice's inscriptions. This book introduces the first of the Old Ones—Merriman Lyon—and develops the responsibility

of the guardian of the Light. The recovery of one item of power is not enough, however, to still the powers of Darkness:

When the Dark comes rising, six shall turn it back; Three from the circle, three from the track. Wood, bronze, iron; water, fire, stone; Five will return, and one go alone. (p. 138)

Cooper uses this chant to develop continuity between the first and second book, *The Dark Is Rising.* The quest for the six signs that form the powerful "Circle of Signs" now becomes the responsibility of eleven-year-old Will Stanton. While born in twentieth-century England, Will has a special responsibility as the seventh son of a seventh son and the last born of the Old Ones whose powers can be used against the powers of Darkness. The relationships between the old powers and the modern hero are shown as Will transcends time, learns the secrets of the Old Ones, and regains the six circles. Early in his quest, his impatience and ignorance cause him to help the forces of Darkness. He swears he will never again use the power unless he has a reason and knows the consequences. His knowledge increases and he finally understands the magnitude of his powers. Will's inner feelings show that he at last realizes his responsibility:

Will realized once more, helplessly, that to be an Old One was to be old before the proper time, for the fear he began to feel now was worse than the blind terror he had known in his attic bed, worse than the fear the Dark had put into him in the great hall. This time, his fear was adult, made of experience and imagination and care for others, and it was the worst of all. In the moment that he knew this, he knew too that he, Will, was the only means by which his own fear could be overcome, and thus the Circle fortified and the Dark driven away. (p. 127)

Greenwitch, the third book of the series, returns the quest to the Grail and the missing manuscript. Two additional books complete the series. In *The Grey King,* Will's quest is the golden harp that has the power to awaken the six sleepers who are instrumental in the forthcoming battle between the Darkness and the Light. The final book, *Silver on the Tree,* brings the Old Ones and characters from the previous books into a final battle between the forces of Darkness and Light.

Cooper has encouraged readers to suspend disbelief by developing a strong foundation in the reality of the twentieth century. The settings are rooted in contemporary times, but the characters may rapidly change centuries. There is a tie, however, between the past and present. For example, in *The Dark Is Rising,* Will needs to go back into the past to recover the Sign of Fire. When he has fulfilled his quest, there is a great crashing roar, a rumbling, a growling, and he is back in the present, where thunder is creating earsplitting sounds. The action is

BEATRIX POTTER'S ILLUSTRATIONS FOR THIS 1902 edition of *The Tale of Peter Rabbit* demonstrate her ability to re-create animal characters with needs and feelings similar to those of young children. Her detailed drawings reflect her knowledge of animals and the English countryside. *The Tale of Peter Rabbit* was the first of a series of books written and illustrated by Potter. Other well-known books include *The Tailor of Gloucester* (1902), *The Tale of Squirrel Nutkin* (1903), *The Tale of Benjamin Bunny* (1904), and *The Tale of Mrs. Tittlemouse* (1910).

believable, and the reader feels that the old ways are actually awakening, their powers alive again.

Readers find powerful themes, characters, and plots in the books that bridge the world between traditional and modern fantasy. The authors who have been successful in this area have spent considerable time researching the world of mythology and fairy tales.

Articulate Animals

Concerned rabbit parents worry about what will happen to their family when new human folks move into the house on the hill, a mongoose saves his young master from a deadly cobra, and a mole and a water rat spend an idyllic season floating down an enchanting river. Humanized animals who talk like people but still retain some animal qualities are among the most popular modern fantasy characters. Authors such as Beatrix Potter and Kenneth Grahame have been able to create animal characters who display a careful balance between animal and human characteristics. This balance is not accidental; successful authors in this category of modern fantasy frequently write from close observations of animal life that result in understanding and loving animals.

Young children are drawn to the strong feelings of loyalty expressed by the animals as they help each other out of dangerous predicaments, stay with friends when they might choose other actions, or protect their human masters while risking their own lives. The memorable animal characters, like all good literature characters, show a wide range of recognizable

traits. Children frequently see themselves in the actions of their animal friends.

Beatrix Potter. "Once upon a time there were four little Rabbits, and their names were—Flopsy, Mopsy, Cotton-tail, and Peter" (p. 3). Children of all ages can identify this sentence as the beginning of an enjoyable story, *The Tale of Peter Rabbit.* Potter, who wrote so knowledgeably about small animals, spent many holidays in the country. Because she enjoyed observing nature and collecting objects, she brought many of her happy experiences back to the city. Included in her collections were drawings that recreated, in considerable detail, her happier life in the country. (See page 582 for a brief biography describing her sheltered and restricted Victorian life in London.) She had small pets, including a rabbit, mice, and a hedgehog, who later became very real in the stories and illustrations in her books for children. Her love for the country continued, and as an adult she purchased a farm that offered stimulation for her stories of articulate animals.

Potter's first book, *The Tale of Peter Rabbit,* began as a letter sent to a sick child. When she later submitted the story to a publisher, it was rejected. She did not let this rejection dissuade her, but had the book printed as an independent publication. When the story was accepted with great enthusiasm by young readers, the publisher asked if he might print the book.

Potter's characters may seem real to children because they show many characteristics that children themselves demonstrate. Peter Rabbit, for example, wants to go to the garden so badly that he disobeys his mother. Happiness, found in a vast store of vegetables, changes rapidly to fright as he encounters the enemy, Mr. McGregor. Children can sympathize with his fright as he tries unsuccessfully to flee. They can also respond to a satisfying ending as Peter narrowly escapes and reaches the security of his mother's love. Children know that such behavior cannot go unpunished. Peter must take a dose of camomile tea to compensate for a stomachache; his sisters feast on milk and blackberries.

The illustrations, drawn with careful detail, complement the story and suggest the many moods of the main character. Peter appears secretive as he stealthily approaches and squeezes under the garden gate, ecstatic as he munches carrots, and hopeless as he reaches the door in the wall and discovers that he is too fat to squeeze under it. In this illustration, his ears hang dejectedly, a tear trickles down his cheek, his paw is clenched in fright against his mouth, and his back paws are crossed in a huddled appearance. These moods, as depicted in the illustrations, are so realistic that children may feel a close relationship with Peter.

The Tale of Peter Rabbit is found in a reissue of the 1902 Warne publication as well as the 1979 edition of *A Treasury of Peter Rabbit and Other Stories,* published by Avenel Books.

Michael Bond. Paddington Bear is another animal character whose warmth and appeal is related to the author's ability to encourage children to see themselves in the actions of the animal. Unlike Beatrix Potter's hero who lives in an animal world, Paddington lives with an English family after they discover the homeless bear in Paddington Station. The family and neighborhood's acceptance of the bear creates a credible and humorous series of stories beginning with *A Bear Called Paddington.* The author's characterization may seem real to children because Paddington displays many childlike characteristics. Paddington often gets himself into trouble, and he tries to hide his errors from people who would be disappointed in or disapprove of his actions. He is hard to communicate with when he is in one of his difficult moods, and like a child, he is often torn between excitement and perplexity. The excitement of preparing the itinerary for a trip in *Paddington Abroad* is balanced with his difficulty in spelling hard words, his difficulty understanding why the bank does not return the same money he put in his savings account, and his final inability to read his prepared map. These difficulties create humorous episodes that are enjoyed by children in the early elementary grades. (Note how closely Paddington's characteristics correspond to characteristics of young children discussed in chapter one.)

Rudyard Kipling. While the majority of the articulate animal stories occur in the woods and farmlands of Europe and America, one series has the jungles of India as a setting. Kipling's early life spent in Bombay, India, had a great influence on his later writing. He spent much time in the company of *ayahs* (nurses) who told him the native tales about the jungle animals. His own young children were the first to hear his most famous stories, told in *The Jungle Book,* published in 1894. Here are the stories of the mancub Mowgli and his brothers, Akela the wolf, Baloo the bear, and Bagheera the panther.

The story "Mowgli's Brothers" is one of the most popular jungle stories. Kipling develops animal characters as diverse as the man-eating tiger, Shere Khan, who claims the young Mowgli as his own and Mother Wolf who demonstrates her maternal instincts as she protects the mancub and encourages him to join her own cubs. The law of the jungle is a strong element in the story as the animals sit in council and decide Mowgli's fate. There is also a strong flavor of the traditional tale; the suspense rises until old Baloo finally speaks for the mancub. Like other articulate animal tales, powerful feelings of loyalty grow as Mowgli saves the life of his old friend, Akela, by placing a branch in the Red Flower pot and producing the dreaded fire.

"Rikki-Tikki-Tavi," another story in this collection, is filled with characters, plot, and language that are excellent for oral story-telling. There are the wicked characters Nag and Nagaina—the deadly cobras who live in the garden. There is the heroic mongoose, Rikki-Tikki, the hunter with eyeballs of flame, the sworn enemy of all snakes. There are also a small boy and his parents who live in the bungalow within the garden.

The action develops rapidly as the two deadly snakes plan their battle against Rikki-Tikki and the humans. After the loyal, heroic mongoose kills Nag, he faces his most deadly peril, a female cobra avenging her mate and protecting her unborn babies. Kipling's language is excellent for the oral tradition. As the tension mounts, Rikki-Tikki asks:

What price for a snake's egg? For a young cobra? For a young king-cobra? For the last—the very last of the brood? The ants are eating all the others down by the melon-bed. (p. 117)

Also in the oral tradition, there is a happy-ever-after ending as Rikki-Tikki defeats his enemy in a last battle. In true mongoose tradition he remains on guard so there will not be another threat in the garden.

Humorous incidents and language that is most effective when shared orally are characteristics of Kipling's *Just So Sto-*

ries. Young children enjoy the language in such favorite tales as "The Elephant's Child" who lives near the banks of the "great, gray-green, greasy Limpopo River."

Kenneth Grahame. There are similarities between the motivational forces behind the development of Kipling's tales and the stories of articulate toads, moles, and water rats created by Grahame. Both authors first told their stories to their young children. Townsend (17), however, suggests that the animals in *The Wind in the Willows* are much farther along the road to humanization than are Mowgli's friends in the jungle.

Grahame creates characters who prefer the idyllic life and consider work a bore; who long for wild adventures; who demonstrate through their actions human frailties, and who are loyal to friends. The idyllic life is exemplified in the lives of Mole and Water-Rat as they explore their river world. Grahame introduces his readers to the Mole's life as spring is penetrating his dark home with a spirit of longing and discontent. As he observes the busy animals around him, he muses that the best part of a holiday is not resting but seeing other animals busy at work. Mole, true to his character, does not work but is lured by the scent of spring. Grahame brings Mole's delight and carefree joy to the reader by describing the scene in careful detail:

He thought his happiness was complete when, as he meandered aimlessly along, suddenly he stood by the edge of a full-fed river. Never in his life had he seen a river before—this sleek, sinuous, full-bodied animal, chasing and chuckling, gripping things with a gurgle and leaving them with a laugh, to fling itself on fresh playmates that shook themselves free, and were caught and held again. All was a-shake and a-shiver—glints and gleams and sparks, rustle and swirl, chatter and bubble. The Mole was bewitched, entranced, fascinated. (p. 6)

Grahame creates credibility for the adventures of his most eccentric character, Toad of Toad Hall, by taking him away from the peaceful surroundings of his ancestral home. In the Wide World, where presumably such adventures could happen, he wrecks cars, is imprisoned, and escapes in a washerwoman's clothing basket. While he is gone, the less desirable animals who live in the Wild Wood, the stoats and the weasels, take over his home. When he returns, his animal friends, brave Badger, gallant Water-Rat, and loyal Mole, help him recapture Toad Hall and tame the Wild Wood. Grahame suggests that a subdued and altered Toad, accompanied by his friends, recaptures his life of contentment along the river, at the edge of the Wild Wood, but far away from the Wide World beyond.

Grahame's writing style, as illustrated by the quote above, creates a visual image of the setting and characterization.

Many children find the text difficult to read; therefore, it may be preferable for adults to share this story orally.

Younger children may be introduced to the various characters in this book by sharing with them picture storybooks that are excerpts from chapters in *The Wind in the Willows*. Beverley Gooding has illustrated *The Open Road* and *Wayfarers All: From the Wind in the Willows* and Adrienne Adams has illustrated *Wind in the Willows: The River Bank,* all suitable for younger readers.

Russell E. Erickson. Students of children's literature may find it interesting to compare the settings, characterizations, and plot developments in Erickson's various Warton toad books, written for younger readers, with Grahame's woodland adventures. When the first book in the series, *A Toad for Tuesday,* was published, the critic for *Booklist* characterized it as a small-scale *Wind in the Willows.* First, the settings in the books are similar. Warton lives in a secure environment, under a stump in the deep woods. There are also places outside this environment filled with danger, unsavory characters, and possibilities for high adventure, if one wants to take the risk. In *Warton and the Traders,* the dangerous place is the bog, inhabited by a wildcat who eats the little creatures of the woodland, snakes who slither through murky waters, and bats who flutter through dark skies. Erikson characterizes the bog as both a dangerous place and, if one is careful, a fine place to live: "but once one learns its ways—such as where to go, and especially where *not* to go—it's a fine place" (p. 19). Second, although Erickson does not develop Grahame's more indepth and complex characterizations, there are similarities. Warton the toad is a loyal friend who is willing to leave his environment either to help a friend or to fulfill his curiosity. His brother Morton is a timid and wary creature who prefers his culinary chores and his placid environment. The wildcat is a ferocious predator who never ceases his attack on the peaceful creatures. Third, like Grahame, Erickson develops credibility for his adventures by taking his characters out of their secure environments. In *Warton and Morton,* Morton convinces his timid brother to leave home in search of culinary delights. During their search they encounter feuding muskrats and a dangerous flood. In *Warton and the Traders,* Warton leaves his peaceful forest to search for his missing aunt. Along the way he encounters wood rats who earn their living as traders, his missing aunt and a wounded fawn, and the dangers of the bog. In true heroic form, he develops a scheme that saves the bog from the fierce wildcat and helps his aunt care for the fawn. In *Warton and the Castaways* the toads are swept away in a flood

Two toads live in a secure environment under a tree stump; high adventure is found when they leave their home.
Illustration by Lawrence Di Fiori on page 6 of *Warton and the Traders* by Russell E. Erickson. Illustration Copyright © 1979 by Lawrence Di Fiori. By permission of Lothrop, Lee & Shepard Books (A Division of William Morrow & Company).

and survive a racoon's pursuit. Friendship is a strong theme in all of Erickson's books.

Robert Lawson. This winner of the Newbery award, the Caldecott Medal, and the Lewis Carroll Shelf Award has created a believable world in which animals retain their individualized characters. Unlike the river world of Mole in *The Wind in the Willows,* this world is influenced by the peculiarities of humans. Lawson (19), like other distinguished authors of articulate animal stories, spent time closely observing animals. In 1936, he built Rabbit Hill on Weston Road in Westport, Connecticut. He says that he had wanted to write a story about the animals who ate everything he planted, the deer who trampled his garden, the skunks who upset his garbage pail, and the foxes who killed his chickens. Instead, when he started to write, he found himself growing fond of Little Georgie, a young rabbit, and the other animals on the hill. He admits that he did not know who wrote the book; it happened naturally.

The resulting book, *Rabbit Hill,* presents the impact on animals from the animals' point of view. This consistent point of view allows Lawson to create believable characters, as the animals on the hill wait expectantly after they learn that new Folks are coming. They wonder if this change will bring about a renewal of older and pleasanter days when the fields were planted, a garden cultivated, and the lawns manicured. But Mother Rabbit fears that the Folks will be lovers of shotguns, traps, poison gases, and worst of all, boys.

Lawson centers much of his book around the exploits of this exuberant rabbit who retains his curiosity and love for a good chase even when his father warns him that parental indulgence and misbehavior can have swift and fatal consequences. Georgie is at first frantic when a dog traps him against Deadman's Brook. Then he is proud when he leaps across the brook, creates a record jump, and outwits the dog.

The new Folks arrive and are definitely on probation; the animals watch carefully and intentionally encounter the Folks to see how they react. The animals believe that all will be well when the owner puts up a sign, "Please drive carefully on account of small animals." They are in doubt, however, when Little Georgie has a dreadful experience with a car on the black road. When the Folks from the hill take the limp rabbit into the house, gloom settles over the animals. Is Georgie alive and, if so, why does he not appear? What terrible experiences are the Folks planning for Little Georgie? The animals learn that the new Folks are considerate and caring; there is a satisfactory ending when the animals pay tribute to their new and gentle Folks on the hill.

George Selden. Like Lawson, Selden loves the Connecticut countryside and creates animals with strong characters. His *The Cricket in Times Square,* however, has an urban setting, the subway station at Times Square. Two animal characters, Tucker Mouse and Harry Cat, are city dwellers. The other animal, Chester Cricket, arrives accidentally, having jumped into a picnic basket in Connecticut and being trapped until he arrived in New York.

Seldon tells their story from the animals' point of view and develops additional credibility by retaining some of each animal's natural characteristics: the city-wise Tucker Mouse lives in a cluttered drainpipe because he enjoys scrounging and does not consider neatness very important; Chester Cricket is a natural musician and prefers playing when the spirit moves him rather than when people want to hear him. The plot of the story develops around Chester's remarkable ability to play any music he hears and the need for returning kindness to the poor owner of the newsstand in the subway. Selden concludes his story with a natural longing that might be felt by anyone taken from his native environment. Chester becomes homesick for autumn in Connecticut and leaves the city to return home. When Tucker asks him how he'll know that he has reached home, Chester reassures him, "Oh, I'll know! . . . I'll smell the trees and I'll feel the air and I'll know" (p. 154).

This is a touching story of friendship, of longing for one's home, and of the love and understanding that can be felt between a young boy and even a tiny insect. Additional stories about these animals are found in Selden's *Tucker's Countryside, Harry Cat's Pet Puppy,* and *Chester Cricket's Pigeon Ride.* (This final book has a large format and illustrations designed to appeal to younger children.)

E. B. White. Charlotte's Web has been identified by Roger Sale (13) as "the classic American children's book of the last thirty years" (p. 258), while Rebecca Lukens (9) uses the book as a touchstone, the story around which she develops her critical standards for literature. This book, therefore, provides a fitting example for an extended discussion illustrating the techniques that an author of fantasy may use to encourage readers to suspend disbelief.

White introduces his characters into the reality of a working farm. Animals are not treated like people or given human characteristics. Instead, there is the harsh reality of a farmer's need to keep only animals that can show a profit. In this setting, Mr. Arable moves toward the hoghouse, with ax in hand, to kill the runt in a newly born litter of six pigs. Still in the realm of reality, it is the farmer's daughter, Fern, who pleads with her father to let her raise the pig. As Wilbur grows, the profitability of the farm again influences Wilbur's fate. Mr. Arable is not willing to provide for Wilbur's growing appetite. Fern again saves Wilbur but without a hint of fantasy; she sells him to Uncle Holmer Zuckerman who lives within easy visiting distance.

Wilbur's new home also begins on a firm foundation of reality as White describes the barn in which Wilbur will live and the afternoons when Fern visits Wilbur. It is on an afternoon when Fern does not arrive that White changes the story from reality to fantasy: Wilbur discovers that he can talk. With this realization, his barnyard neighbors also communicate with him. From this point on, White has laid the framework for the fantasy to follow; he carefully develops the characterization of the animals.

White's characters are consistent in actions, speech, and appearance. Wilbur, for example, frequently complains, and feels lonely, friendless, and dejected. He is a character who must be helped by others' actions. When he discovers that he is being fattened before becoming smoked bacon and ham, he acts with nonheroic behavior, bursts into tears, screams that he wants to live, and cries for someone to save him. It is not Fern who rescues him this time; instead, White answers Wilbur's needs by giving him a barnyard friend, Charlotte A. Cavatica, a beautiful gray spider. Charlotte's character exemplifies quiet manners, intelligence, and loyalty as she reassures Wilbur during their quiet talks, spins the webs that save Wilbur's life, and accompanies him on his trip to the fair.

Templeton, the barnyard rat, also has a character that is revealed through his actions. White describes in detail Templeton's actions as he creeps furtively in his search for garbage, talks sneeringly to the barnyard animals, and eats until he gorges himself. The author verifies this characterization by describing Templeton as having no morals or decency.

Through the reactions of the farm families, White allows readers to suspend disbelief about the possibility of a spider spinning a web containing words. When the local residents react in "joyful admiration" and notify their local newspaper (the *Weekly Chronicle*), White's readers tend to believe this could really have happened.

Even the final, natural death of Charlotte can be accepted by readers, because life and friendship continue through Charlotte's offspring. Wilbur understands this as he welcomes three of Charlotte's daughters to his home:

Welcome to the barn cellar. You have chosen a hallowed doorway from which to string your webs. I think it is only fair to tell you that I was devoted to your mother. I owe my very life to her. She was brilliant, beautiful, and loyal to the end. I shall always treasure her memory. To you, her daughters, I pledge my friendship, forever and ever. (p. 182)

In summary, White uses many techniques that enable readers to suspend disbelief. His characters begin in a real world before they proceed into the world of fantasy. His human characters have no unusual powers; thus, they encourage readers to believe in the action that follows. The settings are authentic and an integral part of the story, and the detailed descriptions allow readers to visualize, feel, and even smell the environment. Finally, the characterization is well developed as it reflects the natures of the animals.

Additional Articulate Animals. Readers may wish to compare White's characterization and creation of a believable story with Dick King-Smith's characterization and development of a believable plot in *Pigs Might Fly.* Like Wilbur, Daggie Dogfoot is the runt of the litter. Unlike Wilbur, Daggie Dogfoot is physically handicapped. As students of children's literature this book they may consider how the author develops a believable character; how he encourages readers to suspend disbelief; how he makes Daggie Dogfoot seem special to his fellow pigs; how he develops the framework for the pig's dream of flying; and how he secures Daggie Dogfoot's life.

Writers of articulate animal fantasies create believable and even heroic characters. *Mrs. Frisby and the Rats of NIMH* by Robert O'Brien is an excellent example of consistent point of view, characterization, setting, and theme in modern fantasy. (See chapter three for a discussion of O'Brien's book.) This story is also apparently credible for readers. Children attending a 1982 summer library program voted the book the most popular. (What influence might the movie have had on the popularity of this book?)

Younger children enjoy articulate animal stories because of the author's use of humor. Beverly Cleary develops humor through imaginative and unusual plots in stories about a mouse named Ralph. In *Ralph and the Motorcycle* Ralph lives with his family at the Mountain View Inn. Humor enters the story when Ralph discovers a boy who owns a toy motorcycle. Of course, Ralph learns to ride. His adventures continue in *Runaway Ralph.* Now Ralph is dissatisfied with life at the old hotel; when he tries to change his life, however, things do not work out as planned. In *Ralph S. Mouse,* the humor increases when Ralph finds himself at school. Cleary's stories are all within the younger child's understanding. Consequently they are good introductions to modern fantasy.

Dolls, Toys, and Inanimate Objects

When children play with dolls or talk to their stuffed animals and pretend to have conversations in return, they frequently demonstrate their belief in the human characteristics they give to their toys. The most memorable stories in this group become believable when they are told from the perspective of the toy or object and include experiences with the children who love them. By telling the experiences from the doll's point of view, an author encourages readers to suspend disbelief and feel what it must be like to live in a beautiful dollhouse or be snubbed by an elegant antique doll. Likewise, this point of view allows the author to develop the dejection of a toy placed on the garbage pile and the elation when he is rewarded for his selfless loyalty. Authors who write from a toy's perspective include such well-known names as Rumer Godden, Margery Williams, A. A. Milne, and Carlo Collodi.

Rumer Godden. Every child who loves dolls knows that a doll is only a thing unless it is loved by a child; with love, the doll becomes real. This is also Rumer Godden's philosophy. She writes books about the dolls who live in her own Observatory House and has her dolls carry on a correspondence with another old family of dolls (3).

By telling the story from the viewpoint of a doll, Godden creates the believable story of a group of small dolls who long to leave a shoebox and live in their own house. The author tells readers in *The Dolls' House* that it is not easy to be a doll. In fact, "It is an anxious, sometimes a dangerous thing to be a doll. Dolls cannot choose; they can only be chosen; they cannot 'do'; they can only be done by; children who do not understand this often do wrong things, and then the dolls are hurt and abused and lost; and when this happens, dolls cannot speak, nor do anything except be hurt and abused and lost. If you have any dolls, you should remember that" (p. 13).

Godden creates dolls who have characteristics just like their human masters; some are strong and unselfish, others are vain and disagreeable. For example, Mr. and Mrs. Plantagenet are quite ordinary dolls with extraordinary hearts; Tottie is an antique Dutch doll with a warm, friendly character; and Marchpane is an elegant nineteenth-century china doll with a vile disposition. These characteristics play an important role as the dolls express their desire for a new home. When an elegant dollhouse arrives, Marchpane declares that the house is rightfully hers and the rest of the dolls are her servants. Godden describes the dolls' increasing unhappiness until a tragedy opens the eyes of the two children who then realize the worth of their dolls. In an ending that suggests justice is related to one's conduct, Marchpane is placed under a glass dome in a museum, and Mr. Plantagenet and Tottie remain in the dollhouse where they return to good times with the children.

Margery Williams. The Velveteen Rabbit is told from the viewpoint of a stuffed toy who lives in a nursery and learns to know his master. Conversations between the rabbit and an old toy horse are especially effective, allowing the author to share her feelings about the reality of toys with the reader. When the stuffed rabbit asks the old, wise Skin Horse what it means to be real, the Skin Horse informs him that "Real isn't how you are made . . . . It's a thing that happens to you. When a child loves you for a long, long time, not just to play with, but REALLY loves you, then you become Real" (p. 17). The horse tells the rabbit that becoming real does not happen all at once; it takes a long time. Usually it happens after the hair has been loved off, the eyes drop out, and the joints are loosened; then, even if the toy is shabby, it does not mind because it is real.

The plot of the story is developed around the growing companionship between the boy and the toy. Children's reactions to this story suggest how meaningful the toy-child relationship is to young children. Teachers and librarians describe younger children's concern when the rabbit is placed in the rubbish pile because he has spent many hours in bed with his master who has scarlet fever. When the nursery fairy appears and turns the toy into a real rabbit, however, children frequently say that this is the right reward for a toy who has given so much love. These reactions suggest the credibility of a story written from a toy's point of view.

Comparisons may be made between the illustrations in three different versions of this text. The original text illustrated by William Nicholson may be compared with recent visual interpretations by Michael Green and by Ilse Plume.

A. A. Milne. Winnie-the-Pooh, or Pooh for short, according to his creator Milne (10), does not like to be called a teddy bear because a teddy bear is just a toy; Pooh is alive. The original Pooh was given to Milne's son, Christopher Robin, on his first birthday. The boy and Pooh became inseparable, playing together on the nursery floor, hunting wild animals among the chairs that became African jungles, and having lengthy conversations over tea. In addition to Pooh, the nursery contained other "real" animals including Piglet, Eeyore, Kanga and Roo. Milne's stories contain all of these nursery animals and a little boy named Christopher Robin. According to Milne (10), when he created Christopher Robin's adventures with the animals, he was thinking not only about his own son but also remembering himself as a boy.

Winnie-the-Pooh and *The House at Pooh Corner* introduce the reader to this unusual bear, his master, and his friends. The books are filled with stories about Pooh and Christopher Robin because Pooh likes to hear stories about himself: "He's that sort of Bear." Milne develops more credibility for the actions in the story by taking them out of the nursery and placing them in the hundred-acre wood where an inquisitive bear can have many adventures. Several stories relate experiences that suggest Pooh's reality: he climbs trees looking for honey and eats Rabbit's honey when he pays a visit. Through the text and illustrations, however, there is no doubt that Pooh is a toy; no real bear would be so clumsy as to fall from branch to branch or become stuck in Rabbit's doorway. Children may feel a close relationship with Christopher Robin because every time Pooh gets into difficulty it is a human child who rescues "silly old bear."

Carlo Collodi (Carlo Lorenzini). The characterization of a wooden marionette who is disobedient, prefers the joys of a playtime land to the rigors of school, and finally learns his lesson and wins his opportunity to become a real boy is similar to the experiences of Collodi, his creator. The Italian author of *Pinocchio* described himself as "the most irresponsible, the most disobedient, and impudent boy in the whole school" (3, p. 74). He also shared a bitter lesson learned in school: "From that day on I persuaded myself that if one is impudent and disobedient in school he loses the good will of the teachers and the friendship of the scholars. I too became a good boy. I began to respect the others and they in turn respected me" (p. 76).

The characterization and plot of *Pinocchio* are similar to these real-life experiences. Pinocchio wants to do only what he wants: he sells his spelling book instead of attending school, he listens to and accompanies a devious fox and cat, he goes to playtime land, and he catches donkey fever. After Pinocchio suffers this bitter lesson, he searches for his creator, Geppetto, who works to restore his health, and he even practices his reading and writing. The author tells the reader through the words of the blue fairy why he is being rewarded:

Because of your kind heart I forgive you for all your misdeeds. Boys who help other people so willingly and lovingly deserve praise, even if they are not models in other ways. Always listen to good counsel and you will be happy." (p. 193)

There are also characteristics in Collodi's writing that are similar to traditional literature. Transformation is used, for example, as Pinocchio proceeds from a wooden figure, to a puppet, to a donkey, back to a puppet, and finally to a human form. This final transformation does not occur, however, until the wooden puppet proceeds through difficult times. The influence of fable may be seen in the recognizable human traits of the cat and the fox (7).

Eccentric Characters, Preposterous Situations, and Exaggerations

Descriptions of eccentric characters, humorous associations with impossible or ridiculous situations, and tongue-twisting language are characteristics of literature that appeal to children. Mary Cordelia Berding (1) found that materials that appeal to a reader's sense of humor include repetition, plays on words, and clever and original expressions. She concluded that the best way to describe a humorous character is through vivid and graphic descriptions of dress, features, or actions. Many stories in this section illustrate these characteristics.

Tongue-twisting sentences describe the Rootabaga Country, vivid descriptions characterize an unusual heroine, and a child travels in a most unusual vehicle, a giant peach. These preposterous situations illustrate to children that reading can be fun.

ISSUE

Should A Literary Classic Be Rewritten to Conform to Society's Changing View of Childhood?

IS PINOCCHIO AN EGOTIStical and self-centered puppet who cannot, as yet, anticipate the consequences of his actions? Or is Pinocchio a lovable mischief-maker who is inherently obedient, totally innocent, and thoroughly well-intentioned? Is Geppetto a parent who displays anger, rage, and frustration when his child is disobedient and displays love and sacrifice when the child is in need? Or is Geppetto a parent who displays only love, support, and self-sacrifice? Richard Wunderlich and Thomas J. Morrissey raise issues related to changing the characters and incidents in Collodi's *The Adventures of Pinocchio* to meet the changing social definition of childhood.[1]

These researchers traced the changing characterizations and incidents found in various editions of Pinocchio since it was first published in 1883. For example, Collodi's Pinocchio was a complex figure; he was egotistical, self-centered, intractable, impudent, and rude. In the 1900s, abridged and condensed editions weakened or changed his nature by omitting episodes or cutting

them. By the 1930s, Pinocchio's mischief became a series of disconnected pranks that made Pinocchio lovable. Likewise, the incident in which Pinocchio and Geppetto are swallowed by a large fish has changed with time. In the original they were swallowed by a shark or dogfish. Later, this fearsome creature became a sea monster, a whale, and "Monstro the Whale" (Walt Disney).

Wunderlich and Morrissey conclude: "Changes in *Pinocchio* manifest changes in the social definition of childhood. And thus a literary classic, written in terms of one perception, has been tragically rejected and rewritten to conform to another" (p. 211).

Students of children's literature may read the different versions of *Pinocchio* and consider the inappropriateness or appropriateness of changes that have been made since the original publication. Are similar changes found in other children's literature classics? If changes are apparent, how do the changes influence characterization, plot development, and theme?

1 Wunderlich, Richard and Morrissey, Thomas J. "The Desecration of Pinocchio in the United States." *The Horn Book* (April 1982): 205–212.

Carl Sandburg. Readers might expect some unusual characters to be the residents of Rootabaga Country where the largest city is a village, Liver and Onions. They are usually not disappointed when they hear Sandburg's *Rootabaga Stories.* These stories, told originally to the author's own children, do lose part of their humor if they are read rather than heard. The alliteration and nonsensical names are hard for children to read themselves, but they are fun to listen to.

Sandburg begins his ridiculous situation by describing how one gets to Rootabaga Country: the rider must sell everything he owns, put "spot-cash money" into a ragbag, go to the railroad station and ask for a ticket to the place where the railroad tracks run into the sky and never come back, and then forty ways farther yet. The author tells the riders they will know they have arrived when the train begins running on zigzag tracks, they have traveled through the country of Over and Under where no one gets out of the way of anyone else, and when they look out of the train windows and see pigs wearing bibs.

The characters in Rootabaga Country have such tongue-twisting names as Ax Me No Questions, Rags Habakuk, Miney Mo, and Henry Hagglyhoagly. The stories also develop plots around tongue-twisting situations. One story about a gold buckskin whincher, for example, develops the power of a charm to control the actions of anyone who wears it. Consequently, when Blixie Bimber puts the charm around her neck, she falls in love with the first man she meets with one *x* in his name (Silas Baxby), then with a man with two *x*'s (Fritz Axanbax), and finally with a man with three *x*'s (James Sixbixdix).

Sandburg's characters frequently rely on alliteration, the repetition of an initial sound, when they talk. When the neighbors see the family selling their possessions, they speculate about where they might be going: "They are going to Kansas, to Kokomo, to Canada, to Kankakee, to Kamchatka, to the Chattahoochee" (p. 6). Likewise, when Gimme the Ax sells all their belongings, he sells pigs, pastures, pepper pickers, and pitchforks. The stories are brief enough to share with children during a short story time, but the uncommon names and the language require preparation by storyteller or oral reader.

Astrid Lindgren. An unusual and vivacious character, who wears pigtails and stockings that are of different colors, has been created by the Swedish author Astrid Lindgren, in *Pippi Longstocking.* The author relies on considerable exaggeration to develop a character who is supposedly the strongest girl in the world. She demonstrates her ability when she lifts her horse onto the porch in her house and when, in *Pippi in the South Seas,* she saves her playmate Tommy from a shark attack. She dives into the water, grabs the shark with both hands, and pulls him out of the water. She flings the shark far out to sea only after scolding him for his terrible behavior and making him promise never to do such a cruel thing again.

Pippi's unconventional behavior and carefree existence appeal to many children. She is a child who lives in a home, Villa Villekulla, all by herself. She sleeps on a bed with her feet where her head should be and decides to attend school because she doesn't want to miss Christmas and Easter vacation.

Other books that continue the adventures of Pippi Longstocking include *Pippi Goes on Board* and *Pippi on the Run.* This final book contains large color photographs that illustrate Pippi's exploits.

Additional Eccentric Characters, Preposterous Situations, and Exaggerations. A housepainter who spends his time dreaming about faraway countries and regretting that he has never hunted tigers in India, climbed the peaks of the Himalayas, dived for pearls in the South Seas, or joined an expedition to the North or South Pole is the unusual character created by Richard and Florence Atwater. Mr. Popper is granted an unusual wish when the Drake Antarctic Expedition sends him a live penguin. This is only the beginning of the excitement in *Mr. Popper's Penguins.* The authors' description of Captain Cook, the penguin, makes him unique. He struts around pompously with his natural black tailcoat dragging behind his feet, prefers to sleep in the refrigerator, and causes havoc as he and Mr. Popper promenade down the avenue. A female penguin, Greta, and a batch of penguin chicks create financial problems and additional preposterous situations. The authors, through their comparisons of the serious manner of Mr. Popper and the ridiculous behavior of his penguins, develop humorous characters.

In tales of modern fantasy, eccentric characters frequently go on absurd journeys. Caractacus Potts, inventor and restorer of an antique car in Ian Fleming's *Chitty Chitty Bang Bang,* is an unusual fellow whose inventions allow him to take a preposterous journey. The author creates a humorous situation by describing inventions that don't work as planned. A candy whistle attracts dogs who demolish a candy factory, and a haircutting machine tears the hair off a customer's head. Finally, Potts purchases an old car that his children love, and his prospects change. He creates a magnificent car with special powers: it can float on the water or sail through the air. Potts and his children and Truly Scrumptious have a fantastic adventure as they follow Baron Bombast's men to Vulgaria, save Grandpa Potts from kidnappers, and free the children of Vulgaria.

While the Potts family traveled to a fantasy kingdom in an unusual car, Charles, Carey, and Paul visit their mother in London and go to a South Sea island merely by turning a brass knob and floating through space on their bed. Mary Norton's *Bed-Knob and Broomstick* is the story of Miss Price, who practices magic, and three children who are entranced by the possibilities of a journey to distant places on their unusual vehicle.

Riding through the air in remarkable cars and on brass beds with glowing knobs may not seem as unusual as floating through the air inside a huge peach propelled by five hundred and two seagulls. This is the fantastic situation created by Roald Dahl in *James and the Giant Peach.* James is an unhappy child who lives with two aunts who mistreat him. Life changes when he becomes the owner of some green magical things that can change his life. When he spills the green things under the peach tree, he thinks that life will go on as miserably as before. Miraculously a peach appears on the top of the tree and grows larger and larger until it is as big as a small house. James crawls inside and discovers unusual characters waiting there: a grasshopper, a ladybug, a centipede, an earthworm, and a silkworm, all many times their normal size. Their adventures begin as the peach rolls away from the yard; James tries to find a way to propel it into the air. With its fresh, original qualities, this story is thoroughly enjoyed by children.

Writers of modern fantasy are frequently influenced by their knowledge of and their admiration for traditional literature. This is seen in the creation of Pamela L. Travers's preposterous nanny, *Mary Poppins*. After almost fifty years Travers has written a new tale about Mary's escapades. The plot in *Mary Poppins in Cherry Tree Lane* revolves around the magical happenings that occur when Mary Poppins and the Banks children go to the park on Midsummer Eve. An interview with Travers (12) reveals a strong relationship between those magical happenings and Travers's background. She identifies the ancestors of Mary Poppins as myths, legends, fairy tales, and nursery rhymes. In addition to a childhood rich in story and poetry, she grew up in a family where imagination and storytelling was important. (Are these influences and traditional literature qualities apparent in the characterization and plot development in *Mary Poppins in Cherry Tree Lane*?)

Strange And Curious Worlds

There are other worlds just as strange as Rootabaga Country or the inside of a giant peach. While reaching the village of Liver and Onions required riding on an unusual train, traveling to the curious world created by Lewis Carroll requires falling down a rabbit hole. James Barrie's "land of lost boys" is entered, not by descending into the earth, but by sprinkling oneself with pixie dust, believing, and soaring into the sky. Roald Dahl's strange world is reached by riding on a chocolate river; Norton Juster's curious land is discovered by getting into a toy car and driving through a tollbooth.

Lewis Carroll. One can get to a very strange and curious kingdom by going slowly down a rabbit hole, following an underground passage, and entering a tiny door into a land of cool fountains, bright flowers, and unusual inhabitants. The guide into this world is also rather peculiar; he is an articulate white rabbit who wears a waistcoat complete with pocket watch.

It may be even more remarkable that this world of fantasy was created by a man who has been described as being dreadfully shy with adults, having a tendency to stammer, and displaying prim and precise habits. Charles Lutwidge Dodgson (Lewis Carroll) was a mathematics lecturer at Christ Church, Oxford, during the sedate Victorian period. Warren Weaver (18) describes the life of this Victorian don: "Dodg-

son's adult life symbolized—indeed, really caricatured—the restraints of Victorian society. But he was essentially a wild and free spirit, and he had to burst out of these bonds. The chief outlet was fantasy—the fantasy which children accept with such simplicity, with such intelligence and charm" (p. 16). Dodgson may have been shy with adults, but he showed a very different personality with children. He kept himself supplied with games to amuse them, made friends with them easily, and enjoyed telling stories.

A story told on a warm July afternoon to three young daughters of the dean of Christ Church made Carroll almost immortal. As the children—Alice, Edith, and Lorina Liddell—rested on the riverbank, they asked for a story and the result was the remarkable tale that later became *Alice's Adventures in Wonderland*. Even the first line of the story is reminiscent of a warm, leisurely afternoon:

Alice was beginning to get very tired of sitting by her sister on the bank and having nothing to do: Once or twice she had peeped into the book her sister was reading, but it had no pictures or conversations in it, "And what is the use of a book" thought Alice, "without pictures or conversations?" (p. 9)

From that point on, however, the day becomes one of wonder as Alice sees a strange white rabbit muttering to himself and follows him down, down, down. This is just the beginning of her adventure into a curious world where the unusual is the ordinary way of life. Size is changed by drinking a substance; strange animals have a "Caucus-race" where there is no beginning and no finish and everyone wins; a hookah-smoking caterpillar gives advice; the Dormouse, the March Hare, and the Hatter have a very odd tea party; the Cheshire Cat fades in and out of sight; and the King and Queen of Hearts conduct a strange trial.

These strange adventures have a broad appeal to children because, according to Weaver (18), childhood is universal and "Something of the essence of childhood is contained in this remarkable book—the innocent fun, the natural acceptance of marvels, combined with a healthy and at times slightly saucy curiosity about them, the element of confusion concerning the strange way in which the adult world behaves, the complete and natural companionship with animals, and an intertwined mixture of the rational and the irrational. For all of these, whatever the accidents of geography, are part and parcel of childhood" (p. 6).

In her reactions throughout the book, Alice reveals a natural acceptance of the unusual. When she finds a bottle labeled "Drink Me," she does so without hesitation. When the White Rabbit sends her to look for his missing gloves, she thinks to herself that it is queer to be a messenger for a rabbit, but she goes without question. During her adventures in this strange land, she does, however, question her own identity. This confusion is expressed in her answer to the Caterpillar when he opens their conversation by asking, "Who are you?" Alice replies, "I—I hardly know, Sir, just at present—at least I know who I was when I got up this morning, but I think I must have been changed several times since then . . . . I can't explain myself. I'm afraid, Sir, because I'm not myself, you see" (p. 23).

The language of Carroll is appealing to children, especially if it is read to them, but they do have difficulty reading the stories for themselves, and some of the word plays are difficult for them to understand. Carroll's version for younger children, *The Nursery "Alice,"* is written as though the author were telling a story directly to children. The introduction to "The Queen's Garden" reads

This is a little bit of the beautiful garden I told you about. You see Alice had managed at last to get quite small, so that she could go through the little door. I suppose she was about as tall as a mouse, if it stood on its hind-legs; so of course this was a very tiny rose-tree: and these are very tiny gardeners. (p. 41)

Carroll is noted for his nonsense words as well as his nonsensical situations. The meanings of some words he claimed even he could not explain; others he did. Myra Cohn Livingston

(8) quotes a letter written by Carroll in which he explains some words in "Jabberwocky":

I am afraid I can't explain "vorpal blade" for you—nor yet "tulgey wood:" but I did make an explanation once for "uffish thought"—It seems to suggest a state of mind when the voice is gruffish, the manner roughish, and the temper huffish. Then again, as to "burble"; if you take the three verbs, "*b*leat," "m*u*rmur" and "war*b*le," and select the bits I have underlined, it certainly makes "burble": though I am afraid I can't distinctly remember having made it that way.

The explanation of the appeal of Carroll's nonsensical characters and fantasy both to himself and to children may lie in a quote from a letter he wrote in 1891:

In some ways, you know, people that don't exist are much nicer than people that do. For instance, people that don't exist are never cross: and they never contradict you: and they never tread on your toes! Oh, they're ever so much nicer than people that do exist!

James Barrie. Peter Pan, the classical flight of the imagination into Never Land, was first presented as a play in 1904. The author begins his fantasy in the realm of reality. He describes the children in their nursery and Mr. and Mrs. Darling preparing to leave for a party. He quickly changes into the world of fantasy when the parents leave the house and enter a house down the street. Peter Pan and Tinker Bell enter the children's bedroom looking for Peter's lost shadow. This is the beginning of an adventure in which the Darling children fly, with the help of fairy dust, to Never Land, that kingdom which is "second to the right and then straight on till morning" (p. 31). There they meet the lost boys—children who fall out of their prams when the nurse is not looking—and discover that there are no girls in Never Land because girls are too clever to fall out of their prams. Along with Peter Pan, who ran away because he didn't want to grow up, the children have a series of adventures in Mermaids' Lagoon, with Tinker Bell, and against their archenemy Captain Hook and his pirates. The children finally decide to return home and accept the responsibility of growing up.

Barrie's descriptions of Mermaids' Lagoon encourage readers to visualize this fantasy land: "If you shut your eyes and are a lucky one, you may see at times a shapeless pool of lovely pale colours suspended in the darkness; then if you squeeze your eyes tighter, the pool begins to take shape, and the colours become so vivid that with another squeeze they must go on fire. But just before they go on fire you see the lagoon. This is the nearest you ever get to it on the mainland, just one heavenly moment; if there could be two moments you might see the surf and hear the mermaids singing" (p. 111).

His settings seem real, and so do his characters; they may be especially real to children who do not wish to grow up. The

A tea party with unusual guests adds to Alice's confusion. From *The Nursery "Alice"* by Lewis Carroll. Illustrated by John Tenniel. Published by Macmillan Publishing Co., 1890, 1979.

reader who does not want to take on the responsibility of adulthood may sympathize with the adult Wendy who longs to accompany Peter Pan but cannot. The book closes on a touch of nostalgia, as Peter Pan returns to claim each new generation of children who are happy and innocent.

Little People

Traditional folktales and fairy tales describe the kingdoms of trolls, gnomes, and fairies; Andersen wrote about tiny Thumbelina who slept in a walnut shell; and Tolkien created a believable world for the hobbit. There are fantasy worlds of little people who closely resemble the human race; they are miniature people living either in their own kingdoms or on the fringe of the larger human society.

Carol Kendall and Mary Norton are authors who bring authenticity to the world of little people. Kendall creates an isolated world inhabited totally by little people. The conflict in one story results from a protest against conformity and danger from an enemy who is small like themselves. There is an allusion to magic when the swords found in the ancient treasure glow to warn of approaching danger. In contrast, Norton creates a group of little people who exist in a human world. Their plots frequently revolve around the characters trying to escape the dangers presented to them from the world of humans.

Carol Kendall. In the year of Gammage 880, readers discover the tranquil and secure valley of the Watercress River. In writing *The Gammage Cup,* Kendall creates a new world, the Land between the Mountains, in which little people live in twelve serene towns with names like Little Dripping, Great Dripping, and Slipper-on-the-Water. The author gives credibility to the land by tracing its history, describing the neat houses, and creating a people who have lived in the valley for centuries.

Through her characters, the author describes two types of valley residents. There are the Periods who display smug conformity as shown by their similar clothing, insistence on neat houses, and similar attitudes and values. In contrast, there are five Minnipins—referred to as "Oh Them"—who insist upon being different. Gummy roams the hills rather than have a suitable job; Curley Green paints pictures and wears a scarlet cloak; Walter the Earl digs for the ancient treasure; Muggles refuses to keep her house organized; and Mingy questions the rulers' authority. The conflict between the two sides reaches a climax when the five Minnipins refuse to conform to one standard and decide that they would rather outlaw themselves, leave their homes, and become exiles in the mountains rather than conform to the Periods' wishes.

Kendall allows nonconformity to save the valley; the Minnipins discover the ancient enemy, the Mushrooms or Hairless Ones, who have tunneled a way into the valley through an old gold mine. These five exiles also rally the villagers and lead the Minnipins in a glorious victory over the enemy. At this point the exiles return to their homes as heroes, and the wisdom of Muggles is finally realized.

Kendall uses similar techniques to encourage readers to suspend disbelief in *The Firelings.* She creates folklore expressed in myths and tall tales; she develops a history engraved on Story Stones; and she describes the government and details of the setting on the slope of Belcher, a volcano. Her intricate description of the Firelings' history sets the framework for the plot. This history describes a previous eruption of Belcher and tells how the people tried to escape through a lost passage, the Way of the Goat. In their past, the people have sacrificed a child to appease the volcano. This began the chain of events that finally allows the Firelings to escape: an unwanted boy runs away because he fears he will be the sacrifice; his actions result in the rediscovery of the Way of the Goat; and the Firelings escape. It is interesting to compare the theme, characterization, and detailed histories and settings in *The Gammage Cup* and *The Firelings.*

Mary Norton. The little people in Norton's stories do not live in an isolated kingdom of their own but are found in "houses which are old and quiet and deep in the country—and where the human beings live to a routine. Routine is their safeguard. They must know which rooms are to be used and when. They do not stay long where there are careless people, or unruly children, or certain household pets" (p. 9). Norton persuades readers to suspend disbelief by developing a foundation firmly planted in reality. The country house is described along with a clock that has not been moved for over eighty years. There are also people living in the house who see and believe in *The Borrowers.*

In addition to grounding the story in reality and having normal characters believe in them, Norton tells her stories through the viewpoint of the characters who are only six inches high. By describing the setting through their eyes, their reactions to the objects around them, and their fear of normal-sized people, the author encourages readers to believe in them. Their size forces them to lead a precarious life by borrowing their needs, food, and furnishings from the human occupants of the house. This need creates danger when the Clock father is seen by a boy. The book reaches an exciting climax as the housekeeper vows to have the Borrowers exterminated by all available means; the rat-catcher arrives complete with dogs, rabbit snares, sacks, spade, gun, and pickax. The author again encourages readers to suspend disbelief through the effort made to catch the little people. It is the boy's reaction, though, as he stealthily takes an ax and desperately tries to dislodge the grating from the brick wall, that convinces readers that there are little people waiting in the shadows trying to escape.

What happens to the Clock family after they are discovered by Mrs. Driver and are forced to escape from the house? The next book in the series, *The Borrowers Afield,* begins as the Clocks move from their apartment to the world of field and hedgerow. There are dangers and excitement as Arrietty discovers "days when the fields were drowned in opal mist and spiders' webs hung jeweled in the hedges" (p. 144). Arrietty meets relatives about whom she has only heard stories and is pleased when her family must again head for the out-of-doors and the freedom she has grown to love. Their continued adventures are found in *The Borrowers Afloat, The Borrowers Aloft,* and *The Borrowers Avenged.*

Additional Stories about Little People. Jane Louise Curry creates a world of perfect little people in a miniature environment where every detail is flawless. The heroine in *Mindy's Mysterious Miniature* purchases an old cobweb-covered dollhouse at a farm auction. The author makes the reader believe in the setting because the furniture is described as too perfect; the scale is too accurate: "You see either the little table isn't doll furniture, or it's made from a kind of wood that doesn't exist . . . the table is made of . . . well, I guess you'd call it miniature wood. But there is no such thing" (p. 39). The mystery persists; the father believes the only solution is that real furniture had been shrunk, but that is also impossible. The mystery deepens when Mindy's neighbor recognizes the house as a replica of her own family house that had disappeared in 1915. When Mindy and her neighbor solve the mystery, they can do nothing about it; they find themselves trapped inside the dollhouse and transported to a miniature village, Lilliput U.S.A. They discover little people, like themselves, who have been living in the miniature house for years. They also find a mad inventor with a machine that can turn real houses and people into miniatures. Mindy provides the solution to their problem and eventually tricks the inventor into returning them to their original size.

These stories are successful because the authors use many of the techniques that encourage readers to suspend disbelief. There is an internal consistency developed as the stories are told through the viewpoint of the little people. Sights, sounds, smells, and experiences seem original and authentic as the reader looks at the world with this new perspective.

Friendly Presences, Ghosts, and Goblins

There may be other presences in a quiet country home aside from Borrowers; there may be friendly presences who love their home and their descendants so much that they return from generations past. There may even be hobgoblins who live in the house to protect it for loved ancestors. But, there may also be creatures of the "Otherworld" whose only joy is creating havoc in a human world. Stories in this section contain elements of folklore and elements from the historic past.

Lucy Boston. The winner of the Lewis Carroll Shelf Award for *The Children of Green Knowe,* Boston uses her own historic manor house at Hemingford Grey near Cambridge as the setting for her stories. In 1939 she purchased this old home, then restored it and the gardens to match their original beauty. The home and way of life experienced by past generations provided ideas for a series of stories written about an old manor house and the friendly presences who return there from generations past.

The first of the series, *The Children of Green Knowe,* introduces the house, its owner Mrs. Oldknowe, her great-grandson Tolly, and the children who have previously lived in the house. Boston describes the house through the eyes of Tolly, a lonely, shy boy who comes to live with his great-grandmother. Through his vision, the reader is encouraged to see an old house with furnishings similar to those found in a castle. The past becomes alive for Tolly as children who have lived in the house in generations past come back to play with each other and bring vitality to the house and gardens. Readers are not surprised by these actions because great-grandmother Oldknowe expects the children to return and enjoys having them visit. The author allows readers to discover the people in the past through the stories Mrs. Oldknowe tells Tolly.

In *Treasure of Green Knowe,* Tolly happily returns to Green Knowe during his school holiday. He cannot wait to see "the others" (he doesn't want to call them ghosts), and spend time in the old home that is "like living in a book that keeps coming true" (p. 22), where "children could play hide and seek from one century into another" (p. 12). He immediately notices, however, that something is gone; his favorite painting of the children from another time is not in the house. Tolly is horrified when he learns that the painting of the children is on exhibition, and worse, his great-grandmother, due to finances, is considering selling it. Tolly learns that in the past the family's jewels were hidden and never found, and he is convinced that he can find them somewhere in the house. He has a marvelous holiday as he searches for the jewels, meets children from the past, and finally discovers the hiding place of the missing treasure.

There is now enough money; his great-grandmother will not need to part with the painting.

Other books in this series include *The River at Green Knowe, A Stranger at Green Knowe,* and *An Enemy at Green Knowe.* In all of the stories, ancestors return because someone wanted to keep their memories alive.

Additional Stories about Friendly Presences, Ghosts, and Goblins. Bumps in the Night can be very frightening, especially if the thunder is clapping and lightning is flashing. In a story for younger children, Harry Allard tells the humorous tale of Dudley Stork who hears something go bump! bump! bump!, feels something wet touch his beak, and hears the television going on and off. When he asks advice from his friend Trevor Hog, he is told he must have a seance. The author describes a night that is just right; thunder and lightning again provide the background. The animals are startled when the medium goes into a trance that produces Donald the Horse. At first they are frightened, but they talk to Donald and discover that he had previously lived in the house; he feels it is lonely being a ghost and asks if he can come and visit again some night. They enjoy each other and no one is ever scared at night again, not even when owls hoot, doors bang, or things bump!

William Hooks's *Mean Jake and the Devils* is a contest of wits between Three Devils—Big Daddy Devil, D.J. or Devil Junior, and Baby Deviline—and Mean Jake, who is forced to wander the swamps because he is not allowed to enter either heaven or hell. The witty dialogue creates more humor than fright during this contest.

Older children who enjoy stories about ghosts and goblins like the humorous pranks of K. M. Briggs's *Hobberdy Dick* as he either helps tenants he likes or interferes with the actions of people he dislikes. Mollie Hunter's creature of the "Otherworld" in *The Wicked One* also provides interesting reading in a story that combines both suspense and some humorous events.

Time Warps

Children who read stories based on time warp themes discover that there are more things in this world than progress and theories about the future. Symbols from the past tie past, present, and future, and heroes and heroines travel through time to a distant past or see a future yet to materialize. Authors use tangible objects and buildings that have an aura of indestructibility; they have witnessed the past and will exist in the future.

The stories may allow children to consider what might have happened in the same place hundreds of years ago or to think about what the future might hold for others who stand on that same spot in the late twenty-first century.

Margaret J. Anderson. History, as well as the future, is not just kings, parliaments, and cathedrals. Instead, according to Anderson, it is the ordinary people, the villagers and the townspeople. Her fantasies deal with these folk; she takes twentieth-century children through time warps where they become involved with the hopes and dangers experienced by the common people of the time.

Anderson was inspired to write her first time warp fantasy when she and her family spent a year in England and lived in Random Cottage, a two-hundred-year-old house. The author develops credibility by beginning *To Nowhere and Back* in the reality of the countryside as a mother and daughter go for a walk and find a cottage with sagging doors and thatched roof. The author describes the house and lane in detail as the two people continue their sightseeing. This description becomes important later, when Elizabeth finds herself drawn back to the same location. This time when she walks down the path, the setting changes. Instead of small fir trees, she sees tall trees with branches that block out the overhead light, the path is well trodden, and the cottage is neither broken down nor deserted. Anderson's ability to depict a setting from another time complete with cottage and a large, loving family makes the experience believable. She allows her heroine to become one of the family when she is touched by the child from the past. Although the two children become one person, Elizabeth can think, view her surroundings, and express her own feelings. She is drawn to the family but frightened by the drudgery, poverty, and ignorance of the time. This ignorance is especially frightening to Elizabeth; the people know nothing outside their own lives and she realizes that this kind of ignorance could cause an evil fear. Ann is also drawn toward the life of the twentieth-century girl who has opportunities to read, write, and learn. Ann makes the decision when the time finally comes for a choice of times in which to live.

Anderson's other time-warp journeys, *In the Keep of Time* and *In the Circle of Time,* take place in Scotland. These stories also begin on a strong foundation of reality. The books contain symbols that tie past, present, and future; tangible objects have an aura of permanence and portray a feeling of having witnessed the passing of time and holding many secrets. In *To Nowhere and Back,* it is the tree-lined path and the old cottages. Within *In the Keep of Time,* it is the ancient Smailholm Tower—a border keep built in ancient times when Scotland was at war with England—that allows the children access to past and future. The same tower plus The Stones of Arden—

an ancient stone circle comprised of massive twelve-foot-high stones—create the opportunity for a journey in time through *In the Circle of Time*. In addition to time symbols, each story contains some occurrence that allows the change to take place: a child is touched by a person from another time; a key glows when the moment is right for the children to walk through a door and enter another time period; and mists encircle the stones in a dense fog when the children are brought into the future.

The characters are believable in Anderson's time warp stories; this is true whether they live in the past, present, or future. The same physical settings are described in detail; readers understand the changes that have taken place over time. Throughout, the power of love, understanding, and friendship among people, even across the years, is a strong theme in Anderson's stories.

Andre Norton. Interests in history, legend, science, and helping children overcome present-day problems are found in Norton's fantasies. Two major areas, fantasies dealing in time warps and science fiction, are included in her popular books.

Norton uses time warp stories effectively to help her heroes and heroines conquer personal problems in their modern lives; they frequently go back in time and successfully overcome a problem. This experience gives them the courage to face a crisis in their own lives. Strong values from the past frequently help children shape their own destinies.

Norton creates credibility by establishing a strong foundation in reality before allowing her characters to enter a time warp. In *Red Hart Magic*, two children, Chris and Nan, resent their parents' marrying, and the problem increases when the parents travel on business and leave the children with an aunt. Life is becoming intolerable—the children are unhappy with each other and with schoolmates who try to bully them. At this point the author allows Chris to find a perfect miniature of an old English inn in a Salvation Army store. The miniature is brought into their home, and the children discover they have shared a most unusual dream. Did they dream or did they go back to the inn during the time of Henry VIII? Did they save a priest from discovery and imprisonment? They go back to the inn three times during different periods in English history. These experiences develop the children's confidence, and they use values developed in their experience to help them solve contemporary problems. Their greatest discovery, however, is when they decide that trying to make a real family is worthwhile.

The foundation of reality in Norton's *Lavender Green Magic* is based on the problems in a family's life: the father is missing in Vietnam, the three children must live with unknown grandparents, and they are the only black children in their classes. The vehicles for a trip in time are found in their grandparents' home and yard. A dream pillow embroidered with two mysterious patterns allows one of the children to dream about how to travel through an overgrown maze planted in 1683. The author encourages readers to suspend disbelief by describing the maze from the children's viewpoint. As they proceed through it, they notice a change: it is no longer cold; it is warm, and flowers are blooming. At the center of the maze is a lovely garden, an old house, and the woman, Tamar, in Puritan attire. The children are happy as they talk to her and accept herbs that she says will fight evil. The author allows the children to discover an evil element in the 1600s when one of the children sleeps on the other side of the pillow. The contrasts are striking as the maze looks different, the bushes appear evil, and the children meet a very different woman, Hagar, at the center of the maze. Through their time travels, the children solve the mystery of the Dimsdale curse, discover that good is stronger than evil, find a way to preserve their grandparents' home, and resolve their own discontent. Norton's stories tie the past with the present because they stress overcoming personal problems.

David Wiseman. Educator and historian David Wiseman combines his knowledge of Cornwall and the burial ground at the mining parish of Gwennap to create a time warp story with a fast plot, memorable characters, and authentic setting. In *Jeremy Visick* the author develps credibility by placing the story into a contemporary setting where twelve-year old Matthew, who is characterized as boyish, lively, naughty, likable, and moody, is drawn to an old cemetery and a tombstone enscribed with the words: "And to Jeremy Visick, aged twelve years, whose body still lies in Wheal Maid" (p. 14). The author ties the plot into mining history during Matthew's discussions with a neighbor who describes the old mines and the disasters that took place over one hundred years ago and during a history assignment that requires students to investigate the Cornish family whose men were killed in the accident. Detailed descriptions of Matthew's interactions with the earlier family, the mine shaft as it would have appeared, the terror created by the accident, and Matthew's frantic search for an escape route from the nineteenth-century accident create a credible and exciting time warp story.

An interest in family history provides the framework that allows Wiseman's heroine in *Thimbles* to move across time as she goes from the present back to 1819. Her discovery of two thimbles—one gold and one worn metal—in her grandmother's trunk creates the tangible objects that tie the past and the present. When she finds herself back in the earlier time, she is using the metal thimble to finish a cap of liberty for a protest march demanding the right to vote. Wiseman's detailed historical settings and concerns of the characters for the issues of the times create a believable time warp fantasy. Wiseman, like many other authors of time warp fantasies, uses the past to help contemporary characters in their personal and social development.

These time-warp stories suggest a positive relationship between people of the past and present. They give children an opportunity to see the continuity in their own lives, a continuity that reaches centuries into the past and moves into the future.

Science Fiction

Authors of modern fantasy discussed so far alter one or more of the literary elements from what is expected in the real world. To create credibility in this altered condition they follow a logical framework that relies on internal consistency, develop detailed settings, allow real characters to accept the fanciful nature of the plot, create a language and a history for the inhabitants, and/or use real objects found in both reality and fantasy. These authors may have relied on magical powers and magical objects to develop their fantasies.

Writers of science fiction also alter literary elements from what is expected in the real world. They, however, rely on hypothesized scientific advancements and technology to create their plots. In order to achieve credibility, science fiction authors provide detailed descriptions of these "scientific facts," describe characters who believe in the advanced technology or the results of advanced technology, and create a world where science interacts with every area of society.

Science fiction written for younger children frequently emphasizes the adventure associated with traveling to distant galaxies or encountering unusual aliens. Stories for older readers frequently hypothesize about the future of humanity and stress problem solving in future societies.

Roland J. Green (5) traces the emergence of the popularity of science fiction from the mid-1800s through the present-day explosion of interest. Jules Verne wrote the first major science fiction in 1863; he constructed his stories around technology and inventions without attempting to develop a society around them. The second major influence occurred in the late nineteenth century with the writings of H. G. Wells. His writings, according to Green, differed from those of Jules Verne in that they included the systematic "extrapolation of social trends to create a detailed picture of a future society, revolutionary inventions, interplanetary warfare, and time travel" (p. 46).

Science fiction writing of the 1920s was influenced by the growth of magazines such as *Amazing Stories,* which expanded until World War II began. The next stage of development occurred, according to Green, in 1938 when John W. Campbell, Jr., became the editor of *Astounding Science Fiction.* His editorship was considered influential; he insisted upon the development of characterization, plausible science and technology, and logical speculation about future societies in all the stories published in the magazine. In addition, he encouraged science fiction writers such as Robert A. Heinlein and Isaac Asimov.

In the 1960s, an increasing number of authors began to write science fiction stories; these were more suited to older children and young adults because the plots often relied on a developed sense of time, place, and space. In the late 1960s, it became a topic of interest for university and high school courses. The media were extremely influential during this period: the movie *2001: A Space Odyssey* and the television program "Star Trek" created a devoted science fiction audience and suggested the imaginative potential of these subjects. This interest is still apparent in the 1980s; audiences flock to pictures such as *Star Wars, The Empire Strikes Back,* and *E.T.* Young people read and reread the paperback versions of these movies. Writers such as Madeleine L'Engle, Ann McCaffrey, and John Christopher are writing high-quality science fiction for young people.

Madeleine L'Engle. Do we all need each other? Is every atom in the universe dependent on every other? These are some of the issues that L'Engle's characters face as they travel the cosmos, face the problems of being different, fight to overcome evil, understand the need for all things to mature, and discover the power of love.

It is interesting to note L'Engle's thoughts about herself as she wrote *A Wrinkle in Time:* "I was trying to discover a theology by which I could live, because I had learned that I cannot live in a universe where there's no hope of anything, no hope of there being somebody to whom I could say, 'Help'!" (20, p. 254). In *A Wrinkle in Time* L'Engle creates characters who help each other. Meg Murry, the daughter of eminent scientists, feels a close relationship with her brother Charles Wallace, who is considered backward and strange by the villagers. In turn, Charles Wallace has very special powers; he can probe the minds of his mother and sister, and he is also extremely bright.

Through the author's characterization of Charles Wallace and Meg, the reader discovers what it is like to be different. Questions and thoughts people whisper about her brother in-

© 1982 Thomas Victor

The Search for Truth

Madeleine L'Engle

LONG AGO WHEN I WAS just learning to read, and the world was (as usual) tottering on the brink of war, I discovered that if I wanted to look for the truth of what was happening around me, and if I wanted to know what made the people tick who made the events I couldn't control, the place to look for that truth was in story. Facts simply told me what things were. Story told me what they were about, and sometimes even what they meant. It never occurred to me then, when I was little, nor does it now, that story is more appropriate for children than for adults. It is still, for me, the vehicle of truth.

As for writing stories for children, whether it's fantasy or "slice-of-life" stories, most people are adults by the time they get published. And most of us adults who are professional writers are writing for ourselves, out of our own needs, our own search for truth. If we aren't, we're writing down to children, and that is serving neither children, nor truth.

I'm sometimes asked, by both children and their elders, why I've written approximately half of my books for children, and I reply honestly that I've never written a book for children in my life, nor would I ever insult a child by doing so. The world is even more confused now than it was when I first discovered story as medium for meaning, and story is still, for me, the best way to make sense out of what is happening, to see "cosmos in chaos" (as Leonard Bernstein said). It is still the best way to keep hope alive, rather than giving in to suicidal pessimism.

Books of fantasy and science fiction, in particular, are books in which the writer can express a vision, in most cases a vision of hope. A writer of fantasy usually looks at the seeming meaninglessness in what is happening on this planet, and says, "No, I won't accept that. There has got to be some meaning, some shape and pattern in all of this," and then looks to story for the discovery of that shape and pattern.

In my own fantasies I am very excited by some of the new sciences; in a *A Wrinkle in Time* it is Einstein's theories of relativity, and Planck's Quantum theory; tesseract is a real word, and the theory of tessering is not as far fetched as at first it might seem. If anyone had asked my grandfather if we'd ever break the sound barrier, he'd have said, "Of course not." People are now saying "Of course not" about the light barrier, but, just as we've broken the sound barrier, so, one day, we'll break the light barrier, and then we'll be freed from the restrictions of time. We will be able to tesser.

In *A Wind in the Door*, I turn from the macrocosm to the microcosm, the world of the cellular biologist. Yes, indeed, there are mitochondria, and they live within us; they have their own DNA, and we are their host planet. And they are as much smaller than we are as galaxies are larger than we are. How can we—child or adult—understand this except in story?

Concepts which are too difficult for adults are open to children, who are not yet afraid of new ideas, who don't mind having the boat rocked, or new doors opened, or mixing metaphors! That is one very solid reason my science fiction/fantasy books are marketed for children; only children are open enough to understand them. Let's never underestimate the capacity of the child for a wide and glorious imagination, an ability to accept what is going on in our troubled world, and the courage to endure it with courage, and respond to it with a realistic hope.

crease Meg's worry. Her father consoles her; he tells her not to worry because her brother Charles Wallace is doing things in his own way and time. After developing a realistic foundation, the author introduces Mrs. Whatsit, Mrs. Who, and Mrs. Which. The children's conversations with these characters show that Mr. Murry is fighting the dark thing—a thing so dark and so evil that it could overshadow a planet, block out the stars, and create fear beyond the possibility of comfort.

The children and their special friends travel in the fifth dimension to a far-distant planet where their father has been imprisoned by the evil power of "It." L'Engle states that this villain is a naked brain because "the brain tends to be vicious when it's not informed by the heart" (18, p. 254). The heart proves more powerful than the evil It; Meg's ability to love deeply saves her father and Charles.

L'Engle continues the battle against evil in *A Wind in the Door,* in which Charles Wallace appears to be dying. Meg and a special neighbor, Calvin, fight against evil and discover why the battle for one small child is so important: "It is the pattern throughout Creation. One child, one man, can swing the balance of the universe" (p. 179). Meg's capacity for love again saves her brother; the balance does not swing toward evil.

In L'Engle's third book about the Murry family, *A Swiftly Tilting Planet,* readers discover the climactic purpose of Charles Wallace's special abilities. A realistic foundation is established as fifteen-year-old Charles and his father construct a model of a *tesseract,* a square squared and then squared again that is considered the dimension of time. Because they can construct it, the reader feels that it must be true. Another credible character adds realism to the story when the phone rings and the president of the United States asks for help.

L'Engle uses an ancient rune to introduce Charles Wallace to this third battle against evil. The rune, designed to call the elements of light and hold back evil, creates within Charles a feeling that he must fight this final danger. As he goes forth, trying to avert tragedy, he is joined by the unicorn Gaudior who is sent to assist him in his perilous journey. Charles Wallace joins the unicorn as they circle the cosmos, riding the wind into the distant past where they find a joy of unity, a lack of disorder. They progress forward in time, however, and the evil tries to overcome them as they come closer and closer to the crucial moment when a decision could change the world. Charles Wallace helps to change history, and tragedy is averted.

The necessity for maintaining the balance within the created order of the cosmos is strongly developed in this book. Anger and love are considered the forces that can influence this balance; anger adds to the hate that the evil Echthros are encouraging to destroy the ancient harmonies; love adds to the ancient harmonies by joining the music of the spheres.

The power of love is a strong theme in this science fiction story. From *A Wind in the Door* by Madeleine L'Engle. Farrar, Straus & Giroux, 1973. Copyright © by Leo and Diane Dillon. Reprinted by permission of Leo and Diane Dillon.

Anne McCaffrey. Pern is the third planet of Rukbat, a golden G-type star in the Sagittarian Sector. When a wildly erratic bright red star approaches Pern, spore life, which proliferates at an incredible rate on the red star's surface, spins into space and falls in thin threads onto Pern's hospitable earth. The spore life, however, is not hospitable to life on Pern; it destroys all living matter. In order to counteract this menace, the colonists in McCaffrey's *Dragonsong* develop a life form indigenous to the planet. These creatures, called *dragons,* have two remarkable characteristics: they can travel instantly from place to place by teleportation, and can emit flaming gas when they chew phosphine-bearing rock. These creatures, when guided by the dragonriders, can destroy the spore before it reaches the planet.

This is the setting in which a young girl has a series of adventures as she fights for her dream. Menolly, who turns fourteen, lives during this time and longs to play the harp and sing. Her father, however, believes this is disgraceful for a woman and forbids her to play her music. She feels that being without music would be worse than braving the planet during Threadfall, and she runs away. She has many adventures, makes friends with nine fire lizards, and even teaches them to sing. The story ends happily: Menolly is discovered by the Masterharper and invited to join him in Harperhall where she will become her life's dream, a harpist.

This dream continues in McCaffrey's sequel, *Dragonsinger.* Menolly learns that she need no longer hide her skill or fear her ambitions:

The last vestige of anxiety lifted from Menolly's mind. As a journeyman in blue, she had rank and status enough to fear no one and nothing. No need to run or hide. She'd a place to fill and a craft that was unique to her. She'd come a long, long way in a sevenday. (p. 264)

Both McCaffrey and L'Engle develop memorable characters who have talents they learn to use and not hide.

John Christopher. The future world envisioned by Christopher in *The White Mountains* is quite different from the world hoped for by today's society. People have lost their free will, and machines called Tripods have taken over. These machines maintain control through a capping ceremony that places a steel plate on the skull, making the wearer docile and obedient. Fourteen-year-old Will Parker is angered by the prospect of an inescapable voice inside his head. Will meets a stranger, who pretends to be a crazy Vagrant, and discovers that a colony of free people lives in the White Mountains far to the south. The stranger gives Will a map, and Will plans his escape. On the way, he is joined by two other youths; they explore the ruins of a great city and marvel at the skill of the ancient ones who built and lived in the now-deserted area. They find they are being followed and must run for their lives or be captured by the dread Tripods. Finally, they reach the relative safety of the White Mountains and join the people who have built a sanctuary there.

Christopher, through Will's feelings, emphasizes the importance of free will. Even though Will is surrounded by the harshness of rock and ice rather than the softness of a sunlit valley, he realizes that he and the people living there have two luxuries:

freedom and hope. We live among men whose minds are their own, who do not accept the dominion of the Tripods, and who, having endured in patience for long enough, are even now preparing to carry the war to the enemy. (p. 184)

A future world in which the earth supports only dust is created in *Dustland.*
From *Dustland* by Virginia Hamilton. Cover illustration by James McMullan. Copyright © 1980 by Greenwillow Books (A Division of William Morrow & Company). Reprinted with permission.

Their plans for carrying the war to the enemy are begun in the next book of the trilogy, *The City of Gold and Lead*. In order to learn more about the Tripods, Will wins an athletic contest and leaves the White Mountain sanctuary to live in the city of the Tripods. He learns about their way of life and escapes with his information. The last book in the series, *The Pool of Fire*, describes the battle against the Tripods. People are finally freed when their controllers are defeated. Humanity, however, has not learned its lesson. Will tries to plan for world unity, but is defeated by the inability of people to agree; quarreling factions make his dream, as yet, impossible. Christopher's stories are exciting, yet sober reminders of what could happen if humanity allows itself to lose the battle for free will.

SUMMARY

Modern fantasy takes children into imaginative worlds where animals and dolls can talk, where wizards cast their spells, and where alien beings live in far-distant galaxies. Modern fantasy must meet the standards of all fine literature and must also develop a point of view to encourage the reader to suspend disbelief; it must create settings that allow the reader to see, hear, and feel the environment; and it must present believable characters. The themes developed by writers of modern fantasy include some very important human values.

Fantasy that bridges the worlds between old and new literature has many elements of traditional literature. The fantasies of C. S. Lewis, J. R. R. Tolkien, and Lloyd Alexander contain elements of mythology. Modern fairy tales by Hans Christian Andersen, Joan Aiken, and Jane Yolen are similar in motif and subject to traditional tales.

Memorable stories about articulate animals depict animals who talk like people but still retain some animal qualities. Literature by Beatrix Potter, Kenneth Grahame, E. B. White, and Robert Lawson suggests an understanding of, and a liking for, animals. It is not only animals who talk. Stories about dolls and toys suggest the imaginative world of a living nursery.

Authors of literature considered classics for children have created strange worlds found at the base of a rabbit hole or at the end of a journey through space propelled merely by trust and pixie dust. Lewis Carroll and James Barrie are two authors who have created such worlds.

Modern fantasy writers also transport children through time warps to experience life through the eyes of realistic people living in the past or to help modern children solve their contemporary problems by effectively solving problems in the past. Science fiction writers may transport readers into new galaxies or futuristic worlds on earth. Heroes and heroines may battle forces of evil by searching for that one moment when a decision could make a difference, or they may rebel against a society controlled by machines. The importance of retaining free will is an important theme in many futuristic science fiction stories.

Suggested Activities for Adult Understanding of Modern Fantasy

- Read Hans Christian Andersen's "The Wild Swans." Compare the plot, characterization, and setting with the Grimms' "The Six Swans." What are the similarities and differences?
- Choose a book written from the point of view of someone who is different from a normal person. What techniques does the author use to encourage readers to suspend disbelief and consider the possibility that the story could happen?
- Discuss "The Chronicles of Narnia" with another adult who has read the books and with a child who has read the fantasies. What are the differences, if any, in the interpretations perceived by the two people?
- Read Joan Aiken's and Jane Yolen's modern fairy tales. Identify the traditional fairy tale motifs found in the stories.
- After reading J. R. R. Tolkien's *Hobbit* or *The Lord of the Rings*, identify common elements and the symbolization found between Tolkien's work and mythology. Consider the use of fate, subterranean descents, denial of death, mortals and immortals, supernatural beings, and the power granted to objects.
- Authors who write about believable articulate animals balance reality and fantasy by allowing the animals to talk but still retain some animal characteristics. Choose an animal character such as Peter Rabbit, Little Georgie from *Rabbit Hill*, or Mole from *The Wind in the Willows*. What human and animal characteristics can be identified? Has the author developed a credible character? Why or why not?

References

1 Berding, Sister Mary Cordelia. "Humor as a Factor in Children's Literature." Cincinnati: University of Cincinnati, 1965. University Microfilm No. 65-12,889.
2 Bettelheim, Bruno. *The Uses of Enchantment: The Meaning and Importance of Fairy Tales*. New York: Knopf, 1976.

3 Commire, Anne. *Something About the Author. Facts and Pictures About Contemporary Authors and Illustrators of Books for Young People.* Detroit: Gale, 1971.

4 De Wit, Dorothy. *Children's Faces Looking Up: Program Building for the Storyteller.* Chicago: American Library Association, 1979.

5 Green, Roland J. "Modern Science Fiction and Fantasy: A Frame of Reference." *Illinois School Journal* 57 (Fall 1977): 45–53.

6 Hedges, Ned Samuel. "The Fable and the Fabulous: The Use of Traditional Forms in Children's Literature." Lincoln: University of Nebraska, 1968. University Microfilm No. 68–18,020.

7 Heins, Paul. "A Second Look: The Adventures of Pinocchio." *The Horn Book.* April 1982, pp. 200–204.

8 Livingston, Myra Cohn. *Poems of Lewis Carroll.* New York: Crowell, 1973.

9 Lukens, Rebecca J. *A Critical Handbook of Children's Literature.* Glenview, Ill.: Scott, Foresman, 1976.

10 Milne, A. A. *The Christopher Robin Story Book.* Illustrated by Ernest H. Shepard. New York: Dutton, 1966.

11 Noel, Ruth S. *The Mythology of Middle Earth.* Boston: Houghton Mifflin, 1977.

12 Philip, Neil. "The Writer and the Nanny Who Never Explain: Neil Philip Meets P.L. Travers, Author of the Mary Poppins Books." *Times Educational Supplement.* (London), 11 June 1982, p. 42.

13 Sale, Roger. *Fairy Tales and After, from Snow White to E. B. White.* Cambridge, Mass.: Harvard University, 1978.

14 Shohet, Richard Matther. "Functions of Voice in Children's Literature." Cambridge, Mass.: Harvard University, 1971, University Microfilm No. 72–297.

15 Sutherland, Zena; Monson, Dianne L.; and Arbuthnot, May Hill. *Children and Books.* Glenview, Ill.: Scott, Foresman, 1981.

16 Tolkien, J. R. R. *Fellowship of the Ring.* Boston: Houghton Mifflin, 1965.

17 Townsend, John Rowe. *Written for Children.* New York: Lippincott, 1975.

18 Weaver, Warren. *Alice in Many Tongues.* Madison, Wis.: University of Wisconsin, 1964.

19 Weston, Annette H. "Robert Lawson: Author and Illustrator." *Elementary English* 47 (January 1970): 74–84.

20 Wintle, Justin, and Fisher, Emma. *The Pied Pipers, Interviews With the Influential Creators of Children's Literature.* New York: Paddington Press, 1974.

Involving Children in Modern Fantasy

EXCITEMENT OF FANTASY DURING PUPPETRY INTERPRETATIONS

ART INTERPRETATIONS OF MODERN FANTASY

A MODERN FANTASY WEB—DEVELOPING A FANTASY INTEREST CENTER

STRATEGIES FOR INVOLVING CHILDREN WITH SCIENCE FICTION

DISCUSSION, CREATIVE DRAMATIZATIONS, AND ARTISTIC INTERPRETATIONS WITH *A WRINKLE IN TIME*

THE WORLD of modern enchantment allows children to discover a magical kingdom by walking through a wardrobe; to eat forbidden lettuce by crawling under a garden gate; to encounter the forces of good versus evil in the disguise of gentle hobbits, cunning dwarfs, wise wizards, and evil dragons. This magic can be extended by providing varied opportunities for children to interact with the settings, characters, and plots found in stories of modern fantasy.

Some of the opportunities for child development through fantasy that this chapter explores include interpreting modern fantasy through puppetry and through art, developing a fantasy interest center, involving children in the world of science fiction, developing interaction activities between science and science fiction, and between social studies and science fiction.

EXCITEMENT OF FANTASY DURING PUPPETRY INTERPRETATIONS

Stories about the youth of Hans Christian Andersen tell readers that his favorite toys were a puppet theater and puppets. Eva Moore's *The Fairy Tale Life of Hans Christian Andersen* (17) recounts the five-year-old watching his father put on puppet plays, the eight-year-old creating his own plays and sewing clothes for the puppets, and the seventeen-year-old putting on puppet shows for the children of Copenhagen. Throughout the book, readers sense how important puppets and the interaction between puppet and fantasy were to Andersen's development. Children today can develop that sense of wonder as they watch puppetry productions or create their own puppets and stage their own productions.

This interaction between puppet and puppeteer has been felt by people throughout history. Puppetry, as a form of creative drama, has a long and varied history. Puppets were found in Egyptian tombs; they were part of rituals in ancient Greece; the Joruri in Japan were extravagant productions; and Punch and Judy shows in England were very popular. Any viewer of twentieth-century television who watches the "Muppets," "Sesame Street," or "Mr. Rogers" can avow to the current popularity of puppets. Such Muppet characters as Miss Piggy and Kermit have even been interviewed on newscasts.

Children often enjoy learning about the history of puppets. Older children can explore informational books on puppetry, or adults can share pictures and illustrations with them. Sources that adults will find useful include Baird's *The Art of the Puppet* (3), which contains colored photographs and information on the history of puppetry; Jeune Scott-Kemball's *Jav-*

anese *Shadow Puppets* (24), which has photographs of the British Museum's collection of puppets; Rene Simmen's *The World of Puppets* (26), which presents a history of puppets; and George Speaight's *Punch and Judy: A History* (27), which includes the history of one type of puppetry production. These books provide historical information and may also stimulate children's interest in puppetry.

This section considers how the literature program can be enriched through the use of puppetry. Included will be ideas for choosing stories that stimulate puppetry, creating the puppets, and children as puppeteers.

Choosing Stories That Stimulate Puppetry

Geraldine Siks, in *Drama with Children* (25), develops a strong case for nurturing children's imagination through literature, drama, music, art, dance, and the spoken word. She says that "a well-planned puppetry project, by its very nature, can serve as an introduction to all the arts, not as separate entities, but as an integrated whole" (p. 177). Siks believes that puppetry projects should start with existing stories that provide the foundation of plot and character upon which the puppet play can be developed. She envisions a logical progression of simple stories, beginning with nursery rhymes, progressing to folktales and fairy tales and modern fantasy, moving on to contemporary stories, and finally writing and creating original scripts.

The characteristics of stories or scenes from stories appropriate for puppetry productions are similar to those of many traditional tales and shorter modern fantasies or scenes from modern fantasies. Nancy Briggs and Joseph Wagner (5) have identified the following characteristics of stories that make them effective for puppetry:

1 A story's structure should be clear and understandable.
2 Stories should contain action that can be shown through the movements and voices of puppet characters. (Facial expressions are not possible with puppets.)
3 The story's pace should be rapid.
4 Stories selected should be those that children will want to repeat; they should be well liked and easily understood.
5 Characters should present challenging, imaginative subjects for puppet construction but should not be impossible to construct.
6 The size of the puppet stage usually determines how many characters can be accommodated; consequently, the story should require that no more characters appear at one time than the stage can accommodate. (Three to five puppeteers are usually all that will fit comfortably behind a stage without the stage collapsing or the players getting in each other's way.)

In addition, if sets are to be added to the puppet theater, the story should require only a few simple ones. There is always a danger in puppetry that children will become so engrossed in making the puppets and the sets that there is no time or emphasis placed upon the actual objective of the puppet production.

Children who have had considerable experience with children's literature and listening to stories told or read by adults often have many ideas about stories to use in puppet presentations. Adults sometimes find it helpful to share some appropriate stories with children and then let them select the story or stories they would like to share with an appreciative audience of their peers.

Besides many of the traditional stories discussed in chapter six, children and adults will find many modern fantasy stories or particular scenes appropriate and enjoyable for puppetry productions. Younger elementary students enjoy creating the Beatrix Potter stories as puppet productions. The interactions and adventures among Mother Rabbit, Flopsy, Mopsy, Cottontail, Peter, and Mr. McGregor make a satisfying puppet play that lets a number of children take different roles. Children have had whole Beatrix Potter festivals; one group put on "Peter Rabbit," while another portrayed the adventures of Benjamin Bunny as he and Peter go back to the garden to retrieve Peter's coat and run into the cat, and a third depicted the confrontation between Nutkin, the squirrel, and Old Brown, the owl. Stories from *Winnie-the-Pooh* are also enjoyable for puppetry. Because there are a number of Pooh stories, children can use their puppets during the creation of several different plots.

Andersen's fantasies are enjoyable sources for lower and middle elementary students. "The Emperor's New Clothes," "The Princess on the Pea," and "The Tinderbox" have all been adapted by puppeteers. The humorous characters and situations in Carl Sandburg's *Rootabaga Stories* are fun to create as puppets and sets as well as to present as puppet plays. Children find that characters such as Jason Squiff with his popcorn hat, popcorn mittens, and popcorn shoes and Rags Habakuk with a blue rat on each shoulder encourage their imagination to soar and create new situations for these characters.

Middle and upper elementary students have recreated many scenes from L. Frank Baum's *The Wizard of Oz* showing Dorothy and Toto whirling through the air and landing in Oz, Dorothy's saving the Scarecrow, the meeting with the Tin Woodman and the Cowardly Lion, the journey through the deadly poppy field, their arrival in the Emerald City, their interview with the wizard, and the exciting encounters with the Wicked Witch of the West.

Joan Aiken's modern fairy tales such as *The Kingdom and the Cave* and Jane Yolen's stories of proud princesses and wicked stepmothers found in *The Moon Ribbon and Other Tales* have also stimulated puppetry presentations. One group of upper elementary students created their own fantasy after reading Yolen's *Dream Weaver*; they pretended to be dream weavers and created puppet plays from the magical threads of their imaginations.

Adults and children can find more ideas for appropriate puppetry stories by reading various books on puppetry plays. For example, Lewis Mahlmann and David Cadwalader Jones's *Puppet Plays for Young Players* (14) contains adaptations of twelve plays including "The Princess and the Pea,"

A simple stage and puppets may increase children's enjoyment of literature.

"Pinocchio," "The Tinderbox," "Alice's Adventures in Wonderland," and "The Wizard of Oz" as well as several traditional fairy tales. These authors have adapted eighteen additional stories in *Puppet Plays from Favorite Stories* (15). This collection contains both traditional and modern fantasy selections. Modern fantasy titles include "The Emperor's Nightingale," "The Elephant's Child," "The Tale of Peter Rabbit," and "The Nutcracker Prince."

Creating the Puppets

The four major types of puppets are hand puppets, rod puppets, shadow puppets, and marionettes. The professional puppeteer or college student who is investigating puppetry may use a wide variety of marionettes and other complex puppets. Younger children, however, who are creating and working with their own puppetry projects will have better results using simple puppets. Hand puppets are usually considered ideal for the beginning puppeteer because they are the easiest to construct and control.

There are a variety of hand puppets that range from stockings or paper sacks placed over the hand to puppets with heads constructed from papier-mâché. A paper-bag puppet is very easy and quick to construct. To make this puppet, children can draw features directly on the bag, allowing the mouth opening to fall on the fold of the bag, or they can cut features from construction paper and glue them onto the bag. Objects such as buttons, yarn, felt, and pipe cleaners can add features to paper-bag puppets.

Paper plates also provide material for easily constructed puppets that can be manipulated by the child's hand. The paper plate is folded in half and features added to the puppet. This folding allows the child to manipulate the puppet's speaking action. Ears can be added to the plate and pipe cleaners glued onto the plate for whiskers.

Boxes of various sizes may be turned into hand puppets. To form the base of a puppet, a box is cut on the sides and folded. Features are then added to the box to create the desired character.

Puppets with papier-mâché heads can be given features that look real. The heads can be formed by using a plastic foam ball, a crumpled newspaper ball, or an inflated balloon as a base. Before the papier-mâché is added to the base, a cardboard tube from paper toweling is placed into the center of the neck. This tube should be wide enough to hold one or two fingers. Newspaper or toweling is then cut into small pieces or strips, dipped into thinned wallpaper paste or glue, and applied over the form until the desired features have been formed.

Paper Bag Puppet: the Owl from *Winnie-the-Pooh*

Box Puppet: Tin Man from *The Wizard of Oz*

cut

fold

Rod Puppet: a Winged Monkey belonging to the Wicked Witch

Paper Plate Puppet: Peter Rabbit

Papier-mâché Head Puppet: the Wicked Witch of the West from *The Wizard of Oz*

Human Puppet: the Cowardly Lion from *The Wizard of Oz*

Puppets Made from Objects

Fire Shovel Guest

Spoon-Licker Guest

Broom Handle Bridegroom

After the head has dried, features can be painted onto the head and hair can be added. A simple garment can then be cut and sewn or glued together to fit over the hand.

Very simple puppets can be constructed by cutting characters from construction paper or cardboard and attaching figures to sticks. The child maneuvers the puppet by grasping the lower end of the rod and moving it across the stage.

Children can actually become human puppets by constructing cardboard shapes or designing box shapes large enough to cover their bodies. Large boxes or cardboard shapes can turn children into the card characters from *Alice in Wonderland,* human characters, or animal characters.

Sometimes stories suggest objects that can be turned into puppets. One group of children created puppets for Sandburg's "The Wedding Procession of the Rag Doll and the Broom Handle and Who Was in It." One child turned a broom into a puppet who was ready for a wedding. He added facial features to a broom, attached a coat hanger just below the face, and placed a shirt and jacket over the coat hanger. The bottom of the broom handle became the stick by which the puppet was maneuvered. A fireplace shovel, tablespoons, dishpans, frying pans, and striped bibs were also turned into puppets. After the children made their puppets and recreated the wedding procession, they created other situations in which their characters played major roles.

Children As Puppeteers

Preparing for a puppet presentation when literature is the stimulus is similar to preparing for other types of creative dramatizations. George Merten (16) recommends that the story should be read several times until the players feel they know it thoroughly. He suggests that the children develop a mental image of the characters, their personalities, and some of their quirks. They should consider the necessary relationships among characters if they are going to portray the plot and characters to an audience. Next, the group should improvise each segment while the adult considers where and when the scene takes place, who is in the scene, what happens in the scene, how the scene moves forward, and the scene's objective. George Latshaw (12) believes the players should go through a three-step improvisation in which they pantomime the scene, then repeat the same scene but add sounds that express the characters' feelings (yawns, giggles, gasps), and finally improvise using dialogue. The final puppet play should be believable to both actors and audience.

Children usually enjoy giving a puppet production several times so that several children can play different parts or all of the children who made a certain puppet character can play that particular part. Many stories discussed earlier have several different scenes so that many children can become involved in the production both as players and audience.

Teachers, librarians, and other adults who work with children find that children will turn many favorite stories into puppet productions if they are given an opportunity to create puppets and even a simple stage on which to perform. Many productions will be very informal, with one or two children putting on a play for their own enjoyment. Whether the production is two children behind a living room sofa or a group of fifth graders staging a more elaborate story for classmates or parents, there is usually a magical quality that transforms the children into storybook characters.

ART INTERPRETATIONS OF MODERN FANTASY

Strange and curious worlds, imaginary kingdoms, animal fantasy, and preposterous situations found in modern fantasy all lend themselves to motivating artistic interpretations. Betty Coody (7) says that "Creative art-literature experiences occur in the classroom when boys and girls are moved by a good story well told or read, when art materials are made available, and when time and space are allowed for experimenting with the materials" (p. 92). (A word of caution: art should allow children to expand their enjoyment of a story through self-expression. It should not be used as a forced activity following the reading of every story.)

The next section considers some artistic interpretations that can be stimulated by the fanciful writings either orally shared with or read independently by children. In addition, modern fantasy selections range from books that interest preschool children through books appropriate for upper elementary and middle school children, and a wide variety of art media may be explored in relation to modern fantasy selections. While these artistic interpretations are discussed in connection with modern fantasy selections, they are also excellent to use with any other literary form.

Mural and Frieze Interpretations

Mural and frieze interpretations encourage children to work in a group in order to create a large picture. A mural is usually made by designing and creating a picture on a long piece of paper that may be placed on the floor or on long tables so that children can work together on it. A frieze is similar to a mural but consists of a long narrow border or band of paper that stretches across a wall or around a room.

The content of the mural is usually planned by the group; the children then decide upon their own responsibilities. Drawings on the mural may be created with paints, chalk, or crayons. Objects may also be cut out of construction paper and added on top of the background paintings. The finished mural is often placed on a large bulletin board or may cover whole sections of a wall or hallway. Murals can depict one setting suggested by a book or can be divided into segments to illustrate different parts of a book.

Stories with vivid descriptions of settings are enjoyable sources of mural subjects for young children. Beatrix Potter's "The Tale of Squirrel Nutkin" has a description of the island in the middle of the lake where the squirrels go to gather nuts. Children have created murals showing a large lake surrounded by a woods, with a tree-covered island in the center. The largest tree is the hollow oak tree, the old brown owl's home. Because the story takes place in the autumn, children can create trees and bushes covered with shades of red, gold, and orange. On the lake, they can paint squirrels sailing toward the island on rafts. One group of children gathered real acorns, autumn leaves, and twigs to add to the mural. Other stories that suggest scenic murals include scenes in the hundred-acre wood in A. A. Milne's *Winnie-the-Pooh;* the river world of Mole, the Wild Wood, and Toad's home at Toad Hall in Kenneth Grahame's *The Wind in the Willows;* and the barn and/or barnyard world of E. B. White's *Charlotte's Web.*

Maps have also been drawn in large mural format to show the travels of various characters in stories. Children have illustrated Little Georgie's journey as he travels across the countryside in search of Uncle Analdas' home in Lawson's *Rabbit Hill.* Chapters three and four in the book describe Little Georgie's journey as he travels to the Twin Bridges, walks briskly down the Hill, moves quietly past the home of the Dogs of the Fat-Man-at-the-Crossroads, runs happily across the High Ridge, leaps over Deadman's Brook, and eventually finds Uncle Analdas's disorderly burrow. Children can illustrate the differences in routes; Little Georgie, influenced by Uncle Analda, travels at a leisurely and cautious pace that keeps them in the shadows of hedgerows, has them circle wide the homes of dangerous dogs, and always has them stop for rests near protective briar patches.

An illustration of a frieze showing the richly carved impressions of people and animals that decorated Greek architecture often interests children and helps them to create their own frieze depicting the important characters and events in a story.

After reading Sandburg's *Rootabaga Stories,* children wanted to create a humorous frieze. One group created a long frieze showing the train and its occupants traveling toward Rootabaga Country. Along the way, children created the land of Over and Under, the country of balloon pickers, the country of circus clowns, the tracks running in zigzags in the land where pigs wear bibs, and the final destination of the village of Liver and Onions.

The characters and their adventures found in Tolkien's *The Hobbit* are fine sources of frieze materials for older children. Likewise, Lloyd Alexander's characters from the "Prydain Chronicles" can be developed into a frieze suggesting the struggles between good and evil.

Collage, Montage, and Mosaic

There are three procedures in art that are produced by gluing other materials onto a flat surface in order to create an artistic interpretation; all three are also enjoyable ways to interpret literature. A collage is made by pasting different shapes and textures of materials onto the surface to create a picture. (See pages 181–82 for detailed suggestions for introducing collage through children's picture storybooks.) Many materials including newspapers, lace paper doilies, velvet, burlap, felt, satin, yarn, tinfoil, rope, buttons, toothpicks, twigs, bark, corrugated paper, tissue paper, and paints should be collected so that children have many things to choose from that will give the desired effect when they are creating collages.

Young children like working with texture and then feeling the results of the different materials on their collage. Potter's *The Tale of Peter Rabbit and Other Stories* is an enjoyable source of ideas and inspiration for collage interpretations. Some younger children created Peter by designing a material jacket, cutting construction paper shoes, and adding a cotton-ball tail and string whiskers. They portrayed him in a gooseberry net made from string or nylon netting and had him peering forlornly at a scarecrow complete with brass-buttoned jacket, hanging shoes, and three-dimensional lettuce plants. Russell Erickson's various Warton toad books suggest a textured woodland setting that is fine for collage.

Other examples of fantasy that children enjoy interpreting through collage include various scenes from Dahl's *James and the Giant Peach,* Aiken's *A Necklace of Raindrops,* and Yolen's *The Girl Who Cried Flowers.*

Montage is the art or process of making a composite picture by bringing together into a single composition a number of different pictures or parts of pictures and arranging them to form a blended whole. Children can create a montage by cutting pictures from magazines or other sources and then mounting them on a surface so that the surfaces overlap. The pictures and the way they are arranged may suggest a feeling, a theme, a mood, or a concept. They may be quite abstract in nature or may rely on concrete symbols to develop a concept. This may be the first time that some children experience an art form that is not necessarily realistic. Through montage, they find that they can select and rearrange pictures and parts of pictures until the result expresses their feelings.

Charlotte's Web is one story that has stimulated the creation of montage. Throughout the book, Templeton, the rat, is portrayed as an animal who "had a habit of picking up unusual objects around the farm and storing them in his home" (p. 45). He collected delectable food scraps: part of a ham sandwich, a chunk of Swiss cheese, and a wormy apple core. Children have developed a montage that suggests the essence of the prized material objects in Templeton's life. After reading Ian Fleming's *Chitty Chitty Bang Bang,* children have created a montage of antique cars and a candy factory.

Older children have created more complex themes; they have used the montage procedure to suggest the battle between good and evil in Tolkien's *Hobbit* or *Lord of the Rings* and Lloyd Alexander's *The Book of Three, The Black Cauldron, The Castle of Llyr, Taran Wanderer,* or *The High King.*

The magical possibilities related to time warp are also stimulating sources for montage. Children have created artistic interpretations suggesting travel from contemporary England into the previous century as described in Margaret J. Anderson's *To Nowhere and Back* or a journey from contemporary Scotland into ancient times or into the future *In the Keep of Time* or *In the Circle of Time.* Because these stories include symbols that tie the past, present, and future, children have used them when creating a montage. For example, a tree-lined path, an old cottage, Smailholm Tower, a stone circle shrouded in mists, and a glowing key enter into the passage between one world and another.

Another topic that can be developed as an effective montage theme is one dealing with friendly presences, ghosts, and goblins. After reading Lucy Boston's *The Children of Green Knowe,* several children created a world of friendly ghosts from the past. After reading Mollie Hunter's *The Wicked One,* another child chose to develop a montage around the possible conflicts between a less benevolent spirit and a man with a fiery temper.

The third technique that children can use to create a picture by attaching objects to a flat surface is mosaic. When creating a mosaic, small pieces of colored objects such as paper, stones, seeds, or wood are glued onto heavy paper, cardboard, or wood that has a design drawn upon the surface. Children

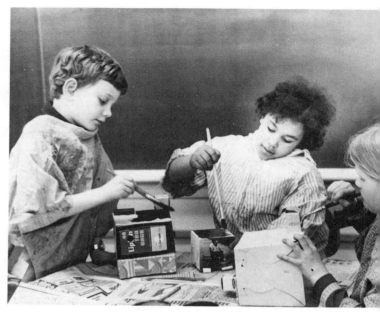

Children are creating settings for dioramas out of boxes and paint.

can select a favorite character from literature, draw the character on the desired surface, select appropriate small objects to fill in the lines, place glue inside the shape, and then attach the objects to the surface. The background may be filled in if desired. Favorite characters for this activity include Margery Williams's *The Velveteen Rabbit,* Milne's characters in *Winnie-the-Pooh,* and Carroll's characters in *Alice's Adventures in Wonderland.*

Papier-Mâché

Children enjoy creating sculptures of their favorite animal or human characters found in the books they read. Papier-mâché characters are created by covering a light form with strips of newspaper or paper toweling that have been dipped into thinned wallpaper paste. Children can make the structural form by inflating a balloon of appropriate size, wadding and taping newspaper into the desired shape, selecting a plastic container that resembles the desired shape, forming the shape from clay, or developing a wire or wire-mesh construction. All these techniques are described in step-by-step detail in Whitman's *A Whitman Creative Art Book, Papier-Mâché* (29).

The statues in the Queen's courtyard in C. S. Lewis's *The Lion, the Witch and the Wardrobe* are interesting subjects for papier-mâché treatments as are Kipling's Mowgli, Rikki-Tikki-Tavi, Father Wolf, Shere Khan, Bagheera, and Baloo in *The*

Jungle Books, or the whale, the camel, the rhinoceros, the elephant, or the armadillo in *Just So Stories.* Any favorite articulate animals provide lively subjects for papier-mâché.

Shadowboxes—Dioramas

Many stories lend themselves to recreations of settings in miniature inside a box or framed on a shelf. The obvious ones are stories about small people or dolls, such as Mary Norton's *The Borrowers* or Rumer Godden's *The Dolls' House.* Children of many ages, and adults as well, are often fascinated by miniatures. Children enjoy collecting small items around their own homes, such as spools, thimbles, bottle caps, and boxes and then turning them into furniture for the Clock family. After reading *The Dolls' House,* children may wish to learn more about the elegant dollhouse described in the book and then choose and create a favorite room for the house. Books such as Barbara Farlie's *All about Doll Houses* (9) illustrate many kinds of dollhouses, period rooms, furniture, and accessory projects. Children can see how beads from a broken necklace could be turned into a lamp, scraps of material turned into curtains and bedspreads, a round bottle top turned into a teapot, a belt eyelet turned into a candleholder, a paper clip turned into a chandelier, an earring turned into a bookend, and a toothpaste cap turned into a cannister.

Robert Lawson's *Rabbit Hill* has several scenes that can be turned into dioramas such as Mother Rabbit's neat burrow home, Uncle Analdas's messy home, and the procession of animals around the garden when they discover "There is enough for all." Numerous scenes are also suggested by Robert O'Brien's *Mrs. Frisby and the Rats of NIMH.* Children can create the inside of the laboratory, Nicodemus's office, the Boniface estate, the toy tinker's truck, and the new colony in Thorn Valley.

The strange and curious world of Carroll's *Alice's Adventures in Wonderland* provides many exciting scenes for dioramas. There is Alice's encounter with the White Rabbit, her conversation with the Caterpillar, her tea party with the Mad Hatter, and her discovery of the Queen's garden. James Barrie's curious worlds in *Peter Pan* are other rewarding subjects; children can create the Darling children's nursery, the flight to Never Land, Mermaid's Lagoon, and Captain Hook's ship.

These scenes are merely suggestive of the many interpretations that children can attempt in using literature to stimulate art work. For many children, art interpretation allows them to interact with their favorite characters in a new way. As suggested earlier, however, they do not need to interpret all of their reading with art projects. For young children, it should be an enjoyable extension of their story, not a general assignment to draw their favorite part. Classrooms and homes that provide a rich background of art materials will encourage children to create many interpretations of their favorite storybook settings and characters.

A MODERN FANTASY WEB—DEVELOPING A FANTASY INTEREST CENTER

University students in children's literature classes can use the webbing process suggested by Donna Norton (20) to identify related topics around a central theme or subject, identify children's books related to the topic, and then develop stimulating activities that encourage children to interact with the characters and situations in these books. One group chose this technique to help formulate and develop a children's literature interest center for the middle elementary grades around the central subject, "Imagine That." After choosing their central, unifying subject, they identified six major categories of modern fantasy that would be appropriate for their "Imagine That" theme (see Figure 7–1).

Next, they identified children's modern fantasy selections that would be suitable for each category. In order to meet interests and reading needs of different students, they identified books that were on several different reading levels or, like *Pinocchio,* had versions of various difficulty levels available. Following their search of the literature, they completed a literature web identifying the books they would use (see Figure 7–2).

With these books in hand and the web developed, the group divided its responsibilities; each student developed an introduction to the books that might captivate children's interests and encourage them to read the books. Next, the students developed four or five different activities to encourage children to interact with the book through art interpretations, creative dramatics, oral discussions, or creative writings. They shared their paragraphs and activities in order to receive feedback from each group member. The motivational paragraphs and directions for the suggested activities were then placed on large cards and put into an attractive fantasy land interest center complete with books, necessary materials, and room to display the completed activities. Because several students were student teaching at the time, they placed the interest center in their classrooms and shared it with children.

Examples of motivational paragraphs and book-related activities developed around three of the six categories in the literature web of interest are shown in Figure 7–3.

The students who developed and used this literature interest center with children found that other children in the class

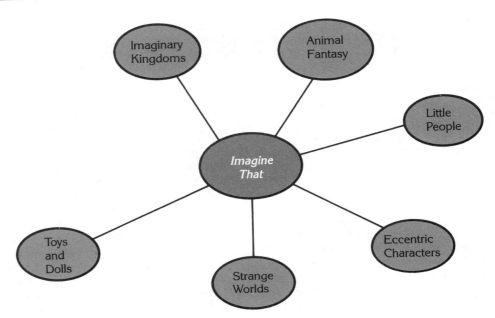

FIGURE 7-1

wanted to read books because of the interest and the activities that were generated. Some activities were teacher led or motivated; others could be done independently by the children.

STRATEGIES FOR INVOLVING CHILDREN WITH SCIENCE FICTION

Science fiction stories have been identified by well-known scientists and writers as strongly motivating their interests in adult occupations. At the beginning of one of his popular "Cosmos" series, scientist Carl Sagan (23) said that at the age of eight he read the stories of H. G. Wells and then went out into the fields, with arms raised, and asked to be transported to Mars. He described his boyhood dreams of flying to the moon and Mars; all were stimulated by reading science fiction. Goddard, the inventor of modern rocketry, read Wells's *War of the Worlds,* while George Lucas, the author of *Star Wars* and *The Empire Strikes Back,* was influenced by stories about Buck Rogers.

In addition to pure enjoyment, science fiction may be used to stimulate interaction between science fiction and science or social studies.

Interaction between Science and Science Fiction

Many science fiction books are based on scientific principles and can be used as springboards for discussions involving critical and creative thinking and for the reinforcement of scientific facts. Children's research skills can be sharpened as they verify the scientific information. Children's appreciation and evaluation of settings in science fiction are also enhanced as they discuss the various books. (Interaction between science and science fiction is a highly motivating subject for gifted and talented programs.)

Several children's literature students and upper elementary and middle school teachers have developed activities that stress the interaction between the science curriculum and the reading of science fiction. One group was stimulated by the suggestions of Dorothy Zjawin (30) who recommended different ways to encourage the interaction between science and science fiction. The students divided into small groups and chose the study of astronomy, the human body, inventions, and changes in natural events including environmental problems, weather, ecosystems, or time. Next, they identified science fiction books that could be shared orally with children or displayed in the library for children to read independently. They then investigated the science curriculum and discovered science-related materials, scientific principles, and topics in current science magazines that could stimulate upper elementary students' interests. Finally, they shared their activities with children. The following are examples of books, discussion topics, and related activities that proved rewarding:

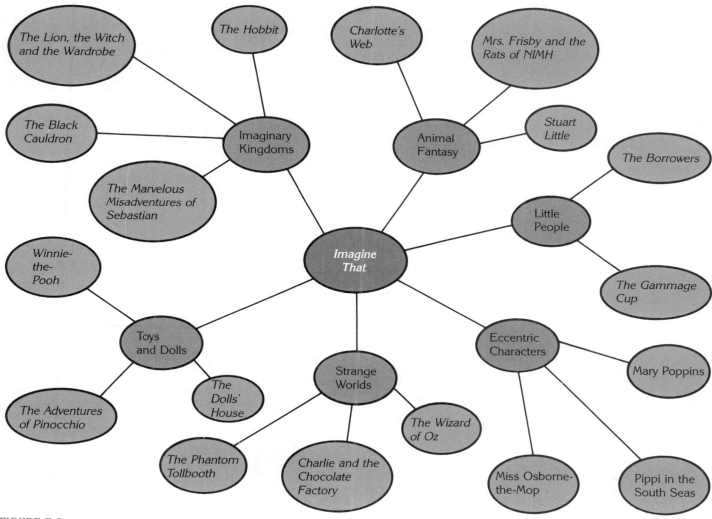

FIGURE 7-2

Astronomy and Science Fiction

Science Fiction to Be Shared with Children

1 Cameron, Eleanor. *The Wonderful Flight to the Mushroom Planet.* Two boys, with the help of a friend, construct a spaceship and travel to a strange planet.
2 Engdahl, Sylvia Louise. *This Star Shall Abide.* A boy learns the secrets of his planetary civilization.
3 Ginsburg, Mirra. *Air of Mars: And Other Stories of Time and Space.* This book contains nine science fiction stories written by Russian authors.
4 Marzollo, Jean and Marzollo, Claudio. *Jed's Junior Space Patrol: A Science Fiction Easy-to-Read.* This intergalactic adventure includes robots and telepathic creatures. (See chapter twelve for nonfiction books about planets and space flights.)

IMAGINARY KINGDOMS

The Lion, the Witch and the Wardrobe by C. S. Lewis.

It's true! A wardrobe leads to another land called Narnia, a land where it always snows but it's never Christmas. Peter, Susan, Edmund, and Lucy discover Narnia and must help break the wicked Snow Queen's spell. The centaurs, beavers, unicorns, and talking horses depend on the Pevensie children and on Aslan, the noble lion.

EXAMPLES OF ACTIVITIES

Pretend you are Edmund's shadow. You ar right there with him in all his adventures. You hear what he says and you know how he feels. Write a character sketch about Edmund from the viewpoint of his shadow. Include the things he does and why you, his shadow, think he does them. How and why does Edmund change? How do you feel about being his shadow? What would you say if you could talk?

With a group of classmates who have read this book, act out "what happened about the statues" for the rest of the class. Refer to chapter sixteen for this exciting adventure.

Choose your favorite part in *The Lion, the Witch and the Wardrobe* (about three pages). Practice reading it; when you are ready, record your selection. Following your recording, tell why this was your favorite part in the book. After everyone is finished, we will all listen to the tapes of *The Lion, the Witch and the Wardrobe.*

Create and construct a box movie using ten scenes in proper sequence from *The Lion, the Witch and the Wardrobe.* Write an accompanying script to narrate the movie. Present your movie to the class.

ANIMAL FANTASY

Mrs. Frisby and the Rats of NIMH by Robert O'Brien

"You must go, Mrs. Frisby," said the owl, "to the rats under the rosebush. They are not, I think, like other rats."

The rats under the rosebush are *not* like other rats. Mrs. Frisby, a mouse, did go to the rats for help, and she did discover their secret. Mrs. Frisby found rats that could read, use machines, and plan a self-supporting rat society. She also found rats that were in great danger. Could tiny Mrs. Frisby help them? Read the book and find out for yourself.

EXAMPLES OF ACTIVITIES

The publisher is searching high and low—it doesn't know what to do. The public is going wild and wants a sequel to *Mrs. Frisby and the Rats of NIMH.* Please help this publisher. Write to the publisher, and tell the editor why you should write *Mrs. Frisby and the Rats of NIMH, Part II.* In your letter tell what you would include in your story.

Choose a friend who has read *Charlotte's Web.* Pretend that you are Nicodemus and your friend is Charlotte. Have a conversation in which you tell each other what it is like to live the life of a rat or a spider. Tell about your best friends, your adventures, and the advantages and disadvantages of being the kind of creature you are. During your conversation, tell each other why you think humans dislike spiders and rats.

Pretend that you are a mouse or a rat. Somehow you have found your way into Ms. (*teacher's name*)'s classroom. You have never seen anything like it. Write about your adventures as you journey through the classroom and meet the people or objects in the room.

STRANGE WORLDS

The Phantom Tollbooth by Norton Juster

Inside the mysterious package that Milo found in his room was what looked like a genuine turnpike tollbooth. But Milo was in for an even bigger surprise when he drove his small electric car through the tollbooth gate. Suddenly, he found himself in The Lands Beyond, the enchanted home of some of the craziest creatures ever imagined. As Milo traveled through this confusing world, he was joined by an ill-mannered little Humbug and a ticking watchfob named Tock. The three characters found themselves drawn into a chain of adventures that led them closer and closer to the forbidden Mountains of Ignorance and black-hearted demons that awaited them there.

EXAMPLES OF ACTIVITIES

Pretend that you are Milo: you just can't believe that you have found The Lands Beyond. You don't want to forget this crazy world that is so different from the one that you know. There must be a way to record your adventures. You decide to keep a diary. Write seven entries in your diary telling about different adventures in the enchanted and confusing world of The Lands Beyond. In your final entry, include any important lessons that you have learned. Bind your entries together and design a cover for your diary.

Choose a friend who has also read *The Phantom Tollbooth* and together prepare a debate to present to the class. One of you is a faithful citizen of Dictionopolis and the other is from Digitopolis. Each of you must try to convince the class that your kingdom is better. Tell the class about the advantages of living where you live and the disadvantages of living in the other place. Defend your own kingdom so that your classmates will choose to live there.

FIGURE 7–3
Motivational Paragraphs and Activities

Discussion Topics and Other Related Activities

1 Discussions were held and speculations were made about the possibility of living in a space colony. How would colonists control their environment? How would they communicate with other colonies? How would they travel between colonies? During the discussions, children were encouraged to let their imaginations soar; they also had to consider scientific principles and the ways authors of science fiction stories had solved these problems. (Films and television programs were also discussed.)

2 Because many science fiction stories take place on other planets, children considered the possibilities of discovering a new planet. Children and teachers shared excerpts from *Science 81* (March 1981), that suggested that astronomers are searching for a possible tenth planet in our solar system. "Astronomers are looking beyond the known edge of the solar system for a planet estimated to be at least five billion miles from the sun, or 50 times further away than Earth" (p. 6). They considered the possible characteristics of such a planet, any life forms that might be there, and wrote their own science fiction stories describing astronomers searching for the new planet, astronauts traveling to the new planet, or space colonists living on the new planet.

3 The above discussion on astronomers searching for new planets led to a discussion about NASA's proposed 430-foot-long orbiting space telescope described in the April 1981 issue of *Science 81*. Children considered what they might discover if they could "peer seven times further into space than ever before, perhaps to the edge of the universe itself" (p. 10).

4 The latest discoveries about the characteristics of other planets and the sun, as discovered by Voyagers 1 and 2 explorations of the solar system and orbiting telescope, were also used to stimulate discussions about science fiction and to consider how these characteristics would affect possible life on the planet or the development of space colonies. Two articles in the January/February 1981 issue of *Science 81*, Bruce Murray's "After Saturn, What?" and J. Kelly Beatty's "No Small Rapture," and an article in *Omni*, Mike Edelhart's "New Sun" (April 1980), provided background information for the teachers as well as illustrations to be shared with children. For example, the following quote by Bruce Murray was used to start a discussion about the environment on Mars: "Robots launched by the United States have changed the imaginary, Earthlike Mars of Percival Lowell into the detailed scientific reality of ancient volcanic mountains, vast chasms, and water-cut channels much larger than any similar features on Earth" (p. 24). Children considered additional characteristics of Mars and compared them with the environments developed in science fiction.

How Could Changes in Natural Events or Environments Affect the Future of Earth or Another Planet?

Science Fiction to be Shared with Children

1 Doyle, Arthur Conan. *The Lost World*. People on earth discover a lost land in which prehistoric animals still live.

2 McCaffrey, Anne. *Dragonsong, Dragonsinger*, and *Dragonquest*. Colonists on Perm create a life form to destroy the spore life that invades the planet and has the ability to destroy all living matter.

3 Snyder, Zilpha Keatley. *Below the Root*. A thirteen-year-old survivor of a society that has experienced devastating destruction sets out to discover a civilization that supposedly lives underground.

4 Hamilton, Virginia. *Dustland*. The air in a future earth time supports only dust and mutant animals and humans.

Discussion Topics and Other Related Activities

1 Students discussed what could happen on earth if prehistoric animals were discovered and then began to multiply rapidly. They considered competition for food, eating habits of various prehistoric animals, conditions necessary for rapid reproduction, and what might happen to plants, smaller animals, and human life. They also considered what could happen if species that are now considered endangered were to multiply rapidly. What changes in the environment might account for the reversal? What would be the consequences for other life?

2 Several science fiction books develop plots around consequences of changes in the earth because of contamination and overpopulation. Discussions and writings were developed around this quote by Joan Stephenson Graf (10): "Global 2000, a presidential report on the future, predicts that between 600,000 and one million plant and animal species will become extinct in 20 years as a result of the expansion of human populations and the exploitation of natural resources. The loss of species, and the biological diversity they represent, is unrecoverable, and the consequences of these losses are impossible to predict" (p. 102).

Another source of scientific facts about endangered plant life and probable consequences is Elizabeth Stark's article "You Can't See the Forests or the Trees" (28). A teacher used this topic to stimulate discussions, beginning with the following quote: "The world's tropics will be bald and barren. With the forest canopy gone, surface temperatures will swing wildly, atmospheric concentrations of carbon dioxide will rise precipitously, and one million species will die. The aftermath of a nuclear war? Not quite. According to a grim report released by the U.S. Interagency Task Force on Tropical Forests, this is what much of the world's forests will look like in less than 50 years if devastation of woodlands continues. . . . What remains of our diminishing tropical woodlands will be gone within 70 years if deforestation in the Third World continues at its present rate" (p. 78).

3 Children considered various environmental problems that are on earth today or problems that could develop due to litter from disabled space ships or other space-traveling vehicles such as Voyager I. Through discussions, they tried to predict and provide various solutions to these problems.

The Influence of Inventions, Machines, and Computers

Science Fiction to be Shared with Children

1 Bethancourt, T. Ernesto. *The Mortal Instruments*. A boy becomes the tool of a sadistic computer.
2 Christopher, John. *The White Mountains*. A futuristic mechanized society forms the setting for the story.
3 Hamilton, Virginia. *The Gathering*. A computer programmed by survivors helps rehabilitate a wasteland.
4 Watson, Simon. *No Man's Land*. A mechanized world causes a boy to rebel.
5 Yolen, Jane. *The Robot and Rebecca and the Missing Owser*. A robot, Watson II, helps solve the mystery of a missing pet.

Discussion Topics and Other Related Activities

1 Children considered changes that had occurred in the world over the last one hundred years due to such inventions as airplanes, automobiles, calculators, computers, and even light bulbs. They speculated about a world without these inventions and a world in which any of these inventions could become too powerful.
2 Children made their own inventions, drew and created models of them, described the purposes and advantages of their inventions, shared them with other children, and speculated what might happen if their inventions became too powerful.
3 Robots such as R2D2 and C3PO in *Star Wars* also fascinate children. They designed their own robot models, de-

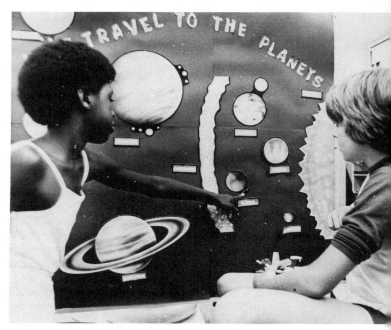

For these children, there is a close relationship between science fiction and astronomy.

scribed capabilities of the robots, and contemplated what other worlds or earth might be like if robots were plentiful or if they became more powerful than their human inventors.

Interaction Between Social Studies and Science Fiction

Not only does science fiction relate to scientific principles and technology, but its authors consider the impact of possible changes such as mechanization, space travel, and life on other planets upon people and societies. Because science fiction is of high interest to many upper elementary students, science fiction and related activities can meet the following four motivational requirements for social studies recommended by John P. Lunstrum and Bob L. Taylor (13):

1 Use materials and approaches that are responsive to and built on student interests.
2 Design and/or use strategies that demonstrate the relevance of the reading task in social studies, focusing on the study and discussion of controversy and the clarification of values.
3 Help students who have negative attitudes toward reading in the social studies and little confidence in their ability to experience success in this area.
4 Encourage students to use language activities, such as role-playing games, and listening more effectively. Arouse curiosity

about the communication process, of which reading is an integral part, and develop interpersonal communication skills. (p. 21)

The way Alan Myers (19) recommends using science fiction in social studies classrooms corresponds with many of these motivational requirements. He says that science fiction has an important position in social studies classes because "broad themes like the nature of government, the merits of different types of social organization, racial hatred, poverty, and exploitation in unfamiliar contexts" (p. 183) can stimulate the debating of issues without being hindered by children's stereotypes. Myers also suggests that through science fiction children acquire a sense of the relationship between cause and effect; in so doing, they can begin to grasp the sweep of history that is so important to any study of social studies.

Many science fiction books lend themselves to the development of debates on issues related to society and social studies. The following issues and books have been used successfully by classroom teachers who were motivating children to consider differing viewpoints during social studies classes:

Issue: People who differ from those around them are frequently misunderstood, feared, and sometimes hated. This treatment is quite different from a belief that fellowship and love are essential ingredients if society is to survive.

1 Key, Alexander. *Escape to Witch Mountain.* Two children from another planet have strange powers. As they search for their identities, they must outwit sinister forces who would like to use their powers.
2 Key, Alexander. *The Forgotten Door.* When a quiet, sensitive boy with unusual powers comes to earth from another planet, he is understood by one family but treated with suspicion and hostility by most of society.
3 L'Engle, Madeleine. *A Wrinkle in Time.* People fear and whisper about Charles Wallace because he is different from the other children in the town; he can communicate without speaking.

Issue: Should society allow its members to have free will? What could happen if people do not strive to retain freedom of choice?

1 Christopher, John. *The City of Gold and Lead.* Will tries to discover the secrets of the Tripod culture by spying from within their major city.
2 Christopher, John. *The Pool of Fire.* People try to set up a new government after defeating the Tripods; dissident groups, however, cannot agree on a unified approach.
3 Christopher, John. *The White Mountains.* People in the twenty-first century are controlled by machines called Tripods. When human members of the society reach the age of fourteen, steel plates are inserted into their skulls so they can be controlled by the state.
4 Watson, Simon. *No Man's Land.* In the future, society has become both extremely mechanized and regulated.

Additional social studies activities that have developed as a result of sharing and discussing science fiction include considerations for planning future cities, exploring the impact on our society from alien visitors, adjusting to different environments, and exploring energy needs in future civilizations.

Because authors of science fiction stories frequently describe futuristic cities either on earth or on other inhabited planets, children enjoy the challenge of creating their own model cities. They can consider what their city would look like and how it would function if they could build it any way that they could choose. One sixth-grade class designed such a city by combining both research into known design possibilities and their own creative imagination. They investigated energy-efficient buildings, transportation systems, sanitation systems, and suburban/urban growth before building their own model city. High-rise office and apartment buildings were included as the most efficient use of urban space, but the buildings were constructed for energy efficiency and beauty. Suburban homes were partially or totally below ground and had solar collectors so that they were energy efficient. Shopping centers made use of below- and above-ground space, with light shafts bringing in light for plants and people. A clean electric mass-transportation system was designed; road systems for private cars were computerized to allow a safe, steady stream of traffic; and moving sidewalks transported people within the urban environment. The sanitation system used a three-phase treatment process that produced drinkable water, and garbage was incinerated by the power plant to provide recycled power. The children also included museums, recreational facilities, parks, trees, and an arboretum. Finally, they considered the issues of controlling growth and how many people would provide an ideal number for their city.

Children have also thought about the impact on their own lives and society if an alien people landed on earth or if space exploration discovered life forms on other planets. Through role playing, they have imagined that first meeting, how they might communicate, and how humans and aliens could function together without destroying either culture. Because programs like "Star Trek" frequently deal with the issue of interfering with another culture, children have also considered the possibility of earth being invaded or colonized by aliens who are far superior intellectually to people on earth, or the reverse situation in which space exploration could discover human life forms who have not progressed as far as earth's civilization.

Children have discussed the impact of various environments on space travelers who are trying to colonize diverse environments. Whole new environments have been constructed within classrooms; children have designed settings that include atmosphere, plants, animals, and land characteristics; new languages have been created; communication systems have been developed; and possible fine arts of a people have been suggested.

The children who created the model city also investigated energy needs in the future; they considered how buildings could become energy efficient and the probability of creating clean synthetic fuels and recycling wastes and water so that natural resources would not be depleted.

The books discussed in this section reflect the many ways that adults may use science fiction to interest children. This final section considers some ideas that may be developed around one book, Madeleine L'Engle's A Wrinkle in Time.

DISCUSSION, CREATIVE DRAMATIZATIONS, AND ARTISTIC INTERPRETATIONS WITH A WRINKLE IN TIME

Discussing L'Engle's text with children can help them focus on characterization, setting, plot development, theme, or style. (This type of discussion can, of course, be developed with any text. The questions suggested here may be used as guidelines when librarians and teachers develop similar discussions.) The following questions are listed in chronological order as the material is found in the text. If an adult wishes to focus on characterization, setting, plot, theme, or style at one time, these questions may be grouped accordingly. They may be used to accompany various parts of the book as suggested by the page or chapter references. Some questions require that children consider information presented at different points in the text and then integrate this information into an answer that requires synthesis. Page numbers are included; an adult leading the discussion may wish to interject text passages as children consider their answers. As the discussion develops, the adult should listen to the children's responses and, if appropriate, encourage divergent thinking. (Divergent questions encourage more than one "correct" answer as children verbalize different interpretations for a story. These questions often require them to consider their own experiences and reactions when they interact with the text.)

Suggestions for Oral Discussion

1 (Characterization). What did Meg's father mean when he told Meg not to worry about Charles Wallace because "he does things in his own way and in his own time"? Was father right? What exceptional behavior did Charles Wallace display? Why was Charles Wallace considered strange and backward by the villagers? Why didn't he want the people in the village to know his real capabilities? (chapter 2)

2 (Plot development, Setting). *Tesseract* is mentioned in several places in the book. Lead a discussion in which the children present ideas about what they think is meant by the word:

p. 21   Mrs. Whatsit informs Mrs. Murry that there is such a thing as a tesseract.

p. 23   Mrs. Murry tells the children that she and their father used to have a joke about a concept called tesseract.

p. 76   The term *tesseract* is described as traveling in the fifth dimension—going beyond the fourth dimension to the fifth dimension. The five dimensions are described as first, line; second, a flat square; third, a cube; fourth, time; and fifth, the square of time, a tesseract in which people can travel through space without going the long way around.

3 (Setting, Style—emotional response to language). Throughout the book, L'Engle makes associations between smells and emotions. Discuss some of these associations: Mrs. Whatsit's statement that she found Charles Wallace's house by the smell; and then her reaction in which she describes how lovely and warm the house is inside (p. 17); or the delicate fragrance that Meg smells when the gentle beast with tentacles relieves her of her pain (p. 175). Encourage children to express their own associations between smells and emotions.

4 (Theme). Mrs. Who told Meg that if she wanted to help her father she would need to stake her life on the truth. Mrs. Whatsit agreed and told the children that their father was staking his life on the truth. What did Mrs. Who and Mrs. Whatsit mean by their remarks (p. 92)? How had Mrs. Whatsit staked her life in the battle against evil (p. 92)?

5 (Characterization, Author's style, Theme). Throughout the book, L'Engle has developed descriptions and associations around "It"; discuss these associations and meanings.

p. 72   "It" is described as a dark thing that blotted out the stars, brought a chill of fear, and was the evil their father was fighting.

p. 88   It is described as evil; It is the powers of darkness. It is being fought against throughout the universe.

The great men of earth who have fought against It include Jesus, Leonardo da Vinci, Michelangelo, Madame Curie, Einstein, and Schweitzer. Discuss how these people fought against darkness and encourage children to identify other people who fought or are fighting against darkness.

p. 108   It makes its home in Camazotz, the most oriented city on the planet, the location of the Central Intelligence Center.

p. 118   The man was frightened about the prospect of being sent to It for reprocessing.

p. 141   It sometimes calls Itself "The Happiest Sadist."

p. 158   It is a huge brain.

p. 170   Meg felt iciness because she had gone through the dark thing.

6 (Characterization, Plot development). Mrs. Whatsit gave each child a talisman in which she strengthened their greatest ability: for Calvin, it was the ability to communicate with all kinds of people; for Meg, it was her faults; and for Charles Wallace, it was the resilience of his childhood (p. 100). How did the children use these abilities throughout the story in their fight against It and in their endeavors to free Mr. Murry? Which ability is most important? Why?

7 (Characterization, Theme, Setting). Why did L'Engle introduce the children to Camazotz by showing them children skipping and bouncing in rhythm, identical houses, and women who opened their doors simultaneously (p. 103)? Why was the woman so frightened about an Aberration? What eventually happened to the Aberration? What is the significance of these actions?

8 (Characterization, Theme). Compare the people living in Camazotz with Meg, Charles Wallace, and Calvin. How does one account for these differences (p. 118)? Could the people living in a city on earth become like the people in Camazotz? Why or why not? Why did the man at Central Intelligence Center tell the children not to fight It so that life would be easier for them? What would happen if everyone took the man's suggestion (p. 121)? What are the consequences of allowing someone to accept all the pain, the responsibility, and the burdens of thought and decision? Would this be good or bad? Give a reason for your answer.

9 (Plot development). What was Meg's reason for saying the periodic table of elements when she was standing before It (p. 161)?

10 (Characterization, Plot development, Theme). What characteristics did Meg have that made her the only one who would be able to go back to Camazotz and try to save Charles from the power of It (p. 195)? What was the only

weapon that Meg had that It did not possess (p. 203)? How did Meg use this weapon to free Charles Wallace? Do any people ever use this weapon? Has anyone here ever used this weapon? Is it a weapon for good or for bad?

Art activities accompanying *A Wrinkle in Time* can stimulate children's interpretations of setting and characterization. Ideally, children can again demonstrate their divergent thinking as they interpret the author's language and descriptions.

Suggestions for Art Interpretations

1 (Characterization, Descriptive language). Mrs. Whatsit goes through several different transformations in the course of the book. Encourage children to illustrate these transformations. Suggestions include Mrs. Whatsit's appearance as a plump, tramplike character in her blue and green paisley scarf, red and yellow flowered print, gold liberty print, red and black bandanna, sparse grayish hair, rough overcoat, shocking pink stole, and black rubber boots (pp. 16–17). Next, the children see her transformed from this rather comical character into a beautiful winged creature with "wings made of rainbows, of light upon water, of poetry" (p. 64). The reader also discovers that Mrs. Whatsit had been a star who gave her life in the battle against It (p. 92).

2 (Setting). The medium is able to show the children visions through her globe. Pretend to be sitting before a magical globe. Draw either the series of visions that the children see or the visions people would like to see if they could ask the globe to show them anything.

3 (Setting). Meg, Mr. Murry, and Calvin travel to a strange planet inhabited by creatures with four arms and five tentacles attached to each hand. The planet also has a different appearance from Earth or Uriel. Create a shadowbox showing the inhabitants and their planet.

Creative drama allows children to interact with the characters in the story, interpret aspects of plot development, and express their reactions to the author's style.

Suggestions for Creative Dramatizations

1 (Characterization). Role-play Mrs. Whatsit's first visit to Charles Wallace's home and Meg's and Mrs. Murry's reactions to her.

2 (Setting, Author's style). Chapter 4 has been used by upper elementary classes to create a Reader's Theater presentation. Children have accompanied their oral readings with music that depicts the mood of the action and setting as Meg describes the light disappearing (p. 56); the sensa-

tions of moving with the earth (p. 58); leaving the silver glint of autumn behind and arriving in a golden field filled with light, multicolored flowers, singing birds, and an air of peace and joy (pp. 59–61); the transforming of Mrs. Whatsit into a beautiful winged creature with a voice as warm as a woodwind, with the clarity of a trumpet, and the mystery of an English horn; and ascending into the atmosphere to observe the moon and then seeing the dark ominous shadow that brought a chill of fear—the dark thing that their father was fighting.

3 (Author's style). Pantomime the passages of pages 56 and 57 when Meg experiences the black thing complete with darkness, the feeling of the body being gone, her legs and arms tingling, traveling through space, and reuniting with Charles and Calvin on Uriel.

4 (Theme, Characterization). Debate the argument between Meg and It, talking through Charles Wallace, found on page 160. Consider the question and encourage one side to take Its view: Like and equal are the same thing; people will be happy if they are alike. The other side will argue Meg's point: Like and equal are two different things; people cannot be happy if they are the same.

5 (Characterization, Extending plot). Pretend that the story continues—role-play the scene in the kitchen after Mr. Murry, Charles Wallace, Meg, and Calvin return home. What would they say to Mrs. Murry and the two boys? What would Mrs. Murry and the boys say to them?

Many other science fiction books encourage creative thinking and imagination. If the stories can inspire other children as they did Carl Sagan, they can open new universes and dimensions for children who discover this form of literature.

SUMMARY

Modern fantasy, proceeding from the marvelous tales of Hans Christian Andersen, to the make-believe land of Lewis Carroll, to the space adventures of Madeleine L'Engle, provides opportunities for many enjoyable experiences in the classroom, home, and library. Modern fantasies, like traditional tales, should be included as part of children's story hours.

Puppetry can be an exciting way to encourage children to interact with the characters in a story. Puppetry nurtures imaginations through the integration of literature, drama, music, art, and dance. The strange and curious worlds, imaginary kingdoms, animal fantasies, and preposterous situations found in modern fantasy lend themselves to motivating artistic interpretations, such as mural and frieze interpretations, collage,

montage, and mosaic interpretations, papier-mâché, and dioramas. Classrooms and homes that provide a rich background of art materials will help children to create many interpretations of their favorite storybook settings and characters.

This chapter described a children's literature interest center, developed around the theme "Imagine That." The interest center included examples of motivational paragraphs and book-related activities around the categories Imaginary Kingdoms, Animal Fantasy, and Strange Worlds.

Science fiction is a source of literature that may be read for pleasure and escape; the stories may also be used to stimulate interaction between science and science fiction or social studies and science fiction.

Suggested Activities for Children's Appreciation of Modern Fantasy

■ Develop a story-hour program that includes several short stories, a major story, and connecting materials appropriate for sharing with a designated age group of children. Decide on a unifying theme around a modern fantasy topic. Combine modern fantasy and traditional literature.

■ Using the criteria for selecting effective stories for puppetry recommended on page 295, compile a list of stories or scenes from longer stories that might be appropriate for children's puppetry productions. After sharing the stories with children, encourage them to select one they would like to develop as a puppetry presentation. Help them decide on the types of puppets they will create and interact with them as they pantomime the story, express the characters' feelings, and add dialogue to their production.

■ With a peer group, investigate one of the methods for artistic interpretation discussed in this chapter—mural, frieze, collage, montage, mosaic, papier-mâché, or diorama. Demonstrate the use of the method to the rest of the class.

■ Share a modern fantasy selection that lends itself to artistic interpretations. Interact with a child or a group of children as they interpret the story through a mural, frieze, collage, montage, mosaic, papier-mâché, or diorama. How did various children decide to interpret the story? Did they interact with setting, characters, or plot? Did they account for all three aspects of the story? Did they develop an abstract feeling or mood, or did they create concrete images? Encourage the children to tell about their artistic interpretations.

■ With a peer group, develop a modern fantasy web of interest around children's literature. For example, webs could be developed around such topics as "Travels in Time, Space, and Imagination" or "Animals as People." Identify books that would be appropriate for the topic. Develop an introduction for each book to stimulate interest in the book. Suggest activities to encourage children to interact with the stories in a variety of ways.

■ Search the science curriculum for topics that could be related to science fiction. Identify appropriate children's science fiction that shows relationships with one of the topics. Develop an oral discussion lesson to share with children. In the lesson, suggest discussion questions and issues that could be used to stimulate creative and critical thinking; relate the science content to the science fiction story.

■ Choose a science fiction book and develop an in-depth plan for sharing the book with children. Include in the plan discussion questions, activities that relate science or social studies, creative dramatizations, artistic interpretations, and creative writing suggestions.

References

1 American Association for the Advancement of Science. "Currents, A Tenth Planet?" *Science 81* 2 (March 1981): 6–7.
2 American Association for the Advancement of Science. "Currents, Last Picture Show?" *Science 81* 2 (April 1981): 7, 10.
3 Baird, Bill. *The Art of the Puppet.* New York: Macmillan, 1965.
4 Beatty, J. Kelly. "No Small Rapture." *Science 81* 2 (January/February 1981): 26–31.
5 Briggs, Nancy E., and Wagner, Joseph A. *Children's Literature through Storytelling and Drama.* Dubuque, Iowa: Brown, 1979.
6 Cacha, Frances B. "Children Create Fiction Using Science." *Science and Children* 15 (November/December): 21–22.
7 Coody, Betty. *Using Literature with Young Children.* Dubuque, Iowa: Brown, 1979.
8 Edelhart, Mike. "New Sun." *Omni* (April 1980): 62–67.
9 Farlie, Barbara L., and Clarke, Charlotte L. *All about Doll Houses.* New York: Bobbs-Merrill, 1975.
10 Graf, Joan Stephenson. "20th Century Arks." *Science 81* 2 (March 1981): 102–4.
11 Green, Roland J. "Modern Science Fiction and Fantasy: A Frame of Reference." *Illinois School Journal* 57 (Fall 1977): 45–53.
12 Latshaw, George. *Puppetry, the Ultimate Disguise.* New York: Rosen, 1978.
13 Lunstrum, John P., and Taylor, Bob L. *Teaching Reading in the Social Studies.* Newark, Del.: International Reading Association, 1978.
14 Mahlmann, Lewis, and Jones, David Cadwalader. *Puppet Plays for Young Players.* Boston: Plays, 1974.
15 ———. *Puppet Plays from Favorite Stories.* Boston: Plays, 1977.
16 Merten, George. *Plays for Puppet Performance.* Boston: Plays, 1979.
17 Moore, Eva. *The Fairy Tale Life of Hans Christian Andersen.* Illustrated by Trina Schart Hyman, New York: Scholastic, 1969.
18 Murray, Bruce. "After Saturn, What?" *Science 81* 2 (January/February 1981): 24–25.
19 Myers, Alan. "Science Fiction in the Classroom." *Children's Literature in Education* 9 (Winter 1978): 182–87.
20 Norton, Donna E. "A Web of Interest." *Language Arts* 54 (November 1977): 928–32.
21 Post, Jonathan V. "Star Power for Supersocieties." *Omni* (April 1980): 44–46, 96–99.
22 Rausen, Ruth. "An Interview with Madeleine L'Engle." *Children's Literature in Education* 19 (Winter 1975): 198–206.
23 Sagan, Carl. *Cosmos,* Public Broadcasting System, October 26, 1980.
24 Scott-Kemball, Jeune. *Javanese Shadow Puppets.* London: British Museum, 1970.
25 Siks, Geraldine. *Drama with Children.* New York: Harper & Row, 1977.
26 Simmen, Rene. *The World of Puppets.* Photographed by Leonardo Bezola. New York: Crowell, 1975.
27 Speaight, George. *Punch and Judy: A History.* Boston: Plays, 1970.
28 Stark, Elizabeth. "You Can't See the Forests or the Trees." *Science 81* 2 (April 1981): 78.
29 *A Whitman Creative Art Book, Papier-Mâché.* Racine. Wis.: Whitman, 1967.
30 Zjawin, Dorothy. "Close Encounters of the Classroom Kind." *Instructor* 87 (April 1978): 54–57.

CHILDREN'S LITERATURE

Aiken, Joan. *The Kingdom and the Cave.* Illustrated by Victor Ambrus. Doubleday, 1974 (I:7–10 R:7). A remarkable palace cat suspects that the Under People are preparing to attack the kingdom of Astalon.

——. *The Wolves of Willoughby Chase.* Illustrated by Pat Marriott. Doubleday, 1963 (I:7–10 R:5). An English country house is the setting for a Victorian melodrama; Miss Slighcarp, the governess, tries to steal a little girl's heritage.

Alexander, Lloyd. *The Black Cauldron.* Holt, Rinehart & Winston, 1965 (I:10+ R:7). Taran and his companions seek to find and destroy the cauldron in which the evil lord creates his warriors, the Cauldron Born.

——. *The Book of Three.* Holt, Rinehart & Winston, 1964 (I:10+ R:5). The first of the Prydain Chronicles. Taran, the assistant pigkeeper, joins forces with the Sons of Don in their fight against evil.

——. *The Castle of Llyr.* Holt, Rinehart & Winston, 1966 (I:10+ R:5). Taran accompanies Princess Eilonwy to a castle where she is expected to learn to be a lady. The adventure increases when she is abducted by the forces of evil.

——. *The Cat Who Wished to Be a Man.* Dutton, 1973 (I:8–10 R:4). The high wizard, Magister Stephanus, owns a cat, Lionel, who asks to be changed into a man. Even though his wish is granted, he retains many catlike characteristics.

——. *The First Two Lives of Lukas-Kasha.* Dutton, 1978 (I:8–10 R:3). Lukas, a carpenter's apprentice, is conjured into a strange land where he is known as the king.

——. *The High King.* Holt, Rinehart & Winston, 1968 (I:10+ R:5). The final book in the Prydain Chronicles. Here are the answers to the purpose of *The Book of Three,* the enchantment of Dyrnwyn, and the future of Taran.

——. *The Kestrel.* Dutton, 1982 (I:10+ R:7). The characters in Westmark face war and corruption.

——. *The Marvelous Misadventures of Sebastian.* Dutton, 1970 (I:10+ R:6). A young musician living in the eighteenth century has a series of adventures.

——. *Taran Wanderer.* Holt, Rinehart & Winston, 1967. (I:10+ R:5) The fourth book of the Prydain Chronicles.

——. *The Town Cats and Other Tales.* Illustrated by Laszlo Kubinyi. Dutton, 1977 (I:8–12 R:6).

Eight tales about cats who succeed in outwitting humans.

——. *Westmark.* Dutton, 1981 (I:10+ R:7). Moral dilemmas and high adventure combine to give a story of good versus evil.

——. *The Wizard in the Tree.* Illustrated by Laszlo Kubinyi. Dutton, 1975 (I:10+ R:6). Mallory, a kitchen maid, encounters Arbican, a wizard, and her life is changed forever.

Allard, Harry. *Bumps in the Night.* Illustrated by James Marshall. Doubleday, 1979 (I:5–8 R:3). In a book for younger children, Dudley Stork is frightened when he hears bumps at night. When he and his friends have a seance, a friendly ghost appears.

Andersen, Hans Christian. *Ardizzone's Hans Andersen.* Translated by Stephen Corrin. Illustrated by Edward Ardizzone. Atheneum, 1979 (I:8–12 R:5). A collection of fourteen fairy tales.

——. *The Emperor's New Clothes.* Retold by Anne Rockwell. Translated by H.W. Dulcken. Illustrated by Anne Rockwell. Harper & Row, 1982 (I:6–9 R:6). Everyone, except a child, is afraid to tell the emperor the truth about his clothes.

——. *Fairy Tales.* Illustrated by Kay Nielsen. Viking, 1981 (I:all). Illustrations reproduced from a 1924 edition in the Metropolitan Museum of Art.

——. *The Fir Tree.* Illustrated by Nancy Ekholm Burkert. Harper & Row, 1970 (I:7–10 R:6). The little tree yearns for a different life; too late, he realizes that he should have enjoyed the beautiful forest.

——. *Hans Andersen: His Classic Fairy Tales.* Translated by Erik Haugaard. Illustrated by Michael Foreman. Doubleday, 1974 (I:7–10 R:7). A collection of eighteen Andersen tales.

——. *Michael Hague's Favorite Hans Christian Andersen Fairy Tales.* Illustrated by Michael Hague. Holt, Rinehart & Winston, 1981 (I:5–8 R:7). A collection of nine stories printed in fairly large type.

——. *The Nightingale.* Translated by Eva Le Gallienne. Illustrated by Nancy Ekholm Burkert. Harper & Row, 1965 (I:all R:7). The emperor learns to value the real nightingale more than the jeweled mechanical bird.

——. *Seven Stories by Hans Christian Andersen.* Illustrated by Eric Carle. Watts, 1978 (I:4–7 R:3). A collection of stories for younger children.

I = Interest by age range;
R = Readability by grade level.

———. *The Snow Queen*. Retold by Amy Ehrlich. Illustrated by Susan Jeffers. Dial, 1982 (I:6–9 R:6). Detailed line drawings suggest a wintry world.

———. *The Snow Queen*. Adapted by Naomi Lewis. Illustrated by Errol LeCain. Viking, 1979 (I:6–9 R:6). An icy Snow Queen is shown against a dark blue background.

———. *The Steadfast Tin Soldier*. Illustrated by Thomas DiGrazia. Prentice-Hall, 1981 (I:6–8 R:6). The toy soldier falls in love with a paper ballerina.

———. *The Swineherd*. Translated by Anthea Bell. Illustrated by Lisbeth Zwerger. Morrow, 1982 (I:8–10 R:6). A princess does not merit the love of a prince.

———. *Thumbelina*. Retold by Amy Ehrlich. Illustrated by Susan Jeffers. Dial, 1979 (I:6–8 R:6). A beautifully illustrated version of the tale about a girl who is only one inch tall.

———. *The Ugly Duckling*. Retold and illustrated by Lorinda Bryan Cauley. Harcourt Brace Jovanovich, 1979 (I:6–8 R:2). The ostracized duckling turns into a beautiful swan.

———. *The Wild Swans*. Retold by Amy Ehrlich. Illustrated by Susan Jeffers. Dial, 1981 (I:7–12 R:7). Finely detailed illustrations develop a fantasy setting.

Anderson, Margaret J. *In the Circle of Time*. Knopf, 1979 (I:9+ R:5). Two children, zhile trying to discover the location of the missing Stones of Arden, are engulfed in the mists of time and find themselves in twenty-second-century Scotland.

———. *In the Keep of Time*. Knopf, 1977 (I:9+ R:6). When the Elliot children place a glowing key into the lock of ancient Smailholm Tower, they step first into the past of the Middle Ages and then into the twenty-second century.

———. *To Nowhere and Back*. Knopf, 1975 (I:9+ R:6). Elizabeth Fenner joins her family in a two-hundred-year-old cottage. She lives the history of the area when she steps back in time and joins a girl who lived in the area one hundred years before.

Atwater, Richard, and Atwater, Florence. *Mr. Popper's Penguins*. Illustrated by Robert Lawson. Little, Brown, 1938 (I:7–11 R:7). Excitement develops when Captain Cook, an Antarctic penguin, is sent to a quiet, dreaming house painter who longs for adventure.

Barrie, James. *Peter Pan*. Illustrated by Nora S. Unwin. Scribner's, 1911, 1929, 1950 (I:8–10 R:6). Wendy, Michael, and John accompany Peter Pan to Never Land where they battle the villainous Captain Hook.

Baum, L. Frank. *The Wizard of Oz*. Illustrated by W. W. Denslow. Reilly, 1956 (I:8–11 R:6). Dorothy has adventures with the Tin Woodman, witches, and other strange beings. Many illustrations of the original 1900 edition.

———. *The Wizard of Oz*. Illustrated by Michael Hague. Holt, Rinehart & Winston, 1982 (I:8–11 R:6). A newly illustrated version of Oz.

Bethancourt, T. Ernesto. *The Mortal Instruments*. Holiday, 1977 (I:10+ R:6). A computer takes control of a boy.

Bond, Michael. *A Bear Called Paddington*. Illustrated by Peggy Fortnum. Houghton Mifflin, 1960 (I:6–9 R:4). Begins a series of adventures after a bear joins a human family.

———. *Paddington Abroad*. Illustrated by Peggy Fortnum. Houghton Mifflin, 1972. (I:6–9 R:4) Paddington plans the family vacation.

———. *Paddington at Large*. Illustrated by Peggy Fortnum. Houghton Mifflin, 1963. (I:6–9 R:4). Paddington has another series of humorous adventures.

———. *Paddington Helps Out*. Illustrated by Peggy Fortnum. Houghton Mifflin, 1961 (I:6–9 R:4). The bear's actions provide humorous episodes.

———. *Paddington Marches On*. Illustrated by Peggy Fortnum. Houghton Mifflin, 1965 (I:6–9 R:4). Continued episodes in bear's life.

———. *Paddington Takes the Air*. Illustrated by Peggy Fortnum. Houghton Mifflin, 1971 (I:6–9 R:4). More about Paddington.

———. *Paddington On Screen*. Illustrated by Barry Macey. Houghton Mifflin, 1982 (I:6–9 R:4). Part of the series of bear stories.

Bond, Nancy. *A String in the Harp*. Atheneum, 1976 (I:10+ R:8). Twelve-year-old Peter discovers an ancient object, the tuning key for the harp of Taliesin, a sixth-century bard. The key allows Peter to experience events in Taliesin's life.

Boston, Lucy M. *The Children of Green Knowe*. Illustrated by Peter Boston. Harcourt Brace Jovanovich, 1955 (I:8–12 R:6). An old English house, a great grandmother, and children who lived in the house during past generations make life happy again for a lonely boy.

———. *An Enemy at Green Knowe*. Illustrated by Peter Boston. Harcourt Brace Jovanovich, 1964 (I:8–12 R:6). A psychology researcher and an evil spirit threaten the existence of Green Knowe.

———. *The Guardians of the House*. Illustrated by Peter Boston. Atheneum, 1975 (I:8–12 R:6). Three carvings in an old house cause a boy to have a series of adventures.

———. *The River at Green Knowe*. Illustrated by Peter Boston. Harcourt Brace Jovanovich, 1959 (I:8–12 R:6). Ancestors from the past visit Green Knowe again.

———. *A Stranger at Green Knowe*. Illustrated by Peter Boston. Harcourt Brace Jovanovich, 1961 (I:8–12 R:6). An escaped gorilla seeks sanctuary at Green Knowe.

———. *Treasure of Green Knowe*. Illustrated by Peter Boston. Harcourt Brace Jovanovich, 1958 (I:8–12 R:6). Tolly finds a treasure hidden in his great-grandmother's house.

Briggs, K. M. *Hobberdy Dick*. Greenwillow, 1977 (I:10+ R:6). An old English manor house in the seventeenth century is the home of hobgoblin Hobberdy Dick and an assortment of ghosts and spirits.

Brittain, Bill. *The Devil's Donkey*. Illustrated by Andrew Glass. Harper & Row, 1981 (I:9–12 R:5). A boy is changed into a donkey when he comes under the spell of Old Magda; his friends help free him.

Cameron, Eleanor. *The Wonderful Flight to the Mushroom Planet*. Illustrated by Robert Henneberger. Little, Brown, 1954 (I:8–10 R:4). Two boys construct and fly a spaceship.

Carroll, Lewis. *Alice in Wonderland*. Illustrated by Marjorie Torrey. Random House, 1955 (I:8+ R:6). Alice goes down the rabbit hole, meets the Cheshire Cat, attends an odd tea party, and witnesses an unusual game of croquet.

———. *Alice's Adventures in Wonderland*. Illustrated by John Tenniel. Macmillan, 1865, 1963 (I:all R:6). The classic tale of an adventure that begins as Alice falls down the rabbit hole.

———. *Alice's Adventures in Wonderland, Through the Looking Glass, and the Hunting of the Snark*. Illustrated by Sir John Tenniel. Chatto, Bodley Head & Jonathan Cape, 1982 (I:all). A reissue of the classic stories celebrates Carroll's 150th anniversary.

———. *The Nursery "Alice."* Illustrated by John Tenniel. Macmillan, 1890, 1979 (I:6–10 R:5). A version of *Alice's Adventures in Wonderland* prepared by Lewis Carroll for younger children.

Christopher, John. *The City of Gold and Lead*. Macmillan, 1967 (I:10+ R:6). In this science fiction story, Will wins an athletic contest so he may go to the city of the Tripods to learn their secrets.

———. *The Pool of Fire*. Macmillan, 1968 (I:10+ R:6). The Tripods are finally defeated, but Will's plans for world unity are hindered by quarreling factions among the people.

———. *The White Mountains*. Macmillan, 1967 (I:10+ R:6). The setting is a time in the future when men are controlled by machines called Tripods. A boy questions this control.

Cleary, Beverly. *The Mouse and the Motorcycle*. Illustrated by Louis Darling. Morrow, 1965 (I:7–11 R:3). Ralph makes friends with a boy who owns a toy motorcycle.

_____. *Ralph S. Mouse.* Illustrated by Paul O. Zelinsky. Morrow, 1982 (I:7–11 R:3). Ralph finds himself in school.

_____. *Runaway Ralph.* Illustrated by Louis Darling. Morrow, 1970 (I:7–11 R:3). Ralph is an unusual mouse who rides a motorcycle and doesn't like his life in an old hotel.

Collodi, Carlo. *The Adventures of Pinocchio.* Illustrated by Naiad Einsel. Macmillan (1892) 1963 (I:7–12). The adventures of a disobedient marionette who eventually learns to be a real boy.

_____. *The Adventures of Pinocchio.* Retold by Neil Morris. Illustrated by Frank Baber. Rand McNally, 1982 (I:7–12). A recent version of the classic story.

_____. *Pinocchio.* Translated by Joseph Walker. Illustrated by William Dempster. Childrens Press, 1968 (I:7–12 R:5). Another version of this well-known story.

Cooper, Susan. *The Dark Is Rising.* Illustrated by Alan E. Cober, Atheneum, 1973 (I:10+ R:8). The last of the Old Ones, immortals dedicated to overcoming the forces of evil, is given the quest of finding six magical signs that will aid the powers of good in their battle against evil.

_____. *Greenwitch.* Atheneum, 1974 (I:10+R:8). The quest continues for the key to the inscriptions on the grail.

_____. *The Grey King.* Atheneum, 1975 (I:10+ R:8). Will Stanton sets out on a dangerous quest against the forces of darkness; he is to regain the golden harp, a thing of power in the battle against evil.

_____. *Jethro and the Jumbie.* Illustrated by Ashley Bryan. Atheneum, 1979 (I:7–10 R:4). Eight-year-old Jethro enlists the help of a jumbie, a spirit of the dead, to convince his older brother that he should take him fishing.

_____. *Over Sea, Under Stone.* Illustrated by Margery Gill, Harcourt Brace Jovanovich, 1965 (I:10+ R:8). Three children go on a quest for "The Grail." They are helped in a battle against evil by the Old Ones, the guardians of the Light.

_____. *Silver on the Tree.* Atheneum, 1977, 1980 (I:10+ R:8). The final battle between the forces of good and evil takes place.

Curry, Jane Louise. *The Birdstones.* Atheneum, 1977 (I:10+ R:7). The discovery of an old stone carved into the shape of a bird leads to an adventure that travels across sixteen hundred years.

_____. *The Magical Cupboard.* Illustrated by Charles Robinson. Atheneum, 1976 (I:8–12 R:4). Felicity, a ten-year-old orphan, discovers the secret of the old cupboard; in 1722, she glimpses the far-distant time, 1976.

_____. *Mindy's Mysterious Miniature.* Illustrated by Charles Robinson. Harcourt Brace Jovanovich, 1970 (I:8–12 R:4). An old dollhouse purchased at an auction causes Mindy and her neighbor to begin an adventure where they meet people who are six inches high.

Dahl, Roald. *Charlie and the Chocolate Factory.* Illustrated by Joseph Schindelman. Knopf, 1964 (I:8–12 R:6). Charlie wins a golden ticket that allows him to explore the fantastic world of Willy Wonka's Chocolate Factory.

_____. *James and the Giant Peach.* Illustrated by Nancy Ekholm Burkert. Knopf, 1961 (I:7–11 R:7). A boy's unhappiness changes when a peach grows large enough to enter.

Dillon, Barbara. *What's Happened to Harry.* Illustrated by Chris Conover. Morrow, 1982 (I:9–12 R:5). Hepzibah the Hateful lures Harry into her kitchen on Halloween and transforms him into a poodle; mischief and humor result.

Doyle, Arthur Conan. *The Lost World.* Random House, 1959 (I:10+   R:7). Prehistoric animals live in a hidden land.

Engdahl, Sylvia Louise. *This Star Shall Abide.* Illustrated by Richard Cuffari. Atheneum, 1972 (I:10+ R:6). A boy in the future learns about his planet.

Erickson, Russell E. *A Toad For Tuesday.* Illustrated by Lawrence DiFiori. Lothrop, Lee & Shepard, 1974 (I:6–9 R:4). An owl captures Warton, but Warton becomes his friend rather than his dinner.

_____. *Warton and Morton.* Illustrated by Lawrence DiFiori. Lothrop, Lee & Shepard, 1976 (I:6–9 R:4). Two toads are separated in the swamp.

_____. *Warton and the Castaways.* Illustrated by Lawrence DiFiori. Lothrop, Lee & Shepard, 1982 (I:6–9 R:4). The toads survive a flood.

_____. *Warton and the Traders.* Illustrated by Lawrence DiFiori. Lothrop, Lee & Shepard, 1979 (I:6–9 R:4). A toad has an adventure when he leaves his secure woodland home.

Fleming, Ian. *Chitty Chitty Bang Bang.* Illustrated by John Burmingham. Random House, 1964 (I:7–11 R:6). A restored car has remarkable properties; it floats and it flies. The car finally takes the family on a fantastic journey to Vulgaria.

Garner, Alan. *Elidor.* Walck, 1967 (I:10+ R:7). Four children explore an old church in England and are drawn into Elidor, a world in the grip of an evil power.

_____. *The Moon of Gomrath.* Philomel, 1979. (I:10+ R:5). A wizard saves the children from the powers of the underworld.

_____. *The Owl Service.* Walck, 1968 (I:10+ R:5). The discovery of an old set of dishes decorated with an owl pattern marks the beginning of some strange events.

_____. *The Weirdstone of Brisingamen.* Walck, 1969 (I:10+ R:5). Two modern English children discover the truth about an ancient legend as they battle witches, troll women, and wolves.

Ginsburg, Mirra. *Air of Mars: And Other Stories of Time and Space.* Macmillan, 1976 (I:10+ R:5). A collection of science fiction written by Russian authors.

Godden, Rumer. *The Dolls' House.* Illustrated by Tasha Tudor. Viking, 1947, 1962 (I:6–10 R:2). Three dolls want a home of their own. Their wish comes true but so does an old enemy's, a truly hateful doll.

_____. *The Mousewife.* Illustrated by Heidi Holder. Viking, 1982 (I:7–10 R:3). A mousewife wishes for adventure and a turtledove longs for freedom.

Grahame, Kenneth. *The Open Road.* Illustrated by Beverley Gooding. Scribner's 1979 (I:7–10 R:7). Based on a chapter from *The Wind in the Willows.*

_____. *Wayfarers All: From the Wind in the Willows.* Illustrated by Beverley Gooding. Scribner's, 1981 (I:7–10 R:7). A picture book version of one of Grahame's chapters.

_____. *The Wind in the Willows.* Illustrated by E.H. Shepard. Scribner's, 1908, 1940 (I:7–12 R:7). Mole, Water-Rat, and Toad of Toad Hall have a series of adventures along the river, on the open road, and in the wild wood.

_____. *Wind in the Willows: The River Bank.* Illustrated by Adrienne Adams. Scribner's, 1977 (I:7–10 R:7). Based on a chapter from *The Wind in the Willows.*

Hamilton, Virginia. *Dustland.* Greenwillow, 1980 (I:10+ R:7). The psychic unit travels into a future time when earth supports only dust and mutant forms of animal and human life.

_____. *The Gathering.* Greenwillow, 1981 (I:10+ R:7). The psychic group of friends go into a domed city of the future which is surrounded by a wasteland.

_____. *Justice and Her Brothers.* Greenwillow, 1978 (I:10+ R:7). Justice and her brothers have powerful psychic powers.

Hiller, Catherine. *Abracatabby.* Illustrated by Victoria de Larrea, Coward-McCann, 1981 (I:7–9 R:4). A boy's pet cat has magical powers.

Hooks, William H. *Mean Jake and the Devils.* Illustrated by Dirk Zimmer. Dial, 1981 (I:9–12 R:6). Three stories about how Mean Jake outwits Big Daddy Devil, Devil Junior, and Baby Deviline.

Hunter, Mollie. *The Wicked One.* Harper & Row, 1977 (I:10+ R:7). A hot-tempered Scotsman and a Grollican, a creature from the Otherworld, have an adventure filled with suspense and humor.

Jones, Diana Wynne. *Charmed Life.* Greenwillow, 1977 (I:10+ R:5). Young Gwendolen Chant is a Coven Street witch. Her life, as well as that of her brothers, changes when they are taken by a stranger to Chrestomanci Castle.

———. *Drowned Ammet*. Atheneum, 1978 (I:10+ R:7). Life-sized dummies known as Poor Old Ammet and Libby Beer are thrown into the harbor every year during the Holland Sea Festival. A boy, born on the day of the festival, discovers the powers of the old gods that are represented by the dummies.

Juster, Norton. *The Phantom Tollbooth*. Illustrated by Jules Feiffer. Random House, 1961 (I:9+ R:8). Milo is given a gift of a tollbooth. When he enters it, he finds himself in the Kingdom of Wisdom.

Kendall, Carol. *The Firelings*. Atheneum, 1982 (I:10+R:6). Author creates a world of little people who live on the edge of a volcano.

———. *The Gammage Cup*. Illustrated by Erik Blegvad. Harcourt Brace Jovanovich, 1959 (I:8–12 R:4). The peaceful existence of a land inhabited by little people is challenged by five nonconformists and an enemy from outside their land.

Key, Alexander. *Escape to Witch Mountain*. Illustrated by Leon B. Wisdom, Jr. Westminster, 1968 (I:8–12 R:6). Two children can communicate without talking, can unlock doors, and make objects move. They search for others like themselves after a sinister man tries to use their powers.

———. *The Forgotten Door*. Westminster, 1965 (I:8–12 R:6). A boy from another planet is not understood by people.

King-Smith, Dick. *The Mouse Butcher*. Illustrated by Margot Apple. Viking, 1982 (I:9–12 R:6). An animal fantasy explores what happens when cats are isolated on an island.

———. *Pigs Might Fly*. Illustrated by Mary Rayner. Viking, 1982 (I:9–12 R:6). The runt of the litter helps his fellow pigs in their time of need.

Kipling, Rudyard. *The Jungle Book*. Doubleday, 1964 (originally 1893, Scribner's) (I:8–12 R:7). A collection of jungle stories including "Mowgli's Brothers," "Tiger-Tiger!" "Rikki-Tikki-Tavi," and "Toomai of the Elephants."

———. *Just So Stories*. Doubleday, 1902, 1907, 1952 (I:5–7 R:5). A collection enjoyed by younger children.

———. *Just So Stories*. Illustrated by Victor G. Ambrus. Rand McNally, 1982 (I:5–7 R:5). New illustrations for the classic stories.

Langton, Jane. *The Astonishing Stereoscope*. Illustrated by Erik Blegvad. Harper & Row, 1971 (I:10+ R:7). Edward and Eleanor discover that they can enter the world of pictures inside the stereoscope.

Lawson, Robert. *Ben and Me*. Little, Brown, 1939 (I:7–11 R:6). The reader is told, through the words of Amos Mouse, about Benjamin Franklin's discoveries and the historical events that were possible because of the assistance of the mouse.

———. *Rabbit Hill*. Viking, 1944 (I:7–11 R:7). The animals on the Hill are waiting expectantly for the new folks. Will they be generous planting folks or will they believe in guns, poison, and dogs?

L'Engle, Madeleine. *A Swiftly Tilting Planet*. Farrar, Straus & Giroux, 1978 (I:10+ R:7). Charles Wallace is now fifteen years old. He travels a perilous journey through time to keep a mad dictator from destroying the world.

———. *A Wind in the Door*. Farrar, Straus & Giroux, 1973 (I:10+ R:7). Strange beings come to enlist the children's aid in the galactic fight against evil. Now Charles's life is at stake; if the children lose, Charles Wallace will die.

———. *A Wrinkle in Time*. Farrar, Straus & Giroux, 1962 (I:10+ R:5). Charles Wallace, Meg Murry, and Calvin O'Keefe accompany Mrs. Whatsit, Mrs. Who, and Mrs. Which on a search for Meg and Charles's father that takes them across the galaxy and leads to combat with an evil darkness that is threatening the cosmos.

LeGuin, Ursula K. *The Farthest Shore*. Illustrated by Gail Garraty. Atheneum, 1972 (I:10+ R:6). Ged, the Archmage of Roke, is placed in final combat against an evil wizard.

———. *Tombs of Atuan*. Illustrated by Gail Garraty. Atheneum, 1971, 1980 (I:10+ R:5). Ged, the wizard, comes to the Tombs of Atuan seeking the missing half of the Ring of Erreth-Akbe. Here, he fights the evil of the Nameless Ones and frees their priestess.

———. *A Wizard of Earthsea*. Illustrated by Ruth Robbins. Parnassus, 1968 (I:10+ R:6). Young Sparrowhawk shows great powers of enchantment. Unhappily, he releases an evil spirit and must hunt it before it destroys Earthsea.

Lewis, C. S. *The Last Battle*. Illustrated by Pauline Baynes. Macmillan, 1956. The final book in the Chronicles of Narnia sees Aslan lead his people into paradise.

———. *The Lion, the Witch and the Wardrobe*. Illustrated by Pauline Baynes. Macmillan, 1950 (I:9+ R:7). Four children enter the magical kingdom of Narnia through a wardrobe. They meet the White Witch and the good lion Aslan and help the good forces overcome the forces of evil. This is one of the "Chronicles of Narnia."

———. *The Magician's Nephew*. Illustrated by Pauline Baynes. Macmillan, 1955 (I:9+ R:7). This sixth book in the chronicles explains how Aslan created Narnia and gave speech to its an-

imals. It also explains the magical properties of the wardrobe.

———. *Prince Caspian, the Return to Narnia*. Illustrated by Pauline Baynes. Macmillan, 1951 (I:9+ R:7). The prince leads his army of talking beasts against the Telmarines.

———. *The Silver Chair*. Illustrated by Pauline Baynes. Macmillan, 1953 (I:9+ R:7). The children complete Aslan's mission; they find the lost prince, help him break an evil spell, and return to Narnia.

———. *The Voyage of the Dawn Treader*. Illustrated by Pauline Baynes. Macmillan, 1952 (I:9+ R:7). Lucy and Edmund, along with their cousin, are reunited with King Caspian of Narnia when they look at a picture of a Narnian sailing ship.

Lewis, Naomi (ed.). *The Silent Playmate: A Collection of Doll Stories*. Illustrated by Harold Jones. Macmillan, 1981 (I:7–9 R:6). An anthology of fantasies, folktales, poems, and realistic stories about dolls.

Lindgren, Astrid. *Pippi in the South Seas*. Illustrated by Louis S. Glanzman, Viking, 1959 (I:7–11 R:5). Pippi continues her hilarious adventures on a south seas island.

———. *Pippi Longstocking*. Illustrated by Louis S. Glanzman. Viking, 1950 (I:7–11 R:5). Pippi lives alone with her monkey and her horse. She does some very unusual things such as scrubbing the floor with brushes tied onto her feet.

———. *Pippi on the Run*. Photographs by Bo-Erik Gyberg. Viking, 1971, 1976 (I:6–10 R:3). Large color photographs accompany the story of Pippi, the strongest girl in the world.

McCaffrey, Anne. *Dragonquest*. Ballantine, 1981 (I:10+ R:6). Continued adventures on a distant planet.

———. *Dragonsinger*. Atheneum, 1977 (I:10+ R:6). Menolly studies under the masterharper of the planet Pern.

———. *Dragonsong*. Atheneum, 1976 (I:10+ R:6). The planet Pern must be protected from the spores that can destroy all living matter.

MacDonald, George. *At the Back of the North Wind*. Illustrated by Arthur Hughes. Dutton, 1871 and 1966 (I:10+ R:6). In an allegorical story Diamond travels in the shelter of the wind to the "Back of the North Wind."

———. *The Princess and the Goblin*. Illustrated by Nora S. Unwin. Macmillan, 1872, 1951 (I:10+ R:9). Princess Irene discovers her fairy godmother spinning magical thread. She is told to follow the thread whenever she might be in danger. She follows it through many adventures.

MacDonald, Reby Edmond. *The Ghosts of Austwick Manor*. Atheneum, 1982 (I:9–12 R:6).

An old dollhouse allows two sisters to go back in time where they discover a family curse.

Marzollo, Jean and Marzollo, Claudio. *Jed's Junior Space Patrol: A Science Fiction Easy-to-Read*. Illustrated by David S. Rose. Dial, 1982 (I:6–8 R:1). Robots and telepathic animals add to the space adventure.

Milne, A. A. *The Christopher Robin Story Book*. Illustrated by Ernest H. Shepard. Dutton, 1966 (I:6–10 R:3). A collection of stories and poems from four Milne books.

———. *The House at Pooh Corner*. Illustrated by Ernest H. Shepard. Dutton, 1928, 1956 (I:6–10 R:3). Pooh builds a house, Tigger comes to the forest, Piglet almost meets the Heffalump, and other stories about Christopher Robin's friends.

———. *Winnie-The-Pooh*. Illustrated by Ernest H. Shepard. Dutton, 1926, 1954 (I:6–10 R:5). Pooh visits Rabbit, hunts woozles, helps Eeyore find his tail, and has other adventures with his nursery friends and Christopher Robin.

Norton, Andre. *Dragon Magic*. Illustrated by Robin Jacques. Crowell, 1972 (I:9–12 R:5). A dust-covered puzzle in an abandoned house casts a strange spell on each of four boys as they travel back to the days of legendary dragons. Each boy learns about his own heritage through four famous dragons—African, Chinese, Scandinavian, and Welsh.

———. *Lavender Green Magic*. Illustrated by Judith Gwyn Brown. Crowell, 1974 (I:9–12 R:6). A magic dream pillow and a maze planted in the 1600s lead three children back to a time when people believed in witches.

———. *Red Hart Magic*. Illustrated by Donna Diamond. Crowell, 1976 (I:9–12 R:4). Chris finds a marvelous miniature of an old English inn. He and his new stepsister discover that the inn has some unusual properties; it takes them back in time.

Norton, Mary. *Are All the Giants Dead?* Illustrated by Brian Froud. Harcourt Brace Jovanovich, 1975 (I:8–10 R:5). James travels to a fairy-tale world and attempts to free the daughter of Beauty and the Beast. He also meets Jack the Giant Killer.

———. *Bed-Knob and Broomstick*. Illustrated by Erik Blegvad. Harcourt Brace Jovanovich, 1943, 1971 (I:7–11 R:6). Three children receive a bed knob that when turned creates a flying machine out of an old brass bed.

———. *The Borrowers*. Illustrated by Beth and Joe Krush. Harcourt Brace Jovanovich, 1952, 1953 (I:7–11 R:3). The Clock family, three little people who live under the floorboards, survive by borrowing items from the household above.

———. *The Borrowers Afield*. Illustrated by Beth and Joe Krush. Harcourt Brace Jovanovich, 1955 (I:7–11 R:4). The Clock family leave their home under the floorboards and escape into the fields.

———. *The Borrowers Afloat*. Harcourt Brace Jovanovich, 1959 (I:7–11 R:4). Fantasy about little people.

———. *The Borrowers Avenged*. Illustrated by Beth and Joe Krush. Harcourt Brace Jovanovich, 1982 (I:7–11 R:4). A new book in the Borrowers series.

———. *The Borrowers Aloft*. Harcourt Brace Jovanovich, 1961 (I:7–11 R:4). Additional tales about small people in a normal world.

O'Brien, Robert C. *Mrs. Frisby and the Rats of NIMH*. Illustrated by Zena Berstein. Atheneum, 1971. (ch. 3).

Park, Ruth. *Playing Beatie Bow*. Atheneum, 1982 (I:10+ R:6). A girl from Sydney, Australia travels in time back to the 1870s.

Potter, Beatrix. *The Tailor of Gloucester, From the Original Manuscript*. Warne, 1969, 1978 (I:5–9 R:8). Text is illustrated with Potter's original drawings.

———. *A Treasury of Peter Rabbit and Other Stories*. Avenel, 1979 (I:3–7 R:6). A collection of favorite stories, including "Peter Rabbit," "Benjamin Bunny," "Squirrel Nutkin," "Two Bad Mice," and "Jeremy Fisher."

Ray, N.L. *There Was This Man Running*. Macmillan, 1981 (I:10+ R:6). A sinister alien causes difficulty for a boy and his deaf sister.

Rodowsky, Colby F. *The Gathering Room*. Farrar, Straus & Giroux, 1981 (I:10+ R:7). Spirits of people buried in the cemetery are friends of a nine-year-old boy.

St. George, Judith. *The Mysterious Girl in the Garden*. Illustrated by Margot Tomes. Putnam, 1981 (I:10+ R:6). Ten-year-old Terrie travels in time back to London in the early 1800s.

Sandburg, Carl. *Rootabaga Stories*. Illustrated by Maud and Miska Petersham. Harcourt Brace Jovanovich, 1922, 1950 (I:8–11 R:7). A series of short nonsense stories about the strange people who live in Rootabaga country, beyond the zigzag railroad, in the villages of Liver and Onions or Cream Puffs.

Selden, George. *Chester Cricket's Pigeon Ride*. Illustrated by Garth Williams. Farrar, Straus & Giroux, 1981 (I:6–9 R:4). Chester goes on a night tour of Manhattan because he misses his country home.

———. *The Cricket in Times Square*. Illustrated by Garth Williams. Farrar, Straus & Giroux, 1960 (I:7–11 R:3). Chester, a cricket from Connecticut, accidentally finds himself in a subway station below Times Square.

———. *Harry Cat's Pet Puppy*. Farrar, Straus & Giroux, 1975 (I:7–11 R:3). Harry experiences problems after he adopts a dog.

———. *Tucker's Countryside*. Farrar, Straus & Giroux, 1969 (I:7–11 R:3). The friends come to Connecticut to help Chester save the meadow.

Selfridge, Oliver G. *Trouble With Dragons*. Illustrated by Shirley Hughes. Addison-Wesley, 1978 (I:7–10 R:6). Three princesses set forth to win an eligible prince; to do so they must first kill a dragon.

Snyder, Zilpha Keatley. *Below the Root*. Illustrated by Alton Raible. Atheneum, 1975. (I:9–12 R:6). A girl searches for a civilization underground.

Stearns, Pamela. *The Mechanical Doll*. Illustrated by Trina Schart Hyman. Houghton Mifflin, 1979 (I:8–12 R:6). A gift of a mechanical doll that dances delights the king but causes difficulty for the court musician. When the doll is broken, the musician gives her a strange new life.

Tolkien, J. R. R. *Farmer Giles of Ham*. Illustrated by Pauline Baynes. Houghton Mifflin, 1978 (I:7–10 R:6). Farmer Giles becomes a hero when he accidentally fires his blunderbuss into a giant's face.

———. *Fellowship of the Ring*. Houghton Mifflin, 1967 (I:12+ R:8) Part of the trilogy enjoyed by older readers.

———. *The Hobbit*. Houghton Mifflin, 1938 (I:9–12 R:6). Bilbo Baggins, a hobbit, joins forces with thirteen dwarfs in their quest to overthrow Smaug, the evil dragon, and regain the dwarf treasure.

———. *The Lord of the Rings*. Houghton Mifflin, 1974 (I:12+ R:8). Part of the trilogy enjoyed by older readers.

———. *The Return of the King*. Houghton Mifflin, 1967 (I:12+ R:8). Part of the trilogy enjoyed by older readers.

———. *Smith of Wootton Major*. Illustrated by Pauline Baynes. Houghton Mifflin, 1978 (I:7–11 R:7). When the baker's new apprentice places a star in the piece of cake eaten by the Smith's son, strange happenings occur.

Travers, Pamela L. *Mary Poppins*. Illustrated by Mary Shepard. Harcourt Brace Jovanovich, 1934, 1962 (I:7–11 R:7). An unusual Nanny arrives with the east wind and changes the life of the Banks family.

———. *Mary Poppins in Cherry Tree Lane*. Illustrations by Mary Shepard. Delacorte, 1982 (I:7–11 R:7). The Nanny returns to give the Banks children a magical happening in the park on Midsummer Eve.

Watson, Simon. *No Man's Land*. Greenwillow, 1976 (I:10+ R:6). Mechanization in the twenty-first century causes a boy to rebel.

Wetterer, Margaret K. *The Giant's Apprentice.* Illustrated by Elise Primavera. Atheneum, 1982 (I:9 –12 R:5). A blacksmith's apprentice is rescued from an evil giant.

White, E. B. *Charlotte's Web.* Illustrated by Garth Williams. Harper & Row, 1952 (I:7–11 R:3). Charlotte, with the help of Templeton the rat, saves Wilbur's life and creates a legend.

_____. *Stuart Little.* Illustrated by Garth Williams. Harper & Row, 1945 (I:7–11 R:6). Mrs. Little's second son is quite different from the rest of the family; he is a mouse. This condition gives him many adventures and finally sends him on a long quest for his dear friend Margalo, a bird.

Williams, Margery. *The Velveteen Rabbit.* Illustrated by Ilse Plume. David R. Godine, 1982 (I:6– 9 R:5). New illustrations for a classic tale.

_____. *The Velveteen Rabbit: Or, How Toys Become Real.* Illustrated by Michael Green. Running Press, 1982 (I:6–9 R:5). Drawings in brown tones create a newly illustrated version of the story.

_____. *The Velveteen Rabbit: Or How Toys Become Real.* Doubleday, 1958. Illustrated by William Nicholson. (I:6–9 R:5). A toy rabbit is given life after his faithful service to a child.

Yolen, Jane. *Dragon's Blood.* Delacorte, 1982 (I:10 + R:7). The planet Austar IV is the setting for a story about a boy who raises a dragon to be a fighter.

_____. *The Acorn Quest.* Illustrated by Susanna Natti. Crowell, 1981 (I:7–10 R:6). The quest is for a golden acorn that could end the famine for the animals.

_____. *Dream Weaver.* Illustrated by Michael Hague. Collins, 1979 (I:8–12 R:5). Seven tales spun by a blind gypsy dream weaver tell of love, death, and loyalty.

_____. *The Girl Who Cried Flowers.* Illustrated by David Palladini. Crowell, 1974 (I:7–10 R:6). Five original fantasies tell about giants, characters with miraculous abilities, and wisdom overcoming adversity.

_____. *The Hundredth Dove and Other Tales.* Illustrated by David Palladini. Crowell, 1977 (I:7 –10 R:6). Seven original fairy tales.

_____. *The Mermaid's Three Wisdoms.* Illustrated by Laura Rader. Collins, 1978 (I:7–12 R:6). A girl with a hearing impairment befriends a mermaid who cannot speak.

_____. *The Moon Ribbon and Other Tales.* Illustrated by David Palladini. Crowell, 1976 (I:7– 11 R:7). Six original stories that are traditional in nature.

_____. *Neptune Rising: Songs and Tales of the Undersea Folks.* Illustrated by David Weisner. Philomel, 1982 (I:7–10 R:6). A collection of stories about undersea beings.

_____. *The Robot and Rebecca and the Missing Owser.* Illustrated by Lady McCrady. Knopf, 1981 (I:8–10 R:5). The year is 2121 and Rebecca's three-legged pet is missing.

Wiseman, David. *Jeremy Visick.* Houghton Mifflin, 1981 (I:10 + R:4). A contemporary Cornish boy goes back in time to discover the location of a boy lost in a mine accident.

_____. *Thimbles.* Houghton Mifflin, 1982 (I:10 + R:4). Two thimbles in an old family trunk provide the ties between the present and 1819 when a girl goes back in time.

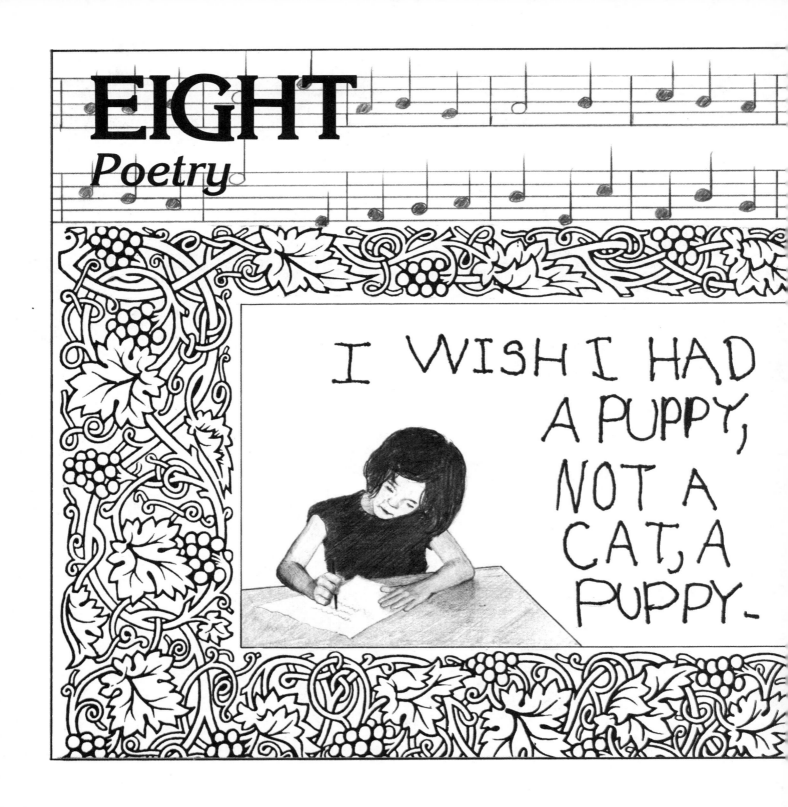

Rhythmic Patterns of Language

Involving Children in Poetry

Rhythmic Patterns of Language

Rainbow Writing

Nasturtiums with
their orange cries
flare like trumpets;
their music dies.

Golden harps
of butterflies;
the strings are mute
in autumn skies.

Vermilion chords,
then silent gray;
the last notes of
the song of day.

Rainbow colors
fade from sight,
come back to me
when I write.

Eve Merriam
Rainbow Writing, p. 3

Poetry, according to Eve Merriam (22), is "Rainbow Writing" because it colors the human mind with the vast spectrum of human experience. Just as the rainbow is a natural phenomenon that inspires an awe of nature, so too may a poem create an awe for words and the expression of feelings. Cecil Day-Lewis (6) agrees. He compares the effect of poetry on words to the effect of sand on pennies; in a miraculous way, poetry brightens words that may have appeared dull or ordinary. Poetry adds a new dimension to the imagination. It often has a musical quality that attracts children and appeals to their emotions. The poet's choice of words can suggest new images and create delightful word plays. When a poet can see and feel from a child's point of view, poetry can provide hours of enjoyment.

There are many poems in this chapter that allow children to see or feel with fresh insights. The value of poetry, characteristics of poems children prefer, criteria for selecting poetry, and the elements and forms of poetry are discussed. The chapter concludes with a discussion of children's poets and the poems they write to create this magical world of the rainbow for their youthful readers.

THE VALUES OF POETRY FOR CHILDREN

When he is most lucky, the poet sees things as if for the first time, in their original radiance or darkness; a child does this too, for he has no choice. He is new in the world, and everything in the world is new to him. (p. 269)

These words by Edwin Muir (25) provide insights into the value of poetry for children. Poetry allows children to experience the world with new understanding and share feelings, experiences, and vision with the poet. Poetry encourages children to play with words, interpret the world in a new way, and realize the images that are possible when words are chosen carefully. Through poetry, children may discover the power imprisoned in words; a power that the poet can release (8).

Jean Le Pere, during a stimulating address to the International Reading Association (13), identified six reasons for sharing poetry with children. First, there is pure enjoyment. Young children begin to discover the enjoyment in poetry by hearing and sharing nonsense poems, Mother Goose rhymes, and tongue twisters. They grow into poetry through such story poems as those written by A. A. Milne. They discover the many exciting forms available to the poet. Second, through poetry, they gain knowledge about concepts in the world around them. They learn about seasons and time and size through the words of the poet. Third, because words play such an important role in poetry, children gain an appreciation for language. Horses not only run, they also clop; not only do kittens jump, they also pounce; and the moon may not only be bright, it may also be a silver sickle. Fourth, through poetry, children identify with characters and situations. With Robert Louis Stevenson, they read about going up in a swing; with Robert Frost, they visualize a snowy evening; and with Karama Fufuka, they vicariously encounter life in an urban black community and may agree that "My Daddy Is a Cool Dude." Fifth, they discover that poetry is a way of expressing a mood. They may have feelings similar to the child's in Charlotte Zolotow's "Nobody Loves Me." The moods expressed in this poem reveal that sometimes it seems as if nobody loves the speaker, and sometimes, as if everybody loves him—feelings that are familiar to all children. Finally, through poetry, children gain insights into themselves and others; many poems develop universal needs and feelings. There also are poems that have been written by other children, and from these children discover that others express feelings poetically and have had experiences similar to their own.

WHAT IS POETRY?

What is this literary form that increases enjoyment, develops appreciation for language, and helps children gain insights about themselves? Poetry is an elusive subject not easily defined; it is not based on fact or easily measured or classified. There is not one accepted definition for poetry. Consider, for example, the following definitions of poetry suggested by poetry critics, poets, and children. Critic Patrick J. Groff (11) suggests that poetry for children is writing that, in addition to using the mechanics of poetry, transcends literal meaning. He states: "The use of original combinations of words is probably the easiest, the best, and the most obvious way to write poetry that transcends the literal and goes beyond a complete or obvious meaning. Consequently, in poetry a word has much more meaning than a word in prose. In the former the emphasis is connotative rather than denotative. Words possess suggested significance apart from their explicit and recognized meanings. It is the guessing element that requires the reader to go below the surface of words, to plumb their literal meanings. Figurative language most often provides the guessing element" (p. 185).

An emotional and physical reaction defined poetry for author Emily Dickinson who related poetry to a feeling: if she read a book that made "her body so cold no fire could warm" her, she knew it was poetry. If she felt physically as if the top of her head were taken off, she also knew it was poetry.

Jerome Judson (12) contends that poetry is words performed. He stresses that the meaning of the words cannot be separated from their sounds. Just as a visual shape is important to the sculptor or painter, the tonal shape is important to the poet. Judson compares the work of the poet to the composition of a musician; in both forms, the total quality is essential.

A thought-provoking definition of what children think poetry is or is not is suggested by poet Harry Behn (3). When he asked children to tell him what poetry should be, one boy replied: "Anything that recites nicely without people . . . people are stories. A poem is something else. Something way out. Way out in the woods. Like Robert Frost waiting in a snowstorm with promises to keep" (p. 159). Other answers suggested the range of what children thought poetry should be: "A poem should be about animals, what you feel, springtime, something funny, anything you see and hear, anything you can imagine. Anything. Even a story!" (p. 159). While these definitions do not agree, they do infer that children have very personal reactions to poetry.

These definitions suggest the importance of an original combination of words, an emotional impact, and the sound of poetry. There is also a visual element in poetry. Some poems are like paintings; they must be seen to be appreciated. Poets may make a statement or increase the impact of their words by carefully arranging the words on the page. Lines are grouped into stanzas, open spaces may emphasize words, an important word may be capitalized, or the arrangement of the whole poem may suggest the subject matter.

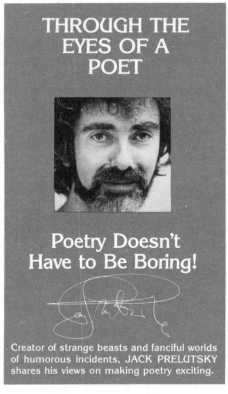
ONCE THERE WAS A teacher who had charge of thirty-three open and eager young minds. One Monday morning, the teacher opened her curriculum book, which indicated that she should recite a poem to her students. She did, and it came out something like this:

> Blah blah the flower,
> blah blah the tree,
> blah blah the shower,
> blah blah the bee.

When she had finished her recitation she said, "Please open your geography books to page one-hundred-thirty-seven."

On Tuesday morning, the teacher (a wonderful person who happened to be rather fond of poetry) decided, on her own initiative, to read another poem to her class. This poem, which was somewhat longer than the first, came out something like this:

> Blah blah blah blah blah blah hill,
> blah blah blah blah blah blah still,
> blah blah blah blah blah blah mill,
> blah blah blah blah daffodil.

Then she said, "Please open your history books to page sixty-two."

She went on like this for the entire week, and by Friday, the children (who knew what was coming when she opened her book of verse) began making peculiar faces and shifting restlessly in their seats. The staunchest aesthetes in the group had begun to lose interest in flowers, bees, and hills etcetera. Many of the children were harboring strange feelings about poetry. They began saying things about poetry to themselves and to each other. Here are some of the things that they said:

"Poetry is boring."
"Poetry is dumb."
"Poetry doesn't make any sense."

The original combinations of words, the sounds of the language, the emotional impact, and the visual images evoked by careful word selection and placement are all essentials of poetry. To be enjoyed, poetry must be savored. Like a painting or a sculpture, it cannot be experienced rapidly; it must be read slowly, even reread several times, if the reader or listener is to be immersed into the sounds and imagery of the poem. In other words, children must have time to see, hear, and feel the world of the poet.

CHARACTERISTICS OF POEMS CHILDREN PREFER

Behn's interview with children suggests that they differ in their definitions of poetry and in their likes and dislikes. These individual interests should be considered when choosing poetry. Samuel French Morse (24) suggests that children's judgment must be respected; he believes they can honestly judge what speaks to their imagination.

Even though some children may have diverse interests and experiences with poetry, students of children's literature will discover valuable information in the research that has investigated children's poetry choices. Several researchers have identified poems that children enjoy and analyzed the subjects and elements in these poems. Ethel Bridge (4) investigated children's poetry preferences in the middle grades and concluded that both boys and girls liked poems related to their own experiences and interests, humorous poems, and poems with elements of rhythm and rhyme. She concluded that because there is a wide range of interests, poetry selections are difficult to categorize according to grade level.

Ann Terry (27) investigated the poetry preferences of children in the fourth, fifth, and sixth grades. She also analyzed poetic elements and form in the poems the children preferred. She concluded the following:

1 Children's enthusiasm for poetry declines as they advance in the elementary grades.
2 Children respond more favorably to contemporary poems than to traditional ones.
3 Poems dealing with familiar and enjoyable experiences are preferred.
4 Poems that tell a story or have a strong element of humor are enjoyed.
5 Children prefer poems with rhythm and rhyme.
6 Among the least popular poems are those which rely too heavily on complex imagery or subtly implied emotion.

"Poetry is about things that don't interest me."
"I hate poetry."

Once there was another teacher with a class of thirty-three young students. She was also a wonderful person with a fondness for poetry. One Sunday evening, she opened her curriculum book and saw that a unit of poetry was scheduled for the next day's lesson. "Hmmmmmm," she mused. "Now what poem shall I share with them tomorrow?" After giving it some careful thought, she settled on a poem about a silly monster, which the poet had apparently created out of whole cloth, and which she thought might stimulate her pupils' imaginations. "Hmmmmmm," she mused again. "Now how can I make this poem even more interesting?" She deliberated a bit more and, in the course of memorizing the poem, came up with several ideas. The next morning, this is what happned:

"Children," she said. "Today is a special day. It is the first day of silly monster week, and to honor the occasion, I am going to share a silly monster poem with you." She held up a small tin can, and continued. "The monster lives in this can, but I am not going to show it to you yet, because I would like you to imagine what it looks like while I'm reciting the poem."

She then recited the poem, and upon reaching the last word in the last line, suddenly unleashed an expanding snake from the can. The children reacted with squeals of mock terror and real delight. Then they asked her to recite the poem again, which she did. Afterward, she had them draw pictures of the silly monster. No two interpretations were alike. The drawings were photographed and later presented in an assembly as a slide show, with the children reciting the poem in chorus. She shared a number of other poems during "silly monster week," always showing her honest enthusiasm and finding imaginative methods of presentation. She used masks, musical instruments, dance, sound effects recordings, and clay sculpture. The children grew so involved that she soon was able to recite poems with no props at all. At the end of the week, these are some of the things her students said about poetry:

"Poetry is exciting."
"Poetry is fun."
"Poetry is interesting."
"Poetry makes you think."
"I love poetry."

7 The majority of teachers in these grades pay little attention to poetry, seldom read it to children, and do not encourage them to write their own poems.

When Terry analyzed the forms of poetry children preferred or disliked, she concluded that narrative poems and limericks were among the most preferred, while haiku and free verse were among the most unpopular. As for poetic elements, Terry found that rhythm, rhyme, and sound were found in the most preferred poems. In contrast, complex imagery and figurative language were elements in the most disliked poems. Her content analysis showed that the most popular poems were humorous, even nonsensical, with most about familiar experiences or animals.

Both Bridge and Terry stress that children should be provided with many experiences that include a wide range of poetry. Terry also recommends that books on poetry should be made accessible to children, listening centers should include tapes and records of poetry, and a rich poetry environment should stimulate children's interest in writing their own poetry.

One reason for the narrow range of poems enjoyed by children may be that poetry is shared with them infrequently. The enjoyment of poetry, like other types of literature, can be increased by an enthusiastic adult who reads poetry to children. Because Terry's research indicates that teachers of older children seldom use poetry with them, enthusiasm for poetry must be stimulated among adults if parents, teachers, and librarians are to share poetry with children.

CRITERIA FOR SELECTING CHILDREN'S POETRY

The previously discussed research suggests some of the characteristics and content of poetry that children prefer. The following list of criteria for selecting poetry is compiled from recommendations by Leonard Clark (5), Patrick Groff (11), Henry Behn (3), Samuel Morse (24), Myra Cohn Livingston (16), and Kinereth Gensler and Nina Nyhart (10):

1 Poems with exciting meters and rhythms are most likely to appeal to young children.
2 Poems for young children should emphasize the sound of language and encourage play with words.
3 Sharply cut visual images and words used in a fresh novel manner allow children to expand their imaginations and see or hear the world in a new way.
4 Poems for young children should tell simple stories and introduce stirring scenes of action.

5 Poems should be selected that have not been written down to children's supposed level.

6 The most effective poems are presented with a careful incompleteness of information so there is room for children to interpret, to feel, and to put themselves into the poems. The degree to which the reader is provoked to find the part that is missing or not understood is another measure of a poem's worth. Does the poem encourage children to extend comparisons, images, and findings?

7 The subject matter should delight children, say something to them, titillate their egos, strike happy recollections, bump their funny bones, or encourage them to explore.

8 Poems should be good enough to stand up under repeated readings.

These criteria refer to many of the elements found in poetry. The next section discusses these elements and gives examples of each from contemporary poems and poems that are considered classics.

ELEMENTS IN POETRY

The poet uses everyday language in different ways to encourage readers to see familiar things in new ways, to draw on their senses, and to fantasize with the imaginative quality of their minds. The poet also uses certain devices to create a medley of sounds, suggest a visual interpretation, and communicate a message to others or himself. Poets may use rhythm, rhyme, sound patterns, repetition, figurative language, and shape in the creation of poetry.

Rhythm

Rhythm, according to the Greek word *rhythmos*, means "to flow." In poetry this flowing quality refers to the whole movement of words in the poem. It is the way sounds, stress, pitch, syllables, and pattern of the language direct and control the ideas and feelings expressed in the poem. The rhythm may have a definite pattern or cadence, or it may be irregular. The rhythm in limericks, for example, is quite structured. Limericks often begin with a similar phrase and include rhyming words at the end of the first, second, and last lines. Free verse, however, usually has a more casual, irregular rhythm.

Poets use rhythm in four quite specific ways. First, rhythm can be used to increase enjoyment of the sounds of language.

Young children usually enjoy the sounds and cadences in nursery rhymes, chants, and nonsensical verse. Rhythm encourages children to join in orally, experiment with the language, and move to the rhythmical sounds of language. Second, rhythm can be used to highlight and emphasize specific words. Poets frequently use stress to suggest the importance of words. Third, rhythm can be used to achieve a dramatic effect. An irregular meter or repeatedly stressed words may immediately attract a listener's or reader's attention. Finally, rhythm can be used to suggest the mood of the poem. For example, there may be a rapid rhythm that suggests excitement and involvement or there may be a slow, leisurely rhythm that suggests a lazy, contemplative mood. David McCord uses rhythm to suggest the sounds a stick might make if a child walked by the fence; it highlights and emphasizes specific words; it attracts and holds attention; and it suggests the mood of the poem.

The Pickety Fence

The pickety fence
The pickety fence
Give it a lick it's
The pickety fence
Give it a lick it's
A clickety fence
Give it a lick it's
A lickety fence
Give it a lick
Give it a lick
Give it a lick
With a rickety stick
Pickety
Pickety
Pickety
Pick

David McCord
Far and Few: Rhymes of the Never Was and Always Is, p. 7

Rhythm is often used to give the listener or reader the feeling of being involved with the poem's action. Gensler and Nyhart (10), who have used poetry to stimulate children's involvement, suggest that the rhythm of a poem works particularly well when it reinforces the poem's content.

Consider, for example, Robert Louis Stevenson's "From a Railway Carriage." The rhythm suggests the dash and rattle of a train as it crosses the country. It is even conceivable that a child might be peering out of the window as the scenery rushes by.

From a Railway Carriage

Faster than fairies, faster than witches,
Bridges and houses, hedges and ditches;
And charging along like troops in a battle,
All through the meadows the horses and cattle:
All of the sights of the hill and the plain
Fly as thick as driving rain;
And ever again, in the wink of an eye,
Painted stations whistle by.

Here is a child who clambers and scrambles,
All by himself and gathering brambles;
Here is a tramp who stands and gazes;
And here is the green for stringing the daisies!
Here is a cart run away in the road
Lumping along with man and load;
And here is a mill and there is a river:
Each a glimpse and gone forever!

Robert Louis Stevenson
A Child's Garden of Verses, 1883

Rhyme

Children apparently receive auditory pleasure from the sounds in poetry. One of the ways a poet can emphasize sounds is through rhyming words. The twenty-five most preferred poems in Terry's study contained a rhyming pattern. Rhyming words may occur at the ends of lines and within lines. Poets of nonsense verse may even create their own words to achieve a humorous, rhyming effect. Consider, for example, Zilpha Keatley Snyder's use of rhyme in "Poem to Mud." The end rhymes—*ooze–slooze, crud–flood,* and *thickier–stickier,*—suggest visual and sound characteristics of mud. The internal rhymes—*fed–spread, slickier–stickier–thickier*—create a tongue-twisting quality.

Poem to Mud

Poem to mud—
Poem to ooze—
Patted in pies, or coating the shoes.
Poem to slooze—
Poem to crud—
Fed by a leak, or spread by a flood.
Wherever, whenever, whyever it goes,
Stirred by your finger, or strained by your toes,
There's nothing sloopier, slipperier, floppier,
There's nothing slickier, stickier, thickier,
There's nothing quickier to make grown-ups sickier,
Trulier coolier,
Than wonderful mud.

Zilpha Keatley Snyder
Today Is Saturday, pp. 18-19

The nineteenth-century authority on nonsense and wit, Edward Lear, created refreshing poems with strong rhyme and rhythm. His "The Owl and the Pussy-Cat" and many other poems published in *The Nonsense Books* reflect both rhyme and rhythm.

Sound Patterns

"The Pickety Fence" and "Poem to Mud" also rely on sound patterns to recreate excitement. In addition to the sounds created by rhyming words, the poets use *alliteration,* the repetition of initial consonants to create sound patterns. Jack Prelutsky uses alliteration to create a humorous poem about a yak. Notice that Prelutsky uses single initial consonants as in *yickity–yackity;* two-letter consonant blends as in *sniggidly–snaggidly;* and three-letter consonant blends as in *scriffity–scraffity.*

The Yak

Yickity-yackity, yickity-yak,
the yak has a scriffity, scraffity back;
some yaks are brown yaks and some yaks are black,
yickity-yackity, yickity-yak.

Sniggidly-snaggidly, sniggidly-snag,
the yak is all covered with shiggily-shag;
he walks with a ziggildy-zaggildy-zag,
sniggidly-snaggildy, sniggidly-snag.

Yickity-yackity, yickity-yak,
the yak has a scriffily, scraffily back;
some yaks are brown yaks and some yaks are black,
yickity-yackity, yickity-yak.

Jack Prelutsky
A Gopher in the Garden, p. 24

"The Yak" is one of the poems selected by Isabel Wilner for *The Poetry Troupe.* (The collection contains over two hundred poems that children have selected for reading aloud.) Additional poems in the "Lingual Gyration" chapter rely on alliteration to create interesting sound patterns. For example, Carolyn Wells's "The Tutor" builds upon the repetition of the beginning sound of *t* as the teacher tries to teach "two young tooters to toot." Mary Ann Hoberman's "Gazelle" stresses the *g* sound. Her four-line poem contains fifteen words beginning with *g.* If a poem has excessive alliteration, a tongue twister results.

Assonance, the repetition of vowel sounds, is another means of creating interesting and unusual sound patterns. Prelutsky uses the frequent repetition of the long *e* sound in the following poem:

Don't Ever Seize a Weasel by the Tail

You should never squeeze a weasel
for you might displease the weasel,
and don't ever seize the weasel by the tail.

Let his tail blow in the breeze;
if you pull it, he will sneeze,
for the weasel's constitution tends to be a little frail.

Yes the weasel wheezes easily;
the weasel freezes easily;
the weasel's tan complexion rather suddenly turns pale.

So don't displease or tease a weasel,
squeeze or freeze or wheeze a weasel
and don't ever seize a weasel by the tail.

Jack Prelutsky
A Gopher in the Garden, p. 19

The sounds of some words suggest the meaning they are trying to convey; *onomatopoeia* refers to words that imitate the actions or things they are associated with. Words such as *plop, jounce,* and *beat* may suggest to children the loud sound of rain hitting the concrete in Aileen Fisher's "Rain." Young children who like to experiment with language may develop their own nonsense words that suggest to them a sound or meaning they are trying to convey. Two poems written by second graders in Gensler's and Nyhart's *The Poetry Connection* (10) incorporate onomatopoeic language. One boy uses consecutive letter *d*s to suggest that rain sounds like a machine gun. A girl uses repetitive words—*lip–lap* and *slip–slap*—to suggest the sound of a waterfall.

Repetition

McCord used considerable repetition of whole lines in "The Pickety Fence"; Prelutsky repeated almost a whole verse in "The Yak." Poets frequently use repetition to enrich or emphasize words, phrases, lines, or even whole verses in a poem. Lewis Carroll, for example, uses repetition to accent his feelings about marvelous soup.

Beautiful Soup

Beautiful Soup, so rich and green,
Waiting in a hot tureen!
Who for such dainties would not stoop?
Soup of the evening, beautiful Soup!
Soup of the evening, beautiful Soup!
   Beau—ootiful Soo—oop!
   Beau—ootiful Soo—oop!
Soo—oop of the e—e—evening,
   Beautiful, beautiful Soup!

Beautiful Soup! Who cares for fish,
Game, or any other dish?
Who would not give all else for two
Pennyworth only of beautiful Soup?
   Beau—ootiful Soo—oop!
   Beau—ootiful Soo—oop!
Soo—op of the e—e—evening,
   Beautiful, beauti—FUL SOUP!

Lewis Carroll
Alice's Adventures in Wonderland, 1865

"Beautiful Soup" is another favorite for oral reading; children find they can recreate that marvelous sound of rich, hot soup being taken from the spoon and placed carefully or noisily into their mouths. Repetition can be found in other poems by Carroll. In "The Mock Turtle's Song," several lines are repeated as the whiting tries to convince the snail to join the dance.

Lullabies shared with young children frequently are enhanced through repetition. Christina G. Rossetti's "Lullaby" uses repetition to suggest a musical quality.

Lullaby

Lullaby, oh, lullaby!
Flowers are closed and lambs are sleeping;
Lullaby, oh, lullaby!
Stars are up, the moon is peeping;
Lullaby, oh, lullaby!
While the birds are silence keeping,
   (Lullaby, oh, lullaby!)
Sleep, my baby, fall a-sleeping,
Lullaby, oh, lullaby!

Christina Rossetti
Sing-Song, 1872

Throughout the long narrative poem "The Song of Hiawatha," published in 1855, Henry Wadsworth Longfellow used the repetition of beginning words in a series of sentences as illustrated by this introduction:

The Song of Hiawatha

Should you ask me, whence these stories?
Whence these legends and traditions,
With the odors of the forest,
With the dew and damp of meadows,
With the curling smoke of wigwams,
With the rushing of great rivers,
With their frequent repetitions,
And their wild reverberations,
As of thunder in the mountains?

I should answer, I should tell you,
"From the forests and the prairies,
From the great lakes of the Northland,
From the land of the Ojibways,
From the land of the Dacotahs,
From the mountains, moors, and fen-lands,
Where the heron, the Shuh-shuh-gah,
Feeds among the reeds and rushes. . . ."

Henry Wadsworth Longfellow
The Song of Hiawatha, 1855

Imagery

Imagery is a primary element in poetry. It encourages children to see, hear, feel, taste, smell, and touch the world created by the poet. A writer appeals to the senses directly through words, sounds, and rhythm and indirectly through the images that recreate the experience and help suggest an emotional response. Poets use figurative language (nonliteral meanings) to clarify, add vividness, and encourage readers to see things in new ways. Several types of figurative language are used in poetry. For the purpose of this discussion, this text will focus on metaphor, simile, personification, and hyperbole.

Metaphors are implied comparisons between two things that have something in common but are essentially different. Metaphors highlight certain qualities in things to make the reader see them in a new way. The poet may compare a flock of birds with change spilling from a pocket, ice skaters with swallows gliding and swooping, or a cat's eyes with changes in the moon.

Similes are direct comparisons between two things that have something in common but are essentially different. The comparisons are considered direct because the words *like* or *as* are usually included in the comparison. For example, the poet may say "the moon is like a silver sickle," "dandelions are like golden nuggets" or "a waffle is like gravel pudding."

Personification allows the poet to give human emotions and characteristics to inanimate objects, abstract ideas, and non-human things. The wind may be given such human qualities as sneakiness, trickery, or the ability to pretend; animals may have human emotions; and chairs may walk around the town just to see the sights.

Finally, hyperbole is the use of exaggeration to create a specific effect. John Ciardi's humorous "Mummy Slept Late and Daddy Fixed Breakfast" suggests that a waffle is so tough that it cannot be cut by a hacksaw or dented by a torch.

Kaye Starbird uses personification to encourage readers to visualize a wind with human characteristics. Notice the reference to sneaky, tricky, and a being that does not die. Imagery also encourages other vicarious sensations such as the feel and the sound of the wind.

The Wind

In spring, the wind's a sneaky wind,
A tricky wind,
A freaky wind,
A wind that hides around the bends
And doesn't die, but just pretends;
So if you stroll into a street
Out of a quiet lane,
All of a sudden you can meet
A smallish hurricane.

And as the grown-ups gasp and cough
Or grumble when their hats blow off,
And housewives clutch their grocery sacks
While all their hairdos come unpinned . . .
We kids—each time the wind attacks—
Just stretch our arms and turn our backs,
And then we giggle and relax
And lean against the wind.

Kaye Starbird
The Covered Bridge House and Other Poems, p. 11

A thirteen-year-old Russian child wrote the following poem that uses simile to compare a new moon with a silver sickle that mows the stars and spreads a golden carpet over the waves. Notice the use of the word *like* in the second line. What are the commonalities between a silver sickle and a new moon?

The Path on the Sea

The moon this night is like a silver sickle
Mowing a field of stars.
It has spread a golden runner
Over the rippling waves.
With its winking shimmer
This magic carpet lures me
To fly to the moon on it.

Inna Miller in *Miriam Morton,
The Moon is Like a Silver Sickle*, p. 28

Judith Thurman uses unusual imagery in *Flashlight,* a collection of her poems. In the introduction to the book, she compares a good poem to a flashlight because a "poem is a flashlight, too: the flashlight of surprise. Pointed at a skinned knee or at an oil slick, at pretending to sleep or at kisses, at balloons, or snow, or at the soft, scary nuzzle of a mare, a poem lets us feel and know each in a fresh, sudden and strong light."

Thurman illustrates her ability with imagery as she compares a flock of flying sparrows to loose change spilling out of a pocket:

Spill

the wind scatters
a flock of sparrows—
a handful of small change
spilled suddenly
from the cloud's pocket

Judith Thurman
Flashlight, p. 16

Other comparisons found in this little book of poems include the Milky Way described as thick white breath in cold air, a flashlight compared to a hound with a yellow eye, eyelids in pretended sleep compared to the wings of a captured moth, balloons described as wild space animals, and clay compared to a clown without bones. The poet's careful selection of words and insightful comparisons can develop what Judson (12) described as meaning which transcends the words. Imagery through poetry can open children's minds to a new world of imagination and allow them to ascend to a different level of consciousness.

In addition to visual images, poetry may appeal to other senses of sound, touch, taste, and smell. David McCord's "The Pickety Fence" may trigger sound images, especially for anyone who has ever struck a fence with a stick. Zilpha Keatley Snyder's "Poem to Mud" creates images of touch as the mud oozes, coats the shoes, and becomes "slipperier," "slickier," "stickier," and "thickier." Aileen Fisher's "The Furry Ones" creates sound and touch images of animals who purr, scurry, snuggle, and are soft, warm, and furry. Contrasting sensations of touch are triggered in the reader's mind by Valerie Worth's "Barefoot." There is the choked, blunt weight of shoes and stockings versus the cool, light sensation of grass and earth on bare feet.

An excellent example of the ability of some poetry to create images in the reader's mind was suggested by a child's response to Myra Cohn Livingston's "I Haven't Learned to Whistle." While reading the poem the child said he felt his lips pucker, his tongue push against his teeth, and his breath blow out. He also "heard" the sickly sound that resulted from his own unsuccessful tries at whistling.

Shape

Poets may place their words on the page to create a greater visual impact and communicate meaning. Line division and shape in poetry can act as silent punctuation marks or add to the meaning of the poem. Lewis Carroll's placement of and division of "Beau—ootiful Soo—oop!" (see page 326) gives the words special emphasis. Likewise, the capitalization of the last few letters emphasizes their importance. The shape of the poem may represent a physical experience as that created by Regina Sauro's "I Like to Swing." The poem is in the form of a pyramid, becoming wider and wider as the sweep of the swing becomes wider and wider.

Poets of the concrete poems discussed later in this chapter (see pages 331–32) shape the words of the poems into the form of a picture to emphasize the desired meaning. David McCord's "The Grasshopper" (see page 343) is an excellent example of a poet's interpretation through shape. Children enjoy discovering that shape may be related to the meaning of the poem and experimenting with shape in their own poetry writing.

FORMS OF POETRY

Is there a form of poetry that is preferable, or are there many different forms of poetry that should be encouraged and shared with children? According to Amy Lowell (17), "Every form is proper to poetry, so long as it is the sincere expression of a man's thought" (p. 7). While adults do not spend time with young children analyzing the form of a poem, it is worthwhile for children to realize that poetry has many different forms; some children do not believe they are reading a poem unless the lines rhyme. In addition, children should be encouraged to write their own poetry; when they write poetry, they enjoy experimenting with the different forms. For such experiments, however, they need to be immersed in poetry and led through many enjoyable experiences with poems. This section takes a brief look at various forms of poetry including limerick, narrative, ballad, concrete poems, free verse, and haiku.

Limericks

The witty, humorous poems called *limericks* are very popular with children. Four of the best-liked poems in Terry's study were limericks. The children liked these poems because they were humorous and contained rhyming words. Limericks are short, funny poems that follow a structured format. They are five-line poems in which the first, second, and last lines rhyme. The third and fourth lines are shorter and rhyme only with each other. The limerick form was popularized by Edward Lear. The following is an example of humorous verse from *A Book of Nonsense.*

FLASHBACK

THERE WAS AN OLD MAN OF THE WEST, WHO NEVER COULD GET ANY REST:
SO THEY SET HIM TO SPIN, ON HIS NOSE AND HIS CHIN,
WHICH CURED THAT OLD MAN OF THE WEST.

AN ARTIST WHO PAINTED birds and reptiles, Lear also entertained children with his absurd poetry and accompanying drawings. These poems entertained without providing instruction. Illustrations and verses in *A Book of Nonsense*, published in 1846, popularized the limerick. Other early nonsense collections of Lear's verses included *More Nonsense* (1872), *Laughable Lyrics* (1877), *Nonsense Botany* (1888), and *Queery Leary Nonsense* (1911).

There was an Old Man with a beard,
Who said, "It is just as I feared!—
      Two Owls and a Hen,
      Four Larks and a Wren
Have all built their nests in my beard."

Edward Lear
A Book of Nonsense, 1846

A yak who was new to the zoo
Made a friend of an old looking gnu;
      Said the gnu to the yak
      "If you'll please scratch my back,
I'll do the same favor for you."

David Ross
Poetry for Children, p. 180

Children enjoy the visual imagery that this poem creates. They can see and laugh at the predicament of a man having all those fowls nesting in his beard. They also enjoy reciting the definite rhythm and rhyme found in the limerick. David Mc-Cord (19) says that for a limerick to be successful it must have perfect rhyming and flawless rhythm.

Several contemporary poets either write limericks or include them in poetry anthologies. David Ross uses a limerick to present the predicament of a gnu who has an itchy back:

Limericks by William Jay Smith are included in his *Mr. Smith & Other Nonsense*. McCord's amusing limericks illustrate the author's ability to play with words and sounds of language. They may also stimulate children to experiment with language. McCord uses limericks in his *One at a Time: Collected Poems for the Young* to describe the form and content of limericks. The descriptions and examples found on pages 176 through 182 can be used to encourage children to write their own limericks.

Narrative Poems

Poets may be expert storytellers; when a poem tells a story, it is called *narrative poetry*. Story poems, with their rapid action and typical chronological order, have long been favorites of children; they are excellent for increasing interest in, and appreciation of, poetry.

A favorite narrative poem of young children is Clement Moore's "A Visit from St. Nicholas," published in 1823. Several illustrators have depicted the poem in picture book format. Tomie de Paola's illustrations for Clement Moore's *The Night Before Christmas* are set in the 1840s (see p. 16 of color insert). This earlier time period seems appropriate for the poem's story line. The book is large enough to share with a group. Another beautifully illustrated version of this poem is Tasha Tudor's *The Night Before Christmas*. Children enjoy listening to the poem and comparing the way two different illustrators have depicted the setting.

Robert Browning's "The Pied Piper of Hamelin," published in 1882, contains many of the characteristics of narrative poems that make them appealing to children. There is the visual quality associated with the villainous rats:

> Rats!
> They fought the dogs, and filled the
> cats,
> And bit the babies in the cradles,
> And ate the cheeses out of the vats,
> And licked the soup from the cook's
> own ladles,
> Split open the kegs of salted sprats,
> Made nests inside men's Sunday
> hats,
> And even spoiled the women's chats
> By drowning their speaking
> With shrieking and squeaking
> In fifty different sharps and flats.

The plot develops rapidly as the townspeople approach the mayor and the council demanding action. Into this setting comes the hero who is visually described:

> And in did come the strangest figure!
> His queer long coat from heel to head
> Was half of yellow and half of red;
> And he himself was tall and thin,
> With sharp blue eyes, each like a pin,
> And light, loose hair, yet swarthy
> skin,
> No tuft on cheek nor beard on chin,
> But lips where smiles went out and
> in—

> There was no guessing his kith and
> kin!
> And nobody could enough admire
> The tall man and his quaint attire:

With rapidity, the council offers the thousand gilders and the piper places the pipe to his lips. The tempo of the poem now resembles the scurrying of rats:

> And out of the house the rats came
> tumbling.
> Great rats, small rats, lean rats,
> brawny rats,
> Brown rats, black rats, gray rats, tawny rats,
> Grave old plodders, gay young friskers,
> Fathers, mothers, uncles, cousins,
> Cocking tails and pricking whiskers,
> Families by tens and dozens,
> Brothers, sisters, husbands, wives—
> Followed the piper for their lives.
> From street to street he piped advancing,
> And step for step they followed dancing,

> Robert Browning
> *The Pied Piper of Hamelin,* 1882

After the efficient disposal of the rats comes the confrontation when the mayor refuses to pay the thousand gilders. In retribution the piper puts the pipe to his lips and blows three notes. Now the poem's tempo resembles the clapping of hands and the skipping of feet as the children merrily follow the piper through the wondrous portal into the mountain.

Contemporary poets also write narrative poems. The most popular poem in Terry's study was a narrative one that told the story of what happened when Daddy fixed breakfast. As adults read this poem by John Ciardi, they may consider why children would thoroughly enjoy the poem. (Notice the poet's use of metaphor and hyperbole.)

Mummy Slept Late And Daddy Fixed Breakfast

> Daddy fixed the breakfast.
> He made us each a waffle.
> It looked like gravel pudding.
> It tasted something awful.

> "Ha, ha," he said, "I'll try again.
> This time I'll get it right." But what I got was in between
> Bituminous and anthracite.

> "A little too well done? Oh well,
> I'll have to start all over."
> That time what landed on my plate
> Looked like a manhole cover.

I tried to cut it with a fork:
The fork gave off a spark.
I tried a knife and twisted it
into a question mark.

I tried it with a hack-saw.
I tried it with a torch.
It didn't even make a dent.
It didn't even scorch.

The next time Dad gets breakfast
When Mommy's sleeping late,
I think I'll skip the waffles.
I'd sooner eat the plate!

John Ciardi
You Read to Me, I'll Read to You, p. 18

Ballads

The ballad is a form of narrative folk song developed in the Middle Ages. These narrative folk songs were told by a bard (the Welsh term for poet) who functioned as a singer, or minstrel, of tales. Through his music, he retold the folk ballads of legend or history. These early ballads are a form of traditional literature and were handed down from minstrel to minstrel through word of mouth. Many old ballads tell heroic tales. When they are read, they have a quality similar to folk songs. Cecil Day-Lewis (6) states that "the meter is simple because the ballads were composed by simple people, and often members of the audience liked to make up additional stanzas. It is a fast-moving meter because a ballad generally had quite a long story to tell, and it was necessary to keep it on the go so that the listeners shouldn't get bored. . . . The ballads are flexible, not only in their meter, but in the way they tell their stories. They tell them in a highly dramatic way; and the dramatic technique they use has something in common with the movies" (p. 57).

The ballad has the following five characteristics: (1) it is a narrative, (2) it is sung, (3) it is a form of folk literature, (4) it focuses on a single incident, and (5) the action, in the form of dialogue and incident, moves rapidly. It is the action in a ballad that carries the interest.

Among the best-known ballads are those about the adventures of Robin Hood. "How Robin Hood Rescued the Widow's Sons," for example, found in William Cole's *The Poet's Tales,* exemplifies the characteristics of the ballad. The lilting lines seem especially appropriate for singing. It is a story of bravery and adventure. The widow tells bold Robin Hood about her three sons who are condemned to die; he exchanges clothes with an old palmer, enters Nottingham town, summons his men, and rescues the sons from the gallows. The action, as suggested by this description, moves rapidly.

Concrete Poems

Concrete means something that can be seen, something real, something physical. When a poet emphasizes the meaning and experience of the poem by shaping it into the form of a picture, it is called *concrete poetry.* Robert Froman has published a book of concrete poems about city street experiences. The words in his *Street Poems* simulate the form of such city experiences as skyscrapers, a brick wall, icicles hanging from a building, and a fire plug. His poem "Dead Tree," from *Seeing Things: A Book of Poems,* is lettered in the shape of a dead tree trunk.

Robert Froman
Seeing Things: A Book of Poems, p. 9

Mary Ellen Solt was inspired to create a poem and a picture about the promise of spring in a forsythia bush. Children should turn this poem on its side to read the thoughts of the author.

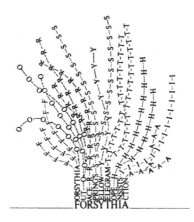

Mary Ellen Solt, ed.
Concrete Poetry: A World View

Children find that concrete poetry is exciting to look at, and also stretches their imagination when they look at concrete objects and write their own picture poems.

Free Verse

Free verse is characterized by lack of rhyme and a less predictable meter. Children are sometimes surprised when they discover that rhyme is not a characteristic of all poetry. In *The Sidewalk Racer and Other Poems of Sports and Motion,* Lillian Morrison has chosen sports and the feelings associated with them as a subject for numerous free verse poems. Skateboards are so popular with children, and they can relate to the author's feelings in the following poem:

> The Sidewalk Racer
> *or*
> On the Skateboard
>
> Skimming
> an asphalt sea
> I swerve, I curve, I
> sway; I speed to whirring
> sound an inch above the
> ground; I'm the sailor
> and the sail; I'm the
> driver and the wheel
> I'm the one and only
> single engine
> human auto
> mobile.
>
> Lillian Morrison
> *The Sidewalk Racer,* p. 12

Haiku

Haiku is a very old form of poetry with specific characteristics: the poem has three lines; the first line has five syllables, the second line has seven, and the final line has five. A modern writer of haiku, Ann Atwood (1), states that haiku, bound within the limitations of approximately seventeen syllables, is paradoxical in nature. "It is both simple and profound, constructive and expansive, meticulously descriptive yet wholly suggestive. And it is the very limitation of haiku that demands the discipline necessary to all art. For with this meager allowance of words, the poet must not be tempted to stop at the right word, but must enlarge his search until the only word is within his grasp" (introduction).

Poems from the great Japanese poets, Issa and Basho, have been translated into English and illustrate how this ancient form of verse has been used to express feelings, experiences, and vision. Richard Lewis (15), in his introduction to a book of haiku by Issa, says, "Every so often there is a man who is not content to allow his life to pass into the silence of mere events. He is compelled, through some means, to express what is within him. He must, rather than remain alone with his thoughts and feelings, share his inner world with others. His response to life, even after he has died, must become part of the lives of those who still live" (p. 7). The poems by Issa and important information about his life are included in Lewis's *Of This World: A Poet's Life in Poetry.*

In haiku, the poet links himself with nature and the moods of earth and the cycles of the seasons. According to Atwood, haiku "is begun by the writer and completed by the reader" (introduction); each experience the power and feeling of the moment. This modern photographer and writer of haiku has combined both her artistic forms in a book of color photographs and poetry, *Haiku: The Mood of Earth.* These poems and photographs must be savored and not read hurriedly. The following example of her haiku accompanies a photograph of a beach scene in which a stream of water is placing its mark upon the land:

> A blank page of sand—
> at the water's cutting edge
> the pattern shaping.
>
> Ann Atwood
> *Haiku: The Mood of Earth,*
> p. 4 unnumbered

All these forms of poetry can be shared with children. Through this experience, they learn that the poet has many ways of expressing feelings and emotions. No one form of poetry is preferable to all others, but as was stated earlier, there are forms of poetry that children seem to prefer.

POETS AND THEIR POEMS

Children and adults who share poetry with children have many poets and poems to choose from. There are older classics: Wadsworth's "Over in the Meadow," Clement Moore's "A Visit from St. Nicholas," and Edward Lear's "The Owl and the Pussy Cat"; there are also many contemporary poets who write about children's feelings and experiences in the twentieth century.

Poets who write for children use subject matter of interest to children. Looking through the books of poetry written for children allows the reader to identify ideas and contents popular with authors of children's poetry. There are humorous poems, nature poems, poems that allow children to identify with characters, situations, and locations, poems that suggest moods and feelings, animal poems, and poems about ghosts, dragons, and magic. Although poets write about many topics, many children's poets select certain subjects to write much of their poetry about. Poets and their poems are discussed in this section as closely as possible according to popular content.

Poems for Starting Out Right

Chapter five discussed the rhymes that are appropriate for early childhood experiences with poetry. Nicholas Tucker (28) says that nursery rhymes are among the best-known literature in America and are appropriate to share with young children because they are made up of easily memorized rhymes and rhythms to help young children master speech. The rhymes encourage children to respond orally as they join in with the rhyme, answer a question formulated by a rhyme, or provide a missing word suggested by the rhyme. Through the words in the rhymes, children discover that words can be manipulated and played with. Tongue twisters and alliteration expand children's delight in the sounds of language. Tucker maintains that characters found in nursery rhymes have important links with children's imaginative life and with antiquity. Children also find a common bond with other children when they share the same nursery rhyme.

Jean Le Pere (13) and Cornelia Meigs (20) believe that nonsense rhymes are the logical successors to Mother Goose rhymes. Meigs feels that the nonsense poems of such great poets as Edward Lear and Lewis Carroll are ideal; they suggest spontaneous fun and emphatic, regular rhythm heightened by alliteration. The nonsense verses convey an absurd meaning or even no meaning at all.

Edward Lear. Edward Lear, introduced earlier as the popularizer of the limerick form, was a friend of Alfred Lord Tennyson, whose work influenced him throughout his life (14). Lear also had many loyal friends among the country's leaders and creative artists; he was welcomed into their homes and became an "Adopt Duncle" to their children. These were the children for whom he wrote his nonsense verses and illustrated them with humorous pictures. These early limericks, along with sketches, were published in 1846 as *A Book of Nonsense.* In his second book, *Nonsense Songs and Stories* published in 1871, he included many nonsense verses and narrative poems.

Lear's rhyming tongue twisters, such as found in his alphabet rhymes, are certainly enjoyed by young children. For example, they can repeat the nonsense words in this alphabet rhyme:

> A was once an apply-pie,
> Pidy,
> Widy,
> Tidy,
> Pidy,
> Nice insidy,
> Apple-Pie!
>
> Edward Lear
> *Nonsense Songs and Stories,*
> 1871 (reissued 1964 as
> *The Complete Nonsense Book*)

Lear's most famous longer humorous poem is probably "The Owl and the Pussy-Cat." Equally enjoyable is the delightful "Teapots and Quails."

Lear's nonsense poems can be found in many anthologies and have also been illustrated in single editions by several well-known illustrators. Six of his limericks were selected to form the text accompanying Janina Domanska's illustrations for *Whizz! The Quangle-Wangle's Hat* was illustrated by Helen Oxenbury, and a recent edition of *The Pelican Chorus & The Quangle Wangle's Hat* was illustrated by Kevin W. Maddison in full-page watercolors. *The Scroobious Pip,* illustrated by Nancy Ekholm Burkert, is a longer, more complex poem that was discovered after Lear's death and completed by Ogden Nash. Older children and adults enjoy this poem and the beautiful illustrations as they speculate about the nature of the Scroobious Pip.

Lewis Carroll. Carroll's works are historical milestones (see pages 53–54) of children's literature and are included in the discussion of modern fantasy (see pages 282–83). His nonsense verses are found in *Alice's Adventures in Wonderland* and *Through the Looking Glass.*

One of Carroll's most famous poems is "Jabberwocky," found in *Through the Looking Glass.* Here are those marvelous nonsense words *brillig, slithy toves,* and *borogoves.* The

The soft brush and ink drawings highlight the mythical nature of the Scroobious Pip.
Specified illustration from *The Scroobious Pip*, by Edward Lear, completed by Ogden Nash, illustrated by Nancy Ekholm Burkert. Illustration Copyright © 1968 by Nancy Ekholm Burkert.

poem is in a lovely single edition illustrated by Jane Breskin Zalben.

A large collection of Carroll's poems, along with illustrations by John Tenniel, Harry Furniss, Henry Holiday, Arthur B. Frost, and Carroll, can be found in Myra Cohn Livingston's compilation of *Poems of Lewis Carroll*. This book also provides considerable information about Carroll (Charles Lutwidge Dodgson).

Laura Richards. It may surprise contemporary children to discover that another well-known author of nonsense poetry is the daughter of Julia Ward Howe, who wrote a beautiful but somber poem, "The Battle Hymn of the Republic." Like the nonsense verse of Lear and Carroll, Richards has shared marvelous words and sounds with children. There are *wizzy wizzy woggums, ditty dotty doggums,* and *diddy doddy dorglums.* There are *Rummy-jums, Viddipocks* and *Orang-Outang-Tangs.* Her collection, *Tirra Lirra, Rhymes Old and New* contains many rhymes that emphasize the sound of language and are good for language development; the rhymes encourage children to play with words. The following is one of her best-loved nonsense poems.

Eletelephony

Once there was an elephant,
Who tried to use the telephant—
No! No! I mean an elephone
Who tried to use the telephone—
(Dear me! I am not certain quite
That even now I've got it right.)

Howe'er it was, he got his trunk
Entangled in the telephunk;
The more he tried to get it free,
The louder buzzed the telephee—
(I fear I'd better drop the song
Of elephop and telephong!)

Laura E. Richards
Tirra Lirra, p. 31

Humorous Poetry

Nonsense and humorous poetry are closely related. Nonsense usually suggests an absurd or impossible situation, but humor deals with amusing or comical happenings that might befall a person or an animal. Many modern poets create poems that range from pure nonsense, to humorous animal situations, to very odd human behavior.

Theodore Roethke. Two collections of Theodore Roethke's poetry, one selected by Beatrice Roethke and Stephen Lushington, *Dirty Dinky and Other Creatures,* and *I Am! Says the Lamb* contain poems for young children. Humor, rhyming elements, repetition, and vivid descriptive words are found in his poems. There are such creatures as Dirty Dinky, a Great Big Lubber, and a Biddly Bear. It seems that children would enjoy being a *piffebob* while *sniggering* or *mocking.*

In addition to humor, there is a moral quality in many of Roethke's poems. He warns readers in one poem that if they are not careful they may be *Dirty Dinky.* Likewise, in "The Kitty-Cat Bird," he tells his readers not to laugh until they have thought about the tale; they could end up like the bird.

Jack Prelutsky. The kingdom of immortal zanies could be the description of the characters and animals who live within the poetry written by Prelutsky. Within the pages of *The Queen of Eene*, children will find such preposterous characters as "Pumberly Pott's Unpredictable Niece," peculiar "Mister Gaffe," "Poor Old Penelope," "Herbert Glerbertt," and the "Four Foolish Ladies" Hattie, Harriet, Hope, and Hortense. The humorous world of animals is contained in the poems in *Toucans Two and Other Poems*. The humorous experiences of a boy and his four friends are found in *Rolling Harvey Down the Hill*. In *The Sheriff of Rottenshot* eccentric characters include Philbert Phlurk, Eddie the spaghetti nut, and a saucy little ocelot. *The Baby Uggs Are Hatching* has poems about such oddly named creatures as sneepies and slitchs. The humor of an unbelievable situation, rhyming words, and rhythm are found in this poem:

Pumberly Pott's Unpredictable Niece

Pumberly Pott's unpredictable niece
declared with her usual zeal
that she would devour, by piece after piece,
her uncle's new automobile.

She set to her task very early one morn
by consuming the whole carburetor;
then she swallowed the windshield, the headlights and horn,
and the steering wheel just a bit later.

She chomped on the doors, on the handles and locks,
on the valves and the pistons and rings;
on the air pump and fuel pump and spark plugs and shocks,
on the brakes and the axles and springs.

When her uncle arrived she was chewing a hash
made of leftover hoses and wires
(she'd just finished eating the clutch and the dash
and the steel-belted radial tires).

"Oh what have you done to my auto," he cried,
You strange unpredictable lass?"
"The thing wouldn't work, Uncle Pott," she replied,
and he wept, "It was just out of gas."

Jack Prelutsky
The Queen of Eene, pp. 10–11

William Jay Smith. Limericks similar to those of Edward Lear are in Smith's *Mr. Smith & Other Nonsense* and *Laughing Time*. An example of this modern poet's use of the limerick is this poem about a strange land:

The Land of Ho-Ho-Hum

When you want to go wherever you please,
Just sit down in an old valise,
And fasten the strap
Around your lap,
And fly off over the apple trees.

And fly for days and days and days
Over rivers, brooks, and bays
Until you come
To Ho-Ho-Hum
Where the Lion roars, and the Donkey brays.

Where the unicorn's tied to a golden chain,
And Umbrella Flowers drink the rain.
After that,
Put on your hat,
Then sit down and fly home again.

William Jay Smith
Laughing Time, p. 8

Mr. Smith & Other Nonsense contains poems about big and little things, imaginary dialogues, and poems about nonsense birds including "The Typewriter Bird." The volume ends with an autobiographical poem, "Mr. Smith." In this poem, the reader learns that Mr. Smith has a gentle disposition, a smooth chin, likes people in arts and sciences, collects hats, has never been to Majorca, and abhors boiled cabbage.

John Ciardi. Two books by a poet who has been both a professor of English and a columnist for *Saturday Review World* are written with a simple vocabulary to appeal to children with beginning reading skills: Ciardi's *I Met a Man* and *You Read to Me, I'll Read to You*. In this second book the author tells the reader, "All the poems printed in black, you read to me" and "All the poems printed in blue, I'll read to you." This collection contains the popular "Mummy Slept Late and Daddy Fixed Breakfast" discussed on pages 330–31. Other popular poems in this book tell about characters such as "Change McTang McQuarter Cat" and "Arvin Marvin Lillisbee Fitch."

Some of Ciardi's poems are better understood by older children; they often contain satirical observations about human behavior or problems of society. Many of these more sophisticated poems are included in *Fast and Slow*. "And They Lived Happily Ever After For a While," for example, tells what happens when two people who live in the Garbage Mountains are married and then build an oxygen tent in order to survive.

N. M. Bodecker. Poems that suggest children should wash their hands with number-one dirt, shampoo their hair with molasses, and rinse off in cider are welcomed by young readers. The humorous questions asked in "Bickering" illustrate Bodecker's ability to use word play to create a humorous verse that is enjoyed by older children.

Bickering

The folks in Little Bickering
they argue quite a lot.
Is tutoring in bickering
required for a tot?
Are figs the best for figuring?
Is pepper ice cream hot?
Are wicks the best for wickering
a wicker chair or cot?
They find this endless dickering
and nonsense and nit-pickering
uncommonly invigor'ing,
I find it downright sickering!
You do agree!

N. M. Bodecker
Hurry, Hurry Mary Dear, p. 13

Both poetry and illustrations provide humor in *Hurry, Hurry Mary Dear.* The title poem depicts a harassed woman who is told to pick apples, dill pickles, chop trees, dig turnips, split peas, churn butter, smoke hams, stack wood, take down screens and put up storm windows, close shutters, stoke fires, mend mittens, knit sweaters, and brew tea. This might not be so bad, but the man who is giving the orders sits in a rocking chair all the time. Finally, Mary has enough—the teapot is placed carefully on the demanding gentleman's head.

Of equal enjoyment are the verses and illustrations in Bodecker's *Let's Marry Said the Cherry.* Word play is again very important; the author shares poems such as "The Lark in Sark," "The Geese in Greece," and "The Snail at Yale."

Other Poets of Humorous Verse. The idiosyncrasies of *Jonathan Bing* create a humorous book of verse by Beatrice Curtis Brown. Through these poems, poor old Jonathan Bing visits the king, displays his manners, does arithmetic, reads a book, dances, catches tea, and finally moves away. All of his actions, however, are a little different from what might be expected.

A banquet of nonsense verse is shared with the reader in Dennis Lee's *Garbage Delight.* The last verse of the title poem suggests what readers are in for if they want to join the feast:

With a nip and a nibble
A drip and a dribble
A dollop, a walloping bite:
If you want to see grins
All the way to my shins
Then give me some Garbage Delight,
    Right now!
Please pass me the Garbage Delight.

Dennis Lee
Garbage Delight, pp. 38–39

A delightful book of humorous verses, *Figgie Hobbin,* by English poet Charles Causley, should appeal to children who enjoy longer nursery rhymes. The subjects of the poems revolve around such characters as "Colonel Fazackerley" as he encounters and outwits a ghost, "Old Mrs. Thing-um-E Bob" as she tries to have her what-you-may-call-it fixed, and his majesty when he refuses nightingales' tongues in favor of *Figgie Hobbin.*

An inn where a rabbit makes the bed and two dragons bake the bread forms the background for the poems in Nancy Willard's *A Visit to William Blake's Inn: Poems for Innocent and Experienced Travelers.* In the introduction to the book she describes her first happy moments when she discovered William Blake's "Tyger, Tyger, burning bright" from his *Songs of Innocence* and *Songs of Experience.* The poems in the book present the odd assortment of guests and human animal characters who work at the inn. The resulting poems create a book that has both nonsense and lyrical poetry. Alice and Martin

The illustrations show some of the odd inhabitants that venture to William Blake's inn.
From *A Visit to William Blake's Inn* by Nancy Willard, illustration © 1981 by Alice Provensen and Martin Provensen. Reproduced by permission of Harcourt Brace Jovanovich, Inc.

Provensen's illustrations complement the mood of the poetry and suggest the characteristics of some of the inhabitants.

One of the most popular children's authors of humorous poetry is Shel Silverstein. Librarians report that *Where the Sidewalk Ends* and *A Light in the Attic* are in considerable demand by young readers. Improbable characters and situations in *A Light in the Attic* include a Quick-Digesting Gink, Sour Face Ann and a polar bear in the Frigidaire. "The Boa Constrictor" from *Where the Sidewalk Ends* is a favorite action poem. Children enjoy acting out the poem as the narrator explains that he or she was swallowed by a boa constrictor.

Anthologies of Humorous Verse. Collections of humorous verse by many different poets have been compiled by William Cole. Poems about wriggling, giggling, noisy, tattling, and naughty children are found in *Beastly Boys and Ghastly Girls.* In *Oh, That's Ridiculous!* there are limericks, two-line poems, and longer verses. More humorous verses are found in Cole's *Oh, What Nonsense!* His anthology *Poem Stew* contains poems written about humorous incidents related to food. The poems include works by such poets as Jack Prelutsky, Myra Cohn Livingston, William Cole, and John Ciardi. Jill Bennett's collection of poems in *Tiny Tim: Verses for Children* includes a variety of jingles and humorous poems written by such authors as William Jay Smith and Conrad Aiken.

Nature Poems

Poets, like children, have marveled at the opening of the first crocus as a promise of spring, have seen new visions in a snowflake, or have stopped to watch a stream of crystal-clear water tumbling from a mountain top. They have understood that people should feel a reverence and respect for nature: not only a special way of looking at nature is required but also a special way of listening to nature.

Aileen Fisher. Fisher presents the feeling and excitement of discovering nature through her poetry. There is a feeling of freshness in Fisher's vision; a feeling of the magic that is possible when a child really looks at nature. Fisher creates images of nature that are real to children and may encourage them to extend these images to other observations. In poems about winter, evergreens after a snowfall wear woolly wraps, snow fills the garden chairs with teddy bears, and footsteps are described as going so quietly the observer thinks they are asleep. Fisher's "Frosted-Window World" allows children to vicariously visit winter's house by going inside a frosted windowpane:

Frosted-Window World

The strangest thing,
the strangest thing
came true for me today:
I left myself beneath the quilt
and softly slipped away.

And do you know
the place I went
as shyly as a mouse,
as curious as a cottontail,
as watchful as a grouse?
Inside the frosted windowpane
(it's rather puzzling to explain)
to visit Winter's house!

How bright it was.
How light it was.
How white it was all over,
with twists and turns
through frosted ferns
and crusted weeds and clover,
through frost-grass
reaching up to my knees,
and frost-flowers
thick on all the trees.

The brightest sights,
the whitest sights
kept opening all around,
for everything
was flaked with frost,
the plants, the rocks,
the ground,
and everything was breathless-still
beneath the crusty rime—
there wasn't any clock to tick
or any bell to chime.
Inside the frosted windowpane
(it's rather puzzling to explain)
there wasn't any Time.

How clear it was.
How queer it was.
How near it was to heaven!
Till someone came
and called my name
and said, "It's after seven!"
And heaven vanished like an elf
and I whisked back, inside myself.

Aileen Fisher
In One Door and Out the Other, pp. 59–60

In the Woods, in the Meadow, in the Sky is another book of nature experiences. Through these poems, children can close their eyes and imagine spring in the form of a pussy willow, sit quietly in the woods and have a rabbit sit beside them, imagine a rain of autumn leaves, or watch a fisherman build a sky net (the fisherman is a spider). They can also imagine more boisterous experiences such as whistling through the woods while experimenting with a whistle made from a twinkling aspen branch, exploring the world from a treetop, or dodging snowballs thrown by the wind. The images are clear and make readers of any age feel that they are seeing a just-discovered dimension in nature.

Byrd Baylor. The closeness felt between the land and the creatures who live upon it is strikingly presented in Baylor's poetry. She tells readers, however, that they must know *The Other Way to Listen* if they are to be fortunate enough to hear corn singing, wildflower seeds bursting open, or a rock murmuring to a lizard. The old man in this poem teaches a child how to learn to listen from the ants, the hills, and the weeds. Instead of starting with big things in nature like mountains and oceans, the child must begin with little things: one seed pod, one horned toad, or one tree. In order to hear nature, the child must also respect the trees, the toads, and the hills. Nature will not talk to people if people feel superior. After a long search, the child is overcome with joy; the oldest sound in the world, the humming of the lava rocks on the hillside, is heard.

The illustrations of Peter Parnall create colorfully illustrated texts that seem attuned to nature and Baylor's poetry. This is especially true in *The Desert Is Theirs,* a poem about Native Americans. The poetry and accompanying illustrations develop the theme that the land is to share; it does not belong only to people but also to spiders, scorpions, birds, coyotes, and lizards. This beautifully illustrated poem tells how Earthmaker created the desert, Spider People sewed the sky and earth together, and Elder Brother taught the people to live in the sun and touch the power of the earth. The reader discovers through this poem that the Papagos learned how to share the earth:

> Papagos try
> not to anger
> their animal brothers.
>
> They don't
> step on
> a snake's track
> in the sand.
>
> They don't disturb
> a fox's bones.
> They don't shove
> a horned toad
> out of the path.
>
> They know
> the land belongs
> to spider and ant
> the same as it does
> to people.

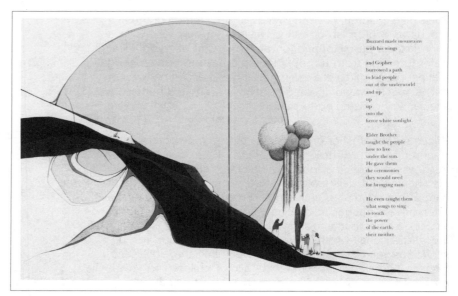

Flowing lines in the illustrations create the mood for poems about the desert.
From Byrd Baylor, *The Desert Is Theirs.* Text copyright © 1975 by Byrd Baylor; Illustrations copyright © 1975 by Peter Parnall. Reprinted with the permission of Charles Scribner's Sons.

They never say,
"This is my land
to do with as I please."
They say,
"We share . . .
we only share."

Byrd Baylor
The Desert is Theirs, p. 15 unnumbered

Additional poems of the desert are found in Byrd Baylor's and Peter Parnall's *Desert Voices.* These poems, written from the viewpoints of desert inhabitants—animal and human—suggest sounds and movements in the desert world.

Ann Atwood.   A love of nature is seen in the two art forms developed by Ann Atwood, mentioned previously. Her books of poetry are accompanied by color photographs that seem to capture the essence of a rippling brook or a fog-shrouded mountain. Both the poems and photographs are designed for savoring leisurely, not reading hurriedly. Many of her poems are written in haiku. In her text, *Haiku-Vision: In Poetry and Photography,* she tells her readers how she believes nature should be observed: "Haiku is the flower of an Eastern culture which for centuries has practiced the unhurried art of gazing. To understand how foreign such a culture is to our own, we have only to imagine ourselves meeting with friends to spend long hours of a night simply 'moon-viewing,' feeling the moon's presence, reflecting . . . remembering . . . imagining . . ." (2, introduction).

In her book, *Fly with the Wind, Flow with the Water,* she has created poems and photographs about things that move in nature, whether the things are birds, waves, breezes, windmills, clouds, gliders, or people. Her introductory poem describes the book's contents and who the poems are about:

This is a book about things
that soar and swing
    and leap and run
    and tumble and swirl
        and flutter and float. . .
It is a book about things that move:
    clouds and creatures
    trees and grasses
    and of course it is about YOU—
running and jumping and wonderfully belonging
    with everything
    that flies with the wind
    and flows with the water

Ann Atwood
Fly with the Wind, pp. 1–2 unnumbered

Other Poets of Nature.   Charlotte Zolotow's poetry is about childhood experiences and nature. An interesting comparison between the effects of illustrations can be made between two collections of her poetry. Both Regina Shekerjian (1970 edition) and Kazue Mizumura (1978 edition) have illustrated *River Winding.* Children find it interesting to discover how two artists have interpreted the same poetry. "Change," in *River Winding,* illustrates how Zolotow is able to bring nature and children's experiences together in poetry:

Change

The summer
still hangs
heavy and sweet
with sunlight
as it did last year.

The autumn
still comes
showering gold and crimson
as it did last year.

The winter
still stings
clean and cold and white
as it did last year.

The spring
still comes
like a whisper in the dark night.

It is only I
who have changed.

Charlotte Zolotow
River Winding, p. 5 (1978 ed.)

Arnold Adoff's *Under the Early Morning Trees* recreates in poetic form a young girl's observances as she goes out into the dawn and explores the line of 100 trees that protect her old farm home from winds, sun, and blizzards. Her eyes and ears are open to nature; she experiences ants working around a rock, hungry beetles leaving their trails in dead wood, a red bird in the tree branches, the noises of animal footsteps through the dry leaves, and the sight of the farm animals who live beyond the hedge. As she goes into the house to begin the day, she feels secure; she knows that the 100-year-old tree hedge will be there tomorrow.

Leslie Norris's poems in *Merlin & the Snake's Egg* are a collection created to cast spells with words. There are poems about such natural phenomena as woodspells, the seasons, moonspells, and the spell of the seeds.

A year in the country, beginning with early April and continuing through the world of melting winter, into the growing seasons with apple-laden trees and new-mown hay in the meadow, and ending with the crimson maple trees and the ice returning to cover the trees is created in Lilian Moore's *Sam's Place, Poems from the Country*. Poems from the country are also the subject of Nancy Dingman Watson's *Blueberries Lavender: Songs of the Farmer's Children*. The title poem in the collection suggests the experience associated with finding wild blueberries and then enjoying them; finally, the children can only laugh through purply lips. The first verse of this poem suggests the feeling of expectation:

Blueberries Lavender

Blueberries lavender, blueberries blue
I will go berrying, Abbie, with you
We'll carry our sugar pails over our arms
And walk through the meadow past orchards and farms
Over the river bridge, orange with rust
Your soft little toe prints are warm in the dust

Nancy Dingman Watson
Blueberries Lavender, p. 2 unnumbered

Robert Frost's lovely poem, *Stopping by Woods on a Snowy Evening*, has been illustrated in large picture book format by Susan Jeffers. The winter setting is depicted through pictures showing the quiet snow-covered woods, animals that blend into the environment, and large downy flakes falling on the man and this magical world.

Anthologies of Nature Verse. Unusual nature photographs by John Earl were the inspiration for a collection of poems selected by Lee Bennett Hopkins. *To Look at Any Thing* is the result of this collaboration between photographer and poetry editor. The photographs are stimulating for children; they try to discover animals or pictures in the fantastic shapes that can be found in close-up photographs of gnarled driftwood, moss-draped branches, and ice-covered rocks. This kind of observation can stimulate the writing of poetry by children. *Moments*, a collection of nature poems selected by Hopkins, contains poems about the four seasons of the year.

Poets may also protest the treatment given the land and suggest the need for living in harmony with nature. Aline Amon's anthology *The Earth Is Sore: Native Americans on Nature* provides thoughtful considerations for what happens to the land.

Identifying with Characters, Situations, and Locations

Poems about experiences that are familiar to children make up one very large category of poetry for children. These familiar experiences may be related to friends or family, they may tell about everyday occurrences, or they may provide insights into the environment of children.

Myra Cohn Livingston. Whether she is writing about whispers tickling children's ears or singing in the night to wake someone up, Myra Cohn Livingston's verses create images and suggest experiences that children can relate to. Consider the problem of this child who has tried but cannot learn to whistle:

I Haven't Learned to Whistle

I haven't learned to whistle.
I've tried—
But if there's anything like a whistle in me,
It stops
Inside.

Dad whistles.
My brother whistles
And almost everyone I know.

I've tried to put my lips together with wrinkles,
To push my tongue against my teeth
And make a whistle
Come
Out
Slow—

But what happens is nothing but a feeble gasping
Sound
Like a sort of sickly bird.

(Everybody says they never heard
A whistle like *that*
And to tell the truth
Neither did I.)

But Dad says, tonight, when he comes home,
He'll show me again how
To put my lips together with wrinkles,
To push my tongue against my teeth,
To blow my breath out and really make a whistle.

And I'll *try!*

Myra Cohn Livingston
O Sliver of Liver, p. 12

Additional poems by Myra Cohn Livingston may be found in *A Crazy Flight and Other Poems*, *Whispers and Other Poems*, and *The Way Things Are: And Other Poems*.

Mary O'Neill. At the Houston Public Library, for example, one of the most popular poetry books for children is O'Neill's *Hailstones and Halibut Bones*. This book presents a visual collection of poems about colors; each poem asks a question about a specific color. This poem answers questions about red:

He will not see me stopping here
To watch his woods fill up with snow.

Detailed lines in the illustrations suggest the woods and the animals hidden there.
Illustration from *Stopping By Woods on a Snowy Evening* by Robert Frost, illustrated by
Susan Jeffers. Illustrations copyright © 1978 by Susan Jeffers. Reprinted by permission of
the publisher, E.P. Dutton, Inc. Text from "Stopping by Woods on a Snowy Evening" from
The Poetry of Robert Frost edited by Edward Connery Lathem. Copyright 1923, © 1969
by Holt, Rinehart and Winston. Copyright 1951 by Robert Frost. Reprinted by permission
of Holt, Rinehart and Winston, Publishers.

What is Red?

Red is a sunset
Blazy and bright.
Red is feeling brave
With all your might.
Red is a sunburn
Spot on your nose,
Sometimes red
Is a red, red rose.
Red squiggles out
When you cut your hand.

Red is a brick and
A rubber band.
Red is a hotness
You get inside
When you're embarrassed
And want to hide.

Mary O'Neill
Hailstones and Halibut Bones, p. 43

This is only the first half of the poem; the author continues
mentioning other things that are red and concludes that red is
both the "giant-est" color and a show-off.

O'Neill has written about another common subject, numbers, in her collection of poems, *Take a Number*. The poems have titles such as "What is One?" Her collection of poems about numbers and about colors can be used to stimulate children to write their own color or number poems.

Valerie Worth. Small common things in the world of children can, according to the poems written by Worth, contain magical qualities. *More Small Poems* describes such experiences as looking at a moth's wing through a magnifying glass, observing a kitten with a stiffly arched back, and seeing and hearing fireworks that spill their colors through the night sky. Additional common objects, seen with uncommon insights, are the subject for Worth's *Still More Small Poems*. The objects written about include grandmother's door with the fancy glass pattern, a kite riding in the air, and rags that are no longer faithful pajamas but crumpled cloth used to wash windows. Something as simple as taking off one's shoes becomes a sensual experience in the following poem.

Barefoot

After that tight
Choke of sock
And blunt
Weight of shoe,

The foot can feel
Clover's green
Skin
Growing,

And the fine
Invisible
Teeth
Of gentle grass,

And the cool
Breath
Of the earth
Beneath.

Valerie Worth
Still More Small Poems, p. 13

Kaye Starbird. Children's honest reactions to such experiences as Mother wanting to jump out of her skin, a friend keeping them waiting once too often, and an obnoxious girl at summer camp are found in Starbird's *The Covered Bridge House.* The poem about the summer camp experience, "Watch Out," describes the exasperation of one girl at Camp Blue Sky when Beverly pulls a series of pranks. Starbird's poetry can also be a lesson to teachers, when she suggests what should not be done when teaching spelling:

The Spelling Test

One morning in a spelling test
The teacher said to Hugh:
"I have a word for you to spell
The word is 'kangaroo.'"
But Hugh was puzzled by the word
Which wasn't one he knew,
So, when he wrote it on the board,
He printed "hannagrue."

"No, No! Go take your seat again,"
The teacher said to Hugh,
"And take along this copy card.
The card says 'kangaroo,'
Then get your pencil out," she said,
"And get your notebook, too.
And write the word a hundred times
And tell me when you're through."

So Hugh did just exacly what
The teacher told him to,
And, when he handed in his work,
The teacher said to Hugh:
"I hope you know your spelling now."
And Hugh said, "Yes, I do,"
Then—walking bravely to the board—
He printed "kannagrue."

Kaye Starbird
The Covered Bridge House and Other Poems, p. 17

Another collection of Starbird's poetry, *The Pheasant on Route Seven,* contains poems about the village of Pleasantsport and its residents, both human and animal. These residents include such characters as the mussy Carey kids and the fancy Clancy kids, the pheasant who left his forest home to stride down the center line of the highway, and Granny Shriver who has survived many experiences in her long life.

David McCord. The poetic genius of McCord was illustrated earlier through his sound poem, "The Pickety Fence." His work has won him numerous honors, including the Sarah Josepha Hale Medal, a Guggenheim Fellowship, and in 1977, the first national award for excellence in children's poetry awarded by the National Council of Teachers of English. Clifton Fadiman (19) said that "David McCord stands among the finest of living writers of children's verse. He is both an acrobat of language and an authentic explorer of the child's inner world" (cover leaf—McCord's *One at a Time*).

Over two hundred of McCord's poems are found in *One at a Time.* Here are the favorite chants like "The Pickety Fence" and "Song of the Train," with the repeated *click-ety, clack*. Here are alphabet verses, riddles, and even poetic conversations. The poems illustrate a variety of contents including animals, children's experiences, nature, and nonsense. The last section of the book, "Write Me Another Verse," attempts to show the reader how to write different poetry forms, including the ballad, the tercet, the villanelle, the clerihew, the cinquain, and haiku. Earlier in the book, there are directions for writing the couplet (two-line verse), the quatrain (four-line verse), the limerick (five-line verse), and the triolet (eight-line verse).

McCord's mastery of shape to enhance the meaning of a poem is illustrated in the following poem:

The Grasshopper

Down
a
deep
well
a
grasshopper
fell.

By kicking about
He thought to get out.
    He might have known better,
    For that got him wetter.
To kick round and round
Is the way to get drowned,
    And drowning is what
    I should tell you he got.

But
the
well
had
a
rope
that
dangled
some
hope.
And sure as molasses
On one of his passes
    He found the rope handy
    And up he went, *and he*

it
up
and
it
up
and
it
up
and
it
up
went

And hopped away proper
As any grasshopper.
                David McCord
                One at a Time, pp. 28–30

Other Poets Who Identify with Characters, Situations, and Locations. Common objects in the environment are the stimuli for Judith Thurman's small poetry book, *Flashlight and Other Poems*. The poems in this collection look at everyday objects and childhood experiences: marbling the colors of an oil slick on the street, sitting around a campfire, and pretending that a closet is really a woods. Thurman's poetry is alive with imagery; she compares the Milky Way with thick breath on a cold, dark night.

The various characters in a family, including grandparents, parents, siblings, cousins, uncles, aunts, and pets, are the subjects of a collection of poems by Shelagh McGee. *Smile Please!* is a family album in poetic form. The first poem introduces the reader to the family; the rest of the poems describe each family member in loving and sometimes humorous terms.

The excitement of riding on a skateboard, running in the women's 400-meter race, or riding the surf is found in Lillian Morrison's poetry collected in *The Sidewalk Racer and Other Poems of Sports and Motion*. Morrison says that she enjoys writing this kind of poetry because "I love rhythms, the body movement implicit in poetry, explicit in sports. I have always believed that the attempt to achieve excellence in either of these fields is both noble and exciting. And there are emotions connected with sports, sometimes a kind of transcendence and beauty one wants to catch. One turns naturally to poetry to express these things" (23, p. 63). (See page 332 for an example of Morrison's poetry, "The Sidewalk Racer.")

Moods and Feelings

Children can learn through poetry that poets, like themselves, experience many moods and feelings. In this section are nostalgic poems as the poet looks back on youthful dreams, poems of despair as the poet remembers a scene once unspoiled, poems of daydreams as the poet leaves the world of reality, and poems of pride and love associated with being black.

George Mendoza. A child's romance with the ocean and his dreams of crossing the China sea or a child's heartache when his beloved river is spoiled by pollution are strong feelings created in Mendoza's poetry. *Poem for Putting to Sea* suggests the fragility of childhood dreams. Through words and illustrations, the reader follows a boy's dream as he finds an old neglected sloop, rebuilds it with planks and love, and launches it into the ocean. The poem takes the reader along with the boy out to sea. Here, it can be calm and dreamy or stormy with waves that claw at the light. As the storm waves increase, the boy and the sloop battle the waves together; the sloop listens to the boy's prayers and sweeps him ashore onto the rocky coast. Although the sloop dies on that rocky shore, the boy is saved.

Mendoza also looks backward in time to create an epitaph for a beloved river that was once in an unspoiled section of Vermont. His feelings are strong in *Goodbye, River, Goodbye* (21). In the foreword to the book, he tells the reader why he feels such despair for the loss of a once lovely place:

Goodbye, River, Goodbye is a song to a river called Battenkill. Streaming through the sun-cliffed meadows and drifting mountain pines of Vermont, the river was my refuge, my window outside the rooms of the real world. Here I went to find the poet in me. Here I followed the trail of a crystal time when I was a boy wandering gypsy banks, and the way back home was another pebble tossed on rippling reflections.

Now the spirit-runs of the river are gone. For the world has reached my soul with its pipes and drains, fountaining my river with its killing filth. I am haunted by a deep despair. Where will I go? There must still be a place. . . .

Patricia Hubbell.

Patricia Hubbell. There is a time, according to Hubbell in *Catch Me a Wind,* when children need to move out of the here-and-now and become someone new, to dream, to do something totally unexpected. Some of these unexpected experiences include riding a carousel freely through a dead town, becoming the gravel that is walked on daily, and contemplating the beginnings of thoughts.

A second book of poems by Hubbell, *8 A.M. Shadows,* represents the experiences of children, their daydreams, and their wishdreams from early morning until bedtime. Thoughts about such subjects as today's secret, first love, and even crabgrass are shared with the reader.

Other Poets Who Develop Moods and Feelings.

Other Poets Who Develop Moods and Feelings. *My Daddy Is a Cool Dude,* by Karama Fufuka, expresses the feelings and experiences of a child who lives in an urban black community. Some poems are filled with emotions of love and joy; others, however, are filled with grief. There are the good times associated with family holidays, the pride felt in a new baby, riding on the "el" train, and respecting a father. There are also the hurt or scary times associated with wanting a bicycle but needing new shoes, living in a creaky old house and listening to the neighbors fighting and Mama crying, or watching the ambulance taking away Jerry Lee's big brother who "o-deed." Fufuka says

about her writing, "In writing these poems I have gone back to my childhood and relived the experiences of those years of growing and learning. I have tried to deal here with both the positive and negative aspects of life which constitute reality for a child in the urban Black community today. I have tried to do so with the honesty of a child and I hope that adult readers of my poems will work to change those negative images for the sake of the children who will inherit our tomorrows" (author's note, 9).

Arnold Adoff's *All the Colors of the Race* contains poems written from the viewpoint of a girl who has black and white parentage. The poems reflect her thoughts and moods as she contemplates her heritage and other experiences in her life.

Anthologies of Moods and Feelings.

Anthologies of Moods and Feelings. *On Our Way* is an anthology of poetry about the pride and love associated with being black. Lee Bennett Hopkins has selected a group of poems that convey the excitement and relevance of being black in today's world. The poems, accompanied by photographs by David Parks, are divided into five sections: "Blackness," "Soul-love," "Four" (people), "Feelings," and "Remembering." The joy of being black is described in the poem "As a Basic" by Linda Porter.

Animals in Poetry

Animals, whether they are teddy bears, cuddly puppies, purring kittens, or the preposterous animals of imagination, hold a special place in children's hearts. Therefore, it is not surprising that many poets have written about animals. Because it is difficult to identify poets who have composed many poems only about animals, this section is divided according to single books by one author or anthologies of animal poems by numerous authors.

Single Books of Animal Poems by One Author.

Single Books of Animal Poems by One Author. The lives of two quite different kinds of cats are told in David Kherdian's verses. His *Country Cat, City Cat* begins with poems about Missak as he explores the country in winter. In the country, he can see sparrows skating on the birdbath, chickadees searching for seeds in the snow, or a flea-bitten dog lounging in front of the garage. He can dance a spring voodoo, seeking the small animals that will not come within his reach, or he can perch on a warm rock and catch the sunshine. In contrast, the city cat sits in a tenement window and stares out of the window at the doves and pigeons on the branches and sidewalks. When he is tired from this, he sleeps peacefully upon a yellow bedspread.

All types of animals are found in Fisher's *Feathered Ones and Furry*. The author shares with children her love for animals. Her title poem expresses her feelings about furry animals.

The Furry Ones

I like
the furry ones—
the waggy ones
the purry ones
the hoppy ones
that hurry,

The glossy ones
the saucy ones
the sleepy ones
the leapy ones
the mousy ones
that scurry,

The snuggly ones
the huggly ones
the never, never
ugly ones. . .
all soft
and warm
and furry.

Aileen Fisher
Feathered Ones and Furry, p. viii

Anthologies of Animal Poems. Within animal anthologies are humorous and serious poems about animals. Children who are fascinated by dinosaurs will enjoy Cole's *Dinosaurs and Beasts of Yore*.

Some poems are about dinosaurs; others consider what would happen if a child had a dinosaur today. The child in Elizabeth Winthrop's story poem, "My Dinosaur's Day in the Park" has his own dinosaur, and the reptile creates some unusual problems as he eats up trees, knocks down a fence, and finally becomes scared of the dark.

Another anthology selected by William Cole is *I Went to the Animal Fair*. Within the text are many old favorites such as Lear's "The Owl and the Pussy Cat" and A. A. Milne's "Furry Bear" as well as some lesser known poems.

Horse lovers will enjoy a recent collection of poems selected by Lee Bennett Hopkins. *My Mane Catches the Wind: Poems about Horses* includes poems on such subjects as the birth of a colt, the beauty of a stallion, and the independence of a horse; they all, however, sing the praises of the horse.

Ghosts, Dragons, and Magic

A shivery Halloween, lonely dark staircases, and empty old houses; these are settings for Lilian Moore's subjects. *See My Lovely Poison Ivy* is a collection of Moore's poems about witches and ghosts. Some are frightening; others, like the "Teeny Tiny Ghost," are not.

Teeny Tiny Ghost

A teeny, tiny ghost
no bigger than a mouse,
at most,
lived in a great big house.

It's hard to haunt
a great big house
when you're a teeny tiny ghost
no bigger than a mouse,
at most.

He did what he could do.

So every dark and stormy night—
the kind that shakes a house with fright—
if you stood still and listened right,
you'd hear a
teeny
tiny
BOO!

Lilian Moore
See My Lovely Poison Ivy, p. 38

In a longer story poem by Peter Meteyard, children can learn about *Stanley the Tale of a Lizard*. While lizards are tiny now, the reader learns that in King Arthur's time they were very big and were called dragons. This poem, with illustrations by Peter Firmin, tells the humorous tale of a timid knight named Sir Lance—a little, who, with the help of a gentle dragon named Stanley, rescues a fair maiden from the black knight.

Poltergeists, zombies, and giants are some scary subjects found in Jack Prelutsky's *The Headless Horseman Rides Tonight*. These poems, with illustrations by Arnold Lobel, suggest the world of the dark sepulcher, the ghostly moor, and the darksome dominion. Other ghostly poems are found in Daisy Wallace's collection, *Ghost Poems*. Tomie de Paola's black and white illustrations depict ghoulies and ghosties, phantomships, and churchyards at night. Children who like stories about ghosts and haunted buildings often enjoy these poems with their vivid, descriptive language.

SUMMARY

Poetry allows children to experience the world with new understanding and share feelings, experiences, and visions with the poet. Reading and sharing poetry is a valuable experience for children since it may be shared for pure enjoyment and also serves the following educational purposes: (1) helps children gain knowledge about concepts in the world around them, (2) develops appreciation for language, (3) allows children to identify with characters and situations, (4) encourages them to share feelings and moods with the poet, and (5) allows them to gain insights into themselves and others.

Writers of poetry rely on several elements when they create poetry. While not all of these elements are found in all poetry, the following elements were discussed in this chapter: rhyme, rhythm, sound, repetition, imagery, and shape. In addition, several forms of poetry including limerick, narrative, ballad, concrete, free verse, and haiku were presented.

Research studies about children and poetry have indicated that children's enthusiasm about poetry declines as they advance in the elementary grades; children enjoy contemporary poems about familiar, enjoyable experiences; they like poems that tell a story or are humorous; they prefer poems that have rhyme and rhythm; they dislike complex imagery; and teachers of older students seldom read poetry to them or encourage the children to write poems.

The poets and their works discussed in this chapter were organized according to poems suitable for fostering a love of poetry; humorous poems; nature poems; poems identifying with characters, situations, and locations; poems about moods and feelings; animal poems; and poems dealing with ghosts, dragons, and magic.

Suggested Activities Designed for Adult Understanding of Poetry

■ Read a poem that relies heavily on rhyming elements. Find the location of the rhyming words (i.e., at the end of the line, at the beginning of the line, within the line). Read the poem orally. What feeling is suggested by the rhyming elements?

■ Look through an anthology of poetry and find some poems that rely on sound patterns to recreate excitement. Prepare for oral presentation a poem that relies on alliteration (the repetition of initial consonant sounds) or asso-

nance (the repetition of vowel sounds). Share the poem orally with a peer group.

■ Locate several poems that develop literal imagery and several poems that suggest figurative imagery. Is there a difference in the interest level of the two types of imagery? Share the poems with a child. Does the child respond in the same way to these types?

■ Compile a list of similes and metaphors found in a poem. What image is the poet trying to suggest? Does the simile or metaphor paint a more effective word picture, a more visual picture, than a realistic word would produce?

■ Compare the subject matter of limericks written by Edward Lear with the subject matter of limericks written by contemporary poets such as David Ross or William Jay Smith. How are they similar? How do they differ?

■ Read several collections of haiku. Based on your reading, tell what Ann Atwood meant when she said that haiku is begun by the writer and completed by the reader?

■ Select one poet of humorous poetry, such as Edward Lear, Lewis Carroll, Laura Richards, Theodore Roethke, Jack Prelutsky, William Jay Smith, John Ciardi, or N. M. Bodecker. Read a selection of their humorous verse. What poetic elements do they use? What subjects do they write about?

■ Compare the content and style of a poet who wrote humorous verse in the beginning of the nineteenth century (e.g., Carroll, Lear) with a contemporary author of humorous verse (e.g., Prelutsky, Bodecker). What are the similarities and differences between the writers in the two time periods?

References

1 Atwood, Ann. *Haiku: The Mood of Earth.* New York: Scribner's, 1971.

2 Atwood, Ann. *Haiku-Vision: In Poetry and Photography.* New York: Scribner's, 1977.

3 Behn, Harry. *Chrysalis, Concerning Children and Poetry.* New York: Harcourt Brace Jovanovich, 1968.

4 Bridge, Ethel Brooks. "Using Children's Choices of and Reactions to Poetry as Determinants in Enriching Literary Experience in the Middle Grades." Philadelphia: Temple University, 1966. University Microfilm No. 67–6246.

5 Clark, Leonard. "Poetry for the Youngest." In *Horn Book Reflections,* edited by Elinor Whitney Field. Boston: Horn Book, 1969.

6 Day-Lewis, Cecil. *Poetry for You.* New York: Oxford, 1947.

7 Deutsch, Babette. *Poetry Handbook: A Dictionary of Terms.* New York: Funk & Wagnalls, 1974.

8 Drew, Elizabeth. *Discovering Poetry.* New York: Norton, 1933.

9 Fufuka, Karama. *My Daddy Is A Cool Dude.* New York: Dial, 1975.

10 Gensler, Kinereth and Nyhart, Nina. *The Poetry Connection, An Anthology of Contemporary Poems With Ideas to Stimulate Children's Writing.* New York: Teachers & Writers, 1978.

11 Groff, Patrick. "Where Are We Going With Poetry for Children?" In *Horn Book Reflections,* edited by Elinor Whitney Field. Boston: Horn Book, 1969.

12 Judson, Jerome. *Poetry: Premeditated Art.* Boston: Houghton Mifflin, 1968.

13 Le Pere, Jean. "For Every Occasion: Poetry in the Reading Program." Albuquerque, N. Mex.: Eighth Southwest Regional Conference, International Reading Association, 1980.

14 Lear, Edward, and Nash, Ogden. *The Scoobious Pip.* Illustrated by Nancy Ekholm Burkert. New York: Harper & Row, 1968.

15 Lewis, Richard. *Of This World: A Poet's Life in Poetry.* Photographs by Helen Buttfield. New York: Dial, 1968.

16 Livingston, Myra Cohn. "Not the Rose . . ." In *Horn Book Reflections,* edited by Elinor Whitney Field. Boston: Horn Book, 1969.

17 Lowell, Amy. *Poetry and Poets.* New York: Biblo, 1971.

18 Lukens, Rebecca J. *A Critical Handbook of Children's Literature.* Glenview, Ill.: Scott, Foresman, 1976.

19 McCord, David. *One at a Time.* Boston: Little, Brown, 1977.

20 Meigs, Cornelia, and Nesbitt, Elizabeth. *A Critical History of Children's Literature.* New York: Macmillan, 1969.

21 Mendoza, George. *Goodbye, River, Goodbye.* New York: Doubleday, 1971.

22 Merriam, Eve. *Rainbow Writing.* New York: Atheneum, 1976.

23 Morrison, Lillian. *The Sidewalk Racer and Other Poems of Sports and Motion.* New York: Lothrop, Lee & Shepard, 1977.

24 Morse, Samuel French. "Speaking of the Imagination." In *Horn Book Reflections,* edited by Elinor Whitney Field. Boston: Horn Book, 1969.

25 Muir, Edwin. "A Child's World Is as a Poet." In *Children and Literature: Views and Reviews,* edited by Virginia Haviland, pp. 269–71. Glenview, Ill.: Scott, Foresman, 1973.

26 Stokes, Anne. *The Open Door to Poetry.* Freeport, N.Y.: Books for Libraries, 1971.

27 Terry, Ann. *Children's Poetry Preferences: A National Survey of Upper Elementary Grades.* Urbana, Ill.: National Council of Teachers of English, 1974.

28 Tucker, Nicholas. "Why Nursery Rhymes?" In *Children and Literature: Views and Reviews,* edited by Virginia Haviland, pp. 258–62. Glenview, Ill.: Scott, Foresman, 1973.

Involving Children in Poetry

SELECTING POETRY TO SHARE WITH CHILDREN

MOVING TO POETRY

POETRY STIMULATES CREATIVE DRAMATIZATIONS

STIMULATING CHILDREN'S INTEREST IN POETRY THROUGH CHORAL SPEAKING

POETRY AND MUSIC

AN INSTRUCTIONAL SEQUENCE THAT STIMULATES CHILDREN TO WRITE POETRY

ENJOYING poems, gaining knowledge about concepts, gaining appreciation for language, identifying with characters and situations, expressing a mood, and gaining insights about oneself and others are all values children realize from poetry. Unfortunately, studies have shown that poetry is not an important part of the elementary curriculum. Jon E. Shapiro (22) says that "Poetry has often been the most neglected component of the language arts curriculum" (p. 91). Ann Terry's (24) research reported earlier verifies this conclusion. She found that over 75 percent of the middle grade teachers in her study read poetry to their children less than once a month. This finding may also relate to the fact that the children in her study reported a decreased interest in poetry as they progressed through the elementary grades.

Several causes have been attributed to this decreased interest in poetry and the neglect of poetry in the elementary curriculum. Shapiro (22) says, "Perhaps one of the reasons for this omission is that unless poetry is a vital factor in one's own life, we know little about it and thus feel uncomfortable in using it in the classroom" (p. 91). The only way for adults to overcome this aversion and to feel comfortable when sharing poetry is to read poetry written by many fine authors, and thus, discover a new or revitalized delight in poetry.

University students in this author's classes often say that their aversion to poetry stems from the way it was presented in their elementary, middle school, and high school classrooms. They fondly remember the rhymes and jingles shared in kindergarten and first grade. Then, they remember forced memorization of poems, analyzing the author's meaning of a poem, and convergent thinking exercises when everyone had to agree with the teacher's analysis of the poem. One student recalled her feelings of terror as every Friday she had to memorize a poem, say it in front of the class, and then had points deducted from her presentation for each error she made.

Other university students, however, described pleasant memories of poetry in their classrooms. They state that their teachers spontaneously shared a wide variety of poetry with their classes. One student remembered a teacher who always had a poem to reflect the mood of a gentle rain, a smiling jack-o-lantern, or a mischievous child. Another student recalled the stimulating environment in her third-grade classroom that encouraged the class to write poems and share them with an appreciative audience. She remembered going outside on a warm spring day, looking at the butterflies and wildflowers in a meadow, listening to the world around her, sharing her feelings with the class, and then writing a poem to express the promise of that beautiful day. Another remembered the enjoyment of choral reading that might be accompanied by rhythm instruments or experimenting with different choral arrangements. Another remembered a librarian who always included poetry in story hour presentations.

After university students explore the various ways of sharing poetry with children, they often sadly conclude that something was left out of their education. This section considers some ways that adults may encourage children to enjoy and experience poetry by moving to poetry, using poetry to stimulate creative dramatizations, developing choral speaking, using music and poetry, and stimulating creative writing of poetry.

MOVING TO POETRY

The rhythm and sound or descriptive subjects of many poems encourage physical responses from children. An observer of children in a playground or park will probably see and hear a scene similar to this one: Two children are swinging a jump rope; the third jumps to the rhythm and the actions in a jumping rope chant such as the following:

> Teddy bear, teddy bear, turn around.
> Teddy bear, teddy bear, touch the ground.
> Teddy bear, teddy bear, close your eyes.
> Teddy bear, teddy bear, be surprised.
> Teddy bear, teddy bear, climb up the stairs.
> Teddy bear, teddy bear, say your prayers.
> Teddy bear, teddy bear, turn out the light.
> Teddy bear, teddy bear, say good night.

Children respond to the rhythm in a jumping-rope chant.

There are many poems that can be read slowly by an adult while children physically respond by prowling, soaring, stomping, and leaping. Valerie Worth's *Small Poems* contains examples of poems that suggest animal movements or the different movements associated with the sun or a firecracker. In *Small Poems,* children can pretend to be a "Cow" moving like a mountain, thumping her hoofs across the pasture; they can be a "Dog" lying down, resting his chin, and sleeping in his loose skin; they can be a "Duck" walking like a toy, wagging his tail, and flicking water drops from his back; they can be a spotted "Frog" quietly sitting or leaping into the water; they can be a "Cat" settling its muscles to prepare for sleep; or they can be the "Sun" leaping like fire or lying quietly on a warm square on the floor.

In Worth's *More Small Poems,* children can become a "Kitten" as she arches her back, dances sideways, tears across the floor, crouches against imagined threats, and pounces with her claws ready. They can become "Sea Lions" as they sink into the water, slide around in circles, and climb snorting and slapping their flippers back onto the rocks. An adult can lead them in a physical response to "Fireworks" as they thud, climb into the air, billow into glowing color, and spill back down toward earth in sliding waterfalls. They can be spectacular in a much quieter way as a "Soap Bubble" that bends into different shapes, rises shimmering into the air, and snaps, only to disappear.

Worth's *Still More Small Poems* encourages children to experience the free flight of a "Kite" as it is torn wildly from a hand and soars and rides through the spring winds; they can become a "Mushroom" pushing up through the soil and spreading its ribs into full bloom; or they can experience going "Barefoot," as their feet emerge from choking socks only to feel the cool clover and gentle blades of grass between their toes.

Children enjoy moving as if they are rockets or airplanes. Leland B. Jacobs's (12) anthology, *Poetry for Space Enthusiasts,* includes several excellent poems that encourage move-

ISSUE

Analyzing Poetry: Help or Hindrance?

WILL CHILDREN ENJOY and understand poetry more if they analyze the meaning and meter, identify figurative language, and define terminology and poetic devices? Or should they be encouraged to have an aesthetic experience with poetry in which they experience the rhythm, sensations, and ideas and interpret it in their own individual ways? The activities suggested in basal readers that include poetry and in literature anthologies designed to be shared with children frequently suggest the importance of such analysis. Teachers or librarians may ask children to read or listen to a poem for the specific purpose of identifying the author's meaning, identifying the theme, locating the similes and metaphors, or identifying the rhyming schemes. Such activities are done in the belief that analyzing poetic devices improves understanding, enjoyment, and writing of poetry.

A contrasting viewpoint is developed by Louise M. Rosenblatt.[1] She maintains that poetry reading should be an aesthetic experience in which children focus upon the cognitive and affective elements such as sensations, images, feelings, and ideas that allow them to have a "lived-through" experience. She believes that focusing children's attention on analysis is detrimental if it is done before they have had many opportunities to experience poetry. She warns that adults who share poetry with younger children should not ask them to focus their attention on specific poetic analysis or hurry them away from a "lived-through" aesthetic experience by too quickly demanding summaries and other types of analysis. Instead, children should be encouraged to savor what was visualized, felt, thought, or enjoyed while they heard or read the poem.

1 Rosenblatt, Louise M. "What Facts Does This Poem Teach You?" *Language Arts* 57 (April 1980): 386–94.

ment. B. J. Lee's "Into Space" takes them from the launching pad, into the countdown, through the blast-off, and into a spinning capsule orbiting the earth and reaching into space. With Alice E. London's "Space Pilot," they zoom past the moon, circle the planets, and bring their rocket back to earth.

Jack Prelutsky's humorous animal poems encourage bodily interpretation of animals of various sizes, speeds, and agility. His *A Gopher in the Garden and Other Animal Poems* (19) contains some very enjoyable poems. Adults can lead children as they progress from "The Shrew," so small it can hardly be seen, to "The Rabbit" hopping and leaping when he hears the slightest sound, to "The Giggling Gaggling Gaggle of Geese" chasing the swans from the lake and stealing the sheep's woolen fleece, to "The Wallaby" bounding with great agility and merriment, and then returning to the moment of new life, as scratching from within "The Egg," they crack the egg and emerge a fluffy goose.

POETRY STIMULATES CREATIVE DRAMATIZATIONS

One of the values of poetry for children noted earlier by Jean Le Pere was encouraging them to identify with characters and situations. Ann Terry also discovered that narrative poems that tell a story were among children's favorite poems. This information may be used by adults to enhance children's enjoyment of the situations found in poetry by encouraging them to use poems to stimulate creative dramatizations (9). For example, after listening to John Ciardi's "Mummy Slept Late and Daddy Fixed Breakfast," children can pantomime the actions or pretend to be the father and the children in a family who are taking part in this breakfast experience. What other dialogue might the father add as he prepares the waffles? How might he try to convince his family to eat the waffles? What might the children say to their father, to each other, and to their mother?

What might happen if the father tried to cook dinner? How would his family respond?

The narrative poem, "The Night Before Christmas," by Clement C. Moore, suggests several scenes that can be dramatized. Children can prepare for the Christmas celebration by trimming the tree and decorating the room; they can imagine the sugarplum dreams and dramatize them; they can reenact Father hearing the clatter of hoofs; they can dramatize St. Nicholas with his reindeer and loaded sleigh as he comes down the chimney, fills the stockings, and laying a finger aside of his nose bounds up the chimney and drives out of sight. This poem has many other dramatic possibilities. Children have created the dialogue for an imaginary meeting between Father or the children and St. Nicholas. What would they say to each other? How would they act? If they could ask St. Nicholas questions, what would they ask? If St. Nicholas could ask questions, what would he want to know? Children have imagined themselves as St. Nicholas going into many homes on Christmas Eve. What was the most unusual experience they had? They have imagined themselves going back to St. Nick's workshop at the North Pole. What kind of a welcome would they receive? If they could plan for next Christmas, what would be the suggestions from the elves, from Mrs. St. Nicholas and from St. Nicholas himself?

Adults have used the nonsensical, humorous situations found in Prelutsky's poems in *The Queen of Eene* to stimulate humorous dramatizations. One group, for example, dramatized the conversation and actions of the "Four Foolish Ladies," Hattie, Harriet, Hope, and Hortense, as they roped a rhinoceros and took him to tea. Then the group imagined and acted out other predicaments that could have been created by the actions of the foolish ladies. "Aunt Samantha" suggests the beginning of a conversation between a lady and a middle-sized rhinoceros who appears mysteriously in her life. A group of children used this situation to create a series of happenings in the life of Aunt Samantha and her new friend. Another group was stimulated by "The Pancake Collector" to create purposes for the pancakes in his collection and to act out several of these unusual suggestions. The final poem in this book, "Gretchen in the Kitchen," has been used for spooky witch scenes at Halloween. The quarts of curdled mud, salted spiders, ogre's backbone, and dragon's blood provide a setting appealing to children who are preparing to be spooks, witches, and black cats.

Another Prelutsky poem that stimulates Halloween dramatizations is "The Ghostly Grocer of Grumble Grove" (presented in Daisy Wallace's *Ghost Poems*) who lives near Howling Hop. The spectacle of a cauliflower poltergeist juggling thinly sliced apples, sausages skipping on ghostly legs, and cornflakes fluttering through the air while being supervised by a ghostly grocer is conducive to creating many animated conversations and surprising happenings.

There are other poems that have been used to stimulate creative dramatizations:

1 "How Robin Hood Rescued the Widow's Sons," a ballad from William Cole's *The Poet's Tales.*
   Robin Hood listens to a sad tale from a widow, exchanges clothes with an old palmer, summons his men, and rescues the sons from the Sheriff of Nottingham's gallows.
2 "Hurry, Hurry Mary Dear," from N. M. Bodecker's book of the same title.
   A harassed woman follows the directions of a demanding man until she has finally had enough.
3 "Jonathan Bing," by Beatrice Curtis Brown.
   Jonathan tries to visit the king and do other tasks; each time his actions are inappropriate for successfully doing the task.
4 Various poems from Kaye Starbird's *The Pheasant on Route Seven.*
   The exploits of residents of Pleasantsport, including Granny Shriver, the Carey kids, and the Clancy kids can be dramatized and suggest additional adventures.
5 "Counter Service," by Robert Froman, found in *Street Poems.*
   Dialogue can be created between people sitting at the counter. For example, between a careful and a fearful person, a correct and a precise person, a nervous and a rigid person, a blank and an unhappy person, and a prudent and a guarded person. These characters can suggest many new dramatizations as children consider what happened to the people to make them appear as described in the poem.

STIMULATING CHILDREN'S INTEREST IN POETRY THROUGH CHORAL SPEAKING

Choral speaking, the interpretation of poetry or literature by two or more voices speaking as one, is a group activity allowing children to experience, enjoy, and increase their interest in rhymes, jingles, and other types of poetry. During a choral-speaking or choral-reading experience, children discover that speaking voices can be combined as effectively as singing voices in a choir. Younger children who cannot read can join in during repeated lines or can take part in rhymes and verses that they know from memory; older children can select anything suitable within their reading ability. Choral speaking is useful in a variety of situations: library programs, classrooms, organizations, and nursery schools.

The main purpose for using choral speaking with elementary children is to increase their enjoyment of poetry and other literature and not to develop a perfect performance, so adults should allow children to enjoy the experience and experiment with various ways of interpreting poetry. Adults should consider the following guidelines identified by Donna Norton (17) when they encourage children to interact in choral arrangements:

1 When selecting materials for children who cannot read, choose poems or rhymes that are simple enough to memorize.
2 Choose material of interest to children. Young children like nonsense and active words; consequently, humorous poems are enjoyable first experiences and encourage children to have fun with poetry.
3 Select poems or rhymes that use refrains, especially for young children. Refrains are easy for nonreaders to memorize and will result in rapid participation from each group member.
4 Let children help select and interpret the poetry. Have them experiment with the rhythm and tempo of the poem, improvise the scenes of the selection, and try different voice combinations and various choral arrangements before they decide on the best structural arrangements.
5 Let children listen to each other as they try different interpretations within groups.

In addition to these guidelines, Barbara McIntyre (16) suggests that adults who work with choral arrangements should understand the different phases through which children should be guided in their choral interpretations of poetry. First, because young children delight in the rhythm of nursery rhymes, they should be encouraged to explore the rhythm in poetry. They can skip to the rhythm found in "Jack and Jill," clap to the rhythm found in "Hickory Dickory Dock," and sway to the rhythm of "Little Boy Blue." They can sense fast or slow, happy or sad rhythms through their bodies. They can explore the rhythm and tempo as they "hoppity, hoppity, hop" to A. A. Milne's poem "Hoppity" (found in *When We Were Very Young*).

The second phase is experimenting with the color and quality of voices available in the choral-speaking choir. McIntyre (16) says that children do not need to know the meaning of *inflection* (the rise and fall within a phrase), *pitch levels* (the change between one phrase and another), *emphasis* (the pointing out of the most important word), and *intensity* (the loudness and softness of the voices), but adults must understand these terms so they can recommend exciting materials that allow children to try different ways of interpreting a poem.

The third phase is understanding and experimenting with different types of choral arrangements, such as refrain, line-a-child or line-a-group, antiphonal or dialogue, cumulative, and unison arrangements. Definitions and examples of each choral arrangement include the following:

Refrain Arrangement

In this type of arrangement, an adult or a child reads or recites the body of a poem; the other children respond in unison when a refrain or chorus is repeated. Poems such as Maurice Sendak's "Pierre: A Cautionary Tale," Lewis Carroll's "Beautiful Soup," and Jack Prelutsky's "The Yak" have lines that seem to invite group participation. A nursery rhyme that encourages young children to participate is "A Jolly Old Pig."

Leader:	A jolly old pig once lived in a sty,
	And Three little piggies she had,
	And she waddled about saying
Group:	"Grumph! grumph! grumph!"
Leader:	While the little ones said
Group:	"Wee! Wee!"
Leader:	And she waddled about saying
Group:	"Grumph! grumph! grumph!"
Leader:	While the little ones said
Group:	"Wee! Wee!"

Line-a-Child or Line-a-Group Arrangement

To develop this arrangement, one child or a group of children reads the first line, another child or children read the next line, and a third child or children read the next line. This arrangement continues with a different child or different group of children reading each line until the poem is finished. Enjoyable poems for line-a-child arrangements include Zilpha Keatley Snyder's "Poem to Mud," Laura E. Richard's "Eletelephony," and Prelutsky's "Pumberly Pott's Unpredictable Niece." The following is a nursery rhyme that can be used to introduce this arrangement:

Child 1 or Group 1:	One, two buckle my shoe;
Child 2 or Group 2:	Three, four, shut the door;
Child 3 or Group 3:	Five, six, pick up sticks;
Child 4 or Group 4:	Seven, eight, lay them straight;
Child 5 or Group 5:	Nine, ten, a good fat hen.

Antiphonal or Dialogue Arrangement

Alternate speaking voices are highlighted in this arrangement; boys' voices may be balanced against girls' voices, or high voices may be balanced against low voices. Poems with a question-and-answer format or other dialogue between two people are obvious choices for antiphonal arrangements. Poems such as Starbird's "The Spelling Test," Milne's "Puppy and I," and the nursery rhyme "Pussy-Cat, Pussy-Cat" are enjoyable dialogue arrangements. Children enjoy chorally reading the lyrics from folk songs. The words of "Yankee Doodle," for example, can be used with boys (or group one) reading each verse and girls (or group two) responding with the chorus. The words from the folk song, "A Hole in the Bucket," present a dialogue between Liza and Henry:

Boys: There's a hole in the bucket, dear Liza, dear Liza,
      There's a hole in the bucket, dear Liza, There's a hole.
Girls: Well, fix it, dear Henry, dear Henry, dear Henry.
      Well, fix it, dear, Henry, dear Henry, go fix it.
Boys: With what shall I fix it, dear Liza, dear Liza?
      With what shall I fix it, dear Liza, with what?
Girls: With a straw, dear Henry, dear Henry, dear Henry.
      With a straw, dear Henry, dear Henry, with a straw.
Boys: But the straw is too long, dear Liza, dear Liza.
      But the straw is too long, dear Liza, too long.
Girls: Then cut it, dear Henry, dear Henry, dear Henry.
      Then cut it, dear Henry, dear Henry, then cut it.
Boys: Well, how shall I cut it, dear Liza, dear Liza?
      Well, how shall I cut it, dear Liza, well, how?
Girls: With a knife, dear Henry, dear Henry, dear Henry.
      With a knife, dear Henry, dear Henry, with a knife.
Boys: But the knife is too dull, dear Liza, dear Liza.
      But the knife is too dull, dear Liza, too dull.
Girls: Then sharpen it, dear Henry, dear Henry, dear Henry.
      Then sharpen it, dear Henry, dear Henry, then sharpen it.
Boys: With what shall I sharpen it, dear Liza, dear Liza?
      With what shall I sharpen it, dear Liza, with what?
Girls: With a whetstone, dear Henry, dear Henry, dear Henry.
      With a whetstone, dear Henry, dear Henry, with a
        whetstone.
Boys: But the whetstone's too dry, dear Liza, dear Liza.
      But the whetstone's too dry, dear Liza, too dry.
Girls: Then wet it, dear Henry, dear Henry, dear Henry.
      Then wet it, dear Henry, dear Henry, then wet it.
Boys: With what shall I wet it, dear Liza, dear Liza?
      With what shall I wet it, dear Liza, with what?
Girls: With water, dear Henry, dear Henry, dear Henry.
      With water, dear Henry, dear Henry, with water.
Boys: Well, how shall I carry it, dear Liza, dear Liza?
      Well, how shall I carry it, dear Liza, how?

Girls: In a bucket, dear Henry, dear Henry, dear Henry.
      In a bucket, dear Henry, dear Henry, in a bucket.
Boys: But there's a hole in the bucket, dear Liza, dear Liza.
      There's a hole in the bucket, dear Liza, a hole.

Cumulative Arrangement

This crescendo arrangement may be used effectively to interpret a poem that builds up to a climax. The first group reads the first line or verse, the first and second group read the second line or verse, and so forth, until the poem reaches its climax. Then, all the groups read together. Edward Lear's "The Owl and the Pussy-Cat" may be read in a cumulative arrangement by six groups; Ciardi's "Mummy Slept Late and Daddy Fixed Breakfast" is also fun for six groups to develop into a climax, as Daddy's waffles become impossible to eat. The nursery rhymes "There Was a Crooked Man" and "This Is the House That Jack Built" are also enjoyable.

Group 1:   This is the house that Jack built.
Group 1,2:   This is the malt
              That lay in the house that Jack built.
Group 1,2,3: This is the rat that ate the malt,
              That lay in the house that Jack built.
Group 1,2,3,
4:            This is the cat,
              That killed the rat, that ate the malt,
              That lay in the house that Jack built.
Group 1,2,3,
4,5:   This is the dog,
              That worries the cat,
              That killed the rat, that ate the malt,
              That lived in the house that Jack built.
Group 1,2,3,
4,5,6:   This is the cow with the crumpled horn,
              That tossed the dog, that worried the cat,
              That killed the rat, that ate the malt,
              That lay in the house that Jack built.
Group 1,2,3,
4,5,6,7:   This is the Maiden all forlorn.
              That milked the cow with the crumpled horn,
              That tossed the dog, that worried the cat,
              That ate the rat, that ate the malt,
              That lay in the house that Jack built.
Group 1,2,3,
4,5,6,7,8:   This is the man all tattered and torn,
              That kissed the maiden all forlorn,
              That milked the cow with the crumpled horn,
              That tossed the dog, that worried the cat,
              That killed the rat, that ate the malt,
              That lay in the house that Jack built.
Group 1,2,3,
4,5,6,7,8,9: This is the priest all shaven and shorn,
              That married the man all tattered and torn,
              That kissed the maiden all forlorn,
              That milked the cow with the crumpled horn,
              That tossed the dog, that worried the cat,

Group 1,2,3,
4,5,6,7,8,9,
10:

That killed the rat, that ate the malt,
That lay in the house that Jack built.
This is the cock that crowed in the morn,
That waked the priest all shaven and shorn,
That married the man all tattered and torn,
That kissed the maiden all forlorn,
That milked the cow with the crumpled horn,
That tossed the dog, that worried the cat,
That killed the rat, that ate the malt,
That lay in the house that Jack built.

Group 1,2,3,
4,5,6,7,8,9,
10,11:

This is the farmer that sowed the corn,
That kept the cock that crowed in the morn,
That waked the priest all shaven and shorn,
That married the man all tattered and torn,
That kissed the maiden all forlorn,
That milked the cow with the crumpled horn,
That tossed the dog, that worried the cat,
That killed the rat, that ate the malt,
That lay in the house that Jack built.

A reverse arrangement may be developed in which all groups begin together; with each subsequent line or verse, a group drops out until only one group remains. William Cole's "I'm Mad At You" works well for this interpretation because the child in the poem starts out in great anger but by the end has let off enough "steam" to feel "like peaches and cream."

Unison Arrangement

In this arrangement, the entire group or class reads or speaks a poem together. This arrangement is often the most difficult to perform, because it may tend to create a singsong effect. For this reason, shorter poems such as Myra Cohn Livingston's "O Sliver of Liver," Lillian Morrison's "The Sidewalk Racer" or "On the Skateboard," and Judith Thurman's "Campfire" are appropriate.

Additional Suggestions for Choral Speaking

Fran Tanner (23) recommends that older children experiment with the effects of grouping their voices according to resonance: light, medium, and dark voices. Through experimentation, children can discover that light voices can effectively interpret happy, whimsical, or delicate parts; medium voices may add to descriptive and narrative parts; while dark voices add to robust, tragic, and heavier material. A poem she recommends for such an experiment is Tennyson's "The Brook":

The Brook

(light)	I slip,
(medium)	I slide,
(dark)	I gloom.
(medium)	I glance.

(light)	Among my skimming swallows;
	I make the netted sunbeams dance
	Against my sandy shallows.
(dark)	I murmur under moon and stars
	In brambly wildernesses;
(medium)	I linger by my shingly bars,
(light)	I loiter round my cresses;
(medium)	And out again I curve and flow
	To join the brimming river,
(dark)	For men may come
(dark and medium)	and men may go,
(all)	But I go on forever.

Librarians, teachers, and other adults who want to identify thematic poetry and choral-speaking arrangements to add enjoyment throughout the year will find it helpful to compile a file of poems that highlight the different seasons or months of the year. One student in a literature class encouraged her fourth-grade students to experiment with many choral arrangements throughout the year and made a file of the poems and the choral arrangements that they enjoyed. She and her students chose their poems from Hazel Fellman's *The Best Loved Poems of the American People* (5), Helen Ferris's *Favorite Poems Old and New* (6), Rosalind Hughes's *Let's Enjoy Poetry* (11), Isabel Wilner's *The Poetry Troupe* (25), and Irving Wolfe's *Music through the Years* (26). The poems in Chart 8.1 include those which were identified to use with each of the months and the choral arrangements used for each one.

POETRY AND MUSIC

The rhythms of poetry and music naturally complement each other. Rhythm instruments, including sticks, bells, tambourines, and blocks, allow children to emphasize the rhythm of a poem and interpret its mood. A group of six-year-olds, for example, thoroughly enjoyed accompanying McCord's "The Pickety Fence" with their rhythm band sticks. They experimented with the sticks until they sounded just like a picket fence being struck by a child hitting it with a stick. They recorded the poem and its accompaniment, and were pleased with the sound interpretation.

Many old ballads and chants have been passed down through the generations in the form of folk songs. They may be listened to, read in choral arrangements, sung, or accompanied by movement, improvisations, and rhythm instruments. Ruth Crawford Seeger's *American Folk Songs for Children—In Home, School, and Nursery School* (21) presents words, accompanying music, and suggestions for interpreting the rhythm and lyrics. The suggestions are a result of

CHART 8—1
The Months in Poetry and Choral Speaking

	Poem	Author	Month	Choral Arrangement
1.	"The Months of the Year"	Sara Coleridge	September	Line-a-Group; each group reads two lines associated with the twelve months.
2.	"September"	Edwina Falls	September	Unison.
3.	"Father William"	Lewis Carroll	September (fun anytime)	Dialogue—two groups; young man and Father William.
4.	"Witch, Witch"	Rose Fyleman	October Halloween	Antiphonal—Adult or group reads questions; second group answers.
5.	"Old Roger"	Anonymous	October Halloween	Refrain.
6.	"Harvest"	M. M. Hutchinson	November Thanksgiving	Cumulative.
7.	"Over the River"	Anonymous	November Thanksgiving	Line-a-Group; six groups.
8.	"In the Week When Christmas Comes"	Eleanor Farjeon	December Christmas	Line-a-Group; six groups.
9.	"Long, Long Ago"	Anonymous	December Christmas	Refrain.
10.	"A Visit from St. Nicholas"	Clement C. Moore	December Christmas	Antiphonal.
11.	"Whispers"	Myra Cohn Livingston	January (snow)	Unison.
12.	"When a Ring's Around the Moon"	Mary Jane Carr	January	Cumulative.
13.	"Dark-Eyed Lad Columbus"	Nancy Byrd Turner	February	Line-a-Group.
14.	"This Land Is Your Land"	Woody Guthrie	February	Refrain.
15.	"March, March Come with Your Broom"	Annette Wynne	March spring	Refrain.
16.	"Faith, I Wish I Were a Leprechaun"	Margaret Ritter	March St. Patrick's Day	Refrain.
17.	"The Umbrella Brigade"	Laura E. Richards	April showers	Line-a-Group.
18.	"Mister Rabbit"	Anonymous	April Easter	Dialogue; Rabbit and Friend.
19.	"Smart"	Shel Silverstein	May (just for fun)	Cumulative.
20.	"Whale"	Mary Ann Hoberman	June (oceanography)	Refrain.
21.	"The Green Grass Growing All Around"	Folk Rhyme	June	Cumulative.

using the materials extensively with young children. The following are taken from Seeger's recommendations (pp. 35–38) for sharing songs with young children.

1 Sing the song first at its natural speed; allow children to experience the impression of the song as a whole rather than analyzing the song.

2 The songs should not drag. Most were originally sung at a lively speed and with a strong metrical accent.

3 The adult who is sharing the songs with young children should sit directly with the children when presenting and singing the songs.

4 Children should be allowed to listen, then interpret the songs at their own leisure.

5 Many folk songs make excellent rhythm band music.

6 Repeat a song many times, especially when using the songs for rhythmic activities.

Music encourages the additional enjoyment of poetry.

7 Include both action songs and listening songs when planning the activities for a session. The changing needs and moods of the children should be considered when making the selections.

8 Do not hurry when moving from one song or activity to another; children frequently derive pleasure from savoring a favorite song or interpreting a song in several different ways. Very young children may need several repetitions before they feel confident enough to join into the activity.

9 Have confidence; be ready with a few "link" songs that draw the children together if there is a need to bring younger children back into the group.

10 Listen to the children, wait, watch, and be ready for them to interpret the words or music. "Give to the child, rather than to the piano, your eyes and attention. Remember that the smallest movement of his fingers may be a thread to follow—a link from one song to the next, or from him to you, or from him to the group—and so from the group back to him again" (p. 38).

Seeger suggests that ballads and other folk chants and songs may be grouped in order to immerse children in a total experience with a subject. For example, children who are fascinated by trains can experience a sequence progressing from the laying of the tracks through meeting someone at the station. This sequence might include the following railroad-related activities: songs and actions or dramatizations. (The music to the songs is found in *American Folk Songs for Children—In Home, School, and Nursery School* and other folk song collections.)

A Railroad Experience

1 Tracks were laid across America by railroad gangs hitting their hammers to the beat of work songs. While reading or

singing the words to the folk song, "This Old Hammer," encourage the children to hammer the tracks in place to the rhythm of the words or music. Large body movement may be encouraged as children pretend to lay their own tracks.

This old hammer
Shine like silver,
Shine like gold, boys,
Shine like gold.

Well don't you hear that
Hammer ringing?
Drivin' in steel, boys,
Drivin' in steel.

Can't find a hammer
On this old mountain,
Rings like mine, boys,
Rings like mine.

I've been working
On this mountain
Seven long years, boys,
Seven long years.

I'm going back to
Swannanoa Town-o,
That's my home, boys,
That's my home.

Take this hammer,
Give it to the captain,
Tell him I'm gone, boys,
Tell him I'm gone.

2   A famous man in folk history, who was also proficient with a hammer, was John Henry. The words to "John Henry" may be sung or read while the children pretend to pick up their twelve-pound hammers and compete with the steam drill in this tribute to a "steel driving man."

3   Children can pretend to be many parts of the train or the various people who work on it as they sing or read "The Train Is A-Coming." They can be engines, passenger cars, coalcars, flatcars, boxcars, and a caboose as they move to the following words:

The train is a-coming, oh yes,
Train is a-coming, oh yes,
Train is a-coming, train is a-coming,
Train is a-coming, oh, yes.

The words can be changed so each child is identified, through repetitive verses, as part of the train.

Jamie is the engine, oh yes,
Jamie is the engine, oh yes,
Jamie is the engine, Jamie is the engine,
Jamie is the engine, oh, yes.

Through

Mary is the caboose, oh yes,
Mary is the caboose, oh yes,
Mary is the caboose, Mary is the caboose,
Mary is the caboose, oh, yes.

Similarly, children can become the different people on the train as each child selects an occupation and then words are improvised to suggest their parts:

Betsy is the engineer, oh, yes,
Betsy is the engineer, oh, yes,
Betsy is the engineer, Betsy is the engineer,
Betsy is the engineer, oh, yes.

4   Children can continue their train movement as they keep their "wheels a-moving and rattling through the land," accompanying the words and music to "The Little Black Train." Also, they can come "a-whistling and a-blowing, and straining every nerve" as they go around curves and up long hills.

5   Finally, they can arrive at the station as they sing, "When the Train Comes Along." To dramatize this song, part of the group can be the train arriving; the remainder can go to the station to meet the train.

Some old ballads that are found in poetry or folk song books have been written and illustrated as picture books. The old English ballad, "The Golden Vanity," begins, "There was a gallant ship, and a gallant ship was she" and has been written in book form and recorded by John Langstaff (14). Children enjoy singing these words as well as reading the words to a musical accompaniment. Langstaff presented his music to children at a recent Children's Literature of the Sea Conference (15). He provided them with background information about sea chanties; he told them that sea chanties were sung by sailors and by early colonists who brought them to America. He described how "The Golden Vanity" had been sung by people in England and Scotland for over three hundred years; then, he enthusiastically encouraged the children to accompany him as he sang several songs, including "The Golden Vanity." When they sang the sea chanty, "Fire Down Below," he encouraged them to use their voices to suggest the rhythmical movement of gathering water in a bucket and then throwing the bucket on the fire:

Fire! Fire! Fire down below,
It's fetch a bucket of water, girls,
There's fire down below.

Other sailing and boat songs that children enjoy include "Blow, Boys, Blow," "Sailing in the Boat," and "The Wind Blow East."

Some of Carroll's poetry has been set to music by Don Harper in *Songs from Alice* (3). Within this book are found some favorite nonsense rhymes such as "Old Father William," "The Lobster Quadrille," "'Tis the Voice of the Lobster," "Beautiful Soup," "Jabberwocky," "Tweedledum and Tweedledee," and "The Walrus and the Carpenter." The music is included in the text so the words can be sung or an accompaniment played to choral renditions. Colorful, humorous illustrations make this an enjoyable book to share with children.

AN INSTRUCTIONAL SEQUENCE THAT STIMULATES CHILDREN TO WRITE POETRY

Donald Graves's (8) research in the development of the writing process suggests that adults must work with children during the writing process rather than after material is completed. Bernice Furner (7) recommends a similar approach but stresses the need for the oral exchange of ideas before children write. Children need a motivational phase before they write, an opportunity to clarify ideas, a transcribing period, and an opportunity to share their poems. An adult sharing poetry-writing experiences with children can use the following sequence, adapted from research by Donna Norton (17).

*An Instructional Sequence for
Creative Poetry Writing*

I. The Stimulation—Motivational Phase
   A. Using ongoing activities
   B. Everyday experiences
   C. A new, adult-introduced experience
II. Oral Exchange of Ideas
   A. Questions and answers extending stimulation activity
   B. Brainstorming ideas, vocabulary, etc.
   C. Claryifying ideas
III. Transcribing Period
   A. Individual dictation of poems to an adult
   B. Individual writing
   C. Teacher interaction to help clarification and idea development
   D. Adult assistance when required

IV. Sharing Poetry
   A. Reading the poetry to a group
   B. Audience development
   C. Making permanent collections
   D. Extending poetry, if desired, to choral reading, art, etc.

Stimulation for Poetry Writing

The three categories of motivational activities suggest numerous topics that can be used to stimulate the writing of poetry. Many ongoing activities already occurring in the classroom, in the library, or in an organization are natural sources of topics for self-expression through poetry. For example, a second-grade teacher used a film that was shown during a social studies unit about farm life to encourage children to observe the characteristics and actions of farm animals and then write about them in poetic form. A Girl Scout leader encouraged her children to describe and write about their feelings following a soccer game; a librarian asked children to write their own color poems after they had shared Mary O'Neill's *Hailstones and Halibut Bones.*

The frequent sharing of poetry has been identified by Gerald Duffy (4) as a very effective way to stimulate children to write poetry. In addition to poetry written by adult authors, university students have stimulated children to write poetry by sharing

The oral exchange of ideas helps children expand and clarify their ideas before writing poetry.

poetry written by other children. They have used, for example, Kenneth Koch's *Wishes, Lies, and Dreams* (13), reading the poems under a certain category to children and then using suggestions developed by Koch to encourage children to write their own poems. Several of these categories include everyday experiences that are common to children and allow them to think of these experiences in new ways. A third-grade teacher encouraged his students to consider all of the wishes they might make if they had the opportunity and then asked them to write a poem expressing those wishes. The following is an example of a third grader wishing for her fondest dreams:

> I wish I had a puppy,
>   not a dog, a puppy
>   not a cat, a puppy
>   not a kitten, a puppy
> I wish I was rich
>   not poor, but rich
>   not a little bit of money, a lot
>   so I'm really rich
> I wish I had a Genie
>   not a pony, a Genie
>   not a pig, a Genie
>   not a pig or a pony
>   a Genie
> I wish I could
> have anything
>   know anything
>   be anything
>   see anything
>   and do anything
>   I wish
>
> Eight-year-old

Many adults encourage children to write poetry by introducing new experiences that allow them to nurture their awareness and their observational powers. They may go for a walk in a flower-strewn park or meadow, listen to the noises around them, smell spring in the air, touch the trees and flowers, describe their sensations with new feelings, and then write a poem about their experience. This poem about bluebonnets resulted from a sixth grader's visual experiences in the out-of-doors.

> *Bluebonnets*
>
> I see the blubonnets growing here
> I wonder where they come from
> they just grow, then disappear.
> I miss them while their gone,
> but I know it won't be long
> until they cover the fields again.

I see them across the field for miles
wondering if its them I see
and not blue dye across the grass
Brilliant and bright reflecting morning dew
Swaying and teetering, as the breeze blows
a promise of spring fills the air.

> Ten-year-old

After a walk in the autumn woods when the children looked at the leaves, listened to the breeze rustling the leaves in the trees, and observed the changing landscape, a middle school child wrote this poem:

> *Woodland*
>
> Cool crisp air calls me
> Late September afternoon
> Crimson, gold, green, rust
> Falling leaves whisper softly
> Come look, what's new in the woods?
>
> Eleven-year-old

Even the sunshine coming into the kitchen window can be used to suggest a poem for some children:

> *Sunshine*
>
> Yellow light shining
> Silently hitting the floor
> As you pull the shade
> Making a weird design
> Upon the kitchen walls
>
> Ten-year-old

Another child contemplated the same sunshine and considered how it changed the environment:

> *The Sunshine*
>
> The sunshine entered the morning
> And birds began to sing.
> The sunshine entered the clouds
> And a rainbow appeared.
> The sunshine entered the afternoon
> And made the evening clear.
> Your smile entered the room
> And sunshine entered my heart.
>
> Eleven-year-old

Other experiences that adults have found successful stimuli for poetry include listening to music, becoming involved in art projects, closely observing and touching objects, looking at and discussing pictures, and considering the various uses for unique objects. One girl described very well how music affected her:

A Song

Something I want to say
But haven't got the words
To say what I feel
The music makes it easy
The music sets me free.

Nine-year-old

A sixth-grade teacher found music to be especially stimulating for her students. She says, "We spent several sessions writing to music such as *Icarus* by Winter Consort and *Night on Bald Mountain* by Mussorgsky. The children let their imaginations soar, they visualized the images created by the music, and wrote their impressions. They especially enjoyed sharing their impressions with each other."

Oral Exchange of Ideas

During an oral exchange of ideas, an adult encourages children to think aloud about the subject. Through brainstorming, for example, children may gain many ideas from each other and experience objects and ideas in a new way. Susan Nugent Reed (20) describes how the poet in the school, Bill Wertheim, encouraged discussion before writing:

The figure of a skeleton in one of the classrooms evolved a lesson about death. Wertheim wrote, "The discussion went from Halloween to skeletons, to fear of skeletons, to monsters, to dying: loss of something and/or someone we love. How it feels to die, how it feels to lose someone you care about." He indicated that the topic first was discussed aloud, then later on paper. For those children who preferred an alternative topic, he suggested writing about coming back to life. Wertheim said it was the most touching lesson he had ever taught and that some children cried. This led to a discusssion about crying, trust, and kindness. He took this opportunity to express the idea that "Crying is OK, even for boys." He said that the children were kind and supportive of one another. (p. 110)

During an outside observational session, children might look at clouds and share their impressions, they might describe the way the light filters through the leaves, or they might close their eyes and describe the sounds they hear.

The librarian who encouraged children to write color poems after listening to Mary O'Neill's poems in *Hailstones and Halibut Bones* asked children to observe colors all around them. They searched for objects that reminded them of the colors and considered their moods as reflected by colors. For example, brainstorming the color white produced some of these associations: white as snowflakes, a winter silence, puffy clouds, a wedding veil, the flash of winning, a frost-covered window, quivering vanilla pudding, heaps of popcorn, a plastered wall, apple blossoms, pale lilac blossoms, sails skimming across the lake, a forgotten memory, fog rising from the marsh, a polar bear, and a gift wrapped in tissue paper. After this experience, children began to look at common objects and feelings with new awareness.

Transcribing Period

Adults frequently help young children write by taking dictation; the children tell an adult their thoughts while the adult writes them down. Parents indicate that even very young children enjoy seeing their creative jingles, rhymes, and poems in print. Many poems written by young children are very spontaneous; they enjoy playing with language and feeling the tantalizing tickle of new words falling off their tongues. One university student told how meaningful it was that her mother had kept a notebook of her early writing experiences with poetry. Another university student, who had had several poems published, felt that it was this early natural poetry composition, written down by his mother, that influenced him in this desire to become a professional writer. Parents who have been successful in this type of dictation have been very careful with their children and have not forced dictation or criticized any thoughts suggested by them. The experience has been a warm, trusting relationship in which children discover that their thoughts can be written down and saved for sharing with themselves and others.

When children have mastered the mechanics of writing, they usually write their own poems. The adult who is working with them, however, still interacts with them as they progress with their writing. The adult can encourage them to reread their poems aloud orally, ask questions to help clarify a problem or an idea, or answer questions pertaining to spelling and punctuation.

Sharing Poetry

The ideal way to share poetry is to read it to an appreciative audience; consequently, many adults encourage children to share their creations with others. Attractive bulletin boards of children's poems may also stimulate children to read each others' poems and write more poems.

Children enjoy making permanent collections from their poems. One teacher had each child develop an accordion-pleated poem book. To construct the book, the children folded large sheets of heavy drawing paper in half, connected several sheets with tape, and printed their poems and an accompanying illustration on each page.

Other classes have made their own books by constructing covers in various appropriate shapes, cutting paper to match

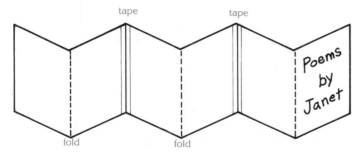

the shapes, and binding the cover and pages together. A group of second graders placed Halloween poems inside a Jack-o-lantern book, fourth graders wrote city poems inside a book resembling a skyscraper, and third graders placed humorous mythical animal poems inside a book resembling a Dr. Seuss beast.

Although it is not necessary to extend writing of poetry to any other activity, children often enjoy using their own poetry for choral-reading arrangements, art interpretations, or dramatizations.

Writing Various Forms of Poetry

Many children enjoy experimenting with writing different types of poems such as limericks, cinquains, and diamantes. Limericks, for example, were found in Ann Terry's research to be among the most enjoyed poetry identified by the children in her study. David McCord's *One at a Time,* discussed previously, describes the content and form of limericks and provides examples that can be shared with children. The nonsense limericks of Edward Lear, David Ross, and William Jay Smith may be used to stimulate these five-line poems that follow this form: lines 1, 2, and 5 rhyme; lines 3 and 4 rhyme.

Line 1 _____

Line 2 _____

Line 3 _____

Line 4 _____

Line 5 _____

After reading and listening to a number of limericks, a sixth grader wrote about and illustrated Mandy's predicament:

> There once was a girl named Mandy
> Whose hair was dreadfully sandy
> She never did wash it
> Instead she did frost it
> The icing made Mandy smell dandy

Eleven-year-old

Brainstorming words that rhyme often assists children when they are completing their rhyming lines.

Cinquains are another form of poetry having specific requirements. These poems help children realize that descriptive words are important when expressing a feeling in poetry. Cinquains also illustrate to children that rhyming words are not necessary when writing poetry. A cinquain uses the following structure:

Line 1:   One word for the title.
Line 2:   Two words that describe the title.
Line 3:   Three words that express action related to the title.
Line 4:   Four words that express a feeling about the title.
Line 5:   One word that either repeats the title or expresses a word closely related to the title.

Sharing cinquains and discussions and brainstorming descriptive words and action words will add to children's enjoyment when they write their own cinquains. The following cinquains were written by middle school children:

Tree

Huge,   woody
Expanding,   reproducing,   entertaining
Leaves   are   colorfully   crisp
Oak

Eleven-year-old

Lasagna

Hot,   delectable
Steaming,   bubbling,   oozing
Always   great   on   Fridays
Paisans

Eleven-year-old

A third form of poetry that has a definite structure is the diamante, the diamond-shaped poem. Poems written in the diamante format progress from one noun to a final noun that contrasts with the first noun. Because this form is more complex than the cinquain, adults find it helpful to describe each line and draw a diagram of the diamante to assist children in seeing the relationships among the lines. The diamante has the following structure:

Line 1:   One noun.
Line 2:   Two adjectives that describe the noun.
Line 3:   Three words that express action related to the noun.
Line 4:   Four nouns or a phrase that expresses a transition in thought between the first noun and the final contrasting noun.
Line 5:   Three words that express action related to the contrasting noun.
Line 6:   Two adjectives that describe the contrasting noun.
Line 7:   One contrasting noun.

Children find it helpful if this poem is also diagrammed:

noun
describing   describing
action   action   action
transition   nouns   or   phrase
action   action   action
describing   describing
noun

In addition to sharing poems before writing them, children find it helpful to brainstorm suggestions for contrasting nouns that could form the framework for the ideas developed in a diamante. One teacher brainstormed with upper elementary students and developed the following contrasts:

sun—moon   summer—winter
tears—smiles   war—peace
day—night   sky—ground
young—old   love—hate
life—death   angel—devil
happy—sad   darkness—light
friends—enemies   boredom—excitement
man—woman   dreams—reality

Next, the group wrote its own poetry. The following poems are examples created by this experience:

Light

Beautiful, bright
Seeing, glistening, refreshing
Light is sometimes blinding
Groping, cautioning, frightening
Evil, insecure
Dark

Ten-year-old

Friends

Happiness, security
Understanding, caring, laughing
Reaching out your hand
Hating, hurting, fighting
Silence, tension
Enemies

Ten-year-old

SUMMARY

Poetry should be a vital part of children's lives, but it has been slighted in many elementary school curricula. Poetry can become an enjoyable part of children's lives if adults consider children's interests, share poems frequently and with enthusiasm, encourage children to experience (not dissect) poetry, and relate poems to children's experiences.

The rhythms and sounds found in many poems encourage physical responses from children. Young children respond to chants and rhymes; other poems encourage them to interpret subjects through bodily movements. Children can also experience poetry through creative dramatizations; narrative poems, nonsensical humorous situations, and holiday themes all lend themselves to creative dramatizations.

Another means of stimulating children's interest in poetry is through choral-speaking arrangements. Children may experiment with different arrangements such as refrain, line-a-child, antiphonal or dialogue, cumulative, and unison. Music is also a means of encouraging children to experience poetry. Rhythm band instruments can complement the rhythm of a poem; old ballads and chants may be used to encourage the interpretation of music and poetry.

Writing and enjoyment of poetry may be encouraged through poets in the school programs. Poetry writing may also be encouraged by providing stimulating experiences that follow an instructional sequence: motivational phase, an oral exchange of ideas, a composing period, and a sharing time. Many children also enjoy writing limericks, cinquains, and diamantes. Published poetry is an effective stimulus for all of these experiences.

Suggested Activities for Children's Appreciation of Poetry

- Develop a card file of poetry that would be appropriate to use with children. Type the poems on cards using a primary type typewriter. On the back of each card list several suggestions for sharing the book with children. Put the cards into a logical categorization.
- Ask children to tell their favorite jumping-rope chants; collect as many of these chants as possible. Share any new chants with children. Ask them why they like and remember such chants.
- Select a series of poems that encourages physical responses from children. Share the poems with a group of children or a peer group. Include poems that encourage children to soar through the air, mimic the movements of an animal, or become something other than themselves.
- Select a poem or a series of poems that encourages creative dramatizations. Plan the steps needed to encourage children to interpret the poetry.
- Choose poems that could be interpreted through choral-speaking arrangements. Select poems appropriate for refrain, line-a-group, antiphonal or dialogue, cumulative, and unison arrangements. Share the poems with a group of children or a peer group.
- Using Seeger's recommendations for sharing songs with children found on pages 355–56, select several songs for an appropriate age group. Share the songs with children or a peer group. Evaluate the group's response to them.
- Following the instructional sequence for creative poetry writing suggested on page 358, develop a lesson plan designed to stimulate children's writing of poetry.

References

1 Baskin, Barbara Holland; Harris, Karen H.; and Salley, Coleen C. "Making the Poetry Connection." *The Reading Teacher* 30 (December 1976): 259–65.

2 Bissett, Donald J. *Poems and Verses to Begin On*. New York: Barnes & Noble, 1967.

3 Carroll, Lewis. *Songs from Alice*. Music by Don Harper. Illustrated by Charles Folkard. New York: Holiday House, 1979.

4 Duffy, Gerald G. "Crucial Elements in the Teaching of Poetry Writing." In *The Language Arts in the Middle School* edited by Martha L. King, Robert Emans, and Patricia J. Cianciolo. Urbana, Ill.: National Council of Teachers of English, 1973.

5 Fellman, Hazel. *The Best Loved Poems of the American People*. New York: Doubleday, 1936.

6 Ferris, Helen. *Favorite Poems Old and New*. New York: Doubleday, 1957.

7 Furner, Beatrice A. "Creative Writing through Creative Dramatics." *Language Arts* 50 (March 1973): 405–8.

8 Graves, Donald H. "Research Update—Language Arts Textbooks: A Writing Process Evaluation." *Language Arts* 53 (September 1976): 645–51.

9 Heinig, Ruth Beall, and Stillwell, Lyda. *Creative Dramatics for the Classroom Teacher*. Englewood Cliffs, N.J.: Prentice-Hall, 1974.

10 Huck, Charlotte. *Children's Literature in the Elementary School*, 3rd ed. New York: Holt, Rinehart & Winston, 1979.

11 Hughes, Rosalind. *Let's Enjoy Poetry*. Boston: Houghton Mifflin, 1967.

12 Jacobs, Leland B. *Poetry for Space Enthusiasts*. Illustrated by Frank Aloise. Champaign, Ill.: Garrard Publishing, 1971.

13 Koch, Kenneth. *Wishes, Lies, and Dreams*. New York: Vintage Books/Chelsea House, 1970.

14 Langstaff, John. *The Golden Vanity*. Illustrated by David Gentleman. New York: Harcourt Brace Jovanovich, 1972.

15 ———. "Sea Chanties." College Station, Tex.: Children's Literature of the Sea Conference, 1981.

16 McIntyre, Barbara M. *Creative Drama in the Elementary School*. Itasca, Ill.: F. E. Peacock Publishers, 1974.

17 Norton, Donna. *The Effective Teaching of Language Arts*. Columbus, Ohio: Merrill, 1980.

18 Peck, Pauline C. "Poetry: A Turn on to Reading." In *Using Literature and Poetry Affectively*, edited by Jon E. Shapiro. Newark, Del.: International Reading Association, 1979.

19 Prelutsky, Jack. *A Gopher in the Garden and Other Animal Poems*. Illustrated by Robert Leydenfrost. New York: Macmillan, 1966, 1967.

20 Reed, Sue Nugent. "Career Idea: Meet the Poet at His Craft." In *Using Literature and Poetry Affectively*, edited by Jon E. Shapiro. Newark, Del.: International Reading Association, 1979.

21 Seeger, Ruth Crawford. *American Folksongs for Children—In Home, School, and Nursery School*. Illustrated by Barbara Cooney. New York: Doubleday, 1948.

22 Shapiro, Jon E. *Using Literature and Poetry Affectively*. Newark, Del.: International Reading Association, 1979.

23 Tanner, Fran. *Creative Communication: Projects in Acting, Speaking, Oral Reading*. Pocatello, Idaho: Clark, 1979.

24 Terry, Ann. *Children's Poetry Preferences: A National Survey of the Upper Elementary Grades*. Urbana, Ill.: National Council of Teachers of English, 1974.

25 Wilner, Isabel. *The Poetry Troupe: Poems to Read Aloud*. New York: Scribner's, 1977.

26 Wolfe, Irving. *Music through the Years*. Chicago: Follett, 1959.

CHILDREN'S
LITERATURE

Adoff, Arnold. *All the Colors of the Race.* Illustrated by John Steptoe, Lothrop, Lee & Shepard, 1982. A girl from a mixed racial parentage reflects on tolerance.

———. *Birds: Poems.* Illustrated by Troy Howell. Lippincott, 1982. Thirty poems about birds.

———. *Eats Poems.* Illustrated by Susan Russo. Lothrop, Lee & Shepard, 1979. Poems that celebrate a love affair with food.

———. *Outside/Inside Poems.* Illustrated by John Steptoe, Lothrop, Lee & Shepard, 1981. Poems that emphasize a boy's hopes and wishes.

———. *Under the Early Morning Trees.* Illustrated by Ronald Himler. Dutton, 1978. Poems revealing a young girl's experiences with nature as she walks around the old farmhouse where she lives.

Aiken, Conrad. *Cats and Bats and Things with Wings.* Illustrated by Milton Glaser. Atheneum, 1965. A collection of sixteen poems about animals. Each poem is illustrated with a large drawing.

Amon, Aline. (comp.) *The Earth Is Sore: Native Americans on Nature.* Illustrated by Aline Amon. Atheneum, 1981. Native American poems reflect the need to live in harmony with nature.

Atwood, Ann. *Fly with the Wind, Flow with the Water.* Scribner's, 1979. Haiku poems about things in nature that swing, soar, leap, run, tumble, swirl, flutter, and float are accompanied by color photographs.

———. *Haiku: The Mood of Earth.* Scribner's, 1971. Beautiful photographs accompany haiku nature poems.

———. *Haiku-Vision: In Poetry and Photography.* Scribner's, 1977. Nature photographs are accompanied by haiku.

Baylor, Byrd. *The Desert Is Theirs.* Illustrated by Peter Parnall. Scribner's, 1975. A poem that stresses the love the Papago Indians have for their desert home.

———. *The Other Way to Listen.* Illustrated by Peter Parnall. Scribner's, 1978. You have to be patient to hear cactuses blooming and rocks murmuring, but it's worth it.

Baylor, Byrd, and Parnall, Peter. *Desert Voices.* Scribner's, 1981. Ten creatures from the desert give their viewpoint of their surroundings.

Bennett, Jill (comp.). *Days Are Where We Live And Other Poems.* Illustrated by Maureen Roffey. Lothrop, Lee & Shepard, 1982. Poems for very young children cover subjects such as playing, eating, and walking.

———. *Tiny Tim: Verses for Children.* Illustrated by Helen Oxenbury. Delacorte, 1982. A variety of poems, including jingles and humorous poems.

Bishop, Elizabeth. *The Ballad of the Burglar of Babylon.* Illustrated by Ann Grifalconi. Farrar, Straus & Giroux, 1968. The story of a criminal who is hunted over the green hills of Rio. Woodcuts illustrate the poem.

Blegvad, Lenore (comp.). *The Parrot in the Garret: And Other Rhymes About Dwellings.* Illustrated by Erik Blegvad. Atheneum, 1982. Twenty-five rhymes that stress the dwellings and their inhabitants.

Bodecker, N. M. *Hurry, Hurry Mary Dear.* Atheneum, 1976. A collection of forty-three humorous poems accompanied by pen sketches.

———. *Let's Marry Said the Cherry.* Atheneum, 1974. A collection of nonsense poems; the poems rely heavily upon word play.

Brown, Beatrice Curtis. *Jonathan Bing.* Illustrated by Judith Gwyn Brown. Lothrop, Lee & Shepard, 1968. Idiosyncrasies and humorous situations create a series of poems about a man who has difficulty performing normal social functions.

Browning, Robert. *The Pied Piper of Hamelin.* Illustrated by Kate Greenaway. Warne Classic, 1888. A reissue of the original poem with delightful illustrations of children by Greenaway.

Carroll, Lewis. *The Hunting of the Snark.* Illustrated by Helen Oxenbury. Watts, 1970. Large, colorful illustrations accompany Carroll's poem.

———. *Jabberwocky.* Illustrated by Jane Breskin Zalben. Warne, 1977. A picture interpretation of Carroll's poem in watercolors.

———. *Poems of Lewis Carroll.* Selected by Myra Cohn Livingston. Crowell, 1973. A collection of poems from *Alice's Adventures in Wonderland* and *Through the Looking-Glass.*

———. *The Walrus and the Carpenter and Other Poems.* Illustrated by Gerald Rose. Dutton, 1969. A collection of Carroll's poems from *Alice's Adventures in Wonderland, Through the Looking-Glass,* and *Sylvia and Bruno Concluded* accompanied by humorous pictures.

Causley, Charles. *Figgie Hobbin.* Illustrated by Trina Schart Hyman. Walker, 1974. Thirteen poems, each illustrated with humorous drawings, tell about such characters as Colonel Fazackerley and King Foo Foo.

Ciardi, John. *Fast and Slow.* Illustrated by Becky Gaver. Houghton Mifflin, 1975. Thirty-four humorous and nonsense poems, including "A Fine Fat Fireman."

———. *I Met a Man.* Illustrated by Robert Osborn. Houghton Mifflin, 1961. A controlled vocabulary creates poetry for beginning readers.

———. *The Monster Den or Look What Happened at My House—and to It.* Illustrated by Edward Gorey. Lippincott, 1966. Humorous poems about what happened when the family was "monstered."

———. *The Reason for the Pelican.* Illustrated by Madeleine Gekiere. Lippincott, 1959.

———. *You Read to Me, I'll Read to You.* Illustrated by Edward Gorey. Lippincott, 1962. Poems for a child to read followed by poems for an adult to read.

Cole, William. *Beastly Boys and Ghastly Girls.* Illustrated by Tomi Ungerer. World, 1964. Poems about naughty and noisy boys and girls.

———. *Dinosaurs and Beasts of Yore.* Illustrated by Susanna Natti. World, 1979. A collection, by different poets, of humorous poems about extinct animals.

———. *I Went to the Animal Fair.* Illustrated by Colette Rosselli. World, 1958. A collection of animal poems by familiar and less familiar poets.

———. *I'm Mad at You!* Illustrated by George MacClain. Collins, 1978. A collection of poems describing and expressing a series of angry thoughts.

———. *Oh, That's Ridiculous!* Illustrated by Tomi Ungerer. Viking, 1972. Nonsense poetry collected from poets noted for their humorous poetry.

———. *Oh, What Nonsense!* Illustrated by Tomi Ungerer. Viking, 1966. A collection of nonsense poems written by many different poets.

Cole, William (comp.). *Poem Stew.* Illustrated by Karen Ann Weinhaus. Lippincott, 1981. A collection of humorous poems related to food.

———. *The Poet's Tales: A New Book of Story Poems.* Illustrated by Charles Keeping. World, 1971. Selections ranging from folk poetry to modern poetry.

———. *The Sea, Ships & Sailors.* Illustrated by Robin Jacques. Viking, 1967. A collection of poems about buccaneers, moods of the sea, ships, songs, storms, under the sea, and sea stories.

Field, Eugene. *Wynken, Blynken and Nod.* Illustrated by Susan Jeffers. Dutton, 1982. The classic poem in a newly illustrated edition.

Fisher, Aileen. *Feathered Ones and Furry.* Illustrated by Eric Carle. Crowell, 1971. Fifty-five poems about furry animals and feathery birds.

———. *In One Door and Out the Other: A Book of Poems.* Illustrated by Lillian Hoban. Crowell, 1969. A collection of poems about childhood experiences.

———. *In the Woods, In the Meadow, In the Sky.* Illustrated by Margot Tomes. Scribner's, 1965. Poems about things in nature, including pussy willows, birds, leaves, trees, meadows, clouds, and sky.

Froman, Robert. *Seeing Things: A Book of Poems.* Crowell, 1974. Several concrete poems are in this collection.

———. *Street Poems.* McCall, 1971. A series of poems shaped like pictures about street objects such as skyscrapers, fire hydrants, and street signs.

Frost, Robert. *Stopping By Woods On a Snowy Evening.* Illustrated by Susan Jeffers. Dutton, 1978. Large pictures illustrate Frost's poem.

Fufuka, Karama. *My Daddy Is a Cool Dude.* Illustrated by Mahiri Fufuka. Dial, 1975. Twenty-seven poems about life in an urban black community as seen through the experience of a child.

Hopkins, Lee Bennett, ed. *Circus! Circus!* Illustrated by John O'Brien. Knopf, 1982. Circus poems by poets such as Jack Prelutsky and Beatrice Schenk de Regniers.

———. *Elves, Fairies, and Gnomes.* Illustrated by Rosekrans Hoffman. Knopf, 1980. A collection of seventeen fantasy poems.

———. *Moments.* Illustrated by Michael Hague. Harcourt Brace Jovanovich, 1980. Fifty poems about the four seasons.

———. *My Mane Catches the Wind: Poems about Horses.* Illustrated by Sam Savitt. Harcourt Brace Jovanovich, 1979. A collection of twenty-two poems about horses written by different poets.

———. *On Our Way.* Photographs by David Parks. Knopf, 1974. A collection of twenty-two poems by Black authors. The subjects include Blackness, Soullove, Four, Feelings, and Remembering.

———. *To Look at Any Thing.* Photographs by John Earl. Harcourt Brace Jovanovich, 1978. Unusual nature photographs are accompanied by appropriate poems.

Hopkinson, Francis. *The Battle of the Kegs.* Illustrated by Paul Galdone. Crowell, 1964. A ballad of the Revolutionary War records the Yankees sending kegs of gunpowder floating down the Delaware toward the British ships.

Hubbell, Patricia. *Catch Me a Wind.* Illustrated by Susan Trommler. Atheneum, 1968. Poems in pursuit of the wind, rain, sunbeams, shadows, and other things that people want to explore.

———. *8 A.M. Shadows.* Illustrated by Julia Maas. Atheneum, 1965. Poems tell about some of the wondering things in a child's day.

Hughes, Ted. *Under the North Star.* Illustrated by Leonard Baskin. Viking, 1981. Poems about northern animals.

Janeczko, Paul B. *Postcard Poems: A Collection of Poetry for Sharing.* Bradbury, 1979. A collection of one hundred poems, brief enough to write on a postcard and share with a friend.

Jones, Hettie. *The Trees Stand Shining: Poetry of the North American Indians.* Illustrated by Robert Andrew Parker. Dial, 1971. A collection of poems from North American Indians accompanied by full-page illustrations.

Jordan, June. *Who Look at Me.* Crowell, 1969. Poems accompany twenty-seven paintings of black American life. Includes notes about the artists.

Kennedy, X. J. *The Phantom Ice Cream Man.* Illustrated by David McPaihl. Atheneum, 1979. Poems about unheard of beasts, including a muddle-headed messer and a giant sloth who gobbles locomotives.

Kherdian, David. *Country Cat, City Cat.* Illustrated by Nonny Hogrogian. Four Winds, 1978. Poems about cats and birds against a background of changing seasons.

Larrick, Nancy. *Piper, Pipe that Song Again.* Illustrated by Kelly Oechsli. Random House, 1965. An anthology of poetry.

———, ed. *When the Dark Comes Dancing: A Bedtime Poetry Book.* Illustrations by John Wallner. Philomel, 1982. Poetry to be read aloud at bedtime.

Lawrence. D. H. *Birds, Beasts and The Third Thing.* Selected and Illustrated by Alice and Martin Provensen. Viking, 1982. Twenty-three poems focus on Lawrence's "Delight of Being Alone."

Lear, Edward. *The Complete Nonsense Book.* Dodd, Mead, 1946. Includes *A Book of Nonsense,* originally published in 1846, and *Nonsense Songs and Stories,* originally published in 1871.

———. *The Nonsense Books of Edward Lear.* New American Library, 1964. Nonsense poems are still enjoyed by children.

———. *The Pelican Chorus & The Quangle-Wangle's Hat.* Illustrated by Kevin W. Maddison. Viking, 1981. Two of Lear's poems are illustrated in full-page watercolors.

———. *The Quangle-Wangle's Hat.* Illustrated by Helen Oxenbury. Watts, 1969. A humorous and colorful choice for children.

———. *Whizz!* Illustrated by Janina Domanska. Macmillan, 1973. Six of Lear's limericks illustrated in picture book format.

———, and Nash, Ogden. *The Scroobius Pip.* Illustrated by Nancy Ekholm Burkert. Harper & Row, 1968. A beautifully illustrated picture book about the wondrous animal that is neither fish nor fowl, insect nor beast.

Lee, Dennis. *Garbage Delight.* Illustrated by Frank Newfeld. Houghton Mifflin, 1978. A banquet of nonsense poems, including such titles as "Quintin and Griffin," "Suzy Grew a Moustache" and "The Big Blue Frog and the Dirty Flannel Dog".

Lewis, Richard. *The Wind and the Rain.* Photographs by Helen Buttfield. Simon & Schuster,

1968. A collection of nature poems written by children.

Livingston, Myra Cohn. *A Circle of Seasons.* Illustrated by Leonard Everett Fisher. Holiday, 1982. Poems about the four seasons.

_____. *A Crazy Flight and Other Poems.* Illustrated by James J. Spanfeller. Harcourt Brace Jovanovich, 1969. Poems to encourage children's imaginations.

_____. *How Pleasant to Know Mr. Lear!* Illustrated by Edward Lear. Holiday, 1982. Includes Lear's poems, art and biographical information.

_____. *Listen, Children, Listen: An Anthology of Poems for the Very Young.* Illustrated by Trina Schart Hyman. Harcourt Brace Jovanovich, 1972. An anthology of over eighty poems written for young children.

_____. *O Sliver of Liver.* Illustrated by Iris Van Rynbach. Atheneum, 1979. A variety of poems, including cinquains, haiku, and poems about nature, holidays, daily life, human relationships, and emotions.

_____. *The Way Things Are: And Other Poems.* Atheneum, 1974. Poems about everyday things.

_____. *Whispers and Other Poems.* Illustrated by Jacqueline Chwast. Harcourt Brace Jovanovich, 1958. Poems about sensory experiences.

_____, ed. *Why Am I Grown So Cold? Poems of the Unknowable.* Atheneum, 1982. Poems about ghosts and monsters.

Longfellow, Henry Wadsworth. *America the Beautiful.* Morrow, 1965. Longfellow's poems accompanied by photographs of different American scenes.

_____. *Paul Revere's Ride.* Illustrated by Paul Galdone. Crowell, 1963. The classic poem illustrated for younger children.

McCord, David. *Away and Ago: Rhymes of the Never Was and Always Is.* Illustrated by Leslie Morrill. Little, Brown, 1974. Poems about familiar places, objects, and experiences.

_____. *Far and Few: Rhymes of the Never Was and Always Is.* Illustrated by Henry B. Kane. Little, Brown, 1952. Includes the popular nonsense poems found in "Five Chants."

_____. *One at a Time: Collected Poems for the Young.* Illustrated by Henry B. Kane. Little, Brown, 1977. A large collection of poems on many subjects.

McGee, Shelagh. *Smile Please!* Prentice-Hall, 1978. Humorous and loving poems about the different members of a child's family.

Mendoza, George. *Goodbye, River, Goodbye.* Photographs by George T. Tice. Doubleday, 1971. A study in ecology, an epitaph for a once-unspoiled river in Vermont.

_____. *Poem for Putting to Sea.* Illustrated by Ati Forberg, Hawthorn, 1972. A lyrical ballad about a boy's dream and the sloop that made him a man.

_____. *The World from My Window.* Hawthorn, 1969. Poems written by children who live in American cities.

Merriam, Eve. *Independent Voices.* Illustrated by Arvis Stewart. Atheneum, 1968. The sayings of Benjamin Franklin, Elizabeth Blackwell, Frederick Douglass, Henry Thoreau, Lucretia Mott, Idea Wells, and Fiorello H. La Guardia written in poetic form by the author.

_____. *Rainbow Writing.* Atheneum, 1976. Poetry designed to color our minds with the vast spectrum of human experience.

_____. *A Word or Two with You: New Rhymes for Young Readers.* Illustrated by John Nez. Atheneum, 1981. Seventeen poems that emphasize rhyming and word play.

Meteyard, Peter. *Stanley, the Tale of the Lizard.* Illustrated by Peter Firnin. Deutsch, 1979. A story poem about a gentle knight and a gentle dragon who rescue a fair maiden from a wicked black knight.

Milne, A. A. *When We Were Very Young.* Illustrated by Ernest H. Shepard. Dutton, 1924, 1952, 1961. Delightful poems about Pooh and hundred-acre wood.

_____. *The World of Christopher Robin.* Illustrated by E. H. Shepard. Dutton, 1958. Poems about a boy and his toy animal friends.

Moore, Clement. *The Night Before Christmas.* Illustrated by Tomie de Paola. Holiday, 1980. Large, brightly colored illustrations in picture book format.

_____. *The Night Before Christmas.* Illustrated by Tasha Tudor, Rand McNally, 1975. Large illustrations of popular Christmas poem.

Moore, Lilian. *Go with the Poem.* McGraw-Hill, 1979. A collection of ninety poems written by outstanding twentieth-century poets.

_____. *Sam's Place, Poems from the Country.* Illustrated by Talivaldis Stubis. Atheneum, 1973. Poems about nature at Sam's place in the Shawangunk Mountains.

_____. *See My Lovely Poison Ivy.* Illustrated by Diane Dawson. Atheneum, 1975. Poems about witches, ghosts, goblins, bats, and monsters.

_____. *Something New Begins.* Atheneum, 1982. Fifteen new poems as well as selections from her previous poems.

Morrison, Lillian. *The Sidewalk Racer and Other Poems of Sports and Motion.* Lothrop, Lee & Shepard, 1977. Poems about sports, including surfing, tennis, boxing, football, skateboarding, and baseball.

Morton, Miriam. *The Moon is Like a Silver Sickle: A Celebration of Poetry by Russian Children.* Illustrated by Eros Keith. Simon & Schuster, 1972. A collection of ninety-two poems written by Russian children.

Norris, Leslie. *Merlin & the Snake's Egg: Poems.* Illustrated by Ted Lewin. Viking, 1978. Poems about woodspells, walking, dogs, darkness underground, ogres, and Christmas animals.

Noyes, Alfred. *The Highwayman.* Illustrated by Gilbert Riswold. Prentice-Hall, 1969. Story poem about a highwayman who risked his life every evening to visit the innkeeper's daughter.

O'Neill, Mary. *Hailstones and Halibut Bones.* Illustrated by Leonard Weisgard. Doubleday, 1961. What is purple? Poems that describe the basic colors.

_____. *Take a Number.* Illustrated by Al Nagy. Doubleday, 1968. Concepts of mathematics are presented in poetry.

Palmer, Geoffrey, and Lloyd, Noel. *Round about Eight.* Illustrated by Denis Wrigley. Warne, 1972. An anthology of poetry written for children eight years old and older.

Pomerantz, Charlotte. *If I Had A Paka: Poems in Eleven Languages.* Illustrated by Nancy Tafuri. Greenwillow, 1982. Poems that rely on foreign words.

_____. *Noah's and Namah's Ark.* Illustrated by Kelly K. M. Carson. Holt, Rinehart & Winston, 1981. Story of Noah told in narrative prose.

Prelutsky, Jack. *The Baby Uggs Are Hatching.* Illustrated by James Stevenson. Greenwillow, 1982. Humorous poems about Grebles, Sneepies, and Slitchs.

_____. *A Gopher in the Garden and Other Animal Poems.* Illustrated by Robert Leydenfrost. Macmillan, 1966, 1967.

_____. *The Headless Horseman Rides Tonight.* Illustrated by Arnold Lobel. Greenwillow, 1980. Twelve scary poems about giants, banshees, poltergeists, and zombies.

_____. *The Queen of Eene.* Illustrated by Victoria Chess. Greenwillow, 1978. Fourteen humorous poems, each illustrated with a funny illustration.

_____. *Rolling Harvey Down the Hill.* Illustrated by Victoria Chess. Greenwillow, 1980. Humorous poems about the adventures of five boys.

_____. *The Sheriff of Rottenshot.* Illustrated by Victoria Chess. Greenwillow, 1982. Humorous poems use a strong rhyming pattern.

_____. *Toucans Two and Other Poems.* Illustrated by Jose Aruego. Macmillan, 1970. Eighteen poems about such animals as zebras, camels, and bees. Large, colorful pictures accompany poems.

Reeves, James. *Prefabulous Animiles*. Illustrated by Edward Ardizzone. Dutton, 1960. Poems about preposterous, unheard of animals.

Richards, Laura E. *Tirra Lirra, Rhymes Old and New*. Illustrated by Marguerite Davis. Little, Brown, 1902, 1955. Over one hundred humorous poems including "Eletelephony" and "Bobbily Boo and Wollypotump."

Roethke, Theodore. *Dirty Dinky and Other Creatures*. Illustrated by Julie Brinckloe. Doubleday, 1973. Poems about creatures, both animal and human.

———. *I Am! Says the Lamb*. Illustrated by Robert Leydenfrost. Doubleday, 1961. Humorous poems and nature poems by the Pulitzer Prize winning author.

Ross, David. *Poetry for Children*. Grosset & Dunlap, 1970. A large collection of poems divided according to seasons, Christmas, tides, creatures of sea and sky, the horizon, spells and enchantments, miracles, miniatures, music, nonsense, limericks, mirth, creatures on land, characters, love poems, men at arms, recollections, and wisdom.

Rossetti, Christina. *Goblin Market*. Illustrated and adapted by Ellen Raskin. Dutton, 1970. A picture book version of the poem originally published in 1862.

Sandburg, Carl. *Rainbows Are Made*. Edited by Lee Bennett Hopkins. Illustrated by Fritz Eichenberg. Harcourt Brace Jovanovich, 1982. A collection of seventy poems.

Saunders, Dennis. *Magic Lights and Streets of Shining Jet*. Photographs by Terry Williams. Greenwillow, 1974. A collection of poems by various writers with accompanying color photographs. Four categories are included: creatures small, weathers and seasons, colors, and sea and shore.

Sendak, Maurice. *Pierre: A Cautionary Tale*. Harper & Row, 1962. A boy learns that he should sometimes care.

Silverstein, Shel. *A Light in the Attic*. Harper & Row, 1981. Humorous poems about such situations as the polar bear in the Frigidaire.

———. *Where the Sidewalk Ends*. Harper & Row, 1974. A collection of humorous poems.

Skofield, James. *Nightdances*. Illustrated by Karen Gundersheimer. Harper & Row, 1981. A boy and his parents go outside on a moonlit night.

Smith, William Jay. *Laughing Time*. Illustrated by Juliet Kepes. Little, Brown, 1955. Humorous poems about animals and people.

———. *Mr. Smith & Other Nonsense*. Illustrated by Don Bologne. Delacorte, 1968. Nonsense verses about things big and little, imaginary dialogues, and nonsense birds.

Snyder, Zilpha Keatly. *Today is Saturday*. Illustrated by John Arms. Atheneum, 1969.

Starbird, Kaye. *The Covered Bridge House and Other Poems*. Illustrated by Jim Arnosky. Four Winds, 1979. Thirty poems about such childhood experiences as jumping rope, hopping after falling on a sky slope, and wondering why no one can get rags from ragweed.

———. *The Pheasant on Route Seven*. Illustrated by Victoria de Larrea. Lippincott, 1968. Poems about the village of Pleasantsport and the people and animals who live there.

Tennyson, Alfred Lord. *The Charge of the Light Brigade*. Illustrated by Alice and Martin Provensen. Golden Press, 1964. A story poem about the cavalry charge against the Russian batteries at Balaclava, 1854.

Thurman, Judith. *Flashlight and Other Poems*. Illustrated by Reina Rubel. Atheneum, 1976. Familiar things such as balloons, closets, and going barefoot are told about in poems.

Viorst, Judith. *If I Were in Charge of the World and Other Worries: Poems for Children and their Parents*. Illustrated by Lynne Cherry. Atheneum, 1981. Poems about everyday situations that frustrate.

Wallace, Daisy. *Fairy Poems*. Illustrated by Trina Schart Hyman. Holiday House, 1980. A collection of poems about leprechauns and fairies.

———. *Ghost Poems*. Illustrated by Tomie de Paola. Holiday, 1979. A collection of seventeen poems about ghosts.

Watson, Nancy Dingman. *Blueberries Lavender: Songs of the Farmer's Children*. Illustrated by Erik Blegvad. Addison-Wesley, 1977. Twenty-eight poems about the experiences important to a farm child: exploring nature, insects, and animals.

Willard, Nancy. *A Visit to William Blake's Inn: Poems for Innocent and Experienced Travelers*. Illustrated by Alice and Martin Provensen. Harcourt Brace Jovanovich, 1981. Poems describing a menagerie of guests.

Wilner, Isabel. *The Poetry Troup*. Scribner's, 1977. An anthology of over two hundred poems selected for reading aloud.

Worth, Valerie. *More Small Poems*. Illustrated by Natalie Babbitt. Farrar, Straus & Giroux, 1976. Ordinary objects such as acorns, soap bubbles, and Christmas lights are subjects of short poems.

———. *Small Poems*. Illustrated by Natalie Babbitt. Farrar, Straus & Giroux, 1972. Poems about ordinary objects.

———. *Still More Small Poems*. Illustrated by Natalie Babbitt. Farrar, Straus & Giroux, 1978. Twenty-five poems about ordinary objects such as doors, rocks, slugs, and mushrooms.

Willington, Louisa Penn. *Aunt Louisa's Rip Van Winkle*. Hart, 1977. A poem based on Washington Irving's story.

Zim, Jacob. *My Shalom My Place*. McGraw-Hill, 1975. A collection of poems about peace, written and illustrated by Jewish and Arab children.

Zolotow, Charlotte. *All That Sunlight*. Illustrated by Walter Stein. Harper & Row, 1967. Sunlight on weeds, flowers, or crickets: all are experiences that create enjoyable poems for young children.

———. *River Winding*. Illustrated by Kazue Mizumura. Crowell, 1978. Same poems as in the following book by this name, but illustrated by a different artist.

———. *River Winding*. Illustrated by Regina Shekerjian. Abelard-Schuman, 1970. Poems that paint images of things seen and remembered for young children.

NINE
Contemporary Realistic Fiction

Window on the World
Involving Children in Realistic Fiction

Window on the World

NEW TERMINOLOGY enters the discussion of children's books as students of children's literature leave the realm of Mother Goose, most picture story books, traditional literature, and modern fantasy. Terms such as relevant books, extreme realism, the problem novel, and everyday occurrences are found in critiques and discussions of the literature. While some books within this genre are among the most popular with older children, they are also among the most criticized and debated among various interest groups, educators, and parents. Issues such as censorship, sexism, violence, alienation from society, racism, and promiscuity are being discussed by concerned adults.

In this chapter we will consider what realistic fiction is and how it is different from stories discussed in other genres, how realistic fiction has changed, why it should be shared with children, the criteria for evaluating realistic fiction, and issues related to realistic fiction.

WHAT IS CONTEMPORARY REALISTIC FICTION?

The term *contemporary realistic fiction* infers that everything in the story, including characters, setting, and plot, could happen to real people living in our contemporary world. Realistic fiction, however, does not mean that the story is true; it means only that it could have happened. Because the word *fiction* is used in the genre, children frequently have difficulty discriminating between modern fantasy, contemporary realistic fiction, and stories that really happened.

There are major differences in authors' techniques, characterization, setting, and plot development between modern fantasy and contemporary realistic fiction. Because authors of modern fantasy use imaginary elements that are contrary to reality, they must encourage readers to suspend disbelief. They may firmly ground the story in reality before they proceed to fantasy; have characters who are firmly grounded in reality accept impossible situations; tell the story from the viewpoint of an unusual being; carefully create and describe new worlds; and develop credibility through real objects that are found or influence the experience in the world of fantasy. All authors, if their stories are credible, must create an internal consistency that complies with all of their previous rules.

Consider, for example, several differences between modern fantasy and realistic fiction that are suggested by Chart 9–1 comparing main characters, setting, plot development, and creating believable stories:

CHART 9–1
Differences Between Modern Fantasy and Contemporary Realistic Fiction

	Modern Fantasy	Contemporary Realistic Fiction
Characters:	Personified toys, little people, supernatural beings, real people who have imaginary experiences, animals who behave like people	Characters who must act like real people Animals who should always behave like animals
Setting:	Past, present, or future Imaginary world May travel through time and space	Contemporary world as we know it
Plot Development:	Conflict may be against supernatural powers Problems may be solved through magical powers	Conflict develops as characters cope with problems such as growing up, survival, family problems, and inner city tensions Antagonists may be self, other family members, society, or nature
Creating Believable Stories:	Authors must encourage readers to suspend disbelief	Authors may rely on "relevant subjects," everyday occurrences, or extreme realism

Two popular animal stories further demonstrate these differences between modern fantasy and contemporary realistic fiction. Consider, for example, Beatrix Potter's fantasy, *The Tale of Peter Rabbit,* and Sheila Burnford's realistic fiction, *The Incredible Journey.* Peter talks, thinks, acts, and dresses like a person. He behaves like an inquisitive, sometimes greedy, and frightened child, who also demonstrates his need for his mother's love and care. While the garden setting is from a realistic world, Peter's home is furnished with human furniture. The conflict develops because Peter demonstrates such believable childlike desires. In contrast, the three animals in *The Incredible Journey* retain their animal characteristics: a trained hunting dog leads his companions across the wilderness; the English bulldog, who is a cherished family pet, seeks people for his food; and the Siamese cat retains her feline independence and characteristics. The author describes a realistic setting in the Canadian wilderness that is also the antagonist. The conflict develops as the animals become lost and face problems as they try to return to their home. The author does not give them human thoughts, values, or other characteristics. The setting is believable and so are the animals that behave as any owner of lost pets might expect them to behave.

In addition to animal stories, popular topics in realistic fiction include living within the family; developing interpersonal relationships between friends, aging adults, and handicapped people; experiencing problems related to growing up, emotional maturity, and self-discovery; surviving under unusual circumstances; solving mysteries; and developing athletic abilities.

HOW REALISTIC FICTION HAS CHANGED

Synonyms for *realistic* include adjectives such as *genuine, lifelike,* and *authentic.* What is lifelike, however, also depends upon the society in which the story takes place. Chapter two, "History of Children's Literature," indicated the degree to which society and society's belief in the concept of childhood influenced children's literature. In the same chapter, the comparisons between fiction reflecting family life written between 1865-1903, 1938-1960, and 1969-1980 suggest how greatly social values, family life, and personal relationships have changed in literature that was considered contemporary for those time periods. A summary of these characteristics illustrates the changes in realistic fiction that have occurred since 1865.

Realistic fiction written between 1865-1903 depicts a strong concern for family; responsibility toward siblings; duty to educate, Christianize, or care for the poor; ambitions centered around Christian goodness and work ethic; male ambitions that stress classic education and manly arts; female ambitions that stress writing, drawing, and playing instruments; respect for law, knowledge, and adult authority; warm, close, stable families that live in an area for generations; strong religious commitment; definite male and female roles; independent males and dependent females; and problems related to overcoming sinfulness and becoming good.

Realistic fiction written between 1938-1960 depicts a strong concern for family; responsibility toward siblings; family unity; strong work ethic; male and female ambitions that are less diverse; respect for law, knowledge, and adult authority; happy, secure, stable families; families that attend church; females more apt to stay at home while father is the breadwinner; both male and female children gaining independence; and few problems.

As mentioned in chapter two, realistic fiction written between 1969-1980 is harder to characterize, but the following characteristics were found in the literature analyzed: children, not parents, may strive to hold family together; older children may be responsible for younger children; families may not include both parents; work ethic is not consistent; career ambitions are not as often set by traditional sex roles; disrespect or fear of law and feelings against war may be found; education and knowledge are not stressed as often as previously; children frequently question adult authority; families are often not stable; some families are happy, but many are disturbed; religion is infrequently mentioned; females work outside the home, father may have left the family, or both parents may work; males and females may be independent; and many problems relate to family disruptions or emotional problems.

Researchers who have analyzed various themes found in children's literature across time periods have also illustrated the changing nature of realistic fiction. John Townsend (23) concluded that the contrasts between the 1950s and late 1960s were striking. The 1950s depicted one of the quietest decades in children's literature, with traditional values maintained and children pictured as part of a stable community in which there was an orderly succession from one generation to the next. Grandparents were pictured as wise, parents were staunch and respected, and childhood was happy and secure. In contrast, he found the literature of the late 1960s inferred an erosion of adult authority and an apparent widening of the generation gap; it was no longer considered self-evident that parents knew best and that children could be guided into accepting the established codes and behavior. In a recent study of themes found in contemporary realistic fiction published in the late 1970s, Jane M. Madsen and Elaine B. Wickersham (13) found that popular themes for younger children dealt with overcoming fear and responsibility. Some situations in the stories were quite different from the typical realistic stories of the past. Stories dealt with overcoming problems related to adoption, divorce, handicaps, and black ancestry.

Themes in contemporary realistic fiction for older children frequently stress children's overcoming family and personal problems as they confront illegitimacy, quarreling or divorcing parents, conflicts between personal ambitions and parental desires, the death of a loved one, deserting or noncaring parents, cruel foster families, and attachments to handicapped siblings. Discovery of self and development of maturity as children face and overcome their fears are other popular themes in stories written for older children. Self-esteem and being true to one's self are frequently stressed in these books.

Terms such as *new realism* and *problem novel* have been coined to define certain segments of this literature. Shelton L. Root (18) defines the new realism as "that fiction for young readers which addresses itself to personal problems and social issues heretofore considered taboo for fictional treatment by the general public, as enunciated by its traditional spokesmen: librarians, teachers, ministers, and others. The new realism is often graphic in its language and always explicit in its treatment" (p. 19).

Some literary critics question the merit of at least portions of contemporary realistic fiction. Sheila Egoff, (6) for example, differentiates between the distinguished realistic novels written since 1960 that have strong literary qualities—including logical flow of narrative; delicate complexity of characterization; style; insights that convey the conduct of life as characters move from childhood, to adolescence, to adulthood; and a quality that touches both the imagination and the emotions (as exemplified by Virginia Hamilton's *The Planet of Junior Brown*)—and the fiction she categorizes as the "problem novel."

Egoff states that the conflict in a realistic novel is integral to the plot and characterization; its resolution has wide applications, and it grows out of the personal vision of the writer. In contrast, she maintains that the conflict in a problem novel stems from the writer's social conscience; this conflict is specific rather than universal, and narrow rather than far-reaching in its significance. Egoff identifies the following characteristics of the problem novel:

1 Problem novels deal with externals, with how things look rather than how things are. Writers begin with a problem rather than with a plot or characters.
2 The protagonist is burdened with anxieties and grievances that grow out of alienation from the adult world.
3 Temporary relief from these anxieties is frequently achieved by an association with an unconventional adult from outside the family.
4 The narrative is usually in first person and its confessional tone is self-centered.
5 The vocabulary is limited and observation is restricted by the pretense that an ordinary child is the narrator.
6 Sentences and paragraphs are short, language is flat, without nuance, and the language may be emotionally numb.

7 There seems to be an obligatory inclusion of expletives.
8 Sex is discussed openly.
9 The setting is usually urban.

CRITERIA FOR EVALUATING CONTEMPORARY REALISTIC FICTION

Contemporary realistic fiction should meet all of the basic criteria for literature developed in chapter three. In addition, Root (18) suggests that the following criteria must be present if contemporary realistic fiction is to develop a story with integrity:

1 The content should be honestly presented; sensationalizing and capitalizing on the novelty of the subject should be avoided.
2 Contemporary realistic fiction should expose those personal and social values central to our culture, while revealing, at the same time, how the overt expression of those values may have changed.
3 The story should allow the reader to draw personal conclusions from the evidence; the personal intelligence of the reader should be respected.
4 Realistic fiction should recognize that today's readers are in the process of growing toward adult sophistication.
5 The language and syntax should help to reveal the background and nature of characters and situations.
6 Contemporary realistic fiction should be written in a hopeful key; it should communicate in an honest way that there is hope in this world.

In addition to these criteria, there are also concerns that should be considered when evaluating books with specific content such as handicaps. These criteria will be presented prior to the discussion of the particular books.

VALUES OF REALISTIC FICTION FOR CHILDREN

One of the greatest values of realistic fiction for children is that many stories are written about children of the same age who have similar interests and concerns. Children like to read about people they can understand. Their favorite authors are frequently those who express a clear understanding of children. Children often say, for example, that Judy Blume really understands what it is like to be a child. As one girl said about *Are You There God? It's Me, Margaret,* "I've read this book five times; I could be Margaret." Another child indicated that *Tales of a Fourth Grade Nothing* described her problems with her younger brother.

Because themes found in realistic fiction cover a wide range of experiences that children are or will be facing, realistic stories about how other children face their problems are popular. A child who is unhappy about his physical appearance may identify with Constance Greene's *The Unmaking of Rabbit,* or the shy child may discover familiar traits in Elizabeth Billington's *Part-Time Boy.* Girls who aspire to professional careers can identify with Winifred Madison's *Call Me Danica.* These heroes and heroines face and overcome their problems while remaining true to themselves.

Children may discover that their problems and desires are not unique and that they are not alone when they read about other children in similar situations. They may feel desolate when their best friend moves away until they discover a new friend with nine-year-old Polly in Mary Stolz's *Cider Days.* If they feel that their dreams differ from their family's, they can discover a comrade in Jess Aarons, a misunderstood boy who longs to be an artist in Katherine Paterson's *Bridge to Terabithia.*

Realistic fiction extends children's horizons by broadening their interests, allowing them to experience new adventures, and showing them different ways to view and deal with problems. They can vicariously live a survival adventure and mature in the process as they read Scott O'Dell's *Island of the Blue Dolphins* or Jean Craighead George's *Julie of the Wolves.* In these books, they may also discover a close relationship between humans and nature. They may discover that life is not always easy as they learn how some children try to cope with an ill mother as in *The Bears' House,* by Marilyn Sachs, or the death of a father as in Vera and Bill Cleaver's *Where the Lilies Bloom.*

Reading about children who are facing emotional problems may help children discharge repressed emotions. Reading may help them cope with their fear, anger, or grief. (*A word of caution:* realistic fiction should *not* be used to replace professional help in situations that may warrant such intervention. Children experiencing severe depression, anger, or grief may require professional help.) Children who are experiencing problems may also seek escape in their reading and not choose literature expressing similar problems. There are, for example, several books about divorce or death that might help children cope with a traumatic period in their lives. The emotions accompanying the death of a pet are explored in Carol Carrick's *The Accident* and Charlotte Graeber's *Mustard.* Constance Greene's *Beat the Turtle Drum* describes the warm relationship between two sisters and the emotions felt by one sister after the other is accidentally killed. Although the characters overcome problems, the authors do not suggest it is easy.

Children can gain insights into their feelings and those of others as they read realistic fiction. In Peggy Mann's *My Dad Lives in a Downtown Hotel,* they may discover that parents as well as children are hurt by divorce. They may also realize the cruelty that is experienced when unthinking or uninformed adults and children attack an illegitimate child, as in Vera and Bill Cleaver's *I Would Rather Be a Turnip,* or when they ridicule a mentally handicapped child, as in Jean Little's *Take Wing.*

Realistic fiction can stimulate discussion and help children share and solve problems. (Using realistic fiction to stimulate discussion, role playing, and other problem solving will be discussed in the second part of this chapter.)

Finally, realistic fiction provides the enjoyment of escape through mystery and animal adventure stories. Children may follow an exciting, interest-holding plot as they try to solve Robert Newman's *The Case of the Baker Street Irregular* or Virginia Masterman-Smith's *The Great Egyptian Heist.* They can pretend to be royalty in an ancient world as they play *The Egypt Game,* by Zilpha Keatley Snyder. Animal lovers can cross the Canadian wilderness with three friends in Sheila Burnford's *The Incredible Journey;* horse lovers can long for Marguerite Henry's *Misty of Chincoteague* or wish to ride the beautiful black horse in Walter Farley's *The Black Stallion;* dog lovers can encourage the blind dog in *The Trouble With Tuck.*

While realistic fiction encompasses some very enjoyable literature for older children, it also contains controversial subjects. Some of the problems faced by heroes and heroines in realistic fiction are accompanied by concerns regarding censorship.

CONTROVERSIAL ISSUES RELATED TO REALISTIC FICTION

The degree to which realistic fiction should reflect the reality of the times leads to controversy as writers create heroes and heroines who face problems relating to sexism, sexuality, violence, and drugs. There is no simple solution; what is considered controversial by one group may not be considered so by another. Realistic fiction has resulted in more controversy and calls for censorship than any other genre; educators must be aware of some concerns in this area of literature.

Sexism

Psychological oppression in the form of sex role socialization clearly conveys to girls from the earliest ages that their nature is to be submissive, servile, and repressed, and their role is to be servant, admirer,

sex object and martyr . . . the psychological consequences of goal depression in young women . . . are all too common. In addition, both men and women have come to realize the effect on men of this type of sex role stereotyping, the crippling pressure to compete, to achieve, to produce, to stifle emotion, sensitivity and gentleness, all taking their toll in psychic and physical traumas.

This position statement by the Association of Women Psychologists (1) stresses the dangers to both females and males when they are expected to live up to the traditional roles created by society and literature. The controversial issue of sexism in children's literature involves not only the exclusion of females from children's books but the stereotyped roles in which females are frequently depicted. Females are often shown as homemakers or as employees in "female" occupations; they possess characteristics that suggest they are passive, docile, fearful, and dependent. The roles of homemakers or employees in traditionally female occupations are not considered negative, but the inference that they are the *only* roles open to women is considered harmful.

People concerned with sexism have evaluated the roles of males and females in children's textbooks, in literature, and in the elementary classrooms. These evaluations are usually harshly critical of the negative forces of sex-role stereotyping. Because a large amount of young children's reading material comes from basal readers, they have also been carefully analyzed. A frequently quoted study, *Dick and Jane as Victims: Sex Stereotyping in Children's Readers* (24) cited considerable bias in basal readers in both quantity and quality of female characters: Stories about boys outnumbered stories about girls, male adult main characters outnumbered female adult characters, and male biographies outnumbered female biographies. The content suggested that boys were more apt to be clever, persistent, heroic, and able to function in a greater variety of roles and occupations. After a study which yielded similar conclusions, Laurel A. Marten and Margaret W. Matlin (14) stated: "Children must see these females engaged in important, active, and independent actions if we wish them to believe that women and men are truly equal. Furthermore, young girls must see competent female role models if we would have them be achieving and self-actualizing. Additionally, young boys should see that males do not have to hide their feelings—they can express their fears and ask for help" (p. 765).

While children's literature selections provide a much wider choice of stories about females and males, critics also denounce sexism in this area. Ramona Frasher (8), for example, reviewed research on sexism and sex role stereotyping in children's literature and identified some current trends. In Newbery award-winning books published prior to the 1970s, male main characters outnumbered female main characters by about three to one. In addition, negative comments about females and stereotyping were common. Frasher's analysis of Newbery winners published between 1971-1980 showed the ratio of male to female was about equal. In addition, female characters tended to be portrayed with more positive and varied personality characteristics and exhibited a greater variety of behaviors. Even though these changes reflect a heightened sensitivity for feminist concerns, Frasher's article identifies three areas that are of major concern: (1) changes are found predominantly in books written for children in middle and late childhood years; (2) the rush to respond to criticism resulted in too many examples of poor or marginal literature; (3) until more authors are able to write with ease about both sexes engaged in a broad scope of activities and exhibiting a range of characteristics, children's literature will remain stereotyped. Frasher's conclusion emphasizes the need for critical evaluation in this area: "The number of books accessible to children is immense; it will take many years of publishing quality nonsexist literature to insure that a random selection is as likely to be nonstereotyped as it is to be stereotyped" (p. 77).

Realistic picture books are also criticized for sexism and sex role stereotyping. Alleen Pace Nilsen (16) analyzed the role of females in 80 Caldecott Medal winners and honor books. She chose picture books because illustrated books are "the ones influencing children at the time they are in the process of developing their own sexual identity. Children decide very early in life what roles are appropriate to male and female" (p. 919). Of the books that were realistic (as compared with fantasy), she found fewer stories having girls as the leading characters. She also compared the number of girl- and boy-centered stories over a twenty-year period; the percentage of girl-centered stories had decreased from a high of 46 percent in 1951–55 to a low of 26 percent in 1966–70. Nilsen does not recommend that children not read these books, but she does suggest that they be provided with books that are equally interesting with females as main characters. She also recommends that artists become aware of the stereotypes they can perpetuate in illustrating books. She points out that in Ezra Jack Keats's *Goggles,* Peter's sister sits on the sidewalk beside a baby and draws pictures while the excitement rages around her. Likewise, in *A Tree Is Nice,* the boys are pictured in the upper branches of the trees; girls are pictured sitting in the lowest branches, waving to boys climbing trees, or sprinkling plants with a watering can.

Many heroines in books for older children behave in nontraditional ways. They reflect characters who have considerable intellectual, emotional, and physical potential. Some of the most memorable girls, including Jo in *Little Women,* Karana in *Island of the Blue Dolphins,* Quennie in *Quennie Peavy* (who insisted that she would grow up to be a doctor, not a nurse), and Harriet in *Harriet the Spy,* are believable and exciting because they are individuals who do not follow stereotypic behavior patterns.

These nontraditional behaviors can, of course, also result in controversy; women's roles and women's rights are political issues with advocates who express strong opinions on both sides. One of the areas that illustrates women's changing roles is the portrayal of the minor characters in a story. Mothers may be sports writers as in Ellen Conford's *The Revenge of the Incredible Dr. Rancid and His Youthful Assistant, Jeffrey;* they may be photographers who travel on assignments and join peace marches accompanied by their daughters as in Norma Klein's *Mom, the Wolf Man and Me.* The newer books suggest that the stereotyped roles of males and females may be changing, as increasingly varied occupations and behavior patterns are found in the books. Teachers, librarians, and parents should be aware, however, that not all people look on these changes favorably.

Sexuality

Today is a time of increasing sophistication and frankness concerning sexuality; television programs and movies portray sexual relationships that would not have been shown to earlier generations of adults, let alone children. Controversial sexuality in children's literature relates to such issues as premarital or extramarital sex, concerns about sexual development, homosexual experiences, and sex eduation.

Several books written for older children describe nontraditional living situations in which a child's mother lives with a male friend. In Stuart Buchan's *When We Lived with Pete,* Tommy and his mother live with Pete who is not ready to get married. In Klein's more controversial *Mom, The Wolf Man and Me,* Theodore spends weekends with Brett's mother, which leads eleven-year-old Brett to ask her mother if she is having sexual relations with him. This results in a frank discussion about sexual intercourse. As might be expected, this book has met with varying reactions. For example, Kean and Personke (11) say, "It should also be remembered that children may be living in homes with, for example, one adult. When this type of awareness informs the teacher's search for good literature, he will be more likely to notice books such as *Mom, the Wolf Man and Me,* which provides children opportunity to read about a warm home environment that differs from the usual pattern" (p. 334). In contrast, several librarians and literature professors at a reading conference (20) were asked about sexuality in

Freedom to Read Versus Censorship of Literature

THE LAST TEN YEARS, AC-cording to James Davis, have produced an increase in the number of organized group efforts to censor children's literature and school textbooks.[1] These groups believe that books which they suspect are capable of subverting children's religious, social, or political beliefs should be censored, and teachers should not be allowed to use the materials in the classroom. Newsletters from organized groups suggest the harmful effects of sharing certain books or books by certain authors with children; many adults maintain that children are more influenced or damaged by "objectionable" materials than are adults[2]; school boards ban books because of objectionable ideas; and lawyers and legislators debate the rights of schools to use certain books or to teach specific content. Rev. Tom Williams, a spokesperson for those who believe library books should adhere to a local community standard, recommends that books should be scrutinized and selected according to a community standard determined by public referendum or by a library board elected directly by the people.[3]

In contrast to this view of censorship, Leanne Katz, coordinator for the National Coalition Against Censorship, maintains that librarians should follow principles of diversity and respect for individual decision making that encourage access to a wide variety of ideas. In Katz's viewpoint, banning books is a "dictatorship over our minds and a dangerous opening to religious, political, artistic and intellectual repression" (4, p. 2). To counter increased efforts for censorship, professional educational journals and professional organizations are responding with articles such as William Palmer's "What Reading Teachers Can Do Before the Censors Come,"[5] and documents such as the American Library Association's *Bill of Rights*,[6] which stresses that the freedom to read is guaranteed by the United States Constitution. Palmer defends the right to read without censorship and suggests the following four-stage approach for educators who may need to defend their use of literature: (1) prepare a rationale for the study of literature, (2) develop community support for freedom to read, (3) prepare a written statement on book and material selection, and (4) have a written policy to handle censorship efforts.

The issue of censorship will in all likelihood continue through the 1980s as concerned adults on both sides of the question argue whether literature and educators should indoctrinate children into the mores and morals of a community or encourage children to expand their ideas and understandings by being exposed to and discussing a variety of books and ideas.

1 Davis, James E. *Dealing With Censorship*. Urbana, Ill.: National Council of Teachers of English, 1978.

2 Woods, L.B. "For Sex: See Librarian." *Library Journal*, 1 September 1978, pp. 1561–67.

3 "Should Librarians Have the Final Say in Selecting Books for the Public Library." *Family Weekly*, 10 January 1982, p. 2.

4 Ibid.

5 Palmer, William S. "What Reading Teachers Can Do Before the Censors Come." *Journal of Reading* 25 (January 1982): 310–14.

6 American Library Association. "The Freedom to Read." *Bill of Rights*. Chicago, Ill.: American Library Association, 1972.

books and reported receiving many negative comments from parents and college students about the sexual discussion and life-style described in Klein's book.

Books describing children's concerns over developing sexuality may also be controversial. For example, the popular *Are You There God? It's Me, Margaret* has been reviewed favorably as a book that realistically conveys preadolescent girls' worries over menstruation and body changes. In 1981, this book was one of several taken from library shelves and burned because of its implied potentially negative influence. In that same year, the national television news showed angry adults criticizing the morality of the book, as well as many others, and the resulting flames of protest.

Other Controversial Issues

Television, movies, and books have all been accused of portraying too much violence. Children's cartoons are often criticized for their excessive violence. Children's books become the object of controversy when they portray what some people define as inappropriate behavior, or when excessive violence is described. Many realistic books containing violence have inner-city settings. For example, Frank Bonham's *Durango Street* describes the hero's bid for survival in a world of grim gang violence where he could be used for "bayonet practice."

Drugs enter into characters' lives in *Durango Street* and create a different world for the father and his friends in Walter Dean Myers's *It Ain't All for Nothin'!* Drug use in children's books is another controversial issue; some people believe children should read about the drug reality in the world around them, while others believe that their minds should not be contaminated by the suggestion of drugs.

Profanity and other objectionable language are also controversial. What is considered objectionable, however, has changed over the years. Mary Q. Steele (21) describes her own experiences with writing: in the 1950s, editors deleted "hecks" and "darns" from manuscripts written for children; now, a more permissive climate encourages authors to write relevant dialogue. This dialogue becomes controversial when young children use profanity or hear the profanity spoken by their elders.

Other issues that can become controversial in children's books include viewpoints on war and peace, religion, death, and racial matters. (Chapter eleven discusses concerns of critics on books about Black Americans, Hispanics, Native Americans, and Asian Americans.)

The question of how "realistic" realistic fiction should be is answered very differently by various groups. Historically, schools and the literature read by children have often been un-

der the pressures of censorship, as differing groups tried to impose their values on all children. While modern censors might laugh at the literary concerns of the Puritans, there is still concern over appropriate subjects for children's literature. When children's books explore sexuality, violence, moral problems, racism, and religious beliefs, they are likely to be thought objectionable by those who believe that children should not be exposed to such ideas. Teachers and librarians need to be knowledgeable about their communities, the subjects that may prove controversial, and the merits of controversial books they would like to share with children. Kean and Personke (11) say that "Even though educators attempt to avoid controversy by selecting only 'safe' books that they believe won't offend anyone, someone is likely to be offended. . . . Everybody has a value position that he considers important and that he thinks the schools ought to perpetuate for his children and for other people's children. When educators have an empathetic understanding of the community, they will be better able to work with parents—helping parents to view the wide range of books that are appropriate for children, rather than telling them which are the 'right' materials" (p. 340).

Rather than avoiding all books that contain volatile topics, Day McClenathan (12) suggests that wholesale avoidance, in addition to encouraging overt consorship, is inappropriate because (1) a book about a relevant sociological or psychological problem can give young people opportunities to grow in their thinking process and to extend experiences; (2) problems in books can provide children who need them opportunities for identification and allow others an opportunity to sympathize with their peers; (3) problems in books invite decisions, elicit opinions and afford opportunities to take positions on issues.

Guidelines for Selecting Controversial Fiction for Children

With these controversial issues in mind, and the need for books that are relevant to the interests, concerns, and problems of today's children, it is necessary that adults who will work with children and books consider some guidelines to use when choosing realistic fiction. McClenathan (12) provides a useful guide for selecting books that might be considered controversial.

1 Know exactly what the problem is and consequently what might be considered controversial. This means you have to really read the book. You can't rely on the opinion of someone else or even on a good review. It's necessary that you, as a member of school and community, be able to appraise specific content in light of the mores of that particular milieu. What might offend in one community would go unnoticed or unchallenged in another.

2 Ascertain the author's point of view and weigh the power of positive influence against exposure to a negatively perceived theme. If

an author writes about the drug culture, for example, but events in the story clearly point up harmful effect of drug use, then reluctance to use the book may result in a missed opportunity for healthy shaping of attitudes.

3 Apply literary criteria to the selection of library books in such a way that vulnerability to the arguments of would-be censors is at least partially reduced by the obvious overall quality of book choices. Occasionally, inferior quality books are selected because they deal with topics having a high interest quotient for middle grade or older children. This sometimes happens with books involving experimentations with sex. The information in such a book may be harmless (or even useful) but the book may fall short of accepted literary criteria. If the book is then targeted because it offends community groups, it will be difficult to defend, and having it in your school collection will suggest that considerations other than literary quality determine choices. In addition to generally accepted literary criteria, you will want to examine books which attempt to counter stereotypes for what can be thought of as the overcorrection syndrome. Sometimes, in a passion to change images, authors will work too hard on the issue itself with the result that plot and characterization suffer.

4 Know and be able to explain your purpose in using a particular book. Have answers ready to the following questions:
   a. Will the topic be understood by the group with which I intend to use the book?
   b. What are some of the merits of this particular book which have influenced me to use it, rather than another book of comparable literary, sociological, or psychological importance?
   c. Is the book an acceptable model in terms of writing style and use of language?
   d. Are my objectives in using this book educationally defensible (e.g., presentation and/or clarification of information, extension of experiences, refinement of attitudes, promotion of reading habits)?

5 In order to clarify and maintain your own sincere objectivity, review and be prepared to discuss both sides of the censorship question. (pp. 33–35)

In addition to these guidelines, adults should also consider the following points when evaluating books that may be controversial:

1 Literature should reflect a sensitivity to the needs and rights of girls and boys without preference, bias, or negative stereotypes. Males should be allowed to show emotions, females should be able to demonstrate courage and ambition. Girls and boys should not be denied access to certain occupations because of their sex. Children should sense that they can be successful in many occupations.

2 If violence is included in the story, does the author treat the subject appropriately? Does the author give the necessary facts? Are both sides of the conflict portrayed fully, fairly, and honestly? Is the writing developed with feeling and emotion? Does the author help children develop a perspective about the subject?

3 Does the story satisfy children's basic needs? Will it provide them with increased insights into their own problems and social relationships?

4 Is the story one that will provide children with enjoyment?

REALISTIC FICTION FOR CHILDREN

The literature in this section is organized according to the content of the stories. The major topics include family life, interpersonal relationships, growing up, animal stories, mysteries, sports stories, and humorous modern fiction. For each topic, the text will focus on literary techniques used by authors in developing credible realistic fiction, such as characterization, plot development, point of view, and theme. The chapter will also stress personality or social developmental aspects so adults may choose and recommend specific types of books for children when they are needed or wanted.

Family Life

Authors depict some of the strongest, warmest family relationships in the family stories of the late 1930s through early 1960s. Students of children's literature may refer to the analysis of family life on pages 63–66 as shown by Elizabeth Enright in *Thimble Summer*, Eleanor Estes in *The Moffats*, Sydney Taylor in *All-of-a-Kind Family*, and Madeleine L'Engle in *Meet the Austins*. Today's children still enjoy the warmth and humor represented by these families. The characters' actions suggest that security is gained by the family working together, each member has responsibility to other members, consideration for others is desirable, and hard times and peer conflicts can be overcome by family unity and loyalty.

Many changes have taken place in the characterization of the American family since the early 1960s. Authors writing in the 1970s and early 1980s often focus on overcoming disturbances as families adjust to a new culture, deal with losing one or both parents, handle the disruption of divorce, solve the problems of an illegitimate child living with a single parent, or include elderly grandparents in the family. Children may be required to live with grandparents or other relatives or face living in foster homes.

Children may realize from reading this literature that there are many types of family units other than the traditional one. They will also see that problems frequently can be solved if family members work together. Even in the most disturbing of

Sydney Taylor creates family stories that show warmth, humor, and strong family relationships.
Cover illustration by Gail Owens. From *Ella of All of a Kind Family* by Sydney Taylor, illustrated by Gail Owens. Copyright © 1978 by Sydney Taylor. Illustrations copyright © 1978 by Gail Owens. Reprinted by permission of the publisher, E.P. Dutton.

relationships, authors often develop a strong need for unity and a desire to keep at least part of the family together.

Family Disturbances. Authors of literature about family disturbances use several literary techniques to create credible plots and characters. The authors frequently focus on realistic situations and feelings that are painful and could be destructive. These situations are usually easily identifiable by readers who may have experienced similar situations, who may have known someone who had such an experience, or may fear they might have a similar experience. The point of view in this literature is frequently developed from the perspective of a child or children who are living the experience. The characterization may develop the vulnerability of the characters, create sympathy for them, and describe how they handle the jolting situations and personal discoveries that affect their lives. The changing reactions of characters to situations and discoveries are frequently used by authors to describe the development of better interpersonal relationships or positive personality changes. Some authors, however, use specific situations or discoveries to allow children to escape from all reality. This latter reaction may be used if an author is trying to make a point about child abuse. Authors may develop a family member as antagonist, or the antagonist may be an uncontrollable outside force such as death of a parent, divorce, or moving to a new location. Authors frequently relieve the impact of painful situations by instilling humor into the characterizations or plot development. Humor may make a situation bearable; it may create sympathy for a character; or it may clarify the nature of the confrontation.

Let us consider how Betsy Byars uses some of these techniques in *The Animal, The Vegetable, and John D. Jones.* First, the author focuses on three children's reactions to changes that are painful and could be destructive. The father of two children, Clara and Deanie, asks a widow whom he loves and her son to share their summer vacation. The confrontation now changes from sibling rivalry and quarrels between the sisters to quarrels with an outside antagonist. The girls focus some of their hostility toward the new situation and the people who share their lives.

John D. is described as a worthy antagonist. He is bright, sophisticated, and conceited; he is writing a book of advice for his inferiors, who, incidently, are all other children. He is also vulnerable and perhaps sensitive; his book is about functioning in a hostile world. Byars describes a series of incidents that emphasize the parents' dilemma, infer their inability to handle the situation, and create sympathy for the characters. Whenever the adults plan a happy excursion something goes wrong: at a cookout the only edible hamburger falls in the sand; during a visit to an amusement park Clara escapes her family only to become sick after riding the Space Cyclone and then seeing John D. with a huge sundae. Although Byars's descriptions of these situations are humorous, there are indications of hostile undercurrents. Byars uses a near tragedy to focus all the characters' attentions on the importance of others. Their reactions indicate that they have learned a great deal about interpersonal relationships.

Carol Lea Benjamin focuses attention on a twelve-year-old girl's fear of losing her father's love in *The Wicked Stepdog*. The author develops sympathy and understanding for Lou's feelings by describing several incidents: Lou's mother left the family because she required seclusion; Lou's father and her new step-mother exclude Lou from their activities; Lou imagines her stepmother is pregnant; and Lou halfheartedly contemplates suicide. The author's first-person narration emphasizes Lou's feelings and reactions which are sometimes painful and sometimes humorous. The author uses Lou's responses to a golden retriever to symbolize her changing feelings. At first she hates walking him. Later, after her father recognizes his neglect, she meets a boy who also walks his dog. Now walking the dog becomes Lou's favorite pastime.

Contrasts in life-styles effectively and humorously introduce the conflict in E. L. Konigsburg's *Journey to an 800 Number*. When Maximillian Stubb's mother remarries Max is forced to stay with his father for a month. At home he proudly contemplates the prep school he will be attending in the fall. Now he must accompany his father and a camel as they perform at a shopping center, a convention, a nightclub, a dude ranch, and a state fair. The author focuses on Max's changing attitudes as he learns to know his father and discovers a great deal about life from his father and the people they meet.

Divorce and/or remarriage of a family member are not the only causes of family disturbances in contemporary realistic fiction. Conflicts and characterization may be developed around the loss of a parent through death or severe illness. Winifred Madison, for example, in *Call Me Danica* focuses on the immigration and adjustment of a family after the father dies and they leave a small village in Yugoslavia to make a new life for themselves in Vancouver, Canada. Conflicts between the family's value system and the personal and social values they encounter are important to the story. Consequently, the author encourages readers to understand the family's values by including family discussions before the father's death, expressing the mother's thoughts that reflect their values, and sharing twelve-year-old Danica's troubled feelings as she tries to adjust to a different way of life while retaining her values. The author develops Danica's character through her worries, reactions, and dreams. She is concerned for her mother because men at the restaurant where her mother is head chef resent working for a woman. She worries because her family seems to be drawing apart with secret problems that they themselves cannot understand. She is discouraged and believes she should give up her dream of becoming a doctor. Finally, she discovers that her own personal dreams are worth working for.

Madison develops strong themes emphasizing the importance of a family working together and the necessity to be persistent and hold to one's dreams. The author does not suggest, however, that the problems are easily solved. The family knows they will need to work together if the restaurant they open is to succeed; Danica realizes she must study hard to earn a medical school scholarship.

This book contains several characteristics that separate it from earlier family stories. The problems that the family must face are covered in depth, the mother faces male bias as she works in a male-dominated environment, and the daughter follows her dream to become a doctor rather than to follow an occupation earlier considered more suitable for women.

The influence of a dead father is important to characterization and plot development in Vera and Bill Cleaver's *Where the Lilies Bloom*. Although the father dies quite early in the plot, the authors create a plausible character who lives by a strong moral and family code. This is clearly developed as he demands that his daughter take pride in the family name, instill that pride in her brothers and sisters, and hold the family together without accepting charity. Later, this promise provides crucial elements in plot development and in fourteen-year-old Mary Call's character development. The authors develop a believable and interesting conflict as Mary Call strains between two forces: her desire to keep her dying father's promise and her own developing realization that she must accept help if she is to gain the knowledge she needs and increase the family's chances for survival. The authors do not develop a story on sentimentality; instead, Mary Call recognizes her father's weaknesses and eventually realizes that his judgment about his oldest daughter and the despised neighbor, Kaiser Pease, was in error. The authors lighten the almost insurmountable odds against survival by adding touches of humor. This is especially true in the sequel, *Trial Valley*. Now a more mature Mary Call copes with both family problems and expectant suitors. (Students of children's literature may find it interesting to compare the characteristics of this contemporary heroine with the Victorian heroine of *The Daisy Chain* discussed in chapter two.)

A family's struggle to survive without a parent is a popular plot in contemporary realistic fiction. Authors may suggest that the experience either strengthens the children, as in *Where the Lilies Bloom*, or causes so many problems that they find it impossible to cope. Two books reflect quite different reactions to the conflict and to children's discoveries in life. For the purpose of comparison, consider Marilyn Sachs's *The Bears' House* and Betsy Byars's *The Night Swimmers*. Both stories are developed around children's striving to cope because of the loss of a parent. In Sachs's story the father deserts the family and the mother is emotionally disturbed. In Byars's story the mother dies and the children are reared by a cowboy singer/composer father who works at night. The final conse-

A child leaves her own harsh reality for the make-believe, dollhouse world.
Illustration from *The Bears' House* by Marilyn Sachs. Copyright © 1971 by Marilyn Sachs. Reprinted by permission of Doubleday & Company, Inc.

quences of each story, however, are very different. Sachs's heroine has so many problems that she cannot cope with reality. Byars's characters learn truth about life and are strengthened.

Sachs's development of a harsh reality is crucial for plot credibility and the final response of the heroine. The author describes the details leading up to the children's problems: five children live in a crowded apartment, the mother is ill, and the father deserts the family. There is a person-against-society conflict as the children demonstrate their distrust of the adult world symbolized by their fear of being placed in foster homes, a need to lie to the social worker, and a distrust of all adults. Sachs contrasts the harsh reality of nine-year-old Fran Ellen's life with the beautiful make-believe place of her fantasies. When she sits in front of the dollhouse in her fourth-grade classroom she can visit the Bear family and sit on Pappa Bear's lap when she feels unhappy. The conclusion of the story illustrates that contemporary realistic fiction may not have a "happy ever after" ending. The story concludes as Fran Ellen withdraws into her make-believe world; she has found her own way to survive in a frightening and bewildering world.

Byars uses a painful and possibly destructive situation to fo-

cus on the heroine's (Retta's) personal and social development and her acceptance of difficult discoveries. Byars chronicles this personal growth and awareness by describing Retta's feelings after her mother's death, describing the moment when she understands her father's career goals (in reaction to her mother's death he composed a hit song, but did not attend to the children), describing her changing feelings as she tries to be a mother to her two younger brothers, and developing her final realization that she must accept her father as he is, not as she would like him to be. The author uses humor to highlight some of these situations and to focus on the painful moments. Retta discovers how a mother should act by observing mothers in the supermarket. She gains cooking skills through television commercials. Retta's and her younger brother Roy's reactions to their own final discoveries may be the most poignant moments in the book. Roy discovers that the Bowlwater Plant is not the enormous and wondrous vegetation of his imagination but is a smelly and ugly chemical factory. At the same time Retta realizes that their father is so obsessed with stardom that he cannot relate to his children in the way Retta would like. Roy expresses their discoveries effectively when he

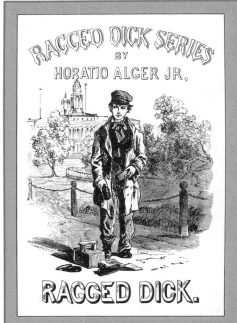

RAGGED DICK SERIES BY HORATIO ALGER JR,

RAGGED DICK.

THE RAGGED DICK SERIES, PUBLISHED IN 1868, TOLD OF THE sad plight of children who tried to survive in a city without family or friends. They often worked long hours in factories or on farms. Many died. Horatio Alger, Jr. wrote the series in the hope that readers would be sympathetic to the cause of poor children and the Children's Aid Society. Since 1854, the Society had been finding homes for these abandoned children.

Horatio Alger's *Frank's Campaign* (1864) was the first of a series of books in which poor American youths went from rags to riches. Other books by the author that have a similar theme include *Fame and Fortune* (1868), *Sink or Swim* (1870), *Strong and Steady* (1871), *Brave and Bold* (1874), *Risen from the Ranks* (1874), and *From Farm Boy to Senator; Being the History of the Boyhood and Manhood of Daniel Webster* (1882).

compares swallowing a hard truth about life with Popeye swallowing his spinach: both experiences make you stronger.

Authors who write about family disturbances such as divorce, a new baby, and illegitimacy frequently develop plausible plots for children by telling the stories from a first person viewpoint. The authors may develop characterization by exploring the changing emotions and reactions of the child characters as they first discover the problem, experience a wide range of personal difficulties and emotions as they try to change or understand the situation, and finally arrive at an acceptance of the situation. Peggy Mann, for example, takes her main character in *My Dad Lives in A Downtown Hotel* through a series of reactions and emotions as he responds to his parents' divorce. First, Joey believes the separation is his fault. The author develops the strength of these feelings through Joey's actions: he makes out a list of promises he will keep if his father returns; he delivers them to his father and tries unsuccessfully to convince him to return. Now Joey's emotional reactions change and he goes through a period when he hates his father and feels very confused. The author suggests that Joey accepts the change in his life when he can enjoy being with his father on their Sunday visits.

Lois Lowry also uses a list to emphasize the strength of a

character's emotions toward a family change and to demonstrate the point where negative feelings change to more positive feelings. Ten-year-old Anastasia in *Anastasia Krupnik* keeps a journal of her loves and hates. The author demonstrates her changing emotions as she thinks about her lists and crosses out certain hates and adds them to the love list. The greatest challenge to her lists and her personal reactions occurs when she discovers a baby is arriving. The author handles Anastasia's self-discovery in a humorous way as she allows this precocious child to discover that a new baby is on the love list, not the hate list.

Vera and Bill Cleaver explore a wider range of emotions and problems in *I Would Rather Be a Turnip*. Their twelve-year-old heroine, Annie, faces change when her eight-year-old illegitimate nephew comes to live with the family. The magnitude of this change is shown by the authors as they compare the before and after life of the main character: she has worked hard to build her reputation and her relationships with best friends only to have everything collapse after her nephew arrives. Now she experiences bigotry as former friends, older people, and fellow church members change in their reactions to the family. Her actions as she tries writing a book, running away from home, and thinking about ways to get rid of her nephew are used by the authors to suggest her dislike and unhappiness. During this time, however, her good humor and independence help her as she learns to know and respect her brilliant nephew. There is a strong theme in this book as the authors suggest that people should not be judged by the circumstances of their birth.

Two authors explore, through their main characters, quite diverse reactions to illegitimacy. Norma Klein creates a close, though somewhat offbeat, relationship between a girl and her photographer mother. The girl accepts her illegitimacy, enjoys their unscheduled life, accompanies her mother on peace marches, and has frank discussions with her. (The frank discussions about premarital sex cause negative reactions in some parents.) It is only when her mother meets the Wolf Man and considers marriage that she is afraid her life will change and unsuccessfully tries to convince them that they should not marry. In contrast, Hila Colman creates a different mother-daughter relationship in *Tell Me No Lies*. When this heroine learns about her birth, she hates her mother for lying and runs away to find her father. The author uses this experience to create an atmosphere in which the girl can understand and forgive her mother. When she finds her father, she discovers he is not like her dreams; in fact, he cannot accept her as his daughter. This is the turning point in the novel that allows her to return home with new understanding. Both of these stories depict changes from the realistic fiction of the 1950s. The authors' development of family structure, life-styles, expressed values, and types of problems reflect contemporary concerns and issues.

The nontraditional family, one made up of members other than one or two parents and their children, plays an increasing role in recent realistic literature. This extended family may include children living with grandparents, other relatives, or foster families.

Authors who write about young children living with grandparents frequently develop settings in which the children's circle of protection increases because of their interaction with older people. Peter Hartling's *Oma*, for example, develops strong relationships between an independent elderly person and a young boy. Young readers can believe in this warm relationship because Hartling develops a character who consistently understands a six-year-old boy: she takes him seriously; she never calls him little man, honey, or kid; she has a sense of humor; she is hard to fool; and she makes life exciting.

Authors who write for older children may develop situations in which main characters express reluctance, or even bitterness and hostility, if they must live with grandparents. In order to create credible plots, the authors usually develop the rea-

sons for the move and the character's reactions. Consider, for example, two quite different reactions as exemplified by Sue Ellen Bridgers's *All Together Now* and Betsy Byars's *The House of Wings*. In the first book, the girl must give up her own plans for the summer and live with her grandparents because her father is in the armed forces and her mother works. Her reactions are similar to many twelve-year-olds. She is at first unhappy, but then makes new friendships and discovers advantages in her summer experience. In contrast, the boy in Byars's novel responds in language filled with hatred and then runs away. The author encourages the reader's belief in this more violent reaction by describing the scene in which the parents leave the boy with his grandfather, without telling him they are going away. In this situation, the author develops a catalyst that draws Sammy and his grandfather together. As the two people discover and care for a blind, wounded crane, the author encourages readers to see the character of the grandfather. He believes in the personal dignity of all creatures and in the right of animals to live in their natural state. Gradually, Sammy realizes that he wants his grandfather to have the same feelings of love toward him as he has toward the animals. Through Sammy's actions and thoughts, the author encourages readers to understand the discovery Sammy has made about himself:

Sammy kept looking at his grandfather in a funny way. He didn't know how it was possible to hate a person in the middle of one morning, and then to find in the middle of the next morning that you loved that same person. (p. 141)

These stories suggest the range of emotions that children may experience when their way of life is interrupted. There is a hopeful note in the stories, however, as children discover the warm relationships that are possible with grandparents or other concerned adults.

Some of the extended family stories written by children's authors do not develop a happy and secure environment. Instead, authors may explore the possibilities of unhappy and even cruel experiences. Consider, for example, the techniques Marilyn Sachs (*A December Tale*) and Marion Dane Bauer (*Foster Child*) use to develop a frightening and sinister environment. Sachs describes in detail the brutality and emotional responses as five-year-old Henry and ten-year-old Myra are rejected by their father and must move from foster home to foster home. This brutality includes systematic beatings and a foster mother who saves the money intended for their care. The children's responses match this extreme behavior: the boy uses offensive language and antisocial behavior, the girl escapes into her own world where she communicates with the

French heroine Joan of Arc. The author concludes the tale as Myra rescues Henry from a beating, takes him out on a snowy December night, and rushes toward the apartment of the only person who has ever been concerned about them, old Mrs. Singer. The fact that no one listens to the children's repeated cries for help makes this story more tragic than many other books dealing with child desertion and abuse. Bauer explores the sinister side of foster family life by describing a situation in which the foster father expresses sexual interest in the girls staying at his farm. Readers realize the danger in this situation when a twelve-year-old and her young friend run away and try to live in her great-grandmother's empty house.

A very different foster home situation is developed by Patricia MacLachlan in *Mama One, Mama Two,* a picture storybook for younger children. The author creates a warm, loving relationship between the foster mother and the child by describing a bedtime story that also tells the reasons for the child's mother not being with her. Unlike Sachs and Bauer, MacLachlan infers a basic trust in society by having a social worker help when the mother asks for assistance, by placing the child in a caring environment, and by allowing the story to end on a hopeful note. Mama One may come home in the spring, but Mama Two will be there until she comes.

Bauer and Sachs develop an environment in contrast with the secure, happy, family life found in the earlier realistic fiction. Children, depending upon their own backgrounds, may have more difficulty relating to such harsh surroundings. One child, after reading Sachs's book, could not believe that a teacher, a relative, or a friend would not come to the children's rescue. As you read Sachs's *A December Tale,* Bauer's *Foster Child,* and MacLachlan's *Mama One, Mama Two* consider each author's possible purpose, how each author developed the setting and the characterization, the antagonist and theme in each story, and the possible responses of readers.

Interpersonal Relationships

As discussed in chapter one, children need friendships and the feeling of security that a best friend can provide. Literature dealing with friendship explores both the joys and sorrows of this unique relationship. There are stories that help develop interracial understanding as writers tell about close friendships between white and black children or white and Hispanic children. Children find that both groups share the same needs and are able to become close, true friends. Some books develop friendships between children who are different from their peers; others suggest that brothers and sisters can be best friends. Still others explore the meaning of real friendship and suggest that best friends should support, rather than hurt,

each other. These stories may help children overcome the disappointment that results when a friend moves or may stimulate a discussion about the meaning of friendship.

Several books in this group explore the relationships between brothers, sisters, or friends and a handicapped child. These stories may help children develop positive attitudes toward the handicapped and may help handicapped children realize that they can overcome their problems. This realization is especially important because mainstreaming brings many special children into regular classrooms for at least a part of the day.

The third type of story in this section deals with relationships between children and aging adults. These stories develop strong relationships suggesting that older people have many worthwhile contributions to make and that they may not be ready to retire to a nursing home.

Finally, there are stories that deal with trauma associated with the death of a loved one. These stories focus on accepting the death of a pet, a friend, or a parent. They explore the varied emotions that children experience as they face this irreversible change in their lives.

An author's development of credible conflict, characterization, and theme are all important considerations in this literature. Authors frequently develop conflict in stories about interpersonal relationships through person-against-self and/or person-against-person conflicts. If a person-against-self conflict is credible, authors allow readers to understand and identify why the character has an inner conflict, how the character handles this conflict, and what causes the conflict to be resolved. This resolution should not be contrived; it should appear as a natural outcome of the story. Contrived endings are frequently found, however, when authors try too rapidly to create happy endings for serious and hurtful situations. If a person-against-person conflict is credible, the author develops both the main character and the antagonist, or opposing force. Readers need to understand why there is conflict between the two forces. Are there differences in values, personalities, or other character traits? The author's characterization should reflect these differences and encourage readers to understand why the characters act and react as they do. The conflicts identified by authors, as well as the ways characters overcome these conflicts, frequently infer the unifying theme in literature about interpersonal relationships. The most successful themes develop naturally as readers glimpse truths about life from the actions of the characters. The least successful themes are created solely for didactic purposes. Let us consider how authors of stories dealing with friendships, handicaps, aging, and death use these various literary techniques.

Friendships. A person-against-self conflict and carefully developed characterization create a credible plot in E. L. Konigsburg's *Jennifer, Hecate, Macbeth, William McKinley, and Me, Elizabeth.* The author encourages readers to understand Elizabeth's inner conflict and need for a friend by emphasizing her shyness: she is a new girl in school, she goes to school alone, and she is afraid she will cry when she walks into her classroom. Elizabeth's shyness and need for a friend are reemphasized through her responses when she meets Jennifer, a very imaginative girl. Even when she does not want to do what her new friend demands of her, she still complies. Later, as she gains confidence in herself, she becomes assertive. The inner conflict is resolved when the friends no longer need the support of their game in which they pretend to be witch and journeyman witch. Now they can be just good friends and act as equals.

Mary Stolz develops a person-against-society conflict as well as a person-against-self conflict in *Cider Days.* The person-against-self conflict develops as Polly faces loneliness after her best friend moves and then learns to respect the courage of a new friend. The person-against-society conflict develops when Polly tries to make friends with a new neighbor, a Mexican girl, Consuela Christina Machado. The author encourages readers to glimpse conflicts caused by racial bias by describing several classmates' reactions to Consuela and her responses to them. Her response to insulting remarks from a classmate also reflects Consuela's pride in her heritage:

My grandmother is Indian. I guess you—I do not recall your name—I guess you think you are making an insult. My grandmother is Indian and beautiful and she has manners. I do not want an apology for my skin color. (p. 38)

This experience helps Polly respect Consuela's courage and encourages Polly to try to become closer to her. Although their home lives and parental values are quite different, the two girls develop a friendship. Through these experiences the author encourages readers to understand the value in different types of friendship.

The attraction between friends whose families are different and the possible resulting turmoil is a popular topic in realistic friendship stories. In *Bridge to Terabithia,* Katherine Paterson uses strong characterization and setting that clarifies the conflict. Paterson effectively contrasts the backgrounds and aspirations of Jess Aarons, the son of a poor country farmer, with Leslie Burke, the daughter of a successful author. Differences in background are clarified through Paterson's description of their families and Jess's reactions when he visits Leslie's family, sees their home filled with records and literature, and listens to their discussions about such topics as French politics and saving the whales. These experiences open a world of imagination and learning never perceived by Jess. The author suggests, however, that the two children have similar aspirations and share a need for friendship. This mutual need reaches fulfillment as they create their own kingdom, a quiet place in the woods where they can create a world more to their liking. This setting, as discussed earlier on pages 88–89, plays an important role in the development of their friendship and in Jess's self-development. Their relationship strengthens Jess to the point that he can cope with Leslie's tragic death that forever alters the Kingdom of Terabithia.

Nina Bawder in *The Robbers* also creates effective characterization and emphasizes important aspects in plot development by contrasting life-styles of two children—one who has lived in the security of his grandmother's apartment in a castle and one who is knowledgeable in the ways of the London streets. When nine-year-old Philip moves to London, life is difficult because his schoolmates tease him about his princely manners and physically attack him. His outlook changes, however, when he becomes friends with Darcy, whose crippled father has been a canal worker. As the two become close friends, Philip discovers that all people do not live in his secure, protected world. Older students may enjoy comparing this book by an English author with books on friendship by American authors. They will discover that the English characters reflect greater concern for class distinction and express feelings of inevitability because of class.

Dealing with Handicaps. Authors who develop credible plots around characters with handicaps frequently describe details related to the handicapping condition, describe feelings and experiences of the handicapped person, and describe feelings and experiences of family members and others who deal with the character. Such characterization and plot development should reflect accuracy, honesty, and sensitivity. Books with these characteristics can provide handicapped children with feelings and situations with which they can identify. Well-written books also help other children empathize with and gain understanding of the handicapped. While these books should be evaluated by literary standards, they should also be evaluated according to their sensitivity. Mary Sage (19) recommends the following criteria when evaluating books concerning the handicapped:

1 The author should deal with the physical, practical, and emotional manifestations of the condition accurately but not didactically.

2 The behavior of other characters in the story should be realistic as they relate to the handicapped individual.

3 The story should provide honest and workable advice to the handicapped character about his or her condition and potential for the future.

In addition, the resolution of conflict may be a special concern in some of this realistic fiction. Does the author concoct a happy ending because he or she believes all children's stories should have happy endings? Or, does the resolution of conflict evolve naturally and honestly? Through fiction which honestly deals with handicaps, readers can empathize with children who are courageously overcoming their problems and with their families who are facing new challenges. Writers of such literature often express the hope that positive attitudes toward the handicapped will be developed through their stories. As mainstreaming brings more handicapped children into the regular classrooms, this goal becomes more important for both children and adults.

Stories set in different historical time periods frequently reflect changing attitudes toward handicapping conditions and provide a basis for discussion with children. Compare, for example, attitudes expressed in Julia Cunningham's story of a mute boy in *Burnish Me Bright* with feelings and attitudes expressed in Larry Callen's *Sorrow's Song*. Cunningham sets her story in a French village of the past. The characterization develops the prejudice, misunderstanding, fear, and even hostility encountered by the boy. Monsieur Hilaire, a retired performer who befriends the boy and brings him into his world of pantomime clarifies reasons behind society's prejudice:

These people you have known are no worse than the others that walk the world but they share with the others a common enemy, and the enemy is anyone who is different. They fear the boy who can't speak, the woman who lives by herself and believes in the curative power of herbs, the man who reads books instead of going to the café at night, the person like me who has lived in the distant differences of the theater. They are not willing to try to understand, so they react against them and occasionally do them injury. (p. 18)

In contrast to the misunderstandings and hatred expressed toward Cunningham's hero are the feelings and attitudes expressed toward Callen's contemporary heroine, Sorrow Nix. Callen explores these various attitudes by describing the reactions of people around the mute girl. Sorrow's best friend, a boy named Pinch, sees her this way: "She is so smart, I don't even like to think about it. She knows words I never heard of. But Sorrow can't use words the way most people can. Sorrow can't talk" (p. 5). Her teacher defends Sorrow and challenges a man who thinks her condition is tragic: "Sorrow Nix is more

normal than the two of us. Don't you do anything that will make her feel otherwise" (p. 56). Pinch's mother considers Sorrow someone special and compares her to a weeping willow, which she considers a very friendly tree. The author, however, does not imply that Sorrow is always happy. She longs to sing, hurts from the remarks and actions of insensitive people, and discovers frustrating terror when she cannot warn Pinch's mother about an approaching copperhead snake. The author parallels Sorrow's special needs with those of an injured whooping crane. When the crane flies away to live its own life, there is a strong feeling that Sorrow has won her own conflict. The author develops a strong theme about individual abilities and not judging people by outward appearances.

Jean Little explores the conflicting emotions of a child with cerebral palsy in *Mine for Keeps*. The author encourages readers to visualize Sally Copeland's mixed emotions as she prepares to leave the Allendale School for Handicapped Children, her home for five years. For as long as she can remember, she has longed to spend more than holidays with her family. She prepares to go home permanently, but worries about fitting in with her energetic family and attending regular school. Sally discovers that her leg braces and crutches do not really make a difference to the people who care about her. The author follows the recommendations for such literature by suggesting that children with physical handicaps have many options open to them. A theme stressing the capabilities of a paraplegic is also developed in Berniece Rabe's *The Balancing Girl*.

Eleanor Spence uses the reactions of her characters in *The Nothing Place* to encourage readers to glimpse the world of whispers and silences. Spence includes reactions of various people as they either ignore or poke fun at twelve-year-old Glen Calder when he suffers a partial hearing loss after an illness. Glen's reactions to his own problems are among the strongest and most compelling. First, the author describes Glen's inability to understand what is happening to him as he changes from an excellent student to one who is unable to understand his assignments:

This was his opportunity to tell the whole story—a rather dismal one of low marks and failure to understand what some of the teachers were saying, especially in the subjects that were new to him. For the first time in his life he actively disliked school. (p. 94)

Next the author develops Glen's changing reactions: he is too proud to complain and ask for help; he struggles along at the back of the room; and he eventually adjusts and decides to wear a hearing aid. Many reactions are explored in this book, including the apparent insensitivity of teachers toward a problem they should have discovered and the parents' tendency to ignore what they did not understand in the hope that the problem would solve itself.

Comparisons between experiences of deaf children and reactions toward deafness in different periods in history may be made with Mary Riskind's *Apple Is My Sign* and Veronica Robinson's *David In Silence*. Riskind's setting is a school for the deaf in the early 1900s—a time when hearing aids are unavailable. The characterizations and conflicts in Robinson's contemporary book are based on her work as a librarian in a school for the deaf. Robinson explores the problems of a child, born deaf, when he moves into a new town and tries to make friends with children who fear him because he is different. The author develops the theme that a person can win the respect of others by proving his own worth as a person.

Jean Little develops a credible world of the visually handicapped by describing a girl's frightening experiences and reactions when letters are blurred, look the same, or even appear to jiggle across the page. This problem is increased in *From Anna* when teachers or family do not recognize the handicap and the child considers herself Awkward Anna who is also slow, slow, slow. The conflict is resolved when Anna's problem is discovered by a doctor who provides her with glasses and enrolls her in a sight saving class. Children can vicariously feel Anna's incredulous joy as, for the first time, she observes the world around her. The depth of her feelings is emphasized as she hesitantly approaches the new class; meets an understanding teacher; discovers words and numbers large enough to read; becomes acquainted with children like herself who do not maliciously tease her, but understand her need to be accepted and to learn; and discovers that she can learn rapidly when the world is not a blur. Her greatest joy comes when she is able to weave a beautiful gift for her parents, a gift that demonstrates her skillful fingers, not the awkward hands that had previously embarrassed her so.

Authors who write plausible books about the relationships between mentally handicapped children and their normal siblings frequently develop conflicting emotions as the normal characters experience both protective feelings and feelings of anger toward the handicapped child. Betsy Byars's characterization develops such conflicting emotions in *The Summer of the Swans*. Sara is a normal teenager who is discontented with her looks, is sometimes miserable for no apparent reason, and is often frustrated with her mentally retarded brother as she loves and cares for him. The author allows readers to glimpse the younger brother's gentle nature as he is fascinated by the swans who glide silently across the lake. Later the swans play a major role in the plot development as he sees them flying by his window at night and follows them into the darkness. The author encourages the readers to understand and sympathize with his confusion as he tries to find the lake, but rapidly becomes lost in a world of tangled bushes, unfamiliar hills, and barking dogs. The nature of the conflict is enhanced when the author describes Charlie's terror at the moment he realizes that he is no longer surrounded by people who keep him safe and well. The true feelings of his aunt and sister are developed through their actions as they discover Charlie's absence. As Sara begins a frantic search, she forgets her personal miseries and concentrates on finding her brother. She even allows a boy whom she had wrongly accused of stealing Charlie's watch to help her search. The police and town people scour the countryside, and Sara and Joe search the densely wooded ravines until they hear the terrified screams of the lost child.

After Sara and Charlie reunite, Sara discovers that she no longer feels miserable; in fact, she feels good about herself. Her concluding thoughts suggest how her summer experiences have changed her whole life:

She suddenly saw life as a series of huge, uneven steps, and she saw herself on the steps, standing motionless in her prison shirt, and she had just taken an enormous step up out of the shadows, and she was standing, waiting, and there were other steps in front of her, so that she could go as high as the sky, and she saw Charlie on a flight of small difficult steps, and her father down at the bottom of some steps just sitting and not trying to go further. She saw everyone she knew on those blinding white steps and for a moment everything was clearer than it had ever been. (p. 140)

Vera and Bill Cleaver's *Me Too* and Jean Little's *Take Wing*, are two other stories that develop a protective relationship between a girl and her mentally handicapped sibling. The children in *Me Too* are twelve-year-old twins, Lydia and Lornie, who is mentally handicapped. The authors explore a range of emotions, including the baffled reactions of their parents, the fearful and angry attitudes of adults toward someone who is different, the cruelty of peers, and the overwhelming desire of Lydia to change her retarded twin. The mentally handicapped child in *Take Wing* is Laural Ross's seven-year-old brother James. James is not as severely handicapped as the children in the previous stories, but he has not been able to learn to read, he has difficulty following directions, and he needs help in getting dressed. Little describes his parents' progress through a series of emotions and beliefs. First, they believe that James is just maturing slowly; later, when he fails kindergarten and first grade, they decide that he is lazy and the teachers are letting him get by without working. Finally, they accept that he *is* different and should be evaluated at a mental health clinic. His older sister Laural, however, knows that James is different, worries about him, takes care of him like a mother, makes her family understand that Jamie needs special help, and then feels rejected when he begins relying on others and doing some things for himself.

This story makes a strong point for schooling for children who are educably mentally retarded and for their prospects for self-sufficiency when they are helped by special teachers who understand their needs. Children reading these stories may understand the emotions of families who have mentally handicapped children and those of the children themselves when they face the often frightening and perplexing world around them.

Being disabled does not mean that an individual is also unable. The books discussed in this section reflect this theme of the International Year of the Handicapped declared by the United Nations in 1981.

Dealing with Aging. When children's literature students evaluate the characterization of elderly people in children's books they frequently discover stereotypes. Denise C. Storey (22) describes a study in which fifth grade children analyzed the elderly characters found in books from their classroom library; they concluded that (1) some elderly people have boring, lonely lives where nothing changes; (2) grandparents in books look older than their own grandparents; (3) the elderly do not work, have fun, or do anything exciting; (4) young people are mean to elderly characters; (5) book characters do not want to listen or talk to the elderly; (6) some elderly are characterized as mean, crabby, overly tidy, fussy, and unfair; (7) the elderly like to remember the good old days or dream of better times; and (8) there are few happy books about the elderly.

Some authors of contemporary realistic fiction are exploring the problems related to aging with greater sensitivity than expressed in books of the past. When evaluating books dealing with aging, books should be selected that show elderly people in a wide variety of roles.

Books dealing with aging for younger children frequently develop close experiences between grandparents and grandchildren. Books such as Tomie de Paola's *Nana Upstairs & Nana Downstairs* (see page 165) and Sharon Bell Mathis's *The Hundred Penny Box* (see page 497) are examples discussed in this text.

Books for older children frequently stress the worthwhile contributions that are still being made by the older person, the warm relationships that can develop between grandparents and grandchildren, and the desire of older people to stay out of nursing homes. Some books are very serious; others develop the theme through a humorous story.

One such book, Eleanor Clymer's *The Get-Away Car*, should appeal to children because it includes humor, mystery,

and adventure. The author's characterization depicts a resourceful, special grandmother who is granddaughter Maggie's idea of a perfect grandmother because she lives by the motto of "fun first, work later." This characteristic is supported as other children from their tenement often join in their outings and their fun. All goes well until Maggie's Aunt Rubey decides that Grandma is not capable of taking care of a young girl; her solution is to put Grandma in a home for the elderly

Humor and mystery add to a story about youth and an older person.
From *The Get-Away Car* by Eleanor Clymer. Copyright © 1978 by Eleanor Clymer. Reprinted by permission of the publisher, E. P. Dutton.

and have Maggie move in with Aunt Rubey. While Aunt Rubey is trying to change their lives, Grandma and the children decide to borrow a car and run away to cousin Esther's home in upstate New York. Along the way, they have many adventures. The story has a satisfying ending as the children solve the mystery of the old black car, a way is found for cousin Esther to restore her formerly beautiful home, and Grandma convinces everyone that she is capable of looking after her granddaughter.

Don Schellie's *Kidnapping Mr. Tubbs* is a more complex book in which the author explores the feelings of the young and the elderly and develops a theme related to human dignity and self-worth. Mr. Tubbs, the nearly one-hundred-year-old cowboy, lives in a nursing home and has neither freedom nor a relative who cares for him. His friends are a teen-age volunteer and A. J., the grandson of the man who shares his room. The young people listen to his wish to visit the ranch in northern Arizona where he worked as a cowboy, the place that gave him happy memories and remembered friends. The young people plot to grant his wish, borrow an old car, "snatch" Mr. Tubbs out of the rest home, and head toward the ranch. The author uses discoveries during the trip to encourage readers to understand the lessons learned by both young and old. Mr. Tubbs discovers that many places he remembers have changed; worst of all, his beloved ranch has been turned into a recreational housing project. The greatest discovery is made by A. J., however, as he realizes that he has always avoided becoming involved with older people because he fears they will die like his early childhood friend. A.J.'s reactions following his personal discovery encourage readers to understand his change in attitude and glimpse the author's theme: A.J. tries to convince Mr. Tubbs that he is not worthless; in fact, he is needed.

In *Queen of Hearts,* Vera and Bill Cleaver create a believable conflict between the generations and develops a many-faceted elderly character by describing the range of feelings expressed toward a seventy-nine-year old grandmother. Wilma considers her grandmother self-sufficient, active, and an adversary who, when crossed, is "more dangerous than gargling with household bleach" (p. 14). Respect is shown Granny by Wilma's younger brother and the elderly next-door neighbor, but respect is not universal. After Granny is injured by a fall, a series of nurses quit because of her bad temper. Likewise, a couple who move in with her disregard her desires, treat her condescendingly, and throw away her possessions. Even Granny's son treats her with exasperation; Granny describes confrontations from his youth that clarify some of the reasons for his reactions.

Through Wilma's interactions with her grandmother, the authors suggest the considerable changes that occur in her developing character. At first she is afraid of Granny; but after Granny's fall, when nurses prove ineffective, Wilma agrees to stay with her because her parents and Granny need help. As the summer progresses, Wilma's feelings toward her grandmother and herself change. A condescending and dictatorial couple replace Wilma in her grandmother's house. Wilma shows concern for her grandmother's feelings and expresses admiration when the elderly lady locks the couple out of her home. Wilma's greatest understanding develops when she realizes the consequences of adults trying to force Granny to be inactive. A more assertive Wilma convinces Granny that there is a market for her delicious baked goods. When Granny becomes useful, her old personality returns.

There is a sad message in the story as Wilma and Granny believe they must hide their activities from nonunderstanding adults. When Granny's son and his wife visit, Granny becomes the "Great Pretender" because the two conspirators feel the son would disapprove of an active, self-fulfilled elderly person. When they leave, the house is filled with a sly, silent laughter that enjoins the heart. By the conclusion, Wilma shocks her parents with her new maturity, a maturity they are not sure they like.

These books, with their diverse attitudes toward elderly people, provide discussion materials that encourage older children to explore the role of elderly people in literature and their own feelings about the elderly.

Dealing with Death.   There are increasing numbers of books in which authors write about themes related to the acceptance of death and the overcoming of emotional problems following the death of a loved one. As might be expected, authors frequently treat the subject differently, depending on the developmental level of the probable readers. Differences in cause of conflict, characterization, resolution of conflict, depth of emotional involvement, and themes are apparent. Let us consider how several authors develop these areas in books written for younger readers, preadolescents, and teenagers. For comparative purposes, consider Carol Carrick's *The Accident,* Charlotte Graeber's *Mustard* and Eve Bunting's *The Empty Window* written for younger readers; Constance C. Greene's *Beat the Turtle Drum* and Peggy Mann's *There Are Two Kinds of Terrible* written for ten- to twelve-year-olds; and Judy Blume's *Tiger Eyes* written for readers in their early teens.

The cause of conflict in two of the books for younger readers is the death of a loved pet. Carrick (*The Accident*) develops plausible conflict and characterization by first developing a bond between a boy and his dog and then exploring Christopher's various emotional responses after his dog is accidentally killed by a truck: he blames the truck driver, himself,

THROUGH THE EYES OF AN AUTHOR

Tom McDonough

The Laughter of Children

Beverly Cleary

BEVERLY CLEARY, recipient of the Laura Ingalls Wilder Award and many children's choice awards, discusses the importance of humor in children's realistic fiction.

ALTHOUGH FOR OVER thirty years I have been absorbed in stories that spring from the humor of everyday life, I try not to think about humor while writing, because of the sound advice given me by my first editor Elisabeth Hamilton, whom I met after writing *Henry Huggins & Ellen Tebbits*. In discussing writing for children, I happened to mention humor. Elisabeth, a forceful woman, interrupted. "Darlin'," she said, "don't *ever* analyze it. Just do it." I have followed her advice. While I am writing, if I find myself thinking about humor and what makes a story humorous, I am through for the day; and that chapter usually goes into the wastebasket, for spontaneity has drained out of my work. Although introspection is valuable to every writer, I find that analyzing my own work is harmful because it makes writing self-conscious rather than intuitive. When I am not writing, however, I find myself mulling over the subject of humor, my kind of humor, and why so many children find it funny.

As a child I would have agreed that humor is "what makes you laugh." I could not find enough laughter in life or in books, so the stories I write are the stories I wanted to read as a child in Portland, Oregon—humorous stories about the problems which are small to adults but which loom so large in the lives of children, the sort of problems children can solve themselves. I agree with James Thurber's statement: "Humor is the best that lies closest to the familiar, to that part of the familiar which is humiliating, distressing, even tragic. . . . There is always a laugh in the utterly familiar."

My first book *Henry Huggins,* a group of short stories about the sort of children I had known as a child, was written with a light heart from memories of Portland. As I wrote I discovered I had a collaborator, the child within myself—a rather odd, serious little girl, prone to colds, who sat in a child's rocking chair with her feet over the hot air outlet of the furnace, reading for hours, seeking laughter in the pages of books while her mother warned her she would ruin her eyes. That little girl, who has remained with me, prevents me from writing down to children, from poking fun at my characters, and from writing an adult reminiscence about childhood instead of a book to be enjoyed by children. And yet I do not write solely for that child; I am also writing for my adult self. We are collaborators who must agree. The feeling of being two ages at one time is delightful, one that surely must be a source of great pleasure to all writers of books enjoyed by children.

By the time I had published five books, several things had happened which forced me to think about children and humor: I had children of my own, twins—a boy and a girl; reviews said my books were hilarious or genuinely funny; a textbook on children's literature said my books were to be read "purely for amusement"; and enough children had written to me to give me some insight into their thoughts about my books.

One phrase began to stand out in these letters from children. Letter after letter told me my books were "funny and sad." Until these letters arrived, I had not thought of *Henry Huggins* as sad. The words, at that time never used by adults in reference to my books, began to haunt me. Funny and sad, or even funny and tragic, describes my view of life. To borrow another phrase from James Thurber, I had chosen "reality twisted to the right into humor rather than to the left into tragedy"—for that is my nature. I feel that comedy is as illuminating as tragedy—more so for younger readers who may be frightened or discouraged by tragedy in realistic fiction.

Abridged from "The Laughter of Children," *The Horn Book* (October 1982): 555–64. Copyright © 1982 by Beverly Cleary.

and his father for not being able to save his dog. The resolution of Christopher's conflict between himself and his father is reached quite rapidly. His father suggests they search for the right stone to mark Bodger's grave. After the marker is placed, his father holds him, and Christopher realizes that his father understands.

Graeber (*Mustard*) develops a closer family relationship as the family shares the sorrow following a fourteen-year-old cat's heart attack and the final decision to let the veterinarian help the cat die in peace. The author focuses on the importance of the pet to a young boy and encourages readers to understand this relationship by describing his disbelief in the cat's ailments and his reactions after the pet dies. When Alex and his father go to the pet shelter to donate some of Mustard's things, Alex declines the offer of a kitten because he does not have room at the moment for anything but memories of Mustard. The au-

A boy faces the realization of his friend's illness.
Illustration by Judy Clifford from *The Empty Window,* by Eve Bunting. Reprinted by permission of Frederick Warne and Co., Inc.

thor encourages readers to understand that this may change, however. Alex states that in another year he may be ready for a pet. This resolution encourages readers to understand that healing takes time, memories are worth retaining, and family members can help each other in times of sadness.

Eve Bunting's picture storybook *The Empty Window* explores a boy's feelings of fear, guilt, and sadness as he faces the death of his best friend. The boy in the story realizes he has been afraid to see his dying friend when he recognizes that the time spent in capturing a wild parrot who lived in the tree outside his friend's window was an excuse for not visiting him. Joe teaches C. G. something about the meaning of life when he thanks him for the parrot but asks him to release it because "once the parrots were free and then someone caught them and caged them, but they go free again. That's why I like them" (unnumbered). The author also suggests an important discovery about people who may be critically ill. C.G. realizes that although Joe is dying he has not changed. They can still sit and talk as they did before.

The two examples of stories written for ten- through twelve-year-olds have more fully developed characters, and deal with the more difficult emotions related to adjusting to the death of a family member. Greene (*Beat the Turtle Drum*) develops the basis for a girl's reactions to her sister's accidental death by describing the warm relationship between ten-year-old Joss and her twelve-year-old sister and best friend Kate. In addition to a best friend relationship, however, there is an undercurrent of hurtful emotion; Kate believes her parents prefer her younger sister. After Joss dies as a result of a fall from a tree, Kate faces both the sorrow of losing a best friend and the inner conflict resulting from her belief that her sister was the preferred child. The author encourages readers to glimpse Kate's inner turmoil when she finally admits her feelings to an understanding relative who responds:

I bet Joss would've felt the same way. If it'd been you, she might've said the same thing. And both of you would've been wrong. I think when a child dies, it's the saddest thing that could ever happen. And the next saddest is the way the brothers and sisters feel. They feel guilty, because they fought or were jealous or lots of things. And here they are, alive, and the other one is dead. And there's nothing they can do. It'll take time Kate. (p. 105)

The resolution of conflict, however, does not happen at that moment. The author, through Kate's reactions, infers that healing takes time. Kate understands that she will receive pleasure from her memories of Joss. In addition, she will, if she has her own children, name a daughter Joss, and tell her children about her sister and the love they shared.

Strong feelings about death are expressed in Peggy Mann's *There Are Two Kinds of Terrible*. The author compares a boy's emotions as he experiences both kinds of terrible: the first is a broken arm from which he would recover; the second is the death of his mother from cancer. This second terrible has no end, no reverse. The author encourages readers to realize the magnitude of these emotions by describing the close relationship with the boy's mother and describing incidents that emphasize his lack of communication with his father. The author explores Robbie's emotional experiences and reactions as he sees physical changes in his mother, attends the funeral, communicates with his close friend, fears the emptiness between himself and his father, briefly blames his mother for leaving him, and finally understands that his father has had an equally terrible experience. This final understanding signifies the resolution of his conflict and is the beginning of a new relationship between father and son. The story ends with a feeling of hope for the future as father and son begin to learn about each other.

The cause of the conflict in Blume's story for older readers (*Tiger Eyes*) is both the sudden, violent death of a parent and a society that creates such violence. The author develops a person-against-self conflict as a teenage girl, Davey, tries to adjust emotionally and physically to the death of her father who was a robbery victim. There is also a person-against-society conflict as the characters respond to and reflect about a society in which there is violent death, vandalism, excessive teen-age tension, and powerful weapons. The author's characterization encourages readers to understand Davey's turmoil, and the depth of her involvement is developed as the author describes her interactions with various people in the story. Blume shows Davey's emotional ties with her father; her physical reactions when she faces peers (she faints at school but cannot tell the nurse her problem); her need for a quiet place to reflect; her interactions with a man dying from cancer; her reactions toward an uncle who will not allow her to take chances but designs weapons at Los Alamos; and her interactions with two friends who are also facing inner conflicts. Davey's conflict is not easily resolved. It takes considerable time before she can face what happened, tell new friends how her father died, and consider her own future. The impression is left, however, that being able to face the future and plan one's life is worth the effort.

The stories discussed in this section deal with irreversible problems that are very difficult to experience. Consequently, children's responses to the books may be quite different and very personal. An eight-year-old said he felt better after reading *The Empty Window*. He had a friend who was very ill; he was pleased that someone else felt like he did. An eleven-year-old,

however, began to read *Two Kinds of Terrible* and then could not finish it. She said she did not want to read a book that reminded her that her mother might die. Several responses by fourteen-year-olds to *Tiger Eyes* demonstrate how very personal reactions to realistic fiction may be. One reader said, "This is not a good book to read in class. You need to be by yourself so you can cry if you want to." Another child said, "It's great. You get into the story and forget everything. I was afraid Davey was going to kill herself, but I thought, Judy Blume wouldn't kill her main character." A third reader advised that the book should be read at one time, otherwise it would be sad. She continued "When you think about the morals in the book they give you a happy feeling." When asked to express these morals the girl answered: "Take a chance on your talents; planning someone's life for them doesn't make them happy; it's always better to face the truth rather than run from it; life is a great adventure; you can't go back in time. So pick up the pieces and move ahead; and some changes happen down inside of you and only you know about them." These responses indicate that a fourteen-year-old grasped many of the complex and multiple themes developed by the author. It is also interesting to note that the themes the reader identified are positive rather than negative glimpses of life.

Growing Up

The growing-up years, as discussed in chapter one, are frequently difficult. Children may be self-conscious about their changing or nonchanging physical appearance or sexuality. They may need to overcome emotional problems in order to develop or recover self-identity. They may need to identify their roles within their changing world. Books that explore children's concerns can stimulate discussion with children facing these same concerns. Books may also let children know that they are not alone, that other children experience and overcome these same problems.

Physical Changes. In order to develop credible problems, authors who write about physical maturity frequently describe an embarrassing physical characteristic and explore the way the character, peers, friends, and family respond to the characteristic and the character. The conflicts in the stories frequently include both person-against-self and person-against-person. Person-against-person conflicts may include peer victimization of the main character or the story may be told from the viewpoint of a child who is part of the peer group. In this latter case the author may develop the consequences of peer victimization by having the peer group turn against the main character. Some problems are resolved through simplistic or humorous means; other resolutions are complex and express the extreme sensitivity of children as they proceed through this period of growing up.

Constance C. Greene uses two different approaches to develop and resolve the conflicts in *The Ears of Louis* and *The Unmaking of Rabbit*. In the first book, Louis responds to the jeers of "Elephant Boy," "Dumbo," and "Stay out of the wind or you will sail to Alaska" by taping his ears to the sides of his head and then wearing a football helmet to try to reduce their size. Because he has a supportive next-door neighbor and a best friend who believes ears are a sign of character, Louis's emotional problems are not severe. The author, however, solves Louis's problem with an overly simplistic solution: when the older boys learn that he can play football, his peers are impressed by his popularity and no longer tease him. In *The Unmaking of Rabbit*, however, the solution cannot be as simple because the author creates more conflict for Paul, an eleven-year-old boy who lives with his grandmother. His peers tease him about his father who deserted him and his mother who visits him infrequently. They also taunt him about his big ears, pink nose, and a tendency to stutter. Although Paul has a loving and supportive grandmother, he longs for a close relationship with friends. The author reveals Paul's true character when he has the opportunity to gain the friends he desires. This is a difficult decision, however, because the overtures are from a gang of boys who want him to help them break the law. The author convinces the readers that Paul has made an important discovery about himself and suggests his appropriate handling of an important moral issue when he decides that a clear conscience is worth more than friends. In this story, the impact of Paul's decision is more important because he faced so many more conflicts than were faced by Louis in the previously discussed book.

The inability to be assertive causes difficulty for eleven-year-old Jeffrey in Ellen Conford's *The Revenge of the Incredible Dr. Rancid and His Youthful Assistant, Jeffrey*. Jeffrey believes that in real life the little guy always is physically whipped: "One of those harsh realities of life you have to face when you're built like me, you're going to spend most of your free time wishing you were built like Clint Eastwood, and the rest of your free time being scared of guys who are" (p. 5). To make matters worse, his mother is the first female sports editor in the county and his father is very self-confident. The bully in Jeffrey's life is a sixth grader twice his size. During months of name calling and teasing, Jeffrey writes stories about how he retaliates against his enemy. The author reveals a great deal about Jeffrey's true character when the bully picks on his only friend and Jeffrey steps in to resolve the problem.

Judy Blume depicts the unhappy world of an overweight child in *Blubber*. The force of peer cruelty is shown when a strong peer leader manipulates her classmates as the children compose a list, "How to Have Fun with Blubber," then force her to say such things as "I am Blubber, the smelly whale of class 206" (p. 72). Blume characterizes the teacher and the principal as ineffective and apparently uncaring, and the indignities continue. The main character realizes the crushing impact of what she has done when she tries to stop the cruelty and her classmates turn on her. Compare Blume's antagonist and characterization with those developed by Jan Greenberg in *The Iceberg and Its Shadow*. Greenberg's main character joins in the victimization of her best friend when a manipulating new girl comes to school. It is not until Anabeth is herself a victim that she realizes the hurtful situation. Children freely admit that this type of peer insensitivity is not uncommon, and they enjoy discussing what could have been done by any of the characters to avoid the emotional disturbances.

Another of Blume's books explores a young girl's developing sexuality. In *Are You There God? It's Me, Margaret*, eleven-year-old Margaret has many questions about the physical changes occurring in her body, including breast development and the onset of menstruation. This topic is also found in Norma Klein's *Tomboy*. Unlike Margaret, ten-year-old Toe does not look forward to bodily changes. While Margaret feared she might be the last girl in her group to menstruate, Toe fears that she is the first. She believes that if her friends discover her secret they will not allow her to join the Tomboy Club; she does not believe a girl mature enough to have a baby can be a tomboy. Toe discovers that the physical changes she fears are also happening to her best friend, and the two girls decide to abandon the club. These books discuss a topic that is very serious to girls approaching maturity.

Emotional Maturity. Authors who write about children's emerging emotional maturity frequently develop a credible antagonist by describing the various forces that create fear and conflict within the person. Consider, for example, Maia Wojciechowska's development of characterization in *Shadow of a Bull*. Manolo is described as the son of a great and supposedly fearless bullfighter who allows people to vicariously cheat death by watching him kill the bull. When the great hero is killed, all of the villagers expect his skills, desires, and bravery to pass on to his son. Now the author exposes the conflict within Manolo as he struggles with the knowledge that the people expect him to be like his father. Manolo believes he is a coward because he has no desire to fight bulls. This conflict increases as the men of the village begin training him in the art of bullfighting. Through the advice of his father's friend, the author helps Manolo see the danger in his own conflict and the necessity to make decisions that are true to himself:

Before he becomes a man, he has many choices to do the right thing, or to do the wrong thing; to please himself, or to please others; to be true to his own self, or untrue to it. (p. 145)

The author creates a strong conclusion with a powerful theme when Manolo learns that real courage is not necessarily found in the bullring but is manifested when a person acts in spite of fear. Manolo shows true bravery by telling the waiting crowd that he does not wish to become a bullfighter; instead, he wants to study medicine. This is a strong story that suggests that there are many types of bravery. Being true to oneself is the most important characteristic of all.

Elizabeth Billington (*Part-Time Boy*) and Maria Gripe (*Elvis and His Secret*) develop characterizations of painfully shy children who interact unsuccessfully with their families and try to make people understand their needs. Billington creates believable characterization through the actions of the shy child's family and his own feelings about himself; his brothers tease him because he is different, his mother worries because she thinks he is lonely, and he worries because he believes his mother does not like him the way he is. It is only through the help of an understanding person outside the family that he begins to develop friendships and self-confidence because he feels accepted for his own worth. Gripe also develops a setting in which a shy child is not understood by his family. She contrasts Elvis's inability to communicate with his family with his ability to communicate with older friends and his grandfather. For example, his parents do not listen to him and his mother prefers being surrounded by the sound of television and the chatter on the telephone. In contrast, his grandfather and older friend encourage him and understand him. His friends reassure him, through their actions, that they feel he is special—because he is Elvis.

A sequel to this book, *Elvis and His Friends,* describes Elvis's experiences as he begins school, makes a new friend, and grows in understanding and independence. He even learns to feel compassion for his insecure mother. Family members frequently recognize themselves in this story about communication problems between children and their parents. The book can be used to improve communication and understanding between generations.

Books that develop plots around physical and emotional maturity differ in several important ways from the realistic fiction of the past. Several authors, for example, infer that the character's own parents are ineffective, are not available, or are

A shy child has difficulty associating with his brothers. Illustration by Diane deGroat from *Part-Time Boy,* by Elizabeth Billington. Reprinted by permission of Frederick Warne and Co. Inc.

unable to understand the child. Current realistic fiction frequently suggests that a person outside the family, an understanding grandparent, or a knowledgeable friend is the most important influence on a child's discovery of self. This is in contrast with literature of the past in which strong parents and caring brothers and sisters provide necessary support. In addition, current books, unlike the earlier family stories, suggest that children have numerous problems as they struggle to grow toward physical and emotional maturity.

Children As Individuals. Publishers are becoming sensitive to the need for literature that does not portray either sex in stereotypic roles. For example, Houghton Mifflin (7) has published the following guidelines for eliminating sex stereotypes in materials published by their company in 1981 and later:

1 Materials should present a balance of both sexes, including female and male protagonists, female and male contributors to society, and females and males in a variety of jobs. Stories should suggest that both men and women can prepare for and succeed in a variety of occupations.
2 Literature should recognize that males and females share the same emotions, personality traits, and capabilities. Both sexes should be included in active pastimes and in solitary pursuits.
3 Sensitivity and taste should be employed when using humor to characterize the sexes.
4 Literature should present a broad range of historical references to women, including contributions of well-known and less well-known women.
5 Where appropriate, legal, economic, and social issues related to women should be included.
6 Historical books should adhere to facts concerning the roles and activities of women in past centuries.

As the roles of females in society shift away from the stereotypes of the past, girl heroines and their mothers reflect these changes. Girls are found who are individuals; they may be brave, they may be tomboys, and they may be unorthodox. Mothers also take on different roles as they often work outside the home; they may even have jobs more demanding than those of their husbands. Whatever roles they play, they are quite different from their sisters Pollyanna and Rebecca. How effectively does the literature adhere to the previous guidelines and how does it differ from realistic fiction of the past?

Consider, for example, the popular contemporary character Ramona, created by Beverly Cleary. Stories of her exploits span the years from the early 1950s into the 1980s. In the earlier *Henry and Beezus,* readers discover that the girls, Beezus and Ramona, are considered worthy playmates even by an active boy such as Henry Huggins. These thoughts at least infer that active pastimes are not usually considered appropriate for girls; girls may not even be considered creative playmates. In later books, however, Ramona quickly comes into her own. In *Ramona the Pest* she is not the stereotypic quiet girl; instead, she is the "worst rester" in kindergarten. By the publication of *Ramona and Her Father* in the late 1970s, the roles of the family members have changed; father loses his job and mother returns to work on a full-time basis. Ramona now humorously tries to help her father through this change in his life. *Ramona and Her Mother* explores a working mother's life as viewed through the point of view of her seven-year-old daughter. By 1981 *Ramona Quimby, Age 8* is "helping" her family while her father returns to college. The "Ramona" books are popular with children who enjoy reading about the exploits of this spunky, humorous girl. Students of children's literature will discover that references to females and male and female roles have changed over the years.

Eleven-year-old Harriet M. Welsch is another heroine whose actions disprove stereotypes. The author, Louise Fitzhugh, uses such adjectives as exceptional, intelligent, and curious when various characters describe her attributes in *Harriet the Spy.* Her actions support these characteristics as she hides in her secret places, observes her neighbors and her classmates, and writes down her observations. The extent of her exceptionality and her independent character is revealed when her classmates find her notebook and organize "The Spy Catcher Club." Now Harriet uses all of her ability to devise a plan to have her friends forgive her. Harriet is not the fainting female of Victorian fiction who must be rescued from her failures by the males in the story. Instead, she is resourceful and highly creative. She is even able to return to her real loves, spying and writing. More tales about Harriet are found in *The Long Secret* and *Sport.*

The exuberant, precocious heroine in Vera and Bill Cleaver's *Lady Ellen Grae* does not accept the feminine role that she thinks is being placed on her by her father and society. The author first describes Ellen Grae's unrestricted life with her artist father and then her reactions when he wants her to leave her beloved Thicket, Florida, and live with her aunt in Seattle and learn to be a lady. At this point she strongly presents her personal philosophy:

I've found, that most things are simply a matter of mental reconciliation, because the mind is elastic—it stretches and can be pulled this way and that. The trick is not to flinch from it. If you do you're a goner before you get started. Mentally, I've reconciled myself to a thousand things: school, being a girl, collard greens, baths. . . But Seattle? Oh, no. No, sir. I, Ellen Grae Derryberry, do not reconcile to things like Seattle. I like it here and here I intend to stay until it's time for me to hop into my grave. (p. 19)

Although the Cleavers develop a plot that allows Ellen Grae to return to her father, she also discovers that there are many things that she doesn't know. Because she doesn't like to be ignorant about anything, she decides that she will learn about them on her own. There is an inference, at least, that she may discover many dimensions of being a woman and not just the confining one she has pictured.

The image of females in realistic fiction of the past frequently suggested that girls play a passive role, not an active role, in plot development. Claudia Kincaid, in E. L. Konigsburg's *From the Mixed-Up Files of Mrs. Basil E. Frankweiler,* plays a very different role as she plans to run away and stay undetected in the Metropolitan Museum of Art. The author reinforces her dominant role as she and her brother arrive safely at the museum, avoid the guards at closing time, discover a way to obtain food, and solve the mystery of the angel statue. This mystery again allows the author to demonstrate the resourcefulness of the heroine. When the two children are given one hour to search the files and discover the answer to the mystery, Claudia tells her impatient brother that five minutes of planning are worth fifteen minutes of haphazard looking. Her techniques prove successful, and they discover the answer to the statue's authenticity.

These books suggest that girls can be effective protagonists. They, like their male counterparts, can have varied emotions, personality traits, and capabilities. Additional strong male and female characters are developed in the survival literature in the following section.

Surviving in Unusual Circumstances.

Leaving the security of home, facing great natural dangers, and not returning home until personal courage has been proven; being lost in the cold, forbidding lands of the Alaskan North Slope or the hot desert surrounding the Grand Canyon and living on nature's bounty; or being cut off from all city services and fleeing an impending crisis are the forceful plots that develop strong personalities in survival literature. These stories are especially popular with older children who enjoy adventure stories.

Authors who have written about survival have described the natural enemy in ways that allow readers to vicariously experience the awesome power of a storm at sea, the loneliness of a deserted island, or the terror felt as floodwaters come closer and closer to the only sanctuary. It is not only the dangers of nature, however, that are developed in the stories. Authors who write about nature also show a love for it; heroes may leave the "civilized" world to experience the satisfaction of living off the bounties of nature, learning about its laws and feeling a kinship with wild animals. Readers may also feel saddened as they discover that in a modern world it may not be possible to return to the basic beauty and challenge of an earlier time.

Authors of survival literature use several literary techniques to create credible plots and characters. Person-against-nature and person-against-self conflicts are frequently used to develop complex and exciting plots. Authors may develop a forceful setting that is the antagonist and the clarifier of the conflict, or the setting may develop a desired mood. Authors' style is also important in survival literature. A careful selection of words and rhythm patterns may increase the imagery and highlight the mood and the action. Finally, authors may rely on a consistent point of view to encourage the reader to believe in the truth of the hero's or heroine's experience. In this section we will consider how authors of survival literature have utilized these techniques.

Jean Craighead George, for example, uses all of these techniques in *Julie of the Wolves.* The strong person-against-nature conflict is developed as she describes the lonesome tundra on which the thirteen-year-old Eskimo girl Mujax (Julie) finds herself after she runs away from home in search of a pen pal in San Francisco. Here is a barren land that stretches for three hundred miles to the Arctic Ocean and for eight hundred miles to the Beaufort Sea. Her only companions on the wind swept slopes are a pack of wolves. The reader's acceptance of her desperate situation is intensified as Mujax desperately studies how the wolves communicate with each other and then tries to use the same signals to let them understand her need for food. The author suggests the awesome loneliness in her plight as Mujax seeks the wolves' friendship as well as their food. Nature, however, is not the only antagonist. George also develops a person-against-society conflict. After Mujax learns to love the wolves and respect her Eskimo heritage, Amaroq, the leader of the wolves, is riddled with bullets from a low-flying plane. Hunters and civilization are infringing upon the Alaskan slope; her beautiful land may not survive. Mujax does not discover a happy solution to this dilemma. Instead, she unhappily concludes "The hour of the wolf and the Eskimo is over" (p. 170).

George's style also increases the reader's acceptance of Sam Gribley's experiences in *My Side of the Mountain.* The diary entries in portions of the book, for example, seem very authentic. They create the feeling that the reader is sharing an autobiographical account of Sam's experiences as he leaves his New York City home and lives off the land in the Catskill Mountains. Detailed descriptions of preparing and storing food, tanning and sewing a deerhide suit, and carving and firing the interior of his hemlock tree home are told in a matter-of-fact manner and resemble the writing of someone keeping a log of his experiences and observations. The detailed descriptions of wild plants that can be eaten and other important survival techniques also infer to readers that Sam prepared carefully for his experiment in nature.

Style and setting as antagonist are again main literary elements used by George to create a memorable and believable survival story in *River Rats, Inc.* Consider, for example, the effect of describing a turbulent rapids in the Colorado River as "a beast with wet claws that clutched, the watery teeth that snapped and swallowed boats" (p. 3). This scene introduces the developing conflict as two boys lose their raft when they attempt to run a falls in the Grand Canyon. George describes the environment in which they must try to survive: the temperatures reach 120 degrees and promising paths may lure the unwary until they are hopelessly lost on the desert. The details of survival in this setting create a credible situation when George describes the lovely canyon and stream, the construction of a shelter, the making of a pumping mill to crush cattail fibers into flour, and the weaving of a fishnet from natural fibers.

The consistent first-person point of view used by Scott O'Dell in *Island of the Blue Dolphins* creates a plausible setting, plot, and main character. When Karana, the young Indian girl who survives a lonely existence on a Pacific Island, tells readers "I will tell you about my island," readers visualize the important features from her viewpoint and believe the description. When she says "I was afraid," the fear seems real; later, her discovery of her brother's body justifies her fear. This first-person viewpoint increases the reader's belief in her personal struggles as she is torn between two forces. Will she adhere to the tribal law that prohibits women from making weapons? Or will she construct the weapons that will probably mean the difference between her life or death? Her inner turmoil heightens the suspense, as suggested by the following quote:

Would the four winds blow in from the four directions of the world and smother me as I made the weapons? Or would the earth tremble, as many said, and bury me beneath its falling rocks? Or, as others said, would the sea rise over the island in a terrible flood? Would the weapons break in my hands at the moment when my life was in danger, which is what my father had said? (p. 54)

Other major decisions are also more meaningful because they are told through Karana's point of view. When she decides to take a tribal canoe and sail in the direction her people sailed, readers believe her turmoil as the canoe begins to leak and she must again make a difficult decision: should she go back and face loneliness or go on and face probable disaster? Karana decides to return to her island and make it as much of a home as she can. O'Dell now emphasizes the small details of days filled with improving shelter, finding food, and hiding supplies against the possibility of her Aleut enemies returning to the island. Her need for companionship is shown when she cannot kill the leader of the wild dogs after wounding him; she takes him to her shelter and cares for him. He regains his health and Rontu, as she names him, becomes her constant companion and defender. In her search for companionship, Karana adds birds to her growing family, clipping their wings so they cannot

fly. Her only human encounter is with an Aluet girl who arrives on the island with a seal hunting party. The girl does not reveal her hiding place and the two spend many hours in conversation, although they do not understand each other's language. Karana again faces loneliness when Rontu dies. Later, Karana discovers a dog that must be Rontu's son and captures and tames him. The story concludes as Captain Nidever finds a girl dressed in a skirt of cormorant feathers standing in front of her island shelter, takes her, the dog Rontu-Aru, and the birds chirping in their cage with him toward the California mainland.

A strong male character who survives an experience with his feared enemy, the sea, and discovers courage on an island is found in Armstrong Sperry's *Call It Courage*. (See page 83 for a discussion of the setting and characterization in this story.)

In *Hills End*, Australian author Ivan Southall tells a story of courage and survival set in Australia's rugged and isolated timber country. The development of a normally peaceful setting as antagonist is necessary for the credibility of this story. The author accomplishes this as he describes two very different settings. First is the peaceful, leisurely scene of villagers leaving town for a picnic and a teacher and seven children exploring caves in hope of discovering aboriginal drawings. The setting remains peaceful as the author describes the excitement as the children discover ancient bones and drawings. The scene changes rapidly, however, when the author describes what has taken place since they entered the cave:

So they came again toward the opening, toward a world of frightening sound and vivid lightning flashes, of bitter cold, of violent wind, of torrential rain and hailstones. The hailstones struck the ledge and bounced and were as big as golf balls. They couldn't approach the opening. They had to stop well back, clear of showering ice and wind-driven rain. The wall beyond was like a block of frosted glass-water, ice, and wind in a mass through which they could not see. (p. 45)

It is into this world that the teacher emerges, telling the children to stay in the cave as she tries to save one who was caught outside. The author creates suspense as he describes the rising water, the children's fear for their teacher's safety, and their concern that the storm's destructive forces may have hurt their parents. The children's decision not to wait but to try to return to their homes is now important to the story. The author has created the setting as antagonist, and the remainder of the plot develops around their dangerous journey and their concern for the people and the town.

Authors of survival literature demonstrate to the student of children's literature effective techniques for developing believable plots and characters who may mature physically and emotionally as they face the challenges of their environment.

The settings in survival stories are integral to the plot development and characterization.

Inner-City Reality.

Inner-City Reality. The problems of overcoming poverty, gang violence, and living without the security of a strong, supportive family are presented by several authors of realistic fiction. While many authors of this literature rely on sensationalism for plot development, authors such as Virginia Hamilton and Walter Dean Myers create inner-city stories with literary merit. One of the strongest inner-city stories that creates memorable characters is Hamilton's *The Planet of Junior Brown*. This is a complex story about brotherhood and learning to live together. The three main characters, all outcasts, live on the fringe of the busy New York City that closes around them. Junior Brown is a talented pianist who should be recognized for his skill, but the fact that he weighs almost three hundred pounds causes people to leave him alone. Consequently, he feels ugly and is afraid of being trapped in small spaces. Buddy Clark is a very intelligent street boy who has lived on his own since the age of nine. The third outcast is Mr. Pool, a former teacher, who is now the school's custodian. He feels that tough black children who know the city streets should be given an opportunity to learn. The rigid school regime, however, caused him to lose heart, give up his teaching job, and return to the school basement. In this basement, however, is a hidden room where he can create a new world and teach the boys.

Hamilton uses the symbolization associated with *planet* to develop each character's place in the story. The first planet, Junior Brown's, is an artistic creation, glazed in black and beige, that hangs suspended from metal rods and spherical tracks attached to the ceiling of the hidden room. While the children in the rooms above go through their normal day, the three outcasts build their solar system, create their planets, and learn about science and each other.

Buddy Clark's planet is not mythical; it is a frightening inner-city reality, a world of homeless boys, hunger, and survival. On his planet, Buddy first learns about personal survival from an experienced street survivor called a planet leader. After he learns the lessons taught by the leader, he becomes a leader with planets and inhabitants of his own to train and supervise.

Hamilton has created a strong character in Buddy Clark by describing his survival and functions in two worlds; in one, he is the protector and the companion of Junior Brown; in the other, he takes care of children, works to feed and clothe them, and is free to create his own planet. Hamilton develops a strong theme as Buddy Clark takes the other outcasts to his own planet in the basement of a deserted house and shares with them his own views of life:

> "We are together," Buddy told them, "because we have to learn to live for each other . . . . If you stay here, you each have a voice in what you will do here. But the highest law for us is to live for one another. I can teach you how to do that." (p. 210)

Two very different worlds are also depicted in Myers's *It Ain't All for Nothin'*. One is the secure world of Tippy's religious, caring grandmother; the other is the violent world of crime and the neglect of his father. The author contrasts these worlds as he describes twelve-year-old Tippy's move from one world to the other when his grandmother becomes crippled by arthritis and can no longer care for herself or her grandson. Myers develops the boy's reactions as he is frightened and angered by his father's use of drugs and his keeping stolen goods and guns in the apartment. In his need to forget, Tippy begins to drink. Life becomes frightening; his father is involved in a robbery during which one of his friends is wounded. Tippy's inner conflicts between the world of his grandmother and the world of his father are emphasized when he debates his own actions. Tippy makes a hard decision when he tells an older friend about the problems in his father's apartment and informs the police. The author suggests that there is hope for Tippy when an understanding man takes custody of him. Tippy decides he will never experience the same troubles with the police as those experienced by his father.

Animal Stories

As discussed earlier in this chapter, the animal stories found in traditional literature and modern fantasy are frequently characterized by animals who talk and act like people or have other magical powers. In contrast, the animal stories in realistic fiction have a strong sense of reality and sometimes tragedy. Realistic animal stories place specific demands upon the author that are not found in fantasy. When evaluating realistic animal stories, the following criteria should be considered.

1 Does the author portray animals objectively without giving them human thoughts or motives?
2 Does the behavior of the animal characters agree with information provided by knowledgeable observers and authorities on animal behavior?
3 Does the book encourage children to respond to the needs of animals or the needs of people to love animals without being too sentimental or melodramatic?

Authors who write credible animal stories frequently develop warm relationships between children and pets. The conflict in such stories often occurs when something happens to disrupt the security of the pet's life. The antagonist may be a physical change in the animal, an environment different from the pet's secure home, or a human character whose treatment of the animal is cruel or even life threatening. Detailed descriptions of the animal's physical changes, the setting that becomes an antagonist, or the cruel human character may encourage children to understand the vulnerability of animals to such forces.

Credible stories about wild animals usually reflect considerable research about animal nature, behavior patterns, and natural habitat. Conflict may be developed when animals face natural enemies, when they are taken from natural surroundings and placed in domestic environments, or when they are hunted or trapped.

Some authors use animal-against-society or animal-against-person conflicts to develop strong themes for animal protection. Other themes stress the personal human development that is made possible because of human interaction with animals. Many authors stress the positive consequences of loyalty and devotion.

Consider, for example, the various techniques used by Theodore Taylor in *The Trouble With Tuck.* Taylor first develops a plausible close relationship between Helen and her golden Labrador, Tuck. Helen's love for the dog and her family's devotion to the dog are strengthened as Taylor describes two incidents in which Tuck saves Helen from harm or possible death: Tuck jumps on a man who attacks Helen while the two are walking in the park, and Tuck rescues Helen after she hits her head on a diving board and sinks to the bottom of the pool. The conflict develops when Tuck, although still a young dog, begins to lose his sight. The author describes the incidents that lead up to the family's awareness: Tuck runs through a screen door when chasing cats, birds land in the yard without demonstrating their characteristic wariness of the dog, and he is unable to adjust when furniture is moved. The reactions of family members when the veterinarian declares that Tuck is going blind and cannot be helped reinforce their devotion for the dog and make plausible their acceptance of Helen's resolution of the problem. When Tuck demonstrates his inability to accept the new restrictions placed on him by chewing his ropes, running in the neighborhood, and damaging woodwork when shut in the house, Helen decides that her pet should not live with these restrictions. Her solution is novel; she calls a trainer for seeing eye dogs and makes an appointment for her parents without telling the trainer that the blind individual is a dog. Although the trainer's initial reaction is negative, the family is finally offered an older seeing eye dog whose master has died. Now the author describes Helen's trials and frustrations as she tries to train Tuck to follow the seeing eye dog. After weeks of disappointment, she is rewarded when Tuck accepts and follows the older dog. This story, based on a true incident, emphasizes determination, loyalty, and human self-confidence that may develop because of animal and human interaction.

A classic book with a notable dog as the main character is Jack London's *Call of the Wild.* First published in 1903, it de-

Photographs depict the changes in a dog's life as he goes from family pet to a working dog in the Klondike.
From *The Call of the Wild,* text by Jack London, photographs by Seymour Linden. Photographs copyright © 1977 by Seymour Linden. Published by Harmony Books (A Division of Crown Publishers, Inc.). Used by permission of Seymour Linden.

picts life in the Klondike during the Alaskan gold rush. The author develops a story of transformation as Buck progresses from a docile pet to a rugged work dog and finally to an animal who is inescapably drawn by the wild cries of the wolf pack. London develops these remarkable changes in Buck by providing details of his life. The credibility of this change is enhanced as the author contrasts Buck's life as a family pet in California with his experiences after he is stolen and brought, raging and roaring, to face the primitive law of the Klondike. London chronicles these experiences and the outward changes that occur in the dog: Buck changes as he reacts to a beating and the fierce fangs of fighting dogs, but retains his spirit; while crossing the countryside in a dogsled harness, he learns by experience as long-suppressed instincts come alive.

This is also the story of the strong bonds between dog and master as Buck, after a succession of sometimes cruel owners, is purchased by John Thornton, a man filled with kindness. Buck apparently feels an adoration for John that causes him continually to return from his wilderness treks until the terrible day when he returns to camp to find that John has been killed. Only then are the bonds between man and dog broken, allowing Buck to roam with the wolf pack:

His cunning was wolf cunning, and wild cunning; his intelligence shepherd intelligence and St. Bernard intelligence; and all this, plus an experience gained in the fiercest of schools, made him a formidable creature as any that roamed the wild. (p. 114)

The wilderness of the eastern mountains of the United States is the location of Jim Kjelgaard's story about a boy and a champion Irish setter. *Big Red* is the ultimate dream of Danny, a mountain boy who longs to raise fine dogs. His dream begins when he accompanies Big Red to a New York dog show where he wins best of breed. Danny is allowed to take Big Red into the wilderness to train him as a partridge dog; the two learn to respect each other, and Danny discovers just how noble and courageous Big Red truly is.

One of the best-known stories (and films) about a boy and his dog is Fred Gipson's *Old Yeller*. The story takes place in the Texas hill country in the late 1860s. It is filled with happy moments as Travis and the big, ugly, yellow dog hunt together and grow to love each other. The story has loyalty and tragedy as Old Yeller saves Travis's mother and his little brother, Arlis, from attacking animals. This last act is also tragic because the rabid wolf bites Old Yeller. Travis discovers the real pain of growing up as his mother asks him to end the life of his beloved pet. Life goes on, and one of Old Yeller's pups wins a place in the family. This story illustrates the loyalty and courage frequently expressed in animal stories.

Another conflict in animal stories results when a family pet, through some accident, is separated from the family and forced to travel and survive in the wilderness. One of the most outstanding of these is Sheila Burnford's *The Incredible Journey*. The setting for the journey is northwestern Ontario, a deeply wooded wilderness with chains of lonely lakes and rushing rivers. As described by the author, it is a natural setting for wild duck, Canadian geese, and lynx, but is hostile for three domestic pets who travel 250 miles in search of their family. The animals retain characteristics that could be described through careful observation. The trained red-gold Labrador retriever, for example, is the leader of the group. This is realistic; he has hunted duck in such territory and would be more knowledgeable about the wilderness. The old English bull terrier, however, retains the characteristics of a pet. He expects attention and food to be provided by people. Consequently, he searches for human help whenever he can. Likewise, the wheat-colored Siamese cat retains her characteristic movements and temperament. The conflict is developed as they face the hostile environment: they experience fatigue and hunger; they encounter unfriendly people; and the old dog is jumped by a bear cub. They face danger when a collapsing beaver dam carries the cat far downstream, and a lynx pursues the cat over treacherous terrain.

As the weary, nearly starved animals approach home, the author shifts the scene to their owners who are also behaving in a believable manner. Their frantic search for news and reports from forest rangers allow the family to discover at least a portion of the experiences of their pets. Children love this story because it describes just what they hope their own pets would do in similar circumstances.

The problems resulting when domesticated pets are allowed to live in the wilds are explored in Helen Griffiths's *Running Wild*. Griffiths develops a boy's dilemma after his dog has puppies; his grandfather takes the first litter away from her. Not understanding his grandfather's reasons, Pablo hides his dog and the second litter in the forest where he feeds them. The dogs mature and return to the wild, killing livestock and terrorizing the farmers in this mountainous region of Spain. The author encourages readers to understand Pablo's error when a wolf pack is killed because the farmers believe that the wolves are responsible for the killing. Pablo feels that he was to blame for the destruction of forest life. His real hope for the future of the wildlife is through the work of his teacher to save the baby wolf cubs, who are being sent to a national game reserve rather than being shot. Readers discover along with Pablo that certain animals are not meant to run wild in the forest; they may become predators and alter the natural life cycle.

BOOKS SUCH AS GIPSON'S *Old Yeller*, Rawlings's *The Yearling* and Sperry's *Call It Courage* have been criticized because they include acts of killing which symbolize the male initiation into manhood. Critics who have labeled such plots as belonging to "the cult to kill" suggest that young men are being conditioned to believe they must perform violent actions or be strong enough to kill even a loved pet if they are to achieve manhood. This male stereotype is suggested by some as being harmful and detrimental to healthy social development. The struggle and strain to live up to such an image is believed to place considerable pressures on males and to suggest that any other behavior is unmanly.

In contrast, other writers suggest that eliminating such acts of violence in children's literature would ignore our literary past with its archetypes found in myth and epic literature. This viewpoint stresses that children should not be isolated from their literary past even though violence may play a key role in the lives of traditional heroes. In addition, eliminating acts of violence from historical fiction would force writers to ignore the harsher realities of life on the frontier and in wilderness areas or the ritualistic rites of passage that are part of many tribal cultures.

Writers of children's literature texts frequently suggest that each act of violence in a book must be interpreted according to the total plot of the story and the changes that occur in the boy and his view of himself and his world.

Horse stories also have qualities that make them a marvelous experience for children. There is usually loyalty and devotion between the horse and owner or someone who longs to be the owner. Frequently, it is the little horse, who may have been laughed at or scorned, who becomes the winner and the beginning of a famous line of horses. There is sadness in many of the stories as both horse and master may need to overcome severe obstacles and even mistreatment before honor is restored.

Two outstanding authors of horse stories are Marguerite Henry and Walter Farley. Henry's stories reflect research and knowledge about horses and their trainers, and several report the history of a breed of horses. One memorable Henry story develops the ancestry of Man o' War, the greatest racehorse of his time. In *King of the Wind*, Henry travels back 200 years to the royal stables of a Sultan of Morocco where Agba, the horseboy, has a dream of glory for a golden Arabian stallion with a high white chest. The story travels from Morocco to France as the Sultan sends six of his best horses to King Louis XV, who rejects the horses who have become thin from their voyage. Agba and the once beautiful Sham are handed over to several degrading and even cruel masters before the English

Earl of Godolphin discovers the boy's plight. Agba and his horse accompany the Earl to his farm in England where Agba's dream and promise to the horse come true. Three of the golden Arabian's offspring win various races and the coveted Queen's purse at Newmarket. When the great Arabian horse, renamed The Godolphin Arabian, stands before royalty, Agba's thoughts flash back to his earlier Moroccan promise:

"My name is Agba. Ba means father. I will be a father to you, Sham, and when I am grown I will ride you before the multitudes. And they will bow before you, and you will be the king of the Wind. I promise it." He had kept his word! (p. 169)

Other enjoyable books by Henry include *Justin Morgan Had a Horse,* the story of the Morgan horse; *Black Gold*, the story of a racehorse and the jockey who brings her to winning form; *Misty of Chincoteague,* the story of the small, wild descendants of the Spanish horses shipwrecked off the Virginia coast; and *San Domingo: The Medicine Hat Stallion,* a story of a Nebraska frontier boy and his affection for an unusual horse. All of Henry's stories reflect an understanding of the nature of horses and the people who feel loving attachments for them.

A beautiful black stallion and his descendents are the chief characters in a series of books written by Walter Farley. The first, *The Black Stallion,* introduces a beautiful wild horse being loaded, unwillingly, onto a large ship. On this same ship is Alec Ramsay who understands and loves horses. The two are brought together as the ship sinks, and the black horse pulls Alec through the waves to a small deserted island. Friendship develops as the two help each other survive, and Alec discovers the joy of racing on the back of the amazing horse. After they are rescued, Alec's friend realizes what a remarkable horse he has; they secretly train the horse for a race between the two fastest horses in the United States. In an exciting climax, the unknown mystery horse wins the race. This story has also been written as a picture storybook illustrated with color photographs from the movie of the same name.

Questions about the black stallion's heritage are answered in Farley's *The Black Stallion Returns.* There are many other stories in the series that focus on the great horse and his notable and courageous descendants.

Griffiths relies on a detailed setting and background information on horses and bullfighting to develop a plausible story in *Dancing Horses.* Without the detailed description of post–Civil War Spain and glimpses of the attitudes of Spanish society, readers would not understand the unrealistic nature of a poor boy's dream or appreciate his struggle. Griffiths's characterization of Francisco depicts a poor Spanish boy whose love for horses grows along with his desire to become a *rejoneador*—a person who fights bulls on horseback. Because of the setting, Francisco's struggles and his need to accept favors and training from the son of a wealthy family seem plausible.

The need for taking responsibility toward the animals in one's care is emphasized in Lynn Hall's *Danza!* The author parallels the recovery of a champion horse, who is injured because of a child's negligence, with the self-discovery of this Puerto Rican boy who believes he cannot live up to his family's expectations. There is an underlying theme against animal cruelty as the author describes the harsh treatment often given to show horses and emphasizes Paulo's need to protect his horse after the horse recovers and enters this competitive world.

Several of the books already discussed stress the vulnerability of animals to changes in their environments or humans who interfere with their way of life. Meindert DeJong explores the impact of negative environmental change and positive human intervention in *The Wheel on the School.* The author introduces several issues related to storks through the questions and investigations of six school children and their teacher in a Dutch fishing village. After they ask "Why didn't the storks

The Black Stallion Picture Book features photographs from the movie.
The Black Stallion. © 1979. United Artists Corporation. All rights reserved. Reprinted with permission.

come to Shora?" they explore the various reasons for the missing storks: the roofs are too steep, there are no trees, there are too many storms, and there is too much salt spray. A plausible situation develops because the children take the problem seriously and work hard to rectify it. Their honest concern suggests to the reader the possibility that this is a vital matter that should be of interest to others. The author also suggests that every effort counts; the children must overcome many obstacles, but a stork family finally accepts the wheel on the schoolhouse roof.

The problems that result for both animals and people when wild animals are tamed are explored in Jean Craighead George's *The Cry of the Crow.* The human conflict in this story set in the Piney Woods of the Florida Everglades develops because Mandy Tressel's family kills crows to save their strawberry crop. Mandy, however, secretly feeds and tames a young crow, the only survivor of her younger brother's gun blast. As Mandy raises the crow, Nina Terrance, she discovers that the crow can imitate some human speech. When the wild crows try to lure Nina away from her human friend, Mandy, knowing that she should encourage the bird to return to the wild, asks her mother's advice. George develops the girl's inner conflicts when she ignores her mother's warnings and decides to keep the bird. The author explores the controversy related to taming wild animals through the neighbors' mixed reactions to the crow; some threaten to poison her, some are intrigued by her speech, and others want to put her in a cage as a tourist attraction. The return home of Mandy's young brother brings the conflict to a climax. When he repeats the same words he said as he killed the crow family, the crow attacks his face. The author suggests Mandy's feelings as she is torn between her love for her pet and her brother, "I'll never feed her again. Mommy was right. She'd be gone now, far, far away, if I hadn't been selfish and dumb. . . . If she hurts you, I'll never forgive myself" (p. 142). When Nina again attacks the boy, Mandy makes the difficult decision that the crow must be killed; the two children realize that they are both responsible for Nina's death.

Mysteries

Footsteps on a foggy night, disappearing people, mysterious strangers, and unusual occurrences woven together into an exciting, fast-paced plot create mystery stories that appeal to older children. One eleven-year-old girl, an avid reader of mysteries, listed the following four characteristics that make a mystery exciting for her: (1) it should have an exciting plot that holds your interest, (2) it should contain suspense, (3) the mystery should have enough clues so that the reader can follow the action, and (4) the clues should be written in such a way that reader can try to discover "who done it." In answer to the question, "What has caused your interest in mysteries?" she replied that she had read *Encyclopedia Brown* in third grade and enjoyed trying to follow the clues. She said that her favorite suspense story was *The House of Dies Drear* (see page 499). This section considers some mysteries that are available for younger and older children.

Mysteries for Younger Readers. The best-known mysteries for young readers are probably contained in Donald J. Sobol's *Encyclopedia Brown* series. The books each contain stories about ten-year-old Leroy Brown who helps his father, the police chief of Idvalle, solve crimes by figuring out the clues. For example, in *Encyclopedia Brown Tracks Them Down*, Leroy

solves the case of the missing ambassador by reviewing the gifts presented to him at a birthday party. In another case, he solves the riddle of the flower can and discovers the identity of the boy who stole a 1861 Confederate coin worth $5,000 by tricking the culprit with a homonym. In *Encyclopedia Brown*

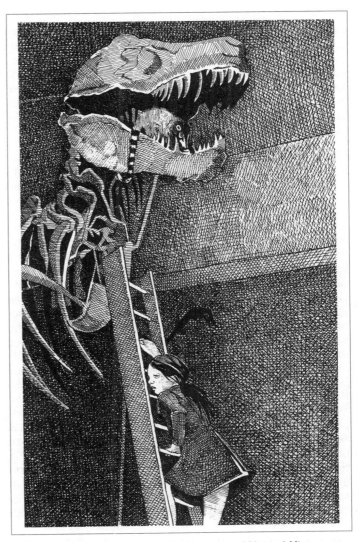

The setting for this mystery is the Museum of Natural History. From *Funny Bananas* by Georgess McHargue. Illustrated by Heidi Palmer. Copyright © 1975 by Georgess McHargue. Copyright © 1975 by Heidi Palmer. Reproduced by permission of Holt, Rinehart and Winston, Publishers.

Sets the Pace there are ten more cases in which young readers can identify the thief or even try to solve the problem of a bully who picks on smaller children. Readers can try to solve each case, because the solutions and the reasoning behind them are provided.

The setting of Georgess McHargue's *Funny Bananas: The Mystery at the Museum* is the Museum of Natural History in New York City. Ben Pollock, whose parents are scientists at the museum, tries to solve the mystery of the vandalized display cases at the museum. The clues include a ransacked kitchen, pieces of strange green bananas found on the floor, a large book that is hollow on the inside, and a feeling of being followed and observed by something that moves close to the ceiling. In addition to the mystery, children can acquire an understanding of how important natural history is in the life of the story's main character.

Mysteries for Older Readers.

Powers of observation play an important role in the mysteries of Robert Newman. A child's ability to observe and deduce clues is frequently as important as the trained skills of Sherlock Holmes, Dr. Watson, or a Scotland Yard inspector. The setting for two mysteries is London in Sherlock Holmes's time. *The Case of the Baker Street Irregular* includes suspense, sinister characters who must be outwitted, and several mysteries that at first seem not to be related but are. The characters include Andrew, a boy who does not know the identity or location of his mother; Mr. Dennison, Andrew's tutor who takes him to London and is then approached by a sinister cab driver and disappears; the Baker Street Irregulars, some poor neighborhood children who sometimes do special jobs for Sherlock Holmes; Screamer, the sister of one of the Baker Street Irregulars who befriends Andrew and helps him rescue Dennison; Holmes, the famous British private detective; and a mysterious woman who asks Holmes to kidnap her own daughter from her husband.

The plot has considerable action as a sinister cab driver apparently kidnaps the tutor and then begins to follow Andrew. A series of other occurrences brings Holmes into the case: an unexplained disturbance at a private club; a lady asking Mr. Holmes to investigate the disappearance of her daughter; and a Scotland Yard inspector seeking Holmes's assistance in solving a series of bomb threats. Andrew accompanies Holmes in the investigation and identifies the seemingly insignificant clues that help unravel the mystery. There is a suspenseful conclusion as Andrew and Screamer follow a hansom cab through the fog to an old warehouse and discover Dennison handcuffed to a chair. With the aid of Holmes, the odd occurrences are shown to be part of the same plot. In a satisfactory ending, Andrew's parentage is solved, and he is reunited with his mother.

Andrew and Screamer are also the main characters in the sequel, *The Case of the Vanishing Corpse*. This book begins at a slower pace as the first few chapters recount the relationships developed in the first story. The pace increases with a series of seemingly unrelated incidents: a young woman disappears, five people notify Scotland Yard about jewelry robberies, and a body discovered by Andrew and Screamer disappears before the inspector arrives. Clues, including a cigarette stub, smudges on a windowsill, an unusual tattoo, and hemp scraps caught in the cracks of a brick wall, help Constable Wyatt, assisted by Andrew and Screamer, solve the case.

Ellen Raskin's several books challenge readers to work out puzzle clues along with often preposterous characters. These clues may be word puzzles, a series of obscurely written messages, or even observations gained through reading. *The Mysterious Disappearance of Leon (I Mean Noel)* is a humorous word puzzle, a game about names. As the story of Leon and Little Dumpling, the heirs to Mrs. Carillon's Pomato Soup fortune, proceeds, Raskin liberally sprinkles clues throughout the text. She informs the reader that there is a very important clue in a particular section or that the reader should use a bookmark to mark the location of Leon's fourteen messages because they contain very important clues. Noel's final words, for example, as he bobs up and down in the water cause the heroine years of searching. What is meant by "Noel glub C blub all . . . I glub new . . ."? When Little Dumpling cannot find Noel, she is convinced that he has amnesia or is hurt and dedicates her life to finding him. Her only clues are his last words and other brief messages. As the years pass, two orphans and an old friend who is a crossword puzzle expert join in the search. The "verifiers," whose motto is "Find the Facts," finally solve the riddle of the last message, discover the identity and whereabouts of Noel, and live happily ever after.

The clue Raskin provides in *Figgs & Phantoms* is "the bald spot." This clue eventually helps Mona Figg discover if she has or has not actually visited Capri, the Figg Family's idea of a perfect heaven.

See page 81 for a discussion of Raskin's *The Westing Game*, which includes many clues that must be worked through before the teams of players solve the mystery.

Zilpha Keatley Snyder's mysteries involve kidnapping, complex games, or mysterious secret environments. *The Famous Stanley Kidnapping Case* involves a family of children who accompany their parents to Italy. For a short time, they lead an idyllic life exploring their large old villa, attending school in a grand Renaissance palace, and becoming acquainted with their neighbors. The pace rapidly increases when kidnappers plan to capture one child and discover instead that they have caught five very unusual children. Imprisoned in an old basement, the children consider the clues to the identity of their masked captors: Who knew that Amanda would go out secretly to meet Hilary if she thought he had written her a note? Where had they seen trucks like the one used in the kidnapping? Where had they heard the motor sounds that occurred when the kidnappers were arriving or leaving? The children solve the mystery and outwit the kidnappers by applying their own unusual personalities to the problem.

Snyder's *The Egypt Game* is a story about creating an ancient world in an abandoned storage yard. In this world, four sixth graders, a fourth grader, and a preschooler learn about ancient Egypt and recreate the altar to the Oracle of Thoth. They rename themselves with ancient Egyptian names, learn to write secret messages in hieroglyphics, and recreate ancient ceremonies. This world is perfect until a murderer enters the neighborhood, causing the children to remain inside and ponder the rumors that are circulating. In an exciting climax, they discover the identity of both the murderer and the person who has answered their questions to the Oracle of Thoth. The author speaks to the needs of many children when she describes how important this world of make-believe was:

It had been a terrific game, full of excitement and mystery and way out imagining, but it had been a great deal more than that. It had been a place to get away to—a private lair—a secret seclusion meant to be shared with best friends only—a life unknown to grownups and lived by kids alone. (p. 197)

Numerous clues and mounting tension create a fast-moving plot in Barbara Corcoran's *You're Allegro Dead*. Instead of the summer camp activities expected by two twelve-year-old girls, the girls glimpse a mysterious intruder and a kidnapping takes place. A doubting camp director and a sympathetic counselor provide mixed adult reactions to the mystery.

These mysteries provide escape and enjoyable reading through their plots and suspense. They allow children to become involved in the solutions through clues and character descriptions. They also suggest that children themselves, if they are observant, creative, and imaginative, can solve mysteries.

Sports Stories

Sports stories rate highly with children who are sports enthusiasts. Some quite reluctant readers will finish a book about their favorite sport or sports hero. However, the majority of these stories are about boys, and few authors write about girls who enjoy participating in sports. Many stories deal with good sportsmanship, the values of sports, overcoming conflicts between fathers and sons, and overcoming fears connected with a sport. Unfortunately, many of the stories are didactic and have familiar plot lines and stock characters.

Most baseball stories are about boys and their excitement over the game or how it helps them solve other problems in their lives. Two books for younger children do suggest that girls are also interested in sports. Sylvia Tester's *Carla-Too-Little* describes Carla's disappointment when her sister claims she is too young for tennis, her brother says she is too small for baseball, her father tells her she must be ten years old to be on his swimming team, and her mother insists that she is too little to be on her softball team. Carla is happy when she is offered the position of bat girl, complete with uniform and some responsibility.

Osmond Molarsky's *Robbery in Right Field* describes the mixed feelings of the town when a girl, who is a prospect for Olympic gymnastics, joins a Little League baseball team. The author develops various attitudes that may be expressed toward girls who want to play "masculine" sports. The majority of these attitudes suggest that the girl is not welcome.

Authors who write about baseball often imply that the sport has therapeutic values. The emphasis in these books is frequently on the role baseball can play in helping children overcome problems at home, develop new friendships, face physical disabilities, or feel accomplishment. Matt Christopher's *The Fox Steals Home*, for example, tells the story of troubled Bobby Canfield as he faces his parents' divorce and the prospect of his father's taking a job far from home. His father and his grandfather have coached him and nicknamed him "Fox." His proudest moment comes when he steals home and demonstrates to his father what a good player he has become.

Likewise, Barbara Cohen's main character in *Thank You, Jackie Robinson,* finds that a mutual interest in baseball allows him to develop a special friendship. This friendship with an older man is especially important; Sam's father is dead, his mother manages an inn, and his sister has no interest in baseball. Alfred Slote, in *Hang Tough, Paul Mather*, writes about a leukemia victim whose greatest interest is baseball. He must face the knowledge that he has a short time to live and that his parents are trying to prevent him from playing to protect him. An understanding doctor helps him play his last season with dignity and courage.

Football is both the major interest and the cause of conflict between father and son in Christopher's *Football Fugitive*. Larry Shope loves football and longs for his father to leave his law practice long enough to watch him play. Larry and his father become closer when Mr. Shope provides legal assistance for a professional football star.

Both Christopher and Slote have written stories about another favorite sport, ice hockey. Christopher's *Face-Off* describes Scott Harrison's love for hockey and his fear that the puck might strike him in the face. Because of this fear, he does not play his best, earning him the disgust of his teammates. Scott overcomes his fear and regains their respect. In Slote's *The Hotshot*, Paddy O'Neill knows that he must be on the Bantam League's all-city team if he is to make the varsity team in high school. When he demonstrates that he can be a team player, not always trying for the goal himself, he is chosen for the team that will play in the state tournament. He is overjoyed, because a win at the state level could lead to the Silver Sticks Tournament in Canada. This book is illustrated with photographs showing different aspects of hockey.

Christopher has written books about two other sports. *The Twenty-One-Mile Swim* describes the frustrations of the son of Hungarian immigrants when he is teased about his small size and his inadequate swimming skills. He decides that he will train for long-distance swimming and challenge twenty-one-mile-long Oshawana Lake. He succeeds, although a foot cramp threatens his success when he has almost reached shore. Another sport popular with many boys provides the excitement in *Dirt Bike Racer*. Twelve-year-old Ron Baker discovers a minibike at the bottom of a lake and decides to restore it. Through a part-time job, he makes friends with a wealthy older man who once raced bikes. Trouble develops, however, when the man's nephew becomes angry because of this friendship. Many boys enjoy these fast-paced sports stories.

There are fewer sports stories with girls as heroines. Frank Bonham's *The Rascals from Haskell's Gym* takes place on the balance beam and the parallel bars. Sissy Benedict is the gymnast who becomes involved in the competition between the Butterflies Gymnastics Club and their arch rivals, Haskell's Raskells. Another story about girls in sports is K. M. Peyton's *The Team,* a book about horses. Ruth Hollis joins an English Pony Club team, prepares her horse for competition, and enters cross-country races. This book will be enjoyable for young riders who have experienced the same thrill during a competitive race.

More sports stories are discussed in the section on biographies in chapter twelve.

Humorous Modern Fiction

Humorous stories, whether involving the world of fantasy or a world of real people living in our contemporary world, are among children's favorites. Authors who write about humorous situations that could happen to real people (these situations and characters may stretch probability) allow children to understand that life can be highly entertaining; it is not always serious. Writers may encourage readers to laugh at themselves and at numerous human foibles. Humorous situations and characterization may be used to highlight real problems and make reading about them palatable.

Many of the sources of humor discussed in chapter five—word play, surprise and the unexpected, exaggeration, and ridiculous situations—are used by authors of humorous modern fiction. Authors, for example, may use a play on words or ideas to create a humorous situation or clarify a character's feelings. Consider Betsy Byars's *The Cybil War,* an entertaining story about a fifth grader who has a crush on a girl. The "war" develops as Cybil Ackerman responds in various ways to Simon's advances, which are intentionally misinterpreted by his best friend. Beverly Cleary uses a twist on the words of a familiar television commercial to create a funny incident in *Ramona Quimby, Age 8.* When Ramona gives her book report she presents it in the style of a television commercial. Her statement, "I can't believe I read the whole thing," causes a hilarious reaction among her classmates. Judy Blume in *The One in the Middle is the Green Kangaroo* uses a humorous analogy to clarify the middle child's feelings: "He felt like the peanut butter part of a sandwich squeezed between Mike and Ellen" (p. 7).

Blume uses a surprising and unexpected situation in *Tales of a Fourth Grade Nothing*. The humorous conflict between two brothers is brought to a climax when the younger boy swallows the older brother's pet turtle. At the hospital the adults are all relieved when the youngster passes the turtle; his brother's main concern, however, is for the turtle. A boy's unusual job and his efforts to keep it a secret from his friends result in an amusing situation in Betty Miles's *The Secret Life of the Underwear Champ.* Larry does not believe that his baseball teammates would understand and support his job modeling underwear for a television commercial.

Exaggeration provides humor in Helen Cresswell's various books in "The Bagthorpe Saga." The series, including *Ordinary Jack, Absolute Zero, Bagthorpes Unlimited,* and *Bagthorpes v. the World,* presents the talented and eccentric Bagthorpes who feel that life is a hilarious challenge. For example, when Uncle Parker wins a Caribbean cruise as a prize in a slogan-writing contest, the competitive Bagthorpes begin to enter every contest imaginable; the result is chaos as the prizes start arriving.

Their competitive spirit continues in *Bagthorpes Unlimited.* The family tries for immortality by creating the great Bagthorpe daisy chain, a chain of daisies 4,750 feet long containing 22,000 daisies that they hope will place them in the *Guinness Book of World Records.* The fame they earn is not, however, what Mr. Bagthorpe had envisioned; instead of being interviewed as a serious writer for a story in *The Sunday Times,* he is photographed on his front lawn surrounded by daisies and enthusiastic chain weavers.

In *Bagthorpes v. the World,* Mr. Bagthorpe is still feeling the trauma of having his one chance at national acclaim whisked away from him by the photograph and article about the incredible daisy chain. The author suggests his frame of mind: "It needed only the slightest nudge, he felt, to topple the balance of his mind and send it plummeting into full-scale schizophrenia or paranoia" (p. 18). The nudge that creates chaos in this episode is the arrival of a bank statement showing that he is overdrawn at the bank by "billions." Even though the overdraft is a mistake, Mr. Bagthorpe feels the world is out to get him. To combat his feelings of doom, he devises a grand survival strategy that he forces upon the other members of the household. In Mr. Bagthorpe's words, "The whole world is ranged up against us out there. But we shall defy it. We shall gird up our loins. We shall survive" (p. 48). It is not, however, until the homemade wine blows up all over the kitchen that Mr. Bagthorpe realizes the error of his plan and ends the self-sufficiency campaign.

In addition to plots filled with humorous exaggerated incidents, "The Bagthorpe Saga" recreates a family overflowing with loyalty and happiness. Children enjoy reading about a family that includes an eccentric grandmother, a precocious and unpredictable cousin, and assorted aunts and uncles. One fourth grader expressed her hope that Helen Cresswell would write more books about the Bagthorpes because her books made children laugh.

Ridiculous situations abound in Cleary's *Ramona Quimby, Age 8.* For example, when Ramona's third grade classmates bring hard boiled eggs to school so they can crack them on their heads, Ramona's mother accidentally gives her an uncooked egg. Sheila Greenwald develops a plot in *Give Us a Great Big Smile, Rosy Cole* around an author/photographer who wrote several information books that chronicled his nieces' accomplishments. Now it is Rosy's turn. Unfortunately she does not have any accomplishments except her definite inability to play the violin. This does not deter her uncle, however. Greenwald depicts the changes in Rosy's life, including the attitude of her music teacher. Several ridiculous situations develop because the uncle wants believable photographs, including one of a recital.

Greenwald's book is characteristic of many humorous fiction stories about people. Although most of the incidents are humorous, the actions of the characters reflect and highlight human foibles. The main characters learn something about themselves as they experience situations that may be more humorous to the reader than to them.

SUMMARY

Popular themes in contemporary realistic fiction include wrestling with fear and responsibility, overcoming family and personal problems in the face of illegitimacy, quarreling or divorcing parents, and conflicts between children's ambitions and their parents' desires. Overcoming problems created by the death of a loved one, problems created by deserting or noncaring parents, and emotions created by handicapped siblings are also found in realistic fiction. Discovery of self and developing maturity are popular themes in stories for older children.

Realistic fiction is especially enjoyable for many children because the stories are written about young people who are the same age, share the same interests, or have the same concerns. Realistic fiction also can help children understand human problems and how people similar to themselves have coped with them. It provides the enjoyment of escape as children read exciting mystery and adventure stories.

Realistic fiction has resulted in more controversy and more calls for censorship than any other type of children's literature. Controversial issues include sexism, sexuality, violence, drugs, profanity and objectionable language, viewpoints on war and peace, religion, death, and racial matters.

Suggested Activities for Adult Understanding of Realistic Fiction

- ■ Sexism in literature, including the harmful sex-role socialization resulting from female- and male-role stereotyping, is a major concern of many educators and psychologists. In a school, public, or university library, choose a random sampling of children's literature selections. If these books were the only sources of information available about male and female roles, what information would be acquired from the books and their illustrations? Is this information accurate?
- ■ Compile an annotated bibliography of books that show both girls and boys in nontraditional sex roles. What is the strength or weakness of each book?
- ■ Compare the professional roles of fathers and mothers in literature published in the 1970s and 1980s with the professional roles of fathers and mothers in literature published in earlier periods. Do the later books illustrate the changing family roles of both men and women? Is there conflict in the story if there is reversal of roles? How is this conflict handled?
- ■ Interview children's librarians in public or school libraries. Ask them to state the guidelines used by the library when

selecting books that might be considered controversial for children. What are the issues, if any, that they feel are relevant in the community? Can they identify any books that have caused controversy in the libraries? If there are such books, how did they handle the controversy?

■ Many realistic fiction books deal with the problems children must face and overcome when they experience separation from a friend, a neighborhood, a parent, or the ultimate separation caused by death. Choose one area, read several books that explore these problems, and recommend the ones that could be shared with younger children and those that might be more appropriate for older children. Explain the decision. Annotated bibliographies such as those found in Joanne E. Bernstein's *Books to Help Children Cope with Separation and Loss* (2) could be helpful in the search.

■ Read a survival story such as *My Side of the Mountain, River Rats, Inc.*, or *Island of the Blue Dolphins*. What writing style or techniques does the author use that allows the reader to understand the awesome power of natural enemies?

■ Compare the characteristics depicted in a modern fantasy story about a specific animal with the characteristics described by an author of a realistic animal adventure about the same animal.

References

1 Association of Women Psychologists. "Statement Resolutions, and Motions." Miami, Fla.: American Psychological Association Convention, September 1970.

2 Bernstein, Joanne E. *Books to Help Children Cope with Separation and Loss.* New York: Bowker, 1977.

3 Blatt, Gloria Toby. "Violence in Children's Literature: A Content Analysis of a Select Sampling of Children's Literature and a Study of Children's Responses to Literary Episodes Depicting Violence." East Lansing, Mich.: Michigan State University, 1972. University Microfilm No. 72–29,931. pp. 358.

4 Carmichael, Carolyn Wilson. "A Study of Selected Social Values as Reflected in Contemporary Realistic Fiction for Children." East Lansing, Mich.: Michigan State University, 1971. University Microfilm No. 71–31, 1972. pp. 224.

5 Egoff, Sheila. "Precepts, Pleasures, and Portents: Changing Emphases in Children's Literature." In *Only Connect Readings on Children's Literature,* edited by Sheila Egoff, G. T. Stubbs, and L. F. Ashley. Toronto: Oxford University, 1980.

6 Egoff, Sheila. "The Problem Novel." In *Only Connect: Readings on Children's Literature,* edited by Sheila Egoff, G. T. Stubbs, and L. F. Ashley. Toronto: Oxford University, 1980.

7 *Eliminating Stereotypes, School Division Guidelines.* Boston: Houghton Mifflin, 1981.

8 Frasher, Ramona. "A Feminist Look at Literature for Children: Ten Years Later." In *Sex Stereotypes and Reading: Research and Strategies.* edited by E. Marcia Sheridan. Newark: International Reading Association; 1982.

9 Hall, Ann E. "Contemporary Realism in American Children's Books." *Choice* (November 1977): 1171–78.

10 Homeze, Alma Cross. "Interpersonal Relationships in Children's Literature from 1920 to 1960." University Park, Pa.: Pennsylvania State University, 1963. University Microfilm No. 64-5366. pp. 222.

11 Kean, John M., and Personke, Carl. *The Language Arts: Teaching and Learning in the Elementary School.* New York: St. Martin's, 1976.

12 McClenathan, Day Ann K. "Realism in Books for Young People. Some Thoughts on Management of Controversy." In *Developing Active Readers: Ideas for Parents, Teachers, and Librarians,* edited by Dianne L. Monson and Day Ann K. McClenathan. Newark, Del.: International Reading Association, 1979.

13 Madsen, Jane M., and Wickersham, Elaine B. "A Look at Young Children's Realistic Fiction." *The Reading Teacher* 34 (December 1980): 273–79.

14 Marten, Laurel A., and M. W. Matlin. "Does Sexism in Elementary Readers Still Exist?" *Reading Teacher* 29 (1976): 764–67.

15 Merla, Patrick. "What is Real? asked the Rabbit One Day." In *Only Connect: Readings on Children's Literature,* edited by sheila Egoff, G. T. Stubbs, and L. F. Ashley. Toronto: Oxford University, 1980.

16 Nilsen, Aileen Pace. "Women in Children's Literature." *College English* 32 (May 1971): 918–26.

17 Noble, Judith Ann. "The Home, the Church, and the School as Portrayed in American Realistic Fiction for Children 1965–1969." East Lansing, Mich.: Michigan State University, 1971. University Microfilm No. 31, 271. pp. 320.

18 Root, Shelton L. "The New Realism—Some Personal Reflections." *Language Arts* 54 (January 1977): 19–24.

19 Sage, Mary. "A Study of the Handicapped in Children's Literature." In *Children's Literature, Selected Essays and Bibliographies,* edited by Anne S. MacLeod. College Park, Md.: Univ. of Maryland College of Library and Informational Services, 1977.

20 Sam Houston Area Reading Conference, Sam Houston State University, February, 1981.

21 Steele, Mary Q. "Realism, Truth, and Honesty." *Horn Book Magazine* 46 (February 1971): 17–27.

22 Storey, Denise C. "Fifth Graders Meet Elderly Book Characters," *Language Arts* 56 (April 1979): 408–12.

23 Townsend, John Rowe. *Written for Children: An Outline of English-Language Children's Literature.* New York: Lippincott, 1974.

24 Women on Words and Images. *Dick and Jane as Victims: Sex Stereotyping in Children's Readers.* Princeton, N. J.: Carolingian, 1972.

Involving Children in Realistic Fiction

INTERACTION with realistic fiction allows children to vicariously survive on uninhabited islands, solve mysteries that mystify even Sherlock Holmes, and ride the wind on the back of a black stallion. These stories also contain some extremely sensitive and controversial subjects and may relate to sexism, violence, death, and nontraditional living styles.

If realistic fiction is to meet children's needs by offering them opportunities to identify with others, extend their horizons, and lead to personal insights, then adults who work with children must be aware of a wide range of realistic fiction and activities that encourage children in this growth.

It is not necessary, or even advisable, to include literature-related activities with all realistic fiction, but some seem very appropriate for this genre. This section considers how realistic fiction may be used to stimulate role-playing experiences that strengthen children's understanding of the world around them and offers suggestions for handling real problems. The text also takes an in-depth look at the development of children's literature units that stress themes of island survival and survival in mountains, canyons, and tundra. In addition to activities and discussions that stress the setting's influence upon the conflicts in the stories, this unit also relates literature to the science curriculum through activities that increase children's understanding of geography and botany.

This chapter also stresses how literature can be used to develop an appreciation for the contributions of females and an understanding of the various roles portrayed by both males and females. Finally, the chapter presents questioning strategies that could be used to accompany realistic fiction or any other genre of literature.

USING REALISTIC FICTION DURING ROLE PLAYING AND BIBLIOTHERAPY

Role playing is an oral creative dramatics activity in which children consider a problem or the possible actions of people and then act out the situations as they believe they might unfold. Laurie and Joseph Braga, in *Learning and Growing: A Guide to Child Development* (5) give several reasons for encouraging role playing with children. First, they stress that role playing helps young children develop an understanding of the world around them. Through playing roles of various people such as teachers, doctors, and police officers, they learn about their world, learn important social skills, and learn about the important contributions of many people in our society. Second, they suggest that children's understanding of various ways to handle problems is enhanced through role-playing experiences in which they focus on common problem situations, play the roles of the people concerned, switch roles to develop understandings of other points of view, and talk about what happened, why it happened, and what they think should be done. The Bragas feel that adults can learn a great deal about children as they listen to responses during role-playing activities and follow-up discussions.

Literature can be the stimulus for involving children in both of these purposes for role-playing activities. For young children, realistic picture books about doctors, dentists, and other neighborhood helpers could be used to encourage them to act out the roles of adults with whom they come in contact. Such role playing could decrease fears by having children experience a role before facing a real situation. Books about families encourage children to role play interactions between different members of a family or the people who might be included in an extended family.

The plots in realistic fiction provide many opportunities for children to role play problem situations. Sutherland and Arbuthnot (16) recommend that literature selected for stimulating, thought-provoking problem situations should (1) contain characters who are well developed and have clearly defined problem situations, (2) have plots that contain logical stopping places so that children can role play the endings, (3) include problems such as universal fears and concerns that allow children to identify with the situations, and (4) include problems that help students develop their own personal value systems.

Adults who use literature in role playing may either choose stories in which a problem is developed to a certain point and then have children role play the unfinished situation, or they may have them role play various solutions to problems after they have read or listened to the whole story.

The steps recommended by Fannie and George Shaftel in *Role-Playing for Social Values* (15) may be used when guiding older children in a literature related, role-playing experience. First, the adult introduces and reads the problem story to the children. During the introduction, children are helped to think about the situation and how it might be solved. Second, children are encouraged to describe the characters in the story; then, parts for the first role-playing situation are chosen. Third, the adult discusses the responsibility of the audience, suggests observations that children could make, and encourages them to consider the reasonableness of the solution. Fourth, players discuss what they will do during the role-playing activity. Fifth, the role-playing problem situation is performed; each person plays the role of the character the person represents. Sixth, the adult leads an after-role-playing discussion, while the audi-

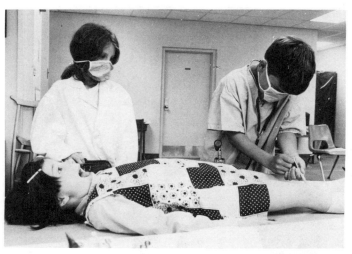

Children learn about their world as they play the roles of doctor, nurse, and patient after reading a story about a hospital.

ence and the characters discuss the actions, consequences, and possible alternative behaviors of the characters. Seventh, the role-playing situation is reenacted using new actions and solutions suggested during the discussion. Eighth, the adult again leads a discussion focused upon the different solutions to the problem. Finally, the children assess the possible outcomes of each portrayal and draw conclusions about the best way or ways to handle the problem.

The realistic fiction selections discussed earlier offer considerable stimulus for role-playing problem situations. The books are organized according to their content, and adults may refer to this source when searching for specific types of situations connected with family life, interpersonal relationships, and physical and emotional maturity. The following books contain problem situations that adults have used to stimulate role-playing experiences:

Family Life

1 Responsibility toward family members and friends, *The Moffats*, by Eleanor Estes. Rufus's friend Hughie feels unhappy during the first day of school. In fact, Hughie runs away, causing Rufus to follow him and persuade him to return. Rufus then helps Hughie return to the school. Ask children to pretend they are Rufus and Hughie. If they were Rufus, what arguments would they use to persuade Hughie to stay in school or return to school?

2 Responsibility toward family members, *Meet the Austins,* by Madeleine L'Engle.

The Austin parents include their children in many important family discussions and stress the importance of sharing family responsibilities. Ask children to pretend that they are family members and role play what they believe is meant by responsibility toward the family. The conflicts between Maggy and various Austin family members are also useful for role playing.

Family Disturbances

1 A family facing difficulties adjusting to a new culture, *Call Me Danica,* by Winifred Madison.

When a family moves from Europe to Canada, several problems must be overcome. Ask children to role play the scene in the restaurant when Mama becomes chef but runs into difficulty because the men do not want to work for a woman. Ask them to consider the feelings of both Mama and the men and to consider the scene in which her children try to convince her that she can open her own restaurant and become her own boss.

2 Problems connected with surviving without a father, *Mama,* by Lee Bennett Hopkins.

Ask children how they could convince Mama that they love her for herself and not for the stolen gifts she brings them.

Interpersonal Relationships

1 The loss of a former "best" friend and the meaning of friendship, *A Secret Friend,* by Marilyn Sachs. Encourage children to empathize with Jessica as she tries to regain Wendy's friendshhip. What would they do and say in that situation?

2 Being accepted by others, *Take Wing,* by Jean Little.

There are many scenes illustrating relationships between a mentally handicapped child and his parents, siblings, and peers. (There are numerous books in the section, "Dealing with Handicaps" (pp. 385–88), that suggest role-playing situations concerning children with physical handicaps, hearing losses, visual and mental handicaps.)

3 Relationships with aging grandparents, *How Does It Feel to Be Old,* by Norma Farber.

Ask children to think about all of the good and bad things suggested in the book that relate to growing old. Have them role play a situation revolving around each person who might have a conversation with grandmother about the positive side of becoming older.

Physical Maturity

1 Overcoming problems related to physical characteristics, *The Ears of Louis* or *The Unmaking of Rabbit,* by Constance Greene.

Encourage children to emphathize with Louis's or Paul's feelings about their big ears. How would they react to taunts of "Elephant Boy" or teasing about a pink nose? Ask them to role play scenes between Louis and his best friend, Louis and his friendly neighbor, Louis and his classmates, and Louis and the older boys who want him to join them for a football game.

2 Overcoming problems related to physical characteristics, *Blubber,* by Judy Blume.

This book contains many episodes of insensitivity between children and the girl who is overweight.

These stories allow children to empathize with characters who have problems that many children in elementary school may experience. Through role playing, they may discover ways to handle problems and increase their sensitivity to the problems of others.

In recent years, reading and interacting with particular books have been suggested as methods for individuals to gain insights into their own problems. *Bibliotherapy,* according to the *Dictionary of Education* (7), means the "use of books to influence the total development, a process of interaction between the reader and literature which is used for personality assessment, adjustment, growth, clinical and mental hygiene purposes; a concept that ideas inherent in selecting reading material can have a therapeutic effect upon the mental or physical ills of the reader" (p. 58). Using this definition, everyone can be helped through reading; bibliotherapy is a process in which every literate person participates at some time. In this context, it is "seen as the self-examination and insights that are gained from reading, no matter what the source. The source can be fiction or nonfiction; the reading can be directed (in settings ranging from reading guidance to formal therapy), self directed, or accidental. The reader might begin reading when actively looking for insights or the insights might come unexpectedly. In any case, the insight is utilized to create a richer and healthier life" (2, p. 21).

Joanne Bernstein, in *Books to Help Children Cope with Separation and Loss* (2), suggests that adults can use books to help children gain insights into their own lives and to help them identify with others if adults are knowledgeable in these areas: (1) knowing how and when to introduce the materials, (2) being sufficiently familiar with the materials, and (3) knowing each child's particular need. Bernstein stresses that if books are used to help children cope with their problems, adults should not force books upon them; instead, they should have a selection of materials from which children choose and then be patient until children are ready to use them. After a book has been read, adults should be available for discussion, or more important, for listening. During a discussion, children can talk about the actions and feelings of the characters in the story, suggest areas in which they agree and disagree with the characters, consider the consequences of the character's actions, and talk about other ways that a problem might be approached. There are other times when an adult should not intrude with any formalized discussion but should be available as someone ready to listen with empathy.

Many books provide additional resources for university students who are interested in bibliotherapy. Bernstein's book contains a bibliography of adult references pertaining to bibliotherapy and an extensive annotated bibliography of children's books that deal with accepting a new sibling; going to a new school; getting used to a new neighborhood; coping with death, divorce, desertion, serious illness, and displacement due to war; and dealing with foster care, accepting stepparents, and understanding adoption.

MORAL DEVELOPMENT IN REALISTIC FICTION

Contemporary realistic fiction contains many moments of crisis when characters make moral decisions. Cheryl Gosa (8) contends that when selecting literature to share with children, if adults expect children to understand the decision-making process of the story characters, they should be aware of the level of the decision that characters are making. In addition, Gosa believes that adults should consider whether or not children are at the stage when they can appreciate that decision. She contends that Lawrence Kohlberg's six stages of moral development (17) are appropriate for categorizing the decision-making processes in realistic fiction. There are no age levels assigned to Kohlberg's stages since individuals of the same age may be reasoning at different stages. Gosa states, "The major implication of Kohlberg's research for children's literature is that a child prior to age ten–twelve is rarely capable of Stage VI decision making (the child conforms to avoid self-condemnation), and unfortunately children's fiction spanning ages two to roughly sixteen is loaded with moral decisions, the majority of which are resolved by Stage VI values even if the protagonist is very young. If Kohlberg is right, and there is good reason to believe he is, fiction containing these high level decisions is meaningless for early character development . . . and beyond the level of their readers" (p. 530).

Students of children's literature may find it valuable and thought provoking to consider the stages of moral decisions represented by the characters in children's books. Chart 9-2 identifies Kohlberg's six stages of development and lists decisions made by characters in books written for children from approximately age four through age twelve.

As can be seen from the chart, the only book in this group that relies on Stage VI decisions is *Queen of Hearts,* which was also written for older readers. These decision-making processes may be used for discussions as children consider the options open to the characters and how they might have responded in similar circumstances. Adults may find it beneficial to analyze the stages in decision making required when choosing appropriate literature.

USING CHILDREN'S INTEREST IN SURVIVAL TO MOTIVATE READING AND INTERACTION WITH LITERATURE

The survival adventures found in realistic fiction have many plots that portray physical survival and increased emotional maturity of the main characters. The plots and strong characterizations encourage children to live these adventures vicariously. The physical characteristics described in the stories show children how to develop an understanding of the importance of setting when it causes major conflicts in the story. University students have used children's interest in physical and emotional survival to develop stimulating literature-related activities to share with children.

Two very interesting instructional activities developed by university students and then shared with classrooms of children centered around the survival theme. One group developed an in-depth literature unit around "Physical and Emotional Survival on Islands." Another group chose "Physical and Emotional Survival on Mountains, in Canyons, and on Arctic Tundra." Each group organized its units by using the webbing process.

Island Survival

The students who chose island survival identified the following books that develop themes around an individual's or a small group's ability to survive physically and grow in maturity because of their experiences:

> *Island of the Blue Dolphins,* by Scott O'Dell
> *Call It Courage,* by Armstrong Sperry
> *The Cay,* by Theodore Taylor
> *The Swiss Family Robinson,* by Johann David Wyss

The group read the books and identified their central theme and the main areas that challenge the character's physical survival. Some were natural environmental characteristics or climatic conditions of the islands caused by their geographical locations; others were survival needs related to other human needs. This central theme and six subtopics associated with survival were identified in the following first phase of the "Survival on Islands" web (see Figure 9–1). During the next phase,

CHART 9—2
Decision Making in Realistic Fiction

Kohlberg's Stages of Moral Development	Ages 4-7 *Send Wendell* by Genevieve Gray	Ages 6-8 *Benjie on His Own* by Joan M. Lexau	Ages 8-10 *Tales of a Fourth Grade Nothing* by Judy Blume	Ages 10+ *Queen of Hearts* by Vera and Bill Cleaver
1. Pre-moral level *Stage I:* Punishment and obedience orientation. Rules obeyed to avoid punishment.		Benjie obeys the big boys, he turns his pockets out to show them he has no money, he is very frightened.	Three-year-old Fudge eats to avoid father's punishment. Nine-year-old Peter believes Fudge would behave if he was punished. Father allows Fudge to be in a commercial so firm does not lose account.	Twelve-year-old Wilma tells her brother not to ring their grandmother's doorbell if he "wants to live tomorrow."
Stage II: Naive instrumental hedonism. The child conforms in order to obtain rewards.			Peter obeys his mother and tricks Fudge so they can go to lunch. Fudge stops complaining when he gets popcorn. Peter's puppy is a reward for his good behavior.	
2. Morality of conventional role conformity. *Stage III:* Good boy morality of maintaining good relations. The child conforms to avoid disapproval.	Six-year-old Wendell happily goes on errands because he loves Mama and likes to help her.	Benjie does not want his grandmother to walk him home after school but he "puts up with it." Benjie promises to be good while grandmother is in the hospital.	Peter does not want to share his room but knows there is no point in arguing with his mother. Peter says thank you for a gift he does not like.	Wilma, with reservations, agrees to stay with her convalescent grandmother because her parents and grandmother need help.
Stage IV: Authority maintaining morality. The child conforms to avoid censure by authorities and resulting guilt.	Wendell's self-esteem increases as his uncle recognizes his worth. He now says he is busy and suggests they send someone else.			Wilma forces herself to accompany an elderly woman into the room of a screaming man in the nursing home.
3. Morality of self-accepted principles. *Stage V:* Morality of contract. A duty is defined in terms of contract, general avoidance of violation of the rights of others.		Benjie wants to ask grandmother to wait for him but does not because he knows it would worry her. Benjie laughs because he knows his grandmother is trying to cheer him up.		Wilma does not want her grandmother forced to accept care from adults who have a condescending attitude toward elderly people. Wilma is happy when her grandmother locks the Screechfields out of the house even though she will need to move back.

CHART 9–2 *(cont.)*

Decision Making in Realistic Fiction

Kohlberg's Stages of Moral Development	Ages 4-7 *Send Wendell* by Genevieve Gray	Ages 6-8 *Benjie on His Own* by Joan M. Lexau	Ages 8-10 *Tales of a Fourth Grade Nothing* by Judy Blume	Ages 10+ *Queen of Hearts* by Vera and Bill Cleaver
Stage VI: Morality of individual principles of conscience. The child conforms to avoid self-condemnation.				Wilma makes the decision, over the objection of her parents, to stay with her grandmother. She feels it is the right action for herself and her grandmother.

the group identified subjects related to each subtopic on the web. The extended web shown in Figure 9–2 was developed by the group.

After finishing the web, the group planned learning activities that encouraged children to develop an understanding of the importance of setting, to realize that setting may cause major conflicts, and to increase their understanding of each identified physical survival topic. The university students also identified many topics listed on their webs that were related to the upper elementary science curriculum. They realized that they could use interesting literature selections to increase children's understanding of scientific principles. They developed activities to stimulate oral language, written language, and artistic interpretations of the plots and characters. The following examples are taken from the physical survival activities developed around the *Island of the Blue Dolphins.* Several activities are included for each main subtopic in the web to allow the reader to visualize the types of physical survival activities that are possible in the classroom. Many of these activities are also approriate for discussion in the library.

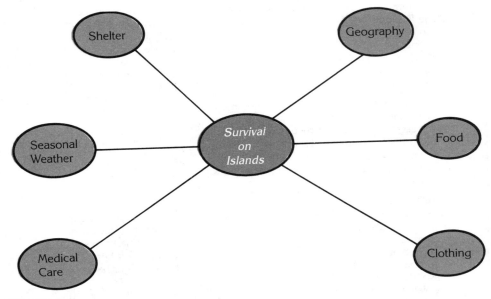

FIGURE 9–1

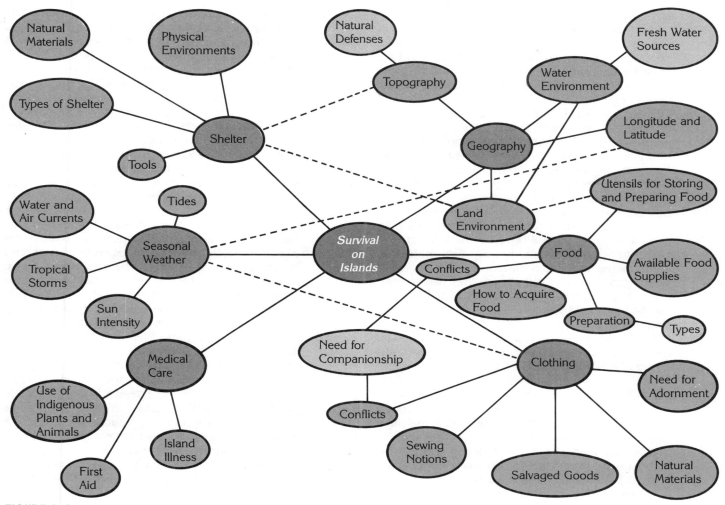

FIGURE 9–2

Physical Survival Activities Developed
Around Scott O'Dell's Island of the Blue Dolphins

I   Seasonal Weather

A. Karana's life revolves around the seasons; she calculates time and the jobs she must do according to the seasons. Lead a discussion with the children that helps them identify the seasons on the island, the characteristics of the seasons, and the reasons for Karana's total involvement in the seasons. O'Dell's text provides many clues to seasonal weather: the flowers are plentiful in the spring because of heavy winter rains; in the spring, the birds leave the island and fly to the north; Karana gathers food for the winter; storms with winds and high waves are described.

B. On a large mural draw the Island of the Blue Dolphins depicting the different seasons and weather conditions described in the book.

C. Pretend to be Karana and write a dairy: include five entries from each season on the island. In the entries, describe seasonal weather and activities during that season.

II. Medical Care
   A. Use of Indigenous Plants and Animals—In the wilderness, accidents or illnesses are dangerous; there are no doctors or drugstores. Read page 96 to find out what Karana used on Rontu's wound. Find this plant (coral bush) in a reference book and consider why it would help Rontu's wound.
   B. First Aid and Use of Indigenous Plants and Animals—Pretend that you and your family are isolated on an island in the Pacific. Consider the minor illnesses or accidents that could easily occur while on the island. For example, sunburn is common in warm climates. Other problems might include poisonous stings, broken legs, stomach upsets, headaches, and wounds. Research some plants, herbs, and other first aid resources that might be found on the island. Make an illustrated island survival book for medical care; include drawings of plants, their medical properties, and sketches of first aid measures. After this is finished, lead a discussion in which the children consider Karana's personal medical needs and how she handled her problems.

III. Clothing
   A. Natural Materials—Karana and her people lived on an island where their only sources of clothing were natural materials—plant and animal—found on the island or in the sea. What garments did Karana make for herself? What natural materials did she use? Divide into groups and investigate the procedures Karana would need to use, and the time involved in making a skirt from yucca fibers, a belt or a pair of sandals from sealskin, an otter cape, or a skirt of cormorant skins. (Even the needle and thread were made from natural sources.) If possible, try making a garment from natural materials. After the natural materials and the procedures are described, lead a discussion to help children develop an understanding of the importance of obtaining clothing in an isolated area and the influence the need to obtain clothing has on the characters' actions. Encourage them to consider how their own lives are different because of the ease of acquiring clothing or the materials for clothing. Children can identify the natural materials available in their environment if they were required, like Karana, to make their clothing from original natural sources.
   B. Natural Materials and the Need for Adornment—Karana and the women of her island wanted flowers and jewelry that would improve their appearance. Ask the group to consider why Karana found satisfaction in making a flower wreath for her hair and for Rontu's neck. Have them investigate the types of flowers that Karana might have used to make her wreath. If possible, ask the children to make their own flower wreaths using flowers in their own locality. Karana was also fond of jewelry. Ask the group to consider the implications of Karana's spending five nights to make a circlet of abalone shells as a present for the Aleut girl, Tutok. Allow children to examine jewelry made from seashells. If possible, have them make their own jewelry from seashells. This can also be an opportunity for investigating the types of seashells that might be available on Karana's island.

IV. Food
   A. Available Food Supplies—Make a list of the foods Karana ate in the story. References are made to the scarlet apples that grow on cactus bushes (tunas) and foods from the sea such as abalones and scallops. Research the possible sources that might be available on a Pacific island. Investigate several cookbooks and make an Island of the Blue Dolphins Cookbook using the foods and seasonings Karana might find.
   B. Utensils for Storing and Preparing Food—How did Karana fix her food? Where did she store the food to preserve it and protect it from animals? Karana had to make all of the utensils and storage containers for her food and water. Draw or make a list of five things Karana had to make in order to cook or store her food. Tell or show how she made these utensils or storage containers. Why was it important that Karana create each item? What could have happened if she had not created ways to store food? What impact did preparing and storing food have on her use of time and the plot of the story?
   C. How to Acquire Food—Women in Karana's village were forbidden to make weapons. What is the significance for Karana when, in spite of her fear, she makes weapons to protect herself and to obtain food? Why did she think of destructive winds when she considered the advisability of making weapons? Draw several weapons that Karana created, explain how she made them, and identify the natural resources she used.
   D. How to Acquire Food and Available Food Supplies—Rontu and Karana encounter and later hunt a devilfish. From the description on pages 103–4 and 118–24 try to determine another name for a devilfish.

Use reference books and pay close attention to the details. Why did Karana spend her whole winter crafting a special kind of spear to hunt the devilfish?

E. Conflicts between Food or Clothing Sources and Need for Companionship—A conflict arises for Karana when she begins to make friends with some animals on the island. What is the significance of her statement on page 156 that she would never kill another otter, seal, cormorant, or wild dog? Encourage children to debate this issue as it could relate to their own lives. (Another topic for debate is the destruction of animals such as the sea otter. Karana decided to stop killing the otters even for a cape and would not tell the white men where the otters were located. Ask children to investigate the controversy connected with killing or saving the sea otter and then, taking a pro or con position, debate the issue.)

V. Geography

A. Topography—Based on Karana's description of the Island of the Blue Dolphins in chapter two and other parts of the book, make a map of the island. The map should include a scale and symbols. To make the scale, the equivalent length of a league must be determined. In her descriptions of where the sun rises and sets, Karana has given the north, south, east, and west directions. Place these symbols on the map. Chart the wind directions on the map. (The island is two leagues long and league wide. A league is equivalent to about three miles. The island looks like a dolphin lying on its side. The tail points toward sunrise, which would be east, and the nose points toward sunset, which would be west.)

B. Physical Environment, Longitude and Latitude—The Island of the Blue Dolphins is real. On a large map or atlas that shows the California coastline try to find San Nicolas, which is located about seventy-five miles southwest of Los Angeles. Identify the longitude and latitude of the island. What is the effect of this longitude and latitude upon the island? Compare a description of San Nicolas in a reference book with the description of the island. Are there any similarities or differences? If someone were marooned on an island, what longitude and latitude would that person choose in order to have a natural environment most advantageous to survival? Write a short story describing the setting and how one would survive on the island.

C. Topography, Physical Environment—Several geographical terms are used in *Island of the Blue Dol-*

phins. Below is a list of some of these terms. To develop an understanding of the geography of the island, define each term as used in the story, find pictures illustrating each term, and draw examples of the terms as they looked on Karana's island. Try to see each one through Karana's eyes. What was the significance of each feature for Karana's survival?

mesa   cliffs   ravine
harbor   canyon   spring
cove

VI. Shelter

A. Types of Shelters, Natural Materials, Physical Environments—In her struggles for survival, Karana constructed both a fenced-in house (pp. 74–76) and a cave dwelling (p. 89). Reread the descriptions of each house and consider Karana's needs when she constructed these shelters. What was the advantage of each type of shelter? How did each shelter relate to the natural materials found upon the island, the physical environment of the island, and the tools that Karana had available for her use? Why did the need for shelter play such an important part in the development of the story and in the use of Karana's time and energy? Choose one of her island shelters and build a model of the shelter. Look at our own environment. If people were isolated in their physical environment without the houses and other buildings that are there at this time, what type of natural shelter would they construct? Write a short story describing the decision-making processes as they think about the type of shelter they will construct. In this story consider the need for protection against seasonal weather changes, natural predators that might harm them or take their food supplies, topography of the land that could be used to their advantage, the proximity of the shelter to life-sustaining food and water supplies, and the availability of building materials and tools needed for construction. Build a model of this shelter.

Similar activities were developed around each island survival book. Discussions and activities stressed the importance of setting in the developing conflict and the effects upon the growth of the characters as they overcame problems connected with setting or loneliness. Comparisons were also made between the various characters, their settings, and their physical and emotional strategies that led to survival. A final activity was developed in which the classroom was set up as an island. Students divided into groups according to shelter, food, clothing, geography, medical care, and seasonal weather. They chose and developed an activity that represented their area of interest during Island Day. Shelters were constructed in which the various interest centers were located. Students shared tool making and cooking experiences. Art and science experiences were used to depict weather, geography, clothing, food and shelter. There was a special demonstration showing possible medical care needed for island survival. While learning about the impact of setting upon characters in survival literature, the students also discovered much about their own environments and how they might conquer their own worlds.

Survival in Mountains, Canyons, and Tundra

Three books by Jean Craighead George stimulated interesting discovery activities related to survival in the mountains of northeastern United States, in a canyon in the southwestern United States, and on the Arctic tundra: *My Side of the Mountain, River Rats, Inc.,* and *Julie of the Wolves.* The stories also stress emotional and personal maturation and physical survival.

After developing a web similar to the one developed for island survival, upper elementary students compared the three different settings according to their geographical locations, topography, longitude and latitude, and physical environments; their natural food supplies; clothing requirements of the main characters; any medical care required and how they resolved this problem; the seasonal changes in weather that influenced the characters' actions; and the types of shelters the characters made out of natural materials. Students compared the actions of the main characters in each story and identified different ways that the characters responded to personal and environmental problems. A large chart (see Chart 9–3) developed by one class helped them define these differences. It contained the categories of Geography, Food, Clothing, Medical Care, Seasonal Weather, and Shelter.

The description of edible foods and their growing locations found in *My Side of the Mountain* and *River Rats, Inc.* relate to topics studied in the science curriculum. To highlight these relationships, students reviewed the types and environmental implications of vegetation that grew along the water and in the desert regions described in *River Rats, Inc.* They identified the edible plants that Joe and Crowbar found in each location and the procedures the boys used to prepare and store the foods. For example, page 70 lists the following water-loving plants that created either a beautiful "Inner Kingdom" or equally important, nourishing foods: cottonwoods, watercress, cattails, monkey flowers, maidenhair fern, wild garlic, and Indian vine.

In *My Side of the Mountain,* they identified the larger trees that covered the slopes of a northeastern mountain—hemlock, oak, walnut, and hickory. They located references to plants that grew next to springs decorated with "flowers, ferns, moss, weeds—everything that loved water" (p. 30). Then, they followed Sam Gribley's search for edible food and his steps in the preparation and methods for storing the food. Some plant foods included hickory nuts and salt from hickory limbs (p. 23), apples (p. 24), walnuts, cattails, arrow leaf (p. 24), bulbs of dogtooth violets (pp. 27–28), dandelion greens (p. 28), strawberries (p. 35), wild garlic, jack-in-the-pulpit roots (p. 45), daisies, inner bark from the poplar tree, acorns (p. 62), sassafras roots (p. 66), pennyroyal, winterberry leaves (p. 67), arrowleaf bulbs, cattail tubers, bulrush roots, and wild onions (p. 81).

Referring to Laurence Pringle's *Wild Foods: A Beginner's Guide to Identifying, Harvesting and Preparing Safe and Tasty Plants from the Outdoors* (11) and Euell Gibbons's *Stalking the Wild Asparagus* (6), they investigated wild plants mentioned by Jean George, read suggestions for identifying and preparing them, compared them with Sam Gribley's identification and preparation, and identified which plants might be found near their own homes. (Warnings were also stressed; many wild plants are dangerous to eat. Therefore, it was recommended that children not eat any plant unless they were accompanied by someone who knew exactly which plants were safe and which were dangerous.)

Because cattails were mentioned in both books and were available near the school, the students gathered them and tried grinding them into flour. They also followed Pringle's suggestions for boiling cattail rhizomes and using them as a potato substitute. This experience increased their empathy toward the characters and the hard work that accompanied survival on natural foods.

This research into natural foods and their preparation was also related to the climatic conditions, geographical locations, and the amount of water available for plants in both stories.

DEVELOPING AN APPRECIATION FOR INDIVIDUALS— IMPROVING SELF-ESTEEM AND UNDERSTANDING

Researchers and writers in educational publications have evaluated the quantity and quality of sexist and nonsexist stories found in children's textbooks and, until quite recently, found them lacking in their portrayal of positive female roles. Myra Sadker and David Sadker (14) say that "a growing body of research . . . attests to loss of female potential as girls go through

CHART 9–3

	Catskill Mountains	Southwest Canyon	Arctic Tundra

Geography
  topography
  longitude and latitude
  physical environment
  fresh water sources			

Food
  available supplies
  how to acquire food
  how to create utensils
  food preparation			

Clothing
  requirements related to environment
  natural materials
  sewing notions			

Medical Care
  major concerns
  first aid
  use of indigenous plants and animals			

Seasonal Weather
  sun intensity
  seasonal storms
  air currents			

Shelter
  requirements due to weather
  requirements due to topography
  natural materials
  types of shelter tools			

school, and many writers have analyzed the way sex stereotyping occurs in classrooms across the country—from sexist teaching patterns to segregated activities. One key way that girls learn to undervalue themselves is through the books they read. When children open elementary school texts, they read most often about the activities and adventures of boys" (p. 231). The research discussed on pages 374–75 attested to the male and female stereotyping that is also found in children's literature.

Children's literature students have identified literature suggesting that females and males do not necessarily act in stereotypic behavior patterns. Books that illustrate nonstereotypic behavioral patterns can help teachers, librarians, and parents who wish to combat stereotypes. Many of the realistic fiction books discussed in the first part of this chapter are excellent sources that illustrate a wide range of behavioral patterns. The following books are categorized according to specific stereotypic behaviors:

1 Girls and boys can overcome great conflicts in nature and survive:
    Female: Scott O'Dell's *Island of the Blue Dolphins*
    Male: Armstrong Sperry's *Call It Courage*
2 Young girls and young boys can be brave and intelligent:
    Female: Beverly Cleary's *Ramona The Brave*
    Male: Eleanor Schick's *Joey on His Own*
3 Girls can be independent and take care of their younger siblings or pets:
    Female: E. L. Konigsburg's *From the Mixed-Up Files of Mrs. Basil E. Frankweiler*
    Female: Theodore Taylor's *The Trouble with Tuck*

4 Girls and boys can be intelligent and curious:
Female: Louis Fitzhugh's *Harriet the Spy*
Male: Donald J. Sobol's *Encyclopedia Brown Sets The Pace*

5 Boys can express feelings of fear. Facing death is not the only way to demonstrate courage:
Male: Maia Wojciechowska's *Shadow of a Bull*

6 Boys can be shy or gentle:
Male: Maria Gripe's *Elvis and His Secret*

These books have led to interesting discussions and comparisons as children learn that both boys and girls can demonstrate a wide range of acceptable behaviors.

DEVELOPING QUESTIONING STRATEGIES WITH REALISTIC FICTION

Guiding Discussions

Not all literature selections should be accompanied by questioning. However, librarians and teachers responsible for encouraging children to think about and react to literature in a variety of ways find it helpful to have a framework for designing questions that assist children in focusing upon certain aspects of a story and upon questions that require higher-level thought processes.

Teachers and librarians who wish to develop such questioning strategies will find assistance in taxonomies of reading comprehension such as the one developed by Benjamin Bloom (4) or Thomas Barrett (1). The questions that follow are examples of the types that can be developed around realistic fiction following the four comprehension levels identified by Barrett: literal recognition or recall, inference, evaluation, and appreciation. They are developed around Katherine Paterson's *Jacob Have I Loved*. The book is appropriate for the upper-elementary and middle-school grades. These questions are only a guide and suggest the types of questions that might be developed around any book. In addition, there are many more questions than a librarian or teacher might choose to focus upon. The number of questions are included to illustrate a variety of examples from each subsection of the taxonomy.

Literal Recognition

Literal recognition requires children to identify information that is stated in the literature. Children may be required to recall the information from memory after reading or listening to a story, or they may locate information while reading a selection. These literal level questions often use words such as *who*,

what, where, and *when*. The following are examples of literal recognition or recall questions:

1 Where does the story *Jacob Have I Loved* take place? When does the story take place? Who are the characters in the story? (recall of details)

2 What was the sequence of events that led Louise to believe that Caroline was the favored child in the family? (recall of sequence of events)
What was the sequence of events that caused Louise to

Nonstereotypic realistic fiction can help children overcome sex stereotypes.

move from an island to a mountain community? (recall of sequence of events)

3 Compare the author's physical description of Louise and Caroline. Compare the way Louise thought the family treated her, with the way she thought they treated her twin sister, Caroline. (recall of comparisons)

4 Describe Louise's response to the story about the birth of the twins, Louise and Caroline.

Why did the people living on the island consider Wallace a coward?

How does Grandma respond to Caroline, to Louise, to Captain Wallace, to her son, and to her daughter-in-law? (recall of character traits)

Inference

When children infer an answer to a question, they must go beyond the information provided by the author and hypothesize about such items as details, main ideas, sequence of events that might have led to an occurrence, and cause and effect relationships. This is usually considered a higher-level thought process; the answers are not specifically stated within the text. Examples of inferential questions include the following:

1 At the end of the book, Joseph Wojtkiewicz says "God in heaven's been raising you for this valley from the day you were born." What do you believe he meant by this statement? (inferring supporting details)

2 What do you believe is the theme of the book *Jacob Have I Loved?* What message do you think the author was trying to express to the reader? (inferring main idea)

3 Think about the Captain Wallace who is such a part of Louise's story. Compare that character with the one who left the island when he was a young man. How do you believe they are alike and how do you believe they are different? (inferring comparisons)

4 If you identified any changes in Captain Wallace, what do you believe might have caused them?

Why do you believe Louise dreamed about Caroline's death?

Why do you believe she felt both wild exultation and then terrible guilt after these dreams? (inferring cause and effect relationships)

5 What do you believe caused Louise to change her mind about wanting Hiram Wallace to be an islander who escaped rather than a Nazi spy? What is Louise saying about herself when she emphasizes the word *escaped?*

Why do you believe Louise became so upset whenever she was called "Wheeze"?

Why do you think Louise was so upset when Call invited Caroline to join Call and Louise during their visit to the captain?

At the end of the book, after Louise has delivered twins to a mountain family, she becomes very anxious over the healthier twin.

Why do you think she gave this advice, "You should hold him. Hold him as much as you can. Or let his mother hold him" (p. 215)?

What does this reaction say about Louise's own character and the changes in character that took place in her lifetime? (inferring character traits)

6 There were several places in the book when the action and outcome of the story might have changed if characters had acted in different ways. (Students can read or listen to the book up to a certain point and predict what the outcome will be.)

At the end of chapter 4, a mysterious man leaves the boat and walks alone toward an abandoned house. Who do you think he is? How do you think this man will influence the story?

At the end of chapter 12, Caroline finds and uses Louise's hidden hand lotion. What do you think will happen after Louise angrily breaks the bottle and runs out of the house?

At the close of chapter 14, the captain has offered to send Caroline to Baltimore to continue her musical education. How do you think Caroline, her parents, and Louise will react to this suggestion?

At the end of chapter 17, Louise and the captain are discussing what she plans to do with her life. Louise responds that she wants to become a doctor but cannot leave her family. Knowing Louise and her family, how do you think the story will end? (predicting outcomes)

Evaluation

Evaluative questions require children to make judgments about the content of the literature by comparing it with external criteria such as authorities on a subject or internal criteria such as the reader's experience or knowledge. The following are examples of evaluative questions:

1 Do you agree that Louise would not have been accepted as a student in a medical college? Why or why not? This story took place in the 1940s; would the author have been able to include the same scene between a woman and a university advisor if the story had taken place in the 1980s? Why or why not? (judgments of adequacy or validity)

2 What do you think the author meant by the reference to the quote, "Jacob have I loved, but Esau have I hated." How does this biblical line relate to the book? Do you think it is a good title for the book? Why or why not? (judgment of appropriateness)

3 Was Louise right in her judgment that her parents always favored Caroline? What caused her to reach her final decision? Do you believe Louise made the right decision when she left the island? Why or why not? (judgment of worth, desirability, or acceptability)

Appreciation

Appreciative questions require a heightening of the sensitivity to the techniques authors use in order to create an emotional impact within their readers. Many of the questions require children to respond emotionally to the plot, identify with the characters, react to an author's use of language, and react to an author's ability to create a visual image through the choice of words in the text. The following are examples of appreciative questions:

1 How did you respond to the plot of the story? Did the author hold your interest? If so, how?
Do you believe the theme of the story was worthwhile? Why or why not? Pretend you are either recommending this book for someone else to read or recommending that this book not be read; what would you tell that person? (emotional response to plot or theme)

2 Have you ever felt, or known anyone who felt, like thirteen-year-old Louise or her twin sister, Caroline? What caused you or the person to feel that way?
How would you have reacted if you were thirteen-year-old Louise? How would you have reacted if you were Caroline? Pretend to be a grown-up Louise in chapter 18 talking with Mother about leaving the island. What emotions do you think your mother would feel when you respond, "I'm not going to rot here like Grandma" (p. 200)? How would you feel when she told you "I chose to leave my own people and build a life for myself somewhere else. I certainly wouldn't deny you that same choice. But . . . oh, Louise, we will miss you, your father and I" (p. 201)? (identification with characters and incidents)

3 How did the author encourage you to see the relationship between the island setting and the mountain-locked valley? Close your eyes and try to picture each setting. How are they alike? How are they different?
Pretend that you are Louise telling Joseph Wojtkiewicz about your island (p. 208). Describe the island so he and his daughters can see a land that is both similar to, and different from, their own valley (imagery).

These examples are not organized according to any sequence for presentation to children, but they do exemplify the range of questions that are considered when the focus is on strengthening the various comprehension abilities. Research does suggest, however, an effective order for presenting comprehension questions to children.

Oral Questioning Strategies That Focus, Extend, Clarify, and Raise Comprehension

Adults find the research reported by Robert Rudell (12) helpful when designing questions that encourage children to focus upon certain aspects of literature. These four strategies that encourage children to focus their attention, extend their answer, clarify a response, and raise the level of response have been proven, according to Ruddell, to be the most significant vehicles for effectively developing children's comprehension. These strategies, combined with questions developed around a taxonomy, provide a useful guide for adults who wish to increase their ability to lead oral discussions that encourage children to respond on several taxonomy levels. Definitions of each strategy and examples of these strategies developed around the literal, inferential, evaluative, and appreciative questions from *Jacob Have I Loved* are given below.

Focusing. Focusing questions allow children to center their attention upon a purpose for listening to or reading a story. This focusing question provides the mental set for the oral discussion that follows and often brings attention to the factual information in a story that must be understood before children can answer an inference question, provide an evaluation of what has been read, or respond emotionally to the theme, characters, and plot.

Extending. If the focus question has not provided the desired answer or included sufficient information, an extending question should be asked so that children can provide additional information on the subject. The extending question is asked on the same subject as the focusing question, and it is at the same comprehension level as the focusing question. Strategies such as "Is there anything else you can tell about the subject" or "Who has another idea about _____" allow an adult to probe further.

Clarifying. A clarifying question encourages children to explain or redefine previous information if the answer is unclear or if they have misinterpreted the question. Children may be asked to return to a previous comment in order to explain or redefine an answer. Sometimes it is necessary to go to a lower level of comprehension in order to clarify a statement. Questions such as "Do you mean that _____" or "Could you explain in more detail what happened to _____?" encourage children to rethink or clarify a point.

Raising. Finally, a raising strategy allows an adult to obtain additional information on the same subject but at a higher level of comprehension. Questions can be asked that shift the focus from a factual to an inferential level of comprehension or from a factual or inferential level to an evaluative or appreciative level.

Examples of Questioning Strategies That Exemplify the Four Strategies.   When using these strategies with the questions from *Jacob Have I Loved,* an adult might need the following sequential order of questioning that progresses from focusing, to extending, to clarifying, to raising:

Focusing: Literal recall of character traits:
Louise's mother and grandmother often tell the story about the birth of the twins. Describe Louise's response to this story.
Extending: Literal recall of character traits:
Who could give another idea about Caroline's refusing to breathe, the midwife trying to get her to breathe, and how happy everyone was when Caroline let out her first cry?
Clarifying: Literal recall of character traits:
Explain in more detail Louise's emotions when she hears about the attention paid to Caroline while she lies in a basket?
Raising from literal recall of character traits to inferring character traits:
At the end of this book, after Louise has delivered twins to a mountain family, she becomes very anxious about the healthier twin. Why do you think she gave the advice "You should hold him. Hold him as much as you can. Or let his mother hold him" (p. 215)? What does this reaction to the baby tell about Louise's character and the changes in her character that took place in her lifetime?
Raising to appreciative comprehension, identification with characters and incidents:
Have you ever felt or known anyone who felt like thirteen-year-old Louise when she listened to the story about her birth and thought "I felt cold all over, as though I was the newborn infant a second time, cast aside and forgotten"? (p. 15)
How would you have reacted if you were Louise and heard this story repeatedly? What experience do you think could make

you feel "cold all over"? If you were Caroline and heard this story?

SUMMARY

Activities suggested in this chapter stress the expansion of children's reactions to realistic fiction through role playing, bibliotherapy, units around survival literature, activities designed to increase an appreciation for the abilities of males and females, and questioning strategies.

The plots in realistic fiction provide many opportunities to role play problem situations, allowing children to learn more about their world and how they might solve problems. Adults may use literature to provide a stimulus for role playing either by reading to a certain point and having children role play the unfinished situation, or by having children role play various solutions to problems after reading or listening to the whole story. Realistic fiction has also been suggested as a means of allowing individuals to gain insights into their own problems through bibliotherapy.

The plots found in survival literature suggest both physical survival and increased emotional maturity of the main characters. The stories also stress the importance of a setting when it may create the major conflicts in the stories. An island survival unit and a unit around survival in mountains, canyons, and tundra suggest the importance of setting and how it may also be used to reinforce the science curriculum.

Researchers recommend that adults counteract stereotypic behavior and occupations found in some basal readers and literature by initiating corrective action, reviewing stories, and providing a balanced portrayal of the contributions and roles of both men and women. Children's literature provides one source of material for creating this balance.

The chapter concluded with examples of questioning strategies developed around a comprehensive taxonomy.

Suggested Activities for Children's Appreciation of Realistic Fiction

■ Using the criteria for selecting appropriate literature for role playing (page 410), develop a file of stories that have problem situations appropriate for elementary school children. Include stories that can be used by reading to a certain point and allowing children to role play possible solutions; also include stories that are more appropriate for role playing after an entire story has been read. Choose a role-playing situation and lead a role-playing activity with either a group of children or a peer group.

- Choose several books written for a specific age level. Analyze the decisions that main characters make according to Kohlberg's stages of moral development on pages 413–14. Discuss the books with several children from the specified age group. Do they understand the decision-making process?

- Choose another survival book listed on the "Survival on Islands" web. Develop instructional activities for the book that correspond with the web. Suggested books include *Call It Courage, The Cay, The Swiss Family Robinson, My Side of the Mountain, River Rats, Inc.,* or *Julie of the Wolves.*

- Review the stories in a basal reader, and evaluate their content according to stereotypic roles for either males or females. Assume that some corrective action might be required if a balanced portrayal of contributions of males and females is to occur, and identify several children's literature selections that could be used to balance a viewpoint. How could the literature be used in an instructional setting?

- Identify a list of children's literature sources that show many behavioral patterns for boys and girls, men and women.

- Develop a bibliography of books that illustrate nonstereotypic behavioral patterns in boys and girls. Write a short summary to describe the behavioral patterns that are shown in each book.

- Choose a realistic fiction book other than *Jacob Have I Loved.* Develop questioning strategies that follow a taxonomy of comprehension such as that developed by Barrett or Bloom.

References

1 Barrett, Thomas C. "Taxonomy of Reading Comprehension." *Reading 360 Monograph,* Lexington, Mass.: Ginn, 1972.

2 Bernstein, Joanne. *Books to Help Children Cope with Separation and Loss.* New York: Bowker, 1977.

3 Blatt, Gloria Toby. "Violence in Children's Literature: A Content Analysis of a Select Sampling of Children's Literature and a Study of Children's Responses to Literary Episodes Depicting Violence." East Lansing, Mich.: Michigan State University, 1972. University Microfilm, No. 72-29,931.

4 Bloom, Benjamin. *Taxonomy of Educational Objectives.* New York: Longmans, 1956.

5 Braga, Laurie, and Braga, Joseph. *Learning and Growing: A Guide to Child Development.* Englewood Cliffs, N. J.: Prentice-Hall, 1975.

6 Gibbons, Euell. *Stalking the Wild Asparagus.* New York: McKay, 1962, 1970.

7 Good, Carter. *Dictionary of Education.* New York: McGraw-Hill, 1969, 1973.

8 Gosa, Cheryl. "Moral Development in Current Fiction for Children and Young Adults." *Language Arts* 54 (May 1977): 529–36.

9 Graebner, Dianne Bennet. "A Decade of Sexism in Readers." *The Reading Teacher* 26 (October 1972): 52–58.

10 Moody, Mildred, and Limper, Hilda. *Bibliotherapy: Methods and Materials.* Chicago: American Library Association, 1971.

11 Pringle, Laurence. *Wild Foods: A Beginner's Guide to Identifying, Harvesting and Preparing Safe and Tasty Plants from the Outdoors.* Illustrated by Paul Breeden. New York: Four Winds, 1978.

12 Ruddell, Robert B. "Developing Comprehension Abilities: Implications from Research for an Instructional Framework." In *What Research Has to Say about Reading Instruction,* edited by S. J. Samuels, pp. 109–20. Newark, Del.: International Reading Association, 1978.

13 Rupley, William; Garcia, Jesus; and Longnion, Bonnie. "Sex Role Portrayal in Reading Materials: Implications for the 1980s." *The Reading Teacher* 34 (April 1981): 786–91.

14 Sadker, Myra Pollack, and Sadker, David Miller. *Now upon a Time: A Contemporary View of Children's Literature.* New York: Harper & Row, 1977.

15 Shaftel, Fannie R., and Shaftel, George. *Role-Playing for Social Values: Decision-Making in the Social Studies.* Englewood Cliffs, N. J.: Prentice-Hall, 1967.

16 Sutherland, Zena, and Arbuthnot, May Hill. *Children and Books.* Glenview, Ill.: Scott, Foresman, 1981.

17 Williams, Norman, and Williams, Sheila. *The Moral Development of Children.* New York: Macmillan, 1970.

CHILDREN'S LITERATURE

Amdur, Nikki. *One of Us.* Illustrated by Ruth Sanderson. Dial, 1981. (I:9–12+ R:5). A blind boy and caring for a rabbit help a girl adjust to a new school.

Bauer, Marion Dane. *Foster Child.* Seabury, 1977 (I:12+ R:6). Twelve-year-old Renny is placed into a foster home when her great-grandmother is taken ill. Problems arise because Pop Beck is attracted to young girls.

Bawden, Nina. *Kept in the Dark.* Lothrop, Lee & Shepard, 1982 (I:10+ R:7). A psychological thriller results when a previously unknown relative returns.

———. *The Peppermint Pig.* Lippincott, 1975 (I:9–12 R:6). Nine-year-old Poll, her mother, and the children move to rural Norfolk, England, when they sell their London home to pay for her boat fare to America.

———. *The Robbers.* Lothrop, Lee & Shepard, 1979 (I:8–12 R:5). Philip leaves the security of his grandmother's rural castle home to live with his remarried father in London. A different background allows him to experience other people's problems.

Benjamin, Carol Lea. *The Wicked Stepdog.* Crowell, 1982 (I:9–12 R:4). A twelve-year-old girl fears she is losing her father's love when he remarries.

Billington, Elizabeth. *Part-Time Boy.* Illustrated by Dianede Groat. Warne, 1979 (I:8–12 R:5). A director of a natural science center helps a ten-year-old accept himself and be accepted by others.

Blume, Judy. *Are You There God? It's Me, Margaret.* Bradbury, 1970 (I:10+ R:6). Eleven-year-old Margaret is at the age when she wonders about the changes that are occurring in her body.

———. *Blubber.* Bradbury, 1974 (I:10+ R:4). The children in the fifth grade start a campaign against a heavier girl in the class. Jill discovers the cruelty of these actions when she becomes the victim.

———. *The One in the Middle is the Green Kangaroo.* Illustrated by Amy Aitken. Bradbury, 1981 (I:6–9 R:2). A second-grade boy, who is a middle child, gains self-esteem when he gets a part in an upper-grade play.

———. *Otherwise Known as Sheila the Great.* Dutton, 1972 (I:9–12 R:6). Ten-year-old Sheila experiences a summer in which she makes friends with a yo-yo champion, gets involved with a day camp drama, and lives through the terrors of swimming lessons.

———. *Tales of a Fourth Grade Nothing.* Illustrated by Roy Doty. Dutton, 1972 (I:7–12 R:4). Peter Hatcher's problem is his two-year-old brother, Fudge. The final insult occurs when Fudge does something dreadful to Peter's pet turtle.

———. *Tiger Eyes.* Bradbury, 1981. (I:12+ R:7). Davy, a fifteen-year-old girl, faces violence and fear.

Bonham, Frank. *Durango Street.* Dutton, 1965 (I:12+ R:5). Gang violence is realistically portrayed as two inner-city gangs cut out their territories.

———. *The Nitty Gritty.* Illustrated by Alvin Smith. Dutton, 1968. (I:12+ R:4). Charlie has conflicts; his father wants him to work and not go to school, and his teacher feels he can become a writer if he will work hard.

———. *The Rascals from Haskell's Gym.* Dutton, 1977 (I:10+ R:6). Two gymnastic teams compete in this story about girls' sports.

Bridgers, Sue Ellen. *All Together Now.* Knopf, 1979 (I:11+ R:7). When a twelve-year-old spends the summer with her grandparents, she finds a new circle of friends.

Buchan, Stuart. *When We Lived with Pete.* Scribner's, 1978. (I:12+ R:6). Tommy Bridge wants a father. He meets two dropouts and learns more about people as he makes the final move that gives him the family he wants.

Bunting, Eve. *The Empty Window.* Illustrated by Judy Clifford. Warne, 1980 (I:7–10 R:3). A boy captures a wild parrot to give to his best friend who has only a short time to live.

Burch, Robert. *Queenie Peavy.* Illustrated by Jerry Lazare, Viking, 1966 (I:10+ R:6). Queenie longs for the day when her father will return from jail but then discovers his true nature. Story of a strong female character.

Burnford, Sheila. *The Incredible Journey.* Illustrated by Carl Burger. Little, Brown, 1960, 1961 (I:8+ R:8). An old English bull terrier, a Siamese cat and a Labrador retriever make an incredible journey through 250 miles of Canadian wilderness as they find their way home to their family.

Byars, Betsy. *After the Goat Man.* Illustrated by Ronald Himler, Viking, 1974 (I:9–12 R:7). Harold Coleman was fat and considered himself the most miserable person in the world. Then he met the Goat Man who was trying to protect his home from an advancing interstate highway.

I = Interest by age range;
R = Readability by grade level.

———. *The Animal, The Vegetable, and John D. Jones.* Illustrated by Ruth Sanderson. Delacorte, 1982 (I:9–12 R:5). Three children come into conflict when their single parents share a vacation.

———. *The Cybil War.* Illustrated by Gail Owens, Viking, 1981 (I:9–12 R:6). Two fourth graders battle for a girl's affections.

———. *The 18th Emergency.* Illustrated by Robert Grossman. Viking, 1973 (I:8–12 R:3). The boys have answers to seventeen jungle emergencies but not an answer to the problem arising from insulting the biggest boy in school.

———. *Good-bye, Chicken Little.* Harper & Row, 1979 (I:10+ R:7). Jimmy feels guilty because he thinks he didn't try hard enough to keep his Uncle Pete from walking across thin ice.

———. *The House of Wings.* Illustrated by Daniel Schwartz. Viking, 1972 (I:8–12 R:3). A transformation takes place as Sammy, with the help of a blind crane, learns to love his grandfather.

———. *The Night Swimmers.* Illustrated by Troy Howell. Delacorte, 1980 (I:8–12 R:5). An older sister tries to care for her brothers while her father works nights.

———. *The Summer of the Swans.* Illustrated by Ted CoConis. Viking, 1970 (I:8–12 R:4). Fourteen-year-old Sara loves and protects her ten-year-old brother who is mentally handicapped. One summer night he goes out alone in search of the wild swans.

Callen, Larry. *Sorrow's Song.* Illustrated by Marvin Friedman. Little, Brown, 1979 (I:8–10 R:3). A young girl who cannot talk takes care of a wounded whooping crane.

Carrick, Carol. *The Accident.* Illustrated by Donald Carrick. Seabury, 1976 (I:5–8 R:4). Christopher experiences a series of emotions after his dog is killed.

Christopher, Matt. *Dirt Bike Racer.* Illustrated by Barry Bomzer. Little, Brown, 1979 (I:10+ R:4). Twelve-year-old Ron Baker finds a minibike at the bottom of a lake and takes a part-time job in order to restore it.

———. *Face-Off.* Illustrated by Harvey Kidder. Little, Brown, 1972 (I:8–12 R:4). Scott Harrison must overcome a tremendous fear for a hockey player; he is afraid the puck will strike his face.

———. *Football Fugitive.* Illustrated by Larry Johnson. Little, Brown, 1976 (I:9–12 R:6). Larry wishes that his father would take an interest in football, the sport that he loves.

———. *The Fox Steals Home.* Illustrated by Larry Johnson. Little, Brown, 1978 (I:8–12 R:6). Bobby is called Fox when he demonstrates his ability to run the bases. Baseball helps him overcome his worries about his parents' divorce.

———. *The Twenty-One-Mile Swim.* Little, Brown, 1979 (I:10+ R:5). A boy of small stature is angered when a boy on the swimming team teases him. He decides that he will train for and swim the twenty-one miles across the lake.

Cleary, Beverly. *Henry and Beezus.* Illustrated by Louis Darling. Morrow, 1952 (I:7–10 R:6). Henry and the girl he finds least obnoxious have a humorously good time even though they must put up with the antics of Beezus's little sister, Ramona.

———. *Mitch and Amy.* Illustrated by George Porter. Morrow, 1967 (I:8–12 R:6). Mitch and Amy are in the fourth grade; they are also twins. This is a humorous story about their everyday experiences.

———. *Ramona and Her Father.* Illustrated by Alan Tiegreen. Morrow, 1977 (ch. 3).

———. *Ramona and Her Mother.* Illustrated by Alan Tiegreen. Morrow, 1979 (I:7–10 R:6). Ramona's mother goes to work; the high and low points in her life are expressed by her daughter.

———. *Ramona the Brave.* Illustrated by Alan Tiegreen. Morrow, 1975 (I:7–10 R:6). Ramona's first-grade teacher does not appear to like students who are different. Ramona has many difficulties until she finally earns a truce with the teacher.

———. *Ramona the Pest.* Illustrated by Louis Darling. Morrow, 1968 (I:7–10 R:4). Ramona enters kindergarten and spreads exasperation into a wider sphere.

———. *Ramona Quimby, Age 8.* Illustrated by Alan Tiegreen. Morrow, 1981 (I:7–10 R:6). Ramona faces new challenges when her father returns to college.

Cleaver, Vera, and Cleaver, Bill. *I Would Rather Be a Turnip.* Lippincott, 1971 (I:11+ R:6). Changes occur in twelve-year-old Annie's life when her illegitimate nephew comes to live with her family.

———. *Lady Ellen Grae.* Illustrated by Ellen Raskin. Lippincott, 1968 (I:8–12 R:6). Eleven-year-old tomboy Ellen Grae Derryberry lives happily with her father. Suddenly, she is told that she must go to Seattle so she can learn to be a lady.

———. *A Little Destiny.* Lothrop, Lee & Shepard, 1979 (I:12+ R:6). Fourteen-year-old Lucy's father dies under questionable circumstances. When Lucy decides to avenge her father's death, she discovers that her destiny is a matter of her own choosing.

———. *Me Too.* Lippincott, 1973 (I:10–14 R:7). Twelve-year-old Lydia and Lornie are twins. Although they look alike, Lornie is mentally handicapped. Lydia tries to educate her sister so that she will not be different.

———. *Queen of Hearts.* Lippincott, 1978 (I:11+ R:6). Twelve-year-old Wilma makes discoveries about herself and her grandmother.

———. *Trial Valley.* Lippincott, 1977 (I:11+ R:5). In a sequel to *Where the Lilies Bloom,* Mary Call struggles to keep the family together.

———. *Where the Lilies Bloom.* Illustrated by Jim Spanfeller. Lippincott, 1969 (I:11+ R:5). Four children, led by fourteen-year-old Mary Call, hide their father's death so they can remain together.

Clymer, Eleanor. *The Get-Away Car.* Dutton, 1978 (I:8–12 R:3). A humorous story about a resourceful grandmother who solves her granddaughter's and her own problems in a satisfactory manner.

Cohen, Barbara. *Thank You, Jackie Robinson.* Illustrated by Richard Cuffari. Lothrop, Lee & Shepard, 1974 (I:10+ R:6). Sam and a sixty-year-old black man become best friends because of their interest in baseball.

Colman, Hila. *Tell Me No Lies.* Crown, 1978 (I:10+ R:5). Twelve-year-old Angela learns the truth about her absent father when her mother decides to remarry; she is illegitimate. She reacts with anger and resentment.

Conford, Ellen. *The Revenge of the Incredible Dr. Rancid and His Youthful Assistant, Jeffrey.* Little, Brown, 1980 (I:10+ R:4). Eleven-year-old Jeffrey Childs who is small and skinny, discovers a way to become a superhero and overcome the class bully.

Corcoran, Barbara. *You're Allegro Dead.* Atheneum, 1981 (I:10+ R:5). The Twelve-year-old friends encounter a mystery at a summer camp.

Creswell, Helen. *Absolute Zero Being the Second Part of the Bagthorpe Saga.* Macmillan, 1978 (I:8–12 R:6). The Bagthorpes began competing in their efforts to win contests.

———. *Bagthorpes Unlimited.* Macmillan, 1978 (I:8–12 R:6). The Bagthorpes try to set a new world record.

———. *Bagthorpes v. the World: Being the Fourth Part of the Bagthorpe Saga.* Macmillan, 1979 (I:8–12 R:6). An overdraft notice from the bank sends the Bagthorpes into a chaotic survival campaign.

———. *Ordinary Jack.* Macmillan, 1977 (I:8–12 R:6). The first book in the series about the humorous Bagthorpes.

Cunningham, Julia. *Burnish Me Bright.* Illustrated by Don Freeman. Pantheon, 1970 (I:8–12 R:8). A mute boy in a French village is taught to pantomime by a retired actor and then is persecuted by the villagers; they believe he is bewitched.

———. *Come to the Edge.* Pantheon, 1977 (I:12+ R:7). A psychological story about a fourteen-year-old boy who must discover the will to love after he has been rejected by both his father and his only friend.

———. *Dorp Dead.* Illustrated by James Spanfeller. Pantheon, 1965 (I:11+ R:7). A complicated psychological novel about an eleven-year-old orphan who faces evil.

———. *The Silent Voice.* Dutton, 1981 (I:10+ R:8). A teenage mute boy is helped by a group of Parisian performers and a famous mime.

DeJong, Meindert. *Shadrach.* Illustrated by Maurice Sendak. Harper & Row, 1953 (I:8–10 R:4). Davie, a boy in the Netherlands, tries to sneak away from his protective mother and grandmother as he plans for his new pet rabbit.

———. *The Wheel on the School.* Illustrated by Maurice Sendak. Harper & Row, 1954 (I:10+ R:6). The children of Shora, Netherlands, wonder why storks never nest in their village. They decide to overcome this problem.

Desbarats, Peter. *Gabrielle and Selena.* Illustrated by Nancy Grossman. Harcourt Brace Jovanovich, 1968 (I:5–8 R:4). A story of interracial friendship in which two children, one black and the other white, decide to exchange places.

Dicks, Terrance. *The Baker Street Irregulars in the Case of the Crooked Kids.* Elsevier/Nelson, 1981 (I:10+ R:6). The youthful detectives capture a ring of juvenile thieves.

———. *The Baker Street Irregulars in the Case of the Ghost Grabbers.* Elsevier/Nelson, 1981 (I:10+ R:6). A haunted house provides the setting.

———. *The Baker Street Irregulars in the Case of the Blackmail Boys.* Elsevier/Nelson, 1981 (I:10+ R:6). A group of London youngsters outwit criminals.

———. *The Baker Street Irregulars in the Case of the Cinema Swindle.* Elsevier/Nelson, 1981 (I:10+ R:6). The hero uses techniques develop by Sherlock Holmes to solve a mystery.

———. *The Baker Street Irregulars in the Case of the Cop Catchers.* Dutton, 1982 (I:10+ R:6). The amateur detectives solve the case of the disappearance of a police sergeant.

Domke, Todd. *Grounded.* Knopf, 1982 (I:9–12 R:5). A sixth grader involves his classmates in a play so he can earn money to build a glider.

Donnelly, Elfie. *So Long, Grandpa.* Translated by Anthea Bell. Crown, 1981 (I:9–12 R:5). A ten-year-old boy and his grandfather look at life and death.

Dubellar, Thea. *Maria.* Translated by Anthea Bell. Illustrated by Mance Post. Morrow, 1982 (I:9–12 R:5). A girl retains her sense of self even though she experiences many family problems.

Enright, Elizabeth. *Thimble Summer.* Holt, Rinehart & Winston, 1938, 1966 (I:7–12 R:5). Nine-year-old Garnet Linden finds a silver thimble that she believes is a good omen for everything good that happens during the summer on her Wisconsin farm.

Estes, Eleanor. *The Moffats.* Illustrated by Louis Slobodkin. Harcourt Brace Jovanovich, 1941 (I:7–10 R:4). The happy Moffat children experience a series of adventures: riding on a freight train, getting lost on a horse-drawn wagon, and moving into a new house.

Farber, Norma. *How Does It Feel to Be Old?* Illustrated by Trina Schart Hyman. Dutton, 1979 (I:5–8 R:2). A grandmother tells her granddaughter about the good and bad experiences related to growing old.

Farley, Walter. *The Black Stallion.* Illustrated by Keith Ward. Random House, 1944 (I:8+ R:3). When a ship burns, a boy and a horse are thrown into the water and the black stallion saves Alec's life.

———. *The Black Stallion Picture Book.* Photographs furnished by United Artists. Random House, 1979 (I:6–8 R:2). A picture storybook version of *The Black Stallion.*

———. *The Black Stallion Returns.* Random House, 1945, 1973 (I:8+ R:3). The true owner of the Black Stallion claims him and takes him back to Arabia. Alec learns the history of the horse and finds himself in the center of a blood feud and an important race.

Fassler, Joan. *Howie Helps Himself.* Illustrated by Joe Lasker. Whitman, 1974 (I:4–8 R:2). A child with cerebral palsy tries very hard to move his wheelchair by himself. Both he and his father are thrilled when he succeeds.

Fitzhugh, Louise. *Harriet the Spy.* Harper & Row, 1964 (I:8–12 R:3). Eleven-year-old Harriet keeps a notebook of observations about people. She gets into trouble with classmates when they find it and read it aloud.

———. *The Long Secret.* Harper & Row, 1965 (I:8–12 R:3). A sequel to the above book.

———. *Sport.* Delacorte, 1979 (I:8–12 R:3). When eleven-year-old Sport inherits $20 million, his mother appears and tries to get the money. Sport is held prisoner in the Plaza Hotel. His friends help in his rescue.

George, Jean Craighead. *The Cry of the Crow.* Harper & Row, 1980 (I:10+ R:5). Mandy finds a young crow whose family has been killed by hunters. She feeds it, tames it, and then must make a choice when the crow attacks the person who hunted the crows, Mandy's brother.

———. *Julie of the Wolves.* Illustrated by John Schoenherr. Harper & Row, 1972 (ch. 3).

———. *My Side of the Mountain.* Dutton, 1959 (I:10+ R:6). Sam Gribley leaves his family in New York City to live for a summer and winter in the Catskill Mountains. He creates a home inside of a rotted out tree and lives off the land.

———. *River Rats, Inc.* Dutton, 1979 (I:10+ R:7). Two boys traveling illegally at night down the Colorado River are shipwrecked when their raft is destroyed. They must survive, with the help of a wild boy, the canyon, and the desert beyond.

Gerson, Corinne. *Son for a Day.* Illustrated by Velma Ilsley. Atheneum, 1980 (I:7–11 R:4). Eleven-year-old Danny leads an exciting life when he discovers and joins "zoodaddies," divorced fathers who bring their children to the zoo on their weekly day together. A humorous story.

Gipson, Fred. *Curly and the Wild Boar.* Illustrated by Ronald Himler. Harper & Row, 1979 (I:10+ R:7). When a wild boar smashes Curly's eighty-pound watermelon that he hoped would win a blue ribbon at the fair, Curly is determined to kill it.

———. *Old Yeller.* Illustrated by Carl Burger. Harper & Row, 1956 (I:10+ R:6). A big yellow dog becomes a loyal member of a Texas family. Old Yeller is bitten by a rabid wolf as he saves the lives of those he loves.

Graeber, Charlotte. *Mustard.* Illustrated by Donna Diamond. Macmillan, 1982 (I:7–10 R:4). A beloved fourteen-year-old cat has a heart attack, and a boy faces his pet's death.

Gray, Genevieve. *Send Wendel.* Illustrated by Symeon Shimin. McGraw-Hill, 1974. (I:3–6 R:4). A boy's family discovers that he is his own person.

Greenberg, Jan. *The Iceberg and Its Shadow.* Farrar, Straus & Giroux, 1980 (I:9–14 R:6). A story of peer manipulation and victimization similar to Judy Blume's *Blubber.*

Greene, Constance. *Al(exandra) the Great.* Viking, 1982 (I:8–12 R:3). A girl's vacation plans are changed when her mother gets pneumonia.

———. *Beat the Turtle Drum.* Illustrated by Donna Diamond. Viking, 1976 (I:10+ R:7). Twelve-year-old Kate describes her warm relationship with her ten-year-old sister, Joss. After an accident the family must cope with Joss's death.

———. *The Ears of Louis.* Illustrated by Nola Langner. Viking, 1974 (I:8–12 R:3). Louis tries many solutions to his big ears before he discovers that he has many desirable characteristics and skills.

———. *The Unmaking of Rabbit.* Viking, 1972 (I:10+ R:5). Eleven-year-old Paul is teased about his big ears and his stuttering. Paul discovers that a certain type of friendship is not worth the risks.

Greenwald, Sheila. *Give Us a Great Big Smile, Rosy Cole.* Little, Brown, 1981 (I:8–10 R:4). Rosy's uncle decides he will base a book on his niece and her violin; humor results.

Griffiths, Helen. *Running Wild.* Illustrated by Victor Ambrus. Holiday, 1977 (I:10+ R:6). A boy discovers the tragic results when two dogs grow wild in the forest.

Gripe, Maria. *Elvis and His Friends.* Illustrated by Harald Gripe. Delacorte, 1973, 1976 (I:9–12 R:4). In a sequel to *Elvis and His Secret,* Elvis goes to school.

———. *Elvis and His Secret.* Illustrated by Harald Gripe. Delacorte, 1972, 1976 (I:9–12 R:5). A shy six year old has difficulty communicating with his parents because they do not listen to him. His best friends who do understand him, are three older friends, including his grandfather.

Haas, Jessie. *Keeping Barney.* Greenwillow, 1982 (I:9–12 R:5). A girl gets a chance to care for a horse and tries to win his devotion.

Hall, Lynn. *Danza!* Scribner's 1981 (I:10–14 R:5). A boy's care for a horse helps his own personal development in a story set in Puerto Rico.

Hamilton, Virginia. *The Planet of Junior Brown.* Macmillan, 1971 (ch. 11).

Hartling, Peter. *Oma.* Illustrated by Jutta Ash. Harper & Row, 1975, 1977 (I:7–10 R:4). A strong relationship develops between a boy and his grandmother as she guides him lovingly toward his own independence.

Hautzig, Esther. *A Gift for Mama.* Illustrated by Donna Diamond. Viking, 1981 (I:8–10 R:4). Sarah mends clothing to earn money for a Mother's Day gift.

Henry, Marguerite. *Black Gold.* Illustrated by Wesley Dennis. Rand McNally, 1957 (I:8–12 R:6). Traces the history of a great racing horse named Black Gold and the trainer and jockey who loved him.

———. *Justin Morgan Had a Horse.* Illustrated by Wesley Dennis. Rand McNally, 1954 (I:8–12 R:6). The story of how Little Bub, the pint-sized stallion who could pull the heaviest logs and run the fastest race, inherited the name of his owner Justin Morgan.

———. *King of the Wind.* Illustrated by Wesley Dennis. Rand McNally, 1948, 1976 (I:8–12 R:6). The story of the great Godolphin Arabian who was the ancestor of Man o' War.

———. *Misty of Chincoteague.* Illustrated by Wesley Dennis. Rand McNally, 1947, 1963 (I:8–12 R:6). Misty is the descendant of the Spanish horses that swam to Assateague Island after a shipwreck. Two children buy Phantom and her colt Misty when they are herded to Chincoteague Island.

———. *Misty Treasury.* Illustrated by Wesley Dennis. Rand McNally, 1982 (I:8–12 R:6). Includes "Misty of Chincoteague," "Sea Star, Orphan of Chincoteague," and "Stormy, Misty's Foal" in one volume.

———. *San Domingo: The Medicine Hat Stallion.* Illustrated by Robert Lougheed. Rand McNally, 1972 (I:9–14 R:4). A boy's greatest joy is his foal with the markings believed sacred by the Indians. The story covers the period of the Pony Express.

Hopkins, Lee Bennett. *Mama.* Knopf, 1977 (I:7–10 R:6). A boy worries about his mother and tries to change her.

Houston, James. *Long Claws: An Arctic Adventure.* Atheneum, 1981 (I:8–10 R:6). Two Eskimo children go across the tundra in order to bring food to their starving family.

Hunt, Irene. *Up a Road Slowly.* Follett, 1966 (I:11+ R:7). The story of a girl's life and the influence of an aunt with whom she stays after her mother dies.

Kjelgaard, Jim. *Big Red.* Illustrated by Bob Kuhn. Holiday, 1945, 1956 (I:10+ R:7). Danny trains a champion Irish setter. Together, the two roam the mountain wilderness, encountering bear as well as partridge.

Klein, Norma. *Mom, The Wolf Man and Me.* Pantheon, 1972 (I:12+ R:6). Eleven-year-old Brett loves her life with her lively unwed mother. Who else can eat when they feel like it, not worry about a strict bedtime, and even go on a peace march to Washington, D.C.?

———. *Tomboy.* Four Winds, 1978 (I:9–12 R:4). Ten-year-old Antonia (Toe) doesn't want to grow up and experience the changes that naturally happen to a girl.

Konigsburg, E. L. *About the B'nai Bagels.* Atheneum, 1969 (I:8–12 R:7). Mark Setzer has special problems with his little league baseball team: his mother is the manager, and his brother is the coach.

———. *From the Mixed-Up Files of Mrs. Basil Frankweiler.* Atheneum, 1967 (I:9–12 R:7). Eleven-year-old Claudia and her younger brother run away to the Metropolitan Museum of Art. While there, they discover a mystery about a statue.

———. *(George).* Atheneum, 1970, 1980 (I:10+ R:7). A story about a multiple personality and how the differences were resolved.

———. *Jennifer, Hecate, Macbeth, William McKinley, and Me, Elizabeth.* Atheneum, 1967, 1976 (I:8–12 R:4). Elizabeth, a lonely only child, meets Jennifer who claims to be a witch. Elizabeth becomes an apprentice witch in this story of interracial friendships.

———. *Journey to an 800 Number.* Atheneum, 1982 (I:10+ R:7). A boy learns to appreciate his father when he spends the summer with him.

———. *Throwing Shadows.* Atheneum, 1979 (I:11+ R:7). A collection of five short stories about people making discoveries about themselves.

L'Engle, Madeleine. *Meet the Austins.* Vanguard, 1960 (I:10+ R:6). The six Austins have a family filled with spontaneous love, understanding, and personal discipline. Into this family enters a disturbed ten-year-old who has just lost her father.

Lexau, Joan M. *Benjie on His Own.* Illustrated by Don Bolognese. Dial, 1970 (I:5–8 R:4). Benjie makes it home from school and helps his grandmother.

Little, Jean. *From Anna.* Illustrated by Joan Sandin. Harper & Row, 1972 (I:8–12 R:5). Nine-year-old Anna lives in a world blurred by poor eyesight until she is diagnosed by a doctor and placed in a special class.

———. *Mine for Keeps.* Illustrated by Lewis Parker. Little, Brown, 1962 (I:8–12 R:4). A girl crippled by cerebral palsy leaves the security of a home for the physically handicapped and returns to her own family.

———. *Take Wing.* Illustrated by Jerry Lazare. Little, Brown, 1968 (I:8–12 R:4). Laurel knows that her seven-year-old brother is different. He cannot learn to read and is slow in learning to take care of himself.

London, Jack. *Call of the Wild.* Photographs by Seymour Linden. Harmony, 1977 (orig. 1903) (I:10+ R:5). The classic story of a brave dog who is stolen from his native California and trained in the harsh reality of the Klondike gold rush.

Lowry, Lois. *Anastasia Again!* Illustrated by Diane deGroat. Houghton Mifflin, 1981. (I:8–12 R:6). Anastasia must adjust to living in the suburbs.

———. *Anastasia at Your Service.* Illustrated by Diane deGroat. Houghton Mifflin, 1982 (I:8–12 R:6). An older Anastasia becomes a housemaid rather than a lady's companion.

———. *Anastasia Krupnik.* Houghton Mifflin, 1979 (I:8–12 R:6). Ten-year-old Anastasia forms a list of "Things I Love" and "Things I Hate" and discovers that eventually all of the items are on one side.

McDonnell, Christine. *Don't Be Mad, Ivy.* Illustrated by Diane deGroat. Dial, 1981 (I:6–9 R:3). A young girl overcomes everyday problems connected with home and school.

McGraw, Eloise Jarvis. *The Money Room.* Atheneum, 1981 (I:10+ R:6). The mystery of possible hidden money adds to a tale of family survival after the father's death.

McHargue, Georgess. *Funny Bananas.: The Mystery at the Museum.* Illustrated by Heidi Palmer. Holt, Rinehart & Winston, 1975 (I:7–9 R:6). Ben Pollack, whose parents are scientists at New York's Museum of Natural History, solves the mystery of the vandalism taking place there.

MacLachlan, Patricia. *Mama One, Mama Two.* Illustrated by Ruth Lercher Bornstein. Harper & Row, 1982 (I:4–8 R:3). A child has a happy foster home experience.

Madison, Winifred. *Call Me Danica.* Four Winds, 1977 (I:11 + R:4). Twelve-year-old Danica and her family immigrate to Canada after her father dies. They must face many adjustments as they discover the importance of working together.

Mann, Peggy. *My Dad Lives in a Downtown Hotel.* Illustrated by Richard Cuffari. Doubleday, 1973 (I:7–10 R:4). A boy experiences many emotions as he discovers that his parents are divorcing.

———. *There Are Two Kinds of Terrible.* Doubleday, 1977 (I:10 + R:5). A boy must face the second kind of terrible, the kind that does not end, when his mother dies from cancer.

Masterman-Smith, Virginia. *The Great Egyptian Heist.* Four Winds, 1982 (I:10 + R:5). Mystery surrounds diamonds found in an Egyptian coffin.

Mauser, Pat Rhoads. *A Bundle of Sticks.* Illustrated by Gail Owens. Atheneum, 1982 (I:9–12 R:5). An eleven-year-old is humiliated by a bully and takes self-defense lessons.

Miles, Betty. *The Secret Life of the Underwear Champ.* Knopf, 1981 (I:9–12 R:5). A boy hides his modeling job from his baseball team.

Myers, Walter Dean. *It Ain't All for Nothin'.* Viking, 1978 (I:10 + R:4). Twelve-year-old Tippy had a secure life with his Grandma Carrie until she became too ill to take care of him. His life changes drastically when he enters his father's world of crime and neglect.

Neville, Emily. *It's Like This, Cat.* Illustrated by Emil Weiss. Harper & Row, 1963 (I:8–12 R:6). David Mitchell has two best friends, an older boy and a stray tomcat.

Newman, Robert. *The Case of the Baker Street Irregular.* Atheneum, 1978 (I:10 + R:6). Kidnappings, bombings, and the mystery of the identity of Andrew's mother bring Andrew and Sherlock Holmes together as they discover the connections and solve the case.

———. *The Case of the Vanishing Corpse.* Atheneum, 1980 (I:10 + R:6). A series of incidents, including jewel robberies, a missing woman, and a disappearing corpse, bring Andrew in contact with Constable Wyatt.

O'Dell, Scott. *Island of the Blue Dolphins.* Houghton Mifflin, 1960 (I:10 + R:6). Twelve-year-old Karana is left on her Pacific island when the tribe leaves in fear of attacking Aleuts. She survives alone for eighteen years before a ship takes her to the California mainland.

Park, Barbara. *Don't Make Me Smile.* Knopf, 1981 (I:9–12 R:5). A ten-year-old boy experiences a series of reactions when his parents tell him they are getting a divorce.

Paterson, Katherine. *Bridge to Terabithia.* Illustrated by Donna Diamond. Crowell, 1977 (ch. 3).

———. *Jacob Have I Loved.* Crowell, 1980 (I:10 + R:7). A twin feels that her sister has deprived her of parental affection and schooling.

Phipson, Joan. *A Tide Flowing.* Atheneum, 1981 (I:10 + R:5). The friendship of a quadriplegic helps a young man cope with his mother's death and his father's rejection.

———. *When the City Stopped.* Atheneum, 1978 (I:10 + R:5). An Australian city is immobilized by a strike that cuts off power, water, transportation, and all other services. Two children experience a world of looters and scavengers.

Rabe, Berniece. *The Balancing Girl.* Illustrations by Lillian Hoban. Dutton, 1981 (I:7–9 R:4). A physically handicapped girl proves she is a capable person.

Raskin, Ellen. *Figgs & Phantoms.* Dutton, 1974 (I:10 + R:5). An unusual family is constantly searching for Capri, their idea of heaven. Mona is afraid her favorite Uncle Florence, a rare book dealer, will find his way there without her.

———. *The Mysterious Disappearance of Leon (I Mean Noel).* Dutton, 1971 (I:10 + R:5). A last message that is only partly recognizable forms a word puzzle allowing the reader to solve the mystery of the disappearing Leon.

———. *The Westing Game.* Dutton, 1978 (ch. 3).

Rinkoff, Barbara. *The Watchers.* Knopf, 1972 (I:10 + R:6). Chris thought he could learn a lot about people by observing them from a distance. He discovers that he doesn't know them as well as he thinks he does.

Riskind, Mary. *Apple is My Sign.* Houghton Mifflin, 1981 (I:9–12 R:5). A deaf boy goes to a school for the deaf; setting is early 1900s.

Robertson, Keith. *In Search of a Sandhill Crane.* Illustrated by Richard Cuffari. Viking, 1973 (I:10 + R:7). Link Keller searches the Michigan wilderness in order to photograph sandhill cranes; during the summer, he learns to respect the fragile beauty of nature.

Robinson, Veronica. *David in Silence.* Illustrated by Victor Ambrus. Lippincott, 1966 (I:8–12 R:7). A boy who was born deaf has difficulty making friends in a new town until one child makes an effort to understand his life.

Roy. Ron. *Where's Buddy?* Illustrated by Troy Howell. Houghton Mifflin, 1982 (I:9–12 R:5). A diabetic boy becomes lost when his older brother does not look after him.

Sachs, Marilyn. *The Bears' House.* Illustrated by Louis Glanzman. Doubleday, 1971 (I:8–11 R:6). An unhappy fourth grader tries to cope with a sick mother and a deserted father.

———. *A December Tale.* Doubleday, 1976 (I:12 + R:7). The brutal world of child abuse is the topic of this book.

———. *A Secret Friend.* Doubleday, 1978 (I:8–12 R:4). Two best friends break their relationship after many years. Jessica goes through many unhappy weeks before she discovers the real meaning of friendship.

Schellie. Don. *Kidnapping Mr. Tubbs.* Four Winds, 1978 (I:12 + R:7). Two young people help an old cowboy who lives in a nursing home visit the ranch that had been so important to him.

Schick. Eleanor. *Joey on His Own.* Dial, 1982 (I:5–7 R:2). A young boy's pride increases when he goes to the grocery store by himself.

Shreve. Susan. *Family Secrets: Five Very Important Stories.* Illustrated by Richard Cuffari. Knopf, 1979 (I:8–10 R:7). A collection of five stories about five different family problems: death of a dog. divorce of an aunt. suicide of a best friend's brother. an ill grandmother. and cheating at school.

Slote. Alfred. *Hang Tough. Paul Mather.* Lippincott, 1973 (I:9–12 R:3). Baseball helps Paul Mather face his life when he discovers that he has an incurable blood disease.

———. *The Hotshot.* Photographs by William LaCrosse. Watts, 1977 (I:8–12 R:3). Paddy learns that it is not always the player who makes the goals who is rewarded on the ice.

Smith. Doris Buchanan. *Kelly's Creek.* Illustrated by Alan Tiegreen. Crowell, 1975 (I:7–10 R:4). A boy with a learning disability discovers that he has special skills when he explores the marsh behind his home.

Snyder, Zilpha Keatley. *The Changeling.* Illustrated by Alton Raible. Atheneum, 1970 (I:10 + R:7). Martha tells about her friendship with a girl who is very different from her own family.

———. *The Egypt Game.* Illustrated by Alton Raible. Atheneum, 1967 (I:10 + R:6). A group of sixth-grade children recreate the land of Ancient Egypt in the abandoned back yard of an antique dealer.

_____. *The Famous Stanley Kidnapping Case.* Atheneum, 1979 (I:10+ R:7). Kidnappers hold the children for ransom in a deserted basement. They solve the mystery of the identity of their kidnappers and escape.

Sobol, Donald J. *Encyclopedia Brown Sets the Pace.* Illustrated by Ib Ohlsson. Scholastic/Four Winds, 1982 (I:7–10 R:5). A new series of cases to solve.

_____. *Encyclopedia Brown Tracks Them Down.* Illustrated by Leonard Shortall. Crowell, 1971 (I:7–10 R:3). The clues and solutions to the cases make it possible for children to try and solve the cases.

Southall, Ivan. *Hills End.* Macmillan, 1962, 1974 (I:10+ R:7). When a violent storm breaks, seven Australian children are separated from their teacher and must face the dangers of floods and a destroyed village.

Spence, Eleanor. *The Nothing Place.* Illustrated by Geraldine Spence. Harper & Row, 1973 (I:10+ R:6). Twelve-year-old Glen loses part of his hearing after an illness. Reactions of family, schoolmates, and the child are explored.

Sperry, Armstrong. *Call It Courage.* Macmillan, 1940 (ch. 3).

Stolz, Mary. *Cider Days.* Harper & Row, 1978 (I:8–12 R:6). Polly makes overtures toward Consuela Christina Machado, the new girl in town. A satisfying story about friendship between children who have different personalities and backgrounds.

_____. *Ferris Wheel.* Harper & Row, 1977 (I:8–12 R:6). Polly Lewis is unhappy when her best friend moves away; she tries to find a new best friend.

_____. *What Time of Night Is It?* Harper & Row, 1981 (I:10+ R:6). Three children face problems when their mother leaves home.

Taylor, Sydney. *All-of-a-Kind Family.* Illustrated by Helen John. Follett, 1951 (I:7–10 R:4). Five girls live with their parents on New York's East Side in 1912. The affectionate family does not have much money but has other strengths holding them together.

_____. *Ella of All-of-a-Kind Family.* Illustrated by Gail Owens. Dutton, 1978 (I:10+ R:5). Ella is now grown-up and must decide whether or not she wants a singing career.

_____. *More All-of-a-Kind Family.* Illustrated by Mary Stevens. Follett, 1954 (I:8–12 R:6). More stories of a New York family in the early 1900s; they begin to grow up and the family, becoming more prosperous, moves to the Bronx.

Taylor, Theodore. *The Cay.* Doubleday, 1969 (I:10+ R:6). A blinded American boy is stranded on a Caribbean Cay with a West Indian native.

_____. *The Trouble With Tuck.* Doubleday, 1981 (I:6–9 R:5). Based on a true incident, the story follows a girl as she trains a blind Labrador to follow a guide dog.

Tester, Sylvia Root. *Carla-Too-Little.* Illustrated by Linda Sommers. Child's World, 1976 (I:4–7 R:4). Carla is discouraged because she is too young to take part in her family's various teams. She feels important when she becomes a bat girl.

Thomas, Ianthe. *Hi, Mrs. Mallory!* Illustrated by Ann Toulmin-Rothe. Harper & Row, 1979 (I:5–8 R:3). Li'l Bits stops to see her good friend Mrs. Mallory every day after school. Then, Mrs. Mallory is not there and her mother explains that she has died.

Vogel, Ilse Margaret. *My Summer Brother.* Harper & Row, 1981 (I:9–12 R:4). A nine year old expresses feelings about mother-daughter rivalry and her first crush.

Wojciechowska, Maia. *Shadow of a Bull.* Illustrated by Alvin Smith. Atheneum, 1964 (I:10+ R:5). The people of the Spanish Village expect Manolo to become a heroic bullfighter like his father. Manolo discovers that true bravery is not always in the bullring.

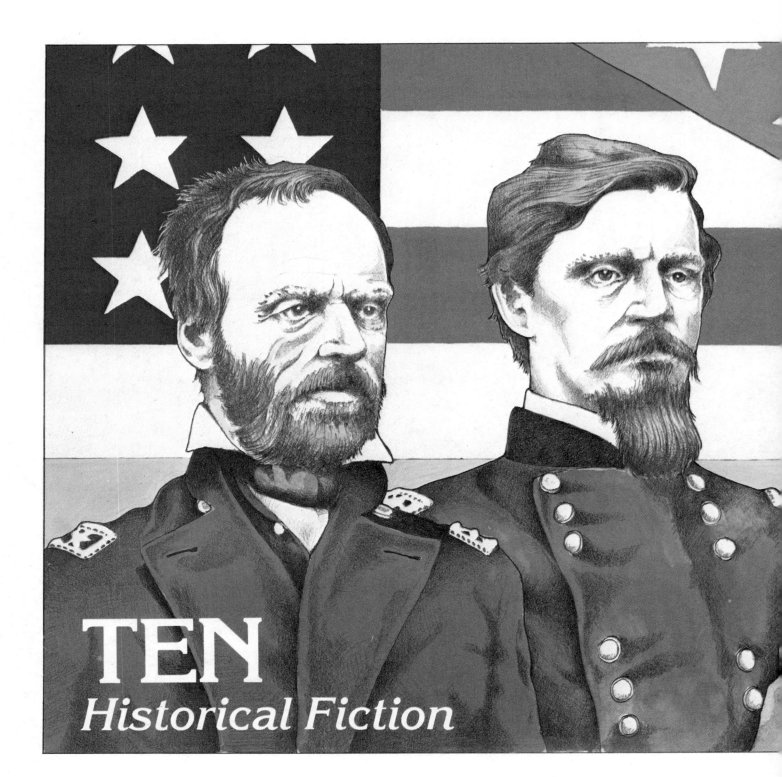

TEN
Historical Fiction

The People and the Past Come Alive

Involving Children in Historical Fiction

The People and the Past Come Alive

VALUES OF HISTORICAL FICTION FOR CHILDREN

CRITERIA FOR EVALUATING HISTORICAL FICTION

SPECIFIC DEMANDS ON AUTHORS OF HISTORICAL FICTION

HISTORICAL FICTION — A CHRONOLOGICAL ORDER OF STORIES AND THEIR PERIODS IN HISTORY

THE THREAD of people's lives weaves through the past, the present, and into the future. Many people have a deep desire to trace their roots back to Europe, Asia, or Africa. What did their ancestors experience? Why did their ancestors travel to America? What were their personal feelings and beliefs? What was life like for the settlers who pioneered the American frontier? Did people of the past have the same concerns as people of the present? Are there solutions for today's problems in past experiences?

Through the pages of historical fiction, the past becomes alive. It is not just dates, accomplishments, and battles; it is people, famous and unknown, who lived during the times and through their actions influenced the course of history. In this chapter, the reader will consider the values of historical fiction for children, the criteria for evaluating historical fiction, some specific demands on the authors of historical fiction, and examples of historical fiction written about different time periods. The last section will tie historical books into a short discussion of historic events for the time period. It is hoped that this will give the reader a better understanding of the sweep of history as portrayed in these books.

VALUES OF HISTORICAL FICTION FOR CHILDREN

Children cannot actually cross the ocean on the *Mayflower* and see a new world for the first time, explore the Americas during the time of Montezuma and Cortés, or feel the consequences of persecution during World War II. They can imagine all these experiences, however, through the pages of historical fiction. With Patricia Clapp's *Constance: A Story of Early Plymouth*, they can imagine they are standing on the swaying deck of the *Mayflower* and seeing their new home. With Julián Escobar in Scott O'Dell's *The Feathered Serpent,* they can imagine they are visiting the palace of the emperor Montezuma and witnessing the emperor's tragic encounter with Cortés. With a twelve-year-old girl and her father in Els Pelgrom's *The Winter When Time Was Frozen,* they can imagine they are given sanctuary in the home of a Dutch farm family during World War II.

As children relive the past through vicarious experiences, they are also reading for enjoyment. Tales based on authentic historic settings or episodes are alive with adventures that appeal to many children. They may follow the adventures of a young girl living on the Wisconsin frontier in Carol Ryrie Brink's *Caddie Woodlawn.* They may read to discover if a girl can successfully hide her identity and pretend to be a man in

Patricia Clapp's *I'm Deborah Sampson: A Soldier in the War of the Revolution.* They may follow the adventures of Jeff Bussey in Harold Keith's *Rifles for Watie* as he tries to find information behind enemy lines during the Civil War.

Children who read historical fiction gain an understanding of their own heritage. The considerable research that precedes the writing of an authentic historic story enables the author to incorporate information about the period naturally into the story. This allows children to gain knowledge about the people, values, beliefs, hardships, and physical surroundings common to a period. They can discover the events that preceded their own century and made the present day possible. Through historical fiction, children can begin to visualize the sweep of history.

As characters in historical fiction from many different time periods face and overcome their problems, readers may discover important universal truths, identify feelings and behaviors that encourage them to consider alternative ways to handle their own problems, empathize with viewpoints that may be different from their own, and realize that history consists of many people who have learned to work together.

The journal of the National Council for the Social Studies, *Social Education* (9), maintains that an emphasis on human relations is a primary criterion for selecting notable books. Through historical fiction, children can discover that all people are dependent upon one another regardless of the time in which they live. They also find that human beings have had similar needs throughout history. They learn that when human relationships deteriorate, the result is usually tragedy. Historical fiction allows children to judge these relationships and realize that their own present and future are tied to the actions of these humans of the past.

CRITERIA FOR EVALUATING HISTORICAL FICTION

When evaluating historical fiction, the teacher must be certain the story adheres to the criteria for excellent literature discussed in chapter three. There are, in addition, some special demands placed on historical fiction, specifically setting, characterization, plot development, and theme.

Setting

Because historical fiction must be authentic in every respect, the development of the setting for the time period is essential. A setting this important to the story is an *integral setting.* Re-

becca Lukens (6) says that an integral setting must be described in details so clear that the reader understands how the story is related to a time and place. This is of particular concern in historical fiction written for children; they cannot visualize the historic periods from memory. The writer must provide this imagery through vivid descriptions that do not overpower plot and characterization.

When writing books for older students, authors have more time to develop integral settings in which the actions and characters are influenced by both time and place. The setting in historical fiction may guide readers into the plot, encourage them to feel the excitement of a time period, and create visual images that encourage them to accept the character's experiences.

In chapter three, the role of setting as an antagonist was discussed. This is a common role for setting in many westward expansion and pioneering books. For example, in Harold Keith's *The Obstinate Land,* the family must overcome drought, hail, and bitter cold. Each new setback strengthens the main character and brings the family and neighbors closer together in their fight to survive. In Honore Morrow's *On to Oregon!,* sleet storms, rugged mountains, swift streams, and natural predators act as antagonists. The description leaves little doubt that the children are confronting a beautiful but awesome adversary. The setting may also be the antagonist in a story set in a city. Carla Stevens develops the 1888 blizzard in New York City into an antagonist in *Anna, Grandpa, and the Big Storm.*

Authors of historical fiction sometimes contrast settings in order to develop the conflict and suggest how the settings influence the characters. This technique is used in both Ann Petry's *Tituba of Salem Village* and Elizabeth George Speare's *The Witch of Blackbird Pond.* Both authors have taken heroines from the warm, colorful Caribbean and placed them in the bleak, somber surroundings of a Puritan village. Time and place then influence how the other characters react to these heroines and how they respond to their new environments.

Although some settings in historical fiction act as antagonists, others create happy, nostalgic moods. This is the result in Cynthia Rylant's picture storybook *When I Was Young in the Mountains.* The illustrations and text allow readers to glimpse the happy growing-up years in the Appalachian mountains of Virginia. This peaceful setting is a world of swimming holes, country stores, and family evenings on the porch. The illustrations help integrate the details of the time period into the story.

Every detail of colonial life is integrated into Esther Forbes's story for older readers, *Johnny Tremain.* The sights, sounds, and smells of revolutionary Boston are integrated into the

The happy days in an Appalachian mountain community are reflected in the illustrations.
Reprinted by permission of the publisher, E. P. Dutton, Inc., From *When I Was Young in the Mountains* by Cynthia Rylant, illustrated by Diane Goode. Illustrations © 1982 by Diane Goode.

characters' daily routines. The reader knows that Johnny sleeps in a loft, wears leather breeches and a coarse shirt, likes the bustling wharf, and is proud of his work in the silversmith's shop. The author has used research collected when writing her Pulitzer Prize-winning biography, *Paul Revere and the World He Lived In,* to develop a fictional book for children that is also authentic in setting. Anne Pellowski, in *Winding Valley Farm: Annie's Story,* integrates Polish customs and descriptions of rural farming practices to create the feeling of an ethnic community during the early 1900s.

Characterization

Authors of historical novels admit that it is sometimes difficult not to develop contemporary actions and values in their heroes and heroines. Geoffrey Trease (15), author of such historical novels as *Saraband for Shadows,* encountered this problem when he wanted a heroine in a story about the Roman Empire to meet a boy and form a friendship. His research showed that the Roman citizens kept their daughters in seclusion and would never have allowed them to associate with a noncitizen's child. He admits that he had to search a long time for a twist in the plot that would resolve this dilemma. Trease believes that "history has all the raw material the novelist needs" (p. 27). Consequently, if the author knows his or her job, facts will not not need to be altered. The actions, beliefs, and values of the characters must be realistic for the time period.

Choosing the main and supporting characters can cause additional problems. Hester Burton (3) says that she never uses a famous person as the pivotal character in her stories and never develops dialogue for a famous person unless there is documentary evidence that the character actually carried on such a conversation or would have held those specific sentiments. She feels it is legitimate to create a historic situation that includes a fictional character. In contrast, she does not believe in placing a famous personage in a fictional adventure. Many authors of historical fiction apparently agree with Burton. This use of fictional characters in historic settings is seen in numerous books. In *Johnny Tremain,* for example, a silversmith's apprentice is the pivotal character, while Paul Revere and Samuel Adams are background characters.

Authors develop characterization through dialogue, thoughts and actions, thoughts of others, and descriptions. While all of these need to appear authentic, the speech of the characters and the language characteristic of a period can cause problems for writers of historical fiction. For example, Harold Keith wanted one of his characters in *The Obstinate Land* to speak with a dialect. He says, "Mattie Cooper's Arkansas dialect was hard to pin down until I had the good fortune to discover old files of the magazine *Dialect Notes,* containing several studies by Dr. J. W. Carr, associate professor of English and Modern Languages at the University of Arkansas, 1901–06" (5, author's notes). This study provided Keith with the words and pronunciation necessary to develop a character whose speech was realistic for the time and location.

Authors of children's historical fiction must be careful, however, not to use so many colorful terms from a period that the story is difficult for a young reader to comprehend.

Plot

Credible plots in historical ficton emerge from authentically developed time periods; the experiences, the conflicts, and the characters' resolution of these conflicts must reflect the times. This is true whether the antagonist is another person, society, nature, or a person facing his or her own dilemmas. Conflict in historical fiction frequently develops when characters leave their own secure or known environments and move into more alien ones. Authors may highlight the problems, the culture, or diverse values of a time period by exploring the conflicts developed because of a character's inner turmoil or societal pressures.

Let us consider, for example, the development of two common conflicts in historical fiction: person-against-self and person-against-society. The heroine's person-against-self conflict in Ann Schlee's *Ask Me No Questions* develops after she moves from London in 1848 to avoid a cholera epidemic. While living with her aunt and uncle, Laura uncovers a neighbor's sinister activities. Although he is supposedly training children acquired from the workhouses, Laura discovers children who are starving and ill. The author develops a person-against-self conflict as Laura faces her own moral dilemmas. Should she help the children even if she must steal food from her own relatives and then lie about her actions? The dilemmas in this story based on a true incident seem believable because of the author's descriptions of Laura's discoveries. For example, Laura discovers children eating pig slops in her aunt's barn. The author's descriptions of Laura's formidable aunt who has strong Victorian attitudes toward children illuminate reasons for Laura's conflict.

Scott O'Dell develops a credible person-against-self conflict in *The Captive* by developing and describing the moral dilemmas faced by a young Jesuit seminarian as he leaves his Spanish homeland in the early 1500s and accompanies an expedition to the Americas. The author describes the Jesuit's faith and his desire to bring Christianity to the Indians of New Spain, his turmoil when he discovers the real motives behind the Spaniards' actions, his refusal to betray the Indians, his pondering over his inability to change the Mayan people, and his final justification for his own grasping for power by impersonating a Mayan god. The various characterizations help readers understand both good and bad human motives. O'Dell's detailed descriptions of the incidents that cause the main character's moral dilemmas and the character's responses to these dilemmas create credible conflict for the time period.

Personal moral dilemmas created by prejudice are explored in William H. Hooks's *Circle of Fire.* The author depicts a 1925 North Carolina setting in which a white boy and his two black friends try to prevent a Ku Klux Klan attack on Irish gypsies. The author develops additional believable personal conflict when the eleven-year-old boy discovers that his father, who he loves and respects, is probably involved in the Klan.

Each of these stories also develops plausible person-against-society conflicts. The conflict in *Ask Me No Questions* is possible because of Victorian attitudes about children and the place of at least lower-class children in society. Much of the conflict in *The Captive* develops because of human greed and a society that supposedly permits human exploitation. Likewise, the conflict in *Circle of Fire* develops because of prejudice.

Authors who develop credible person-against-society conflicts must describe the values and beliefs of the time period or the attitudes of a segment of the population in such as way that readers will understand the nature of the antagonist. In Ann Petry's *Tituba of Salem Village* and Patricia Clapp's *Witches' Children: A Story of Salem,* the authors describe the building hysteria that results in the final trial for witchcraft. The potentially deadly nature of the antagonist is emphasized in Kathryn Lasky's *The Night Journey* because a Jewish family must plan and execute a dangerous flight from czarist Russia. The plot seems more credible because a contemporary family believes these memories would be so painful that the great grandmother should not be encouraged to remember her own experiences.

Well-developed person-against-self and person-against-society conflicts help readers understand the values expressed during a time period and the problems, moral dilemmas, and issues faced by the people. Authors frequently use these conflicts and their resolution to develop themes in historical fiction.

Theme

The theme in historical fiction, as in any story, should be worthwhile; it should be as relevant in today's society as it was in the historical period being represented. The themes in many historical fiction books are basic and have been relevant for humans throughout their existence.

The search for freedom, for example, is found in literature from all time periods. This theme is found in Rosemary Sutcliff's stories of tribal Britons seeking freedom from a conquering tribe or the invading Roman armies. It is found in the desire of a slave in Haugaard's *A Slave's Tale* when he longs to return to his native land. The desire for religious freedom is dominant in stories about the settlers of Plymouth Colony; the desire for political freedom is found in stories of the revolutionary period. A desire for personal freedom appears in many books about the Underground Railroad before and during the Civil War.

Love of the land and the independence provided by it are powerful themes in books about westward expansion. Families leave relatives and the protection of established communities to face unknown dangers to acquire homesteads. Children inherit their parents' dreams and fight hostile environments to retain the land.

There are also themes of loyalty and honor in all historical periods. People are loyal to friends and follow them on difficult quests; they are loyal to their principles and defend them; and they are loyal to families and may even avenge their deaths or dishonor.

The cruelty and futility of war are also found in stories from all periods. A boy in the English Civil War discovers the realities of war, and a boy during the American Civil War cannot understand the divisions within his own family. Stories of wartime frequently develop the theme of conscience. This is seen when a Quaker boy, living up to his beliefs, refuses to fight in the Revolutionary War and is persecuted by both sides. It is also found in the Separatists' village as the people declare their nonviolent beliefs. Wartime stories develop the theme that people cannot sit back and allow another group to be persecuted without interfering. This theme is found, for example, in many stories about the Holocaust.

These themes are relevant to human understanding whether they are in stories set in medieval England, colonial America, revolutionary America, Europe during World War II, or contemporary America.

Important Questions

The following questions summarize the criteria that should be considered (in addition to considerations of literary quality raised in chapter three) when evaluating historical fiction:

1 Is the setting authentic in every detail?
2 Are details integrated into the story so that they do not overwhelm the reader or detract from the story?
3 If the setting is the antagonist, are the relationships between characters and setting clearly developed?
4 Do the characters' actions express values and beliefs that are realistic for the time period?
5 Is the language authentic for the period without relying on so many colorful terms or dialect that the story is difficult to understand?

6 Do the experiences, the conflicts, and the characters' resolutions of conflicts reflect what is known about the time period?
7 Is the theme worthwhile?

SPECIFIC DEMANDS ON THE AUTHORS OF HISTORICAL FICTION

The authors of the selections discussed in this chapter can be placed in two categories. First, there are authors who actually lived the experiences they are writing about or knew someone who lived through them. In contrast, other authors write about historical periods far removed from their personal experiences. To gather their data, they must rely on sources of information far different from the person who remembers vividly the people and the minute details of the setting.

Consider first the demands on the authors who lived through these experiences. One of the most famous is Laura Ingalls Wilder, the author of the "Little House" books. She actually lived in the big woods of Wisconsin; traveled by covered wagon through Kansas; lived in a sod house in Minnesota; and shared her life with Pa, Ma, Mary, and Carrie when they finally settled in South Dakota. While these books sound as if they were written immediately after an incident occurred, they were not. The stories relate Laura's life from 1870 through 1889 but were not written until much later, between 1926 and 1943. The ability to remember is a considerable requirement. Through her remembrances, she has recreated her own loving family in order to share her experiences.

Just as the experiences of the frontier are vivid for those who lived them, so are the more recent days of World War II. Laura's experiences were predominantly happy, but days of exile, hiding, or escape evoke quite different memories. Several authors lived through the Holocaust and have written about their lives during this period. In 1972 Johanna Reiss published the story of her experiences as a Jewish child hidden by Dutch Gentiles. According to the publishers of *The Upstairs Room,* Reiss (11) "did not set out to write a book about her experiences during the Second World War; she simply wanted to record them for her two daughters, who are now about the age she was when she went to stay with the Oastervelds" (p. 197). When she started to write, she discovered how much she remembered, things that she had never talked about with anyone because they were too painful. To reinforce this memory, she took her children back to Usselo, Holland. While there, she visited the Dutch family and looked again at the upstairs room and the hiding place within the closet. Such memories create demands on the writer that may be more painful than ordinary experiences.

Authors such as Carol Ryrie Brink wrote about relatives' experiences. In *Caddie Woodlawn*, Brink recreates the story of her grandmother, Caddie Woodhouse, and her grandmother's family. She relates in the author's note to the book (2) that she lived with her grandmother and loved to listen to her tell stories about her pioneer childhood. Brink says:

It was many years later that I remembered those stories of Caddie's childhood, and I said to myself, "If I loved them so much perhaps other children would like them too." Caddie was still alive when I was writing, and I sent letters to her, asking about the details that I did not remember clearly. She was pleased when the book was done. "There is only one thing that I do not understand," she said. "You never knew my mother and father and my brothers—how could you write about them exactly as they were?" "But, Gram," I said, "You told me." (p. 283)

It is impossible, of course, for contemporary authors to have lived in earlier times or even to have known someone who lived during many of the historical periods, so they must use other resources in researching their chosen time periods. Hester Burton (3), a well-known writer of historical fiction with a British setting, says:

Ideally I should be so knowledgeable that I have no need to turn to a book of reference once I have actually started writing the book. I should be able to see clearly in my mind's eye the houses in which my characters live, the clothes they wear, and the cars and carriages and ships in which they travel. I should know what food they eat, what songs they sing when they are happy, and what are the sights and smells they are likely to meet when they walk down the street. I must understand their religion, their political hopes, their trades—what is most important—the relationships between different members of a family common to their particular generation. (p. 299)

To acquire this much knowledge about a time period demands considerable research. Some authors have chosen to research and write about one period; others have written books covering many different times. An author who has made brilliant contributions in stories written about a specific time period is Rosemary Sutcliff. John Townsend (14) says that in the area of serious historic novels Sutcliff stands above the rest. He believes that her most important contributions are the books set in Roman Britain. Sutcliff's thorough knowledge of the history of the period is expressed in her introductions to her books. For example, in *Song for a Dark Queen* (13), she presents the historic happenings that influence the incidents in the book. Next, she describes how, after reading T. C.

Lethbridge's *Witches* and *Gog-Magog,* she theorized that the Iceni were a matriarchy, thus creating the plot for her story. Finally, she lists the sources that provided her with background information for the story.

Reading about any of the well-known authors of historical fiction whose books are noted for authentic backgrounds reveals that hundreds of hours are spent researching county courthouse records, letters, old newspapers, and history books, conducting personal interviews, and visiting museums and historic locations before the story is written. The author must then write a story that develops plot and character without sounding like a history textbook. In addition, authors must carefully consider the many conflicting points of view that may surround particular events. Writing excellent historical fiction is a very demanding task.

HISTORICAL FICTION—A CHRONOLOGICAL ORDER OF STORIES AND THEIR PERIODS IN HISTORY

Two authors stress the importance of historical fiction in developing human understanding. Joan W. Blos believes the role of literature is "tying together the past, the present, and the promise of the future in a tale that confirms human bonds" (1, p. 375). Geoffrey Trease (15) also believes that historical fiction should be relevant to current problems. When choosing a subject for historical fiction, he considers the historical period, or person, or event and the immediate modern significance of the story. Literature critic Rebecca Lukens (6) stresses the need for understanding the similarities and differences in people from other times and places. Lukens maintains that before readers can accept other times and places as believable, they must first believe that the characters are human beings like themselves. In addition, in order to understand a different time period or culture, they must see the particular differences between their own lives and those of other people.

Special demands are also placed on students of children's literature and adults who share historical fiction with children when they try to tie past, present, and future together. They must understand at least some of the history around a time period if they are to evaluate the literature from that period and share it effectively with children. This section will discuss the literary selections according to a procedure developed by Donna Norton (8). Following a three-year study, Norton found that university students' understanding, evaluation, and utilization of historical fiction improved if students in children's literature courses discussed the historical fiction in chronological order, briefly identified the actual historical happenings of the time period, identified major themes found in literature written about a specific period (this is not meant to suggest that there are not multiple themes found in the literature), discussed the implications of recurring themes, identified how authors developed believable plots for the time period, and discussed the modern significance of the literature. In order to assist in the study of historical fiction, this chapter follows an order similar to the one used during Norton's study. It is hoped that this framework will assist readers of historical fiction as they discuss the literature in children's literature classes, extend the time line to other periods, or consider historical fiction during individual contemplation. Chart 10–1 presents this order and the main themes developed in each period.

The Ancient World

The early Egyptian culture spanned more than 4000 years. Powerful Pharaohs, with the help of vast numbers of slaves, built pyramids and temples to themselves and their gods. The

Egyptian dynasties overcame political and religious conflicts, as well as outside invasions, to become by 1600 B.C. a strong and prosperous military state. In 332 B.C. Egypt was conquered by Alexander the Great and later by the Romans.

Toward the close of Egyptian rule a great power was developing in Rome that would eventually conquer and maintain an empire greater in size than that achieved by Alexander the Great. During the early days of Roman expansion there were attempts to assimilate the foreign populations. This tendency did not last, however, as expanding Roman rule became harsher and harsher.

England before the birth of Christ was inhabited by tribes ruled by chiefs; the members of one tribe, the Iceni, were also known as "Horse People." During this time, it was not uncommon for warring tribes to conquer each other's people, land, and other holdings. In 55 B.C., the tribes had to contend with an outside invader when Julius Caesar tried to add Britain to the Roman Empire. He overcame the Belgic tribes of the south but could not overrun the more powerful tribes to the north. One hundred years later, Emperor Claudius succeeded in adding Britain to the Roman Empire. The Iceni, along with other

CHART 10–1
Themes in Historical Fiction

4000 B.C. The Ancient World	Personal Conscience
Loyalty to Friends and Country	**1692 Impact of Salem**
There are Consequences for Blind Hate	Freedom from Persecution
Hate, Not Man, Is the Enemy	**1776 Revolutionary War**
Love Is Stronger Than Hate	Freedom is Worth Fighting For
Man's Search for Freedom	Strong Beliefs Require Strong Commitments
Loyalty to Family and Friends	**1780 Early Expansion—North and West**
Light Extends Beyond One's Lifetime	Love for the Land
Darkness Threatens to Destroy Light	Consequences of Hatred and Prejudice
A.D. 1000 Vikings Travel the Seas	**1861 Civil War**
Man's Search for Freedom	Tragedy of War
Man's Search for Land	Personal Conscience Does Not Allow Humans to Kill
Consequences of Greed	Others
Bravery	Search for Freedom
Loyalty to Family and Friends	**1860s Pioneer America**
1500 Medieval Europe Through Early Exploration	Love for The Land
Man's Search for Riches	People Need Each Other
Importance of Crusades	**1929 Depression**
Consequences of Greed	Striving for Survival
Consequences of Human Ignorance	Prejudice and Discrimination Are Destructive Forces
Ability Should Not Be Judged by Physical	**1939 World War II**
Appearance	Freedom from Religious Persecution
1620 Beginnings of America and England at War	Freedom Is Worth Fighting For
Freedom from Religious or Political Persecution	Hatred and Prejudice Are Destructive Forces
Tragedy of War	

tribes, came to make their peace with Claudius. Roman legions were left behind to subdue the people and keep peace among the tribes. This Roman dominance lasted until about A.D. 410.

Authors who write credible stories about this ancient world frequently tell their stories from the viewpoint of a slave or a person who is under the harsh rule of a conqueror. Through these viewpoints, which may express strong feelings and emotions, the authors encourage readers to glimpse both personal and societal conflicts. Strong themes emerge as the characters fight for their beliefs and personal freedom and/or overcome strong negative feelings that could destroy them.

Consider, for example, the literary techniques Eloise McGraw uses in *Mara, Daughter of the Nile*. The author tells her story set in ancient Egypt from a slave's viewpoint. Glimpses of various strata of Egyptian life emerge as the character interacts with shopkeepers, slaves, soldiers, and royalty. Royal intrigue and conflict develop as Mara is first hired to spy for the queen and then for the king. Through the author's development of Mara's character as she changes from a dishonest slave to a girl who endures torture rather than betray her new friends and the rightful Pharaoh, readers gain an understanding of a strong theme: loyalty to friends and country is more important than personal safety.

Elizabeth George Speare focuses upon Israel during Roman rule in *The Bronze Bow.* She develops a view of the harsh rule of conquest by telling the story through the viewpoint of a boy who longs to avenge the death of his parents. (His father was crucified by Roman soldiers, and his mother died from grief and exposure.) Daniel bar Jamin's bitterness is intensified as he joins a guerrilla band and nurtures his hatred. His own person-against-self conflict comes to a turning point when he almost sacrifices his sister because of his hatred. The author encourages readers to understand Daniel's real enemy when Daniel talks to Jesus. Jesus makes Daniel realize that hate, not Romans, is the enemy. In fact, the only thing stronger than hate is love. The author shows the magnitude of Daniel's change at the close of the story; he invites a Roman soldier into his home.

Rosemary Sutcliff uses a real twenty-century-old British mystery as a basis for a historical novel. The magical Uffington White Horse has raced over the British Berkshire Downs for over two thousand years. What force, in approximately 100 B.C., motivated the carving of this beautiful animal? Who was the sculptor who could recreate a horse alive with movement and power? This mystery motivated Sutcliff's search for answers; *Sun Horse, Moon Horse* is her version of how this horse, still visible today, came to be carved on the high downs.

In this tale, Sutcliff tells the story of the Iceni tribe before the Roman invasion. She develops believable characters who, through their actions and desires, express strong feelings of tribal loyalty, honor, and a fierce desire for freedom. Sutcliff develops the theme "man's search for freedom" by comparing the peaceful days when the tribe dreams of finding new horse runs, with the days following their capture by another tribe who covets their land and horses. In this turbulent time, they decide

The symbol for the Iceni expresses the desire for tribal freedom. From *Sun Horse, Moon Horse* by Rosemary Sutcliff. Text © 1977 by Rosemary Sutcliff. Decorations copyright © 1977 by The Bodley Head. Reprinted by permission of the publisher, E. P. Dutton.

that they must hold together and wait for their chance for freedom. It is a boy's strong desire for freedom for his people, combined with his artistic talents, that gives the tribe its opportunity for freedom. Readers are encouraged to believe in the boy's longing for freedom for his tribe through his agreement with the conquering chieftain, his actions during the carving of the horse, and his final sacrifice. Consider, for example, the scene where he agrees to complete the carving of the conquering tribe's sun horse symbol if, after he has completed the carving, his people can go free. But, he does not only carve the symbol of his enemies, he also includes the moon horse, the symbol for his own tribe. His final actions develop the strongest belief in his desire for tribal freedom and his belief in the symbolization of the moon horse: upon completion of the carving, he asks that his own life be sacrificed upon the horse. This action, he believes, will add the necessary life and strength to his carving. Sutcliff reaffirms the tribe's loyalty and admiration for the boy through feelings expressed by the new leader of his people:

Heart-brother . . . wait for me in the Land of Apple Trees. Whether it be tomorrow, or when I am Lord of many spears in the north, and too old to sit a horse or lift a sword, wait for me until I come. And do not be forgetting me, for I will not forget you. (p. 106)

The Iceni tribe's futile effort to stem the tide of Roman conquest is the subject of another book by Sutcliff, *Song for a Dark Queen.* The year is A.D. 62, over 150 years after the tribe left the Berkshire Downs in search of new horse runs. The leading character is a queen rather than a male chieftain. (The Iceni leadership does not go from father to son, but down the moonside, or "womanside.") Sutcliff develops the belief in a strong female leader who could rule her tribe through the descriptions of her early training and her reactions when her tribe is conquered by the Romans. She has been trained from early childhood to lead men in battle, and she heads a revolt that almost succeeds in overpowering Roman rule and defending ancient tribal culture. Her efforts fail; the Ninth Legion overpowers her, and her tribe is placed firmly under Roman dominance. The author's theme of the importance of freedom is emphasized by the queen's actions. She decides to sacrifice her own life rather than be a captive.

Sutcliff's *Frontier Wolf* and *The Lantern Bearers* are set in a later Britain; one that has been invaded by and ruled by Roman legions for several hundred years. The author tells these stories from the viewpoints of Roman soldiers or former soldiers. In *Frontier Wolf* she paints a vivid picture of a remote Roman outpost in northern Britain and a young centurion's problems as he tries to understand and lead a group of British tribesmen

who have volunteered to serve Rome. The importance of understanding people and local customs is exemplified by comparisons between the behaviors of centurion Alexios Flavius Aquila and a dictatorial commander who visits the outpost.

In *The Lantern Bearers.* the setting is at the end of Roman rule, as the last of the Roman troops are withdrawn from Britain, chaos is beginning as old alliances dissolve, and the "wolves of the sea" invade Britain. Sutcliff tells the story from the viewpoint of a Roman, Aquila, who sees his sister captured by roving invaders, their father killed by the Saxons, and their property destroyed. Sutcliff uses this setting to develop themes about the importance of light and darkness in human lives. Aquila's heart is first filled with darkness and despair as he discovers what it is like to be a slave, and then he escapes, only to search for the man who betrayed his father. Light, the force that goes beyond one's lifetime, is finally discovered by Aquila when he realizes he has the greatest riches of all: a wife who foresook her own people to be with him, and a son who stood beside him, risking disgrace. Even though uncertainty and war lay ahead, Sutcliff concludes her book on a hopeful note:

I sometimes think that we stand at sunset. . . . It may be that the night will close over us in the end, but I believe that morning will come again. Morning always grows again out of darkness, though maybe not for the people who saw the sun go down. We are the Lantern Bearers, my friend; for us to keep something burning to carry what light we can forward into the darkness and the wind. (p. 250)

Students of children's literature may wish to consider how and why the following themes developed by authors who write about the ancient world relate to the historical happenings:

1 It is important to be loyal to friends and country.
2 There are dangerous personal consequences associated with blind hatred.
3 Hate, not men, is the greatest enemy.
4 Love is stronger than hate.
5 Humans will search for freedom.
6 Light extends beyond one's lifetime.
7 Darkness threatens to destroy the light that extends beyond life.

Are there any other time periods in history when these themes might have special significance? Are the themes significant in our contemporary world?

Vikings Travel the Seas

Long black galleys sailing out from the fjords of the Scandinavian coast, men with names like Eric the Red or *Magnus the*

Fair, and the icy domain of the Norse god Odin are part of the Viking heritage. Between the fifth and ninth centuries, the Vikings, or inletmen, were using their seamanship to travel the northern seas toward Iceland and Greenland. Stories tell of their raids against the people living along the coasts of England and Scotland. In about A.D. 1000, these Norsemen made their greatest voyage, journeying across 3,000 miles of uncharted ocean and landing on the North American continent. Although they did not make a lasting settlement in "Vinland," they proved their remarkable seamanship. Each of these periods in Viking history provides fertile seeds for storytelling.

Were the Vikings bold heroes or bloodthirsty raiders? Authors who write about the Viking period develop both loyal and honorable heroes who strive for human freedom, and evil, treacherous men who kill and enslave. Vivid descriptions are important for these characterizations. Conflicts develop as free men search for land, slaves search for freedom, humans ponder their own beliefs, or worshipers war over the superiority of the ancient god Odin or the new Christian God. The ways characters overcome these conflicts illustrate various human values characteristic of the time period.

The settings in literature of the Viking period frequently stress the sea's importance. The sea is not usually an antagonist but provides the means to expand the Viking world.

Erik Christian Haugaard has written two enjoyable stories about the Viking period. In *Hakon of Rogen's Saga,* Haugaard describes an island setting and develops the importance of the sea for the Vikings and for Hakon, a young Viking boy. The sea does not confine, instead it is the road that leads everywhere and is the reality from which Hakon's dreams are made. Haugaard develops a fast-paced plot as the island is attacked by his father's enemies, and Hakon is left to the mercies of an uncle who wishes to steal his birthright. Fleeing for his life, Hakon hides in a secret cave on the island. It is during this time that the boy's thoughts and actions reveal his own feelings about courage, strength, and freedom. He realizes that if he can be alone without fear no one can call him weak even if he is not yet strong enough to wield a sword. The actions of a few loyal men on the island and of a freed slave help him recapture the island and his birthright. Haugaard suggests through these actions that freedom is the greatest birthright that anyone can have. Hakon's belief in freedom is reinforced when he takes over the rule of the island, his men swear loyalty to him, and he declares, "I swear that on Rogen shall rule only justice. That no man shall fear his tongue nor his thought, but each man shall live in peace" (p. 113).

The second book by Haugaard, *A Slave's Tale,* extends the story of Hakon and Helga, the young slave girl. This story is told

In Viking tales, the sea is the highway to adventure. From *Hakon of Rogen's Saga* by Erik Christian Haugaard. Copyright © 1963 by Erik Christian Haugaard. Reprinted by permission of Houghton Mifflin Company.

from the viewpoint of the slave whom Hakon frees after he becomes the island's ruler. The slave's experiences and her growing loyalty to Hakon are made believable through the author's descriptions of her early life when her mother raised her and Hakon, of her close attachment to him, and the unpleasant times when she was beaten and life was a struggle against weariness, pain, and hunger. Haugaard's contrasts between these two time periods help the reader understand Helga's feelings of loyalty toward Hakon. The importance of freedom is reinforced by both action and thought throughout the story. Helga is a willing slave to Hakon because he did not treat her as a slave; she has freedom of both spirit and body. When Helga is freed, however, she says that a slave cannot be freed by words only. Along the way, she learns that being born free is not everything: "That you were born free is the gift of the gods and your parent's luck. It gives you neither honor nor dishonor. What you become, this alone shall you be judged by" (p. 116).

Several books for older children tell the story of the Vikings' Atlantic voyage in search of new lands. Henry Treece's *Westward to Vinland* contains tales of Eric the Red as he is exiled first to Iceland and then to Greenland. It also includes the journeys of Leif the Lucky as he goes west and discovers a rich American coast. In this story, the hostility of the Indians, whom the Vikings call Skraelings, and quarrels among the settlers force the Vikings to return to Greenland.

Viking stories usually have settings in Norway, the North Atlantic, Greenland, Iceland, or the British Isles. The Vikings, however, also traveled down Russian rivers, to the Baltic Sea, and east to Constantinople. This journey is the setting for *Blood Feud* by Rosemary Sutcliff. In this tale, an English boy, Jestyn, is captured by a raiding party and taken to a slave market in Dublin, where he is approached by several Vikings. Sutcliff's description of the approaching Vikings is especially effective because it is told from the point of view of the frightened boy who has heard and believed terrible stories about the Vikings:

The men who stood there glancing me over were the true Viking kind that I had heard of in stories and been told to pray God I might never see in life. Men with grey ring-mail strengthening their leather byrnies, iron-bound war-caps, long straight swords. One had a silver arm-ring, one had studs of coral in the clasp of his belt, one wore a rough wolf-skin cloak. (p. 14)

Jestyn's belief encourages readers to believe in his experience and the vision he is seeing. Sutcliff's vivid descriptions of the boy's reactions to being purchased for six gold pieces and a wolfskin and to wearing the hated thrall ring of a slave help the reader understand his feelings. When Jestyn concludes that his master is a good man and worthy of his loyalty, readers are also encouraged to believe in his worth. The remainder of the book stresses the theme of honor toward parents and loyalty between friends as the Viking and his now loyal friend search for the murderer of the Viking's father.

Consider how and why the following themes developed by authors who write about the Viking times relate to the historical happenings of the time period. If there are similarities or differences between themes developed in literature on the ancient world, what might account for them? Are these themes significant in our contemporary world?

1 Land is important; humans will go through numerous hardships to acquire land for personal reasons or for the glory of their country.
2 Humans will search for freedom.
3 Freedom is a state of mind as well as the body.
4 Courage of the heart is as important, if not more important, than physical ability.
5 Greed is a powerful and threatening human characteristic.
6 Loyalty to noble friends and family is one of the highest human character traits.
7 Only one's deeds live on after death.

Medieval Europe Through Early Exploration

The Roman Empire has ended in western Europe, the Vikings have invaded and raided western and eastern Europe, and a period of feudalism is beginning in western Europe. Heavily armored knights live in fortified castles, and Gothic churches are being built in the cities. This is a time of conflict between the church and various rulers; it is also the time of the Crusades. The Hundred Years' War between France and England is causing pain and suffering; so is the great plague, or black death, that ravages cities and towns. By the end of the medieval period, there is considerable interest in exploration: Columbus discovers America, and Cortez begins his conquest of the Aztecs. Previously unknown cultures—the Mayas, the Aztecs, and North American Indians—are discovered and then are frequently exploited or irreversibly changed. By the 1500s, theaters are being built in England and crowds enjoy the works of the playwright, William Shakespeare.

Authors who write credible stories about the medieval period frequently develop detailed settings of castle life or a humble cottage existence. Characterizations include the development of values, beliefs, and reactions to personal or physical problems. The settings in stories of exploration may encourage readers to visualize a Mayan temple, an Aztec city, or a native American village. Antagonists reflect the beliefs, knowledge, and historic happenings. Consequently, antagonists may be suspicion, ignorance, prejudice, or greed; sickness or war; or the personal dilemmas that must be faced and resolved in a changing world. Through the resolutions of problems, higher values are also expressed.

Marguerite DeAngeli, in *The Door in the Wall,* uses a castle setting to depict the life of ten-year-old Robin, who is expected to train for knighthood. The plot has an unusual twist when Robin is stricken with a mysterious ailment that paralyzes his legs. The door in the title of the story now becomes symbolic as a monk gives unhappy Robin difficult advice: "Thou hast only to follow the wall far enough and there will be a door in it" (p. 16). This symbol is very important in the story; DeAngeli develops the plot by tracing Robin's search for his own door.

Other doors in Robin's wall and the need for preparation to find them are developed by the author when Robin is helped by the monk who guides his learning, encourages him to carve and to read, and expresses the belief that his hands and his mind must be taught because they represent other doors in the wall. The reference to the door occurs again; Robin worries that as a cripple who walks with crutches he will be useless. His father's friend, Sir Peter, reassures him by saying that if a person cannot serve in one way, there will be another means of serving: a door will always open.

FLASHBACK

THE HISTORICAL NOVEL BECAME POPULAR IN THE 1800s WITH the publication of stories by Sir Walter Scott and Charlotte Yonge. Scott's story of medieval English life, *Ivanhoe* (1820), was frequently used as a school assignment for older children. Other popular books by Scott included *The Lady of the Lake* (1810), *Waverly: Or, 'Tis Sixty Years Since* (1814), *Rob Roy* (1818) and *Tales of the Crusaders* (1825). Yonge's historical books including *The Little Duke* (a boyhood story of Richard the Fearless, 1854), *Richard the Fearless* (1856), and *The Lances of Lynwood* (1855), and her series of "Cameos from History" (1850s–1890s) published in *The Monthly Packet* provided vicarious adventure, relaxation, and a sense of history to Victorian children.

Robin proves his worth to himself and the castle when Welsh forces attack. He escapes the enemy sentry and obtains help from the neighboring castle. Readers are encouraged to understand the importance of being accepted for what one is rather than being rejected because of a handicap when Robin's father congratulates him:

The courage you have shown, the craftsmanship proven by the harp, and the spirit in your singing all make so bright a light that I cannot see whether or not your legs are misshapen. (p. 120)

Many children enjoy this beautiful story about a child who finds a door in his wall. One girl said that it was her favorite book because she liked the way Robin overcame his problem and was happy with his life. The theme is especially appropriate for teaching positive attitudes about the handicapped.

Another book that develops more severe problems related to living with a handicapping condition in medieval Europe is Gloria Skurzynski's *Manwolf*. The author builds a plot around the symptoms of a rare skin disease—hair grows on skin exposed to the sun, and scarring creates an animal appearance—and a superstitious people's reactions to anyone who has this disease. The belief in werewolves and the personal tragedy that results from such a belief are shown by the attacks on a

young boy and his mother's attempts to protect him. The lifelong battle against prejudice is suggested by the mask his father wears to hide his own features from the superstitious people.

Strong person-against-self conflicts, settings that depict Mayan and Aztec cultures, and themes that illustrate the human consequences of greed are all found in Scott O'Dell's historical novels based on the Spanish conquest of Mexico in the early 1500s. O'Dell's *The Captive* and his sequel, *The Feathered Serpent,* focus not so much on events of the time period, but on the moral dilemmas facing the main character.

Person-against-self conflicts are developed as a young, idealistic Jesuit seminarian, Julián Escobar, leaves his secure homeland in Spain and joins an expedition to New Spain. O'Dell develops these conflicts and illustrates the main character's changing ideals and values by describing Julián's decisions, his reactions to the Spaniards' behaviors, his own ponderings about right and wrong, his discoveries about himself and others, and his various actions toward the Mayas and their culture.

Consider, for example, the changing characterization as Julián proceeds from an idealistic student to a man who takes on the role of a powerful Mayan god. First Julián is convinced by a

Spanish nobleman, Don Luis, that he should leave Seville and the prospect of becoming a secure village priest to go to New Spain where he could be a powerful saver of souls. Julián's first moral dilemma oocurs when, on the ocean voyage, he questions Don Luis's motives for choosing a young seminarian rather than an older priest. Now Julián debates the morality of slavery after he realizes that Don Luis wants to enter the slave trade. Later, Julián again questions the human motives for the expedition. Don Luis's treatment of the Indians suggests he wants to enslave and exploit them, not save their souls. Doubts enter Julián's mind as he questions whether he has the spirit or the patience to spread the Christian faith.

Throughout both books, O'Dell encourages readers to glimpse personal conflicts as Julián gradually perceives that the Spaniards are motivated by greed rather than the rewards from spreading Christianity. O'Dell explores changes in Julián by stressing the changing conflicts in his own life: Should he take on the role of the mythical Kukulcán to save his own life and bring his views to the Mayas? Should he advise attacking a neighboring city before his own Mayan city is attacked? How should he respond to the rites of sun worship? Why did God permit both good and evil?

Julián's defense of his inability to change the Mayas and his own actions demonstrate changes in his character and how he resolves his own moral dilemma. In *The Feathered Serpent*, for example, he thinks back to Augustine's teachings and concludes that evil exists because God wills it. Therefore, the worship of idols and human sacrifice are beyond his control. Julián does admit, however, that this argument may be only in defense of his own actions.

The author's descriptions of Mayan and Aztec cities and temples and other aspects of their cultures encourage readers to understand that an advanced civilization inhabited the Americas long before European exploration and settlement. Readers may also ponder the right of one culture to destroy another culture whose citizens worship different gods and possess riches desired by a foreign power.

A different perspective on the time period and the consequences of exploration is developed in Joyce Rockwood's *To Spoil the Sun*. The author emphasizes the Cherokee culture, personal development and family relationships within the tribe, and the disaster that follows a smallpox epidemic brought by Spanish explorers. See page 507 for a discussion of Rockwood's book.

Some of the themes chosen by authors of historical fiction with settings in medieval Europe or the Americas in the 1500s focus on harsh realities; others are more positive in nature. Consider how and why the following themes relate to the time period. Are there similarities or differences between these themes and themes from either different historic periods or contemporary stories?

1 A physical handicap does not reduce a person's capabilities.
2 People can overcome their handicaps.
3 People should be accepted for what they are.
4 Human ignorance has severe consequences.
5 Human greed is a strong motivational force and has severe consequences.
6 Prejudice is a destructive force.
7 Moral dilemmas must be faced and resolved.
8 Humans will search for riches.
9 Loyalty to family and tribe is one of the highest character traits.

Beginnings of America and England at War

The first half of the seventeenth century brought disruptions in England that affected not only England but also America. The persecution of religious groups, the desire to escape the tyranny of a king and his taxes, and a desire for freedom caused many Englishmen to dream of, and seek a new life on, America's shores. The *Mayflower* was the first of the pioneer ships to bring immigrants from Europe to settle the Plymouth Colony in America. Their's was not, however, an easy conquest of a wilderness. The sponsors did not provide sufficient supplies, the first winter was filled with sickness and starvation, and the new settlers were apprehensive about the Indians who lived beyond their settlement.

While a young colony is trying to survive, ominous clouds are gathering over England. In 1640 there is conflict between Charles I and Parliament; rumors abound; alliances are both openly and secretly made. Will the hatreds break out into civil war? In 1642, the king sets up his standard at Nottingham, and war begins with the king holding Oxford and Parliament controlling London. One of the strongest leaders to emerge from the Parliament commanders is Oliver Cromwell, an ordinary man but a great military organizer. There is also conflict between religious groups; the king has taken a Catholic bride, and supporters of Parliament are staunchly Protestant.

Authors who write about the Mayflower and the settlement of Plymouth frequently focus upon the reasons for leaving England and hardships faced by the Pilgrims. Patricia Clapp, for example, tells the story of the early settlement of New England through the point of view of a fourteen-year-old girl in *Constance: A Story of Early Plymouth*. Because she did not want to leave her cherished London, her first view of the new

THROUGH THE EYES OF AN AUTHOR

Making the Past Come Alive

Patricia Clapp

Graduate of Columbia University's School of Journalism and author of books set in an earlier America, PATRICIA CLAPP discusses the importance of experiencing with and reacting to her protagonists in historical fiction.

AS THE WRITER OF HIStorical novels, the most rewarding comment I can receive from a young reader is "I felt as if I was there!" Then I know that the book has achieved what I worked for, an immediacy and realism that make the past as alive to the reader as the present in which he lives.

I can only create that immediacy and realism by being there myself. I don't mean checking out the location by visiting the place, although I do that too, whenever I can. I mean feeling the emotions, smelling the air, tasting the food, wearing the clothes—being there. That probably explains why most of my books are written in the first person. I become Constance Hopkins, or Elizabeth Blackwell, or Deborah Sampson, or Mary Warren, and write the story as I live it.

This is not to say that months of research don't precede every book. They do, and I love every minute of them. But what I absorb must become a natural part of the narrative, not paragraphs of exposition which most young people skip over as quickly as possible. For example, there is no need to describe the pastry of the 1780's by giving the recipe for Maid of Honor Tarts when Deborah Sampson makes them. It is enough to mention the succulent ingredients, the sugar and butter, the ground almonds and sherry wine, the currant preserves spread in the bottoms of the patty pans. The reader knows as well as Deborah and I how delicious they will taste.

The same holds true with physical responses. I must be there, experiencing and reacting with my protagonist. When Deborah sits alone by a campfire, weeping as she tries to pry a British musket ball from her shoulder with her army jackknife, we suffer together because we are one. When Mary Warren is caught in the thick web of 17th century superstition she struggles with terrified helplessness, and I struggle with her. When Constance Hopkins seeks escape from the confusion in her heart by walking deep into the Plymouth woods and hacking fiercely at small branches to be used for kindling, kicking them into a pile, feeling her hair caught and tumbled by encroaching twigs, I feel the same sting of cold pine-scented air on my face and the same quick rushing of blood as the axe bites into the wood.

It is an exciting way to live. To move back to whatever era interests me, to live there and then, to know the people and their problems and triumphs. My world is wide and timeless. There is a brief but difficult transition when I cover my typewriter, push my chair back, and return to what some people refer to as "the real world," but there is always the knowledge that I can, at will, retreat into some long-ago time. When a young person tells me "I felt as if I was really there," I know I have taken him traveling with me.

world from the deck of the *Mayflower* is an unpleasant one. Clapp encourages readers to understand the various viewpoints of the Pilgrims by contrasting Constance's view of a bleak and and unfriendly land with other views of excitement and anticipation expressed by her father, William Bradford, John Alden, and Miles Standish. Clapp's vivid descriptions of Constance's first encounter with Samoset, her feelings of resentment toward doing "womanly" tasks, and her grief when she sees friends struggle and die during the first long winter encourage readers to understand the many facets of Constance's character. Clapp demonstrates the changes in Constance's feelings toward America when, six years after her first disappointing view of America, she marries and she and her husband decide they will begin their life together in the new world. Through the course of the story, Clapp develops a high-spirited girl who grows stronger as she faces and learns to enjoy her new life.

A picture storybook for young children brings the colonial setting of New Amsterdam to life. Arnold Lobel's *On the Day Peter Stuyvesant Sailed into Town* provides a humorously illustrated account of this occasion. When Stuyvesant arrived on the American shore in 1647, he found a town near collapse. The streets were reverting to weeds, animals ran freely, garbage littered the settlement, houses were falling into disrepair, and the walls of the fort were crumbling. Stuyvesant considered this abominable and quickly told the settlers to improve their town. He was so successful that the next ten years produced a city that doubled in size and was as neat as any Dutch community in Europe. The pictures in this book help children visualize the setting of sailing ships, colonial dress and homes, and Dutch windmills.

Authors who place their settings in England during the English Civil War frequently develop themes related to the tragedy of war. The character development often explores the influences that shape a person's growing awareness of the reality of war. Haugaard, for example, uses the war setting to develop such changing attitudes toward war in *A Messenger for Parliament*. The war is seen through the point of view of eleven-year-old Oliver Cutter who has his own conflicts: his mother is dying and his father is a ne'er-do-well braggart. After his mother dies, he follows his father into war without understanding his own feelings or realizing what is involved. Haugaard effectively encourages readers to understand Oliver's changing feelings as he talks to other boys about the glory of war and describes it in terms of a game. When the boys joke about taking swords and money from dead soldiers, however, Oliver begins to understand the realities of war:

Till now I had not thought that the taking of a sword or a dagger on the battlefield would mean robbing the dead. Though I had seen the sacking of Worcester, war seemed to me still a game. Jack's words made me feel the fear I had not felt before. It came creeping like the shadows of twilight. (p. 64)

Haugaard shows the attitude changes of his main character by having him observe a battle and see the sufferings of war. He still does not understand the differences between the warring sides. Oliver matures rapidly in this harsh time. He is finally given the responsibility of getting a message through to Cromwell. After long days of walking, danger, and hiking, he reaches Cromwell's home and delivers the message. Cromwell is pleased with young Oliver's bravery and spirit and tells him that with allies such as Oliver on Parliament's side, there is nothing to fear. Oliver has made a true friend, and Cromwell asks him to be his personal messenger. Oliver is very proud when the soldiers call him "Cromwell's boy."

In the sequel, *Cromwell's Boy*, Oliver is now a much older thirteen. He rides a horse well, does not divulge secrets, and looks inconspicuous and unimportant. His ability to serve Cromwell extends beyond messages as he goes into the dangerous stronghold of the king's army as a spy. Even his flight from Oxford is dramatic; he rescues a friend whose father is imprisoned as a traitor and escapes on the powerful stallion of an Irish lord. The author suggests the lessons that Oliver has learned by using a flashback in which he remembers his earlier life. When Oliver as a grown man reminisces about his youthful promises and experiences, he concludes:

In my youth there was little time for dreams. Life challenged me early. The leisure to reflect was not my lot; tomorrow was ever knocking on the door of today with new demands. It made me resourceful and sharpened my wit, but the purpose of life must be more than just to survive. You must be able—at least for short moments—to hold your precious soul in your hands and to contemplate that gift with love and understanding. (p. 1)

The themes chosen by authors who write about England and America during the early 1600s frequently stress the importance of freedom and the tragedies of war or persecution. Consider the following themes. Why are they developed during this time period? Some themes have been mentioned before, others are new.

1 People want freedom from religious or political persecution; they are willing to face hardships for this freedom.
2 People must work together if they are to survive.
3 Overcoming problems can strengthen character.
4 War creates human tragedy.
5 Life is more than survival.

Impact of Salem

In the late 1600s, many people living in Massachusetts and Connecticut were accused of witchcraft. The famous witch-hunt of 1692 in Salem started when a doctor stated that the hysterical behavior of several teenage girls was due to the "evil eye." Within six months, twenty persons were sentenced to death and one hundred and fifty were sent to prison. Boston minister Cotton Mather was one of the clergymen who preached the power of the devil and the need to purge the world of witchcraft. Persons charged with witchcraft were pardoned in 1693 when Sir William Phipps, royal governor of the Bay Colony, said that the witch-hunt proceedings were too violent and not based upon fact. Belief in witchcraft faded in the 1700s with scientific understanding of previously frightening phenomena.

The conflict in stories set in this short period of American history is usually person-against-society. Authors frequently take their characters out of an environment in which the society is not an antagonist and place them in a hostile environment. Now common behavior patterns can create suspicion. For example, is a person a witch because she brews tea from herbs to give to the ill? Does spinning thread faster and better prove a person is a witch? Does speaking to a cat indicate witchcraft? These are the charges that face the heroine in Petry's *Tituba of Salem Village.*

Contrasts in setting suggest the drama that follows. Petry describes two slaves living in comparative freedom by a sparkling sea on the coral-encrusted coastline of Barbados. The setting changes rapidly from their tropical home to the dark ship. The characters also shift from a fairly permissive owner to the solemn dark-clothed minister from Boston who buys Tituba and her husband. Even their first meeting is ominous; Tituba backs away from a tall, thin shadow that blots out the sun and covers her body. The change in setting is complete as the author describes the house in Salem. When Reverend Parris, his family, and their two slaves approach the house, they are greeted with rotten eggs on the doorstep and neglected buildings, and a general gloom surrounds and permeates the house. It is not only the setting that proves ominous. People mutter threats, teenage girls become hysterical, and townspeople testify that Tituba can transform herself into a wolf or travel without her body.

Tituba's crime is not witchcraft, but simply that she is more capable and intelligent than many of the people around her. This book develops insights into the consequences of inhumanity, regardless of time or place. The reader is encouraged to see and feel the danger in mass accusations and the fear of people to defend what they know is right. Compare Petry's characterization and plot development with Clapp's *Witches' Children: A Story of Salem.* Clapp tells the Salem experience through the viewpoint of a bound girl.

Tituba was noticed and suspected because she was a talented slave, but others who were "different" were also objects of this cruel obsession. The heroine in Speare's *The Witch of Blackbird Pond* also comes from Barbados, but her life is quite different from Tituba's. Contrasts between the people in her earlier childhood environment and the people in New England encourage readers to anticipate the building conflict. On Barbados Kit was raised by a loving grandfather who taught and encouraged her to read history, poetry, and plays. After his death, however, Kit travels to New England to live with her aunt. Several experiences on the ship suggest that her former lifestyle may not be appropriate for the new world. For example, when she tries to discuss Shakespeare with a fellow passenger, he is shocked because a girl should not read such things: "The proper use of reading is to improve our sinful nature, and to fill our minds with God's holy word" (p. 28). An even harsher response occurs after she jumps in the water and swims to rescue a child's doll. (It is believed that only the guilty are able to stay afloat.) When her actions in the Puritan village remain consistent with her earlier behavior, she raises the suspicions of the townspeople. Consider, for example, how the following actions might be viewed by her grandfather or the people of the village: she brings seven trunks filled with colorful clothes; she teaches children to read by writing frivolous verses such as "Timothy Cook, Jumped over the brook"; she has children act out stories from the Bible; and she becomes friendly with Hannah Tupper, a Quaker, who the villagers believe is a witch. It is this friendship with Hannah Tupper that creates the greatest conflict for Kit. Sickness breaks out in the town, and the people believe they are bewitched; Hannah is blamed. Kit risks her life to warn her friend, and they escape before the cottage is burned by angry men. Kit's action incurs the wrath of the settlement; she is arrested for witchcraft. The charges brought against her are similar to those brought against Tituba. Unlike Tituba, Kit has friends and family who stand by her and assist in her acquittal. She learns that it is important to choose your friends and then stand by them.

Both heroines are courageous, spirited, and honorable. The authors develop strong person-against-society conflicts because neither is considered different or suspected of witchcraft until she is taken out of her environment and placed in different circumstances. Both remain true to their beliefs, however, even when faced with hostility and superstition, and are examples of voices that cry out against the injustices around them. Because of their actions, a few people realized the consequences of blind, superstitious fear and hatred.

Consider the following themes developed in the literature of the Salem witch-hunts. What are the consequences of inhumanity and persecution developed in other time periods? What historic events coincide with such persecution?

1 Inhumanity and persecution are frightening and destructive forces.
2 People seek freedom from persecution.
3 Moral obligations require some people to defend others' rights.

The Revolutionary War—Heroes, Famous and Unknown

The inhabitants of the thirteen colonies came from different countries and had differing sympathies and practices. They did, however, have several strong antagonisms in common. First, they shared a fear of the native Indians. Second, they went through a period when they shared a dread of French conquest. Finally, they were in conflict with the British crown. In England, the oppressed and oppressor were in close proximity because of the social system; this was not true in America. The oppressor was now far away, and people could gather together to develop a sense of unity against a common enemy.

A series of demands made by the British government hastened the uniting of the colonies. In 1763, Britain tried to raise money in the colonies by passing the Stamp Act. Another intolerable act was the demand that British soldiers be quartered by the colonists. The final outrage occurred in 1773 when several ships bearing tea from London's East Indian Company arrived in Boston Harbor. The Bostonians would not accept the shipment; they refused to pay taxes without the right to vote for those who would represent them. Colonists disguised as Indians boarded the ships and dumped the tea into the harbor. The British Parliament responded by closing Boston Harbor, blocking it from trade. Sympathies were now in accord with the goal of freedom, and Samuel Adams and others like him rallied the colonists in support of this cause. The eight years from 1775 through 1783, beginning with Paul Revere's ride and ending with the Treaty of Paris, were a vibrant, dynamic time in American history.

This period was rich in the history of both great and common people. Elizabeth Yates (17) provides an excellent description of the people who fought in the Revolution:

They were the Founding Fathers who framed and signed the Declaration of Independence; the statesmen who inflamed and inspired public opinion; the patriots whose names and deeds live in history books. And they were those who lived in small towns and villages and on distant farms, who thought and talked about events and made their feelings known: men who left their stock and crops and marched off to fight because they were convinced of the rightness of the stand that had been made, women who took over the work of the farms along with the care of their homes and families. Their names made no news. They did no particular acts of heroism, except as the living of each day was heroic in itself. Hard work they knew well, and hardship they could endure. Giving their lives or living their lives, they were as much the foundation of the new nation as were those whose names have long been known. (p. 6)

While famous people are found in the backgrounds of much historical fiction written for children, the common people are the heroes and heroines of most of the books. There are generally two types of stories written about the revolutionary period: some tell about family members who stay home while fathers and brothers go to war; others deal with the lives of the boys, men, and even women who became actively involved in the war itself.

The best-known story of this period is Forbes's *Johnny Tremain.* The setting is superb, with Forbes using the same authenticity in this story as she did in her Pulitzer prize-winning *Paul Revere.* Paul Revere and Samuel Adams play an important part in *Johnny Tremain,* but the silversmith's apprentice and other unknown boys like him are the heroes. It is through the observances, actions, and thoughts of the apprentice that Forbes develops the issues of the times, the values of the people, and the feelings about freedom. Johnny discovers the political thinking of the time when he sends messages for the secret Boston Observers, rides for the Boston Committee of Correspondence, and attends church with the printer and listens as the minister preaches sermons filled with politics and anger against taxation without representation. He learns that without printers the cause of liberty would be lost. The author's style also enhances the authenticity of the time period. The language and excerpts from speeches made by revolutionary leaders create believable settings and characters. Consider, for example, the following speech calling the rebels to action:

Friends! Brethren! Countrymen! That worst of Plagues, the detested tea shipped for this Port by the East Indian Company, is now arrived in the Harbour: the hour of destruction, of manly opposition to the machinations of Tyranny, stares you in the Face; Every Friend to his Country, to Himself, and to Posterity, is now called upon to meet. (p. 107)

Johnny is one of the men disguised as Indians who throw the despised tea into Boston Harbor. He knows the anger and resulting unity when the harbor is closed by British troops. He is there as the alarm is spread, and men march for Concord.

Unhappily, he is also there when his best friend dies. He makes the discovery that a sixteen-year-old is considered a boy in times of peace but a man in times of war. As a man, he has the right to risk his life for what he believes.

An unusual character in the Revolutionary War is the heroine in Clapp's *I'm Deborah Sampson: A Soldier in the War of the Revolution.* Based on a true incident, this is the tale of a girl who sees her adopted brothers go off to war and one of them die. She believes so strongly in the need to fight that she disguises herself as a man, joins a regiment of soldiers, travels with them across the countryside, and is wounded. Her greatest fear when she is wounded is that her identity will be discovered. Deborah is a strong, memorable character who vividly lives in the pages of Clapp's story. (See pages 84–86 for a discussion of characterization.)

Most school children know about Paul Revere's ride, but Gail E. Haley has chosen a not-so-famous ride to share with younger readers. *Jack Jouett's Ride* takes place in 1781 and tells a tale of equal daring. This time, a young rider discovers that Tarleton and his troop of Green Dragoons are riding toward Charlottesville to capture Thomas Jefferson, Patrick Henry, and other leaders of the Revolution. Jack saddles his horse, moves out into the night, and rides across meadows and thickets to spread the alarm. This picture storybook, with its vivid illustrations and less complex language, will appeal to young children and help them share in the flavor of this historic period.

These authors establish believable plots by creating detailed descriptions of the settings, adhering to known issues and expressed values of the times, and telling the stories through the viewpoint of the common people involved in the developing conflict.

Consider the themes and the historic facts from this period. Why do you think the following themes are developed in the literature? How and why are these themes similar or different from themes in other war time periods?

1 Freedom is worth fighting for.
2 Strong beliefs require strong commitments.

Early Expansion—North and West

As more and more settlers came to America, the need for additional land became evident. Many settlers looked beyond the shores of New England and Virginia and headed into the rolling, tree-covered hills to the west or north. These settlers had something in common: they sought freedom and land and had considerable courage. Some settlers developed friendly relationships with Indian tribes; others experienced hostilities.

Detailed illustrations of the setting help younger readers visualize the historic period.
From *Jack Jouett's Ride* by Gail E. Haley. Reprinted by permission of Viking Penguin, Inc.

It was not uncommon for settlers to be captured by Indians and taken into the tribe, sold as slaves, or held for ransom. Many abductions, however, were in retaliation for attacks against the Indians. Missionary groups also had an impact on pioneer and Indian relationships. The Moravians, for example, taught their ways to the Indians.

Stories about early pioneer expansion are popular with children who enjoy vivid characters and rapid action. The young characters may be popular with children because they frequently show extraordinary courage and prove they can be equal to adults. There are also strong family bonds in many of the stories. The focus may be on everyday experiences or on tense drama. Authors frequently develop vivid descriptions of the new land that encourage readers to understand why a family is willing to give up a secure environment to live on a new frontier. There are also person-against-self conflicts as characters face moral dilemmas such as racial prejudice.

Alice Dalgliesh's *The Courage of Sarah Noble* is an excellent story for young children. (Sarah, according to the author, did exist.) Dalgliesh encourages readers to visualize the courage that even an eight-year-old can demonstrate when she accompanies her father to their new land in Connecticut. The author uses the words her mother says as they leave to highlight times of great stress: "Keep up your courage, Sarah Noble!" (p. 2). These words come back to Sarah repeatedly as they journey into the wilderness. She says them when the wolves howl in the forest, when she is surrounded by strange Indian children, and when her father leaves her with friendly Indians so that he can travel back to Massachusetts.

This is a story of friendship and faith as well as courage. The author develops the theme, the need to help others, through the actions of the characters; Sarah and her father help each other, and they develop strong ties with an Indian family.

Friendship is believable in *The Courage of Sarah Noble,* because the family lives this philosophy. An Indian family invites Sarah to stay with them, encourages her to eat their food, makes her deerskin moccasins, and treats her like a daughter.

Blos's *A Gathering of Days, A New England Girl's Journal, 1830–32* is set on a New Hampshire farm between 1830 and 1832. The story is written in journal format by a fictional thirteen-year-old, Catherine Hall. Blos says that within this story she tried to develop three types of truthfulness: "the social truthfulness of the situation, the psychological truthfulness of the characters, and the literary truthfulness of the manner of telling" (1, p. 371). Consequently, the characters are similar to those who, drawn by unknown artists, stare from New England portraits. Likewise, the tone of the story is similar to *Leavitt's Almanac,* written for farmers, with the form and style found in journal writings of that period.

Blos's style of writing and the first person point of view make believable characters. Readers are encouraged to visualize many aspects of life in the early 1800s as the heroine states her feelings about raising the children and caring for her father. She faces her own moral dilemmas as she ponders issues such as slavery and breaking the laws of the state. The author clarifies these issues as Catherine and her friends help a runaway slave and contemplate the rights and evils of slavery as well as the morality of bringing him a quilt and food.

The wilderness to the north and the island-scattered coast of Maine have enchanted several authors and provided the settings for historical fiction books for young children. Rachel Field develops a strong love for Maine through historical fiction. According to Ruth Hill Viguers (16), "The strong sense of place had its roots in her love and intuitive understanding of a region where the somber, icy months of winter are long and spring comes late but so suddenly that almost overnight it seemed, the earth turned from bleakness to vehement green" (p. vii).

Love for this land and a willingness to withstand considerable hardships to keep the land are emphasized in *Calico Bush.* as Marguerite, a "bound out" girl, learns to admire both the land and its people. The story is told through the point of view of a French girl who at first has difficulty adjusting to the environment. Several plausible characteristics of the pioneers are also developed through their reactions to her: they are shocked when she dances the *pavane* and astonished when she longs to celebrate Christmas. This longing results in her eventual saving of the family. When she can bear her need to hear traditional French carols no longer, she goes into the spruce woods on Christmas Eve and sings "Noel! Noel! Noel!" An Indian approaches and answers her in French. She is so moved that she gives him a cherished gilt button. This action is important to the plot as it allows a noncontrived method for saving the family. Months later, when their cabin is surrounded by Indians, Marguerite goes out and offers them food. The French-speaking Indian is there, wearing the gilt button. The Indians accept the food and go in peace. Marguerite's decision to stay with the family rather than go back to France or to Quebec allows readers to understand the depth of her feelings for the family and the land she has grown to love.

Speare, in *Calico Captive,* develops a story around the capture of settlers by Indians. She effectively shows how her main character changes as a result of being captured. Speare introduces Miriam Willard by describing a happy girl who is thinking about her new calico dress and an invitation to Boston. This carefree mood changes rapidly as Miriam is kidnapped by an Indian raiding party and held for ransom in Montreal. Miriam's personal conflicts are shown as she worries about the other captives, including her sister and the baby born on the trail; her reactions of horror when her young nephew willingly runs with the Indian boys; and her responses to the wealthy French family who take her into their home as a servant. The author uses conversations with Pierre, a *coureur des bois,* to allow Miriam to learn more about the Indians and begin to question her own prejudices.

A western captive story began in 1850, when a group of Mormons left Illinois to travel by wagon train into Utah and New Mexico. One by one the wagons withdrew until only the Oatman family remained on the trail. At about the same time, some Tonto Apache women and children who were berry picking were attacked by three white men; the women were killed, and two Indian girls were taken as slaves. One of the captured girls escaped and took the news back to the camp. A raiding party was sent out to avenge the Indian women.

These events provided the background for Evelyn Sibley Lampman's *White Captives.* This story relates what happens when the Oatman family becomes the *pinda Lickoyi,* or "white eyes," whom the Apaches are seeking. Like their Indian counterparts, the family, except for the two girls, is massacred. The girls are taken to the Apache village to replace the two Indian girls.

This captivity story includes considerable information about the Indian viewpoint and way of life. Because the girls were slaves for two different Indian tribes, comparisons can be made between the hunting, nomadic life of the Apache and the more settled life-style of the Mohave who planted fields and harvested crops. The author effectively brings Indian spiritual beliefs into the story when ceremonies are completed before the planting of crops and when an Indian shares the great Mohave dream with the girls. The girls' reactions to this story characterize the belief held by many pioneers: they are shocked, because the dream of a great flood and the finding of sanctuary at the top of a sacred mountain is similar to the Biblical story of Noah. Lampman informs the readers that after the oldest girl's rescue (the younger girl died in captivity), she told her story to a minister, Mr. Stratton. He published the story, *Captivity of the Oatman Girls, Being an Interesting Narrative of Life among the Apache and Mohave Indians,* in 1857. The book was popular and sold over 25,000 copies. Lampman states that "In a small way, the book probably did as much to turn public sentiment against the Indians as *Uncle Tom's Cabin* did against Negro slavery" (p. 177). *White Captives,* written over one hundred years later, presents a fairer view of the hardworking Indian and the reasons behind the captivity.

The heroine in *Calico Captive* lost some of her fear of the Indians but also wanted to return home to live among her own people. In contrast, her young nephew rapidly learned Indian ways and seemed to prefer the Indian life-style. Some children who were captured by Indians returned to their homes; others spent their entire lives with the Indians. Lois Lenski's *Indian Captive: The Story of Mary Jemison* tells the true story of a Pennsylvania girl who was captured by Indians at the age of twelve. Although the author develops considerable conflict as Mary adjusts to the new life, she finally decides that the Senecas are her people and chooses to stay with them. The author allows the readers to visualize Mary's inner turmoils and her love for her adopted people as she makes this final decision.

At that moment she saw Old Shagbark looking at her, his brown eyes overflowing with kindness and understanding. He knew how hard it was for her to decide. . . . She saw the Englishman, too. His lips were smiling, but his eyes of cold gray were hard. Even if she were able to put all her thoughts into words, she knew he would never, never understand. Better to live with those who understood her because they loved her so much, than with one who could never think with her, in sympathy, about anything. . . . Squirrel Woman's scowling face and even Gray Wolf's wicked one no longer held any terrors, because she understood them. (p. 268)

The previous books were written through the viewpoint of white women or children who had tragic experiences. There are, however, several stories about this period written from an Indian perspective. The tragic *The Valley of the Shadow,* by Janet Hickman, tells of a true incident involving a group of Moravian teachers and their Indian converts who both chose to live peaceful lives. The story may be more plausible and horrifying to readers because it is told through the viewpoint of a young Indian who believes in the gentle ways of his Moravian teachers. Consider, for example, Tobias's confusion when a white captain scornfully tells the Indians:

The Moravians have made you Christians, so they say, and taught you to read and write, and made you all proud of yourselves. . . . Let me tell you, boy, just let me tell you—Before all this is over, it won't make the least difference whether you can read or write or say your prayers like white men. All the words in the world won't keep the Moravians and their Indians out of trouble now. (p. 56)

Tobias's confusion increases as the Moravians and Indians are forced to leave their homes and march westward through the Ohio Territory to the Sandusky River. On the one hand, his father and the Bible speak to him of righteousness, but he feels that the ways of righteousness and wickedness are so wound together in most people that they cannot be told apart. The most dramatic scene occurs when Tobias and a group of Indians return to their old community to harvest crops. They are captured by Virginia "Long Knives," placed in the mission house, and systematically massacred. This scene seems extremely believable because Tobias describes the sounds he hears as he hides in a cellar below the mission house. Later, Tobias returns to the Moravian teachers to learn their ways, thus hoping to understand what has happened to his people. After the horror, he discovers that he is a man, no longer a boy: he has "walked through the valley of the shadow of death."

The author ends the book on a hopeful note as Tobias decides to live up to his father's hopes. "Good hopes, he thought, were filled from within; the cherry buds on the hill above the White Woman's River would swell and burst from the inside out, come sun or rain or even spring snow. He would live in a Shawano town without taking up all the old ways" (p. 214).

The themes in this section are quite varied depending on the perspective developed by the various authors and the age level of the readers. Consider the following themes. Why do you think they were chosen by authors who write stories about this period? What themes are found in different time periods? Are the themes significant today?

1 Friendship and faith are important human characteristics.
2 People long for their own land and the freedom ownership implies.
3 People will withstand considerable hardships to retain their dreams.

4 Strong family bonds help physical and spiritual survival.
5 Prejudice and hatred are destructive forces.
6 The greatest strength comes from within.
7 Moral obligations require personal commitment.

The Civil War Years

Before the Civil War, hundreds of thousands of blacks were captured, brought by slave ships from Africa, and sold on the auction block. Many people in both the North and the South believed that slavery was immoral, but they had not been able to pass laws against it. However, they were able to assist slaves in their flight toward Canada and freedom. This was a dangerous undertaking, especially after the passage of the Fugitive Slave Act in 1850, when it became a crime for anyone, in either the North or the South, to conceal or help a runaway slave. Handbills offering rewards for the return of the described slaves added to the danger by urging "slave-catchers" to hunt for any suspected runaways. Because of the dangers and the need for secrecy, a network of people dedicated to assisting fugitive slaves was established, linking North and South. This network included safe hiding places and people who led the fugitives on each part of the journey. This network came to be

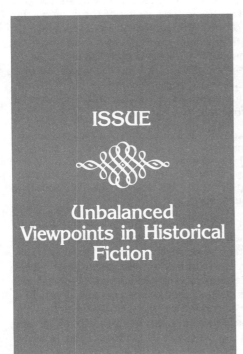

ISSUE

Unbalanced Viewpoints in Historical Fiction

THE REPORTING OF HIStory may change depending upon the viewpoint of the author. This is equally true in the writing of historical fiction. It is frequently noted, for example, that too many frontier books are told from the white settlers' perspective rather than from the perspective of Native Americans. In this context, it is feared that children will not realize the hardships experienced or the contributions made by Native Americans. Common adventures told from the white settlers' perspective include kidnappings of white children, wagon trains attacked by warring Indian tribes, settlements attacked and burned, settlers rescued by soldiers, and stories of frontier heroes who created their reputations as Indian fighters. Some critics believe that historical fiction about this period should include more stories told from the Native American perspective. These stories might include Indian children who were kidnapped by white settlers or place a greater emphasis upon the reasons for the kidnapping of the white children; portray the numerous peaceful tribes who lived in harmony with settlers; and emphasize the diversity between various Indian tribes.

Students of children's literature may consider issues related to the viewpoints of authors and the consequences of unbalanced narratives of other time periods; for example, early explorers, Roman invasion of Britain, religious freedom and settlement of America, the Revolutionary War, the Civil War, and World War II.

known as the Underground Railroad, and the people who fled toward Canada were often called "North Star People."

Conflicts between northern and southern interests that emerged during the Constitutional Convention increased into the 1860s. Now the United States, because of the outbreak of the Civil War, was torn apart. Allegiances were drawn, not only between states, but also within families. It was therefore possible for brother to fight against brother.

Strong human drama emerges from this historic period. Authors may focus upon slavery and experiences during captivity or the fugitive slaves' search for freedom. Other writers choose to tell about the impact of war on young soldiers or the hardships and conflicts felt by those who remain at home. The impact on humans may be developed through person-against-self conflicts as the main characters wrestle with their own consciences, consider moral obligations, or discover the human tragedy associated with slavery and war. Society may be the antagonist as characters face broader prejudices and hatred. Authors who create credible plots must not only consider the historic happenings but also the conflicting social attitudes of the times. The themes developed in this literature reflect strong human values as writers express the need for personal freedom, ponder the right of one person to own another, consider the tragedies of war, and question the killing of one human by another.

The attitudes expressed toward blacks create special problems for authors who write about slavery. How accurate should they be? Should they reflect attitudes and circumstances of the times? Should they use terms that were used during the time but are considered insensitive and offensive today? James Collier and Christopher Collier, a history professor, consider this issue in their authors' note in *Jump Ship to Freedom*. Specifically, they consider the use of the word *nigger*. Although the word is not used today, would avoiding the term in dialogue in a novel about slavery distort history? The authors chose to use the term to illustrate the main character's change in attitude as he develops self-respect and self-confidence. In addition they used the term to highlight the social attitudes of the other characters in the book. Those who use the term express racial bias toward blacks; those who do not are concerned with the rights and self-respect of all humans. Consider, for example, how the slave Daniel uses the word. At first he refers to himself as a nigger. He considers himself unintelligent, inferior to whites, and unable to think of himself as a person. He allows other people's opinions to reinforce these beliefs. Self-realization develops slowly as Daniel discovers he can develop and carry out a plan to recover his father's confiscated funds, be resourceful and escape, associate with people who consider him capable and

slavery immoral, meet his moral obligations to his mother, and fight for his rights. After he makes these personal discoveries, he refuses to call himself nigger.

The cramped quarters of a slave ship and its chained human cargo provide the setting for Paula Fox's *The Slave Dancer*. The story is told from the point of view of a thirteen-year-old boy from New Orleans who is kidnapped for the purpose of playing his fife on a slave ship. When Jessie recovers from the shock of his own abduction, he cannot understand why the captain needs someone to play music. Upon reaching Africa, Jesse learns about the trade in human "Black Gold," and discovers that, in their greed for trade goods, native chiefs sell their own people and those kidnapped from other tribes. Jessie hears the "cold dead clang of metal striking wood" (p. 72) and sees the first black captive struggling over the railing and dropping on the deck. During four long nights, longboats deposit their cargoes, men and women who are half-conscious from the pressure of bodies and bruised from the ankle shackles. The detailed setting and descriptions of the conditions seem believable: Jessie describes the holds as pits of misery, is horrified by the low regard for human life, and is shocked when prisoners who die are thrown overboard. Jessie learns the reason for having him aboard when slaves are dragged on deck and forced to dance; a dead or weak slave cannot be sold for profit, and dancing is believed to keep their bodies strong.

This book has stirred considerable controversy. The fact that slaves are not treated like human beings or even given names has been criticized. Many college students who read it, however, say that for the first time they realize the true inhumanity of slavery. The author reveals the impact of the experience on Jessie by flashing ahead in time. Even years later, the sound of music creates a vivid memory as described in Jessie's thoughts:

For at the first note of a tune or a song, I would see once again as though they'd never ceased their dancing in my mind, black men and women and children lifting their tormented limbs in time to a reedy martial air, the dust rising from their joyless thumping, the sound of the fife finally drowned beneath the clanging of their chains. (p. 176)

A book written for young children explains the purposes of the Underground Railroad. F. N. Monjo's *The Drinking Gourd* tells of a family that is part of the Underground Railroad and their role in helping a fugitive slave family escape. Even though this is an "easy-to-read" book, it illustrates the importance of one family's contributions, with dialogue between father and sons disclosing the purpose of the Railroad. Young readers also experience excitement and danger as Tommy accompa-

The illustrations capture the role of the fugitive slave.
Illustration (pp. 34–35) from *The Drinking Gourd* by F.N. Monjo. Pictures by Fred Brenner.
An I CAN READ History Book.
Pictures copyright © 1970 by Fred Brenner.
Reprinted by permission of Harper & Row, Publishers, Inc.

nies his father and an escaping black family on the next part of their journey.

The impact of the war years is also a subject in historical fiction of the 1800s. As idealistic young men see the horrors of war, they come to realize that it is not a glamorous time of brass bands, horses ridden by men in fine uniforms, and heroic battles led by banner-carrying leaders. This change of viewpoint is frequently shown in books written about fighting soldiers. Janet Hickman's *Zoar Blue* illustrates the emotional effects of war when the younger members of the Separatists group in Zoar, Ohio, defy their elders and enlist in the Union army. The author encourages children to understand the conflict of these young men as the characters discuss Lincoln's call for troops, debate their need for loyalty to the constitutional government, and discuss the teachings of their church that stress that men of conscience do not fight each other. The author emphasizes these personal conflicts through the mockery of outsiders who taunt them about playing tunes with a piano while ''braver'' men play tunes with cannons. After they join the army, they are still in conflict as they prepare for their first battle. This conflict is emphasized as John questions if he could pull the trigger against any man:

He had learned the Principles too well, perhaps. A Separatist could not murder any enemy, much less, one supposed, a countryman. How was it possible to follow the Principles and be a soldier too? There was no way to make sense between the war and such arguments. He had tried. (p. 54)

The men long for the peace and stability of their old community while they are gone from Zoar. The author develops several sides of the personal conflict by describing the residents of Zoar, their grief for their sons, their physical sacrifices, and the changes in the soldiers after they return home. Hickman develops strong person-against-self and person-against-society conflicts in which the characters face problems because their personal values conflict with the spirit of the times.

In Keith's *Rifles for Watie,* the conflict occurs in the western United States behind both Union and Confederate lines. Jeff Bussey, who lives in Kansas in 1861, is horrified when bushwhackers threaten to kill his father; this experience sends him to Fort Leavenworth to join the Union army. Jeff learns about war on the battlefields of Oklahoma and Missouri. The conflict is based, according to the author, on the story of the Indian Watie who led the Cherokee Indians on raids behind the Union lines. The idea for Watie's trying to acquire repeating rifles is based on the fact that Northern manufacturers sold firearms to the seceding states; the resulting gun traffic became a national scandal.

One of the finest books to depict the wartime hardships and conflicts of family members who remain at home is Irene Hunt's *Across Five Aprils*. The beginning conflict is effectively introduced as a family in Southern Illinois debates the issues related to the war and chooses its allegiances: Matt Creighton, the head of the family, argues that a strong union must be maintained; the majority of his sons agree with him; one argues that people in the South should be able to live without government interference. The author develops a strong personal conflict as Jethro, the youngest boy, is emotionally torn between two beloved brothers, one who joins the Union army and another who fights for the Confederacy. The consequences of hatred are illustrated when young toughs burn the Creightons' barn and put oil into their well because of the family's divided allegiances. The author allows readers to glimpse a different view of people when the neighbors guard the farm, help put in the crops, and rebuild the barn. This is a touching story of a heroic family's overcoming their problems at home and awaiting news of fighting sons. Although there is disagreement, strong family ties are maintained. These ties are emphasized through a family member's actions. When the son fighting for the South learns that one of his brothers was killed at Pittsburg Landing, he sends a message to his mother: "Ma— Bill wants that I shood tell you this—he was not at Pittsburg Landing. That bullet was not fired by him" (p. 205).

Those words help children visualize the real tragedy of the Civil War: brothers fought against brothers and neighbors against neighbors. Children may begin to understand the dreams of freedom and the hopes in the future that kept men alive. Like Jethro, they may realize that life goes on, and by the final April, clouds begin to lift and promises of new life are in the air.

Consider the following themes developed by authors who write about the pre-Civil War and the Civil War period. Why are so many of the themes related to overcoming great human and societal conflicts? How do these themes relate to the historic happenings and values expressed during the times? Are they appropriate for the time period? What other time periods, if any, reflect similar themes? If there are other time periods, what do they have in common with the Civil War period? Are any of these themes significant in contemporary life and literature?

Strong personal values conflict with society in this Civil War story. Reprinted with permission of Macmillan Publishing Co., Inc. from *Zoar Blue* by Janet Hickman. Copyright © 1978, Janet Hickman.

1 Moral obligations must be met even if one's life or freedom is in jeopardy.
2 Moral sense does not depend on the skin color; it depends on what is inside a person.
3 People should take pride in themselves and their accomplishments.
4 Prejudice and hatred are destructive forces.
5 Humans will search for freedom.
6 Personal consience may not allow humans to kill others.
7 Strong family ties will help people persevere.

Pioneer America

Frontiers were extending farther and farther west, and wagon trains of brave pioneers were giving up settled towns and farms in the East to acquire land in the West. The Homestead Act promised free land to settlers willing to stake their claims and develop the new land. Stories of rich earth in fertile valleys caused families to break away from their roots and travel several thousand miles over prairies and mountains to reach Oregon. Others dreamed of rich prairie land that did not need to be cleared of rocks or timber, and covered wagons carried many of them into the Oklahoma Territory. Whether the pioneers stopped in the Dakotas or went along the Oregon Trail, the journey was perilous. They fought nature as they battled blizzards, dust storms, mountain crossings, and swollen rivers. They fought people as they met unfriendly Indians, outlaws, and cattle ranchers who did not want them to farm. Some demonstrated noble human qualities as they helped each other search for new land and made friends with the Indians. Others demonstrated greed and prejudice in their interactions with other pioneers and Native Americans.

Stories about pioneer America are very popular with children as exemplified by the continuing interest in books such as Laura Ingalls Wilder's "Little House" series. Three types of historical fiction emerge when viewing stories written about this period: adventure stories in which the characters cross the prairies and mountains; family life stories in which families build and live on their pioneer homestead; and stories in which there is interaction between Native Americans and pioneers or Native Americans and military forces. Authors who write about crossing the continent frequently explore reasons for moving and strong feelings for the land. Self-discovery may develop in younger characters as they begin to understand their parents' motivation and values. Detailed descriptions of settings allow readers to glimpse the awesome continent and understand the nature of the antagonist. Stories set on the homestead often develop warm family relationships as the family seeks to achieve its dream. Like earlier stories about Native Americans and colonial settlers, these Native American and pioneer stories include tales of captive children and stories that depict harsh treatment given to various Indian tribes as their way of life is forcibly altered.

Barbara Brenner's *Wagon Wheels* is an enjoyable book for young readers. Based on fact, it tells about a black pioneer family who leaves Kentucky after the Civil War and moves to Kansas to receive land under the Homestead Act. This story develops friendly relationships with members of an Indian tribe; without their help, the settlers would have starved. Young children enjoy the story because it shows that pioneer children were courageous: three boys survive a prairie fire and travel over one hundred miles to join their father. This is one of the few books written about blacks as a part of the frontier experience.

Honore Morrow develops a pioneer story about a family's dream for rich land in Oregon. This book for older children recreates the Sager family's experience as they leave Missouri in 1844 and head west. *On to Oregon!* is more than an adventure story about a family crossing the continent. It is about thirteen-year-old John who, after his parents die on the trail, becomes head of the family and leads his brothers and sisters on to Oregon. It is the story of a boy who is inspired by his father's dream—one that is hard to achieve. With a thousand miles of treacherous mountains, canyons, and rivers yet to cross, the people in the wagon train do not want the responsibility for the Sager children; they want them to go back east. The author shows the strength of the father's dream by describing John's actions as he refuses to forfeit his father's dream; he works out a scheme so that the people will think he is traveling with Kit Carson. The children secretly pack their goods on oxen and head out on the lonely trail. Now the antagonist becomes the natural environment. Morrow develops believable and awesome antagonists by describing the children's experience with severe weather, the treacherous Snake River, the loss of supplies, friendly and hostile Indians, hunger, and sickness. The author effectively contrasts the treacherous mountains and the warm, gentle valley in Oregon where the children will wait until John is old enough to homestead the land.

Morrow encourages readers to understand the importance of reading about westward expansion through historical fiction and the contributions of the people who made expansion possible. Consider, for example, the possible impact of the author's closing statements:

You and I will never hear that magic call of the West, "Catch up! Catch up!" We never shall see the Rockies framed in the opening of our prairie schooner and tingle with the knowledge that if we and our fellow immigrants can reach the valleys in the blue beyond the mountains and there plow enough acreage, that acreage will belong forever to America. (p. 235)

The obligations associated with responsibility and the power of a father's beliefs combine to create strong pioneer characters and plot in Louise Moeri's *Save Queen of Sheba*. The author develops physical and emotional trials after twelve-year-old King David and his young sister Queen of Sheba (named after biblical characters) survive a Sioux Indian raid and set out alone across the prairie in hopes of finding the wagons that separated from their portion of the train. The author effectively demonstrates the strength of King David's feeling of responsibility by developing his varied emotional responses. First, he feels hopeful; he found his young sister alive and there are a few items in the burned wagons that increase their chances for survival. Later, he feels a consuming need to catch up with the wagons. This need is so strong that he forgets why they were going to Oregon. Then he is faced with a severe moral dilemma: his sister is lost. Although he feels compelled to go on and outwardly believes that it will be impossible to find her, he goes back and searches. It is during these emotionally and physically draining experiences that King David's memory of his father emerges and gives the boy the strength to continue. The author reveals the emotional ties between the boy and his father when the children reach their destination:

Three men rode over the crest of the hill. The rider in the lead—his face half covered with bandages and one arm in a sling—was Pa. And when he saw Pa there—tall on a tall black horse—King David knew why he had gone back to save Queen of Sheba. (p. 16)

For another view of the western trails, younger children enjoy Sibyl Hancock's *Old Blue.* This story, based on a true incident, tells about a boy's experience on an 1878 cattle drive. The hero of the story is actually an intelligent steer who can find the right direction even in a storm. This book probably appeals to younger readers because many young children experience dreams about being cowboys in the old West.

The power of the family's working together to conquer outside dangers and build a home filled with love and decency is found in many books of this period. One author in particular has enabled children to vicariously experience family life on the frontier. Laura Ingalls Wilder, through her "Little House" books, recreated the world of her frontier family from 1870 through 1889. The "Little House" books sold in the millions and received literary acclaim. A popular television series also introduced the Ingalls family to millions of new friends.

The first book, *Little House in the Big Woods,* takes place in the big woods, seven miles from Pepin, Wisconsin. Unlike those in many other pioneer stories, this setting is not antagonistic. Although the woods are filled with bears and other animals, the danger never really enters the log cabin in the clearing. Any potential dangers are inferred through Pa's stories about his adventures in the big woods, told in the close family environment inside the cabin. Other descriptions of family activities also suggest that the environment, while creating hard work for the pioneer family, is not awesome or dangerous: they clear the land, plant and harvest the crops, gather sap from the sugar bush, and hitch up the wagon and drive through the woods to Grandpa's house. Wilder's development of a close family environment allows her to focus upon the characters and their interactions within the Ingalls family. Pa's actions, for example, infer that he is a warm, loving father. After working all day he has time to play the fiddle, play mad dog with the children, and tell them stories. Likewise, Ma takes care of their physical needs but also helps them create paper dolls. The impact of what it means to live in the relative isolation of the frontier where a family must be self-sufficient is also inferred by the children's actions and thoughts: they feel secure when the attic is hung with smoked hams and filled with pumpkins; they are excited when they get new mittens and a cloth doll for Christmas; and they are astonished when they visit a town for the first time and see a store filled with marvelous treasures.

In the rest of the books, Laura and her family leave the big woods of Wisconsin to live in the prairie states. In *Little House on the Prairie,* they travel by covered wagon to Kansas. Their next home, described in *On the Banks of Plum Creek,* is a sod house in Minnesota. Here, they meet Nellie Oleson and her parents who own Oleson's store. They go to a one-room school, build a fish trap, have a grasshopper invasion, worry when Pa must walk three hundred miles to find a job, and live through a blizzard.

Their next move takes them to Dakota Territory in *By the Shores of Silver Lake.* In the Dakotas, they have *The Long Winter.* Wilder's description of the winter in the next book, *Little Town on the Prairie,* encourages modern children to see the experience:

All winter long, they had been crowded in the little kitchen, cold and hungry and working hard in the dark and the cold to twist enough hay to keep the fire going and to grind wheat in the coffee mill for the day's bread. All that long, long winter, the only hope had been that sometime winter must end, sometime blizzards must stop, the sun would shine warm again. (p. 3.)

In the little town of De Smet, South Dakota, Laura gets her first job; she earns twenty-five cents a day and her dinner when she sews shirts. Unselfishly, she saves this money to help send her sister Mary to a college for the blind in Vinton, Iowa.

The last books are about a grown-up Laura. In *These Happy Golden Years,* she is fifteen and takes a teaching job in a rural school twelve miles from home. This is a challenge; many students are taller than she. There are many happy moments, however. She meets Almanzo Wilder, and every Friday evening he brings her home in his sleigh. Laura and Almanzo are married in *The First Four Years* and begin life together on a prairie homestead. One reason children like these books so much may be the feeling of closeness they have with Laura.

Another loving frontier family is presented in Brink's *Caddie Woodlawn*. The time and setting are similar to the first "Little House" book; both take place in the last half of the nineteenth century in Wisconsin. In fact, Caddie lived south of Menomonie, approximately thirty miles north of where Laura was born. Laura wrote her own story, but Brink wrote of her grandmother.

Brink (2) says, "Gram represented kindness and good sense, justice tempered by humor, and love and security" (p. 284). These are the qualities that children discover in *Caddie Woodlawn*. She is a warm-hearted tomboy who loves to play in the woods and along the river with her brothers to the despair of her mother and older sister. She is also a friend of the Indians. One dramatic event occurs when she overhears some men plotting to attack their Indian neighbors. She jumps on a horse, rides through the night woods, and warns her friend, Indian John. Caddie's experiences differ from present-day ones, but her worries about growing up are similar to those of any girl, no matter when she lives. With Caddie, children know that everything will be all right: "When she awoke she knew that she need not be afraid of growing up. It was not just sewing and weaving and wearing stays. It was a responsibility, but, as Father spoke of it, it was a beautiful and precious one, and Caddie was ready to go and meet it" (p. 251).

Keith is an author who wrote about this period by combining personal experiences and careful research, including personal interviews with people who lived on the Oklahoma frontier and researching newspaper files and historic journals. His experiences were similar to Brink's in that they were told by two grandfathers who pioneered farms in the Cherokee strip. Keith's book, *The Obstinate Land*, tells about Fritz Romberg and his family when they leave south Texas in 1893 to homestead on the Oklahoma prairie. There is an underlying theme similar to other stories of westward expansion: the dream of owning a farm without being obligated to anyone.

The author encourages the reader to see the land for the first time through the reactions of three people. Their contrasting feelings about the land are consistent with Keith's characterizations; Father is excited because it's a land without timber, stumps, or rocks that's "shouting to be farmed" (p. 2). Fritz, the thirteen-year-old, is "exhilarated by the lonely magnificence of the country, and the sense of freedom it inspired. It was like being in a boat on the ocean with no land in sight" (p. 2). The mother, Freda, looks at the land with sadness: "You can look a long way and see nothing" (p. 3). She has torn up her roots, left her relatives, left her small daughter in a distant cemetery, and traveled to an unknown land.

Keith develops effective plots in *The Obstinate Land* because he relies upon both historic conflicts of the time period and the natural environment. The first type of conflict is reflected by the family's clash with a sooner family (people who illegally crossed the boundaries before the strip was open to homesteaders) who claims the land that father desires. Another more important historic conflict develops, however, as a neighboring cattle rancher tries through legal and illegal means to drive them off the land. Nature becomes the strong antagonist during a series of disasters: Fritz's father dies as a result of the hard winter, and there are several years of crop failures due to hail, grasshoppers, and drought.

The author develops themes around the need for humans to help each other, the use of legal rather than illegal means to win battles, and a strong love for the land. Keith's descriptions of the isolated homestead that is open to attack by outlaws, unfriendly cattle ranchers, or natural forces develops the vulnerability of the homestead and people living apart. He effectively contrasts these mishaps with times, when working together, the homesteaders save each other or make it possible to withstand the consequences of crop failure. The final actions of Keith's main character allow readers to grasp the significance of frontier justice. Instead of resorting to frontier vigilante action, Fritz takes a rancher to court. Now the law forces the rancher to repay Fritz for crops ruined when cattle roved illegally across his fields. The ranchers' disbelief at such an event infers, however, that the law was not the usual way to settle disagreements. A strong love for the land is depicted by the human endeavors and sacrifices necessary to keep and develop it. For example, every time the family considers moving they think of their original dream and decide to stay. This attitude is reflected in Fritz's final feeling of self-worth:

Fritz was proud of having been able to endure against the stiff challenge thrown out by the land and the elements. He had hung on tenaciously and won. The more he sacrificed and the harder he had worked, the more he came to appreciate himself. The struggle had broadened his character and made him a man. (p. 209)

The setting for Scott O'Dell's *Carlota* is California in the mid 1800s. Carlota is a strong and independent daughter of Don Saturnino, a Californian whose ancestors came from Spain. O'Dell explores the conflicts that could occur between people who believe that a woman should play a very feminine role and others who encourage a different behavior. For example, the roles that her father hopes she will play are inferred by her actions and his encouragement of these actions: she rides her black stallion, not like a lady with a sidesaddle, but like a man, riding at top speed around the ranchero; she races horses with the neighbors, brands cattle, and accompanies her father on dangerous trips as they seek treasure from a sunken ship. A different role for the time period is inferred by Carlota's grandmother's strong reactions to her behavior. The author develops Carlota's inner conflicts when she rides out with the men to ambush the American army and wounds a young soldier. She must deal with her feelings of compassion and, in so doing, defy her father. Readers are encouraged to believe in her compassion because she takes the American back to the ranchero and nurses him back to health. Her strength of character is ultimately tested and demonstrated when she manages the ranchero after her father dies. Like other memorable heroines, Carlota grows in self-understanding and discovers inner strength.

A Spanish Basque boy's experience as he reaches self-understanding on a Western sheep ranch is explored in Ann Nolan Clark's *Year Walk*. See page 514 for a discussion of this book.

The West Texas frontier of the 1860s provides the setting for Patricia Beatty's *Wait for Me, Watch for Me, Eula Bee*. The story centers around the capture of two farm children by Comanche and Kiowa Indians, the subsequent escape of the older boy, the changing loyalties of the very young girl as she learns to love her Comanche foster parent, and her final rescue by her brother. Beatty's descriptions of camp life, food, travel, and behavior create a vivid picture of the period. Her author's notes list the sources for her information on Comanche and Kiowa tribes and their treatment of captives. While the author's descriptions and characterization depict the Comanches as leading a harsh life built on raiding and warfare, there is also a strong feeling for the value of children. The developing love between the little girl and her Indian foster parent exemplifies a warm, loving relationship. There is also a very sad feeling expressed in the book: when two cultures have little understanding of each other, the results can be tragic.

A tragic period in Navaho history, 1863–1865, is the setting for O'Dell's *Sing Down the Moon*. The story of the three hundred mile forced march which culminates in the Navahos being held prisoner at Fort Sumner is told through the viewpoint of a Navaho girl, Bright Morning. The author effectively uses both descriptions of physical settings and characterizations to depict the harsh human tragedy. For example, contrasts are made between the Navahos' home, the beautiful Canyon de Chelly with its fruit trees, green grass, sheep, and cool water and the harsh wind-swept reality of the landscape around Fort Sumner. The greatest tragedy does not result from the loss of their home, however. It is, rather, the story of what happens to people who lose their spiritual hope. Through Bright Morning's analysis the reader begins to understand the consequences when people lose everything that is important to them. Bright Morning does not give up her dream of returning to her beautiful canyon and O'Dell creates a thought-

A warm relationship develops between a pioneer child and her Indian captor.
Front jacket painting by Jeff Geary of *Wait for Me, Watch for Me, Eula Bee* by Patricia Beatty. Copyright © 1978 by Patricia Beatty. By permission of William Morrow & Company.

provoking, bittersweet ending. Bright Morning and her husband escape and return to her hidden valley. It is as she remembers it: the blossoms are on the trees, a sheep and a lamb are there, the land is green, and the tools she hid from the soldiers are waiting. There is also a menacing shadow over their happiness. Readers cannot forget that the Navaho family is hiding from the soldiers they saw on the horizon.

Many authors who write about this period stress the quest for and love of land. Consider the following themes developed in the literature about pioneer America. How do the themes correspond with the historic happenings? What other periods have similar themes? What are the similarities between times with similar themes?

1 Humans have moral obligations that must be met.
2 People have strong dreams of owning land.
3 Families can survive if they work together.
4 People need each other and may work together for their mutual good.
5 Battles can be won through legal means rather than unlawful actions.
6 Hatred and prejudice are destructive forces.
7 Without spiritual hope, humans may lose their will to live.

The Depression

The next stories take place in the early 1900s and during the Great Depression years, which began in 1929. Depression stories may stress both physical and spiritual survival as a family strives to maintain pride and independence.

Authors who write about this period frequently explore the hardships related to the Depression. Person-against-society conflicts may develop as characters face and try to resolve financial hardships, loss of jobs, or racial conflicts. Person-against-self conflicts emerge as characters consider the moral dilemmas resulting from changes in their lives. Strong person-against-self and person-against-society conflicts often develop when authors explore causes for and consequences of racial prejudice.

Mildred D. Taylor's *Roll of Thunder, Hear My Cry* explores both the subtle and explicit racial prejudice expressed toward many blacks in rural Mississippi. Consider, for example, the subtle discrimination developed by the author: Cassie and her brother excitedly await new books only to receive badly worn, dirty castoffs from the white elementary school. The final insult for Cassie's younger brother occurs when he reads the chronological history stamped on the inside cover of his book: on its twelfth date of issue, it is listed in very poor condition and the race of the student is listed as "nigra." The impact of this discrimination as well as many facets of the children's characters

ISSUE

Should Historical Fiction Reflect the Attitudes of the Time Period?

THE SEARCH FOR AUTHENTICITY in setting, character development, attitudes, and actions for a historical time period, and a sensitivity toward racial perspectives result in conflicts and issues for authors, publishers, and reviewers of historical fiction for children. Should historical fiction reflect the attitudes and circumstances of the times? Or should historical fiction reflect the changing attitudes toward people of all races? These issues become especially critical when historical fiction is reviewed by literary critics and various interest groups. *Sounder* by William H. Armstrong is an example of historical fiction that has been both acclaimed for literary merit and criticized for its portrayal of a black family. Literary acclaim is exemplified in the awarding of the Newbery medal in 1970. However, *Sounder* has been denounced by some critics because they believe it emasculates the black man and destroys the black family by showing it as spiritless and submissive rather than actively fighting injustice. In contrast, other critics maintain that the book authentically depicts the poverty, ignorance, and attitudes of the times; consequently, the family members acted in the only way possible. A similar debate centers around the depiction of black characters in Paula Fox's 1973 Newbery medal winner *The Slave Dancer*. Students of children's literature should consider this issue and the implications for writers, publishers, and selectors of literature when they read historical fiction that depicts Black Americans, Oriental Americans, and Hispanics.

are expressed by their reactions. First, they refuse the books. Then Cassie is perplexed because the teacher does not understand their indignation. The children in the school retaliate, however, when they create a minor accident for the bus driver who consistently and intentionally splashes the children's clothes with dirty water as he drives the white children to their separate school. (There is no bus service for the black school.) After the children secretly deepen one of the puddles, the bus breaks an axle and its riders must walk.

Other forms of discrimination developed by the author are not as subtle, however. The author describes an experience with night riders and burnings. Now fear, rather than indignation and humiliation, are the feelings expressed. Varying attitudes of these characters toward both whites and blacks are explored in Taylor's sequel, *Let the Circle Be Unbroken*. Through the expressed feelings and actions of the characters, readers glimpse the shaping of attitudes of blacks toward whites as well as whites toward blacks. For example, Cassie's family avoids whites, considers friendship with a white lawyer different from friendships with their black neighbors, and expresses disbelief when it is discovered that one of the Logan relatives has a white wife.

The family in *Roll of Thunder, Hear My Cry* owns their own land, the mother has graduated from a teacher's college, and the children consistently attend school. They experience injustice, but a warm, loving environment helps protect and strengthen them. The experiences in William H. Armstrong's *Sounder* are harsher and filled with tragedy. The author depicts the poverty of the family and the tragedy that follows by describing a sharecropper's cabin, one of a number scattered across the vast fields of the landlord, and the consequences when the father steals a ham to feed his hungry family. Armstrong vividly describes the scene as the father is handcuffed, chained, and taken to jail. The futility of protest is suggested as Sounder, the family's faithful coon dog, tries to save his master and is wounded by the sheriff's shotgun. Comparisons between the two incidents are developed as both the father and Sounder are gone: the father to jail and then to a succession of chain gangs, Sounder to the woods to heal his wounds. A strong bond between man and dog is inferred as Sounder returns, a crippled skeleton of his former self; he does not bark, however, until six years later when his master returns. The master is not his former self, but crippled from a prison quarry dynamite blast. The two old friends are physically and emotionally tired and have only a short life together. The final vision of the two friends is one of remembered strength as the son, grown to manhood, recalls his father and the faithful dog as they were before the tragic happenings:

The pine trees would look down forever on a lantern burning out of oil but not going out. A harvest moon would cast shadows forever of a man walking upright, his dog, bouncing after him. And the quiet of the night would fill and echo again with the deep voice of Sounder, the great coon dog. (p. 116)

As students of children's literature read *Sounder* they may wish to consider two quite different viewpoints in evaluation and criticism. One is negative. Because the dog is the only character in the family with a name, many critics believe that the book infers that the characters are not human and need not be respected as human beings. In addition, the black family is characterized as submissive and spiritless. The other viewpoint argues that the family should be nameless because the tragedy depicted in the story was one shared by many poor black sharecroppers during that period. In this latter view, tragedy is seen as a strong bond between all people who experience injustice. Readers may consider both aspects and form their own evaluation as they read the book.

Roosevelt's fireside chats, a father who mends his shoes with folded paper, and a twelve-year-old's dreams of having her own suitcase so she can travel are all found in Greene's *Dotty's Suitcase*. A sense of the hardships of the time is created when the author describes Dotty's friend's family who must move to find work, the tragedy of the friend's father's death, and the experiences of a man who loses both wealth and family because of the Wall Street crash. Other details related to the Depression are developed through the radio programs they enjoy ("The Singing Lady" and "Little Orphan Annie"), the cost of food, and the worries of children and adults. Dotty longs to escape from the Depression by obtaining a suitcase and traveling with money she hopes to acquire. Her true character is exposed when she finds the money and the suitcase and gives the money to her friend's family. The author encourages readers to understand Dotty's changing feelings and her self-discovery caused by comparing her life with her friend's. Dotty discovers that she is rich compared to her friend: she has enough to eat, her father has a job, and she has a radio.

The themes developed in literature set in the Depression highlight both negative and positive human attitudes and values. Consider the following themes found in the literature. How do the themes relate to the historic happenings? Are these themes found during any other time period in historical fiction?

1 Humans will strive for the survival of physical body and human spirit.
2 People cannot survive without human spirit.
3 Prejudice and discrimination are destructive forces.

4 There is a bond between people who experience injustice.
5 Monetary wealth does not create a rich life.

World War II

In 1933, Hitler took power in Germany, the last Disarmament Conference was dissolved, and Germany resigned from the League of Nations. In 1935, Hitler reintroduced conscription and recommended rearmament contrary to the Treaty of Versailles. Along with a rapid increase in military power came an obsessive hatred of the Jewish people. In March 1938, Hitler's war machine began moving across Europe. Austria was occupied, and the imprisonment of Jews began. A year later, the Nazis occupied Czechoslovakia, and Albania also fell. World War II became a reality when Poland was invaded on September 1, 1939.

The 1940s saw the invasion of Norway, Belgium, and Holland; the defeat of the French army; and the heroic evacuation of British soldiers from Dunkirk. These years, from the start of the invasions through the defeat of Hitler's forces in 1945, provided many tales of both sorrow and heroism. There are moving stories about the Jewish flight, exile, and imprisonment, and of the people who bravely fought for the freedom of their countries.

Authors who write children's literature with a World War II setting frequently focus on the Jewish experience in exile, the Japanese experience in internment centers, or the perseverance of people in occupied lands. Because some of these stories are written by people who lived similar experiences, they tend to be emotional. The authors often create vivid conflicts by describing characters' fears and the nature of the setting and antagonists. Authors may explore the human consequences of war and/or prejudice by having characters ponder why their lives are in turmoil, by describing the various attitudes and actions expressed toward the main characters, by describing various emotional and physical reactions experienced during wartime, and by revealing what happens to the characters or their families as a consequence of war. As might be expected, the themes include the consequences of hatred and prejudice, the search for religious and personal freedom, and the role of personal conscience and obligations toward others.

The terrible crimes of the Holocaust are widely known by adults and children alike. Stories of brave Jewish exiles and the people who helped them have often been written from first-hand experience. From these stories, children sense the bewilderment and terror of a time when innocent people were the subject of irrational hatred and persecution.

Esther Hautzig, in *The Endless Steppe: A Girl in Exile,* tells her experiences as she and her family are transported from their comfortable home to a labor camp in Siberia. Hautzig effectively contrasts Esther's home and the labor camp to define the powerful changes influencing her life. In her home she is surrounded and protected by the wealth and love of her prominent family. In contrast, Siberia includes back-breaking work in the gypsum mines, lack of privacy in the empty wooden living quarters, near starvation, and cold and sickness made worse because of lack of boots or warm clothing. More than one side of the experience is developed, however, as Esther describes her happier feelings during trips to the *baracholka* (the stalls around the village square where produce from the collective farms is sold) and her opportunity to attend school and read books. Other emotions reveal the harsh reality of their lives: Esther feels accomplishment when she can knit a sweater and receive a pail of potatoes and some milk as payment; heartbreak is felt when the family discovers that their relatives and friends left behind in Poland were exterminated by the German invaders. Hautzig's characterizations and plot development create a strong story of individual and family survival despite great peril.

While Esther experienced pain in a cold, bleak land, Johanna experienced terror in an upstairs room. While Esther walked through the cold snow, Johanna could not leave a bedroom for over two years. Johanna Reiss tells her story of World War II in *The Upstairs Room.* The author allows readers to glimpse varying consequences of prejudice and hatred as the heroine hears news of the war and asks why Hitler hates her people; she is barred from restaurants and the public school; and she learns that many Jewish people are being taken to forced labor camps. The obligations of one human to another are developed when a Dutch family offers to hide the children and Johanna and her sister move to their country farm. The strength of this commitment is emphasized when the author describes the danger of this act for both the Dutch family and the children as the farmer builds a secret space in an upstairs closet to provide a hiding place. At first Johanna does not understand why they must hide, but gradually she realizes their serious predicament as word of the Holocaust spreads.

The author's style and first-person point of view create several scenes that show the breathless fear of the children as they wait in the cramped closet. Consider, for example, the effect of the following passage:

Footsteps. Loud Ones. Boots. Coming up the stairs. Wooden shoes. Coming behind. Sini put her arms around me and pushed my head against her shoulder. Loud voices. Ugly ones. Furniture being moved. And Opoe's protesting voice. The closet door was thrown open.

Hands fumbled on the shelves. Sini was trembling. She tightened her arms around me. I no longer breathed through my nose. Breathing through my mouth made less noise. (p. 149)

Both girls are brave during this unsuccessful search by Nazi troops. The family who protects them is equally brave. Their strength comes from their strong feelings of moral decency toward other people.

The story ends happily; Canadian troops liberate the town, and at last, Johanna and her sister may leave their room. This is a powerful story of the experiences of common people during German occupation. There has been some criticism of this book for children because of the realistic dialogue in which members of the farm family use swear words.

In addition to tales of exile and hiding, there are tales of escape from Germany. Using personal experiences to provide details, Judith Kerr tells about a Jewish family who flees Germany before Hitler's election in 1933. *When Hitler Stole Pink Rabbit* allows readers to glimpse the impact of taking away freedom of speech: Papa, who writes newspaper articles against Hitler, escapes to Switzerland before he can be arrested. His family later joins him there. They discover how close their escape was when they learn that their property, including Anna's stuffed pink rabbit, has been confiscated by the Nazi government.

A more difficult escape is experienced by Lisa Platt and her family in Sonia Levitin's *Journey to America.* Like Judith Kerr's father, Papa escapes from Germany and goes to America. His family, too, must leave Germany, their flight taking them to Switzerland and difficult times before they can join Papa. In these books, the families show considerable courage in times of great danger. Although they must leave wealth, possessions, and friends behind, there is an underlying theme that everything will be all right if they can be together.

Readers may glimpse the widespread impact of the Holocaust when they read stories with other settings but similar conflicts. For example, Aranka Siegal's *Upon the Head of the Goat: A Childhood in Hungary 1939–1944* chronicles a nine-year-old girl's experiences from the time she hears about Hitler until her family boards a cattle train to Auschwitz. A burned and broken tree provides a symbolic setting for the stories in Benjamin Tene's *In the Shade of the Chestnut Tree.* In earlier years children play around a green, vigorous tree in the Warsaw ghetto. Readers may consider any symbolic meanings related to the use of the tree: years later, the author returns to find his friends no longer there, the city destroyed, and the tree black from destruction. There are, however, green shoots growing through the charred bark. Comparisons between the consequences of prejudice expressed during different times may be made by reading Kathryn Lasky's *The Night Journey.* In Lasky's book a contemporary girl discovers the consequences of prejudice when her great grandmother tells about her escape from Russia in 1900. After reading these stories, children often are concerned about the implications of not acting when other people are unjustly accused of crimes.

The Jewish people weren't the only ones to live through persecution and fear. Many children are surprised to read stories about the American treatment of Japanese Americans during World War II. Two books by Yoshiko Uchida tell about a Japanese American family after the bombing of Pearl Harbor. (Although the stories are fictional, many of the experiences are similar to those of Uchida when she and her family were sent to a relocation center in Utah and then released.) In *Journey to Topaz,* the author traces Yuki's experiences following the attack on Pearl Harbor. First, her father, who is a businessman, is taken away. Then Yuki, her mother and older brother are sent to a temporary center and then on to a permanent internment center, Topaz, in Utah. The author creates vivid pictures of the internment camps by describing such things as latrines without doors, the wind blowing across the desert and into the barracks, and the waiting lines of people. The fear of people from both sides is climaxed when the grandfather of Yuki's best friend goes searching for arrowheads and is shot by a guard who believes he is trying to escape. The conflict within members of the family is developed when Yuki's brother, wishing to prove his loyalty to America, joins a Nisei Army Volunteer Unit.

Yuki's story continues in *Journey Home.* Readers are encouraged to understand the effect of Topaz on Yuki as she describes her nightmares and recurring thoughts. In this book, the family returns to Berkeley only to discover distrust, difficulty finding work, and anti-Japanese violence. However, the family is characterized by hope and strength, not bitterness. Furthermore, not all people show distrust. Through her experiences, Yuki discovers that coming home is having everyone she cares about around her; it is a matter of the heart and spirit. Some other World War II stories create adventurous plots. For example, Marie McSwigan's *Snow Treasure* is based on a true 1940 incident in which nine million in Norwegian gold bullion (thirteen tons) is slipped past Nazi sentries and shipped to Baltimore. The unusual twist is that children, on their sleds, were able to get the bullion past the Nazi troops to a boat hidden in a fiord. It is a tale of daring, courage, secrecy, and cooperation. Children enjoy this story because it demonstrates how important even the work of young children can be when they all work together to preserve their country.

A Norwegian fishing boat in 1940 is the setting for Dale Fife's adventurous story, *Destination Unknown.* The author's

Children demonstrate that they can be courageous even during times of peril.
From *Snow Treasure* by Marie McSwigan. Copyright 1942 by E. P. Dutton & Co., Inc. Renewal © 1970 by Kathryn McSwigan Laughlin.

vivid descriptions recreate a twelve-year-old boy's experiences after he stows away on a boat only to discover that the occupants are seeking America, not returning to Norway or going to England. Especially effective are the descriptions of his reactions to the ocean, his shipboard assignments, the welcome in the United States, and his reactions to New York.

The themes found in the World War II historical fiction for children resemble themes found during other times of great peril. Consider the following themes. How do they relate to the historical happenings? What are characteristics of other historic periods that have similar themes?

1 Humans will seek freedom from religious and political persecution.
2 Prejudice and hatred are destructive forces.
3 Moral obligation and personal conscience are strong human forces.
4 Freedom is worth fighting for.
5 Family love and loyalty help persons endure or survive catastrophic experiences.

SUMMARY

Historical fiction provides a means for children to live vicariously in the past. While they are learning about the experiences of others, they are also reading for enjoyment and gaining understanding of their heritage. Through historical fiction, children can discover that all people are dependent upon one another regardless of the time in which they live. They also discover that people have had similar human needs throughout history; historical fiction allows them to judge human relationships and realize that their present and future are tied into the relationships of times past.

Historical fiction is evaluated according to the criteria used for any fine literature, but there are several specific demands placed on these writers. The settings are integral to the story and must be authentic in every respect. Settings function as antagonists. This is common in pioneer stories. The actions, beliefs, and values of the characters must be realistic for the period. The plots must be credible for the time period. The experiences, the conflicts, and the characters' resolution of these conflicts must reflect the times. The themes in historical fiction should be worthwhile and relevant both in today's society and in the historical setting. These themes frequently stress humans' search for freedom, love for land, loyalty and honor, and the cruelty and futility of war. Considerable research is necessary before an author can write credible historical fiction.

The literature discussed in this chapter followed a chronological period from the ancient world in 4000 B.C. through the world at war in the late 1930s and early 1940s. Themes for each historical period were emphasized.

Suggested Activities for Adult Understanding of Historical Fiction

■ Find an example of historical fiction written for beginning readers and another written for older readers. Compare the settings. Can they both be described as *integral settings?* If the book written for younger children does not provide as many details as the one for older children, has the author used any other medium to relate these details to the reader? For example, compare Arnold Lobel's setting in *On the Day Peter Stuyvesant Sailed into Town* with Esther Forbes's setting in *Johnny Tremain.*

■ Locate a story such as Honore Morrow's *On to Oregon!* in which the setting takes on the role of antagonist. How has the author developed the realization that the setting is the antagonist? How do the characters overcome these obstacles of nature? What happens to the characters as they face and overcome the antagonist?

■ Writers of historical fiction often place famous persons into the backgrounds of their stories, while the pivotal character is usually fictional. Read a story such as Erik Christian Haugaard's *Cromwell's Boy* and compare the roles of the little-known eleven-year-old Oliver Cutter with the well-known Oliver Cromwell. Why did the author choose a little-known person as the main character?

■ Writing an excellent historical fiction novel requires considerable research by the author. Choose several authors of historical fiction and investigate the sources they used.

■ Read the acceptance speech of a Newbery award-winning author of historical fiction (1). What were the author's reasons for choosing to write about that period in history? Does the author discuss the sources used?

■ Using the "Themes in Historical Fiction" chart on page 440, make a list of historical literature that develops each theme during a selected time period.

References

1 Blos, Joan W. "Newbery Medal Acceptance." *The Horn Book* 56 (August 1980): 369–73.
2 Brink, Carol Ryrie. *Caddie Woodlawn.* Illustrated by Trina Schart Hyman. New York: Macmillan, 1935, 1973.
3 Burton, Hester. "The Writing of Historical Novels." In *Children and Literature: Views and Reviews,* edited by Virginia Haviland, pp. 299–304. Glenview, Ill.: Scott, Foresman, 1973.
4 Haugaard, Erik Christian. *Hakon of Rogen's Saga.* Boston: Houghton Mifflin, 1963.
5 Keith, Harold. *The Obstinate Land.* New York: Crowell, 1977.
6 Lukens, Rebecca J. *A Critical Handbook of Children's Literature.* Glenview, Ill.: Scott, Foresman, 1976.
7 Miles, Betty. "Joan W. Blos." *The Horn Book,* (August 1980), 374–77.
8 Norton, Donna E. "A Three-Year Study Developing and Evaluating Children's Literature Units in Children's Literature Courses." A paper presented at the College Reading Association, National Conference, Baltimore, Maryland, October, 1980.
9 "Notable Children's Trade Books in the Field of Social Studies." *Social Education* 42 (April 1978): 318–21.
10 Parker, Arthur C. Introduction to *Indian Captive,* by Lois Lenski. New York: Lippincott, 1941.
11 Reiss, Johanna. *The Upstairs Room.* New York: Crowell, 1972.
12 Segel, Elizabeth. "Laura Ingalls Wilder's America: An Unflinching Assessment." *Children's Literature in Education* 8 (Summer 1977): 63–70.
13 Sutcliff, Rosemary. *Song for a Dark Queen.* New York: Crowell, 1978.
14 Townsend, John Rowe. *Written for Children.* New York: Lippincott, 1974.
15 Trease, Geoffrey. "The Historical Story: Is It Relevant Today?" *The Horn Book* (February 1977): 21–28.
16 Viguers, Ruth Hill. Foreword to *Calico Bush,* by Rachel Field. New York: Macmillan, 1966.
17 Yates, Elizabeth. *We, The People.* Illustrated by Nora Unwin. Hanover, N.H.: Regional Center for Educational Training, 1974.

Involving Children in Historical Fiction

COLONIAL TIMES THROUGH THE REVOLUTIONARY WAR

IMPACT OF SALEM

PIONEER AMERICA

AMERICAN HISTORY IN FOLK SONGS

THE EXCITEMENT of plot and characterization and the authenticity of much historical fiction make it a natural source of enjoyment and learning. Anne Troy (13) says that for children "history is one of the areas where fiction seems to be preferable and many times nearly replaces textbooks" (p. 473). Her rationale is that children acquire the idea that history is people rather than merely a series of events. Children can learn to love and respect history when they vicariously share the experiences of a character with whom they identify. Through experiences, they can surround themselves with the flavor and spirit of the times. They also visualize how real people are affected by the times during which they live.

Troy suggests that in addition to the individual reading of historical fiction, adults can bring history to life by reading historical fiction aloud to students, encouraging dramatic presentations of short scenes, and using literature in pleasant ways to develop attitudes, feelings, and general concepts about history. She also warns that this should be done with great care, without pressure or preaching, so that literature does not become "too much of a teaching-learning medium which could turn children off to all literature for fun" (p. 474).

A writer of historical fiction, Geoffrey Trease (12), makes a strong case for using it to add new meaning and excitement to social studies:

So even in the context of social studies, the historical story has an important part to play, and it would be wasteful not to utilize all that the writer has so painstakingly researched and made available to children in an attractive form. (p. 28)

Thus, historical fiction allows children to learn about the continuity of events, understand human relationships, and immerse themselves in the settings characteristic of specific times.

Another author of historical fiction, Alberta Wilson Constant (11), stresses the desirability of allowing children to be immersed in a book:

One of the best things that you can do for children is to teach them how to escape into a book. Let them be for a while somebody else. Let them stand with their feet on the cobblestones of Paris with Jean Valjean and hear the pursuing steps of police inspector Javert; let them walk into the jungle of Mowgli and hear the cry of their hero the panther and the long howl of the mother wolf. Show them how to mount the winged horse Pegasus and let him carry them away. He will bring them back safely. They'll be better, and they'll be stronger for the journey. (p. 23)

Constant believes that it is equally important for children to be immersed in the American past, as they feel the joy and challenge of new frontiers, the pride of human self-sufficiency, and the fun of being a pioneer child.

COLONIAL TIMES THROUGH THE REVOLUTIONARY WAR

Celebrations throughout the United States commemorated the bicentennial of our country in 1976. The bicentennial stimulated interest in searching for our roots and learning more about the early colonial days and the Revolutionary War. Carol Gay (6), discussing the importance of sharing a sense of the colonial past with children, says that this task can be effectively approached through the following activities: (1) sharing with children the same stories that Puritan children read, (2) en-

couraging children to take a penetrating look at a historical figure, and (3) inviting students to compare the values and problems of colonial times with those of contemporary times. While these activities would be meaningful for any time period, this section will consider some ways to accomplish each of these goals with literature related to colonial days.

Sharing Books Read by Colonial Children

What books were available to the colonial children in the 1600s and 1700s? What books did they read at school and at home? One of the most common books referred to in colonial literature and used in colonial education was the hornbook. (Reproductions are available through The Hornbook, Inc., Boston, Massachusetts.) The original hornbooks included a thin piece of three-by-five inch wood on which was a printed paper, covered with a transparent sheet of yellowish horn. This covering was fastened down by tacks. The hornbook contained the alphabet, vowel-consonant and consonant-vowel combinations, the Lord's Prayer, and sometimes Arabic numerals. It was designed to teach a colonial child to read and spell.

Another book mentioned frequently in the literature of colonial times is the *New-England Primer* (3). (This primer came out in many editions over the years and is available in a reissued text.) The chapbooks popular in England were also found in the colonies. Some of these had didactic messages; other such as "Tom Thumb," "Reynard the Fox," "Jack the Giant Killer," and "Robin Hood" were entertaining. These stories are available today. A very influential book written during the seventeenth century was John Bunyan's *Pilgrim's Progress;* both children and adults enjoyed following Christian on his perilous journey as he searched for salvation. Other popular books of earlier times that may be shared with contemporary children include *Babes in the Woods* (reissued in Frederick Warne's edition of Randolph Caldecott's *Picture Book No. 1),* John Newbery's *The History of Little Goody Two Shoes,* and Daniel Defoe's *Robinson Crusoe.* Reading from these books or listening to stories read from them allows children to develop a close relationship with characters from the past. It is exciting to discover that today they laugh at, or are excited by, the same plots and characters that fascinated children over two hundred years ago.

Taking a Penetrating Look at a Historical Figure

Older elementary and middle school children can learn about the process of scholarly research used by historical novelists or biographers when they recreate a day in the life of a colonial leader such as Benjamin Franklin, Patrick Henry, Thomas Jefferson, George Washington, or Paul Revere. While many

A boy learns about colonial children by reading a book read by children in the 1600s.

historical fiction books discussed earlier develop fictional stories about the common people, many others also refer to their leaders. For example, Esther Forbes's *Johnny Tremain* includes frequent mention of revolutionary leaders. Children can do research on these historical figures because considerable information about them is available.

The first step is to identify a figure about whom there is sufficient source material. With the person selected, the class can break into smaller research groups, each to work on a different period in the person's life. Next, as many reference materials as possible should be accumulated. In addition to biographies, information about the person's home, any speeches or writing by the person, reproductions of the front page of a newspaper that might have been available at that time, and a copy of the *Farmer's Almanac* listing the weather conditions for the period would all be valuable resources. Each group should develop a composite picture of what the historic figure did during the chosen period; this should include the person's thoughts, writings, actions, associations, concerns, and so on.

Gay (6) says that children should gain two values from this activity: They should experience such a close intimate look at a day from the past that the person and the place will come alive for them, and they should gain an awareness about how research uncovers the past. This understanding of the human qualities of the past is important to children; it is through such understanding that they become aware of "those human qualities that persevere through each century and bind the past and the present together" (p. 15).

Comparing the Values and Problems Depicted in Colonial Times with Those Set in Other Historic Times

Historical fiction written in colonial times creates two types of problems and their related values. The stories written around the earlier colonial period stress a search for religious and political freedom, as the colonists fight the tyranny of a hated government and brave the frequent miseries associated with starting over in a new land. There is danger; the colonists face disease and even starvation in order to fulfill their dream of freedom and new land. Some characters, such as Patricia Clapp's *Constance: A Story of Early Plymouth,* must make personal adjustments as they first long to return to a beloved home, then battle the role mandated by their society, and finally discover love for their new land. Much of this literature written around the Revolutionary War period stresses the battle for freedom. Other books, however, develop the characters' understanding of the tragedy of war, show the personal and emotional problems associated with characters following their conscience during wartime, or explore destructive forces related to war or hatred.

Books may be found that develop similar problems and values but have settings in different time periods. Students may discuss these problems and values, compare and relate them to current experiences. A few examples of historical fiction that may be used to stimulate this discussion are listed below:

Humans have a need for political and religious freedom. They will go through many hardships in search of freedom.
Colonial Times: Clapp's *Constance: A Story of Early Plymouth;* Speare's *The Witch of Blackbird Pond*
Czarist Russia: Lasky's *The Night Journey*
World War II: Fife's *Destination Unknown;* Siegal's *Upon the Head of the Goat: A Childhood in Hungary 1939–1944;* Uchida's *Journey Home*

Sometimes a person must fight or risk freedom to save what he believes in.
Colonial Times: Forbes's *Johnny Tremain;* Clapp's *I'm Deborah Sampson: A Soldier in the Revolution*
Post-Revolutionary Times: Collier's *Jump Ship to Freedom*
Civil War: Hunt's *Across Five Aprils*
World War II: McSwigan's *Snow Treasure*

War and hatred are destructive forces.
Colonial Times: Hickman's *The Valley of the Shadow*
English Civil War: Haugaard's *Cromwell's Boy*
Civil War: Hickman's *Zoar Blue*
World War II: Reiss's *The Upstairs Room*

When children see and discuss the relationships among values that have been held across time periods, they also begin to discover some major values that people have held throughout recorded history. They realize that these same values are also important today.

Using Creative Dramatizations to Stimulate Interest in Colonial America

Many exciting dramas unfold in the pages of historical fiction written about the colonial period, especially about Revolutionary War days. Jone Wright and Elizabeth Allen (20) describe a creative dramatization with sixth graders in which the group reenacted Paul Revere's ride. They added an interesting dimension to this activity with comparative dramatizations; one group dramatized Longfellow's poem "Paul Revere's Ride," while the second dramatized the ride as told by Jean Fritz in *And Then What Happened, Paul Revere?* (5) and Louis Wolfe in *Let's Go with Paul Revere* (19). This second group also verified additional facts about Revere's ride by reading a magazine article (1). After the group members read and discussed their sources, they pantomimed various actions and planned the scenes they wanted to include. The following scenes were developed for each group:

Poetry Group

1 Paul talking to his friends about hanging the signal lights.
2 Paul rowing alone across the river.
3 Paul waiting on the opposite shore for the signal to be hung.
4 Paul galloping alone through the countryside: 12:00 P.M., Medford; 1:00 A.M., Lexington; 2:00 A.M., Concord.
5 Paul galloping on through the night.

Authentic Sources Group

1 Patriots giving the signal.
2 Patriots rowing Revere across the river.
3 Paul Revere warning patriots at Cambridge and Concord.
4 British soldiers capturing and releasing Paul Revere.

After the two dramatizations, the children discussed the differences observed between the two presentations and drew some interesting conclusions about the romanticizing of history and the researching of historical data.

"The worst of Plagues, the detested tea shipped for this Port by the East Indian Company, is now arrived in the Harbour" (p. 107). With these words, the colonists were told that they must rally to the cry for freedom if they wanted to repeal the hated taxation-without-representation laws. This scene from *Johnny Tremain* is another natural subject for creative dramatizations. The following scenes depicting the Boston Tea Party could be dramatized:

Boston Tea Party from Johnny Tremain (Esther Forbes)

1 Samuel Adams asking the printer to duplicate the placard announcing the tea shipment.
2 Johnny Tremain going from house to house, using the secret code, notifying the Observers that there would be a secret meeting.
3 The meeting of the Observers and a decision being reached about the tea.
4 The meeting in front of Old South Church, with Josiah Quincy talking to the crowd and Samuel Adams giving the message that the tea would be dumped.
5 The colonists throwing the tea into Boston Harbor.

IMPACT OF SALEM

Incidents of unreasonable fears and unjustified persecutions appear throughout history. The historical fiction books written about the late 1600s provide stimulating sources for oral discussion, creative dramatizations, values clarification, writing, understanding setting, understanding characterization, and comparing literary works that develop similar themes. Ann

Petry's *Tituba of Salem Village* is about a slave and Elizabeth George Speare's *The Witch of Blackbird Pond* is about a teenage white girl; both experience the impact of witch-hunts and unjustified persecution. These stories are excellent for discussion and comparison. The teacher of a sixth-grade class mapped the following discussion and learning possibilities for using *Tituba of Salem Village* and *The Witch of Blackbird Pond* with her students:

Dramatization: Tituba

Dramatize the family approaching the gloomy house in Salem Village and meeting Goody Good.
Recreate the scene in which the children bring in the fortune-telling cards and try to convince Tituba to read their fortunes.
Dramatize the court scene, including the witnesses against Tituba and the appearance of Samuel Conklin who comes to her defense.
Interview Tituba, her husband, the minister, Betsy, Abigail, and Samuel Conklin. How does each describe the experiences leading up to the trial? How do they feel about the results of the trial? Are they pleased when Tituba is free?

Dramatization: Kit

Dramatize Kit's first meeting with her relatives.
Recreate the Dame's school and Kit providing instruction for her six students.
Role play the conversations between Kit and the Quaker woman, Hannah Tupper, who lives in the meadow.
Dramatize the scenes during which Kit is accused of witchcraft, is taken as a prisoner to the shed, stands trial for witchcraft, and is freed because Prudence demonstrates her reading skills.

Developing Characterization: Tituba

How did each of these people see Tituba and feel about her?
Her former owner in Barbados
The minister
The minister's wife
Betsy and Abigail
Dr. Griggs
The residents of Salem Village
Samuel Conklin
Tituba

Developing Characterization: Kit

How did each of these people see Kit and feel about her?
Kit's grandfather

Matthew Wood
Aunt Rachel
Reverend Gershom Bulkeley
William Ashby
Judith and Mercy
Goodwife Cruff
Hannah Tupper
Nat Eaton
Kit

Importance of Setting: Both Books

Compare the jewellike setting of Barbados with Tituba's description of the house in Salem and Kit's description of the colorless Puritan village.

Why do you believe both authors chose to take their heroines from tropical islands to very different locations?

What might have happened in each story if Kit and Tituba had remained in Barbados?

Values Clarification: Tituba

Why did Tituba's former owner decide to sell her two dear companions? Do you believe her reason was good? Why or why not?

Why do you believe Abigail encouraged the other girls to try and put Betsy in a trance?

What special skills did Tituba have that made her different from the people in Salem Village? Why would the people hate and fear her?

Why do you believe the minister did not come to her defense or pay her jail fees?

Why was Samuel Conklin the only one to come to Tituba's defense? How did he demonstrate his faith in her?

Values Clarification: Kit

Why did Kit's grandfather want her to read and discuss plays? Why do you think the Puritans reacted so differently to her desire to read such material?

Why do you believe Kit enjoyed going to the meadow and visiting Hannah Tupper? Why were the villagers afraid of both the meadow and Hannah Tupper?

What makes Hannah Tupper different from the villagers? Why would the people fear her?

What made Kit Tyler different from the villagers? Why would people fear her?

What was the difference between the way Goodwife Cruff felt about her daughter Prudence and the way Kit felt about Prudence? Who was right? How would Prudence's life have been different if Kit had not helped her? Why do you think Kit helped Prudence? Why do

you think Kit didn't speak out in court about Prudence, even if her answer might have helped her own case?

Why do you believe Kit's friend, "dear dependable William," did not come to her defense at the trial? Why did Nat Eaton risk his own liberty to testify for her?

Personal Response: Tituba

How would you have felt if you had been Tituba and had been forced to leave your homeland? What would your reaction have been to your new family and the people of the village?

Have you ever known anyone or read about anyone who was feared or disliked because that person was different from others? Has this ever happened to you? When?

Personal Reponse: Kit

Who helped you when you needed help? If you had been Kit, would you have risked your safety in order to help both Hannah Tupper and Prudence Cruff? Why or why not?

Have you ever felt like Kit? When?

Which story did you like better? Why?

Were you satisfied with the ending of each story? Why or why not? If you could change either story, how would you change it?

Do you believe a story about such personal persecution could be written about a heroine today? What would be the cause of the persecution? How might the heroine solve her problem?

Writing: Both Books

Pretend that you are either Tituba or Kit. Choose a period of time from the story and write your experiences in a journal format.

Pretend to be a villager living in Salem Village who has relatives in England. Write a letter to these relatives telling them about what has been happening in Salem.

Pretend to be a twentieth-century writer developing a script for a television "You Are There" program. Write the script for either a reenactment of the trial of Tituba or Kit Tyler.

Related Literature

Historical fiction books with settings from other time periods that also develop themes of fear and unjustified persecution:

Suspicion toward, and persecution of, Christian Indians who lived in peace in a Moravian village: Janet Hickman's *The Valley of the Shadow*.

Suspicion toward, and persecution of Navaho Indians: Scott O'Dell's *Sing Down the Moon.*

Suspicion toward, and persecution of, Jewish people during World War II. Johanna Reiss's *The Upstairs Room;* Esther Hautzig's *The Endless Steppe: A Girl in Exile;* Judith Kerr's *When Hitler Stole Pink Rabbit;* Sonia Levitin's *Journey to America;* Aranka Siegal's *Upon the Head of the Goat: A Childhood in Hungary 1939–1944.*

PIONEER AMERICA

Most children are fascinated with that time in U.S. history when courageous men, women, and children were struggling across the country on foot, on horseback, or in covered wagons. They like to hear about children who rode on canal barges, floated on rafts down the Ohio, or traveled on steamboats down the Mississippi. They also enjoy vicariously experiencing with the pioneers the frontier years after the covered wagons had been unloaded and the family began its new life in a sod house or a log cabin.

Teachers of social studies find this period exciting. They use the fiction of the pioneer period to help children develop closer ties with the past, understand the relationships between past and present values, understand the physical environment of the time, and discover the links between the pioneer past and the present. Ways of developing these understandings range from sharing an individual story with children through developing total units that encourage children to identify with the period through music, art, stories, games, foods, values, home remedies, and the research of historic characters. This section presents some interesting ways of sharing the pioneer past with children.

Introducing Pioneer America to Children

In order to immerse children in the physical environment of the time and to stimulate their curiosity, objects can be shown that were important, for both survival and pleasure, to a pioneer family. These objects can include quilts, tools (hammer, nails, spade, hoe, grindstone), tallow candles, lengths of cotton cloth, wooden buckets, iron pots, skillets, earthenware jugs, tin lanterns, dried herbs, food (a barrel of flour; yeast; dried beans, peas, and corn; salt; sugar; dried apples; a slab of bacon), seed corn, cornhusk dolls, a treasured china-head doll, a yoke, a churn, a spinning wheel, a fiddle, a log cabin (made from Lincoln Logs), and pictures of pioneers.

In addition to objects appropriate for the time being studied, there should be displays of historical fiction such as those discussed earlier in this chapter; books that might have been read by pioneer children; books on pioneer art, music, and crafts.

One teacher introduced some third-grade students to the pioneer period by dressing in pioneer style, greeting the students at the classroom door, and taking them on a classroom tour. By enthusiastically presenting artifacts, the teacher excited the children and made them want to know more. The following are examples of learning experiences teachers have used to encourage children to learn about the people who lived in pioneer America.

Values from the Past

Children can learn about the past and relate it to the present when they identify the values held and problems overcome by characters living in pioneer America. These values and problems and their solutions can be compared with those of today. The pioneer period is filled with stories that stress love of the land; the need for positive relationships among family members, neighbors, pioneers, and Indians; the struggle for survival; and the need for bravery. The following experiences encourage children to clarify their own values as well as those of others:

Love of the Land

1 Pioneers were drawn to the West because of the opportunity to own rich farmland. Some people left their homes in the East when their land no longer produced good crops. Others traveled to the West because they wanted more room or fewer neighbors. Still others acquired the free land provided under the Homestead Act. After reading one of the books that place this strong emphasis on the land (i.e., Honore Morrow's *On to Oregon!;* Barbara Brenner's *Wagon Wheels;* Harold Keith's *The Obstinate Land*), ask students to identify the reasons these pioneers had for moving and any conflicts that family members felt when they were deciding whether or not to move.

At this point, role playing could help clarify the attitudes of pioneer family members. Ask the students to imagine that the year is 1862 and they are living on a small New England farm. They are sitting with their family at the evening meal when suddenly their uncle runs into the room with a paper in his hand. The paper is a notification of the Homestead Act and information about what this act will provide.

Their uncle is ready to sell his farm, pack a few belongings, and travel to the West in a covered wagon. He wants his brother's family to join him. Suggest that the students role play the reactions of the different family characters

Announcing The

HOMESTEAD ACT

The West Wants FARMERS

Rich Prairie Land Yours For Improvement
160 Acres of Public Land
FREE to Anyone Over 21
Who Will Live On The Land For Five Years

and decide whether or not they should go. Based on common characteristics found in historical fiction stories, the characters might express these concerns:

Mother: She knows that her husband wants to own a better farm, but her family lives in the East; she doesn't want to leave them. In addition, she has lost one child who is buried on the old farm. She is also concerned about living on the frontier away from a church, a school, and the protection of close neighbors.

Father: He is unhappy with his rocky farm and the poor production it has provided. He has dreamed of a farm with rich soil that could produce better crops and support his family.

Twelve-Year-Old Son: He is filled with the excitement of a new adventure. He wants to see new lands and Indians. In addition, he is not displeased with the prospect of leaving school for a while.

Seven-Year-Old Daughter: The farmhouse is the only home she has ever known; her friends and relatives live in the surrounding countryside. She wants to please her father but she doesn't know what to expect in a land that far from home.

The students could consider each person's arguments and decide if they would have moved to a new land. They can continue by talking about what they would take with them if they decided to homestead. Finally, the discussion can be drawn into the present time. Do people still have a strong loyalty to the land? Do they want to own their own land? Encourage children to provide reasons for their arguments.

2 The desire for unspoiled land as well as adventure can be placed into a modern framework by having students pretend their families are moving to a wilderness area in Alaska. Why would they want to move? Why would they not want to move? What problems do they think they would encounter before moving? How would they solve them? What problems would they encounter in the Alaskan wilderness? How would they solve them? Finally, do they believe these problems and their solutions are similar to those experienced by pioneers?

Human Relations

1 Many pioneer books present different ways of dealing with the Indians and diverse attitudes toward them. The only solution given in many books is a battle between the Indians and white men. In contrast, Alice Dalgliesh's *The Courage of Sarah Noble* presents a family who settles on land for which the Indians have been given a fair price; they have also been allowed to retain their right to fish in the river. Sarah's father believes that all people must be treated fairly. Encourage children to discuss the reasons for various actions, the beliefs of the pioneers, and the consequences.

2 After children have read the "Massacre" and "Ambassador to the Enemy," chapters in Carol Ryrie Brink's *Caddie Woodlawn,* ask them to discuss the decision made by the settlers to attack the Indians because they thought the Indians were going to attack them. Why did the settlers reach their decision? Was it accurate? Why or why not? Then, ask the students to place themselves in Caddie's role. If they were Caddie would they have warned the Indians? Why or why not? What might have been the results if Caddie had not made her evening ride? Finally, bring the discussion to contemporary times. Ask the students if there are times when people today might decide to act out of fright rather than out of knowledge? What events would they consider important enough to risk their own safety?

3 The pioneer books also include many stories of people's need to help others. Neighbors and family members help each other and provide moral support during times of crisis. The "Little House" series, by Laura Ingalls Wilder, has many incidents of family support and working with the neighbors. Fritz and his neighbor in Keith's *The Obstinate Land* help each other till the soil, plant crops, guard fields against the dangers of marauding cattle, and share the necessities of survival. Encourage children to discuss the values of positive human relationships during both pioneer and contemporary times.

ISSUE

❦

Does Watching Television Influence the Reading of Literature?

BOTH EDUCATORS AND parents express mixed reactions to the issues related to television viewing. The positive viewpoint stresses the many films, plays, and stories that can deepen children's understanding of a variety of literature and introduce them to new ideas, background information, and literary forms. Television shows such as "Little House on the Prairie" are cited for their ability to provide historical backgrounds and stimulate children to read Wilder's books. On the other hand, many people claim that children watch so much television that their literature reading decreases and their reading achievement declines. Critics of television viewing by children may also be concerned with such related topics as television and aggression, child development, child psychology, and sociology.

To illustrate the spectrum of materials that have been written on the subject, Diane Erbeck compiled an annotated bibliography of recent articles that discuss the positive and/or negative aspects of television viewing.[1] The balanced presentation of articles suggests that the issues related to television viewing have not been resolved. Does television discourage or encourage reading of literature? Does watching television promote passivity? Can literature in book form compete with the visual stimulation found in the adoption of a story for television?

Results reported from a television-related school project sponsored by the Home and School Association of Hawes Elementary School in Ridgewood, New Jersey[2] suggest some of the problems connected with televi-

sion. A group of parents and teachers felt that students wasted too much of their time watching television. Children in the fourth, fifth, and sixth grades agreed to turn off their televisions for one week and keep a diary of their reactions and activities. School officials reported astonishment at the reactions of the families: "The Hawes experiment was supported almost unanimously by the students. But school officials, accustomed for years to parental railing about the perils of television for youthful viewers, were stunned to find that many mothers and fathers balked at being without television" (p. 1). Reports of the activities carried on by students did not indicate that there was a considerable increase in either reading of literature or school achievement.

A point of view frequently stressed by educators is that television can have positive effects on children if there is planned interaction with others to counter passivity. Iris Tiedt[3] suggests that a literature film adds visual interpretation to a book, stimulates interest in reading the book, stimulates oral discussion, and extends children's imaginations. Television viewing can be positively used by having children study how a literature presentation differs in film or print and discuss and critically evaluate what they see or hear. While there seems to be no clear research evidence on the effects of television on literature reading and appreciation, it may be the quality of the television programs and the quality of the interaction that is essential if television is not to have a detrimental influence on literature reading.

---

1 Erbeck, Diane M. "Television and Children: A Pro/Con Reading List." *Top of the News* 37 (Fall 1980): 47–53.
2 Mayer, Jane. "Some Cried A Lot, But Youths Survived Week Without TV." *The Wall Street Journal,* 6 January 1982, pp. 1, 21.
3 Tiedt, Iris. "Input, Media Special." *Language Arts* 53 (February 1976): 119.

The Pioneer Environment

Pioneer stories are rich in descriptions of the homes, crafts, store goods, food, transportation, books, and pleasures that occupied the people of this time.

Amusements of the Pioneer Family

Allowing children to take part in the same experiences that entertained pioneer children is a good way to help them feel closer to their counterparts in the past. For example, Wilder's *Little House in the Big Woods* describes these happy moments that can be recreated with children:

1   For a special birthday treat, Pa played and sang "Pop Goes the Weasel" for Laura. Some of her happiest memories were related to Pa's fiddle. Other songs mentioned in the book are "Rock of Ages" (the fiddle could not play weekday songs on Sunday) and "Yankee Doodle."
2   The family traveled through the woods to a square dance at Granpa's house. At the dance, the fiddler played and the square-dance caller called the squares for "Buffalo Gals," "The Irish Washerwoman," and "The Arkansas Traveler."
3   After the day's work was finished, Ma would sometimes cut paper dolls for the girls out of stiff white paper and make dresses, hats, ribbons, and laces out of colored paper.
4   In the winter evenings, Laura and Mary begged Pa to tell them stories. He told them about "Grandpa and the Panther," "Pa and the Bear in the Way," "Pa and the Voice in the Woods," and "Grandpa's Sled and the Pig." Enough details are included in these stories so that they can be retold to children.

A School Day with the Pioneer Family

A day in school for pioneer children (if a school was available) was quite different from a contemporary school day. The historical fiction stories, and other sources, provide enough information about school, books read, and parables memorized to interest children and recreate a school day that emphasizes spelling, reading, and arithmetic.

Modern children may be surprised that Ma in Wilder's *On the Banks of Plum Creek* considered three books on the subjects of spelling, reading, and arithmetic among her "best things" and gave them solemnly to the girls with the advice that they care for them and study faithfully. Likewise, Fritz in Keith's *The Obstinate Land* sold his most prized possession to pay for the schooling of his brother and sister. In addition, these children had to ride sixteen miles on one pony every day in order to get to and from school.

1   A number of early textbooks and other stories have been reissued in their original form and can be shared with children. For example, children can read the rhyming alphabet; practice their letters; and learn to read words of one, two, three, four, and five syllables from the *New England Primer* (3).
2   Pioneer children also read and wrote maxims to practice their handwriting or as punishment for bad behavior. Joan W. Blos's *A Gathering of Days: A New England Girl's Journal, 1830–32* tells of this experience in the 1830s and lists some maxims that were written, such as

> To thine own self be true.
> Give to them that want.
> Speak the truth and lie not.

3   Additional methods of instruction are described in other stories. Marguerite De Angeli's *Skippack School* (1750) mentions the spelling bee, reciting verses, and receiving sugar pretzels as a reward for learning. Carol Ryrie Brink's *Caddie Woodlawn* describes an 1860 method for memorizing the multiplication tables; the children sang them to the tune of "Yankee Doodle." Recreating a typical school day during which children read from the primer, recite and copy parables, have a spelling bee, and sing their multiplication tables would help them visualize the pioneer child's life and develop an understanding that education was considered important in earlier times.

A Day in the General Store

The country store was also very different from the contemporary department store or large shopping mall. It fascinated children, however, just as department stores create excitement in today's children. Laura's first experience in a general store is described in *Little House in the Big Woods*. This store included bright materials, kegs of nails, kegs of shot, barrels of candy, cooking utensils, plowshares, knives, shoes, and dishes. In fact there was just about everything.

1   A source of information about the kinds of materials that might be available to a pioneer family in the late 1800s is a reissue of an early Sears, Roebuck and Co. catalogue (10). Through these pages, children can acquire an understanding of the merchandise available and the fashions of the day. They can use the information found in these sources either to recreate a child-sized general store in one corner of the room or create miniature stores in boxes.

Pioneer Chores
Wash on Monday
Iron on Tuesday

Mend on Wednesday
Churn on Thursday
Clean on Friday
Bake on Saturday
Rest on Sunday

The pioneer setting in historical fiction seems real when children reenact chores.

1   While people may not keep this kind of a work schedule today, the daily activities of the pioneer family associated with the house and other outside responsibilities are of interest to children. Preparing food is mentioned in many stories. Because pioneer families could not go to the local store for supplies, they needed to prepare their own. Churning butter is one activity that children enjoy doing. A simple recipe for butter that children can make easily is given below:

½ pint whipping cream
¼ teaspoon salt
Pint jar with tight cover

Pour the ½ pint of whipping cream into the pint jar. Seal the cover tightly onto the jar. Shake the jar until the cream turns to butter. Remove the lid, pour off the liquid, and work out any excess liquid. Add salt and stir it into the butter. Remove butter from jar and shape it.

According to Laura in *Little House in the Big Woods,* Ma was not always satisfied with white butter. Children may wish to experiment with the technique Ma used to add a yellow color to the butter. She rubbed a carrot over a pan that had nail holes punched across the bottom. She placed the soft, grated carrot into a pan of milk, then warmed the mixture and poured it into a cloth bag. When she squeezed the bag, bright yellow milk ran from the cloth and was added to the cream in the churn (p. 30).

2   Because pioneer families had no refrigerators or freezers, they had to find other ways to preserve their foods. If they lived in the North, they used nature's icebox in the winter. In *A Gathering of Days: A New England Girl's Journal, 1830–32*, children read about chopping off a frozen wedge of soup and heating it in the kettle. Other stories describe the feeling of well-being when the pantry, shed, attic, and cellar were filled with food. In contrast, great concern was experienced when only the seed corn remained between the family and starvation. Children learn about different ways the pioneers preserved fruits and vegetables by reading Eliot Wigginton's *The Foxfire Book* (18); children enjoy drying their own apples and then having them for a special snack.

The people in pioneer fiction become alive for children who cannot actually live on a prairie homestead. Children can sing the same songs pioneer children sang, dance to the music of a pioneer fiddle, listen to the pioneer storyteller, imagine they attend a pioneer school, imagine they go to the general store, and do the chores of the homestead.

Significance of American Trails in Westward Expansion

Deep ruts across a sea of prairie grass, markers along a river crossing, and scars created by oxen hooves sliding down the rock side of a canyon were the pioneer equivalent of modern interstate highways. Like highways, these trails were important for moving passengers and commerce across the country; without them, the West could not have been opened for expansion. It is hard to imagine a thousand men, women, and children, with two hundred covered wagons, heading across the prairies, deserts, and mountains to reach California or Oregon.

Children can discover additional information about the trails referred to in historical fiction books by reading Bruce Grant's *Famous American Trails* (8). They can discuss the purpose for the trails (i.e., cattle drives, wagon trails, fast movement of mail), the locations of the trails, the physical hardships found along the trails, forts built along the trails, and distances covered by the trails. They can draw a large U.S. map, place on it the major westward trails, and then trace, using different colored pencils, the routes taken by pioneers in various historical fiction books. The following books provide enough descriptions of locations to be of value in this activity:

Alice Dalgliesh, *The Courage of Sarah Noble*—Westfield, Massachusetts, to New Milford, Connecticut, by foot and horseback, 1707.

Honore Morrow, *On to Oregon!*—Missouri to Oregon by covered wagon, horse, and foot, 1844.

Evelyn Sibley Lampman, *White Captives*—Illinois to Santa Fe Pass, by wagon train divided as some went to Salt Lake City, Utah, and others traveled south to Socorro on the Rio Grande, 1851.

Clyde Robert Bulla, *Riding the Pony Express*—Pony Express trail from St. Joseph, Missouri, to Sacramento, California, 1860.

Laura Ingalls Wilder, "Little House" books—Pepin, Wisconsin, to Kansas, to Minnesota, and to Dakota Territory near De Smet by covered wagon, 1870s.

Research Skills

Many historical fiction books describe the sources used by the authors to develop the setting and the authenticity of a period. Encouraging children to choose a specific time period and location and then discover as much as possible about the people and their times will help them develop respect for research skills and gain new insights into the period.

In one class, children researched their own small city during the late 1800s. The group investigated documents at the historical society; searched old newspapers; found old family albums, journals, and letters; searched documents at the courthouse; interviewed people whose relatives had lived in the town during that time; read references to discover information about fashions, transportation, and food; and located buildings that would have existed during that time. After they had gathered this information, they pretended that they were living a hundred years earlier and wrote stories about themselves; the stories contained only authentic background information.

Additional Activities Related to Pioneer American Literature

1   Have the children pretend that they are newspaper reporters sent from an eastern paper to discover what living on the frontier is really like. Encourage them to write news stories that will be sent back to the newspaper. In addition, have them pretend that they can take a tintype to accompany their stories; have them draw pictures of the scenes they would like to photograph.

2   Many pioneers moved to the West because they received encouraging letters from friends and relatives. Have children write letters to friends or relatives and telling the Easterners why they should or should not sell all their property and move to _____.

3   Several historical fiction books such as Joan W. Blos's *A Gathering of Days: A New England Girl's Journal, 1830–32* are written in journal format. Allow children to select a hero or heroine from a historical fiction story and write several journal entries for a specific period in the story.

4   Many scenes from the pioneer period in historical fiction may be dramatized. An example is the scene when Marguerite made the Maypole and shared the experience with the Indians in Rachel Field's *Calico Bush*. The experiences of Sarah Noble in playing and living with the Indian family when her father leaves her to return for his wife is another interesting scene to dramatize.

Culminating Activity for Pioneer America

Children enjoy sharing their knowledge about pioneer days with parents or other children. Consequently, a pioneer day can be planned in which they display pioneer objects, food, arts and crafts; demonstrate songs or dances learned; and share information gained, creative writing completed, and art projects made during their study of pioneer life and historical fiction.

AMERICAN HISTORY IN FOLK SONGS

Just as historical fiction presents a panorama of American history, folk songs from the different periods present a picture of the common people during that time. The books discussed frequently refer to characters listening to, singing, or playing music. Several songs have been suggested as a means of making the pioneer period live for today's children.

One very exciting historical unit used with children combined folk music, historical fiction, and social studies. Singing or square dancing to the music of the times allowed the children to share a memorable, enjoyable experience that was similar to that of the characters in the historical fiction books. In addition, the words in the songs brought a new understanding about the essence of the time. Chart 10–2 lists folk songs from different historical periods.

The folk songs in the chart, and information about the historical struggles of the times, can be found in the following books: C. A. Browne's *The Story of Our National Ballads* (2), Edith Fowke and Joe Glazer's *Songs of Work and Protest* (4),

CHART 10–2
Folk Songs

1754 and 1776	"Yankee Doodle"—symbolic of the struggle for freedom.
1796–1800	"Jefferson and Liberty"—Jefferson pledged to repeal the Sedition Act.
Early 1800s	"Blow Ye Wings in the Morning"—whaling industry along the eastern seaboard.
1825–1913	"Low Bridge Everybody Down"—mule drivers on the Erie Canal.
1841–1847	"Patsy Works on the Railroad"—Irish workers completing railroad in eastern United States.
1850s	"Sweet Betsy from Pike"— taking a covered wagon to California.
1850s	"Go Down Moses"—freedom song of the black slaves.
1850s	"Oh, Freedom"—freedom song of the black slaves.
1859	"John Brown's Body"—attack on garrison at Harper's Ferry to capture arms and liberate slaves.
1861	"The Battle Hymn of the Republic"—Julia Ward Howe watched the campfires of the Union Army.
1872	"John Henry"—a steel-driving man drilling the Big Bend Tunnel on the Chesapeake and Ohio Railroad.
1888	"Drill, Ye Tarriers, Drill"—dynamiters blasting their way through the mountains as the railroads crossed the continent.
1870–90	"The Old Chisholm Trail"—herding cattle from San Antonio, Texas northward.
1897	"Hallelujah, I'm a Bum"—hoboing on the open road.
Early 1900s	"Sixteen Tons"—coal mining song.

Tom Glazer's *A New Treasury of Folk Songs* (7), and Carl Sandburg's *The American Songbag* (9).

The teacher who developed this historical song and literature unit with fourth-grade children divided the historical periods into the following time periods: Revolutionary War, Early Expansion, Civil War, and Pioneer America. He collected many books on different levels of reading ability: some were shared orally with the group; others were read by the children. Literature that he identified for the Revolutionary War period included the following: Patricia Clapp's *I'm Deborah Sampson: A Soldier in the War of the Revolution;* Esther Forbes's *Johnny Tremain*; and Leonard Wibberley's *John Treegate's Musket* (14), *Peter Treegate's War* (15), *Sea Captain from Salem* (16), and *Treegate's Raiders (17).*

Historical fiction books that were used with the early expansion period included Rachel Field's *Calico Bush,* Honore Morrow's *On to Oregon!* and Joan Blos's *A Gathering of Days: A New England Girl's Journal, 1830–32.*

Historical fiction books for the Civil War period included Marguerite DeAngeli's *Thee, Hannah!,* Harold Keith's *Rifles for Watie*, Janet Hickman's *Zoar Blue*, and Irene Hunt's *Across Five Aprils.*

Historical fiction books about pioneer America included Brink's *Caddie Woodlawn,* all of Wilder's "Little House" series, and Harold Keith's *The Obstinate Land.*

In addition to historical fiction books, the teacher used biographies of famous people from the time period (see chapter twelve) and other informational books about the period from the Revolutionary War through the days of pioneer America. The students involved themselves in history; they sang the songs of the people, acted out scenes from the stories, made artifacts such as cornhusk dolls, wrote creative stories, and investigated the historical periods.

One day, the children sat in a circle on the floor and sang folk songs from the Civil War period. After they sang each song, some children shared their experiences. They pretended to be slaves, seeking freedom by way of the Underground Railroad; Separatists in Ohio deciding if they should or should not fight in the Civil War; and different members of Matt Creighton's family, who were now home from the war, sharing their experiences from *Across Five Aprils.* Both the teacher and the children thoroughly enjoyed the experience and gained considerable information about their American heritage and literature reflecting this heritage. When evaluating their experience, the children indicated that they had never had such an enjoyable time learning social studies. The characters of the past actually lived for these children, and the pleasures that may be gained from reading were discovered.

SUMMARY

Children can learn to appreciate and respect history when they share vicarious experiences with characters with whom they can identify. This enjoyment can be enhanced by encouraging children to read and allowing them to become immersed in historical fiction, providing opportunities for them to listen to historical fiction, encouraging dramatic presentations of short scenes, and using historical fiction in pleasant ways to bring new meaning and excitement to social studies.

Children can experience colonial times by reading and listening to books about colonial children, taking a penetrating

These children recapture the feeling of pioneer America by singing the folk songs that were common during the time.

look at a historical figure, comparing the values and problems depicted in colonial times with those of contemporary times, and taking part in creative dramatizations in order to stimulate interest in colonial America.

Pioneer America is an especially exciting period for many elementary children. Historical fiction helps children develop closer ties with the past, understand the relationships between pioneer values and present values, and understand the physical environment of that time. Adults can help children develop these understandings by sharing individual stories with children or developing total pioneer America units. Children can involve themselves in the time period through music, art, games, foods, drama, home remedies, living conditions, and researching western expansion trails.

Students can personally discover the research skills that are necessary to write credible pioneer historical fiction by investigating sources available to them in their hometowns. They can write journal entries and creative stories about time periods that they can investigate.

Folk songs depicting a specific historical period can also increase appreciation of historical fiction and the people of the past. Sharing songs that were sung by the common people of the time allows children another means to experience history

vicariously. The vivid music and exciting plots of historical stories help to emphasize that reading and sharing literature can be very enjoyable.

Suggested Activities for Children's Appreciation of Historical Fiction

- Historical fiction has been suggested as a source for translating the information found in sterile textbooks into vivid spectacles of human drama. Choose an appropriate level social studies or history text, list the content and time periods covered in the text, and identify historical fiction that could be used to stimulate children's interest and understanding of that content or time period.

- With a group of children or a peer group, compare the information found in the textbook (see first activity) with the background information discovered in the historical fiction books. Do the two sources agree? If they do not, research other sources in order to discover which are correct. If they do agree, discuss which source more vividly describe history and what makes those sources more meaningful.

- One value of reading historical fiction is the development of an understanding that there are human qualities that persist through each century and tie the past to the present. Use Chart 10-1, Themes in Historical Fiction (see p. 440), and the theme summaries at the end of each section of the first part of this chapter and share literature from several periods with children. Lead a discussion that helps them identify the human values expressed in those time periods. Allow them to discuss whether these values are still accepted by people today and if they think the values will still be important in the next century. Why or why not?

- Discussions of controversial issues have been identified as one method of creating a "springboard" strategy that allows children to become involved in stimulating debates. Historical fiction has numerous characters who took stands on controversial issues. The plots of many historical fiction stories are developed on issues that were considered controversial during that time period. Identify several books from a time period and find paragraphs that state these issues. Develop a list of provocative questions that could be used when sharing this material with children. For example, in the Revolutionary War period, some literary characters believed that freedom was worth fighting for no matter what the consequences, others believed that the colonies should stay loyal to England, and still others felt that all killing was wrong.

- Encourage children to select one controversial issue found in historical fiction, pretend to be on the side of one group or another in the story, do additional research on the issue, and take part in a debate.
- In order to discover how vividly the setting can be presented in historical fiction, allow children to draw detailed pictures after they have read or listened to a story. To increase their appreciation of the settings described in some books, allow them to draw the setting described in an excellent historical book as well as an inadequately described setting. Discuss the differences for the reader and for the writer. Which one is more meaningful to the reader? Which one is more demanding on the author? Why?
- Select a scene from historical fiction that has both memorable characters and an exciting plot. With a group of children or peers, develop the scene into a creative dramatization.
- Select the folk songs that were popular during a specific period in history. Listen to and read the words and sing the songs. What conflicts, problems, or values are presented through the lyrics? Are the same themes found in historical fiction of that time period?

References

1 Armstrong, O. K. "The British are Coming! Great Moments in U.S. History." *Reader's Digest* 106 (April 1975): 187–98.
2 Browne, C. A. *The Story of Our National Ballads.* Edited by Willard Heaps. New York: Crowell, 1960.
3 Ford, Paul Leicester. *The New-England Primer.* New York: Columbia University, Teachers College, 1962.
4 Fowke, Edith, and Glazer, Joe. *Songs of Work and Protest.* New York: Dover, 1973.
5 Fritz, Jean. *And Then What Happened, Paul Revere?* New York: Coward-McCann, 1973.
6 Gay, Carol. "Children's Literature and the Bicentennial." *Language Arts* 53 (January 1976): 11–16.
7 Glazer, Tom. *A New Treasury of Folk Songs.* New York: Bantam Books, 1961.
8 Grant, Bruce. *Famous American Trails.* Chicago: Rand McNally, 1971.
9 Sandburg, Carl. *The American Songbag.* New York: Harcourt Brace Jovanovich, 1927.
10 *Sears, Roebuck and Co., Consumers Guide.* 1900. Reprint. Northfield, Ill.: DBI Books, 1970.
11 Toothaker, Roy E. "A Conversation with Alberta Wilson Constant." *Language Arts* 53 (January 1976): 23–26.
12 Trease, Geoffrey. "The Historical Story: Is It Relevant Today?" *The Horn Book* (February 1977): 21–28.
13 Troy, Anne. "Literature for Content Area Learning." *The Reading Teacher* 30 (February 1977): 470–74.
14 Wibberly, Leonard, *John Treegate's Musket.* New York: Farrar, Straus & Giroux, 1959.
15 _____. *Peter Treegate's War.* New York: Farrar, Straus & Giroux, 1960.
16 _____. *Sea Captain From Salem.* New York: Farrar, Straus & Giroux, 1961.
17 _____. *Treegate's Raiders.* New York: Farrar, Straus & Giroux, 1962.
18 Wigginton, Eliot. *The Foxfire Book.* Doubleday, 1975.
19 Wolfe, Louis. *Let's Go with Paul Revere.* Putnam, 1964.
20 Wright, Jone P., and Allen, Elizabeth G. "Sixth-Graders Ride with Paul Revere." *Language Arts* 53 (January 1976): 46–50.

CHILDREN'S LITERATURE

Armstrong, William H. *Sounder.* Illustrated by James Barkley. Harper & Row, 1969 (ch. 11).

Beatty, John, and Beatty, Patricia. *Who Comes to King's Mountain?* Morrow, 1975. (I: 11–14 R: 6). Fourteen-year-old Alexander MacLeod is first loyal to the king, then becomes a patriot as he joins Francis Marion, the Swamp Fox, during the Revolutionary War.

Beatty, Patricia. *Eight Mules from Monterey.* Morrow, 1982 (I:10 + R: 6). The Ashmores cross the California mountains in 1916.

———. *Wait for Me, Watch for Me, Eula Bee.* Morrow, 1978 (I: 12 + R: 7). Thirteen-year-old Lewallen and three-year-old Eula Bee are the only survivors of a Comanche Indian raid on their Texas home. The children are taken captive, and the girl grows to trust an Indian brave.

Blos, Joan W. *A Gathering of Days: A New England Girl's Journal, 1830–32.* Scribner's, 1979 (ch. 3).

Brenner, Barbara. *Wagon Wheels.* Illustrated by Don Bolognese. Harper & Row, 1978 (ch. 5).

Brink, Carol Ryrie. *Caddie Woodlawn.* Illustrated by Trina Schart Hyman. Macmillan, 1935, 1963, 1973. (I: 8–12 R: 6). Twelve-year-old Caddie lives with her family on the Wisconsin frontier in 1864.

Bulla, Clyde Robert. *Riding the Pony Express.* Illustrated by Grace Paull. Crowell, 1948 (I: 6–10 R: 3). In 1800, Dick travels from New York to St. Joseph, Missouri, to be with his father. He learns about the Pony Express and even carries the mail when his father is injured.

Clapp, Patricia. *Constance: A Story of Early Plymouth.* Lothrop, Lee & Shepard, 1968 (I: 12 + R: 7). The story begins in November 1620; Constance stands on the deck of the *Mayflower,* seeing America for the first time. This is the story of the first few years of the Plymouth Colony.

———. *I'm Deborah Sampson: A Soldier in the War of the Revolution.* Lothrop, Lee & Shepard, 1977 (ch. 3).

———. *Witches' Children: A Story of Salem.* Lothrop, Lee & Shepard, 1982 (I:10 + R:7). A bound girl tells about the hysteria that takes over Salem in 1692.

Collier, James, and Collier, Christopher. *Jump Ship to Freedom.* Delacorte, 1981 (I:10 + R:7). A slave obtains his and his mother's freedom.

Crofford, Emily. *A Matter of Pride.* Illustrated by Jim La Marche. Carolrhoda, 1981 (I:9–12 R: 6). A ten-year-old girl tells her viewpoint of the depression as experienced on an Arkansas cotton plantation.

I = Interest by age range;
R = Readability by grade level.

Dalgliesh, Alice. *The Courage of Sarah Noble.* Illustrated by Leonard Weisgard. Scribner's, 1954 (I: 6–9 R: 3). In 1707 Sarah keeps up her courage as she and her father go through the wilderness and meet Indians. She then stays with the Indians when her father returns for her mother.

DeAngeli, Marguerite. *The Door in the Wall.* Doubleday, 1949 (I: 8–12 R: 6). Robin lives in England during the time of Edward III. He overcomes a mysterious ailment that cripples his legs.

———. *Skippack School.* Doubleday, 1939 (I: 6–9 R: 5). The story of a schoolboy in Pennsylvania in 1750.

———. *Thee, Hannah!* Doubleday, 1940. (I: 6–8 R: 4). Hannah is a young Quaker girl living in Philadelphia before the Civil War. The book illustrates the simple life of a family of Friends.

Ellison, Lucile Watkins. *A Window to Look Through.* Illustrated by Judith Gwyn Brown. Scribner's, 1982 (I: 7–9 R: 4). Author depicts two years of a family's life in Mississippi during the early 1900s.

Field, Rachel. *Calico Bush.* Illustrated by Allen Lewis. Macmillan, 1931, 1966 (I: 9 + R: 6). A French girl accompanies a family as they become pioneers on the Maine coast. Her friendliness toward Indians saves the family.

Fife, Dale. *Destination Unknown.* Dutton, 1981 (I :10 + R: 6). A twelve-year-old boy stows away on a Norwegian fishing boat in 1940 and sails to safety in America

Forbes, Esther. *Johnny Tremain.* Illustrated by Lynd Ward. Houghton Mifflin, 1943 (I: 10–14 R: 6). A silversmith's apprentice lives through prerevolutionary days and early wartime in Boston.

Fox, Paula. *The Slave Dancer.* Illustrated by Eros Keith. Bradbury, 1973 (I: 12 + R: 7). In 1840, a kidnapped fife player joins the crew of a slave ship. As they pick up human cargo and place the slaves in the ship's hold, Jessie experiences the misery of the slave trade.

Gray, Elizabeth Janet. *Adam of the Road.* Illustrated by Robert Lawson. Viking, 1942, 1970 (I: 8–12 R: 6). A young minstrel has many adventures as he learns his art, tries to recover his dog from thieves, and concludes that the minstrel's life is the finest of all in the England of 1294.

Greene, Constance C. *Dotty's Suitcase.* Viking Press, 1980 (I: 8–12 R: 4). During the depression, a twelve-year-old girl longs to acquire a suitcase and travel to exotic places. She discovers what it means to be a friend.

Haley, Gail E. *Jack Jouett's Ride*. Viking, 1973, 1976 (I: 6–10   R: 4). A picture storybook tells the tale of Jack Jouett as he rides to warn Thomas Jefferson, Patrick Henry, and Benjamin Harrison that the British are coming to arrest them.

Hancock, Sibyl. *Old Blue*. Illustrated by Erick Ingraham. Putnam, 1980 (I:7–9   R: 3). Based on historical information on a lead steer and a trail drive in 1878.

Haugaard, Erik Christian. *Cromwell's Boy*. Houghton Mifflin, 1978 (I: 11 +   R: 5). Oliver is a messenger for Cromwell and Parliament. He is also sent as a spy into the king's stronghold.

_____. *Hakon of Rogen's Saga*. Illustrated by Leo and Diane Dillon. Houghton Mifflin, 1963 (I: 9–12 R: 6). When the Viking island is attacked and his father is killed, Hakon flees from his wicked uncle before his loyal followers help him regain his birthright.

_____. *A Messenger for Parliament*. Houghton Mifflin, 1976 (I: 11 +   R: 7). The year is 1641; England is approaching civil war. Oliver, an eleven-year-old, follows the Parliamentary army and is responsible for sending an important message to Cromwell.

_____. *A Slave's Tale*. Illustrated by Leo and Diane Dillon. Houghton Mifflin, 1965 (I: 8–12 R: 4). In this sequel to *Hakon of Rogen's Saga*, a slave tells her side of the story, including her adventures as she sails to distant lands.

_____. *The Untold Tale*. Illustrated by Leo and Diane Dillon. Houghton Mifflin, 1971 (I: 10 + R: 6). This is the story of the war between Denmark and Sweden, written from the viewpoint of a boy who experienced it.

Hautzig, Esther. *The Endless Steppe: A Girl in Exile*. Crowell, 1968 (I: 12 +   R: 7). A true story of a Jewish girl and her parents who are exiled to Siberia during World War II.

Hickman, Janet. *The Valley of the Shadow*. Macmillan, 1974 (I: 10 +   R: 6). Moravian missionaries convert a group of Indians; they try unsuccessfully to live in peace during the days of the Revolutionary War. The story is told through the eyes of Tobias, a confused young Indian in search of answers.

_____. *Zoar Blue*. Macmillan, 1978 (I: 9–14   R: 4). The Civil War did not allow Separatists to remain isolated. The young men of Zoar, Ohio, abandon their church's teaching and enlist in the Union army.

Hooks, William H. *Circle of Fire*. Atheneum, 1982. (I:10 +   R:6). A boy and his friends try to prevent a Ku Klux Klan attack.

Hunt, Irene. *Across Five Aprils*. Follett, 1964 (I: 10 +   R: 7). Jethro Creighton must become the man of the family when his brothers go to war and his father has a heart attack. Jethro has brothers fighting on both sides of the conflict.

Keith, Harold. *The Obstinate Land*. Crowell, 1977 (I: 12 +   R: 7). In 1893, a thirteen-year-old Fritz Romberg and his family move to the Oklahoma prairie to homestead a farm. Fritz becomes head of the family and tries to overcome many problems.

_____. *Rifles for Watie*. Crowell, 1957 (I: 12 +   R: 7). In 1861, Jeff Bussey joins the Union army at Fort Leavenworth, Kansas. Watie is the Cherokee Indian who leads Indian raids behind Union lines.

Kerr, Judith. *When Hitler Stole Pink Rabbit*. Coward-McCann, 1972 (I: 8–12   R: 3). Anna and her family escape from Hitler's Germany and go to Switzerland and France before they move to England. This is a lighter, happier story than most escape tales.

Lampman, Evelyn Sibley *White Captives*. Atheneum, 1975 (I: 11 +   R: 7). In 1850, a family is attacked by Apaches who are retaliating against an attack by whites in which Indians are killed and taken captive. Two girls, the only family survivors, are taken to live with the Indians. The Indian viewpoint is presented.

Lasky, Kathryn. *The Night Journey*. Illustrated by Trina Schart Hyman. Warne, 1981 (I:10 + R: 6). A nine-year-old girl learns about her great-grandmother's escape from Czarist Russia in 1900.

Lenski, Lois. *Indian Captive: The Story of Mary Jemison*. Lippincott, 1941 (I: 10 +   R: 7). Mary Jemison, called the White Captive of the Genesee, is captured by Senecas. The book tells of her experiences and concludes with her decision to stay with the Senecas rather than go back to a white settlement.

Levitin, Sonia. *Journey to America*. Illustrated by Charles Robinson. Atheneum, 1970 (I: 12 + R: 6). The story tells of a Jewish family's courage as they escape from Germany to America.

Lobel, Arnold. *On the Day Peter Stuyvesant sailed into Town*. Harper & Row, 1971 (I: 4–8   R: 3). A picture storybook describing the New Dutch director-general's appointment to New Netherland.

McGraw, Eloise Jarvis. *Mara, Daughter of the Nile*. Coward-McCann, 1953 (I: 10 +   R: 6). An Egyptian slave learns that loyalty is important in a story of royal intrigue.

McSwigan, Marie. *Snow Treasure*. Illustrated by Mary Reardon. Dutton, 1942 (I: 8–12   R: 4). In this retelling of a real incident, Norwegian children smuggled $9 million of gold bullion past Nazi sentries to a Norwegian freighter bound for America.

Moeri, Louise. *Save Queen of Sheba*. Dutton, 1981 (I: 10 +   R: 5). A twelve-year-old boy and his young sister cross the prairie alone after their wagon train is attacked.

Monjo, F.N. *The Drinking Gourd*. Illustrated by Fred Brenner. Harper & Row, 1970 (I: 7–9   R: 2). This "I can read" history book designed for younger readers tells about a family on the Underground Railroad that helps slaves seeking freedom in Canada.

Morrow, Honore, *On To Oregon!* Illustrated by Edward Shenton. Morrow, 1926, 1948, 1954 (I: 10 +   R: 6). In 1844, the Sager family left their home in Missouri and traveled west toward Oregon. On the way, both parents die and the fate of the seven children is left in the hands of a thirteen-year-old boy who takes over as head of the family.

O'Dell, Scott. *The Captive*. Houghton Mifflin, 1979 (I: 10 +   R: 6). A young Spanish seminarian witnesses the exploitation of the Mayas during the 1500s.

_____. *Carlota*. Houghton Mifflin, 1977 (I: 9 +   R: 4). A girl faces her own feelings when she fights beside her father in California during the Mexican War.

_____. *The Feathered Serpent*. Houghton Mifflin, 1981 (I: 10 +   R: 6). In a sequel to *The Captive*, the seminarian takes on the role of the Mayan god Kukulcán and witnesses the arrival of Cortés.

_____. *Sing Down the Moon*. Houghton Mifflin, 1970 (ch. 11).

Pelgrom, Els. *The Winter When Time Was Frozen*. Rudnik, Maryka, and Rudnik, 1980. (I:8–12   R:5). A World War II story set in Holland.

Pellowski, Anne. *Winding Valley Farm: Annie's Story*. Illustrated by Wendy Watson. Philomel, 1982 (I: 9–12   R: 6). The setting develops Polish customs and an ethnic community in rural Wisconsin during the early 1900s.

Petry, Ann. *Tituba of Salem Village*. Crowell, 1964 (I: 11 +   R: 6). A talented, sensitive slave is forced to leave her homeland in Barbados and is brought to Salem in 1692. She is part of the famous Salem Witch Trials.

Phelan, Mary Kay. *The Story of the Louisiana Purchase*. Illustrated by Frank Aloise. Crowell, 1979 (I: 12 +   R: 7). In 1803 the territory of a young nation was doubled.

Reiss, Johanna. *The Upstairs Room*. Crowell, 1972 (I: 11 +   R: 4). This is a true story of a Jewish girl's experience as she is hidden by a Dutch farm family during World War II.

Rockwood, Joyce. *To Spoil the Sun*. Holt, Rinehart & Winston, 1976 (ch. 11).

Rylant, Cynthia. *When I Was Young in the Mountains*. Dutton, 1982 (I: 4–9   R: 3). A young girl remembers her life in the Appalachian mountains.

Sandin, Joan. *The Long Way to a New Land.* Harper & Row, 1981 (I: 7–9 R: 3). A family leaves Sweden in 1868 and emigrates to America.

Schlee, Ann. *Ask Me No Questions.* Holt, Rinehart & Winston, 1982 (I: 10 + R: 6). In a London 1848 setting, Laura faces moral issues related to feeding hungry children.

Siegal, Aranka. *Upon the Head of the Goat: A Childhood in Hungary 1939–1944.* Farrar, Straus & Giroux, 1981 (I: 10 + R: 7). Nine-year-old Piri tells about her experiences during the Holocaust.

Skurzynski, Gloria. *Manwolf.* Houghton Mifflin, 1981 (I:10 R 7). A rare disease causes people in medieval Poland to believe a boy is a werewolf.

Speare, Elizabeth George. *The Bronze Bow.* Houghton Mifflin, 1961 (I: 10 + R: ?). A boy's hatred of the Romans is affected after he meets Jesus.

_____. *Calico Captive.* Illustrated by W. T. Mars. Houghton Mifflin, 1957 (I: 10 + R: 6). After an Indian raid, Miriam Willard and her sister's family are forced to march north to an Indian village and then to Montreal.

_____. *The Witch of Blackbird Pond.* Houghton Mifflin, 1958 (ch. 3).

Stevens, Carla. *Anna, Grandpa, and the Big Storm.* Illustrated by Margot Tomes. Houghton Mifflin, 1982 (I: 6–9 R: 3). Seven-year-old Anna experiences a blizzard in New York City during 1888.

Sutcliff, Rosemary. *Blood Feud.* Dutton, 1976 An English boy is carried away in a raid and sold into slavery. He and his Viking master become friends and avenge the death of the Viking's father.

_____. *The Eagle of the Ninth.* Illustrated by C. Walter Hodges. Walck, 1954 (I: 11 + R: 8). The Ninth Legion marches into northern Britain to deal with the tribes; they disappear. Years later, the son of the missing commander solves the mystery and reclaims the missing symbol of the legion, their golden eagle.

_____. *Frontier Wolf.* Dutton, 1981 (I: 10 + R: 8). A Roman centurion leads a band of British warriors during the English Roman period.

_____. *The Lantern Bearers.* Illustrated by Charles Keeping. Walck, 1959 (I: 11 + R: 7). Britain is at the end of Roman rule. Saxon invaders try to break up the struggling British leaders.

_____. *The Silver Branch.* Illustrated by Charles Keeping. Walck, 1958 (I: 10 + R: 8). Two kinsmen, Flavius, an officer of the legion, and Justin, a surgeon in the Roman army, uncover a plot to overthrow the Emperor.

_____. *Song for a Dark Queen.* Crowell, 1978 (I: 10 + R:6). The year is A.D. 62, and Boudicca has inherited the leadership of her people as they fight against the invading Roman armies in Britain.

_____. *Sun Horse, Moon Horse.* Illustrated by Shirley Felts. Dutton, 1978 (I: 10 + R: 6). The time is preRoman Britain in 55 B.C. The people are the Iceni, who are great horsemen. A boy becomes chief after his tribe is invaded; he draws a horse on the chalk downs, allowing his people to go free.

Taylor, Mildred D. *Let The Circle Be Unbroken.* Dial, 1981 (I: 10 R: 6). The author continues the story of the family in *Roll of Thunder, Hear My Cry.*

_____. *Roll of Thunder, Hear My Cry.* Illustrated by Jerry Pickney. Dial, 1976 (ch. 11).

Tene, Benjamin. *In the Shade of the Chestnut Tree.* Translated from Hebrew by Reuben Ben-Joseph. Illustrated by Richard Sigberman. Jewish Publication Society of America, 1981 (I: 10 + R: 6). Author explores growing up in Warsaw during the years prior to World War II.

Trease, Geoffrey. *Saraband for Shadows.* Macmillan, 1982 (I: 10 + R: 7). Set in the time of Charles I, the hero tries to uncover a plot to murder his friend, Lord Ravenswood.

Treece, Henry. *Viking's Dawn.* Illustrated by Christine Price. Criterion, 1956 (I: 10–14 R: 7). Harold joins the crew of the Viking ship *Nameless* as her warrior captain, Thorkell Fairhair, sets sail to plunder the coasts of Scotland and Ireland.

_____. *Westward to Vinland* Illustrated by William Stobbs. Phillips, 1967 (I: 8–12 R: 4). Incidents from "Erik the Red" and "The Greenland Saga" are told. The book begins with a journey from Norway in A.D. 960, includes Greenland in A.D. 981, and Vinland in A.D. 1001.

Uchida, Yoshiko. *Journey Home.* Illustrated by Charles Robinson. Atheneum, 1978 (I: 10 + R: 5). In a sequel to *Journey to Topaz,* twelve-year-old Yuki and her parents return to California and try to adjust.

_____. *Journey to Topaz.* Illustrated by Donald Carrick. Scribner's, 1971 (I: 10 + R: 5). A Japanese American family is evacuated from California and held in an internment camp in Utah.

Wilder, Laura Ingalls. *By the Shores of Silver Lake.* Illustrated by Garth Williams. Harper & Row, 1939, 1953 (I: 8–12 R: 6). The Ingalls move again to the Dakota Territory.

_____. *The First Four Years.* Illustrated by Garth Williams. Harper & Row, 1971 (I: 8–12 R: 6). Laura and Almanzo spend their first four years of marriage on a South Dakota homestead.

_____. *Little House in the Big Woods.* Illustrated by Garth Williams. Harper & Row, 1932, 1953 (I: 8–12 R: 6). A warm family story told through the viewpoint of a girl who lived on the Wisconsin frontier. First story in series.

_____. *Little House on the Prairie.* Illustrated by Garth Williams, Harper & Row, 1935, 1953 (I: 8–12 R: 8). The Ingalls move to Kansas.

_____. *Little Town on the Prairie.* Illustrated by Garth Williams, Harper & Row, 1941, 1953. (I: 8–12 R: 8). Laura has her first job.

_____. *The Long Winter.* Illustrated by Garth Williams, Harper & Row, 1940, 1953 (I: 8–12 R: 6). A blizzard causes the Ingalls family great discomfort.

_____. *On the Banks of Plum Creek.* Illustrated by Garth Williams. Harper & Row, 1937, 1953 (I: 8–12 R: 6). The Ingalls move to Minnesota.

_____. *These Happy Golden Years.* Illustrated by Garth Williams. Harper & Row, 1943, 1953 (I: 8–12 R: 6). Laura becomes a teacher and meets her future husband.

Yates, Elizabeth. *We, The People.* Illustrated by Nora Unwin. Regional Center for Educational Training, 1974 (I: 8–12 R: 4). A young father leaves his family to fight in the Revolutionary War. The story is about the family who stayed behind.

ELEVEN
Multiethnic Literature

從一個孩子的眼中

Our Rich Mosaic

Involving Children in Multiethnic
 Literature

Our Rich Mosaic

A HEIGHTENED sensitivity to the needs of all people in American society has led to the realization that the literature program should include literature by, and about, members of all cultural groups. Literature is considered an appropriate vehicle to build respect across cultures, sharpen sensitivity toward individuals, and improve self-esteem. Laura Fisher (11), as well as many other educators and critics of children's literature, asks whether the multiethnic literature available for children will serve the dual purposes of heightening a minority child's self-esteem and creating a respect for the individuals, the contributions, and the values of the culture.

Many of the successful multiethnic literature programs that have met these goals have accomplished them either through preservice or inservice education that stressed evaluating, selecting, and sharing multiethnic literature (20). The tasks related to developing such programs are enormous. Universities are beginning to require courses in multiethnic education that often include selecting and using multiethnic literature. Until all educators are trained, school districts must provide inservice instruction so that teachers and librarians can select and use materials that will create an atmosphere in which all children can respect one another. One of the most formidable tasks is becoming familiar with the available literature and other materials. Library selection committees, teachers, and administrators must all become involved in this process.

It is for these reasons that this text contains a separate chapter on multiethnic literature. The purpose is not to isolate the literature and contributions of an ethnic minority but to place the literature in a more usable context for librarians, educators, and parents who wish to select and share these materials with children or develop multiethnic literature programs.

DEFINITION OF MULTIETHNIC LITERATURE

Multiethnic literature, according to Ruth Kearney Carlson (6), is the literature about a minority ethnic group with values and characteristics different from the typical white Anglo-Saxon middle-class values and characteristics of persons living in the United States. Multiethnic literature usually consists of four major categories: literature about Black Americans; Native Americans*; Hispanics, including Mexican Americans, Puerto

*The term *Native Americans* will be used wherever possible to denote the people historically referred to as *American Indians*. The term *Indian* will be used to name tribes and sometimes interchangeably with Native Americans.

Ricans, and others of Spanish descent; and Asian Americans, including Chinese Americans, Japanese Americans, Korean Americans, and Vietnamese Americans.

VALUES OF MULTIETHNIC LITERATURE

Well-written multiethnic literature, like other quality literature, provides enjoyment for the reader or the listener. In addition to the enjoyment of reading and sharing a good book, there are other values for children whether or not they are members of an ethnic minority. The following values of multiethnic literature have been identified as important by Ruth Kearney Carlson (6) and Esther C. Jenkins (16):

1 Through multiethnic literature, minority children realize that they have roots in the past through a cultural heritage of which they can be proud; their own culture has made important contributions to the United States and to the world.
2 By developing pride in their heritage, children improve their self-concept and develop a sense of identity.
3 Learning about other cultures allows all children to understand that people who belong to ethnic groups other than their own are real people with feelings, emotions, and needs similar to their own.
4 Reading about other cultures, including their poetry, philosophies, and products of their imagination and creativity, helps children expand their own understanding and realization that all cultural groups have made contributions in these areas.
5 Children discover that while all people may not share their personal beliefs and other cultures may respect different value systems, individuals can and must learn to live in harmony.
6 Through multiethnic literature, children of the majority culture can learn to respect the contributions and values of the minority; they learn historical contributions made by people in both the United States and the world.
7 By enjoying the traditional folk literature of ethnic minorities, children can identify with the people who created and passed down the stories through centuries of oral tradition.
8 Through the multiethnic stories, children broaden their understanding of geography and natural history as they read about cultural groups living in various areas.
9 The wide range of multiethnic themes helps children develop an understanding of sociological change.
10 Reading about minority members who have achieved or successfully solved their own problems helps raise the aspiration level of children who belong to a minority.
11 Reading books about ethnic minorities helps children develop a sense of social sensitivity; all people are human beings who should be considered as individuals, not stereotypes.

THE IMAGES OF ETHNIC GROUPS IN LITERATURE OF THE PAST

Through their selections of books and instructional materials, educators have been accused of telegraphing messages about minorities to children. Bettye I. Latimer (18) makes a very strong case for this view when she says: "If your bulletin boards, your models, and your authority lines are White, and I am Black, Latino or Native American, then you have telegraphed me messages which I will reject" (p. 156). She maintains that white children are filled with a distorted image of society and not prepared to value its multiracial character when they are surrounded with literature that either presents minorities stereotypically or as invisible by omitting them entirely. Latimer stresses that because of the smaller number of books written about minorities, librarians, teachers, and other adults are likely to accept all books with a picture of a minority child without carefully evaluating the stories and the stereotypes they might be fostering. She believes that adults who work with children and literature should reeducate themselves to the social values that books pass on to children. To do this, they must learn to evaluate and assess books written about children from all ethnic backgrounds.

This chapter first considers the images of different ethnic groups that have been portrayed in children's literature of the past and then discusses the criteria for evaluating literature for today's children.

Blacks in Literature of the Past

Only recently have we come to understand that certain books, because of their illustrations, themes, characterizations, and language, can perpetuate a stereotype or result in psychological damage or discomfort to children. According to Barbara Bader (2), this idea was not advanced publicly until the 1940s when there were growing objections to the use of certain illustrations and stereotypes in literature. Considerable changes have taken place since that time.

''Why are they always *white* children?''

The question came from a five-year-old Negro girl who was looking at a picturebook at the Manhattanville Nursery School in New York. With a child's uncanny wisdom, she singled out one of the most critical issues in American education today: the almost complete omission of Negroes from books for children. Integration may be the law of the land, but most of the books children see are all white.

But the impact of all-white books upon 39,600,000 white children is probably even worse. Although his light skin makes him one of the world's minorities, the white child learns from his books that he is the kingfish. There seems little chance of developing the humility so urgently needed for world cooperation, instead of world conflict, as long as our children are brought up on gentle doses of racism through their books.

THE ABOVE QUOTES FROM AN ARTICLE IN THE September 11, 1965 issue of *Saturday Review* (p. 63) are from one of the early and frequently quoted articles that criticized the omission of black characters in books for children. Nancy Larrick's "The All-White World of Children's Books" reported the results of a study that analyzed children's trade books published over a three-year period. Most books published during this time showed blacks outside of the continental United States or before World War II—only four-fifths of one percent of the books told stories about contemporary black Americans. In addition, most books that included black characters depicted them as slaves, sharecroppers, or other types of menial workers. Larrick's article in a prestigious publication may have had considerable impact on future publications.

Several researchers have investigated the image of Black Americans both in popular and recommended children's literature. They researched such concerns as stereotypes, the attitudes expressed toward black characters, and the importance of these characters in the literature. Dorothy May Broderick (3), for example, analyzed literature published between 1827 and 1967. She reported that the personal characteristics of blacks portrayed in these books suggested that they (1) were not physically attractive, (2) were musical, (3) combined religious fervor with superstitious beliefs, (4) were required to select life goals that would benefit black people, and (5) were dependent upon white people for whatever good things they could hope to acquire. After evaluating the books published during this period, Broderick concluded that black readers would find little in them to enhance pride in their heritage; further, if these books were their only contacts with blacks, whites would develop a sense of superiority.

In investigating whether or not changes in attitudes toward blacks had occurred in more recent times, Julie Ann Carlson

(5) compared the literature of the 1930s with that of the 1960s. She discovered that considerable changes in attitudes toward black characters had occurred between the two time periods. Although 15 percent of the books analyzed from the earlier period mentioned black characters, these characters tended to be stereotyped. In contrast, only 10 percent of the books analyzed in the later period mentioned black characters, but they tended to be presented either as individuals with a racial problem or some universal problem. She concluded that there were indeed changes in attitudes between the two periods. Likewise, Betty M. Morgan (19) found that the number of books with blacks as the main characters had increased markedly in recent years.

The number of books with black main characters is increasing, but Latimer (18) is concerned with the disproportionate numbers that deal in any way with black people. She cites a three-year survey of trade books published in the mid-1960s showing that about one percent of all books published during that time by sixty-three publishers dealt with black people. She extended her research into books published in the 1970s. She estimated that of the 2,000 to 3,000 children's books published annually, about one percent involve blacks. She concludes this finding with an important concern for librarians, teachers, and parents:

This low statistical probability is frightening. It means that the average child, White or Black, will have only one out of 100 chances to read a book that is integrated. It means that only one out of every 100 books in a classroom or library will represent Blacks. (p. 154)

If the probability that many of these books may represent stereotypes is added to this observation, this again lowers the chances of children reading books that would raise their expectations or develop positive attitudes. Consequently, evaluating and selecting books about the black experience becomes very important.

Native Americans in Literature of the Past

The Native American has not fared any better than the Black American in the literature of the past. Mary Gloyne Byler (4) contends:

There are too many books featuring painted, whooping, befeathered Indians closing in on too many forts, maliciously attacking "peaceful" settlers or simply leering menacingly from the background; too many books in which white benevolence is the only thing that saves the day for the incompetent childlike Indian; too many stories setting forth what is "best" for American Indians. (p. 28)

Authorities analyzing the image of the Native American in literature of the past identified many negative stereotypes characteristic of a large percentage of the literature. Laura Herbst (15) identifies three stereotypes common in literature featuring these peoples: Native Americans are often characterized as savage, depraved, and cruel; they may be characterized as noble, proud, silent, and close to nature; or they are depicted as inferior, childlike, and helpless. Such stereotypes are often reinforced by terms and comparisons suggesting negative and derogatory images. A white family, for example, may be said to consist of a husband, a wife, and a child; members of Native American or Indian families, in contrast, may be called bucks, squaws, and papooses. Even their language is often described as snarling, grunting, or yelping. Characters are frequently dehumanized and compared with animals. *The Matchlock Gun,* by Walter Edmonds, compares the nameless Indians to trotting dogs, sniffing the scent of food. The frequent depersonalization of the Native American by not giving the characters names has been criticized as implying that the people are not individuals, or even full-fledged human beings.

In addition to stereotypes about Native American people, Laura Herbst (15) identifies three ways in which their culture has been portrayed in novels of the past. First, it may be considered inferior to the white culture. In this situation, the author may treat the abandonment of the Indian way of life as an improvement for them. Characters often make this gain by going to white schools or taking on the values of the white culture, thus abandoning their own culture and even their own people. A frequent theme in such literature is that white people must be responsible for remaking the Indian into an image acceptable to western European immigrants. Second, the culture may be depicted as valueless, consequently stripping both the culture and the individuals of respect. The rich diversity of the culture may be ignored and one glorifying violence presented. A common practice in literature from the past is the grouping of Indians into a story without any understanding that Native Americans in the Northwest had ceremonies, artistic skills, cultural values, and life-styles different from those living in other localities. Finally, the culture may be implied to be quaint or superficial, without depth or warmth. It is common for white characters to ridicule or scorn customs that have great spiritual significance to the Indians. Sacred ceremonies, medicine men, ancient artifacts, and traditional legends may be scorned as belonging to "heathen savages." Any of these portrayals of a culture is offensive and would not elevate Indian children's self-esteem or develop favorable attitudes in non-Indian children. There are more current books, however, especially those written by Native American authors or authorities, that are sensitive to the heritage and individuality of the Indians.

Hispanics in Literature of the Past

Betty M. Morgan (19) concluded from her study that the number of books with minority people as main characters has increased since World War II, but she also found that this was true only for books either about Black Americans or Native Americans. Consequently, there are far fewer books about Hispanic or Asian American people.

Both the lack of children's literature about people of Mexican American or Puerto Rican descent and the negative stereotypes found in some of the literature have been criticized. At one children's literature conference, Mauricio Charpenel (7), consultant to the Mexican Ministry of Education, reported that there are very few stories written for or about Mexican or Mexican American children. He was especially concerned about poetry; he said that while Latin American writers create and publish beautiful poetry, these poems are not shared with Mexican American children in the United States. Both teachers and librarians at the conference expressed concern about the need for literature that would appeal to Mexican American children and create positive images of their heritage.

The Council on Interracial Books for Children (8) has been very critical of Mexican American literature. After analyzing 200 books, the council concluded that there was little in the stories to enable children to recognize a way of life, a history, or a set of life circumstances. The report was critical of the tediously recurring theme of poverty as if it were a "natural facet of the Chicano condition" (p. 57). Another highly criticized theme is the tendency for problems to be solved not by the efforts of Mexican Americans but by the intervention of an Anglo. The council felt also that these problems had been treated superficially.

There are even fewer books written about Puerto Rican Americans, and the majority of these have been criticized for their lack of literary merit and overuse of a predominantly inner-city, New York ghetto setting.

Asian Americans in Literature of the Past

With few books published in this category, researchers who have tried to evaluate Asian American books have had small numbers from which to choose. In 1976, the Asian American Children's Book Project identified sixty-six books with Asian American central characters; most of these books were about Chinese Americans. The members of the project concluded that, with only a few exceptions, the books were grossly misleading; they presented stereotypes of Asian Americans suggesting they look alike, they all choose to live in "quaint" communities in the midst of large cities, and they cling to "outworn, alien" customs. The books were also criticized because they tended to measure success by the extent to which Asian Americans have assimilated white middle-class values; or they implied that hard work, learning to speak English, and keeping a low profile will overcome adversity and lead to success.

BLACK LITERATURE

If literature is to contribute to developing positive attitudes and respect for individuals across cultures, children need many opportunities to read and listen to high-quality books that portray the desired image. Because few books are written with an ethnic minority perspective and many stories develop negative stereotypes, there is need to evaluate this literature carefully. While ethnic literature must meet the same criteria demanded of any fine book, there are some specific suggestions for evaluating books about each ethnic minority. This section considers criteria for evaluating black literature and then suggests some fine black literature—traditional, realistic fiction, or factual—that can be shared with children in order to develop positive attitudes and enjoyment of a literary heritage.

Evaluating Black Literature

The Children's Literature Review Board developed an excellent list of criteria for evaluating books written with a black perspective. This list, reported in Latimer's *Starting Out Right: Choosing Books about Black People for Young Children* (17, pp. 7–12), includes the following criteria:

1 Has a black perspective been taken into consideration? There should be no stigma attached to being black; the characters should not conform to old stereotypes. The dignity of the characters should be preserved.

2 How responsible is the author in dealing with issues and problems? Is it an honest presentation, with problems presented clearly but not oversimplified? Must a black character exercise all the understanding and forgiveness?

3 Do the black characters look natural? This is especially crucial in picture books; characters should not have exaggerated features.

4 Will the young reader realize he is looking at a black person, or do the characters look *gray*? (*Gray* refers to a merely darkened version of Caucasian-featured characters.)

5 Is the black character a unique individual, or only representative of a group?

6 Does clothing or behavior perpetuate stereotypes of blacks as primitive or submissive?

7 Is the character glamorized or glorified, especially in a biography? Some situations may be glorified, others ignored, resulting in an unreal and unbalanced presentation.

8 Is the setting authentic? Can the child recognize it as an urban, suburban, rural, or fantasized situation?

9 Does the author have a patronizing tone?

10 Is the black character used as a vehicle to get a point across, so that the character becomes a tool of literary exploitation and acts artificial rather than real?

11 How are black characters shown in relationship to white characters? Is either placed in a submissive or inferior role without justification? Is the white person always shown as the benefactor?

12 If dialect is used, does it have a purpose? Does it ring true and blend naturally with the story, or is it used as an example of "substandard" English?

13 If the story deals with historical or factual events, how accurate is it?

14 If the book is a biography, are both the personality and accomplishments of the main character shown?

Traditional Black Literature

Traditional folk literature, the tales originally handed down through centuries of oral storytelling, includes many of the stories most enjoyed by children. In experiencing the traditional tales, they discover the rich literary heritage of the Black American, gain a respect for the creativity of the people who originated the stories, develop an understanding of the values of these originators, and share an enjoyable experience that has entertained others in centuries past. Modern writers of contemporary realistic fiction often have their characters tell an African tale in order to develop a closer relationship to and understanding of the black child's African heritage. The black children in the stories often ask older family members or friends to tell stories so that they can feel closer to their roots. Sharing the beautiful traditional tales with children of all backgrounds can develop these beneficial values.

Ruth Kearney Carlson (6) identifies three types of oral traditional black tales that can be shared with children:

1 African folktales that are indigenous to various countries on the African continent.

2 Folk literature that was transported to one of the Caribbean islands and then altered in the new setting.

3 Folk literature that originated in the plantation areas of the United States.

This section discusses the traditional tales that originated in Africa and those that originated in the plantation areas of the United States. An example of a tale altered in the new setting concludes the discussion of African traditional tales.

African Traditional Tales. Black Americans often told the traditional African tales that came to America with their ancestors. Many contemporary stories about the black experience include traditional tales from the African heritage. Virginia Hamilton's *The Time-Ago Tales of Jahdu,* for example, begins with Mama Luka sitting in her little room in a "good place called Harlem." With her is young Lee Edward, who is sitting on the floor with his eyes "tight shut" so that he can imagine Jahdu, the mischievous but heroic subject of Mama Luka's tales. Jahdu is a mysterious being who lives high atop the Mountain of Paths in the only gum tupelo tree in the pine forest. He is also the subject of four tales in this delightful book.

The tales explain how Jahdu learned that he had power, how he got into difficulties with and overcame the giant Trouble, how he was filled with mischief, and how he became himself. This last story is filled with black pride and hope, as Jahdu discovers the secret of turning himself into other forms. He becomes a tall building but cannot move, a cat who is always hungry, and a taxicab on whose seats people sit too hard. Finally, he reaches Harlem where he sees a small black boy running and making noise. Because black is Jahdu's favorite color, he decides to become a strong black child.

This story speaks of the pride felt by the strong black child as he grows bigger and bigger. It concludes with Lee Edward's feelings after hearing the story: "Lee Edward imagined Jahdu's changing from a strong, black boy into a bigger, stronger boy" (p. 62). He thinks about the pride that was always in Jahdu's face and he realizes, "I can have the pride and the power, too" (p. 62). Additional Jahdu tales that stress that black is beautiful are found in Virginia Hamilton's *Time-Ago Lost: More Tales of Jahdu.*

Traditional values reflected in the folklore from several African cultures are found in Harold Courlander's *The Crest and the Hide: And Other African Stories of Heroes, Chiefs, Bards, Hunters, Sorcerers, and Common People.* This collection of twenty tales from such cultures as the Ashanti, the Yoruba, the Swahili, and the Zulu develop the human values of wisdom, friendship, love, and heroism as well as some behaviors that are not respected, including foolishness and betrayal.

There are several beautifully illustrated books containing single black African folktales written for children of all ages. Jan Carew's *The Third Gift* suggests the traditional values respected by the Jubas as they acquire the most important gifts that can be given. According to this lovely legend, "in long-time-past days," the black prophet Amakosa, leader of the Jubas, gathered his people who were threatened with extinction and led them to the base of a tall mountain. He told them that when he was gone, the young men should climb the Nameless Mountain. The one who could climb the highest and bring back a gift of wonders would be the new leader. One young man reached the top and returned with the gift of work; he ruled for a long time and his people prospered. When it was time for him to die, the young men again went to the mountain top to seek a gift, and the one destined to rule returned with the gift of beauty. Through his rule, the Juba country became very beautiful. When young men climbed the mountain for the third time, the gifts brought back were the most important ones of all: fantasy, imagination, and faith. These traditional values are highlighted in the tale: "So, with the gifts of Work and Beauty and Imagination, the Jubas became poets and bards and creators, and they live at the foot of Nameless Mountain to this day" (p. 32).

Children of the Sun, also by Carew, concerns the birth of the sun's twin boys, Makunaima, "a rebellious, haughty child with wild fires burned in the depths of his eyes," and Pia, the gentle one. In this story of values clarification, the two children are asked by the great spirit to choose between being good men and being great men. Makunaima chooses greatness, eventually disobeys his father, and is destroyed. Pia chooses to be good and hopes to bring peace and harmony to humans. According to the tale, his mother still waits for Pia to finish his task.

Peace and harmony are two values developed in this African tale. From *Children of the Sun* by Jan Carew. Illustrations Copyright © 1980 by Leo and Diane Dillon. Reprinted by permission of Little, Brown and Company.

Weaving curtains of mist and rainbows around her, she weeps for her lost sons. Her tears run down the cliff-face of the mountain, flowing into rills, brooks and rivers, and the sea carries them to the shores of the whole world. (p. 35 unnumbered)

This traditional tale suggests that the black heritage includes a longing for peace and harmony, although they may require long years to attain. The black heritage, as developed in Rosa Guy's *Mother Crocodile,* also values the knowledge of the elders. This folktale from Senegal expresses the traditional value that the advice of the elders is important and should be taken seriously.

The African folktales provide explanations for many natural phenomena. Verna Aardema's *Why Mosquitoes Buzz in People's Ears* explains why mosquitoes are constantly noisy. Written as a cumulative tale, it is excellent for sharing orally with children. It suggests a rich language heritage and a respect for storytelling. (See page 161 for a discussion of the language in this folktale and page 127 for a discussion of Leo and Diane Dillon's outstanding illustrations.)

Who's in Rabbit's House? is an unusual Masai tale written in the form of a play performed by villagers for their fellow townsfolk. It is retold by Verna Aardema and illustrated by Leo and Diane Dillon. The repetitive words add to the vivid descriptions, and the dialogue suggests the rich African language heritage. Humor and trickery abound as Rabbit discovers that her hut has been taken over by the mysterious Long One who eats trees and tramples elephants. Added humor results when the animals at the lake try to help, but each solution would destroy her hut. Jackal collects sticks to build a fire, Leopard claws the roof, Elephant decides to trample it, and Rhinoceros wants to hoist it into the lake with his horn. Frog finally finds a solution; she curls a large leaf into a horn, impersonates a cobra, and frightens the Long One out of the hut. The play ends humorously as a long green caterpillar crawls timidly out of the hut.

This is an excellent tale to stimulate creative dramatizations with children. They enjoy the repetition of words, which is characteristic of African tales; the jackal trots off *kpata, kpata,* the leopard jumps *pa, pa, pa,* and the frog laughs *dgung, dgung, dgung.* They also enjoy creating the animals' masks. Language, actions, masks, and a humorous, active plot combine to create an enjoyable story for sharing in a dramatic presentation.

Another folktale rich in the language of the African storyteller is Gail E. Haley's *A Story, a Story.* This tale about Ananse, the spider man, repeats key words to make them stronger. The story develops the personal value of wit in overcoming difficulties. Ananse seeks the stories from the powerful sky god and the god laughs: "How can a weak old man like you, so small, so small, so small, pay my price" (p. 6 unnumbered)? Ananse fools the god and is able to capture the leopard of-the-terrible-teeth, Mmboro the hornet who-stings-like-fire, and Mmoatia, the fairy whom-men-never-see. As a reward for bringing these gifts to this god, Ananse is given the stories that previously belonged only to the god. From this story, children can gain an understanding of the importance of storytelling on the African continent. This importance for storytelling is reinforced in Aardema's *Tales From the Story Hat: African Folktales*. Each of the nine tales from West Africa is represented by an object dangling from the storyteller's hat.

Spider stories are very popular in African folk literature. Joyce Cooper Arkhurst retells six of them in *The Adventures of Spider: West African Folktales*. The stories are good for sharing orally with children. They explain how the spider acquired his thin waist, why he lives in ceilings, how he came to have a bald head, why he lives in dark corners, and how the world received wisdom. Arkhurst says that Spider is a favorite character in West African stories.

These beautifully illustrated traditional African tales represent some of the strongest and most noble values attributed to humanity. Children discover that there is both pride and hope in being a strong black child. African people respect and honor the three greatest gifts that have been given to humanity: the need to work for prosperity, the need for beauty to foster an environment, and the need for imagination and faith that allows people to become creators. Children also discover that the black heritage includes a longing for peace and harmony and the willingness to strive long years to attain this goal. Finally, they find that the black heritage is filled with a rich language and a respect for storytelling.

Some of the tales incorporate characters and language from a new environment into the stories recalled from the African homeland. Priscilla Jaquith's *Bo Rabbit Smart for True: Folktales from the Gullah* contains four stories collected from the islands off the coast of Georgia and South Carolina. The storytellers, whose ancestors came from Angola and the Bahamas, speak with a lilt similar to calypso and include words from Africa and Elizabethan English and dialect from the British provinces. Language and subject matter reflect the changes in folktales as the people add elements of their current life-style while retaining important elements from the past.

Black American Tales.

The most famous collection of black folktales originating in the southern United States are the Uncle Remus stories originally collected by Joel Chandler Harris. These are the tales of that crafty Br'er Fox; he tries to trap Br'er Rabbit first by constructing a tar baby and then by throwing him into the briar patch. But that "monstrous clever beast," Br'er Rabbit, always uses his cunning and survives. This cunning is especially apparent as Br'er Rabbit tells Br'er Fox in Jane Shaw's *Uncle Remus Stories*, "Bred and born in a briar-patch, Br'er Fox—I was bred and born in a briar-patch! And with that he skipped out just as lively as a cricket in the embers" (p. 17). These stories suggest that the Black American can overcome great adversity because of humor, cunning, and intelligence.

Other memorable animals in this book include Old Man Terrapin, Br'er Wolf, and Br'er Bear. The large illustrations and short stories are appealing to young children; however, because the stories are written in dialect, they may prefer to listen to them rather than read them. A standard English version of the tales is Joel Chandler Harris's *The Adventures of Brer Rabbit*.

Virginia Haviland's *North American Legends,* in a section titled "Black American Tales," contains five stories identified by place of origin. Included in the book are "The Tar Baby" (West Virginia), "How Ole Woodpecker Got Ole Rabbit's Conjure Bag" (Missouri), "The Conjure Wives" (southern), "Wiley and the Hairy Man" (Alabama), and "Jean Sotte" (Louisiana). William J. Faulkner's *The Days When the Animals Talked* (10) presents background information on Black American folktales, how they were created, and their significance in American history.

John Henry, the great black hero of American folklore, is characterized as a "steel-driving" man. Ezra Jack Keats has written and illustrated an attractive edition, *John Henry: An American Legend*. John Henry, born with a hammer in his hand, is a real folk hero who accomplishes such seemingly impossible tasks as turning a huge broken paddle wheel and saving a ship from sinking, laying more railroad track than many men combined, hammering out a dangerous dynamite fuse and saving the men from a cave-in, and challenging and beating a steam drill in a race until he finally dies "with his hammer in his hand." The large, colorful illustrations in this book suggest the power and heroism of this American legend.

A longer version is Harold W. Felton's *John Henry and His Hammer.* According to legend, on the night John Henry was born, the moon stood still and then went backward while it grew bigger and redder; the stars stood still, and then went backward as they grew bigger and whiter; the great strong river stopped, turned, and flowed uphill. This moon, as red as a hero's blood, signaled that something powerful had come into the world; that power was a strong black baby named John Henry. This book concludes with the words and music to the folk song, "John Henry." This song and legend could be shared during social studies to relate the history of the railroads to children.

Realistic Black Literature for Younger Children

The realistic fictional stories written for young children deal mainly with black children faced with problems common to all young children. There are themes of overcoming jealousy, adjusting to a new baby, the need for attention, sibling rivalry, relationships with an elderly person, and overcoming family problems. Children from all ethnic backgrounds can realize from these books that black children have the same needs, desires, and problems that other children have. In addition, they may learn that they too may solve their problems in similar ways.

John Steptoe's *Stevie* tells about Robert, a happy young boy who is the center of his mother's attention. His conflict begins when his mother cares for another child whose mother works. Steptoe's illustrations and text describe the increasing tension; toys are broken, and the younger child insists on having his own way. However, after Stevie moves away, Robert remembers the good times they had together and decides that Stevie was "a nice little guy," just like a little brother. This warm story demonstrates a common universal emotion.

The varied relationships between a father and his two sons are featured in Steptoe's *Daddy Is a Monster . . . Sometimes.*

The illustrations show two different reactions by the same father. While he is nice most of the time, he can turn into a monster with "teeth comin out his mouth" and hair on his face when his sons fight over the teddy bear, play with their food at a restaurant, are extra messy or noisy, and when they have an accident in the house. Daddy concludes that: "I'm probably a monster daddy when I got monster kids." This book has been praised for the strong father-son relationships it develops; literature about a black experience often shows a family without a father.

Steptoe's subjects in his books for young children could be any children who have problems at home, are jealous of another child, or have a father who is sometimes unhappy with their behavior. The language and the illustrations make it a black experience. According to Karen Johnson (12), "The thing about *Stevie* that makes it black is the language. There is a cadence to the way this language is written" (p. 102). The dialect follows the criteria for black literature because it rings true and blends naturally with the story.

A too-crowded apartment and the birth of a baby are the problems that must be solved in June Jordon's *New Life: New*

A father, as shown in this illustration, may express a wide range of emotions.
Specified illustration from *Daddy Is a Monster . . . Sometimes* by John Steptoe (J.B. Lippincott Company).
Copyright © 1980 by John Steptoe.

Room. The author emphasizes the emotions three children feel as they learn about the baby: they are frightened about the idea of a baby, they are angry because they will have to share their small space with another person, and they are insecure about what will happen to them. The author has the children solve their own problems by finding a new use of space in a bedroom; the solution is accomplished in a humorous and cooperative manner. This book also depicts a strong family unit in which both the father and mother make suggestions but allow the children to solve their own problems of bedroom space creatively.

Everett Anderson's Nine Month Long, by Lucille Clifton, deals with adjusting to a stepfather and preparing for a baby. The illustrations and text convey the unhappiness of a child whose mother cannot share as many experiences with him as before; he even wonders if she will love him as much when the baby is born. The illustrations suggest family warmth as his mother and father reassure him, and Everett decides that they have enough love to share with another family member.

The developing love between a young boy and a very old family member is the theme of Sharon Bell Mathis's *The Hundred Penny Box.* The author develops a universal need for love and understanding as Michael's great-great-Aunt Dew moves into his home. The relationship is made closer because Michael understands Aunt Dew's need to keep her beloved possessions, including an old, broken box containing one hundred pennies, one for each year of Aunt Dew's life. When Michael's mother threatens to burn the old box, Aunt Dew explains its importance: " 'It's my old cracked-up, wacky-dacky box with the top broken, them's my years in that box,' she said. 'That's me in that box' " (p. 19).

Michael understands that if she loses the box, she also loses herself. However, he must convince his mother of Aunt Dew's needs. This is a tender story about the warm relationships that can develop between generations.

The desire to own something special is the plot of Osmond Molarsky's *Song of the Empty Bottles.* Thaddeus's longing begins when he hears Mr. Andrews sing and play the guitar at Neighborhood House. The problem develops when Mr. Andrews offers to give Thaddeus lessons, but the boy does not have the money to buy a guitar. Thaddeus decides to solve his problem by collecting and selling empty bottles and old newspapers. He develops the best understanding of his own worth when he writes a song about empty bottles, and Mr. Andrews pays him for his song. This is a satisfying book for children who understand that there can be several ways to solve a problem.

In addition to these stories for young readers, several other books were discussed in chapters four and five. For example,

the picture storybooks by Ezra Jack Keats tell about varied experiences of young black children. The integrated family is the subject of the picture storybook *Black Is Brown Is Tan* while *Gabrielle and Selena,* by Peter Desbarats, tells the story of friendship between a white and a black girl.

Realistic Black Literature for Children in Middle Elementary Grades

Many stories for children in the middle elementary grades are written by authors—black and white—who are sensitive to the black experience. Some themes, such as the discovery of oneself, the need to give and receive love, the problems experienced when children realize that the parents they love are getting a divorce, and the fears associated with nonachievement in school are universal and suggest that all children may have similar needs, fears, or problems. Other themes, such as the searching for one's own roots in the African past, speak of a special need by children to know about their ancestry and the people who made up their past.

Virginia Hamilton's *Zeely* is a warm, sensitive story about an imaginative girl who makes a remarkable discovery about herself and others when she and her brother spend the summer on Uncle Ross's farm. Early in the story, Hamilton develops the imaginative quality of her heroine as Elizabeth is not satisfied with the status quo; she calls herself Geeder, renames her younger brother Toeboy, renames her uncle's town Crystal, and calls the road cracking its surface Leadback. The plot is enhanced as the imaginative Geeder sees her uncle's neighbor, Miss Zeely Tayber. The author describes her appearance in detail: she is thin and stately in a long smock that reaches her ankles, she is over six feet tall, her expression is calm and filled with pride, she is the color of rich Ceylon ebony, and she has the most beautiful face Geeder has ever seen.

The sight of the mysterious Miss Zeely intrigues Geeder. She watches as Miss Zeely walks proudly down the road to care for her father's prize hogs, and as she guides the hogs down the road to the market without losing her majestic, ladylike appearance. The greatest excitement occurs when Geeder discovers a photograph of a Watusi queen; the woman in the picture looks exactly like Miss Zeely. Geeder is sure her mysterious neighbor is a queen; she must have royal blood. Geeder is swept up in her fantasies and shares her beliefs with the village children.

It is Miss Zeely who allows Geeder to make her greatest discovery. As they talk, she realizes that it is fine to dream, but it is greater to be yourself. Her experience helps her see everything in a new way. She realizes that Miss Zeely is a queen, not like the ones in books with their servants, kingdoms, and wealth, but the kind who is a lady, who always does her work better than anybody else. She realizes that what counts is what a person is inside. When the author shares Geeder's final thoughts about her wonderful summer and her discovery that even stars resemble people, readers understand just how much wisdom she has gained:

Some stars were no more than bright arcs in the sky as they burned out. But others lived on and on. There was a blue star in the sky south of Hesperus, the evening star. She thought of naming it Miss Zeely Tayber. There it would be in Uncle Ross' sky forever. (p. 121)

Like Geeder, ten-year-old James in Paula Fox's *How Many Miles to Babylon?* dreams of African royalty. Unlike Geeder, he knows that *he* must be a long-lost prince whose ancestors had been chained and marched across the land to boats that took them to a new country. James even fantasizes that instead of being taken to the hospital, his mother has traveled to Africa to plan for his celebrated return. When he goes to the basement of a dilapidated house to dress and dance like the African princes in photographs, he encounters a harsh reality. Instead of adoring subjects, he is discovered by a gang who earns money by stealing valuable dogs and returning them to their owners for the advertised rewards. James is terrified when they force him to approach a luxury apartment house and solicit jobs walking dogs. James and the dogs are taken to a deserted amusement park where the gang waits for the newspapers and the rewards. James sees the Atlantic Ocean for the first time and begins to understand a different reality; he knows that there is no way that his gravely ill mother could have crossed such a fearsome body of water.

The author encourages readers to understand the strength of James's character and his ability to face reality by describing James's thoughts and actions when he plots his escape. James does not merely look out for his own safety; instead, he feels obligated to take the dogs with him and return them to their owners. As he leaves the hiding place, he does not allow the thought of a long walk to discourage him. Instead, he remembers his aunt's advice: Think about something or do it—a person cannot do both. James reaches home and finds that his mother has returned. She is not, as he once hoped, dressed in a long white robe. As he looks at her and thinks about who he really is, she seems to read his mind and answers his question. With loving arms, she holds out her hands saying, "Hello Jimmy." He knows he is not a prince, but he has also discovered much about himself. Fox has created a strong person in his own right, a person who can solve his own problems, not a stereotype who is dependent upon others.

Another book that explores a character's personal discovery and strength of character is *Sister,* by Eloise Greenfield. (Eloise Greenfield has won several awards for her contributions to children's literature, including the Irma Simonton Black Award and a citation from the Council on Interracial Books for Children.) The words of the school song sung in *Sister* are characteristic of the themes found in her books:

We strong black brothers and sisters
Working in unity,
We strong black brothers and sisters,
Building our community,
We all work together, learn together
Live in harmony
We strong black brothers and sisters
Building for you and for me. (p. 69)

A book of memories written by Sister, whose real name is Doretha, is the means by which she reviews her life and discovers who she is and how she came to be that person. This is a perceptive story about a frightened young girl. People say she looks like her older sister Alberta, but she does not want to grow up and act like sad, rebellious Alberta who always made their mother cry. As Doretha waits and wonders if her older sister will return, she rereads her Doretha Book—a book written about special times written in special colors. The author lets readers understand Doretha's background and feelings by sharing the experiences that molded the "colors of her life." Greenfield effectively uses this technique to develop Doretha's character by listing the experiences and accompanying feelings that she identifies as important: the special book in Daddy's school remembrances, her grandfather's way of fighting pain, her teacher's prejudice, her discovery of the Ndugu Na Ndada School (Swahili for "brothers and sisters"), and her discovery that her sister needs to laugh without being hurt. After she finishes reading her journal, she realizes that she has seen herself and the others who helped her gain her strength. The author suggests that while her personal book is a book of hard times, it is also a book of loving times—the times that "rainbowed" their way through those harder times. She decides that these are the times she will remember and also the times she will share with her older sister. Doretha no longer fears being like her sister; her memory book has helped her realize "I'm me."

Another problem that can cause emotional difficulties for children of any race or nationality is the fear associated with the inability to learn to read. In *Nellie Cameron,* Michele Murray successfully develops the unhappy emotional responses of nine-year-old Nellie by tracing the development of Nellie's feelings and contrasting her feelings during athletic experiences with those during reading classes. Nellie remembers her first-grade teacher who made her feel "too dumb to live" when she made a mistake, and her promotion to second grade when she read with the "dumb" kids. Nellie's conflicting emotions and feelings of self-worth are suggested by comparing weekends and weekdays; she never wants Sunday to end because there is "Monday morning like a slap at the beginning of the week" (p. 17). These comparisons continue as she enters school; she enjoys playing games in the school yard because she is better than the "fast" third graders. Equally revealing are the comparisons between the way Nellie thinks the teachers see her and the way she sees herself. It is only the teachers who think she is "dumb"; Nellie knows she can do numbers and is better than her schoolmates when playing games.

Nellie's character also shows a strong feeling about reading, a wistful determination to succeed. She considers reading a mountain that she cannot climb; she can see that the top is beautiful but does not know how to reach it. The rest of the story shows Nellie's experience as she tries to reach her mountain top. The contrasts between the teachers who did not understand her and her response to Miss Lacey, the teacher in the reading clinic, also reveal Nellie's feelings about herself and her school experiences. She is amazed when Miss Lacey talks to her about herself and then writes her words down so that she can read them back. Nellie approaches the room, breathing quietly so as not to destroy this exciting chance and thinks to herself:

Nobody had ever cared enough for her words to do anything with them but let them vanish into the air. Now she felt funny inside as she thought of those words kept forever in Miss Lacey's room. Not that they were such good words. She would do better. But this was something. (p. 78)

Nellie's problems are not all solved by her improving reading skills; she still must overcome her feelings about her gifted brother and the respect he receives from their parents. Although she wants this kind of attention, she decides that she has accomplished a goal. She is no longer frightened about her inability. This story carries a strong message for educators and parents who work with children.

The stories recommended in this section have varied settings. Like the total American population, some of the characters live in rural areas, some in suburban areas, and others in the harsher surroundings of inner-city neighborhoods. All of the characters, however, are real people. The authors have preserved the dignity of the characters without stigma or stereotype. These stories are also enjoyable and contain human emotions that appeal to all children.

Realistic Black Literature for Older Children

Outstanding realistic fiction written for older readers is characterized both by strong characters and strong themes. The themes in these stories include searching for human freedom and dignity, learning to live together for the benefit of humanity, tackling problems personally rather than waiting for someone else to do so, survival of the physical body and the human spirit, and the more humorous problem of living through a girl's first crush.

Virginia Hamilton reveals considerable information about the history of slavery and the work of the Underground Railroad in her suspenseful contemporary story, *The House of Dies Drear*. She skillfully presents this background through the conversations of a black history professor and his son who are interested in the history of the pre–Civil War mansion they are about to rent. The family travels to Ohio, and Thomas's father tells him about the wealthy abolitionist who built the house and helped many slaves toward freedom. The author hints at the suspense to follow as Thomas learns that Dies Drear and two escaped slaves were murdered; there are rumors that the abolitionist and the slaves haunt the old house and the hidden tunnels below.

Readers of mysteries will enjoy this suspenseful book. Hamilton provides details for a setting that seems perfect for the mysterious occurrences that begin soon after the family arrives:

The house of Dies Drear loomed out of mist and murky sky, not only gray and formless, but huge and unnatural. It seemed to crouch on the side of a high hill above the highway. And it had a dark, isolated look about it that set it at odds with all that was living. (p. 26)

There is more mystery and suspense; the family tries to discover who or what force entered the locked house as they slept and placed strange triangles, portions of a Greek cross, on the walls. Who ransacked the kitchen, plastering food all over the floor and walls? Was it a warning from old Mr. Pluto, the caretaker who lived in a cave on the property? Or was it a warning from the ghosts who didn't want strangers living there? Thomas and his father make an exciting discovery, a secret room behind Mr. Pluto's cave. The mystery is solved in a fast-paced conclusion in which Thomas and his father play the roles of slave ghosts complete with chains and phosphorous tape outlining their facial features. (Compare the presentation of information about slavery in Hamilton's book with the Belinda Hurmence's time travel fantasy about slavery in *A Girl Called Boy*.)

Virginia Hamilton writes about the black experience with a universal appeal that speaks to readers of any ethnic heritage.

I AM A WRITER FOR YOUNG PEOPLE. Before that, I am a writer for myself. I enjoy what I do, which I call "puzzling out" ideas. Solving is as natural for me as eating or sleeping. I tend to think through problem situations of living and the process of life itself in terms of stories.

I write especially for young people, because I have come to cherish particularly fond memories from my own childhood. My rural childhood was wonderfully free and exciting, often mysterious, which is the way I will always remember it. And through acts of imagination, I am able to transpose the sense of my somewhat isolated early life experiences into books for the young.

I write also because creating is what I do easily and what I care to do best of all. I believe I have something unique to show and tell, that I can put words together in a way that is new and different from the way anyone else would put them together. It would be wonderful if people would think of me simply as a writer, for I believe adults can enjoy my books as well as children. I wish we would dispense of categories that tend to separate us.

The reading young people that I know show as much intelligence, as much imagination as many of the adults I know, and perhaps a good deal more readiness to enter into something that is imagined or made up, and to live a story. Young people are not just teenagers—another category—but individuals who will read books they like and have heard about. They will read them when they feel like it and when they are ready to read—if and when books are made available to them. This last is so important. For we can't expect our young people to become sophisticated readers, able to judge the good from the not so good book if they do not have open and free access to all kinds of books for their age. Thus, the child in the all-white suburb or the child in the all-black neighborhood should not be limited in reading because of their social and racial environment. One nice thing about America is its library system and the accessibility of all kinds of books

Her strong characterizations in *The Planet of Junior Brown* were discussed in chapter nine. Another of Hamilton's strong characters learns that choice and action lie within his power in *M. C. Higgins, the Great.* The enemy in this rural mountain story is the spoil heap remaining from strip mining, an oozing pile that threatens to swallow the house and even the hero's mother's beloved sunflower. Mayo Cornelius Higgins does not take any action at first; instead he sits on top of his forty-foot steel pole and fantasizes ways to take his family to safety. When the "dude" comes into their lives, M. C. imagines that the man will turn his mother into a singing star, allowing the family to leave the mountain. The most influential outsider is a young wanderer, Lurhetta, who teaches M. C. that he does not need to dream of solutions—he can find them himself. In a conclusion that separates reality fron fantasy, M. C. decides that since he has to live on the mountain, he will build something big between himself and the spoil heap:

There began to take shape a long, firm kind of mound. The children fed it. M. C. shoveled and Ben packed it. In the immense quiet of Sarah's Mountain late in the day, they formed a wall. And it was rising. (p. 278)

A rural story for older readers is much lighter in tone than the previously discussed books. Bette Greene's humorous *Philip Hall Likes Me. I Reckon Maybe* is set in Arkansas. The characters are Philip Hall, the smartest boy in the class, and Beth Lambert, the eleven-year-old girl who has her first crush. The author creates considerable humor as Beth tries to maneuver experiences that she can share with Philip. She is even a little suspicious that he may not be the smartest child in the class; she may be letting him win. The two work together to solve the mystery of her father's missing turkeys, and they set up the "Elizabeth Lorraine Lambert and Friend Veg. Stand." They are in direct competition, however, when both of them raise a calf to show at the annual Randolph County Fair. When Beth's calf wins, Philip's first reaction is shame; then he feels the unfamiliar emotions related to losing. Beth solves their problem when she invites him to be her partner in the square-dancing contest; as friends and partners, they can win or lose together. Philip finally admits what Beth has been longing to hear:

"Sometimes I reckon I likes you, Beth Lambert," he said as we touched hands and together ran toward the lights, the music, and the microphone-amplified voice of Skinny Baker. (p. 135)

Other stories for older readers were discussed in chapter ten. Mildred D. Taylor's *Roll of Thunder, Hear My Cry* and William Armstrong's *Sounder* are also about the black experience.

to the young people who cannot afford to buy them.

In my childhood, comic books were what my brothers and sisters and friends, all country children, had to read. Who had books? Only the public libraries. Occasionally, we were given books for Christmas. I recall a glorious, huge book of Cinderella with marvelous, full color illustrations. But comic books were what we read after school (and during school, hidden behind our primers!), before bed and under the covers. And yet, it wasn't *what* we read that was important. It was the growing, developing habit of reading that would turn us into literate adults.

Therein lies the key to literacy and reading well. No substantial gains can be made on the problem of literacy in this country until we understand that young people must learn the *habit* of reading. Reading has to become as fundamental to young lives as television has become, and as essential as eating or sleeping.

Young people read for entertainment. A book of fiction entertains by offering solace, excitement, relaxation, encour-agement and escape. That escape allows the young person to find the strength and new ways to cope with her own reality when she returns to it. In so-called *realistic* fiction, the escape and encouragement come from a sense of parallel in finding a true, recognizable portraiture of real life. The reader watches as the fictional person copes with the real life situation there. When the ending is happy or resolved, the reader feels reassured.

An image occurs to me. A book follows. Something puzzles me in terms of the image and I begin writing it down. Puzzling out the plot of a book from one or two vague images is something I find extremely pleasant to do. Not only must I solve, but I am interested in having others investigate my solutions, my books. Communicating is as important to me as puzzle-solving. It is an integral part of the whole puzzle. It is necessary that I write and offer books outward to the public. The response of readers, young people, to my books makes my calling worthwhile. The hundreds of wonderful letters, sweet and silly, critical and sad, closes the circle.

Writing for the young is as rigorous as I imagine teaching the young would be. My books are full, sometimes complex, because I believe young peoople are equally full, growing toward complexity. What I attempt to bring them is life's range of possibilities, in situations and in terms of language that most of the time, they will find comprehensible. In my fictions, fictional people become real as they live as best they can. Through living, they learn to change and to grow. Learning to live to the utmost, living in harmony, learning that life is ultimately what each of us is given, and what we do with our lives is what I am concerned with in my stories.

The challenge for me, the writer, is to deal with all that I consider to be the real world by creating a youth literature that beyond entertaining, shows compassion, hope and humor. I try to provide ways of thinking, ways of opening young minds to possibilities.

The characters in these stories meet the criteria for outstanding characterization in literature: they are memorable individuals; they are real people who face the best and the worst that life offers. As in the literature for young readers, the stories reflect varied settings and socioeconomic levels. If children read a variety of the literature, there is no suggestion that blacks as a group belong to one socioeconomic level. The main character may be the son of a highly educated college professor or the son of a destitute sharecropper. The realistic stories for older readers do, however, reflect a harsher realism in the black experience, whether in the history of black people or in contemporary life. These stories may portray an inner-city existence and survival that is very different from a middle-class experience. In an Associated Press story (1), Fred Crawford, the director of Emory University's Center for Research and Social Change, reflects on the experiences of poor black children who live in the inner city:

Black children often are not supervised, not because of deliberate neglect or lack of concern by their parents, but simply because life at the poverty level forces them to be on their own. We talk about vulnerability in the black kids, but is has been a necessity, a pattern for a long time. These kids are different from white people in that they frequently have to do more things by themselves.

Books such as Hamilton's *The Planet of Junior Brown* and *How Many Miles to Babylon?* by Paula Fox reflect this way of life. The children in the stories, however, reflect pride in their individuality and in their decisions to be themselves. The characters' courage and determination are inspirations to all.

Nonfiction Books about the Black Experience

Because two of the strongest purposes for sharing black literature with children are to raise the aspirations of black children and develop an understanding of the contributions of Black Americans for nonblack children, biographies should play an important role in the multiethnic literature program. There are biographies of black leaders and artists that tell children about the contributions they have made and the problems they have had to overcome.

The life of nineteenth-century freedom fighter Frederick Douglass can be found in several biographies. Lillie Patterson's *Frederick Douglass: Freedom Fighter* is a dramatic encounter with the statesman's life in slavery, his protest against slavery, his escape from the slave masters and then the slave hunters, his work on the Underground Railroad, and his championing the rights of not only blacks but also Chinese, Irish, and women. Another biography about this same period in

Douglass's life is Margaret Davidson's *Frederick Douglass Fights for Freedom.*

A twentieth-century freedom fighter who is comparable to Frederick Douglass is black leader Dr. Martin Luther King, Jr. Gloria D. Miklowitz's *Dr. Martin Luther King, Jr.* traces the development of King's feelings about slavery and injustice; his education; his experiences with prejudice; his campaign that his people join the NAACP and register to vote; his dedication to the boycotts, sit-ins for freedom, and peaceful marches on Washington; his receiving *Time*'s Man of the Year Award, the Nobel Peace Prize, and the Medal of Freedom; and finally, his tragic assassination on April 4, 1968.

A biography of another black leader written for young readers is Arnold Adoff's *Malcolm X.* This book traces his life from his days as a hustler in Harlem, through his experiences in jail, and into the experiences that began to change his life and gave him reasons for his later dedication. Adoff stresses how and why Malcolm X urged blacks to be proud of their heritage and themselves.

All children do not want to be political leaders; some may long to be artists or other professionals. Midge Turk's *Gordon Parks* presents the life of an internationally known photographer, poet, and musician whose fame came because he could portray his sensitivity to the black experiences in Harlem with his camera. This book also depicts the discrimination that Gordon Parks experienced along with his success.

Several picture books for children of all ages show different aspects of the African heritage. Nonny Hogrogian's illustrations let children share the sights seen by an African child in Leila Ward's *I Am Eyes—Ni Macho.* The title of the book means "I am awake"; it also means "I am eyes." What the child sees with her eyes suggests some of the wondrous and unusual animals of Africa. There are long-necked giraffes ambling through tall grass, elands and elephants strolling across the land, camels resting in a desert oasis, birds soaring above Mt. Kilimanjaro, colorful flamingos standing in a pond, and butterflies fluttering. The illustrations leave the impression of a beautiful and varied country.

Donn Renn's photographs and Tom Schactman's text accompany a Masai boy and girl as they progress through a typical day in *Growing Up Masai.* Readers are given a better understanding of the Masai culture and the daily life and aspirations of the people when they glimpse the culture through the experiences of children.

The customs and traditions of twenty-six African peoples are shown through Leo and Diane Dillon's beautiful illustrations and Margaret Musgrove's text in *Ashanti to Zulu.* This un-usual alphabet book reinforces the understanding that the African continent has a rich heritage of culture and tradition. The illustrations, where possible, show a man, a woman, a child, their living quarters, an artifact, and a local animal. (See page 108 for a discussion of the illustrations in this book.)

The books discussed in this section have broad appeal for children and a wide range of content. When shared with children, such books contribute toward positive self-images and respect for individuals across cultures, and do much to lessen the negative stereotypes common in black literature of the past. The emergence of outstanding authors who write about the black experience with sensitivity and honesty has provided more excellent books about the black minority than are available about other minorities in the United States.

NATIVE AMERICAN LITERATURE

The copyright dates listed in the annotated bibliography at the end of this chapter show that the majority of recommended books about Native Americans have been published quite recently. Few copyright dates precede the 1970s, thus indicating an increase in books written with an Indian perspective. Many are beautifully illustrated traditional Indian tales, and several have won Caldecott awards. Native Americans themselves have written notable books. In addition, such writers as anthropologist Joyce Rockwood have used their knowledge of Indian cultures to write about an authentic Indian past. The lovely poetry written by Byrd Baylor and the Indian tales she collected increase understanding of the Indian values and heritage. There are fewer stories, however, about contemporary Indian main characters than about contemporary black characters. Consequently, most children have few opportunities to read about Indian children facing problems in today's world.

Evaluating Native American Literature

Native Americans have often been romanticized, misrepresented, and their lives and cultures ignored or distorted in children's literature of the past. Stereotypes such as the noble or ignoble savage and the characterization of good Indians as ones who have taken on the characteristics and values of white society while abandoning their own were commonly found in children's stories.

The following criteria are compiled from the references listed previously on the images of Native Americans in children's literature, and from concerns identified by Anna Lee Stensland (21):

1 Are the Indian characters portrayed as individuals with their own thoughts, emotions, and philosophies? The characters should not conform to stereotypes or be dehumanized.

2 Do the Indian characters belong to a specific tribe, or are they grouped together under one category referred to as *Indian?*

3 Does the author recognize the diversity of Indian cultures? Are the customs and ceremonies authentic for the Indian tribes?

4 Is the Indian culture respected, or is it presented as inferior to the white culture? Does the author believe the culture is worthy of preservation or that it should be abandoned? Must the Indian fit into an image acceptable to white characters in the story?

5 Is offensive and degrading vocabulary used to describe the characters, their actions, their customs, or their lifestyles?

6 Are the illustrations realistic and authentic, or do they reinforce stereotypes or devalue the culture?

7 If the story has a contemporary setting, does the author accurately describe the life and situation of the Native American in today's world?

Traditional Tales of Indians of North America

Jamake Highwater's *Anpao: An American Indian Odyssey* compares the teller of Indian tales to a weaver whose designs are the threads of his personal saga as well as the history of his people. These stories have been passed from one generation to the next and were often borrowed from another tribe. Highwater says that the stories have no known authors:

They exist as the river of memory of a people, surging with their images and their rich meanings from one place to another, from one generation to the next—the tellers and the told so intermingled in time and space that no one can separate them. (p. 239)

Highwater recounts the task of preserving and transmitting Indian stories as described by the Santee Dakota, Charles Eastman. Writing of his own boyhood, Eastman said that very early in life Indian boys assumed the task of preserving and transmitting their legends. In the evening, a boy would listen as one of his parents or grandparents told a tale. The following evening, the boy would often be required to repeat the story. The household became his audience and either criticized or applauded his endeavors.

In the introduction to a collection of traditional Indian tales, Byrd Baylor's *And It Is Still That Way: Legends Told by Arizona Indian Children*, the author says that Indians had a high regard for the storytellers; no one was supposed to go to sleep while the storyteller was speaking. Consequently, when the storyteller paused, the audience signaled that they were listening. The Papagos repeated the last word they had heard; the Hopis answered with a soft sound. When the stories are told today, they are told with a feeling that they are not out of the past and finished; rather, the storyteller frequently ends with "It can happen like that now," "We still know such things," or "And it is still that way." There is respect for everything that went before and still touches people today.

The Indians of North America evolved a mythology that explained the origins of the universe and other natural phenomena. According to Virginia Haviland (14), they believed in

supernatural forces and their legends told of culture heroes and shape-shifters who used magic. Animals had power to turn into people and people into animals. The animal stories, like animal folklore of many other countries, are often humorous, and the characters are accomplished tricksters. (p. 13)

Researchers and writers alike are increasingly interested in traditional Indian literature. There are many beautifully illustrated traditional tales in both single volumes and anthologies that draw upon the tales passed down from tribes across the North American continent.

Single Edition Traditional Tales. Native American tales often explain how the wonders of nature came to be. Gerald McDermott's *Arrow to the Sun, a Pueblo Indian Tale* illustrates the Indian's reverence for the sun. In this tale, the Pueblo Indians explain that the lord of the sun sent the spark of life to the earth where it entered the pueblo of a maiden. This spark created Boy who came to live in the world of humans. Boy did not have an easy life, however; people mocked him because he had no father. In his desire to discover his father, Boy left home and traveled through the world until he found Arrow Maker who changed him into an arrow and sent him through the heavens toward the mighty lord of the sun. Here he had to prove that he was the rightful son. To do this, he had to pass through four chambers: the Kiva of Lions, the Kiva of Serpents, the Kiva of Bees, and the Kiva of Lightning. After successfully passing through these trials, he was filled with the power of the sun, and returned to the world of humans, bringing the spirit of the sun to men. (See pages 109–10 for a discussion of the illustrations.)

In the days of the long-ago time, when people and animals could talk together, but before fire was brought to their tribes, there lived an Indian boy who, according to Paiute legend, had Coyote as his friend and counselor. It was Coyote, in Margaret Hodges's *The Fire Bringer: A Paiute Indian Legend,* who helped the boy find and return fire from the Burning Mountain. This tale is an excellent example of a "why" tale that explains an animal's characteristics. The conclusion shows how many Native American storytellers suggested their stories were true:

And this is the sign that the tale is true. All along the Coyote's thin sides the fur is singed and yellow to this day, as it was by the flames that blew backward from the brand when he brought it down from the Burning Mountain. (p. 31)

(Compare this tale with William Toye's *The Firestealer,* a tale about how Nanabozho gave fire to the people.)

Horses are greatly prized in many Indian tales. Paul Goble's *The Girl Who Loved Wild Horses* is a beautifully illustrated story of an Indian girl who understands and loves wild horses; she leads the herd to the river to drink, finds them the choicest grass, locates shelter for them during blizzards, and looks after them when they are injured. After she and the herd are pursued by thunder and lightning and reach safety, she is invited by the leader of the wild horses to live with them. According to the tale, it is believed that she became one of the wild horses. Again, there is a relationship between the past and the present as the story ends with these words:

Today we are still glad to remember that we have relatives among the Horse People. And it gives us joy to see the wild horses running free. Our thoughts fly with them. (p. 25)

(See page 92 for a discussion of the language used in this book and pages 106–7 for a discussion of Paul Goble's illustrations.) In *The Gift of the Sacred Dog,* Goble presents a folktale explaining how horses were given to humans.

Native American tales frequently include transformation; this transformation may be used by a trickster or it may explain a close kinship with animals. Both uses of transformation are found in John Bierhorst's *The Ring in the Prairie: A Shawnee Legend.* A young Shawnee hunter turns himself into a mouse to creep closer to a beautiful maiden who descended from the sky. He returns to his human form and captures his heart's desire. His final transformation suggests a close relationship between humans and animals. The young hunter brings one of each kind of bird and animal he kills to his wife's family, the star people.

When the star people choose their animals or birds, they are changed into that creature. The young hunter and his family each choose a white hawk's feather, immediately become white hawks, spread their wings, and soar to earth where they

The loon is rewarded with beautiful markings in this Native American tale.
From *The Loon's Necklace* by William Toye, illustrated by Elizabeth Cleaver, copyright © 1977 by Oxford University Press Canada. Reprinted with permission of the publisher.

still live. Another strong value is found in this tale: the Shawnee demonstrates strong family ties and love for his family.

Another lovely tale that shows respect for the wisdom of animals, an animal's reward for a good deed, and a human transformed into an animal form is William Toye's *The Loon's Necklace.* This tale explains how the loon was transformed from a black and white bird into one with lovely shell markings around his neck and white markings across his feathers.

Repetitive language in the form of a cumulative folktale provides an enjoyable tale for listening and encouraging oral language in Betty Baker's *Rat Is Dead and Ant Is Sad.* In addition, this Pueblo tale stresses the consequences that may develop when characters reach the wrong conclusion.

Collections of Traditional Tales. Virginia Haviland's anthology, *North American Legends,* contains a collection of Native American and Eskimo tales identified by location. One story that is interesting to compare with other tales using the same theme is "The Indian Cinderella" from the Northeastern woodlands of the United States. In this version, a great Indian warrior, Strong Wind, says that he will marry the first maiden who can see him arriving home; this is difficult, however, because he has the power of invisibility. In the village lives a great chief with three daughters; the older girls are jealous and cruel, while the youngest is gentle and loved by all. She is dressed in rags, her hair is cut short, and her face has been burned by her sisters. When the older girls try to identify the object that draws Strong Wind's sled, they must lie because they cannot see him. However, the youngest girl says that she cannot see anything. Strong Wind rewards her for telling the truth and allows her to see that his sled is drawn by the rainbow and his bowstring is the Milky Way. The cruel sisters are punished when they are turned into aspen trees. This story, found in many other cultures, reflects how strongly the specific culture is woven into the oral tradition.

Highwater has combined a number of traditional Indian tales in *Anpao: An American Indian Odyssey*. The tale begins "In the days before the people fled into the water . . . [when] there was no war and the people were at peace" (p. 15). During this time, Anpao travels across the great prairies, through deep canyons, and along wooded ridges in search of his destiny. Along the way, he observes the diverse cultures and customs of many different tribes. His odyssey illustrates the diversity of land, life-styles, and folk history found within the Indian culture of North America. Of Blackfeet-Cherokee heritage, Highwater heard most of the stories included in Anpao as a boy attending powwows, from friends, or in his travels across America researching Indian tales for his books. He expanded his early interest in Indian legends and earned degrees in cultural anthropology and comparative literature. In the conclusion of Anpao, he expresses a desire to share these tales with others who do not share his heritage: "Many of us are prepared to sail to the strange places in time and in space; perhaps Anpao will address itself to that audience and become a personal journey for readers who wish to sail from one world to another" (p. 246).

Emerson and David Coatsworth compiled a collection of sixteen Ojibway tales in *The Adventures of Nanabush: Ojibway Indian Stories*. Nanabush, a very powerful spirit of the Ojibway world, can turn himself into an animal, a tree stump, or a leaf; he has both supernatural abilities and human frailties. The tales in this collection include the story of how Nanabush created the world. In this flood and creation story, the Serpent People cause the water to rise in retaliation for Nanabush's destruction of two of their people. Anticipating their reactions, Nanabush builds a large raft, places it on top of a mountain, and invites the animals to join him as the water rises. After they float on the raft for a month without sighting land, Nanabush realizes that the old world has been submerged forever. In or-

der to get substance out of which he can create a new world, he first sends the loon to the old world to retrieve mud. When the loon is successful, he sends the beaver and then the muskrat. The muskrat returns with a few particles of sand out of which Nanabush forms a tiny globe. After he breathes life into the globe, he places it on the water next to the raft and commands it to grow. The globe revolves until it is large enough to contain Nanabush and all the animals. That, according to the Ojibway tale, is how the world of today was created.

An interesting anthology of Navaho, Hopi, Papago, Pima, Apache, Quechan, and Cocopah stories to share with children is Baylor's *And It Is Still That Way*. This collection is especially meaningful to children because the stories were told to the author by Arizona Indian children. Baylor asked children at reservation schools to choose their favorite story—the best story they had ever heard—told to them by someone in their tribe. The stories and drawings by the children were divided into six categories: Why Animals Are the Way They Are, Why Our World Is Like It Is, Great Troubles and Great Heroes, People Can Turn into Anything, Brother Coyote, and There Is Magic All Around Us. Baylor's *God on Every Mountain* is a collection of Southwest Indian tales about the sacred mountains.

Christie Harris's *The Trouble with Adventurers* is a collection of five tales from Northwest Coastal tribes and one told by a white man who was captured by the Indians. The author includes a map indicating the geographic locations of the stories. There are heroic tales of brave hunters as well as humorous stories of trickery. It is interesting to compare the tales because five are told from a Native American perspective while one is told from a white captive's perspective. Additional tales from the Northwest tribes are found in Gail Robinson's *Raven the Trickster: Legends of the North American Indians*.

These tales, in both single editions and collections, highlight Indian storytellers' magic with their beautiful illustrations. They show that the North American continent had original traditional tales that were centuries old before European settlers arrived. They comprise a heritage to take pride in and to pass on to future generations.

Indian Literature in Poetic Form

Songs, chants, and poems are very important in the Indian culture. Many poems express reverence for creation, nature, and beauty. According to Carlson (6), the Indians created poetry for a purpose. They considered a song or a poem important because they believed there was power in the word. Songs were often created as a part of a ceremonial ritual with the symbolism portrayed through dance.

The beauty of both ancient Indian poetry and contemporary poetry about Indian experiences are found in literature that can be shared with children. An interesting resource book that shares the music of the Indian with children of many cultures is John Bierhorst's *A Cry from the Earth: Music of the North American Indians*. According to the author, Indians throughout North America shared a belief in the supernatural powers of music. It was used to cure disease, bring rain, win a lover, or defeat an enemy. Many Indians today sing the songs for pleasure and to express pride in their heritage. The text includes words and music for many songs, including songs of prayer, magic, and dreams; songs to control the weather; and music to accompany various dances. There are greeting songs, love songs, a Hopi flute song, a Hopi sleep song, a Cherokee lullaby, and a Kwakiutl cradlesong. Music, words, and dance steps are included so that children can recreate the Indian love of music and a respect for this heritage. The wide range of subjects around which songs were created suggests an Indian heritage that is rich in variety, not one concerned mainly with violence.

Baylor has expressed her love and concern for the people and the land of the Southwest in a series of books written in poetic form. Two of them ponder the secrets of prehistoric Indians as seen through their drawings left on canyon walls and pottery. *Before You Came This Way* recaptures the people who lived in some long ago age—the Cliff Dwellers, the wanderers, and the hunters who left their messages on the canyon walls. They drew the birds, the deer, the rabbits, and the coyotes that inhabited their lives. Across these canyon walls, battles rage and people dance and search for new hunting grounds. Although the pictures have been battered and dimmed by exposure to rain, winds, and age, they are still visible. Tom Bahti's illustrations, based on rock drawings found in Arizona, New Mexico, and western Texas, inspire feelings of awe and respect for an ancient culture.

The same writer-illustrator team collaborated on *When Clay Sings*. The designs on the ancient shards of pottery created by the Anasazi, Mogollon, Hohokam, and Mimbres cultures of the Southwest are the models for the illustrations and suggest the culture and capability of ancient artisans. According to Baylor, "Indians who find this pottery today say that everything has its own spirit—even a broken pot . . . . They say that every piece of clay is a piece of someone's life. They even say it has its own small voice and sings in its own way" (cover summary).

This voice found in nature and the ability to hear it is the theme of another perceptive book by Baylor. *The Other Way to Listen* suggests that listeners who have the ability can hear the wildflower seeds bursting, the hills singing, and the rock murmuring. The special relationship between the Papago Indians and their desert land is the topic of *The Desert Is Theirs*. Illustrations by Peter Parnall suggest the majesty of the desert and the Indians' respect for it in these books. (See pages 338–39 for a discussion of Baylor's poems.)

In a third book, *Hawk, I'm Your Brother,* Baylor and Parnall capture a young Indian's dream of soaring over canyons, floating on the wind, and wrapping himself in the wind while facing the sun. The Indian boy's desires are emphasized by his decision to capture a young hawk, learn his secret of flying, and become its brother. The captured hawk, however, pulls against the restraining string, beats his wings against his cage, and calls to his free brothers soaring in the canyon. Because Rudy Soto loves the hawk and does not wish to see him unhappy, he returns him to the Santos Mountain, the place of his birth. There, the hawk rises in splendor and the boy and his hawk brother call back and forth to each other. The author suggests that while Rudy has his feet on the ground, he feels as if he is soaring through the air with his friend. He never mentions his brother to anyone, but the people know that he has changed: his eyes flash like the eyes of a young hawk; the sky is reflected in his eyes.

A Pima Indian tale provides the content for Baylor's poetic rendition in *Moonsong*. Baylor's text explains how Coyote was born of the moon. It is interesting to compare Ronald Himler's interpretation of Baylor's text in the *Moonsong* illustrations with Parnall's illustrations in *The Desert Is Theirs, Hawk, I'm Your Brother,* and *The Other Way to Listen*. Himler's harsher charcoal drawings create a different mood of the desert and the inhabitants.

Masks from various Indians of North America are the source for illustrations and text in Baylor's *They Put on Masks*. Ancient Indians believed that there was great power in a mask; it could change them into the spirit of anything. Masks allowed them to speak with the fierce gods of sun, rain, thunder, and lightning. Baylor's lyrical text presents the spirit of Eskimo masks made from visions in dreams and decorated with ivory, reindeer hair, and porcupine quills. Ingram's illustrations depict the masks of the Northwestern Coastal Indians, carved in wood and decorated with hammered copper and fur; the twisted "False Face" masks of the Iroquois, carved to break the ancient spell against evil spirits and cure illness; and the Apache masks, painted with the colors of the four sacred directions—north designated by white, east by black, south by blue, and west by yellow. The colorful, authentic illustrations modeled after real Indian masks provide a source for study of the culture. The book ends with an enticing challenge to children reading the book: what kind of mask would their mask be, what kind of songs would their mask bring out of them, and what dances would their bones remember? This book reinforces the desirable understanding that the Indians have a diverse culture and great artistic tradition.

A poetic tale of Indian life by Ann Nolan Clark depicts a warm relationship between a small Papago girl and her grandmother as they travel *Along Sandy Trails* to pick the fruits of the desert. Full-color photographs vividly portray the desert beauty as the pair look at cactus in bloom; ocotillo branches tipped with firelike blossoms; quails progressing with quick, small, elegant steps; and giant cactus, tall and stark against the summer sky. They fill their baskets with fruit from the giant cactus and return home content after a day filled with viewing the pleasure found from a desert in bloom.

A year in the life of a Navajo girl is the subject for Ramona Maher's poems in *Alice Yazzie's Year*. The everyday experiences of a modern Navaho girl's bringing a lamb into the hogan, watching bulldozers transform her world, and visiting Los Angeles and San Francisco are shown. The author develops Alice's conflicting emotions as she sees wonderful things in the city but is concerned because no one really listens to her. In the last month of her year, Alice wants to learn to weave the Navaho way, the way her grandmother showed the world of clouds, animals, and Mother Earth. The text concludes with four pages of notes about the Navaho country and the Navaho way of life written by Carl N. Gorman, Director of Navajo Resources and Curriculum Development, Navajo Community College, Tsailie, Arizona.

The literature in poetic form develops a diverse culture made up of many people who have a reverence for beauty, for nature, and for freedom of thought. Some books develop a respect for ancient artisans and the art they created. There is a feeling of ancient ancestry of a proud people who have lived on this continent for centuries.

Historical Fiction about Native Americans

Joyce Rockwood has applied her study of anthropology, with its emphasis on the history of the Cherokee Indians, to create a portrayal of the traditional Indian life of the early 1500s. Steeped in information about the Cherokee culture, *To Spoil the Sun* is also a story of personal development and family relationships. The story spans two generations of experiences and viewpoints and shows the maturation of a Cherokee girl named Rain Dove as she and her people endure tragic events associated with the coming of the Spaniards to the eastern seaboard of the United States.

The story begins as omens foretell a change in the life of Rain Dove's village. A hawk captures a snake in winter and is struck dead by the reptile's fangs. There is thunder in the winter and the sacred warriors' tree burns, causing the tribe to believe that Thunder has abandoned his warriors. The author uses each omen to suggest a tragic happening to the Chero-

kee leaders. When the ancient fire is mysteriously extinguished, the leader of the tribe calls the people to council:

Beloved people of the Seven Clans! My heart is in pain and my eyes are filled with tears! The breath has gone out of Quail Town! Our town lies in the valley like a corpse in its bed! There is no heartbeat in the center! The fire has gone out! (p. 10)

With the final omen, the people feel that the circle is complete; there may be no sanctuary for the Cherokees.

The author develops the story through Rain Dove's life as she discovers the significance of the omens: she faces crucial decisions about marriage, experiences the dreaded smallpox brought to the tribe by the conquistadors, witnesses the death of family and friends, and assists the tribe as they try to reestablish their village. Although the surviving Cherokees move to a new area and build a new village, the shadow of the change that will result from the white man's coming follows them and waits for its momentous effect to be felt. Rockwood concludes with an afterword that emphasizes her feelings about the importance of these background events in American history:

These are events which have never been regarded as greatly significant in our history books, and perhaps they never will be. They are but obscure sentences in the first paragraph of the story we tell about ourselves. And the Indians, so momentously affected by these "minor" events are never glimpsed by us at all. This book, then, is about a people who lived and died on the other side of history, just beyond our view. (p. 180)

The author uses her knowledge of Cherokee culture to write a lighter, more humorous story of a young Cherokee boy living in 1750. *Groundhog's Horse* tells of a boy who loses his horse when Creek Indians steal it and leave a message signifying that they have taken it to Rabbit-town. Even worse, the warriors do not consider Groundhog's horse important enough to retrieve. Instead of being able to go on the trail with a loud whoop, Groundhog decides he must "sneak away like a weasel" and find his horse himself. He stealthily plans his trip, stores cornmeal in a pouch, locates his extra pair of moccasins, and waits for clouds to cover the moon so that he can move unnoticed across a clearing to the cornfield. When he is alone in the wilderness, his stomach churns, he thinks longingly of his family and home, and he procrastinates as he tries to think of a plan. Finally, "with bravery fluttering faintly in his heart," he approaches the sleeping Rabbit-town and the house with his horse Midnight hobbled out in front. Surprisingly, he finds not only the horse but a young Cherokee boy who has been captured by the Creeks and adopted into a family to replace their own son. After a series of adventures, Groundhog's horse finds the way home, and the boys are reunited with their anxious families. Rockwood weaves tradition and history naturally into the story, but the overwhelming feeling is one of human relationships and the personalities of the characters. Unlike many Indian story characters, these Indians laugh, and they have names and individual personality traits and desires. Children can learn a great deal about Cherokees as well as enjoy a humorous adventure.

Through these stories, children can experience Indian characters who have personal thoughts and emotions and live within a family as well as a tribe. They will also begin to understand the impact of the white people on the Indian way of life. (Additional historical stories about the Indian relationships with the white settlers are discussed in chapter ten in this text.)

Modern Realistic Fiction about Native Americans

Many contemporary stories about Native American children express conflict between the old and new ways. Frequently, children must decide whether to feel reverence for or abandon their heritage; many story endings allow children to honor the old ways but live with the new ones. Some stories show life on a modern reservation; others depict famiilies who have left the reservation to live in cities. The universal needs of all individuals are shown as characters search for their identities or express a need for love. There is often hostility expressed toward white business people who have been unfair to the families involved, but other stories develop strong friendships between people from two different backgrounds.

Virginia Driving Hawk Sneve has written several books for young readers about modern Indian boys and their families who live on reservations in western South Dakota. She writes of this setting with knowledge, because she spent her own childhood on the Rosebud Sioux reservation in South Dakota. Her first book, *Jimmy Yellow Hawk,* was awarded first prize in its category by the Council on Interracial Books for Children. Jimmy Henry Yellow Hawk, whose nickname is Little Jim, attends the reservation school where Miss Red Owl is the teacher. Little Jim considers her special because she is one of the first Indians from the reservation to graduate from college and return to work with her people. She is also special because she understands and respects the Indian ways. The author recreates the everyday experiences of an Indian boy as he helps his father on their ranch, takes part in a rodeo, searches for a horse on Red Butte, and attends the annual Dakota Reservation Pow Wow. Children also discover that, like themselves, Little Jim can have a personal goal in life: he wants his classmates and his family to stop calling him "Little" Jim. He plans his strategy, accomplishes his goal, and earns the name of Jimmy. His classmates no longer tease him about his name, and more important, he feels grown-up.

Two other books by Sneve have settings in western South Dakota. *High Elk's Treasure* ties the past into the present with a flashback to the year 1876 when the Sioux are brought to the reservation following the defeat of General Custer at the Battle of the Little Big Horn. There is great excitement when one hundred years later High Elk's descendants discover a pictograph of the Battle of the Little Big Horn that is later authenticated by an expert from the university. The author develops a strong feeling for the past and pride in heritage throughout this book.

A third book by Sneve, *When Thunder Spoke,* also has a tie with the past, the past of the thunders that spoke from the sacred butte and an ancient coup stick recovered from its burial place there. There is conflict in this story between old and new ways and between the whites and the Indians. The author develops this conflict in values through each character's reactions after Norman, a Sioux boy, uncovers an ancient coup stick. His grandfather treats it reverently, considering it a sacred object; his mother rejects it as a heathen symbol; and his father warns that no one should make fun of grandfather or the old ways. In order to help Norman overcome his confusion, his grandfather tells him that it is possible to honor the old ways and live with the new ways.

The characters in *When Thunder Spoke* express hostility toward the white man. This hostility is felt when Norman says that the white trader has been cheating him for years, giving Norman candy rather than money for his agates. In addition, the tourists are identified only as white men who wish to take the Indian's relics. When Norman expresses his concern about the white man's ways to his grandfather, he is again given advice by the older man: "When you find something good in the white man's road, pick it up. When you find something bad, or something that turns out bad, drop it and leave it alone" (p. 76). This expressed conflict and mistrust of the white man is often found in contemporary Indian literature, especially literature written for older children.

Nanabah Chee Dodge writes about the tender relationship between a revered grandmother and a child. *Morning Arrow,* a ten-year-old Navaho boy, lives in Monument Valley, Utah, with his partially blind grandmother. They live in a *hogan* ("house everlasting"), with the door facing east toward the rising sun. Both Morning Arrow and his grandmother revere the beauty of the valley. The author emphasizes these feelings through the descriptions of the almost blind grandmother:

Soon the days will turn warm and the sunrises will please my eyes— such beauty I can't miss. And there will be sunsets to paint the buttes dusty red. Each bush will cast a giant shadow and all the shadows will march into the valley. (p. 12)

The author suggests the devotion between Morning Arrow and his grandmother as he longs to replace his grandmother's shawl, tattooed with holes. His solution produces a sensitive story about a boy growing up and making major decisions. The white man who runs the reservation trading post enters into the solution to Morning Arrow's problem; unlike the trader in *When Thunder Spoke,* he is honest and does not try to cheat the boy and his grandmother. This story was awarded first prize by the Council on Interracial Books for Children.

The search for identity in a contemporary world, the conflict between the Indian and the white worlds, and the death or retention of an ancient, honorable heritage are themes found in Evelyn Sibley Lampman's realistic fiction. The setting for *The Potlatch Family* is the northwestern Pacific Coast, the home of Chinook Indians whose lineage includes chiefs who were proud of their culture. Lampman's heroine, Plum Longor, does not feel this pride. Instead, the author describes her feelings of rejection as her schoolmates ridicule her because of her father's weakness for alcohol. This conflict in values between the old and new is voiced by Plum's younger brother who says that the only way that Indians can make whites look up to them is to be superior in sports.

The author's interjection of the older brother, Simon, and his determination to revive knowledge of and pride in their Chinook heritage causes Plum to consider her conflicting emotions. After involving their family and neighboring Indians in research, they plan and perform a traditional potlatch celebration to demonstrate to the townsfolk that they have a cultural heritage worth preserving. Simon expresses this feeling as he tells his people that their ancestors had a culture of their own, and their lives did not consist of waving tomahawks and painting faces. The author expresses pride in heritage as Simon states:

We survived in a wilderness, unassisted by the white world . . . . We made our own tools, provided adequate shelter, manufactured clothing, found food and made our own entertainment. We had our own laws and entertainment. We have nothing to be ashamed of. The potlatch is one of our ancient customs, . . . We're not doing it only for the whites who will come to see it. We're doing it for ourselves, to remind us of our forefathers. (p. 105)

While some tribal members, including Plum, are hesitant at first, they become enthusiastic as the first potlatch performance is acclaimed by the audience. As word spreads and the celebration is favorably covered by a large city newspaper, the performers acquire the feeling of unity and pride that Simon had hoped for. The proceeds from the performances are used to encourage capable Indian youths to complete a college ed-ucation. Toward this end, the Simon Longor Scholarship Fund is founded.

These stories suggest some conflicts in the contemporary Indian child's life as well as some solutions that the characters have found. Flashbacks develop strong ties with an ancient heritage and the fact that some authors are concerned with developing strong self-esteem and respect for this heritage. As mentioned earlier, however, there are few books written with a contemporary Indian perspective.

Informational Books about Native Americans

Some informational books about Native Americans stress the importance and variety of Indian festivals, the skills that were used by the Indians, the Indian history, the Indians' fight for their sacred lands, and the importance of their contributions.

Many Indian tribes across the United States retain their ancient customs and celebrations by holding festivals. Paul Shower's *Indian Festivals* describes some of them: the Green Corn celebration of the Seminole Indians of Florida; the Shalako festival of the Zuni Indians honoring the rain spirits; the Sun Dance performed by the Utes, Shoshones, Crees, Sioux, and Cheyennes; the Eskimo celebration following a successful whale hunt; and the fair sponsored by various plains Indians at Anadarko, Oklahoma. These Indian festivals are a time for worship and remembering sacred customs. The illustrations clarify the text and encourage children to visualize these celebrations.

It is not only the festivals that are considered sacred; Indian tribes often have land that has been considered sacred for centuries. Marcia Keegan's *The Taos Indians and Their Sacred Blue Lake* reports the history of the Pueblo Indians of Taos, New Mexico, and their struggle to regain the sacred Blue Lake and the surrounding 48,000 acres in the Sangre de Cristo Mountains from the U.S. government. Accompanying photographs illustrate the sacred land, the people of the Taos Pueblo, and their celebration when the land was returned to them in 1971.

In *Before Columbus* Muriel Batherman uses information revealed by archaeological explorations to present and discuss the daily life of earlier North American inhabitants. The text and illustrations show dwellings, clothes, tools, and customs.

Skills and knowledge held by the Indians are described in Tillie S. Pine and Joseph Levine's *The Indians Knew.* The text, written in a highly illustrated format for younger readers, presents each area of knowledge first, followed by how this information is used today. Finally, an experiment is described that allows young readers to discover that the information is correct.

Photographs, as in this book about Taos Indians, are especially effective for depicting settings and people.
From *The Taos Indians and Their Sacred Blue Lake* by Marcia Keegan (New York: Messner, 1972). Copyright © 1972 by Marcia Keegan. Reprinted by permission.

The Indians also gave the world a very important food product. Christopher Columbus, returning from the new world, told about maize, a grain the Indians grew. Aliki's *Corn Is Maize: The Gift of the Indians* traces the history of corn in text and illustrations. Children can discover how corn is planted, cultivated, and harvested. The probable history of corn is traced from the discovery of five-thousand-year-old tiny ears of corn found in a cave in Mexico through its improvement into the large ears grown today. Illustrations show how Indians of Mexico and North America planted, stored, and used corn. The text concludes with illustrations of the Pilgrims learning about maize from the Indians and of the many products that are derived from corn.

Broader contributions of North and South American Indians are explored in Alice Hermina Poatgieter's *Indian Legacy: Native American Influences on World Life and Culture*. In addition to agricultural contributions, the author discusses Native American contributions to culture and democratic attitudes.

Biographies about Native Americans

The historical biographies are about Indians who are well known because of their relationships with white settlers. The

biographies of contemporary Native Americans include the life stories of a famous ballerina and a well-known athlete. Because increasing aspirations of children and respecting contributions of people are two of the values of reading multiethnic literature, biographies are important. Here again, there are fewer biographies about Native Americans than there are about Black Americans.

Maria Tallchief, by Tobi Tobias, is the biography of a prima ballerina born in Fairfax, Oklahoma. Her grandfather, Peter Big Heart, had been chief of the Osage Indian tribe. Maria demonstrated considerable musical talent from the time she was a small child and was encouraged by her mother. At a young age, she began the long, grueling study necessary for success on the concert stage. At a concert she gave at age twelve, she played the piano during the first half and danced during the second half. "That concert, she said, showed how she felt inside. She was split in half between the two things she loved most. One day she would have to choose between them" (p. 10). Maria made her decision, and the ballet world was the richer for her choice. She studied ballet in Los Angeles with the great Russian teacher, Mme. Bronislava Nijinska. Later, she joined the Ballet Russe de Monte Carlo in New York. She was the first ballerina in more than one hundred years to dance with the Paris Opera Ballet. She joined the New York City Ballet and later the American Ballet Theatre.

Tobias stresses that Maria Tallchief was always proud of her Indian heritage, as illustrated by her refusal to use a stage name. She was also honored when the Osage Indians celebrated her success by elevating her to the role of Indian Princess and giving her the title Wa-Xthe-Thonba.

Maria worked hard at her profession until she felt she needed to give more time to her young daughter and husband. In 1966, she "hung up her toe shoes" and returned home to her family. This biography suggests the pride of a worldrenowned artist in her Indian heritage as well as the contributions she made and worldwide acclaim that she merited.

Thomas Fall has written a biography for young children about the life of the great athlete and Olympic hero, *Jim Thorpe*. The book chronicles the life of this Fox Indian from the time he was a young child living on a ranch in the Oklahoma Territory until he became a famous athlete. The story describes his unhappiness in school after his twin brother died, his discovery of football at the Haskell Institute in Kansas, his experiences at the Indian school at Carlisle Pennsylvania, his success on the United States Olympic Team of 1912, the loss of his medals because he had played professional baseball, and his success as a professional football and baseball player. The author stresses both the problems he overcame and the hard work required of him before he became a champion athlete. This biography may be of interest to today's children because Thorpe's medals were awarded posthumously in 1982.

There are biographies of two famous Indians in history. *Squanto: The Indian Who Saved the Pilgrims,* by Matthew G. Grant, is an illustrated biography of the Wampamoag Indian who played an important role in the lives of the Plymouth settlers. *Sacajawea, Wilderness Guide,* by Kate Jassem, is the biography of the Shoshone Indian woman who accompanied the Lewis and Clark Expedition across the Rocky Mountains to the Pacific Ocean. The book is illustrated and appropriate for young readers.

Additional literature about Native Americans may be found in Anna Lee Stensland's *Literature by and about the American Indian* (21).

HISPANIC LITERATURE

In this category stories are included showing a Mexican, a Spanish, and a Puerto Rican heritage. People of Hispanic descent are the major minority group in the United States, but relatively few children's books have been written about them. In addition, there is an imbalance in the types of stories available. The award-winning picture storybooks, for example, tend to be about Christmas celebrations. The award-winning novels are about a small segment of the Spanish American population, the sheepherders of Spanish Basque heritage, whose ancestors emigrated to America before the regions became part of the United States. Although folktales and poetry are available for adults, a shortage of children's literature exists.

ISSUE

Are Authors, Editors, and Publishers Responding to the Critical Reviews About Hispanic Literature?

THE LACK OF CHILDREN'S literature about Hispanic populations and Hispanic cultures and the negative stereotypes found in the available literature are frequently criticized. In a 1981 issue of *Top of the News,* Isabel Schon contends that the "overwhelming majority of recent books incessantly repeat the same stereotypes, misconceptions, and insensibilities that were prevalent in the books published in the 1960s and the early 1970s" (1, p. 79). Schon supports this contention by reviewing books published in 1980 and 1981 that develop the stereotypes of poverty, children's embarrassment about their backgrounds, distorted and negative narratives about pre-Columbian history, and simplistic discussions of serious Latin American problems.

In this review Schon contrasts two books about pre-Columbian cultures. The first, Brenda Ralph Lewis's *Growing Up in Aztec Times*[2] is cited as a book that perpetuates a lack of appreciation for a culture and uses stereotypic terms as "savage" Aztecs, "behaved like barbarians," "ferocious nature," and "superstitious" to describe the people. In contrast, Elizabeth Gemming's *Lost City in the Clouds: The Discovery of Machu Picchu*[3] describes Hiram Bingham's discovery of spectacular monuments and achievements of the Incas. This book is recommended as one that portrays both the achievements of a people and accurate historical incidents.

Schon ends her article with a plea that young readers in the United States need to be exposed to more distinguished books about Hispanic peoples and cultures rather than books that perpetuate misconceptions and negative impressions.

1 Schon, Isabel. "Recent Detrimental and Distinguished Books About Hispanic People and Cultures." *Top of the News* 38 (Fall 1981): 79–85.

2 Lewis, Brenda Ralph. *Growing Up in Aztec Times.* North Pomfret, Vermont: Batsford, 1981.

3 Gemming, Elizabeth. *Lost City in the Clouds: The Discovery of Machu Picchu.* New York: Coward, 1980.

Evaluating Hispanic Literature

When evaluating Hispanic literature, the reviewer must be concerned with many of the previously discussed criteria. There are a few additional points that are specifically characteristic of Hispanic literature because of the stereotypes inherent in some literature of the past. The following list may be used when evaluating literature about Hispanics:

1   Does the book suggest that poverty is a natural condition for all Hispanics? This is a negative stereotype suggested in some literature.
2   Are problems handled individually, allowing the main characters to use their own efforts to solve their problems? Or are all problems solved through the intervention of an Anglo American?
3   Are problems handled realistically or superficially? Is a character's major problem solved by learning to speak English?
4   Is the cultural information accurate? Are Mexican American, Mexican, or Puerto Rican cultures realistically pictured? Is the culture treated with respect?
5   Do the illustrations depict individuals, not stereotypes?
6   Is the language free from derogatory terms or descriptions?
7   If dialects are portrayed, are they a natural part of the story and not used to suggest a stereotype?
8   Does the book have literary merit?
9   If the Spanish language is used, are the words spelled and used correctly?

Mexican and Spanish Heritage

Many books for children develop strong connections between the people and their religious faith. Celebrations such as La Posada suggest this cultural heritage, while the respect for freedom is stressed through the celebration of Cinco de Mayo. Spanish vocabulary is also interspersed in many stories, allowing children to associate with a rich language heritage. (However, misspelled Spanish words and words used incorrectly have appeared all too often in this type of book. These errors have understandably caused criticism.) Several books are more factual, developing the Spanish heritage that existed on the North American continent long before the United States became a nation. These stories suggest that Americans with a Spanish ancestry have a heritage worthy of respect and of sharing with others.

Folktales. A traditional tale developing a strong connection between the Mexican people and their religious faith is Tomie

de Paola's *The Lady of Guadalupe.* According to legend, the Lady of Guadalupe, now the patron saint of Mexico, appeared to a poor Mexican Indian on a December morning in 1531. Juan Diego, "He-who-speaks-like-an-eagle," was walking toward the Church of Santiago when he saw a hill covered with a brilliant white cloud. Out of the cloud came a gentle voice calling Juan's name and telling him that a church should be built on that site so that the lady could show her love for Juan's people, the Indians of Mexico. When Juan approached the bishop with his message, however, he was not believed. Juan returned and pondered why he, a poor farmer, would be chosen to carry such an important message to someone as noble as the bishop. The lady appeared to Juan twice more, each time reassuring him that he was her chosen servant. On Juan's third visit to the bishop, he was believed because he brought with him a visual sign from the lady: his rough cape had been changed into a painting of the lady. The church was built on the location, and the cape with its miraculous change was placed inside the structure.

de Paola says that he has had a lifelong interest in the legend of the Lady of Guadalupe. His drawings, based on careful research, depict the dress and architecture of sixteenth-century Mexico.

Verna Aardema's translation of *The Riddle of the Drum: A Tale from Tizapán, Mexico* depicts a folktale with universal motifs: a king with a marriageable daughter challenges suitors to a task; on the way to the palace, the suitor meets four people with exceptional skills; the king adds additional tasks after the first is completed; and the suitor's extraordinary abilities allow him to win the princess. The tale also reflects a strong Spanish heritage, respect for the language, and beauty in architecture and costumes. The names are Spanish, counting is in Spanish, the foods are Mexican, and Tony Chen's illustrations depict an earlier Mexican culture. The author includes a pronunciation guide for Spanish words and a glossary of meanings.

Picture Books for Younger Children. Leo Politi has written and illustrated a number of award-winning picture storybooks about Mexican American children living in southern California. His *Song of the Swallows* tells the story of a young boy whose dear friend is the gardener and bell ringer at the Mission of San Juan Capistrano. The author shares history with the reader as the gardener tells Juan the history of the mission and about *las golondrinas,* the swallows who always return to the mission in the spring, on Saint Joseph's Day, and remain there until late summer. Juan learns to love both the plants and the birds and creates a garden in which he hopes to attract a family of swallows. When two swallows flutter into his garden and build a

Spanish architecture enriches the illustrations for a Mexican folktale.
From *The Riddle of the Drum: A Tale from Tizapán, Mexico* by Verna Aardema, illustrated by Tony Chen. Illustrations copyright © 1979 by Tony Chen. Reprinted by permission of Four Winds Press (A Division of Scholastic Book Services).

nest, Juan's wish is fulfilled. Politi's illustrations recreate the Spanish architecture of the mission and demonstrate a young boy's love for plants and birds.

The Christmas season with the Posada celebration is one of the most important holidays in the Spanish American tradition. Two other picture storybooks by Politi center around this important occasion. *Pedro, the Angel of Olvera Street* is the story of a boy who lives on Olvera Street in Los Angeles. Pedro loves his street with its red-tiled pavement and old adobe houses, the *puestos* ("shops") with their colorful wares, the smell of his favorite foods, the Mexican songs played on his

grandfather's violin, and best of all, the friendly people who live there. His greatest happiness occurs when he is chosen to lead the Posada procession and the singing of Christmas songs. Politi's illustrations depict the square, the artisans at work (e.g., blacksmith, sandal maker, glassblower, candle maker, pot maker, and silversmith), and the colorful Posada celebration. Two songs that may be shared with children are included in this book.

Politi's other picture storybook about the Christmas celebration is *The Nicest Gift.* The hero of this story, Carlitos, lives with his family and his dog, Blanco, in the barrio of East Los Angeles. He accompanies his mother as she goes to the *mercado* (the "marketplace") to buy foods and other goods for the holiday. Unhappily, Blanco is lost at the market. The best gift occurs on Christmas Eve when Blanco finds Carlitos. This book is filled with Spanish terms associated with the celebration.

Marie Hall Ets and Aurora Labastida's *Nine Days to Christmas, a Story of Mexico,* tells of a kindergarten child who is excited because she is going to have her own special Christmas party complete with piñata. The illustrations show Ceci as she looks at the piñatas outside the factory, goes to kindergarten, plays with her dolls, plays in the patio of her home, visits the park, chooses her piñata at the market, fills the piñata, joins the Posada procession, and watches her beautiful piñata broken at the party. Ceci is unhappy until she sees a star in the sky that resembles her piñata. Children relate to the girl's feelings and learn about the Mexican celebration of Christmas when they read this book. This story also depicts a middle-class family who lives in an attractive city home. Children can see that poverty is not the natural condition of all people with a Spanish heritage.

While the majority of books for younger children about Spanish American celebrations concentrate on the Christmas holidays, the celebration of Cinco de Mayo, the commemoration of May 5, 1862, when the Mexican army defeated the French army, is also a major holiday. June Behrens's *Fiesta!* is a nonfiction book describing the modern-day celebration of this holiday. Photographs show a Mexican American festival where music is played by a mariachi band, costumed dancers perform traditional Mexican dances, and young and old enjoy the celebration. Photographs also illustrate children at school as they learn about and participate in the Cinco de Mayo activities. The book closes with a message from the author suggesting that Americans of all heritages have shared an experience and become good amigos.

Historical Fiction for Children in Middle and Upper Elementary Grades. A book with a more documentary approach to

Spanish American history and life in the United States is Marian L. Martinello and Samuel P. Nesmith's *With Domingo Leal in San Antonio 1734.* Published by the University of Texas Institute of Texas Cultures at San Antonio, the book depicts a day in the life of a young Spanish boy who traveled with his family from the Canary Islands through Mexico to the Villa de San Fernando on the banks of the Rio San Antonio de Padua. It is based on research about the "people who lived and events which did or could have occurred in the Villa de San Fernando, the mission and the presidio of San Antonio in 1734" (p. 8). This book strengthens the understanding of a lengthy Spanish heritage in the southwestern United States. It also demonstrates that people of Spanish ancestry were living on the North American frontier.

The setting for another book stressing Spanish heritage, Ann Nolan Clark's *Year Walk,* is the sheep-ranching region of Idaho in the early 1900s. In order to research the Spanish Basque background of the book, Clark interviewed Basque families living in the Pyrenees. After researching Basque history, traditions, culture, and language, she visited, during different times of the year, a sheep ranch in the area where the Basques settled in Idaho. She saw lambing, shearing, and the sheepherders on the trails with their dogs, mules, and sheep. Her research, along with her knowledge of the western mountains, creates a story with a strong respect for the contributions of Spanish Americans.

Clark develops a strong Basque background by beginning her story in Spain as a Basque family considers the request of Pedro, a Spanish Basque immigrant who is godfather to their son, Kepa. Pedro asks that Kepa come to America as an apprentice sheepherder. Clark describes Kepa's experience as he leaves his family in the Spanish Pyrenees and travels to Boise, Idaho, where his godfather owns a vast ranch with many sheep. The author suggests what it means to be a Basque sheepherder as she describes Kepa's lonely experience as he guides 2,500 sheep to a safe grazing destination 400 miles from the ranch. During this time, he loses the guidance of the old sheepherder who was to train him, bears the lonely weeks with only a dog and a mule for company, fights coyotes and rattlesnakes, and saves his sheep from flash floods.

Clark encourages readers to understand how much the experience has affected Kepa as he descends the slopes and thinks about how he has changed and considers the hard decision that he still must make: Will he be a sheepherder of a flock in Spain or in America? When he decides to stay with his godfather, the conversation between the two indicates their reverence for the close family feelings that are part of the Basque heritage.

Joseph Krumgold's *... And Now Miguel,* based on a full-length documentary film feature, is the story of the Chavez family who has been raising sheep in New Mexico since before it became part of the United States; prior to that time, their ancestors raised sheep in Spain. The author tells the story from the viewpoint of the middle child, Miguel, who, unlike his older brother, is too young to get everything he wants and, unlike his younger brother, is too old to be happy with everything he has. Miguel has a secret wish to accompany the older family members when they herd the sheep to the summer grazing land in the Sangre de Cristo Mountains. With the help of San Ysidro, the patron saint of farmers, Miguel strives to make everyone see that he is ready for this responsible journey. When he is allowed to accompany his elders on the drive and reaches the summer camp, he feels the greatest of pride in his family's traditions and in his own accomplishments:

In this place many men named Chavez had come. Those I could remember, and then my grandfather as well. And my father, Blas and my uncles, Eli and Bonifacio. And my brothers, Blasito and Gabriel. And now, watching the shining world as I knew it would look when I came to this place, I stood, Miguel. (p. 244)

Krumgold visited the real Miguel and his family when the original film was produced; he celebrated saints' days with the family and observed all the important functions of a sheep ranch. He grew to know a closely knit family with a proud heritage going back to ancient Spain.

Although these stories are interesting, well written, and develop an understanding of the Basque heritage, they also focus attention on the need for greater variety in the literature. There is a lack of contemporary realistic fiction, biographies, and historical stories about Hispanic Americans.

Puerto Rican Literature

Adults and children who are looking for excellent literature stressing the traditional Puerto Rican heritage, information about the Puerto Rican culture, or contemporary experiences of Puerto Ricans in America are disappointed by the lack of available stories. The beautifully illustrated traditional tale *The Rainbow-Colored Horse* presents an example of the traditional heritage and implies a rich store of folktales that could be written for children. In the other stories to be discussed, the first has a strong male character who solves a problem and buys his mother a longed-for Christmas gift. The second story has a memorable female character.

Folktales. Pura Belpré's *The Rainbow-Colored Horse* is a Puerto Rican tale written in the manner of a traditional folk tale.

The tale includes motifs found in tales from other cultures: two "superior" sons cannot solve a problem (the fields are mysteriously trampled); the quietest and gentlest son solves the problem (a rainbow horse is in the field); the youngest son is granted three wishes if he will not capture the horse; a king offers his daughter's hand in marriage to anyone who can meet a challenge (while riding a horse at full gallop, the winner must toss balls into the princess's lap); the supernatural horse makes it possible for the hero to pass the test. The tales suggest a universality in folktales and the people who tell them and enjoy them. The Spanish names and the inclusion of Spanish phrases create a strong Spanish heritage.

Realistic Fiction. A ten-year-old boy's longing to give his mother a Christmas gift and relieve the cold and loneliness of a new land creates a touching story in Joan M. Lexau's *José's Christmas Secret.* The reasons for the family's misfortunes are made believable as the author describes changes that happen soon after they arrive in New York City from Puerto Rico: José's father dies, his mother must find a job, and their funds are quickly depleted. Their family and friends who might have helped them are in a distant land, and José feels that his family is surrounded by uncaring strangers. In order to buy a warm blanket for his mother, José gets a job selling Christmas trees. His earnings do not grow rapidly enough to buy the gift until, on Christmas Eve, he takes a tree to a busy street. In order to drive away the cold and bolster his courage, he remembers his mother's advice: "When you feel like crying, sing—sing the tears away" (p. 41). José begins singing Christmas carols and attracts a crowd who follow him to the Christmas tree lot and buy the remaining trees. He now has enough money to buy a warm red blanket. He has also discovered that the big city is not as cold and lonely as he had previously imagined.

Many of the problems experienced by a family from a different culture are expressed in this book. For example, José's mother undergoes the frustration of trying to learn a new language rapidly. She also has feelings of accomplishment: although her husband has died, her new job allows her to walk with pride without needing welfare. Close family ties and concern for the children's welfare are shown as José and Tomás, his younger brother, are *niños de casa* ("children of the home") who are not allowed to go anywhere except to school without their mother. Strong values are apparent when the children feel guilty about keeping José's job a secret from their mother. Time concepts are frustrating, and they feel they live by the clock as if they were machines. Names also create a problem when teachers do not understand the Puerto Rican way of writing a name:

A young boy discovers that singing sells Christmas trees. Illustration from the book *José's Christmas Secret* by Joan M. Lexau. Illustrations by Don Bolognese. Copyright © 1963 by Joan M. Lexau. Reprinted by permission of The Dial Press and E.P. Dutton.

The teacher had been new and it was hard for her to understand that the last name was the name of the mother and the name in the middle that of the father. But after many Puerto Rican parents had argued with her about it, she had at last understood. (p. 36)

Unlike José, Nicholasa Mohr's eight-year-old *Felita* has lived in her New York City neighborhood for as long as she can remember. The author develops Felita's love for her neighborhood through her actions: She walks down the street and can greet everyone by name; her dearest friends live in the apartments on the block; she loves the old stores that face the street; and her grandmother, Abuelita, lives nearby. Conflict results when her father decides that the family must move to a better neighborhood where the schools are better and the threats of gang violence are decreased. The author describes the reactions of the people in the new neighborhood as they call Felita names, tear her clothes, and tell her to move away. Her mother is shocked by the children's attitudes and tells Felita that she must not hate because that could make her as mean inside as the people who are attacking her. She advises Felita:

Instead you must learn to love yourself. This is more important. To love yourself and feel worthy, despite anything they might say against you and your family! That is the real victory. It will make you strong inside. (p. 39)

When violence against the family continues and no one offers to help them, they move back to the old neighborhood. The author explores Felita's various feelings and reactions as she experiences anger, sorrow, and humiliation, and finally regains her feelings of self-worth. With her grandmother's help, Felita returns to her happy, lively self, secure in the surroundings of her warm, loving family and friends. The neighborhood and the people seem real in *Felita,* perhaps because Mohr was born and grew up in a similar neighborhood in New York City.

Information on the history and contributions of Puerto Ricans, Mexican Americans, and Cubans is discussed in Milton Meltzer's *The Hispanic Americans.* The author explores the influence of Spaniards as a result of exploration and colonization. Then he considers the development of the political, economic, and cultural status of Hispanic Americans. The author's chapter on the harmful influences of racism provides thought-provoking discussion material for older readers.

ASIAN AMERICAN LITERATURE

There are few highly recommended books written from an Asian American perspective. The widest range of Asian American experiences can be found in the works of Laurence Yep, who writes with sensitivity about Chinese Americans who, like himself, have lived in San Francisco, California. His characters overcome the stereotypes associated with Asian American literature, while the stories integrate information about the cultural heritage into the everyday lives of the people involved. His literature has received the International Reading Association's 1976 Children's Book Award and a Newbery Honor Book award.

An Asian American girl solves her own problems in this mystery. From Eleanor Estes, *The Lost Umbrella of Kim Chu.* Text copyright © 1978 Eleanor Estes. Illustrations copyright © 1978 Jacqueline Ayer. Reprinted with the permission of Atheneum Publishers.

Evaluating Asian American Literature

The Council on Interracial Books for Children (9, pp. 87–90) has developed the following criteria for evaluating Asian American literature:

1 The book should reflect the realities and way of life of the Asian American people. Is the story accurate for the historical period and cultural context of the story? Are the characters from a variety of social and economic levels? Does the plot exaggerate the "exoticism" or "mysticism" of the

customs and festivals of the Asian American culture? Are festivals put into the perspective of everyday activities?

2 The book should transcend stereotypes. Are problems handled by the Asian American characters or is benevolent intervention from a white person required? Does the character have to make a definite choice between two cultures or is there an alternative in which the two cultures can mingle? Do the characters portray a range of human emotions or are they docile and uncomplaining? Is there an obvious occupational stereotype in which all Asian Americans work in laundries or restaurants?

3 The literature should seek to rectify historical distortions and omissions.

4 The characters in the book should avoid the "model" minority and "super" minority syndromes. Are characters respected for themselves or must they display outstanding abilities to gain approval?

5 The literature should reflect an awareness of the changing status of women in society. Does the author provide role models for girls other than as subservient females?

6 The illustrations should reflect the racial diversity of Asian Americans. Are the characters all look-alikes, with the same skin tone and exaggerated features such as slanted eyes? Are clothing and settings appropriate to the culture depicted?

Books about Asian Americans

(Folktales from several Asian countries are discussed on pages 217 to 221 in chapter six, "Traditional Literature." These books may be used to develop the traditional values.) The guilt and fear that can result when a child takes a parent's prized possession without permission and then loses it are feelings experienced by all children. The prized possession in Eleanor Estes's *The Lost Umbrella of Kim Chu* is not ordinary; it is an elegant black umbrella with a secret compartment in its handle. The umbrella has great significance for Kim Chu's father; it was presented to him when he won first prize for the dragon he designed for the New Year's Day parade.

Children can sympathize with Kim Chu as she takes and then loses the umbrella; they can vicariously feel her excitement and apprehension as she travels to unknown parts of New York City, her relief as she proves the umbrella is hers by opening the secret compartment, and her elation as she excitedly retells her story to her family. Together with Kim Chu, children realize that it is truly "a happy day that begins bad but ends happy!" (p. 84).

While this book refers to cultural celebrations and the setting of Chinatown, it does so through the perspective of everyday activities. In addition, children can relate to Kim Chu; she is not stereotyped, she displays a range of emotions, and she successfully solves her own problems.

Laurence Yep's literature covers a wide range of Chinese American experiences in both historic times and themes. His works begin in the early 1900s when many Chinese are leaving their homes and families to seek their fortunes in the United States; they extend to the modern world of a Chinese American girl who knows little about her heritage as she tries to adjust to life in San Francisco's Chinatown; and they relate an experience of a modern Chinese American boy who must adjust to life outside his beloved Chinatown.

Dragonwings provides a story rich in Chinese traditions. The characters are strong people who retain their values and respect for their heritage as they seek a new future while adjusting to a new country. The setting is San Francisco in 1903. It is to the "town of the Tang people" that eight-year-old Moon Shadow comes after leaving his mother in the Middle Kingdom (China). He is filled with conflicting emotions when he first meets his father and joins his dream for the future. Even the stories he has heard about his new country cause him to speculate: some call it the land of the demons; others call it the Land of the Golden Mountain. Moon Shadow discovers his father's nature when he receives gifts from the Tang Men; they give him clothing and things for the body, but his father gives him a marvelous, shimmering kite shaped like a butterfly, a gift designed to stir the soul. Moon Shadow also discovers that his father is a friend and a guide when he joins the Company, a group of Chinese men who band together for mutual help and protection. He learns the necessity for mutual protection as anti-Chinese sentiment is expressed toward the group and toward himself. Moon Shadow also learns that his stereotype of the white demons is not always accurate. When he and his father move away from the Company's protection, Moon Shadow meets and talks to his first demon. Instead of being ten feet tall, with blue skin, and a face covered with warts, she is a petite lady who is very friendly and considerate. As Moon Shadow and his father get to know this Anglo-Saxon lady and her family, they all gain respect for each other. When they share knowledge, the father concludes: "We see the same thing and yet find different truths."

This book is based on a true incident of a Chinese American who builds and flies an airplane. In the book, Moon Shadow joins his father in his dream to build a flying machine. Motivated by the work of Orville and Wilbur Wright, Moon Shadow's father builds an airplane, names it *Dragonwings,* and soars off the cliffs overlooking San Francisco Bay. Having achieved his dream, he decides to return to work so his wife can join him in America.

Just as Moon Shadow discovered that his stereotype of the demon white people was in error, readers also discover that stereotypes of Chinese Americans are incorrect. This book is especially strong in its coverage of Chinese traditions and beliefs. For example, readers learn about the great respect that is felt for the aged and dead; family obligations do not end when a family member has retired or died. As Moon Shadow seeks to educate his white friend about the nature of dragons, readers discover the traditional Chinese tales about a benevolent and wise dragon who is king among reptiles, emperor of animals. Readers realize the strong value of honor as they join the doubting Company who come to pull *Dragonwings* up the hill for its maiden voyage. They do not come to laugh at or applaud a heroic venture but to share in their friend's perceived folly; if the Tang men laugh at Moon Shadow's father, they will laugh at a strong body of people who stand beside each other through times of adversity and honor. Children who read this story learn about the contributions and struggles of the Chinese Americans and the prejudice felt toward them.

Yep's *Child of the Owl* presents another vivid character who learns to look deep within herself to discover who she is. When Casey joins her grandmother in San Francisco's Chinatown, she discovers that she knows more about racehorses (her father is a gambler) than she does about her heritage. By attending Chinese school, talking with her grandmother, going to Chinese movies, and visiting Chinatown she begins to understand and respect her heritage. She is especially moved by her first Chinese movie; she discovers that Chinese are people who can be brave or sad. Yep, through Casey, develops a strong rationale for knowing about one's heritage:

I realized then that you don't have to believe in the stories. You don't even have to believe in the gods they're about; but you ought to know those stories and the gods and also know your ancestors once believed in them and tried to model their lives after certain good spirits. (p. 114)

Casey is a strong Chinese American female character who is an individual, not a stereotype. Yep has given her an alternative in her discovery of her heritage; she can respect and understand it and still live with her past experiences. In contrast to Casey, the boy in Yep's *Sea Glass* faces the unhappy experience of leaving Chinatown and learning to live in a non-Chinese community. This book contains less information about the Chinese heritage than the other two stories. Instead, it is about a boy who tries to fulfill his father's dreams of great athletic ability. With the help of an old Chinese uncle, Craig learns to respect himself and convinces his father that old dreams must be taken seriously. Yep deals effectively with the stereotype that sports is an avenue Asian Americans must use if they are to win the respect of their white peers.

The setting of Ann Nolan Clark's *To Stand Against the Wind* is wartime Vietnam. As the story begins, eleven-year-old Elm, a refugee living in America, is helping his grandmother, older sister, and Old Uncle prepare for the traditional Day of the Ancestors when those who have recently died are honored and remembered. As the head of the household, Elm must record the family history and tell his descendants about a country they may never know. His thoughts go back, and he remembers the beautiful countryside, the rich delta of the Mekong River that had been his ancestors' home for uncounted centuries. The author creates a believable experience as he describes Elm's memories and compares them with the last time he saw his village. Instead of the beautiful land he sees burned villages, bulldozed ground, and destroyed dikes. Elm remembers his father who loved the land and their happy family who lived together in the hamlet. He remembers Sam, the American reporter, who often visited them to learn about the Vietnamese. As the war progresses, Elm's thoughts turn to sadder visions. He remembers the male members of his family going off to fight, Sam's description of the fall of Saigon, and that terrible day when his village was accidentally bombed by American planes. Now his mother, his grandfather, his friend Sam, and his father and brother are dead. Elm and his remaining family travel to America where they are sponsored by a church group. This realistic story about a sad chapter in the life of a people concludes as Elm seeks to express his memories. The only words that seem appropriate, however, are from a proverb that his father had taught him: "It takes a strong man to stand against the wind" (p. 132).

If children are to learn about the cultural heritage and the contributions of the Asian American people, as well as discover the similarities between Asian and non-Asian Americans, more high-quality literature about Asian Americans is needed. Because biographies and autobiographies are especially good both for raising aspirations and enhancing understanding about the contributions and problems of individuals, it is appropriate to include biographies of Asian Americans in the literature written for children.

SUMMARY

Multiethnic literature helps minority children realize that they have roots in the past through a cultural heritage of which they can be proud. Through this literature, children who do not belong to that ethnic group can discover that all cultural groups have made contributions, and that all people have similar feelings and emotions. However, literature of the past has been criticized because of negative stereotypes. Researchers have identified such stereotypes in literature about Black Americans, Hispanic Americans, Native Americans, and Asian Americans. Criteria for selection are suggested to assist adults who are responsible for selecting literature for children.

The literature discussed develops strong traditional values such as respect for elders, love for beauty, respect for imagination, and a longing for peace and harmony. Many of the stories also reflect additional information about the culture and the language. Contemporary realistic stories emphasize similarities as well as differences among people. Stories with historical settings provide insights into values, behaviors, and contributions. There is a need, however, for a wider variety of multiethnic literature.

Suggested Activities for Adult Understanding Of Multiethnic Literature

- Collect several examples of children's literature written before 1960 that have black characters in the stories; compare these books with books written after 1975. Using the criteria to evaluate children's literature recommended on pages 492–93, compare the black image suggested by the literature of the two time periods.

- Bettye Latimer surveyed trade books published in the mid-1960s and the 1970s and concluded that about one percent of the books involved black characters. Choose a recent publication date, select the books that have been chosen as the best books of the year by the School Library Journal Book Review Editors or some other group that selects outstanding books. Tabulate the number of books that are about Black Americans, Native Americans, Hispanics, or Asian Americans. What percentage of the books selected as outstanding literature include minority characters?

- Many African tales have characteristics such as repetition of words that make them appealing for oral storytelling. Select several traditional African tales and identify the characteristics that make them appropriate for storytelling or oral reading.

- Choose an outstanding author such as Virginia Hamilton or Laurence Yep and read several of that author's books. What quality in the literature makes the plot and the characters memorable? What themes can be identified in the writer's work? Is there a common theme throughout all the writing?

- With a group of your peers, choose an ethnic literature area discussed in the chapter. Select five books that develop the eleven values of multiethnic literature discussed on page 489. Also select five books that do not develop the same values. Share the books and rationale for selecting them with the rest of the class.

- Compare the characterizations of Native Americans found in children's literature published before 1960 with the characterizations of Native Americans in books published after 1975. How would the Native Americans as either individuals or a group of people be described if this literature were the only contact with Native Americans? Has there been a change in characterizations between the literature of the two periods?

- There are several books listed in Latimer's *Starting Out Right: Choosing Books about People for Young Children* (17) that the Children's Literature Review Board does not recommend because of stereotypes, unacceptable values, or terms used in relationship to the characters. Read one of these books, such as David Arkin's *Black and White*, Florine Robinson's *Ed and Ted*, Shirley Burden's *I Wonder Why*, Anco Surany's *Monsieur Jolicoeur's Umbrella*, May Justus's *New Boy In School*, or William Pappas's *No Mules*. Are the review board's recommendations accurate? Why or why not?

- There are several classics, or old standards, in children's literature that have been praised by some, but criticized by others. In the area of literature referring to black experiences, Marguerite De Angeli's *Bright April* has been criticized because of the way April is subjected to prejudice and the prescribed formula for success that the story implies. Likewise, Ingrid and Edgar D'Aulaire's *Abraham Lincoln* has been criticized for overromanticizing Lincoln's life and depicting both black and Indian people in terms of the "white man's burden." Read one of these books. Discuss your reactions with your peers.

References

1 Associated Press News Release. "Blacks' Poverty Tied to Child Deaths." Bryan, Texas: *Eagle*, January 31, 1981 p. 3A.
2 Bader, Barbara. *American Picturebooks from Noah's Ark to the Beast Within*. New York: Macmillan, 1976.
3 Broderick, Dorothy May. "The Image of the Black in Popular and Recommended American Juvenile Fiction, 1827–1967." New York: Columbia University, 1971, University Microfilm No. 71–4090.

4 Byler, Mary Gloyne. "American Indian Authors for Young Readers." In *Cultural Conformity in Books for Children*, edited by Donnarae MacCann and Gloria Woodard. Metuchen, N.J.: Scarecrow, 1977.

5 Carlson, Julia Ann. "A Comparison of the Treatment of the Negro in Children's Literature in the Periods 1929–1938 and 1959–1968. Storrs, Conn.: University of Connecticut, 1969, University Microfilm No. 70–1245.

6 Carlson, Ruth Kearney. *Emerging Humanity: Multi-Ethnic Literature for Children and Adolescents.* Dubuque, Ia.: Brown, 1972.

7 Charpenel, Maurico. "Literature about Mexican American Children." Children's Literature Conference, College Station, Tex.: Texas A&M University, 1980.

8 *Council on Interracial Books for Children.* "Chicano Culture in Children's Literature: Stereotypes, Distortions and Omissions." In *Cultural Conformity in Books for Children*, edited by Donnarae MacCann and Gloria Woodard. Metuchen, N.J.: Scarecrow, 1977.

9 _____. "Criteria for Analyzing Books on Asian Americans." In *Cultural Conformity in Books for Children*, edited by Donnarae MacCann and Gloria Woodard. Metuchen, N.J.: Scarecrow, 1977.

10 Faulkner, William J. *The Days When The Animals Talked.* Illustrated by Troy Howell. Chicago: Follett, 1977.

11 Fisher, Laura. "All Chiefs, No Indians: What Children's Books Say about American Indians." *Elementary English* 51 (February 1974): 185–89.

12 Granstrom, Jane, and Silvey, Anita. "A Call for Help: Exploring the Black Experience in Children's Books." In *Cultural Conformity in Books for Children*, edited by Donnarae MacCann and Gloria Woodard. Metuchen, N.J.: Scarecrow, 1977.

13 Hall, Robert L., and Lederer, Richard. "Literature and the Minority Student." *Independent School Bulletin* 33 (May 1974): 50–52.

14 Haviland, Virginia. *North American Legends.* Illustrated by Ann Strugnell. New York: Collins, 1979.

15 Herbst, Laura. "That's One Good Indian: Unacceptable Images in Children's Novels." In *Cultural Conformity in Books for Children*, edited by Donnarae MacCann and Gloria Woodard. Metuchen, N.J.: Scarecrow, 1977.

16 Jenkins, Esther C. "Multi-Ethnic Literature: Promise and Problems." *Elementary English* 50 (May 1973): 693–99.

17 Latimer, Bettye I. *Starting Out Right: Choosing Books about Black People for Young Children.* Madison, Wis.: Wisconsin Department of Public Instruction, Bulletin No. 2314, 1972.

18 _____. "Telegraphing Messages to Children about Minorities." *The Reading Teacher* 30 (November 1976): 151–56.

19 Morgan, Betty M. "An Investigation of Children's Books Containing Characters from Selected Minority Groups Based on Specified Criteria." Southern Illinois University, 1973, University Microfilm No. 74–6232.

20 Norton, Donna E. "The Development, Dissemination, and Evaluation of a Multi-Ethnic Curricular Model for Preservice Teachers, Inservice Teachers, and Elementary Children." New Orleans: International Reading Association, National Conference, April 1981.

21 Stensland, Anna Lee. *Literature by and about the American Indian.* Urbana Ill.: National Council of Teachers of English, 1979.

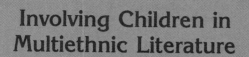

Involving Children in Multiethnic Literature

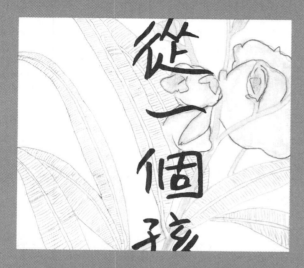

PROVIDING BALANCED LITERATURE
OFFERINGS

DEVELOPING MULTIETHNIC LEARNING
EXPERIENCES WITH CHILDREN

DEVELOPING AN APPRECIATION FOR THE
BLACK AMERICAN CULTURE

DEVELOPING AN APPRECIATION FOR THE
NATIVE AMERICAN CULTURE

DEVELOPING AN APPRECIATION FOR THE
HISPANIC AMERICAN CULTURE

DEVELOPING AN APPRECIATION FOR THE
ASIAN AMERICAN CULTURE

PEOPLE FROM ALL ETHNIC
BACKGROUNDS HAVE SIMILAR
FEELINGS, EMOTIONS, AND NEEDS

EDUCATORS are concerned with both the quality and quantity of ethnic materials available for sharing with children. They are also concerned with the teaching strategies used in developing positive attitudes toward ethnic minorities. Geneva Gay (9) says that the major ethnic minorities in the United States, including Hispanics, Black Americans, and Native Americans, "are the students most directly involved in and affected by dilemmas of cultural conflict in the classroom. Academically, they are the ones served most unsuccessfully by educational institutions" (p. 47). Authorities in multiethnic studies are very critical of the role played by schools in transmitting cultural values. Gwendolyn Baker (3), for example, says that little planning has been given to the process of multicultural education. She maintains that both college students and teachers require training in the concepts to be developed, the objectives to be achieved, the knowledge about various cultures, and the integration of multicultural concepts at all levels of education.

Following a study that attempted to change the attitudes of children toward Hispanic Americans, Shirley Koeller (14) concluded:

Evidence of these negative attitudes by children suggests a need for inter-group education, a need for curricula dealing with recognition and respect for our multi-cultural society, and a need for teachers trained in dealing with inter-group education. The crucial role of the teacher in influencing attitudes is widely acknowledged; adequate training of teachers is vital. (p. 334)

There is also support in the research for developing a multiethnic program that has a strong literature component. Frank Fisher (7), for example, asked fifth graders to read children's literature that developed favorable images of Native Americans. One group read the stories without discussion, a second read the stories and then took part in discussions led by an adult, while a third did not use the literature in any way. The greatest change in positive attitudes resulted in the group who both read and discussed the literature. Similar results were reported by Herbert Frankel (8) and Carol S. Schwartz (28). Results of these studies seem to imply that while reading literature is somewhat helpful for changing attitudes, it is more beneficial when combined with subsequent activities.

This section considers many types of activities that can heighten the positive value of excellent multiethnic literature. Many of the suggestions are a result of multiethnic research conducted by Donna Norton, Blanche Lawson, and Sue Mohrmann (18, 19) in both university and elementary classrooms. The results of this three-year research project indicate that college students, classroom teachers, and elementary children can improve their attitudes toward Black Americans, Native Americans, and Hispanic Americans if multiethnic literature and literature-related activities are encouraged by placing them in the curriculum and if teachers are provided instructions in selecting this literature and developing teaching strategies that can be used to accompany it. In contrast, this research also indicates that merely placing the literature in the classroom, without subsequent interaction, does not change children's attitudes.

PROVIDING BALANCED LITERATURE OFFERINGS

One of the greatest values of all good literature is a momentary glimpse of the glow of humanity when one experiences the problems and purposes, the hates and the hurts, and the values, dignities, and human worth of another human being who is both similar to and different from oneself. (p. 3)

This value expressed by Ruth Kearney Carlson (5) can be encouraged by the literature program if children have an opportunity to read a wide range of multiethnic and nonethnic books. (Although many educators are critical of the lack of multiethnic literature in the classroom, a well-balanced program should not consist exclusively of multiethnic literature any more than it should consist totally of fantasy or nonfiction. Children need experiences with many types of literature.)

A well-balanced literature program includes literature about all ethnic minorities as well as literature that shows a variety of aspirations, socioeconomic levels, occupations, and human characteristics. This literature should avoid negative stereotypes, allow children to see similarities and differences among people, and develop an understanding that children live in a culturally heterogeneous nation.

DEVELOPING MULTIETHNIC LEARNING EXPERIENCES WITH CHILDREN

Norton's research (18,19) has identified a series of steps that help preservice and inservice teachers create effective multiethnic learning experiences that also bring about positive attitudes in the adults developing the materials and in the children using them. These steps include the following:

1 Identify values that children can gain from multiethnic literature.

2 Investigate methods for determining and improving children's attitudes toward contributions of all people.
3 Identify traditional cultural values that may be highly valued in the literature and in the children's heritage.
4 Develop criteria for evaluating multiethnic literature.
5 Evaluate multiethnic literature available in libraries.
6 Select children's literature that provides positive multiethnic viewpoints.
7 Develop ethnic cultural webs that illustrate the varied subjects to be covered in the multiethnic literature study.
8 Develop instructional strategies and activities that encourage appreciation for ethnic contributions and an understanding of the similarities and differences between ethnic groups.

All of these steps are included in either the first part of chapter eleven or in this section. Each ethnic group discussed will be introduced with a cultural web developed by college students taking a children's literature course. The same students then created learning activities that developed the concepts identified on the webs.

DEVELOPING AN APPRECIATION FOR THE BLACK AMERICAN CULTURE

Using Black Traditional Tales—Adding Authenticity to Storytelling

The marvelous traditional tales of Africa are natural sources of materials for storytelling; they can appear more authentic, however, and increase children's understanding of this cultural heritage if African storytelling techniques discovered by folklore researchers are followed. There are suggestions for story selections, opening sentences, storytelling styles, and closing techniques that can be adapted by adult storytellers or children.

Story Selections. Descriptions of storytellers from West Africa provide ideas for selecting a story from a number of possibilities. Mary Kingsley (13), during her travels through Africa, discovered story minstrels who carried nets resembling fishing nets that contained objects such as bones, feathers, and china bits. When the listener chose an object, the storyteller would tell a story about it. Another interesting technique required the storyteller to wear a hat with articles suspended from the brim. A listener again would select an intriguing item, and the story

FIGURE 11–1

would begin. (See the cover of Verna Aardema's *Tales from the Story Hat: African Folktales*.)

These techniques can easily be used to help children select the story or stories they want to hear and stimulate their interest. Cardboard cutouts, miniature objects, or real items that suggest a character or animal in a story can be chosen. The items shown in Chart 11–1 are suggestive of the objects and the stories they represent.

Story Openings. Storytellers from several African countries introduce stories by calling out a sentence that elicits a response by the audience. For example, Philip Noss (21) relates that the following is a common story starter from Cameroon:

Storyteller:	Listen to a tale! Listen to a tale!
Audience:	A tale for fun, for fun.
	Your throat is a gong, your body a locust; bring it here for me to roast!
Storyteller:	Children, listen to a tale, a tale for fun, for fun.

If an adult or a child prefers to use an opening statement and response in an African language, this Hausa opening from Nigeria, identified by A. J. Tremearne (33), can be used:

Storyteller:	Ga ta, ga ta nan.
	(See it, see it here.)
Audience:	Ta zo, muii.
	(Let it come, for us to hear.)

If the stories are from the West Indies, one of these introductions identified by Elsie Clews Parsons (23) would be appropriate:

(1) Once upon a time, a very good time
   Not my time, nor your time, old people's time
(2) Once upon a time, a very good time
   Monkey chew tobacco and spit white lime

These openings can be used with any of the African traditional tales previously described, or they can be used to introduce a series of folktales. For example, Verna Aardema's humorous *Who's in Rabbit's House* seems particularly appropriate for an introduction stressing a tale for fun. An enjoyable series of folktales might include why tales such as Aardema's *Why Mosquitoes Buzz in People's Ears* and "How Spider Got a Thin Waist" in Joyce Arkhurst's *The Adventures of Spider*. Another series might include hero or trickster tales.

Styles of African Storytellers. The style of the traditional African storyteller, still found in many African countries today, can be characterized as a lively mixture of mimicking dialogue, body action, audience participation, and rhythm. Storytellers mimic the sounds of animals, change their voices to characterize both animal and human characters, develop dialogue, and encourage their listeners to interact with the story. They may also add musical accompaniment with drums or other rhythm and string instruments such as thumb pianos. Anne

CHART 11–1
Introducing Traditional Tales with Objects

	Object	Association	Traditional Tales
1	A flower	Receiving the gift of beauty.	Jan Carew, *The Third Gift*
2	A cardboard rainbow	Pia is trying to bring harmony to human world, while his mother weaves curtains from rainbows.	Jan Carew, *Children of the Sun*
3	A rabbit and a hut	Someone has taken possession of rabbit's house.	Verna Aardema, *Who's in Rabbit's House?*
4	The mosquito	The mosquito was not always noisy.	Verna Aardema, *Why Mosquitoes Buzz in People's Ears*
5	A large spider	How did spider get a thin waist?	Joyce Arkhurst, *The Adventures of Spider*
6	A box containing stories	How stories came to earth.	Gail Haley, *A Story, A Story*
7	A gum tupelo tree	The home of the mysterious, mischievous Jahdu.	Virginia Hamilton, *The Time-Ago Tales of Jahdu*

Pellowski (25) says that music and rhythm are important additions to African storytellers:

Taken as a whole, all storytelling in Africa, whether folk, religious, or bardic, whether in prose or poetry, seems to be strongly influenced by music and rhythm. It is rare to find stories that do not have some rhythmical or musical interlude or accompaniment, using either the voice, body parts, or special instruments. (p. 116)

Because children enjoy interacting with a storyteller and interpreting tempos with drums or other musical instruments, this is a natural addition to storytelling that can increase appreciation and understanding of traditional African tales. Stories such as Aardema's *Why Mosquitoes Buzz in People's Ears* and *Who's in Rabbit's House?* with their strong oral language patterns and varied animal characterizations can effectively introduce this traditional African style.

Ending the Story Time.   Just as African storytellers used interesting story beginnings, they also often used certain types of story endings. If the story was dramatic, it could end with the Hausa *Suka zona* ("they remained") or the Angolan *Mahezu* ("finished"). If the story was an obvious exaggeration from the West Indies, the storyteller might choose this ending:

> Chase the rooster and catch the hen
> I'll never tell a lie like that again.

Storytellers from the West Indies also provided an appropriate ending for humorous folktales:

> They lived in peace, they died in peace
> And they were buried in a pot of candle grease.

Children enjoy recreating the atmosphere of traditional African tales. Black American children, however, take special pride in the stories and the exciting ways they can be presented to an audience. Both adults and children can tell them and then discuss the traditional African approaches to storytelling and how these approaches enhanced the enjoyment for both storyteller and listeners. After the stories are told, they may be constantly read by students. Mohrmann (19), who used folktales with eighth graders with low reading ability, indicated that the children had never enjoyed reading materials as much as they enjoyed these African folktales. In working with children, Norton found that elementary children enjoy the folktales and their enrichment through traditional means of storytelling (19).

An Ananse the Spider Festival

Many folktales from West Africa include a character called Ananse, the spider, or Kwaku (Uncle) Ananse. He is the main hero in a series of stories from the Ashanti tribe in which animals speak and act as humans. These stories usually teach a moral or account for the origin of things. According to Harold Courlander (6), Ananse is also a cultural hero, often a buffoon, who is endlessly preoccupied with outwitting the creatures of the field and forest, people, and even the deities. He is an adversary in endless contests with his community. He is shown with a range of personalities: sympathetic, wise, cunning, predatory, greedy, gluttonous, and unscrupulous. There are moral teachings in many of his defeats that suggest he was humiliated or punished because of unacceptable behavior. As a cultural hero, some of his escapades result in creating a natural phenomenon such as the moon or beginning institutions, traditions, or customs. He has frequent encounters with the Sky God, Nyame, and the earth deity, Aberewa.

The Ashanti people, according to Gerald McDermott (15), have a long, established culture:

The Ashanti have had a federation, a highly organized society, for over four hundred years. Still, today as long ago, the Ashanti are superb artisans. They excel as makers of fine metal work and as weavers of beautiful silk fabric. Into this fabric they weave the rich symbols of their art and folklore—Sun, Moon, Creation, Universe, the Web of the Cosmos, and Anansi, the Spider. (p. i)*

Because the Ananse tales and Ashanti proverbs incorporate many black traditional personal values—wit, strength, verbal ability, achievement, and the attainment of a distinctive personality—they are excellent sources to stimulate discussions and enjoyment. The following ideas were developed with fourth-grade students who enjoyed the Ananse stories so much that they created a festival and shared some of the exciting activities they had experienced, art work they had created, creative writings of their own Ananse stories, knowledge of the Ashanti culture, and how the roots of present-day Black Americans may go back to the Ashanti culture:

1 The first Ananse tale shared with the group was Haley's *A Story, A Story* (the book that created the interest in reading additional Anansi stories) that tells how the "Spider Stories" of Africa were created. After the reading of the story, children talked about the importance of storytelling, the beauty of the repetitive language that allowed them to visualize an Anansi who was "so small, so small, so small" and a leopard so powerful that he had to be tied "by his foot, by his foot, by his foot, by his foot." The teacher

---

*Variant spellings—Ananse or Anansi—exist for this character.

shared the fact that African storytellers often repeated words to make them stronger. They also discussed the descriptive language connected with animals' names, such as the leopard "of-the-terrible-teeth." Finally, they discussed the wit, verbal ability, and trickery suggested by Ananse's actions in trapping the animals and acquiring the box of stories from Nyame, the Sun God.

2 The next series of stories shared were Joyce Cooper Arkhurst's *The Adventures of Spider*. The book was introduced in this way: "In the book, *A Story, A Story,* you learned how Ananse was given all the stories by the Sky God. This book contains some of the stories that are said to have been stories of Ananse the spider. In this book, however, he is just called Spider."

The titles of the Ananse stories found in the book were then written on the chalkboard:

"How Spider Got a Thin Waist"
"Why Spiders Live in Ceilings"
"How Spider Got a Bald Head"
"How Spider Helped a Fisherman"
"Why Spiders Live in Dark Corners"
"How the World Got Wisdom"

The class was divided into five groups of five children each after they discussed the probable contents of the listed stories and decided which story they wanted to share through dramatization or other visual approach. (If there are not enough children, or if some stories are not selected, they can be read aloud to the class or made available during free reading time.) Various methods of dramatizing their stories included pantomime, a puppet show, a play, reader's theater, a flannelboard story, and a box movie theater. The children in each group read their stories (each group read the stories orally because there were not enough books for each child to have a copy) and decided how they would share their stories with their audience. Activities for the next few class sessions revolved around the children preparing puppets, flannelboard characters, and so forth, and practicing their stories. The teacher went from group to group, giving assistance when required.

Each group presented its story to the rest of the class. After each presentation, the teacher led a discussion in which the children considered the characters, the moral suggested, and the traditional values found in the story.

3 Gerald McDermott's *Anansi the Spider: A Tale from the Ashanti* stimulated the creation of a mural which depicted the six wondrous deeds performed by Ananse's sons—See Trouble, Road Builder, River Drinker, Game Skinner, Stone Thrower, and Cushion—as they tried to save their father from a terrible danger.

4 In order to show where the Ananse tales originated, the children made a large map of Africa and identified the areas in western Africa where the Ashanti live. They also showed the movement of the tales from Africa to America. During the discussion of the movement of Ashanti traditions to the United States, several children showed an interest in tracing cultural roots and learning more about these people.

5 Margaret Musgrove's *Ashanti to Zulu: African Traditions* was shared in order to observe the cultures of the various African tribes and compare them with the Ashanti culture. The children described what they saw in each picture: beautiful designs in fabrics, intricate jewelry, clothing, animals, artifacts, and characteristics of geography. Pictures from other sources were also shared.

6 Ashanti proverbs were chosen from Harold Courlander's *A Treasury of African Folklore* (6). The teacher led a discussion, and the children talked about the fact that many cultures have wise sayings that have been passed down from generation to generation. They listed some of the proverbs they knew, and discussed the meaning of each. Then some Ashanti proverbs were introduced, the meanings discussed, and similar proverbs in their own families were listed:

Only birds of the same kind gather together.
Regrets are useless.
A man with no friends has no one to help him up.

7 Children wrote their own Ananse stories.

8 They compared contemporary writings about animal characters that are given human characterizations with the Ananse characters. Examples include Snoopy and Woodstock in "Peanuts," Heathcliff, and Winnie-the-Pooh.

9 On the day of the festival, the class invited their parents into a room decorated with their Ashanti projects. Their parents observed their creative dramatizations, read their writings, saw their art work, and listened to other information they had discovered about the Ashanti culture and Ananse the Spider.

Other Creative Dramatizations Using Traditional Folktales

The Ananse tales suggest the types of creative dramatizations that can result from sharing folktales with children. Because Aardema's Masai tale *Who's in Rabbit's House?* is written and illustrated in play form, it is easily adapted to the classroom.

The story's strong animal characters shown behind large masks, the lively repetitive words describing their actions and the series of short scenes that build up to an exciting but humorous climax create a story that children enjoy reenacting. A second-grade teacher read the story to the children and then discussed how it could be performed as a play. The children identified the characters and made large paper-sack masks to represent each animal: Rabbit, Jackal, Leopard, Elephant, Rhinocerous, Frog, and Caterpillar. Simple props were created, including a cardboard box (large enough to hold a crouching child) made to look like a hut with a door that opened and closed, sticks for Jackal to build a fire, and a large leaf that Frog could turn into a horn.

The children discussed how the animals would act in each scene. The teacher reminded the children that African storytellers are very good mimics of animal sounds and movements; consequently, they should try to create realistic animals through their voices and body movements. Next, the teacher read each scene and the children acted the part of each animal character. They were leopards attacking the hut with their claws, elephants showing how easily they could trample the hut, or intelligent frogs using their wits to trick the intruder into leaving the hut. Finally, they took turns being players and audience as they created the play with each player's interpretation of the animal characters.

Other teachers and librarians have used different ways to present this story through dramatizations. For example:

1 An adult read the dialogue, and children pantomimed the actions.

2 Children combined choral reading with the creative dramatizations; as the audience, they spoke the part of the feared Long One each time he refused to leave the hut and continued to threaten Rabbit. This was very successful because children could react as players and audience, both highly involved in the presentation.

3 Students became human puppets by drawing large cardboard shapes that covered their bodies with only their faces visible through an opening, or they turned large boxes into animals and placed them over their own bodies. The production was put on as a puppet show, but without the puppet theater.

Sharing and Discussing a Black American Folktale—John Henry

The tall tale of the steel-driving man, John Henry, as a poem, a song, or a longer narrative can stimulate many creative activi-

ties. Teachers have used the tale in its various forms with children in all elementary grades. In the lower grades, children listen to the story and discuss the large illustrations in the picture book *John Henry,* by Ezra Jack Keats. The language of the book makes pleasant listening while children discover that American folklore heroes are from different ethnic backgrounds. Through the story and pictures, they can gain an understanding of a tall tale and the kinds of actions a hero is supposed to perform. They can discuss other folk heroes such as Davy Crockett and Paul Bunyan; they can compare the remarkable feats of each hero and decide how much of each hero's story is exaggerated.

"John Henry" in poetic form makes a good choral presentation. Classes have tried the poem as a refrain arrangement in which a leader reads the opening lines of each verse while the class enters in on each of the repetitive lines, such as "He laid down his hammer and he died." Each verse can also be read in a cumulative arrangement (see pages 351–54 for descriptions of different types of choral arrangements) in which one group begins the first verse, the second joins in on the second verse, and a third joins in on the third verse. This arrangement continues until the poem is complete.

Older children may want to learn more about the history of the railroad, how tracks were laid by work gangs, and how the steam drill changed railroad construction. One group, for example, investigated the purposes of work songs and identified songs sung by railroaders and other types of workers. These work songs or chants were done as choral readings while the group pantomimed the actions of a work gang. One such chant, used by black Americans laying track, has a line chanted by the leader while the crew rests. It is followed by a response while the crew works in unison. The "shack-a-lack-a" response is an imitation of the sound made by the pieces of track as they are pushed into line with long metal poles:

Leader:	Oh boys, can't you line her?
Gang:	shack-a-lack-a
Leader:	Oh boys, can't you line her?
Gang:	shack-a-lack-a
Leader:	Oh boys, can't you line her?
Gang:	shack-a-lack-a
Leader:	Every day of the week we go linin' track (16, p. 19).

(Work songs from different periods in American history are also excellent sources of information about our country's history and its people. See page 479 for a selection of songs and the historical periods when they were used.)

Because there are several versions of the John Henry tale, the books, poem, and song can be compared. Is the story the same in each version? Are the illustrations alike or different? Which version is the most effective? Why?

Creative writing can be encouraged as children write their own work chants and tall tales. One class pretended that John Henry was a contemporary hero and wrote about the heroic deeds he could do if he lived in their lifetime. Stories described him saving the nuclear reactor at Three Mile Island, rescuing people from the upper floors during a hotel fire, and completing work on a superhighway or a skyscraper. Illustrations accompanying the stories showed John Henry as a strong man who was also concerned with the lives of the people around him.

Other classes have used tales about John Henry to stimulate creative drama. Scenes from John Henry's life that are good for this purpose include the following:

1 John Henry's birth when the moon stood still and went backward, the stars stood still and went backward, and a mighty river flowed uphill.
2 John Henry's early life. (One class speculated about what extraordinary things he might have done as a child.)
3 John Henry's job on a riverboat when he saved the ship from sinking.
4 John Henry's work on the railroads, the tunnel cave-in, and his saving of men's lives.
5 The race between John Henry and the steam drill.

Additional Strengths Found in Black Folktales and Ways in Which They Can Be Shared with Children

The following activities have been very effective in elementary classrooms and during library story time:

1 The strong sequential development of the cumulative tale in Aardema's *Why Mosquitoes Buzz in People's Ears* makes this story appropriate for a feltboard presentation. The story can be told by an adult using the felt characters and then retold by children. The cumulative language with its considerable repetition also makes the story appropriate for choral speaking. The teacher or librarian can read the beginning of the story and encourage children to join in as the repetition begins.
2 The Swahili alphabet, words, and numbers in two books by Muriel Feelings provide stimulation for children to learn some African words and more about African culture. While these books are not folktales, they can be used effectively either with a folktale presentation or for learning more about the culture. Although these books are picture-alphabet and picture-number books, an eighth-grade teacher reported that the students thoroughly enjoyed learning to count and say other words in Swahili. *Jambo Means Hello* presents the alphabet plus appropriate words and pictures depicting the culture; *Moja Means One* allows children to count up through ten. Children enjoy counting culturally related objects in the pictures and then using Swahili numbers in other situations.

Appreciation Study of Famous Black Americans

Increasing aspirations of black children and increasing respect for the contributions of blacks in American history are both values suggested by multiethnic studies. The Multiethnic Research Advisory Council that worked with Norton (19) on the development of multiethnic studies stated that one of its chief concerns was the inclusion of ethnic contributions throughout the years, not only during Black Awareness Week or other ethnic unit. This advisory council, made up of educators and community leaders who themselves were minority members, stressed the desirability of including literature that allowed children to investigate and share contributions made by Americans from all ethnic backgrounds. Nonfictional books and biographies about Black Americans discussed in this chapter and chapter twelve suggest a few of the many contributions of Black Americans to politics, medicine, science, literature, music, art, and sports. The following learning experiences were developed by children's literature students or research project members and then either incorporated into a school curriculum or shared with classroom teachers and librarians for inclusion with history, science, literature, art, music, or sports.

1 Have the children search the literature and develop a time line illustrating the contributions of famous Black Americans in history. Develop a bulletin board that illustrates the time line and displays literature selections that tell about the people.
2 Ask children to share their reactions after reading a biography about Martin Luther King, Jr. Have them interview parents and other adults about the goals of the late civil rights leader.
3 When studying the Civil War, read literature about Harriet Tubman and Frederick Douglass. Re-enact scenes from the literature.
4 After reading a biography about George Washington Carver, have students prepare a presentation to be given to the U.S. Patent Office requesting a patent.

5 After reading a biography, perform "A Day in the Life of
   ____."
6 Share literature written by black authors. Discuss the contributions and styles of such authors as John Steptoe,
   Sharon Mathis, Eloise Greenfield, and Virginia Hamilton.
7 After reading biographies or stories about black musicians, share and discuss their music.
8 Read biographies of black athletes and discuss records
   set or other contributions.
9 After reading literature about the contributions and lives of
   Black Americans, create a "What's My Line" game in
   which a panel of children asks questions while another
   group answers.
10 Using a "Meet the Press" format, ask children to take roles
   of famous Black Americans or reporters who interview
   them. Prepare for the session by reading literature.

Similar activities can be developed highlighting the contributions of Native Americans, Hispanics, and Asian Americans.

DEVELOPING AN APPRECIATION FOR THE NATIVE AMERICAN CULTURE

Using Native American Traditional Tales—Adding Authenticity to Storytelling

Native Americans, like African storytellers, developed definite
styles in their storytelling over centuries of oral tradition. Storytelling was an important part of earlier Indian life, and stories
were carefully passed down from one generation to the next. It
was quite common for Indians to gather around a fire or sit
around their homes while listening to stories. The storyteller
sessions frequently continued for long periods as each tribesman in turn told a story. Children have opportunities to
empathize with members of the culture when they take part in
storytelling activities that more closely resemble the original
experience.

Story Openings. Several collectors of tales and observers of
storytellers have identified opening sentences that characterized Indian storytelling. These openings may also be used
when presenting Indian stories to children. Franc Newcomb
(17), for example, found that many Navaho storytellers
opened their stories with one of these tributes to the past:

(1) In the beginning, when the world was new
(2) At the time when men and animals were all the same and
    spoke the same language

A popular beginning with the White Mountain Apache was

"long, long ago, they say."

Children can also search through stories from many Native
American tribes and discover how interpreters and translators
of traditional Indian folktales introduced their stories. They can
investigate further and find the exact story openers a certain
tribe would be likely to use. Then, they can use those openings
when telling stories from that tribe.

Storytelling Styles. The storytelling style used by various Indians of North America was quite different from the style described earlier for African storytellers. Melville Jacobs (12) described the style of Indians of the Northwest as being terse,
staccato, and rapid. It was usually compact with little description, although the storytellers might use pantomime and gestures to develop the story. Gladys Reichard (26) found that the
Coeur d'Alene Indians used dramatic movements to increase
the drama of their tales.

The listening styles of the Indian audiences were also quite
different from the participation encouraged by African storytellers. Children were expected to be very attentive and not interrupt the storyteller. Their only response might be the Hopi's
repetition of the last word in a sentence, or the Crow's responsive *E!* ("yes") following every few sentences. This response,
according to Byrd Baylor (4), was a sign that the audience was
attentive and appreciative. Children in classroom and library
story times may also enjoy using these signs that they are listening.

Morris Opler (22) discovered an interesting detail about
Jicarilla Apache storytellers that can be used to add authenticity and cultural understanding to Indian storytelling. Storytellers gave kernels of corn to children during story time. Because
corn was very important, it was believed that if children ate the
corn during the storytelling they would remember the content
and the importance of the stories.

Ending the Story Time. Melville Jacobs (12) says that Clack-
ama Indians ended many stories by telling an epilogue about
an Indian's metamorphosis into an animal, bird, or fish. Most
of the stories also had a final ending that meant "myth, myth"
or "story, story." Jicarilla Apache storytellers sometimes ended
their stories by giving gifts to the listeners because they had
stolen a night from their audience.

Teachers and librarians have found that adding authentic
storytelling techniques is an excellent way to increase understanding and respect for a cultural heritage. In addition, they
stimulate discussions about traditional values. After children
have taken part in both Native American and African traditional

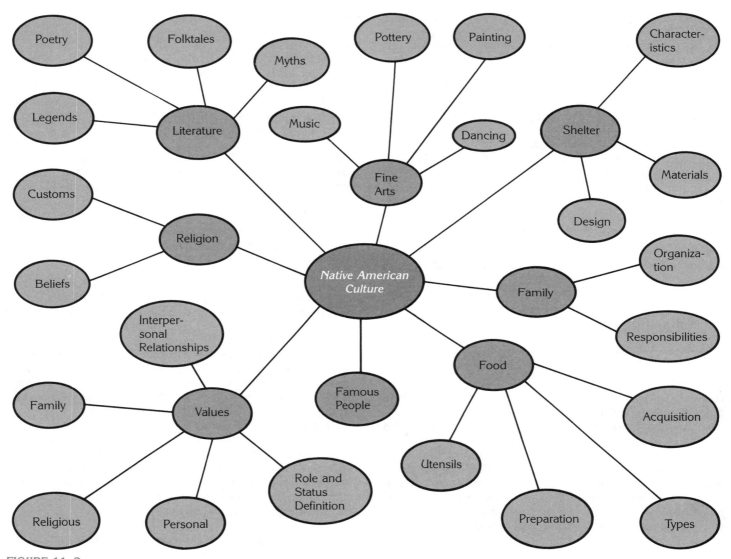

FIGURE 11–2

story times, they can also compare the oral traditions of both groups and discuss the beauty and style of each form.

Stimulating Creative Writing through Native American Folklore

The imagery found in Native American folktales is closely related to nature. The wind may suggest a ghost; the sky, a bowl of ice; the moon, a man smoking a pipe; sun rays, the earth maker's eyelashes; twinkling stars, a bird flying slowly; shooting stars, a bird darting swiftly; or the sun, a yellow-tipped porcupine. These marvelous images may be found in Indian lore collected throughout the United States; they are excellent sources that stimulate children to look at nature in a different way and then write their own stories using imagery and illustrations to suggest the relationship. One book that teachers have used to stimulate this type of writing is Natalia Belting's *Whirlwind Is a Ghost Dancing*. Teachers have shared this collection of Indian lore from many different tribes, discussed the images suggested, looked at the illustrations depicting the images, and then gone outside to observe nature for themselves. Children have been encouraged to look at their environment in new ways, try to picture relationships between the unknown and the known, sketch their interpretations, and take notes about what they experience. When they return to the classroom, they have turned their observations and sketches into creative, imaginative stories.

The pourquoi tales of the Native American, with their stress on telling how things in nature came to be, are another excellent source for stimulating children to write their own tales. One class, for example, wrote pourquoi tales after reading Bernice G. Anderson's *Trickster Tales from Prairie Lodgefires*. These stories appeal to the children as they tell about a half-Medicine Man and half-trickster character who is characterized as tall, lanky, and ungainly with thinning hair that hung like a frayed rope over his bony shoulders. He understood and spoke the language of the wind, people, birds, and even plants. Trickster had special powers that enabled him to turn himself into an animal, another person, or to cause others to do amazing things. Anderson's collection includes thirteen of these tales that provide answers to such questions as "Why Rabbits Have Only a Little Fat," "Why the Bob-Cat Stays in the Woods," and "Why Crows Are Black." The children wrote their own collection of "why" tales with Trickster as the main character, illustrated their stories, and placed them together in their own book. The book's preface includes Anderson's warning that these tales should only be told at night because as Trickster said: "If you ever tell stories or make jokes about me in the daytime, I'll hear you, and I won't like it. At night while I am asleep, you may talk about me all you please. But not in the daytime. Remember that!" (p. 93). (Another interesting activity using these Native American trickster tales is to compare them with the African tales of Ananse, the spider.)

Two other Indian folktales that have been very successful in stimulating creative writing are William Toye's *The Loon's Necklace* and Byrd Baylor's *And It Is Still That Way*. After sharing *The Loon's Necklace*, which explains how the loon was transformed from a common black and white bird to one with beautiful markings that resemble a shell necklace, children have considered many other birds and animals that have beautiful markings and written stories suggesting how they might have been rewarded with their beautiful plumage or coats. Examples include how the monarch butterfly acquired its beautiful black and orange markings, how the raccoons acquired their masklike appearance, and how the pheasant acquired its beautiful, colorful plumage.

Baylor's *And It Is Still That Way: Legends Told by Arizona Indian Children* has been used by teachers who are encouraging children from many different cultures to interview older adults or write down stories they themselves have been told. This book includes favorite stories told to Arizona Indian children by their families and other members of their community. It has been used in many classrooms to interest children in becoming recorders of stories that have been handed down in their own families. One teacher asked the class to record their favorite stories told by their grandparents or other older adults who came from a specific culture. The stories were divided according to culture and printed into a multiethnic folktale book for the class. Another teacher of older children asked students to interview older residents of the community and write down any stories they remembered that had been handed down from generation to generation in their own families. These stories were then recorded and made into a book. Children discovered the enjoyment found in storytelling and also discovered the importance of handing down a cultural heritage.

Sharing and Discussing One Book—Sing Down the Moon (Scott O'Dell)

Sing Down the Moon is based on a tragic time in Navaho history spanning 1863–65. The story begins during a beautiful spring in Canyon de Chelly when life seems promising. Then the U.S. government sends Colonel Kit Carson to the canyon to bring the Navahos to Fort Sumner, New Mexico. In order to force the Indians' surrender, the troops destroy the crops and livestock, then drive the Navahos to the fort. This three-hundred-mile journey is known as *The Long Walk*. While at Fort Sumner, more than fifteen hundred Indians died, and many others lost their will to live.

1 *Discussion:* The creation stories of the Navahos refer to creating the mountains as "singing up the mountains." What is the significance of Scott O'Dell's title *Sing Down the Moon?* What happened to the Navaho way of life during the years depicted in the story? Why did the government force the Indians to leave their home? If people today were Navahos living at that time, how might they feel? How might a soldier feel?

2 *Ceremonies:* When it was time for Bright Morning to become a woman, the tribe prepared for the Womanhood Ceremony.

Investigate the ceremonies celebrated by Navaho Indians. In groups, demonstrate one ceremony to the rest of the class. Explain its purpose.

3 *Folk Medicine Beliefs:* When Tall Boy was wounded, Bright Morning rode to the village to get the Medicine Man. The Medicine Man used the juice of mottled berries to treat his wound. Many medicine men effectively used herbs and berries to cure the sick.

Using resource materials such as Joe Graham's *Grandmother's Tea, Mexican Herbal Remedies* (10), research the various plants that might cure illness. Many of these herbs and plants have significant pharmacologic values. Identify the plants that have the greatest value and the illnesses that they can cure. Discuss the importance of medicine men, the reasons they were respected within the tribe, and what knowledge was required.

4 *Weapons and Tools:* Tall Boy made a lance to use against the Long Knives. The only materials he had to work with were those available in nature.

Find other weapons and tools the Indians used. Review how they made them and draw a picture of each. Choose an Indian weapon or tool and write instructions about how people would make this tool or weapon if they were Indians. Explain its purpose to the class. Bright Morning steps on a spear and breaks it when her son reaches out toward a young lamb. Discuss the symbolic meaning of this action.

5 *Setting:* Many clues in *Sing Down the Moon* suggest the environment in which Bright Morning and her tribe live. For example, O'Dell develops a visual image as he describes the canyons:

The stone walls of the canyons stand so close together that you can touch them with your outstretched hand. (p. 1)

He describes the rain through Bright Morning's thoughts:

At first it was a whisper, like a wind among the dry corn stalks of our cornfield. (p. 2)

Even the streams are suggested to have a voice of their own:

The stream sounded like men's voices speaking. (p. 53)

These descriptions of the environment also suggest the Navaho's respect for nature, characteristics of their environment, and whether they were a hunting or a farming tribe. Discuss the significance of the descriptions in O'Dell's language. How does the author feel about the Navahos? Search for other examples of visual language in the book that describe the various environments experienced by the Navahos as they leave their canyon and go to

Fort Sumner. Compare the canyon environment with that at Fort Sumner. Draw a picture illustrating both locations.

Describe two environments, one that is lovely and would be enjoyable to live in and one that would not be enjoyable. Draw a picture illustrating each; describe the pictures using language that will allow someone else to visualize them.

Art Interpretations Stimulated by Native American Literature

The traditional Indian folktales and realistic literature provide many opportunities for artistic interpretations. The books have vivid language and visual interpretations of cave paintings, pottery designs, ceremonial masks, sand painting, jewelry, dolls, descriptions of dwellings or clothing, woven rugs, basket weaving, and totem poles. All of these contributions to our artistic heritage may be developed with class projects, scouting groups, or individual children. The following ideas are examples of artistic interpretations used effectively with children in elementary classrooms.

Children enjoy listening to a Native American storyteller.

The designs found in cave paintings and on shards of ancient Indian pottery not only stimulate children to chronicle events in ways similar to those used by early Indian tribes but also suggest that the Indians' ancient culture existed long before the Europeans arrived. Teachers have used Baylor's *Before You Came This Way* for discussions about the animals common to the ancient Indians, plants used by them, and events that were important in their lives. They have encouraged children to carve, paint, and draw pictures resembling those found on cave walls on stone or rough paper. Murals have been made filling bulletin boards with the ancient happenings of people who lived in an area during ancient times. Children have also designed a pictorial story of their own lives for others to see. One teacher presented this problem to the class:

Our class is trying to discover a way to make people who may come to our land thousands of years from now understand what we look like, what we respect, what we do. They probably will not be able to read our writing, but we can leave them a message through carvings and paintings. (The group discussed how this could be done and considered the Indian drawings they had seen and talked about.) Pick out the most important things you want to tell these visitors from another time and draw your own story.

Another of Baylor's books, *When Clay Sings,* has been used to motivate the creation of clay pottery and the drawing of designs on the pottery. In another classroom, after reading and discussing this book, the teacher provided the following background information and had the children do a clay project:

The Indians dug their clay for pottery from pits and added fine white sand and crushed pieces from old pots to the clay. This clay was then mixed, water was added, and the clay was kneaded by hand until it was smooth as dough. For the base of the pot, a lump of clay was patted into the bottom of a broken bowl. Long ropes of clay were rolled out and then coiled around the base. The walls inside and outside of the pots were rubbed carefully to make them smooth. The pots were then placed in the sun to dry. After they were dry, fine red clay was rubbed over the pots. When they were dried again, they were put in a fire and baked until ready to use.

The class then made pottery from clay provided by the teacher. The designs suggested by the illustrations in *When Clay Sings* were used to carve decorations into the pottery.

The beautifully illustrated masks found in Baylor's *They Put on Masks* have been used to learn more information about the masks' significance, learn about the songs and ceremonial dances that accompanied many masks, and make masks that resemble those illustrated or make up children's own creative masks about something important to them. An upper elementary class investigated the masks and found additional sources that described how masks could be made from paper, cardboard, and papier-mâché. They adopted the directions found in Chester Jay Alkema's *Masks* (1), Kari Hunt and Bernice Carlson's *Masks and Mask Makers* (11), G. C. Payne's *Adventures in Paper Modeling* (24), and Laura Ross's *Mask-Making with Pantomime and Stories from American History* (27) in order to make masks characteristic of those created by different Indian tribes. Activities similar to those suggested for developing an appreciation for famous Black Americans are also appropriate for encouraging children to respect the contributions of Native Americans.

DEVELOPING AN APPRECIATION FOR THE HISPANIC AMERICAN CULTURE

Hispanic Customs

Children's literature written about Mexican, Mexican American, or Spanish customs stresses two customs in particular: La Posada, celebrated at Christmas, and celebrations connected with weddings. Christmas celebrations are found in Marie Hall Ets's *Nine Days to Christmas: a Story of Mexico,* Politi's *The Nicest Gift,* and Ann Nolan Clark's *Paco's Miracle.* Teachers report that younger children find La Posada with its traditional piñatas to be especially enjoyable.

A book such as *Nine Days to Christmas* is usually used to stimulate an interest in the holiday and its related customs. After sharing the book with children, teachers and librarians have asked Mexican American children to share their own Christmas celebrations and to decide if they are anything like the one described in the book. Librarians and teachers have shared the following background information with the children. The word *posada* means "inn" or "lodging house"; La Posada refers to Mary and Joseph's pilgrimage to Bethlehem. The celebration, which originated in Spain, is still celebrated in Mexico and in parts of the United States. The traditional celebration begins on December 16 and ends on the evening of December 24 (the nine days to Christmas). Nine community families usually entertain each other on the first eight evenings of the celebration. During this celebration, eight families form a procession leading to the home of the ninth family. The participants, carrying lighted candles and singing, beg for admit-

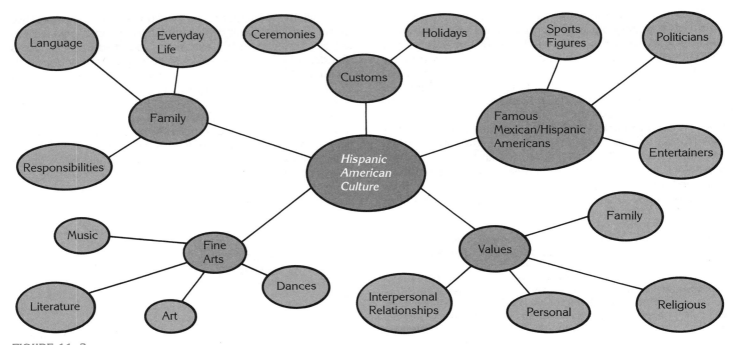

FIGURE 11–3

tance, but as Mary and Joseph were refused at the inn, they are also refused entrance. After this symbolic refusal, the families are invited inside for a celebration. The home may be decorated with a nativity scene, and a piñata is usually found on the patio. The piñata, which contains a clay pot filled with candy, is made out of papier-mâché. Children are blindfolded, turned in circles, given a stick, and are given turns hitting the piñata until it is broken and the candy falls out.

On Christmas Eve, the most important ceremony takes place: the procession is led by a young girl dressed as Mary and a young boy dressed as Joseph. On this last evening, the pilgrims are not refused admittance to the inn but are welcomed into the home or other community building. In addition to the piñata, fireworks, flowers, and lanterns often enhance the celebrations. This is a happy occasion, filled with singing, dancing, and laughter.

Adults usually follow this discussion of the Christmas celebration with other stories that describe the holiday and then help children have their own celebration with a children-made piñata and other decorations such as lanterns and tissue paper or crepé paper flowers that are illustrated or mentioned in the stories. In public schools, it is usually the piñata, the sing-

ing, the dancing, and the food that are stressed, not the religious reenactment of the Christmas Eve procession.

A star piñata, for example, can be made by inflating a balloon that expands to about eleven inches and then covering it with four layers of newspaper strips that have been dipped into starch or paste. A 3-inch circular area is left uncovered at the

Children learn about Hispanic customs and traditional celebrations by taking part in dramatizations.

stem end of the balloon for the piñata opening. Five star points are made by cutting and forming cones from three thicknesses of newspaper. The cones are made by overlapping the straight edges and cementing or taping them together. Around the bottom edges of the cones one-inch cuts are made, and the cones are pasted to the piñata form. After the form has dried, the balloon is deflated, and the shape is decorated with rows of colored, ruffled crêpe paper. Tassels can be cut from colored paper and added as decorations to the cone tips. The opening is filled with individually wrapped candy and unbreakable toys, it is tied by a rope to a tree branch or beam, and the children have their own piñata party.

Children can compare their piñata party with the ones described in the children's literature selections and with different Christmas celebrations observed in the United States and in other parts of the world.

Paco's Miracle, by Ann Nolan Clark, not only describes the Christmas celebration but also describes traditions centered around the wedding ceremony that originated in Spain. As Paco attends a fiesta when the family accepts the new husband, he also discovers the traditional value placed on items that have been handed down from generation to generation

and the various customs related to the wedding celebration. In this book, the author discusses customs that began in Spain, accompanied Spaniards to Mexico, and then traveled with settlers as they journeyed up the Royal Road to the mountains of New Mexico. These traditional customs can lead to lively discussions and dramatizations that enhance an understanding of historic customs, customs that are still carried on in much the same way as in earlier times, and compare present-day observances and those of the past.

Magdalena Benavides Sumpter (31) states that

weddings have always been an important part of a culture, signaling, as they do, one of the most significant events in a person's life. Special rituals and ceremonies surround the acts of courtship and matrimony, and although wedding customs may vary from country to country—and change through the years—their meaningfulness and sentimental value to the participants remains as constant as human nature. (p. 19)

She describes the wedding traditions and suggests activities that may be used with children in *Discovering Folklore through Community Resources.*

Following dramatizations or discussions about the traditional ceremony, children can compare the traditional Mexican wedding ceremony with a contemporary Mexican American wedding ceremony. Are there any similarities? They can also compare this traditional ceremony with wedding customs in other cultures. What are the similarities and differences? Children can interview their parents, grandparents, and older people living in their community to learn about wedding customs they have experienced or heard about. Children enjoy making some of the traditional Mexican foods discussed in the various books and mentioned in the wedding celebration.

Sharing And Discussing One Book— . . .And Now Miguel (Joseph Krumgold)

1 *Motivation:* Ask students if there has ever been anything they wanted to do very badly but were told by their parents they had to wait until they were older. Talk about some of the things the children mention. Discuss the possible reasons why they would have to be older to do those things. Then explain that this book is about a twelve-year-old boy who wants something; the story is about how he goes about getting what he wants.

2 *Procedure:* Because it will take several days to read the book, the activities listed can be used following the appropriate reading selection. The book can be read aloud to children or silently if there are enough copies. If each child

has a copy, the beginning of the chapter could be read aloud with the remainder read silently.

3 *Setting:* Chapter one describes the setting of the story in detail. Prepare a map of New Mexico showing the Sangre de Cristo Mountain Range, the Rio Grande River, the city of Taos, and the San Juan Mountain Range. Show the cliffs of the San Juan Range going down to the Rio Grande. Have the children locate and label each map detail. Then have them trace the migration of the sheep as described by Miguel in chapter one. The beginning chapters also mention the following landforms: cliff, mountain, mesa, plain, canyon, and arroyo. Collect pictures to show examples of each type of landform. Discuss characteristics of each picture and how the characteristics relate to the section in the story.

In chapter two, Miguel says that he must take his winter clothes to wear in the mountains even though it will be summer. Have the children speculate on the reasons for the differences in temperature between the plain and the mountains. Using reference books, have a group of children find the temperature ranges for New Mexico. Have them check other areas where there is a plain and nearby mountains so differences in temperature according to elevation can be checked. Lead them into a generalization on the effect of elevation on temperature and on Miguel's plans.

4 *Characters:* Miguel comes from a large, multigeneration family. Starting with Grandfather Chavez, have children make a genealogical chart of the Chavez family. Then have them make a chart of their own family.

The life of the Chavez family revolves around the life cycle of the sheep. Review the cycle with the children: winter on the mesa, back to the ranch in early spring for the birth of the lambs and the shearing, and into the mountains for the summer. Discuss the importance of sheep to the Chavez family and how sheep influence the life-style and desires of each family member.

Ask the children to imagine they are Miguel and planning their trip into the mountains. They will be gone all summer—they must take everything with them. Have them list everything they will need and defend why they would use valuable space on the pack mule to take each item.

Using a diary format, ask the children to pretend that they are Miguel and write their feelings and experiences as they try to convince the family that they are old enough to accompany the men to the summer pasture.

5 *Values:* Mutual cooperation and dependence within the family are important values stressed in the book. Discuss how each family member contributes to its welfare.

Another value developed is the strong integration of religious beliefs in daily life. There are references to this value throughout the book, but it is particularly strong beginning with chapter eight in which Miguel explains about San Ysidro to the reader. Grandfather Chavez is the embodiment of the values, whereas Eil has seemingly rejected the religious values.

DEVELOPING AN APPRECIATION FOR THE ASIAN AMERICAN CULTURE

Using Asian Traditional Tales—Adding Authenticity to Storytelling

A Japanese style of storytelling that is especially interesting to children is the *kamishibai*—an outdoor form of storytelling with pictures. Although it is not as old as the African and Native American techniques discussed, this style is different from either the African or Native American traditions.

Story Opening. Keigo Seki (29) identified an opening sentence that is often used in Japanese storytelling and can add an authentic flavor to the tales, especially if the storyteller begins the story in Japanese:

> Mukashi, mukash
> (Long, long ago)
> Aro tokoro ni
> (In a certain place)

Storytelling Style. Kamishibai was performed by men who had a collection of about four stories that were illustrated on cards and shown in a wooden boxholder resembling a miniature stage. The stories were illustrated on a series of picture cards and then placed in a wooden holder about one foot high and eighteen inches wide. The front of the theater had flaps that opened to reveal the stage. The cards fit into a slot in the side of the box; the storyteller pulled the sequentially placed cards out of the box; the text was written on the back of the card that preceded the picture that was currently showing on the stage. (The title was the first card removed and placed in the back of the box, the text that accompanied the next picture was on the back of the title card. This procedure continued with each card as the story unfolded in pictures and words.)

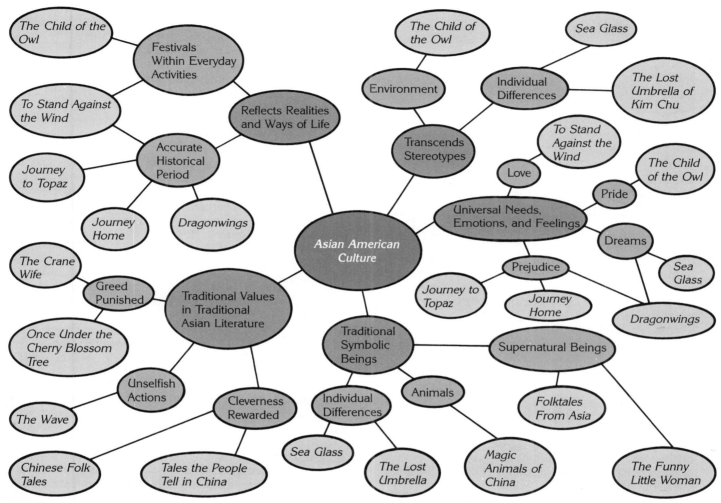

FIGURE 11—4

Anne Pellowski (25) describes how influential kamishibai storytelling has been in Japan:

Considering the impact that the kamishibai had on children's literature and the fact that the same publishers who produced the cards were also later producing children's books, it is no wonder that one of the most popular formats for children's picture books in Japan is the horizontal style reminiscent of the kamishibai" (p. 145).

Developing a Japanese Kamishibai Presentation. A kamishibai storytelling experience with its boxholder and picture cards is an enjoyable way for children to illustrate a story, retell the story, and also experience how folktales may be enjoyed among Japanese children. One group of children recreated a kamishibai theater out of a heavy cardboard box. They first cut a viewing opening in the front of the box. Next, they cut flaps that could open and close across the front of the stage and attached them to the front sides of the box so the flaps could be in either an open or closed position. Then, they cut an opening in the sides of the box so that the cards could be placed inside. Identical openings were placed on either side so that the openings would provide support for the pictures viewed on the stage. The side openings were made a little taller than the front openings so that each card would be framed by the center stage.

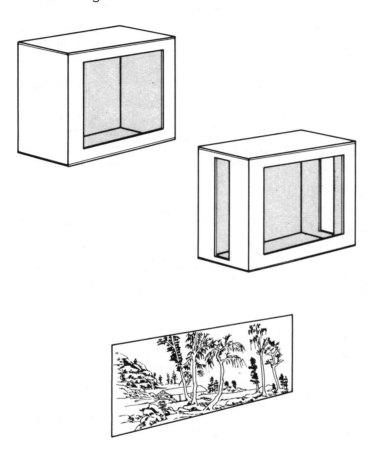

Next, tagboard cards were cut to fit inside the theater. The cards were a few inches wider than the theater so the storyteller could grasp them easily and remove them at the proper time. They were also slightly shorter than the side opening so they would go in and out easily.

The group chose a Japanese folktale to illustrate on the kamishibai picture cards. Arlene Mosel's *The Funny Little Woman* was selected for the first production, because the group wanted to illustrate the characters including the wicked Oni (demons who live in underground caverns) and the old woman who is kidnapped and forced to cook for the Oni. They

selected the scenes they wanted to illustrate, selected from this list the scene or scenes each one would draw (the original kamishibai presentations usually ranged from six to twenty scenes), and completed the drawings. They put the cards in sequence, including a title card for an introduction. Then, like authentic *kamishibai* storytellers, they wrote the dialogue for each card on the back of the card preceding it. They placed the cards in the theater and told the story to an appreciative audience. (As each card was removed, it was placed at the back of the box, so the storytellers would have their cues in front of them.)

This activity is especially appropriate for small groups, because each group can select a particular Japanese tale, prepare it for presentation, and present the story to the other groups. In that way, children can be both storyteller and audience. Other Japanese tales that make fine kamishibai presentations include Margaret Hodges's *The Wave* and Sumiko Yagawa's *The Crane Wife.*

PEOPLE FROM ALL ETHNIC BACKGROUNDS HAVE SIMILAR FEELINGS, EMOTIONS, AND NEEDS

One value of sharing multiethnic literature with children is to increase their understanding that those who belong to ethnic groups other than their own are real people with feelings, emotions, and needs similar to theirs. Elaine M. Aoki (2) says that literature can contribute to children's development of values. Consequently, she feels that adults must lead children in active discussions about those values. She says that this discussion should not be a didactic lesson but should help children gain positive attitudes toward all people. She identifies two steps that should be included. First, the discussion should help children focus on understanding others by having them take the viewpoint of a character in a story. When they are that character, they can consider what they would have done under similar circumstances; they can also consider how they would have felt if they had been that character. Second, they can search for elements within the story that are related to their own experiences. They can identify times when they had the same feelings, emotions, or needs as expressed by the characters in the story.

Many multiethnic books, especially those written for young children, have themes suggesting that children have more similarities than differences. These books can stimulate discussions in which children relate similar experiences they may have had, tell how they handled similar problems, suggest how

A child learns to value the contributions of a culture different from his own.

they would feel if they had a similar experience, and relate ways they might respond to similar circumstances. For example, after reading John Steptoe's *Stevie,* children can talk about how they would feel if a younger child came to their room and broke their toys, how they would solve this problem if they were Stevie, and the feelings they might experience if the child were no longer there. They can discover from discussing Lucille Clifton's *Everett Anderson's Nine Month Long* that feelings of jealousy over a baby are universal.

There are also many books for older readers that suggest universal needs, emotions, and feelings. The following books can be used to stimulate discussions around the topics suggested:

1 Experiencing prejudice creates strong emotions:
   Laurence Yep's *Dragonwings* (Chinese American)
   Nicholasa Mohr's *Felita* (Puerto Rican)
   Evelyn Sibley Lampman's *The Potlatch Family* (Native American)
   Gloria D. Miklowitz's *Dr. Martin Luther King, Jr.* (Black American)
   Mildred Taylor's *Roll of Thunder, Hear My Cry* (Black American)

2 People all have dreams that influence their lives:
   Laurence Yep's *Dragonwings* and *Sea Glass* (Chinese Americans)
   Joseph Krumgold's *...And Now Miguel* (Spanish American–Basque)
   Virginia Driving Hawk Sneve's *High Elk's Treasure* (Native American)

Rose Sobol's *Woman Chief* (Native American)
Michele Murray's *Nellie Cameron* (Black American)
Paula Fox's *How Many Miles to Babylon?* (Black American)

3 Discovering one's own heritage brings pride to the individual:
   Laurence Yep's *Child of the Owl* (Chinese American)
   Evelyn Sibley Lampman's *The Potlatch Family* (Native American)
   Virginia Hamilton's *Zeely* (Black American)

4 People can have strong feelings of love toward older family members:
   Ann Nolan Clark's *To Stand Against the Wind* (Vietnamese)
   Miska Miles's *Annie and the Old One* (Native American)
   Sharon Bell Mathis's *The Hundred Penny Box* (Black American)

SUMMARY

Educators are concerned with the teaching strategies used in classrooms to develop positive attitudes toward ethnic minorities as well as the quality and quantity of multiethnic literature available for sharing with children. Research indicates that reading literature is somewhat helpful for changing attitudes, but it is more beneficial to combine the reading with subsequent activities such as discussions, creative dramatizations, and other activities that stress the values and contributions of the culture. A well-balanced multiethnic literature program includes literature that shows people with a variety of aspirations, from different socioeconomic levels, with different occupations, and a range of human characteristics. The literature should avoid stereotypes, allow children to see similarities as well as differences among people, and develop an understanding that children live in a culturally heterogeneous nation.

Suggested Activities for Children's Appreciation of Multiethnic Literature

■ With a peer group, choose an ethnic group discussed in this chapter. Create a cultural web that can be used to identify important subjects that can be investigated through literature and literature-related activities.

■ Choose African, Native American, or Asian traditional tales. Prepare an appropriate story opening, storytelling style, and story ending that reflects the authentic traditional presentation of the tales. Share the stories with a group of children or a peer group.

■ Choose an African tribe other than the Ashanti. Suggest stories and other learning experiences that would allow children to develop an appreciation for its culture.

■ Search a social studies or history curriculum and identify Black Americans, Native Americans, Hispanic Americans, or Asian Americans who have made contributions during the time periods or subjects being studied. Identify literature selections that include additional information about those individuals and their contributions.

■ Develop a time line showing the chronology of famous Black Americans, Native Americans, Hispanic Americans, and Asian Americans. Identify literature that may be used with the time line.

■ Develop a "What's My Line," a round-table discussion, or a "Meet the Press" activity that stresses the contributions of famous Black Americans, Native Americans, Hispanic Americans, or Asian Americans.

■ Choose a Native American story and develop a series of discussion questions that would allow children to gain insights into the Indian culture as expressed in the book.

■ Develop a lesson that encourages children to appreciate the Indian artistic heritage; suggestions include creating masks, pottery, sand painting, and weaving.

■ Prepare the directions for a Native American dance; present the dance to a group of children or a peer group. Include the purpose for the dance and identify the Indians who created the dance.

■ Research one of the Mexican American, Puerto Rican, Latin American, or Asian American customs described in the literature. Plan an activity, such as a creative dramatization, that would allow children to experience the custom.

References

1 Alkema, Chester Jay. *Masks.* New York: Sterling, 1971.
2 Aoki, M. Elaine. "Are You Chinese? Are You Japanese? Or Are You Just a Mixed-Up Kid?—Using Asian American Children's Literature." *The Reading Teacher* 34 (January 1981): 382–85.
3 Baker, Gwendolyn C. "The Role of the School in Transmitting the Culture of All Learners in a Free and Democratic Society." *Educational Leadership* 36 (November 1978): 134–38.
4 Baylor, Byrd. *And It Is Still That Way.* New York: Scribner's, 1976.
5 Carlson, Ruth Kearney. *Emerging Humanity, Multi-Ethnic Literature for Children and Adolescents.* Dubuque, Ia.: Brown, 1972.
6 Courlander, Harold. *A Treasury of African Folklore.* New York: Crown, 1975.

7 Fisher, Frank L. "The Influences of Reading and Discussion on Attitudes of Fifth Graders toward American Indians." Berkeley, Calif.: University of California, 1965, University Microfilm.
8 Frankel, Herbert Lewis. "The Effects of Reading the Adventures of Huckleberry Finn on the Racial Attitudes of Selected Ninth Grade Boys." Philadelphia: Temple University, 1972, University Microfilm.
9 Gay, Geneva. "Viewing the Pluralistic Classroom as a Cultural Microcosm." *Educational Research Quarterly* (Winter 1978): 45–49.
10 Graham, Joe. *Grandmother's Tea, Mexican Herbal Remedies.* San Antonio: Institute of Texan Cultures, 1979.
11 Hunt, Kari, and Carlson, Bernice W. *Masks and Mask Makers.* Nashville, Tenn.: Abingdon, 1961.
12 Jacobs, Melville. *The Content and Style of an Oral Literature: Clackamas Chinook Myths and Tales.* Chicago: University of Chicago Press, 1959.
13 Kingsley, Mary. *West African Studies.* 1899. Reprint, 3d ed. New York: Barnes and Noble, 1964. pp. 126–27.
14 Koeller, Shirley. "The Effect of Listening to Excerpts from Children's Stories about Mexican-Americans on the Attitudes of Sixth Graders." *Journal of Educational Research* 70 (July 1977): 329–34.
15 McDermott, Gerald. *Anansi the Spider: A Tale from the Ashanti.* New York: Holt, Rinehart & Winston, 1972.
16 Metcalfe, Ralph E. "The Western African Roots of Afro-American Music." *The Black Scholar* 1 (June 1970): 16–25.
17 Newcomb, Franc J. *Navajo Folk Tales.* Santa Fe: Museum of Navajo Ceremonial Art, 1967. p. xvi.
18 Norton, Donna E. "The Development, Dissemination, and Evaluation of a Multi-Ethnic Curricular Model for Preservice Teachers, Inservice Teachers, and Elementary Children." New Orleans International Reading Association, April 1981.
19 Norton, Donna; Lawson, Blanche; and Mohrmann, Sue. *A Multi-Ethnic Reading/Language Arts Program.* College Station, Tex.: Texas A&M University Research Project, 1981.
20 Norvell, Flo Ann Hedley. *The Great Big Box Book.* Photographs by Richard W. Mitchell. New York: Crowell, 1979.
21 Noss, Philip A. "Description in Gbaya Literary Art." In *African Folklore,* edited by Richard Dorse, pp. 73–101. Bloomington, Ind.: Indiana University Press, 1972.
22 Opler, Morris Edward. *Myths and Tales of the Jicarilla Apache Indians.* Memoirs 31. New York: American Folklore Society, 1938. pp. viii–ix.
23 Parsons, Elsie Clews. *Folktales of Andros Island, Bahamas.* New York: American Folklore Society, 1918. pp. xi–xii.
24 Payne, G. C. *Adventures in Paper Modeling.* New York: Warne, 1966.
25 Pellowski, Anne. *The World of Storytelling.* New York: Bowker, 1977.
26 Reichard, Gladys A. *An Analysis of Coeur d'Alene Indian Myths.* 1947. Reprint. Philadelphia: American Folklore Society, 1969, 1974. p. 26.

27 Ross, Laura. *Mask-Making with Pantomime and Stories from American History.* New York: Lothrop, Lee & Shepard, 1975.

28 Schwartz, Carol S. "The Effect of Selected Black Poetry on Expressed Attitudes toward Blacks of Fifth and Sixth Grade White Suburban Children." *Dissertation Abstracts International* 33 (1973): 6077-A.

29 Seki, Keigo, ed. *Folktales of Japan.* Translated by Robert J. Adams. Chicago: University of Chicago, 1963. p. xv.

30 Sleator, William. *The Angry Moon.* Illustrated by Blair Lent. Boston, Mass.: Little, Brown, 1970.

31 Sumpter, Magdalena Benavides. *Discovering Folklore through Community Resources.* Illustrated by Santa Barraza. Austin, Tex.: Dissemination and Assessment Center for Bilingual Education, Education Service Center, Region XII, 1978.

32 Toelken, Barre. "The 'Pretty Languages' of Yellowman: Genre, Mode and Texture in Navajo Coyote Narratives." In *Folklore Genres,* edited by Dan Ben-Amos, p. 155. Austin, Tex.: University of Texas, 1975.

33 Tremearne, A. J. *Hausa Superstitions and Customs: An Introduction to the Folklore and the Folk.* 1913. London: Reprint.: Frank Cass, 1970 (pp. 10–11).

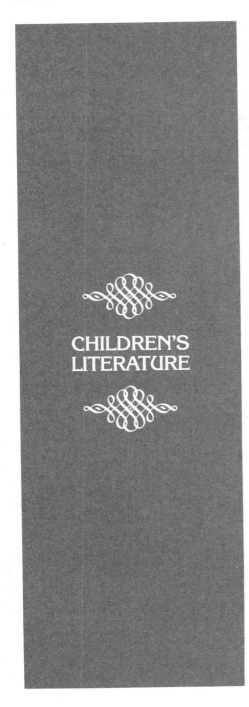

CHILDREN'S LITERATURE

Asian American Literature

Asian Culture Centre for UNESCO. *Folktales from Asia for Children Everywhere.* Weatherhill, 1977 (ch. 6).

Clark, Ann Nolan. *To Stand Against the Wind.* Viking, 1978 (I:11+ R:4). An eleven-year-old Vietnamese boy prepares for the traditional Day of the Ancestors. Although he now lives in the United States, his memories return to the beautiful land of his birth before it is destroyed by war.

Estes, Eleanor. *The Lost Umbrella of Kim Chu.* Illustrated by Jacqueline Ayer. Atheneum, 1978. Nine-year-old Kim Chu and her family live in New York City's Chinatown. The adventure begins when Kim takes a prized umbrella to the library without her father's permission. When someone takes the umbrella, she travels on an El train and the Staten Island Ferry trying to retrieve it.

Hodges, Margaret. *The Wave.* Illustrated by Blair Lent. Houghton Mifflin, 1964 (ch.4).

Mosel, Arlene. *The Funny Little Woman.* Illustrated by Blair Lent. Dutton, 1972 (ch. 4).

Yagawa, Sumiko. *The Crane Wife.* Illustrated by Suekichi Akabas. Morrow, 1981 (ch 4).

Yep, Laurence. *Child of the Owl.* Harper & Row, 1977 (I:10+ R:7). Casey must leave her father and live with her grandmother in Chinatown. She discovers that she knows little about her own heritage. While living with her grandmother, she learns to respect her heritage and most important, how to look deep inside herself.

———. *Dragonwings.* Harper & Row, 1975 (I:10+ R:6). In the year 1903, eight-year-old Moon Shadow leaves his mother in the Middle Kingdom (China) to join his father in the Land of the Golden Mountain (America). Moon Shaow experiences the "town of the Tang people," the San Francisco earthquake, and his father's building a flying machine.

———. *Sea Glass.* Harper & Row, 1979 (I:10+ R:6). Craig leaves San Francisco's Chinatown and moves to a small town in California. He faces problems as he tries to make his father understand his desires.

Black Literature

Aardema, Verna. *Bringing the Rain to Kapiti Plain: A Nandi Tale.* Illustrated by Beatriz Vidal. Dial, 1981 (I:5–8). A cumulative tale from Kenya tells how a herdsman pierces a cloud with his arrow and brings rain to the parched land.

———. *Tales from the Story Hat: African Folktales.* Illustrated by Elton Fax. Coward-McCann 1960 (I:5–8 R:6). Nine West African stories correspond with the carvings that dangle from the story hat.

———. *Who's in Rabbit's House?* Illustrated by Leo and Diane Dillon. Dial, 1977 (I:7+ R:3). A Masai folktale illustrated as a play performed by villagers wearing masks.

———. *Why Mosquitoes Buzz in People's Ears.* Illustrated by Leo and Diane Dillon. Dial, 1975 (ch. 3).

Adoff, Arnold. *Black Is Warm Is Tan.* Harper & Row, 1973 (I:5–7). A story in poetic form about an integrated family.

———. *Malcolm X.* Crowell, 1970 (I:7–12 R:5). A biography of the black leader, including information about his early life, his experiences as a hustler in Harlem, and the changes that took place in his life.

Arkhurst, Joyce Cooper. *The Adventures of Spider: West African Folktales.* Illustrated by Jerry Pinkney. Little, Brown, 1964 (I:7–12 R:6). A collection of West African folk tales.

Bertol, Roland. *Charles Drew.* Illustrated by Jo Polseno, Crowell, 1970 (I:7–9 R:3). A biography about the scientist who pioneered a method for preserving blood.

Campbell, Barbara. *A Girl Called Bob and A Horse Called Yoki.* Dial, 1982 (I:9–12 R:5). An eight-year-old girl saves a horse from the glue factory.

Carew, Jan. *Children of the Sun.* Illustrated by Leo and Diane Dillon. Little, Brown, 1980 (I:8+ R:6). Twin boys, the children of the sun, search the world to discover the values they wish to live by.

———. *The Third Gift.* Illustrated by Leo and Diane Dillon. Little, Brown, 1974 (I:7+ R:7). A beautifully illustrated tale of how the Jubas gained the gifts of work, beauty, imagination and faith.

Clifton, Lucille. *Everett Anderson's Friend.* Illustrated by Ann Grifalconi. Holt, Rinehart & Winston, 1976 (I:3–7 R:3). Everett Anderson is at first disappointed when the new neighbor is a girl, but discovers that girls can be good friends.

———. *Everett Anderson's Nine Month Long.* Illustrated by Ann Grifalconi. Holt, Rinehart & Winston, 1978 (I:3–7 R:3). Everett Anderson has a new daddy, and his mother is expecting a baby. He decides that they have enough love to share with another.

I = Interest by age range;
R = Readability by grade level.

Courlander, Harold. *The Crest and the Hide: And Other African Stories of Heroes, Chiefs, Bards, Hunters, Sorcerers and Common People.* Illustrated by Monica Vachula. Coward-McCann, 1982 (I:8+ R:5). The book includes twenty tales from the Ashanti, Swahili, Lega, Tswana, and Yoruba cultures of Africa.

Davidson, Margaret. *Frederick Douglass Fights for Freedom.* Scholastic, 1968 (I:7–10 R:3). A biography of the nineteenth-century black leader, including his experiences as a slave, his escape, and his work on the Underground Railroad.

DeKay, James T. *Meet Martin Luther King, Jr.* Illustrated by Ted Burwell. Random House, 1969 (I:7–12 R:4). Stresses the magnitude of Martin Luther King's work and the reasons he fought against injustice.

Desbarats, Peter. *Gabrielle and Selena.* Illustrated by Nancy Grossman. Harcourt Brace Jovanovich, 1968 (I:5–8). A black girl and a Caucasian girl share a close friendship.

De Trevino, Elizabeth Borton. *I, Juan de Pareja.* Farrar, Straus & Giroux, 1965 (I:11+ R:7). Story is based on the true characters of the seventeenth-century Spanish painter, Velazquez, and his black African slave, Juan de Pareja.

Feelings, Muriel. *Jambo Means Hello: Swahili Alphabet Book.* Dial, 1974 (ch. 5).

———. *Moja Means One: Swahili Counting Book.* Illustrated by Tom Feelings. Dial, 1971 (ch. 5).

Felton, Harold W. *John Henry and His Hammer.* Illustrated by Aldren A. Watson. Knopf, 1950 (I:7–10 R:4). The talltale of the American folk hero who inspired the railroad work song.

Fox, Paula. *How Many Miles to Babylon?* Illustrated by Paul Giovanopoulos. White, 1967 (I:8+ R:3). Ten-year-old James lives with three aunts in a tenement house in New York City. James discovers the truth about who he really is during a frightening experience when he is abducted by a gang of boys.

Fufuka, Karama. *My Daddy Is a Cool Dude.* Illustrated by Mahiri Fufuka. Dial, 1975. (I:7–9).

Greene, Bette. *Philip Hall Likes Me. I Reckon Maybe.* Illustrated by Charles Lilly, Dial, 1974 (I:10+ R:4). Beth Lambert experiences her first crush. A humorous book set in the Arkansas mountains.

Greenfield, Eloise. *Sister.* Illustrated by Moneta Barnett. Crowell, 1974 (I:8–12 R:5). Thirteen-year-old Doretha reviews the memories written in her book starting when she was nine.

———. *Talk about a Family.* Illustrated by James Calvin. Lippincott, 1978 (I:8–11 R:2). Three children discover that sometimes the shape of a family changes, and nothing they do can change the pattern.

Guy, Rosa. *Mother Crocodile.* Illustrated by John Steptoe. Delacorte, 1981 (I:5–9 R:6). A folktale from Senegal, West Africa stresses that advice of the elders should be heeded.

Haley, Gail E. *A Story, A Story.* Atheneum, 1970 (ch. 3).

Hamilton, Virginia. *The House of Dies Drear.* Illustrated by Eros Keith. Macmillan, 1968 (I:11+ R:4). A contemporary, suspenseful story about a family living in a home that was a station on the Underground Railroad.

———. *M. C. Higgins, the Great.* Macmillan, 1974 (I:12+ R:4). M.C. dreams of fleeing from the danger of a strip mining spoil heap but decides to stay and build a wall to protect his home.

———. *The Planet of Junior Brown.* Macmillan, 1971 (I:12+ R:6). Three outcasts from society create their own world in a secret basement room in a schoolhouse. Buddy Clark, a strong, street-wise boy, discovers that the secret of living on the planet is to live for one another.

———. *Time-Ago Lost: More Tales of Jahdu.* Illustrated by Ray Prather. Macmillan, 1973 (I:6–11 R:2). Additional Jahdu tale about a mischievous being.

———. *The Time-Ago Tales of Jahdu.* Illustrated by Nonny Hogrogian. Macmillan, 1969 (I:6–11 R:3). Four stories are told about the powerful, mischievous being who lives at the top of the Mountain of Paths.

———. *Zeely.* Illustrated by Symeon Shimin. Macmillan, 1967 (I:8–12 R:4). Geeder is convinced that her tall, stately neighbor is a Watusi queen. Geeder discovers Zeely's identity and also discovers her own.

Harris, Joel Chandler. *The Adventures of Brer Rabbit.* Illustrated by Frank Baber. Rand McNally, 1980 (I:8+ R:6). A standard English version of 31 stories from Harris's collection.

Hurmence, Belinda. *A Girl Called Boy.* Houghton Mifflin, 1982 (I:10+ R:6). A black girl goes back in time to 1853 and experiences slavery.

Jaquith, Priscilla. *Bo Rabbit Smart for True: Folktales from the Gullah.* Illustrated by Ed Young. Philomel, 1981 (I:all R:6). Four tales from the islands off the Georgia coast.

Jordon, June. *New Life: New Room.* Illustrated by Ray Cruz. Crowell, 1975 (I:6–8 R:5). Three children living with their parents in a two-bedroom apartment must make room for a new baby.

Keats, Ezra Jack. *John Henry: An American Legend.* Pantheon, 1965 (I:6–9 R:4). A picture storybook of the tall tale about the baby who grew up to be a steel-driving man.

McDermott, Gerald. *Anansi the Spider: A Tale from the Ashanti.* Holt, Rinehart & Winston, 1972 (I:7–9). A colorfully illustrated African folktale.

Mathis, Sharon Bell. *The Hundred Penny Box.* Illustrated by Leo and Diane Dillon. Viking, 1975 (I:6–9 R:3). Great-great-aunt Dew had a special box containing one penny for each of her 100 years. Young Michael loved to hear her tell the story of each penny and understood how important her old things were in her life.

Miklowitz, Gloria D. *Dr. Martin Luther King, Jr.* Grosset & Dunlap, 1977 (I:8–12 R:3). A biography of the black leader describing his feelings about civil rights, his crusade for equal rights, and his many accomplishments that led to the Nobel Peace Prize and Man of the Year award.

Molarsky, Osmond. *Song of the Empty Bottle.* Illustrated by Tom Feelings. Walck, 1968 (I:8+ R:5). A young boy works to buy a guitar.

Murray, Michele. *Nellie Cameron.* Illustrated by Leonora E. Prince. Seabury, 1971 (I:8–12 R:3). Nellie Cameron's desire is to learn to read. She gets her chance when a reading clinic and an understanding teacher are now found in Room 111.

Musgrove, Margaret. *Ashanti to Zulu.* Illustrated by Leo and Diane Dillon. Dial, 1976 (ch. 4).

Patterson, Lillien. *Frederick Douglass: Freedom Fighter.* Garrard, 1965 (I:6–9 R:3). The biography of a great black leader as he escapes first from his slave masters and then from slave hunters.

Schactman, Tom. *Growing Up Masai.* Photographs by Donn Renn. Macmillan, 1981 (I:8–10 R:5). Photographs and text describe the daily activities and aspirations of a Masai boy and girl.

Shaw, Jane. *Uncle Remus Stories.* Illustrated by William Backhouse, Collins, n.d. (I:8+ R:6). Thirteen of the tales originally collected by Joel Chandler Harris in a simpler form.

Steptoe, John. *Daddy Is a Monster . . . Sometimes.* Lippincott, 1980 (I:4–7 R:3). Two children, Bweela and Javaka, remember the times when their daddy gets angry and takes on his monster image.

———. *Stevie.* Harper & Row, 1969 (I:3–7 R:3). Robert is unhappy when Stevie plays with his toys and wants his own way. When he leaves, however, Robert realizes how much fun they had together.

Taylor, Mildred D. *Roll of Thunder, Hear My Cry.* Dial, 1976 (I:10+ R:6). A Mississippi family in 1933 experiences night riders, burning, and humiliating experiences but retain their independence and their pride.

Turk, Midge. *Gordon Parks.* Illustrated by Herbert Danska. Crowell, 1971 (I:7–10 R:3). Biography about the black photographer, poet, and musician.

Wagner, Jane. *J. T.* Photographs by Gordon Parks, Jr. Dell, 1969 (I:7–11 R:6). Ten-year-old J. T. discovers himself as he cares for a battered cat and interacts with people in his inner-city neighborhood.

Ward, Leila. *I Am Eyes, Ni Macho.* Illustrated by Nonny Hogrogian. Greenwillow, 1978 (I:3–7 R:1). An African child wakes to the marvelous sights of her land.

Weik, Mary Hays. *The Jazz Man.* Illustrated by Ann Grifalconi. Atheneum, 1966 (I:7–10 R:6). When the Jazz Man moves into the apartment with the wonderful yellow walls, life seems to change for a crippled boy living in Harlem. Then Zeke's mother leaves, and his daddy doesn't come home.

Hispanic Literature

Aardema, Verna. *The Riddle of the Drum: A Tale from Tizapán, Mexico.* Illustrated by Tony Chen. Four Winds, 1979 (I:6–10 R:3). The man who marries the king's daughter must guess the kind of leather in a drum.

Behrens, June. *Fiesta!* Photographs by Scott Taylor. Children's, 1978 (I:5–8 R:4). Photographs of the Cinco de Mayo fiesta celebrating the occasion when the French army was defeated by the Mexican army.

Belpré, Pura. *The Rainbow-Colored Horse.* Illustrated by Antonio Martorell. Warne, 1978 (I:6–10). Three favors granted by a horse allow Pio to win the hand of the Don Nicanor's daughter.

Clark, Ann Nolan. *Paco's Miracle.* Illustrated by Agnes Tait. Farrar, Straus & Giroux, 1962 (I:8–12 R:3). Paco learns to love a family in nearby Santa Fe and discovers their customs.

———. *Year Walk.* Viking, 1975 (I:10+ R:7). A Spanish Basque sheepherder faces loneliness as he takes his 2,500 sheep across the desert into the high country. He also faces the challenges and becomes a man.

de Paola, Tomie. *The Lady of Guadalupe.* Holiday, 1980 (I:8+ R:6). A traditional Mexican tale about the Lady of Guadalupe, the patron saint of Mexico, who appeared to an Indian in 1531.

Ets, Marie Hall, and Labastida, Aurora. *Nine Days to Christmas, a Story of Mexico.* Illustrated by Marie Hall Ets. Viking, 1959 (I:5–8 R:3). Ceci is excited; she is going to have her first Posada with her own piñata. This book has lovely illustrations of the Mexican Christmas holiday.

Krumgold, Joseph. *. . .And Now Miguel.* Illustrated by Jean Charlot. Crowell, 1953 (I:10+ R:3). Miguel Chavez is a member of a proud sheep-raising family. His great wish is to go with the sheepherders to the Sangre de Cristo Mountains.

Lexau, Joan M. *José's Christmas Secret.* Illustrated by Don Bolognese. Dial, 1963 (I:6–10 R:2). Ten-year-old José, his mother, and brother spend their first cold and lonely Christmas in New York away from Puerto Rico.

Martinello, Marian L., and Nesmith, Samuel P. *With Domingo Leal in San Antonio 1734.* The University of Texas, Institute of Texas Cultures at San Antonio, 1979 (I:8+ R:4). Results of research investigating the lives of Spanish settlers who arrived in Texas in the 1730s.

Meltzer, Milton. *The Hispanic Americans.* Photography by Morrie Camhi and Catherine Noren. Crowell, 1982 (I:9–12 R:6). The author discusses the influence in America of Puerto Ricans, Chicanos, and Cubans.

Mohr, Nicholasa. *Felita.* Illustrated by Ray Cruz. Dial, 1979 (I:9–12 R:2). Felita loves her neighborhood with all her friends better than any other place in the world. Then, her father decides they should move to a new neighborhood.

Politi, Leo. *The Nicest Gift.* Scribner's, 1973 (I:5–8 R:6). Carbitos lives in the barrio of East Los Angeles with his family and his dog Blanco. There are many Spanish words in the text and illustrations of the barrio.

———. *Pedro, the Angel of Olvera Street.* Scribner's 1946 (I:4–8 R:4). Pedro lives on Olvera Street in Los Angeles. He loves the shops on the street, especially during Christmas.

———. *Song of the Swallows.* Scribner's, 1949 (I:5–8 R:4). Juan lives in Capistrano, California. His special friend is the gardner and bell-ringer at the Mission of San Juan Capistrano. Excellent illustrations of Spanish architecture.

Native American Literature

Aliki. *Corn Is Maize: The Gift of the Indians.* Crowell, 1976 (I:6–8 R:2). A history of corn, how it grows, and how it was first used.

Anderson, Bernice G. *Trickster Tales from Prairie Lodgefires.* Illustrated by Frank Gee. Abingdon, 1979 (I:8–14 R:6). These tales tell why the rabbits have only a little fat, why prairie dogs are brown, and why crows are black.

Baker, Betty. *Rat Is Dead and Ant Is Sad.* Illustrated by Mamoru Funai. Harper & Row, 1981 (I:6–8 R:2). A cumulative tale based on a Pueblo Indian tale stresses the consequences of reaching the wrong conclusions.

Batherman, Muriel. *Before Columbus.* Houghton Mifflin, 1981 (I:6–9 R:5). Illustrations and text present information about North American inhabitants revealed from archaeological explorations.

Baylor, Byrd. *And It Is Still That Way: Legends Told by Arizona Indian Children.* Scribner's, 1976 (I:all R:3). This is a collection of tales told by Native American children.

———. *Before You Come This Way.* Illustrated by Tom Bahti. Dutton, 1969 (I:all). Poetry describes the Indian petroglyphs on the canyon walls of the Southwest.

———. *The Desert Is Theirs.* Illustrated by Peter Parnall. Scribner's, 1975. (I:all). The life of the Papago Indians is captured in illustrations and text.

———. *God On Every Mountain.* Illustrated by Carol Brown, Scribner's, 1981 (I:6–10 R:5). Southwest Indian folktales about the sacred mountains.

———. *Hawk, I'm Your Brother.* Illustrated by Peter Parnall. Scribner's, 1976 (I:all). Rudy Soto would like to glide through the air like a hawk, wrapped up in the wind.

———. *Moonsong.* Illustrated by Ronald Himler. Scribner's, 1982 (I:all). Written in poetic style, this Pima Indian tale tells how coyote was born of the moon.

———. *The Other Way to Listen.* Illustrated by Peter Parnall. Scribner's, 1978. (I:all). If one listens carefully, nature is heard.

———. *They Put on Masks.* Illustrated by Jerry Ingram. Scribner's, 1974. (I:all). The masks of the Eskimo, Northwest Coast, Iroquois, Apache, Hopi, Zuni, and Yaqui are presented in verse and illustrations.

———. *When Clay Sings.* Illustrated by Tom Bahti. Scribner's, 1972. (I:all). A poetic telling of the ancient way of life stimulated by designs on prehistoric Indian pottery found in the Southwest desert.

Belting, Natalia. *Whirlwind Is a Ghost Dancing.* Illustrated by Leo and Diane Dillon. Dutton, 1974 (I:all R:3). A poetic text depicting the lore of such tribes as the Dakota, Maidu, Shoshoni, Bella Coola, Zuni, Tlingit, Makah, Yana, Pawnee, Iroquois, and Crow.

Bierhorst, John. *A Cry from The Earth: Music of the North American Indians.* Four Winds, 1979 (I:all). A collection of Indian songs of North America.

———. *The Ring in the Prairie, A Shawnee Legend.* Illustrated by Leo and Diane Dillon. Dial, 1970 (I:all R:6). One of the most skilled Indian hunters discovers a mysterious circle in an opening in the forest.

Brown, Dee. *Tepee Tales of the American Indian.* Holt, Rinehart & Winston, 1979 (I:6–12 R:5). Stories are grouped according to animal stories, trickster tales, heroines, and ghost stories.

Bulla, Clyde Robert, and Syson, Michael. *Conquista!* Illustrated by Ronald Himler. Crowell, 1978 (I:6–10 R:2). Relates a story of how a young Indian boy might have experienced his first horse at the time of Coronado.

Clark, Ann Nolan. *Along Sandy Trails.* Photographs by Alfred A. Cohn. Viking, 1969 (I:all). Beautiful color photographs of the desert accompany a poetic text about a young Papago Indian girl and her grandmother gathering the fruits of the desert.

Coatsworth, Emerson, and Coatsworth, David, comps. *The Adventures of Nanabush: Ojibway Indian Stories.* Illustrated by Francis Kagige. Atheneum, 1980 (I:8+ R:6). Sixteen tales told by Ojibway tribal elders. Nanabush is one of the most powerful spirits of the Ojibways.

Dodge, Nanabah Chee. *Morning Arrow.* Illustrated by Jeffrey Lunge. Lothrop, Lee & Shepard, 1975 (I:7–10 R:3). Morning Arrow is a ten-year-old Navaho boy who lives with, and is devoted to, his partially blind grandmother.

Fall, Thomas. *Jim Thorpe.* Illustrated by John Gretzer. Crowell, 1970 (I:7–9 R:2). An illustrated biography of the great athlete from the Sax and Fox Indian tribe.

Field, Edward. *Eskimo Songs and Stories.* Illustrated by Kiakshuk and Pudlo, Delacorte, 1973 (I:8–12). Poems based on songs and stories collected by the Danish explorer Knud Rasmussen.

Goble, Paul. *The Gift of the Sacred Dog.* Bradbury, 1980 (I:all R:6). The Sioux tale about how the horse was given to the people.

———. *The Girl Who Loved Wild Horses.* Bradbury, 1978. (ch. 4)

Grant, Matthew G. *Squanto: The Indian Who Saved the Pilgrims.* Illustrated by John Nelson and Harold Henriksen. Publications Associates, 1974 (I:6–9 R:3). A simple biography of the Wampamoag Indian who was first kidnapped by English explorers and then helped the settlers at Plymouth Colony.

Harris, Christie. *The Trouble With Adventurers.* Illustrated by Douglas Tait. Atheneum, 1982 (I:10+ R:6). A collection of stories drawn from the Northwest Coast tribes.

Haviland, Virginia. *North American Legends.* Illustrated by Ann Strugnell. Collins, 1979 (I:8+ R:6). An anthology of myths, legends, and tales of North America including stories of the Native Americans and Eskimos; stories of black Americans; tales brought by European immigrants; and American tall tales.

Highwater, Jamake. *Anpao: An American Indian Odyssey.* Illustrated by Fritz Scholder. Lippincott, 1977 (I:12+ R:5). Anpao journeys across the history of Indian traditional tales in order to search for his destiny.

———. *Moonsong Lullaby.* Photographs by Marcia Keegan. Lothrop, Lee & Shepard, 1981 (I:all). Color photographs show the animals and other activities as the moon watches.

Hodges, Margaret. *The Fire Bringer: A Paiute Indian Legend.* Illustrated by Peter Parnall. Little, Brown, 1972 (I:7–10 R:6). According to the Paiute Indian tale, Coyote led the Paiutes on a dangerous quest for fire.

Jassem, Kate. *Sacajawea, Wilderness Guide.* Illustrated by Jan Palmer. Troll Associates, 1979 (I:6–9 R:2). An illustrated biography of the Shoshone Indian woman who accompanied the Lewis and Clark Expedition across the Rocky Mountains to the Pacific Ocean.

Keegan, Marcia. *The Taos Indians and Their Sacred Blue Lake.* Messner, 1972 (I:8–12 R:7). This information book presents the Taos Indians of New Mexico and their struggle to regain their sacred Blue Lake and the land around it.

Lampman, Evelyn Sibley. *The Potlatch Family.* Atheneum, 1976 (I:10+ R:4). A veteran changes his family's life when he returns with ideas about ways of reviving the Chinook Indians' respect for their own heritage.

———. *Squaw Man's Son.* Atheneum, 1978 (I:10+ R:7). The setting is Oregon during the time of the Modoc War of 1872–73. A boy is caught in the struggle between settlers and Indians.

McDermott, Gerald. *Arrow to the Sun, a Pueblo Indian Tale.* Viking, 1974 (ch. 4).

McGraw, Jessie Brewer. *Chief Red Horse Tells About Custer: The Battle of Little Bighorn—An Eyewitness Account Told in Indian Sign Language.* Elsevier/Nelson, 1981 (I:8+). Historical background and a glossary of Indian terms add to a story based on Indian pictographs.

Maher, Ramona. *Alice Yazzie's Year.* Illustrated by Stephen Gammell. Coward-McCann, 1977 (I:all). Poems that follow the experiences of a Navaho girl as she lives through her year.

Miles, Miska. *Annie and the Old One.* Illustrated by Peter Parnall. Little, Brown, 1971 (I:6–8 R:3). Annie's love for her Navaho grandmother causes her to prevent the completion of a rug that she associates with the probable death of her grandmother.

O'Dell, Scott. *Sing Down the Moon.* Houghton Mifflin, 1970 (I:10+ R:6). A young Navaho girl tells of the 1864 forced march of her people.

Poatgieter, Alice Hermina. *Indian Legacy: Native American Influences on World Life and Culture.* Messner, 1981 (I:10+ R:7). Author presents North and South American Indian contributions to democratic attitudes, agriculture, and culture.

Pine, Tillie S., and Levine, Joseph. *The Indians Knew.* Illustrated by Ezra Jack Keats. McGraw-Hill, 1957 (I:6–9 R:4). A factual book about knowledge of the Indians.

Robbins, Ruth. *How the First Rainbow Was Made.* Parnassus, 1980 (I:6–9 R:6). A California Indian tale tells how Coyote got the Old Man Above to make the first rainbow.

Robinson, Gail. *Raven the Trickster: Legends of the North American Indians.* Illustrated by Joanna

Troughton. Atheneum, 1982 (I:8–12 R:6). Nine tales from the Northwest Indian tribes.

Rockwood, Joyce. *Groundhog's Horse.* Illustrated by Victor Kalin. Holt, Rinehart & Winston, 1978 (I:7–12 R:4). A young Cherokee boy's horse is stolen by the Creeks in 1750. No one will rescue the horse so he decides to rescue it himself. A warm, humorous story.

———. *To Spoil the Sun.* Holt, Rinehart & Winston, 1976 (I:10+ R:8). The story of traditional Cherokee life in the early 1500s. There is a strong sense of Cherokee culture in this story.

Schweitzer, Byrd Baylor. *One Small Blue Bead.* Illustrated by Symeon Shimin. Macmillan, 1965 (I:all). An old man sitting around a prehistoric campfire ponders the possibility of other humans besides themselves. Only one tribesman, a young boy, shares his belief.

Showers, Paul. *Indian Festivals.* Illustrated by Lorence Bjorklund. Crowell, 1969 (I:7–10 R:3). Describes festivals of the Seminoles, Zunis, Eskimos, Plains Indians, and Indians of the mountain regions.

Sneve, Virginia Driving Hawk. *High Elk's Treasure.* Illustrated by Oren Lyons. Holiday, 1972 (I:8–12 R:6). A dream beginning in the autumn of 1876 is renewed in the 1970s when Joe High Elk's family expands the herd of palomino horses.

———. *Jimmy Yellow Hawk.* Illustrated by Oren Lyons. Holiday, 1972 (I:6–10 R:5). Awarded first prize in its category by the Council on Interracial Books for Children, this story is about a contemporary Sioux boy who lives on an Indian reservation in South Dakota.

———. *When Thunder Spoke.* Illustrated by Oren Lyons. Holiday, 1974 (I:8–12 R:4). A fifteen-year-old Sioux boy finds a coup stick, a relic from the Indian past. Strange changes in the family fortune resulted when the stick was placed in their home. Was the stick the cause of their good luck?

Sobol, Rose. *Woman Chief.* Dial, 1976 (I:10+ R:5). A fictional account of the only woman in the Crow nation who reached the title of chief and sat in the council meetings.

Tobias, Tobi. *Maria Tallchief.* Illustrated by Michael Hampshire. Crowell, 1970 (I:7–12 R:4). A biography of the great prima ballerina who was also an Osage Indian.

Toye, William. *The Firestealer.* Illustrated by Elizabeth Cleaver. Oxford, 1979 (I:4–7 R:5). The tale tells how Nanabozho gave fire to his people and how he turned autumn leaves to a flame color.

———. *The Loon's Necklace.* Illustrated by Elizabeth Cleaver. Oxford, 1977 (I:all R:5). This tale explains how the loon received the lovely shell markings around its neck and across its wings.

TWELVE
Nonfiction: Informational Books and Biographies

From How To to Who's Who

Involving Children in Nonfictional
Literature

From How To to Who's Who

CURIOSITY and the need to make discoveries about the ever-expanding children's world are strong motivational forces. Books that encourage children to seek answers, look at the world in a new way, discover laws of nature, and ponder the consequences of human actions on the animal world meet many needs of growing children.

Through informational books, such as Oxford Scientific Films' *The Butterfly Cycle,* children may see the emergence of a caterpillar from an egg and discover facts stranger than fiction. While reading Bernie Zubrowski's *Bubbles, a Children's Museum Activity Book,* they may become excited about an experiment and discover scientific principles by making and observing bubbles. They may be motivated to observe a bird family carefully by seeing close-up photographs of a mother bird preparing the nest and the babies growing to maturity while reading Geraldine Lux Flanagan's and Sean Morris's *Window into a Nest.*

There are biographies that allow children vicariously to view a new land from the deck of the Santa Maria, go into the African wilderness with a brave and determined woman, and live through a stormy sea thundering over the balsa raft, *Kon Tiki.* They are able to march at the head of a troop of French soldiers with Jeanne d'Arc, thirst for knowledge with a boyish Lincoln, and struggle for civil rights with Andrew Young. They may question the old truths with Copernicus or feel exhilaration with Maria Mitchell when she discovers a new comet. They may realize the loneliness and seclusion of Beatrix Potter and experience the creation of Peter Rabbit.

VALUES OF NONFICTION

"I am curious." "It is easier to find the answer from reading than it is to ask my teacher." "I want to learn to take better pictures." "I want to learn about a career I might enjoy." "I don't believe that information." "I like reading the books." All of these reasons were given to this author by children who were asked why they read nonfictional books. The range of answers also reflects the many values of nonfiction for children.

Literature that fills the need for information is of great value to children. There are thousands of nonfiction books that provide information on hobbies, experiments, the nature of how things work, the characteristics of plants and animals, and the lives and contributions of people.

Gaining knowledge about the world is a powerful reason for reading informational books. Glenn O. Blough (3), professor of Science Education and author of science books for children, says that it should be emphasized that the fact that information grows and ideas change is no excuse for not expecting children and young people to learn from science. While the great supply of information may be somewhat discouraging, and the fluctuation of ideas disconcerting, neither is an excuse for remaining ignorant of the world we live in, or not understanding the methods by which knowledge grows. (p. 420)

Many recently published books contain information on timely subjects that children hear about on television or radio or read about in newspapers. For example, in the late 1970s and early 1980s, when there was much interest in the development of the space shuttle, children could find more information by reading Franklyn M. Branley's *The Story of the Space Shuttle, Columbia and Beyond.* Children could see the inside of the shuttle and the space lab through labeled diagrams, photographs, and text. Additional information could be obtained about proposed space projects. An interest in space exploration might extend to questions about comets and meteors that could be answered by reading Seymour Simon's *The Long Journey From Space.* Likewise, in the mid-seventies, when interest about the treasures of Tutankhamun was especially intense because of the traveling museum exhibition, children could learn about this remarkable archaeological discovery in Irene and Lawrence Swinburne's *Behind the Sealed Door: The Discovery of the Tomb and Treasures of Tutankhamun.* Photographs of actual objects found in the tomb added authenticity to children's discoveries.

Another value of reading informational books is their stimulating nature because well-written informational books provide opportunities for children to experience the excitement of discovery. New doors of self-discovery are opened for children if the books also contain step-by-step directions for experiments that children can do to reinforce a principle or make a new discovery. For example, they may make discoveries about the life cycle of the popcorn plant and learn about basic principles of botany when they read and do the experiments in Millicent E. Selsam's *Popcorn.* They may discover the importance of fibers and the insulation quality of wool or how cotton or wool can be spun by hand by reading and following Vicki Cobb's directions in *Fuzz Does It!* They may rediscover the great contributions to communications developed by Morse and Marconi; children, too, feel the excitement of inventing a telegraph or telephone as they follow Irwin Math's directions in *Morse, Marconi, and You, Understanding and Building Telegraph, Telephone and Radio Sets.*

Children who read about subjects such as botany or zoology and make their own discoveries are exposed to a third value of informational books: they are introduced to the scientific method. They discover, through firsthand experience and reading about the work of scientists, how these people observe, experiment, compare, formulate and test hypotheses, draw conclusions, or withhold them until more evidence is uncovered (3). When children do experiments, they also become familiar with the instruments used by scientists.

As children learn about and become comfortable with the scientific method, they gain an appreciation for the attitudes of people who use this method. Children discover the importance of careful observation over long periods of time, the need for gathering data from many sources, and the requirement that scientists, whatever their field, should not make conclusions before all the data have been collected. For example, Seymour Simon's *The Secret Clocks, Time Senses of Living Things* relates the varied experiments and the careful observation of German scientist Gustav Kramer as he investigated the ability of birds to pinpoint their destinations when they migrate thousands of miles to the south or the north. That an archaeologist may spend years in meticulous search before making a significant discovery is developed in the story of Howard Carter in the Swinburnes' *Behind the Sealed Door: The Discovery of the Tomb and Treasures of Tutankhamun.* Even after archaeological discoveries are made, long hours of careful work are necessary so that information is not lost during the initial excitement of discovery. Children may also learn that a person's achievement is not always his or hers alone; success often depends upon work completed earlier by others.

Informational books allow children to explore on their own, whetting their curiosity so that they want to learn more about a subject. Curiosity is a strong motivator, and parents and educators need to provide books and materials that help children explore their environment and make discoveries about subjects that interest them. A high school student who likes to read nonfiction and informational books emphasizes this curiosity-satisfying potential of books:

I enjoy reading to answer my own curiosity. Fictional books don't have the information that I want. I am more interested in real things. When I was in first grade, astronomy was the first science that interested me; the more I read, the more I learned I didn't know. As I became older I read a lot of books about the stars, space exploration, and theories about the black hole. I discovered that reality is stranger and more exciting than any fiction could be. I could not take fiction and transfer it into the real world; factual books help me learn about the real world.

Some books stimulate readers' enthusiasm to duplicate an experiment reported in a book. For example, many children and adults are eager to carry on their own research after they see the exciting photographs in Geraldine Lux Flanagan and Sean Morris's *Window into a Nest.*

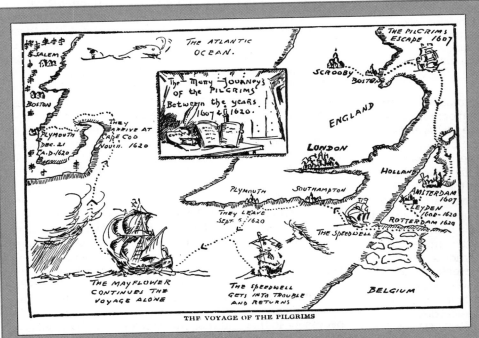

THE VOYAGE OF THE PILGRIMS

FLASHBACK

THE FIRST NEWBERY MEDAL was awarded in 1922 to an informational book that traced the steps in the development of the human race from prehistoric times to the early twentieth century. Hendrik Willem Van Loon's *The Story of Mankind* is also noteworthy because the author dealt with ideas and acts that greatly influenced the human race rather than focusing primarily on dates and picturesque incidents. At the time of its publication the book was praised for its comprehensiveness, taste, and humor. The book was credited with changing the writing of informational books; authors were encouraged to write books that presented learning as an exciting process.

Informational books can also encourage children to develop critical reading and thinking abilities as they learn to evaluate what they read. As they read books on the same subject written by different authors, they may compare and evaluate the objectivity, truthfulness, and perspective of various authors; they may determine the qualifications of the authors to write on a particular subject; and they may check copyright dates to see if the information is current. For example, various views on using chimpanzees in captivity might be considered following the reading of Anna Michel's *The Story of Nim: the Chimp Who Learned Language,* Joan Hewett's *Watching Them Grow: Inside a Zoo Nursery,* and Linda Koebner's *From Cage to Freedom: A New Beginning for Laboratory Chimpanzees.*

Nonfictional materials encourage children to stretch their minds, enlarge their vocabularies, and stimulate their imaginations. New thoughts and ways of looking at the world are possible when children are involved in an in-depth study of a subject. When they read Hope Ryden's *The Little Deer of the Florida Keys,* they may discover the perilous balance between animals, the environment, and humans. They may begin to think of ways their own generation could conserve animal and plant life and natural resources. When they read informational books, they may find that there are differing views of problems and their solutions and of appropriate life-styles. Many well-written informational books expand children's vocabularies by introducing the meanings of new words, including technical terms. Meanings of technical terms are often enriched through photographs or detailed illustrations. For example, *Glaciers: Nature's Frozen Rivers* by Hershell H. and Joan Lowery Nixon introduces terms such as *crevasses* in the text: "The cracks that are found in the ice are called crevasses. They can be very deep and wide and dangerous, or very shallow" (p. 23). One of the deep crevasses is then shown in a photograph on the same page. The definition is followed by a detailed discussion of crevasses. Books also stimulate children's imagination by allowing them to think of new possibilities and creative ways to use or look at the world. Anyone who has observed young children playing with a box has seen the creative and imaginative toys they can develop. Flo Ann Hedley Norvell's *The Great Big Box Book* stimulates the imagination of young children as they consider all the fascinating toys that can be created out of large boxes and then extends their imagination even more as they think of new uses for a box. Likewise, Paul Berman's *Make-*

Believe Empire: A How-to Book encourages children to make a town out of boxes and cans, feed the townspeople with crops grown in flower pots, and create laws to govern the people.

Reading about the achievements of others may increase children's aspirations. For example, reading about athletes who overcame adversity in Vernon Pizer's *Glorious Triumphs: Athletes Who Conquered Adversity* may result in children daring to achieve. They may be inspired to strive for their own achievements when they read Jean Lipman and Margaret Aspinwall's *Alexander Calder and His Magical Mobiles*, Tobi Tobias's *Arthur Mitchell*, or Margery Facklam's *Wild Animals, Gentle Women*. When children discover that there are still many unanswered questions, they may choose to become involved in this vital search for knowledge.

Finally, educators and parents must not forget that one of the greatest values in informational books and biographies is enjoyment. Many children who make new discoveries, become involved in the scientific process, or read because of curiosity are also reading for enjoyment. In fact, enjoyment is often the primary reason children read such nonfictional literature as biographies, histories of the ancient world, and photographic essays of animal life.

EVALUATING INFORMATIONAL BOOKS

Guidelines suggested by several science associations concerned with the education of elementary school children provide valuable information for the librarian, teacher, or parent responsible for selecting informational books for children. These guidelines are addressed to science books but are equally valid for all types of informational books. The following guidelines are taken from recommendations made by the National Science Teachers Association (11) and the American Association for the Advancement of Science (16). The books mentioned will be discussed in detail in a subsequent section of the chapter.

All Facts Should Be Accurate

This guideline includes more than the obvious need for all materials to be factually accurate. The evaluator can ask several questions in order to judge the extent of the text's accuracy.

Does the Author Have the Scientific Qualifications to Write a Book on the Particular Subject? Laurence Pringle, an author of biological and environmental books, for example, studied wildlife conservation at Cornell University and at the University

of Massachusetts, where he earned a master's degree. Dorothy E. Shuttlesworth, author of *To Find a Dinosaur,* has been on the staff of the American Museum of Natural History in New York and the editor of *Junior Natural History,* a magazine for young people. Many books, however, do not provide any background information about the author, or the information provided is useless for evaluating an author's qualifications.

Are Facts and Theory Clearly Distinguished? Children should know if something is a fact, if it is a theory that has not been substantiated, or if it is a theory that is impossible to prove because of limited information. For example, Jack Denton Scott clearly differentiates between fact and theory in *The Book of the Goat.* During his discussion of the ancestry of the goat, he says: "One fact is certain: the goat has been with us a long time" (p. 8). He then traces the known historical record of the goat and compares this record with that of the dog. He carefully separates fact from controversial conjecture: "Despite the combined knowledge of archaeologists (who study materials from past civilizations), osteologists (who study ancient bones), and historians, controversy exists regarding which is the oldest of our friends, the goat or the dog" (p. 10). Scott then presents the evidence compiled by osteologists and archaeologists.

Are Significant Facts Omitted? The above example shows how an author should present enough significant facts so that the text is accurate. For example, specialized animal books that give complete life histories are valuable because they help children understand the evolution of a species, its characteristics, and the need, if any, for its protection. Again, Scott's books do this: they begin with the ancient history of the species, continue into its behavior, and if the animal is endangered, provide information about human efforts to preserve it. This progression of historic through current information is found in *Loggerhead Turtle: Survivor from the Sea* and *Return of the Buffalo.*

Are Differing Views Presented on Controversial Subjects? Subjects such as ecology often have proponents on both sides of the issue. In *Natural Fire: Its Ecology in Forests,* Pringle presents viewpoints supporting the benefits of forest fires and those that consider forest fires as detrimental. Francine Jacobs presents arguments of a group that desires uncontrolled human expansion and those of a group that fights for the protection of the environment in *Africa's Flamingo Lake.* While both authors have definite viewpoints, they do more than present one side of the issue. If there is author bias, the author should identify that it is a personal point of view and not necessarily a universally held position. Sometimes, just one sentence will interject author bias into what otherwise is a factual presentation or controversial views. For example, Ann E. Sigford, in *Eight Words for Thirsty,* follows her discussion of the problems between farmers who need water for irrigation versus townspeople who need water with this statement:

Someone has to pay the high cost of desert water, and that someone is the American people. The CAP was born in a time when farming seemed to be the only way a state could be developed. Today, however, farming contributes only about 7 percent of Arizona's income. It does not seem smart to spend so much to earn so little. (p. 77)

Is the Information Presented without Relying on Anthropomorphism? While it is perfectly acceptable for authors of fantasy to write about animals who think, talk, act, and dress like people, authors of informational books should not ascribe thoughts, motives, or emotions to plants and animals. When authors attach human behavior to an animal, the book is no longer considered accurate. A writer of animal information books should describe the animals in terms that can be substantiated through careful observation. For example, Jack Denton Scott in *The Book of the Pig* describes an incident in which a boar consistently unlatched a gate and took the runt of a litter out into a meadow until he was no longer a runt. Instead of giving the pig human reasons for his actions, Scott states: "Was the boar Andy exhibiting pig instinct or pig intellect when he "adopted" Sawyer? We don't know, but a five-year research program at the University of Kentucky found that pigs not only are the smartest of all farm animals but are also more intelligent than dogs, mastering any trick or feat accomplished by canines in much shorter time" (p. 31). Scott continues to describe pigs in terms of information gained from observation and research.

Is the Information as Up to Date as Possible? Because knowledge in some areas is changing rapidly, copyright dates for certain types of informational books become very important. It is not only knowledge, however, that changes with time. The chapters in this book on the history of literature and realistic fiction show that attitudes and values also change. Comparing older factual books with those with recent copyright dates is one way to illustrate how attitudes and biases change. No educator or publisher today would condone the information about Native Americans that is presented in *Carpenter's Geographical Reader, North America* (4) published in

1898. The chapter on Indians contains information that is not only untrue, but highly offensive. For example, note how Indians are introduced: "What queer people they are, and how sober they look as they squat or stand about the depots, with their merchandise in their hands!" (p. 290). A baby on the next page is described in these terms: "Notice that hole in its top and the odd little brown head peeping out of it. That is an Indian baby, or papoose. See how sober it is. It turns its head about, but it does not cry" (p. 291). In the same chapter, the historical background of the Indians is described: "The savage Indians were in former times dangerous and cruel foes. They took delight in killing women and children. They hid behind rocks and bushes to fight. . . . They used tomahawks to brain their victims, and delighted in torturing their captives and in burning them at the stake" (p. 293). Information about Australian "natives" is just as biased in Charles Redway Dryer's *Geography, Physical, Economic and Regional* (7), published in 1911, while V. M. Hillyer's 1929 text, *A Child's Geography of the World* (10), says that the most curious animals in Africa are not the animals but the people. Children's literature students may not realize how outdated, misinformed, and biased informational books can be until they discover books such as these that influenced the thinking of children who attended school earlier in this century.

Stereotypes Should Be Eliminated

Does the Book Violate Basic Principles against Racism and Sexism? The quotes from the books discussed in the preceding paragraph violate principles against racism. Contemporary books, while not depicting such biases, may still suggest stereotypes through inclusion or exclusion of people in certain professions. For example, are both males and females shown in illustrations depicting interest in science or science professions? The illustrations in Shuttlesworth's *To Find a Dinosaur* show that both boys and girls can be interested in searching for fossils. In addition the illustrations show that black and white children can be youthful fossil hunters.

Illustrations Should Clarify the Text

Are Illustrations Accurate? Do the illustrations add to the clarity of the text? When photographs and drawings are included, they should be accompanied by explanatory legends keyed directly to the text to allow children to expand their understanding of the principles or terminology presented. Millicent E. Selsam's *The Amazing Dandelion,* for example, contains photographs of cross sections of a dandelion that identify the ovary, pappus, petal, anther tube, style, pollen, and stigma. As children read the technical terms in the text, they can easily locate the corresponding parts of the dandelion in the photographs. Well-illustrated texts are very important in books that encourage experimentation. For example, Irwin Math's *Morse, Marconi, and You: Understanding and Building Telegraph, Telephone and Radio Sets* provides the young experimenter with detailed drawings of each experiment described in the book.

Analytical Thinking Should Be Encouraged

Do Children Have an Opportunity to Become Involved in Solving Problems Logically? Are they encouraged to observe, gather data, experiment, compare, and formulate hypotheses? Are they encouraged to withhold judgment until enough data have been gathered or enough facts explored? Books that demonstrate scientific facts and principles should encourage children to do more experiments on their own. They should also stress the value of additional background reading. Seymour Simon's *The Secret Clocks, Time Senses of Living Things* encourages readers to become involved with the principles of biological time clocks by providing step-by-step directions for experiments with bees, animals, plants, and themselves. The book concludes with a list of books and magazine articles appropriate for additional reading.

Organization Should Aid Understanding

Is the Organization Logical? Are ideas broken down into easily understood component parts? Authors often use an organization that progresses from the simplest to the more complex, or from the familiar to the unfamiliar, or from early to later development. Bernie Zubrowski's *Bubbles, A Children's Museum Activity Book,* for example, proceeds from simple experiments using straws to form different-sized bubbles to complex experiments with hexagon bubbles. By building on simpler experiments, the author encourages children to understand the concepts before they do the more difficult experiments.

Are Organizational Aids Included? Reference aids such as a table of contents, index, glossary, bibliography, and list of suggested readings can encourage children to understand the need for, and use of, reference skills. While books for very young children do not include all these aids, they are helpful for older children. Ruth Karen's *Feathered Serpent, the Rise and Fall of the Aztecs,* for example, has a table of contents and

a detailed map showing the archaeological sites at the beginning of the book. At the conclusion are guides to Aztec Mexico, a pronunciation guide, a glossary, and a detailed index including cross-references.

Style Should Stimulate Interest

Is the Writing Lively and Not Too Difficult for the Age of the Children? The vivid style of Scott, for example, creates the visual imagery and suggests the sound of a cormorant rookery in *The Submarine Bird:*

Rookeries come alive at dawn. The rustling of feathers, hoarse gruntings, and some sounds resembling coughing signal that the colony is about to begin its day. Time is spent foraging for fish, feeding the young, perching on rocks, drowsing, often sitting with wings outstretched. On the water beneath the rocky outcropping, the young frolic in swimming and diving practice sessions. (p. 30)

Hope Ryden is another author whose lively writing style creates a visual image. In *The Little Deer of the Florida Keys,* she creates an image of entangled trees that form a perfect hiding place:

Like the enchanted forest that surrounded Sleeping Beauty's castle, mangrove trees protect the beautiful keys they encircle. The savage force of hurricanes that blow in suddenly from the sea is weakened by a mangrove thicket of branches and roots. In centuries past, raiding pirates could not navigate ships through such a snarl of trees. And more recently, hunters intent on killing the deer that inhabit these islands were thwarted when the little creatures took shelter in a maze of curved roots. (p. 7)

Writers can also clarify concepts when they use comparisons to help explain complex ideas or startling facts. Pringle in *Dinosaurs and Their World* develops comparisons between known objects or animals and unknown animals when he describes dinosaurs:

Imagine a seventy-foot-long animal weighing more than a dozen elephants. . . . However, not all dinosaurs were huge. Some were only as big as automobiles. Others were as small as rabbits. . . . There were skinny dinosaurs that looked like ostriches. There were armored dinosaurs, built like army tanks. (p. 9)

In summary, the following questions should be considered when evaluating informational literature:

1 Are the facts accurate?
2 Does the author have the scientific qualifications to write a book on the particular subject?
3 Are facts and theory clearly distinguished?

4 Are significant facts omitted?

5 Are differing views presented on controversial subjects?

6 Is the information presented without relying on anthropomorphism?

7 Is the information as up to date as possible?

8 Does the book violate basic principles against racism and sexism?

9 Are the illustrations accurate?

10 Do children have an opportunity to become involved in solving problems logically?

11 Is the organization logical?

12 Are organizational aids included?

13 Is the writing lively and not too difficult for the age of the children?

Authors of credible informational literature create books that meet many of these guidelines. Consider in the following section how authors of books on history and geography, laws of nature, experiments and discoveries, and occupations and hobbies develop credible books that may stimulate and inform readers.

HISTORY AND GEOGRAPHY

Authors who write about the ancient world may develop credible books by citing the latest information gained from their own or others' research, including findings by paleontologists and archaeologists, and by describing details in such a way that readers can visualize an ancient world. Because readers cannot verify facts about the ancient world through their own experiences, authors may compare known facts from ancient times with known facts from the contemporary world, include drawings that clarify information, and/or use photographs of museum objects or archaeological sites. The factual data in literature on the contemporary world may be made credible by citing research; quoting authorities; quoting original sources; and providing detailed descriptions of the setting, circumstances, or situations. Photographs are frequently used to add authenticity.

The Ancient World

With scientists as detectives and fossils as clues, twentieth-century children can experience the thrill of discovering clues about the earth's distant past and the animals that inhabited it. Children often become enthusiastic amateur paleontologists as they learn about dinosaurs in books, study about them in museums, search for fossilized footprints or bones, and make

dinosaur models. The excitement of scientists in the field, the discoveries of paleontologists, and photographs from on-site locations are all used by Dorothy Shuttlesworth in *To Find a Dinosaur*. Many of these photographs show on-site discoveries of dinosaur bones or fossils. The photographs, which include pictures of both boys and girls, illustrate that both sexes may be interested in this branch of science and encourage the realization that there are still many discoveries to be made about the earth's past. The author encourages child involvement by including directions for making castings from fossils and models of dinosaurs. Other books that explore the subject of dinosaurs are Pringle's *Dinosaurs and Their World* and Helen Roney Sattler's *Dinosaurs of North America*.

William Mannetti's *Dinosaurs in Your Backyard* may encourage critical evaluation, speculation, and additional reading. The author challenges some previous theories about dinosaurs and provides new interpretations suggesting that birds are feathered dinosaurs, dinosaurs may have been warm blooded, and some dinosaurs that were previously believed to be water inhabitants spent most of the time on land. Through the author's choice of terminology, however, he implies that these theories are accepted by all authorities. He does not refer to opposing viewpoints or discuss how the same evidence has been interpreted by others. Knowledgeable readers may be stimulated to search for various interpretations and read the latest research and theories.

Archaeologists in North America have investigated many of the 10,000 Aztec ruins scattered from Guatemala northward to the United States border. Ruth Karen, in *Feathered Serpent: The Rise and Fall of the Aztecs*, develops the thesis that a great civilization also flourished in North America. Her text, written for older children, is divided into three parts: a history of the Aztec civilization; a fictionalized story, "The Life of a Girl Called Windflower and the Death of a Boy Named Hungry Coyote," based on Aztec history; and a documentation of recent archaeological discoveries including the summer palace of Cortez and a major Aztec temple site at Cholua, "with pyramids so ambitious in scale they match the pyramids in Egypt" (p. 169). One of the strengths of this text is the description of six vantage points that can be visited in order to gain firsthand knowledge of the Aztec people. By tying the past to the present, children may envision the possibility of making significant archaeological discoveries in the twentieth century. In addition, texts such as this provide positive materials for multiethnic studies. Children may discover that the Aztec civilization is part of a strong North American heritage. Comparisons may also be made between the history of the Aztec civilization as presented by Karen and the details and settings developed in Scott O'Dell's histori-

ISSUE

Content Bias in Information Books: Creationism Versus Evolutionism

A STUDY REPORTED IN *Publishers Weekly* found the increasing controversy over literature content was most prevalent in contemporary fiction.[1] The content found in textbooks and informational library selections, however, were the second and third most frequently challenged. Over 95 percent of the reported challenges sought to limit rather than expand the information and points of view expressed in the literature. Objections to content centered around broad ideological questions such as the theory of evolution, creationism, and secular humanism.

Creationism versus evolutionism is receiving renewed interest as creationists claim materials centering on evolution deny students their religious beliefs. In contrast, evolutionists claim that creationism is a religious subject without scientific support. This debate extended into state legislatures and courts as states such as Arkansas and Louisiana passed laws specifying that creationism must be taught in conjunction with evolution. These laws, however, were challenged in the courts and overruled. The issue remains a topic of concern.

These challenges to material content and instructional practices have considerable monetary and program content significance. The Louisiana state science supervisor, Don McGehee, estimated the cost of introducing creationism into the schools at about seven million dollars. Most of this money will be needed for texts and other informational literature that develop the creationist theory. The cost for materials and instruction, according to McGehee, will be drawn from other educational programs.

This debate will probably increase as librarians, educators, parents, and publishers consider issues surrounding purchases for libraries and the need for, or restriction against, a variety of viewpoints in informational literature.

1 Mutter, John. "Study on School Censorship Finds Cases on Rise." *Publishers Weekly*, 7 August 1981, p. 12.

cal fiction, *The Captive* and *The Feathered Serpent,* discussed in chapter ten.

Readers who enjoy traditional literature and historical fiction set in medieval times and adults who would like to recreate medieval festivals should find Madeleine Pelner Cosman's *Medieval Holidays and Festivals: A Calendar of Celebrations* rewarding. The chapters are organized according to festivals characteristic of each month. Her detailed directions for costumes, games, settings, and recipes are easily followed and not too difficult to reproduce. The content should be helpful for librarians, teachers, and other adults who are interested in giving children a feeling for earlier times and cultures.

Authors may trace the history of a common item to show its importance in diverse cultures and across different time periods. Chris and Janie Filstrup's *Beadazzled: The Story of Beads,* for example, traces the history of beads from ancient times to the present. The authors effectively develop the importance of beads by describing and illustrating their use for such varied purposes as calculating, counting prayers, money, and ornamentation. The beauty of beadwork is highlighted by color illustrations. Because the illustrations show beadwork from different time periods, they reinforce the authors' thesis that many cultures have created works of art and useful objects from beads. The authors encourage readers to experiment with beadwork by including detailed directions for bead craft projects and sources where beads can be obtained.

The Modern World

Many informational books help develop an understanding of the varied people, their struggles, and their contributions that made an impact on history. For example, Suzanne Hilton focuses on the early years of American history in *We the People: The Way We Were 1783–1793*. The author creates an authentic and lively history of America by incorporating quotations from actual sources such as letters, newspapers, and diaries. These original quotes clarify the attitudes of the people and the issues of the times; consequently, there is a feeling that history is people rather than dates.

Effective authors of informational books that relate historical events often clarify their subjects by presenting important details in chronological order. For example, Richard Snow in *The Iron Road: A Portrait of American Railroading* uses a logical ordering of events to trace the development of the railroad in the United States from the founding of the Baltimore and Ohio Railroad in 1827, through the great age of the steam engine, through the replacement of steam with diesel power, and finally, to the demise of the railroad's importance. Older children who are fascinated by railroads and their history will enjoy the accompanying photographs.

The cry of "Gold" in 1898 created a great change in a land that previously had been peaceful and isolated, populated by trappers, Indians, and wild animals. Margaret Poynter's *Gold Rush! The Yukon Stampede of 1898* describes the people who abandoned their jobs and businesses in the United States to travel to rugged Alaska. The author, whose parents and maternal grandparents were Alaskan pioneers, uses her knowledge of the period to describe these frantic, adventuresome days. Old photographs add authenticity by showing prospectors hitting the trail, panning for gold, sluicing the gold, climbing the Chilkoot Pass in winter, and walking through downtown Skagway in 1898.

A former researcher for ABC news, Elizabeth Levy, and co-author Tad Richards depict the history of coal miners and the development of their union in *Struggle and Lose, Struggle and Win: The United Mine Workers*. The authors capture the readers' interest by beginning with a startling fact: America is so rich in coal deposits that the Arab nations seem energy poor in comparison. Next, they take the readers back to a time before the unions, a time when working conditions were hazardous and unprofitable. In a style that resembles investigative journalism, the authors present many details to back their argument and describe the plight of the miners. Consider the following example in which they describe the miners' helplessness:

There was no way out of this maze for the miner. He needed a job, so he worked in the mines. The company saw to it that his rent and food were more than he could afford so he borrowed money on next week's pay. The company eventually got back all the money they paid out in wages through high rents and high prices at their stores. Their workers were thus never able to leave the company, and could never demand more money or better working conditions because they were always in debt. (p. 4)

This book tells about the struggles between the miners and the mine owners, the violence that often accompanied these disputes, the emergence of the early labor leaders, and the rise of John L. Lewis, the most powerful president of the United Mine Workers.

Highly emotional periods in history are difficult to present objectively. Seymour Rossel, however, approaches *The Holocaust* with a historian's detachment. He traces Hitler's rise to power; describes the harassment, internment, and extermination of many Jewish people; and discusses the Nuremburg trials. The author effectively uses quotations from original sources such as diaries and letters to allow readers to visualize the human drama and draw their own conclusions.

Another emotional period is presented in Daniel S. Davis's *Behind Barbed Wire: The Imprisonment of Japanese Americans During World War II*. The author clarifies the situation by exploring attitudes expressed toward Japanese Americans before and after the attack on Pearl Harbor. He effectively presents the human consequences of internment by describing changes in family structure, changes in geographical locations, and legal procedures for reparation of property. Both the Rossel and Davis texts may provide sources for comparing and evaluating setting and background information for the World War II historical fiction discussed in chapter ten.

Some authors explore various cultures by doing in-depth studies on one person or family. Investigative reporter, photographer and author David Mangurian creates an accurate view of Indian life in Latin America in his *Children of the Incas*. He adds authenticity to his book by describing his travels through Latin America and his experiences with the people. The author's style, told in first person, seems very believable to children. Consider, for example, his reasons for writing this book: "I went to Coata for the first time to photograph Indian life for UNICEF. For years I had photographed Indians in Latin America. But I had never really gotten to know any. The only way you get to know people is by sleeping in their homes, eating their food, and living their routine" (p. 3). Mangurian creates additional authenticity by telling the story from the viewpoint of thirteen-year-old Modesto. The author's recorded text and his photographs create a story of a proud, cheerful people who are bravely struggling to obtain the bare necessities. The photographs show Indian children playing together, living with loving parents, attending school, working in the handicraft center, visiting the plaza, and working with their sheep and crops.

Photographs showing daily lives of the people add authenticity to a book about Latin America.
Reprinted by permission of Four Winds Press, a division of Scholastic Inc. from *Children of the Incas* by David Mangurian. Copyright © 1979 by David Mangurian.

Modesto's words describe his longing to leave this area, which is one of the poorest regions of the world, and move into a city where he hopes to study to become an engineer; this profession would allow him to build schools, parks, and streets and to develop electricity and water for his town, Coata. Modesto ends his story with his belief that although he does not know what heaven is like, he believes it must be a city where no one is hungry, there are enough fruits, and no water problems. After children read this book, they have a better understanding of life in a culture that has descended from the once powerful Inca civilization.

Exceptional photographs document the lives of the Tasaday, a Stone Age Philippino people, in John Nance's *Lobo of the Tasaday*. By focusing on Lobo, a ten-year-old boy, the author creates a vivid picture of their social organization, living conditions, and beliefs.

Quite a different environment is captured in Jack Demuth's photographs for Patricia Demuth's *Joel: Growing Up a Farm Man*. The midwestern farm environment and the responsibility of being a farmer are vividly portrayed as the author describes in detail such activities as delivering calves, caring for the pigs, and repairing farm machinery. Because the author focuses

upon the responsibilities and observations of a thirteen-year-old boy, young readers may gain a clearer understanding of farm life in America.

LAWS OF NATURE

Effective books written about the laws of nature encourage children to observe nature, to explore the life cycles of animals, to consider the impact of endangered species, to experiment with plants, to understand the balance of the smallest ecosystem, and to explore the earth's geology. In order to create effective and credible books authors must blend fact into narrative; facts about animals, for example, need to be gained from observation and research. Close-up photography is especially effective for clarifying information and stimulating interest. Photographs may illustrate what happens inside an egg or a nest and follow the life cycle of an animal or a plant. Labeled diagrams may clarify understanding. Maps may show natural habitats of animals, migration patterns of birds, or locations of earthquakes. If authors present new vocabulary or concepts it is helpful if they define the terms, illustrate with diagrams or photographs, and proceed from known to unknown information. Clearly developed activities that encourage children to observe and experiment add to the potential of the book. A bibliography, an index, and list of additional readings are helpful.

Animals

Authors who write effectively about land invertebrates (earthworms), insects, amphibians and reptiles, mammals, and birds must clearly develop their facts without giving their animals human qualities and emotions. Because books about animals are popular with many different age groups authors must consider the experiential backgrounds of their readers as they develop new concepts.

Consider, for example, the techniques used by two authors who have written about earthworms for different age levels. In *Twist, Wiggle, and Squirm: A Book About Earthworms,* Pringle encourages children to discover and explore the different kinds of earthworms by identifying their body segments, feeding habits, and value to plants. He gives readers step-by-step directions for capturing an earthworm, discovering its sensitivity to light and locating the bristles, or setae, on each segment. This simplified text and emphasis on doing an activity appeals to many younger readers. In a more advanced text, *The Amazing Earthworm,* Lilo Hess uses photographs to illustrate characteristics of unusual earthworms, develops new terminology through the context of the book, and encourages children to carry on certain experiments with worms so that they can answer questions or reaffirm statements made in the text. One photograph of a man holding a twelve-foot-long Australian earthworm effectively develops the concept of length. Other photographs, however, lose some of their value because they are not labeled.

Color photography is used effectively by Oxford Scientific Films. *The Butterfly Cycle,* for example, is useful at several levels: the introduction presents pertinent background information on the egg, larva, pupa, and adult stages of the butterfly. This is followed by almost full-page color photographs illustrating close-up, enlarged details of each stage (see p. 16 of color insert). Photographs showing the transparent quality of the eggs with the dark head of the caterpillar visible, followed by the caterpillar eating its way out of the egg, are especially interesting; they may allow children to make observations about an aspect of nature that they have not previously seen. Short captions under each photograph identify the actions occurring in the photograph. The life of another insect is developed in a similar way by Oxford Scientific Films in *Bees and Honey.*

Authors of informational books may entice children's interests by challenging them to compare their capabilities with those found in nature. Tom Walther in *A Spider Might,* for example, encourages children to understand the remarkable capabilities of spiders by asking readers if they think they could jump twenty times their own length. He suggests they try, and then describes and illustrates how the zebra spider can easily jump twenty times its length.

Seymour Simon, who has had over twenty books selected as outstanding Science Trade Books for Children, effectively presents facts about snakes, dispels some myths about them, and provides detailed observational suggestions for readers. For example, in *Discovering What Garter Snakes Do,* written for younger readers, he provides detailed directions for safely capturing a garter snake, carrying it home, handling it, constructing an escape-proof cage, and then caring for it. Less familiar snakes are described in *Meet the Giant Snakes.* The author increases readers' understanding of size through comparisons with familiar objects: a boa constrictor is as long as a car, the African python is as long as a station wagon, while the anaconda and reticulated python are each as long as a school bus. Simon describes the characteristics of these giant snakes and provides straightforward facts without assigning human feelings or motivations to them. (This practice of providing human characteristics to animals is called *anthropomorphism.*) Consider, for example, his description of the python's incubation of her eggs: "Every once in a while she shivers and muscular waves move up and down her body. Scientists think that these movements heat up her body and this warms the eggs" (p. 13). He concludes by refuting some of the legends and tales about giant snakes. The important role played by poisonous snakes as well as advice on what to do if a person is bitten is included in Simon's *Poisonous Snakes.*

The ability of photographs to illustrate a point is shown in Joanna Cole's *A Snake's Body.* Jerome Wexler's series of photographs showing a python capturing and swallowing a chick effectively shows how the snake's body allows it to acquire food.

The British zoologists who write and photograph books for Oxford Scientific Films use their considerable photographic skills to present lifelike illustrations in *Common Frogs.* The four-page introductory text presents specific information about the frog's characteristics and life cycle and is followed by large close-up colored photographs described with brief sentences. Close-up views of eyes, web-footed hind legs, jumping frogs, mating in water, growing eggs, tadpoles hatching from eggs, changing stages of the tadpoles, and full-grown frogs are outstanding.

Writing Natural History for Young Readers

Jack Denton Scott

Naturalist, former war correspondent, spokesman for endangered species, and recipient of numerous awards for outstanding science trade books for children, author JACK DENTON SCOTT discusses his beliefs about writing children's nonfictional books.

DEMANDS ARE PRECISE: Be accurate. Be relaxed; write fluently; never write down to your readers; never try to write up either. Know your audience; also know your subject; but even if you do know it, research it so that you will know perhaps more than you or anyone else will want to know. Put these all together and they may be an axiom for writing nonfiction for your readers.

But there is more: There can be no cloudy language; writing must be simple, crisp, clear. This, in fact, should be a primer for all writing. Children demand the best from a writer. If young readers become bored, confused, puzzled by style, or showered with a writer's self-important, complicated words you've lost readers. Young readers instinctively shy away from the pretentious and the phony.

In the dozen photo-essays that photographer Ozzie Sweet and I have produced for Putnam and our brilliant editor, Margaret Frith, we have worked with one object in mind: Entertain and inform. We believe that children want to learn; and everyone knows that they want to be entertained. We have tried to do this with clarity in words and with dramatic but thoughtfully conceived photographs by perhaps the most talented man with the camera in the U.S.

We have also introduced our series of books to children with a new technique. Action, constant movement, words flowing into photographs, photographs flowing into words, no labored captions, no slowing of pace. Almost a cinematic technique. This is difficult, demanding that photographer and writer work closely together.

I, personally, also have the belief that too much weird way-out fiction is pushed at children. (I have nothing against fiction; in fact I also write adult fiction.) But children have their own vivid and creative imaginations that they bring to their reading. One 10-year-old boy wrote me that while he was reading our book, *Canada Geese,* he actually flew south with the geese. I bet he did. I *hope* he did.

Ozzie Sweet and I also object to violence in children's literature; it's boring, it's burdensome and it's unwanted by children. I write of the free, wild creatures and try to give children straight information that will interest them and educate them, staying away from cuteness or giving animals or birds human traits which, of course, they don't have. There is an entire essay on our shrinking world and what wildlife means to children, wildlife thay may not even be around when our readers become adults.

Finally, we believe that children who are forming habits and outlooks that will serve them forever are more important than adult readers and we feel fortunate that we have the opportunity to give them worthwhile subjects to think about. Thus we choose those subjects carefully for our intelligent and demanding audience. Ask any librarian or teacher. They know children's standards better than anyone. And thank God for librarians and teachers! Without them the darkness of ignorance would close in much more quickly than it is doing at present, pushed by television which creates non-readers and a growing careless attitude toward the written word—by adults, of course. Not children. They still are excited about good books and receptive to the well written word. Ozzie Sweet and I shall continue to try to give them the best we have.

Jack Denton Scott and photographer Ozzie Sweet have collaborated to give children several outstanding books on mammals. Because their work exemplifies many of the characteristics of outstanding informational books for children, we will consider several of the techniques used by Scott in *The Book of the Pig*. First, he skillfully blends facts into narrative. Information from animal experts, naturalists, and observations of a pig farmer are all included. When developing the pigs' characteristics he refers to facts gained from observation and research. Consider, for example, his support for pigs' intelligence, cooperativeness, and cleanliness. He provides examples of pigs' adaptability, research demonstrating intelligence and meaning of the sounds pigs utter, photographs of pigs walking or playing with people, and proof that young pigs try to keep their farrowing pen clean. The author uses frequent comparisons to help readers understand the pig's nature and development. For example, a family who raise pigs "romp with their piglets as they would with puppies" (p. 9). Later the author cites research that claims that a newborn "piglet's mobility is equivalent to that of a 2½-year-old child" (p. 20). The author develops the meaning of new vocabulary through the text. There are frequent sentences such as "The mother, or sow . . ." (p. 15), "giving birth to, or farrowing . . ." (p. 19). The photographs enhance the text and frequently add warmth and humor. When the text indicates that "pigs really are in clover" (p. 7), a photograph shows piglets in a flower-dappled meadow. Likewise, when the text describes the young pigs lying in the meadow with their ears up like a group of bunnies, a photograph illustrates the image.

Wild mammals, their contributions, and their survival are topics in two other books by Scott and Sweet. The life of the prairie dog is explored in *Little Dogs of the Prairie*. Accuracy and interest is developed through photographs taken on the Pine Ridge Indian Reservation in South Dakota, where the largest collection of prairie-dog towns in the United States exists. Scott describes the contributions of prairie dogs and then argues for their control and protection by means of responsible population control rather than mass extermination by poisoning. Another prairie animal, the buffalo, is presented in Scott and Sweet's *Return of the Buffalo*. Scott uses statistics to develop his points on survival and to demonstrate the plight of the buffalo whose once vast herds were reduced from 60 million to 541 animals in the 1800s. Scott uses these facts, as well as the efforts of some people to protect the buffalo, to support preservation of an endangered species.

Scott Barry is another author who develops a plea for the protection of animals that once roamed the North American continent. He develops his viewpoint in *The Kingdom of the Wolves* by depicting the wolf as a powerful, intelligent, social animal that does not deserve the reputation suggested in fairy tales. His argument seems credible because he describes seven years of working with and observing wolves. Children who have read Jean George's *Julie of the Wolves* may enjoy reading Barry's description of wolf-body language and the wolves' lives on the Alaskan tundra.

Bighorn sheep are other animals whose numbers have decreased drastically since the 1800s. Kay McDearmon's *Rocky Mountain Bighorns* explores their habits, size, feeding habits, mating, and birth. The text is enhanced by photographs taken by Dr. Valerius Geist while he was doing field research in Banff National Park in the Canadian Rockies; his experiences while observing and becoming friendly with the bighorns add credibility and warmth to the text. This book concludes with a plea to preserve Rocky Mountain bighorns.

The need for preservation of unusual animals is a popular theme in informational books. Hope Ryden uses numbers and history to support her argument that the key deer, animals no larger than big dogs, should be preserved. She traces their existence from the twenty-five identified in the early 1900s to the increasing herd that is now protected due to a ten-year crusade by conservationists. Ryden's language in *The Little Deer of the Florida Keys* creates a vision of a world not only filled with mangrove thickets, tropical birds, and alligators but also endangered by the poacher's rifle and the bulldozers of land development. The photographs evoke readers' sympathy and appreciation by showing rare images of the small deer in their tropical environment. The author develops the human struggle for this survival by describing the long crusade to identify the deer as different from the mainland deer and to establish a sanctuary for the animals. A different approach to animal survival is developed by Barbara Ford in *Alligators, Raccoons, and other Survivors: The Wildlife of the Future*. She contrasts the traits of surviving animals and the human use of their environment with the traits and environmental use of animals that did not survive.

Depending upon their purposes and points of view, authors may approach the subject of monkeys, apes, and chimpanzees quite differently. For example, Nina Leen's purpose in *Monkeys* is general information with some consideration for extinction. Consequently she includes a short description of each primate's habitat, use of prehensile tail, preferred foods, vocalization, sleeping habits, grooming, family relationships, and any danger of extinction. In *Watching Them Grow: Inside a Zoo Nursery*, Joan Hewett uses photographs to depict the life of a young chimpanzee living in the nursery of the San Diego Zoo. Photographs and text inform children how the primates are cared for, how they need and respond to affection, and how they move from crib to cage. There is an emphasis on the important work done by zoo employees.

Books by Anna Michel and Linda Koebner report the results of chimpanzee research. Although both authors stress the human interaction with chimps, the points of view, purposes of the research, and underlying concerns are quite different. Michel's *The Story of Nim: The Chimp Who Learned Language* reports Dr. Herbert Terrace's research in which he tries to teach a chimpanzee to recognize and use words in sign language. Photographs showing Nim interacting with people add a sense of authenticity to the thesis. Koebner's *From Cage to Freedom: A New Beginning For Laboratory Chimpanzees* presents a more cautious and skeptical view of using chim-

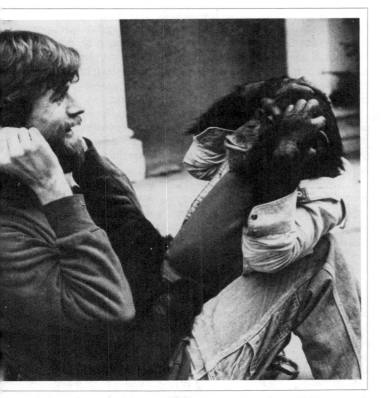

Photographs show Nim and researcher identifying parts of the body.
Photograph Copyright © 1980 by Herbert S. Terrace. Reprinted from *The Story of Nim,* by Anna Michel, photographs by Susan Kuklin and Herbert S. Terrace, by permission of Alfred A. Knopf, Inc.

panzees for experimental purposes. Her book reports results from a grant obtained to investigate if formerly caged chimps can learn to survive without humans and eventually breed in their environment. The complexity of this undertaking is made plausible when the author describes the chimps' problems and how she helped them learn to survive. Some of these survival skills are as basic as teaching them how to drink water. The author's presentation and concern for the chimps implies another issue: Do laboratory purposes warrant the capture of African chimpanzees even though they may become an endangered species?

Several books on animals may be especially appropriate for younger readers because the subjects are common and readers can verify the authenticity of the text. For example, Joanna Cole's *A Cat's Body* explores characteristic cat behaviors such as pouncing, reacting to moving objects, reacting when angry, and purring. The text with its photographs may encourage children to observe their own pets. The humorous and lovable-appearing rabbit in Lilo Hess's *Diary of a Rabbit* may appeal to children who have seen rabbits or read stories about them. The text, written in diary format, includes considerable information about rabbits and their care.

Another book that can stimulate younger children's observational powers is Millicent Selsam's *How to Be a Nature Detective.* The text, combined with Ezra Jack Keats's illustrations, encourages children to search for and identify animal tracks.

Simon encourages children to interact in *Animal Fact/ Animal Fable* by using a guessing game format. First, he presents a common belief about animals; the belief is stated through a humorous illustration with a short caption. Then, readers are asked to predict whether it is fact or fable. Finally, they turn the page to find the answer, which includes information about why scientists think the belief is either fact or fiction (see p. 16 of color insert).

Several books explore the birth process of a specific mammal. Numerous photographs are usually used to clarify the text. For example, Joanna Cole presents the birth of miniature dachshund puppies in *My Puppy Is Born.* Jerome Wexler's photographs show the pregnant dog going into her box, the emergence of the first puppy born inside a sac, and the mother tearing the sac and licking the puppy. The growth of the puppies is followed during their first eight weeks as they are unable to see or hear, as they nurse, and then as they open their eyes and become strong enough to take their first steps. Readers observe the puppies' first teeth, their exploration of a new world, and the moment when one puppy is old enough to become a pet. Another book on the same subject is Camilla Jessell's *The Puppy Book.*

Authors of informational books have written books about birds ranging from the common barnyard fowl to exotic tropical birds. Through these books students of children's literature can observe various techniques that authors use to create interest for young children and how they develop new concepts and clarify subjects for older children. In *Five Nests,* a simply written book for young children, Caroline Arnold describes the nests of five different kinds of birds and how the birds take care of their young. The illustrations show common birds such as robins and redwing blackbirds. The book may appeal to younger children because it stresses how baby birds are cared for: both parents may care for the babies, only the female or male may care for them, sometimes brothers and sisters care for the babies, and sometimes parents let other birds care for their babies. Arnold concludes, "There are many different ways that birds care for their babies. Each way is a good way" (p. 31). This book has a simple index that can encourage children to use reference skills.

In *Window into a Nest,* a book for older children, Geraldine Lux Flanagan uses and describes more sophisticated observational technique to reveal the stages in chickadee nesting and hatching behavior. The text describes the placement of a concealed camera into an observational opening in a wooden birdhouse. The photographs clarify behavioral patterns such as floor hammering before nest building, reactions of alarm when an intruder peers into the house, struggles with straw brought into the home, and the feeding ceremony between male and female. The behaviors explored are more complex than those presented in Arnold's book for younger children. Flanagan's text, the winner of the London Times Educational Supplement Senior Information Book Award for 1975, shows the careful research that should go into scientific investigation.

Close-up photography is especially effective in books written about evolving embryos. Several books clarify this development by allowing readers to see what happens inside an egg. For example, Oxford Scientific Films' *The Chicken and the Egg* is an excellent book for younger children that allows them to observe a developing chick embryo inside an egg. Colored photographs by George Bernard and Peter Parks follow the embryo as major changes occur. The photographs are so detailed that viewers see an embryo covered with skin, feathers, and a chick ready to hatch. Likewise, the photographs in Hans-Heinrich Isenbart's *A Duckling Is Born* show different stages in the embryo of a duck.

Patricia Lauber takes advantage of children's curiosity and encourages interaction with the text in *What's Hatching out of That Egg?* Text and photographic clues allow readers to speculate about the identity of the animal that is hatching from an egg. The author encourages readers to become involved with problem solving by first deciding what they believe the animal is, then turning the page to discover if they are correct. The various eggs belong to ostriches, alligators, spiders, frogs, octopuses, penguins, salmon, sea turtles, caterpillars, monarch butterflies, pythons, and platypuses. This book encourages children to search for visual and written clues before making a decision.

The large flying birds and exotic water birds have interested a number of eminent science writers, researchers, and photographers. Because the birds and environment may be new to younger readers, many books for younger children develop much of the content through photographs. Max Alfred Zoll's *A Flamingo Is Born,* for example, uses pictures to help chronicle the life of a flamingo from the time its parents build the mud nest in the water until the mother lays one egg that both parents care for. Large black and white photographs by Winifred Noack tell the story for young children who can understand and enjoy the birds even without reading the text. In contrast, Francine Jacobs's *Africa's Flamingo Lake,* written for older children, emphasizes more abstract concepts such as the conservationist's struggle to preserve Nakuru Lake, the support for four hundred kinds of birds and the greatest flamingo population in the world. The author allows readers to ponder the issues involved by contrasting the viewpoints and efforts of conservationists with the viewpoints and interests of people who want to develop the area. Children who enjoy reading Jean George's ecological mystery *Who Killed Cock Robin?* can discover that the people of Kenya had to investigate and solve many of the same problems as those found in the northeastern United States. Like the robin in the fictional account, the flamingo is an ecological weather vane in this book depicting the realities of wildlife.

Scott and Sweet, who created fascinating books on mammals, have also developed books on large birds. Through photo essays and accompanying text they provide historical background and describe the behaviors and characteristics of several birds. In *That Wonderful Pelican,* for example, Scott traces the birds back 70 million years and then discusses their life in their present home in the National Wildlife Refuge on Pelican Island, Florida. Similar photo essays are developed about the American stork, often referred to as the *wood ibis,* in *Discovering the American Stork,* and the egret in *Discovering the Mysterious Egret.*

In *The Submarine Bird* photographs are used to effectively substantiate research that traces the cormorant back through

Detailed photo essays allow children to observe natural settings, behaviors, and characteristics of egrets.
From *Discovering the Mysterious Egret* by Jack Denton Scott, photograph copyright © 1978 by Ozzie Sweet. Reproduced by permission of Harcourt Brace Jovanovich, Inc.

its probable connection with Jurassic Age reptiles. Photographs of reptilelike offspring reinforce this connection between reptiles and cormorants.

Because Scott includes various theories about birds and describes research, older children may discover the importance of distinguishing between fact and theory in informational books. For example, various theories about the migrating habits of geese are presented in *Canada Geese*. The author reinforces his factual information by describing studies such as the "Stellar-Orientation System" that tested the star-map theory of how the geese are able to find exact locations and follow exact routes year after year. Other theories discussed include sensitivity to barometric pressures in the atmosphere and magnetic stimuli. This inclusion of research and separating fact from theory are two important criteria in the evaluation of children's informational books.

Plants

Informational books on plants may be especially rewarding for children if they develop clear details in logical order, include diagrams and photographs that illustrate terminology, and encourage children to become involved in learning. Because Millicent E. Selsam uses many of these techniques, her books provide worthwhile examples. In *Bulbs, Corms, and Such,* consider how the author and photographer Jerome Wexler develop children's understanding of plant characteristics by proceeding from the familiar to the unfamiliar. When introducing bulbs, a cross section of an onion is photographed with the fleshy leaves that store food and stem labeled. Next, the unfamiliar daffodil bulb is introduced and sectioned to illustrate the similarities between the onion and the daffodil. The flower bulb is enlarged for easier identification. Children are then encouraged to plant a bulb and observe its growth. The text and photographs inform readers how they can plant a bulb in a glass container and observe the development of roots, leaves, and flower buds. The discussion of the daffodil explains that the formation of several new bulbs at the end of the season ensures that the life cycle will begin again the following spring. The book concludes with directions for growing begonias, cannas, daffodils, dahlias, gladioli, hyacinths, lilies, and tulips.

In *The Amazing Dandelion,* Selsam effectively introduces the considerable reproductive potential of the dandelion by showing photographs of two fields: one has a single dandelion plant and another, a few years later, is covered with dandelions. Then, she attracts readers' attention and speculation as she asks how the dandelion is able to spread so quickly. Why is it one of the most successful plants? The text and photographs answer this question by tracing the life cycle of the dandelion. Several experiments also encourage children's involvement in learning about why the dandelion is so successful in its reproduction. Step-by-step directions accompanied by photographs are also found in other books by Selsam. In *Popcorn* the author describes how to sprout seeds in a glass, transplant them into a garden or container, pollinate the corn, and wait for it to reach maturity.

Another example of an informational book that develops concepts about plants through chronological order and personal experience is Patricia Lauber's *Seeds Pop! Stick! Glide!* The text and Jerome's Wexler's photographs help children understand the many different ways that seeds travel and disperse. Consider, for example, the presentation of Queen Anne's lace. The photographs and accompanying text proceed in chronological order from a plant with many small flowers, to its appearance in early winter, and finally to what happens when the dried plant opens and closes its umbrella. The author encourages children's involvement in the discovery process; she describes an experiment they can do that resembles the plant's changes in nature.

The "Let's-Read-and-Find-Out Science Book" series contains several books that allow children to explore the world of plants. For example, Phyllis S. Busch's *Cactus in the Desert* encourages them to learn about a variety of cacti from the tall saguaro to the tiniest pincushion. The text emphasizes the ability of cacti to store water and survive in dry climates. In order to help children perceive height and quantity, the illustrations compare the cactus with known quantities: the height of a saguaro cactus is compared to ten people standing on each other's shoulders; the amount of water evaporating from a regular tree is illustrated as being about 320 quarts compared with less than a glass from a cactus. The book concludes with suggestions for cacti that can be raised at home and recommendations for their care.

The Earth's Ecology

The planet earth is one ecosystem—a place in nature with all its living and nonliving parts. There are, however, much smaller ecosystems within it; ecosystems that are small enough for children to observe and gain new understandings about the balance of nature. Pringle is one of the excellent authors who write about both familiar and unfamiliar ecosystems. In *City and Suburb; Exploring an Ecosystem,* for example, Pringle describes and encourages students to observe an environment that is familiar to many children. He entices older children's interest by describing how a city, which may be similar to their own, affects its surroundings: heat islands, air pollution beyond the city, dying trees, and adapting plants and animals. Pringle encourages children to discover these changes and a possible abundance of plants and animals by searching their own environments, including cemeteries, vacant lots, parks, and sidewalk cracks. Many children who read this book and then explore their own environments are amazed at the variety of plants, insects, mammals, birds, and snakes found within their city. Discussions may also make them aware of the problems created by the urban environment.

Children may discover the forest ecosystem through Pringle's *Into the Woods: Exploring the Forest Ecosystem* as he shows the various forest layers, the animals and plants that live in each layer, and how each is an important part of the forest's energy cycle. The part that fire plays in the ecology of the forest is considered in Pringle's *Natural Fire: Its Ecology in Forests.* Children may gain a new perspective on forest fires when they read the last two chapters in which their benefits are presented. This is an interesting subject for debate as students investigate differing points of view about forest fires and then present and defend their viewpoints.

Fire is not the only beneficial event in the life cycle of the forest. In *Death Is Natural,* Pringle shows that death is also a necessary part of life; it makes life possible for succeeding generations. Through the discussion of death, children discover answers to some important questions: Why is death necessary? What happens to a living thing after it dies? How does the death of one animal or plant affect others of its kind? These questions can stimulate discussions among students. Children also discover that dead plant material is a vital link in the food chains in fields, forests, and marshes in *Chains, Webs, and Pyramids: The Flow of Energy in Nature.* In this book, Pringle explains methods that ecologists use to trace the flow of food energy in nature. Children learn that they also play a part in the flow of food energy. Pringle's books encourage additional study as they contain many reference aids such as an index, glossary, and a list of related readings.

Simon's *The Secret Clocks, Time Senses of Living Things* is another good book for children's literature students to evaluate. This author uses several techniques to interest children and help them investigate and understand the biological or "internal clocks" (a term identified by the research of German scientist Gustav Kramer) that help plants and animals survive. First he stimulates interest in the subject by posing a series of questions: "What makes the clock of an animal or plant run so accurately? What sets these biological clocks and keeps them going? Do animals somehow learn to keep time, or do they depend upon changes in their surroundings? What factors work to keep a plant on time?" (p. 8). Next, he uses the questions to develop a logical organization and he describes how scientists and nature observers have investigated these questions, discoveries they have made, and new questions that have resulted from the discoveries. Finally, he involves children in the learning process; he describes step-by-step directions for experiments with biological clocks of plants, animals, and humans that children can perform. Related readings are suggested.

It is not only biological time clocks that aid the survival of animals and plants. Morphology—the size, shape, and structure of living things and how these factors relate to daily life and evolution—is also important in nature. Dr. Dorothy Hinshaw Patent, a zoologist, discusses such topics as the significance of different kinds of skeletons, blood systems, types of structures used for moving, muscles, chewing and digestive organs, communicative organs, and reproductive organs. *Size and Shapes in Nature—What They Mean* includes photographs, drawings, an index, and a reference list of both books and magazine articles that will assist older children in investigating this topic.

Earth and Geology

Because the results of earthquakes are frequently seen on television, this is a subject that interests many children. Simon's *Danger from Below: Earthquakes—Past, Present, and Future* provides a comprehensive coverage of the subject. It begins with a history of devastating earthquakes and their causes as regarded by ancient people. The text also discusses the latest discoveries about how and why earthquakes occur, and how scientists are working to monitor their intensity and to predict where and when they will occur. The text is clarified by illustrations: photographs of actual earthquake damage show their destructive power, and maps illustrate the plates of the earth's crust and identify places where earthquakes are likely to happen. Both the Richter Scale and the Modified Mercali Intensity Scale are explained. The author appeals to children's concern for their own safety; a very useful concluding chapter tells readers what safety precautions they should take during and after an earthquake. Students of children's literature may find it interesting to compare this book written for older students with Hershell and Joan L. Nixon's book for younger students, *Earthquakes: Nature in Motion*. Readers of Simon's and the Nixons' books may enjoy comparing their descriptions with the experiences described by the main characters in Laurence Yep's *Dragonwings* as they live through the great San Francisco earthquake.

Technical terms in geology informational books may be difficult for children to understand unless authors clarify the terms with photographs and/or drawings. Written descriptions of terms such as cirques, hanging valleys, stalactites, and stalagmites may prove quite bewildering to children who have not seen these formations. The Nixons, for example, in *Glaciers: Nature's Frozen Rivers* show through photographs different classifications of glaciers and illustrate their ability to alter land formation. In addition, many of the examples are from areas where children might visit: hanging valleys are shown in Yosemite National Park and bowl-shaped cirques in Glacier National Park. The work of glaciologists is described as well as a history of the ice ages when glaciers covered northern portions of the earth. The authors bring a contemporary perspective to the study of glaciers; the text concludes with contemporary benefits of glaciers from the past and ways that people are using, or are trying to benefit from, the vast water supply contained in glaciers and icebergs. This same team of writers collaborated on another book about forces that shape the earth in *Volcanoes: Nature's Fireworks;* it was selected in 1978 as an Outstanding Science Trade Book for Children.

The photographs in the above book present a beautiful world of lofty peaks, carved valleys, and waterfalls. There is an equally fascinating world that children may discover if they have the opportunity to travel beneath the earth's surface. Geraldine Sherman's *Caverns, a World of Mystery and Beauty* discusses what explorers find when they go into this incredible world. Photographs by Julian Messner clarify the descriptive text and illustrate the exciting formations that may be found in a cavern.

Many books discussed in this section encourage children to observe nature, to become involved in experiments, and to be conservationists.

EXPERIMENTS, DISCOVERIES, AND HOW THINGS WORK

Several books in the previous section described experiments children could perform with plants or animals. There are also books designed specifically to stimulate children to learn through experimentation. Within this category are books that answer children's questions about discoveries of the past and present and books that provide explanations about how many kinds of machines actually work. Authors may clarify their texts through detailed step-by-step directions, carefully labeled diagrams, photographs that illustrate concepts, and content that proceeds from the simple to the complex or from the known to the unknown.

Experiments

Books that encourage children to experiment help them open the doors of discovery and become excited by the scientific process. The books, however, must have clearly written directions and should build on previous knowledge. For example, in

Bubbles, a Children's Museum Activity Book, by Bernie Zubrowski, the author states that experimenting with bubbles can not only be fun but can also encourage children to examine and discover some of the shaping forces of nature that scientists also study. The author helps children build concepts upon the foundation of previous knowledge because the book's organization proceeds from the simple to the more complex.

The first experiment is to make bubbles using a drinking straw. Subsequent experiments deal with making gigantic bubbles, bubble sculptures, geometric shapes, domes, and bubble houses; experimenting with bubbles as structural units; creating bigger building blocks; measuring bubbles; shrinking bubbles; observing different characteristics of bubbles; and discovering mathematical relationships and investigating light rays. Zubrowski's questioning style encourages children's interaction with the author as they make scientific discoveries. For example, after they have made the first bubble, the author says, "When you have a bubble, touch it with a wet finger, then with a dry one. What happens when you use the dry finger?" (p. 11). Zubrowski then explains why bubbles break when they come in contact with dry places. He also explains how some of the subsequent experiments, such as with domes, are used by architects and scientists.

The diagrams illustrate the relationships between the bubble and its practical application. For example, the dome experiment illustration shows a bubble dome beside an architect's drawing of a building dome. The text encourages children to expand their knowledge of bubble domes by using the shapes they have already discovered to "design your future house using bubbles as your model. With bubbles you can study the ways the walls intersect, the most natural relationships between large bubble rooms and small ones, and the ways that they join together. You can invent all kinds of special arrangements" (p. 34). The book concludes with a list of references for explorations with soap film. The content of another Zubrowski book, *Messing Around With Water Pumps and Siphons,* appeals to many young children.

Vicki Cobb, whose background includes a master's degree in science, teaching science, and creating a science television show, has created a challenging book for older students. *Bet You Can't, Science Impossibilities to Fool You* is written in a format that first presents a challenge, such as "Bet you can't flip a newspaper into the air with a ruler!" Next, the steps for the experiment are described so that children can meet the challenge. Finally, the scientific principle behind the experiment is revealed. The science impossibilities deal with gravity, mechanics, fluids, logic, energy, and perception. A table of contents and an index help the reader find information.

Discoveries

Books on discoveries range from those describing principles of past discoveries to the latest space or computer technology. Some books combine information about discoveries with experiments designed to help children understand and duplicate earlier experiments. One such book for older students is Irwin Math's *Morse, Marconi and You, Understanding and Building Telegraph, Telephone and Radio Sets.* The text describes the invention of these communication devices and shows how to perform experiments that demonstrate the principles involved. Diagrams illustrating the necessary materials and procedures for the experiment are included. Proceeding from the simple to the complex, readers begin with a basic understanding of the nature of electricity and progress through the development of the telegraph, the first telephone, a wireless system, and the radio. The text includes a table of contents, lists of illustrations, suggested further readings, and an index. Later experiments become quite complex, but it is difficult to put an age level on this book because many young science enthusiasts are fascinated with building the devices described and illustrated.

The development of the revolutionary silicon chips that make possible the minicomputer, calculator, digital watch, and other microelectronic devices is described in Stanley L. Englebardt's *Miracle Chip: The Microelectronic Revolution.* The author helps children understand the changes that have taken place in microelectronic technology. For example, photographs compare the sizes of early transistors and vacuum tubes with today's chip that can hold 3,000 separate transistors. The author ties the present into the future by presenting some fascinating possibilities for using the miracle chip to improve life in the future: computers developed for medical care and supermarket use, individually programmed computers for each student, microprocessors to help the handicapped, and a multipurpose telephone system.

Discoveries obtained from space exploration have greatly increased human knowledge. Informational books on space and space travel should reflect this expanded knowledge. Copyright dates may therefore be a very important consideration when selecting books. An attractive, almost wordless book recreates the drama of July 20, 1969, when Neil Armstrong first stepped on the moon. Erich Fuch's *Journey to the Moon* depicts the eight-day mission of Apollo 11 from launch until splashdown. This book, for younger children, has two pages of print describing the mission, followed by paintings without text.

Ten years after the moon landing, the major emphasis in space travel shifted to developing a space shuttle. Dr. Franklyn

M. Branley's *The Story of the Space Shuttle, Columbia and Beyond* traces the development of the shuttle and the anticipation that it will be used for travel when space colonies have been developed. The text is complemented by drawings of the components of the shuttle, photographs of Skylab, and diagrams and illustrations of proposed space colonies. Branley, former chairman of the Hayden Planetarium in New York City, has written many science information books for children.

Simon's readable *The Long View into Space* takes young readers, through words and photographs, from the earth into the far reaches of outer space. In the text accompanying the photographs, Simon uses facts and concepts known to children to develop new understanding about the universe. Consider, for example, how the author uses known information to help readers understand distances in space. In order to help children understand the reason for not measuring space distances from earth to the planets in miles, he tells them that it would be like "trying to measure the distance between New York and London in inches" (p. 4 unnumbered). Similarly, he uses children's knowledge of the time it would take a spaceship to travel to the moon to develop the concept of distances: the same spaceship that could reach the moon in a few days would require more than a year to travel close to the sun. To help children understand size, a large photograph of the sun is compared to an earth the size of a period on the page. Numbers are also related to known time frames. Children are informed that if they wanted to count the over 100 billion stars in the Milky Way, it would take them 3,000 years, counting one star each second. Another of Simon's space books, *The Long Journey From Space,* effectively tells what we know about comets by using old photographs to show comets in history and current photographs of Halley's Comet. The comparisons between the times are striking and help readers understand the considerable increase in technology and knowledge.

How Things Work

Several informational books respond to children's curiosity about how common home appliances and bigger machines actually work. These books usually contain detailed diagrams or photographs accompanying two or three pages of descriptive text. While the readability and interest level are usually considered upper elementary and above, many much younger children ask questions about how percolators, dishwashers, or Thermos bottles work. Therefore, parents may find these books helpful when answering questions asked by young children. (One mother said that her six-year-old son's favorite book was one containing diagrams of machines at work.) Two

such informational books are Michael Pollard's *How Things Work* and Robert Gardner's *This is the Way It Works: A Collection of Machines.* Pollard's text describes the workings of larger machines: helicopters, jet engines, rockets, steam engines, diesel engines, elevators, and televisions. Detailed drawings and colored photographs clarify the text. Gardner's book emphasizes many objects or machines that are found around the house: mechanisms related to light, appliances, electric apparatus, and machines used in medicine and recreation. The illustrations are all diagrams. Both texts contain indexes.

Where is the longest, the highest, or the most expensive bridge? What did the first bridge probably look like? Who were the first great bridge builders? What changes have taken place in bridge construction? These are some of the questions answered in Scott Corbett's *Bridges*. Both bridges and their builders are discussed. Drawings help clarify the terminology and illustrate kinds of bridges from the early suspension bridges, to Roman arches, to medieval fortified bridges, to covered New England bridges, to railroad trestles, and finally, to the great twentieth-century bridges.

Proceeding from the simple to the complex, an important technique in books that explain concepts, is used by Anne and Scott MacGregor in *Domes: A Project Book*. The authors develop concepts related to physical stress and the construction of domes. They begin with simple igloos and proceed to cathedrals. Models for domes and directions for building them encourage children to experiment.

Photographs may illustrate and clarify the steps in demolishing a building as well as building it. Elinor Horwitz's *How to Wreck a Building* follows the demolition of an elementary school from the time the crane operator strikes the building until the debris is loaded into dump trucks.

Michael Berenstain's *The Castle Book* appeals to children who want to know about where their favorite fairy tale characters might have lived or are fascinated with medieval life. Its strength lies in the cutaway illustrations that allow children to picture the various parts of castles, some of which had the appearance of small cities. Children can visualize the life of the inhabitants as they travel from the dungeon, up the stone stairs to the kitchen and guard rooms, through the great hall where musicians and jugglers entertained, up to the royal chamber where ladies wove tapestries, and finally to the top of the watchtower. They can see blacksmiths working at their trade, boys training for knighthood, and peasants tending livestock. Several types of castles are pictured along with a discussion about their purposes and routines. Older children who would like to learn more about castles may refer to Sheila Sancha's *The Castle Story.* This comprehensive text gives detailed descriptions of castles and includes a map of castle sites, a glossary of terms, a bibliography, and an index.

Several books help children understand contemporary structures and how they work. Peter Schaaf's *An Apartment House Close Up,* for example, shows photographs of architectural features, typical rooms, elevators, and heating facilities found in an apartment house. The book would be meaningful to children living in a city apartment. The content includes some areas that are not always accessible to tenants.

Byron Barton's *Airport* is an excellent picture book for younger children. The large, colorful pictures answer many questions about airports and airline travel. The text has a logical organization; it follows passengers from their arrival at the airport to boarding the plane. A cutaway illustration is especially effective; it places the interior of the plane in proper perspective for the viewers.

Many books discussed in this section answer children's questions about how common and uncommon objects and machines work. Others encourage children to become involved in their own experiments and learn scientific principles through the scientific method. The books in the next section also encourage children to become actively involved in areas that interest them.

HOBBIES, CRAFTS, AND HOW-TO BOOKS

One of the main reasons for reading identified by older elementary school children is to learn more about their hobbies and interests. One educator who asked children how teachers could improve children's enjoyment of reading was told that teachers should ask them about their hobbies and help them find books about them (12). Books are available on almost every hobby or craft. The more useful books contain clearly understood directions, provide guidelines for choosing equipment or other materials, or provide interesting background information.

One such book, Glen and Eve Bunting's *Skateboards: How to Make Them, How to Ride Them,* provides step-by-step instructions for making a skateboard that would sell for over thirty dollars if purchased. There are also photographs showing skateboard maintenance and suggestions for riding. The directions for riding progress from beginning through advanced skills and on to competitive skateboarding. The steps are illustrated with photographs of skateboarders performing. The book stresses safety and using good judgment when skateboarding.

Two books that explore running are Frank and Jan Asch's *Running with Rachel* and Carol Lea Benjamin's *Running Basics. Running with Rachel* describes how a young girl takes up running after meeting a lady jogging on the road. Warm-up and warm-down exercises and the importance of wearing the right shoes and eating proper food are discussed. Photographs of a young runner illustrate the exercises. *Running Basics* provides a more in-depth coverage of jogging. It includes advice on getting started, running techniques, warm-up exercises, attitudes, equipment, endurance, and first aid.

Jill Krementz, a documentary photographer, has written several books with photographs about young people who have chosen hobbies that they hope to extend into professional or competitive status sports. The dedication needed for success in a sport is shown in *A Very Young Skater.* The photographs illustrate Katherine Healy's rigorous schedule as she practices, takes lessons, and prepares for competition. Krementz's *A Very Young Rider* is a photographic essay about a ten-year-old girl, Vivi Malloy, who hopes to become a member of the U.S. Olympic team. Krementz has also accompanied dancers, gymnasts, and circus performers. The pictures effectively present the joys as well as the day to day struggles.

Young photographers may be stimulated by Krementz's beautiful black and white photographs. If they need advice in taking pictures and developing and printing black and white photographs, they can find instructions in Edward E. Davis's *Into the Dark, a Beginner's Guide to Developing and Printing Black and White Negatives.* This text includes information on setting up a home darkroom and step-by-step directions for developing negatives, making contact prints, and printing enlargements. A bibliography and index are included. Miriam Cooper's *Snap! Photography* appeals to some younger photographers because it includes examples of photographs taken by children.

Jim Arnosky, an illustrator for *Rod and Reel,* uses his considerable knowledge of fishing to create a credible and useful book for young fishermen. *Freshwater Fish and Fishing* includes clearly stated directions on tying a fly and making lures, detailed illustrations showing types of fish, and advice on how to catch fish.

One large box and a child's imagination can result in creating a horse, a castle or even a supermarket. Flo Ann Hedley Norvell's *The Great Big Box Book* presents seventeen projects described with easily followed step-by-step directions. Each direction is numbered and illustrated in an accompanying drawing or photograph. Young children, with a little help, will have hours of fun making and playing with an Indian tepee, a castle, a log cabin, a spaceship, or an artist's easel. Of interest to the slightly older child is Paul Berman's *Make-Believe Empire: A How-to Book.* Simple instructions and accompanying drawings show young construction workers how to build a city

Detailed directions and photographs of finished projects help children create items out of boxes.
Photograph by Richard W. Mitchell from *The Great Big Box Book* by Flo Ann Hedley Norvell. Photographs copyright © 1979 by Richard Warren Mitchell. By permission of Thomas Y. Crowell, Publishers.

from cans, boxes, and wood; how to construct a navy; and how to create their own laws and documents.

Children who read frontier books or survival stories may be interested in discovering more about their foods and food preparation. Barbara M. Walker's *The Little House Cookbook: Frontier Foods from Wilder's Classic Stories,* for example, presents frontier foods written about in Wilder's "Little House" stories. The author says that she has searched for authentic recipes by reading the writings of Wilder and her daughter Rose, pioneer diaries, and local recipe collections. Her purpose for sharing this collection with children is the hope that they will rediscover basic

connections among the food on the table, the grain in the field, and the cow in the pasture. Between the winter and dried apples, the summer and tomatoes, the autumn and fresh sausage. Between the labors of the pioneers and the abundance we enjoy today. Between children and their elders. Between the preparation of a meal and the experience of love. (p. xv)

The author has used liberal excerpts from the "Little House" books and the original Garth Williams illustrations in discussing the foods and their preparation.

Readers often ask how the heroes in Jean George's *My Side of the Mountain* and *River Rats, Inc.* could identify and live off the wild foods discussed in the two books. Pringle's *Wild Foods: A Beginner's Guide to Identifying, Harvesting and Cooking Safe and Tasty Plants from the Outdoors* discusses many of these wild plants. The author's credentials are valid. He studied wildlife conservation at Cornell University and has been the editor of *Nature and Science,* a children's science magazine published by The American Museum of Natural History. The book discusses common, edible wild plants that are easily identified. The plants are presented in the order in which they appear in nature, beginning in early spring. The book gives general information about each plant, descriptions of locations, detailed descriptions and drawings of plant identification, information about the edible parts, how the plant should be harvested, and recipes. The plant drawings by Paul Breeden, an artist whose illustrations have appeared in *National Geographic, Audubon,* and *Smithsonian* magazines, are especially effective and clarify differences between edible plants and poisonous plants that resemble them.

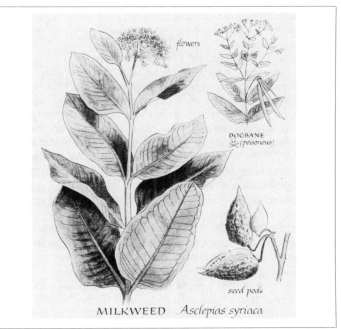

Detailed comparisons of wild plants help readers distinguish the poisonous from the nonpoisonous.
Reprinted by permission of Four Winds Press, a division of Scholastic Inc. From *Wild Foods* by Laurence Pringle. Illustrations © 1978 by Scholastic Inc. Text copyright © 1978 by Laurence Pringle.

Pets usually interest children. When that pet is a gerbil, a snake, or a hamster, however, children may not know how to take care of it. *Care of Uncommon Pets,* written by veterinarian William J. Weber, answers questions about handling, housing, feeding, breeding, and caring for unusual pets. Each chapter, which may be read independently, is divided into the previously listed subheadings and concludes with related readings. The chapter shows how to construct a cage. This book should provide valuable information for children who want one of these uncommon pets or for teachers who have rabbits, mice, guinea pigs, or snakes in their classrooms.

These books encourage children to consider new hobbies or to learn more about existing ones. Children discover that some hobbies may even lead to a career.

BIOGRAPHIES

Writers of biographies have a vast pool of real characters from which to choose. There are brave men and women who conquer seas, discover new continents, and explore space. There are equally brave and intelligent men and women who fight discrimination, change lives through their ministering or inventions, and overcome handicaps in their efforts to achieve. The way writers of children's literature choose to portray these figures, however, changes with historic time periods. During the eighteenth and nineteenth centuries biographies reflected the belief that literature should teach children and save their souls. Jon C. Stott (13) concludes that there were many "biographies of good little children who died early and went to Heaven and of bad little children who died early and went to Hell" (p.177). M. Ione Taylor (14), in a study of biographies, found this earlier didacticism was gradually reduced and current biographies are more concerned with appealing to children's imagination, their need for realism, and their response to humor.

Gertrude B. Herman (9) relates children's understanding of biography to the changes in their own development. She maintains that until children are about eight years old they have difficulty stepping out of their own time and space to explore the lives of real people who they may never meet. Herman believes that children in the fourth through sixth grades read biographies with increasing understanding and self-identification as long as the books are about people they are interested in and the author has written in a lively style that holds children's interest. Herman believes it is

the adolescent who is finally ready for causes, for heroes and heroines . . . and for all those fascinating persons who are not necessarily mod-

els of perfection, but who are human beings through whose doubts and triumphs, courage or villainy, victories or defeats, young people may try on personalities, life styles, and modes of thought and commitment. It is in investigating, in shifting and winnowing facts and ideas, in empathizing with the deeds and sufferings of others that growth is helped along—intellectual, emotional, and spiritual growth. It is through this integrative function that biography and autobiography, honesty presented with literary and artistic merit, can make important contributions to self-integration and social realization. The testimony of many individuals over many years supports a conviction that young people have much to gain from reading about real human beings in all their complexity, with all their sometimes troubled lives. (p. 88)

As with realistic fiction, there are differences of opinion about the content of children's biographies. Several authors have criticized biographies that avoid controversial facts about people's backgrounds, including sensitive areas about their political beliefs or their private lives. William Anderson and Patrick Groff (1) in *A New Look at Children's Literature* discuss the taboos imposed by society upon biographies written for children. These taboos often are against writing about infamous people or showing the "dark, unsavory, or undistinguished side" of a great person's life.

Jean Fritz (8), a well-known author of historical biographies for young children, says:

Biographies have for the most part lagged behind other types of children's literature, bogged down, for one thing, by didacticism. Famous men and women must be shown in their best colors so children can emulate them. The idea of emulation has been a powerful factor in determining the nature of biography for children; you see the word over and over again in textbooks and courses of study. And I think it has done great harm in distorting history and breeding cynicism; the great men are all gone, the implication is. Because history is old, educators are often guilty of simply repeating it instead of taking a fresh look at it. Because if is complicated, they tend to simplify by watering down material for children, whereas children need more meat rather than less, but selected for their own interests. This, of course, involves original research, a great deal of it, which twenty years ago, I think was rather rare in children's biographies. (p. 125)

Students of children's literature now find more biographies that develop many sides of a person's character. Readers may discover, through biographers such as Fritz, that heroes and heroines are real. They can, like other humans, demonstrate negative qualities. It may, in fact, be easier to emulate someone who is a believable human being.

Evaluating Biographies for Children

Like other literature, biographies should be evaluated according to the criteria for good literature discussed in chapter three.

THROUGH THE EYES OF AN AUTHOR

On Writing Biography

Jean Fritz

JEAN FRITZ, biographer of early American patriots, creates believable characters by admitting their foibles as well as their strengths.

THE REASON FOR WRITING biography for children is the same as for writing biography for adults: to explore human behavior; to come to grips with specific characters interrelating with their specific times. This is not as obvious as it sounds. It was once a commonly held assumption (one that still persists in some quarters) that biographies written for children should portray idealized heroes and heroines, models held up by the adult world to inspire children to attain virtue and, by implication, its concomitant rewards. Furthermore, according to some educators, the motivation of characters should not be examined, only their deeds.

Such an approach, it seems to me, is dull, unrealistic, and unfair. Children look for clues to life. They want the truth, they need the truth, and they deserve it. So I try to present characters honestly with their paradoxes and their complexities, their strengths and their weaknesses. To do this, I involve myself in as much research as I would if I were writing a biography for adults.

Contrary to what I call "old-fashioned" biography for children, I do not invent dialogue. I use dialogue only when I can document it. If the text is meaty enough, I do not think that children need facts dressed up in fictional trimmings. Indeed, children welcome hard, specific facts that bring characters to life—not only the important facts but those small vivid details that have a way of lighting up an event or a personality. Had I been present, for instance, to hear Patrick Henry give his famous "liberty or death" speech, I would certainly have been impressed by his dramatic oratory, but I would also have remembered the man in the balcony who became so excited, he spit a wad of tobacco into the audience below. The trivial and the significant generally travel hand in hand and indeed I suspect that most people find that memory of trivial off-the-record detail serves to nail down memory itself. I think of history and biography as *story* and am convinced that the best stories are the true ones.

Due to their specific nature, there are some additional concerns that should be considered. The quote by Fritz suggests that authors also have special demands placed on their writing and research abilities. Authors and adults who select biographies for children are concerned with the accuracy of the information, the worthiness of the subject, and the balance between fact and story line.

Accuracy—Where Did the Facts Originate? Biographies have a special responsibility to be accurate and authentic as they depict person and setting. This task is so important and demanding that May Hill Arbuthnot and Dorothy M. Broderick (2) say:

An author who undertakes the writing of a biography should be prepared to spend months, and probably longer, in study and research before he touches his typewriter. He should read what recent historians have written, and he should go back to the time when his hero was alive, and read what he wrote and what others of the period wrote about him. (p. 225)

In addition to careful research, biographer Olivia Coolidge (5) says that the author of biographical literature must also distinguish a fact from a judgment because

a good biography is also concerned with the effect its hero has on other people, with environment and background, with the nature of the great man's achievements, and their value. I find that I examine facts in all these and many other spheres before I form judgments and that it needs great care to do what sounds quite easy, namely to distinguish a fact from a judgment. (p. 146)

She concludes her concern over fact and judgment by saying:

It simply seems that I need to know everything possible—because knowledge may affect judgment or because I am not yet really certain what I shall use or omit. In other words, I find it necessary to have a habit of worrying about facts, small or large, because my buildings are made up of these bricks, stones, or even pebbles. (p. 148)

An author's search for accuracy should include a wide range of sources. It is helpful if the author includes a bibliography in the book. Leonard Wibberley's note at the end of his biography of Thomas Jefferson (15), for example, illustrates the variety of sources that an author relies on in his research. His bibliography includes numerous books about Jefferson, a book written by Jefferson's great-granddaughter, and sources of information about figures around Jefferson including Aaron Burr, John Marshall, and James Madison. Other authors often mention their research in historical societies, newspaper records, diaries, and letters. Frequently, they visit the actual locations. Even the simple biographies for young children must be authentic in their facts and illustrations because young children acquire considerable knowledge about a time or a setting from the illustrations rather than from detailed descriptions.

A Worthy Subject and a Believable Human. The subject of a biography should be worth reading about just as it should be worthy of the author's meticulous research and time spent in writing. Has the subject made a significant accomplishment or a discovery that should be shared? Will children have a better understanding of the complexities of human nature, both good and bad, after they have read the book? Will they discover that history is made up of real people when they read the book? Will they appreciate the contributions of their ancestors or their heritage through the life of the person in the biography?

If children are to discover that history or science or politics is made up of real people, these people must be believable. Just like the people children know, subjects must have many-faceted characters: they may have good and bad characteristics, they may be liked and disliked. Fritz, for example, has written a series of historical biographies that suggest that our revolutionary leaders were very human. Patrick Henry is presented as a practical joker who did not appreciate school in his youth, while Samuel Adams is found to be a man who was not afraid to speak out against the British but who refused to ride a horse.

Balancing Fact and Story Line. Writers of biographies for young children must balance the requirement for accuracy with the requirement of a narrative that appeals to young children. Through her selection of humorous facts, for example, Fritz develops plots and characters that present information in a story format.

Writers of biographies for older children usually include considerable factual detail. Because the books are longer, pertinent background details, facts, and people who influenced the subjects' values and decisions can be developed. For example, Ronald Syme's *Toussaint: The Black Liberator* develops the island setting that led to violence, the conditions experienced by slaves on Haiti, the career changes as Toussaint progressed from a slave to a free leader of the black revolt, and the political and military leaders of the time who influenced his actions and led to his imprisonment and death. However, the facts in books written for older children should be written in a lively style that produces believable characters who almost come to life.

Biographical Subjects

The subjects of biographies written for children range from early explorers of the new world who sailed uncharted seas to contemporary explorers who face the challenges of space exploration as they seek the moon and beyond. There are political heroes and heroines who spoke out against oppression and became leaders in time of need. There are great achievers who have made contributions in science, art, literature, and sports. There are also common people who express uncommon courage and warmth in their daily struggle for survival.

The biographies under the categories of explorers, political heroes and heroines of the past and present, and achievers in science are discussed in a chronological order so that students of children's literature can better understand the times within which these people lived, and compare books written about similar time periods or identical characters.

Explorers—"To Seek New Worlds For Gold, For Praise, For Glory" (Walter Raleigh). Stories of monsters lurking in unknown waters and dog-headed people as well as vast riches waiting in the fabulous Indies rang in the great halls and crowded streets of fifteenth-century Europe. Educated people were beginning to agree that the world was round, rather than flat, and a few men believed they could reach the Indies by sailing due west rather than traveling the long, arduous overland trail that crossed thousands of miles of deserts and mountains. The man of the times, Christopher Columbus, who persevered in his quest for financial backing and a crew who would accompany him on his search for the Indies is the subject of many biographies. These books range from short, highly illustrated books designed to be read to young children to the longer versions that describe Columbus's trials in being accepted, his triumphs after his initial discovery, and the final disappointments that plagued him until his death. These biographies differ in literary style, focus, amount of detail, and the development of Columbus's character. Consequently they are good for evaluation and comparison.

Let us consider several differences in biographies by Alice Dalgliesh, Ingri and Edgar Parin D'Aulaire, Piero Ventura, David Goodnough, and Jean Fritz. The simplest of these five biographies is Dalgliesh's *The Columbus Story.* The writer's style is characterized by short sentences and repetitive language. For example, she introduces readers to Columbus's growing desire to go to sea with these words:

Mystery, danger, adventure—what exciting words! Christopher wanted more than ever to be a sailor. The wind that ruffled his red hair seemed to call to him, 'Come!' 'Come, come, come!' The waves that lapped the wharves said it over and over. (p. 3 unnumbered)

The author focuses upon three incidents in Columbus's life: his unsuccessful pleas to the king of Portugal, his successful pleas to the queen of Spain, and his first voyage to America. Large illustrations by Leo Politi provide additional detail. This simpler version does not develop the problems and disappointments that later plague Columbus's life.

The D'Aulaires' *Columbus,* written for slightly older children, does not conclude with Columbus's triumphant return to Spain but continues with his subsequent voyages to America. The authors' inclusion of details about plots against Columbus, his disfavor at the Spanish court, his arrest as a traitor to Spain, and his disenchantment because he had not discovered the passage to the Indies develops quite a different character than the Dalgliesh version. Because of the inclusion of

This highly illustrated text captures the setting for a biography about Columbus.
From *Christopher Columbus,* by Piero Ventura, based on the text by Gian Paolo Ceserani. Copyright © 1978 by Random House, Inc. Reprinted by permission of the publisher.

more information, readers visualize a character who did not understand the magnitude of his discovery. The authors' description of Columbus reinforces this image:

Old and tired, Columbus returned to Spain from his fourth and last voyage. While he was searching in vain, the Portuguese had found the seaway to the East by sailing south around Africa. Now Columbus stood in the shadow. (p. 54)

The focus of Ventura's *Christopher Columbus,* based on the text by Gian Paolo Ceserani, is upon a pictorial account of Columbus's version of his adventures. Detailed drawings depict the city of Genoa, the fleet sailing from Palos, the interior of the Santa Maria, typical clothing worn by each crew member, the Bahamas as they looked in 1492, an Indian village on the coast of Cuba, the plants discovered in the new world, and the fort built by the crew.

Goodnough's *Christopher Columbus* provides more information on Columbus's search for funds; the major emphasis is on his early seafaring years and his efforts to persuade Portuguese and Spanish royalty to back his exploration and his first voyage. Fritz's *Where Do You Think You're Going, Christopher Columbus?* is written in a lighter style that appeals to many children. She has also added background information that creates a lively history inhabited by real people. For example, Queen Isabella

was so religious that if she even found Christians who were not sincere Christians, she had them burned at the stake. (Choir boys sang during the burning so Isabella wouldn't have to hear the screams). (p. 17)

The main emphasis in this book is on events that occurred during Columbus's four voyages. Fritz ends her book with useful notes that clarify some points and an index of people and locations discussed in the book.

Illustrations help readers visualize the ancient lands, the different cultures, and the new discoveries discussed in biographies of explorers. With the same fine detail as developed in the Columbus biography, Piero Ventura illustrates Gian Paolo Ceserani's text for *Marco Polo.* This pictorial account traces Marco Polo's travels from Venice, to China, and back to Europe. The detailed pictures recreate the bustle of a European port, the active life in the Chinese court, the inventions found in China, and the value of spices and silks. The illustrations and text create a feeling of time and place and the importance of Marco Polo's discoveries.

In the 1500s, a new excitement was stirring in Spain as suggested by author William O. Steele. Notice how the author in *The Wilderness Tattoo: A Narrative of Juan Ortiz* uses strong visual images to develop this excitement:

The Admiral of the Ocean Sea had burst through the unknown and the darkness and swept away forever the lurking watery horrors of the Atlantic Ocean from men's minds. A new-found land lay to the west of Europe. And it belonged to Spain. (p. 23)

This is the background in which Steele places his hero, seventeen-year-old Juan Ortiz as he joins the 1527 Spanish expedition of Panfilo de Narvaez when it sails from Spain to explore Florida. The author develops a fast paced plot as he describes Juan's radically changing life. Consider, for example, the impact and importance of this series of events: Juan and three friends are captured by Timucuan Indians on the shores of Tampa Bay. Juan, whose life is spared, becomes a slave of an Indian chief and then escapes to join a neighboring village where he is eventually adopted into the tribe. Because of his affection for the Indian people who have given him a new life, he experiences mixed emotions when he learns that Spanish explorers are near the village. His desire to see his homeland again causes him to seek their company. However, Juan finds himself in a new role: the leader of the expedition, Hernando de Soto, seeks his aid as an interpreter. De Soto rejoices over Juan's abilities: "This interpreter puts a new life into us in affording the means of our understanding these people, for without him I know not what would become of us" (p. 177). For the next two years, until the time of his death, Juan Ortiz marched westward across southern America. Steele's writing is a highly readable account of the period and the people involved. The historical framework of the book is enhanced by the author's introduction of "Interludes" at strategic places in the biography. These eight short sections report historical facts that clarify the story's action. Sixteen old prints showing early artists' portrayals of the time period also add interest.

All explorers do not try to discover new lands; some search for proof that will lend credibility to their own theories. *Thor Heyerdahl: Viking Scientist,* by Wyatt Blassingame, is the biography of a man who believed strongly that the Pacific Islands had been populated by pre-Columbian Indians who had sailed from South America. In order to disprove the critics who claimed that balsa rafts would become waterlogged and sink long before they could reach their destination, Heyerdahl built a balsa raft, *Kon Tiki* (named after an ancient Polynesian god), and with five friends sailed 4,000 miles from Peru to the Polynesian islands of the South Pacific. The author creates a believable character as he develops the background that caused Heyerdahl to become interested in the origins of the early inhabitants of the Polynesian islands and why he believed they came from South America: trade winds and currents move from east to west; words like *Tiki* are common to both Indians of Peru and native Polynesians; similar stone terraces are

A contemporary explorer searches for the origins of the Polynesian culture.
Jacket art by Linda Lenkowski from *Thor Heyerdahl: Viking Scientist* by Wyatt Blassingame. Reproduced by permission of the publisher, Elsevier/Nelson, a Division of Elsevier-Dutton Publishing Co., Inc.

found in both locations; and the skulls of Polynesians are long, similar to those of the Indians, rather than round like Asian people. Children can also vicariously accompany the crew of the *Kon Tiki* on their perilous voyage through storms and pounding waves on a great reef before they reach their destination.

Two biographies of modern-day explorers relate the lives of people who have chosen to explore space. Mitchell R. Sharpe's *It Is I, Sea Gull, Valentina Tereshkova, First Woman in Space* is the life of the Russian cosmonaut, who, on June 16, 1963, became the first woman to orbit the earth. Photographs of her training and experiences add credibility and interest. An autobiography of an astronaut may seem more exciting and plausible than if the story were told by someone else. Michael Collins's *Flying to the Moon and Other Strange Places* includes photographs of early jets, fighting planes, astronauts in training, and the moon, which should interest children who enjoy reading about astronauts and space exploration. His descriptions of his journey aboard Gemini and Apollo demonstrate that exploration is still possible.

Political Heroes and Heroines of the Past and Present. Throughout history, men and women have been willing to speak out in favor of strongly held beliefs, although those beliefs might endanger their lives; to defend their country's position if they believe it is correct; and to defend their people's right to freedom. Biographies about national political heroes vary in their inclusion of facts about the characters. Some authors suggest by their reporting of only worthy personal traits that the characters are saintly. Other authors develop well rounded characters who demonstrate a more believable range of human emotions and personal traits.

It is helpful if students of children's literature read several biographies, from differing perspectives, about the same person. This experience helps clarify the importance of the focus and tone chosen by the authors. For example, after reading three books about a political leader, one of this author's students commented that she could have been reading about three different people. Because the authors each had a specific purpose in writing their biographies, each author's choice of incidents and tone of writing created a different bias in the reader.

1776. Some very exciting biographies for young children are Fritz's stories of Revolutionary War heroes. Her characters seem to come alive through her inclusion of little-known information that makes them seem real to children. Through these books children discover that heroes, like themselves, have fears, display good and bad characteristics, and may be liked by some and disliked by others. Fritz, for example, adds humor to *Where Was Patrick Henry on the 29th of May?* by developing the theory that unusual things seem to happen to him on the date of his birth. Her characterization of Henry suggests a many-sided character: a practical joker; a man filled with "passion for fiddling, dancing, and pleasantry"; and a lawyer with a gift for oratory.

In *Why Don't You Get a Horse, Sam Adams?* Fritz portrays a man who is a fierce advocate of a free America; but he is also a man who refuses to ride a horse. This mistrust of horses causes him to walk through Boston and even hide in a swamp when he flees the British. It is not until John Adams convinces him that his country's honor and his own are at stake that he agrees to get on a horse; in statues, statesmen are always shown riding horses. Fritz illustrates a humorous conclusion: Samuel Adams, complete with padded drawers to prevent saddle sores, rides triumphantly into Philadelphia. Three other books about Revolutionary War heroes include *And Then*

The illustrations in Fritz's biographies complement the realistic and often humorous behavior of the characters.
Reprinted by permission of Putnam Publishing Group from *And Then What Happened, Paul Revere,* text copyright © 1973 by Jean Fritz, illustrations copyright © 1973 by Margot Tomes.

What Happened, Paul Revere?, Will You Sign Here, John Hancock?, and *What's the Big Idea, Ben Franklin?*

Heroes, however, are not the only subjects of Fritz's biographies for children. In *Traitor: The Case of Benedict Arnold* the author characterizes a man who wanted to be a success and a hero, but developed into a notorious villain of the Revolutionary War. Notice how Fritz introduces her character, interests the readers in the forthcoming happenings, and prepares the readers for dramatic changes in a man: "Benedict Arnold succeeded beyond anyone's wildest expectations — 'the bravest of the brave,' George Washington called him in 1777. Yet three years later he was described as 'the veriest villain of centuries past,' and no one would have argued with that" (p.7). The incidents Fritz chooses to include develop many sides to Arnold's character and encourage readers to understand why he chose to join forces against his country.

Most of the biographies about colonial American figures deal with the contributions and lives of men. Women are included in the biographies of great political heroes, but their roles are usually minor. One book that focuses on contributions of great American women is *Demeter's Daughters: The Women Who Founded America 1587-1787* by Selma R. Williams. It is a lengthy text for older students that contains biographical sketches of women of the period; the sketches are written to illustrate various aspects of society and the patterns of colonial life. The book is divided into six parts: the early settlement of America; the family including law and marriage, childhood and education; political stirrings including witchcraft; the later colonial period; women during the Revolutionary War; and women's search for equality. This book is too complex and lengthy to appeal to many children, but it is a valuable source of material about the role of women in the founding of America.

1791. In lands other than the United States, political leaders were calling for freedom against oppression. In Haiti, in the mid- to late eighteenth century, leaders were concerned with the oppression of slaves. Ronald Syme in *Toussaint: The Black Liberator* effectively contrasts the beauty of the setting with the unhappiness of the black residents. Consider, for example, the following contrasts in terms and resulting images: "The whole island of Haiti, from its lofty blue mountain ranges to the graceful white shores, was a smoldering mass of cruelty, oppression, and racial hatred that betrayed its natural loveliness. A rebellion destroying the existing way of life was inevitable" (p. 18). The major portion of this biography focuses on Toussaint's rise until he rallies his people to fight against French, Spanish, and English armies. The author develops a strong character who, even after his arrest and imprisonment in France, expresses his defiance and dreams for freedom. This desire for freedom is felt in Syme's use of strong images: "You may have felled the Tree of Liberty in Saint Dominque, which was myself, but its roots plunge deeply into the soil. They will soon grow again" (p. 180).

1725–1801. Fiery words and bold leadership were not the only ways to fight oppression. Elizabeth Yates's *Amos Fortune, Free Man* is an example of a man who expresses love through gentle action. Through the character's thoughts, through his treatment of others, and through his actions, Yates creates a consistent character who lives by his beliefs; a man who helps others and feels his life should make the way better for those who follow him. These words on his tombstone erected in 1801 suggest the strength of his character: He "was born free in Africa, a slave in America, he purchased liberty, professed Christianity, lived reputably, and died hopefully" (p. 181).

1750–1826. Older students can experience an in-depth view of Thomas Jefferson's life through Leonard Wibberley's four-volume biography. These volumes are *Young Man from Piedmont, the Youth of Thomas Jefferson; A Dawn in the Trees, Thomas Jefferson, the Years 1776 to 1789; The Gales of Spring, Thomas Jefferson, the Years 1789 to 1801;* and *Time of Harvest, Thomas Jefferson, the Years 1801 to 1826.* Wibberley's own comments detail the research that went into this work and his eventual realization of Jefferson as a man rather than a distant myth: "During that time I have come to know Jefferson (or to believe that I know him) rather better than I know many of my closest contemporaries.... When I started this biography Jefferson was for me a remote and somewhat cold figure. I now feel a great warmth for him and a closeness to him that I believe will last the rest of my life" (*Time of Harvest*, p. 165). It is hoped that children will feel this same warmth after they read the book.

1809–1865. The best-known biographer of Abraham Lincoln is probably Carl Sandburg. His *Abraham Lincoln: The Prairie Years* is the source for the information he used to write his biography for children, *Abe Lincoln Grows Up.* Through this book, children discover a young backwoodsman who is starved for books, wanting to learn, to live, and satisfy his hunger for knowledge. They discover his feelings about books from such dialogue as, "The things I want to know are in books; my best friend is the man who'll get me a book I ain't read" (p. 135). Books did more for young Abe than for others as Sandburg says:

It seemed that Abe made the books tell him more than they told other people.... Abe picked out questions....such as "Who has the most right to complain, the Indian or the Negro?" and Abe would talk about it, up one way and down the other, while they were in the cornfield pulling fodder for the winter. (p. 135)

1824–1863. The most famous Native American of his time is the subject of Betsy Lee's *Charles Eastman, The Story of an American Indian.* The author focuses this biography on the influences that combined to make Eastman a spokesman for his people, including the forced leave from Minnesota; his medical education; and his efforts to provide medical treatment, better living conditions, restore broken treaties, and encourage Indians and whites to respect the Indian culture. Lee says that after the Indians were granted religious freedom in 1934

Charles's message was finally heard, at long last his people would have a voice of their own. Charles Eastman, perhaps more than anyone else, kept Sioux culture and tradition alive during the silent years from 1890 to 1934. Much of what we know today about the American Indian we owe to him. (p. 62)

The contributions and life of Charles Eastman make an excellent addition to multiethnic literature.

1900s. Biographies written for younger readers and for older readers differ in tone, focus, choice of content, amount of detail, and development of character. Because of the range in intended audiences, biographies about political leaders who rose to power in the 1900s provide an opportunity to compare authors' techniques and content.

First, consider several "Crowell Biographies" written for younger readers: Ophelia Settle Egypt's *James Weldon Johnson,* Jane Goodsell's *Eleanor Roosevelt,* and Ruth Franchere's *Cesar Chavez.* The books share several common features. Readability levels that range from second to fourth grades indicate the books are meant for children's independent reading. The books contain numerous illustrations. The authors focus on very positive characteristics and situations.

Egypt's biography of the Civil Rights leader, author, and educator, *James Weldon Johnson,* is a good example of author's tone (the author's attitude toward the character). The author's choice of content and descriptions of Johnson create a feeling of admiration and affection. The reasons for her feelings are revealed in the text. She says that her admiration and affection for Johnson may be traced to her early childhood and the pride she felt when singing Johnson's "Lift Every Voice and Sing." She was also "his most ardent fan" when she was a young instructor at Fisk University where Johnson was a professor.

Jane Goodsell's biography of *Eleanor Roosevelt* focuses on personality development and the changes that allow Mrs. Roosevelt to overcome personality conflicts and eventually succeed. Goodsell's characterization of young Eleanor shows her as shy, lonely, and often bored. These personality characteristics are overcome, however. The author focuses on Eleanor's adult role as an assistant to her husband in his political career, a crusader for her beliefs, and a worker for the United Nations. Goodsell does not include any materials that hint at the personal unhappiness developed in adult biographies.

Ruth Franchere's *Cesar Chavez* focuses on the Mexican American political leader's struggles to develop the National Farm Workers Association and gain political and economic power for Mexican Americans. The author develops sympathy for Chavez's undertakings by showing pictures of the poor living conditions of a migrant family and providing details related to Chavez's schooling. His family moved so often that he attended thirty-six schools while acquiring an eighth-grade education. Franchere's choice of content infers information about Chavez's concerns and values: he tries to organize classes where Mexicans can learn to read and write English; he works for Mexican American voter registration; and he organizes the 1968 grape boycott in order to demand better pay and living conditions for migrant workers.

Next consider the following books written for an older audience: James Haskins's *Andrew Young: Man With A Mission,* Edward F. Dolan, Jr.'s *Adolf Hitler: A Portrait in Tyranny,* Barbara Silberdick's *Franklin D. Roosevelt, Gallant President,* and Margaret Davidson's *The Golda Meir Story.* The longer format allows authors to include more details and develop more information about the historical period. As inferred by the descriptive terms in the titles, readers would expect to find differences in tone. One of these books differs markedly; it is not the biography of a political hero.

Haskins's biography of the first Black American to become ambassador to the United Nations, *Andrew Young: Man With A Mission,* focuses not only on Young's achievements but also on problems he faced overcoming prejudice. By including his setbacks as well as his accomplishments, readers gain a clearer understanding of Young's character, his struggles for civil rights, and his role as clergyman, legislator, and ambassador.

The subject matter in Dolan's biography for older readers, *Adolf Hitler: A Portrait in Tyranny,* exemplifies the belief that children should read about the villains in history as well as the heroes. As reflected in the title, the author's tone is not affec-

tionate, praiseworthy, or noncritical. Instead he refers to a "frightening period in the past" that should be shared with children so they will be able to recognize "dangers" in the present and the future. One of his techniques for illustrating this point is to include times during Hitler's life when his rise to power might have been prevented. The author develops the historical period and places Hitler's rise to power within this context. Dolan's characterization includes Hitler's shrewdness in analyzing the German people and his ability to select people who advocated his viewpoint. The details about the Holocaust and Hitler's suicide provide a look at a terrifying period.

The tone and characterization in Silberdick's *Franklin D. Roosevelt, Gallant President* is in contrast to that created by Dolan. The author focuses upon Roosevelt's ability to overcome physical disabilities during his rise to power. Because the author also chooses to focus upon Roosevelt's political accomplishments, there is neither an in-depth look at his private life or the inclusion of viewpoints that might be considered critical.

Davidson develops a broader characterization of a political leader in *The Golda Meir Story.* For example, experiences from her childhood are related to achievements as an adult. The author does not infer that Meir's private life was always happy; instead her marital problems are discussed. There is natural drama in the biography as Meir faces both the problems and rewards of leadership. As prime minister she leads her country during the Yom Kippur war. On a happier occasion she meets with Anwar Sadat.

There are many sources of information about these modern political figures. Consequently, children can verify factual information in the biographies or extend an interest by reading more about a political leader. When children do a library search, they discover some of the techniques used by biographers.

Achievers—Science, Arts, Literature, and Sports. There are exciting stories of men and women who felt a need to question, to investigate, and to find answers to their questions. Many of these people made achievements during times when their questions and findings were in conflict with the accepted ideas of the time. There are both great men and great women who were first in their fields. There are writers and illustrators of children's literature who share with readers their own creative processes, and there are sports heroes and heroines who can excite children who want to achieve in sports.

The first four biographies discussed in this section form a natural continuum and illustrate how the discoveries or theories of one scientist build upon work previously completed.

They also demonstrate the need for careful research by authors who are concerned with developing these relationships. In Galileo's biography, for example, the author refers to Galileo's interest in the Copernican theory. In the biography of Maria Mitchell, the author discusses Mitchell's strong respect for the work of Copernicus and Galileo and the strength that allowed them to pursue truth, although it was dangerous at that time. The story of Mitchell also suggests that the theories of Charles Darwin support Mitchell's astronomical observations. Children may discover an interrelationship among the sciences and realize that new discoveries are often made possible because of the careful work of earlier scientists.

In fifteenth- and sixteenth-century Europe, questioning or challenging the writings of earlier scientists and the scientific ideas accepted by the church could result in charges of heresy, imprisonment, or even death. In this climate of inquisition, however, people emerged who dared to question, investigate, and theorize. In *Dance of the Planets: The Universe of Nicolaus Copernicus* Nancy Veglahn creates a vivid picture of the times and the man who questioned the traditional view that the earth was the center of the universe and the sun spun around it. The author focuses on Copernicus's years of study: years when he puzzled over the positions of the planets, when he grasped the significance of Columbus's voyages, and when he questioned the old "truths" but did not consider himself a heretic. Consider, for example, the effect of this straightforward language as Copernicus thinks about his own beliefs:

He was no heretic. It simply seemed to him that human beings should not presume to understand God completely, or even the creations of God. Why could not the Almighty make a universe that was larger, more complex, more amazing than anyone had yet imagined? (p. 54)

The Copernican theory was declared false by the church and Copernicus's writings were condemned for 200 years, but his theories greatly influenced the astronomers and mathematicians who followed him. One scientist, Galileo Galilei, is the subject of Sidney Rosen's biography *Galileo and the Magic Numbers.* Rosen suggests the reasons for Galileo's questioning by describing the influence of his father who taught him, "Do not be afraid to challenge authority at any time, if a search for truth is in question. This is not the easy path in life, but it is the most rewarding" (p. 50). Because of the author's detailed descriptions, children are able to vicariously accompany Galileo as he looks through his invention, the first telescope of astronomical value, and sees the moon's surface dotted with depressions like craters of volcanoes. Through the author's description of Galileo's emotions, children are encouraged to believe his elation as he discovers the truth of

Copernicus's theory; and his bitterness as he is charged with heresy and imprisoned. They are encouraged to believe his strong will as he reaffirms "in spite of what they forced me to say, the earth will continue to move on its path about the sun" (p. 205).

The theories of both Copernicus and Galileo had a strong influence on one of the foremost astronomers in American history, Maria Mitchell. Helen L. Morgan's biography, *Maria Mitchell, First Lady of American Astronomy,* presents not only a person in quest for knowledge but a woman who had to overcome the prejudices of her time against females in higher education and particularly in the sciences. The author describes how she gained knowledge about Mitchell's personal life: Morgan stayed in Nantucket only a block from the Atheneum Library where Mitchell spent so many hours; she read her diaries, letters, and notebooks; she visited her home, library, and observatory; and she read the files of the Nantucket Inquirer and the Nantucket Historical Association. Because of the author's detailed descriptions, readers can almost see Maria as a young girl learning about astronomy at her father's side. They are encouraged to believe her exhilaration in 1847 when she looks into her telescope and observes a new comet, they can believe her pride when she receives the medal from the king of Denmark in honor of her discovery, and they can understand her excitement when she is appointed the first woman astronomy professor at Vassar College.

The author develops two personal struggles and strong beliefs in this biography: Mitchell felt strongly about the right to question and the right of women to have equality with men. This first belief is demonstrated in the author's description of Mitchell's most memorable experience in Rome, as she visits the site of Galileo's trial before the inquisition:

Maria could imagine it all and knew how much it must have hurt Galileo to recant his belief after seeing proofs of it in the heavens. The petty restrictions of his later life, when he was ill and blind, were unpleasant but could not equal the despair he must have known in publicly denying his belief. She felt that she was on sacred ground where she walked near the place where he had suffered. (p. 104)

The author focuses upon Mitchell's struggles by describing in detail the following incidents: Mitchell's personal criticism when she states to her classes that Darwin's theory of evolution fits into her concept of the universe; the disapproval she receives when she argues against discriminatory treatment of women faculty members; and the bigotry she experiences when she fights for the equal rights of women. Her beliefs in women's rights are reinforced through excerpts from a speech in 1876 when she was president of the Women's Congress.

Consider how the author uses this quotation to combine her educational background and her personal philosophy: "I have so long believed in woman's right to a share in the government that it is like the first axiom I learned in geometry—a straight line is the shortest distance between two points" (p. 123). This is a strong biography that allows children to follow the development of a human being from a rather shy girl to a strong advocate searching for truth and equality.

One of the reasons that Irwin Shapiro's biography, *Darwin and the Enchanted Isles* may appeal to middle elementary school children is the author's development of a character who does not always like the school subjects that are recommended. Instead of liking mathematics, Latin, and Greek, he finds his real interest lies in the observational walks he takes with a professor who is a naturalist. The most interesting part of this biography follows Darwin's years of discovery when, as a naturalist, he joins the crew of the *Beagle* to observe, collect,

Questions about life on an isolated island motivate a famous scientist.
Reprinted by permission of Coward, McCann & Geoghegan, Inc. from *Darwin and the Enchanted Isles* by Irwin Shapiro. Illustrations copyright © 1977 by Christopher Spollen.

and make notes of plants, animals, and geological characteristics of South American countries and the southern islands. The author develops the focus of Darwin's study and asks readers to speculate about the results of his research by stating questions that haunt Darwin: Because he has seen the face of the earth changing, could plants and animals also change? Why were there so many different kinds of species? Why were the plants and animals of the Galapagos different in some ways from those found in South America, but alike in other ways? What was the reason for their change? Through his search, study, and driving need for the facts to substantiate his theory of natural selection or survival of the fittest, students can discover that long years may go into the process of scientific inquiry. In this book, children discover that Darwin, like others whose theories were contrary to accepted thought, received tremendous criticism as well as fame.

During the years that Darwin was growing up in England and observing natural history, another naturalist was studying and drawing birds in America. Barbara Brenner's *On the Frontier with Mr. Audubon* is based, according to the author, on an unedited diary of Audubon's travels during 1820 and 1821 when he and a young assistant, Joseph Mason, traveled down the Mississippi and Ohio Rivers to find and draw birds. The author also used information from Alice Ford's *John James Audubon* and Audubon's other writings. The resulting biography is in the form of a new journal, one that could have been written by the assistant. Brenner says that almost every incident in the book actually happened, but the conversations are fictional, based on the facts found in the research. The book is illustrated with black and white drawings of Audubon's work and photographs from original sources showing flatboats on the river and people and places discussed in the book.

In 1891, it was unheard of for a woman to attend the Sorbonne University for the purpose of earning a doctorate in physical science. This did not deter a famous woman scientist. Veglahn's *The Mysterious Rays: Marie Curie's World* tells about the long years of laboratory work as Marie and Pierre Curie conduct experiments with pitchblende in their efforts to isolate a new element, radium. Veglahn concludes her biography with added information about the two Nobel Prizes awarded Marie Curie, the beneficial uses of radium, and the tragedy related to the damage done to the Curies by the unsuspected radiation from the radium.

Margery Facklam's *Wild Animals, Gentle Women* is a collection of short biographical sketches of eleven women who have spent their lives studying animal behavior, ethology. The book includes such people as Belle Benchley, former director of the San Diego Zoo; Jane Goodall, the scientist who became famous because of her work with chimpanzees; and Karen Pryor, a research scientist who specializes in behavorial studies with porpoises. The last chapter discusses ethology as a profession. Suggestions are made concerning appropriate education, developing writing skills, learning photography, learning first aid, and becoming involved with Outward Bound or similar programs.

Children can discover the motivational forces behind the artists who illustrate some of their books through autobiographies written and illustrated by the artists. In *Self-Portrait: Erik Blegvad,* the artist tells how he received a love for the sea from his father. He illustrates through his drawings how he used this love of the sea in his early work. Children also discover that he lived in a house filled with paintings, drawings, and art books. The artist tells about his first commissions as an artist and shows through his own work the changes it has undergone through the years. Children find information about another award-winning illustrator in *Self-Portrait: Margot Zemack.* In this autobiography, children may understand the influence of growing up during the depression and drawing pictures to make one laugh. Several sides of the character are revealed as she is given a Fulbright Scholarship, marries author Marve Zemack, raises a family, and draws pictures that allow her to create "her own theater and be in charge of everything"— actors, sets, costumes, and lighting. *Self-Portrait: Trina Schart Hyman* is another autobiography by the same publisher. The highly illustrated text and Hyman's selection of important and memorable episodes from her life create a rewarding reading experience.

Through photographs of Isamu Noguchi's sculpture in Tobi Tobias's *Isamu Noguchi: The Life of a Sculptor,* children can see a variety of his work: museum pieces in bronze, ceramic, marble, and cast iron; light sculptures; aluminum sculptures; playground sculptures; and foundations. The author stresses the artist's feelings about his work and how he approaches a new project. The work of artist Alexander Calder is discussed in text and illustrations in David Bourdon's *Calder: Mobilist, Ringmaster, Innovator.* Here are hanging mobiles, wire sculptures, animal toys, wooden sculptures, ink drawings, miniature circuses, motorized mobiles, and oil paintings. The photographs in Jean Lipman and Margaret Aspinwall's *Alexander Calder and His Magic Mobiles* provide an excellent example of this artist's creations. Children receive a feeling about the requirements of being an artist and what it is that stimulates artistic creativity.

The fine arts also include music and dance. *The Boy Who Loved Music,* by Joe and David Lasker, covers an incident in Joseph Haydn's life that led to the composition of a symphony

An elegant eighteenth-century setting provides a background for a biography about Joseph Haydn.
From *The Boy Who Loved Music* by Joe Lasker and David Lasker. Illustrations copyright © by Joe Lasker. Reprinted by permission of Viking Penguin Inc.

with a surprise ending. Joe Lasker's illustrations create the mood of elegant eighteenth-century Europe at the time of Prince Miklos Esterhazy. The drawings showing the fashions and life at court are especially informative. Children can see the artist's interpretations of the summer palace, an opera being performed, a country fair, hair styles that may be two feet tall, a masked ball, and a hunt.

A biography of a twentieth-century musician is provided in Bill Gutman's *Duke: The Musical Life of Duke Ellington.* This book not only encompasses the life and achievements of Duke Ellington from his early childhood when he gained a "sense of pride in his heritage" through his musical contributions, it also is the story of jazz as it evolved in black America. The author traces jazz from the ragtime era, to the swing of the 1940s, to the recognition that it is appropriate for the concert stage. Photographs accompanying the text show Ellington and his orchestra on different bandstands and with famous performers such as Ethel Waters, Benny Goodman, and Count Basie.

A highly illustrated biography of a famous dancer is found in Tobias's *Arthur Mitchell.* For young readers, the story describes the experiences of a young black dancer as he tries to enter into the world of classical ballet, a field in which few blacks had found acceptance. The author develops Mitchell's numerous struggles by describing his problems in meeting the demands of ballet at the High School of Performing Arts, his dancing with the New York City Ballet where he had to overcome audience prejudice, his dancing in a lead role developed especially for him, and his desire to form an all-black classical ballet company where young black dancers could practice and perform. His Dance Theatre of Harlem, which began in an empty Harlem garage, is now internationally known and provides training for hundreds of black dancers.

Children particularly enjoy the circus. The life of the most famous man in circus history, *P.T. Barnum,* is found in an easy-to-read biography by Anne Edwards. The author creates a humorous story, by including lively anecdotes and by describing a man who loved spectacular entertainment and enjoyed making people laugh. Readers can follow this showman as he begins his career with the oldest woman alive—a 161-year-old lady who claimed to be George Washington's nurse; organizes a circus—The Greatest Show on Earth; brings the first Punch and Judy show to America; shows the smallest man in the world—twenty-four-inch Tom Thumb; and joins James Anthony Bailey in a partnership. Marylin Hafner's humorous illustrations complement the text.

Creating believable situations out of make believe is also important for authors of children's books. Children who loved the delightful characters Peter Rabbit, Squirrel Nutkin, and Benjamin Bunny may enjoy learning more about the author in Dorothy Aldis's *Nothing Is Impossible: The Story of Beatrix Potter.* Aldis pictures the isolation of Potter's childhood by describing her Victorian English home and the influence of her parents. The author contrasts this restrictive atmosphere with the happier days when she spends her summers in the country, observes animals, and fills notebooks with sketches. Readers can identify the possible motivation for her later books as she writes in her journal and does paintings of small pets she brings back from the country. Many children enjoy knowing that she wrote and illustrated *Peter Rabbit* to amuse a five-year-old child who was ill with rheumatic fever. Quotes from Beatrix Potter's journal add to the credibility of the biography. For example, she explains why she wrote the stories: "One of the loves of my life has always been animals. Children and gardens, too. That's all" (p.144). Later, she explains why her characters may seem so real: "I remember I used to half believe and wholly play with fairies when I was a child. What heaven can be more real than to retain the spirit-world of childhood" (p.154). The biographer portrays a Victorian woman who was

hampered by the constraints of society, but still allowed her imagination, determination, and talent to provide her with enjoyment. (See pages 273–74 for a discussion of Beatrix Potter's literature.)

Children who are sports enthusiasts also enjoy reading about the people they see on television or those whose records

The humorous illustrations seem appropriate for a biography about a circus personality.
Reprinted by permission of G. P. Putnam's Sons from *P. T. Barnum* by Anne Edwards. Illustrations copyright © 1977 by Marilyn Hafner.

they would like to duplicate. A collection of short biographies about athletes who had to overcome handicaps, reversals, and obstacles is found in Vernon Pizer's *Glorious Triumphs: Athletes Who Conquered Adversity.* Such athletes as Barney Rose, 1933 lightweight boxing champion of the world; Ben Hogan, professional golfer; Carole Heiss, Olympic gold medalist; Jerry Kramer, football player for the Green Bay Packers; and Althea Gibson, tennis professional, are included.

The lives of hockey greats are presented in Edward F. Dolan and Richard B. Lyttle's *Bobby Clarke,* Marshall and Sue Burchard's *Sports Hero: Phil Esposito,* and Howard Liss's *Bobby Orr: Lightning on Ice.* These books are enhanced with photographs of the hockey players and their teammates.

Biographies about sports stars may be easily dated because of rapidly changing stardom and changing team memberships. Many children who are sports enthusiasts, however, enjoy reading almost everything about their favorite sports heroes.

Additional biographies about sports heroes are found in chapter eleven, "Multiethnic Literature." Sports stories are also included in chapter nine, "Contemporary Realistic Fiction."

People Who Have Persevered. Biographies are not always written about the lives of famous people. Many times the courage and perseverance of ordinary people create excellent stories. One such book is David Kherdian's *The Road from Home: The Story of an Armenian Girl.* This story about the author's mother, Vernon Dumehjian, is one of courage, survival, and hope: the author tells about his mother's experiences in the Armenian quarter of Azizija, Turkey, and on the road as a refugee when in 1915 the Turkish government decided to eliminate its Armenian people by deporting them to the Mesopotamian desert or killing them. Kherdian tells of days spent in a caravan on the march, days of weakening physical condition, days of not knowing where her destination would be, and days of sadness when family members died from cholera. There are also days of hope; Vernon meets kind people who provide her with an education while she waits to return to her home. The security of home does not last long, however, as fighting resumes between Turkey and Greece. When Vernon's aunt is approached by a family whose Armenian American son wants a wife to join him in America, she finally finds a means of becoming safe and realizes her wish to go to America. Children could compare this book with other stories on similar subjects in the historical fiction chapter.

Another author who develops a theme related to the joy and sorrow of being human is Bernard Wolf. His *In This Proud Land: The Story of a Mexican American Family* is about a family rather than an individual. This book is a photographic essay about a Mexican American family who supplement their income by migrating from Pharr, Texas, to work in the sugar beet fields in Minnesota. The photographs and text show warm family relationships and children who work at part-time jobs to help their family financially. This is not only a story of a poor family striving to earn a living, it is also a story of proud people attempting to educate their children and create a better life for them. The photographs show the poor living conditions experienced by some families, and the Hernandez family in their home, at school, at work, and as they travel north from Texas. Wolf ends his story with these words:

In this proud land there are many Americas. There is an America of inequality and racial prejudice. There is an America of grave poverty, despair, and tragic human waste. And yet because of people like the Hernandez family, there is also an America of simple courage, strength, and hope. (p. 95)

Another book that traces a family's experiences is Eloise Greenfield and Lessie Jones Little's *Childtimes: A Three-Generation Memoir.* The book is divided into three parts: a Black American grandmother, mother, and daughter tell about their growing-up experiences. The time period ranges from the late 1800s through the 1940s. Both Greenfield and Little are well-known children's authors. The authors conclude their autobiographies with this poignant remembrance:

It's been good, stopping for a while to catch up to the past. It has filled me with both great sadness and great joy. Sadness to look back at suffering, joy to feel the unbreakable threads of strength. Now, it's time for us to look forward again, to see where it is that we're going. Maybe years from now, our descendants will want to stop and tell the story of their time and their place in this procession of children. A childtime is a mighty thing. (p. 175)

These words also provide a fitting conclusion to biographies written for children. What better purpose is there for sharing biographies with children than allowing them to feel good, to catch up to the past, and to experience the sadness and great joy of other people's lives.

SUMMARY

There are many values for children who read nonfictional materials. They gain knowledge about the world they live in, they are stimulated in their search for discovery, and they are introduced to the scientific method and gain an appreciation for people who use it. They are also encouraged to develop critical thinking abilities, they may increase their own aspirations, and they may gain considerable enjoyment.

When evaluating informational books for children, the facts should be accurate, stereotypes should be eliminated, and illustrations should be accurate and clarify the text. The text should encourage analytical thinking, its organization should be logical and helpful, and the style should be lively and not too difficult for the age of the children.

Informational books discussed in the chapter include history and geography; animals, plants, earth's ecology, and earth and geology; experiments, discoveries, and how things work; and hobbies, crafts, and "how-to" books.

Biographies, in addition to meeting the criteria for all good literature, should be worthy of authors' meticulous research and of the time children spend in reading, and should be written so that the characters are believable.

Suggested Activities for Adult Understanding of Informational Books and Biographies

- Select the work of an outstanding author of informational books for children such as Millicent E. Selsam, Seymour Simon, or Laurence Pringle. Evaluate the books according to the criteria listed on pages 553–54. Share with the class the characteristics of the books that make them highly recommended.

- Select several informational books that include many illustrations. Evaluate the illustrations according to the value of the explanatory legends presented next to the illustrations, the accuracy of the illustrations, and the possibility that they will stimulate children's interest in the subject.

- Choose several informational books that exemplify the encouragement of logical problem solving. Share the books with a peer group and present a rationale for the belief that these books will encourage logical problem solving.

- Search the elementary social studies or science curriculum on a given grade level. With a peer group, develop an annotated bibliography of informational books that would reinforce the curriculum and stimulate the acquisition of additional information.

- In order to write accurate information, differentiate fact from opinion, and provide authentic background information, biographers must research many sources. Select a writer of biographies for children and identify the sources that were used in the research of a book. Do you believe these sources were sufficient? Why or why not?

- Choose someone who has had several biographies written about him or her. Read several interpretations of that person's life. Compare the biographies as to content, accuracy of information, sources of references indicated by the author, balance of the facts with story line for young readers, intended audience for the biography, and author's style.

- Select a well-known author who has written several biographies for older children, such as Ronald Syme, and another biographer who has written several biographies for younger children, such as Jean Fritz. What techniques does each author use in order to write a biography that would appeal to a specific age group?

- Select a content area, such as science or social studies, that is taught in an elementary or middle school grade. Identify from the curriculum names of men and women who are discussed in that content area. Develop an annotated bibliography of literature on a subject such as biology that could be used to stimulate interest in the subject and provide additional information about the contributors.

References

1 Anderson, William, and Groff, Patrick. *A New Look at Children's Literature.* Belmont, Calif.: Wadsworth, 1972.

2 Arbuthnot, May Hill, and Broderick, Dorothy M. *Time for Biography.* Glenview, Ill.: Scott, Foresman, 1969.

3 Blough, Glenn O. "The Author and the Science Book." *Library Trends* 22 (April 1974): 419–24.

4 Carpenter, Frank G. *Carpenter's Geographical Reader, North America.* New York: American Book, 1898.

5 Coolidge, Olivia. "My Struggle with Facts." *Wilson Library Bulletin* 49 (October 1974): 146–51.

6 Doughty, Frances. "Responsibilities of Reviewers." *Library Trends* 22 (April 1974): 443–51.

7 Dryer, Charles Redway. *Geography, Physical, Economic, and Regional.* New York: American Book, 1911.

8 Fritz, Jean. "Making It Real." *Children's Literature in Education* 22 (Autumn 1976): 125–27.

9 Herman, Gertrude B. " 'Footprints on the Sands of Time': Biography for Children." *Children's Literature in Education* 9 (Summer 1977): 85–94.

10 Hillyer, V. M. *A Child's Geography of the World.* Illustrated by Mary Sherwood Wright Jones. New York: Century, 1929.

11 National Science Teachers Association. "Outstanding Science Trade Books for Children in 1981." *Science and Children* (March 1982): 48.

12 Roettger, Doris. "Reading Attitudes and the Estes Scale." Paper presented at the 23rd Annual Convention, International Reading Association, Houston, Texas, 1978.

13 Stott, Jon C. "Biographies of Sports Heroes and the American Dream." *Children's Literature in Education* 10 (Winter 1979): 174–85.

14 Taylor, M. Ione. "A Study of Biography as a Literature Form for Children." Bloomington, Ind.: Indiana University, 1970, University Microfilm No. 71-11, 353 pp 119.

15 Wibberley, Leonard. *Time of the Harvest, Thomas Jefferson, the Years 1801–1826*. New York: Farrar, Straus & Giroux, 1966.

16 Wolff, Kathryn. "AAAS Science Books: A Selection Tool." *Library Trends* 22 (April 1974): 453–56.

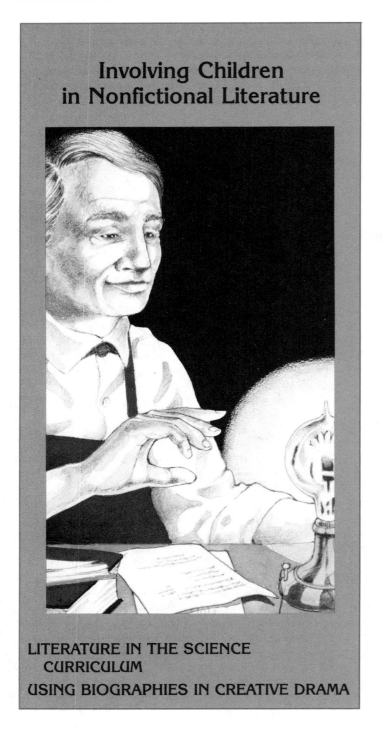

Involving Children in Nonfictional Literature

LITERATURE IN THE SCIENCE CURRICULUM

USING BIOGRAPHIES IN CREATIVE DRAMA

STIMULATING learning experiences can result from informational books and biographies that contain factual, authentic interpretations written in a style often more exciting than content area textbooks. Because many of the informational books previously discussed relate to the science curriculum, they can be used to increase children's enjoyment and understanding of science-related topics. This chapter presents ways to help children acquire such abilities related to content areas as using parts of the book, locating sources of information, understanding science vocabulary, reading for exact meaning, evaluating science literature, and applying learnings to practical problems.

The lively dialogue, confrontations between people and ideas, and the joys and sorrows connected with discovery and achievement found in many biographies are natural sources for creative dramatizations and discussions. Activities developed around biographies will suggest ways that people of the past and present can be made to seem realistic to contemporary children.

LITERATURE IN THE SCIENCE CURRICULUM

Several values of informational books identified earlier relate to the science curriculum. The interesting books such as those by Simon, Selsam, and Pringle allow children to experience the excitement of discovery; through experiments stimulated by books such as Selsam's *Popcorn* and Simon's *The Secret Clocks, Time Senses of Living Things,* they can observe, experiment, compare, formulate hypotheses, test hypotheses, draw conclusions, and evaluate their evidence. Children can become directly involved in the scientific method. Through the experiments and information found in books, children learn about the world of nature. Because many informational books that deal with science subjects have greater depth of coverage than science textbooks, these materials are valuable for extending knowledge and understanding.

Illa Podendorf (4) says that there are communication abilities such as graphing, illustrating, recording, and reporting that are especially important to science. She believes that an author of science information books should use these communication abilities often when writing science materials. She also says:

At an early age children are able to read and interpret graphs and can present their own ideas and findings in graphic form. A trade book which provides such experiences is a valuable addition to their literature. Any opportunity to help children get experience in interpreting data and making predictions from recorded data should not be overlooked. Such experiences often result in activities in which children can become actively involved. (p. 428)

However, the nature of science materials—with their heavier concentration of facts and details, new scientific principles to be understood, and new technical vocabulary—may cause reading problems for children who are accustomed to the narrative writing style. David L. Shepherd (6) identifies the following three types of reading that students face in the content area of science: (1) science textbooks that tend to be technical and require a careful, slow, and analytical reading; (2) assigned readings in scientific journals, popular science magazines, and books on scientific research that may contain many small but important interrelated details that require analytical reading; and (3) nontechnical scientific materials found in biographies of scientists, newspapers, and popular magazines reporting scientific findings that are easier to read and understand. The majority of the science-related informational books discussed earlier fall under the categories of reading requirements for numbers two and three above.

The excellent informational materials on science-related topics may be used to encourage children's development of both the reading abilities needed for science-related materials and the development of science-related concepts. This section considers ways that teachers, parents, and librarians may use science-related informational books to stimulate children's minds and increase vital abilities needed for science. The web, "Using Science Informational Books," shown in Figure 12–1 suggests the multiple purposes that may be gained from using informational books with children. For the object of this text, we will consider those purposes that relate to both the study of literature and the content areas: using parts of the book, locating sources of information, understanding science vocabulary, reading for exact meaning, seeing author's organization, and evaluating science materials. Specific books are mentioned but they are only examples of the numerous books that can be used in the classroom. Children's literature students may wish to extend this web to include additional informational books. (The book titles on the web are shortened due to space limitations.)

Using Parts of a Book

Both librarians and teachers provide instruction in how to use the valuable aids provided by authors of many informational books. Science informational books reinforce the ability to use parts of a book, because many books contain a table of contents, a glossary, a bibliography of further readings, and an index. Children can use the table of contents to locate a specific chapter in an informational book. They can discover the type of information provided in the index, locate a chapter, and search through it to discover if the subject is covered there. For example:

1 Find the chapter describing how to make a walkie-talkie space helmet in Flo Ann Hedley Norvell's *The Great Big Box Book* (chapter 7, p. 36).
2 Find the chapter about a space colony in Franklyn M. Branley's *The Story of the Space Shuttle, Columbia and Beyond* (chapter 5, p. 65).
3 Find the chapter on tubers in Millicent E. Selsam's *Bulbs, Corms, and Such* (chapter 3, p. 32).
4 Find the chapter "Snakes in Fact and Fancy" in Seymour Simon's *Discovering What Garter Snakes Do* (chapter 8, p. 44).
5 Find the chapter "Seven Helpless Chicks" in Geraldine Lux Flanagan's *Window into a Nest* (chapter 8, p. 62).

Pringle's books usually have a glossary of technical terms, an index, and a list of further readings that can add information on a subject. These books can be used to reinforce the importance of each part of the book, the kind of information that is available, and the use of each locational aid. As children read *City and Suburb: Exploring an Ecosystem; The Gentle Desert: Exploring an Ecosystem;* or *Natural Fire: Its Ecology in Forests,* they can use the glossary that provides definitions for the technical terminology in each book including words such as *climate, ecosystem, environment,* and *habitat.* In these books, they can find subjects in the index and find the information on the correct page in the text. These indexes are especially useful, because an asterisk beside a page number indicates that a photograph or drawing is on that page. Children may see how rapidly they can find subjects in the index and then find them in the text. For example, find the page number for magpies in *City and Suburb: Exploring an Ecosystem.* Is it a picture or text? Find magpies in the book. In the list of further readings in each book asterisks indicate materials that are fairly simple. The easier references include magazines such as *Ranger Rick's Nature Magazine* and *Natural History* as well as other children's books on the topic. The more difficult books provide information for a highly motivated child or one in an accelerated program.

Locating and Using Sources of Information

The lists of references at the back of many informational books provide a logical source of materials to show children how to use a library card catalog for more information. The sources

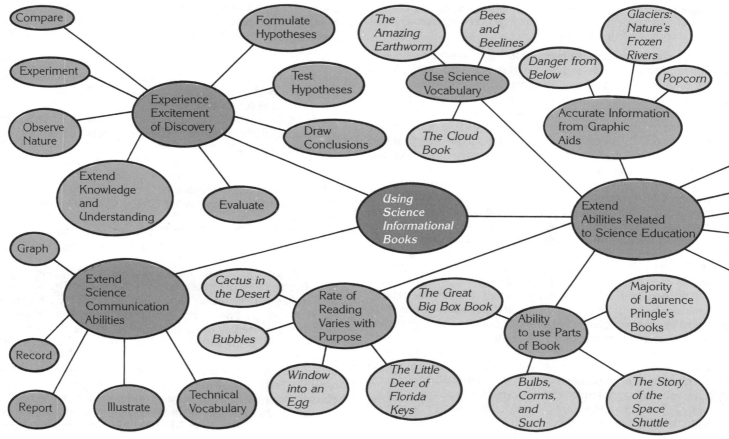

FIGURE 12–1

can be found in the library card catalog under an author card, a title card, and a subject card. For example, one additional source listed in *City and Suburb: Exploring An Ecosystem* is Pringle's *Into the Woods: Exploring the Forest Ecosystem.* Children learn and reinforce library location skills by learning how to find this book or other informational books under three types of cards, as shown in Figure 12–2. Children can also discover related reading materials while looking for a particular reference in the card catalog.

Using Science Vocabulary

The glossary in many informational books is also a source of additional information about the meaning of technical termi-

nology found in the book. Authors of informational books for children often present the meaning of new words through the context of the texts. This technique should be demonstrated to children, and they should try to understand the meaning of the word. Lilo Hess in *The Amazing Earthworm* uses contextual clues to suggest the meaning of scientific terms:

The earthworm is a *terrestrial* animal, which means it lives on land; yet it has not accomplished true land status, since it is restricted to an underground existence—a life of burrowing in damp soil. (p. 10)

The author uses a similar technique to give the meanings of *segmented worms* (p. 7), *invertebrates* (p. 8), *setae* (p. 10), *nocturnal* (p. 13), *castings* (p. 15), *phototropic* (p. 20) and *hermaphrodite* (p. 23).

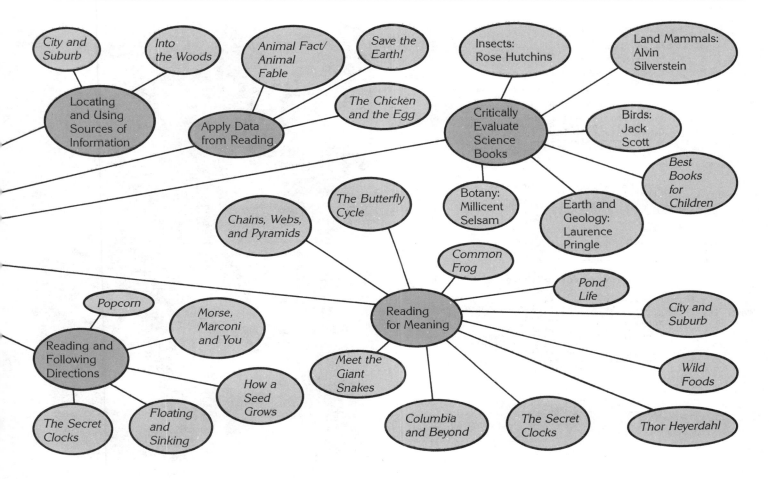

Authors also clarify the meanings of technical terminology through photographs, diagrams, and charts. Even books written for young children often clarify meanings of technical terminology by including labeled drawings. An illustration by Aliki, in Judy Hawes's *Bees and Beelines*, shows the directions a bee moves when flying a "round dance" and a "waggle." This illustration is followed by four pages of drawings that resemble a map of a bee's flying actions when it leaves the hive to search for nectar. Arrows are included in the drawings so that children can follow the bee's movement. When parents or teachers share the book with children, they should help them to follow the directions of the arrows and tell what is occurring in the drawings. (This book is a "Let's-Read-and-Find-Out Science Book.")

Another "Let's-Read-and-Find-Out Science Book" for young children that includes labeled diagrams clarifying technical terminology is Hawes's *Ladybug, Ladybug, Fly Away Home*. Ed Emberley's illustrations not only appeal to young children but also include large drawings of ladybugs with various labeled parts such as *body, shield, head, eye, jaws, palps, feelers, claws,* and *sticky pads*. These drawings are especially effective with young children because the author explains that the drawings are magnified by showing an actual ladybug on a human finger on the same page that an enlarged drawing is introduced. Parents and teachers may use the book to encourage children to look through a magnifying glass and identify the same body parts that are shown in the enlarged, labeled drawings. Children frequently want to draw and label their own illustrations.

AUTHOR CARD

```
QH
541.5    Pringle, Laurence P.
.F6         Into the woods: exploring the forest
P74      ecosystem [by] Laurence Pringle. New
         York, Macmillan [1973]
            54 p. illus. 23 cm.
            SUMMARY: Explains the interdependency
         of plants and animals and examines
         man's role in protecting this
         ecological balance.
            Bibliography: p. 51.



            1. Forest ecology--Juvenile
         literature.  I. Title
```

TITLE CARD

```
            Into the woods: exploring the forest
               ecosystem
QH
541.5    Pringle, Laurence P.
.F6         Into the woods: exploring the forest
P74      ecosystem [by] Laurence Pringle. New
         York, Macmillan [1973]
            54 p. illus. 23 cm.
            SUMMARY: Explains the interdependency
         of plants and animals and examines
         man's role in protecting this
         ecological balance.
            Bibliography: p. 51.



            1. Forest ecology--Juvenile
         literature.  I. Title
```

SUBJECT CARD

```
            FOREST ECOLOGY--JUVENILE LITERATURE.
QH
541.5    Pringle, Laurence P.
.F6         Into the woods: exploring the forest
P74      ecosystem [by] Laurence Pringle. New
         York, Macmillan [1973]
            54 p. illus. 23 cm.
            SUMMARY: Explains the interdependency
         of plants and animals and examines
         man's role in protecting this
         ecological balance.
            Bibliography: p. 51.



            1. Forest ecology--Juvenile
         literature.  I. Title
```

FIGURE 12–2

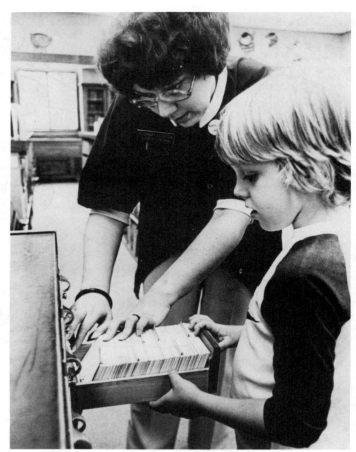

A librarian helps a child locate informational books listed in a book's reference list.

Tomie de Paola's *The Cloud Book* also presents the technical names for clouds through text description and humorous illustrations. Drawings show *cirrus, cumulus,* and *stratus* clouds; *cirrocumulus* and *cirrostratus* clouds; *altostratus* and *altocumulus* clouds; and *nimbostratus, stratocumulus,* and *cumulonimbus* clouds. Because many children are curious about the changing cloud formations they see in the sky, this book can be used to introduce the technical terms for the clouds observed. Drawings and bulletin boards on which different types of clouds are labeled are excellent extensions of this knowledge. A bulletin board created to extend the vocabulary in the book might look like one made by a group of fifth-grade children (see Figure 12–3).

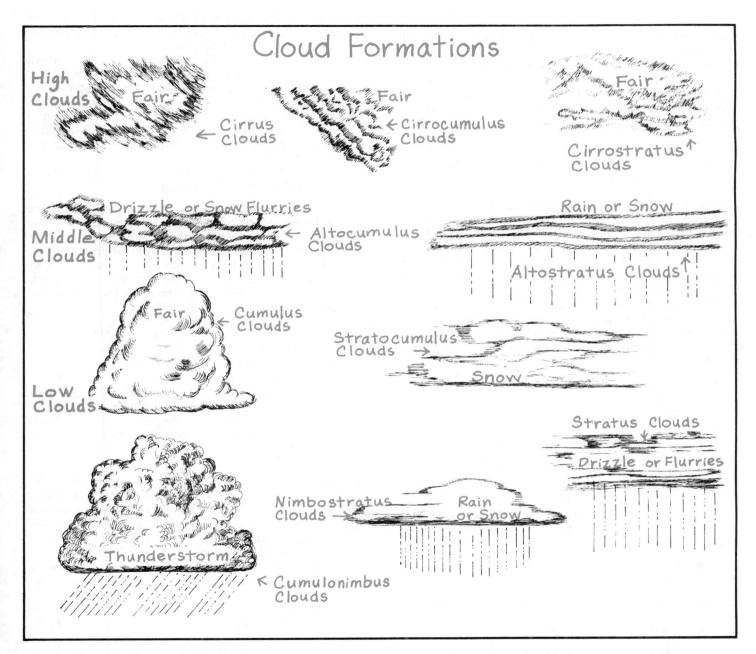

Cloud Formations

High Clouds — Fair — Cirrus Clouds

Fair — Cirrocumulus Clouds

Fair — Cirrostratus Clouds

Middle Clouds — Drizzle or Snow Flurries — Altocumulus Clouds

Rain or Snow — Altostratus Clouds

Low Clouds — Fair — Cumulus Clouds

Stratocumulus Clouds — Snow

Stratus Clouds — Drizzle or Flurries

Nimbostratus Clouds — Rain or Snow

Thunderstorm — Cumulonimbus Clouds

FIGURE 12–3

Reading for Exact Meaning

A major reason that many students give for reading scientific informational books is to acquire facts; therefore, comprehending the author's exact meaning is often important. Unlike the writings that stress make-believe, scientific informational books are based on accuracy. Children often need encouragement to note main idea and supporting details, and to see organization. Reading methods books usually include several chapters on these comprehension abilities, but a few approaches will be considered that allow content area teachers and parents to reinforce and encourage these abilities through informational books.

Noting Main Ideas. Short, fact-filled paragraphs as well as paragraph and chapter organization provide considerable materials for the content area teacher who is trying to enhance children's ability to find the main idea. Because many informational books written for children have the main idea as a topic sentence at the beginning of the paragraph, one technique that has been helpful to many teachers is to have children read a paragraph or a series of short paragraphs and then visualize the author's organization of the material according to main idea and important details. (This technique may also help them evaluate if the author uses a logical organization.) A typical paragraph may follow this organization:

Main Idea
   Supporting Details
   Supporting Details
   Supporting Details

Simon's writing tends to follow this structure. Consider how to use this diagram with material from *Meet the Giant Snakes* to help children identify the main idea, supporting details, and evaluate whether or not the organization is logical. On page 13 of Simon's book is a paragraph that describes how the python, unlike other snakes, cares for her young. If this paragraph were arranged like the above diagram, it would look something like this:

A giant python is unusual because she cares for her young.
   She pushes her eggs into a pile.
   She coils her body around the eggs.
   She stays on the nest until the eggs are hatched in about ten
     weeks.
   She leaves her nest only for water.

Children can discover that each of the important details supports the idea that the giant python takes care of her young. This main idea can also be turned into a question; children can decide if the rest of the paragraph answers these questions: Does the giant python take care of her young? How does the giant python take care of her young?

The same book introduces a series of paragraphs by asking the question, "How does a giant snake find food to eat?" (p. 15). Each of the succeeding paragraphs answers some question about the giant python's eating habits. Children find that they will get the main idea from the three following pages if they read to answer the introductory question. This should be demonstrated to children so that they can use this important comprehension aid.

There are other activities that can be done using informational books that also stress the main idea:

1 If the informational material contains subheadings, ask children to turn each subheading into a question and read to answer the question. For example, in Branley's *The Story of the Space Shuttle, Columbia and Beyond,* the author uses subheadings to indicate each section of the shuttle. Children could turn each of the following subheadings into questions and then read to answer their specific questions:

Columbia in Orbit (chapter 1)

The Flight Section
The Cargo Bay
Orbiter Engines
The Main Engines
The Solid-Rocket Boosters
The Orbit-Maneuver Engines
The Reaction-Control or Thrust Engines
Heat Control

2 The results of an experiment may be the main idea. After children have read the results of an experiment or finished their own experiments, ask them to relate the purpose and the findings of the experiment in one or two brief sentences. Literature sources could include the following:
  a. Dr. Frank Brown's experiments with fiddler crabs, oysters, and potatoes, described on pages 37–41 in Simon's *The Secret Clocks, Time Senses of Living Things.*
  b. Gustav Kramer's experiments with migration of birds described on pages 24–29 in Simon's *The Secret Clocks, Time Senses of Living Things.* Graphic aids may be incorporated with these experiments by having children illustrate the steps taken during the completion of these experiments.

Noting Supporting Details. The outlines discussed earlier stressed the main idea and important details. When the main idea was turned into a question, or questions, each of the items listed provided an important detail that supported the main idea. Many important details in a science informational book may refer to characteristics of animals or plants: size, color, number, location, or texture. Have the children listen to or read a description from a science informational book and draw a picture that shows the important details. This activity also provides them with graphic aids. The following descriptions are examples of sources that could be used:

1 The description of *Kon Tiki* found on pages 44–45 in Wyatt Blassingame's *Thor Heyerdahl: Viking Scientist.*
2 The description of leaves found in Laurence Pringle's *Wild Foods: A Beginner's Guide to Identifying, Harvesting and Cooking Safe and Tasty Plants from the Outdoors:* maple leaves (p. 24), cattails (pp. 63–64), and milkweed (pp. 103–4).

3 Descriptions of city and suburb ecosystems in Pringle's *City and Suburb: Exploring an Ecosystem:* the city made by people (p. 3), how the automobile changed open land (p. 7), weeds growing in vacant lots (p. 34).

Seeing Author's Organization. The sequence of events and the author's organization of information are often critical in science content areas. When evaluating informational books a logical organization is also critical. Many books emphasize the life cycle of plants or animals, the correct steps to use in following an experiment, or the chain of events that occurs. These books can be used to help children increase their ability to note scientific organization, and to evaluate the author's ability to develop logical organization. The following activities could be used with informational materials:

1 Number of steps identified in the butterfly's life cycle. Read Oxford Scientific Films' *The Butterfly Cycle.* Identify, draw,

Children discuss the purposes and findings of an experiment motivated by an informational book about seeds.

or list and then number the four stages in the life cycle of the butterfly.
a. the egg (drawing)
b. the caterpillar or larva (drawing)
c. the chrysalis or pupa (drawing)
d. the adult butterfly (drawing)

2 Number of steps identified in the life cycle of the frog. Read Oxford Scientific Films' *Common Frogs.* Identify, draw, or list and number the stages in the frog's cycle.
a. eggs at bottom of pond (drawing)
b. eggs rise to surface for about two weeks (drawing)
c. eggs hatch into tadpoles with tails (drawing)
d. legs develop on tadpole (drawing)
e. tadpole's tail has vanished and tadpole is transformed into frog (drawing)

3 The food chain is another item in nature that can be used to help children understand the sequential order from smallest to largest or from plants, to animals, to humans. Have children draw the described links in food chains, progressing from plants to various animals then humans. A book for young children that illustrates this cycle is Herbert H. Wong and Matthew F. Vessel's *Pond Life: Watching Animals Find Food.* A book for older children that can stimulate interest in the energy chain is Pringle's *Chains, Webs, and Pyramids: The Flow of Energy.* The chains discussed include simple links that go from plants to man or from grass to mouse to snake to hawk. Others are more complex; many chains are joined and criss-crossed to form a web. Webs are described for a dry chaparral forest in California and a salt marsh. Have children draw the various chains and webs. They may also consider the food chains that surround them or that provide their own energy. Bulletin boards could also be made showing various food or energy chains, webs, or pyramids.

Evaluating Science Materials

The ability to evaluate requires developing critical thinking abilities. Critical reading and thinking go beyond factual comprehension; they require weighing the validity of facts, identifying the problem, making judgments, interpreting implied ideas, distinguishing fact from opinion, drawing conclusions, determining the adequacy of a source of information, and suspending judgment until all the facts have been accumulated.

Helen Huus's (3) list of questions that students should ask about the author and the content of the material can help children evaluate both the author and the content of scientific informational books. For example, students should ask the following questions about the authors:

A Guide for Critical Evaluation of an Author
1 Why did the author write this book?
Was it to present information?
Was it to promote a point of view?
Was it to advertise?
Was it to propagandize?
Was it to entertain?
2 How competent is the author to write an article on this topic for this purpose?
What is the author's background?
What is the author's reputation?
Does the author have any vested interests in this topic?
What is the author's professional position?

In order to evaluate authors of informational books critically (this list and activity are excellent for all informational books, not just those related to science), children should have access to many books by different authors and biographical information about the authors. One teacher of upper elementary students divided the class into five research groups according to a category of interest each group chose to investigate. The categories included authors who wrote the books about botany, birds, earth and geology, land mammals, and insects.

Next, each group used John T. Gillespie and Christine B. Gilbert's *Best Books for Children, Preschool through the Middle Grades* (1) in order to identify authors who have written at least three books in their chosen category. For example, under botany, the group chose the following authors:

Anne Dowden—Three books
Rose E. Hutchins—Three books
Joan Elma Rahn—Three books
Millicent E. Selsam—Five books

Similarly, the group working with birds selected these authors:

Olive L. Earle—Three books
Roma Gans—Four books
John Kaufman—Four books
Jack Scott—Four books

The group working with earth and geology specified the following authors:

Ramona Gans—Four books
Delia Goetz—Five books
Laurence Pringle—Three books

The group working with land mammals chose the following authors:

Gladys Conklin—Four books
Irmengarge Eberle—Four books
Michael Fox—Three books
Russell Freedman—Three books
Alice L. Hopf—Five books
Sylvia Johnson—Three books
Laurence Pringle—Three books
Jack Scott—Three books
Millicent E. Selsam—Five books
Alvin Silverstein—Five books
Seymour Simon—Three books

The group working with insects named these authors:

Gladys Conklin—Eight books
Rose E. Hutchins—Eight books
Robert McClung—Four books

Next, they found as many of the books as possible in the library. These books included each author's most recent publications on the subject. They read the information about the author on the dust jacket or elsewhere in the book and searched for biographical data, and magazine or journal articles written by the author. Then, they evaluated the author's background, and read and reread the books, searching for each author's point of view and purpose for writing the book.

After the children had carefully read the books, they evaluated the content of the materials. For this evaluation, they referred to a list of content suggestions recommended by Huus (3) and placed the suggestions into an evaluative guide.

A Guide for Critical Evaluation of the Content
1 Does the author include all the necessary facts?
2 Are all the facts presented accurately?
3 Is the information recent?
4 Are the facts presented logically and in perspective?

In addition to reading the books, they read background information from science textbooks, encyclopedias, and magazine or journal articles. They checked the copyright dates of the materials; scrutinized the photographs, graphs, charts, and diagrams; and tried to evaluate whether the author had differentiated fact from opinion. If they found that there was more than one viewpoint on the subject, they tried to discover if the author had presented both.

Finally, each group presented their information on the authors and their books to the rest of the class. Children not only learned how to evaluate informational books and authors critically but also learned much about the content area and the procedures that writers of informational books should go through as they research their subjects.

Several authors of science informational books develop themes related to endangered species and ecology. These books can provide stimulating sources for topics of debate and independent research. The criteria for evaluating author and content that have been given earlier should also be used here. In addition, students should test the validity of an argument presented in written materials. Willavene Wolf (8) lists the following steps:

1 Strip the argument of any excess words or sentences.
2 Be sure students have access to all the premises upon which the author's conclusion may rest.
3 Determine whether the author is referring to all of a group, some of a group, or none of a group.
4 After students have stripped the argument to its basic framework, identified all of the premises (both stated and assumed), and transformed the premises, they are then in a better position to determine if the conclusion logically follows from the premises.

Children can independently evaluate if the author's conclusion is logical and supported by facts. They can also enter into debates: they can choose to take different sides of an issue presented by an author, research outside sources, and develop the contrasting viewpoints. For example, Jack Denton Scott's *Little Dogs of the Prairie* can be used for a debate on the plight of the prairie dogs. One upper elementary class used information in Scott's book to provide the framework for their debate. They chose sides in the issue, completed additional research, and presented their positions in debate format. They included this basic information from Scott's book:

Debate Subject: Protection of Prairie Dogs Versus Total Extermination

Points for Protection:

1 At the end of the nineteenth century, there were 600,000 square miles of prairie dog towns occupied by 5 billion prairie dogs. In the 1980s, the prairie dog is vanishing.
2 Naturalists claim prairie dog burrows benefit groundwater accumulation as water can penetrate the hard soil of prairies through the tunnels.
3 Naturalists claim soil carried to the surface by prairie dogs breaks down into helpful soluble forms.
4 Naturalists claim poisoning prairie dogs sets off a chain reaction in which many other animals die.
5 Scott claims people gain an immeasurable aesthetic value from observing prairie dogs.

Children apply knowledge gained from informational books during an environmental project.

6 Naturalists claim that prairie dogs come to an area after it has been overgrazed by cattle, horses, or sheep.

Points for Extermination:

1 Cowboys and ranchers consider the prairie dog burrows dangerous to horses and riders.

2 Ranchers claim prairie dogs destroy grazing land, making it unfit for cattle, horses, and sheep.

3 Ranchers claim prairie dogs eat grasses that should be reserved for livestock.

Other books about animals that have been endangered because of human hunting include Scott's *Return of the Buffalo* and *Loggerhead Turtle: Survivor from the Sea,* Scott Barry's *The Kingdom of Wolves,* and Hope Ryden's *The Little Deer of the Florida Keys.*

Some animals are not endangered because people hunt or poison them; instead, it is human pollution or land development that has endangered their survival. Books on this subject can spark debates as children consider if the interests of people are in opposition to the interests of animals or if the protective measures designed for animals also protect human life. Books that can be used for this purpose include Francine Jacob's *Africa's Flamingo Lake,* Robert M. McClung's *America's Endangered Birds: Programs and People Working to Save Them,* and the biography, *Thor Heyerdahl: Viking Scientist,* by Wyatt Blassingame.

Applying Data from Reading to Practical Problems

After children have critically evaluated the subjects of water, land, and air pollution discussed in informational books, they may be interested in evaluating the extent of pollution in their own environment. An informational book that can spark this kind of critical evaluation through experimentation and observation is Betty Miles's *Save the Earth! An Ecology Handbook for Kids.* Several projects that appeal to third and fourth graders include planning a new town to make the best possible use of land, recording air pollution by placing several cards covered with a thin layer of petroleum jelly outside in different locations and noting after twenty-four hours the pollution that has collected on the cards, and tracking water pollution in their own neighborhood, town, or city.

This last project reinforced observation, critical evaluation, and graphic interpretation abilities when a fourth-grade class identified various waterways in their town and made notes about pollution they found as they walked beside several creeks, a lake, a river, and a pond. When they returned to school, they used their notes to draw a large map of the waterways and marked on the map any pollution they found. Next, they filled in the type of building or human activity that was near the pollution. They could not more closely evaluate possible causes of water pollution in their own town. When the students discovered a definite problem, they took pictures of the evidence, wrote letters to the newspaper, made "clean up the waterways" posters, and asked people to make pledges to clean up their waterways.

Adults can encourage children to relate their reading to experiences and observations in their daily lives. In addition, children can link new applications of science principles to their previous knowledge. Helen Huus (3) emphasizes the desirability of encouraging children to place new learning into a personal context. A reader, according to Huus, fails to obtain the greatest pleasure, enjoyment, and even knowledge from his efforts unless, in the doing he gives something of himself. He must amalgamate the total into his own background of information, what the psychologists call his "apperceptive mass," and reorganize his ideas to accommodate his new learnings, his attitudes, or his feelings. In this reorganization, he gains new insights—sees the same things from a different point of view, sees aspects hitherto not noticed, savors the color and texture of a word or phrase, stores away a new visual image, or feels empathy with characters he has previously ignored or misunderstood. (p. 164)

Deciding whether information about animals is fact or fantasy is another way for children to apply data from reading to a practical problem. Several informational books discussed previously refer to animal facts versus fables, legends, or people's erroneous opinions. These books can stimulate children's investigations into other people's perceptions of truth about animal behavior and into literature to discover other animal fables. A second-grade teacher, for example, read Simon's

Animal Fact/Animal Fable to her students and interested them in interviewing people to discover what they believed about animal characteristics or behaviors. Because the students had often incorrectly identified a statement as fact or fable they wondered whether other children or even their parents would know the correct interpretation of statements such as "blind as a bat" that are often stated as truths. This led to a discussion during which the teacher wrote on the chalkboard the questions the children developed from the statements in Simon's book. (See Figure 12–4).

The teacher typed and duplicated the questionnaire so that all children had their own copies. They talked about how to ask questions and how to tally responses in the yes or no column. They questioned other classes, parents, and other adults. The next day they counted the number of tallies and put their totals on a big chart. In addition to an enjoyable activity, they used oral communication skills and discovered how opinion polls are conducted.

	Yes	No
1 Are bats blind?	///	//
2 Do bees sting only once?		
3 Are owls wise?		
4 Does the archer fish shoot food?		
5 Can a turtle leave its shell?		
6 Does a wolf live alone?		
7 Can some fish climb trees?		
8 Does a cricket tell the temperature with its chirp?		
9 Are elephants afraid of mice?		
10 Do cats have nine lives?		
11 Can a porcupine shoot his quills?		
12 Can a dog talk with his tail?		
13 Do ostriches hide their heads in the sand?		
14 Will goats eat just about anything?		
15 Do bulls become angry when they see red?		
16 Do snakes charm their prey?		
17 Do camels store water in their humps?		
18 Do snakes bite with their tongues?		
19 Will rats leave a sinking ship?		
20 Do raccoons wash their food before they eat?		

FIGURE 12–4

Discussions can also be developed with children that encourage them to observe and analyze differences among behavior of real animals, behavior of real animals depicted in informational books, and behavior of the same animals depicted in folktales and modern fantasy. For example, a caged chicken might be brought into the classroom for observational purposes. Children could observe the eating, sleeping, movement, and clucking behavior of the chicken. They could also observe the chicken's appearance. This factual observation could then be compared with the presentation of chickens in an informational book such as *The Chicken and the Egg*, by Oxford Scientific Films. Finally, children could consider the behavior of chickens in folktale versions such as Paul Galdone's *The Little Red Hen*. They might discuss differences in behavior and identify different purposes for writing and reading the two types of literature. Children can write their own books similar to Simon's *Animal Fact/Animal Fable* but illustrate and describe characteristics of real animals instead of fantasy animals. Other observations and discussions might be stimulated by comparing a caged mouse to the informational book *House Mouse*, by Oxford Scientific Films, and either of Beverly Cleary's fantasies, *The Mouse and the Motorcycle* or *Runaway Ralph*.

USING BIOGRAPHIES IN CREATIVE DRAMA

The biographies of significant people of the past and present are filled with lively dialogue, confrontations between new ideas and society, and the joys connected with discovery. Consequently, the plots suggest many opportunities for creative drama, as children relive the momentous experiences in people's lives. Children can pretend to be various characters in history and pantomime their actions and responses, they can create "You Are There" dramas based on scenes of scientific or historic significance, and they can devise sequence games based on the most significant incidents in a person's life. They can also create imaginary conversations between two people from the past or present or from different time periods who have some common traits but were never able to communicate because of time or distance. The following ideas are only samples of the types of creative drama that can result from using biographies in the classroom.

Pantomiming Actions

Jean Fritz's stories of Revolutionary War heroes, with their portrayal of the humorous and human side of the characters,

are excellent sources for pantomime. For example, an adult can read the book *Where Was Patrick Henry on the 29th of May?* and ask children how Patrick Henry acted and how they would act if they were Patrick Henry. The story can then be read a second time as children pantomime all of the actions. There is another way to approach this dramatization: After listening to or reading the book, children can identify and discuss scenes they would like to depict and then pantomime each scene. Children have identified the following scenes as being of special interest in Patrick Henry's life:

Scenes from Patrick Henry's Life

1 Going fishing with a pole over his shoulder.
2 Going hunting for deer or possum, with a rifle in his hands, accompanied by a dog at his heels.
3 Walking barefoot through the woods, lying down while listening to the rippling of a creek or the sounds of birds singing and imitating their songs.
4 Listening to rain on the roof, his father's fox horn, and music of flutes and fiddles.
5 Teaching himself to play the flute when he is recovering from a broken collarbone.
6 Listening to his Uncle Langloo Winston making speeches.
7 Waiting for the school day to end.
8 Playing practical jokes on his friends, including upsetting a canoe.
9 Trying to be a storekeeper without success.
10 Attempting to be a tobacco farmer.
11 Attending court and discovering that he liked to watch and listen to lawyers.
12 Beginning his law practice and not finding many clients.
13 Defending his first big case in court and winning.
14 Arguing against taxation without representation as a member of Virginia's House of Burgesses.
15 Delivering his "give me liberty or give me death" speech at St. John's Church.
16 Governing Virginia.
17 Hearing the news that the Continental army has defeated the English troops at Saratoga, New York.
18 Speaking against the enactment of the Constitution of the United States and for individual and states' rights after the war is over.
19 Retiring on his estate in western Virginia.

These nineteen scenes may also be developed into what Ruth Beall Heinig and Lyda Stillwell (2) describe as a sequence pantomime game. This game involves careful observation by all players who must see and interpret what someone else is doing and at the correct time, according to directions written on their own cue card, stand and perform the next action. (Players must be able to read to do this pantomime activity.) Cue cards for the nineteen scenes from Patrick Henry's life would now be developed. The first cue card would look approximately like this:

> You begin the game.
>
> Pretend that you are a young, barefoot Patrick Henry happily going fishing with a pole over your shoulder.
>
> When you are finished, sit down in your seat.

The second card would read:

> Cue: Someone pretends to be a young Patrick Henry going fishing with a pole over his shoulder.
>
> You are a young Patrick Henry happily going hunting for deer or possum, with a rifle in your hands and accompanied by a dog running at your heels.
>
> When you are finished, go back to your seat.

The rest of the scenes, written in a similar manner, would also be placed on cards. It is helpful if the cue and the directions for the pantomime are written in different colors. The cards are mixed and distributed randomly. There should be at least one cue card for each player, but more scenes may be added if a whole class is doing the activity. If there are fewer players, either the number of scenes can be reduced or each player can receive more than one cue card. Children should be asked to watch carefully and wait for each player to complete the pantomime. It is helpful if the adult or leader has a master cue sheet containing all the cues in correct sequential order so that cueing can be accomplished if a pantomime is misinterpreted, children seem uncertain, or the group loses its direction. Heinig and Stillwell suggest that in order to involve as many children as possible, large groups may be divided into three small groups. Each small group pantomimes a set of identical cue cards independently. A child might act as leader of each group and follow the master sheet.

Incidents in the lives of other Fritz heroes, related in *And Then What Happened, Paul Revere?*, *Why Don't You Get a Horse, Sam Adams?*, and *What's the Big Idea, Ben Franklin?* also make enjoyable pantomime dramas. All of the scenes described may also encourage oral interpretations, as children may add dialogue to their impersonations.

Incidents in the lives of famous scientists also provide material for pantomimes. Several scenes from Nancy Veglahn's *The Mysterious Rays: Marie Curie's World* that lend themselves to pantomime include the following:

Scenes from Marie Curie's Life

1   Shivering as she works in her cold laboratory at the University of Paris.
2   Thinking of her childhood on her way to the market, and observing people who remind her of earlier times.
3   Happily holding her baby as she has a few relaxed moments away from the laboratory.
4   Tediously grinding pitchblende until she has 100 grams, and then testing it.
5   Vacationing with her husband, Pierre, after long hours of work.
6   Excitedly discovering that the powder she and Pierre have been working with was 330 times more active than uranium.
7   Moving to a large laboratory, a dirty building resembling an abandoned barn; preparing the laboratory and beginning to experiment with pitchblende the in hope of reducing it to a pure sample of radium.
8   Working long hours over a caldron, heating and stirring pitchblende, and showing her fatigue and frustration over the inability to collect a sample of radium without any trace of other substances.
9   Producing pure radium on March 28, 1902.
10   Receiving the degree of Doctor of Physical Science on June 25, 1903.
11   Receiving the Nobel Prize in November, 1903 (jointly with Pierre), but being too ill and overworked to attend the ceremonies.

Children can pantomime the actions of dancers as in *Arthur Mitchell,* by Tobi Tobias; the actions of musicians as in *Duke: The Musical Life of Duke Ellington,* by Bill Gutman, or *The Boy Who Loved Music,* by David Lasker; the actions of a skater as in *A Very Young Skater,* by Jill Krementz; and the actions of athletes as in *Sports Hero: Phil Esposito,* by Marshall and Sue Burchard, and *Wesley Paul, Marathon Runner,* by Julianna A. Fogel.

"You Are There" Creative Dramatizations

Biographies allow children to experience some very exciting moments in history through the emotions, words, and contributions of the people who created these moments. Consequently, reenactments of those scenes can allow children to experience the excitement and realize that history is made up of real people and actual incidents.

A group of seventh graders chose to return in time to Rome in 1632, during the cruel days of the Inquisition. Their "You Are There" drama, based on Sidney Rosen's *Galileo and The Magic Numbers,* begins after Galileo has published his *A Dialogue on the Two Great Systems of the World* and is facing an angry Pope Urban. The following scenes illustrate the outline of events depicted by the group:

1 The announcer prepares the audience: "You are there; the year is 1632; Galileo is facing an angry Pope Urban. The pope's face is reddened in anger, his eyes are flashing venom. He is pounding his fists on the arms of the papal throne. Shouting, he declares:
'That scoundrel! That ingrate! We try to befriend him. And how does he repay us? By doing all this behind our back! Well this time he has gone too far! Let him take care! It is out of our hands now. This is a matter for the Holy Office!'" (p. 192). With these words, the slow process of the Inquisition begins. Galileo's enemies are winning, and he is to be charged with heresy.

2 Next, the announcer, the action, and the dialogue take the audience back to Florence: Galileo waits anxiously with his health failing, his fever returning, and his eyesight failing.

3 A scene in October is described and enacted as the inquisitor of Florence appears at Galileo's door with a summons; Galileo has thirty days in which to appear before the Holy Office in Rome.

4 The scene shifts to April 12, 1633; Galileo is summoned to the Inquisition chambers. Galileo is exhaustively questioned and threatened with torture for many days until he finally signs a document confessing his wrongdoing; he then feels shame and guilt for his weakness.

5 On June 21, Galileo discovers that signing the document is not sufficient; he is to be tried for heresy before ten cardinals who will be his judges. The scene shows a bent, graying Galileo in front of the men dressed in red cloaks and hats sitting about a great semicircular table. The questioning begins as the judges ask Galileo whether he does, indeed, believe that the earth moves about the sun. Silence hangs over the hall as the judges await Galileo's response.

6 On June 22, 1633, the scene shows Galileo dressed in the shirt of penitence, awaiting the verdict of the Inquisition. A hush falls over the hall; Galileo, kneeling before the cardinals, listens to the long document of charges read against him. At last, he hears the words that crush all hope:
"But in order that your terrible error may not go altogether unpunished, and that you may be an example and a warning to others to abstain from such opinions, we decree that your book, *Dialogue on the Two Great Systems of the World,* be banned publicly; also, we condemn you to the formal prison of this Holy Office for an indefinite period convenient to our pleasure. So we, the subscribing and presiding cardinals pronounce!" (p. 202)

Galileo and the Magic Numbers contains vividly described settings, characters, and enough dialogue so that children can develop a realistic "You Are There" drama. This can be done informally with an announcer only setting the stage and the actors developing the dialogue as they proceed, or some actual dialogue may be chosen from the book. The seventh-grade group chose a combination of these two approaches; they felt that their "You Are There" production was more authentic when some of the author's words were included.

Other "You Are There" episodes could be created around Christopher Columbus's meeting with Queen Isabella, his discovery of America, or his return to the Spanish court. The April 30, 1860, confrontation between scientists who wished to discredit Darwin, and Thomas Huxley and Robert Chambers, who supported Darwin's theory, is another dramatic moment in history (found in Irwin Shapiro's *Darwin and the Enchanted Isles*).

Imaginary Conversations Between People of Two Time Periods

Children enjoy contemplating what historic personalities who have similar viewpoints or opposite beliefs might say to each other if they had the opportunity to meet. Because this is impossible except through imagination, chidren can be motivated to read biographies in order to enter into such conversations. For example, an exciting conversation could result if Maria Mitchell (Helen S. Morgan's *Maria Mitchell, First Lady of American Astronomy*), Charles Darwin (Shapiro's *Darwin and the Enchanted Isles*), and Galileo (Rosen's *Galileo and the Magic Numbers*) could meet. Children can consider what questions each person might ask the others, interests and viewpoints that the three would probably share, and any differences of opinion they might express. After they have discussed these points, they can role-play a meeting between these figures. What advice could Galileo give Mitchell when she knew she must defend her teaching before the Vassar Board of Trustees? Would Galileo see a relationship between his discoveries of an earth that revolves around the sun and Darwin's work on the evolution of man, or would he believe that the work and publications of Darwin were heresy? Would Darwin empathize with Galileo's shame after his work was banned? Galileo worried about how history would view him; how would he discover nineteenth-century scientists felt about his work? Different children can present their views through the role-playing format; the class or group can then discuss what they believe the most likely responses would be and why they believe these responses would occur.

Other historical biographical characters might have stimulating conversations if they could meet with world figures of the 1980s. What views would emerge if Patrick Henry could share his opinions on states' rights and the rights of the individual with those of the current president of the United States? If children have read the informational book *Struggle and Lose, Struggle and Win: The United Mine Workers,* by Elizabeth Levy and Tad Richards, they can consider the similarities and differences of the experiences that John L. Lewis and Lech Walesa, leader of Poland's Solidarity Union movement, might discuss.

When children read in order to role-play a character's actions, express a character's feelings, or state dialogue that the character might express, they interact with the character at a human level and will often read until they feel empathy with that character and the historic time period.

SUMMARY

Most children find the writing style of informational books and biographies far more interesting than that of content area textbooks. Such books can provide many opportunities for stimulating children's learning experiences.

Many informational books relate to the science curriculum and provide valuable materials for helping children acquire abilities important for science education. Two types of informational materials relate specifically to the science curriculum: books on scientific topics and research that contain many small but interrelated details requiring analytical reading; and nontechnical materials, such as biographies of scientists and literature reporting scientific principles and findings, written in a style that is easier to read and understand.

In this chapter, activities are suggested so that parents, teachers, and librarians can assist children in increasing their ability to understand and enjoy science-related literature.

Biographies often include lively dialogue, confrontations between new ideas and society, and the joys and sorrows connected with discovery. Activities are suggested that allow children to interact with literature and the biographical characters through creative drama. Pantomime, "You Are There" dramatizations, and imaginary conversations between people of two time periods are suggested for creative thinking, empathizing with people in history, and developing the understanding that biographies are written about real people.

Suggested Activities for Children's Understanding of Informational Books and Biographies

- Identify the parts of a book that are necessary if children are to use informational materials at a particular grade level effectively. Choose a particular part of a book such as table of contents, index, glossary, or bibliography of further readings; select several informational books that can be used to encourage the development and use of these book aids. Prepare an activity that increases children's understanding of that part of the book.
- Visit a public or school library. What reference aids are available to assist children in their search for nonfictional materials? Explore the relationship between the author card, the title card, and the subject card in the library card catalog. Is the information on cards or computerized? Ask librarians how they help children find information.
- Choose several books by authors who have effectively presented the meaning of new technical terminology through the text or photographs, diagrams, and charts. Share the books with a peer group and make suggestions as to how you would use the books with children.
- Search through a science or social studies curriculum to identify the graphic aids that children at a particular grade level are expected to use, understand, or develop themselves. Develop an annotated bibliography of informational books by authors who have included accurate, clearly understandable graphic aids. Include page numbers for each aid you identify.
- Choose a reading for exact meaning requirement for science-related materials (pp. 592–94). Using a science-related book, other than one of those discussed in this chapter, develop a lesson that would encourage children to note the main idea of a selection, identify supporting details, or note the author's organization.
- Select an informational book that encourages children to perform an experiment in order to develop an understand-

ing of a scientific principle. Perform the experiment as directed. Are the directions clearly stated? Should they be modified or clarified to use with children? Make any necessary modifications and encourage a child to perform the experiment. Follow each step of the experiment and discuss the scientific principle with the child.

■ Develop a lesson that encourages children to evaluate what they read critically, including the author's purpose for writing the book, the author's competency, and the adequacy and accuracy of the content.

■ Prepare a pantomime-sequencing game that identifies both the cue and the directions for the pantomimed activity. Share the game with a peer group or a group of children.

■ Select a biographical incident that you believe would make an excellent "You Are There" creative dramatization. Identify the introductory scene and circumstances, the consecutive scenes to use, the characters to be involved, and the questions to be asked of children while guiding their discussion and development of the drama.

■ Select several biographies written about the same person. Plan a discussion that encourages children to consider the strengths and weaknesses of each biography.

References

1 Gillespie, John T., and Gilbert, Christine B. *Best Books for Children, Preschool through the Middle Grades.* New York: Bowker, 1978, 1981.
2 Heinig, Ruth Beall, and Stillwell, Lyda. *Creative Dramatics for the Classroom Teacher.* Englewood Cliffs, N.J.: Prentice-Hall, 1974.
3 Huus, Helen. "Critical and Creative Reading." In *Developing Comprehension Including Critical Reading,* edited by Mildred A. Dawson, pp. 163–65. Newark, Del.: International Reading Association, 1968.
4 Podendorf, Illa. "Characteristics of Good Science Materials for Young Readers." *Library Trends* 22 (April 1974): 425–31.
5 Roettger, Doris. "Reading Attitudes and the Estes Scale." Paper presented at the 23rd Annual Convention, International Reading Association, Houston, Tex., 1978.
6 Shepherd, David L. *Comprehensive High School Reading Methods,* 3rd ed. Columbus, Ohio: Merrill, 1982.
7 Thomas, Ellen Lamar, and Robinson, H. Alan. *Improving Reading in Every Class.* Boston: Allyn & Bacon, 1972.
8 Wolf, Willavene. "The Logical Dimension of Critical Reading." In *Developing Critical Reading,* edited by Mildred A. Dawson, pp. 166–69. Newark, Del.: International Reading Association, 1968.

CHILDREN'S LITERATURE

Informational Books

Ancona, George. *Dancing Is.* Dutton, 1981 (I:6–12 R:5). Photographs and text describe different dances such as the Highland Fling.

Arnold, Caroline. *Five Nests.* Illustrated by Ruth Sanderson. Dutton, 1980 (I:5–8 R:1–2). Nesting characteristics of five birds are illustrated and described in simple terminology.

Arnosky, Jim. *Freshwater Fish and Fishing.* Four Winds, 1982 (I:8–12 R:5). Text includes information about trout, perch, and pike and how to catch them.

Asch, Frank, and Asch, Jan. *Running with Rachel.* Photographs by Jan Asch and Robert M. Buscow. Dial, 1979 (I:7–10 R:3). A young girl explains how she became interested in running, how she feels when she runs, and the importance of comfortable running shoes, warm-up exercises, and the right foods.

Barry, Scott. *The Kingdom of Wolves.* Putnam, 1979 (I:9+ R:6). The author, through the use of photographs and text, pleads for the protection of wolves. He describes the life of the wolf and wolf pack.

Barton, Byron. *Airport.* Crowell, 1982 (I:3–8). Large illustrations follow passengers as they get ready to board the plane.

Benjamin, Carol Lea. *Running Basics.* Illustrated by Carol Lea Benjamin. Photographs by M. Beth Brennan. Prentice-Hall, 1979 (I:9–12 R:6). Eight topics are covered, including reasons for running, conditioning, clothing, and injuries.

Berenstain, Michael. *The Castle Book.* McKay, 1977 (I:5–8 R:5). Contains detailed drawings of various types of castles.

Berman, Paul. *Make-Believe Empire: A How-to Book.* Atheneum, 1982 (I:8–12 R:6). Directions are given for creating a city, a navy, and other objects needed for one's own kingdom.

Bester, Roger. *Fireman Jim.* Crown, 1981 (I:5–10 R:4). Photographs and text follow a twenty-four hour-day in the life of a New York City firefighter.

Bitter, Gary G. *Exploring With Computers.* Messner, 1981 (I:4–6 R:5). Explains use of computers and encourages readers to do activities such as reading a punch card.

Bluestone, Naomi. *"So You Want to Be a Doctor?" The Realities of Pursuing Medicine As a Career.* Lothrop, Lee & Shepard, 1981 (I: 10+ R:6). A doctor discusses what it means to be a medical student, an intern, and a resident.

Bonners, Susan. *A Penguin Year.* Delacorte. 1981 (I:6–9 R:3). The life of the Antarctic penguin is shown in watercolors.

Branley, Franklyn N. *Floating and Sinking.* Illustrated by Robert Galster. Crowell, 1967 (I:4–7 R:2). A Let's-Read-and-Find-Out Science Book describes experiments.

————. *The Story of the Space Shuttle, Columbia and Beyond.* Collins, 1979 (I:8+ R:6). The text, illustrations, and photographs trace the development of the space shuttle and suggest how it will be used in the future.

Brown, Marc. *Your First Garden Book.* Atlantic-Little, 1981 (I:5–9 R:4). Text includes over thirty simple projects that introduce children to gardening.

Bunting, Glenn, and Bunting, Eve. *Skateboards: How to Make Them, How to Ride Them.* Harvey, 1977 (I:9+ R:6). Photographs and text describe making, maintaining, and riding skateboards.

Busch, Phyllis S. *Cactus in the Desert.* Illustrated by Harriet Barton. Crowell, 1979 (I:7–9 R:3). Information is provided on a range of different cacti from the pincushion to the saguaro. Details are also included about taking care of a cactus.

Cobb, Vicki. *Fuzz Does It!* Illustrated by Brian Schatell. Lippincott, 1982 (I:6-12 R:6). Author explores various fibers, their sources, and uses.

———— and Darling, Kathy. *Bet You Can't, Science Impossibilities to Fool You.* Illustrated by Martha Weston. Lothrop, Lee & Shepard, 1980 (I:10+ R:6). A series of scientifically impossible challenges are described.

Cole, Joanna. *A Cat's Body.* Photographs by Jerome Wexler. Morrow, 1982 (I:6–12 R:4). Photographs and text show how a cat responds when pouncing, angry, etc.

————. *A Horse's Body.* Photographs by Jerome Wexler. Morrow, 1981 (I:2–6 R:5). Text and photographs explain the horse's anatomy.

————. *My Puppy Is Born.* Photographs by Jerome Wexler. Morrow, 1973 (I:7–9 R:2). Text and photographs follow the birth of puppies through their first eight weeks of life.

————. *A Snake's Body.* Photographs by Jerome Wexler. Morrow, 1981 (I:8–10 R:4). Photographs and text describe the anatomy of a python.

Cone, Ferne Geller. *Crazy Crocheting.* Illustrated by Rachel Osterlof. Photographs by J. Morton Cone. Atheneum, 1981 (I:9–12 R:5). Instruc-

I = Interest by age range;
R = Readability by grade level.

tions are given for a range of projects, including finger puppets.

Cooper, Miriam. *Snap! Photography.* Messner, 1981 (I:3+ R:5). Photographs, diagrams, and text provide an introduction to photography.

Corbett, Scott. *Bridges.* Illustrated by Richard Rosenblum. Four Winds, 1978 (I:10+ R:6). A history of bridges and the men who built them spans the time between prehistoric bridges through twentieth-century structures.

Cosman, Madeleine Pelner. *Medieval Holidays and Festivals: A Calendar of Celebrations.* Scribner's, 1981 (I:9+ R:6). Medieval holidays for each month discussed and described.

Davis, Daniel S. *Behind Barbed Wire: The Imprisonment of Japanese Americans During World War II.* Dutton, 1982 (I:10+ R:7). The author examines the facts leading up to the internment of Japanese Americans and how their lives were altered.

Davis, Edward E. *Into the Dark, a Beginner's Guide to Developing and Printing Black and White Negatives.* Atheneum, 1979 (I: 10+ R:7). An extensive coverage of beginning photography including setting up a darkroom, taking pictures, and developing the film.

Demuth, Patricia. *Joel: Growing Up a Farm Man.* Photographs by Jack Demuth. Dodd, Mead, 1982 (I:9+ R:6). Photographs and text reveal how a thirteen-year-old learns to be a farmer.

de Paola, Tomie. *The Cloud Book.* Holiday, 1975 (I:6–9 R:4). Ten clouds, their shapes, and how they forecast weather are explained in text and illustrations.

———. *The Popcorn Book.* Holiday, 1978 (I:3–8 R:5). Illustrations and story present facts about popcorn.

Englebardt, Stanley L. *Miracle Chip: The Microelectronic Revolution.* Lothrop, Lee & Shepard, 1979 (I:10+ R:8). Text describes the development of the miracle chip used in minicomputers.

Fenner, Carol. *Gorilla, Gorilla.* Illustrated by Symeon Shimin. Random House, 1973 (I:7–10 R:4). The text describes the early life of a gorilla and his capture and confinement in a zoo.

Fields, Alice. *Satellites.* Illustrated by Mike Tregenza. Watts, 1981 (I:8 + R:4). Presents a history of satellites, including uses, launching, and discoveries.

Filstrup, Chris, and Filstrup, Janie. *Beadazzled: The Story of Beads.* Illustrated by Loren Bloom, Warne, 1982 (I:10+ R:6). Text traces the history of beads from ancient civilizations through contemporary times.

Flanagan, Geraldine Lux, and Morris, Sean. *Window into a Nest.* Houghton Mifflin, 1975 (I:9+ R:8). Excellent, detailed account of the life of a pair of chickadees from the time they build their nest until the babies leave the nest.

Ford, Barbara. *Alligators, Raccoons, and Other Survivors: The Wildlife of the Future.* Morrow, 1981 (I:9+ R:6). Text describes how animals have survived in spite of human encroachment.

Freedman, Russell. *Farm Babies.* Holiday, 1981 (I:4–8 R:2). Photographs and text show young farm animals in the spring.

Fuchs, Eric. *Journey to the Moon.* Delacorte, 1969 (I:4–9 R:5). Two pages of text are followed by twelve pages of drawings that illustrate the stages of Apollo II from launching, to the landing on the moon, to splashdown and recovery.

Gardner, Robert. *This is the Way It Works: A Collection of Machines.* Illustrated by Jeffrey Brown. Doubleday, 1980 (I:10+ R:7). Diagrams and text describe how various tools and machines work.

Goldin, Augusta. *Straight Hair, Curly Hair.* Illustrated by Ed Emberley. Crowell, 1966, 1972 (I:4–8 R:2). A Let's-Read-and-Find-Out Science book explores properties of human hair.

Goor, Ron and Goor, Nancy. *Shadows: Here, There, and Everywhere.* Photographs by Ron Goor. Crowell, 1981 (I:6–10 R:4). Authors suggest experiments with shadows.

Graham, Ada, and Graham, Frank. *The Changing Desert.* Illustrated by Robert B. Shetterly. Scribner's, 1981 (I:9–12 R:6). Text explores problems in the desert, including vehicles, water, overgrazing.

Greenfeld, Howard. *Bar Mitzvah.* Illustrated by Elaine Grove. Holt, Rinehart & Winston, 1981 (I:9–12 R:5). Text provides background and traditions of this Jewish ceremony.

Gross, Ruth Bevlov. *What Is That Alligator Saying?* Illustrated by John Hawkinson. Hastings, 1972 (I:4–8 R:2). The author explains how different animals can communicate with each other.

Hartman, Jane E. *Armadillos, Anteaters, and Sloths: How They Live.* Holiday, 1980 (I:10+ R:6). Discusses the anatomy, physiology, and life-styles of animals that may be the most primitive mammals in North America.

Hawes, Judy. *Bees and Beelines.* Illustrated by Aliki. Crowell, 1964 (I:4–8 R:3). A Let's-Read-and-Find-Out Science Book explores flight of bees.

———. *Ladybug, Ladybug, Fly Away Home.* Illustrated by Ed Emberley. Crowell, 1967 (I:4–8 R:3). A Let's-Read-and-Find-Out Science Book encourages children to view the ladybug.

Heilman, Joan Rattner. *Bluebird Rescue.* Lothrop, Lee & Shepard, 1982 (I:9–12 R:6). Provides reasons for decline of the bluebird and suggestions for conservation groups.

Hess, Lilo. *The Amazing Earthworm.* Scribner's 1979 (I:8 + R:7). The earthworm's five hearts, small brain, and taste buds are described. The ecological importance of this animal is stressed as well as the danger from insecticides.

———. *Diary of a Rabbit.* Scribner's, 1982 (I:9–12 R:6). Includes information on different breeds and the care of rabbits as well as a five-month diary about one rabbit.

Hewett, Joan. *Watching Them Grow: Inside a Zoo Nursery.* Photographs by Richard Hewitt. Little, Brown, 1979 (I:7–12 R:6). Photographs and text show what happens in the nursery at the San Diego Zoo.

Hilton, Suzanne. *We the People: The Way We Were 1783–1793.* Westminister, 1981 (I:10+ R:7). Explores such subjects as education, living conditions, and culture.

———. *Who Do You Think You Are? Digging for Your Family Roots.* Westminister, 1976 (I:10+ R:7). Young genealogists discover how to trace their own family trees.

Horwitz, Elinor Lander. *How to Wreck a Building.* Photographs by Joshua Horwitz. Pantheon, 1982 (I:9–12 R:5). A former student describes the procedures used to demolish an elementary school.

Hunt, Patricia. *Koalas.* Dodd, Mead, 1980 (I:8–10). Photographs depict the life of the Koalas.

———. *Tigers.* Dodd, Mead, 1981 (I:8–10 R:4). The Bengal and Siberian tigers are described.

Huntington, Harriet E. *Let's Look at Cats.* Doubleday, 1981 (I:9–12 R:5). Photographs show various members of the cat family.

Isenbart, Hans-Heinrich. *A Duckling Is Born.* Translated by Catherine Edwards Sadler. Photographs by Othmar Baumli. Putnam, 1981 (I:4–8 R:3). Describes the life cycle of ducks.

Jacobs, Francine. *Africa's Flamingo Lake.* Photographs by Jerome Jacobs. Morrow, 1979 (I:9+ R:7). Author visits Lake Nakuru in Kenya, home of the largest number of flamingos in the world.

Jessell, Camilla. *The Puppy Book.* Metheun, 1980 (I:8–12). Follows the birth, in photographs, of nine Labrador puppies.

Jordan, Helen J. *How a Seed Grows.* Illustrated by Joseph Low. Crowell, 1960 (I:4–8 R:2). A Let's-Read-and-Find-Out Science Book gives directions for experimenting with seeds.

Kalb, Jonah, and Kalb, Laura. *The Easy Ice Skating Book.* Illustrated by Sandy Kossin. Houghton Mifflin, 1981 (I:7–12 R:5). Beginning ice skating skills such as stopping, gliding, and spinning are described.

Karen, Ruth. *Feathered Serpent: the Rise and Fall of the Aztecs.* Four Winds, 1979 (I:10+ R:9). Text includes both the history of the Aztec civilization and a description of where the best Aztec archeological sites may be viewed.

Koebner, Linda. *From Cage to Freedom: A New Beginning for Laboratory Chimpanzees.* Dutton, 1981 (I:9+ R:5). Scientists follow laboratory chimps after they are released on a Florida island.

Kohl, Herbert. *A Book of Puzzlements: Play and Invention with Language.* Schocken, 1981 (I:10+ R:7). A large collection of word games, including anagrams, hieroglyphics, and crossword puzzles.

Krementz, Jill. *A Very Young Rider.* Knopf, 1977 (I:7–12 R:3). Ten-year-old Vivi Malloy hopes to be a member of the Olympic team one day. Photographs and text describe her preparation as she is taught dressage and jumping.

———. *A Very Young Skater.* Knopf, 1979 (I:7–12 R:4). Ten-year-old Katherine spends several hours every day preparing for her desired goal of being an accomplished skater. Excellent photographs.

Lasky, Kathryn. *Dollmaker: The Eyelight and the Shadow.* Photographs by Christopher G. Knight. Scribner's, 1981 (I:9+ R:5). A doll that will be a collector's item is described in text and photographs.

Lauber, Patricia. *Seeds Pop! Stick! Glide!* Photography by Jerome Wexler. Crown, 1981 (I:8–10 R:4). Discusses the many ways that seeds travel.

———. *What's Hatching out of That Egg?* Crown, 1979 (I:7–10 R:2). A science mystery asks children to discover the identity of eleven animals that hatch out of eggs.

Leen, Nina. *Monkeys.* Holt, Rinehart & Winston, 1978 (I:7–12 R:5). Photographs showing monkeys, apes, and great apes.

Levy, Elizabeth, and Richards, Tad. *Struggle and Lose, Struggle and Win: The United Mine Workers.* Photographs by Henry E. F. Gordillo. Four Winds, 1977 (I:10+ R:7). The text traces the history of miners from preunion days through the work of John L. Lewis.

Linsley, Leslie. *Air Crafts: Playthings to Make and Fly.* Photographs by Jon Aron. Lodestar, 1982 (I:9–12 R:6). Six how-to activities for objects such as a boomerang and a skate sail that can be made to move through air.

McClung, Robert M. *America's Endangered Birds: Programs and People Working to Save Them.* Illustrated by George Founds. Morrow, 1979 (I:9+ R:6). Six endangered birds: the whooping crane, the bald eagle, the brown pelican, the California condor, the Kirtland's warbler, and the ivory-billed woodpecker.

McDearmon, Kay. *Foxes.* Dodd, Mead 1981 (I:9–2: R:5). Lives of the red fox, the gray fox, the kilt fox, and the Arctic fox are explored.

———. *Rocky Mountain Bighorns.* Photographs by Valerius Geist. Dodd, Mead, 1980 (I:9+ R:6). Pictures and text describe the habitat, behavior, physical characteristics, and need for protection of the bighorn sheep.

MacGregor, Anne, and MacGregor, Scott. *Domes: A Project Book.* Lothrop, Lee & Shepard, 1982 (I:9+ R:7). Text traces history of domes and includes models for building one.

Mangurian, David. *Children of the Incas.* Four Winds, 1979 (I:7–12 R:3). Photographs and text illustrate the life of a thirteen-year-old boy who lives in the highlands of Peru.

Mannetti, William. *Dinosaurs in Your Back Yard.* Atheneum, 1982 (I:9+ R:6). The author considers some new theories about dinosaurs.

Marcus, Rebecca. *Being Blind.* Hastings, 1981 (I:9–12 R:6). The author documents many aspects of blindness such as inventions to help blind people, problems, and solutions.

Math, Irwin. *Morse, Marconi and You, Understanding and Building Telegraph, Telephone and Radio Sets.* Scribner's, 1979 (I:10+ R:10). Describes discovery of telegraph, telephone, and radio sets and detailed directions for building each one.

———. *Wires and Watts: Understanding and Using Electricity.* Illustrated by Hal Keith. Scribner's, 1981 (I:10+ R:10). Describes experiments with electricity.

Michel, Anna. *The Story of Nim: The Chimp Who Learned Language.* Photographs by Susan Kuklin and Herbert S. Terrace. Knopf, 1980 (I:8+ R:6). The story of the research study that resulted in a chimpanzee learning to identify and use 125 signs in sign language.

Miles, Betty. *Save the Earth! An Ecology Handbook for Kids.* Illustrated by Claire A. Nivola. Knopf, 1974 (I:8+ R:5). Text contains activities designed to help children explore their environment.

Millard, Anne. *Ancient Egypt.* Illustrated by Angus McBridge, Brian and Constance Dear, and Nigel Chamberlain. Warwick, 1979 (I:9+ R:6). Provides background information about the Egyptian civilization that lasted from 3118 B.C. to 31 B.C.

Milton, Joyce. *Here Come the Robots.* Hastings, 1981 (I:8–10 R:4). A collection of stories about robots in space and in other exploration.

Nance, John. *Lobo of the Tasaday.* Pantheon, 1982 (I:9–12 R:5). Photographs and text follow a Filipino boy whose people lived in the Stone Age.

Nixon, Hershell, and Nixon, Joan Lowery. *Earthquakes: Nature in Motion.* Dodd, Mead, 1981 (I:8–10 R:5). Describes what, how, and why related to earthquakes.

———. *Glaciers: Nature's Frozen Rivers.* Dodd, Mead, 1980 (I:9+ R:6). Text and photographs describe glacier formation, different types of glaciers, results of glaciers, and use of glaciers for water supplies and electric power.

———. *Volcanoes: Nature's Fireworks.* Dodd, Mead, 1978 (I:7–10 R:5). Discusses causes of volcanoes.

Norvell, Flo Ann Hedley. *The Great Big Box Book.* Photographs by Richard W. Mitchell. Crowell, 1979 (I:5–9 R:5). Directions for making playthings out of large boxes.

Oxford Scientific Films. *Bees and Honey.* Photographs by David Thompson. Putnam, 1977 (I:all R:4). Photographs follow bees through the process of making honey.

———. *The Butterfly Cycle.* Photographs by John Cooke. Putnam, 1977 (I:all R:5). Text describes, in photographs and words, the life cycle of the cabbage white butterfly. Excellent color photographs show enlarged eggs and body parts.

———. *The Chicken and the Egg.* Photographs by George Bernard and Peter Parks. Putnam, 1979 (I:all R:4). Characteristics of chickens are discussed. Marvelous photographs show changes in the chick embryo growing inside the egg.

———. *Common Frogs.* Photographs by George Bernard. Putnam, 1979 (I:all R:5). Beautiful photographs depict the life cycle of the frog.

———. *House Mouse.* Photographs by David Thompson. Putnam, 1978 (I:all R:5). Photographs depict the life of adult mice and their babies.

Patent, Dorothy Hinshaw. *Sizes and Shapes in Nature—What They Mean.* Holiday House, 1979 (I:10+ R:8). Explores the significance of the structure of living things in their ability to relate to daily life and evolution.

Pettit, Florence H. *The Stamp-Pad Printing Book.* Photographs by Robert M. Pettit. Crowell, 1979 (I:10+ R:6). Directions are included for carving and printing and then using a stamp pad to create several projects.

Pollard, Michael. *How Things Work.* Larousse, 1978 (I:10+ R:7). Contains facts, diagrams, and photographs detailing how large machines work.

Poynter, Margaret. *Gold Rush! The Yukon Stampede of 1898.* Atheneum, 1979 (I:9+ R:6). The lure of the Yukon gold rush and the people who searched for gold are reported by a descendant of Alaskan pioneers.

Pringle, Laurence. *Chains, Webs, and Pyramids: The Flow of Energy in Nature.* Illustrated by Jan Adkins. Crowell, 1975 (I:9–12 R:6). Author describes how the sun's energy is changed to food energy in plants and then flows from one living thing to another in food chains.

_____. *City and Suburb: Exploring an Ecosystem.* Macmillan, 1975 (I:9–12 R:7). The author suggests places that the reader can explore in a city, looking for plants and animals; he discusses how a city affects its surroundings.

_____. *Death Is Natural.* Four Winds, 1977 (I:9–12 R:6). The author suggests that death in nature is an essential part of life.

_____. *Dinosaurs and Their World.* Harcourt Brace Jovanovich, 1968 (I:8–12 R:6). Describes how scientists over the last fifteen years have discovered what life was like millions of years ago.

_____. *Frost Hollows and Other Microclimates.* Morrow, 1981 (I:9–12 R:7). Author describes causes of microclimates, their effect on plants and animals, and their influence on buildings.

_____. *The Gentle Desert: Exploring An Ecosystem.* Macmillan, 1977 (I:9–12 R:6). Explores the land forms, climates, soils, and life found in the North American desert.

_____. *Into the Woods: Exploring the Forest Ecosystem.* Macmillan, 1973 (I:8–12 R:4). Explores the forest's energy cycle and encourages readers to respect the valuable ecosystem.

_____. *Natural Fire: Its Ecology in Forests.* Morrow, 1979 (I:9–12 R:7). Develops the position that fire in the forest is not now considered as detrimental as formerly believed.

_____. *Twist, Wiggle, and Squirm: A Book about Earthworms.* Illustrated by Peter Parnall. Crowell, 1973 (I:6–9 R:2). The author explains how earthworms live, how they mate, and what they eat.

_____. *Vampire Bats.* Morrow, 1982 (I:9–12 R:6). Author discusses bats that feed on blood rather than insects.

_____. *Wild Foods: A Beginner's Guide to Identifying, Harvesting and Cooking Safe and Tasty Plants from the Outdoors.* Illustrated by Paul Breeden. Four Winds, 1978 (I: 10+ R:7). Includes information on identifying safe wild foods and recipes that may be used in their preparation.

Purdy, Susan Gold. *Jewish Holiday Cookbook.* Watts, 1979 (I:10+ R:5). The text contains information on the Jewish holidays and recipes describing some dishes that might be served during the holiday.

Rossell, Seymour. *The Holocaust.* Watts, 1981 (I:9+ R:6). Author examines Germany in the 1930s, Hitler's dictatorship, the Nuremberg trials.

Ryden, Hope. *The Little Deer of the Florida Keys.* Putnam, 1978 (I:8–12 R:4). The characteristics, habitat, and fight for survival of a deer no bigger than a large dog are depicted in photographs and text.

Sancha, Sheila. *The Castle Story.* Crowell, 1982 (I:10+ R:7). A reference that includes considerable information about types of castles.

Sattler, Helen Roney. *Dinosaurs of North America.* Illustrated by Anthony Rao. Lothrop, Lee & Shepard, 1981 (I:9+ R:6). In addition to discussions about various dinosaurs, the text includes theories about extinction.

Schaaf, Peter. *An Apartment House Close Up.* Four Winds, 1980 (I:all). Black and white photographs showing the various parts of an apartment house: windows, doors, hallways, elevators, rooms, windows, and heating.

Schlein, Mariam. *Lucky Porcupine!* Four Winds, 1980 (I:6–9 R:4). A porcupine's movements are followed, and campers discover signs of porcupine visits.

Scott, Jack Denton. *The Book of the Goat.* Photographs by Ozzie Sweet. Putnam, 1979 (I:9+ R:5). The goat is presented as a valuable animal that is intelligent and useful to humans.

_____. *The Book of the Pig.* Photographs by Ozzie Sweet. Putnam, 1981 (I:8–10 R:4). Author develops the characteristics and history of the pig.

_____. *Canada Geese.* Photographs by Ozzie Sweet. Putnam, 1976 (I:9+ R:6). Text discusses the migration habits of the Canadian geese as they fly from Canada to their southern feeding area in the Mississippi Valley.

_____. *Discovering the American Stork.* Photographs by Ozzie Sweet. Harcourt Brace Jovanovich, 1976 (I:9+ R:7). Photographs and text describe the habits, habitats, and unique qualities of the American stork.

_____. *Discovering the Mysterious Egret.* Photographs by Ozzie Sweet. Harcourt Brace Jovanovich, 1978 (I:9+ R:7). The background history and details of mating, nesting, and feeding are developed through photographs and text.

_____. *The Gulls of Smuttynose Island.* Photographs by Ozzie Sweet. Putnam, 1977 (I:9+ R:7). A photographic essay of the gulls that have a rookery ten miles off the Maine and New Hampshire coasts.

_____. *Little Dogs of the Prairie.* Photographs by Ozzie Sweet. Putnam, 1977 (I:9+ R:6). Pictures and text present the life of the prairie dog and the contributions it makes to the prairie.

_____. *Loggerhead Turtle: Survivor from the Sea.* Photographs by Ozzie Sweet. Putnam, 1974 (I:9+ R:6). Text and pictures follow the loggerhead turtle as she buries her eggs, the eggs hatch, and the turtles return to the sea.

_____. *Moose.* Photographs by Ozzie Sweet. Putnam, 1981 (I:8–10 R:5). Discusses physical characteristics and behavior of moose.

_____. *Return of the Buffalo.* Photographs by Ozzie Sweet. Putnam, 1976 (I:9+ R:6). Photographs of buffalo herds and the text report the return of the buffalo that became almost extinct in the 1800s.

_____. *The Submarine Bird.* Photographs by Ozzie Sweet. Putnam, 1980 (I:9+ R:6). A photographic essay of the cormorant, a bird whose rookeries are found on small islands off the coast of New England.

_____. *That Wonderful Pelican.* Photographs by Ozzie Sweet. Putnam, 1975 (I:9+ R:7). A picture-essay of the pelicans that live on Pelican Island, Florida.

Selsam, Millicent E. *Bulbs, Corms, and Such.* Photographs by Jerome Wexler. Morrow, 1974 (I:7–10 R:3). An introductory text that allows children to see and experiment with some general principles of botany.

_____. *How to Be a Nature Detective.* Pictures by Ezra Jack Keats. Harper & Row, 1958, 1963 (I:5–8 R:4). Encourages children to identify animals by observing their tracks.

_____. *Plants We Eat.* Photographs by Jerome Wexler. Morrow, 1981 (I:10+ R:5). Presents the history and development of plants as food.

_____. *Popcorn.* Photographs by Jerome Wexler. Morrow, 1976 (I:7–10 R:4). The history of popcorn and the life cycle of the plant are developed in text and photographs.

_____, and Wexler, Jerome. *The Amazing Dandelion.* Morrow, 1977 (I:7–10 R:4). The life cycle of the dandelion is presented in text and photographs.

Sherman, Geraldine. *Caverns: A World of Mystery and Beauty.* Photographs by Julian Messner, 1980 (I:8–12). Photographs and discussion describing what an explorer might find inside a cavern.

Shuttlesworth, Dorothy E. *To Find a Dinosaur.* Doubleday, 1973 (I:9+ R:7). What did dinosaurs look like? What discoveries have scientists made from the bones and fossils from the past? Children discover what it is like to be a paleontologist.

Simon, Seymour. *Animal Fact/Animal Fable*. Illustrated by Diane de Groat. Crown, 1979 (I:5– R:3). A humorous presentation of animal beliefs that are not always true: bats are blind, an owl is wise, wolves live alone.

––––––. *Danger from Below: Earthquakes—Past, Present, and Future*. Four Winds, 1979 (I:10+ R:6). Information developed through text, photographs, diagrams, and maps tells where earthquakes occur, why they occur, and how they are measured.

––––––. *Deadly Ants*. Illustrated by William R. Downey. Four Winds, 1979 (I:8–12 R:6). The characteristics of two dangerous ants, the fire ant and the army ant, are developed in considerable detail.

––––––. *Discovering What Garter Snakes Do*. Illustrated by Susan Bonners. McGraw-Hill, 1975 (I:7–10 R:3). Describes characteristics of garter snakes, and how to capture them, care for them, and observe them at home.

––––––. *The Long Journey From Space*. Crown, 1982 (I:9+ R:6). Old and new photographs trace history and changes in comets.

––––––. *The Long View into Space*. Crown, 1979 (I:all R:5). A photographic essay depicting the moon, the sun, planets, stars, nebulas, and galaxies.

––––––. *Meet the Giant Snakes*. Illustrated by Harriet Springer. Walker, 1979 (I:7–10 R:5). Characteristics of pythons and boa constrictors are presented in text and illustrations.

––––––. *Poisonous Snakes*. Illustrated by William R. Downey. Four Winds. 1981 (I:7–10 R:5). Discusses important role of poisonous snakes, where they live, and their behavior.

––––––. *The Secret Clocks, Time Senses of Living Things*. Illustrated by Jan Brett. Viking, 1979 (I:9+ R:6). Explores the biological time clocks of plants, animals, and humans. Step-by-step experiments involve students in research.

––––––. *The Smallest Dinosaurs*. Illustrated by Anthony Rao. Crown, 1982 (I:5–9 R:6). Seven small members of the Coelurosauria, or hollow, lizard family are presented.

––––––. *Strange Creatures*. Illustrated by Pamela Carroll. Four Winds, 1981 (I:7–10 R:5). Presents twenty-two animals who act or look strange, or have other extraordinary abilities.

Smith, Howard E. *Balance It!* Photographs by George Ancona, Four Winds, 1982 (I:9–12 R:6). Pictures illustrate how to make a mobile, a letter scale, and other things that balance.

Snow, Richard. *The Iron Road: A Portrait of American Railroading*. Photographs by David Plowden. Four Winds, 1978 (I:10+ R:7). The history of railroads is traced from its beginning in the United States.

Steiner, Barbara. *Biography of a Bengal Tiger*. Illustrated by Lloyd Bloom. Putnam, 1979 (I: 8–12 R:4). The setting for this biography is the grasslands of India; the story tells of the life cycle of a tigress and her cubs.

Swinburne, Irene, and Swinburne, Lawrence. *Behind the Sealed Door: The Discovery of the Tomb and Treasures of Tutankhamun*. Sniffen Court, 1977 (I:all R:5). Beautiful photographs help children visualize the treasures buried in 1334 B.C.

Tinkelman, Murray. *Rodeo: The Great American Sport*. Greenwillow, 1982 (I:8–12 R:5). Black and white photographs illustrate each event in a rodeo.

Walker, Barbara M. *The Little House Cookbook: Frontier Foods from Laura Ingalls Wilder's Classic Stories*. Illustrated by Garth Williams. Harper & Row, 1979 (I:8–12 R:7). The author presents authentic pioneer recipes for the foods discussed in the Laura Ingalls Wilder books.

Walther, Tom. *A Spider Might*. Sierra Club/Scribner's, 1978 (I:all R:5). The natural histories, habits, and characteristics of the spiders found living near people are shown. Spiders are compared to humans.

Weber, William J. *Care of Uncommon Pets*. Holt, Rinehart & Winston, 1979 (I:all R:5). A veterinarian shares information about caring for rabbits, guinea pigs, hamsters, mice, rats, gerbils, frogs, turtles, snakes, and parakeets.

Weiss, Harvey. *Hammer and Saw: Introduction to Woodworking*. Crowell, 1981 (I:9–12 R:6). Author discusses through text and illustrations some step-by-step-directions for beginning woodworking.

Wong, Herbert H., and Vessel, Matthew F. *Pond Life: Watching Animals Find Food*. Illustrated by Tony Chen. Addison-Wesley, 1970 (I:6–9 R:3). Explores the food chain in a pond.

Zoll, Max Alfred. *A Flamingo is Born*. Photographs by Winifred Noack. Putnam, 1978 (I:7–12 R:4). Black and white photos follow the development of a flamingo from egg stage until the chick acquires its feathers.

Zubrowski, Bernie. *Bubbles, A Children's Museum Activity Book*. Illustrated by Joan Drescher. Little, Brown, 1979 (I: 8+ R:5). Experiments designed to help children discover information about bubbles.

––––––. *Messing Around with Water Pumps and Siphons*. Illustrated by Steve Lindblom. Little, Brown, 1981 (I:5–8 R:3). A Children's Museum Activity Book that encourages children to experiment.

Biographies

Aldis, Dorothy. *Nothing is Impossible: The Story of Beatrix Potter*. Drawings by Richard Cuffari. Atheneum, 1969 (I:10+ R:6). The biography of writer Beatrix Potter.

Blassingame, Wyatt. *Thor Heyerdahl: Viking Scientist*. Elsevier-Dutton, 1979 (I:8+ R:5). The story of the scientist who built and sailed the *Kon Tiki*.

Blegvad, Erik. *Self-Portrait: Erik Blegvad*. Addison-Wesley, 1979 (I:all R:5). A short autobiography written and illustrated by an artist of children's books.

Bourdon, David. *Calder: Mobilist, Ringmaster, Innovator*. Macmillan, 1980 (I:10+ R:7). Photographs and text describe the work of a noted artist.

Brenner, Barbara. *On the Frontier With Mr. Audubon*. Coward-McCann, 1977 (I:8–12 R:3). This story describes a trip down the Ohio and Mississippi rivers, when John James Audubon and his assistant sketched birds.

Burchard, Marshall, and Burchard, Sue. *Sports Hero: Phil Esposito*. Putnam, 1975 (I:7–10 R:3). Explores Phil Esposito's hockey career from a child playing in Canada through his experiences with the Chicago Black Hawks and the Boston Bruins.

Collins, Michael. *Flying to the Moon and Other Strange Places*. Farrar, Straus & Giroux, 1976 (I:10+ R:6). An autobiography written about the experiences of the astronaut who was part of the team to travel to the moon.

Dalgliesh, Alice. *The Columbus Story*. Illustrated by Leo Politi. Scribner's, 1955 (I:5–8 R:3). A picture book version of Columbus's first voyage to America.

D'Aulaire, Ingri, and D'Aulaire, Edgar Parin. *Abraham Lincoln*. Doubleday, 1939, 1957 (I: 8–11 R:5). This book for young children covers details in Lincoln's life from his birth to the end of the Civil War.

––––––. *Benjamin Franklin*. Doubleday, 1950 (I:8–12 R:6). A colorfully illustrated biography of Benjamin Franklin from boyhood through his diplomatic career.

––––––. *Columbus*. Doubleday, 1955 (I:7–10 R:5). A colorfully illustrated biography that includes Columbus's struggles for recognition and his four voyages to America.

Davidson, Margaret. *The Golda Meir Story*. Scribner's, 1981 (I:9–12 R:6). Traces Meir's life through the Yom Kippur war and her tenure as prime minister.

Dolan, Edward F. *Adolf Hitler: A Portrait in Tyranny*. Dodd, Mead, 1981 (I:10+ R:7). Author covers Hitler's rise to power, the days of World War II, the facts of the Holocaust, and Hitler's suicide.

II, the facts of the Holocaust, and Hitler's suicide.

——, and Lyttle, Richard B. *Bobby Clarke.* Doubleday, 1977 (I:10+ R:5). A biography of the hockey star of the Philadelphia Flyers.

Edwards, Anne. *P. T. Barnum.* Illustrated by Marylin Hafner. Putnam, 1977 (I:5–9 R:3). The life of the greatest circus showman presented in an easy-to-read biography.

Egypt, Ophelia Settle. *James Weldon Johnson.* Illustrated by Moneta Barnet. Crowell, 1974 (I:5–9 R:3). A Black American author, educator, lawyer, and diplomat who started the first black newspaper in the United States.

Facklam, Margery. *Wild Animals, Gentle Women.* Illustrated by Paul Facklam. Harcourt Brace Jovanovich, 1978 (I:10+ R:6). Includes information on the lives of eleven women who have studied animal behavior. The author gives information on how a student can prepare for a profession in ethology.

Fogel, Julianna A. *Wesley Paul, Marathon Runner.* Photographs by Mary S. Watkins. Lippincott, 1979 (I:6–9 R:4). A nine-year-old boy describes his training for, and running in, marathons.

Franchere, Ruth. *Cesar Chavez.* Illustrated by Earl Thollander. Crowell, 1970 (I:7–9 R:4). Illustrated biography of Chavez's struggles to improve the pay and living conditions for migrant workers.

Fritz, Jean. *Stonewall.* Illustrated by Stephen Gammell. Putnam, 1979 (I:10+ R:6). A biography of a famous Civil War general, Thomas Jackson.

——. *And Then What Happened, Paul Revere?* Illustrated by Margot Tomes. Coward-McCann, 1973 (I:7–10 R:5). A humorous biography of the Revolutionary War hero.

——. *Traitor. The Case of Benedict Arnold.* Putnam, 1981 (I:8+ R:5). The life of the man who chose the British cause in the Revolutionary War.

——. *What's the Big Idea, Ben Franklin?* Illustrated by Margot Tomes. Coward-McCann, 1978 (I:7–10 R:5). A biography of the inventor, ambassador, and co-author of the Declaration of Independence.

——. *Where Do You Think You're Going, Christopher Columbus?* Illustrated by Margot Tomes. Putnam, 1980 (I:7–12 R:5). Fritz's style creates a believable background for Columbus's four voyages.

——. *Where Was Patrick Henry on The 29th of May?* Illustrated by Margot Tomes. Coward-McCann, 1975 (I:7–10 R:5). This is a humorous telling of incidents in Patrick Henry's youth and political career.

——. *Why Don't You Get a Horse, Sam Adams?* Illustrated by Trina Schart Hyman. Coward-McCann, 1974 (I:7–10 R:5). A humorous story about Samuel Adams, his refusal to ride a horse, and his final decision to ride.

——. *Will You Sign Here, John Hancock?* Illustrated by Trina Schart Hyman. Coward-McCann, 1976 (I:7–10 R:5). The story covers the rise to fame of a charming Revolutionary War hero who was also on George III's Dangerous Americans list.

Goodnough, David. *Christopher Columbus.* Illustrated by Burt Dodson. Troll Associates, 1979 (I:8–12 R:6). An illustrated life of Columbus including his early experiences with the sea.

Goodsell, Jane. *Daniel Inouye.* Crowell, 1977. Daniel Inouye, the first Japanese American congressman, grew up in a part of Hawaii that was not a tourist paradise but instead an island slum area. Story also tells of his hard work and fighting during World War II.

——. *Eleanor Roosevelt.* Illustrated by Wendell Minor. Crowell, 1970 (I:7–10 R:2). Eleanor's life as a shy child is discussed as well as her years in the White House and her work after her husband's death.

Greenfield, Eloise, and Little, Lessie Jones. Childtimes: A Three-Generation Memoir. Crowell, 1979 (I:10+ R:5). Three black women—grandmother, mother, and daughter—tell about their childhood experiences.

Gutman, Bill. *Duke: The Musical Life of Duke Ellington.* Random House, 1977 (I:10+ R:6). The life of Duke Ellington and a discussion of jazz from 1899 to 1974.

——. *The Picture Life of Reggie Jackson.* Watts, 1978 (I:5–9 R:2). A picture story of the experiences of the baseball player.

Haskins, James. *Andrew Young: Man with a Mission.* Lothrop, Lee & Shepard, 1979 (I:12+ R:7). The story of the first Black American ambassador to the United Nations.

Hyman, Trina Schart. *Self-Portrait: Trina Schart Hyman.* Addison-Wesley, 1981 (I:9–12 R:5). The artist tells how she developed as an artist; illustrations help tell her story.

Kheridan, David. *The Road from Home: The Story of an Armenian Girl.* Greenwillow, 1979 (I:12+ R:6). In 1915, an Armenian girl experiences the horrors of the Turkish persecution of Christian minorities.

Lasker, Joe, and Lasker, David. *The Boy Who Loved Music.* Illustrated by Joe Lasker. Viking, 1979 (I:all R:6). An eighteenth-century story of Joseph Haydn and a new symphony.

Lee, Betsy. *Charles Eastman, the Story of an American Indian.* Dillon, 1979 (I:8–12 R:5). A biography of a famous doctor, writer, and worker for Indian rights.

Lipman, Jean, and Aspinwall, Margaret. *Alexander Calder and His Magical Mobiles.* Hudson Hills, 1981 (I:9+ R:). The text begins with artist's early work and includes work in wood, bronze, wire, and mobiles.

Liss, Howard. *Bobby Orr: Lightning on Ice.* Illustrated by Victor Mays. Garrard, 1975 (I:8–12 R:4). The hockey star's story begins when he is a young player in Canada and follows him into professional hockey where he was voted the best defenseman in the league.

Manes, Stephen. *Pictures of Motion and Pictures that Move: Eadweard Muybridge and the Photography of Motion.* Coward-McCann, 1982 (I:9+ R:6). A photographer in the late 1800s invents the zoopraxiscope, a machine which projected moving images.

Morgan, Helen L. *Maria Mitchell, First Lady of American Astronomy.* Westminister, 1977 (I:12+ R:7). Covers the years from childhood when she learns astronomy from her father through her years as first woman astronomy professor at Vassar.

Patterson, Lillie. *Sure Hands, Strong Heart, The life of Daniel Hale Williams.* Illustrated by David Scott Brown. Abingdon, 1981 (I:10+ R:5). Biography of a black physician who worked for interracial hospitals.

Pizer, Vernon. *Glorious Triumphs: Athletes Who Conquered Adversity.* Dodd, Mead, 1966, 1968, 1980 (I:12+ R:8). Includes a collection of brief biographies about sports personalities who have overcome some problem; Babe Didrikson, Gordie Howe, Ben Hogan, and Althea Gibson are included.

Rosen, Sidney. *Galileo and the Magic Numbers.* Illustrated by Harie Stein. Little, Brown, 1958 (I:10+ R:6). A story about the astronomer and mathematician who invented the first telescope.

Sandburg, Carl. *Abe Lincoln Grows Up.* Illustrated by James Daugherty. Harcourt Brace Jovanovich, 1926, 1928, 1954 (I:10+ R:6). The first nineteen years of Lincoln's life are developed by a well-known writer and biographer.

Shapiro, Irwin. *Darwin and the Enchanted Isles.* Illustrated by Christopher Spollen. Coward-McCann, 1977 (I: 8+ R:6). Born in England in 1809, Charles Darwin later visited the Galapagos Islands where he discovered life forms that substantiated his theory on the evolution of animals.

Sharpe, Mitchell R. *It is I, Sea Gull: Valentina Tereshkova, First Woman in Space.* Crowell, 1975 (I:10+ R:6). The early life, training, and career of the Russian woman cosmonaut.

Silberdick, Barbara. *Franklin D. Roosevelt, Gallant President.* Feinberg, 1981 (I:9–12 R:6). This biography focuses upon Roosevelt's accomplishments.

Steele, William O. *The Wilderness Tattoo: A Narrative of Juan Oritz.* Harcourt Brace Jovanovich, 1972 (I:10+ R:6). Juan Oritz was a Spanish explorer who lived with the Florida Indians and then joined de Soto's expeditions as an interpreter.

Syme, Ronald. *Toussaint: The Black Liberator.* Illustrated by William Stobbs. Morrow, 1971 (I:12+ R:8). Toussaint, a former slave, rises to power in Haiti as he leads an uprising against French, Spanish, and English troops.

Tobias, Tobi. *Arthur Mitchell.* Illustrated by Carol Byard. Crowell, 1975 (I:7–9 R:5). Arthur Mitchell had a dream: to study and dance classical ballet. Describes the founder of the Dance Theatre of Harlem.

———. *Isamu Noguchi: The Life of a Sculptor.* Crowell, 1974 (I:10+ R:6). Background information and photographs of the work of a famous Japanese American sculptor.

Veglahn, Nancy. *Dance of the Planets: The Universe of Nicolaus Copernicus.* Illustrated by George Ulrich. Coward-McCann, 1979 (I:10+ R:6). The story of the astronomer who in 1507 developed the theory that the earth revolved around the sun.

———. *The Mysterious Rays: Marie Curie's World.* Illustrated by Victor Jahasz. Coward-McCann, 1977 (I:10+ R:6). The long years of dedicated experimentation are explored that provided the foundation for the Curies' discovery of radium.

Ventura, Piero. Based on text by Gian Paolo Ceserani. *Christopher Columbus.* Random House, 1978 (I:all R:6). A picture biography of Columbus's voyage to America.

———. Based on text by Gian Paolo Ceserani. *Marco Polo.* Illustrated by Piero Ventura. Putnam, 1982 (I:all R:6). A picture biography of Marco Polo's travels.

Wibberley, Leonard. *A Dawn in the Trees, Thomas Jefferson, the Years 1776 to 1789.* Farrar, Straus & Giroux, 1964 (I:12+ R:6). The second part of a four-volume biography.

———. *The Gales of Spring, Thomas Jefferson, the Years 1789 to 1801.* Farrar, Straus & Giroux, 1965 (I:12+ R:6). The third part of a four-volume biography.

———. *Time of the Harvest, Thomas Jefferson, the Years 1801 to 1826.* Farrar, Straus & Giroux, 1966 (I:12+ R:6). The final volume in a four-part biography.

———. *Young Man from Piedmont, the Youth of Thomas Jefferson.* Farrar, Straus & Giroux, 1963 (I:12+ R:6). The first of a four-volume biography.

Williams, Selma R. *Demeter's Daughters: The Women Who Founded America, 1587–1787.* Atheneum, 1976 (I:12+ R:7). A history of women in America that includes biographical sketches of women, well known and otherwise, whose contributions made the settlement of America possible.

Wolf, Bernard. *In This Proud Land: The Story of a Mexican American Family.* Lippincott, 1978 (I:all R:4). Photographs and text follow a family from the Rio Grand Valley to Minnesota for summer employment.

Yates, Elizabeth. *Amos Fortune, Free Man.* Illustrated by Nora S. Unwin. Dutton, 1950 (I:10+ R:6). The life of a man who is captured by slave traders in Africa and brought to Boston. There, he is purchased by a Quaker who educates him and provides him a trade.

Zemach, Margot. *Self-Portrait, Margot Zemach.* Addison-Wesley, 1978 (I:all R:8). An autobiography of an illustrator of children's books.

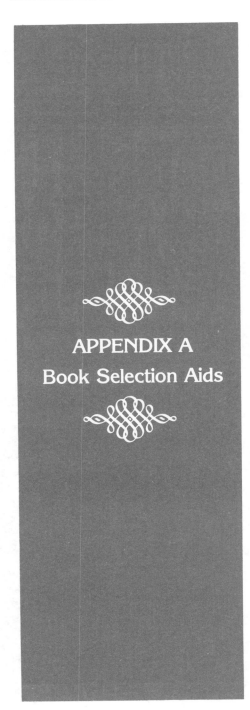

**APPENDIX A
Book Selection Aids**

Books

AAAS Science Book List for Children, 3rd ed., comp. by Hilary J. Deason. American Assoc. for the Advancement of Science, 1972

A to Zoo: Subject Access to Children's Picture Books. Bowker, 1982.

About 100 Books: A Guide to Better Intergroup Understanding, comp. by Ann G. Wolfe. American Jewish Committee, 1972.

Adventuring with Books: A Booklist for Pre-K-Grade 8, ed. by Mary Lou White. National Council of Teachers of English, 1981.

American Indian Stereotypes in the World of Children: A Reader and Bibliography, Scarecrow Press, 1982.

Best Books for Children: Preschool Through the Middle Grades, ed. by John T. Gillespie and Christine B. Gilbert. Bowker, 1978, 2nd ed. 1981.

Best Books on Health for Children, ed. by Pat Azarnoff. Bowker, 1982.

The Best in Children's Books: The University of Chicago Guide to Children's Literature 1966–1972, ed. by Zena Sutherland. The University of Chicago Press, 1973.

The Best in Children's Books: The University of Chicago Guide to Children's Literature 1973–1978, ed. by Zena Sutherland. The University of Chicago Press, 1980.

The Best of Children's Books: 1964–1978: with 1979 Addenda, ed. by Virginia Haviland. Library of Congress, 1980.

The Best of the Best, 2nd ed., ed. by Walter Scherf. Bowker, 1976.

Bibliography on Disabled Children, Canadian Assoc. of Children's Librarians' Committee on Library Service to Disabled Children. Canadian Library Assoc., 1982.

The Black Experience in Children's Books, Barbara Rollock. New York Public Library, 1974, 1979.

The Bookfinder: A Guide to Children's Literature About the Needs and Problems of Youth Aged 2–15, Sharon Spredemann Dreyer. American Guidance Service, 1981.

Books and the Teenage Reader: A Guide for Teachers, Librarians and Parents, 2nd ed., G. Robert Carlsen. Harper & Row, 1980.

Books for the Gifted Child, ed. by Barbara Holland Baskin and Karen H. Harris. Bowker, 1980.

Books for the Teen Age, 1982 Annual. New York Public Library, 1982.

Books for Today's Young Readers: An Annotated Bibliography of Recommended Fiction for Ages 10–14, comp. by Jeanne Bracken. Feminist Press, 1982.

Books in American History: A Basic List for High Schools and Junior Colleges, 2nd ed., ed. by John E. Wiltz and Nancy C. Cridland. Indiana University, 1981.

Books, Materials and Services for the Teenage Problem Reader, ed. by Ellen V. LiBretto. Bowker, 1981.

Book Waves: A Compilation of Reviews of Books for Teenagers, Bay Area Young Adult Librarians, Fremont, Calif., 1981.

Canadian Books for Young People, 3rd ed., comp. by Irma McDonough. University of Toronto Press, 1980.

Children's Authors and Illustrators: An Index to Biographical Dictionaries, 3rd ed., ed. by Adele Sarkissian. Gale, 1981.

Children's Books: Awards and Prizes, comp. by the Children's Book Council (revised periodically).

Children's Books in Print. Bowker (annual).

Children's Books in the Rare Book Division of the Library of Congress: Author-Title and Chronological Catalogs. Rowman and Littlefield, 1975.

Children's Books of International Interest, 2nd ed., ed. by Virginia Haviland. American Library Assoc., 1978.

Children's Books of the Year 1981, Barbara S. Smith. Watts, 1982.

Children's Books of the Year 1982, The Child Study Children's Book Committee. Bank Street College, 1982.

Children's Books Too Good to Miss: Revised Edition 1979, May Hill Arbuthnot, et al. University Press Books, 1980.

Children's Catalog, 14th ed., ed. by Richard H. Isaacson and Gary L. Bogart. Wilson, 1981.

Choosing Books for Children: A Commonsense Guide, Betsy Gould Hearne. Delacorte, 1981.

A Comprehensive Guide to Children's Literature with a Jewish Theme, Enid Davis. Schocken, 1981.

Easy Reading: Book Series and Periodicals for Less Able Readers, Michael F. Graves, Judith A. Boettcher, and Randall A. Ryder. International Reading Assoc. 1979.

The Elementary School Library Collection: A Guide to Books and Other Media, 13th ed., ed. by Louis Winkel. Bro-Dart, 1982.

Emerging Humanity: Multi-Ethnic Literature for Children and Adolescents, Ruth Kearney Carlson. Brown, 1972.

Folklore: An Annotated Bibliography and Index to Single Editions, comp. by Elsie B. Ziegler. Faxon, 1973.

Fun for Kids: An Index to Children's Craft Books, Marion F. Gallivan. Scarecrow Press, 1981.

The Great Lakes Region in Children's Books: A Selected Annotated Bibliography, ed. by Donna Taylor. Green Oak Press, 1980.

Guide to Reference Books, 9th ed., ed. by Eugene P. Sheehy. American Library Assoc., 1976.

Guide to Reference Books for School Media Centers, 2nd ed., ed. by Christine Gehr Wynar. Littleton, Colo.: Libraries Unlimited, 1981.

Guide to Reference Books: Supplement, 9th ed., ed. by Eugene P. Sheehy. American Library Assoc. 1980.

A Hispanic Heritage: A Guide to Juvenile Books About Hispanic People and Cultures, Isabel Schon. Scarecrow Press, 1980.

Index to Fairy Tales, 1949–1972, Including Folklore, Legends and Myths in Collections, Norma Olen Irland. Faxon, 1973.

Index to Poetry for Children and Young People: 1970–1975, ed. by John E. Brewton, G. Meredith Blackburn, and Lorraine A. Blackburn. Wilson, 1978.

Index to Young Readers' Collective Biographies, ed. by Judith Silverman. Bowker, 1975.

Indian Children's Books, Hap Gilliland, Billings, Mont.: Montana Council for Indian Education, 1980.

Junior High School Library Catalog, 4th ed., Wilson, 1980 (annual supplements).

Learning About Aging, The National Retired Teachers Assoc. and the American Assoc. of Retired Persons. American Library Assoc., 1981.

Let's Read Together: Books for Family Enjoyment, 4th ed., comp. by Assoc. for Library Service to Children, Let's Read Together Revision Committee. American Library Assoc., 1981.

Literature by and about the American Indian: An Annotated Bibliography, Anna Lee Stensland. National Council of Teachers of English, 1979.

Matters of Fact: Aspects of Non-Fiction for Children, Margery Fisher. Crowell, 1972.

Mexico and Its Literature for Children and Adolescents: Special Studies No. 15, comp. by Isabel Schon. Arizona State University, 1977.

More Juniorplots: A Guide for Teachers and Librarians, ed. by John T. Gillespie. Bowker, 1977.

A Multimedia Approach to Children's Literature: A Selective List of Films, Filmstrips, and Recordings Based on Children's Books, 2nd ed., ed. by Ellin Greene and Madalynne Schoenfeld. American Library Assoc., 1977.

Multimedia Library: Materials Selection and Use, James Cabeceiras. Academic Press, 1982.

Notable Children's Books, 1940–1970, comp. by Children's Service Division. American Library Assoc., 1977.

Notable Children's Books, 1971–1975, comp. by 1971–75 Notable Children's Books Re-evaluation Committee, Assoc. for Library Service to Children. American Library Assoc., 1981.

Notes from a Different Drummer: A Guide to Juvenile Fiction Portraying the Handicapped, comp. by Barbara Baskin and Karen Harris. Bowker, 1977.

Periodicals for School Media Programs: A Guide to Magazines, Newspapers, Periodical Indexes, rev. ed., comp. by Selma Richardson. American Library Assoc., 1978.

Reading for Young People: The Great Plains, ed. by Mildred Laughlin. American Library Assoc., 1979.

Reading for Young People: The Middle Atlantic, ed. by Arabelle Pennypacker. American Library Assoc., 1980.

Reading for Young People: The Midwest, ed. by Dorothy Hinman and Ruth Zimmerman. American Library Assoc., 1979.

Reading for Young People: The Northwest, ed., by Mary Meacham. American Library Association, 1981.

Reading for Young People: The Rocky Mountains, ed. by Mildred Laughlin. American Library Assoc., 1980.

Reading for Young People: The Southeast, ed. by Dorothy Heald. American Library Assoc., 1980

Reference Books for Children, comp. by Carolyn S. Peterson and Ann D. Fenton. Scarecrow Press, 1981.

Science Books: A Quarterly Review, American Assoc. for the Advancement of Science.

Special Collections in Children's Literature, ed. by Carolyn W. Field. American Library Assoc., 1982.

Starting Out Right: Choosing Books about Black People for Young Children, ed. by Bettye Lattimer. Wisconsin Department of Public Instruction, 1972.

Subject Guide to Children's Books in Print. Bowker (annual).

The World of Books for Children: A Parent's Guide, Abby Campbell Hunt. Sovereign, 1979.

Periodicals Containing Information on Children's Books

Appraisal: Children's Science Books. Children's Science Book Review Committee, Harvard Graduate School of Education.

Book Review Digest. Wilson.

Bookbird. International Board on Books for Young People, International Institute for Children's Literature.

The Booklist. American Library Association.

The Bulletin of the Center for Children's Books. Graduate Library School, University of Chicago Press.

The Calendar. Children's Book Council.

Canadian Children's Literature: A Journal of Criticism and Review. Canadian Children's Literature Assoc., Canadian Children's Press.

Childhood Education. Assoc. for Childhood Education International.

Children's Literature. Temple University Press.

Children's Literature in Education. APS Publications.

The Horn Book Magazine. Horn Book.

Interracial Books for Children. Council on Interracial Books for Children.

Language Arts. National Council of Teachers of English.

The Lion and the Unicorn. Department of English, Brooklyn College.

Media and Methods. North American Publishing.

The New York Times Book Review. New York Times.

Parents' Choice: A Review of Children's Media—Books, Television, Movies, Music, Story Records, Toys and Games. Parents' Choice Foundation.

Phaedrus: An International Journal of Children's Literature Research. Phaedrus, Inc.

Previews: Non-Print Software & Hardware News & Reviews. Bowker.

Publishers Weekly. Bowker.

School Library Journal. Bowker.

School Media Quarterly. American Assoc. of School Librarians, American Library Assoc.

Science Books: A Quarterly Review. American Assoc. for the Advancement of Science.

Science and Children. National Science Teachers Assoc.

Teacher. Macmillan Professional Magazines.

Top of the News. Assoc. for Library Service to Children and the Young Adult Services Division, American Library Assoc.

The Web. Center for Language, Literature, and Reading, The Ohio State University.

Wilson Library Bulletin. Wilson.

APPENDIX B
Professional Reading

Additional References*

Aaron, Shirley L. *A Study of Combined School-Public Libraries.* Chicago: American Library Assoc., 1980. The author discusses the feasibility of combining public and school libraries.

Andersen, Hans Christian. *Fairy Tales.* Illustrated by Kay Rasmus Nielsen. New York: Viking, 1981. This is a reproduction of a 1924 edition.

Boner, Charles, trans. *Andersen, Hans Christian.* New York: Schocken, 1981. Kate Greenaway's original drawings for *The Snow Queen* are reproduced.

Bratton, J. S. *The Impact of Victorian Children's Fiction.* Barnes & Noble Imports, 1981. The author explores Victorian literature written for moral instruction.

Butler, Dorothy. *Babies Need Books.* New York: Atheneum, 1980. Characteristics of children age one through five are discussed and stories that will stimulate their development are presented.

———. *Cushla and Her Books.* Boston: Horn Book, 1980. The life of a handicapped child is changed through literature.

———, and Clay, Marie. *Reading Begins at Home: Preparing Children for Reading Before They Go to School.* Exeter, N.H.: Heinemann Educational, 1982. Includes suggestions for parents and a list of recommended books.

Butler, Francelia, ed. *Children's Literature.* Vol. 8. New Haven, Conn.: Yale University Press, 1980. The text includes fourteen essays on children's literature.

———. *Children's Literature,* Vol. 9. New Haven, Conn.: Yale University Press, 1981.

———. *Children's Literature,* Vol. 10. New Haven, Conn.: Yale University Press, 1982.

Carr, Jo, comp. *Beyond Fact: Nonfiction for Children and Young People.* Chicago: American Library Assoc., 1982. A collection of previously published essays on nonfiction, science, history, and biography.

Chambers, Nancy, ed. *The Signal Approach to Children's Books.* Metuchen, N.J.: Scarecrow Press, 1981. A collection of articles from the British literature journal are included.

Colwell, Eileen. *The Magic Umbrella and other Stories for Telling.* Lawrence, Mass.: Chatto, Bodley Head & Jonathan Cape, 1981. Includes information on how to tell stories to children.

Cope, Dawn, and Cope, Peter. *Humpty Dumpty's Favorite Nursery Rhymes.* New York: Holt, Rinehart & Winston, 1981. Reproductions of nursery rhyme postcards that were popular in the early 20th century.

Coplan, Kate. *Poster Ideas and Bulletin Board Techniques: For Libraries and Schools,* 2nd ed. Dobbs Ferry, N.Y.: Oceana, 1981. Illustrations and directions for developing bulletin boards are developed in school and library settings.

Crane, Walter. *An Alphabet of Old Friends and the Absurd ABC.* New York: Metropolitan Museum of Art, 1981. Reproductions of two of Walter Crane's toy books.

Davies, Ruth Ann. *The School Library Media Program: Instructional Force for Excellence,* 3rd ed. New York: Bowker, 1979. Discusses the future of the school media program.

Donelson, Kenneth L., and Nilsen, Alleen Pace. *Literature for Today's Young Adults.* Glenview, Ill.: Scott, Foresman, 1980. Authors discuss literature written for students between twelve and twenty.

Egoff, Sheila. *The Republic of Childhood: A Critical Guide to Canadian Children's Literature in English,* 2nd ed. New York: Oxford University Press, 1975.

———. *Thursday's Child: Trends and Patterns in Contemporary Children's Literature.* Chicago: American Library Assoc., 1981. Includes a series of essays about fantasy, picture books, realistic fiction, and poetry.

Emmens, Carol A., ed. *Children's Media Market Place,* 2nd ed. New York: Neal–Schuman, 1982. This reference includes information about publishers, periodicals, and bookstores.

*These references provide additional adult sources. They are not referenced at the end of the preceding chapters.

Engen, Rodney. *Kate Greenaway: A Biography.* New York: Schocken, 1981. A biography of the English artist.

Franklin, Linda Campbell. *Library Display Ideas.* Jefferson, N.C.: McFarland, 1980. Bulletin board and book display ideas are developed around monthly and other themes.

Goldstein, Ruth M., and Zornow, Edith. *Movies for Kids: A Guide for Parents and Teachers on the Entertainment Film for Children,* rev. ed. New York: Ungar, 1980. Recommends 430 films suitable for children.

Hearne, Betsy, and Kaye, Marilyn, eds. *Celebrating Children's Books: Essays on Children's Literature in Honor of Zena Sutherland.* New York: Lothrop, Lee & Shepard, 1981. Text contains twenty-three essays.

Hicks, Warren B. *Managing the Building-Level School Library Media Program: School Library Media Program; School Media Centers; Focus on Trends and Issues, No. 7.* Chicago: American Library Assoc., 1981. Discusses trends and the management system in the media center.

Jacobs, Joseph, comp. *English Fairy Tales: Being the Two Collections, English Fairy Tales and More English Fairy Tales.* Lawrence, Mass.: Chatto, Bodley Head & Jonathan Cape, 1980. Versions of Jacobs's tales published in the 1890s.

Jenkins, Peggy Davison. *The Magic of Puppetry: A Guide for Those Working with Young Children.* Englewood Cliffs, N.J.: Prentice–Hall, 1980. Illustrations and text present the instructions for making more than forty puppets.

Jenkinson, Edward B. *Censors in the Classroom: The Mind Benders.* Carbondale, Ill.: Southern Illinois University Press, 1980. Reviews censorship cases and discusses factors contributing to censorship.

Kellman, Amy. *Guide to Children's Libraries Outside the United States.* Chicago: American Library Assoc., 1982. A helpful location reference for libraries.

Knox, Rawle, ed. *The Work of E. H. Shepard.* New York: Schocken, 1980. Samples of Shepard's work and an outline of his life are published to celebrate the hundredth anniversary of his birth.

Kohn, Rita T., and Tepper, Krysta A. *Have You Got What They Want? Public Relations Strategies for the School Librarian—Media Specialist: A Workbook.* Metuchen, N.J.: Scarecrow Press, 1982. Discusses various public relations strategies that may be useful to the librarian.

Lamme, Linda Leonard, ed. *Learning to Love Literature: Preschool through Grade 3.* Urbana, Ill.: National Council of Teachers of English, 1981. Guidelines for developing a literature-based curriculum.

Lanes, Selma G. *The Art of Maurice Sendak.* New York: Harry N. Abrams, 1980. In an illustrated text, the author discusses Sendak's books, recurring themes, and early influences on his work.

Leonard, Charlotte. *Tied Together: Topics and Thoughts for Introducing Children's Books.* Metuchen, N.J.: Scarecrow Press, 1980. Presents ideas for book discussions, displays, and program planning.

Lystad, Mary. *From Dr. Mather to Dr. Seuss: 200 Years of American Books for Children.* Cambridge, Mass.: Schenkman, 1980. The author examines the changing values expressed in children's literature.

Meggendorfer, Lothar. *The City Park: A Reproduction of an Antique Stand-Up Book.* New York: Viking, 1981. A reproduction of an 1887 mechanical picture book.

Moore, Vardine. *The Pleasure of Poetry with and by Children: A Handbook.* Metuchen, N.J.: Scarecrow Press, 1981. Includes poems and suggestions for sharing them with children.

Opie, Iona Archibald, and Opie, Peter. *A Nursery Companion.* New York: Oxford University Press, 1980. A reproduction of a collection of nineteenth century alphabets, verses, and grammars.

Paterson, Katherine. *Gates of Excellence: On Reading and Writing Books for Children.* New York: Elsevier/Nelson, 1981. Includes speeches and book reviews by the Newbery author.

Peterson, Carolyn Sue, and Hall, Brenny. *Story Programs: A Source Book of Materials.* Metuchen, N.J.: Scarecrow Press, 1980. Develops suggestions for library programs for preschool and primary children.

Philip, Neil. *A Fine Anger: A Critical Introduction to the Work of Alan Garner.* New York: Putnam/Philomel, 1981. The author traces the development of Garner's work.

Polette, Nancy, and Hamlin, Marjorie. *Exploring Books with Gifted Children.* Littleton, Colo.: Libraries Unlimited, 1980. Units are developed around style, theme, character, and setting in books by L'Engle, Konigsburg, Paterson, Alexander, Lenski, and the Cleavers.

Potter, Beatrix. *Beatrix Potter's Americans: Selected Letters.* Edited by Jane Crowell Morse. Boston: Horn Book, 1982.

Preiss, Byron, ed. *The Art of Leo & Diane Dillon.* New York: Ballantine Books, 1981. Text and illustrations provide a review of the Dillons' works from the 1950s to the present.

Prostano, Emanuel T., and Prostano, Joyce S. *The School Library Media Center,* 3rd ed. Littleton, Colo.: Libraries Unlimited, 1982.

Rees, David. *The Marble in the Water: Essays on Contemporary Writers of Fiction for Children and Young Adults.* Boston: Horn Book, 1980. Explores similarities and differences in British and American children's literature and includes essays by well-known authors.

Schwarcz, Joseph H. *Ways of the Illustrator: Visual Communication in Children's Literature.* Chicago: American Library Assoc., 1982. Discusses illustrations in children's books.

Scott, Dorothea Hayward. *Chinese Popular Literature and the Child.* Chicago: American Library Assoc., 1980. Author discusses oral and literary heritage of the Chinese people.

Shannon, George W. B. *Humpty Dumpty: A Pictorial History.* La Jolla, Calif.: Green Tiger Press, 1981. Text develops the history of Humpty Dumpty.

Silverman, Eleanor. *101 Media Center Ideas.* Metuchen, N.J.: Scarecrow Press, 1980. The ideas in the text are from the Demonstration Media Center for New Jersey.

———. *Trash into Treasure: Recycling Ideas for Library Media Centers.* Metuchen, N.J.: Scarecrow Press, 1982. Inexpensive ideas for the library.

Spiegel, Dixie Lee. *Reading for Pleasure: Guidelines.* Newark, Del.: International Reading Assoc., 1981. Discusses the development of a recreational reading program.

Taylor, Mary M., ed. *School Library and Media Center Acquisitions Policies and Procedures.* Phoenix, Ariz.: Oryx Press, 1981. Examines the selection process in media centers and presents the rationale for comprehensive selection policies.

Thomason, Nevada Wallis, ed. *The Library Media Specialist in Curriculum Development.* Metuchen, N.J.: Scarecrow Press, 1981. A collection of articles about the role of the media specialist.

Trelease, James. *The Read-Aloud Handbook.* New York: Penguin, 1982. Presents practical suggestions for sharing books orally with children.

Vandergrift, Kay E. *Child and Story: The Literary Connection.* Edited by Jane Anne Hannigan. New York: Neal-Schuman, 1981. Explores literary form, elements of the story, and practical suggestions for using literature.

Van Orden, Phyllis. *The Collection Program in Elementary and Middle Schools: Concepts, Practices, and Information Sources.* Illustrated by William R. Harper. Littleton, Colo.: Libraries Unlimited, 1982. A guide for elementary and middle school libraries.

White, Gabriel. *Edward Ardizzone: Artist and Illustrator.* New York: Schocken, 1980. Text includes samples of Ardizzone's work, discussion of his style, and information about his personal life.

Yolen, Jane. *Touch Magic: Fantasy, Faerie and Folklore in the Literature of Childhood.* New York: Putnam/Philomel, 1981. Yolen stresses the importance of folklore in stimulating children's emotional and intellectual growth.

APPENDIX C
Notable Children's Films

The Film Evaluation Committee of the Association for Library Service to Children, the American Library Association, identifies films that demonstrate an especially commendable quality, reflect respect for children's intelligence and imagination, and encourage children's interests. Lists of notable films (NF) are published in *The Booklist* (Chicago: American Library Association). Dates indicate the year in which they were identified as notable.

The Amazing Cosmic Awareness of Duffy Moon. Time-Life Multimedia, New York NF 1978 (ages 8–12). A humorous and suspenseful film based on Jean Robinson's *The Strange But Wonderful Cosmic Awareness of Duffy Moon.*

Angel and Big Joe. Bert Salzman. Learning Corporation of America, New York, NF 1977 (ages 8–12). A telephone lineman and a Chicano migrant worker develop a warm friendship.

Aquarium. Bob Gronowski, Bill Walker, and Mel Waskin. Perspective Films, Chicago, NF 1980 (ages 6–12). Sea creatures are filmed in color photography.

Boy and a Boa. Renato Stola. Phoenix Films, New York, NF 1977 (ages 6–12). A boy's pet boa constrictor causes problems when it escapes in a library.

The Bridge of Adam Rush. Daniel Wilson. Time-Life Multimedia, New York, NF 1977 (ages 8–12). A twelve-year-old boy in colonial Pennsylvania learns to cooperate with his stepfather.

Butterfly. Nico Crama. Carousel Films, Los Angeles, NF 1977 (ages 8–12). The last butterfly on earth fights problems of pollution.

Charlie Needs a Cloak. Gene Deitch. Weston Woods Studios, Weston Woods, Conn., NF 1979 (ages 5–10). The film is adapted from the book by Tomie de Paola.

Chick Chick Chick. Robert and Michael Brown. Churchill Films, New York, NF 1977 (ages 4–10). A hatching egg, chicks, and barnyard life are accompanied by bluegrass music.

Christmas Lace. George Mendeluk and Linda Sorenson. Encyclopaedia Britannica Educational Corp., Chicago, NF 1980 (ages 9–12). Nineteenth century Quebec is the setting for a story about a thief and a lace maker.

Claymation. Will Vinton. Pyramid Films, Santa Monica, Calif., NF 1980 (ages 9–14). Techniques of clay animation are presented.

The Concert. Claude and Julian Chagrin. Pyramid Films, Santa Monica, Calif., NF 1977 (ages 6–12). A fantasy turns a crosswalk into a piano keyboard.

Fire! Witold Giersz. Encyclopaedia Britannica Educational Corp., Chicago, NF 1979 (ages 6–12). Traces life in a forest before, during, and after a fire.

The Flashettes. Bonnie Friedman and Emily Parker Leon. New Day Films, Franklin Lakes, N.J., NF 1979 (ages 9–14). An inner-city documentary about a girls' track team.

Floating Free. Jerry Butts. Pyramid Films, Santa Monica, Calif., NF 1980 (ages 6–12). A film of the 1977 World Frisbee Championship.

Hardware Wars. Ernie Fosselius and Michael Wiese. Pyramid Films, Santa Monica, Calif., NF 1980 (ages 6–12). A satire of *Star Wars* in which the hero and heroine battle a giant waffle iron and a toaster.

I'll Find a Way. Beverly Shaffer. National Film Board of Canada, The Media Guild, Solana Beach, Calif., NF 1979 (ages 8–14). The conduct of a physically handicapped girl persuades others that she is an ordinary child.

Kuumba: Simon's New Sound. Carol Munday Lawrence. Beacon Films, Norwood, Mass., NF 1980 (ages 4–10). A boy invents a steel drum during a carnival in Trinidad.

Little Tim and the Brave Sea Captain. Weston Woods Studios, Weston, Conn., NF 1978 (ages 4–8). A boy and a sea captain experience a storm in Edward Ardizzone's story.

Luke Was There. Learning Corporation of America, New York, NF 1978 (ages 9–14). The film is based on Eleanor Clymer's story about an unhappy boy who discovers that some adults care.

Lullaby. Cyörgy Csonka. International Film Bureau, Chicago, NF 1979 (ages 3–8). A lullaby sung in Hungarian provides a musical background for a dreamlike setting.

Me and Dad's New Wife. Time-Life Multimedia, New York, NF 1978 (ages 9–14). Based on Stella Pevsner's *A Smart Kid Like You.*

Mr. Frog Went A-Courting. Evelyn Lambart. National Film Board of Canada, Films Incorporated, Wilmette, Ill., NF 1977 (ages 3–6). The folk song is illustrated with animated cutouts.

Metamorphosis. Catherine Mercier and Timothy Wallace. Texture Films, New York, NF 1979 (ages 6–12). A young girl marvels at the metamorphosis of a butterfly.

Mighty Mouse and the Quarterback Kid. Harry Bernsen and Alex Karras. Time-Life Multimedia, New York, NF 1979 (ages 9–14). A twelve-year-old boy wants to be a photographer, but his father wants him to play football.

The Morning Spider. Julian and Claude Chagrin. Pyramid Films, Santa Monica, Calif., NF 1977 (ages 6–12). Julian Chagrin and troupe mime insect life.

Nature Adventure. Dan Gibson. Universal Education and Visual Arts, University City, Calif., NF 1977 (ages 8–14). Animals and birds are photographed in their wilderness setting.

Nikkolina. Glen Salzman and Rebecca Yates. Learning Corporation of America, New York, NF 1980 (ages 8–14). A girl makes a difficult decision when family loyalty conflicts with her desire to enter a skating competition.

Nicky: One of My Best Friends. McGraw-Hill Films, New York, NF 1978 (ages 9–14). A documentary that shows how a blind and partially paralyzed boy is similar to other children.

Rag Tag Champs. Robert Chenault. ABC Wide World of Learning, New York, NF 1980 (ages 8–14). The story of a boy and a baseball team based on Alfred Slote's *Jake.*

Really Rosie. Weston Woods Studios, Weston, Conn., NF 1978 (ages 5–9). The story is based on Maurice Sendak's character.

Red Ball Express. Steve Segal. Perspective Films, Chicago, NF 1977 (ages 6–12). Images of wheels, tracks, and trains are drawn on film.

Rookie of the Year. Larry Elikann. Time-Life Multimedia, New York, NF 1977 (ages 8–14). A girl faces problems when she becomes a substitute player during the Little League Championships.

The Sand Castle. Co Hoedeman. National Film Board of Canada, New York, NF 1979 (ages 5–12). Sand creatures build a castle and play upon it.

The Shopping Bag Lady. Bett Salzman. Learning Corporation of America, New York, NF 1977 (ages 9–14). A teenage girl becomes sensitive to the needs of a homeless older woman.

Snow Monkeys of Japan. John LePointe. ACI Media, New York, NF 1977 (ages 9–14). Snow monkeys in Tokyo are shown as they care for themselves. The film stresses the dangers of extinction.

Spaceborne. Philip Dauber and Tom Valens. Pyramid Films, Santa Monica, Calif., NF 1979 (ages 6–12). Presents footage from a space mission.

Taleb and His Lamb. Amiram Amitai. Barr Films, Pasadena, Calif., NF 1977 (ages 9–14). A Bedouin boy runs away rather than sell his lamb.

Tangram. Alan Slater. Pyramid Films, Santa Monica, Calif., NF 1977 (ages 6–12). A ballet is performed by the pieces of a Chinese puzzle.

Tap Dance Kid. Evelyn Barron. Learning Corporation of America, New York, NF 1980 (ages 8–14). An eight-year-old boy challenges his parents' wishes when he wants to be a tap dancer. Based on Louise Fitzhugh's *Nobody's Family is Going to Change.*

Veronica. Beverly Schaffer. National Film Board of Canada, Media Guild, Solana Beach, Calif., NF 1980 (ages 6–10). A documentary about a Polish-Canadian child who lives above her parents' bakery.

APPENDIX D
Book Awards

A wards for outstanding children's books are presented yearly by organizations, publishers, and other interested groups. These awards have multiplied since the instigation of the Newbery Award in 1922. The following lists include the books, authors, and illustrators who have received the Caldecott Medal and honor awards, the Newbery Medal and honor awards, the Children's Book Award, the Hans Christian Andersen International Medal, or the Laura Ingalls Wilder Medal. Following this list are examples of additional awards presented in the United States, Canada, and the United Kingdom. Complete lists of book award winners, including United States, British Commonwealth, and international awards, are found in *Children's Books: Awards and Prizes,* compiled and edited by the Children's Book Council. An annotated bibliography of Newbery and Caldecott books is available in *Newbery and Caldecott Medal and Honor Books,* compiled by Linda Kauffman Peterson and Marilyn Leathers Solt, 1982.

Caldecott Medal and Honor Awards

The Caldecott awards, named after a British illustrator of children's books, Randolph Caldecott, are granted by the Children's Services Division of the American Library Association. The medal and honor awards are presented annually to the illustrators of the most distinguished picture books published in the United States. The first Caldecott Medal and honor awards were presented in 1938.

1938 *Animals of the Bible* by Helen Dean Fish, ill. by Dorothy P. Lathrop, Stokes
Honor Books: *Seven Simeon: A Russian Tale* by Boris Artzybasheff, Viking; *Four and Twenty Blackbirds: Nursery Rhymes of Yesterday Recalled for Children of To-Day* by Helen Dean Fish, ill. by Robert Lawson, Stokes

1939 *Mei Li* by Thomas Handforth, Doubleday
Honor Books: *The Forest Pool* by Laura Adams Armer, Longmans; *Wee Gillis* by Munro Leaf, ill. by Robert Lawson, Viking; *Snow White and the Seven Dwarfs* by Wanda Gág, Coward; *Barkis* by Clare Newberry, Harper; *Andy and the Lion: A Tale of Kindness Remembered or the Power of Gratitude* by James Daugherty, Viking

1940 *Abraham Lincoln* by Ingri and Edgar Parin d'Aulaire, Doubleday
Honor Books: *Cock-a-Doodle Doo: The Story of a Little Red Rooster* by Berta and Elmer Hader, Macmillan; *Madeline* by Ludwig Bemelmans, Simon & Schuster; *The Ageless Story,* by Lauren Ford, Dodd

1941 *They Were Strong and Good* by Robert Lawson, Viking

Honor Book: *April's Kittens* by Clare Newberry, Harper

1942 *Make Way for Ducklings* by Robert McCloskey, Viking
Honor Books: *An American ABC* by Maud and Miska Petersham, Macmillan; *In My Mother's House* by Ann Nolan Clark, ill. by Velino Herrera, Viking; *Paddle-to-the-Sea* by Holling C. Holling, Houghton; *Nothing at All* by Wanda Gág, Coward

1943 *The Little House* by Virginia Lee Burton, Houghton
Honor Books: *Dash and Dart* by Mary and Conrad Buff, Viking; *Marshmallow* by Clare Newberry, Harper

1944 *Many Moons* by James Thurber, ill. by Louis Slobodkin, Harcourt Brace Jovanovich
Honor Books: *Small Rain: Verses from the Bible* selected by Jessie Orton Jones, ill. by Elizabeth Orton Jones, Viking; *Pierre Pigeon* by Lee Kingman, ill. by Arnold E. Bare, Houghton; *The Mighty Hunter* by Berta and Elmer Hader, Macmillan; *A Child's Good Night Book* by Margaret Wise Brown, ill. by Jean Charlot, W. R. Scott; *Good Luck Horse* by Chih-Yi Chan, ill. by Plato Chan, Whittlesey

1945 *Prayer for a Child* by Rachel Field, ill. by Elizabeth Orton Jones, Macmillan
Honor Books: *Mother Goose: Seventy-Seven Verses with Pictures* ill. by Tasha Tudor, Walck; *In the Forest* by Marie Hall Ets, Viking; *Yonie Wondernose* by Marguerite de Angeli, Doubleday; *The Christmas Anna Angel* by Ruth Sawyer, ill. by Kate Seredy, Viking

1946 *The Rooster Crows . . .* ill. by Maud and Miska Petersham, Macmillan

Honor Books: *Little Lost Lamb* by Golden MacDonald, ill. by Leonard Weisgard, Doubleday; *Sing Mother Goose* by Opal Wheeler, ill. by Marjorie Torrey, Dutton; *My Mother Is the Most Beautiful Woman in the World* by Becky Reyher, ill. by Ruth Gannett, Lothrop; *You Can Write Chinese* by Kurt Wiese, Viking

1947 *The Little Island* by Golden MacDonald, ill. by Leonard Weisgard, Doubleday

Honor Books: *Rain Drop Splash* by Alvin Tresselt, ill. by Leonard Weisgard, Lothrop; *Boats on the River* by Marjorie Flack, ill. by Jay Hyde Barnum, Viking; *Timothy Turtle* by Al Graham, ill. by Tony Palazzo, Viking; *Pedro, the Angel of Olvera Street* by Leo Politi, Scribner's; *Sing in Praise: A Collection of the Best Loved Hymns* by Opal Wheeler, ill. by Marjorie Torrey, Dutton

1948 *White Snow, Bright Snow* by Alvin Tresselt, ill. by Roger Duvoisin, Lothrop

Honor Books: *Stone Soup: An Old Tale* by Marcia Brown, Scribner's; *McElligot's Pool* by Dr. Seuss, Random; *Bambino the Clown* by George Schreiber, Viking; *Roger and the Fox* by Lavinia Davis, ill. by Hildegard Woodward, Doubleday; *Song of Robin Hood* ed. by Anne Malcolmson, ill. by Virginia Lee Burton, Houghton

1949 *The Big Snow* by Berta and Elmer Hader, Macmillan

Honor Books: *Blueberries for Sal* by Robert McCloskey, Viking; *All Around the Town* by Phyllis McGinley, ill. by Helen Stone, Lippincott; *Juanita* by Leo Politi, Scribner's; *Fish in the Air* by Kurt Wiese, Viking

1950 *Song of the Swallows* by Leo Politi, Scribner's

Honor Books: *America's Ethan Allen* by Stewart Holbrook, ill. by Lynd Ward, Houghton; *The Wild Birthday Cake* by Lavinia Davis, ill. by Hildegard Woodward, Doubleday; *The Happy Day* by Ruth Krauss, ill. by Marc Simont, Harper; *Bartholomew and the Oobleck* by Dr. Seuss, Random; *Henry Fisherman* by Marcia Brown, Scribner's

1951 *The Egg Tree* by Katherine Milhous, Scribner's

Honor Books: *Dick Whittington and His Cat* by Marcia Brown, Scribner's; *The Two Reds* by William Lipkind, ill. by Nicholas Mordvinoff, Harcourt Brace Jovanovich; *If I Ran the Zoo* by Dr. Seuss, Random; *The Most Wonderful Doll in the World* by Phyllis McGinley, ill. by Helen Stone, Lippincott; *T-Bone, the Baby Sitter* by Clare Newberry, Harper

1952 *Finders Keepers* by William Lipkind, ill. by Nicholas Mordvinoff, Harcourt Brace Jovanovich

Honor Books: *Mr. T. W. Anthony Woo: The Story of a Cat and a Dog and a Mouse* by Marie Hall Ets, Viking; *Skipper John's Cook* by Marcia Brown, Scribner's; *All Falling Down* by Gene Zion, ill. by Margaret Bloy Graham, Harper; *Bear Party* by William Pène du Bois, Viking; *Feather Mountain* by Elizabeth Olds, Houghton

1953 *The Biggest Bear* by Lynd Ward, Houghton

Honor Books: *Puss in Boots* by Charles Perrault, ill. and tr. by Marcia Brown, Scribner's; *One Morning in Maine* by Robert McCloskey, Viking; *Ape in a Cape: An Alphabet of Odd Animals* by Fritz Eichenberg, Harcourt Brace Jovanovich; *The Storm Book* by Charlotte Zolotow, ill. by Margaret Bloy Graham, Harper; *Five Little Monkeys* by Juliet Kepes, Houghton

1954 *Madeline's Rescue* by Ludwig Bemelmans, Viking

Honor Books: *Journey Cake, Ho!* by Ruth Sawyer, ill. by Robert McCloskey, Viking; *When Will the World Be Mine?* by Miriam Schlein, ill. by Jean Charlot, W. R. Scott; *The Steadfast Tin Soldier* by Hans Christian Andersen, ill. by Marcia Brown, Scribner's; *A Very Special House* by Ruth Krauss, ill. by Maurice Sendak, Harper; *Green Eyes* by A. Birnbaum, Capitol

1955 *Cinderella, or the Little Glass Slipper* by Charles Perrault, tr. and ill. by Marcia Brown, Scribner's

Honor Books: *Book of Nursery and Mother Goose Rhymes,* ill. by Marguerite de Angeli, Doubleday; *Wheel on the Chimney* by Margaret Wise Brown, ill. by Tibor Gergely, Lippincott; *The Thanksgiving Story* by Alice Dalgliesh, ill. by Helen Sewell, Scribner's

1956 *Frog Went A-Courtin'* ed. by John Langstaff, ill. by Feodor Rojankovsky, Harcourt Brace Jovanovich

Honor Books: *Play with Me* by Marie Hall Ets, Viking; *Crow Boy* by Taro Yashima, Viking

1957 *A Tree Is Nice* by Janice May Udry, ill. by Marc Simont, Harper

Honor Books: *Mr. Penny's Race Horse* by Marie Hall Ets, Viking; *1 Is One* by Tasha Tudor, Walck; *Anatole* by Eve Titus, ill. by Paul Galdone, McGraw; *Gillespie and the Guards* by Benjamin Elkin, ill. by James Daugherty, Viking; *Lion* by William Pène du Bois, Viking

1958 *Time of Wonder* by Robert McCloskey, Viking

Honor Books: *Fly High, Fly Low* by Don Freeman, Viking; *Anatole and the Cat* by Eve Titus, ill. by Paul Galdone, McGraw

1959 *Chanticleer and the Fox* adapted from Chaucer and ill. by Barbara Cooney, Crowell

Honor Books: *The House That Jack Built: A Picture Book in Two Languages* by Antonio Frasconi, Harcourt Brace Jovanovich; *What Do You Say, Dear?* by Sesyle Joslin, ill. by Maurice Sendak, W. R. Scott; *Umbrella* by Taro Yashima, Viking

1960 *Nine Days to Christmas* by Marie Hall Ets and Aurora Labastida, ill. by Marie Hall Ets, Viking

Honor Books: *Houses from the Sea* by Alice E. Goudey, ill. by Adrienne Adams, Scribner's; *The Moon Jumpers* by Janice May Udry, ill. by Maurice Sendak, Harper

1961 *Baboushka and the Three Kings* by Ruth Robbins, ill. by Nicolas Sidjakov, Parnassus

Honor Book: *Inch by Inch* by Leo Lionni, Obolensky

1962 *Once a Mouse. . .* by Marcia Brown, Scribner's

Honor Books: *The Fox Went Out on a Chilly Night: An Old Song* by Peter Spier, Doubleday; *Little Bear's Visit* by Else Holmelund Minarik, ill. by Maurice Sendak, Harper; *The Day We Saw the Sun Come Up* by Alice E. Goudey, ill. by Adrienne Adams, Scribner's

1963 *The Snowy Day* by Ezra Jack Keats, Viking

Honor Books: *The Sun Is a Golden Earring* by Natalia M. Belting, ill. by Bernarda Bryson, Holt; *Mr. Rabbit and the Lovely Present* by Charlotte Zolotow, ill. by Maurice Sendak, Harper

1964 *Where the Wild Things Are* by Maurice Sendak, Harper

Honor Books: *Swimmy* by Leo Lionni, Pantheon; *All in the Morning Early* by Sorche Nic Leodhas, ill. by Evaline Ness, Holt; *Mother Goose and Nursery Rhymes* ill. by Philip Reed, Atheneum

1965 *May I Bring a Friend?* by Beatrice Schenk de Regniers, ill. by Beni Montresor, Atheneum

Honor Books: *Rain Makes Applesauce* by Julian Scheer, ill. by Marvin Bileck, Holiday; *The Wave* by Margaret Hodges, ill. by Blair Lent, Houghton; *A Pocketful of Cricket* by Rebecca Caudill, ill. by Evaline Ness, Holt

1966 *Always Room for One More* by Sorche Nic Leodhas, ill. by Nonny Hogrogian, Holt

Honor Books: *Hide and Seek Fog* by Alvin Tresselt, ill. by Roger Duvoisin, Lothrop; *Just Me* by Marie Hall Ets, Viking; *Tom Tit Tot* by Evaline Ness, Scribner's

1967 *Sam, Bangs & Moonshine* by Evaline Ness, Holt

Honor Book: *One Wide River to Cross* by Barbara Emberley, ill. by Ed Emberley, Prentice

1968 *Drummer Hoff* by Barbara Emberley, ill. by Ed Emberley, Prentice

Honor Books: *Frederick* by Leo Lionni, Pantheon; *Seashore Story* by Taro Yashima, Viking; *The Emperor and the Kite* by Jane Yolen, ill. by Ed Young, World

1969 *The Fool of the World and the Flying Ship* by Arthur Ransome, ill. by Uri Shulevitz, Farrar

Honor Book: *Why the Sun and the Moon Live in the Sky: An African Folktale* by Elphinstone Dayrell, ill. by Blair Lent, Houghton

1970 *Sylvester and the Magic Pebble* by William Steig, Windmill

Honor Books: *Goggles!* by Ezra Jack Keats, Macmillan; *Alexander and the Wind-Up Mouse* by Leo Lionni, Pantheon; *Pop Corn and Ma Goodness* by Edna Mitchell Preston, ill. by Robert Andrew Parker, Viking; *Thy Friend, Obadiah* by Brinton Tur-

kle, Viking; *The Judge: An Untrue Tale* by Harve Zemach, ill. by Margot Zemach, Farrar

1971 *A Story—A Story: An African Tale* by Gail E. Haley, Atheneum

Honor Books: *The Angry Moon* by William Sleator, ill. by Blair Lent, Atlantic-Little; *Frog and Toad Are Friends* by Arnold Lobel, Harper; *In the Night Kitchen* by Maurice Sendak, Harper

1972 *One Fine Day* by Nonny Hogrogian, Macmillan

Honor Books: *If All the Seas Were One Sea* by Janina Domanska, Macmillan; *Moja Means One: Swahili Counting Book* by Muriel Feelings, ill. by Tom Feelings, Dial; *Hildilid's Night* by Cheli Duran Ryan, ill. by Arnold Lobel, Macmillan

1973 *The Funny Little Woman* retold by Arlene Mosel, ill. by Blair Lent, Dutton

Honor Books: *Anansi the Spider: A Tale from the Ashanti* adapted and ill. by Gerald McDermott, Holt; *Hosie's Alphabet* by Hosea Tobias and Lisa Baskin, ill. by Leonard Baskin, Viking; *Snow White and the Seven Dwarfs* translated by Randall Jarrell, ill. by Nancy Ekholm Burkert, Farrar; *When Clay Sings* by Byrd Baylor, ill. by Tom Bahti, Scribner's

1974 *Duffy and the Devil* by Harve Zemach, ill. by Margot Zemach, Farrar

Honor Books: *Three Jovial Huntsmen* by Susan Jeffers, Bradbury; *Cathedral: The Story of Its Construction* by David Macaulay, Houghton

1975 *Arrow to the Sun* adapted and ill. by Gerald McDermott, Viking

Honor Book: *Jambo Means Hello: A Swahili Alphabet Book* by Muriel Feelings, ill. by Tom Feelings, Dial

1976 *Why Mosquitoes Buzz in People's Ears* retold by Verna Aardema, ill. by Leo and Diane Dillon, Dial

Honor Books: *The Desert Is Theirs* by Byrd Baylor, ill. by Peter Parnall, Scribner's; *Strega Nona* retold and ill. by Tomie de Paola, Prentice

1977 *Ashanti to Zulu: African Traditions* by Margaret Musgrove, ill. by Leo and Diane Dillon, Dial

Honor Books: *The Amazing Bone* by William Steig, Farrar; *The Contest* retold and ill. by Nony Hogrogrian, Greenwillow; *Fish for

Supper* by M. B. Goffstein, Dial; *The Golem: A Jewish Legend* by Beverly Brodsky McDermott, Lippincott; *Hawk, I'm Your Brother* by Byrd Baylor, ill. by Peter Parnall, Scribner's

1978 *Noah's Ark* by Peter Spier, Doubleday

Honor Books: *Castle* by David Macaulay, Houghton; *It Could Always Be Worse* retold and ill. by Margot Zemach, Farrar

1979 *The Girl Who Loved Wild Horses* by Paul Goble, Bradbury

Honor Books: *Freight Train* by Donald Crews, Greenwillow; *The Way to Start a Day* by Byrd Baylor, ill. by Peter Parnall, Scribner's

1980 *Ox-Cart Man* by Donald Hall, ill. by Barbara Cooney, Viking

Honor Books: *Ben's Trumpet* by Rachel Isadora, Greenwillow; *The Treasure* by Uri Shulevitz, Farrar; *The Garden of Abdul Gasazi* by Chris Van Allsburg, Houghton

1981 *Fables* by Arnold Lobel, Harper

Honor Books: *The Bremen-Town Musicians* by Ilse Plume, Doubleday; *The Grey Lady and the Strawberry Snatcher* by Molly Bang, Four Winds; *Mice Twice* by Joseph Low, Atheneum; *Truck* by Donald Crews, Greenwillow

1982 *Jumanji* by Chris Van Allsburg, Houghton

Honor Books: *A Visit to William Blake's Inn: Poems for Innocent and Experienced Travelers* by Nancy Willard, ill. by Alice and Martin Provensen, Harcourt Brace Jovanovich; *Where the Buffaloes Begin* by Olaf Baker. ill. by Stephen Gammell, Warne; *On Market Street* by Arnold Lobel, ill. by Anita Lobel, Greenwillow; *Outside Over There* by Maurice Sendak, Harper

1983 *Shadow* by Blaise Cendrars, ill. by Marcia Brown, Scribner's

Honor Books: *When I Was Young in the Mountains* by Cynthia Rylant, ill. by Diane Goode, Dutton; *Chair for My Mother* by Vera B. Williams, Morrow

The Newbery Medal and Honor Awards

The Newbery award, named after the first English publisher of books for children, John Newbery, is granted by the Children's Services Division of the American Library Association. The medal and honor awards are presented annually for the most distinguished contributions to children's literature published in the United States. The first Newbery Medal and honor awards were presented in 1922.

1922 *The Story of Mankind* by Hendrik Willem van Loon, Liveright

Honor Books: *The Great Quest* by Charles Hawes, Little; *Cedric the Forester* by Bernard Marshall, Appleton; *The Old Tobacco Shop: A True Account of What Befell a Little Boy in Search of Adventure* by William Bowen, Macmillan; *The Golden Fleece and the Heroes Who Lived before Achilles* by Padriac Colum, Macmillan; *Windy Hill* by Cornelia Meigs, Macmillan

1923 *The Voyages of Doctor Dolittle* by Hugh Lofting, Lippincott

Honor Books: No record

1924 *The Dark Frigate* by Charles Hawes, Atlantic/Little

Honor Books: No record

1925 *Tales from Silver Lands* by Charles Finger, Doubleday

Honor Books: *Nicholas: A Manhattan Christmas Story* by Anne Carroll Moore, Putnam; *Dream Coach* by Anne Parrish, Macmillan

1926 *Shen of the Sea* by Arthur Bowie Chrisman, Dutton

Honor Book: *Voyagers: Being Legends and Romances of Atlantic Discovery* by Padraic Colum, Macmillan

1927 *Smoky, the Cowhorse* by Will James, Scribner's

Honor Books: No record

1928 *Gayneck, The Story of a Pigeon* by Dhan Gopal Mukerji, Dutton

Honor Books: *The Wonder Smith and His Son: A Tale from the Golden Childhood of the World* by Ella Young, Longmans; *Downright Dencey* by Caroline Snedeker, Doubleday

1929 *The Trumpeter of Krakow* by Eric P. Kelly, Macmillan

Honor Books: *Pigtail of Ah Lee Ben Loo* by John Bennett, Longmans; *Millions of Cats* by Wanda Gág, Coward; *The Boy Who Was* by Grace Hallock, Dutton; *Clearing Weather* by Cornelia Meigs, Little; *Runaway Papoose* by Grace Moon, Doubleday; *Tod of the Fens* by Elinor Whitney, Macmillan

1930 *Hitty, Her First Hundred Years* by Rachel Field, Macmillan

Honor Books: *Daughter of the Seine: The Life of Madame Roland* by Jeanette Eaton, Harper; *Pran of Albania* by Elizabeth Miller, Doubleday; *Jumping-off Place* by Marian Hurd McNeely, Longmans; *Tangle-coated Horse and Other Tales: Episodes from the Fionn Saga* by Ella Young, Longmans; *Vaino: A Boy of New England* by Julia Davis Adams, Dutton; *Little Blacknose* by Hildegarde Swift, Harcourt Brace Jovanovich

1931 *The Cat Who Went to Heaven* by Elizabeth Coatsworth, Macmillan

Honor Books: *Floating Island* by Anne Parrish, Harper; *The Dark Star of Itza: The Story of a Pagan Princess* by Alida Malkus, Harcourt Brace Jovanovich; *Queer Person* by Ralph Hubbard, Doubleday; *Mountains Are Free* by Julia Davis Adams, Dutton; *Spice and the Devil's Cave* by Agnes Hewes, Knopf; *Meggy Macintosh* by Elizabeth Janet Gray, Doubleday; *Garram the Hunter: A Boy of the Hill Tribes* by Herbert Best, Doubleday; *Ood-Le-Uk the Wanderer* by Alice Lide and Margaret Johansen, Little

1932 *Waterless Mountain* by Laura Adams Armer, Longmans

Honor Books: *The Fairy Circus* by Dorothy P. Lathrop, Macmillan; *Calico Bush* by Rachel Field, Macmillan; *Boy of the South Seas* by Eunice Tietjens, Coward; *Out of the Flame* by Eloise Lownsbery, Longmans; *Jane's Island* by Marjorie Allee, Houghton; *Truce of the Wolf and Other Tales of Old Italy* by Mary Gould Davis, Harcourt Brace Jovanovich

1933 *Young Fu of the Upper Yangtze* by Elizabeth Foreman Lewis, Winston

Honor Books: *Swift Rivers* by Cornelia Meigs, Little; *The Railroad to Freedom: A Story of the Civil War* by Hildegarde Swift, Harcourt Brace Jovanovich; *Children of the Soil: A Story of Scandinavia* by Nora Burglon, Doubleday

1934 *Invincible Louisa: The Story of the Author of 'Little Women'* by Cornelia Meigs, Little

Honor Books: *The Forgotten Daughter* by Caroline Snedeker, Doubleday; *Swords of Steel* by Elsie Singmaster, Houghton;

ABC Bunny by Wanda Gág, Coward; *Winged Girl of Knossos* by Erik Berry, Appleton; *New Land* by Sarah Schmidt, McBride; *Big Tree of Bunlahy: Stories of My Own Countryside* by Padraic Colum, Macmillan; *Glory of the Seas* by Agnes Hewes, Knopf; *Apprentice of Florence* by Ann Kyle, Houghton

1935 *Dobry* by Monica Shannon, Viking

Honor Books: *Pageant of Chinese History* by Elizabeth Seeger, Longmans; *Davy Crockett* by Constance Rourke, Harcourt Brace Jovanovich; *Day on Skates: The Story of a Dutch Picnic* by Hilda Van Stockum, Harper

1936 *Caddie Woodlawn* by Carol Ryrie Brink, Macmillan

Honor Books: *Honk, the Moose* by Phil Stong, Dodd; *The Good Master* by Kate Seredy, Viking; *Young Walter Scott* by Elizabeth Janet Gray, Viking; *All Sail Set: A Romance of the Flying Cloud* by Armstrong Sperry, Winston

1937 *Roller Skates* by Ruth Sawyer, Viking

Honor Books: *Phoebe Fairchild: Her Book* by Lois Lenski, Stokes; *Whistler's Van* by Idwal Jones, Viking; *Golden Basket* by Ludwig Bemelmans, Viking; *Winterbound* by Margery Bianco, Viking; *Audubon* by Constance Rourke, Harcourt Brace Jovanovich; *The Codfish Musket* by Agnes Hewes, Doubleday

1938 *The White Stag* by Kate Seredy, Viking

Honor Books: *Pecos Bill* by James Cloyd Bowman, Little; *Bright Island* by Mabel Robinson, Random; *On the Banks of Plum Creek* by Laura Ingalls Wilder, Harper

1939 *Thimble Summer* by Elizabeth Enright, Rinehart

Honor Books: *Nino* by Valenti Angelo, Viking; *Mr. Popper's Penguins* by Richard and Florence Atwater, Little; *"Hello the Boat!"* by Phyllis Crawford, Holt; *Leader by Destiny: George Washington, Man and Patriot* by Jeanette Eaton, Harcourt Brace Jovanovich; *Penn* by Elizabeth Janet Gray, Viking

1940 *Daniel Boone* by James Daugherty, Viking

Honor Books: *The Singing Tree* by Kate Seredy, Viking; *Runner of the Mountain*

Tops: The Life of Louis Agassiz by Mabel Robinson, Random; *By the Shores of Silver Lake* by Laura Ingalls Wilder, Harper; *Boy with a Pack* by Stephen W. Meader, Harcourt Brace Jovanovich

1941 *Call It Courage* by Armstrong Sperry, Macmillan

Honor Books: *Blue Willow* by Doris Gates, Viking; *Young Mac of Fort Vancouver* by Mary Jane Carr, Crowell; *The Long Winter* by Laura Ingalls Wilder, Harper; *Nansen* by Anna Gertrude Hall, Viking

1942 *The Matchlock Gun* by Walter D. Edmonds, Dodd

Honor Books: *Little Town on the Prairie* by Laura Ingalls Wilder, Harper; *George Washington's World* by Genevieve Foster, Scribner's; *Indian Captive: The Story of Mary Jemison* by Lois Lenski, Lippincott; *Down Ryton Water* by Eva Roe Gaggin, Viking

1943 *Adam of the Road* by Elizabeth Janet Gray, Viking

Honor Books: *The Middle Moffat* by Eleanor Estes, Harcourt Brace Jovanovich; *Have You Seen Tom Thumb?* by Mabel Leigh Hunt, Lippincott

1944 *Johnny Tremain* by Esther Forbes, Houghton

Honor Books: *The Happy Golden Years* by Laura Ingalls Wilder, Harper; *Fog Magic* by Julia Sauer, Viking; *Rufus M.* by Eleanor Estes, Harcourt Brace Jovanovich; *Mountain Born* by Elizabeth Yates, Coward

1945 *Rabbit Hill* by Robert Lawson, Viking

Honor Books: *The Hundred Dresses* by Eleanor Estes, Harcourt Brace Jovanovich; *The Silver Pencil* by Alice Dalgliesh, Scribner's; *Abraham Lincoln's World* by Genevieve Foster, Scribner's; *Lone Journey: The Life of Roger Williams* by Jeanette Eaton, Harcourt Brace Jovanovich

1946 *Strawberry Girl* by Lois Lenski, Lippincott

Honor Books: *Justin Morgan Had a Horse* by Marguerite Henry, Rand; *The Moved-Outers* by Florence Crannell Means, Houghton; *Bhimsa, the Dancing Bear* by Christine Weston, Scribner's; *New Found World* by Katherine Shippen, Viking

1947 *Miss Hickory* by Carolyn Sherwin Bailey, Viking

Honor Books: *Wonderful Year* by Nancy Barnes, Messner; *Big Tree* by Mary and Conrad Buff, Viking; *The Heavenly Tenants* by William Maxwell, Harper; *The Avion My Uncle Flew* by Cyrus Fisher, Appleton; *The Hidden Treasure of Glaston* by Eleanore Jewett, Viking

1948 *The Twenty-One Balloons* by William Pène du Bois, Viking

Honor Books: *Pancakes-Paris* by Claire Huchet Bishop, Viking; *Le Lun, Lad of Courage* by Carolyn Treffinger, Abingdon; *The Quaint and Curious Quest of Johnny Longfoot, The Shoe-King's Son* by Catherine Besterman, Bobbs; *The Cow-tail Switch, and Other West African Stories* by Harold Courlander, Holt; *Misty of Chincoteague* by Marguerite Henry, Rand

1949 *King of the Wind* by Marguerite Henry, Rand

Honor Books: *Seabird* by Holling C. Holling, Houghton; *Daughter of the Mountains* by Louise Rankin, Viking; *My Father's Dragon* by Ruth S. Gannett, Random; *Story of the Negro* by Arna Bontemps, Knopf

1950 *The Door in the Wall* by Marguerite de Angeli, Doubleday

Honor Books: *Tree of Freedom* by Rebecca Caudill, Viking; *The Blue Cat of Castle Town* by Catherine Coblentz, Longmans; *Kildee House* by Rutherford Montgomery, Doubleday; *George Washington* by Genevieve Foster, Scribner's; *Song of the Pines: A Story of Norwegian Lumbering in Wisconsin* by Walter and Marion Havighurst, Winston

1951 *Amos Fortune, Free Man* by Elizabeth Yates, Aladdin

Honor Books: *Better Known as Johnny Appleseed* by Mabel Leigh Hunt, Lippincott; *Gandhi, Fighter Without a Sword* by Jeanette Eaton, Morrow; *Abraham Lincoln, Friend of the People* by Clara Ingram Judson, Follett; *The Story of Appleby Capple* by Anne Parrish, Harper

1952 *Ginger Pye* by Eleanor Estes, Harcourt Brace Jovanovich

Honor Books: *Americans Before Columbus* by Elizabeth Baity, Viking; *Minn of the Mississippi* by Holling C. Holling, Houghton;

The Defender by Nicholas Kalashnikoff, Scribner's; *The Light at Tern Rock* by Julia Sauer, Viking; *The Apple and the Arrow* by Mary and Conrad Buff, Houghton

1953 *Secret of the Andes* by Ann Nolan Clark, Viking

Honor Books: *Charlotte's Web* by E. B. White, Harper; *Moccasin Trail* by Eloise McGraw, Coward; *Red Sails to Capri* by Ann Weil, Viking; *The Bears on Hemlock Mountain* by Alice Dalgliesh, Scribner's; *Birthdays of Freedom*, Vol. 1, by Genevieve Foster, Scribner's

1954 *. . . and now Miguel* by Joseph Krumgold, Crowell

Honor Books: *All Alone* by Claire Huchet Bishop, Viking; *Shadrach* by Meindert DeJong, Harper; *Hurry Home Candy* by Meindert DeJong, Harper; *Theodore Roosevelt, Fighting Patriot* by Clara Ingram Judson, Follett; *Magic Maize* by Mary and Conrad Buff, Houghton

1955 *The Wheel on the School* by Meindert DeJong, Harper

Honor Books: *The Courage of Sarah Noble* by Alice Dalgliesh, Scribner's; *Banner in the Sky* by James Ullman, Lippincott

1956 *Carry on, Mr. Bowditch* by Jean Lee Latham, Houghton

Honor Books: *The Secret River* by Marjorie Kinnan Rawlings, Scribner's; *The Golden Name Day* by Jennie Linquist, Harper; *Men, Microscopes, and Living Things* by Katherine Shippen, Viking

1957 *Miracles on Maple Hill* by Virginia Sorensen, Harcourt Brace Jovanovich

Honor Books: *Old Yeller* by Fred Gipson, Harper; *The House of Sixty Fathers* by Meindert DeJong, Harper; *Mr. Justice Holmes* by Clara Ingram Judson, Follett; *The Corn Grows Ripe* by Dorothy Rhoads, Viking; *Black Fox of Lorne* by Marguerite de Angeli, Doubleday

1958 *Rifles for Watie* by Harold Keith, Crowell

Honor Books: *The Horsecatcher* by Mari Sandoz, Westminster; *Gone-away Lake* by Elizabeth Enright, Harcourt Brace Jovanovich; *The Great Wheel* by Robert Lawson, Viking; *Tom Paine, Freedom's Apostle* by Leo Gurko, Crowell

1959 *The Witch of Blackbird Pond* by Elizabeth George Speare, Houghton

Honor Books: *The Family Under the Bridge* by Natalie Savage Carlson, Harper; *Along Came a Dog* by Meindert DeJong, Harper; *Chucaro: Wild Pony of the Pampa* by Francis Kalnay, Harcourt Brace Jovanovich; *The Perilous Road* by William O. Steele, Harcourt Brace Jovanovich

1960 *Onion John* by Joseph Krumgold, Crowell

Honor Books: *My Side of the Mountain* by Jean George, Dutton; *America is Born* by Gerald W. Johnson, Morrow; *The Gammage Cup* by Carol Kendall, Harcourt Brace Jovanovich

1961 *Island of the Blue Dolphins* by Scott O'Dell, Houghton

Honor Books: *America Moves Forward* by Gerald W. Johnson, Morrow; *Old Ramon* by Jack Schaefer, Houghton; *The Cricket in Times Square* by George Selden, Farrar

1962 *The Bronze Bow* by Elizabeth George Speare, Houghton

Honor Books: *Frontier Living* by Edwin Tunis, World; *The Golden Goblet* by Eloise McCraw, Coward; *Belling the Tiger* by Mary Stolz, Harper

1963 *A Wrinkle in Time* by Madeleine L'Engle, Farrar

Honor Books: *Thistle and Thyme: Tales and Legends from Scotland* by Sorche Nic Leodhas, Holt; *Men of Athens* by Olivia Coolidge, Houghton

1964 *It's Like This, Cat* by Emily Cheney Neville, Harper

Honor Books: *Rascal* by Sterling North, Dutton; *The Loner* by Ester Wier, McKay

1965 *Shadow of a Bull* by Maia Wojciechowska, Atheneum

Honor Books: *Across Five Aprils* by Irene Hunt, Follett

1966 *I, Juan de Pareja* by Elizabeth Borten de Treviño, Farrar

Honor Books: *The Black Cauldron* by Lloyd Alexander, Holt; *The Animal Family* by Randall Jarrell, Pantheon; *The Noonday Friends* by Mary Stolz, Harper

1967 *Up a Road Slowly* by Irene Hunt, Follet

Honor Books: *The King's Fifth* by Scott O'Dell, Houghton; *Zlateh the Goat and Other Stories* by Isaac Bashevis Singer,

Harper; *The Jazz Man* by Mary H. Weik, Atheneum

1968 *From the Mixed-Up Files of Mrs. Basil E. Frankweiler* by E. L. Konigsburg, Atheneum

Honor Books: *Jennifer, Hecate, Macbeth, William McKinley, and Me, Elizabeth* by E. L. Konigsburg, Atheneum; *The Black Pearl* by Scott O'Dell, Houghton; *The Fearsome Inn* by Isaac Bashevis Singer, Scribner's; *The Egypt Game* by Zilpha Keatley Snyder, Atheneum

1969 *The High King* by Lloyd Alexander, Holt

Honor Books: *To Be a Slave* by Julius Lester, Dial; *When Shlemiel Went to Warsaw and Other Stories* by Isaac Bashevis Singer, Farrar

1970 *Sounder* by William H. Armstrong, Harper

Honor Books: *Our Eddie* by Sulamith Ish-Kishor, Pantheon; *The Many Ways of Seeing: An Introduction to the Pleasures of Art* by Janet Gaylord Moore, World; *Journey Outside* by Mary Q. Steele, Viking

1971 *Summer of the Swans* by Betsy Byars, Viking

Honor Books: *Kneeknock Rise* by Natalie Babbitt, Farrar; *Enchantress from the Stars* by Sylvia Louise Engdahl, Atheneum; *Sing Down the Moon* by Scott O'Dell, Houghton

1972 *Mrs. Frisby and the Rats of NIMH* by Robert C. O'Brien, Atheneum

Honor Books: *Incident at Hawk's Hill* by Allan W. Eckert, Little; *The Planet of Junior Brown* by Virginia Hamilton, Macmillan; *The Tombs of Atuan* by Ursula K. Le Guin, Atheneum; *Annie and the Old One* by Miska Miles, Atlantic-Little; *The Headless Cupid* by Zilpha Keatley Snyder, Atheneum

1973 *Julie of the Wolves* by Jean Craighead George, Harper

Honor Books: *Frog and Toad Together* by Arnold Lobel, Harper; *The Upstairs Room* by Johanna Reiss, Crowell; *The Witches of Worm* by Zilpha Keatley Snyder, Atheneum

1974 *The Slave Dancer* by Paula Fox, Bradbury

Honor Book: *The Dark Is Rising* by Susan Cooper, Atheneum

1975 *M.C. Higgins, the Great* by Virginia Hamilton, Macmillan

Honor Books: *Figgs & Phantoms* by Ellen Raskin, Dutton; *My Brother Sam Is Dead* by James Lincoln Collier & Christopher Collier, Four Winds; *The Perilous Gard* by Elizabeth Marie Pope, Houghton; *Philip Hall Likes Me. I Reckon Maybe* by Bette Greene, Dial

1976 *The Grey King* by Susan Cooper, Atheneum

Honor Books: *The Hundred Penny Box* by Sharon Bell Mathis, Viking; *Dragonwings* by Lawrence Yep, Harper

1977 *Roll of Thunder, Hear My Cry* by Mildred D. Taylor, Dial

Honor Books: *Abel's Island* by William Steig, Farrar; *A String in the Harp* by Nancy Bond, Atheneum

1978 *Bridge to Terabithia* by Katherine Paterson, Crowell

Honor Books: *Ramona and Her Father* by Beverly Cleary, Morrow; *Anpao: An American Indian Odyssey* by Jamake Highwater, Lippincott

1979 *The Westing Game* by Ellen Raskin, Dutton

Honor Book: *The Great Gilly Hopkins* by Katherine Paterson, Crowell

1980 *A Gathering of Days: A New England Girl's Journal 1830–32* by Joan Blos, Scribner's

Honor Book: *The Road from Home: The Story of an Armenian Girl* by David Kherdian, Greenwillow

1981 *Jacob Have I Loved* by Katherine Paterson, Crowell

Honor Books: *The Fledgling* by Jane Langton, Harper; *A Ring of Endless Light* by Madeleine L'Engle, Farrar

1982 *A Visit to William Blake's Inn: Poems for Innocent and Experienced Travelers* by Nancy Willard, Harcourt Brace Jovanovich

Honor Books: *Ramona Quimby, Age 8* by Beverly Cleary, Morrow; *Upon the Head of the Goat: A Childhood in Hungary, 1939–1944* by Aranka Siegal, Farrar

1983 *Dicey's Song* by Cynthia Voigt, Atheneum

Honor Books: *Blue Sword* by Robin McKinley, Morrow; *Dr. DeSoto* by William Steig, Farrar; *Graven Images* by Paul

Fleischman, Harper; *Homesick: My Own Story* by Jean Fritz, Putnam's; *Sweet Whisper, Brother Rush,* by Virginia Hamilton, Philomel.

Children's Book Award

The Children's Book Award is presented annually by the International Reading Association to a children's author whose work shows unusual promise. The award was established in 1975.

1975 *Transport 7-41-R* by T. Degens, Viking
1976 *Dragonwings* by Lawrence Yep, Harper
1977 *A String in the Harp* by Nancy Bond, Atheneum
1978 *A Summer to Die* by Lois Lowry, Houghton
1979 *Reserved for Mark Anthony Crowder* by Alison Smith, Dutton
1980 *Words by Heart* by Ouida Sebestyen, Little
1981 *My Own Private Sky* by Delores Beckman, Dutton
1982 *Good Night, Mr. Tom* by Michelle Magorian, Harper & Row

Hans Christian Andersen International Medal

This international award was established in 1956 by the International Board on Books for Young People. It is presented every two years to a living author and a living artist whose total works have made an outstanding contribution to children's literature. A committee of five members, each from a different country, judges the selections.

1956 Eleanor Farjeon (Great Britain)
1958 Astrid Lindgren (Sweden)
1960 Erich Kästner (Germany)
1962 Meindert DeJong (United States)
1964 René Guillot (France)
1966 Author: Tove Jansson (Finland); Illustrator: Alois Carigiet (Switzerland)
1968 Authors: James Krüss (Germany); Jose Maria Sanchez-Silva (Spain); Illustrator: Jiri Trnka (Czechoslovakia)

1970 Author: Gianni Rodari (Italy); Illustrator: Maurice Sendak (United States)
1972 Author: Scott O'Dell (United States); Illustrator: Ib Spang Olsen (Denmark)
1974 Author: Maria Gripe (Sweden); Illustrator: Farshid Mesghali (Iran)
1976 Author: Cecil Bodker (Denmark); Illustrator: Tatjana Mawrina (Union of Soviet Socialist Republics)
1978 Author: Paula Fox (United States); Illustrator: Svend Otto S. (Denmark)
1980 Author: Bohumil Riha (Czechoslovakia); Illustrator: Suekichi Akaba (Japan)

Laura Ingalls Wilder Medal

The Laura Ingalls Wilder award, named after the author of the "Little House" series, is presented every five years by the American Library Association, Children's Book Division, to an author or illustrator whose books have made a lasting contribution to children's literature. The award was established in 1954 and is restricted to books published in the United States.

1954 Laura Ingalls Wilder
1960 Clara Ingram Judson
1965 Ruth Sawyer
1970 E. B. White
1975 Beverly Cleary
1980 Theodor Geisel (Dr. Seuss)

Examples of Additional Book Awards for Children's Literature

Amelia Frances Howard–Gibbon Medal, Canadian Library Association, is awarded annually to a Canadian illustrator for outstanding illustrations in a children's book published in Canada. First presented in 1971.

Boston Globe/Horn Book Awards, Boston Globe, Boston Mass., are awarded annually, since 1967, to an author of fiction, an author of nonfiction, and an illustrator.

The Canadian Library Awards, Canadian Library Association, are given annually to a children's book of literary merit written by a Canadian citizen and to a book of literary merit published in French. First presented in 1947 (Canadian citizen) and 1954 (French publication).

The Carnegie Medal, British Library Association, is awarded annually, since 1936, to an outstanding book first published in the United Kingdom.

Charles and Bertie G. Schwartz Award, National Jewish Welfare Board, New York, is awarded annually to a book that combines literary merit with an affirmative expression of Jewish thought. Established in 1952.

CIBC Award for Unpublished Writers, Council on Interracial Books for Children, New York, awards the United States writer from a racial minority whose manuscript best challenges stereotypes, supplies role models, and portrays distinctive aspects of a culture. Given for the first time in 1969.

Jane Addams Children's Book Award, Jane Addams Peace Association and the Women's International League for Peace and Freedom, New York, is given annually, since 1953, to honor the book that most effectively promotes peace, world community, and social justice.

The Kate Greenaway Medal, British Library Association, is awarded each year to the most distinguished work in illustration first published in the United Kingdom. Established in 1956.

Mildred L. Batchelder Award, American Library Association, Children's Services Division, Chicago, is given annually to the publisher of the most outstanding book originally issued in a foreign language. First awarded in 1968.

National Book Awards, Association of American Publishers, New York, are given annually to United States authors whose books have contributed most significantly to human awareness, national culture, and the spirit of excellence. Established in 1969 (Children's Literature Division).

William Allen White Children's Book Award, William Allen White Library, Kansas State Teachers College, Emporia, Kansas, is given annually, since 1953, to an outstanding children's book selected by Kansas children.

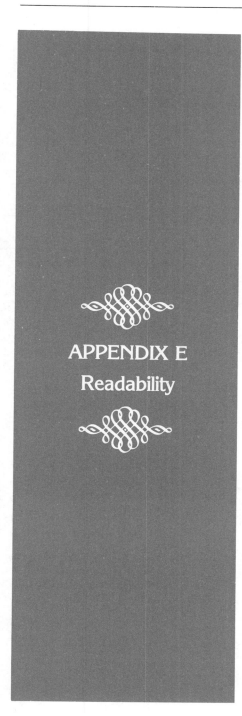

APPENDIX E
Readability

The books in the annotated bibliographies have been evaluated according to approximate reading levels. This information is important for teachers, librarians, and parents who are interested in selecting or recommending books that children can read independently. There are several readability formulas that may be used to determine readability levels. The books in this text were evaluated according to the following Fry Readability Graph:

Average Number of Syllables per 100 Words

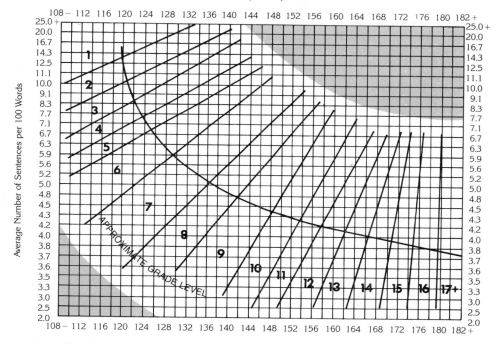

From Edward Fry, "Fry's Readability Graph: Clarifications, Validity, and Extension." *Journal of Reading* 21 (Dec. 1977): 249. The journal is published by the International Reading Association.

The Fry Readability Graph shown above calculates a book's reading level by the following method:

1 Select three 100-word passages, one each from the beginning, middle, and end of the book. Count proper nouns, initializations, and numerals in these 100-word selections. For example, "We went to the circus in Sarasota, Florida" counts as 8 words.

2 Count the total number of sentences in each 100-word passage. Estimate the number of sentences to the nearest tenth of a sentence. Average the total number of sentences in the beginning, middle, and ending passages so that you have one number to represent the number of sentences per 100 words.

3 Count the total number of syllables in each of the three 100-word passages. You will find it faster to count syllables if you tabulate every syllable over one in each word, then add this number to 100 at the end of the passage. For example:

$$\overset{1}{\text{Jim}}\ \text{was}\ \text{planning}\ \text{to}\ \text{take}\ \text{a}\ \overset{1}{\text{camping}}$$
$$\overset{2}{\text{vacation}}\ \text{in}\ \text{the}\ \overset{1}{\text{high}}\ \text{country.}\ (17\ \text{syllables})$$

Now, find the average total number of syllables for the three 100-word passages.

4 Plot on the graph the average number of sentences per 100 words, and the average number of syllables per 100 words. The example shown in the chart places the reading level of *Stuart Little* at fourth grade, with 9.2 average number of sentences per 100 words and 127 average number of syllables per 100 words.

Readability formulas assume that shorter sentences and fewer syllables in words result in easier reading materials. In contrast, long sentences and numerous multisyllabic words are thought to be more difficult to

Source		
Stuart Little (E.B.White)	Sentences per 100 words	Syllables per 100 words
100-word sample page 6	6.3	116
100-word sample page 72	10.5	136
100-word sample page 125	10.7	129
Total	27.5	381
Average	9.2	127

read. While this is often true, the adult should be aware that readability formulas do not take into consideration such factors as the difficulty of the concepts presented, or the child's interest in a particular subject. Although readability formulas are useful, they should not be used without examining a book for difficult conceptual content, difficult figurative language, and stylistic or organizational pecularities that might cause comprehension problems. In addition, the adult should note a book's content and interest value, since a child may be able to read a book that would otherwise be at his frustration level if he is interested in the subject.

APPENDIX F
Publishers and Their Addresses

Ars Edition, Inc.
Box 121
Massapequa Park, N.Y. 11762

Abelard-Schuman Junior Books
Div. of Harper & Row Pubs., Inc.
10 E. 53rd St.
New York, N.Y. 10022

Abingdon Press
Div. of United Methodist Publishing House
201 Eighth Ave. S.
Nashville, Tenn. 37202

Addison-Wesley Publishing Co., Inc.
Reading, Mass. 01867

Aladdin
Div. of Atheneum Publishers
597 Fifth Ave.
New York, N.Y. 10017

Atheneum Publishers
Div. of The Scribner Book Co.
597 Fifth Ave.
New York, N.Y. 10017

Beginner Books
Div. of Random House, Inc.
201 E. 50th St.
New York, N.Y. 10022

Bobbs-Merrill Co., Inc.
Subs. of Howard W. Sams & Co., Inc., Pub-
    lishers (ITT Publishing)
Box 558
4300 W. 62nd St.
Indianapolis, Ind. 46206

Bradbury Press, Inc.
2 Overhill Rd.
Scarsdale, N.Y. 10583

Cambridge University Press
32 E. 57th St.
New York, N.Y. 10022

Carolrhoda Books, Inc.
241 First Ave. N.
Minneapolis, Minn. 55401

Celestial Arts
231 Adrian Rd.
Millbrae, Calif. 94030

Childrens Press
Div. of Regensteiner Publishing Enterprises,
    Inc.
1224 W. Van Buren St.
Chicago, Ill. 60607

Child's World, Inc., The
980 N. McLean Blvd.
P.O. Box 989
Elgin, Ill. 60120

Clarion Books
Juvenile Div. of Ticknor & Fields
52 Vanderbilt Ave.
New York, N.Y. 10017

William Collins Pubs.
Collins Wm, Sons & Co. (Canada) Ltd.
100 Lesmill Rd.
Don Mills Ont., M3B 2T5 Canada

Coward, McCann & Geoghegan, Inc.
Member of The Putnam Publishing Group
200 Madison Ave.
New York, N.Y. 10016

Criterion Photocraft Co.
6 E. 39th St.
New York, N.Y. 10016

Crowell-Collier
Macmillan Publishing Co., Inc.
Subs. of Macmillan, Inc.
866 Third Ave.
New York, N.Y. 10022

Crowell/Lippincott Junior Books
10 E. 53rd St.
New York, N.Y. 10022

Thomas Y. Crowell Co.
Harper & Row Publishers, Inc.
10 E. 53rd St.
New York, N.Y. 10022

Crown Publishers, Inc.
One Park Ave.
New York, N.Y. 10016

Delacorte Press
One Dag Hammarskjold Plaza
New York, N.Y. 10017

Dell Publishing Co., Inc.
Subs. of Doubleday & Co., Inc.
One Dag Hammarskjold Plaza
New York, N.Y. 10017

Deutsch, Andre
E. P. Dutton, Inc.
2 Park Ave.
New York, N.Y. 10016

The Dial Press
One Dag Hammarskjold Plaza
New York, N.Y. 10017

Dillon Press, Inc.
500 S. Third St.
Minneapolis, Minn. 55415

Dodd, Mead & Co.
79 Madison Ave.
New York, N.Y. 10016

Doubleday & Co., Inc.
245 Park Ave.
New York, N.Y. 10167

E. P. Dutton, Inc.
2 Park Ave.
New York, N.Y. 10016

Elsevier-Dutton
Div. of E. P. Dutton, Inc.
2 Park Ave.
New York, N.Y. 10016

Elsevier/Nelson Books
Div. of E. P. Dutton, Inc.
2 Park Ave.
New York, N.Y. 10016

Faber & Faber, Inc.
99 Main St.
Salem, N.H. 03079

Farrar, Straus & Giroux, Inc.
19 Union Sq.
New York. N.Y. 10003

The Feminist Press
Box 334
Old Westburg, N.Y. 11568

Follett Publishing Co.
Div. of Follett Corp.
1010 W. Washington Blvd.
Chicago, Ill. 60607

Four Winds Press
50 W. 44th St.
New York, N.Y. 10036

Funk & Wagnalls, Inc.
53 E. 77th St.
New York, N.Y. 10021

Garland Publishing, Inc.
136 Madison Ave.
New York, N.Y. 10016

Garrard Publishing Co.
1607 N. Market St.
Champaign, Ill. 61820

Godine Press, Inc.
David R. Godine Publisher, Inc.
306 Dartmouth St.
Boston, Mass. 02116

Golden Press, Inc.
The Golden Quill Press
Francestown, N.H. 03043

Greenwillow Books
Div. of William Morrow & Co., Inc.
105 Madison Ave.
New York, N.Y. 10016

Grosset & Dunlap, Inc.
Subs. of Filmways, Inc.
51 Madison Ave.
New York, N.Y. 10010

Hamish Hamilton
Box 57
North Pomfret, Vt. 05053

Harcourt Brace Jovanovich, Inc.
757 Third Ave.
New York, N.Y. 10017

Harmony Books
Div. of Crown Publishers, Inc.
One Park Ave.
New York, N.Y. 10016

Harper & Row Publishers, Inc.
10 E. 53rd St.
New York, N.Y. 10022

Harvey House Publishers
20 Waterside Plaza
New York, N.Y. 10010

Hastings House Publishers, Inc.
10 E. 40th St.
New York, N.Y. 10016

Hawthorn Books, Inc.
Div. of E. P. Dutton
2 Park Ave.
New York, N.Y. 10016

Holiday House, Inc.
18 E. 53rd St.
New York, N.Y. 10022

Holt, Rinehart & Winston, Inc.
383 Madison Ave.
New York, N.Y. 10017

Houghton-Mifflin Co.
One Beacon St.
Boston, Mass. 02107

Houghton-Mifflin/Clarion Books
Houghton-Mifflin Co.
One Beacon St.
Boston, Mass. 02107

Hudson Hills Press, Inc.
30 Rockefeller Plaza

Suite 4323
New York, N.Y. 10112

Human Sciences Press, Inc.
72 Fifth Ave.
New York, N.Y. 10011

Jewish Publication Society of America
117 S. 17th St.
Philadelphia, Pa. 19103

Alfred A. Knopf, Inc.
Subs. of Random House, Inc.
201 E. 50th St.
New York, N.Y. 10022

Larousse & Co., Inc.
Affiliate of Librairie Larousse USA, Inc.
572 Fifth Ave.
New York, N.Y. 10036

Lerner Publications Co.
241 First Ave. N.
Minneapolis, Minn. 55401

J. B. Lippincott Co.
Subs. of Harper & Row Publishers, Inc.
E. Washington Sq.
Philadelphia, Pa. 19105

Lippincott Junior Books
10 E. 53rd St.
New York, N.Y. 10022

Little, Brown & Co.
34 Beacon St.
Boston, Mass. 02106

Lodestar Publishing
3075 W. Seventh St.
Los Angeles, Calif. 90005

Lothrop, Lee & Shepard Books
Div. of William Morrow & Co., Inc.
105 Madison Ave.
New York, N.Y. 10016

McGraw-Hill Book Co.
1221 Avenue of the Americas
New York, N.Y. 10020

Macmillan Publishing Co., Inc.
Subs. of Macmillan, Inc.
866 Third Ave.
New York, N.Y. 10022

Mayflower Books
W. H. Smith Publishers, Inc.
Subs. of W. H. Smith & Sons, Ltd.
112 Madison Ave.
New York, N.Y. 10016

Julian Messner, Inc.
Div. of Simon & Schuster
Simon & Schuster Bldg.
1230 Avenue of the Americas
New York, N.Y. 10020

Methuen, Inc.
Subs. of Associated Book Publishers Ltd.
    (UK)
733 Third Ave.
New York, N.Y. 10017

William Morrow & Co., Inc.
Subs. of The Hearst Corp.
105 Madison Ave.
New York, N.Y. 10016

The New American Library, Inc.
Subs. of The Times Mirror Co.
1633 Broadway
New York, N.Y. 10017

Oxford University Press, Inc.
200 Madison Ave.
New York, N.Y. 10016

Pantheon Books, Inc.
Div. of Random House, Inc.
201 E. 50th St.
New York, N.Y. 10022

Parents Magazine Press
Div. of Gruner & Jahr USA, Inc.
685 Third Ave.
New York, N.Y. 10017

Parnassus Press
6421 Regent St.
Oakland, Calif. 94618

Penguin Books
Div. of Viking Penguin, Inc.
625 Madison Ave.
New York, N.Y. 10022

S. G. Phillips, Inc.
305 W. 86th St.
New York, N.Y. 10024

Philomel Books
Member of The Putnam Publishing Group
200 Madison Ave.
New York, N.Y. 10016

Platt & Munk Publishers
Div. of Grosset & Dunlap
51 Madison Ave.
New York, N.Y. 10010

Prentice-Hall, Inc.
Englewood Cliffs, N.J. 07632

Price/Stern/Sloan Publishers, Inc.
410 N. LaCienega Blvd.
Los Angeles, Calif. 90048

G. P. Putnam's Sons
Member of The Putnam Publishing Group
200 Madison Ave.
New York, N.Y. 10016

Rand McNally & Co.
8255 Central Park Ave.
Skokie, Ill. 60076

Random House, Inc.
201 E. 50th St.
New York, N.Y. 10022

Regional Center for Educational Training
45 Lyme Rd.
Hanover, N.H. 03755

Reilly, William A.
P.O. Box 63
6 Crest Dr.
Dover, Mass. 02030

Schocken Books, Inc.
200 Madison Ave.
New York, N.Y. 10016

Scholastic Book Services
Div. of Scholastic Inc.
50 W. 44th St.
New York, N.Y. 10036

Scholastic Four Winds
Four Winds Press
50 W. 44th St.
New York, N.Y. 10036

Charles Scribner's Sons
Div. of The Scribner Book Cos., Inc.
597 Fifth Ave.
New York, N.Y. 10017

Scroll Press, Inc.
559 W. 26th St.
New York, N.Y. 10001

The Seabury Press, Inc.
815 Second Ave. N.
New York, N.Y. 10017

Simon & Schuster
The Simon & Schuster Bldg.
1230 Avenue of the Americas
New York, N.Y. 10020

Sniffen Court Books
% Atheneum Publishers
597 Fifth Ave.
New York, N.Y. 10017

Stemmer House Publishers, Inc.
2627 Caves Rd.
Owings Mills, Md. 21117

Time-Life Books, Inc.
Subs. of Time, Inc.
Alexandria, Va. 22314

Troll Associates
320 Route 17
Mahwah, N.J. 07430

Unicorn/Dutton
E. P. Dutton, Inc.
Unicorn Press
2 Park Ave.
New York, N.Y. 10016

Vanguard Press, Inc.
424 Madison Ave.
New York, N.Y. 10017

Viking Press
Div. of Viking Penguin, Inc.
526 Madison Ave.
New York, N.Y. 10022

Walck, Henry Z., Inc.
Div. of David McKay Co., inc.
2 Park Ave.
New York, N.Y. 10016

Walker & Co.
Div. of Walker Publishing Co., Inc.
720 Fifth Ave.
New York, N.Y. 10019

Wanderer Books
Div. of Simon & Schuster
The Simon & Schuster Bldg.
1230 Avenue of the Americas
New York, N.Y. 10020

Hill & Wang
Div. of Farrar, Straus & Giroux, Inc.
19 Union Sq., W.
New York, N.Y. 10003

Frederick Warne & Co., Inc.
2 Park Ave.
New York, N.Y. 10016

Franklin Watts, Inc.
Subs. of Grolier, Inc.
730 Fifth Ave.
New York, N.Y. 10019

John Weatherhill, Inc.
157 E. 69th St.
New York, N.Y. 10021

Western Publishing Co., Inc.
850 Third Ave.
New York, N.Y. 10022

The Westminster Press
Unit of The United Presbyterian Church in the
    U.S.A.
925 Chestnut St.
Philadelphia, Pa. 19107

Albert Whitman & Co.
560 W. Lake St.
Chicago, Ill. 60606

Windmill Books, Inc.
Affiliate of and Co-publisher with Simon &
    Schuster
The Simon & Schuster Bldg.
1230 Avenue of the Americas
New York, N.Y. 10020

Windmill/Dutton
E. P. Dutton, Inc.
2 Park Ave.
New York, N.Y. 10016

Alan Wofsy Fine Arts
150 Green St.
San Francisco, Calif., 94111

SUBJECT INDEX

Illustrations are indicated by boldface. The color insert appears between pages 122–23.

Dear Reader:

Writing *Through the Eyes of a Child* has been a very exciting task, and I hope that you have enjoyed reading it. The relationship between author and reader is very special, and I would like to nurture it by receiving your comments about the text. That way I can improve the 2nd edition based on your suggestions.

Name _____   Date _____

School _____   Instructor _____

Department _____   Title of Course _____

Address _____   Course # _____

_____   Your Major _____

1. What did you like most about *Through the Eyes of a Child?* (Content: topics covered, length, depth and organization. Pedagogy: examples, writing style, A/B format, issues, art, annotated bibliography, etc.)

_____

_____

_____

_____

2. What did you like least? _____

_____

3. Which chapters were most exciting, and why? _____

_____

_____

4. Which were least exciting, and why? _____

_____

5. Do you plan on keeping this book for your professional library? _____

_____

_____

PLEASE TAPE, DO NOT STAPLE

6. If you were writing the 2nd edition of *Through the Eyes of a Child,* what would you change to make it even better?

____

____

____

____

May Merrill quote you? ______ YES ______ NO

Thanks for your help,

Donna Norton

FOLD HERE

CUT PAGE OUT

NO POSTAGE NECESSARY IF MAILED IN THE UNITED STATES

BUSINESS REPLY MAIL

FIRST CLASS PERMIT NO. 284 COLUMBUS, OHIO

POSTAGE WILL BE PAID BY ADDRESSEE:

Donna Norton
℅ Chris Cole, College Division
Charles E. Merrill Publishing Co.
Box 508
Columbus, Ohio 43216